SETTING ALL THE CAPTIVES FREE

McGILL-QUEEN'S NATIVE AND NORTHERN SERIES
(In memory of Bruce G. Trigger)

Sarah Carter and Arthur J. Ray, Editors

1 When the Whalers Were Up North
Inuit Memories from the Eastern Arctic
Dorothy Harley Eber

2 The Challenge of Arctic Shipping
Science, Environmental Assessment, and Human Values
Edited by David L. VanderZwaag and Cynthia Lamson

3 Lost Harvests
Prairie Indian Reserve Farmers and Government Policy
Sarah Carter

4 Native Liberty, Crown Sovereignty
The Existing Aboriginal Right of Self-Government in Canada
Bruce Clark

5 Unravelling the Franklin Mystery
Inuit Testimony
David C. Woodman

6 Otter Skins, Boston Ships, and China Goods
The Maritime Fur Trade of the Northwest Coast, 1785–1841
James R. Gibson

7 From Wooden Ploughs to Welfare
The Story of the Western Reserves
Helen Buckley

8 In Business for Ourselves
Northern Entrepreneurs
Wanda A. Wuttunee

9 For an Amerindian Autohistory
An Essay on the Foundations of a Social Ethic
Georges E. Sioui

10 Strangers Among Us
David Woodman

11 When the North Was Red
Aboriginal Education in Soviet Siberia
Dennis A. Bartels and Alice L. Bartels

12 From Talking Chiefs to a Native Corporate Elite
The Birth of Class and Nationalism among Canadian Inuit
Marybelle Mitchell

13 Cold Comfort
My Love Affair with the Arctic
Graham W. Rowley

14 The True Spirit and Original Intent of Treaty 7
Treaty 7 Elders and Tribal Council with Walter Hildebrandt, Dorothy First Rider, and Sarah Carter

15 This Distant and Unsurveyed Country
A Woman's Winter at Baffin Island, 1857–1858
W. Gillies Ross

16 Images of Justice
Dorothy Harley Eber

17 Capturing Women
The Manipulation of Cultural Imagery in Canada's Prairie West
Sarah A. Carter

18 Social and Environmental Impacts of the James Bay Hydroelectric Project
Edited by James F. Hornig

19 Saqiyuq
Stories from the Lives of Three Inuit Women
Nancy Wachowich in collaboration with Apphia Agalakti Awa, Rhoda Kaukjak Katsak, and Sandra Pikujak Katsak

20 Justice in Paradise
Bruce Clark

21 Aboriginal Rights and Self-Government
The Canadian and Mexican Experience in North American Perspective
Edited by Curtis Cook and Juan D. Lindau

22 Harvest of Souls
The Jesuit Missions and Colonialism in North America, 1632–1650
Carole Blackburn

23 Bounty and Benevolence
A History of Saskatchewan Treaties
Arthur J. Ray, Jim Miller, and Frank Tough

24 The People of Denendeh
Ethnohistory of the Indians of Canada's Northwest Territories
June Helm

25 The Marshall Decision and Native Rights
Ken Coates

26 The Flying Tiger
Women Shamans and Storytellers of the Amur
Kira Van Deusen

27 Alone in Silence
European Women in the Canadian North before 1940
Barbara E. Kelcey

28 The Arctic Voyages of Martin Frobisher
An Elizabethan Adventure
Robert McGhee

29 Northern Experience and the Myths of Canadian Culture
Renée Hulan

30 The White Man's Gonna Getcha
The Colonial Challenge to the Crees in Quebec
Toby Morantz

31 The Heavens Are Changing
Nineteenth-Century Protestant Missions and Tsimshian Christianity
Susan Neylan

32 Arctic Migrants/Arctic Villagers
The Transformation of Inuit Settlement in the Central Arctic
David Damas

33 Arctic Justice
On Trial for Murder – Pond Inlet, 1923
Shelagh D. Grant

34 The American Empire and the Fourth World
Anthony J. Hall

35 Eighteenth-Century Naturalists of Hudson Bay
Stuart Houston, Tim Ball, and Mary Houston

36 Uqalurait
An Oral History of Nunavut
Compiled and edited by John Bennett and Susan Rowley

37 Living Rhythms
Lessons in Aboriginal Economic Resilience and Vision
Wanda Wuttunee

38 The Making of an Explorer
George Hubert Wilkins and the Canadian Arctic Expedition, 1913–1916
Stuart E. Jenness

39 Chee Chee
A Study of Aboriginal Suicide
Alvin Evans

40 Strange Things Done
Murder in Yukon History
Ken S. Coates and William R. Morrison

41 Healing through Art
Ritualized Space and Cree Identity
Nadia Ferrara

42 Coyote and Raven Go Canoeing
Coming Home to the Village
Peter Cole

43 Something New in the Air
The Story of First Peoples Television Broadcasting in Canada
Lorna Roth

44 Listening to Old Woman Speak
Natives and Alternatives in Canadian Literature
Laura Smyth Groening

45 Robert and Francis Flaherty
A Documentary Life, 1883–1922
Robert J. Christopher

46 Talking in Context
Language and Identity in Kwakwaka'wakw Society
Anne Marie Goodfellow

47 Tecumseh's Bones
Guy St-Denis

48 Constructing Colonial Discourse
Captain Cook at Nootka Sound
Noel Elizabeth Currie

49 The Hollow Tree
Fighting Addiction with Traditional Healing
Herb Nabigon

50 The Return of Caribou to Ungava
A.T. Bergerud, Stuart Luttich, and Lodewijk Camps

51 Firekeepers of the Twenty-First Century
First Nations Women Chiefs
Cora J. Voyageur

52 Isuma
Inuit Video Art
Michael Robert Evans

53 Outside Looking In
Viewing First Nations Peoples in Canadian Dramatic Television Series
Mary Jane Miller

54 Kiviuq
An Inuit Hero and His Siberian Cousins
Kira Van Deusen

55 Native Peoples and Water Rights
Irrigation, Dams, and the Law in Western Canada
Kenichi Matsui

56 The Rediscovered Self
Indigenous Identity and Cultural Justice
Ronald Niezen

57 As affecting the fate of my absent husband
Selected Letters of Lady Franklin Concerning the Search for the Lost Franklin Expedition, 1848–1860
Edited by Erika Behrisch Elce

58 The Language of the Inuit
Syntax, Semantics, and Society in the Arctic
Louis-Jacques Dorais

59 Inuit Shamanism and Christianity
Transitions and Transformations in the Twentieth Century
Frédéric B. Laugrand and Jarich G. Oosten

60 No Place for Fairness
Indigenous Land Rights and Policy in the Bear Island Case and Beyond
David T. McNab

61 Aleut Identity
Tradition and Modernity in an Indigenous Fishery
Katherine L. Reedy-Mascher

62 Earth into Property
Aboriginal History and the Making of Global Capitalism
Anthony J. Hall

63 Collections and Objections
Aboriginal Material Culture in Southern Ontario, 1791–1914
Michelle A. Hamilton

64 These Mysterious People
Shaping History and Archaeology in a Northwest Coast Community
Susan Roy

65 Telling It to the Judge
Taking Native History to Court
Arthur J. Ray

66 Aboriginal Music in Contemporary Canada
Echoes and Exchanges
Edited by Anna Hoefnagels and Beverley Diamond

67 In Twilight and in Dawn
A Biography of Diamond Jenness
Barnett Richling

68 Women's Work, Women's Art
Nineteenth-Century Northern Athapaskan Clothing
Judy Thompson

69 Warriors of the Plains
The Arts of Plains Indian Warfare
Max Carocci

70 Reclaiming Indigenous Planning
Edited by Ryan Walker, Ted Jojola, and David Natcher

71 Setting All the Captives Free
Capture, Adjustment, and Recollection in Allegheny Country
Ian K. Steele

SETTING ALL THE CAPTIVES FREE

Capture, Adjustment, and Recollection in Allegheny Country

IAN K. STEELE

McGill-Queen's University Press
Montreal & Kingston • London • Ithaca

ISBN 978-0-7735-4184-9 (cloth)
ISBN 978-0-7735-8989-6 (ePDF)
ISBN 978-0-7735-8990-2 (ePUB)

Legal deposit third quarter 2013
Bibliothèque nationale du Québec

Printed in Canada on acid-free paper that is 100% ancient forest free (100% post-consumer recycled), processed chlorine free

This book has been published with the help of a grant from the Canadian Federation for the Humanities and Social Sciences, through the Awards to Scholarly Publications Program, using funds provided by the Social Sciences and Humanities Research Council of Canada. This book has been published with the help of a grant from the J.B. Smallman Publication Fund, Faculty of Social Science, Western University.

McGill-Queen's University Press acknowledges the support of the Canada Council for the Arts for our publishing program. We also acknowledge the financial support of the Government of Canada through the Canada Book Fund for our publishing activities.

Library and Archives Canada Cataloguing in Publication

Steele, Ian K., 1937–, author
Setting all the captives free : capture, adjustment, and recollection in Allegheny country / Ian K. Steele.

Includes bibliographical references and index.
Issued in print and electronic formats.
ISBN 978-0-7735-4184-9 (bound).
ISBN 978-0-7735-8989-6 (ePDF).
ISBN 978-0-7735-8990-2 (ePUB)

1. Indians of North America – Wars – 1750–1815 – Prisoners and prisons. 2. United States – History – French and Indian Wars, 1754–1763 – Prisoners and prisons. 3. Indian captivities – Allegheny River Valley (Pa. and N.Y.) – History – 18th century. 4. Allegheny River Valley (Pa. and N.Y.) – History – 18th century. I. Title.

E199.S74 2013 973.2'6 C2013-903964-3
C2013-903965-1

Set in 10/13 Baskerville 10 Pro
Book design/typesetting by Garet Markvoort, zijn digital

For

KAITLYN, THOMAS, TAYLOR, AND JANET

With so many promising tomorrows still
to convert into treasured yesterdays

CONTENTS

Illustrations, Maps, and Tables xi
Preface xiii
Introduction 3

PART 1: CAPTURED IN "PEACETIME" 9

1 Taken along Warriors' Paths 13
2 Taking Traders, 1745–54 33
3 Colonial Soldiers Take Captives, 1754 54

PART 2: CAPTURED IN WAR 73

4 Taken in Raids, 1754–59 77
5 Taken in Sieges and Surrenders, 1756–58 117
6 Taken in Battles, 1755–59 127
7 Indian War with Traders and Soldiers, 1763–65 142
8 Indian War with White Settlers, 1763–65 163

PART 3: CAPTIVITY, CONVERSION, AND ESCAPE 185

9 Trails into Captivity 187
10 Allegheny White Indians 198
11 Escaped 231
12 The Bereft 250

PART 4: SETTING ALL THE CAPTIVES FREE 259

13 Diplomacy of Gift Exchange, 1756–62 263
14 Redeemed and Exchanged, 1745–62 290
15 Forced Return of Captives 309
16 Imperial Moment, 1765 340

PART 5: AFTERWARDS AND AFTERWORDS 351

17 Restoring and Revising Identities 355
18 Captivating Accounts, 1755–1826 384

Conclusion 429
Tables 435
Abbreviations 437
Appendix: Named Captives Taken on the Allegheny Frontier, 1745–65 439
Notes 553
Index 675

ILLUSTRATIONS, MAPS, AND TABLES

ILLUSTRATIONS

1 Robert Stobo's smuggled drawing of Fort Duquesne, 1754 67
2 Silver medal struck to commemorate raid on Kittanning 105
3 "Old Selim," engraved from a lost Charles Willson Peale portrait, 1789 247
4 "Colonel Peter Schuyler, Patron of Captives in Canada" 297
5 "A Survey of That Part of the Country through which Colonel Bouquet Marched in 1764" 321
6 "The Indians Giving a Talk to Colonel Bouquet" 346
7 "The Indians Delivering Up the English Captives to Colonel Bouquet" 348
8 Statue of Mary Jemison at Letchworth Park, New York State, 1910 426

MAPS

1 Allegheny Country, 1754 10
2 Allegheny Country, 1755–63 75
3 Allegheny Country, 1763–65 147

TABLES

1 Victims of Allegheny conflict, by status, 1745–54 435
2 Victims of Allegheny warfare, by status, 1755–62 435
3 Victims of Pontiac's War, by status, 1763–65 436
4 Victims of Allegheny warfare, by status, 1745–65 436

PREFACE

This study began as a companion to *Betrayals: Fort William Henry and the "Massacre"* and was intended to provide comparisons between the better-studied captivities of New Englanders and those of Pennsylvanians and Virginians taken in Allegheny country during the same Seven Years' War. I hope this purpose has, to some extent, been accomplished. The project mushroomed as soon as it became clear that very little had been assembled about individual Allegheny captives; there is nothing remotely comparable to the ancient and valuable two-volume *New England Captives Carried to Canada*, by Emma Lewis Coleman (Portland, ME: Southworth, 1925–26). Rather than accept the sensible conclusion that a serious study of Allegheny captivity could not be done, I began to build a database of the captives, ransacking colonial newspapers, archival collections, printed narratives, letters, monographs, local folklore, and genealogical websites, to learn more about as many as possible of those captured in Allegheny country between 1745 and 1765. Those killed have been studied as well because those who witnessed the killing of their families knew how little of their previous lives could ever be recovered, and because the numbers of those killed can usefully be compared with the numbers captured in various circumstances. There was also no satisfactory rationale for confining the study to British colonials, as Coleman had done, so Indian, British, French, and Canadian captives have been included among "all the captives," as have traders, warriors, soldiers, farmers, and their wives and children.

Admittedly, it is radical to place captives at the middle of a study of a crucial generation in the contest for Allegheny country. Numerous familiar topics are minimized, distorted, or ignored in focusing on a chance collection of ordinary people who became vulnerable bellwethers of the relations among families, ethnicities, colonies, and empires caught in collision, confusion, and compromise. Such a novel approach is justified only by what it reveals.

Although Emma Coleman's work would surely have been easier in the age of the computer, I have often wondered whether mine has been. Those familiar with good database programs will appreciate that the wealth of readily accessible information and statistics has ruined many more clever ideas than it has supported, and may even have added more time to the preparation of this book than it has saved. Yet one of the enduring fascinations has been the opportunity to switch readily from the emotive detail of individual captivities to the sobering general statistics, and then attempt to write an accessible analytical study that is not overwhelmed by either. Readers can decide whether the result is, to paraphrase E.F. Schumacher, history as if people mattered.

The database (in SPSS) reports as many as thirty-nine variables concerning 6,130 people captured or killed in Allegheny warfare between 1745 and 1765. A major limitation of this database is that many of these victims were unnamed. Two-thirds of the 3,343 people killed, either in these attacks or within five days of capture, were not named, but the dates, locations, ages, gender, status, and numbers of those involved allow for some confidence that none of the cases are duplicated. The statistics on the number captured, the timing and place of capture, and the ratios of killed-to-captured are offered with confidence. Of the 2,788 captives taken, fully 695 (25%) are without recorded names or other adequate identifying information. All these unnamed are included in the 1,078 whom I have identified as "missing." Some 511 of those returned from captivity were not identified by name either, and these are included among the 1,709 captives whose fate is known (see table 4). However, it is not possible to tell how many of the 695 unnamed at capture were among the 511 returned without their names being reported. It is also likely that the number of "white Indians" is underreported, but it is impossible to tell by how many. The overall number of cases is therefore likely exaggerated, at least a little. Where record linkage between capture and fate are not required, as in the study of the time, place, and method of capturing or returning captives, this database is more reliable.

A mountain of debts of gratitude have been gathered in the long preparation of this work, during which some libraries and archives have changed their names, and some scholars and librarians have died. Western University (formerly the University of Western Ontario) has supported this research in numerous ways, and essential research funds have also come from the Social Science and Humanities Research Council of Canada, and from the Ley and Lois Smith Research Fund.

Publication has been assisted by the Awards to Scholarly Publications program of the SSHRC, the J.B. Smallman Fund at Western University, and the endowed Joanne Goodman Lectures "established by Joanne's family and friends to perpetuate the memory of her blithe spirit, her quest for knowledge, and the rewarding years she spent at Western University."

Scholars who have been particularly helpful include Jay Cassel, Regna Darnell, Frederick Dreyer, George Emery, Joseph Ernst, Allan Greer, Thomas Guinsburg, Ron Hoffman, Adrienne Hood, José Igartua, Daniel Richter, Nancy Rhoden, Timothy Shannon, Wolfgang Splitter, Scott Stephenson, Darryl Stonefish, and Neil Whitehead, as well as the anonymous assessors of articles published along the way and readers of the book manuscript. Jon Parmenter and Brendan Carnduff were excellent research assistants in the early stages of the project, and Elizabeth Mantz, David Murphy, Maureen Ryan, and Walter Zimmerman have been particularly helpful librarians at Western University for decades. The librarians and archivists of what are now Library and Archives Canada, the British Library, and the National Record Office of Great Britain have been most helpful with inquiries and copying. Brian Dunnigan of the Clements Library at the University of Michigan and Nelson Lankford at the Virginia Historical Society have been particularly helpful, as have the staff there and at the American Antiquarian Society, Haverford College, the Library of Congress, the New Jersey Archives, the Pennsylvania State Archives, and the Historical Society of Pennsylvania. The network of archival resources, reading rooms, and websites of the Church of Jesus Christ of Latter-Day Saints has been of great assistance with access to microfilmed local records and genealogical searches. George Emery and Tom Guinsburg kindly read and improved the entire manuscript, and Hertha Steele has once again protected readers and myself from numerous irrelevant complexities, as well as infelicities and errors. Philip Cercone and Robert Lewis of McGill-Queen's University Press have helped greatly. Persisting errors are, of course, the exclusive property of the author and should not be reproduced without express permission.

A portion of chapter 1 appeared as "The Shawnee and the English: Captives and War, 1753–1765," in *The Boundaries between Us: Natives and Newcomers along Frontiers of the Old Northwest, 1750–1850*, ed. Daniel Barr (Kent, OH: Kent State University Press, 2006), 1–24, copyright of 2006 by the Kent State University Press, reprinted with permission. Thanks also to the *Journal of Canadian Studies/Revue d'études canadiennes*, the

Journal of the Canadian Historical Association, and *Ethnohistory* for permission to reprint earlier versions (2005 and 2006) of parts of chapters 6, 3, and 1 respectively. For permission to reproduce illustrations, I am grateful to the Pennsylvania State Museum, Harrisburg, PA; the New Jersey Historical Society, Newark, NJ; and the Annenberg Rare Book and Manuscript Library, University of Pennsylvania, Philadelphia, PA.

SETTING ALL THE CAPTIVES FREE

INTRODUCTION

What can be learned by putting captives at the center of a study of the cultural and military war for Allegheny country in the middle of the eighteenth century? The intensive study of American captives has never concerned those from this particular region, and the rich military history of this contested region has paid scant attention to captives. There were stark cultural differences concerning the taking, treatment, and return of captives that should reward more careful discrimination, and be watched for continuities and adaptations, as well as comparisons with New England, New York, and southern colonial borderlands.[1] In a short generation, Allegheny country went from relative peace to a flashpoint for global war, and finished with a fierce conflict exclusively between the region's Indians and its white traders, soldiers, and settlers. By learning as much as possible about all the captives of all the contending groups, and analyzing their capture, adaptation, and fate, it is hoped that our understanding of the events, the captives, and the consequences will be greatly improved. If this approach yields enough, it should invite replication concerning other cultural borderlands.

A Delaware Indian living in the Susquehanna Valley in 1755 reportedly declared war on his German neighbor by saying, "We are Allegheny Indians and your enemies. You must die."[2] Then he killed his neighbor and migrated, with his new captives, across the Allegheny Mountains to Kittanning. In this study Allegheny country refers to the region within a two-hundred-mile radius of what became, in very quick succession, Shannopintown, Fort Trent, Fort Duquesne, Fort Pitt, and then Pittsburgh. At the beginning of the eighteenth century, the Alleghenies, or "endless mountains," with their pinched valleys, scrub lands, and marshes, thoroughly separated the richer valleys of the Susquehanna and Shenandoah Rivers in the east from those of the Ohio and Muskingum Rivers in the west. This had been something of a no-man's-land between the Iroquois and the Algonquians, a place haunted by memories of earlier wars, broken peaces, and unreturned captives.

Iroquois, Delaware, and Shawnee migrants began re-peopling this relatively empty land in the 1720s, forming rather dispersed and often multitribal villages. These Indian refugees and hunters already had plenty of experience with colonial Europeans. Canadians and British colonials soon came to trade, and then to scout or fight for land, drawing French and particularly British regular soldiers into their intensifying contest. Although first contact was an ancient memory, this became another kind of "new world," where no culture dominated and all had to devise and evolve, once again, strategies to cope with unwelcome "others."

In the decade before major warfare in the region, people sometimes attempted to control situations by taking captives and hostages, and their practices affected numerous decisions made during the next decade of wars. There were three distinct ways in which captives were taken between 1745 and 1755, and each deserves separate discussion (chapters 1–3). Iroquoian and Shawnee warriors traditionally proved themselves and reinforced their communities with endemic, long-range, small-scale raids against the Catawba or Cherokee, raids that brought captives, martial honor, and some friction with white settlers who increasingly encumbered the intervening "Warriors' Path." There was no Ohio Indian trade in white captives like that which persisted even in peacetime for the Abenaki and Iroquois on the southeastern borders of Canada. There was no British colonial trade in Indian captives in Ohio country, as there had been earlier in Virginia and the Carolinas – a small mercy that meant that whites had virtually no interest in taking Indian captives at all. As Canadian traders faced increasingly effective competition in upper Ohio country, they supported their government in bluntly warning Pennsylvanian and Virginian traders out of the region. Ohio Indians generally refused Canadian invitations to attack these British colonial traders, but Canadian fort commanders won their trade war in Allegheny country by taking the region's second type of captives, Pennsylvanians, who were confined and sent to France as illegal traders. The third type of captivity came as Canadians and Virginians confronted each other as soldiers in 1754, in famous little incidents at the forks of the Ohio, in Jumonville Glen, and at Fort Necessity. They were initially reluctant to take prisoners outside of war, but soon took both prisoners and military hostages. The confused and anomalous position of some of these captives persisted until the fall of New France in 1760.

Once the Seven Years' War began, for the Shawnee in the fall of 1754, for British colonials in the summer of 1755, and for the French and British in the spring of 1756, dozens and then hundreds of captives and prisoners were taken each year. On the face of it, taking captives and agreeing to go as a captive were major ameliorations in what was not total war. European-trained soldiers were proud of their humanity toward each other in taking, maintaining, and returning prisoners in accordance with detailed agreements. British colonial authorities, trying to stiffen local resistance against Indian attacks, demonized Indians as taking captives as slaves, an evocative claim that masked the fact that they were taking no Indian captives themselves. Indians who had shown little interest in taking or keeping white captives during peace were suddenly taking captives as a central feature of their war.

The tactical aspects of capture have been too easily ignored, as though training in hunting with firearms was adequate preparation for capturing prisoners alive and unharmed. Taking captives was very different in a raid, a siege, or a battle, and those significant differences and evolving tactics can best be examined by treating them separately (chapters 4–6). The cadence of raids charted the phases of the borderland war, which was declared with raids and ended only when the raids ceased. Surrender after a siege could represent a sane and trusting negotiation between people still capable of killing each other, or the desperation of those caught in a burning stockade. Was captivity in Allegheny battles the most difficult to accomplish, for both captor and captive? Comparisons are worth exploring between the few captures in General Edward Braddock's defeat of 1755, those in Major James Grant's defeat a few miles away in 1758, and those in the crushing of Commandant François-Marie Le Marchand de Lignery's Ohio forces at the battle of La Belle Famille the following year. It is valuable to count those killed in all of these forms of fighting, to notice the different ratios between the killed and the captured, and to watch for change over time.

The Ohio Indians' war with British traders, soldiers, and white settlers between 1763 and 1765 reveals Indian priorities and preferences most clearly because they were then unencumbered by French or Canadian influence. The launch of war against traders and soldiers (chapter 7) was strikingly different from 1755, and the changes can easily be read through the taking of captives. The war against white settlers (chapter 8) was a resumption after five years of truce, but continuities were accompanied by various new strategies and tactics. Did Indian warriors maintain their preoccupation with taking captives when: some of their villages already held many captives, their enemies persisted in taking no Indian captives at all, and atrocities were accumulating on both sides? Throughout the study of these wars, it will be valuable to calculate –

by age, gender, occupation, and situation – the varying and changing odds of being captured rather than killed. The taking of captives can be expected to serve as a sensitive barometer of the changing confidence, purposes, and relative strength of contending groups.

Deliberate transformation of captives began with the trauma of most captures and the seemingly arbitrary killings that followed on the trail into captivity. A noisy infant who could betray the whereabouts of a party would be killed, as would a bold or obstreperous captive who might kill in attempting to escape. With or without the influence of confiscated alcohol, captors occasionally fought over captives with deadly consequence. A subdivided major raid could result in too many captives to be effectively guarded during retreat or resistance to a counterattack, or too many may have been captured for the supply of food that had been cached earlier or taken in the raids. A captive might not be able to keep up on a long journey, hurried along by captors anxious to outpace those in pursuit. The trauma of witnessing these deaths was among the very hard initial lessons of Indian re-education (chapter 9). Whereas colonial and European captors made fewer efforts to convert captives than had been characteristic of New France earlier, most Ohio Indian captors took people to adopt and convert into "white Indians." Learning just how many captives, and of what ages and genders, became fully and permanently adapted to Indian life will test the commonly held assumptions about the success of this re-education (chapter 10). Age, gender, and race could be expected to affect captivity, conversion, and escape. Those who became white Indians can be compared to those who escaped, indicating not only how many, but also what kinds of, captives risked their lives to reverse their initial acceptance of captivity (chapter 11). How enduring were the adaptations to Indian ways in captives who were eventually returned to a colonial society that had become less tolerant because of the wars? There are few records that confirm either the understandable anguish of the spouses, parents, and kin of those taken captive, or the strenuous and even suicidal efforts made to find, join, or recover captives (chapter 12). What can be learned is more than enough to challenge those who think that the sensibilities of "affective family relations" had not yet been imported to this brutal country.

Efforts to set the captives free, and their results, deserve special attention. Quakers promoted the first efforts as soon as Pennsylvania declared war in 1756, prompting incredulity from Delawares and derision from non-Quaker Pennsylvanians, Virginians, and newly arrived British soldiers. Yet Pennsylvania's expensive diplomacy produced a truce with the North Branch Delaware, even if few captives were returned. The new British Indian Affairs Superintendency, overseen and funded by the British Army, took control of a series of expensive conferences, and the gift exchanges there eventually became a thinly veiled traffic in captives. Did a British Army that loudly denounced ransom come to pay large sums for diplomatic gifts that freed a surprising number of captives (chapter 13)? The sums expended by George Croghan in these conferences helped to provoke the infamous retrenchment that is so often judged unconscionable, and a major provocation for the war of 1764–65. Private ransom, in Indian country or in New France, was another method of recovering captives, though it was fraught with many hazards. The formal exchanges of captured military personnel between the Government of Canada and the British Army brought back a few other Allegheny captives (chapter 14). The success and limits of each of these diplomatic methods to recover captives can be measured and compared.

The option of using force to recover captives was often tempting and always dangerous. The price and accomplishments of "hot pursuit," and the notorious Kittanning raid on an Indian village containing many white captives, reveal some of the predictable problems. The most dramatic large-scale recovery of captives came with the British-led 1764 punitive expedition to the Muskingum Valley, where a substantial force sought to intimidate Delaware, Shawnee, and Mingo into surrendering all their captives, and even their *métis* children, thereby dismembering families and taking some captives in the name of redeeming them (chapter 15). How was this bloodless imperial accomplishment perceived by the Indians, by those liberated, by the British military, and by those leading colonials who were at that moment preoccupied with the Stamp Act crisis (chapter 16)? And what have historians and folklorists chosen to remember and forget about this expedition led by Colonel Henry Bouquet?

The redeemed captives were never entirely free. The "red colonials" who returned from captivity faced suspicions, expectations, and challenges. Recovering or inventing identities required different things of white and *métis* children, youths, soldiers, civilian men and women, and slaves (chapter 17). Writing their captivity narrative was part of returning for very few captives, but recounting became part of family and local history and legend. The varied and changing purposes and audiences for captivity accounts, published during the lifetime of survivors, helps explain the shape of some accounts, and the eclipse of interest in others. With enough information, it becomes possible to test the narratives and discover those severely distorted by third parties, and those that were entirely fictitious (chapter 18). These distinctions may matter a little less to literary scholars interested in the popularity of these iconic American classics than it does to those of us who persist in attempting to separate facts from the myths, which have often been more consequential.

Following the early Allegheny captives, from the few rather accidental captures of the 1740s to the last survivor's interview in 1837, affords insights into unexpected humanity amid horror, the compulsions and plasticity of cultural identity, and the memories of captivity that affected thousands of captives and captors and helped root a particularly American preoccupation with individual freedom. The wondrously varied captivity accounts, published and unpublished, continue to defy their purposeful users and abusers.

PART 1

CAPTURED IN "PEACETIME"

In the first half of the eighteenth century, Algonquian, Iroquoian, and European migrants brought a range of incompatible and evolving habits and beliefs into the recently unpopulated Allegheny Mountains and upper Ohio Valley. Their disparate martial histories included conflicting assumptions and practices concerning the taking of enemies and aliens. Even more interesting, there were three separate ways of taking and treating captives in the decade before open war began in 1754. Intertribal raids, the capture of rival traders, and the clashes between the French and English colonial militaries offered distinct precedents, habits, and arguments that would not only became entangled but were complicated further by the subsequent arrival of European regulars.

Small-scale raids against relatively distant southern enemies were rites of passage for young male Iroquois, Delaware, and Shawnee and routes to honor and status for all warriors. When other war did not intrude, this belligerence was the ultimate hunt that animated peacetime for martial people. A major objective of these raids was to take Catawba or Cherokee captives who might be adopted as full members of the community, kept as servants, traded, given to allies, or tortured to death. Occasionally, raiding parties traveling this Warriors' Path (see map 1) came into conflict with British colonials, and relations were further complicated by French-allied Canadian Iroquois participants who took the occasional English captive back to Canada for adoption or ransom.

English and French fur traders had come to upper Ohio villages since the 1730s. These traders were potential hostages representing economic, political, and religious cultures that were known to compete seductively with Indian values. Surprisingly few traders were robbed, captured, or killed through bloody-minded opportunism or retaliation for perceived wrongdoings, and more English traders were eventually

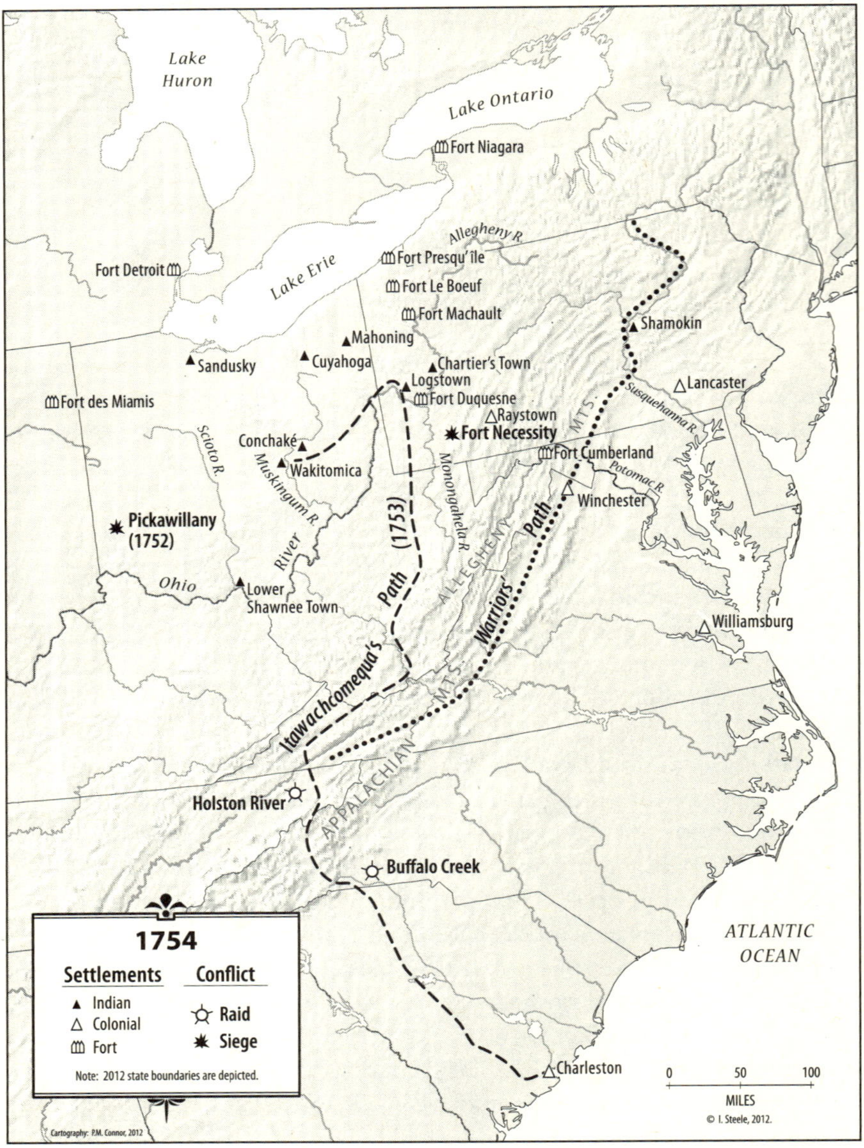

Map 1 Allegheny Country, 1754

harmed as proof of Indian alliance and friendship with the French. A new type of captivity was emerging. From the mid-1740s, the French compensated for their lagging competitiveness in trade by asserting claims of sovereignty in the region, and by offering gifts to warriors who captured and delivered Pennsylvanian traders. A few traders were captured, presented to French post commanders, treated as illegal traders, and sent to jail in Canada and France.

Colonial soldiers and militiamen also invaded the region after 1748, bringing martial inheritances that reached back to the ferocities of Reformation Europe and had been adapted through generations of belligerence and coexistence with Indians. Virginian and Canadian rivals clashed here for the first time, meeting each other in little parodies of the sieges and surrenders that were regular features of western European war. The colonial militaries, fighting in peacetime, were understandably hesitant about taking prisoners of war, but a few of their prized hostages remained captive during the ensuing war. Colonial captains and commandants, as well as Indian raiders, all took captives in peacetime, and helped to provoke the Seven Years' War.

1

Taken along Warriors' Paths

On a hilltop north of Shamokin, overlooking the main Iroquoian Warriors' Path to the south, two posts stood in the 1730s, each topped with a skull. These were defiant Catawba historical markers, countering the region's numerous Iroquoian painted posts that boasted of victorious raids that had yielded prisoners and scalps. In this case, Catawba captives, already far from home, had turned on their Iroquois captors, killed at least two of them, and, though in the territory of their enemy, had taken the time to erect this mocking memorial. It is equally interesting that the Iroquois, who claimed intimidating power over the Delaware and Shawnee inhabitants of this locality, chose not to take down this symbol of their own vincibility.[1] The skull-topped posts at Shamokin are gone, as are the prisoners and scalps from innumerable raids that were even less evident to the intruding white keepers of longer-lasting records.

Inflicting casualties is a universal military method, and suffering no casualties in return may be a widespread attending prayer, but Indians were unlike Europeans in deliberately shaping their warfare to take captives and scalps, while avoiding all casualties themselves. Whether in sieges, battles, or raids, the tactical purpose was usually to surprise and segregate a portion of the opposing group, to overwhelm them, and to measure victory in the number of prisoners and scalps taken. Particularly after the introduction of effective firearms, this martial objective precluded any participation in suicidal frontal assaults of the sort that Europeans undertook to gain control of a stockade or battlefield. Indians seldom conducted large-scale campaigns of extermination; in such campaigns, captives could be taken only at the end of the final fight because warriors were individually responsible for guarding their own prisoners. Iroquoians and Algonquians developed and displayed their martial skills most frequently through their surprise raids on distant enemies. The small scale of most of these raids, and the long distances traveled, allowed for an endemic hostility that seldom constituted a major threat to either their communities or their wide-ranging hunters.[2]

Captives and scalps were tangible proofs of success that enhanced individual and communal martial reputations and built solidarities among warrior cohorts, tribes, and alliances. Missionary David Zeisberger reported that an eighteenth-century Delaware would immediately become a captain if he "has the good fortune not to lose a man of his troop in six or seven engagements and to bring scalps and prisoners to the camp."[3] If there were losses, and these were not matched by at least an equal number of prisoners, the blameworthy leader would not lead again. According to one Shawnee chief, any warrior hoping to become a war chief needed to prove himself by participating in twelve raids into enemy territory, successfully leading four of these. An attack was considered successful only if the entire raiding party returned unhurt and brought back at least one scalp or prisoner.[4] These Shawnee also believed that the Catawba had been their enemies since creation, and some older Shawnee remembered that the Catawba had deserted the Indian alliance in the Yamasee War (1715–17), bringing on a defeat that drove the Savannah branch of the Shawnee into exile from the river that still bears their name.[5] These were Delaware and Shawnee customs, but the route to the status of warrior chief was not fundamentally different from that required by most of their Indian allies and enemies.

Scholars have argued (at least for the Six Nations of the Iroquois) that these attacks were intended to yield captives who would restore populations ravaged by warfare or disease. Certainly in the Iroquois tradition of the "mourning war," the Catawba practice of "crying blood," and the Delaware intent to capture a replacement for a fallen relative, it was imperative to take captives to avenge deaths and, on the decision of female elders or grieving relatives, either to torture such captives to death or, increasingly, to adopt them in order to replace those lost. To replace warriors who fell in battle, the most prized captives were enemy warriors, who either provided a cathartic spectacle of endurance unto death or fulfilled their adoptive role in the place of the fallen. Since Indian warriors fought by a code "in which running was preferable to dying, but dying was preferable to surrendering,"[6] a live enemy warrior was a rare prize. Younger male adoptees could be favored, and even rise to prominence. For instance, Mohawk chief Theyanoguin (Chief Hendrick) was an adopted Mohegan captive, and a young Catawba captive, Tanaghrisson, rose on the Ohio peripheries of Iroquoia as the Half-King.[7] It seems clear that captured warriors were too few to expand populations significantly, or to restore the large numbers lost to major epidemics.

It might be argued that the endemic raids also captured women and children and that they could better adapt to the host communities. However, the largest additions to the population of the Six Nations in the seventeenth century had not come from endemic minor raids on distant enemies, but in two other ways. Successful major wars against nearer rivals, the Iroquoian-speaking Huron, Petun, Neutral, and Erie tribes, destroyed these communities completely and brought thousands of captives who became Iroquois at least to some degree. The other significant method of population recovery was the adoption of entire peoples who were refugees, like the Susquehanna and Tuscarora; this provided major expansions of Iroquois communities, including warriors anxious to battle against old enemies and to prove themselves within their new Six Nations communities.[8] The results of raids need not conform to their initial purposes or subsequent justifications, but it is very hard to see that major additions to population were even hoped for in such honor raids, though losses of people in raids certainly provoked revenge.

Europeans sought to expand, channel, and pervert Indian belligerence for their own purposes, though long-range raids continued to be deliberate, even defiant, demonstrations of Indian independence in war and diplomacy. The Spanish, French, and English had all encouraged slaving raids that were remembered by peoples who came to inhabit Allegheny country in the eighteenth century. The range of such slave trading can be illustrated by the Pawnee. From their homeland in the center of the continent, they were taken as slaves toward both coasts. Without ever seeing Pawnee country, Spanish colonials acquired Pawnee slaves from Indian neighbors.[9] As early as 1670, the Illinois were capturing many Pawnee and Sioux and trading them to the Ottawa for French trade goods, and the Ottawa, in turn, sold these slaves to the French, as did the Illinois directly.[10] This trade led the Canadians to refer to all Indian slaves as *panis*. Pawnee slaves were also known among the English and the Iroquois before 1760, and they both adapted readily to owning *panis* thereafter.[11]

The English had earlier pursued the largest known Indian slave trade north of the Rio Grande. Equipping Westo allies as slave raiders in the 1670s, the white settlers of South Carolina had acquired slave laborers for local plantations and for sale to West Indian buyers. As the Westo grew stronger, the Carolinians armed a rival group of Shawnee refugees, who had been expelled from their Ohio homeland by Iroquois attacks. These "Savannah" defeated the Westo and sold these slavers into English colonial slavery.[12] English interest in Indian slavery waned after the Tuscarora (1711–13) and Yamasee (1715–17) Wars demonstrated the dangers of enslaving Indians and confirmed a growing English colonial preference for African slaves, who had no armed kin nearby. Although by the 1750s slaving was not part of the English interest in Indian raids, a South Carolina Assembly, desperate for volunteers in the midst of the Cherokee War (1759–61), reverted to earlier methods by decreeing that all Indian captives became the slaves of their captors.[13]

French interest in Indian slaves had also faded by the 1730s in Louisiana and in the Illinois settlements, but not in New France, where Indian slaves remained a source of labor, and *panis* were part of French diplomatic and legal settlements in the *pays d'en haut*.[14] As late as 1748, Canadian settlement of intercultural murder cases involved compensation paid in *panis*.[15] The persistent Indian slave trade into Canada, the continuing social and legal status of Indian slavery in the English colonies, and the inheritance of slaving and raiding among the Iroquois, Shawnee, and Delaware would all affect the martial culture of those who resettled in the upper Ohio Valley.

Decades after European interest in Indian slaves had lessened, English and French geo-political ambitions and fears revived their encouragement of Indians raids. Canadian governors were consistent supporters of southern raids by Canadian Iroquois communities for at least three reasons: these raids deflected Iroquois aggression away from New France and its allies; the raids reinforced the kinship between Kahnawake Iroquois and their Six Nations relatives in New York, a kinship that helped insulate New France from attacks; and most importantly, these raids disrupted the relations of the Six Nations of the Iroquois with the Catawba and the Cherokee, all of whom were supposed allies of the English.[16] This provocative aspect of Canadian policy would be a harbinger of the Seven Years' War in Allegheny country.

Canadians had long since developed another trade in captives, the purchase of white New England captives from Indian allies. By offering bounties on scalps and prisoners, Canadian governors encouraged their allies, particularly those who lived in the "converted villages" around Montreal, to join campaigns or launch their own raids against neighboring English colonies. In addition to this official traffic in captives who often became prisoners of war, individuals and religious orders "redeemed" white captives from Indian mission villages as a charity and a source of labor needed when war took so many Canadian men from their farms for extended militia service. Those redeemed became the equivalent of indentured servants, working off what might be the inflated price of their redemption with years of labor, or through ransom paid by their relatives, parishes, or even some colonial governments.[17] This traffic in white captives was not evident in the western borderlands before 1753, but would frame the treatment of numerous captives taken there subsequently.

Canadian Iroquois could combine their quest for Catawba or Cherokee captives with the incidental capture of saleable whites taken on the way home from long-range raiding. For instance, a French-speaking young white woman arrived in Philadelphia from Trois-Rivières after a brief captivity with "French Indians" and a decade of servitude to a Canadian master who had purchased her. Known as either Elizabeth Steal or Tell, she reported being one of three young girls who had been captured from her aunt's school somewhere on the Pennsylvania frontier in the early 1740s. In 1753 her Canadian master received a letter, which neither he nor she could read. It revealed that her mother had somehow located her missing daughter through Albany traders. After much pleading, Elizabeth's master freed her, and Canadian governor Ange Duquesne de Menneville, Marquis Duquesne, gave her a pass and a *métis* guide, allowing her to retrace the path of the letter as far as Albany, and her guide to do a little spying. There she learned that her mother's letter had originally come from Pennsylvania, and she journeyed on, evidently through the charity of strangers. In Philadelphia this French-speaking teenager faced a new challenge that would be shared by many returning captives. She failed to find either her remarried mother, whose new surname she could not remember, or any relatives of her dead father. The *Pennsylvania Gazette*, in sympathetically reporting her story in October of 1754, wondered "whether she may not be mistaken with regard to the Province she was made Prisoner from, which is not to be wondred at, considering how young she was when taken."[18] She may well have become, once again, a servant in a household of strangers.

British colonial authorities encouraged honor raids as adjuncts to their own campaigns in the Tuscarora War (1711–13), the Yamasee War (1715–17), and the Cherokee War (1759–61).[19] Additionally, Sir William Johnson was far from alone in supporting small-scale honor raids as an outlet for belligerence that might otherwise erupt in more-valued areas. After 1763, some intertribal raiding was still encouraged by the British as a way of reducing and dividing Indians' opposition to white invasion of their lands.[20]

Yet Indian honor raids created many more problems than they solved for British colonial governments, leading some to oppose them entirely. Iroquois heading south down the Warriors' Path expected hospitality and reinforcement from the Delaware and Shawnee living in the Susquehanna Valley. Farther south, in the Shenandoah Valley, a disparate group of Europeans had settled since the 1730s, and Virginia claimed sovereignty over them. Iroquois war parties expected food and sometimes lodging, in friendship if not in tribute, from these new British allies encroaching on their Warriors' Path. Cattle and hogs were the first major cash crops of this frontier economy, and they were also food that could not easily be hidden from hungry Iroquois hunters, who might butcher animals themselves if uncooperative locals refused to offer food. As the value of lands along the Warriors' Path increased, colonial governments were anxious to simplify land acquisition by first supporting and then buying out Iroquois pretensions, and then calling on the Iroquois to evict other resident Indians.

A number of minor incidents had culminated in a striking confrontation in December 1742. A party of twenty-one Onondaga, including war captain Jonnhaty, had been joined by seven Oneida in a raid against the Catawba that autumn. At John Harris's ferry (Harrisburg), they obtained the now-routine magistrate's pass, which entitled them to unmolested travel, and the occasional free meal, in Pennsylvania. When they entered Virginia, they could not find a magistrate to extend their license and, after farmers refused them food, they killed cattle and hogs. As they progressed down the Shenandoah Valley, they were shadowed by a growing number of angered white locals. There are contradictory surviving accounts of who fired first and who fled, but, when the brief encounter was over, eight Virginians and four Iroquois were dead. When the returning Onondaga told their version of the story to Shawnee and Delaware at Great Island above Shamokin, there was very serious talk of war. The Pennsylvania government initiated a diplomatic reconciliation that proved successful, and Virginia sent gifts and apologies.[21]

Although the infamous Treaty of Lancaster of 1744 is rightly remembered as the occasion on which the Six Nations accommodationists sold their dubious title to vast tracts of Allegheny and Ohio lands, thereby disgusting their Shawnee and Delaware allies, the treaty was also an attempt to prevent further clashes between Virginian settlers and the Iroquois along the Warriors' Path. Onondaga chief Canasatego, speaking for the Iroquois, accused the Virginians of violating an earlier agreement that gave the Iroquois free access west of the Blue Ridge Mountains, and therefore the whole of the Shenandoah Valley. They now agreed that the Warriors' Path would run along the foothills of the Allegheny "Great Mountains," which formed the western edge of that wide valley. These colonial governments thus accepted the raids on the Catawba as legitimate, or at least unavoidable, and admitted that earlier English efforts to make peace between the Catawba and the Iroquois had failed completely.[22]

There was bound to be continuing trouble in South Carolina, even if there were fewer serious incidents for a time along the new Warriors' Path. South Carolina's government had not been part of the Lancaster conference, and could not have appreciated the results. Most of the northern raiders came into Carolina in quest of Catawba scalps and prisoners, or they attacked South Carolina's Cherokee trading partners. Attacks on these allies of South Carolina, even when they did not involve direct clashes with colonials, meant the loss of negro or Indian slaves, the disruption of local alliances and trade, and accidental violence. A redefined Warriors' Path only made these raids by northerners easier, and the Carolina government continued its attempts to have them stopped.

A Catawba-Iroquois peace was needed to end these raids, and it proved very difficult to achieve. The Catawba had been reinforced by various Siouan-speaking peoples seeking protection against raiders early in the eighteenth century, and low-level hostilities with the Iroquoians had already lasted for at least three decades. The Catawba heard the "crying blood" of those killed by northern enemies and sought to consolidate their multi-ethnic nation and gain revenge as well as the trophies of battle.[23] If Catawba success against the Six Nations motivated their persistence in this war, it also attracted new northern enemies in quest of the special honor of success against the valiant Catawba. The Catawba's martial reputation also meant that South Carolina governors wanted to secure these allies in the British interest, and end this war between Britain's premiere Indian allies. In 1751, a Catawba delegation of six, led by King Hagler and accompanied by Carolina representative William Bull, finally sailed north to meet the Iroquois at Albany.

Although paid well to be accommodating, the Iroquois remained cautious. They agreed to make peace if the Catawba returned all their Iroquois prisoners within a year. Claiming, disingenuously, that "Nothing now remained, but the mutual Exchange of Pris[oner]s, which was what they always observed in making Peace," the Iroquois imposed an impossible and humiliating requirement that they were never inclined to observe themselves. The white authorities who funded the meeting wanted to believe it was a success, and they celebrated the peace of 1751 in New York and Charleston. The negotiators had not even achieved a truce, for poorly identified northerners, who may have been from the Six Nations alliance or from the Iroquois allies in New France, continued the raids. Young Six Nations warriors may have been bent on proving themselves regardless of what sachems thought they could promise. Only one Iroquois captive was returned with the much smaller and less prestigious Catawba delegation that came north the following year, a small gesture toward a peace that had evaporated even before its concluding ceremonies were performed. Raiding parties from the north only increased in size and peripheral belligerence, and raiding against the Cherokee resumed as well.[24] Once a pattern of raiding was established, it could not be ended by the promises of wise and accommodating sachems.

There were three incidents during 1753, all linked to honor raiding, that reveal much about the raiding, the trading of captives, and the coming of war. Kahnawake raiders came down the Warriors' Path southward to Cherokee country late in the autumn of 1752, just as Canada was preparing to launch its military invasion of Ohio country.[25] Canadian authorities had recently shown particular interest in capturing English traders, who could become profitable additional prizes in honor raids against the British-allied Cherokee (see chapter 2). Yet matters were not quite that simple for the Kahnawake, who long dominated an illicit trade between Canada and Albany that was vulnerable to any intensification of Anglo-French hostilities. According to a Kahnawake trader known as Susanna, interviewed by the Albany Indian Commissioners the next summer, a party of sixty-eight Kahnawake warriors had set off against the Cherokee late the previous year, and had found some in what would later become Kentucky. Shots were exchanged, a Kahnawake was wounded, and Pennsylvania traders who were with the Cherokee were captured.[26] Susanna insisted that the captors had been ridiculed when they returned home, being chided as "old women and Breakers of the Peace." Susanna was reassuring her Albany trading partners, of course, but perhaps all honor raids were not equally honorable, and this one had left one warrior wounded and had taken adult male captives who were linked to a needed illicit trading partner.[27]

The captured traders themselves reported that seven of them had been robbed, stripped, and beaten on 26 January 1753; only James Lowery escaped, naked, and his fellows erroneously presumed that this prominent Pennsylvania trader had frozen to death.[28] Lowery's six companions were taken to Fort des Miamis and, after twenty-seven days in confinement, were sent on to Detroit. Commandant Pierre-Joseph Céloron de Blainville, the veteran frontier commander best known for leading the 1749 expedition to expel English traders from Ohio country, was finally seeing success. He bought two of these captive traders, Jacob Evans and Thomas Hyde, to demonstrate official support for capturing Pennsylvania traders who, finding Ohio country increasingly unsafe, had begun venturing a little farther south. Céloron sent all six of the captives on to Montreal with the returning Kahnawake.[29] The four captives still belonging to the Kahnawake were ransomed and home within eighteen months; Evans and Hyde were sent to France.[30]

The second, and more serious, incident of 1753 involved the capture of six Shawnee warriors in South Carolina. The Catawba had been attracting new enemies from the north, and white South Carolinians had become increasingly nervous about possible violence against themselves. In May of 1751, four white people had been killed by Shawnee in the geographic center of South Carolina.[31] A "gang of Northern Indians" murdered a white settler within thirty-five miles of Charleston in April of 1753, prompting South Carolina's veteran governor, James Glen, to issue a proclamation offering £100 to anyone who captured or killed any of those involved in the murder. The proclamation also offered £50 to those who captured or killed any "other Northern Indians who shall come into our Settlements after the Expiration of Three Months, unless such Indians shall have in their Company some white Man, and be coming down on any Business or Message to this Government." Late in May the militia had been called out again after a band of northerners had attacked local Indians. The son of a prominent Creek ally, Red Coat King, was killed early in June by northern Indians, "the usual Token being left near the dead Body i.e. an Eagle's feather and some Beads." Amid rising fears, word arrived that the French were launching their major military initiative into the Ohio Valley, and were urging Indians there to turn against the English.[32]

Six Shawnee warriors, from distant Wakitomica (Waketummaky, Lapitchuna) on the idyllic Muskingum River in Ohio country,[33] would be caught in this fear-drenched South Carolina environment. More Shawnee had become pro-British during the previous decade,[34] though they had also accumulated a great deal of resentment against the Six Nations of the Iroquois. This raid was independent of, and contrary to, the lame Six Nations' truce with the Catawba. After "a pipe dance" that included ample liquor, the party set off with horses and several rifled guns, evidence of adaptability, status, and prosperity. The expedition was also armed with a bundle, which featured a belt of black wampum and prized buffalo-hair "prisoner ties" for expected captives. The bundle included silver bracelets and a silver cross, currency that suspicious English interrogators would construe as marks of French influence.[35] The leader was Itawachcomequa (the Pride), who had been prominent in a pro-French 1745 attack on Pennsylvanian traders.[36] By early 1752, however, he had become pro-English, and his war party of 1753 was later called "the Flower of their Nation for Courage and Activity," by Pennsylvania's lieutenant governor, James Hamilton, and leaders of the pro-English faction, who were sorely needed in Ohio country during the rapidly developing confrontation with the French.[37] A Shawnee spokesman would later refer to Itawachcomequa as "a noted Man among the Shawonese, a great Warrior and a true Friend to the English."[38]

Although seven of the Shawnee warriors turned back during the difficult mountain journey they had taken because of recent incidents along the Warriors' Path, the persevering six reached the southeastern corner of South Carolina within about six weeks (see map 1). Thirty South Carolina militiamen surrounded these six Ohio Shawnee found in a farmhouse near the Salkehatchie River. The Shawnee agreed to surrender their weapons and be conducted to the governor "under the Care and Protection of a Party of our Militia, rather than as Prisoners of War, that they may go without Fear" as the sympathetic Lieutenant Governor William Bull explained in sending them on to Governor Glen in Charleston. Bull added, "I have treated them kindly, for which they seem very thankful, and told them they are a going to hear your Excellency's Talk."[39] This "capture" was understood by the Shawnee as a negotiation, for Shawnee warriors did not surrender to whites; none would be captured by the British Army, colonial regiments, or militia in the twelve years of war after 1754. If these Shawnee had shown any belligerence at all, the militia would have killed and scalped them, receiving the same bounty as if they had brought in live captives who could threaten both their lives and their explanations.

Itawachcomequa and his companions might have expected to fare well because they understood some English, regarded themselves as British allies, surrendered their weapons without inflicting any casualties, were supported by a lieutenant governor's sympathetic letter, and were escorted to a diplomatic meeting during Governor Glen's declared three-month period of grace. The initial reception in Charleston was not encouraging. In an item widely reprinted in the British colonies, the *South Carolina Gazette* of 18 June 1753 described "some Northern Indians, lately taken and brought to Town by Capt. David Godin's Company of Militia," hoping other militias would act similarly and "soon clear the Country of these French and Northern Indians that have for some Years past infested this Province."[40] Glen immediately ordered the Shawnee to prison and then, together with his council, questioned them individually. The council heard that Itawachcomequa was still willing to declare, "I am a Friend to all the People here. I am a Shavanah and loyal to the English." The youngest Shawnee, a teen captured with his father, offered the frankest statement of the warriors' purpose. The youth admitted that they had come to capture Catawba prisoners, but had taken none. He also pointedly noted that white people had promised his group freedom if they went to talk with the governor. Another Shawnee prisoner said that the entire war party had been drunk when they set out and that some had turned back when they sobered. Other prisoners' explanations less wisely included their intended visit to pro-French Shawnee who had recently migrated to live among the Creek.[41]

Strangers captured by chance during peacetime were judged worth exploiting, rather than simply setting them free. In deciding to hold the Shawnee in prison, Glen was violating Indian understandings of hospitality, diplomacy, and dignity. Indian hospitality between allies, who were regarded as fictive kin, presumed at least a fair sharing of the host's resources and conditions, during visits that might extend for weeks or months. Diplomacy presumed that those who were invited to hear the governor talk, and who had displayed good faith in surrendering their weapons, had even more reason to expect good treatment; diplomats were to be respected, and violations had prompted wars. Indian dignity was thoroughly violated by close confinement, which was regarded as worse than death.[42] Incarceration was the most humiliating outcome possible for warriors who had traveled so far to confirm and enhance their reputations. The Carolina governor and council admitted that "there are not any positive Proof that they had actually killed any of our People," but kept the Shawnee in jail for nearly a month before deciding what to do with them. Although apparently ignorant of the degradation he was inflicting, Glen did voice concern to the Commons House of Assembly two weeks later: "I should be sorry that any of them should die in Prison, [and] I think the sooner we get rid of them, the better."[43]

Early in October, after the six Shawnee had been imprisoned for nearly four months, Glen wrote James Hamilton, Pennsylvania's lieutenant governor, sending along two of the captives. Glen asked Hamilton to invite Ohio Shawnee headmen down to Philadelphia or to send "some proper Person" home with the two returnees to explain the terms under which the other four would be released.[44] Glen's terms included having the Shawnee return all "our friendly Indians or Mustee Slaves," noting that northern raiders were carrying off "such of our Slaves as had the least Tincture of Indian Blood in them." The six Shawnee had become prisoners without being charged; four of them were now held hostage by a British colonial government willing to act on the too widely shared assumption that one alien could be punished for the behavior of inadequately identified others.

Within two months, news of their brethren's capture had reached the Ohio Shawnee. Although there is no record of Shawnee efforts to recover captured warriors, the Shawnee regarded this entrapment and incarceration in peacetime as outrageous.[45] In September of 1753, at conferences with uninformed and evasive Virginians and Pennsylvanians at Winchester and Carlisle respectively, Shawnee and their Delaware neighbors asked those governments to intervene to secure the release of the Shawnee captives in Charleston. The Ohio Mingo leader Scarouady, who regarded the Shawnee raid, the imprisonments, and these diplomatic petitions all as violations of the Iroquois diplomatic overlordship that he and Tanaghrisson were trying to embody, threatened to go to Charleston himself to retrieve those he regarded as errant Shawnee subordinates. Perhaps Scarouady should have been allowed to proceed, but he was persuaded not to leave the Ohio Valley at this critical time. The lieutenant governors of Pennsylvania and Virginia did write Glen, asking about these troubling Shawnee.[46]

Before the ship carrying the two returning Shawnee had left Charleston for Philadelphia, three of the four remaining Shawnee hostages escaped from the watch house "by cutting out one of the Iron Barrs of a Window, and bending two others." Outside assistance, perhaps even help from the Ohio Valley, was never identified; inside connivance to be rid of a problem that now included at least one very sick prisoner was never admitted. The South Carolina council curtly explained to Virginia's lieutenant governor, Robert Dinwiddie, "through the Negligence of the Centinel [they] escaped out of the Prison, and as they have not been retaken, have[,] as we suppose, bent their Course to their own Country."[47] At least publicly, Governor Glen did not give up easily, offering a few more details when he sought the help of Creek chiefs in recovering his hostages. Again Glen offered the European perspective on imprisonment as a legitimate and common precaution, and emphasized that the prisoners had been well treated, and given good beef and corn or bread every day and rum "very often." Despite these kindnesses, Glen complained, three had decided to escape, and one of these died in the woods soon afterward. The casualty was Itawachcomequa, who had died either in the woods or in jail. Glen asked the Creek to inquire about the escapees, especially among the recently transplanted Shawnee community, and to return the fugitives to him. He projected his own values upon the lone Shawnee hostage who remained in custody and may have been ill, claiming that he "thought it dishon[o]urable to go and still continues here."[48]

The two Shawnee whom Glen sent to Philadelphia arrived in mid-November, and, after a month's delay because one of them had "a bloody Flux," they were escorted home by John Patten, an established Indian trader and recently returned captive of the French in Ohio country, in Canada, and in France.[49] Patten's assignment was to see these Shawnee through Pennsylvania, and then pick up Andrew Montour and George Croghan, frontier traders, brokers, and translators. Once this party had crossed the Allegheny Mountains, they were to proceed to Shannopintown at the forks of the Ohio to find Scarouady and Tanaghrisson. Although Tanaghrisson was the Iroquois Confederacy's "Half-King" in the region, these two Mingo leaders were increasingly on their own because the confederacy confirmed its declared neutrality and refused to resist the new French intrusions in the upper Ohio Valley in 1753. As he had done before, Hamilton deliberately preferred to work through these Mingo leaders, hoping to consolidate a useful Iroquoian dominance analogous to that which the Six Nations had claimed over Pennsylvania lands they had previously sold from under Shawnee and Delaware inhabitants. The two Mingo chiefs were to receive Hamilton's formal message and a validating string of wampum, and then the whole party was to proceed down the Ohio to Lower Shawnee Town at the mouth of the Scioto River.[50] Scarouady and Tanaghrisson would conduct an Iroquoian-style meeting with principal Shawnee leaders, conveying the messages of Glen and Hamilton with appropriate dignity. Then the Mingo and Pennsylvanians would release the two healthy and reclothed Shawnee captives in return for compliance with Glen's terms.

A grateful Shawnee community would supposedly witness the continuing strength of the Iroquoian Covenant Chain, give up their captives taken in Carolina, and confirm their own loyalty to the English.

Along with this proposed drama, Hamilton secretly instructed Patten to measure the road from Carlisle to Shannopintown carefully, in order to see whether this increasingly contested site was within the Pennsylvania grant. Reliable information concerning Ohio country had become scarce that year because the fort-building French had discouraged, diverted, expelled, or arrested all Pennsylvanian traders. So Hamilton instructed Patten to: observe the numbers, arms, and loyalties of the Mingo, Delaware, Shawnee, Wyandot, and Miami; discover what the French and the Virginians had been doing in the region; gather details of the whiskey trade and traders; and discreetly investigate the insolvent George Croghan as manager of substantial presents sent to the Indians by the Governments of Virginia and Pennsylvania. Patten was to keep a journal, but destroy it if he became sick or in danger.[51] Returning these Shawnee was intended to provide an amateur Pennsylvania spy with camouflage in what had quite suddenly become hostile country.

Hamilton's expectations met deflating reality as soon as Patten and the two Shawnee caught up with Croghan and Montour, who were already at Shannopintown. Croghan had just learned that George Washington's quixotic diplomatic mission to warn the French away from the upper Ohio Valley had failed, and that the new French Fort Le Boeuf was soundly built, fully provisioned, and, even in winter, was manned by about a hundred soldiers and fifty workmen. The French had also completed Fort Presqu'île and were expected to build another fort at Logstown in the spring. Croghan later claimed that between Shannopintown and Logstown he had been forced to spend £46 on gifts for the disgruntled pair of Shawnee he was taking home.[52] Patten and his enlarged party proceeded, less than triumphantly, down the Ohio Valley only as far as Logstown, where Shawnee warriors seized both Croghan and Montour, on whose heads the French had recently fixed a good price. However, upon recognizing their two returning friends, the Shawnee sacrificed the French bounty and released Croghan and Montour. The next day a party of seventeen Canadian marines camped nearby and promptly captured John Patten while he was spying on them. Tanaghrisson stormed into the French officer's tent and gained the inept spy's release.[53] In Croghan's self-interested retelling, nothing could be done for the next ten days because the Shawnee were drunk. Then the French concluded their inebriating visit with a one-day council, distributed presents, and called on the locals to stand aside while their "Father" dealt with the British, whom "he will not suffer to live or tread on this River Ohio."[54]

Patten's group had spent a humiliating twelve days in Logstown before they could finally begin their ceremony to return the two captive Shawnee warriors. Croghan delivered the official messages, which included confirmation of the escape of the three other Charleston captives from jail, and heard a soothing initial response from Tanaghrisson, supposedly on behalf of the silent Shawnee and Delaware. The most important speech of this week-long council was a considered reply to Hamilton and Dinwiddie, delivered by Tanaghrisson together with a belt and eight strings of wampum, and endorsed by seven Mingo and Delaware chiefs.[55] These chiefs agreed with the general messages received from the governors, with the pointed exception of a suspicious addition that would have benefited both Croghan and Patten by proposing land grants for traders whose goods had earlier been stolen. The Indian reply had obvious omissions. They did not thank the governors for the return of the two Shawnee, did not reciprocate by returning any captives, did not pledge any legation to Charleston, and did not indicate any proposed restraint on raiding into the Carolinas.[56] It is also noteworthy that no Shawnee endorsed this message, though the Delaware names indicate that declining to do so was not merely diplomatic deference to the Iroquois. The Pennsylvania government promptly hid Patten's diary, since lost, and the assembly rejected his unwelcome map of Pennsylvania's troubled frontier.[57]

Meanwhile, angry Ohio Shawnee were going to war over an incident that historians have routinely ignored or underestimated. News that Ohio Shawnee had proclaimed a "perpetual war" against the English was first recorded by Canadian lieutenant Joseph-Gaspard Chaussegros de Léry, a sixteen-year veteran of frontier war and diplomacy who was at the Lake Erie outpost of Chatakoin on New Year's Day, 1755. Over a drink, Huron courier Le Glorieux explained that the Shawnee were furious with the English for imprisoning several of their warriors in Charleston, and had distributed war belts, including one to the Huron.[58] Léry was puzzled at this reversal of the recent warming trend in Shawnee-English relations and, like historians subsequently,[59] could not believe that a distant imprisonment of a few warriors could ignite a war from Ohio country.

Yet this incident was precisely what Indian diplomats and captives insisted upon when asked the origin of the Ohio Indian war against

British America. Trader John Kennedy had already heard the story before he was captured in July of 1754.[60] Christian Delaware Moses Tattamy, in providing sympathetic Quakers with an account of Indian complaints in 1756, started with:

> In the beginning of the present Troubles & soon after I receiv'd Intelligence that the Shawanese in Revenge for some of their People being put into Prison by the Virginians had begun to commit Hostilities in Virginia & invited the Delaware to join them. Several of the young Warriors of the Delaware Nation who being driven from the Forks of Delaware now lived at Allegheny join'd with them & strengthened them without consulting their Chiefs. By the Persuasion of these and the Shawanese most of their Nation were soon brought over & induced to turn their Hatchet against their Brethren the English & the French being there & also declaring against the English they joined with them.[61]

Tattamy might be forgiven for presuming the Shawnee had been provoked by Virginians rather than Carolinians, given the course of the Shawnee war, but for him the imprisonment explained the revenge. Mohawk sachem Little Abraham presented the same Shawnee explanation clearly, with no Shawnee present, when he addressed a Pennsylvania conference in the spring of 1757.[62]

At the crucial Easton peace conference of October 1758, the bold Oneida orator Saghughsuniunt (Thomas King) reminded the English that "you gave the first Offence; For in Time of Profound Peace, some of the Shawanese passing through South Carolina to go to War with the[ir] Enemies, were taken up and put in Prison; ... and one who was an Head Man of that Nation, lost his Life, and the others were severely used." The eloquent Mingo Ackowanothio reinforced the argument, blaming French priests for seducing the Shawnee to that side of the war, but insisting that this had been possible only because the Shawnee were "wrong'd in Carolina, and Imprisoned, and had their Chief hanged or put to death in a cruel manner."[63] Even in 1764, during what the Ohio Shawnee considered a continuation of the same war, they told the British once again: "That it is altogether yr own Faults, formerly when a Number of our Nations was going to War agt our Enemies the Catabas and was oblig'd to travel through your Country, then you laid Violence on some of our Warriors & killed them."[64] For Indian diplomats justifying the Shawnee war against the English, and fixing the blame on the latter, the captivity in Charleston was their consistent explanation.

It was not only clever and self-interested Indian diplomats who told the English that the Charleston captivity had provoked the Ohio Shawnee to war. Two Shawnee warriors captured by the Cherokee in 1757, and interrogated by Pennsylvanian officers at Fort Lyttleton, were additional voices with exactly the same understanding of events. When asked why the Shawnee and Delaware were attacking the English, captured Shawnee warrior Wauntaupenny answered clearly, "by Reason of their People's being taken and imprisoned by the white People in Carolina." Succomabe, a Chickasaw who had lived with the Shawnee for about three years before being captured along with Wauntaupenny, was interrogated separately. Although the Shawnee had been at peace when he had joined them, "some time after he came to them, they concluded on a War, & the Reason whereof was, Some of the Shawonese were taken in Carolina and put in Prison."[65] The assumption that the captivity was an intolerable violation of Indian mores, and an entirely adequate provocation for war, was obvious to the Huron, Mohawk, Oneida, Mingo, Chickasaw, and Shawnee. It was also eventually admitted even by George Croghan, in private. In his 1759 survey of the western Indians, he said of the Shawnee: "They consist of about three hundred fighting Men [who] were steady in the British Interest all last War, but inveterate Enemies this, owing to some of their People being put in Goal [*sic*] at Charles Town, the chief Man of the Party (a Man more particularly attached to the British Interest than any other in the Nation) Dead."[66]

The confinement of six Shawnee had much more impact on the coming war than did the capture of six Pennsylvania traders and their detention in Canada. In September of 1754, while some relatives of Itawachcomequa were pledging peace and receiving condolence gifts from the Pennsylvania government,[67] others were attacking the Carolina settlement of Buffalo Creek on South Carolina's Broad River. The raiders returned without casualties and with trophies to distribute; they had killed and scalped sixteen recently established white settlers, and thirteen others were missing and presumed captured. Carolinians could not identify the attackers in what they considered the unprovoked "Buffalo Creek Massacre," but the Cherokee reported that the raiders had been Shawnee.[68] The Shawnee did not join a French war as bloodthirsty opportunists, as has been too easily presumed, and the Shawnee would disappoint the French when asked to participate in ventures not seen as part of their own war of revenge.[69] A prisoner of the Delaware reported in 1756 that the Shawnee were then being led by Itawachcomequa's relative, the Delaware war captain Kageshquanohel (the Pipe).[70] The Shawnee had begun what would become six decades of intermittent battle with the "Long Knives," a contest sustained by new grievances and mutual atrocities but one that had been triggered by the Charleston imprisonments of 1753.

Less is known about linked incidents later in 1753 that became part of Virginia's march to war in the Ohio Valley. In October, Thomas Cooper left several children at home alone on his farm on the South Branch of the Potomac River. The children heard their twelve-year-old brother yell twice, but neither they nor a search party found anything except an undecipherable note left on a piece of birch bark stuck in a forked stick beside a path. Indian traders could not read it, but claimed to know that it was from "French Indians."[71] Not long thereafter Robert Foyle, his wife, and five children were killed and scalped in their cabin about seventy miles farther west, where for two years they had been developing one of the first Virginian farms near the Monongahela River.[72] Before hearing of the Foyles' murders, George Washington had made inquiries about the Cooper boy while on his diplomatic mission to Fort Le Boeuf. He learned that a party of northern Indians had passed through the Delaware-Mingo town of Kuskuski, with the Cooper boy and white scalps (presumably those of the Foyles). Jacques Legardeur de Saint-Pierre, commanding at the new French Fort Le Boeuf, admitted "that a Boy had been carried past ... but pretended to have forgot the Name of the Place that the Boy came from & all the Particulars, tho' he Question'd him for some Hours as they were carrying him past."[73] On his way home, Washington met a group of about twenty agitated warriors, who had just canceled their raid southward after coming across the scalped bodies of the Foyles, dead for some time, eaten at by animals, and scattered around what had been their farmyard. This war party had turned back, fearing that they might be attacked by white avengers, and they blamed the Ottawa for the killings.[74]

The captured Cooper boy and the murdered Foyles would become martyrs in the Virginia lieutenant governor's attempt to rouse a reluctant people to fight the French over distant Ohio lands claimed by prominent Virginians, including himself, through the Ohio Company. Dinwiddie, presuming support from the Virginia House of Burgesses, had already commissioned George Washington and William Trent to raise two companies of soldiers for the Ohio Valley. He told the Burgesses and the council, on 14 February 1754, of the capture of Pennsylvania traders on the Ohio River, but doubtlessly realized the limited appeal of fighting to avenge Pennsylvanian trading rivals whose pacifist government refused to avenge itself: "Add to the aforementioned unjustifiable insults of the French, the cruel and barbarous murder, in cool blood, of a whole family of the dominion, man, wife, and five children, no longer ago than last month; and very lately, a poor man, on the south branch of Potowmack, robbed of his son. These depredations were said to be done by the French Indians; but, if I be rightly informed, some of the French Subjects always go with the Indians on these Incursions, and are both Privy to, and Instigations of their Robberies and Murders." Dinwiddie was just beginning an appeal that included more extravagant rhetoric of hypothetical rapes and real murders.[75] Dinwiddie's hyperbole was unrestrained by any concern for who the killers, captors, or victims had been. We cannot know what happened at the Foyles' farm late in 1753, but random or provoked violence was increasingly likely between Indians heading for war and settlers resenting or refusing to provide the hospitality that seemed like extortion on the farms they were struggling to build along warpaths they did not understand.

These incidents of 1753 reflected and exacerbated rising tensions between Indians and settlers, but they were not the only types of intercultural entanglements that resulted from Indian honor raids. In March of 1754, an Onondaga search party was in Schenectady, New York, looking for two captured Catawba women who had escaped. These Onondaga were quick to point out that the women had been captured five years earlier, long before the Iroquois-Catawba truce. The Onondaga had tracked their escapees down the Mohawk Valley and, suspecting that they were headed for Albany and New York, asked the Albany Commissioners for Indian Affairs to "order, that no sloop takes them in, and if you hear of them, that you will confine them, till the Govr. meets with the Five Nations."[76] Since the Catawba and the Onondaga were both British allies, both escapees and pursuers could ask for help. In this case, the commissioners were able to reply that they had not seen the captives, and suggested that they had likely escaped overland through the Susquehanna Valley.

Later that year, the commissioners were petitioned by a dozen Cherokee who had just escaped from the Canadian Iroquois at Kahnawake. In this case, there was no hesitation in supporting the Cherokee allies who had accomplished the largest escape of the entire generation. The commissioners gave them a travel license, a guide, and a letter exhorting all to help them, and by early in 1755 these Cherokee had reached Philadelphia. There they were given lodging, clothing, and an escort as far as John Harris's place, from which they could make their way home down the Warriors' Path.[77]

The English would not stay entirely ignorant of the raiding between their allies during the next decade. In September of 1755, Virginia militiamen halted a small party of Seneca returning through the Shenandoah Valley with Catawba scalps and prisoners. After two days of escorted travel, fighting erupted when the Virginians sought to disarm the Seneca. Two Catawba captives regained their freedom here, but a militiaman and two Seneca were killed and a young Seneca captured. "This gave great offence, and the more so as it was upon the Warriors road and we were in perfect Peace with our Brethren."[78] The English seldom witnessed the conflict between their allies quite as directly as Quaker trader James Kenny did a few years later. A Mingo raiding party, returning through Fort Pitt with Cherokee scalps and prisoners, displayed an English medal taken from one of the killed Cherokee. Kenny also recognized one of the Cherokee captives, "being a Tall Spair fellow who had been out this way, helping ye English a few years ago & was known by some of ye Soldiers here who Spoke to him."[79] No one dared to intervene, though it was thought that one of the captives would soon be burned to death.

The Warriors' Path, so confidently rerouted in 1744, had again become clogged with incidents that proved it could not be insulated, despite considerable efforts to do so. In the supposedly peaceful year of 1753, seven Pennsylvania traders were captured in a Kahnawake raid on the Cherokee, six Shawnee were captured in South Carolina, seven members of the Foyle family were killed, and young Cooper was captured in Allegheny borderlands. The capture of Pennsylvania traders confirmed French belligerence in a trade war, and the Pennsylvania government responded characteristically, seeking to redeem the captives but avoiding retaliation. The incident involving the Shawnee raiding party displayed the high martial value placed on taking enemy captives, the warriors' abhorrence at being taken captive by allies, and a misguided British propensity to take Indian hostages. The incident prompted revenge, launching a Shawnee-British colonial war that would be bitter, if intermittent, and continue long after the colonial period. The killing and capture of Virginians prompted no sustained hunt for the survivor or the culprits, but became an emotive part of selling the coming Virginian war for the upper Ohio Valley.

2

Taking Traders, 1745–54

The Kahnawake capture of six Pennsylvania traders in 1753 may have been incidental to their traditional raid on the Cherokee, but these captors had reason to hope for gratitude from the governor of Canada. Increasing numbers of Canadian and Pennsylvanian traders, backed by strikingly different levels and kinds of government support, were competing in Ohio country during the 1740s for the furs and deerskins gathered by Shawnee, Miami, Delaware, Mingo, and Wyandot communities. There were many signs that the Pennsylvanians were winning the contest, with a better supply of goods at lower cost. The Canadian traders, who included some post commanders, had every personal reason to support their government's new assertion of sovereignty in the Allegheny-Ohio Valley. The Canadians encouraged Indians to plunder their rivals, and could offer alternate markets and supplies of European goods as well as effective defensive alliances against retaliation. The Canadians escalated their attack by arresting English traders, by buying traders from Indians willing to capture them, and by funding and organizing an attack on the pro-English trade center at Pickawillany in 1752. The Canadians launched the war on traders, introducing a kind of captivity different from that familiar to Indians in the region.

Most English traders arrived in Allegheny country as outsiders, benefiting from Indian hospitality to strangers and building relationships with their customers by fair dealing and gift exchanges that would gain some the status of fictive kin. Unlike French traders in the upper Ohio Valley and English traders there later, these Pennsylvania traders are not known to have married into Shawnee, Delaware, or Mingo communities before 1765.[1] There were no supporting troops or forts for refuge or supply, like those the French already had at Detroit, Fort des Miamis, and Ouiatenon, and those they intended to build much closer. Traders were always outnumbered by their hosts and could easily become hostages during years of unsettling Anglo-French intrusion and competition. A trader's pack train or canoe convoy, outward-bound with trade goods or returning with the pelts accumulated in months of trading, made a tempting target for robbery, for forcible adjustment of unfavorable terms of trade, or for personal revenge. Given that many trading sessions were reportedly drenched in mind-numbing quantities of alcohol, the possibility of robbery, captivity, or murder was real, but incidents were very rare.

Indians who migrated into the upper Ohio Valley in the first half of the eighteenth century brought assumptions and traditions, as well as personal remembrances and needs, that regulated their relations with European traders. A code of Indian hospitality to peaceable strangers had survived innumerable distressing experiences, and was reinforced by real and fictive cross-cultural kinship with some traders. Hunters wanted dependable sources of guns, gunpowder, and shot as well as liquor and other less-than-essential manufactures, just as traders needed trustworthy suppliers to whom they could advance credit with confidence that they would be repaid in skins and furs. It was equally true that angered and well-armed hunters, long familiar with the ways of the traders, could take swift, effective, and culturally approved reprisals. The murder of Pennsylvania trader John Armstrong and two of his servants early in 1744, after a dispute about repayment of a debt, was a retaliation against a perceived injustice.[2]

The capture and killing of traders during the contentious decade before the war revealed much about changing assumptions. Capturing a trader was not a martial accomplishment, and such captives were not candidates for torture or full adoption. In sharp contrast to the explosion of Shawnee and Delaware attacks on Pennsylvania traders that would initiate a war a decade later, the Indian communities were cautious, even as French encouragement and visible power increased. Indians regarded such captures as declarations of war, and the French found it necessary to induce Indians from outside the region to undertake raids that disrupted their rivals' trade and diplomacy. When a few Ohio Delaware announced that they had joined the Canadians by offering captured Pennsylvania traders, they were effectively selling white captives. How did the taking of traders in peacetime, like the rather different captures of warriors and soldiers, contribute to the coming of war and the complexities of intercultural captivity?

Peter Chartier, a Shawnee-French *métis* trader, can be said to have initiated political violence against traders in the upper Ohio Valley. His father, Martin Chartier, had been one of several renegade Canadians who became part of the trading network of Jacques Le Tort and James

Logan, the factotum of Pennsylvania's proprietary interests and eventually baron of the Susquehanna Valley "Indian trade." On Martin's death in 1718, Peter had inherited both a 300-acre Susquehanna trading post at Conestoga Creek and a crushing debt to Logan. Logan promptly seized all Peter's property, evicted him, and installed an English trader in his place, though Peter continued to trade upriver on credit from his father's old trading post. Peter was following Shawnee kin and customers when he migrated in 1728 to a town on the lower Allegheny River that Pennsylvanians soon called Chartier's Town.[3]

Peter Chartier and his Shawnee kin and neighbors traded with both Pennsylvanians and Canadians, seeking relative independence, fairness in trade, and advantages in diplomacy. His ties with Pennsylvania seemed firm, and his influence was valued. In 1734 Chartier, then about forty, was enthusiastically described as working for the interests of Pennsylvanians and "Very Ready on all acc[oun]tts to Do all the Service hee Can, and as hee has the Shawanise Tongue Very perfectt and [is] well Looktt upon among them, hee may Do a greatt Deale of Good."[4] Six years later, he refused to go to Canada to meet the governor and thwarted a plan to have his Shawnee community move closer to French-controlled Detroit. He acquired property in western Pennsylvania once again in 1740 and was one of twenty-one traders licensed by Pennsylvania for the Indian trade in 1744.[5] This licensing occurred a year after Thomas Penn had already voiced some suspicions about both the Shawnee and Chartier. Nonetheless, Lieutenant Governor George Thomas followed the proprietor's lead in advocating caution, fearing that the Shawnee, "whose perfidious blood partly runs in Chartier's veins," would seek revenge on Pennsylvania traders if Chartier was harmed.[6]

As was becoming customary in most Indian communities that were positioned between English and French trading rivals, there were pro-French clans and factions among the Shawnee of the upper Ohio Valley. By 1731 some Ohio Shawnee had been trading with Canadians, had visited Montreal to seek help against their Mingo rivals, and had reportedly flown a French flag at Chartier's Town. Attempts by Pennsylvania and the Six Nations to call these Shawnee back to Pennsylvania failed completely. Although Chartier declined to visit Montreal in 1740 and was not entirely trusted there, his background led him to be cultivated by Canadian traders and officials as "their countryman."[7]

In April of 1745, a year after Anglo-French warfare had resumed elsewhere, Chartier advertised his decision to join the French before a well-armed gathering of Shawnee, said to number between 400 and 600, including chief Nucheconer (Neucheconno), as well as Missemediqueety (Big Hominy) and Itawachcomequa. These Shawnee stopped Pennsylvania traders James Dunning and Peter Tostee as they and six of their employees were bringing deerskin-laden canoes homeward past Chartier's Town. With a few Canadian witnesses, Chartier claimed to act on the authority of his new captain's commission from the governor of New France. Dunning was an appropriate target; he had traded in the region for two decades and had previously been accused of brutality by some Shawnee.[8] Tostee was another veteran fur trader who was then working for his more successful protégé, George Croghan, himself being threatened with similar arrest and confiscation by a French delegation at Cuyahoga at that very time.[9] The robbery of Tostee and Dunning was not simply a squalid attack on Chartier's trading rivals. This was public political theatre, enacted before Canadian and Shawnee witnesses, assembled by a mixture of curiosity, interest in plundering traders, and support for the pro-Canadian stance Chartier had come to embrace. Given the ambiguities of this contested "country between," and Peter Chartier's own reputation in all quarters, this was a clear and public declaration of hostility and of alliance. The unnamed Canadian witnesses were almost certainly traders, and the event was plausible only as a calculated risk that Canadians would reliably supply trade goods and buy these stolen deerskins and others gathered subsequently.[10]

Robbing Dunning and Tostee also indicated the lack of Shawnee interest in white captives. The eight Pennsylvanians were robbed of goods later valued at £1,600, but were physically unharmed and promptly released. Although the leaders of these Shawnee may have intended such a measured and profitable anti-English gesture before Canadian witnesses, either these leaders had uncharacteristic control over all those attending or none of these people were willing to take the opportunity to avenge any grievances, even against Dunning. The prompt release of the traders is particularly revealing. The Shawnee evidently saw no reason to keep any of these prisoners as adoptees or as hostages, or to send them to the French at Detroit in exchange for presents. Admittedly, such captives could be troublesome, and alien men were of limited value as additions to a Shawnee community. A captive woman could be taught to grow about four times as much corn as she would eat, but additional male hunters did not increase the game available. These Shawnee were not yet selling or giving captives as political trophies or inviting their ransom by Canadians, who could then require the "liberated" to work in order to repay their benefactors. Although this Anglo-French war had enhanced the Abenaki and Iroquois trade in English captives in the St Lawrence River Valley, there was no Canadian farming in the upper Ohio region, and no traffic in white captive labor from there to Detroit, to Illinois country, or to the St Lawrence River Valley. Given different Indian priorities, the five years from 1744 to 1748 might have been years of profitable retribution in Allegheny country, against unfair English traders, and against European frontier farming families who settled on Indian lands. It is valuable to notice that this had not happened. Although Ohio Indians were armed by European traders throughout their war, with the notable exception of Chartier and the Miami of Pickawillany, Indians did not take European traders captive.

Evidently Chartier's Shawnee just missed a lucrative opportunity, for Paul-Joseph Le Moyne de Longueuil, Canadian commandant and trader at Detroit, was anxious to acquire those eight Pennsylvanian captives.[11] Within days of receiving news of their capture, Longueuil sent a party of Canadians to bring in the Pennsylvanians, but by the time the Canadians reached Chartier's Town, none were found. However, Chartier reveled in the validation that these French visitors provided. He planted a French flag, heard Longueuil's martial letter read, and was encouraged by a war dance performed to show support for the French war. Chartier also extracted a barrel of gunpowder from the visitors, whom he maneuvered into staying for two weeks. This Canadian delegation then set out on an extensive Ohio Valley tour, a precursor to the larger and more famous Céloron de Blainville expedition of 1749, visiting Shawnee, Delaware, and Miami settlements on the Allegheny, Ohio, and Miami Rivers, seeking to oust English traders and to support the French, but accomplishing neither.[12]

Perhaps Chartier's challenge to the Pennsylvanians had been easier because the people of Chartier's Town were in the process of migrating westward to join Shawnee kin in the Scioto Valley and to be close enough to trade with the French at Fort des Miamis, though not as close as the French wished. In any case, Chartier's Town was abandoned before the end of 1745. Most of the group followed Nucheconer and settled on the lower Scioto River at Sonnontio. In less than two years, Itawachcomequa and Missemediqueety were at Logstown convincing Pennsylvania representatives that they now repudiated Chartier's attack. By 1753 Itawachcomequa was leading pro-English Shawnee warriors on their fateful journey from Wakitomica to Charleston, South

Carolina. Chartier and his personal following had settled briefly on the Scioto, before he and as many as 185 Shawnee warriors and their families followed an earlier Shawnee migration south to live with the Creeks in what would eventually became Alabama.[13]

The Pennsylvanians initially sought compensation for their robbed traders via the Covenant Chain with the Six Nations. Lieutenant Governor Thomas sent experienced diplomat Conrad Weiser to Onondaga, where he insisted that the Six Nations overlords were responsible for the safety of traders in Ohio country, but he failed to gain any Six Nations support to capture Chartier or to obtain restitution. The Six Nations joined the English and some Shawnee in denouncing Chartier, but did nothing more than mention the matter to the governor of New France, who said he had heard nothing of the attack.[14] Pennsylvanian traders were beginning to learn that Ohio country was effectively beyond their empire or that of the Six Nations, and local diplomacy seemed the only hope for protecting traders.

Chartier's migration southward drastically weakened the French faction among the remaining Ohio Shawnee, and his choice quickly came to be seen as ill-advised. Although the fall of Louisbourg later in the summer of 1745 was far away, and the British blockade of French ports was even more remote, the impact of disrupted shipping on the Indian allies of New France was prompt and severe. The maritime war in the North Atlantic curtailed the delivery of European trade goods to Canada, raised French prices, and shrank French diplomatic gifts to Indian allies. Six Nations legates happened to be in Montreal when news of the fall of Louisbourg arrived, and the governor gave them a noticeably smaller present than expected, "giving for reason that the English had blocked up the River so that their Vassels [*sic*] cd. not get in." Few Ohio Shawnee had been firm French allies, and by 1747 most of them had moved closer to the English in trade and diplomacy, and were associated with both the anti-French Choctaw "Revolt" of 1746–49 and the Wyandot-Ojibwa-Miami "Indian Conspiracy of 1747."[15]

Mounting disillusionment with the French erupted in incidents of Indian violence against Canadian traders throughout the *pays d'en haut*, attacks that the Canadians came to call the "Conspiracy of 1747." Some shift to the English was predictable, but George Croghan repeatedly went beyond his cautious pacifist Pennsylvanian government in encouraging Huron chief Orontony and the Wyandots and Mingos of the Cuyahoga Valley to attack the French. Orontony became a leading figure in a broader alliance, building connections with a disgruntled faction within the French-allied Miami and, less directly, with Ohio Delaware and Shawnee who were also attempting to assemble a broad anti-French alliance involving the Choctaw and the Creeks. Orontony also had allies among dissident Ottawa and Ojibwa farther north.[16] Orontony's Wyandots killed five Canadian traders at Sandusky, and stole furs that undoubtedly were sold through George Croghan. Ojibwa attacked two large fur-laden canoes on Lake Huron, killing all eight Canadians in one canoe, and causing the loss of the fur cargo in the other. In another episode, Saginaw Ottawa led by Agouachimagand killed three Canadian traders. Memeskia, chief of the Piankashaw band of the Miami, led a raid that took temporary control of Fort des Miamis (Kekionga), confiscating most of the trade goods and furs, and capturing eight Canadian traders. This was the only incident in 1747 in which Indians took prisoners, apparently to influence Miami opinion rather than to bargain for French diplomatic concessions or to blunt retaliation.[17]

The ransacking of Fort des Miamis was the boldest of the assaults of 1747, and would have the broadest consequences. Memeskia was a clan chief among the Piankashaw band of the Miami who had lived on the lower Wabash River. He had become well enough known for his interest in trade with the English for them to call him "Old Briton," whereas the French preferred simply to translate his Miami name as "La Damoiselle," the unpredictable dragonfly. In 1745 he and his community had resettled on the upper Maumee River, where the majority of the Miami bands lived and traded with the French at nearby Fort des Miamis. Although the Miami were comparatively independent French allies involved in a large fur trade, Memeskia remained a dissident who favored trade with the English.[18] The fort had been attacked while the commandant and the leading Miami chiefs, Wisekaukautshe (Piedfroid) and Janet, were away at Detroit. Two of the captives were released promptly, and the others after negotiations with the returned Miami chiefs. Most of the stolen trade goods were also returned. Although this attack was bloodless, and tempered by pro-French leaders of the entire Miami tribe, the outspoken Memeskia had risen to prominence through aggression, diplomacy, and economic opportunities that he had found in defiance of the general Miami council.[19]

Like others involved in these attacks and expecting French retaliation, Memeskia moved physically and diplomatically to strengthen his ties with both the Six Nations and the English.[20] Memeskia's community moved about seventy-five miles to the southeast, establishing

Pickawillany and attracting not only the Wea and Piankashaw bands but, over the next three years, also most of the Miami from Kekionga. Memeskia's new town contained forty to fifty warriors by 1749, and 400 families the following year. The diplomatic defenses for this anti-French community were built, less effectively, on the anticipated support of the Six Nations of the Iroquois and the British colonies, a situation that brought sudden prominence for Iroquoian Mingo chiefs Tanaghrisson and Scarouady. However, the Six Nations council resolutely maintained its official neutrality and bluntly refused a request for help from all those Ohio communities that were challenged by the French.[21]

As early as April 1747, the pro-English Mingo and Shawnee had approached Pennsylvania, seeking to add the dissident Miami to their own new alliance.[22] Tanaghrisson and Scarouady had initial success with the Pennsylvanians, who provided substantial presents, and interlocking alliances that were agreed to at the new council fire at Logstown in 1748, where three Miami, including Memeskia's nephew Asepansa (the Raccoon), presumed to sign for the entire Miami nation. The alliance was accompanied by a thriving trade involving as many as 300 Pennsylvania traders in the Ohio region, a third of whom worked for George Croghan.[23] Virginians behind their new Ohio Company also began to show diplomatic interest in the community that Tanaghrisson and Scarouady seemed to represent, though the Virginians sought land more than trade. With what seemed solid English support, a substantial party of Ohio Indians was assembling its own diplomatic identity under Mingo leadership.

The French responses to the attacks of 1747 were both conciliatory and belligerent, and all responses came to involve captives. The prevailing "middle ground" custom for dealing with murders in the *pays d'en haut* began with the offending community offering hostages until the killers could be found. Once some or all of the killers had surrendered, the hostages were released and a negotiation was begun to establish the compensation required to "cover the dead" and gain the release of the killers. Compensation usually included offering Indian war captives, taken or purchased, in order to gain a pardon for the killers. These Algonquian conventions usually meshed fairly well with Iroquoian assumptions about replacing the dead. At Detroit in January 1748, Longueuil began cooperating in this conventional process of accepting gifts, releasing hostages, and pardoning "rebels."[24]

However, the new French governor of New France, Roland-Michel Barrin, Marquis de La Galissonière, refused to treat these killings according to the customs of the *pays d'en haut*. He demanded that all the murderers be sent down to Quebec, and then made his own addition to the customary compensation required: the offending communities were also to provide two British captives for every Frenchman who had been killed.[25] This exorbitant demand can be dismissed as the blunder of an inexperienced and overconfident new governor, but it also reveals both a ready French acceptance of captives as currency and a European distinction between murders that were individual acts of violence and those considered to be coordinated acts of rebellion against a monarch's pretensions. Those seeking to negotiate with the French on behalf of captured Ottawa leader Agouachimand, and two of his men, saw their initial gift of a beaver robe and a slave accepted at Fort Niagara, but the three prisoners were not released there or in Montreal. The Ottawa found their own way to save their kin from incarceration or worse. The outmaneuvered governor later recounted, in resigned wonderment, that, as these prisoners were being escorted from Montreal to Quebec, "those three men, without arms and with manacles on their feet, killed or drowned eight well armed men, and having cut their irons with an axe on the bows of the canoe, escaped ashore and thence into the woods." It would be three years before this and other embarrassments caused by ineffectual French belligerence were buried by the governor's announcement of a general amnesty.[26]

Although most of the violence of 1747 had occurred in the Great Lakes region, the most aggressive and sustained French response was directed farther south, against English traders and their Indian customers in the Ohio Valley, and particularly against those Miami who were leading the defection of their people to the English and thereby endangering both a major French fur trade and a preferred route between Canada and Louisiana. In 1749 the Ministry of Marine met the new threat of the Ohio Company of Virginia by transferring the oversight of all French interests east of Illinois country from Louisiana to Canada.[27] The assertion of this new authority began with a punitive expedition led by an experienced Canadian officer of the *troupes de la marine*, Pierre-Joseph Céloron de Blainville, who had led the successful expedition against the Chickasaws in 1739. His new force consisted of 255 colonial militia, regulars, and Indians. The principal interpreter for the expedition was Philippe-Thomas Chabert de Joncaire (Nitachinon), a renowned trader, interpreter, and broker who had been raised among the Six Nations Seneca; he was the Frenchman with the most influence among the Iroquois.[28] The expedition proceeded from Montreal via Niagara, Lake

Erie, and the upper Allegheny River. Cuyahoga, the only place in this region where Frenchmen had been murdered in 1747, was not even on the itinerary.

At the first council, held at the new Seneca village of Paille Coupée (Broken Straw) on the upper Allegheny, Céloron delivered the Canadian governor's order that all relations with the English were to cease. On 6 August 1749, at abandoned Chartier's Town, the expedition met six Pennsylvania traders bound homeward with 50 horses and 150 packs of furs. Although their packs were inspected, these Pennsylvanians were not robbed, as Dunning and Tostee had been four years earlier; they were merely hurried on their way with a letter to Pennsylvania's lieutenant governor, announcing a prohibition on all English trade on the Ohio River and its tributaries.[29] The next day, at "Queen" Aliquippa's Seneca village near the forks of the Ohio, six more Pennsylvania traders were expelled. Céloron had to be more diplomatic downriver at Logstown, "this village of hostiles," where he found the British and French flags flying side by side. The ten Pennsylvania traders agreed to leave, but "obviously were firmly resolved to do nothing of the kind as soon as our backs were turned."[30]

Céloron's reception farther down the Ohio River at Lower Shawnee Town was more openly hostile. On hearing of the approach of the Canadian force, the inhabitants had hastily erected a stockade, and Joncaire and a companion were fired upon as they approached to arrange a meeting, leaving three bullet holes in the flag they carried. These two were seized by the Shawnee, reportedly with intent to burn them, but they were released on the intercession of a local Iroquois chief.[31] Céloron summoned the five Pennsylvania traders then in the town, ordering them out and giving them yet another copy of the letter to Lieutenant Governor James Hamilton. "Although Céloron had orders to pillage the goods of the English traders, he was not strong enough for that, as they were well established in the village, and sustained by the savages."[32] Céloron had expected a reinforcement of Ottawa warriors from Detroit to join him for the anticipated difficulties of the next stage of his mission, but only four messengers arrived to report that others could not be convinced to come and challenge the Miami.[33]

Céloron's wearying expedition then headed for Pickawillany, expelling only two traders, as most of the English traders had already left for the season. Céloron had orders to move these Miami back to Fort des Miamis and French influence. He began negotiations with a substantial present and forgiveness for what he claimed was the fault of the English traders, but he gained no more than vague promises. Once Céloron's own Miami interpreter arrived, Memeskia refused to meet with the French at all.[34] Céloron returned to Quebec after issuing a ban on English traders, expelling a few of them, and leaving lead plates and plaques that were indicators of a very insecure French suzerainty. He had found the Indians unsympathetic and the English traders well established and easily underselling the French. He suggested that force would be very expensive to apply and even more expensive to sustain. Céloron had not confiscated Pennsylvanian property, as Indians had done to both Canadians and Pennsylvanians earlier. He had not taken prisoners or hostages, though two of his own people were briefly held by the Shawnee. Nonetheless, Céloron had warned the English repeatedly and threatened more drastic employment of French power if the English traders returned. His trip, report, and subsequent decisions all helped escalate the conflict.[35]

The continuing strength of Pennsylvania traders' influence among the Indians of the upper Ohio Valley was clear from their continuing safety in the wake of Céloron's heavily armed blustering and his rejected suggestions to Indians that they rob and oust the English traders. Within two months of Céloron's visit, Croghan led a group of English traders back to Pickawillany to erect a stockaded trading post.[36] Prominent Pennsylvania trader John Lowery, one of five Pennsylvania brothers continuing their father's trade to the Ohio, died there after an unidentified Indian exploded a keg of gunpowder near him. Europeans were not sure whether this was an accident, an act of private vengeance, or a political murder, but the Miami of Pickawillany made no such distinctions. When a French-Miami *métis* trader named Pacane arrived in Pickawillany from Fort des Miamis as a supposed refugee, Memeskia rightly suspected he was a spy, but English traders objected to his execution. Memeskia cleverly applied the *pays d'en haut* murder ritual; he turned Pacane over to the Lowery family as a hostage until John Lowery's escaped murderer was given up.[37] Although the "murderer" was not found, Pacane was freed a few weeks later.

Commandant Longueuil's next initiative against the English traders at Pickawillany was to sponsor Indians willing to raid into that area and take English traders captive. In May of 1750, seven northern Indians came upon Morris Turner and Ralph Kilgore in a travelers' cabin about twenty-five miles from Pickawillany. These two hired hands of Pennsylvania trader John Fraser were on their way back to Pickawillany to retrieve deerskins; all three of them were working for one of

Croghan's partnerships.[38] The initially friendly meeting, in which both parties evidently understood each other, changed suddenly when the Indians seized the two, took their wampum and silver, and announced that they would be taken to "their French father" at Detroit, who had supplied ammunition and tobacco to encourage this attack. Upon the party's arrival at Detroit, Longueuil called a council of local Indians and publicly rewarded the captors with 10 gallons of brandy and 100 pounds of tobacco. For Longueuil, if not for the captors, this transaction represented the importation into the Ohio Valley of a practice current in New France, the purchase of English captives who had been taken by Indians while the colonies remained nominally at peace. To begin working off their "ransom," Turner and Kilgore hoed, harvested, and did other "country work" on a nearby farm during the next three months. Near the end of this period, they were visited by a soldier from the garrison who spoke English. He recounted being taken prisoner himself by the Catawba, who took him to Williamsburg, where he had been civilly treated and released, and he remembered kind entertainment in Philadelphia and New York while making his way back to Canada. He added, supposedly as a confidence, that a major French force was to subdue the Ohio Valley Shawnee and Wyandots the next year, and that $1,000 had been put on the heads of George Croghan and James Lowery.

Longueuil, replaced by Céloron as Detroit's commandant, set off for Montreal with a party that included his purchased servants, Turner and Kilgore. At Niagara they saw Joncaire and a substantial supply of presents and military stores that confirmed that there were major French preparations for the *pays d'en haut*. Turner and Kilgore escaped from their sleeping guard and made their way from Oswego to New York and Philadelphia, spreading their warnings. They informed the Pennsylvania Council and Assembly, and learned of the assembly's response, which amounted to a gift and three wishes. The gift was more presents for the Ohio Indians in what was becoming a war of presents that Pennsylvania could win. The Quaker-controlled assembly's three peaceable and economical wishes were deflective: Ohio Indians should come closer together for their mutual defense, New York should contribute more to counteract growing French influence both at Onondaga and on the Ohio River, and the Pennsylvania proprietors should pay to defend what were their personal claims to the still-distant western frontier.[39]

The escape of Turner and Kilgore, late in the summer of 1750, postponed the question of how such purchased captives would have been dealt with officially, in peacetime, by the Government of New France. The case of John Patten and his companions would not answer this precise question, but did clarify what would happen to English traders "arrested" by Canadian officials after the warnings of 1749. Just as Turner and Kilgore were escaping, John Patten was setting out from his home in Wilmington, Delaware, bound for Pickawillany. He had several years' experience in the Ohio trade, and was established enough to take along two hired men, a string of packhorses, and some £650 sterling worth of trade goods. The three took the Raystown route to Shannopintown and Logstown, and then went overland to the headwaters of the Muskingum River, and followed Whitewoman's Creek to Whitewoman Town, both named for former captive Mary Harris. (She had been captured at Deerfield in 1704 at age nine, and adopted by the Kahnawake, and had then settled in what would become Whitewoman Town with her Kahnawake husband and their several children; a white woman was unusual enough in this region to be a landmark.)[40] Patten's horse train crossed the Scioto River and went on to Pickawillany, the town that French officials were calling the center of a "republic of renegades." Since British colonial traders had initially built the fort, traders like Patten were afforded huts within it. Patten set off alone from there with a smaller stock of goods to trade at a canoe portage some sixty-five miles to the northeast, and then followed up what seems to have been an invitation from the French commander of Fort des Miamis.[41]

Patten later claimed that, since the British and French were at peace, he had entered the French fort without apprehension, and was outraged when arrested.[42] Patten was sent under guard to Detroit, to Céloron de Blainville himself, who already had three other Pennsylvanians in custody: Thomas Burk, Luke Erwin, and Joseph Faulkner (Fortiner). A party of Canadian soldiers had arrested these three while they were trading at Cuyahoga.[43] Patten was told that he was arrested for violating the complete prohibition on British traders in Ohio country, the prohibition that Céloron had repeatedly announced in writing to Lieutenant Governor Hamilton the previous year. These four were aliens arrested by French commanders, not captives "redeemed" from Indians. They were considered criminals, and imprisoned rather than required to work off a ransom. After more than four months in loose confinement at Detroit, these traders were sent under heavy guard to Montreal, and imprisoned there on short rations.[44] Recently arrived Governor General Jacques-Pierre de Taffanel de La Jonquière, together with the governor of Montreal and other city officials, twice interrogated the traders individually. Patten insisted that he had a Pennsylvania license to trade, which was in his hut in Pickawillany. He once again denied hearing anything of Céloron's prohibition against British traders in the Ohio Valley.[45] The four captives were sent on to Quebec before La Jonquière answered an inquiry about them from Governor George Clinton of New York. La Jonquière claimed that these traders knew of Céloron's prohibition, and were distributing gifts to foment anti-French sentiment; at the same time, he feigned surprise that British officials were concerned about such vagabonds and *coureurs de bois* who supposedly traded without licenses.[46] Although Britain, France, and their colonies were at peace, the harassment of these four merchants was not just a matter of petty extortion, though their goods had been confiscated; the Canadian government was enforcing a claim to the Ohio Valley.

Three of the four arrested traders were shipped to France after a brief detention in Quebec. Joseph Faulkner (Fortiner), too ill to be sent to France, reportedly won his own freedom after changing his religion and marrying a local girl.[47] The other three prisoners reached La Rochelle in November, and were sent to prison in handcuffs. French authorities thought it "proper that they be left there," and did not expect a British protest, as none had ever been made about five venturers from Virginia who had been captured in Louisiana in July 1742.[48] However, the Ohio Valley was not Louisiana, as the inconclusive Anglo-French boundary-negotiating commission was discovering in Paris. Patten later claimed that sympathetic La Rochelle townspeople protested against the rough treatment of the captives and "how contrary it was to the Laws in Time of Peace & to humanity."[49] Although the captives promptly wrote Lord Albemarle, the British ambassador in Paris, it was only after a protest from London, including copies of the correspondence between Clinton and La Jonquière, that the three captives were released. There was no apology, no compensation for trading or personal losses, and no French assistance to get home. English trade in Ohio country was being punished. Patten and Burk went to Paris and, with the help of Albemarle, reached London. With proprietor Thomas Penn's help, Patten was back in Philadelphia in September 1752, just over two years after he had left his Delaware home for the west. The Pennsylvania Assembly gave him £30 in assistance, not compensation. Patten gave them a written account of his travels, together with a map.[50]

Pennsylvania's traders would stop going to the Ohio Valley, but not until seven months after Patten's arrest. In the interim, traders led by George Croghan distributed official gifts from Pennsylvania and

Virginia, and received the protection of their flattered Indian recipients. Within weeks of Patten's capture, Croghan had called a conference of traders and Indians at the new Wyandot town of Conchaké on the Muskingum River, where English colors flew. The assembled learned that some Shawnee had been attacked on the Scioto River by a party of French and French-allied Indians, who had killed one and captured three others. The Shawnee pursued the attackers, and took at least four French prisoners. Two of these, traders La Mirande and Ste Marie, were sent to find and return the murderers, while the Shawnee held Le Mirande's wife and the other Frenchman as hostages. The two traders returned with presents and assurances that the Illinois had not been involved in the initial attack. The Shawnee woman and children captured in the initial raid were apparently held by Indians, and they were returned with apologies within two months.[51] English connections among the Shawnee seemed to be growing.

Croghan and Virginian Christopher Gist were in Pickawillany in February 1751, negotiating a bold treaty that the Pennsylvania Assembly would refuse to ratify. At Logstown three months later, Croghan lied to Miami chiefs in claiming that Pennsylvania had ratified this treaty, and he confronted Joncaire when he arrived with forty Six Nations warriors. Joncaire gave Croghan a version of the familiar letter for the Pennsylvania governor repeating Céloron's orders, and blustered in vain that the locals should oust these English. Privately, he admitted that the French would achieve nothing there without a major investment in force. Croghan's ascendancy seemed complete, as he and Andrew Montour, despite a French bounty on their heads, were joined by ten Pennsylvania traders as witnesses at a public conference they held with Mingo, Delaware, Shawnee, Wyandot, and Miami legates, where they distributed Pennsylvania's latest present, and heard the Mingo leader Tanaghrisson berate Joncaire for the capture of English traders on Indian land. Although there were still at least five Canadian traders among the Shawnee, this was the time, Secretary Richard Peters would remember fondly, when "Croghan & others had store houses on the Lake Erie all along ye Miami River, & up & down all the fine Country watered by ye Branches of ye Miamis, Sioto, & Muskingham Rivers & upon the Ohio from Buckaloons an Indian Town near its head to below ye Mouth of ye Miami River an Extent of 500 miles on one of ye most beautiful Rivers in ye world."[52]

Under Governor La Jonquière (1749–52), French attention was shifting from the Pennsylvania traders to the Indians who protected them, and especially to Memeskia at Pickawillany. At Quebec, Kaskaskia, New Orleans, and Paris, Memeskia was reported to have revived Orontony's ambitions, heading an increasingly intertribal "republic of renegades" that was said to reach from St Joseph to the Illinois River, and that was determined to trade only with the English and to oust the French. This overreaction led to a clumsy use of force, after diplomacy and bribery had both failed. In the summer of 1751, Céloron was instructed to assemble a force to destroy Pickawillany. The expedition aborted when, as had occurred two years earlier, Detroit allies and most mission Indians from Quebec refused to proceed, either because they had links to the Miami or because they were reluctant to provoke this group. Nonetheless, a small party of seventeen Nipissing, accompanied by an Ottawa, a Potawatomi, and marine officer François-Marie Picoté de Belestre, did raid Pickawillany while most of its inhabitants were hunting, and took two Piankashaw scalps. In a wave of reprisals by the Piankashaw and their relatives, at least ten French were killed and four captured; it is noteworthy that the Miami killed two black slaves, who would have been regarded elsewhere as valuable prizes. Some thirty Miami warriors were killed, and the French initially thought they had captured four "rebels" as well. The policy of attacking allies of the English had only revealed French weaknesses and increased Indian support for the "rebels."[53]

Although direct French action against the English themselves was the new approach of the third governor of New France within seven years, Ange Duquesne de Menneville, Marquis Duquesne, the discarded strategy was about to have its biggest success. On the morning of 21 June 1752, some 240 Ottawa and Ojibwa warriors from the Michilimackinac region, accompanied by Lieutenant François-Xavier de St Ours of the *troupes de la marine* and by Ottawa-French *métis* cadet Charles-Michel Mouet de Langlade,[54] surprised the women of Pickawillany, who again were working in their cornfields while their men were away hunting. Fifteen Indians and seven English traders managed to reach the stockade, and resisted effectively for several hours. During the ensuing siege, at least nine attackers and five defenders were killed, including Memeskia; the attackers had also captured a number of Piankashaw women and as many as three additional English traders. Wanting to avoid the added casualties that would come with an assault on the stockade, the attackers proposed a ceasefire and parley. Langlade announced that they had a commission from the governor of New France, on two wampum belts, inviting them "to kill all such Indians as are in Amity with the English, and to take the Persons and effects of all such English Traders as they could meet with, but not to kill any of them if they could avoid it." To accomplish part of this objective, they proposed to exchange their Piankashaw women captives for the English traders still within the fort. The defenders agreed to surrender the whites, the beaver pelts, and the wampum in the fort on condition there would be no further violence and "all be at their Mercy." Thomas Burney, a Pennsylvania blacksmith who was successfully smuggled out of the fort, conceded that these "instructions were in some measure obeyed."[55]

The martial conventions of these northern Ottawa hunters deserve some attention. The Indian defenders of the stockade and the captured Indian women were allowed to go free, despite the Canadian governor's supposed instructions and the fact that the attackers had at least nine casualties to avenge. Some twenty-five families of Pickawillany "rebels" immediately agreed to return with the victors to resettle at Kekionga. As a ritual of victory, Memeskia's body was cooked and eaten at the scene, as was the heart of a trader killed in the fighting. Andrew Browne and Alexander MacDonald were both killed and scalped after the siege; at least one of them had been severely wounded and was summarily killed, which was often done as an act of mercy but usually perceived by whites as an atrocity. There were no claims of torture and no adoptions, though an Ojibwa chief was among those killed in the siege. The five surviving captive Pennsylvania traders claimed losses of £1,400 in trade goods and thirty horses killed by Ottawa and Ojibwa hunters, who apparently were not interested in using horses to carry off their loot. Although the recently announced French bounties were identical for either English scalps or prisoners, the Ottawa and Ojibwa delivered the prisoners, rather than their less troublesome scalps, to Detroit.[56]

Although Canadian boasts that Langlade and St Ours led the attackers must be treated with some skepticism, subsequent treatment suggests that the two Canadian officers had acquired the five captive traders in the surrender. The captives were sent to Montreal and Quebec, where they later complained they had not been questioned at all, and spent two and a half months under harsh conditions in the Quebec jail. They were then shipped to La Rochelle, where they endured even worse jail conditions until released by the efforts of Ambassador Albemarle. The French claimed that they had intended to prosecute the five for carrying on a contraband trade. Four of the five were back in Philadelphia within a year of their capture. By then, Virginia's lieutenant governor had reported that "All the English Traders have left the Ohio in a great Panick, being affraid of being cut off."[57] The destruction of Pickawillany was the decisive deterrent for English traders, and the lack of any English military response discouraged all their Indian allies.

The Ohio Delaware response to the intensifying Anglo-French trade rivalry was varied. Delaware had migrated west from the Susquehanna Valley since the 1720s, and remained neutral traders in deerskins rather than declared partisans in the increasingly belligerent diplomacy of the late 1740s. Approximately 700 families had gradually migrated into eight Ohio Valley villages, leaving perhaps 200 Delaware families still living on the upper Susquehanna River. If the Delaware migrants to the Ohio Valley were escaping European encroachment and Six Nations bullying, they nonetheless continued to trade with Pennsylvanians and to live near Mingo and Shawnee who did likewise. It was not until early in 1753 that some of these Delaware were forced to become involved in the Anglo-French contest. In keeping with the general advice of both Céloron and Joncaire, a force of 1,500 Canadians and Indians refurbished Fort Presqu'île and moved inland to build Fort Le Boeuf and to establish an advance post under Joncaire at Venango on the Allegheny River. Whereas Delaware living farther down the Allegheny River remained neutral, the village of Ticastoroga, nearest Venango, was divided. One faction lodged the first formal protest against the French invasion, and others followed prominent Munsee Delaware chief Custaloga (Pankanke) in actively cooperating with the French. Custaloga was the recognized keeper of the Delaware-French wampum belts by 1753, when he refused to turn them over to Tanaghrisson and George Washington as they challenged the French at Fort Le Boeuf.[58] In addition to hunting to provide meat for the French, these Munsee helped refit John Fraser's abandoned house for Joncaire, and hired out their horses to transport construction materials for building Fort Le Boeuf. Although Custaloga would later supply the Virginians with some useful information about French military strength, he more often provided the French with information about English movements.[59]

This French intrusion-in-force rightly alarmed the few straggling Pennsylvanians who were still among the Delaware. John Fraser abandoned the gunsmith shop he had run at Venango for years, and his servant William Wilson was the last to flee. However, not all of the English escaped. John Trotter and his servant, James MacLaughlin, were seized the next day by Custaloga, who publicly confirmed his new alliance with the French by handing these prisoners over to the veteran Canadian commander, Paul Marin de La Malgue. Marin accepted Custaloga's prisoners, who were also his trading competitors, and followed what was becoming his government's convention for dealing with arrested English traders. He sent them to Canada and France, where they were jailed in La Rochelle for a month, and then released without trial.[60]

Custaloga had been the first of the Delaware chiefs to declare himself openly for the French, and it was eight months before another Delaware chief followed suit. The following April, after the English had already surrendered their primitive "fort" at the forks of the Ohio and it was being rebuilt as Fort Duquesne, a party of Delaware led by English John came to trade at Christopher Gist's Ohio Company post just a few miles up the Monongahela River. Trading degenerated into a violent dispute and the capture of four traders, Andrew McBriar, Nehemiah Stevens, John Kennedy, and Elizabeth Williams, all of whom worked for the Lowery brothers. Elizabeth Williams is the only Pennsylvanian woman known to have been trading on this frontier at the time, but this fact prompted no special interest or treatment from her captors. Andrew McBriar had earlier escaped capture at the fall of Pickawillany, but he was less fortunate this time. Williams and McBriar, together with Stevens and Kennedy, who was wounded in the dispute, were taken to what had just become, within the week, the functional new French Fort Duquesne. This fort immediately became the principal mart for such English prisoners as Ohio Indians sought to sell. The Delaware apparently offered the three healthy prisoners for sale within the hearing of Captain Robert Stobo, a Virginian military officer held hostage since the capture of Fort Necessity, for the exorbitant price of 40 pistoles (about £16 sterling) each.[61] When Stobo asked the commandant to intervene, Céloron replied that the prisoners belonged to the Delaware. Nonetheless, there must have been a transaction that eventually put the captives into Céloron's hands, and he sent them on to Quebec, from whence they were transported to France. The wounded Kennedy had been allowed to convalesce near Fort Duquesne. He escaped after thirty-five days only to be recaptured, returned to Fort Duquesne, and sent in chains on the now familiar trip to Quebec and, after more than two years in the prisoners' house there, on to France. Kennedy went from being a criminal to being a prisoner of war after the formal Anglo-French declarations of May 1756; he was exchanged only after an Anglo-French prisoner cartel in August 1757.[62] English John may have initiated a trade in captives at Fort Duquesne that resembled one conducted by the Abenaki at Montreal, but the French on the Ohio River were arresting "criminals," not buying laborers for the price of their ransom.

The majority of the seventy-two European traders attacked by Indians in the Ohio–Great Lakes region between 1745 and 1754 survived.

This general picture masks a surprising difference between French and English traders. Seventeen Canadian traders were killed in the 1747 tumult by Wyandot, Ottawa, and Ojibwa, and only eight were captured, and the fate of five others is not known. English traders had no military support, yet they fared much better. Only six were killed, and all thirty-four of those captured by Indians and Canadians are known to have survived.[63]

Perhaps the most striking feature of this unsettling decade, of shifting alliances and encouragement to attack traders, was that Ohio Indians showed even less interest in taking white traders than they had in taking white captives along the Warriors' Path. The Shawnee and Delaware of Ohio country were neutral or allied with the Pennsylvanian traders and frontier farmers they might have been expected to resent. Most Ohio Indians declined the lucrative invitation to become bounty hunters for the French. Chartier's party of Shawnee had held Dunning and Tostee only momentarily in 1745, as other Shawnee did Joncaire and a companion in 1749. The Shawnee held two French traders in 1751, as hostages for the return of three of their people captured by the French. Memeskia's Miami were the only participants in the conspiracy of 1747 who had taken captives, and the captures and releases were related to internal Miami politics. Memeskia also disposed of the spy Pacane by offering him to the Lowerys as a murder hostage. None of the Ohio Delaware are known to have taken a trader captive before the spring of 1753. It was not Ohio Indians but intruding Nipissing, Ottawa, and Ojibwa who took captives near Pickawillany in 1750 and 1752. Despite substantial and repeated French encouragement and offers to become alternative suppliers, Ohio Indians showed little interest in taking English captives. This challenges all the tidy explanations about subsequent captures, which are said to have: satisfied long-held resentments about lost homelands, punished Europeans for their trading offences, added to comparatively small Indian communities competing for control of this contested region, or produced profits when captives were sold or gifted to other Indian or European communities. Although Ohio Indians would soon be willing to travel hundreds of miles and risk death to take white captives and scalps, this radical change in behavior cannot be explained simply by citing the real grievances that had been there throughout the previous decade.

In the colonial traders' own war for the Ohio Valley between 1745 and 1754, the French were supported by a government that demonstrated a growing interest in capturing English traders.[64] Longueuil had missed his quarry in 1745, but later sponsored the capture and "redemption" of Turner and Kilgore, put them to work on a Detroit farm, and was taking them to Montreal when they escaped. Céloron took no prisoners on his 1749 tour, but he expelled some English traders and warned the rest. The arrest of John Patten and fellow traders in 1750, and their imprisonment in France, was intended to oust Pennsylvanian traders, or at least to raise their risks and costs. Although metropolitan French laws against illegal traders were used to arrest English traders on the Ohio River in peacetime, the captures were few, and all were eventually released without trial. They had, of course, been severely punished by loss of goods and belongings, by imprisonment in Canada and France, and by their release an ocean away from home. More decisive, in a French commercial victory that stayed just short of war, was the destruction of Pickawillany, where Indians who traded with the English were attacked, and their leader killed, and where Pennsylvanian traders were captured and sent to France. This bold and unanswered strike was a warning to others allying themselves with pacifist Pennsylvania, or expecting support from the Six Nations. It left the Miami as rather reluctant French allies in the ensuing war, dominant in only one major raid, at Vause's Fort, which degenerated into a costly siege.[65] Pennsylvania traders had a government that was unwilling to fight, either with legal pretensions or with troops, and lacked the interest or ability to capture Canadian traders.

The French, who needed to alter the terms of trade by disrupting the more competitive Pennsylvanians, were the only ones who actively sought to capture traders in the decade before 1754.[66] Although they captured only nine English traders themselves, and received only ten more from their allies and clients, the French were advertising their interest in captives, and establishing patterns for their treatment that would be transformed by war. The French had won momentary dominance in the trade of the upper Ohio Valley, but the British would soon challenge it. Most Ohio Indians had not helped the French win their initial victory, though the Delaware chiefs Custaloga and English John had taken and given the captives who marked alliance with the French by the summer of 1754. Yet traders and victims of long-range Indian raiding were not the only captives taken in the waning months of peace; colonial soldiers captured each other on different terms, in actions that even more clearly brought them to war.

3

Colonial Soldiers Take Captives, 1754

As Virginians and Canadians belligerently confronted each other in Ohio country for the first time, they did so as soldiers, not as traders. Paul Marin de La Malgue brought an army of Canadian *troupes de la marine* and militia to the upper Ohio Valley in 1753 to build military forts. The ambitions of the Ohio Company of Virginia, a land company more than a trading company, would need defending by Virginia's new regiment. In the contested upper Ohio borderlands, these colonials began fighting while their colonial and imperial governments remained formally at peace. The Virginia government eventually drew the British government into the contest, by building, defending, and surrendering forts, however makeshift. Three well-known incidents in the first half of 1754 put colonial soldiers in the hands of their rivals: Virginian ensign Edward Ward surrendered an incomplete fort at the forks of the Ohio River; George Washington captured the survivors of Joseph Coulon de Villiers de Jumonville's party; and then he surrendered Fort Necessity a few weeks later. It is worth noticing how these soldiers, captured in peacetime, were treated by their colonial and Indian opponents. Conventions applied to these "hostages" would echo throughout the coming war.

Despite the reputation of their culture-shifting and itinerant *coureurs de bois*, Canadians had long since built the string of defensible trading forts that linked their Great Lakes bases and protected their Wabash River route to Louisiana, while skirting the less valued upper Ohio country at a considerable distance. In contrast, there were no English forts on Pennsylvania's Allegheny-Ohio frontier in 1753. Pennsylvanians had traded in these Ohio woods without any defensible refuge and, like the more venturesome white settlers on isolated Susquehanna Valley farms, were dependent upon the hospitality or tolerance of Indians who were usually better armed than themselves. It was Virginians supporting their new Ohio Company who had built what would become the nearest English trading fort and storehouse, Fort Cumberland, at Will's Creek in Maryland.

Admittedly, the earlier French forts were less alien to Indians for being commanded by veteran Canadian officers of the *troupes de la marine*, whose experience in the area, awareness of local conventions, and personal trading interests moderated the application of the wishes of the French noblemen who usually governed New France. With the English traders driven from the upper Ohio in 1753, the new French forts there could be expected to offer welcome trade goods available closer than Detroit or the Wabash Valley forts. Nonetheless, the new forts of the upper Ohio, and especially what became Fort Duquesne, were heralds of a European warfare that could either run parallel to, or conflict with, Indian martial interests and values, including conventions about the taking of captives, their treatment, and their return.

The Canadian invasion had begun decisively in 1753, when an army of 2,400 militiamen and *troupes de la marine*[1] built and garrisoned the stockaded forts of Presqu'île and Le Boeuf, and built a wagon road between them that linked Lake Erie to the Allegheny River headwaters of the Ohio. Montreal-born Marin had spent most of the preceding thirty years as an officer and trader at upper Great Lakes posts; at sixty-one he worked himself and many in his army to death completing this ambitious assignment. When Custaloga decided to become the first Delaware chief to support the French publicly, he did so by capturing and offering them two Pennsylvania traders. Marin may have seen himself as a military gentleman who despised the alien traders he imprisoned; more likely, he also saw his captives as traders who were competing too successfully with himself and his backers in the Indian trade. In any case, these captives were rival traders, not soldiers, and his action was policing, not war.[2]

Indian settlers in the upper Ohio Valley were understandably suspicious of these latest intrusions, and they had long been familiar with forts and garrisons. At least some of the Shawnee, Miami, Delaware, and Mingo, for whom "first contact" was an ancestral memory, still occasionally stockaded villages themselves. The Shawnee had stockaded Lower Shawnee Town at the approach of Captain Pierre-Joseph Céloron de Blainville's expedition in 1749, and the Piankashaw Miami had done the same for their defiant center of English trade at Pickawillany that same year. Shawnee and Piankashaw had also traded furs and talk with the French at Forts Vincennes, Ouiatenon, des Miamis, and

Detroit. The Delaware and Mingo had visited the strong French fort at Niagara and had heard dissident Seneca grumble about it as an invasion of their territory.

Indian protests against the Canadian invasion of the upper Ohio Valley came from a variety of sources. After Marin's outward-bound army had been seen on Lake Ontario, Mohawk leader Theyanoguin (Hendrick) complained angrily to New York authorities that the Covenant Chain had been broken by British neglect. Ohio Seneca leader Tanaghrisson, who had recently emerged as the leader of pro-English Indians in the upper Ohio and saw this role evaporating, made three futile protests that were brushed aside by Marin and his successor, and these rejections were more humiliating because they were witnessed by Tanaghrisson's fellow Seneca who were with the Canadians as hunters. Pennsylvania authorities and merchants had misled Tanaghrisson with presents that seemed to reinforce the promises of mutual defense made in recent treaties. However, Pennsylvania's lieutenant governor, James Hamilton, could not push his Quaker-dominated assembly, or the colony's increasingly cautious English proprietors. Hamilton resigned himself to doing nothing more belligerent than encouraging the hitherto-rival Virginians as they confronted the Canadians.[3]

It was Virginians' objections to the new French forts that precipitated war. Lieutenant Governor Robert Dinwiddie's 1753 summons to the French to leave Ohio country was as quixotic as Céloron de Blainville's demand, four years earlier, that the English leave. Yet Dinwiddie's message, delivered by the ambitious twenty-one-year-old George Washington to Marin's unimpressed successor, was preliminary to more forceful objections. The Ohio Company storehouse at Will's Creek became the base for their invasion, and by January 1754 a newly raised company of Virginian soldiers under trader-turned-soldier Captain William Trent were at the mouth of Redstone Creek on the Monongahela River, where they built "a strong Square Log House with Loop Holes sufficient to have made a good Defence with a few men and very Convenient for a store House where stores might be lodg'd in order to be transported by water."[4] The contenders were closing in on the strategic forks of the Ohio River; the Virginians were now less than 50 miles south, and the Canadians were fortified some 100 miles north and were negotiating to build a fort at Logstown, just 20 miles downstream to the west of the forks.

Tanaghrisson, humiliated into a very pro-English stance, formally laid the first log of "Fort Trent," an Ohio Company storehouse at the forks of the Ohio, in February 1754. Ensign Ward led the forty-one Virginian soldiers and workmen constructing something similar to the Redstone Creek blockhouse, but, on hearing that a major French force was approaching, Ward and Tanaghrisson oversaw the hasty construction of a stockade around the new storehouse. This was to be the first of two indefensible Virginian stockades built that year, and each formal surrender was itself a claim to sovereignty that had just been overpowered.

Captain Claude-Pierre Pécaudy de Contrecoeur, backed by at least 500 *troupes de la marine* and Canadian militia with eighteen cannon, formally summoned Ward to surrender pathetic Fort Trent on 16 April 1754. Contrecoeur was a thirty-year veteran of the frontier military, had been commandant at Fort Ste Frédéric in 1742, and had been second in command on Céloron's 1749 tour, but he was also a "wise and prudent" second-generation Canadian seigneur.[5] In an unwritten but "civilized" surrender that avoided bloodshed on either side, Ward's group of eight ex-traders and thirty-three soldiers were allowed to retreat to Redstone Creek, bearing their small arms and the tools they had refused to sell. This arrangement did not quite amount to the latest "honors of war," but these Virginians were certainly being treated as soldiers, and not as rival traders, who would have been arrested.[6] Contrecoeur had gained control of the forks, and humanity coincided with good sense in limiting immediate casualties and further friction with the English. Tanaghrisson departed from the stockade with the defeated, and railed against the French in vain; he was the only Indian directly involved in this intercolonial incident, though others would certainly hear of it. Contrecoeur immediately began building Fort Duquesne on this site. Within a week, Pennsylvanian trader-captives Elizabeth Williams, Andrew McBriar, Nehemiah Stevens, and John Kennedy became the first of at least 139 captives who would be brought to the new fort in its five years of existence, and they were promptly transported to Canada.[7] The distinction made at Fort Duquesne between illegal traders and rival soldiers could not have been clearer.

Whereas the more numerous Canadians had focused their displeasure on English traders rather than soldiers, and had followed orders to maintain the fiction of peace, the Virginians were pursuing a more openly belligerent policy intended to recover the initiative. Washington's men were improving a road from Will's Creek to the Monongahela at Redstone Creek, intent on bringing cannon and reinforcements against Fort Duquesne. Although Dinwiddie's instructions to Washington had urged him to stay on the defensive, they authorized him to restrain anyone seeking to "disrupt the Works or interrupt our Settlmts … & in Case of resistance to make Prisoners of or kill & destroy them."[8] Tanaghrisson prepared the battleground in more immediate ways. On 23 May 1754 he sent Washington a warning that a French "army" had left Fort Duquesne to confront him. Five days later Tanaghrisson guided Washington's detachment on a night expedition that found the French camp and ambushed Jumonville's substantial scouting party, leaving ten Canadians and one Virginian dead and twenty-one Canadians captured.

The Jumonville incident was a skirmish in peacetime, and was bound to have consequences. Washington's diary indicates Tanaghrisson's role in planning the attack, and commanding the final scout, and it notes that all the attackers had approached the camp "in Indian fashion."[9] Washington recorded simply that, once positioned, he gave the order to fire, and the fighting continued for a quarter of an hour, during which ten French were killed, including Jumonville. He mentioned that the Indians scalped the dead Frenchmen and took most of their weapons. In his report to Dinwiddie, Washington offered a similar and even shorter version of the fighting than he had confided to his diary.[10] He claimed to have convinced Tanaghrisson and those few Indians with him to join the Virginians in attacking the French. Washington again made no mention of any preliminary summons or shots from the French, any French request for quarter, or any explanation of how the killing stopped. He stated only that he sent the prisoners to Winchester because he and his officers were convinced that the pretense of a diplomatic mission was a cover for a force that was spying and preparing to call for reinforcements. "It was too great an indulgence to send them back." Washington portrayed himself as firmly in charge throughout, and was apparently untroubled by unavoidable comparisons with his own little summons-and-spying mission that had been met with French civility a few months earlier. Washington promised the surviving officers, Pierre-Jacques Druillon de Macé and Michel Pepin *dit* La Force, "all the favour that's due to Imprison'd Officer's [*sic*]." It was only several days later, amid boastful comparisons between the Virginians and their opponents, that Washington mentioned that seven Indians had fought with the Virginians, whereas others merely "servd to knock the poor unhappy wounded in the head and beriev'd [*sic*] them of their Scalps."[11]

Soldiers could have difficulty ending their killing. Europeans who surrendered during or after a battle took much greater risks than those surrendering from defensive positions. European commanders routinely sent their cavalry to slaughter defeated enemies who were fleeing a battlefield, and any granting of "quarter" on a battlefield had traditionally included no promises beyond the preservation of life. Indians could not understand why those who had just been trying to kill them were suddenly to be saved, apparently because they asked. Not surprisingly, there were witnesses who suggested that things had not been so simple in what became Jumonville Glen. For instance, three pro-French witnesses insisted that Washington ordered his men to fire while a translator with Jumonville was attempting to read Jumonville's summons aloud.[12]

The first English colonial newspaper "account from the westward," which has been overlooked by scholars, gives a very full, illuminating, and plausible description. It begins with the questionable claim that some of the French fired first, killing a Virginian, and that then Washington's men returned fire, killing seven or eight Frenchmen,

> on which the Rest took to their Heels; but the Half-King, and his Indians, who lay in Ambush to cut them off in their Retreat, fell upon them, and soon killed and scalped Five of them. Monsieur Le Force finding that they were all likely to lose their Lives under the Hands of the Savages, called to his Men, and advised them to surrender to the English; they immediately, with great Precipitation, ran towards the English, flung down their Arms, and begg'd for Quarter. Major Washington interposed between them and the Half-King, and it was with great Difficulty that he prevented the Indians from doing them further Mischief, the Half-King insisting on Scalping them all, as it was their Way of Fighting, and he alledged that those People had killed, boiled, and eat [*sic*] his Father, and that the Indians would not be satisfied without all their Scalps; however, Major Washington at Length persuaded him to be content with what Scalps he had already got. One of those Five which were killed and scalped by the Indians, was Monsieur Jumonville, an Ensign, whom the Half-King himself dispatched with his Tomahawk.[13]

This account has plausibility and may well have come from an eyewitness. Parts of it are corroborated by two second-hand accounts.[14] French officers retold an English deserter's report that Tanaghrisson had killed Jumonville when the fighting ended, after expressing surprise that "You are not dead yet, my father."[15] It is puzzling that Washington's cryptic accounts of the Jumonville incident never included either Tanaghrisson's execution of Jumonville or his own negotiations to acquire and preserve the captives. Washington's genteel self-fashioning could be trumped by a stronger desire to appear in command.

Druillon and his captured comrades immediately claimed to be part of a peacetime diplomatic party, and they supported their claim by producing a written summons from Contrecoeur ordering the Virginians out of the Ohio Valley. However, Jumonville's group had been too large simply to be carrying a message and had included no Indians to hunt, scout, or to broker the contact. They had spent several days in the area and had camped so as to hide their whereabouts. Washington's pre-emptive and deadly peacetime ambush would be reported and protested as assassination.

Washington's attack needed justification, as would the holding of the prisoners whom Washington represented as spies. Dinwiddie, who had no military experience, was apparently comfortable with holding these prisoners in jail, though anxious to claim to his British superiors that the Virginians were merely auxiliaries to the Indians and had not disturbed the Anglo-French peace.[16] Ensign Druillon had been the only wounded Frenchman to survive the skirmish, and he was granted the European privileges given a captured officer, including parole, despite his insistence that he was not a prisoner of war. After aborted negotiations to exchange him, Druillon spent parts of the next year at liberty in Williamsburg and Baltimore, and then sailed in an English merchantman to Bristol in June of 1755. In England he was not considered a prisoner of war and was sent home to France.[17] By 1756 he was back in Canada, and served actively until Montreal surrendered five years later.[18]

Most of Washington's other captives were released early in the spring of 1755. Two cadets and ten other soldiers, who all likely came from France, had been sent to England. Two of these soldiers later complained that they had been poorly fed while in a Virginian prison, during a rough voyage to London in March of 1755, and while held there aboard another ship for more than three months. They had been confined but had not been made to work for their subsistence, either as crewmen aboard the homeward-bound English merchantman or on the naval vessel in the port of London, and they admitted that their poor food was the same as that of the ships' crews. However, their rations had been vindictively withheld for four days after news of General

Edward Braddock's defeat reached London late in August 1755, forcing them to live on food smuggled to them by sympathetic Catholics. Despite heightening diplomatic tensions, and a British naval attack on French ships in the Gulf of St Lawrence, these captives of a colonial skirmish were given new clothes and allowed to board the packet boat for Calais at the end of September 1755.[19]

The other Canadian captives, with the notable exception of La Force, were sent home slowly by way of Martinique, where a British colonial ship could combine this mission with some illicit trading and spying. These six Canadians were back in Canada by the end of October 1755.[20] All these captivities had ended while the colonies and empires were still formally at peace. The captors made no claims against the French for prisoner maintenance expenses, as they would have done if this had been part of European wartime exchanges.[21]

La Force was the prize captive of the incident, and would never get home. He was an officer in the *troupes de la marine*, a trader, an accomplished linguist, and an influential woodland diplomat, who should not have been risked on a mission to the Virginians that had not even included Indians.[22] Washington immediately claimed that releasing "La Force, I really think, w'd tend more to our disservice than 50 other Men," a self-congratulatory judgment later confirmed from Fort Duquesne and Quebec.[23] Dinwiddie ordered La Force brought to Williamsburg, and warned the escort to "Look on him as a cunning, designing man, and therefore require double care."[24] Dinwiddie was no soldier, but he knew he was mistreating an officer who had been promised the usual privileges. This should have included a parole of honor, which he was not granted, and freedom from imprisonment, as well as an allowance. Dinwiddie readily called this captive "a most wicked fellow" and said that the Virginia Council had begged that La Force be kept as a close prisoner.[25] La Force was held in prison in Williamsburg until after the fall of Niagara and Quebec, though he attempted to escape repeatedly and once succeeded briefly. After five years in a Virginia prison, he was finally sent to New York in November 1759, with the Virginians and General Jeffrey Amherst thinking of exchanging him only for their own remaining hostage of 1754, Captain Jacob Van Braam.[26] Captain Anthony Wheelock, General Amherst's trusted commissary for prisoners, doubted La Force's self-description as a "Captain of Provincials" who had no company, but reported that "he must be something or other & having been so long Prisoner & being at Jamaica [New York] I cou'd not avoid sending him up" to Crown Point for exchange.[27] Amherst, who had gradually developed anxiety about Canadian marine officers, stopped La Force, and kept him in custody for another full year.[28] Determined to keep all captured *troupes de la marine* officers out of the war, Amherst not only refused to exchange them, but also interpreted the 1760 surrender of Canada as authorizing his eventual shipping of these officers to France, rather than allowing them to return home to Canada. In December of 1760, La Force, after six and a half years in custody, was sent to France with more than 500 French regulars and marine officers. There is no surviving evidence that La Force ever returned to North America.[29]

In diplomatic terms, the taking of prisoners in the Jumonville affair had been a disproportional Virginian response to Contrecoeur's humane treatment of Ward's little band, but the Canadians had an opportunity to reply in kind just over a month later, when Washington surrendered Virginia's second hastily assembled stockade, Fort Necessity. Contrecoeur had prepared a force of 500 Canadians and 11 Indians to avenge the killing of Jumonville and gave the command to Jumonville's elder brother, Louis Coulon de Villiers, who had just arrived from Montreal with reinforcements, including 130 mission Indians. After a long and very divided Indian council that was worried about causing a war that would disrupt trade, 90 of these mission Indians decided to join the retaliatory expedition. Only 6 or 7 Ohio Indians, including English John, joined this attack force.[30] Washington's 300 soldiers, armed with muskets, bayonets, and nine swivel guns, would normally have been expected to defend a fortified position readily against 600 men attacking without cannon. What apparently began as a European-style open-field battle very quickly became a small-arms exchange, with the Virginians quite exposed within their low-lying stockade and surrounding two-foot-deep trenches, which were rapidly filling with rainwater. The Canadians and Indians were sniping from the better cover of the nearby woods. In this day-long battle, the Virginians suffered five times as many casualties as their opponents. Nonetheless, Villiers's Indian allies were losing enthusiasm for this kind of fight, and he proposed a parley.[31]

In the first minutes of that Fourth of July, two colonial soldiers who had never been to Europe and had just spent a wet day fighting in what both must have seen as the middle of nowhere, signed a formal and decidedly European capitulation document. The terms were prepared by or for Villiers, who had never fought Europeans or colonials, though he was a hardened veteran of warfare against the Chickasaw and Fox. He had also commanded Fort des Miamis from 1750 to 1753, where he confined John Patten and at least six other English traders before sending them off to imprisonment in Canada.[32] Villiers's importation of European martial values into the capitulation may have owed something to François Le Mercier, his second in command, who was a veteran French regular officer and now an artillery officer and engineer in the *troupes de la marine*.[33] Le Mercier knew what the honors of war were, but he had also been with Contrecoeur at Ward's surrender a season earlier, where no written document had been thought necessary.

George Washington, ambitious to be a regular officer like his elder half-brother, was at least familiar with current European siege conventions from accounts in his newspaper, the *Virginia Gazette*. His immediate advisor on martial niceties in this sodden wilderness outpost was Jacob Van Braam, a former lieutenant in the Dutch army and teacher of French in Virginia, now serving as a captain in the Virginia Regiment and as Washington's translator.[34] Captain James Mackay, a British regular officer and veteran of Georgia border warfare, who had joined Washington just in time for the siege, also signed the revealing terms of surrender. The English signers, perhaps hampered by their ignorance of French, by water drops on the paper, by poor light, or by the fact they were in a hopeless situation, were not much worried about the agreement's preamble, which stated that the French force never intended to disrupt the continuing peace between the Crowns and sought only to avenge the assassination of Jumonville and to hinder English settlement on lands of the king of France.[35] Once again, the French insisted that the peace was continuing despite this formal surrender of a fortification.

Villiers, who noted in his journal that it was not normal to take prisoners in peacetime and that they were a drain on provisions even during war,[36] allowed the defeated garrison to return to Virginia, taking all their baggage except the artillery. They were to have the "honors of war" granted to defeated European enemies whose resistance had invariably lasted much longer than a single day. This meant that the defeated Virginians could retreat without being taken as prisoners, could march out of the fort carrying their small arms, with drums beating and regimental flags flying, and could be accompanied by one of their own swivel guns on its carriage. This was all *au courant* in western Europe, though not the added clause that stated these privileges were granted "to convince them we treat them as Friends."[37] The Virginians were even allowed to cache their belongings, having no surviving draft animals, and to place a guard over these belongings until they could be removed.

In return for such generous terms, Villiers took two hostages to ensure that his main demand was met, the prompt return to Fort Duquesne of the French and Canadian prisoners taken in the Jumonville incident. Although such hostage taking was unusual in this borderland,[38] it had a long history in Europe and on the Atlantic, as well as in America. The very last time that the British would provide the French with diplomatic hostages in Europe had occurred only six years earlier, when two British peers were given as hostages to ensure the return of Cape Breton to the French.[39] In the most recent Anglo-French maritime war, between 1744 and 1748, fully one-third of prize vessels taken by privateers were ransomed, and one or two of a captured ship's officers were usually surrendered as hostages until the ransom was paid.[40] We do not know whether Washington and his officers worried much about whether they had the power to promise the return of Druillon and his comrades, but the defeated officers had little difficulty deciding to offer as hostages the only two unmarried captains of the Virginia Regiment, Van Braam and Robert Stobo, neither of whom had been born in Virginia.[41] The English were also to strike their colors, to surrender the fort, and to give their "parole d'honneur" that they would not rebuild there or anywhere west of the mountains for a year. This adapted another common European convention that had parolees promise not to fight for a year, but the governor of New France was understandably upset by the implication that the Virginians could return in a year to contest the Ohio Valley, as they would.[42]

Nearly 100 Indians who had assisted the victors were not part of these surrender negotiations, and were not paid except in loot, and the overwhelming majority of them were familiar with the profits made selling war captives in New France. Although Villiers guaranteed not to harm the retreating Virginians, he wisely added that the French would "restrain, as much as shall be in our Power, the Indians who are with us." He was admitting that Indians were independent allies, and he knew they would not be impressed with these very alien and illogical terms after a firefight in which one of them was killed and two were wounded.[43] Villiers confessed to his diary that, though the Indians had faithfully obeyed his commands, they now thought themselves entitled to booty. He hurried to have the English artillery smashed, the stockade destroyed, and his force moved out to prevent "the disorder which could undoubtedly follow."[44] Indians took or destroyed much of the English baggage, and killed and scalped two of the seriously wounded and three others who were evidently drunk and asleep.[45] The terrified Virginians fled, leaving much baggage, including one of their flags and Washington's own revealing journal.

When Indians later offered Villiers ten English prisoners they had taken, he offended these allies and confirmed the values he shared with his enemies. He ordered the ten released to join their retreating fellow soldiers, and sent six Canadian militiamen along as what proved to be an inadequate escort. While this party was traveling to catch up with the retreating Virginians, the Indians decided to strip these ten prisoners (they had not been asked to return their clothes), killing and scalping three who likely resisted. This brought the number of Virginians killed after the surrender to eight. Understandably, the Canadian militiamen chose not to escort seven naked surviving soldiers to Washington's column, but let them go on alone.

After the French forces returned to Fort Duquesne, they discovered that the Indians had taken six additional prisoners, perhaps the baggage guard or six of the seven just released naked, and had made them run a gauntlet. Still held hostage at Fort Duquesne three weeks later, Stobo claimed that a total of ten prisoners, all taken after the surrender, were for sale at 40 pistoles apiece. Contrecoeur insisted that their Indian captors were willing to part with only two of them. He handled this gift more diplomatically than had Villiers; apparently he held the two until after the Indians had dispersed, and then returned them to Virginia.[46] Seven other Virginians captured in this incident were reportedly taken to Canada by their Indian captors.[47] The Canadian-domiciled Indians, who had accompanied Villiers into this battle with some reluctance, eventually had between six and thirteen prisoners and eight scalps to mark their participation in the capture of Fort Necessity. They acquired these by pointedly rejecting the alien "honors" that the colonials had embraced in the capitulation agreement.

It might seem puzzling that the Virginians did not immediately claim that the terms of the capitulation were violated, and that Lieutenant Governor Dinwiddie still intended to fulfill the surrender terms. He sent all twenty-one of the Jumonville prisoners, under escort, westward from Fort Cumberland early in August 1754.[48] Villiers' "escape clause" about the Indians, in the widely reprinted capitulation terms, might have satisfied French consciences but does not explain this Virginian reaction. Did Dinwiddie hear nothing of these violations in the initial reports of Washington and MacKay, and why were no depositions taken from those involved? Virginian soldiers who survived the bloody and humiliating aftermath of the capitulation would certainly share accounts of Indian treachery around their campfires. Admittedly, the safety of Stobo and Van Braam would have been compromised if the capitulation had been repudiated, though Washington was soon unjustly accusing Van Braam of incompetence or even duplicity as the translator of the terms by which Washington admitted to assassinating Jumonville.[49] Virginia's lieutenant governor initially intended to use the formal capitulation to attract British and Virginian support, to recover the hostages, and to spy on the Canadians at the forks of the Ohio River.

This plan changed abruptly when Dinwiddie received copies of Stobo's two impressive smuggled letters and a detailed plan of Fort Duquesne (see illustration 1), delivered by trusted Indians.[50] Stobo revealed that Virginians involved in the capitulation were being held captive by Indians, that La Force was greatly missed by the French and should not be released even if Stobo and Van Braam suffered, and that Fort Duquesne was vulnerable to an attack, which he outlined. Dinwiddie changed his mind, ending what had been a way to conclude the incident, and taking a more belligerent route. He sent an express to bring back the French prisoners, who were already beyond Winchester and heading for Will's Creek. La Force was returned to prison in Williamsburg, and the others were held in Winchester and then Alexandria.[51] New instructions to Colonel James Innes, commanding at Winchester, called for an attempt to exchange Druillon and the two cadets for the two Virginian captains held hostage. This was a fairly plausible exchange, but only if both sides accepted that the capitulation had been violated and was invalid. On Dinwiddie's orders, Innes wrote Contrecoeur that the taking of captives after the capitulation had been a violation of "the Law of Nations and against all the rules and regulations of war even among the Turks,"[52] and that the capitulation was therefore invalid. Any French claims that the captured Virginians belonged only to the Indians were countered by noting that Tanaghrisson had wanted to claim all the Frenchmen taken in the Jumonville incident.[53] Contrecoeur presumed the English messenger was spying, and kept him from seeing the fort in daylight and from meeting with Stobo. Contrecoeur replied that the capitulation had been honored because the French made every effort to restrain the Indians, and because he knew of only one captive with the Abenaki who had not been recovered and sent on to Virginia. Yet Contrecoeur

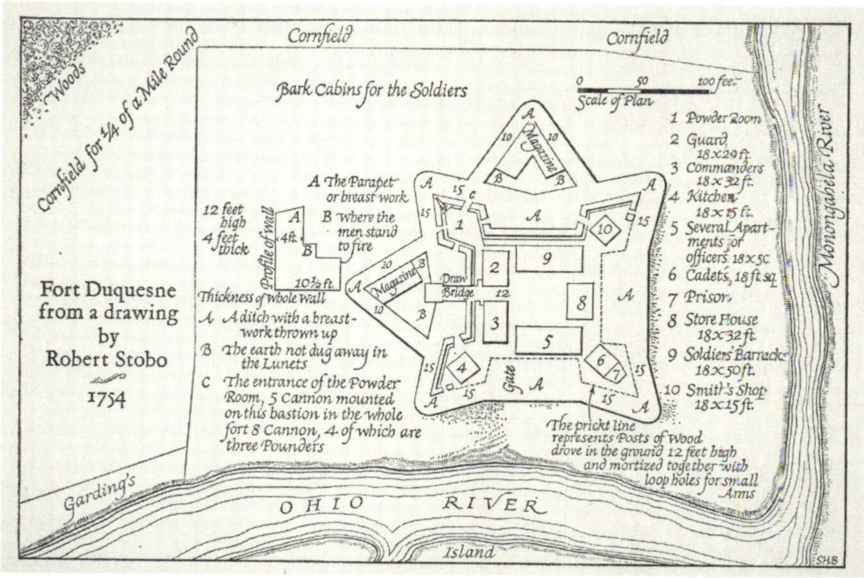

1 Robert Stobo's smuggled drawing of Fort Duquesne, 1754. Robert C. Alberts, *The Most Extraordinary Adventures of Major Robert Stobo* (Boston, MA: Houghton Mifflin, 1965), 100.

knew the Virginians would not honor the terms of the capitulation. The day the Virginian messenger left Fort Duquesne to return to Winchester, both Stobo and Van Braam were escorted north to Detroit and eventually to Montreal and Quebec.[54]

Robert Stobo's eventful captivity reveals much about the importation into Canada of European perceptions of military hostages and prisoners of war. Although Stobo later claimed that, as a military neophyte, he had no idea what the duties of a hostage were and no one in long-peaceful Virginia knew either, his companion knew very well. Under interrogation, Van Braam admitted that a hostage should not act against the interests of his hosts if afforded liberties, but if imprisoned he may act as a regular prisoner of war, attempting to write home or to escape. Stobo and Van Braam were officers initially treated very well at both Fort Duquesne and Quebec; they were given small allowances and the freedom of the town of Quebec and the Indian villages, and were allowed to socialize freely.[55]

The courtesies to Stobo diminished once Governor Ange Duquesne de Menneville, Marquis Duquesne, a professional French naval officer who was personally generous to captives,[56] was replaced at the end of July 1755 by the first and only Canadian-born governor of New France, Pierre-François Rigaud, Marquis de Vaudreuil. Circumstance had changed as well. Braddock's offensive was a major escalation, and rumors that Stobo had smuggled out letters and a plan of Fort Duquesne had been published in London and Paris newspapers, with which Vaudreuil confronted Stobo.[57] The hostages were briefly jailed, and then restored to some freedom while Vaudreuil awaited the French court's reply to his request that the English captains be tried for treason. The trial, held in Montreal in November 1756 and featuring none other than Céloron de Blainville as prosecutor, readily acquitted Van Braam and found Stobo guilty because his incriminating letters and map of Fort Duquesne had subsequently been found among the captured papers of General Braddock.[58]

Yet the Stobo case was not that simple. Like Dinwiddie and Innes, Stobo would argue that the capitulation at Fort Necessity had been violated by the French, thereby turning him from a hostage into a conventional European prisoner of war. Van Braam was less sure that the terms had been violated, because Villiers had done what he could to restrain the Indians. General Louis-Joseph de Montcalm's aide-de-camp, Louis-Antoine de Bougainville, asked what hostages became when the agreement they represented had been violated. He also wondered whether the capitulation was invalid if Washington had no power to pledge the return of those captured in the Jumonville incident. "In this case these hostages become no more than ordinary prisoners, who are not, I believe, subject to any punishment for trying to serve their country. It is up to those who hold them to see that they do not have the means."[59] Although Canadian judges found Stobo guilty of treason and ordered him beheaded, the French court had stipulated that he was not to be executed.[60] Whatever Vaudreuil, Céloron, or Villiers thought of the matter, to say nothing of any Indian told this fantastic story, Stobo was a military officer protected by European convention and by some well-placed new Canadian friends. He escaped twice from his rather comfortable confinement before finally succeeding in a harrowing third escape down the St Lawrence River with a small party of other prisoners in the summer of 1759.

Already promoted to major while in captivity, Stobo was treated as a returned hero with a handsome £1,000 gratuity, a dubious 9,000-acre Ohio land grant, and a precedent-setting gift of full pay during captivity that was eventually granted to all captured soldiers of the Virginia

Regiment.[61] Stobo was brazen enough to petition successfully for the double pay that he claimed was usually awarded to hostages, though he had acted as a prisoner of war in spying and escaping, and had claimed to be a prisoner of war at his trial.[62] On the recommendation of William Pitt, Stobo was awarded a captaincy in Amherst's own British regiment, the 15th Foot.[63] Fellow hostage Jacob Van Braam was not released until Canada's surrender in September 1760; he was not given double pay, but was given all his back pay, a gratuity of £500, a 9,000-acre Ohio land grant awarded to captains in Virginia's 1754 campaign, and a recommendation that helped him become a captain in the Royal American Regiment. He would eventually mortgage the dubious Ohio land grant to help buy his retirement farm in Wales, not in Virginia.[64] Both hostages had been rewarded by Virginia, but more by the British Army, which then became their lives.

The Virginia House of Burgesses refused to compensate one of its veterans of 1754, John Ramsey,[65] and his case is suggestive of a wider issue with "captured" soldiers. Ramsey claimed, when petitioning for his back pay of £66 in May of 1763, that he had been taken prisoner in the battle of Fort Necessity and held in cruel captivity by Indians for five and a half years. On returning to Virginia in 1761, he had rejoined the Virginia Regiment. Having investigated his claim, as was routine in such cases, a Burgesses' committee admitted his continued membership in the Virginia Regiment but reported that he had "behaved in a cowardly dastardly manner," and had previously deserted once, and again gone missing. In one of his smuggled letters from Fort Duquesne, Stobo said, "This man is the cause of our misfortunes" since he deserted the day before the battle and informed the enemy of the location and numbers of Washington's force.[66] In denying Ramsey's petition as unproven, the Burgesses recorded that it was not clear "whether he was taken prisoner, or voluntarily surrendered himself, or fled to the enemy."[67] Throughout the ensuing war, soldiers tended to return from captivity in pairs, answering such inevitable questions by corroborating each other's accounts and thereby avoiding the potentially fatal charge of desertion.

Virginians, Canadians, and Indians made noteworthy distinctions when capturing each other in 1754. The Canadians consistently treated all captured soldiers entirely differently from all captured traders. No captured traders were released, whether initially taken by Indians or by French garrisons. Capturing American colonial traders provoked no military response; no martial honor or reciprocity was involved or expected. However, when taken as soldiers with Ensign Ward, several veteran traders were immediately released. The contest between Virginian and Canadian soldiers escalated during 1754 from taking no captives in Ward's surrender to Washington's capture of all the survivors in the Jumonville incident, which was answered by the taking of hostages at Fort Necessity's surrender. The restraint of European military convention, and the reciprocity it was intended to generate, was noticeable in the actions of both the awkward young Virginian colonel and the more experienced Villiers. Indians fighting with Washington at Jumonville Glen or against him at Fort Necessity showed no inclination to regard soldiers any differently than other captives. Killing or selling any who had "surrendered" was the choice of their captor. John Ramsey was the only soldier who claimed to have been kept captive by Indians, and his story was not believed. Allegheny Indian communities had been raiding each other for captives to adopt, but were not adopting white captives in the decade before 1755.

Another distinction, between a hostage and a prisoner of war, was recognized by the British and French officers and the French court, which taught Canadians this distinction in refusing the execution of Robert Stobo. La Force was a captured officer jailed throughout most of his captivity, and, having attempted to escape several times like Stobo, he was acting like a prisoner of war. Yet Dinwiddie and Wheelock called him a hostage, presumably because he was taken outside of war, and claimed that he could be exchanged only for a hostage. Like the Virginians earlier, Amherst ignored the distinction and refused to release or exchange La Force, who was sent to him in 1759. As a captured *troupes de la marine* officer in the custody of the British Army, he lived more comfortably on Long Island for a year before being sent to France in what amounted to a major exchange of prisoners of war.[68] The idea that a hostage was to be awarded more privileges than a prisoner of war had been violated, but would resurface in the cases of Indians taken hostage in 1764.

The clearest and most consequential distinction was that being made between colonials and Indians in this new social environment. Intertribal raiding and slave trading had established a culture of captivity understood by colonials. Delaware leaders Custaloga and English John used the capture and transfer of English traders to signal their new alliance with the French. It is interesting that these captives were to be sold or given as gifts, but the Delaware were not then adopting captives, in sharp contrast with what would happen after 1755. The treatment of prisoners was also a sensitive and reliable measure of the limits of colonials' influence over their Indian allies. Tanaghrisson had disregarded Washington's grant of quarter to survivors of a skirmish. Washington never mentioned Tanaghrisson's execution of Jumonville, perhaps because it was a violation of his own offer of quarter, which he had not been able to enforce. Washington did not reveal this story even when widely accused of assassinating Jumonville himself. The more experienced Villiers considered Indians to be independent allies who neither negotiated nor signed the surrender terms, and were not bound by them. He acknowledged and accepted this distinction in his journal and in the terms offered at Fort Necessity. It is telling that the attack on Virginians retreating from Fort Necessity was not the result of ignorance, inexperience, or oversight by some recently arrived French commander. This was a distinction made by an experienced Canadian frontier commander, at the head of an overwhelmingly colonial force, who still recognized that even mission Indians were allies who would seek their own trophies and booty, including captives. Once again Washington did not include any mention of this violation of his surrender. Villiers and Washington were colonials who imported European understandings of honor and surrender to this new battleground. Their differing colonial perspectives did not prevent both of them from considering what their Indian allies did as beyond their control, beyond their responsibility, and in Washington's case, even beyond their version of what happened.

The taking and treatment of captives in the decade after 1745 was a consequential feature of the coming of war in Allegheny country. Intertribal raiding had reinforced a culture of captivity that was understood by white colonials, and the capture of six Shawnee allies provoked a war that would precede, parallel, and outlast the colonial wars. The French capture of English traders after 1749 was an effective, and largely forgotten, assertion of political and economic claims against the English, but it had very limited success in encouraging local Indians to take Pennsylvania traders captive for profit. Ohio Indians' violence against Canadian traders in 1747 was more ferocious than anything they undertook against English traders. In 1754, Delaware leaders Custaloga and English John used the capture of English traders to signal their alliance with the Canadians, as Peter Chartier had done earlier. The direct military contest between the Virginians and the Canadians escalated during 1754, revealing a sharp difference in French attitudes to English soldiers compared to traders, and the ready acceptance of current European military conventions by colonials. These European military conventions were flatly rejected by all Indian allies. Indian initiatives at Jumonville Glen and Fort Necessity displayed the limits of colonials' influence over their Indian allies concerning prisoners. In the various clashes of the decade before 1755, Ohio Indians showed very little interest in taking white captives, and no interest in taking them for adoption into their own communities.

The decade before 1755 saw escalating violence in Allegheny country, and killing was as likely as capture. Although the numbers were small, and the evidence is incomplete, it is noteworthy that Indian victims were more likely to be captured than killed in this period. For comparison with later periods, it is useful to summarize the fate of victims by status (see table 1). Traders comprised one-quarter of the victims, but were twice as likely to be captured as killed. Soldiers, most of whom faced each other in minor contests, were as likely to be captured as killed. White settlers were least likely to be victims, but these victims were more likely to be killed than would be evident between 1755 and 1765.

PART 2

CAPTURED IN WAR

As they had done before 1755, combatants in Allegheny country continued to take one prisoner for each person they killed during the Seven Years' War (see table 2) and the Anglo-Indian War of 1763–65 (see table 3). Captors chose to hold people who could readily have been killed in what was a contest to preserve and strengthen settlements of one's own culture, and to thwart rivals. Despite the claims of vocal survivors and their historians, the captured were those who did not resist much, and few captives attempted to escape. Undoubtedly, there were some who valued liberty more than life (as the warrior code tried to prescribe on all sides), or who feared captivity more than death (as the tellers of horrific tales intended), and these included many who died fighting or trying to escape, as well as some who did escape. Yet the unending celebration of these few escaped as paragons of liberty should not obscure the fact that, despite major cultural differences, the taking and keeping of captives was widespread, and a major amelioration of what has been inaccurately described as total war.[1]

A captive was taken because of quick decisions by both captor and captive, decisions usually made in very tense and dramatic circumstances, where culturally nurtured preconceptions could overwhelm the very limited information then available about each other. Allegheny Indians had shown little interest in white captives before 1755 and had little market for them thereafter, but war caused them to fight with their customary emphasis upon raiding for captives.[2]

For European military officers, reciprocity of civilities to higher-status prisoners had long allowed those who killed for a living to regard themselves as gentlemen, and by 1750 a shared system for capturing and treating all enemy soldiers, distinguished carefully by rank, had evolved in western Europe and was relatively easily extended to include colonials, but not Indians.[3] In the entire decade between 1755 and 1765, the British Army is known to have captured only one warrior in arms, though it took twenty hostages in negotiations. This single warrior was captured by a Highlander at Bushy Run, and was sardonically reported as having "received his quietus after a little examination." Two Potawatomi chiefs were held hostage during negotiations at Detroit in 1763, and accidentally became prisoners of war after Pontiac violated the agreed terms. These chiefs were eventually exchanged for nineteen captive British soldiers.[4] Even in this second war, when their enemies were all Indians, the British Army was not taking Indian combatants as captives.

French colonials who joined Indian allies in war could impress their hosts by taking or buying white captives,[5] but colonials of the British empire were more familiar with bounties on scalps than bounties on Indian captives.[6] The very few Indians who were captured by colonials had a short life expectancy if they did not escape. As a consequence of these very different martial practices, the taking of captives was extremely unequal in these wars. British colonials, who took very few captives themselves, developed culturally defensive myths about the nature and meaning of captivity amongst Indians.

Because circumstances could do so much to affect the taking of captives, this analysis separates captures into five related chapters. The raids, sieges, and battles of the Seven Years' War in Allegheny country afforded very different opportunities to take captives. Raids dominated these borderlands in the Seven Years' War, and chapter 4 can be read as a general narrative of the war there. There were few sieges and battles on the Allegheny frontier, but each type of action (chapters 5 and 6) provided very different incentives and opportunities to take prisoners. All those white settlers, traders, soldiers, and Indians killed or captured in Allegheny country during the Seven Years' War are worth considering in comparison to each other, and to the victims of the war that followed.

The British and Indian War of 1763–65 (a.k.a. Pontiac's War) is worth examining separately. It involved neither French nor Canadian forces, did not include European intercolonial captures, and occurred in an altered political and cultural landscape. However, like the previous war, this one began with the capture of traders, and included sieges of frontier garrisons and two sizable battles (chapter 7). Although the focus upon traders and garrisons was different in this war, it also featured renewed raids on colonial frontier settlements (chapter 8). How was the taking and treatment of captive white traders, soldiers, and settlers

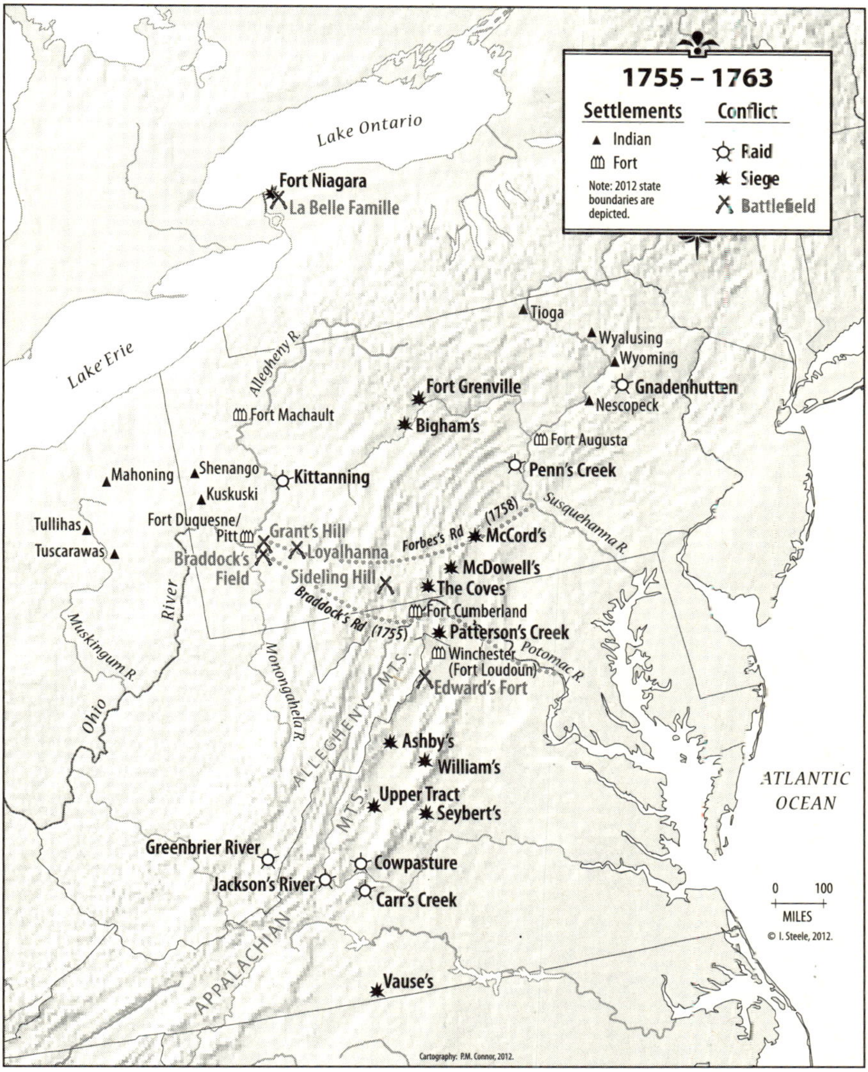

Map 2 Allegheny Country, 1755–63

in this war affected by experiences from the earlier war? In what ways was the shorter war a culmination, a replay, or a sequel to two decades of taking captives across Allegheny frontiers?

Learning how Allegheny captives were taken, by whom, and where also casts new light on well-known military actions of these two wars, adds to our understanding of Indian captors fighting with and without European allies, and measures whether the accumulating experiences led to a murderous spiral that affected willingness to take captives or "to go as captives."

4

Taken in Raids, 1754–59

Although the military events that came to resonate in European retellings of this Allegheny war were the battles and sieges, these were certainly not the essence of the war as lived in the region. For "back country" white settlers, the later 1750s were a time of soul-wrenching, family-destroying chaos that overwhelmed many who lived, died, or were captured in Allegheny country, and the panic and rumor spread much farther than the attacks. For Indians of the Allegheny borderlands, the raiding war provided victories, honors, and booty, and succeeded in expelling white intruders from a wide swath of recently lost farming and hunting lands. Raids declared war, and measured the pulse of the conflict, and the end of the raids was the only meaningful indicator of the end of the war.

To comprehend this chaos, sufferers readily came to assume that all this mayhem was orchestrated as part of a single war between the French and the English, and therefore had both a single source and a single solution. The French and Indian War could be seen as a united whole by a Scots-Irish frontiersman plotting revenge against Indian "reivers" in Pennsylvania, or by a Canadian governor drafting reluctant militiamen for service in the far-off Ohio Valley or appropriating the successes of independent Indian raiders more than five hundred miles away. Imperial and colonial authorities who lavished money and lives on building Fort Duquesne, or on its destruction, and who otherwise tried to convince their subjects to sacrifice local for more general objectives, all argued that this was a single unified imperial war. In this telling, the Indians were portrayed as clever opportunists, deluded dupes, or the faithful allies of the French. Any reckless young Canadian ensign accompanying an Indian raiding party was reported by the furious survivors as a "French officer," and therefore the embodiment of the hypocrisy of a nation that pretended to teach western European martial civilities. Canadian governor Pierre-François Rigaud,

Marquis de Vaudreuil, too readily considered the same teenager to be a Canadian hero said to have been in charge of the raid. A Virginian land surveyor and a Pennsylvanian trader were equally quick to exaggerate when claiming to represent their king in acts of greed, revenge, self-promotion, or self-defense. Even Indian sachems and war chiefs portrayed the war as a unified conflict under European sponsors when Indians and Europeans conferred. Indians often exaggerated their own dependency, either to solicit gifts from allies, or to excuse their attacks on erstwhile friends and trade associates. Consequently, though the Allegheny war started before the European courts decided, exploded at times that served no European military schedules, and seemed to end long before the Europeans made peace, the French and English easily came to be seen as overseeing a unified war.

However, Indians of the upper Ohio and Susquehanna Valleys were usually fighting their own parallel wars, using the Anglo-French conflict to extract necessary weapons and supplies from grateful allies and using these resources to challenge and reverse European encroachment on their lands. There was no known multitribal or pan-Indian alliance in 1755 to reclaim ancestral lands from Europeans who were, as an aged Ohio Delaware said in 1758, like pigeons; "where one lands there are soon a thousand."[1] The Shawnee, the separatist Iroquoian Mingo, and the related but distinct Ohio and Susquehanna Delaware all fought for their own purposes on their own schedules, were led by their own war chiefs while drawing allies and opportunists from the other groups, and were fed and directed by their own anger, rumors, and casualties. As we attempt to understand who was raiding where and when, their captives can be the best clues to the changing shape of this confusing, gruesome little war.

Capture in a raid was a quick but complex event, involving the assumptions, actions, reactions, and calculations of both the captor and the captive. Although much is known, or readily conjectured, about why Indian war against white frontiersmen centered on swift and deadly raids for scalps and captives, much less has even been asked about exactly how these captives were taken. The flintlock musket was intended to kill or maim, not to take healthy animals or enemies. This musket needed to be fed with powder and shot that usually bound the user to European suppliers whose wartime prices were higher, and included alliance. Indian communal and individual hunting provided the skills to stalk, to shoot, and to kill opponents at a distance, but exactly how did these skills assist Indians in capturing live enemies unharmed?

What calculations, emotions, and circumstances determined who was killed and who was captured in raids on individual frontier farmsteads? There is some evidence that Indians preferred to use edged weapons, at least in capturing isolated individuals by surprise.[2] Edged weapons were quieter than guns and did not need reloading, but they could not be used as a threat against an opponent with a loaded gun or a drawn sword, or against someone strong and quick enough to turn the knife against its wielder. These were among the various reasons why men who encountered Indian raiders were less likely to be captured than were women or children.

The Indian warrior who first took hold of a captive usually acquired clear and personal rights: to take the life or scalp of this captive on the trail, to be recognized as a successful warrior on arrival in his home village, and, in some cases, to dispose of this captive by gift or exchange. The captive was a prized form of property in a culture that valued the sharing of property rather than its hoarding.[3] The choice to take a prisoner rather than a scalp could be based on personal psychology and history, on tactical considerations, or on immediate guesses at the strength, health, personality, or usefulness of the captive. The captor's attending responsibility was to supervise his captive personally until delivered to the village, which meant that active raiding, for a scalp, for a more valuable prisoner, or for other loot, usually ended once a captor had taken a prisoner.

Colonial regular regiments and militiamen were initially neither well trained nor experienced, but both training and experience could prepare these fighters to take as captives those Euro-American enemies who indicated their surrender by throwing down their weapons and asking for quarter, as Michel Pepin *dit* La Force's men had done in Jumonville Glen. Scouting parties were sometimes assigned to take a captive as their primary tactical purpose. These captors were often entitled to some bounty for a captured enemy, and colonial forces were likely to take fellow Europeans, or enslavable Africans, as prisoners. Indians were less likely to surrender, and colonial captors were also less likely to take an Indian captive, aside from isolated cases of "protective custody" as war began.[4] Late in 1755, Conrad Weiser lamented that "back inhabitants" were terrorizing friendly Indians, who feared "being killed by a mob." When the people of Paxton had the singular fortune to capture an Indian, Weiser hurried out to interrogate him, but was too late: "(shocking to me) they shott him in the midst of them, scalped him and threw his Body into the River."[5]

People captured outside formal sieges have too easily been portrayed as victims without any choice in the matter. Certainly, Indians captured some farmworkers and travelers by complete surprise, overpowering and securing them instantly, and adult male captives were prone to explain their capture this way. However, more had been initially captured in their homes. Some believed that surrendering to Indians without fighting gave them a better chance of survival, and they feared the prospect of captivity less than they feared death. Indians certainly did not share the curious European convention that allowed people to fight first and, when that failed, ask for and expect quarter. European colonial women and children were taken captive in disproportionate numbers partly because they were perceived as less likely to resist dangerously, and/or thought themselves unable to do so. There was often an initial choice to fight or surrender, a choice that might have been impulsive or calculated, but was derived from a personal sense of what was expected, or from understandings about captivity and escape that varied more widely than colonial authorities wished. Local tales of captivity and escape were supplemented in some places by newspaper and pamphlet narratives of captivity, offering very ambiguous lessons throughout the war.[6] Few Indians were taken captive by whites because most Indians encountered were warriors trained to prefer death to captivity, because captors feared that such captives would be dangerous to secure, and because these captives would confer little renown, and even some suspicion, upon the captor. Indian captives were not objects for any formal colonial rituals of torture or adoption, and could not profitably be exchanged.

The first Allegheny raiding war went through four discernible phases. Before and after General Edward Braddock's failed invasion of 1755, Indians declared war by attacking unsuspecting Virginian families working on the most isolated backwoods clearings. This initial phase of surprise attacks, on people who had neither prepared nor fled, came a little later to Pennsylvania. The second phase and climax of the raiding war came in 1756, when French support and involvement peaked and raiders began to meet more serious resistance and even counterattack. A third phase was discernible by 1757, when the devastated no-man's-land had expanded on both sides, and the best targets had retreated behind developing defenses; raids against settlements declined in size and frequency. Raids became even less frequent in the last phase of the raiding war, after the spring of 1758. White settlers were still the primary targets, but more of the casualties were colonial regulars, rangers, militiamen, and warriors. As General John Forbes's army mobilized that year, to redo Braddock's work, raids became more closely identified with this European contest, where captives were taken by scouts to gain information, and where major raids by regulars and their allies were directed against their opponents' strongholds. Delineating and exploring these four phases invites comparisons that indicate the changes, as well as the relentless Indian focus on taking captives.

PHASE ONE

The first phase of the raiding war began in September 1754, and then spread gradually during the following year along a 500-mile front from the Roanoke to the Delaware Rivers. Shawnee and Delaware war parties repeatedly declared war with a surprise attack upon frontier farmers who evidently still expected to be spared from the war even months after Braddock's defeat. In these initial attacks, raiders found unsuspecting families at their farming, so capture was relatively easy, food was plentiful, and war parties returned home untroubled by rescuers, ranger patrols, or the intervention of garrisons of yet-to-be-built forts. Guns and gunpowder, which did not keep well beyond a year or two, had been acquired in peacetime trade, without the higher prices and diplomatic strings that would be attached once the Europeans were at war. Here were ideal conditions in which to exercise the skills of long-range raiding, and to take what prisoners they wanted by surprise, with minimum risk of fouling the victory by losing a companion.

Shawnee, with a few Delaware and Nottaway neighbors and sympathizers, began the war with their retaliatory attack on the Buffalo Creek community in South Carolina's Broad River Valley in September 1754. Although few details of this raid have survived, it apparently came as a complete surprise, with the raiders killing sixteen and capturing fourteen, without suffering any casualties in return – the Shawnee definition of a completely successful raid. One captured young man escaped the following day, but could identify his alien captors only as part of a larger party of "French Indians."[7] This "Buffalo Creek Massacre" was reported in the Charlestown newspaper as part of a stream of details about French aggression at Jumonville Glen and Fort Necessity, and about Indian raids on the New York frontier. Although Cherokee promptly told an English trader that the Shawnee had been involved at Buffalo Creek, it was a full year before Governor James Glen of South Carolina had confirmation, when he learned that two children taken in the raid were among some Shawnee who had recently migrated south to live with the Creeks.[8] News of the Buffalo Creek raid was welcomed in New France, and Governor Ange Duquesne de Menneville, Marquis Duquesne, was quick to claim he had shamed the Shawnee into finally avenging their insulting loss of 1753.[9] Although this attack opened the raiding war, it could be seen as an isolated horror by those who did not know that, even if it was sufficient revenge on South Carolina, it was just the beginning of a wider Shawnee war with the English.

The Shawnee had clearly signaled that this initial raid was a declaration of war against all the English, and particularly against Virginians. As the escaped youth had learned in his single day of captivity, the Buffalo Creek raiders were part of a larger war party. Although encumbered with captives and heading home via the New River, this larger group took the time and risks to attack Virginians at their out-settlement on the Holston River. They killed three men in this poorly recorded incident, men living on land that was claimed by the Shawnee and by other tribes.[10] The victims' neighbors, like the Virginia governor, regarded these as murders in peacetime, acts of French-inspired savagery like the murders of Robert Foyle's family in the same region nine months earlier.[11] Samuel Stalnacker, who ran the trading post in this first Virginia community beyond the Blue Ridge Mountains, knew better. He was unharmed in the attack, and later recalled having been warned to leave by these "Northern Indians" who claimed the area.[12]

It seems at least an efficient coincidence that Indian and English colonial opponents paired off quickly as the Seven Years' War began on this frontier, bringing the Shawnee to focus on Virginia, and the Delaware to be preoccupied with Pennsylvania. Land grievances, Virginian intrusions into Shawnee country, and military practicalities may all have helped angry Shawnee to target the Virginians as their primary English enemy. Virginian place names, like Shawnee Cabins and Shawnee Springs in the vicinity of Winchester, certainly indicated that the Shawnee had lived there in recent times, and in the 1750s the South Branch of the Potomac River was still called the Wappatomaka.[13] However, little written evidence survives of any specific Shawnee land claims made in Virginia, and defensive Quaker pioneers in the Shenandoah Valley had earlier insisted that they were unable to discover the specific Indian owners of their lands.[14] The Shawnee also knew that Virginian hunters and settlers were intruders and competitors in the Ohio Valley and in Kentucky, where the French still referred to the Cumberland River as the "Chaouanon," their name for the Shawnee.[15]

Delaware lands and history had been in what became Pennsylvania, and theirs was in part a civil war between neighbors, with Ohio Delaware assisting their kin to capture people and provisions while ousting strangers from lands Delaware had recently inhabited.[16] These raiders were often known to their victims by sight and name. With or without a negotiated agreement with the Delaware, the Shawnee concentrated on Virginia, thereby allowing separate target areas for loot and captives, and limiting intertribal rivalries over command and rewards without excluding considerable cooperation. Their opponents reinforced this arrangement, allowing them to focus attention as well. Scots-Irish immigrants to Virginia and Pennsylvania recognized clan raiding particularly well from their experiences in Ulster, where they had lived on lands confiscated from other unreconciled natives. Scots-Irish could match the Shawnee and Delaware in sustaining blood feuds, even if they did not reciprocate with a revival of the English borderers' older tribal habit of "bride stealing" or with the Highlanders' clan remembrances of capturing and incorporating children after killing their parents.[17] Scots-Irish would "fort-up" rather than flee, with the result that in Cumberland County, for instance, almost all the 6,000 white inhabitants were Scots-Irish by the end of the war.[18]

Although the winter of 1754–55 had been quiet, by its end the Canadian garrison at Fort Duquesne was already on alert for signs of Braddock, and patrols were sent out "to prevent Desertions, get intelligence, and prevent our [English colonial] Indian Trade." In March one patrol captured three Virginians who had gone west to Redstone Creek to recover tools cached the previous spring after Ensign Edward Ward's surrender at the forks of the Ohio River. A month later three Virginia "woodboys" were surprised over their campfire by a mounted patrol of eighteen that approached them in three columns, two of Indians and one of Canadians. The overwhelmed woodboys hurried to surrender to the Canadians, and the Indians confiscated the horses that the woodboys claimed they had come west to retrieve after Indians had stolen them the previous summer. Escorted to Fort Duquesne for interrogation, these young captives were grilled about Braddock's preparations and were assured that the French could not return their horses because this was "intirely an Indian War, in which they act only as auxilarys." They were also told that they would have been kept as slaves if they had chosen to surrender to the Indians. Nonetheless, it was the Canadians, not the Indians, who threatened to hang the youths if they came west again. As they were neither traders nor soldiers, the three were escorted east by the next patrol to leave the fort, and released. At least this was the story they told to the commander of Fort Cumberland, the Wills Creek fort that was becoming the English colonial counterpart to Fort Duquesne.[19]

By May of 1755, Captain Claude-Pierre Pécaudy de Contrecoeur at Fort Duquesne was deliberately seeking prisoners who might provide better information about Braddock's approaching army. The varying fate of these captives depended upon their status and their captor. A Kanesatake Mohawk and two Delaware set up a blind near Bedford, Pennsylvania, and fired on two traveling road builders. One was killed, and eighteen-year-old James Smith was thrown from his horse and immediately captured by the Canadian Mohawk. Smith recalled being taken to Fort Duquesne and severely beaten by a gauntlet of warriors before being taken into the fort "for doctoring" and interrogation.[20] He was reclaimed by the Canadian Mohawk, whom he never named, and was adopted by this community. A more prized captive was Iroquoian Half-King Scarouady, who was apparently scouting for Braddock when taken by a patrol of eighty-seven Indians accompanied by twelve Canadian cadets. The Indians immediately took control of what might well have been their own staged negotiation, and they forced the disgusted Canadians to release the captive to his kinsmen, who set him free.[21] Braddock's "head scout," soldier John Walker, was a third captive, taken by a patrol that he later described as consisting of four Frenchmen and four Shawnee. He became a prisoner of the Canadians, was interrogated at Fort Duquesne, and was then sent to Montreal and Canadian servitude, and would be a soldier-prisoner of undeclared war until he escaped.[22]

Most of the Shawnee and Delaware remained uncommitted to the French until well after Braddock's defeat, though individual Delaware and Shawnee had been involved in earlier captures. Contrecoeur complained on 21 June 1755 that he had great difficulty persuading the Shawnee and Delaware to attack the English; out of some 267 Indians who participated in five of his own recent scouts, there had been only 12 Shawnee and 2 Delaware in total.[23] Additionally, only 3 Shawnee and no Delaware are known to have been among the 637 Indians who fought alongside the Canadians in the Battle of the Monongahela on 9 July.[24] The Shawnee were already busy in their own war, joined by a number of Ohio Delaware who had not yet launched their war into Pennsylvanian borderlands.

What is known of four raids into Virginia just prior to Braddock's defeat suggests that they were part of the Shawnee war, into which they were drawing a few Ohio Delaware.[25] Shawnee and Delaware attacked the Virginia frontier in mid-June, while Braddock's army was still proceeding effectively westward. Lieutenant Governor Robert Dinwiddie, desperate to rouse Virginians and their British colonial neighbors to defend the western interests of Virginian land speculators, including himself, was likely correct in claiming that the attacks were by two linked raiding parties totaling 130, but there is no evidence to support his contention that they were "French and Indians." The attackers stayed well away from Braddock's army, suggesting the French were not in charge. The raiders followed the Great Kanawha–New River route again, divided into two groups, one of which revisited the Holston River on 18 June, killing five and taking two captives, this time including trader and militia captain Samuel Stalnacker. Stalnacker, who rented lands called "Colonel Patton's Indian Field Estate" and had ignored the earlier Shawnee warnings, was being treated generously in being captured at all.[26] Four days after this Holston River raid, Shawnee and Delaware were again attacking vulnerable targets a little closer to Fort Cumberland, killing three and capturing eight.[27] The other Shawnee raiding party apparently attacked white settlers farther east, at Patterson's Creek, leaving eleven dead plus at least two missing and presumed captured. These raiders then attacked isolated farmsteads along the North River in Augusta County, killing seven and this time taking ten captives before heading west. Disrupting life anywhere near Braddock's supply lines certainly would have pleased the French, and may have been suggested, but neither Fort Cumberland nor the roads to it were among the targets, and no captives were taken who could provide the French with military information. Each war party had struck twice, with impunity, taking more prisoners on the second strike before heading home.

Something of the dynamics of capture early in the war was evident in the contrasting experience of two families attacked on the North River. John Bingeman, his wife, and their son Adam were all killed, and Adam's wife, Katherine, their daughter, and a nephew all became Shawnee captives, soon to be separated from each other. No eyewitness account remains, but John Bingeman was remembered as a strong man who vigorously attempted to defend his family and was even said to have killed two Indians in doing so.[28] At least one of the three Bingemans killed that day, and perhaps all of them, had died fighting. In contrast, John Freeling's family, attacked at the same place and time, were afforded very different treatment. John, his wife Peggy, and their five young children were all captured without any bloodshed. Perhaps John had calculated that resistance was futile; in any case, his captors did not prove murderous. John and Peggy Freeling were one of the few couples caught in this war who are known to have spent their long Indian captivity together. Moreover, at least three of their children were still near them in Lower Shawnee Town a decade later, at which time John and Peggy would return to Virginia.[29]

The Shawnee raided southwestern Virginia again in each of the three months after Braddock's defeat, hitting settlements at the Greenbrier, New, and Holston Rivers. The opportunity for complete surprise was gone; at least one Shenandoah Valley preacher had already called for a day of fasting and prayer because local sinners had brought on "wars and many murders committed by the savage Indians on the back inhabitants."[30] Some prayed, many fled, and some "forted up" their houses to resist more effectively. It was not by chance that the Shawnee took risks to target Colonel James Patton, owner of the "Indian Field Estate" that Stalnacker had leased on the Holston River, a legate at the 1752 Logstown conference that revealed the Iroquois betrayal of 1744, a member in the belligerent Virginia House of Burgesses, Augusta County's lieutenant and militia colonel, and the leading patentee of 200,000 acres.[31] Patton had stopped at the Ingles farm at Draper's Meadows near the headwaters of the New River, and had stayed behind to refresh himself after sending on the rest of the government's convoy of ammunition and military supplies. The observant Shawnee then attacked, and Colonel Patton was said to have fought several assailants with his sword before being killed. This attack bore signs of change in the war and in the taking of captives, because pursuit of the raiding party was now presumed. Five people had been captured there, including Mrs Mary Ingles, her two young sons, and her sister-in-law. The four killed were the fighting colonel, a man riding by who could have promptly alerted pursuers, an infant whose cries would have done the same, and an older woman who would have encumbered rapid travel.[32] Although captured ten months after the Shawnee began their war and three weeks after Braddock's defeat, Mary Ingles did not regard herself as in a war, and claimed not to recognize the meaning of the Shawnee attack on Colonel Patton. She would not learn much Shawnee in her two months as a prisoner in Lower Shawnee Town, but she later confirmed that there were no expected signs of the French there, and she saw no torture or killing. For her chronicler, this calm somehow indicated "the casual and mercenary motives of these Shawnees, who had perpetrated the massacre more to gain booty and to display their courage than to start a blood feud."[33]

There were some signs of Virginian settler resistance before the end of August 1755, though a party of about fifty Shawnee and Delaware raiders was still able to surprise white settlers in an isolated new Virginian settlement on the Greenbrier River, killing eight, taking five captives, and driving off 500 head of cattle. Cattle had been offensive weapons in the white intruders' peaceful advance onto Indian lands, and were particularly so in the isolated valleys of the Appalachian Mountains, where "pioneers" since the 1730s had felt safe enough to scatter themselves and their herds.[34] What the Delaware intended to do with this herd is unclear, but these raiders soon had a small reversal of fortune. Two of the captives were assigned to help two Delaware warriors to drive the cattle and some horses westward. Captive Hugh McSwain killed both the Delaware in their sleep, removed the bells from the freed cattle, and returned to Fort Cumberland with his German fellow captive, together with the guns, matchcoats, and scalps of the Delaware.[35] Meanwhile, the main party of Shawnee and Delaware failed in its attack on some fifty-nine people who retreated into one fortified house, and two Shawnee were killed in an unsuccessful attack upon another.[36] The white settlers who had not fled on news of war were beginning to adapt effectively, and war parties were not yet burning houses full of people.

The final attack on Virginians that season, by 150 Shawnee and Delaware warriors, bore marks of things to come. There was evidently more French material support, and the attackers were likely accompanied by at least two Canadians. The force broke into smaller groups to harass settlements near Fort Cumberland that still supplied the garrison. The fort had been near the edge of Euro-American settlement but was now more isolated, for many of the white settlers of western Augusta and Frederick Counties had left in the previous year. In their largest raid to date, the Shawnee struck Patterson's Creek again on 1 October, killing forty-two and capturing twenty-eight.[37] The Ohio Delaware conducted their first known separate raid here, in an attack near Fort Cumberland, killing two soldiers and taking thirteen prisoners.[38]

In the five months ending in early October 1755, after which raids on Virginia were suddenly suspended, the Shawnee and their Delaware allies had prompted the wholesale evacuation of much of Augusta County, had killed sixty-nine Virginians and captured fifty-five, and had lost five warriors. The ratio of killed to captured was less ferocious than it would become, but more deadly than the advantages of surprise attacks might have allowed. A frustrated Lieutenant Governor Dinwiddie denounced the Augusta County militia as cowards and threatened to confiscate the land of anyone who would not defend it. Through the House of Burgesses, he established bounties of £10 on Indian scalps, with no premium for captives over scalps, and he raised more ranger companies.[39] He solicited the help of the Cherokee, much of which would be squandered in the abortive Sandy Creek expedition. None of this bluster was what caused the Virginia frontier to calm over the ensuing winter. The Shawnee had been conducting their own war in their own season, and their raiding season ended in October, when these warrior-hunters shifted back to hunting, where they took no prisoners.[40]

The Ohio Delaware conversion to war came after a long history of fairly peaceful coexistence with European settlers and missionaries in Pennsylvania. Long since gone from most of the river that bore their name, these Delaware had migrated first to the Susquehanna Valley, where the depressing process of orderly dispossession had soon been repeated. Those who had migrated again to the tributaries of the upper Ohio River were drawn to farm and hunt in the hills and fertile bottom lands, and also sought to escape capricious white and Iroquois interference. For many Ohio Delaware, resentments against the English were greater, older, and more personal than their anger at the recently intruding French. They had little living tradition of intertribal raiding for scalps and prisoners, compared to their Mingo and Shawnee allies, had few experienced war chiefs, and were soon reviving, improvising, and inventing their martial tradition.[41] They would prove at least as ferocious as other raiders, and more varied and unpredictable as captors, and they were more inventive than ritualistic in torture, mutilation, and the markers left with those they killed.

The most prominent Ohio Delaware in 1755 was Shingas, one of the three nephews of Chief Allumapees (Sassoonan) who were known to whites as the Delaware "Royal Family." Shingas himself had long since moved to the upper Ohio Valley, where the Six Nations had unwisely "appointed" him king of the Delaware in 1752. The gesture had failed to rein in these Ohio Delaware, who were effectively independent of both their Six Nations overlords and the Pennsylvania government. As Shingas later explained, he had been inclined toward the more familiar English rather than the French until he and five other Delaware, Shawnee, and Mingo chiefs had interviewed General Braddock in the spring of 1755. The chiefs offered to help the English to drive out the invading French, on condition that Ohio country be restored to its Indian inhabitants. Braddock was apparently peremptory, if clairvoyant, in asserting that "No Savage Should Inherit the Land."[42] After Braddock's defeat, and the failure of Mingo diplomacy in Philadelphia early in August 1755, most of the Ohio Delaware went over to the French. The first Delaware blow had been to join the Shawnee and Canadians in a raiding party of 150 that attacked near Fort Cumberland at the end of September. Delaware were predominant, and included Shingas, Tewea (Captain Jacobs), and Tamaqua (Beaver). After returning from this raid, three leading Ohio Delaware war captains (Tewea, Captain Will, and Captain John Peter) and Shingas himself "were supplied and sent out by the French Commander at Fort Du Quesne against Pennsylvania."[43] The Ohio Delaware war had independent origins, but was directly linked to the French at its outset.

A tense quiet had pervaded the Pennsylvania frontier in the three months after the defeat of General Braddock, during which Pennsylvanians hoped for continuing exemption from the unprecedented Shawnee raids into neighboring Virginia and Maryland. Some Pennsylvania frontier settlers had already abandoned their Cumberland County farms and ripening crops, moving east in anticipation that the war would spread from Virginia. Rumors were rampant, and relations between Indians and Euro-Americans became more strained.[44] Near the end of August 1755, "woodsmen" brought three Indian women, two men, and a boy to the commander of the British Army, Colonel Thomas Dunbar, who had precipitously withdrawn the survivors of Braddock's army into very early winter quarters in Pennsylvania. Dunbar confessed that he did not know what to do with these Indians, and could not distinguish Indian friend from foe. After consulting a staunch Iroquois ally, Dunbar released the prisoners, "and hope I have acted right."[45] European settlers in the Susquehanna Valley soon had similar difficulties in distinguishing friend from foe, and most would not act with Dunbar's circumspection.

For all Delaware, their friends, and the Pennsylvania authorities, the drift to war was complicated by the two remaining centers of Delaware settlement on the Susquehanna River, both shared with Shawnee. One was in the Shamokin–Big Island region around the river's forks, and the other was on the North Branch around Wyoming. Six Ohio Delaware and four Shawnee visited the settlement on Big Island, announcing that they came from Shingas, that the Ohio Delaware and Shawnee had taken up the French hatchet, and that Pennsylvania was about to be invaded. They invited the Susquehanna Delaware to join them, presenting two scalps (likely those of the soldiers killed in the recent attack near Fort Cumberland), and warned those who did not join to get out of the way. English allies and informants Scarouady and Andrew Montour hurried to Big Island to confirm this news and then headed to Philadelphia to sound the alarm. While these two were on their way east, as were numerous Virginian refugees fleeing by way of the Susquehanna, Delaware and Shawnee gathered at Shamokin to consider and reject Shingas's message and the scalps that embodied their Ohio kinsman's invitation to war.

While this group of Susquehanna Delaware were deciding against war at Shamokin, others declared war on their Euro-American neighbors by joining in a well-chosen attack on Penn's Creek, just fifteen miles to the south, on 16 October.[46] This was a local Indian grievance, at the northern boundary of a fraudulent recent Iroquois land sale, and on land that was already occupied by some twenty-five European families.[47] The most detailed account of the attack, ostensibly by two young girl captives, reveals the peculiarities of a raid in which fourteen local Delaware attacked unsuspecting neighbors at leisure over three days. Eight Delaware approached Jean Jacques Le Roy's place, killed him, took his children captive, and set fire to his house. Two of the Delaware then went to the next farm, and leisurely smoked a pipe with Barbara and Regina Leininger's father before killing him. The captured girls could later name each of the eight Delaware who had attacked these families. None of Leininger's three children escaped to carry news of this declaration of war. This terrifying truth became clear enough when John Harris, Thomas McKee, and forty other armed local white settlers came to investigate and to bury the fourteen bodies. Because they now distrusted even their firmest Indian allies, Scarouady and Montour, Harris's mounted party ignored their clear warning and rode into an ambush laid by 120 warriors, all of whom were not locals. The ambush left four of Harris's party killed, and four more drowned in the Susquehanna while trying to escape.[48]

It is curious that belligerent Susquehanna Delaware in this war party took any prisoners at all in the Penn's Creek attacks. These inexperienced raiders held captives who were living proof that their captors had attacked their white neighbors, as well as being a burden during the captors' own migration and resettlement. Ten of the captives taken at Penn's Creek, including two of Leininger's daughters, were displayed at several Delaware villages up the West Branch of the Susquehanna, before being taken farther west. In this instance, both captors and captives were migrating to Shingas's town of Kittanning on the Allegheny River. Going over to the French initially meant going over the Allegheny Mountains for these Susquehanna Delaware, and could mean a particularly hard captivity for those forced to go with them.[49]

Ohio Delaware, led by Shingas and Tewea accompanied by some Shawnee and Mingo, brought the war to Cumberland County, Pennsylvania, at the end of October 1755, killing at least six, and capturing twenty-eight.[50] The target was again well chosen to answer Delaware grievances, as the attack surprised and disrupted settlements on unpurchased Indian lands in the three neighboring valleys of Great Cove, Little Cove, and Conollaways (Tonoloway) Creek. The attackers once again declared war on yet another isolated micro-settlement, this time by leaving a tomahawk embedded in the body of David McClelland.[51]

Tewea's personal capture of William and Elizabeth Fleming of Conollaways, which lasted only hours before they escaped to have their story publicized throughout the northern British colonies, reveals unique and telling aspects of capture in the initial, surprise, phase of the conflict. William Fleming, heeding a warning that other locals had discounted,[52] was riding home to protect his wife when two Delaware leapt from behind trees, grabbed his horse's bridle, ordered him in "good English" off his horse, and then offered a handshake "very compaisantly" and said he must go with them. Frozen in terror, Fleming was clapped on the shoulder several times by his captors and urged not to be fearful, for they would not hurt him as long as he would cooperate "and promise to stand by them, in Case they should be attacked by the English in our future Proceedings." Fleming's first test was to tell which houses were most defenseless, as "they were afraid to venture on Houses that had many Inhabitants." Tewea and his companion, named Jim, were Ohio residents, not local Delaware attacking their neighbors. Fleming wished to appear helpful without being so, but Tewea promptly became suspicious and more hostile. Fleming then admitted that his own house and pregnant and unsuspecting wife, Elizabeth, were nearby, claiming that "all my Concern was for her." Tewea confessed a need for a woman to bake bread for them, and said she would be safer with them than with other attackers, for Tewea's general "orders" were "to spare none but young Men and young Women."[53]

Such a surrender was bought with compliance, as was soon demonstrated more starkly. They had to pass the home of the Hicks family, eight strong, on the way to the Flemings' place. As they passed by, the Delaware noticed two of Hicks's sons come out of the house. One was surprised and captured, screaming piteously, and the other fled back to the house. No one came out of the Hicks house, doubtlessly fearing a large war party, and the two Delaware with their two captives proceeded on towards the Flemings' farm. Whereas Fleming "had the Policy to counterfeit a chearful Behaviour," young Hicks would not be quiet and "continued Obstinate to the last Degree"; he lasted less than a mile. Fleming was tied to a tree, and then Jim killed Hicks with several tomahawk blows. The horrified Fleming was told, "with an Air of Insult, nothing but my good Behaviour for the future could save me from the same Treatment." When Fleming "introduced my Guests" to his wife, he warned her of the need for cheerful cooperation. Fleming's message, which would be published in Lancaster within two months and reprinted in pamphlets and newspapers soon thereafter in Philadelphia, New York, and Boston, was that going quietly was best.[54]

What did Fleming's captors want? Tewea and Jim ransacked the Fleming house, taking what his victims thought was everything of value, and then loading William with a sack of meal (an odd choice unless Tewea was serious about the bread making), and Elizabeth with a bundle of clothes. When the party was leaving the Fleming house, the buildings were set afire, apparently as an afterthought. They then revisited the now-empty Hicks house,[55] and took tools, bread, cheese, dried peaches, and tobacco before burning the house, barn, and "several Barraks of Grain." Delaware were not yet burning people alive in their houses, but were destroying the buildings that symbolized the hated occupation the warriors were ending. Elizabeth Fleming escaped and, looking down from a hilltop the next day, "saw so many Houses in a Blaze that I almost concluded the whole Province was in Flames."[56]

What captors took was not a fair measure of why they came. It was a conversation about motives between Tewea and Elizabeth Fleming, during the only evening of the Flemings' captivity, that made their narrative an instant and compelling propaganda piece, subtitled "Wherein it fully appears, that the Barbarities of the Indians is owing to the French, and chiefly their Priests." Tewea not only claimed that General Braddock had slighted the Indian chiefs at that crucial meeting, but also added that Braddock "threatened to destroy all the Indians on the Continent, after they had conquered the French." Tewea further claimed that he was now under French orders to bring all his captives to the Ohio Valley, where they would not be turned over to the French but "you shall live well, and be given as Kindred to our Friends." William Fleming remained suspicious and speculated that "so far as I could learn," the Indians were offered French bounties for scalps and prisoners. Yet the central damning passage from the conversation was Tewea's response to Elizabeth's question about the shedding of innocent blood. She was reportedly told that "the French were better off than the English, for they had a great many old Men among them that could forgive all their Sins, and these Men had often assured the Indians it was no Sin to destroy Hereticks, and all the English were such." As though to excuse the Delaware slightly, and damn the French more, William Fleming reported that Tewea and Jim assured him that his wife would not be molested because doing so would affront "their God," leading to death in war, and they offered the suggestion that this moral difference was the reason for the bad luck of the English. If the Delaware were being ironical or chiding the Flemings about their religion or morals, which supports the authenticity of the conversation, the Flemings did not record any retort.[57]

Delaware still living in the Susquehanna Valley communities were now under irresistible pressure to choose sides. Most of those living in and near the intertribal community of Shamokin saw their neighborhood dissolved by the anger of some and the fear of all that they would be victims of Indian intimidation or of reprisals by frustrated Pennsylvanians unable to identify or catch their Indian attackers. As winter came, Shamokin residents went off to hunt, but they were not coming back; by spring the village of more than 300 had been abandoned and burned, and by summer the Pennsylvania government had built its premier new fort, Fort Augusta, near the site.[58]

The easier choice for Shamokin's displaced residents would have been to accept the invitation presented at Big Island, to join the anti-English raids that answered local grievances, and to take themselves and their captives to the growing community at Shingas's Kittanning settlement on the Allegheny River. Arriving too late in the year to grow any crops, these Susquehanna Delaware refugees could add guns to the winter hunt, and hope to survive on kin generosity, looted grain and cattle, and perhaps some French supplies. Their recent history and knowledge of Pennsylvania's geography, people, and languages, as well as their need to prove themselves and gain acceptance in this new setting, all encouraged them to support and join the raiding.

It is striking that most of the Susquehanna Delaware did not make this obvious choice to go west. Instead, they moved some twenty-five miles up the North Branch of the Susquehanna River to the Delaware village of Nescopeck, a little closer to their overbearing Six Nations "nephews," but not so close as to be free from the intimidation of their French-allied kin from Shamokin and the Ohio Valley. If the refugees who arrived at Nescopeck hoped they had moved far enough to escape the fighting, they were soon disappointed. Early in October, Delaware and Shawnee warriors from the Ohio, likely accompanied by some Shamokin refugees, attacked east of the Susquehanna for the first time, bringing the war to Lancaster and Berks Counties. These initial raids were a surprise, but did not involve the taking of numerous unsuspecting captives or the gathering of looted goods and livestock; these raids were markedly more ferocious than other first strikes, and only two of the first twenty-six victims are known to have been taken prisoner.[59] These attackers from Ohio country may have killed more people here to force local kin into the war, or because the raiders anticipated that their long, fast-paced journey home would be harder with captives. Some former Shamokin residents may also have been taking their more personal revenge. There is no evidence that unusual levels of resistance provoked this intensity. If some Nescopeck residents joined these raids, they had no incentive to take captives either. Nescopeck was overcrowded with new Delaware refugees to be fed that winter, and needed no surviving witnesses from the nearby Euro-American settlements of Lancaster, Berks, and Northampton Counties.

Thirty miles farther up the North Branch, the Shawnee-Delaware town of Wyoming was also rapidly being transformed. This settlement had been home to the peaceable and accommodating Shawnee chief Paxinosa and to the Delaware "king" Nutimus, with the neutral Six Nations of the Iroquois as overlords not far upriver. Some of the Iroquois had considered it valuable to have these compliant Indians forming a North Branch buffer between themselves and the expanding Pennsylvanian settlements, but other Iroquois repeatedly made land sales that aborted such plans and alienated the Delaware.[60] As recently as 1754 the Iroquois had forced converted Delaware and Munsee Moravians to leave the thriving farming community they had helped build at Gnadenhütten over the previous decade, and to bring their skills (but not the Moravian religion) to Wyoming. Teedyuscung, nephew of Nutimus, was among the less pious and more influential of those moving from Gnadenhütten to Wyoming.[61] Anger at the Iroquois and the whites to whom they sold land would increase mightily in Wyoming once it became known that some Iroquois had sold the Wyoming Valley itself to the Susquehanna Company of Connecticut in 1754. As the Allegheny war spread eastward, Teedyuscung built up a following among the angry and dispossessed that soon made him the effective headman of a sizable village that was becoming anti-English and anti-Iroquois. These Delaware, and the Minisink Munsee and Mahicans who joined them, may have totaled nearly 200 fighting men who would extend the war eastward to the Delaware River by the end of 1755.

The North Branch Delaware war began with a deadly attack on several farmsteads near Tulpehocken in Berks County, where a Delaware village had been overtaken by white settlement over the previous generation.[62] Investigating militia found that six white men, one woman, and four children had been killed, as was one of the Delaware raiders. A nine-year-old girl was found alive, but scalped, as were all the dead. The bodies of two of the men indicated torture or at least mutilation. "Caspar Spring's Brains were beat out, had two cuts in his Breasts, was shot in the Back, and otherwise cruelly used, which a Regard for Decency forbids mentioning." No whites were reported missing, and no prisoners were known to have been taken. "The Horses and Cattle are in the cornfields, and every thing is in the utmost Disorder."[63] This was an amateurish attack unlike initial attacks elsewhere: one warrior was killed and scalped, and the attackers took the time to torture or mutilate at the attack site, burned no buildings, and evidently took neither prisoners, food supplies, nor cattle. The raiders, furious but inexperienced, were attackers from nearby, who may have been bonding in killing, but they left no sign that they had a larger strategy or even a place of refuge.[64]

The next attack by the North Branch Delaware was an equally deadly descent on an even more vulnerable target. The war faction at Wyoming sent its first raiding party to attack in Northampton County, where they destroyed the unarmed Moravian mission settlement at Gnadenhütten, until recently the home of a number of Wyoming residents, including Teedyuscung himself.[65] The raiders knocked on the mission house door as fourteen Moravian missionaries were eating, and then fired as soon as the door was opened, killing ten in the mission house, which they promptly set ablaze, and the Delaware took only one captive. Meanwhile, the mission's Delaware and Mohican converts had scattered into the woods; seventy-three of them kept their faith and headed south to the Moravian mission station at Bethlehem. They were among the 232 Delaware "who lived near the white people" and were reported at Wyoming to have been captured by the whites. Although there was no internment of Indians as this war began, there were 556 Indians who had sought refuge in the three major Moravian settlements by the end of the year.[66] These refugees were clinging to a multicultural past, and putting their faith in the Moravians and their God. Two months later, Lieutenant Governor Robert Hunter Morris appointed John Ross to take other Christian Indian refugees then in Philadelphia out to the proprietor's Conestoga manor in Lancaster County and construct and provision a settlement for them and for others then at Harris's Ferry. Although these friendly Indian refugees were not formally confined, Morris pointed out that the locals "may not be well disposed" and that stragglers or drunks would be in danger of death.[67]

Other Delaware at Gnadenhütten put their inherited culture first, and belatedly joined Teedyuscung at Wyoming.[68] Although the Moravian missionaries responded with continuing hospitality to displaced Indians, the raid had accomplished the purpose of making many Indian converts abandon hope of an intercultural future. This ferocious rejection was marked by refusal to take more of the Moravian missionaries captive, as might easily have been done if their captors were seeking diplomatic advantage or holding hostages to dissuade counterattack. By burning the Moravians alive in their mission home, these raiders displayed a contemptuous, and effective, tactic that was rare so early in the war.

Teedyuscung and his followers soon became the most desperate and deadly Delaware in the war, and they were fighting on their own. After their first raids in November 1755, Teedyuscung's community moved farther up the North Branch of the Susquehanna River to the Iroquois-Delaware village of Tioga, and was promptly and predictably warned by Sir William Johnson and the Six Nations to cease raiding.[69] As an upstart headman, Teedyuscung had no incentive to migrate to join the Ohio Delaware with his prisoners, and had no safe place to keep them. He gained an endorsement from the pro-French faction among the Chenussio Seneca, but his later dealings with the French at Forts Niagara and Duquesne were disappointing. A captive reported that no French or French Indians visited Tioga while he was there. This increasingly hungry community, without the fresh and fertile fields that were home to the Ohio raiders, did not even undertake a winter hunt in what would have been dangerous Iroquois woods. When the year ended, Teedyuscung personally led thirty warriors, including seven relatives, in an attack on several Northampton County farms, all within the bounds of the old Walking Purchase. At least ten people were killed and four captured in these raids, and three days later the raiders fought a skirmish near Gnadenhütten, where five Delaware and fourteen Pennsylvania militiamen died.[70]

Raiders' initial advantages had lasted until the end of 1755, indicating how isolated colonial borderers were and had vainly hoped to remain. Delaware and Shawnee captors had the advantage of surprise, and access to isolated families, they captured food supplies that could sustain a war party and its captives on the trail, and they were able to retreat without facing any effective interception or pursuit. Sixteen warriors had been killed in raids, marring victory in Indian eyes but doing nothing to mitigate the sense of utter defeat felt by their helpless enemies. Despite the particularly deadly Delaware attacks in northern Pennsylvania, the year's raids left nearly as many people captured (216) as had been killed (226).[71] These raids were nowhere near as deadly as Braddock's battle, in which at least thirty-one were killed for every one captured (538:17), and the moderation of that year's raids would not be matched again in this war or the next.

PHASE TWO

The great advantages of the first raids were bound to fade. British colonial settlers were abandoning the region in great numbers, creating a buffer of vacant fields and woods that could be reclaimed by Indians and deer, but these Indians would soon have no cattle, grain, or people available for relatively easy capture. As Indians and whites both began moving farther apart to relative safety, raiders had to travel farther, needing more supplies and taking more risks. There were already some signs that raiders were facing increasing resistance. Four Shawnee were killed while attacking fortified houses in Augusta County, Virginia, seven died in raiding farther east, and four Delaware died in a skirmish with pursuing Pennsylvania militia.[72] The Governments of Virginia and Pennsylvania finally responded with ranger patrols, major forts, and support for garrison houses. These measures would not stop raids, but they increased the likelihood that war parties would be pursued or counterattacked.

The year 1756 saw the peak of the raiding war in the Allegheny borderland, and it truly became a French and Indian war. One scholar has cataloged 102 attacks in Pennsylvania and Virginia during that year, and these ranged over the entire front from Northampton County, Pennsylvania, to the New River farmsteads of southwestern Virginia.[73] The midwinter attacks of Teedyuscung's hungry Delaware meant that raiding occurred every month; nearly half of the attacks of 1756 occurred in the first four months. Even for Teedyuscung, whose independent war included eight attacks in January, this was becoming a more unified French and Indian war. Delaware from his village at Tioga visited Kittanning that winter, displaying scalps they were carrying to Fort Duquesne to obtain a reward that they later judged to be inadequate. Ohio Delaware visited kin in Tioga in March, bringing along captive John Coxe, whom they left there. His account confirmed that the Tioga settlement was very hungry, that several prisoners had starved to death, and that few prisoners were being taken. Some Delaware there were talking openly of preferring peace to starvation. The tortured negotiation of a peace between Pennsylvania and Teedyuscung had already begun, and something approaching a ceasefire gave relief to Northampton County residents after April.[74] By June, most of the surviving captives had been moved from Tioga to the Ohio Valley, where Shawnee, Delaware, and Wyandot communities were not only planning joint raids, but were also contemplating moving farther down the Ohio River together to share hunting and planting grounds in the Muskingum and Scioto Valleys.[75]

Intertribal cooperation increased for Ohio raiders, and the Canadians at Fort Duquesne became more influential as the sole suppliers of the essential gunpowder and shot, either as trade goods for hunters or as inducements and rewards for hunters willing to join raids that might serve French strategic purposes. What had been three distinguishable Indian raiding wars against the colonists of Pennsylvania and Virginia in the fall of 1755 now coalesced through French and intertribal diplomacy and the bonding of warriors who had shared recent fighting experiences. In 1756 the French at Fort Duquesne still had the reputation gained against Braddock as well as the supplies necessary to recruit for raids, and to encourage the Shawnee and the Ohio Delaware in their own attacks.[76]

The Canadians also organized, funded, and contributed *troupes de la marine* officers for a few attacks that involved Miami, Potawatomi, Ottawa, and Huron allies. Some of these Canadians were young ensigns who were, despite their instructions, more volunteers than commanders of Indian raiding parties. Others were seasoned Canadian veterans of the *pays d'en haut* who had borderland military reputations and could assemble forces with some loyalty to themselves and sometimes even induce Indian raiders to risk their lives against fortified opponents. In the strategic highlights of the summer of 1756, senior officers led the sieges and negotiated the surrenders of Vause's Fort and Fort Granville. Raiders that year faced longer journeys, suffered more deaths and wounds in fighting better-prepared opponents, found proportionally fewer women, children, or valuables available for capture, and were more likely to be pursued in their retreat into the Allegheny Mountains.

The context was also changing because of the way Virginian and Pennsylvanian settlers and their governments belatedly responded to the attacks of 1755. Many colonial borderers had fled the frontier, or sent their families eastward, as news of the first frightful attacks spread and was embroidered to justify flight. The population of Augusta County, Virginia, fell by nearly 20 per cent between 1755 and 1757, and the western half of the county was virtually deserted.[77] Desperate to slow this flood of refugees who abandoned militias, clogged roads, and diverted supplies, Lieutenant Governor Dinwiddie not only charged cowardice, but also declared that abandoned farms would be considered forfeit; returned captives would be among those made landless by this proclamation. The number of men fit to bear arms in Cumberland County, Pennsylvania, may not have fallen from 3,000 to 100 in the year ending in April 1756, as reported, but some 928 farms were abandoned in this county by the end of 1757.[78] A swath of Allegheny borderland ranging from 50 to 200 miles wide had been reclaimed by Shawnee and Delaware raiders, and was marked by burned-out farmsteads.

Those frontier farmers who did not flee began "forting up" on their own, before their governments provided any assistance. Determined Euro-American settlers fortified stronger houses and grist mills with reinforced walls, firing slits, and stockades. Neighboring families, militia, and even small parties of rangers or provincial soldiers gathered at these strengthened farmhouses in times of trouble. Raiders adjusted their tactics quickly, announcing their presence by a surprise attack on a few field workers but only after laying an ambush for those expected to flee toward the garrison houses. The fortified houses became increasingly isolated and were never effective obstacles to raiding, but some potential captives were protected there, and patrols or garrisons of armed militiamen or provincial regulars might be there in sufficient numbers to challenge, intercept, or pursue raiders returning home. The garrison houses themselves, usually named after the resident family, were sometimes attacked, as were McDowell's Fort in Pennsylvania, Stoddart's Fort in Maryland, and Williams's Fort in Virginia, all in late February and early March of 1756. Five were killed and six captured near Stoddart's Fort in what was a loose blockade rather than a siege.[79]

Shingas led a raiding party of about fifty Ohio Delaware with similar intentions near McDowell's Fort, but they were counterattacked on 29 February before they chased the militiamen into the fort. Four militia and a warrior died in fighting that the defenders considered their successful defense against a siege.[80]

It may not be a coincidence that the Canadians became more involved as the English frontiersmen fortified. Commandant Jean-Daniel Dumas at Fort Duquesne ordered, funded, and provided Canadian officers to "lead" attacks. An ensign who accompanied one such party had been ordered to attack magazines that supplied Fort Cumberland, disrupt convoys, and take prisoners who could provide information.[81] In at least two cases, it was Canadians who negotiated the surrender of forts, and Canadians involved in raids were awarded some of the captives, who were usually moved along to New France. Stockaded Ashby's Fort on Patterson's Creek was besieged briefly by one large war party, and, after a parley that evidently did not involve Canadians, the attackers moved on to the similarly constructed Cock's Fort on the Little Cacapon River, which was attacked but not captured.[82] A night battle between Captain John Fenton Mercer's Virginian rangers and these Delaware near Edward's Fort left Mercer among the twenty-six dead, who included nine Delaware; predictably, no prisoners were taken by either side in this skirmish.[83] These raids into Virginia helped isolate Fort Cumberland, but the results could not have satisfied either Dumas or the Indians.

Ohio Delaware led by Tewea displayed another Indian tactical change when they set fire to Williams's Fort, Virginia, early in March. Seven men, three women, and eight children were in the house when it was set alight.[84] With this tactic, the garrison house changed from a minor obstacle for raiders to an ideal place to capture fleeing people, though setting a substantial fire was risky against vigilant defenders and never as simple as shooting flaming arrows. Ohio Delaware under Shingas burned McCord's Fort in Cumberland County, Pennsylvania, at the beginning of April 1756; twenty-seven persons were initially reported missing there, though five escaped and one was killed during a major skirmish between the captors and luckless militia four days later.[85]

Canadian *troupes de la marine* were more numerous and prominent in the capture of three other colonial fortifications that summer. It is not clear whether the Canadians were thought necessary to organize, sustain, and direct Indian efforts in a war that was becoming more deadly and less profitable, but the French supplies needed to encourage Indian allies were becoming scarce, and joining the raids was another form of encouragement. In mid-June seven Canadians and twenty Delaware burned Bigham's Fort at the junction of Pennsylvania's Tuscarora and Juniata Rivers, killing five and taking eighteen captives.[86] Vause's Fort, south of the James River in Virginia, was also attacked that month. After a particularly fierce defense, which left at least thirty-two Indians, three Canadians, and two Virginians dead, the attackers successfully set fire to the stockade. Before the fire went out of control, the defenders negotiated surrender. The surrender of Vause's Fort, and of Pennsylvania's Fort Granville a month later to a "French and Indian" raiding force led by François Coulon de Villiers, will be examined more fully later as examples of captivity by way of siege and surrender.[87] These attacks were also features of a raiding war that had lost most of its softest targets.

If the European settlers' defensive measures were forcing raiders into a new kind of war, so were the belated actions of British colonial governments. The Government of Virginia had been fighting for over a year before the wave of Indian attacks finally prompted the more serious pursuit of some measures and the initiation of others. Lieutenant Governor Dinwiddie may have ranted against the cowardly militia, but he told the British government bluntly, early in 1756, that his wartime borderland was 300 miles long and nearly 200 miles wide, making it impossible for militias from the more settled parts of the colony to respond effectively.[88] The Virginia Regiment was still undermanned despite attempts to draft both vagrants and militiamen, whose own units routinely dissolved in the face of emergency. Nonetheless, patrols of rangers from this regiment stiffened militias in defense of some private forts and in several skirmishes that disrupted and diverted raiders.[89] Although the Virginia Regiment had manned only nine forts by the summer of 1757, in addition to Maryland's Fort Cumberland, a string of eighty-one private and public stockades and forts now attempted to protect Virginia's frontier.[90]

Pennsylvania's political leaders were much more cautious and divided than were Virginia's, but they finally decided on war in the spring of 1756. Early in January private individuals in Philadelphia had been allowed to offer $350 each for the heads of Shingas and Tewea, Delaware leaders who were still seen as criminals responsible for alienating Pennsylvania's Indians.[91] Within days a broader scalp bounty, without any premium for live captives, was being considered. When Pennsylvania finally went to war with the Delaware in April, the governor proclaimed a bounty of $150 on Indian male captives over twelve years of age, pledging $130 for their scalps. Conrad Weiser argued in vain that this was not sufficient distinction to encourage the taking of Indian captives, given the risks and troubles. The difference in the bounties offered for a woman Indian prisoner ($130) and for her scalp ($50) was more substantial, but no Indian women were reported captured during the war.[92] Pennsylvania had no militia, but, by the summer of 1756, its volunteer regiment had three undermanned battalions expected to garrison, and patrol from, an ambitious string of publicly funded new forts. Thirteen forts, focusing on devastated Northumberland and Cumberland Counties, were projected and twelve were being built at that time, but even then, most of them were isolated, being well beyond the people they were intended to protect, and were inoffensively consuming the lion's share of the colony's limited military manpower and funding. By the end of the year, one of these forts had been surrendered and six had been abandoned as indefensible. Some twenty-four private garrison houses that survived the attacks of that summer became more integrated with the government's efforts, being taken over completely, or at least having provincial troops stationed there on occasion.[93] As in Virginia, the forts and garrison houses did not stop the raids, but they diverted some raiders, and challenged others. With the raids penetrating well to the east of the forts, these garrisons could, if informed quickly, intercept raiding parties as they returned home.

The colonies of Virginia, Maryland, and Pennsylvania each attempted a single and separate raid to counterattack their Ohio enemies in 1756. Virginia was the first to organize some 350 men, guided by Cherokee, who were to travel up Sandy Creek and attack Indian towns on the Ohio River. The expedition set off in mid-February, but was plagued by fractious leaders, bad weather, unexpectedly rough terrain, and tragically inadequate supplies. Within a month the attempt collapsed far from its enemies or objectives, leaving the conscripted militiamen seething and the Cherokee convinced that the English were hopeless.[94] The Cherokee were, however, drawn into familiar raiding of their own, where they were more successful.[95] A small Maryland party on a similar mission left Fort Cumberland late in April. The leader was killed in a skirmish when the group had progressed only a few miles, and the project immediately collapsed.[96]

The only significant counterattack by colonials in the Allegheny raiding war was the Pennsylvania regiment's raid on Kittanning on 8 September 1756, which reveals much about the limits of such an undertaking, and the views of captives and captivity from both sides. Any attack on a settlement thought to contain more than 100 of your own captured people was inherently reckless. One of the few conventions shared by Indians, colonials, and imperial troops was that anyone holding prisoners could be expected to kill these captives when attacked.[97] The expedition's leader was not even instructed on what to do with recovered captives.[98] Despite the rhetoric about recovering captives, the attack on Kittanning was a desperate counterstrike to inflict some damage on the Ohio Delaware and to improve the shattered morale of Pennsylvanian colonials who had endured a year of relentless, unanswered frontier raids. Prominent frontier land speculator, proprietary surveyor, and former assemblyman John Armstrong was the lieutenant colonel of newly raised Pennsylvania regulars on the expedition.[99] They supposedly knew their target well from former captives, including John Baker, who had escaped from Kittanning seven months earlier and now accompanied the attack in which he would be killed. Kittanning straddled the Allegheny River some thirty miles upstream from Fort Duquesne. On the west side lived Shingas, then the premier Ohio Delaware war leader, together with his supporters and most of the English captives. The target of the early morning surprise attack was, instead, thirty unstockaded cabins on the east side of the river, where Tewea, more widely known among whites as Captain Jacobs, and his smaller community lived. Tewea had been the leading Delaware war captain in the destruction of Fort Granville, where Armstrong's brother had died only weeks earlier.[100] Although the 300 attackers outnumbered all of Kittanning's warriors by nearly three to one, the raiders' objective had quickly shrunk to burning Tewea's settlement and cornfield, recovering a few captives held there, and withdrawing before Shingas's warriors or a nearby French patrol could become involved. Like Indians attacking defenders in garrison houses in Pennsylvania, this raid soon centered on burning people in their houses.

The Pennsylvanian view of taking Indian prisoners soon seemed clear enough. The fighting centered upon the cabins from which a surprised Tewea and his companions were soon defending themselves effectively. Armstrong reported that his offer of quarter was defiantly rejected by a man who shouted what could have served as an Amerindian warrior motto: "he was a Man and wou'd not be a Prisoner." When warned that he would be burned, he replied that he could eat fire, and that "he did not care, for he wou'd kill four or five before he died." Armstrong also noted that one defender, "to shew his Manhood, began to Sing," and a squaw who began to cry was ordered to be silent.[101] Both sides understood these rituals. Even before Pennsylvanian losses mounted and the threat of being cut off by Delaware reinforcements became serious, Armstrong's forces were making no efforts to take Delaware prisoners. Some Delaware were killed trying to escape their burning houses, but none were captured. The Delaware lost fourteen people, including Tewea and his wife; the Pennsylvanians had at least nineteen men killed, and at least two captured, and fourteen others were initially declared missing.[102]

Revenge against the English prisoners already held by the Delaware at Kittanning might have been expected. At least one captive had been wounded by Pennsylvanian gunfire. At hearing the first gunshots, the people of Shingas's settlement sent all their women, children, and captives (including all five who have left written accounts) some ten miles away to safety. Perhaps the attackers were not yet known, but the inclusion of the captives in this retreat is a reminder that they were considered parts of Delaware families, rather than threats to them or aliens useful as human shields. After the siege and pursuit were over, and their losses known, the Delaware took a limited but ferocious revenge. Although fourteen Delaware, including a celebrated chief, had been killed, the vengeance fell on three people. One was Mrs Alexander McAllister, taken captive in the burning of Bigham's Fort three months earlier and the only adult among four captives who had just been rescued by the Pennsylvanians and then retaken by the Delaware. In the only reported case of formal torture of a woman on this frontier, Mrs McAllister was stripped, bound to a stake, and tortured to death with hot irons.[103] Paul Broadly, another captive who evidently attempted to escape during the raid, was also caught and tortured to death.[104] The other victim was a Pennsylvanian soldier, Thomas Burke, taken in the skirmish in which Mrs McAllister was recaptured. His torture climaxed, and ended abruptly, when he was forced to drink molten lead. Cruel inventiveness rather than traditional ritual marked these and other incidents of Delaware torture; a warrior culture was being recovered, borrowed, and invented. The other captives were assembled and forced to witness these tortures, and were expected to learn from them, but none of these captives were otherwise punished in retaliation.[105] More surprising was the fate of Lawrence Donahue, a Pennsylvanian soldier captured in the Delaware pursuit of the fleeing raiders. Donahue survived nearly eight years of Delaware captivity before being returned to Colonel Henry Bouquet at the Muskingum River in 1764.[106]

In desperation, the Pennsylvanians had begun fighting like their enemy. Pennsylvanians claimed they offered quarter, which was refused; they then took scalps, as government bounties encouraged them to do,

2 Silver medal struck to commemorate raid on Kittanning. Courtesy of the State Museum of Pennsylvania, Pennsylvania Historical and Museum Commission.

and burned their enemies in their homes. Pennsylvanians, whose government had reluctantly abandoned pacifism only months earlier, had just burned women and children at Kittanning, had taken no prisoners, and had recovered very few of their own, half of whom were retaken by the Delaware that same day. The Kittanning medal (see illustration 2) congratulated Pennsylvanians on a much-needed, if dubious, victory and reassured the victorious that they were still civilized Europeans. The outrageous claim was made that the raid had brought Teedyuscung to seek peace.[107] The only significant success of the Kittanning raid has been underestimated. The attack displayed that the Allegheny River villages were no longer secured by the mountains or by the French at Fort Duquesne.[108] Kittanning was promptly abandoned, and the Delaware moved west and established themselves on the Beaver River at Kuskuski, Salt Lick, and relocated Mahoning (Mahoning II), and farther west at Tuscarawas near the headwaters of the Muskingum River. Downstream a little at Wakitomica, new Delaware arrivals were enlarging the Shawnee settlement as well.[109] Like the initial raids of 1755 against Euro-Americans farther east, the Kittanning raid widened the no-man's-land of abandoned settlement by another fifty miles and, for a short time, caused more Allegheny Delaware to migrate than to raid in revenge.

It was the Shawnee, more than the Ohio Delaware, who pressed the war that autumn.[110] They attacked Virginia's Jackson River settlements once again, taking twenty-nine captives and killing thirteen. It was

Shawnee who raided in Cumberland County, Pennsylvania, and their captives included George Brown, a child who would one day become a Shawnee war chief.[111] Although the Ohio Delaware were raiding less, they were alert and on the defensive. A raiding party of eight Catawba and five Virginians attacked the remnant of the Shawnee settlement at Chartier's Creek at the end of 1756, killing and scalping three or four Shawnee. The Catawba expressly wanted a live captive, and the attackers persisted in this quest long enough to be caught by pursuing Delaware, Shawnee, and Canadians. In the ensuing fighting, and in a chance encounter with a large French and Indian war party returning to Fort Duquesne, three of the Catawba were killed and one was captured. Two Virginians, at least one of whom was wearing his hair in Catawba fashion, were captured and three others killed.[112] The raid was not a success by Catawba or Virginian standards, but it did indicate again that counterattack was possible, and that the upper Ohio Valley Indian sanctuary had become unsafe.

The changed circumstances, strategies, and tactics of the raiding war, and the intensifying quests for revenge affected casualties and captures in 1756. Some 525 people were killed in that year of fighting, and 395 were captured. Known Indian casualties increased dramatically that year, as at least 98 Indians died fighting fortified white settlers, colonial armies, or each other. Catawba and Cherokee had resumed their traditional raids against Shawnee and Mingo enemies, sometimes accompanied by British colonial allies, who also attempted their own raids. Four Canadians were killed accompanying Indian raids into Virginia, and none were captured. The British Army avoided casualties completely on this frontier in 1756, while militia and colonial regulars died and were captured in burned-out garrison houses, skirmishes, or incidents near the forts they garrisoned. Three soldiers were killed for every one taken. In contrast, forty-nine warriors were killed for every one of them captured, and it was only Indian opponents who took Indian captives.[113] The raiding and skirmishing war had become more deadly in 1756.[114]

PHASE THREE

The raiding war changed markedly again in 1757 and the first half of 1758. Although the overall number of reported attacks continued the pace of the previous year,[115] there were fewer victims and more of the attacks were clustered into a clearer seasonal rhythm. There were very few attacks in the first quarter of 1757 for three reasons: snow was uncommonly deep in the mountains that winter; smallpox was widely reported among garrisons, and among white and Indian settlers;[116] and the North Branch Delaware had suspended raids amid serious peace negotiations with Pennsylvania. In retrospect, both years had a clearly defined raiding season, with one-quarter of all raids occurring in April, and two-thirds between April and July. In September Shawnee focused again upon southwestern Virginia, but there were only a few small raids during the remainder of the year. This stronger seasonal pattern suggests that warrior-hunters were operating closer to their own cultural norms, of dispersed winter hunting and a season of war that paralleled the women's farming season.

The French and Canadian role in the raiding faded, as was implied by the clearer seasonal rhythm of the raids. French supplies had become so scarce that Fort Presqu'île was abandoned in April, and its hungry garrison had to walk and hunt its way to Fort Niagara.[117] There were no major attempts on frontier forts or garrison houses in 1757, another sign of diminishing Canadian involvement. More Canadians became victims in Allegheny country, but this change did not reflect increased involvement. There were two incidents in which Indian raiders disagreed with, and abandoned, their Canadian companions. M. de Montisambert, who had been prominent in the expedition that burned McCord's Fort the previous year, led the largest joint raiding party, of more than 200, against Fort Cumberland early in June 1757. However, Montisambert fell ill, and the expedition promptly broke into small raiding parties that instead attacked Virginian settlements near Winchester, the South Branch of the Potomac River, and neighboring Conococheague. Thirteen Canadians, including three young officers, were heading back to Fort Duquesne alone when they were attacked by a party of fifteen Cherokee and five Virginia regulars. In the skirmish, Cherokee chief Swallow was killed, as were three Canadians; three more Canadians were granted quarter, but two of them were promptly killed by the Cherokee.[118] The capture of Canadian ensign Michel La Chauvignerie Jr, who wandered in to surrender himself at Fort Henry in September after being lost in the woods, may have involved another disagreement, or at least a miscommunication, between Indians and Canadian fighters.[119]

Although black slaves were usually absent in accounts about this Allegheny war, two incidents in 1757 reveal interesting choices made by blacks. François, a French slave at Fort Duquesne, escaped, bringing

Lieutenant Governor Dinwiddie valuable information about French preparations.[120] He was granted his freedom, which was easily done because he had no Virginian owner. An unnamed black slave girl was caught in the attack on Alexander McKeasey's farm near Tom's Creek, Maryland. Her master had been killed, and his son captured, and she was being "taken away by the hand" when she set the dogs on her liberators and fled.[121] Only three identified black soldiers are known to have been captured in the Allegheny war, one remained missing, and two were returned at Detroit when that Canadian garrison surrendered. Slavery proved to be a protection against death; only one black was reported killed, whereas twenty-two were captured.[122]

During 1758 more than 500 Cherokee became seriously involved as raiders in their parallel war into Ohio country, in joint raids with Virginians, and then as guides and scouts for the relentless Forbes expedition that distracted, diverted, and outlasted the raiding against English frontier settlements by Indians allied with the French. A two-month winter respite in the raiding war ended when an Overhill Cherokee raiding party, led by Attakullakulla (Little Carpenter) and the Great Warrior of Chota, attacked the Miami and their Canadian allies. The Cherokee surprised and killed six members of a Canadian military patrol, and went on to kill six Miami and capture one Miami woman and two "Frenchmen" in a related incident. The victors, who had been encouraged by the English at Fort Loudoun (Vonore, Tennessee), were given a generous welcome there on their way home. The fort's commander, Captain Paul Demeré, was able to get a deposition from one of the French prisoners, but lamented, "I would have given a Price for the Prisoners, but if I had mentioned one word about it, then, they would have stoke [struck] them on the Head that Moment."[123] Cherokee and Catawba allies of the English again attacked Ohio Indian communities in April, killing seven and taking five captive.[124]

Although this increased Cherokee and Catawba support was most welcome to the English, and doubtlessly affected Shawnee and Delaware raiding plans, there were soon major difficulties in distinguishing friend from foe. In Virginia's Bedford County, in May, parties of Indians "which cald themselves Sumtimes Cherokees and sumtimes Shonees" were taking provisions, horses, and valuables from farmsteads in peremptory and recognizable Warrior Path fashion, and confronting angry militia. In one instance, the warriors identified themselves as Shawnee and challenged the militiamen to fight for the horses they had taken. Three Indians and a white settler were killed in one resulting firefight, and sixteen Indians were killed and six militiamen went "missing" in another. These Cherokee-impersonating Shawnee were disrupting Anglo-Cherokee cooperation, and left the battlefield without taking any prisoners.[125] The British Army could not distinguish its allies either, and Bouquet's standing orders for Fort Lyttleton were that "no Party Guard, Centry or any Person belonging to the Army are to fire upon any Indians without they are first fired upon." The attempt to distinguish allies as those wearing yellow feathers or ribbons, or those carrying their matchcoats on a pole, could have been helpful only very briefly.[126] The Cherokee would become disillusioned with the British war effort for many reasons, but the Shawnee impersonators had helped this process.

The spring of 1758 marked the final full season of major attacks on civilians on the Virginia and Pennsylvania frontiers, and these focused on two areas, York County, Pennsylvania, and along the South Branch of Virginia's Potomac River.[127] Although west of the Susquehanna River, York County had been relatively protected from the raiding war that ravaged neighboring Cumberland County, little local fortification was undertaken, and York County leaders were very active in recruiting to support military efforts elsewhere. Six captives were taken in York County in July 1757, but no deaths had been reported before the two surprising and well-recorded raids of April 1758.[128] An unusual raiding party, of six Shawnee and four "Frenchmen," who may have been scouting for information about the British Army assembling to attack Fort Duquesne, evidently finished their spying with an attack on the well-established Jamieson (Jemison) farm on Marsh Creek, in western York County. Mary Jamieson, then fifteen, was a captive who went on to become famous as the Seneca "white woman of the Genesee," and her recollections sixty-five years later provide colorful details of the attack. The early morning raiders surprised and secured her father in his yard, shot and killed another man arriving on horseback (and likely to ride off to sound the alarm), and then took the unresisting women and children from the house. What was most unusual was what Mary recalled happening over the next two days. Eight of the eleven captives were killed by their captors, including all the adults and five of the eight children. Mary remembered this as resulting from Shawnee fear of Virginian pursuers, and these captors may have taken too many captives to control on a long journey through an increasingly abandoned but better-defended area. This small raid, which became iconic in American memory, resulted in the deliberate killing of more captured children than occurred in any other attack in this entire borderland war.[129] It cannot be known whether the capture of the Jamiesons was an unscheduled trophy hunt at the insistence of the Shawnee guides, or whether the tactical killing of prisoners was at the insistence of Canadians trapped far behind enemy lines.

It was not simply that a spying expedition had drawn raiders so far that the return with captives would be difficult and deadly. All the easy targets were farther east now. Thirteen Ohio Delaware attacked in the same county eight days later, and a young sawmill operator was unable to defend his family from enemies who "mostly all Spake English, one spake as good English as I can."[130] After a child discovered the approaching warriors, and ran screaming into the millhouse, the Delaware rushed the door. They were initially driven back, but the surprised defenders were without powder or shot and now inside a thatch-roofed wooden mill that could readily be burned. Richard Bard (Baird), his wife, Katherine, his cousin Thomas Potter, and four children became captives of Delaware who promised to spare their lives, and three other captives had already been captured outside. Thirteen captors had ten prisoners, a better ratio than at the Jamiesons'. Yet Thomas Potter, who had wounded one cutlass-wielding attacker with his own weapon, was killed later that morning, and Richard's seven-month-old child, who may have been endangering the captors by crying, was killed and scalped within a few miles of the looted and burned mill. Predictably, the raiders found themselves closely pursued after they passed through the gap into Path Valley in Cumberland County. Captive Samuel Hunter, who had trouble keeping up, was killed soon thereafter, and chronicler Richard Bard soon escaped. These daring raiders had eluded the borderland garrisons and patrols in attacking into York County, but faced the real prospect of being intercepted on their way home. The Shawnee and Delaware who killed so many of their captives on the trail were, not surprisingly, engaged in their last raids here.

The other center of the final raids of the spring of 1758 was, by way of contrast, along the South Branch of the Potomac, where raids had become endemic. Whether or not the party of about fifty Shawnee, Delaware, Wyandot, and Mingo warriors knew this was their last raid, it had a couple of unusual features. At the New River gap, they broke into smaller groups, as was customary, with half of them attacking the Cowpasture settlement at the headwaters of the James River for what was the fourth time in less than a year. Loot would be limited unless captives were the purpose. Four men were killed resisting the raiders this time, and fifteen captives were taken, including Barbara Conrad and five of her children. Although the raiders were not being pursued, casualties among their captives were again uncommonly high, and, as in York County, the killed included children. Isham Bernat, our only captive-witness, soon lost a nephew, who died "because he was cross & troublesome." Another captive boy died accidentally when he slipped beneath the belly of a horse to which he had been tied for a speedier retreat. The raiders still had eleven captives when they returned to their rendezvous at the New River, and might have been expected to head home. Instead, the group split up for additional raiding, killing three and capturing three more on the Roanoke River before the entire group returned to the Ohio River. It was at the Ohio that both Isham Bernat's son and an old woman captive who had endured the journey so far were both killed.[131] There may have been a serious dispute about the distribution of the captives at this point, as there was no visit to Fort Duquesne, where the French might have given some gifts to help broker a redistribution of captives and scalps.

The Shawnee raiding war climaxed in April of 1758 with the burning of two stockades at Upper Tract Fort and Seybert's Fort, on the South Branch of the Potomac, where forty-two were killed and thirty-eight captured. Virginians went on high alert. No one realized that these two strikes, which will be examined more closely as sieges, would be followed by a five-year suspension of raids on the Virginia frontier. Within ten days of the fall of Seybert's Fort, Rev. Samuel Davies gave his famous sermon, to a less than enthusiastic Virginian militia, denouncing the "Barbarities and Depradations a mongrel Race of Indian Savages and French Papists have perpetrated upon our Frontiers." He went on to conjecture wildly that "Now, perhaps some tender delicate Creature may be suffering an involuntary Prostitution to savage Lust; and perhaps debauched and murdered by the same Hand" or more plausibly that "Now some helpless Children may be torn from the Arms of their murdered Parents, and Dragged away weeping and wringing their Hands, to receive the Education among Barbarians, and to be formed upon the Model of a ferocious Indian soul."[132] Davies did not instill effective new military zeal in Virginians; the un-negotiated truce began because Indians and Canadians became preoccupied with the 6,000-man British Army that was beginning its march to Fort Duquesne.

The raiding war had slowed a little in 1757 and early 1758. Most raiding parties were smaller than in 1756, and fewer were killed or captured.[133] Colonial soldiers, on both sides, were a large proportion of the smaller group of victims, and soldier-victims were usually killed rather than captured. Indian warriors were only half as likely to be victims of the borderland as in the previous year, and more of them were captured. Cherokee and Catawba were now fighting Shawnee and Delaware, opponents who were more able and prepared to take Indian captives. The most unusual capture of Indians occurred at Winchester in July 1757, when a group of ten Indians posing as Cherokee approached the garrison. Indian superintendent Edmond Atkin realized that they were not all Cherokee, and were not who they said they were; he had them all imprisoned as possible spies. Atkin soon feared for their health in jail and, in an echo of 1753, particularly feared that one of them might die in custody; they were released ten days later.[134] Fewer civilians were as vulnerable as earlier, but they were just as likely to be captured as killed. Civilian men remained more than twice as likely as women to be victims (127:48) and were still likely to be killed, though not nearly as likely as soldiers. For the first time in the war, adult women who were attacked were as likely to be killed as captured. Perhaps more of the women who persevered on the frontier farms into 1757 were prepared to fight back, and were treated accordingly. Although the killing of captives on the trail increased in 1758, children were still much more likely to be captured than killed.

PHASE FOUR

Forbes's invasion of 1758 was preceded and accompanied by a scouting duel that centered on taking captives. By mid-summer the English forces needed information badly, but were increasingly cautious; any information gathered was less important than the fear of having an informed scout captured by the French. When Colonel John Armstrong, of Kittanning fame, and veteran Indian trader James Dunning proposed scouting the trail to Fort Duquesne, General Forbes was so anxious to avoid the capture of any well-informed person that he aborted the plan, claiming that a hundred soldiers plus Indian scouts would be the minimum escort necessary.[135] It was mid-September before Major James Grant's nightmare scout-in-force went out, was defeated, and provided the French with most of the thirty-four captives taken in this battle.

Commandant François-Marie Le Marchand de Lignery at Fort Duquesne had been much more desperate for information. Small parties went out regularly to take a prisoner, and they focused upon capturing strays near English forts. In mid-July a herdsman with the Virginia

Regiment near Fort Cumberland was captured, and another was killed and "mangled," as was a soldier of the "grass guard." The next day another French-related scouting party killed two and captured one near Raystown, Pennsylvania, as the French simultaneously sought information about both likely routes for Forbes's forces. Cherokee scouts near Fort Duquesne intercepted another French spying party, and brought back two scalps but no prisoners.[136]

In mid-August six Indians, who spoke English fluently, captured another prisoner near Raystown. They did not take him to Fort Duquesne, but questioned him repeatedly over two days, taking special interest in the artillery accompanying the invading army, and then released him.[137] In this instance, Delaware were gathering their own intelligence, and signaled this fact by releasing their captive. Early in September, small parties of Indians attacked British and colonial soldiers out hunting, taking yet another captive.[138] Commandant Lignery at Fort Duquesne had generally succeeded in the contest for information.

As his supplies dwindled, Lignery needed to feign strength in hope of stalling Forbes's army for the winter. Although Lignery had accurate knowledge of the overwhelming threat, provisions were so short that he had to send his Illinois contingent home. His victorious Ottawa and Wyandot allies had already left, and the well-informed local Delaware were not only releasing a captive, but were also listening to a British peace mission. In these trying circumstances, Lignery gave Captain Charles Philippe Aubry command of a force of more than 1,000 men, three-quarters of them Canadians, to attack the much larger British Army at Loyalhanna. En route they encountered and overwhelmed a sizable English colonial scouting party, killing at least twelve.[139] However, one wounded French soldier was captured by the fleeing English, and the bold French attack, which required complete surprise, was abandoned.[140]

A much more useful captive was taken exactly a month later by 500 of Washington's troops sent to pursue French and Indian raiders who were again harassing Loyalhanna.[141] After chasing off the French and Indians, the Virginians found and captured three people who evidently had nothing to do with the raid: a Delaware woman, a Delaware man, and an "Englishman" named William Johnson, who plausibly claimed he had been captured by the Delaware in Lancaster County the previous year.[142] While captors and captives were sharing the warmth of a fire, they were suddenly attacked at dusk. Before either side learned that the other was Virginian, thirty-seven soldiers had been killed in the confused skirmish. When interrogated, Johnson was threatened with death as a traitor and promised a reward if he gave what proved to be accurate information about the state of Fort Duquesne. Johnson reported that the Illinois troops had withdrawn, the Indians were leaving, and Fort Duquesne was very weak. Johnson's testimony proved central in encouraging the English to postpone going into winter quarters, forcing Lignery to demolish Fort Duquesne on 21 November, and move his command to Fort Machault. Johnson was much less fortunate in his second captivity than he had been in his first. He was not treated as a recovered civilian, but as a renegade caught amid a bloody skirmish. The promise made to him was broken and the threat carried out; this most useful of informers was hanged as a traitor.[143]

The Indian raiding war against borderland farmers had seemingly ended in the spring of 1758, though the raiding between the British and the French armies, each with Indian allies, continued well into the summer of 1759. The Pennsylvania regulars, left to garrison the makeshift defenses at a new Fort Pitt the previous winter, had scouts out to the north but gained no prisoners. A major attack against Fort Machault at the end of March aborted after the expeditions' supply convoy was attacked, and another substantial raid failed miserably.[144] Canadian and Indian scouts and spies were more successful, taking two soldiers and killing five others near Fort Pitt in March.[145] From Fort Machault, Lignery organized attacks on British supply trains, killing soldiers and capturing several teamsters and horse wranglers. In preparation for a larger counterattack against Fort Pitt or Fort Ligonier (Loyalhanna), Lignery had scouts capture prisoners, officers recruit Indian support, and messengers call *troupes de la marine* from the Illinois and militia from Detroit. By early July 1759, Lignery had about 1,000 men together, but they would all be diverted to attempt the relief of besieged Fort Niagara. There, removed from the Allegheny country they had been contesting, the Ohio contingent of the Canadian forces was completely demolished.

One frightening postscript reminded Virginians that some Shawnee still had their own war. In October of 1759, eighteen months after the last raids on white settlers, a war party came from the Scioto Valley to attack the Carr's (Kerr's) Creek settlement near Jackson River in Augusta County. One report even claimed that two Frenchmen were with the Shawnee in an attack in which seven were killed and thirteen captured. Local militia and a detachment of rangers from tiny Fort Dunlop gave chase, eventually catching up with the retreating war party and their captives. In the confused night skirmish, the rescuers triumphed, recovering nine of the captives, seventeen horses laden with loot, a number of abandoned scalps, and a quantity of coin. Was this a sizable raid by dissidents to defy the truce makers after the fall of Fort Niagara and Quebec, was it a raid to satisfy a pent-up quest for honor raiding, or was it well-organized robbery with violence that ended poorly even though no Shawnee were killed? Perhaps it was all three. The retreating warriors had been surprised, but it is noteworthy that they did not kill their prisoners, either when attacked or later; all four captives who were not recovered that night were surrendered five years later to Colonel Bouquet's army at the Muskingum.[146]

The Allegheny raiding war had lasted five years, from the first Shawnee attack on Buffalo Creek to their last raid on Carr's Creek,[147] during which the Virginians gave the Shawnee an undeserved reputation for ferocity and perfidiousness. The Shawnee spoke a language that few English borderlanders could even identify, they were led by war chiefs whose names remained unknown, they lived safely beyond the reach of all English counterstrikes, and they seemed to have joined the French in a war for blood and booty. They routinely undertook raids more than 300 miles from the safety of their settlements in the fertile middle Ohio country. Captives were added to their villages readily, and needed little supervision because successful escapees faced a formidable odyssey in returning home through the upper Ohio Valley and the Alleghenies. The Shawnee took more than three times as many people captive as they killed in the belligerent generation between 1745 and 1764. However, there is no surviving evidence that this was because white colonists showed less resistance than to the Delaware. Terrified victims had limited information, but some must have suspected that the Shawnee were willing to take more captives than were the Delaware.[148] The Ohio Shawnee added at least 327 captives and converts to their communities, and perhaps as much as 24 per cent to their total population.[149] Although the majority of these captives were eventually returned, more than 100 may have lived out their lives with the Shawnee.[150]

The raiding war of 1754 to 1759 was conducted much more effectively by Indians than by their white imitators, and more captives were taken this way than any other. Amongst victims whom the English would regard as nonmilitary, more are known to have been captured or missing (822) than killed (765). For all their horror, raids on white settlers were noticeably less deadly than the Allegheny war in general, where two died for each one taken, where soldiers and militiamen were four times more likely to be killed rather than captured, and where Indians were seven times more likely to be killed rather than captured. Yet there was variation in the deadliness of Indian raids on white settlers. White borderlanders had one captured for each one killed in the first phase of the war, when surprise attacks were numerous and community resistance minimal. The raiding war climaxed in 1756, with more colonial resistance, more Canadian involvement, and some particularly desperate Delaware raiders. Three times as many Indians were killed in 1756 as in any other year of the war,[151] and five white settlers died that year for every three captured. Surprisingly, this increased ferocity did not continue or accelerate. More civilians were captured than killed in raids undertaken between the beginning of 1757 and the middle of 1758. In the last eighteen months of the raiding war, when attacks were more likely to be against military targets, fewer civilians were attacked, and they were even more likely to be captured than killed.[152] The waning of Canadian support had coincided with the 1757 reversion to the previous norm, and may have been a factor; Canadians had favored more "strategic" and dangerous targets. Avenging warriors who abhorred captivity themselves may have seen the captives they took as less worthy than those who died fighting, though there is not direct evidence of this. As will be seen, captives were readily adopted into Indian families, and most who left remembrances reported good treatment. It is even possible that whites' relentless insistence on the return of captives, which became their central diplomatic concern and even a precondition of peace talks, may have added value to the taking of captives. More captives were taken in raids than in successful sieges, or in battles, but these very different contexts deserve separate discussion.

5

Taken in Sieges and Surrenders, 1756–58

Although sieges had been a major part of the prewar maneuvering of both Virginians and Canadians, they were not part of local Indian warfare in Allegheny country before 1756. It had been northern Ottawa and Ojibwa allies, led by Ottawa-Canadian *troupes de la marine* cadet Charles Langlade, whom the Canadians had induced to destroy the Piankashaw stockade at Pickawillany in 1752. As they went to war, Shawnee, Delaware, and Mingo raiders were intent upon the quick and casualty-free taking of adoptable captives, scalps, or loot; besieging fortified buildings, or "log pens," was of no interest. Regardless of the eventual outcome of any firefight at a stockaded private "garrison house" or colonial government fort, attackers would likely suffer some casualties, making the raid inherently unsuccessful. If a siege occupied attackers for hours, there could be even more casualties once colonial rangers or militia arrived to relieve the besieged or pursue the retreating Indians and their captives. It is easier to understand why Indian raiders avoided sieges than to understand why they attacked any garrison houses.

Historians of colonial strategy have dismissed the garrison houses, and the provincial forts strung along Pennsylvania's and Virginia's retreating frontiers, as failing to stop the Indian raids. Surely their primary purpose was to protect those who gathered there. The most determined white frontiersmen, including the Scots-Irish who had brought clan memories of raiding, bride-stealing, and adoption of captured children with them from their homelands, refused to flee and defended themselves by "forting up." Neighbors worked together to strengthen better-built farmhouses and mills by reinforcing walls and adding stockades with firing slits. Communities and governments had built at least 150 garrison houses and provincial forts in the frontier districts of Pennsylvania, Maryland, and Virginia by 1758.[1] Families, militia, and parties of rangers or provincial soldiers gathered at these refuges when trouble was expected or had begun. Unlike the provincial forts built by authorities who sought to stabilize the region, the garrison houses were not always located strategically. However, if the garrison houses were intended primarily to protect those who gathered there, it seems sensible to consider how well they served this purpose.

Shawnee and Delaware raiders usually bypassed garrison houses, as their defenders hoped, and fewer than one in ten was ever attacked. However, Indians promptly worked these forts into their tactics. One method was to disperse hidden warriors to form a loose blockade surrounding a fort, as they did at Stoddart's Fort in Maryland. Shots were then fired, and these or a settler's alarm horn sent frightened settlers hurrying toward the fort, and toward the well-placed warriors who easily ambushed them.[2] A raiding party of about fifty Ohio Delaware under Shingas may have had similar intentions near McDowell's Fort on 29 February 1756, but were discovered. Four militia and a warrior died in fighting that the colonials considered a successful defense against besiegers; for the Delaware, this was a skirmish that ended once their opponents had recovered their strong defensive position.[3]

A second Indian tactic was to lure soldiers from one fort into an ambush as they responded to an attack on another garrison house in the neighborhood. At ranger Captain John Ashby's fort, four miles south of the Potomac River on Patterson's Creek, Tewea led a Delaware raiding party that lured a detachment out of the house, killing six and capturing two soldiers. Two weeks later a larger party returned and called on Ashby to surrender. Apparently, the two sides met, Ashby stalled by claiming that he was not authorized to surrender, and the Delaware let him send a messenger to his superiors.[4] Naturally, the besiegers did not wait for a reply, but moved to a fort twelve miles to the east, which they attacked but did not capture.[5] Such a sustained Indian presence was bound to result in skirmishes. A scouting party of fifteen, which included French ensign Alexandre Dagneau Douville, was surprised by Virginia militia in the same vicinity at that time. Douville was killed and scalped, and his captured instructions from the commandant of Fort Duquesne confirmed the Canadian priority of attacking convoys, depots, and stockades as well as gathering information and prisoners.[6] A larger night battle occurred near Edward's Fort on 18 April when Captain John Fenton Mercer led forty to fifty Virginian regulars out of this fort in pursuit of Delaware seen nearby. Seventeen Virginians, including their commander, were killed in a skirmish less than two miles from the fort, as were as many as nine of the Delaware.[7]

The more obvious Indian tactic against wooden strongholds was to burn them. This was never a simple matter of launching flaming arrows, and there were risks in trying to pile combustible dry wood and pine knots against stockades. Stockades of freshly cut logs were hard to set on fire. The early attempt to burn Coombes's Fort, in southern Cumberland County, failed when the few defenders managed to kill the fire with soap suds.[8] The first effective use of fire against wooden forts in Virginia came with the destruction of Williams's Fort early in March 1756.[9] A party of about thirty Delaware, led by Tewea, rafted across the Potomac thirty miles below Fort Cumberland, and attacked a small stockade protecting seven men, three women, and eight children. Once Williams's Fort was set afire, the three women and two of the men managed to escape. Five men died there; the eight children were missing and presumed captured.[10] That summer Tewea would boast to captive Peter Walker that "he would take any fort that would catch fire."[11] Fire could transform considerable defenses into death traps that allowed warriors to capture those fleeing. In such circumstances, the siege became a more attractive Indian tactic, and any negotiated surrenders favored the attackers.

The Ohio Delaware attacked more garrisoned houses in the spring of 1756, but the results were uneven. Colonial troops and militia were now better prepared to respond to news of attacks and were willing to pursue raiders, even if captives were put at risk. A war party led by Shingas watched McCord's Fort until its militiamen were called away, and then attacked after killing the only two remaining men. After capturing and plundering the ground floor, they set fire to the house, forcing down those who had fled upstairs. Twenty-seven women and children were captured readily and marched over "the Blue Mountain." Four days and about twenty-five miles later, on Sideling Hill, the group was caught by a company sent in pursuit from Fort Lyttleton. The pursuing militia attacked, and the Delaware immediately scattered. While the rescuers untied their relieved neighbors and kin, the Delaware surrounded the entire group and began firing from dense cover. When this unequal skirmish between Delaware rifles and militia muskets ended, twenty-one militiamen and three Delaware were dead; the Pennsylvanians had recovered only five captives, and they had killed another accidentally.[12]

The next three sieges of the summer of 1756 were clear demonstrations that the Canadians' reputation and resources were at their best, and Indian allies were drawn into the strategies sketched in Douville's captured instructions. In the first major expedition, eight Canadians joined Tewea and nineteen other Delaware in what was intended as a June attack on George Croghan's well-fortified compound (Fort Shirley) in Cumberland County's remote Juniata Valley. Finding their preferred target too well defended, this Delaware-Canadian force went down the valley to attack Bigham's Fort. Although no first-hand account of the capture survives, it is likely that the Delaware once again set fire to a stockaded house, forcing its occupants to flee without negotiation. The bodies of three were found outside the burned fort, and twenty-two survivors became captives. In this case, Canadians had joined a Delaware siege, apparently without affecting its method, brokering the outcome, or acquiring any captives.[13]

While the Delaware-Canadian force attacked Bigham's at the northern end of this war zone, a Shawnee-Miami-Canadian force was attacking more than 250 miles to the south, at Vause's Fort in southwestern Virginia. Veteran Canadian fur trader and soldier François-Marie Picoté de Belestre, commander at Fort des Miamis, personally recruited a force of about 150 Miami and Shawnee, and 25 Canadians.[14] Picoté de Belestre and this sizable force traveled more than 400 miles along the Shawnee raiding routes to the headwaters of the Roanoke River, and Virginia's southernmost fortification. Significant French provisioning must have supported a group that was too large to have subsisted by hunting.

Ephraim Vause (Voss, Vaus) and his family had a substantial frontier ranching operation, with workers who included at least one negro slave and two Indian "servants." One captive had been taken nearby the previous summer, and Vause had fortified his isolated home early.[15] The next June, Shawnee scouts took another prisoner and some cattle, presumably to feed Picoté de Belestre's approaching war party. Despite this warning, only eleven Virginia militiamen were there with Captain John Smith when the Shawnee-Miami-Canadian force surrounded the fort on 25 June 1756. According to the independent accounts of Smith and his ensign, Peter Looney, there was an eight-hour daytime firefight that left at least thirty-two Indians, three Canadians, and two Virginians dead. These uncommonly persistent attackers finally succeeded in setting the blockhouse ablaze. Both Smith and Looney separately reported that they surrendered after the fire went out of control. However, surrender would have been hard to negotiate at this point, and the sequel and Smith's unconfirmed claim to have agreed to terms both suggest that the surrender may have occurred a little earlier.[16]

If the Indians' losses were anything like those reported, their known behavior in victory must be regarded as very restrained. They discovered that they had been fighting a mere nine surviving militiamen, six of whom were injured. The victors promptly killed one of John Smith's sons, who was likely the most seriously wounded. Understandably, Smith regarded this as a violation of the quarter granted, though his opponents would have viewed the killing as expediency, if not mercy. A total of twenty-three captives, including Vause's family and servants, were taken. No captives were reported as molested until after the victorious party divided their spoils on the trail several days later, and headed for their own towns. Smith and his surviving son, Joseph, went with Picoté de Belestre back to Fort des Miamis before being sent to Canada, and then to England, where Smith was celebrated and formally exchanged. Ensign Peter Looney went with the Shawnee, who soon killed one old man who could no longer travel. The Shawnee warriors tortured one captured militiamen, named Cole, to death. It is not clear why he was chosen, but the motives would have included avenging their own losses.[17] This killing occurred before the party reached Lower Shawnee Town; if there were Canadian witnesses to this burning, as Looney claimed, they were no longer in charge. It is noteworthy that the other five surviving militiamen became prisoners of the Indians, and all were eventually repatriated.[18] Looney reported no further killings when he arrived in Lower Shawnee Town. Aside from the torture of Cole and the killings of wounded John Smith Jr and the older man, the quarter granted by Picoté de Belestre to the defenders of Vause's Fort had been honored by both the Indians and the Canadians. Although less is known about the fate of the civilian captives, at least three stayed with the Indians, and four are known to have returned to Virginia.[19]

The greatest puzzle in the capture of Vause's Fort was that the Indians persisted in attacking after incurring heavy losses. The result may well have been regarded by the Indians as a "bad success" that was not worth the casualties. According to one report that cannot be confirmed, Picoté de Belestre spoke to the Shawnee chiefs as the victorious war party separated and headed home, attempting to sustain their interest in driving the English out of Virginia. He claimed, "You told me Virginia Men could not fight, but I did not find it so." He admitted being "disappointed by a small Company of Men, ten or eleven, which kept me the best Part of a Day very hot engaged, and killed me near 40 Men." He pleaded, "I hope this piece of bad Success will not discourage you to go with me again; for I am resolved to force down into their Country, till we drive them into the Sea." He promised more plunder, including negroes, a vast recovered hunting ground, and French trade that would be much cheaper when brought by sea to the Chesapeake.[20] The Shawnee were evidently not convinced. They went back to their own war, and when they took forts again two years later, they did it their own way. For the Miami, participation in the attack on Vause's Fort remained their only major contribution of the entire Allegheny war.

The most successful Indian-Canadian siege of a British colonial fortification on the Allegheny frontier occurred a month later. Fort Granville was the northwest anchor of the three major forts (Granville, Shirley, and Lyttleton) built by the Pennsylvania government to protect settlers of western Cumberland County.[21] Built to command a narrow pass on the Juniata River, and designed to accommodate a garrison of seventy-five, this stockade included two corner blockhouses and mounted two swivel guns but evidently had no cannon. On 30 July 1756, just after a large detachment left the fort to protect harvesters, what can properly be called a French and Indian force of fifty-five attacked the fort and its twenty-four Pennsylvania regulars. Tewea, who had scouted and tested Fort Granville after his success at Bigham's Fort the previous month, had a personal stake in this attack. Two years earlier he had sold nearby land to a trader friend, who then broke a promise not to bring in settlers; Tewea had burned them out and moved to Kittanning. Now he was back again, with thirty-two Delaware and Shawnee, and they were joined by twenty-three *troupes de la marine* led by François Coulon de Villiers, younger brother of Louis de Villiers and of the late Joseph Coulon de Villiers de Jumonville.[22] Even for Europeans willing to launch suicidal direct assaults, odds of two-to-one were inadequate for attacking secured defenders, and the Delaware were not given to suicidal attacks. After a day and night of ineffective sniping, the attackers succeeded in approaching part of the wall at night through a ravine that gave them cover. Setting fire to dry brush, including resinous pine knots, against part of the stockade, the attackers burned a hole through the wall. Lieutenant Edward Armstrong, commander of the garrison, was one of the two who were killed while putting out the fire. By one report, it was the Indian who killed Armstrong who then shouted in English, "Surrender You English Dogs, or else you shall be burnt or eaten."[23]

In what sounds like a parody of European siege convention, the wall had been breached, defenders had suffered casualties in this breach, and then the attackers shouted an offer of quarter if the surviving defenders surrendered. Sergeant John Turner, now in command of an increasingly vulnerable and outnumbered garrison, and anxious to protect dependents, including his own wife and her five children, promptly surrendered by opening the gates of the fort. Villiers may have offered quarter, but it worked only because the Shawnee and Delaware agreed. The victors took everyone prisoner, left a jocular message on a nearby post, and then supposedly burned the fort as something of an afterthought.[24]

The fate of those granted quarter is instructive. The victors initially brought all twenty-nine captives to Kittanning, Tewea's base on the Allegheny River, rather than to Fort Duquesne. During the five-day trek, one of the wounded could not go on, and was unceremoniously killed and scalped. Within hours of arriving at Kittanning, the victors burned Sergeant John Turner to death. Had he said or done something since capture? One report claimed that he was killed because he had beaten one of the attackers with a stick sometime before the war, and another report claimed he had killed the Delawares' friend Simon Girty Sr in order to marry his wife.[25] As the one who decided to surrender Fort Granville, Turner was certainly not selected by the Delaware as a brave and worthy warrior fit to undergo extensive torture, and he was not killed in revenge for Indian losses in the siege, for there had been none. Whatever the reasons, the man who had accepted a Delaware or Canadian offer of quarter was the only one who did not get it. Turner, like Cole, died in what was then being seen as a Delaware and Shawnee practice of torturing one captive in the wake of each surrender. If the Canadians had acquired this sergeant from a British colonial regiment as their own prize, he would have been forwarded to Canada and France. But Turner would have had no great value in the trade of men by rank as practiced in European military exchange, even compared to the self-styled major John Smith, whom the Canadians had been allowed to keep for themselves after the conquest of Vause's Fort. The fate of captives was not determined by the casualties inflicted by defenders at Vause's Fort, who were much more effective than the defenders of Fort Granville.

After killing Turner at Kittanning, the war party and its twenty-eight remaining captives moved on to Fort Duquesne, where the Canadians and Indians had a predictable, if unspecified, dispute over the captives. Despite their sizable contribution to the war party, there is no evidence that the Canadians acquired any of these prisoners.[26] The fate of fifteen of the captives is known, suggesting a significant role for the Shawnee in the attack. Of the nine captives who eventually escaped, at least four escaped from the Shawnee at Logstown. When Mary Girty-Turner and four of her children were returned, three of these captives came from the Shawnee, one from the Delaware, and one from the Seneca.[27]

The successful siege of Fort Granville had been conducted in a way that misled Sergeant Turner to believe he could surrender to Canadians who could protect those who accepted the promised quarter. The fate of those captured suggests that the Indians had been dominant and eventually took complete control of the prisoners.[28] It is noteworthy that soldiers of a garrison that had shot at the attackers, ineffectively, for nearly twenty-four hours were accepted as prisoners in keeping with the capitulation. For the Canadians, the victory meant not only that the humiliated Pennsylvania government did not rebuild Fort Granville, but also that it abandoned Fort Shirley and Patterson's Fort as well, moving its Cumberland County frontier defense line a full forty miles eastward to Carlisle, Shippensburg, and Fort Augusta. European settlers who had thus far refused to leave their frontier farms, now abandoned an excellent harvest and fled eastward.[29] The destruction of Fort Granville also prompted the Pennsylvanians to undertake their only offensive of the war, the inglorious raid on Kittanning already discussed, where they killed Tewea, who had been involved in burning Williams's Fort, Bigham's Fort, and Fort Granville within the previous six months.

Despite the success of the attack on Fort Granville, there were no more sieges on the Pennsylvania frontier in this war, and none in Virginia for nearly two years. Tewea was gone, as were Canadian supplies needed to provision major multi-ethnic forces and give the Canadians some leverage in proposing targets. The counteroffensive of the Pennsylvanians against Kittanning had disrupted Ohio Delaware participation in the war that fall, and caused them to migrate westward. When the two last sieges of the Indian war were undertaken, in the spring of 1758, they were the ventures of the Shawnee, attacking in their southern sector of the borderland, in Augusta County, Virginia.

The particularly deadly finale, or postscript, to siege warfare on the Virginia frontier was the puzzling attacks on Upper Tract Fort and Seybert's Fort in April 1758. Without Canadians to offer support and their version of courageous resolution, a Shawnee-Delaware force of about fifty warriors targeted two well-manned little stockades on the upper reaches of the Potomac River's South Branch. Had easier targets become so difficult to find that raiding parties were willing to take much higher risks by traveling farther and by attacking forts? Upper Tract Fort was garrisoned by twenty-one rangers, accompanied by four of their wives and four children. The attackers surprised and promptly set fire to a stockade bristling with adult male defenders.[30] All the men and two of the women died, either in the gunfire, in escape attempts, in the flames of the fort, or perhaps after surrendering. Only two women and four children were taken captive.[31] Although it seems very unlikely that forty bodies were found at the site, as some claimed, any number of

Indian casualties may have provoked the slaughter of all the captured soldiers. These Shawnee and Delaware may also have taken few captives because they were intent on a second strike. Although they already had unacceptable casualties themselves, the raiders could proceed knowing that none had escaped their attack to sound the alarm and gather pursuers.

The same war party, minus the dead and those who had already taken captives that day, proceeded south about ten miles to attack stronger-built Seybert's Fort the next morning. Local tradition claims that the seventeen rangers there, under Captain Jacob Seybert, were completely surprised. Although the absence of pursuing militia confirms that word of the previous day's fight had not reached fifteen miles north to Waggener's Fort, the shots may well have helped draw the total of thirty-three other people into Seybert's Fort that day. Surviving evidence is very weak, but there was resistance during which both sides took some casualties, and negotiations were followed by surrender. All surviving members of the garrison, except Stephen Blankinship, were apparently killed upon surrender, thirty-one women and children were captured, and the fort was burned.[32] Fourteen-year-old James Dyer[33] escaped nearly two years later from captivity on the Muskingum River, and left his family with a vague and exaggerated story of treachery and murder after surrender.[34] Whatever provoked these sieges, they had brought some predictable casualties among the attackers, and ended in the execution of almost all the men who surrendered. Forty-two people were killed and thirty-eight captured in these last two sieges of the war, a survival rate no better than that of people attacked in their homes. In these final attacks, the Shawnee added their ferocious postscript to the war against garrison houses, just as their attack on Carr's (Kerr's) Creek six months later was their finale to the raiding war. The Shawnee reputation as the first to make war and the last to make peace was established. Although the Shawnee played little part in the sieges of forts when war resumed five years later, they had demonstrated a method that could succeed at a price.

These two Shawnee sieges of 1758 were particularly deadly, but there is overwhelming evidence that elsewhere the frontier stockades and forts had moderated the loss of lives. Physician and minister Joseph Doddridge combined frontier experience and historical research when commenting in 1824 that garrison houses "answered the purpose, as the Indians had no artillery. They seldom attacked, and scarcely ever took one of them."[35] Fewer than one in ten was attacked at all. At least four forts were defended well enough for attacks to be aborted, and, at the five stockades that were set afire and destroyed, casualties among the defeated were surprisingly light.[36] Including colonial soldiers killed in the course of these five sieges, the dead numbered 18, whereas 105 were taken captive. Where quarter is known to have been granted, at Vause's Fort and Fort Granville, even colonial regular troops were taken into Indian captivity, though the severely wounded were killed and one soldier was subsequently tortured to death in each case. The chances of surviving in an attacked stockade, aside from Upper Tract Fort and Seybert's Fort, were five times better than the chances of being killed there. This was a much higher survival rate than among those who were attacked in battle or in raids in this borderland, where the general casualty rate was two killed for each one captured.

6

Taken in Battles, 1755–59

There were only three battles in the Allegheny borderlands between 1755 and 1759, and battles were not a good place for acquiring or becoming a captive. Assuming that death was preferable to surrender, Indian warriors seldom sought, nor were offered, quarter in battle. Although the deliberate killing of prisoners of war was becoming less common in western European warfare, it was still easier to be killed than to be taken prisoner.[1] Victors routinely unleashed cavalry to slaughter the fleeing rather than to herd bothersome resource-draining prisoners. In the Allegheny woodlands, at the little ambush of Joseph Coulon de Villiers de Jumonville's party or the defeat of General Edward Braddock's army, those who fought could not expect to be taken prisoner. Wherever Indian, colonial, and European warriors engaged in battle together, successful surrender would be particularly difficult.

Only three engagements in the region and time period might be called battles: the defeat of General Edward Braddock's army (1755); the defeat of Major James Grant's expedition (1758); and the defeat of Commandant François-Marie Le Marchand de Lignery's Ohio forces at La Belle Famille (1759). The coalition of forces among the victors was different in each case, and the leadership was not always effective, or clear to their opponents. The margin of victory was not always the same, which would affect those seeking or granting quarter. The risks of escorting prisoners to secure bases differed, as did the potential value of those captured. These varying circumstances may explain the variety of outcomes, or there may have been some evolution in the tactics for taking or becoming captives in battle.

As Braddock's army followed the Virginian route to the forks of the Ohio River, the French were particularly anxious to take captives for information; they had no one nearly as well positioned as captive Robert Stobo had been, reporting the previous year from captivity within Fort Duquesne itself. In the month before Braddock's battle of 9 July 1755, the French captured at least thirty-five, while the English captured no one. Most of these captives could provide no strategic information, though those taken near Will's Creek and Patterson's Creek may have seen movement of troops and supplies. The Shawnee were already raiding the Virginia frontier on their own account, but four of their warriors joined with four Canadians in a reconnaissance that captured John Walker, one of Braddock's chief scouts. James Smith, a young road builder, was captured in Cumberland County, Pennsylvania, about the same time by a Kahnawake and two Delaware, and he was taken briefly to Fort Duquesne "for doctoring" and interrogation. The capture of Mingo chief Scarouady, the Iroquois Half-King and leading Indian ally and scout for the English, was another part of the French quest for captives with information; his immediate release by his Iroquoian captors annulled this success.[2]

In apparent contrast to the French, Indian combatants who won the deadliest battle of the Allegheny borderland in the entire Seven Years' War seemed to show very little interest in taking captives. Braddock's defeat was a spectacular victory for some 637 Indians, and the supporting cast of 108 *troupes de la marine* and 146 Canadian militia. The victory was won by Ottawa, Ojibwa, Wyandot, Potawatomi, and Iroquois warriors, with very few Shawnee and even fewer Delaware.[3] British and colonial casualties are believed to have been 516 killed and 461 wounded out of a force of some 1,450 men, a casualty rate of 67 per cent, which made this an unequalled disaster in the annals of European battles of this era.[4] Yet the victory was not quite as easy or complete as the myths have insisted. Indian hunter-marksmen supposedly shot for about three hours, from cover, at a mass of supposedly terrified, huddled, and unprotected redcoats. Although they may have inflicted more than one injury per victim, they succeeded in killing an average of fewer than one redcoat each.[5]

It is initially puzzling that fewer than twenty were taken captive, meaning that about thirty soldiers were killed for every one captured, a horrific ratio compared to the rest of this war in the Allegheny Mountains. Europeans on both sides had certainly lost control of this battle, which makes the dearth of prisoners even more striking. The British regulars, fearing "Barbaras Usage" and seeing some scalping of the dead early in the battle, may have resolutely fought to their death rather than consider surrendering.[6] It is also likely that anyone asking for quarter, in English or French, would be ignored by his enemies and exposed as a coward to his comrades. The massive casualties and minimal captures suggest that, for all of their success, the eventual victors were unable to employ their familiar tactic of segregating and disarming groups of their opponents for capture. Indians may have found the British persistence incomprehensible and felt their own victory against so many aliens was very long in coming. The battle also ended without much opportunity to capture fleeing soldiers who could have been: used to help haul away the astonishing booty, paraded or tortured amid village victory celebrations, offered in gift exchanges to Captain Claude-Pierre Pécaudy de Contrecoeur at Fort Duquesne, sold at Fort Niagara, held for eventual ransom in a mission village in Canada, or adopted to strengthen tribes by incorporating youths or "women of the regiment." The battle ended suddenly in a disorganized but generally effective British retreat across the Monongahela River, allowing 461 wounded to escape death or captivity. An immensely valuable baggage train was abandoned to be plundered by those who claimed it first, but only the severely wounded were left to be killed and scalped with the rest of the dead on that hastily abandoned battlefield.[7]

If the dynamics of the battle minimized the number of captives taken, the capture of women was certainly anomalous. At least seven of a maximum of twenty-eight "women of the regiment" who were with this advanced force, if Braddock's orders had been obeyed, became captives. Were they nursing the wounded and dying in what became isolated and exposed places, or were these the women who stayed at this task when the battle ended and/or were left behind during the retreat? Those women captured were likely unarmed, and not resisting dangerously. In any case, Indian attackers took at least one woman in four captive.[8]

Official French reports do not mention prisoners at all, and it is likely that the Canadians took none and that Indians gave very few to the French at Fort Duquesne. A French regular officer, who assembled a credible general account of the battle, preserved one private account stating that twenty prisoners were taken, including seven women and girls.[9] This is the highest estimate of prisoners taken, and it can reasonably be reconciled with some other accounts. A less reliable source, a French officer known as J.C.B., claimed that the Indians took sixteen prisoners away to their villages.[10] Two captured women with the 44th Regiment, Mrs Agnes Hamilton and Mrs Miller, left second-hand accounts. While still held captive in an Indian village near Detroit a year later, Agnes Hamilton told a fellow captive that she knew of fourteen captives taken by Indians in Braddock's defeat. Two "being badly wounded, and their Wounds offensive, occasioned by the Heat of the Weather, the Savages knocked them in the Head."[11] Mrs Miller reported being trapped under the severely wounded Sir Peter Halket near the end of the battle and being forced to watch the hasty killing of the wounded and mutilation of the dead. She saw few captives taken: two women of the 44th Regiment (Agnes and herself), five women of the 48th Regiment, some "women of the Artillery" who were not numbered, and a male servant of Colonel Thomas Gage taken shortly after the battle, supposedly after he had been sent back to look for his master's horse. According to Mrs Miller, who was freed by December 1757, she was sold at Fort Niagara by her shrewd Indian captors; her ransom cost her two years of service plus the ten guineas she had sewn into her petticoat. She worked off her ransom as a servant of a French officer at Fort Toronto and then of his wife in Montreal. Mrs Miller was released at the end of her indenture and returned, probably via a cartel ship, to England. She claimed that the others of her little group, apparently including Agnes Hamilton, were kept by the Indians. Once she had come into French hands, Mrs Miller had been treated like a typical New England civilian captive of Indians, those who had been sold or "redeemed" into service in New France while France and England were still at peace. Since she completed her indenture in wartime, she had to wait for repatriation in a cartel ship.[12]

Three additional accounts suggest the range of possible experiences in captivity after such a battle. One of Mrs Miller's companions, supposing that her husband was killed in the slaughter, reportedly married a French subaltern during her captivity, and they had a son. Taken prisoner once again in the English capture of Fort Niagara in July 1759, this woman chose not to take her son to Montreal immediately, as article 4 of the terms of surrender explicitly allowed, but instead took this clause's other option: "those women who choose to follow their husbands are at liberty to do it." She was supposedly undeterred by the same article's insistence that this offer did not apply "to those women who are his Brittanic Majesty's subjects."[13] When this little Anglo-French family was paraded through Albany with the rest of the captured garrison, the wife was discovered by her first husband, who had survived Braddock's defeat and now learned that his wife had as well. As the *Pennsylvania Gazette* concluded the story, "He immediately demanded her, and after some Struggles of Tenderness for her French Husband, she left him, and closed again with her First: Tho' it is said the French Husband insisted on keeping the Child, as his Property, which was consented to by the Wife and First Husband."[14] Whatever happened to this woman's life thereafter, hers had not been the typical tale of Allegheny captivity.

Crosby Eger, of the Virginia Regiment, is the only soldier known to have survived capture after Braddock's defeat. Four years later his sad petition was carefully investigated by a Virginia House of Burgesses that included his former commander.[15] Eger reported receiving several wounds in the battle, and apparently came into Canadian hands promptly, perhaps for "doctoring," for he mentioned nothing of an Indian captivity. He was moved from fort to fort until he was imprisoned at Quebec. He was then sent to England in a flag of truce ship, and spent two months in hospital there. The ship bringing him back to America was captured by a French privateer, and the unfortunate Eger was imprisoned in Bordeaux, France, for six months. Three and a half years after capture, Eger returned to Virginia "now destitute and rendered incapable of providing for himself and family." His petition was investigated and believed, and he was granted £15.[16]

Another riveting tale, still entirely unconfirmed, has been readily accepted by generations of leading historians as true and iconic. Forty-five years after Braddock's defeat, Kentucky frontiersman James Smith published memoirs of his captivity. He had been taken as a teenager working on a Pennsylvania military road, badly beaten in running a gauntlet of warriors at Fort Duquesne, and taken into the fort "for doctoring" and interrogation. He was still there the day Braddock was defeated, and would vividly describe the fate of some of the captives:

> About sundown I beheld a small party coming in with about a dozen prisoners, stripped naked, with their hands tied behind their backs, and their faces and parts of their bodies blacked; these prisoners they burned to death on the bank of the Allegheny river, opposite to the fort. I stood on the fort wall until I beheld them begin to burn one of these men; they had tied him to a stake, and kept touching him with firebrands, red-hot irons, &c, and he screamed in a most doleful manner; the Indians, in the mean time, yelling like infernal spirits.

Another half-century after Smith's memoires, Winthrop Sargent would supplement them with implausible horrors that included boiling whiskey being poured down the victim's throat.[17]

Smith's tale is not very convincing. He mentioned that, before leaving the ramparts in sorrow and disgust, he had seen a single soldier being burned. No other witness at Fort Duquesne that day made any mention of this horror. No British regulars left tales of this supposed event to fuel their revenge or to discourage desertion, and nothing was said of this incident by anyone else anxious to vilify or denounce the French or Indians during the forty-five years before Smith's account was published. A captured Virginian named Staut (Stott or Stuart) was able to report on other events at Fort Duquesne that day, but he reported no such burning, nor did Mrs Miller, held by Indians near Fort Duquesne that day.[18] In Iroquois and Shawnee societies, such major torture rituals would have been conducted amid victory celebrations in home villages after approval by prominent matrons.[19] Indian warriors camped at Fort Duquesne might well have had prisoners run a vicious gauntlet, or have tortured a victim to death in revenge for losses, but there are no other reports of such numbers of captives being burned to death in this warrior camp. Smith's account, which is so rich a source regarding his adopted life among the Kahnawake, deserves to be questioned concerning this eyewitness tale. Perhaps some later event was being conflated, or perhaps a couple of generations of fighting to confiscate Kentucky from the Shawnee seemed more justified if such a burning had occurred.

Yet some captives taken in this battle may well have been burned. In a third-hand account of the life of her admired Seneca husband, Hiokatoo, Mary Jemison is made to say, "At Braddock's defeat he took two white prisoners, and burnt them alive in a fire of his own kindling."[20] This cryptic comment does not suggest burning in a village ceremony; Hiokatoo's victims would likely have been soldiers and could have been tortured to death somewhere near Fort Duquesne.

The combatants and the course of the Battle of the Monongahela had made the taking of prisoners unlikely. The Canadians from Fort Duquesne were not in charge at the end of this battle and, aside from their quest for information in the month before the battle, had not shown much interest in taking English soldiers as prisoners in what was not yet a declared war. Contrecoeur had not been collecting trophy captives, recruiting among them, or using them to exchange for his own people. It is noteworthy that women were prominent among those prisoners taken, though few women accompanied their army's advance force.[21] If not sold to the Canadians, women were usually more manageable and more useful as captives. British soldiers were not much use as adoptees: they needed constant watching as captives prone to escape, and most did not adapt easily to Indian community life. At this time, Indians had no sizable market for captives at Fort Duquesne or Detroit; Indians familiar with the Canadian captive trade rightly took those for sale directly to Fort Niagara.

Fort Duquesne escaped Braddock's threat and went on to became the supply center of the ensuing Canadian war in Allegheny country. Fort Duquesne remained an unavenged humiliation for the British Army, and the perceived source of endless guerilla raids against which Virginians and Pennsylvanians were nearly defenseless. The renewed British drive against Fort Duquesne in 1758 was ultimately successful, but this systematic approach included one more major defeat even closer to the destination than Braddock had been.

Major James Grant, a well-respected officer of the Montgomery Highlanders regiment, led regulars and colonials on a major raid out of the British Army's advance base at Loyalhanna to gain prisoners and information at Fort Duquesne and to retaliate for recent harassment by Indians. Offensive maneuvers misfired, as did plans to draw the defenders of Fort Duquesne out into an ambush, and Grant's force became disorganized and was overwhelmed by a counterattack by some 950 *troupes de la marine* and 550 Indian allies on 14 September 1758.[22]

Some 292 of Grant's 800-man contingent were initially reported killed or missing, including 22 of the 37 officers involved. The 258 killed represented a slightly lower proportion of the force (31%) than had those killed with Braddock (36%), but this time one prisoner was taken for every seven soldiers killed, compared to approximately one in thirty in Braddock's case. In reporting on the battle, Colonel Henry Bouquet commented optimistically, "The Frenchmen did not try to kill, but to make prisoners: and it seems that for the first time they have shown humanity."[23] In the confused fighting, Grant himself, along with a dozen desperate men outnumbered by Indians, surrendered to Canadian officers who arrived in time to offer them quarter. With Fort Duquesne nearby to hold prisoners, and with prisoners of war now routinely sent to Quebec for eventual exchange, the predominant *troupes de la marine* were interested in taking prisoners, especially high-ranking officers. The recent fall of Louisbourg and the strength of General John Forbes's threatening army may also have encouraged a show of humanity in the hope that it would be reciprocated. Indians took prisoners in this battle as well. In the years since 1755, Indians had become more familiar with redcoats, including those in kilts, and individuals and small groups of them were comparatively easy to isolate and overwhelm in this confused woodland battle of 1758, and in the subsequent rout of the British. Isolated soldiers could seek quarter without the scrutiny of officers and the witness of peers, and then hope for a monopoly on the story of what had happened to them. A Virginian soldier of George Washington's company reported being captured alone by a group of

Indians, robbed of his money and musket, and tied with a rope "round the middle," while his captors pursued others. He was not the only one who reported escaping captivity when his captors were fired upon and scattered.[24]

When more than a third of the British detachment failed to return, Colonel Henry Bouquet of the Royal American Regiment, the veteran Swiss officer in command at Loyalhanna, wrote a polite letter to the commandant of Fort Duquesne, inquiring about his missing men and trusting that the wounded had been treated well. In a show of imported military ritual, Bouquet sent an ensign, two sergeants, a drummer, and thirty privates in a party to carry a flag of truce to the Canadian fort, to drum for a parley, and to deliver the letter. Commandant François-Marie Le Marchand de Lignery had fought irregular warfare for thirty years as a *troupes de la marine* officer, had been prominent in the defeat of Braddock and as commander at Fort Duquesne, and had subsequently fostered numerous raids into Virginia and Pennsylvania.[25] Yet in 1758 he could still respond with a ready assurance that the soldiers he had just captured were given the "civil and humane treatment" that had always been the French code, and that he had sent his prisoners on to Canada for their comfort and safety. Displaying the conventional military class-consciousness, Lignery named each of the seven captured officers, noting that he had not been able to recover one Virginian ensign, Thomas Gist, from the Wyandot.[26] Lignery used the opportunity to inquire, in turn, about François-Louis Picoté de Belestre, an officer captured by the Cherokee, "your savages."[27] Nothing whatever was said of the enlisted men with Grant, though twenty-eight of them had been taken. Bouquet concluded the exchange of notes, and the accompanying spying, by replying that "it gives me and I dare say it must give you great pleasure to see ... the European and Christian usages prevail here."[28] The six captured officers who had come into Canadian hands, including Major Grant, would be among prisoners exchanged via Crown Point, New York, thirteen months later.[29] If one of the motives for humanity toward these prisoners was the hope of reciprocity in converse circumstances, the Canadian officer contingent at Fort Duquesne invested their charity well.

Indians took and kept as many as twenty-eight prisoners of their own in defeating Grant's expedition, and, according to the two surviving captivity accounts, the captured had included wounded soldiers. Although Canadians and Indians had cooperated in fighting for the previous four years, they still disagreed about the distribution and fate of prisoners. One Pennsylvanian teen already held in Fort Duquesne reported, "After the rout of Grant's army the French and Indians quarreled over the division of the spoils. The Indians grew so angry that they retired from the Fort, crossed the river and returned to their villages."[30] Ensign Thomas Gist of the Virginia Regiment, who was wounded and captured in the battle, hinted at similar friction. His Wyandot captor took Gist home to a village near Detroit, after the surgeon at Fort Duquesne refused to dress Gist's wounds.[31]

Comparing the defeats of Braddock and Grant must be done cautiously but can be suggestive. Both defeated forces were composed of regulars and colonials who were surprised and enveloped by rapidly moving Indian warriors accompanied by Canadian *troupes de la marine*. Ohio Delaware and Shawnee, who took hundreds of captives in the war, had been all but absent against Braddock but were prominent in Grant's defeat. Both battles had high casualty rates for the defeated, but more captives were taken from Grant's much smaller force. Canadian officers gave "quarter" to small clusters of soldiers who surrendered with Majors Grant and Andrew Lewis. Three years of formal war had intervened between the two battles, and thousands of prisoners had been taken from other borderlands of Canada in the interim, including the defeated garrisons at Fort Oswego and Fort William Henry. Some prisoners had been formally paroled, and most had been sent to Canada for imprisonment and eventual exchange there or in Europe. Braddock's soldiers had fought for nearly three hours as a rapidly thinning but connected red line along their new road, a battle that did not isolate individuals who might seek quarter free of white witnesses. Grant's soldiers soon became dispersed, if not lost, in dense and unfamiliar woods. In this circumstance, Indians could chase down and tie up individual captives, who now had recognized value as trophies, commodities, or adoptive kin, and the captors could later bargain about transferring some prisoners to the Canadians.

The Anglo-French battle for Allegheny country did not end with Lignery's demolition of Fort Duquesne on 24 November 1758; it ended at the battle of La Belle Famille seven months later and 200 miles away.[32] Early in 1759, Lignery had begun gathering a large force of Indians, *troupes de la marine*, and militia at Fort Machault (Venango), for a major counteroffensive against Fort Pitt and Loyalhanna, both of which had recently been denuded of British regulars. The vulnerable 200-man garrison of Pennsylvanians left at what was now called Fort Pitt would be thoroughly drained of provisions by a large Indian conference held there, at Indian insistence, early in July 1759. However, Lignery's plans changed suddenly on 12 July with the arrival of orders to relieve besieged Fort Niagara. He convinced nearly 1,000 Indians to join 400 Detroit militiamen and 300 militia and *troupes de la marine* from Canada and Illinois.[33] As this relief force approached its destination, the Indians accompanying Lignery had secret discussions with the Iroquois, who were there in comparable numbers demonstrating their renewed commitment to the English besiegers of Fort Niagara. Indians had become increasingly reluctant to slaughter each other in this white man's war, and the talks led to the effective neutrality of nearly all the Indians during the battle of 24 July 1759.[34]

Lignery's remaining force promptly signaled that European martial conventions could not be presumed. They "cut off" an isolated working party of the Royal American Regiment early that morning, and most of them were killed and scalped; their corpses were dismembered, and body parts were mounted on stakes positioned to intimidate their living comrades.[35] In the main action later that morning, Lignery's remnant force failed to fight their way through an ambush by a well-positioned detachment of 500 British and New York regulars. After decisive volleys of disciplined musketry, the victors gave quarter to some of the French, including the mortally wounded Lignery, Captain Charles Philippe Aubry, who had led the Illinois contingent of *troupes de la marine*, and marine cadet Pierre Hertel de Montcour. Montcour's fate displayed the vulnerability of those who surrendered in battle, where survival could depend on many independent judgments. A Six Nations warrior, a friend of Montcour, was with the British forces and saw him captured. Reportedly to save his friend from what he saw as the ultimate humiliation of captivity and "to prevent them from making you suffer," he killed Montcour himself with a single tomahawk blow.[36]

As French survivors fled the battlefield, the Iroquois joined the British and New York regulars in pursuit. One British officer reported that the Six Nations "took many scalps, tho' I don't hear that they behaved with great Inhumanity to the Prisoners," even against those *troupes de la marine* whom he tellingly called "partisans."[37] Another witness saw the same scene rather differently. As soon as they sensed that the French were losing, the Iroquois "fell on them like so many Butchers, with their Tomahawks and "Long Knives," hooping and shouting, as if Heaven and Earth were coming together, and kill'd Abundance of the Enemy ... Whether the barbarities at Fort William Henry and Ohio, has influenced any of our Troops to encourage the Savages is uncertain; but sure it is, that most of the French that came from Venango are Encouragers of such Cruelties, and I hope at this Time they have Satisfaction."[38] Fully 250 (36%) of Lignery's 700 companions were killed in what was, proportionally, as deadly as Braddock's defeat. Indians, colonials, and regulars all regarded the slaughter of fleeing enemies as a legitimate conclusion to battle, and historians have agreed. There were no accusations of a "massacre" at Fort Niagara.

General Jeffrey Amherst was not present, but boasted that, after the barbaric treatment of the Royal American patrol earlier that morning, "One would have thought it would be difficult ... to have Stopt the Men from following the Example, but I am assured they did not hurt a Man that was Prisoner."[39] At least ninety-six are known to have been captured, making the chances of being captured rather than killed nearly one in three, much better than the odds in the two earlier battles for the west. It is not known whether veteran Canadian and Illinois frontier fighters knew the words and gestures to surrender successfully to Iroquois warriors. The warriors knew some of the Canadians they were chasing, and they knew the value of captives both from their own tradition and from years of raiding sponsored by their friend and paymaster Sir William Johnson, who was by chance in command of the English forces at Niagara.[40]

After the consequent surrender of Fort Niagara the next day, Johnson gave priority to a separate but parallel negotiation with his Iroquois allies, including the reapportioning of the 96 prisoners and some 150 scalps taken in the battle. As both superintendent of Indian affairs and commander of the victorious, he had every reason to press for recovery of all captured French and Canadians in order to limit French influence in Iroquois villages. Moreover, Johnson was a recently minted baronet who followed military and social convention in making a priority of recovering all French officers and cadets held captive by the Iroquois. He also knew that the Iroquois would not be content without some prisoners, for at least three warriors had been killed and five had been wounded in the course of the siege. Johnson recorded, "The officers I with difficulty released from them [the Iroquois], by ransom, good words, &c." It is not recorded whether his "&c." included trading enlisted men captured by the British, in order to acquire from the Iroquois the last of the surviving Canadian officers.[41] Admittedly, these well-known Canadian officers could have been more influential than other French prisoners if left among the Iroquois. Johnson's military and social concern for rank meshed well with his diplomatic concern as superintendent of Indian affairs.

The Iroquois were rewarded very well, according to their custom, for modest losses. They had more than 150 scalps and at least a few prisoners. Colonial newspapers reported that the Mohawk had insisted upon their share of those captured at La Belle Famille, but next to nothing is known of the identity or fate of such prisoners. There were initial rumors that "Those that were taken in the wood fight near Niagara are still there among our Indians, with above 300 scalps, and are also to come down [to New York City]."[42] Nearly six months later Amherst sent an agent into Iroquoia to recover several French and Canadian prisoners taken at Niagara.[43] Five others taken by the Iroquois are known to have subsequently escaped because they were recaptured by the British Army and became its prisoners of war.[44] Fully twenty-five years later, a prominent US legation, including James Madison and the Marquis de Lafayette, were surprised to discover that one of their Oneida bearers spoke excellent French. He was Nicholas Jordan, born in Longpré-les-Corps-Saint, a village on the Somme River. He mentioned that he and a number of other Frenchmen had come into Oneida hands during the Seven Years' War. He said that all of the others in his group had been burned at the stake, but that he was saved by a sachem's daughter who had recently lost her husband; her "dowry" supposedly included scalps. Jordan was gilding his story, but he may have been a survivor of the Niagara events of 1759, and he was not the only Frenchman later found living among the Oneida, the only Six Nations community that was strongly anti-British during the American Revolution.[45]

The nineteen *troupes de la marine* officers recovered by Johnson did not sign the humane terms of surrender negotiated with the Fort Niagara garrison the day after the decisive battle, but they would enjoy a remarkably long and comfortable captivity under those terms. Of some thirty officers with Lignery, seven had been killed in the battle, Montcour had been killed upon capture, and only three had escaped. Lignery, who had fought in all three of the major battles for the west, would die of his wounds this time, attended by a British surgeon. The eighteen other captured officers included some of the most famed and feared names along English Allegheny frontiers: Villiers,[46] Legardeur de Repentigny,[47] Marin de La Malgue,[48] Montigny,[49] Douville,[50] Niverville,[51] and La Chauvignerie.[52] These notorious "partisans," who would have been summarily killed upon capture in Europe,[53] were given almost all of the privileges of the other captured French officers. New York's lieutenant governor, James De Lancey, recognized "these great Partisans and Chief Leaders of the Indians," and insisted that they be scattered among the towns of eastern Long Island and required to stay within a half-mile of their chosen lodging unless accompanied by a magistrate. Yet De Lancey advanced each of them $50, and they received mail and their pay from Canada.[54] Although they had been separated from their men, these officers were allowed to borrow money without limit, as though they were providing necessities to a company of subordinates in accordance with a recent cartel negotiated between the British and French in Europe. One of the more difficult aspects of their eventual repatriation was finding ways to pay the extravagant expenses of two of these marine officers without provoking a refusal of the accounts by auditors in France.[55]

The French regular officers of the Niagara garrison and captured militia officers were exchanged along with most of their men within six months; they would fight in the final campaign in defense of Canada. However, General Amherst refused to exchange captured *troupes de la marine* officers, whom he had come to regard as particularly dangerous. Not only were they held until after the fall of Canada, but even then General Amherst refused petitions, supported by his own trusted commissary of prisoners, to allow any of these men to be treated as new British subjects or even to return to their native Canada temporarily before being sent to France in December of 1760.[56]

Word of the defeat at La Belle Famille and the fall of Fort Niagara brought the immediate end of French power in Allegheny country. Captain Pierre Robineau de Portneuf, left in command at Fort Presqu'île, learned the news in less than a week and immediately sent a flag of truce to William Johnson. Portneuf urged every consideration for the captured officers, and evidently ordered the evacuation of Forts Machault (Venango), Le Boeuf, and Presqu'île itself. Salvaged stores were sent on to Detroit, anything else of interest was given to the Indians, and each of the forts was burned between 6 and 12 August 1759. Two passing Shawnee told the garrison of Pennsylvania regulars at Fort Pitt that the last three French forts in the region had been destroyed, and that the evacuated garrisons were withdrawing to Detroit. The previous week had seen both the last major attack on a British supply train and a decisive Indian conference with George Croghan, as William Johnson's deputy superintendent of Indian affairs. Some 300 Ohio Indians, with Delaware chief Tamaqua (Beaver) prominent among them, agreed to a truce.[57]

It may well be coincidence that the proportion of victims known to have been taken prisoner increased notably with each of these three battles: from 1.3 per cent of those with Braddock to 4.3 per cent of those with Grant, and then to 16.7 per cent of those with Lignery. This improvement occurred despite the fact that the proportion of the defeated who were killed in battle remained comparable.[58] The Indians who defeated Braddock did not have favorable conditions for taking captives, and the Ottawa and Ojibwa who predominated had previously not shown much interest in adding Euro-American captives to their hunting, fishing, and gathering communities. Shawnee and Ohio Delaware assisted in defeating Grant in a dispersed woodland battle, and these communities had been systematically gathering Euro-American captives for four years. The Iroquois who pursued the leaderless survivors of Lignery's rout seized an opportunity to take captives within their "mourning war" tradition, while impressing the English with their newfound commitment. They were also pursuing some men they knew would be prized by the British commander, the sometime Mohawk chief Sir William Johnson. Battles exposed few noncombatants to capture and, except in a rout, limited opportunity or incentive to take enemies captive. Nonetheless, at least 154 captives had been taken in the region's three major battles, proof that – even during these bloody contests for survival and scalps – it was sometimes possible to take and be taken captive in battles involving Indians, colonials, and imperial troops.

In the raids, sieges, and battles of the Allegheny war of 1755–59, and in minor incidents over the next three years of uneasy truce, at least 2,400 people were killed, and some 900 were known to be either captive, or missing and presumed captured. Soldiers accounted for three-quarters of those killed, and 70 per cent of these soldiers died in the three battles. Nearly eight soldiers were killed for every one known to have been captured. Traders were not a focus of Indian attack and had fled this war zone under French harassment before the war began; only two are known to have been killed during the entire war.[59] European settlers of all ages and both genders were the largest group taken captive, and were the only sizable group less likely to be killed than captured or reported missing. Casualties among Indians were much fewer than among soldiers, but members of either of these groups were much more likely to be killed than captured. For white settlers or soldiers, the forts and garrison houses had proven to be by far the safest places to be defeated, with one killed for every five captured. Those caught in raids were as likely to be killed as captured. In the three major battles, six were killed for every one captured, but this figure included the odds of one captured for every thirty killed in Braddock's defeat. The Allegheny victims of the Seven Years' War can be graphically represented (see table 2), and compared with the previous period (see table 1) and with Pontiac's War (see table 3).

None of these outcomes could have been known, or easily predicted, by captors or captives. Indians took many more captives than did other combatants and, despite relentless misrepresentation, were certainly not engaged in wars of extermination. Indian raiders tended to avoid attacking forts or garrisoned houses, for good reasons, though these became places where they and their allies would take numerous captives. White settlers who insisted on staying in the borderlands during the war certainly increased their risks, but those of them who forted up greatly improved their chances of survival. Those who resisted militia duties or recruitment into provincial or British regiments probably increased their odds of surviving in direct conflict, though many men died defending their farmsteads. Some captives were taken in each of these circumstances, and submitting to captivity was a sane alternative to dying in combat.

Although the Indian raiding war of 1755–58 was usually separate and parallel to the imperial contest, this was always a French and Indian war to some degree. Canadians actively recruited Indian allies on occasion, joined in some raids, sieges, and battles, and supported raiders with arms and ammunition or with provisions for warriors and their families. The garrison commander at Fort Duquesne hosted numerous conferences, and occasionally served as broker/arbitrator in disputes over captives, even giving compensation to ease settlements between allies. He received a few captives from Indians as gifts, and purchased/ransomed others, who were usually sent to Montreal for eventual exchange. "Civilized" conventions about the taking of prisoners led the French, their English enemies, and historians to expect that these views somehow moderated a presumed Indian "barbarity." This supposition has been challenged here, and can be tested further by comparing captivities in the French and Indian War with those of the subsequent Anglo-Indian War of 1763–65.

7

Indian War with Traders and Soldiers, 1763–65

Captive taking was not a part of the preliminaries of war in 1763, as it had been for warriors, traders, and soldiers in the years 1753–55. After a long, uneasy truce, Indians launched a war in 1763 that was both entirely new and a resumption of the previous war. The Indian war with British traders and soldiers was new in extent and intensity; the Indian war on European settlers, discussed in the next chapter, was a resumption of a familiar war. Traders, soldiers, and white settlers had all been captured on Allegheny frontiers in the Seven Years' War, and both the taking and the treatment of each of these categories of captive in the next war reveal much about what remained essential, what had been learned from the previous fighting, and what was fundamentally different.

British and British colonial officialdom insisted that the Seven Years' War had ended in Allegheny country with the burning of Fort Duquesne in November 1758, though the final ratification of this imperial peace did not come for nearly five years. The British claimed that the Shawnee, Delaware, and Mingo had agreed to peace at Easton and Fort Pitt in 1758. Although the terms of this conditional agreement were never met by either side, British officials regarded all Indian reticence to return captives, or other Indian resistance to white intrusion, as a violation of the "peace." The extent to which traders and soldiers were repeatedly surprised by Indian attacks in the spring of 1763 indicates that they had come to presume peace and had long since relaxed their vigilance. Those outraged by the Indian attacks in the spring of 1763 saw themselves as in a new war.

However, there had never quite been peace. European settlers who persevered in the Allegheny borderlands were aware that most captured and missing kin and neighbors had not been returned despite repeated promises, isolated attacks still occurred, and there were unsolved murders of both whites and Indians. Indians were equally aware that the English were ignoring their pledge to withdraw from Fort Pitt, and that competing white hunters, land-hungry settlers, and abusive traders were all violating promises that had been made. In the summer of 1764, a Shawnee spokesman would remind the British that the previous eleven years constituted a single war, started by the imprisonment of those Shawnee warriors in Charleston back in 1753: "it is altogether yr own Faults ... Brethren, you have this War, asked for a Peace, but don't blame us, but yourselves for our prosecuting the war against you as we have done."[1]

People had been killed or captured during the truce, and it was seldom clear how far these were instances of random violence in a lawless borderland or remnants of a still-smoldering war. One Indian family of four was killed near Carlisle early in 1760; Indians blamed whites, and the Pennsylvania government proclaimed a reward for apprehending the killers, but they were never caught.[2] (There was, of course, no question of providing hostages until the killers were found, as was Indian custom.) The Anglo-French war definitely continued near Fort Presqu'île that summer, where small British patrols twice clashed with French and Indian war parties from Detroit.[3] In the second of these, a British soldier was killed and two were taken captive and brought to Detroit. They were held there for three months, and released only when a British force finally arrived to accept the French surrender of Detroit and to send the forty-two Canadians of this garrison off to New York as prisoners of war.[4]

Horse stealing had become a new Indian sport by the summer of 1759, and there were predictable casualties in clashes between military "grass guards" and Indian horse thieves. Capturing horses was not quite like capturing people, but it became a test of daring that profitably diverted some aggressive warriors in this time of suspended belligerence and also helped slow the building and supplying of intrusive British fortifications.[5] By 1761 the situation had become so serious that Colonel Henry Bouquet embargoed all trade with the Delaware, Shawnee, and Mingo until these communities returned captured people as well as stolen horses.[6]

English authorities had become increasingly anxious to preserve calm in the west amid "blood stains on the road" between Indians and whites. When a Mingo was killed while stealing horses near Fort Ligonier, William Johnson and his deputies sought to forestall retaliation by offering condolence ceremonies and gifts at both Fort Pitt and Detroit.[7] When prominent Delaware Ticasso (Thomas Hickman) was killed by a colonial at Salt Licks on the Tuscarawas River, George Croghan took condolences and a small gift to his family, and Lieutenant Governor James Hamilton offered a reward for the capture of those involved and soon claimed to have a man in custody.[8] A revenge attack planned by Ticasso's brother was slowed by gifts from conciliatory Moravian Delaware, and then ended by the more substantial gifts and arguments of a legation of Quakers and Delaware.[9] Traditional Mingo, Wyandot, and Shawnee raids against the Cherokee also resumed that year, and these attacks left at least a dozen Indians killed and four captured.[10] Once again, such raiding led to incidental killing of colonial frontiersmen, though this time the outrage subsided as soon as Croghan pointed out that the three men killed by the Shawnee in the spring of 1761 were "two half Breed Cherrokes and a Mustee or half Molota."[11]

General Jeffrey Amherst, who had been anxious to assert British authority by prosecuting Indians for any serious crime, gained no reputation for himself or his army from the only case in the west that came to trial.[12] Near Fort Presqu'île a couple of Indian slaves killed their new master, English trader William Clapham Jr. These *panis*, a man and a woman, were reportedly "assisted" by several Ottawa, who promptly confiscated all of Clapham's goods, burned his papers, and may even have arranged to have the killers turned over to the British commander at Detroit, Major Henry Gladwin. With the two accused in custody, Amherst and Johnson both pressed Gladwin for a military trial and exemplary public punishment of the perpetrators of this first murder in the vicinity since the British arrival. The imprisoned man escaped custody, and, after waiting in vain for the recapture, Gladwin had the woman accomplice tried by court martial, found guilty, and publicly hanged at Detroit in April of 1763. Whether the British were losing their horses and then offering condolence gifts upon the death of a horse thief, encouraging the diversion of Indian aggression against the Cherokee, or inflicting their lame judicial power over a hapless *panis* accomplice, these authorities were repeatedly asserting strength but more clearly revealing weakness.[13] In January of 1763, Amherst confessed to Gladwin that precautions needed to be taken against "an Enemy, and Such the Indians, in some Degree, must always be Lookt upon, altho' it is unnecessary to Let them know it."[14]

Ohio Indian communities had become increasingly disgusted with the English by 1762, and conciliators were fading from tribal leadership. Chief Tamaqua (Beaver) and his Delaware kin visibly lost influence after his brother Menatochyard (Delaware George) died and his brothers Pisquetomen and Shingas both withdrew from public affairs.[15]

Other Delaware voiced their angry intent to fight, and dissident Shawnee raided the Virginia frontier in January 1762, capturing no prisoners but taking three scalps and being suspected in two other frontier killings.[16] Throughout the year, Alexander McKee continued what proved to be vain efforts to recover captives still held by the Shawnee, captives held for at least five years. At the end of March 1763, George Croghan was still waiting for the promised return of captives by the Shawnee. By this time rumors of the renewed war had reached the most western posts.[17]

Two events of the next month triggered the resumption of open war. On the night of 19 April 1763, Teedyuscung, the Delaware chief who had led the North Branch Delaware into the previous war and out of it, died in a very suspicious fire that consumed all twenty buildings of his Wyoming settlement. Two days later, Christian Frederick Post arrived at Fort Pitt to report that Netawatwees (Newcomer), who had become the most influential leader of the Ohio Delaware, "was struck dumb for a considerable time" upon hearing the news that France had ceded all lands east of the Mississippi River to the British in the Peace of Paris, and then he declared that "ye English was grown too powerfull & seemd as if they would be too strong for God himself." Alexander McKee, who was among the Shawnee when word of the peace arrived, reported that they, too, were stunned and angry.[18]

Although the tensions, grievances, and simmering hostilities of the truce all linked the renewed fighting to the recent war, some vital changes could be expected to affect the taking of captives. The Anglo-French rivalry, which had given Indians considerable leverage with European customers, suppliers, and diplomats, was over, though Ohio Indians denied this fact even as its damaging consequences were becoming obvious.[19] The French were gone as allies, and all but gone as patrons and trading partners. Without French war objectives to accommodate, Indians could avoid some of the sustained and deadly actions that had marked earlier joint Indian-French sieges. Warriors could now take prisoners at will, and withdraw when enough prisoners were taken to bring honor to the victors and provoke the flight of terrified white survivors from disputed lands. The French were also gone as a market for captives who had been valued for information, for labor, or as prisoners of war useful in military exchanges.

Although the Shawnee, Delaware, and Mingo of the Ohio again allied with fighters from farther north, these allies were now Anishinabeg, not French. It was these Ottawa, Ojibwa, and Potawatomi who began the fighting around Detroit in May of 1763 and spread it into much of the *pays d'en haut*. The Anishinabeg had occasionally raided in Allegheny and Ohio country before and during the earlier war, when these outsiders came to be accepted by the Delaware, Shawnee, and Mingo as ferocious former enemies who had become fellow allies of the French and Canadians.[20] These Anishinabeg allies, unlike the Canadians, could not reliably offer any quantity of arms, ammunition, trade goods, or provisions, and they were direct rivals for the spoils of war. The Anishinabeg also had fewer pretentions about managing war in Allegheny country than had the French. The Ohio Indians now needed to find their own arms, ammunition, and provisions in order to sustain both their raids and their families while they were away fighting. The strategy and tactics required to gain supplies could affect the taking or keeping of captives for communities that already including at least 524 white captives not returned by the end of the truce.

The new battlegrounds pressed perilously close to Ohio Indian settlements, which would affect both the willingness to take captives and the opportunities for escape (see map 3). Although Indians had migrated west from the uppermost Ohio River to the valleys of its Beaver, Muskingum, and Scioto tributaries, captors and captives were now much closer to the English in less forbidding country. The British Army had overcome the mountain buffer in defeating the French, and in the spring of 1763 the British military were at Pittsburgh and the Allegheny River forts, as well as the formerly French forts farther north that linked Detroit to Ouiatenon on the Wabash River. The experience of the previous war in northern Pennsylvania suggested that aggrieved Indian near-neighbors would take fewer captives.

The new war was also haunted by the bitter Cherokee War (1759–61) in the southern Appalachian Mountains,[21] though the Cherokee War had not visibly disrupted the Anglo-Indian truce that held farther to the north and few northern warriors took the Warriors' Path against the Cherokee.[22] English traders in Cherokee towns had been summarily killed to launch war there. Cherokee raids into neighboring English colonies had been belatedly countered with punitive British Army expeditions – imperial overreach that destroyed empty Cherokee towns and ripening crops. The British had held hostage an entire Cherokee

Map 3 (*facing page*) Allegheny Country, 1763–65

1763 – 1765
Settlements
Indian
Colonial
Fort
Conflict
Raid
Siege
Battlefield
Note: 2012 state boundaries are depicted.
Cartography: P.M. Connor, 2012.
© I. Steele, 2012.
0
50
100
MILES
Fort Michilimackinac
L'Arbre Croche
Lake Huron
Lake Michigan
Lake Ontario
Lake Erie
Fort Edward Augusta/La Baye
Upper Mississippi River
Bloody Run
Detroit
Point Pelee
Fort St Joseph
Fort Sandusky
Fort Miami
Fort Ouiatenon
Fort Niagara
Devil's Hole
Kanestio
Allegheny R.
Fort Presqu'ile
Fort Le Boeuf
Fort Venango
Salt Licks
Fort Pitt
Bushy Run
Bouquet's Route (1764)
Tuscarawas
Muskingum R.
Fort Ligonier
Fort Bedord
Carlisle
Path Valley
Susquehanna R.
Juniata River
Auqvauge
Fort Augusta
Wyoming
Conestoga
Scioto R.
Upper Shawnee Town
Chillicothe
Lower Shawnee Town
Ohio River
Wabash River
Bulltown
Monongahela R.
Potomac R.
ALLEGHENY MTS
Staunton
Fort Dinwiddie
Greenbrier River
Jackson River
Upper James River
ATLANTIC OCEAN

diplomatic mission early in the war, and soldiers had murdered all twenty-two of them to avenge the killing of the commander of Fort Prince George. The war had included pitched battles between regulars and Cherokee and the siege and surrender of the major British garrison of Fort Loudoun (Venore, Tennessee), which was followed by the violation of agreed terms. The Cherokee had become increasingly short of both gunpowder and grain by the second year of their war, and had negotiated a peace that included a boundary line and the subsequent return of captives by the Cherokee.[23] Even though the Cherokee did not join either side when the Ohio war resumed in 1763, their war had shown that Indians could force the surrender of a major fort, that seasoned British regulars could inflict severe damage in punitive raids on agrarian Indians, that Indians needed a reliable source of gunpowder to sustain a war beyond two years, and that captives held by Indians were both vulnerable and highly valued by both sides.

How did earlier experiences and new circumstances affect the taking of captives in the war of 1763–65? The Indian war in Allegheny country exploded with attacks on both traders and stockaded little garrisons and major forts, and would include several pitched battles between Indians and regulars. These attacks reflected what was new in context and motivation. Studying the capture of traders and soldiers demonstrates the changes and invites close comparisons with the earlier war.

English traders caught in the Ohio Valley and Great Lakes region in the spring of 1763 were the clearest proof that renewed warfare was not widely anticipated or discussed, and that Indians' view of English traders had been entirely revolutionized in the preceding decade. English traders were among the causes of violence this time, rather than the preferred business partners of the early 1750s who were protected by their Indian customers and forced to flee only because of Canadian harassment. Spring was the end of the "winterers'" trading year, when the trade goods, including guns and ammunition, had already been sold and the furs and skins were being sent eastward. In the spring of 1763, unlike 1745 or 1753, Indians who confiscated English furs would have a limited market for them. Some Delaware and Mingo timed their first attacks so well that they negotiated suspiciously large sales of pelts for English gunpowder at both Fort Pitt and Fort Augusta in May.[24] Once the attacks on traders and forts were reported, the only welcoming fur mart was the French garrison and trading fort at Fort Chartres on the Mississippi, where even increased trade could not absorb all the pelts gathered to the east and north.[25]

Traders were accustomed to being outnumbered by their Indian customers, and were much more likely to surrender than to fight.[26] Therefore, Ohio Delaware and Shawnee could easily have captured familiar traders to declare war in May of 1763. However, anger over the restrictions on trade and high prices were among the motives for the war, and these grievances were vented directly against the traders. Thomas Calhoun, a prominent Pennsylvania trader with the Delaware on the Muskingum River, was the only trader known to have been formally "warned" to leave. Late on the night of 27 May, six Delaware chiefs, including Shingas, Tamaqua, and Daniel, visited Calhoun's camp at Tuscarawas, presented a string of wampum, and gave exaggerated accounts of initial Indian martial successes farther north. They also reported the recent killing of all five of one trader's party, at nearby Salt Licks, without mentioning that Delaware had killed them.[27] The Delaware may still have been divided about going to war, and these chiefs may have been genuine in warning Calhoun's group, while urging them to leave all their goods and weapons and flee under Delaware escort. This escort evaporated when Calhoun, fellow trader Thomas Copeland, and their twelve workers reached Beaver Creek and Delaware led by Kitchi (Turtle Heart) attacked. A packhorseman escaped and brought the first report to Fort Pitt. He was sure that the warning and attack had been coordinated, and that his companions had all been killed. Although Calhoun and two others escaped within the next two days, the other ten were apparently killed.[28] With or without a warning, three other traders and their workers had also gathered at the mouth of Beaver Creek, waiting for canoes and escape. Delaware reportedly attacked this group of ten, killing six. In the last week of May 1763, Ohio Delaware had attacked three parties of traders, killing as many as twenty-one, and capturing only two. Taking familiar English traders captive was certainly not a priority.

Traders farther down the Ohio River were attacked by the Shawnee, who were even less willing to take prisoners. Very little detail survives, but three men were killed on the river, and eight in Lower Shawnee Town. Mathew McCrea and one servant were killed at the Salt Licks on the Scioto River, with four others missing and presumed killed. Three employees of Thomas Mitchell were killed at Wakitomica. No traders were reported taken prisoner by the Shawnee, though one came into their hands later.[29] By any comparison with their earlier warfare, and especially their earlier treatment of traders, the Delaware and Shawnee were ferocious against traders in May of 1763.

Ironically, proportionately fewer traders are known to have been killed farther north in Anishinabeg country around Pontiac's fierce and frustrated multitribal siege of Detroit. Wyandot captured two traders' flotillas on the Detroit River in the latter half of May 1763.[30] A month later a large Detroit-bound flotilla could still be caught by surprise as they put ashore at the mouth of the Grand River and were attacked by Ojibwa, who killed several and captured fourteen.[31] Wyandot captured three traders' caravans near Sandusky, and all thirty-two men were missing, including Michael Teaffe, who had been robbed in the same region when war began a decade earlier, and another trader, whom the Wyandot would return to Detroit after a year of captivity.[32] Veteran trader Hugh Crawford had led another eight-man trading party that was attacked on the lower Maumee River on 14 May. Although six were initially reported killed, Crawford and four of the others eventually escaped or were released at Detroit.[33]

If a trader's chances of being captured, rather than killed, were better around Detroit than in the Ohio Valley, the chances of deliberate violence after capture were higher, too, as the fate of John Welch illustrates. Five Canadians in sympathy with Pontiac had left Detroit for Illinois, with an Indian escort, in mid-May. At the mouth of the Maumee River, they met, lured ashore, and captured John Welch, his five servants, and their cargo of pelts and skins. The captors then divided into two groups. One group took four of the captured, whom they soon killed, and continued on to Illinois country with the confiscated furs. Three of the Canadians took their share of the booty, including John Welch, back to Detroit. When the Ottawa of Detroit heard of this, they confiscated the pelts, killed Welch, and insisted that the Canadians "had no business with any Plunder, but that it belonged entirely to the Indians."[34] Another trader, who had been captured by Wyandot warriors, was also hidden for a time by a Detroit Canadian. When discovered, he was fated for burning by the Ojibwa, but was apparently freed as insane after he threw hot gruel in the face of a tormentor.[35] Another merchant at Fort St Joseph, who also survived the war, thanked God and a man he called Louison Chavalie for hiding him for four days when this fort was destroyed, the garrison killed, and two other traders sent captive to Illinois country.[36] Alexander Henry, at Michilimackinac, was another trader who was protected during a massacre, owing his life to a *panis* woman who was a slave of Charles Langlade.[37]

Not only were more English traders attacked in 1763 than at any time in the previous generation, but these traders were now twice as likely to be killed. Sixty-four British American traders and their servants were reported killed in May and June 1763, and ninety-eight were captured or then considered missing.[38] The picture darkened further when most of the traders captured or missing in Pontiac's War never returned and were eventually presumed dead. The known dead and presumed dead came to number 124 traders, and only 43 are known to have escaped or been released. Led by the energetic and self-serving George Croghan, who had been making land claims to compensate for trading losses since as early as 1753, traders and the heirs of some of the dead became the "suffering traders" who would eventually gain £85,000 worth of compensation in awards of Ohio Indian lands.[39] Most Allegheny traders who survived attack, personally and financially, did not become major players in the revived Indian trade after 1765. They would find more profit in using what and whom they knew to speculate in land for themselves, for land companies, or for the Crown.

Sieges of garrisons in this war contrasted markedly with those of the previous decade. Pennsylvania did not revive its own frontier forts at all.[40] New garrisons of British regular soldiers farther west had not been particularly suspicious of Indians, routinely allowed them into their forts in numbers, and proved almost as easy to surprise and overwhelm as were traders in the first weeks of the war. Paltry garrisons of fifteen unsuspecting Royal American musketeers and an ensign may have symbolized distant power, but these were weak, isolated, cannonless, and flammable stockades. Without experience or adequate resources for effective Indian diplomacy, the junior army officers who led these British intruders were at best ignorant and irritating substitutes for the absent French "father." The garrisons were accustomed to having numerous Indians attending in order to trade and confer, so simple ruses were effective in capturing these posts. Eight of the nine captured posts fell without anything resembling a siege. At most of the garrisons, soldiers could be taken captive relatively easily if the Anishinabeg, Wyandot, Miami, and Seneca considered British soldiers worth capturing. These were very different situations from the unsuccessful larger sieges of Forts Pitt and Detroit, the last of which became an anomalous six-month duel, with captives playing major roles.

Three British posts in the Detroit region were captured easily during the first three weeks of the Detroit siege. Ensign Christopher Pauli was smoking a pipe with seven Wyandot and Detroit Ottawa in the fort at Sandusky when, on a signal, he was seized and the entire garrison and attending merchants were killed. Pauli was taken to Pontiac's camp, given to the Ojibwa, and supposedly "made a very good Indian" who was adopted and treated well until allowed to escape.[41] A week after the capture of Sandusky, Ensign Francis Schlosser was the victim of a similar ruse at Fort St Joseph, where thirteen men of the garrison were killed by the Potawatomi. Schlosser, two soldiers, and three traders were taken captive. At Fort Miami, Ensign Robert Holmes was aware of impending trouble, but was lured out of the fort by his Miami mistress and promptly killed, and his sergeant was captured when he investigated. The garrison, after deliberating without their officers, surrendered on being promised quarter. Nine were then killed and five taken captive.[42] In the easy capture of these three forts, by allies of Pontiac attacking with his emissaries present, four soldiers were killed for every one captured. These casualties were deliberate executions, though the captivity rate for soldiers was comparable to that in the earlier war, and to that for traders in the spring of 1763. Although Pontiac was already using captives as pawns in negotiations at Detroit, captive soldiers were not valued much in these three instances.

Early in June three more outposts, Ouiatenon, Michilimackinac, and Green Bay, were captured, but the outcomes were quite different. Lieutenant Edward Jenkins had been at the remote Wabash River fort of Ouiatenon for more than a year when he complained, at the end of May, that Canadian traders were disturbing Indian relations with wild talk of a great French military expedition coming from Louisiana. His dim view of local Canadian traders changed abruptly a few days later. Jenkins and part of his garrison were conferring with an Indian council outside the fort when they were suddenly taken captive by local Kickapoo, Mascouten, and Miami. The captors claimed that other tribes were pressuring them to act, which seems likely from the sequel. Canadian traders, known only as Maisonville[43] and Lorrain, intervened to offer wampum for the lives of the captured soldiers, and may have suggested that the captives be taken to the last remaining French fort in the region, Fort Chartres. Jenkins was able to write his commanding officer a letter, delivered by Lorrain, and the captives were kept in French houses at Ouiatenon until eventually taken to a surprised and helpful commandant at Fort Chartres, who held them in comfortable captivity in Illinois country. By the following spring they were all back on active duty.[44]

Fort Michilimackinac was no mere blockhouse, but a settlement of some fifty houses, including those of English and French traders, many of whom were in the fort and protected by a garrison of thirty-seven men and officers led by Captain George Etherington. The local Ojibwa numbered about 2,000, and about 1,250 Ottawa lived at L'Arbre Croche, some thirty miles west of the fort; both of these communities had frequented the fort during the three years since the English garrison replaced the French.[45] There were some grievances here, a preference for the French, who had been trading and preaching there for ninety years, and foreknowledge that Pontiac intended to attack Detroit. However, the carefully planned fury at Michilimackinac had its puzzles. The Ojibwa played their now-famous lacrosse game for hours on the morning of 2 June 1763, as they had done on the previous few days, before capturing the curious and unwary commander and swarming into the fort with hatchets that women had concealed under their blankets. There may have been some resistance, some immediate surrenders, and some mercy to acquaintances, and French traders protected a few individuals like Ezekiel Solomon and Alexander Henry, who was not captured by the Ojibwa until two days later. The attackers immediately killed Lieutenant John Jamet, and all fifteen soldiers of the watch, and merchant Warren Tracy, who had joined in resisting the intruders. However, Alexander Henry's vivid recollections were misleading: the Ojibwa were not "cutting down and scalping every Englishman they found."[46] They captured eighteen soldiers and five English traders, in addition to five *panis* slaves of the latter. Although Captain Etherington later noted that no French inhabitants or traders were attacked, it is more curious that the Ojibwa took so many captives.

The Ojibwa had not burned Michilimackinac or massacred all the soldiers. Although they wanted the English out and the French returned, their anger and resentment evidently had limits.[47] The Ojibwa then effectively looted the fort, with some collusion by French traders, and angered their rival Ottawa by excluding them from both their plan and the booty. Although the Ojibwa killed at least five more soldiers after the initial attack,[48] the Ottawa confiscated or successfully negotiated for control of most survivors and the fort. Etherington had somehow managed to confiscate two canoe-loads of merchandise brought in by unsuspecting traders from Montreal, and he made their entire cargo a strategic present to the helpful Ottawa. Led by Charles Langlade, Ottawa-Canadian warrior and trader, and by Father Pierre Du Jaunay, the popular veteran Jesuit missionary, the Ottawa succeeded in gaining control over all but four of the surviving soldiers.[49] The war began very differently for the more remote detachment at Green Bay, where Lieutenant James Gorrell followed orders from Etherington and took his fourteen men, escorted by ninety supportive Menominee across the lake to join Etherington's redeemed survivors in the Ottawa village of L'Arbre Croche.[50] The Ottawa escorted these captive soldiers to an astonished British Army at Montreal that summer.

The English had been cleared from the upper posts of Ouiatenon and Green Bay without any violence, and from Michilimackinac with less violence than might have been expected. It was only after the six garrisons had fallen in the vicinity of Detroit and the remote reaches of the *pays d'en haut*, that the Seneca annihilated two forts that had marked the French approach to upper Ohio country back in 1753. The dissident Chenussio Seneca, pro-French in the earlier war and resentful of General Amherst's unauthorized land grants around Fort Niagara, had been advocating violent Indian resistance since early in 1761. The campaign they led did not proceed from Lake Erie southward, spreading a Detroit example, but rather took the reverse route, beginning with the burning of Fort Venango (16 June) and Fort Le Boeuf (18 June) before they joined Pontiac's expeditionary force farther north at the siege of Fort Presqu'île (19–21 June).

The Seneca campaign was in defiance of the Six Nations alliance with the English and the influence of William Johnson in Iroquoia, and these circumstances did not encourage the taking of prisoners. A large party of Seneca came to Venango in feigned friendship on 16 June, were allowed into the fort, and soon took Lieutenant Francis Gordon captive and killed his entire garrison. Gordon was forced to write out a list of Indian grievances and was then burned to death with the fort.[51] Within two days, the Seneca went north and attacked Fort Le Boeuf. Ensign George Price and his thirteen men managed to get into a defensible blockhouse and watch other buildings burn. Convinced that they could not hold off their attackers, Price and seven of his men escaped during the night. Six of the garrison, and one woman, did not escape and were presumed killed.[52] If the Seneca had planned to attack three posts seriatim, as seems most likely, their unwillingness to take any captives at Venango and Le Boeuf left them unencumbered as they went on to Presqu'île.

Presqu'île was the only Allegheny garrison where a siege ended in surrender. After hearing of both the attack on the convoy at Point Pelee and the destruction of Sandusky, Ensign John Christie had two weeks to prepare his post for its final defense.[53] The Presqu'île blockhouse was reinforced, outbuildings and combustible fascines removed, roofs prepared for the expected fire arrows, and water barrels readied. The Seneca, fresh from two victories, were outnumbered by a much larger force from Detroit, which included Wyandot, Ottawa, Ojibwa, Potawatomi, and Fox, making up an attack force of about 250. These warriors employed siege techniques that included log and mobile breastworks, trenches, tunnels under the palisade, and dominance in musketry, as well as increasingly effective fire arrows that soon confined the defenders to their sturdy blockhouse. As water to fight the fires was used up, the garrison successfully tunneled from their blockhouse to the well in the parade.[54] With overwhelming numbers of attackers now within the fort, no prospect of reinforcement, and inadequate water to fight more fires, Christie responded to a midnight invitation to talk. A former English captive, now with the Wyandot, conveyed proposed terms that would allow the garrison to withdraw. A ceasefire continued on the morning of 22 June, when soldiers who were sent to continue the negotiations confirmed the rapid progress of the attack against the blockhouse. Although the surviving soldiers later insisted, in circumstances where they were subject to military discipline, that the garrison overwhelmingly favored continuing the fight, Christie met with two chiefs, likely including at least one Wyandot, and agreed to surrender.

In their understanding of the translated oral surrender, the garrison thought they were free to go to the nearest surviving English post. It is clear that these terms were not honored, but exactly what did happen is difficult to know. The precise size of the garrison is uncertain, though twenty-five men and two women can be accounted for. None of the defenders were reported killed during the siege, but several attackers died.[55] Christie reported that he, four soldiers, and a woman became prisoners of the Wyandot. Two of these soldier-captives were killed on arrival in the Wyandot village at Detroit, likely to avenge the deaths of warriors in the siege.[56] The Wyandot delivered Christie, the woman, and one soldier to Major Gladwin at Detroit less than three weeks later as part of negotiations there. Christie had, as the reported terms had promised, been delivered to the nearest surviving British post. The third survivor of this Wyandot captivity was likely Conrad Wagner, who was still living with the Potawatomi four years later.[57] Christie claimed that the rest of the garrison was taken captive by other tribes involved. Six additional captives from this garrison were delivered at Detroit over the next ten months.[58]

Christie had not seen everything that happened as he was taken captive, and another part of the story soon appeared in the *Pennsylvania Gazette*. Four days after the capitulation, a correspondent at Fort Pitt wrote, "Just now came in a Soldier from Presque-Isle, who affirms that the Place was attacked, and had been defended for two Days, when the Indians undermined the Block-house, on which the Garrison capitulated, with Liberty to come here; but the Indians fell upon them, and, as he supposes, massacred them all."[59] The soldier was young Benjamin Gray of the Royal American Regiment, who had just run more than 110 miles, finding both Le Boeuf and Venango burned-out ruins along his way. Having run for his life, he then had to testify for it with an explanation that countered any intimation of desertion. Gray's interrogators and newspaper readers would find his account plausible, recalling the infamous attack on the paroled garrison at Fort William Henry in 1757. However, the next day, five more exhausted men and a woman arrived at Fort Pitt to correct Gray's story, and to report that two more refugees who were unable to continue had been left along the way.[60] How had these nine escaped after such an overwhelming Indian victory? Perhaps they were near the front of the surrendered garrison as it prepared to set out for the now-destroyed Fort Le Boeuf. No witnesses ever claimed that anyone had been killed immediately after the capitulation, though Gray heard one woman scream. The nine who ran for Fort Pitt escaped as the rest of the surrendered garrison were taken captive. In the victorious Indians' plausible version of the event, recorded in red paint on a sixty-foot post erected near the site, they claimed to have taken eighteen prisoners. At least this was the reading of the post by New York rangers who were there a month later.[61] Only two of the twenty-seven persons who surrendered to Indians after this siege, in which several warriors died, are known to have been killed. The tribes from around Detroit had demonstrated some restraint at Presqu'île, a show of humanity in the face of temptations that even their Seneca allies did not violate, and one that their British enemies never acknowledged.

In the well-known explosion of hostility against soldiers in nine captured forts, Indians are known to have captured eighty-two, nearly as many as the eighty-six they killed. This general record was comparable to the results of attacks on all fortified places in the previous war, and was markedly more humane than the treatment of soldiers in the previous war. Yet Indian communities varied widely in their willingness to take soldier-captives. The Ojibwa hunters, with limited practical uses for captives and few ceremonial traditions that focused upon them, took a surprising number of soldiers captive at Michilimackinac, and saw the Ottawa protect even more. The Miami treated soldiers taken in the capture of their fort more ferociously, killing four for each one kept as a captive. Of the Iroquoians involved, the Wyandot killed all but the commander at Sandusky, in contrast to their relatively benign treatment of traders they captured nearer Detroit. The Seneca dissidents who took Forts Venango and Le Boeuf were clearly the most ferocious, killing every soldier they encountered.

The siege of Detroit was the inspiring first strike that became a most remarkable and sustained anomaly in Indian warfare and the taking of captives. Woodland Indians were not organized politically, socially, economically, or culturally to sustain a six-month multitribal siege of a fort that was resolutely defended by a substantial garrison with canon, naval support, and adequate supplies. Pontiac had come to lead angry and alienated Indians because of his outstanding oratorical skills and his combined Ottawa-Ojibwa roots. The easiest part may have been rousing warriors and their supporting communities with the nativist message of the Delaware prophet Neolin, with a Delaware invitation to avenge the murder of Teedyuscung, and with rising anger at the preposterous new European claims to own and exchange the entire region. Even assembling a force of at least 800 Ottawa, Ojibwa, Wyandot, and Potawatomi for a few days, in support of a plan to take Detroit by surprise, was complicated by rivalries and cautious factions. Holding this force together for a siege once the ruse failed would require much more skill and good fortune. Captives came to play an uncommon role in sustaining the siege.

The day before Pontiac attempted to surprise the garrison, 300 Ojibwa warriors sprang their own trap north of Detroit. A ten-man party from the fort had been sounding Lake St Clair for days when they were lured ashore and fired upon; four died and six were captured. That evening, amid heavy drinking from the "stores" of the captured boat, warriors ate parts of a body. John Rutherfurd, one of the captured who was forced to witness this fearsome feast, would later rather serenely recall that this was "practiced only by some of the Indian nations to the northward ... not for want of food, but as a religious ceremony, or rather from a superstitious idea that it makes them prosperous in war."[62] His first night in captivity was full of terror and death threats, but he was promptly adopted. At the end of the month, the Ojibwa surprised two bateaux on the St Clair River, capturing all nineteen soldiers and boatmen, plus one woman.[63] It was then that Rutherfurd's master took him very briefly to Detroit.

Pontiac's evolving perspective on captives may have prompted Rutherfurd's master to withdraw quickly back to Lake St Clair with his captive. Hoping for a quick surrender, Pontiac had opened negotiations with a suspicious Major Gladwin on 9 May and even provided two Potawatomi chiefs as the demanded hostages for the safe return of Gladwin's negotiators, Captain Donald Campbell and Lieutenant George McDougall. Pontiac kept these negotiators as prisoners, and thereby abandoned his own hostages, but this unique exchange left prominent prisoners with each side, and indicated a potential use for prisoners at the very outset of hostilities.[64] Amid the inconclusive fighting at the fort over the next two weeks, Pontiac did not gain direct control over many other captives. The Ojibwa of Lake St Clair already had a number of captives, the Wyandot captured two parties of traders downriver, and even Canadians were claiming captives they had taken on the Maumee River. Captives were not yet escaping to carry information to the besieged nearby, but Pontiac wanted tactical control of the captives to intimidate the garrison, and to negotiate. His execution of trader John Welch on 14 May was a brutal display of power, or perhaps a sign of weakness. When the Wyandot victors at Sandusky arrived with a welcome supply of ammunition and provisions, they turned their sole captive over to the Ottawa in Pontiac's camp, where Ensign Christopher Pauli was severely beaten in a gauntlet, made to yell so the besieged might notice or even be drawn out to intervene, and then given as a bridegroom to a recent widow.

The use and abuse of captives reached a terrible climax on 29 May, when a flotilla of eight bateaux was rowed up the Detroit River to Pontiac's camp, bringing military supplies, ample liquor, and captives. The bateaux, part of a major convoy escorted by ninety-five Queen's Rangers under Lieutenant Abraham Cuyler, had been bound for Detroit but was ambushed the day before at Point Pelee. During a fierce skirmish ashore and Wyandot pursuit of the fleeing bateaux on Lake Erie, Cuyler and thirty-seven others escaped, a comparable number were killed, and at least twenty-three were captured.[65] The Wyandot had proven once again that well-managed canoes were faster than the reloading of muskets.[66] In Pontiac's camp that evening, drunken warriors tortured at least eleven soldiers with brutal gauntlets, wounding with arrows and gun flints, amputations, and the burning to death of those who survived these other tortures. If it was intended to provoke the horrified Detroit garrison into a rash sortie, or to weaken their resolve to resist, this gruesome carnival did not work. If it helped to bond warriors to each other and their cause, it occurred before serious problems of building and holding the alliance together were as evident as they would soon become. If it was spontaneous violence that Pontiac encouraged, condoned, or merely tolerated, he would be made to bear some responsibility for it within a month.

Although June began well for Pontiac, he received a startling public rebuke from a party of victors who denounced the wanton killing of captives.[67] Kinonchamek, son of the pre-eminent Ojibwa chief Minweweh (Minavana), led a delegation of fifteen Ojibwa and Ottawa who arrived from Michilimackinac on 18 June, without bringing any of the expected reinforcements. They were accompanied by Jesuit missionary Pierre Du Jaunay, observing on behalf of the Ottawa of L'Arbre Croche. The next day Kinonchamek told the assembled chiefs, and several visiting Ohio Shawnee and Delaware legates, about the lacrosse game that had ended in the capture of Fort Michilimackinac, and the sending of the captured garrison to Montreal. Celebrating how honorably they had acted, and falsely claiming to have limited their killing entirely to the battle for control of the fort, Kinonchamek then pointedly accused Pontiac and his allies of killing and eating captives after they had been brought into camp, and also of abusing French settlers. A Wyandot chief went further, speaking for his community and the Delaware, when he noted that the prophet Neolin, who may have been in attendance, had relayed the Master of Life's message that "it is all right to kill during battle, but afterwards, and when one has taken prisoners, it is no longer of any value; nor is it to drink the blood or eat the flesh of men." This chief asked his listeners to follow the French example, of keeping enemy prisoners for exchange. He then concluded that his community would not join Pontiac in the war, as they had intended, because it was being conducted in a way that offended both the Master of Life and the French "Great Father," whose return was eagerly anticipated.[68]

Pontiac made no reply to these criticisms, and his allies reportedly remained silent as well. Kinonchamek may have been offering an excuse for his community's unwillingness to join Pontiac at Detroit, and may have been pressured or coached by Langlade's Ottawa, who might more correctly have made the claim to have respected all prisoners. French civilians at Detroit, tired of being pillaged for food and drink by a host of bullying warriors, would agree with these sentiments. Assuming the critics had not intended to embarrass themselves, it is particularly revealing that they could give such lectures on the humane treatment of prisoners to an intertribal assembly of warring chiefs.[69]

The return of captives became a bellwether of Pontiac's stalled siege. The Potawatomi, like the Wyandot, had been wavering in their support for Pontiac, and offered Gladwin three captured soldiers in exchange for their two chiefs held hostage. Gladwin readily accepted the return of the ensign Schlosser and two soldiers, but surrendered only one chief, No-Kaming, and went on to acquire sixteen more captives in exchange for Chief Big Ears.[70] The Wyandot surrendered fourteen of the twenty captives brought in by various parties talking peace with Gladwin during July.[71] By the end of the month, French settlers had bought at least a few soldier-captives as well.[72] These captives were being bought and returned in defiance of Pontiac, who had returned none, an indication that both his control and wider support for the siege were waning.

It was common for Indians to execute captives who attempted to escape, and Pontiac had gone further by threatening to kill all captives if any escaped. Captain Donald Campbell, who had heard and passed along this threat, then failed in his own escape attempt when fellow hostage Lieutenant George McDougall freed himself on 2 July.[73] Surprisingly, Pontiac imposed no punishment whatever upon his premier captive. However, two days later a British detachment sallied from the fort to clear threatening new Indian positions, and one casualty of the resulting skirmish was a nephew of prominent Saginaw Ojibwa headman Wasson. Not only had this warrior been killed and scalped, but his body was reportedly cut to pieces by a furious soldier. Wasson led the angered Ojibwa, who retaliated by killing Pontiac's captive, Captain Campbell. Pontiac and the Ottawa, in turn, sought to kill the most prominent Ojibwa-held captive, Ensign Christopher Pauli. At this point Pauli managed to escape into Fort Detroit, evidently with Ojibwa help.[74]

Although a total of nine captives escaped during July, there were still "upwards of fifty" whom Rutherfurd thought were held in the vicinity of Detroit at month end.[75] Neither side took any prisoners during or after Captain James Dalyell's failed counterattack on the last day of July, and Pontiac and his allies had more losses than Gladwin did in the spasmodic fighting over the next three months.[76] The arrival in August of 200 Ojibwa with the Grand Saulteur gave new resolve to what then became approximately 1,000 besiegers. There were no more reports of the torture or killing of captives near Detroit, even though ten more captives escaped before Pontiac lifted the siege at the end of October.

Four battles, or major skirmishes, occurred during this Anglo-Indian war: Point Pelee, Bloody Run, Bushy Run, and Devil's Hole. In the skirmish at Point Pelee, ninety-five Queen's Rangers, led by Lieutenant Abraham Cuyler, exchanged a volley of musket fire on the beach, and then took to bateaux that allowed some to escape, but also allowed the pursuing Wyandot to kill others or take captives if they chose, and they chose to take at least twenty-three captives. The three other battles of this war were more typical of the deadly open encounters between Indians and British regulars. Two months after escaping, Cuyler was among 247 fresh British troops who left besieged Detroit for a night attack on Pontiac's relocated camp. Both sides in this siege leaked information readily, and Pontiac knew of the attack in time to prepare a very effective ambush. In the resulting battle of Bloody Run, twenty-five British were killed, including the raid's commander, Captain James Dalyell, some forty British were wounded, and nine Indians were killed. The British retreat eventually became orderly, and no prisoners are known to have been taken on either side.[77]

In a major two-day battle near Fort Pitt less than a week later, between Colonel Henry Bouquet's relief force and the Delaware, Shawnee, Wyandot, and Mingo who ambushed them, about fifty British were killed, and Indian losses were comparable. In the limited pursuit of the retreating Indians, a Highlander took the only known prisoner, who was examined before being summarily killed.[78] There is no surviving evidence that the Indians took any prisoners. The same is true of the Chenussio Seneca double ambush in September, when they attacked an escorted British supply train at Fort Niagara and then the reinforcements who responded to the alarm. The worst British losses of the war occurred here, where the Seneca killed and scalped seventy-two soldiers without any known losses of their own, and without taking any prisoners.[79] Excluding the water battle off Point Pelee, Indians took no prisoners in the battles of this war, and the British took only one, and then killed him. If refusal to take captives in immediately obvious battle victories was a sign of anger, fury, or hatred, this war was even more furious than the last.

More soldiers are known to have been killed in Pontiac's War than were traders.[80] Whatever their complaints about traders, Indians deemed soldiers the primary enemy, and fifteen of them were the only people tortured to death. It is particularly difficult to guess the fate of the ninety-two soldiers who were last reported as missing, since desertion was a major problem that could be masked by presuming the missing were captured. Five soldiers were killed for every two known to have been captured, which was better than the odds for traders in this war, and much better than soldiers' odds in the previous war, when eight soldiers were killed for each one known to have been captured. It is also noteworthy that ninety-three British and colonial soldiers are known to have survived captivity, seventy-four of whom were exchanged, ransomed, or otherwise returned by their captors.[81] Despite the obvious targeting of soldiers, the accumulated grievances from the Seven Years' War, and the absence of a European ally, Indians were more likely to spare a soldier than in the previous decade.

The taking and treatment of traders and soldiers were clearly different in the war of 1763–65. Violence began with widespread and deadly attacks on English traders in the Ohio Valley. This contrasts sharply with Ohio Indian treatment of English traders in the coming of war between 1748 and 1754, when almost all resisted the temptation to plunder these vulnerable targets. In the war between Indians and garrisons, the survival rate for defeated soldiers was better than earlier, and Pontiac's unique negotiations with Gladwin may have enhanced the value of soldier-captives in spite of some horrid abuses of them. The Seneca were by far the most ferocious in fighting soldiers, killing ninety-four soldiers while taking no prisoners at all where they operated independently in two sieges and in the slaughter at Devil's Hole. They dissented from the Anglo-Iroquois alliance, they were early promoters of this war, and they likely remembered William Johnson's earlier insistence that they humiliate themselves by returning all their captives in 1759. The Delaware and Shawnee were prominent in the killing and capture of traders as the war opened, but their new war against soldiers was limited to participation in the unsuccessful siege of Fort Pitt, the battle of Bushy Run, and minor harassment along military communication lines. What they had learned from the previous war and the loss of French patronage is better measured by their renewed war on white settlers.

8

Indian War with White Settlers, 1763–65

Raids on white settlers were not an Indian priority in the war that began in May of 1763, though the rapid white resettlement of the borderlands during the last years of truce had effectively retaken lands the Indians had emptied in the previous war. Ohio Shawnee and Delaware played no part in the dramatic conquests of British military posts that spring, except for the loose blockade of Fort Pitt and an abortive attack upon it at the end of July.[1] For these Indians, war had begun with unprecedented attacks on traders in Ohio country, and then reverted to familiar raids against borderland farmers. The military roads cut by the armies of General Edward Braddock and General John Forbes on their way to what became Fort Pitt attracted new white settlers interested in economic opportunity, and these people now became particularly accessible targets for Indian raiders using these same roads in 1763 and 1764. White intruders' farms and herds may still have been in the early stages of recovery, but the families themselves were back on contested ground, accompanied by newcomers. Once the fighting began, people would again evacuate some areas, but those who did not flee included numerous women and children. The resettlers had not anticipated war, and, like the traders and soldiers, they could be taken by surprise as before. With more than 500 previous captives absorbed into their communities, the raiders now knew much more about the benefits and problems attending this process. In tactical positions comparable to those of the earlier war, were as many white settlers captured, and were those chosen for captivity different from those taken previously?

In the spring of 1763, Hannah Dennis escaped from Wakatomica and walked more than 250 miles home. Widowed and childless from the Shawnee raid on Virginia's James River in which she had been captured six years earlier, Dennis had adapted quickly to life with the Shawnee and had even established herself as a wise woman of medicines and spells. It is not known, but can be suspected, that news or rumors of Shawnee attacks on traders prompted her to flee. Dennis spent a wearying twenty days ascending the waterways of the upper Ohio, the Great Kanawha, and the Greenbrier Rivers before she was found, starving, exhausted, and lame, near the Virginian frontier at the Levels, one of two resettlements on the Greenbrier River since 1761.[2] In this remote corner of expanding southwestern Virginia, far from Braddock's Road, the settlers on the Greenbrier and Jackson Rivers did not know that war had begun at Detroit more than a month earlier, and that traders had already been killed in the Ohio Valley. No witnesses or subsequent legends claim that Dennis announced the outbreak of this war.

A sixty-man Shawnee party, led by war captain Cornstalk, was a month behind Hannah Dennis, not pursuing a fugitive so much as launching war. The Shawnee with Cornstalk used the same ruse to destroy each of two unsuspecting Greenbrier settlements, about fifteen miles apart. The Greenbrier ran beside the warpath used by Ohio war parties raiding the Cherokee or Catawba, and white intruders were familiar with Indian war parties, who had to be accommodated.[3] Here was an ideal opportunity for the Shawnee to take as many captives as they wished in the act of declaring war. After "banquets" at Muddy Creek and at the Levels, the Shawnee killed the heads of three families and took twenty-seven captives. Leaving a small guard over these traumatized captives, whom feisty Jennet Clendennin claimed she could not rouse to resist, the raiders went on to Jackson River. Warned by a rider who had escaped from the Levels, the Jackson River resettlers had fled. The war party went some thirty miles farther east to Carr's (Kerr's) Creek, where the last Shawnee raid of 1759 had ended unsatisfactorily in a battle with militia and rangers; this time they captured seven women and children.[4] Cornstalk's raiders had obliterated white resettlement on the Greenbrier, and had avenged themselves at Carr's Creek. Despite the unusual strategy of attacking three targets in turn, the Shawnee priority was to take captives in each case. In ideal circumstances of complete surprise, they had killed three and taken thirty-three captives, all without suffering any losses; thirty of these thirty-three captives lived with the Shawnee for sixteen months and are known to have been surrendered as part of peacemaking.[5] Shawnee experience with captives during and after the previous war, and British pleas and threats about returning captives, had certainly not discouraged the Shawnee from taking white settler captives again.

The Ohio Delaware raiding war against Pennsylvania frontier settlers began earlier and proved more deadly than the Shawnee attacks, hitting first at white settlers near the hated forts. A former colonel of Pennsylvanian troops and four of his hired hands were killed on 28 May 1763 at his farm a few miles southeast of Fort Pitt. No captives were taken, and two who succeeded in fleeing this sudden slaughter reported that the Wolf, an Ohio Delaware war chief, had led the attackers.[6] As fighting began around Fort Ligonier two weeks later, Mary Means and her mother were captured while fleeing to the fort. The Delaware captors were more intent on attacking the fort, so they tied these two to a tree, where, hours later, they were freed and guided to safety by a Delaware acquaintance, a warrior named Maiden Foot. This act of kindness was eventually returned, and is still celebrated, but neither the capture nor the release reflected the general shape of the deadly Delaware offensive.[7] A few of the white settlers who had flooded into Fort Bedford on first reports of attacks returned too soon to their farms on nearby Dunning Creek. After their wounded dog returned to the fort, a search party found that eleven people had been killed and scalped, with a spear left in one mangled body to declare a war that no one doubted had begun. The twelve-man garrison of the Royal American Regiment at Fort Bedford had difficulty protecting seven peaceable Indian prisoners, supposedly held in the fort for their own safety, from dozens of infuriated local inhabitants.[8]

The next Ohio Delaware attack was even more ferocious, and occurred farther east along the military road between Fort Pitt and Carlisle. Shemokin Daniel, who had been a double-agent in the previous war but had repeatedly voiced his enmity for those who had driven his people from the Susquehanna Valley, led eighteen warriors in two days of killing white settlers and pursuers in the Juniata Valley. In three attacks on busy farmsteads, the Delaware killed a dozen people, including women and children. One warrior was killed, and a wounded boy was the only captive taken. In two engagements with pursuing posses of local militia, when taking captives was even less likely, Shemokin Daniel's force killed ten and lost a second warrior. Although the deaths of two warriors would negate the Delaware sense of victory, their opponents were certain that they had been thoroughly defeated by a deadly enemy that had killed twenty-two people and taken only one captive.[9]

The siege of Fort Pitt and the subsequent battle with the relief force at Bushy Run were distractions from raiding white settlements, and affected the raiding that was undertaken. The Delaware of the upper Ohio Valley were assisted by Shawnee, Mingo, and Potawatomi in a siege that began gradually, became an open exchange of gunfire from 22 June 1763, and continued unevenly for six weeks. During the siege, warriors, who were not expecting to return soon to their villages, sporadically attacked farmsteads in the neighborhood and eastward, killing almost all their victims, including women and children. By mid-July, two soldiers and twenty-seven farmers, including ten children, had been killed in the "Department of Fort Pitt." Only two men and two women were taken captive, and three of these four escaped or were released promptly.[10] The raids led by Cornstalk and Shemokin Daniel were very different from each other, though they both occurred during the siege of Fort Pitt, and the raids likely represented more profitable alternatives for some Ohio warriors. After the bloody battle of Bushy Run in early August, warriors had battle deaths to avenge, but found the British soldiers more wary and better ensconced in their forts. In such circumstances, Ohio Indians could be expected to launch raids of increased size, frequency, and deadliness. One major, and likely multitribal, raid was launched into northern Virginia almost immediately after Bushy Run.

Although there is no surviving evidence that these raiders came on horseback, horses were a major part of their loot, and horses changed the raiding. The stealing and trading of horses at the garrisons had increased Indian familiarity with the management, use, and value of horses. The first raiders after Bushy Run attacked farmsteads between Fort Cumberland and Winchester, where there were plenty of horses. Horses allowed the warriors to take more loot and move more quickly. Killing a total of six men in two separate attacks, the warriors also took a dozen captives, who likely hauled less and ate better going westward than was usual in their circumstances.[11] Horses affected the route and pace of travel west, but they also left tracks. Three mounted "hot pursuit" parties of Virginia volunteers and Hampshire County militia were able to follow the tracks, and, in one instance, could even hear the sound of horse bells. Captors who had traveled as much as 120 miles west after their attack tended to relax, even to the point of leaving their guns unloaded. Virginians surprised three separate groups from this large war party, killing a total of five Indians and recovering four captives, more than thirty horses, as well as guns and plunder. No captives were reported killed by either side in these skirmishes, but the danger to captives was serious.

Eleanor Ryan and her brother were teens taken by what became a fourth fragment of this mounted war party returning west. They all took cover at one point and watched a large and noisy group of pursuers pass by. Meanwhile two captors stood over the Ryans, prepared to kill them if they made a sound. Although the horses had not alerted these pursuers, this part of the war party then killed their horses and took a safer, if more tortuous, route over the mountains, one that proved fatal for Eleanor's brother after the teens escaped.[12]

Pennsylvania's lieutenant governor, James Hamilton, proudly told his assembly on 12 September 1763 that "for the two last Months, Gentlemen, We have been so happy that our Frontiers have been very little, if at all, infested by the Enemy," and he suggested that Colonel Henry Bouquet's success at Bushy Run and Pennsylvania's raising of 700 troops in addition to the Fort Augusta garrison were the reasons.[13] He was very soon to learn that Pennsylvania's calm had already been shattered four days earlier, not on the western edges of Cumberland County, but at a Quaker farm deep in Berks County. According to the boy who escaped, eight heavily armed warriors were welcomed and offered food in friendship. Yet the warriors killed the man, his wife, and two sons, taking only one daughter captive. These Ohio Delaware went on to another nearby farm, where they found six children in the house while the parents were working in their ripened field. Presented with another opportunity to take prisoners with little risk, the attackers killed four of the young children and took only two prisoners. This war party was pursued and exchanged gunfire with provincial troops, and the fleeing Indians left the two children, still tied together but unharmed, as well as loot, including a saddle. This was likely the same war party that regrouped to capture a mother and three of her children the following day, after leaving her three other children scalped alive.[14] The Indians had killed ten, and had taken only one captive in their first attack, two in their second, and four in their last. In mid-November there were three more attacks in quick succession, east of Bedford and at Great Cove, in which six were killed and ten taken.[15] A pursuit party lost the trail in new-fallen snow, but found the body of one child who had been killed because it was unable to keep up the pace of retreat necessitated by this hot pursuit.

The Delaware of the North Branch of the Susquehanna River followed their own schedule, once again, and were surprisingly slow to avenge recent brutalities and insults. Connecticut migrants claimed the Wyoming Valley, where Teedyuscung had recently settled with support of both the Pennsylvania government and the Six Nations. Both patrons joined Teedyuscung in denouncing what they saw as the New Englanders' fraudulent intrusion, but neither offered Teedyuscung any practical help. After repeatedly turning back loggers and expelling settlers of Connecticut's Susquehanna Company, Teedyuscung was mysteriously burned to death in a fire that simultaneously consumed all twenty buildings of his village on the night of 19 April 1763.[16] Survivors scattered, and Teedyuscung's eldest son, baptized as Johann Jacob but known as Captain Bull, was with those who joined Nutimus and other refugees at the Indian community on Big Island, on the Susquehanna's West Branch. In August a drunken group of militia murdered four Delaware Indians associated with the Moravians, including Captain Bull's cousin.[17] There was no evidence that the Indians of Big Island were involved in that summer's raids on the Pennsylvania frontier, but fearful and infuriated white survivors and frustrated soldiers demanded an attack on this nearby Indian settlement. The next month Colonel John Armstrong, of Kittanning fame, led a rowdy scalp-hunting expedition that found the settlement on Big Island completely deserted; they burned all the houses and the ripening crops. Captain Bull had been burned out again, and this time the English certainly did it.[18]

Like his father in 1755, Captain Bull launched a belated, separate, and short campaign in northeastern Pennsylvania, where he had no obvious place or resources to take care of prisoners. Bull's objectives were not as obviously political as his father's; the targets of October 1763 were chosen to avenge two specific and egregious wrongs, not to build political and diplomatic capital. The first strike was to avenge the four wanton murders of Delaware kin two months earlier. Officers of the Pennsylvania forces that had killed Captain Bull's kin[19] were spending a night at an inn eight miles north of Bethlehem, where the host and his wife had a history of encouraging violence against Indians. At the first opening of the inn's front door on that October morning, twenty Delaware attacked, exchanging gunfire with the militia officers, and eventually killing them, as well as tavern workers and chance witnesses. One Delaware and nineteen whites died, including nine children; none were known to have been captured.

Within a week Captain Bull and a much larger war party, said to number 135, attacked the Connecticut settlers at Wyoming (Cushietunk, later Wilkes-Barrie). The attackers may not all have been Delaware, for they numbered more than twice those associated directly with the leader. The Chenussio Seneca, who had been fomenting anti-English action for at least two years, were supportive, and ended up with captives from this raid; they may have been directly involved as well. The raiders completely destroyed the settlement, and their fury included torture of some of the fifteen killed there and one captive burned alive later.[20] Nine captives were taken, but only five of them are known to have survived their captivity. The fate of eight additional people remains unknown. Wyoming Valley was as empty of human inhabitants as it had been after Teedyuscung's village had been destroyed six months earlier. There would be two skirmishes in Northampton County between Indians and soldiers over the next winter, but there were no more serious attacks on white farmers there.[21] Captain Bull's revenge in Northampton County had ended, though his special vilification by Sir William Johnson, who sought to obscure the role of the Chenussio Seneca in this campaign and in the wider war, had only begun.

Indian raiding of Allegheny farmsteads stopped during the winter hunting months of 1763–64, but white attacks on Indian neighbors did not. The notorious Paxton Boys slaughtered twenty innocent Conestoga wards of the government in December, sparking a noisy political controversy, but no arrests.[22] To meet his own political and diplomatic needs, Sir William Johnson encouraged and sponsored two very untraditional attacks by the Iroquois against their kin, the Susquehanna Delaware, who were the nearest and weakest allies of Pontiac. Johnson put a bounty on the heads of warring Delaware chiefs, including Captain Bull and Squash Cutter, and provided arms, repair of arms, ammunition, and war paint for two Iroquois raids. Oneida chief Saghughsuniunt (Thomas King), who had earlier been an eloquent speaker for angry Delaware, led the smaller of the two war parties, consisting of ten Oneida and Tuscarora. On 9 March 1764, they surprised nine Delaware heading for war in western Pennsylvania, killing and scalping a nephew of Squash Cutter and taking three prisoners to the Oneida town of Oquaga. The *Pennsylvania Gazette*, like Johnson and the Susquehanna Delaware, saw the potential significance of this single killing: "the Indians being once engaged in Blood, must carry on the War with great Alacrity, as the rest will never forgive them, nor will they probably stop till they have destroyed these troublesome People, who have annoyed all the Northern Frontiers, both in the last War and since."[23] In the face of this, some Delaware would flee and others negotiate.

More than 140 Iroquois and a number of rangers, including Andrew Montour and William Johnson's son, John, had set off in February on a larger and stranger raid. They went to Montour's own village of Auqvauge and spent several days there. Most likely, they invited the Great Island Delaware to talks, as a party of leading Delaware soon camped nearby. Seven Delaware chiefs, including Captain Bull, were taken captive when they visited the Auqvauge settlement. The next morning, the

Iroquois surprised the Delaware encampment and captured eleven men, eight women, and three children. The deception used to capture these Delaware was followed by greater deceptions in Johnson's accounts of what happened. The trickery of the capture was forgotten, and the event presented as a brave and characteristic dawn attack against a Delaware village. The number captured was soon inflated from twenty-nine to forty-one. Subsequent burning of nearby deserted settlements, including Kanestio, where Captain Bull had been living, was represented as a measure that had driven inveterate enemies south and west, when it had actually reinforced the hostility of enemy Delaware who had fled north to an embarrassingly friendly reception among Cayuga and Seneca. The other strenuous, but less successful, deception was the effort by William Johnson, New York governor Cadwallader Colden, and General Thomas Gage to link the captured enemy with the Pennsylvania Quaker peace party.[24]

What happened to the thirty-two captives of these two raids, the largest group of Indian captives taken in either war? Six of the seven Delaware chiefs captured by Montour's deception were not brought to William Johnson at all; "their King Attyatawitsera" and Yaghkapoose (Squash Cutter) were given to the dissident Chenussio Seneca, who also welcomed other Delaware refugees from Johnson's raids.[25] The other twenty-six captives were brought to Johnson Hall, and one man and a woman "were Buffeted, and Bruised much by their own sort 'till rescued by Sir Wm's direction." Johnson, as the sponsor of the raids, distributed one wounded warrior, three children, and eight women, plus wampum, and he was given one Delaware woman prisoner as a personal gift.[26] He distributed clothing for warriors, their families, and their Delaware prisoners. Captain Bull and thirteen other adult male captives were sent to Albany, where the commander "Honor'd Capt. Bull wth. the Heavyest Irons that cou'd be got & all the rest are likewise in Irons & Confined in one of the Cellars under the Hospital."[27] Their humiliation continued for more than a year while they were jailed in Albany and then in New York city. In negotiating peace with the Delaware in June 1765, Johnson promised that those still held in jail in New York would be released.[28] By one report, Captain Bull and his fellow captives were given a choice of hanging or exile beyond the Allegheny Mountains. He and some forty other Delaware migrated, not to their Ohio Delaware kin, but to Frederick Eice's settlement on the Cheat River west of Virginia. They established Bulltown in the vicinity, were later accused of killing eight members of a frontier family, and died in the white revenge raid known as the Bulltown massacre of 1774.

The Genesee Seneca did not give Johnson any of their leading Delaware "captives," but turned over three others: a negro, a white renegade, and a Delaware known as Roger. Johnson sent them to jail in Albany, but feared they would be released by the court for lack of white evidence against them. Legally, these prisoners were in three different categories, and Johnson, General Gage, and Governor Colden gathered information and then decided what to do with each of them. The negro was Sam Tony, a slave who had escaped from Maryland a generation earlier and had become a prominent anti-English influence among the Indians, most recently in the polyglot town of Otsiningo. He was readily seen by whites as a harbinger of some dangerous Indian-negro alliance. General Gage decided he was "a cursed fellow" to be sold into slavery again, this time in the West Indies.[29] The white captive sent to Albany was Frederick Eice's son John, whom Johnson rightly claimed had been taken captive in Virginia as a lad years earlier. Johnson did not yet know that eight members of the Eice family had been captured nine years earlier in Virginia or that all the others were still in Ohio country, and now with the Shawnee. Frederick Eice had been away from home when his entire family, save one son, had been captured; he became an angry dissident who challenged English passersby and, as noted, hosted Captain Bull and his people when they were released from jail later in 1765. The John Eice then in Albany's jail had become influential among the Delaware and may, like Roger and Sam Tony, have been taken in the Iroquois attacks on the Delaware and then given to the Seneca. In any case, John Eice was a British subject with no charges and no white witnesses to speak against him. After some discussion between Johnson, Colden, and Gage, it was agreed that Gage would send John Eice to indentured servitude in Pensacola or the West Indies.[30]

The fate of the Delaware named Roger is not known: he may have suffered the same fate as Sam Tony, or that of Captain Bull and the other Delaware in a New York prison at the time. What is clear is that he was treated neither as an accused criminal nor as a prisoner of war. Major Henry Gladwin out at Detroit might hold enemy Indian hostages for exchange, and Captain Lewis Ourry at Bedford could talk vaguely of exchanging prisoners, but higher military or civilian authorities did not.

During the winter of 1763–64 the Delaware in the Muskingum Valley were hunting and clearing land for a safer new town and its cornfield. Seventeen-year-old captive Mathias Warren reported that the warriors were conserving their limited supplies of gunpowder by hunting with bows and arrows, and they were assembling provisions for their families in preparation for leaving with a major intertribal force to burn hated

Fort Pitt.[31] This attack never occurred, but the preparations served well for the launch of the last major raids of the war.

The first strikes in the spring of 1764, both on 20 March, revealed a clever new tactic. Nineteen warriors attacking in Pennsylvania's Path Valley captured Agnes Davidson, her infant daughter, and three unrelated children, evidently without a fight. A dozen warriors set off westward with these five captives, luring pursuers, who left the neighborhood unprotected.[32] Meanwhile the other seven members of the raiding party spent the next two days burning seven houses, along with their accompanying barns, and killing livestock. Surviving accounts report no one killed, though three "death mallets" were found at the scene, as war was being declared once again on the white intruders and their livestock. These farms may have been deserted, for a newspaper noted, "These fresh Troubles greatly discourage the poor People, who intended to return early in Spring to their deserted Habitations." The "hot pursuit" by militia, which was now routine in both Pennsylvania and Virginia, had just been exploited by the Indians.

The first raid into Virginia in 1764 might best be described as armed robbery with violence. Ten unidentified Indians bypassed Virginia's frontier settlements to attack the upper James River home of wealthy planter David Cloyd on 20 March, killing his son, mortally wounding his wife, ransacking his house and his liquor supply, taking four negro slaves captive, and escaping with substantial loot, including more than £137.18.0 in gold and silver coin. Twenty-two militiamen and neighbors gave chase and caught up with the raiders, killing one Indian and recovering the four slaves, many of the household goods, and all of the coin.[33] Two weeks after the attack on Cloyd's plantation, three men were found dead near Warm Springs in southwestern Virginia, and it was noted that they were killed with arrows. In the same area and at about the same time, five Delaware and Shawnee surprised and captured Mrs Kincade and her three children.[34] She remembered a very quick and efficient attack, in which the Indians used the bedding as sacks to fill with clothing, taking a saddle and two guns as well as the captives.[35]

The final thunder of the war with white settlers may well have been the result of the preparations with which Warren had been forced to help on the Muskingum River. At least three nearly simultaneous attacks struck Bedford and Cumberland Counties in Pennsylvania, and Frederick County in northern Virginia, and a large force once again hit the Jackson River Valley farther south, with a rather surprising focus on Fort Dinwiddie. Some reports claimed that the large multitribal force was initially led by a Canadian. They struck first at a large party of farmers working together near the fort. The "french Man from Wacatomacky" was almost certainly not in charge in this attack, when the Indians killed sixteen and took fifteen prisoners – enough to end the raid for some warriors. Part of the war party may have listened to the Canadian when they then surrounded Fort Dinwiddie and exchanged gunfire with the garrison for several hours. There are no reports of attempts to negotiate a surrender or to burn the fort. The attackers then divided into a number of smaller parties varying in size from three to thirty warriors, who attacked isolated farmsteads over a wide range of the Virginian and southwestern Pennsylvanian frontiers during the next three weeks. In this period, there was very little harassment of the major forts.[36]

The duration of this climactic wave of violence did not reduce warriors' interest in taking captives, though thirteen people were burned to death in three Cumberland County homes by attackers who took no prisoners.[37] The war parties killed fewer than they captured (45:57), but the sustained offensive allowed militia and rangers time to mobilize, pursue, and fight with war parties that had taken captives. In the resulting skirmishes, five in the war parties were killed, including the Canadian. Under pressure, the pursued warriors killed eight of their prisoners, and nine others were able to escape. The Ohio Indians' war on European settlers petered out thereafter. As the Pennsylvania regiment mustered at Carlisle in July, to meet Bouquet's regulars and begin the push west to the Ohio Indian towns, small parties of Ohio Delaware attacked farther west in Cumberland County, killing four and losing a warrior in a skirmish that freed the only prisoner taken. The most notorious of these attacks, one denounced as cowardly by fellow Delaware, was on a schoolhouse on Conococheague Creek not far from Pennsylvania's Fort Loudoun, on 26 July 1764. Schoolmaster Enoch Brown was killed and scalped, as were nine of his students, and four others were taken captive.[38] Three raids into northern Virginia in the autumn, in which fifteen were killed and eleven taken captive, brought the raiding war against white settlers to an end.

The war between the Ohio Indians and Allegheny white settlers was the part of Pontiac's War that was most like a rerun of the previous war; both raiders and targets included people for whom this was a return to an unfinished struggle in familiar country. Although not the center of Pontiac's War, at least 255 white settlers were killed, a few more than the soldiers killed, and a settler was nearly as likely to be captured as killed. The fifteen months of raiding were more fatal for white farming families than had been average during the previous war.[39] Civilian men were nearly twice as likely as women to be victims in Pontiac's War and four times as likely to be killed as captured, as was the case in the Seven Years' War. Adult women were as likely to be killed as captured, as had been true ever since "hot pursuit" became routine in these borderlands, and the women who stayed or ventured into the war zone may have become more resistant to capture since they knew that so many had not been returned during the truce.[40]

Amid the ferocity of Pontiac's War, in which at least 160 white settlers of all ages were captured and another 74 are known only as "missing," there were noticeable changes, especially for children. No European settlers were tortured after capture, as occurred rarely in the earlier war, but 16 died and 23 were rescued in the now-routine "hot pursuit." Only 14 escaped, but fully two-thirds of civilian captives were returned, and only 3 of those returned had been captives for more than the two years of this war. This may help explain why young Adam Brown was the only captive taken in this war who is known to have stayed with his captors to became a white Indian, compared to at least thirty of those taken in the previous war. There may have been some change in the education and attitudes of colonial children ages seven to fifteen, and/or in the attitudes of their potential captors. Numbers are small, but two children of that age were captured in Pontiac's War for every one killed, whereas three were captured for every one killed in the previous war, and the more deadly trend was stronger in attacks on girls than boys.[41] The chances for victims known to be six or younger were also worse in Pontiac's War, when one was captured for every one killed in raids or on the trail; nearly three such young children were captured for every one killed in the previous war.[42]

Blacks were seldom caught in the Allegheny border wars, but more were taken in Pontiac's War than earlier, and none are known to have been killed during raids. Like their captors, we do not always know whether these were slaves, escaped slaves, or freemen. Trader John Welch had six black servants with him when captured: one escaped, another was missing, and the other four were deliberately killed after capture. These four are the only blacks known to have been killed in the war. Of ten others captured during Pontiac's War, five are known to have stayed with their captors, the four from David Cloyd's plantation were recaptured and returned to their owner, and Sam Tony was sold into slavery in the West Indies.

Very few Indians were captured by British or colonial troops or militia in Pontiac's War, as was also the case earlier. However, in both the Cherokee War and the war named for Pontiac, local British commanders initially followed habits and interests in taking both captives and hostages from their primary opponents, and, when negotiating peace, the British forced Indian communities to provide hostages without reciprocity. At Detroit in May 1763, as has been discussed, Gladwin took two Potawatomi chiefs hostage and, after the terms of the exchange had been violated, held them as prisoners of war for more than a month before exchanging them for nineteen captive British soldiers. (This exchange rate would have embarrassed British soldiers familiar with intensely detailed schedules of exchange by status.)

The unusual story of two Cayuga families, the Hudsons and the Conaways, peaceably growing corn on an island in the Susquehanna River near Carlisle as the war began, is more complicated and instructive. Early in June 1763 local militia brought John Hudson, Samuel Conaway, their wives, and their four children to Captain Lewis Ourry, the Royal American officer in charge at Fort Bedford. Unlike Colonel Dunbar, who had released Indians brought in by locals back in 1755, Ourry confined the eight as prisoners. Although noncombatants of an allied tribe, Ourry reported that they had been "lurking here last Winter." Both the Cayuga Conaway and the Mohican-Cayuga Hudson had some Delaware relatives, but Hudson managed to bring with him written testimonials concerning some of the white captives he had helped to return in 1756 and 1760. Despite the lack of any evidence or legitimate pretext for what was an unsoldierly detention of women and children, Ourry lectured his victims on his own humanity, adding that "the way of the English is not to kill or hurt their Prisnors, but to exchange them."[43] George Croghan soon arrived, worried that the imprisonment of these allied Iroquois might have severe diplomatic consequences. He re-examined the prisoners and suggested that Hudson be sent as a spy while his family was held as surety and cared for in the fort.

Even before this suggestion reached Colonel Henry Bouquet or General Jeffrey Amherst, Ourry reported that an unsuccessful Indian attack near the fort "has added greatly to the Panick of the People. With difficulty I can restrain them from murdering the Indian Prisoners."[44] Unwarranted detention had unintentionally become protective custody. Amherst's comment on using Hudson as a spy was predictable: "My Opinion with regard to the Indians that are in our power, is, that they should Remain as prisoners; as I am Convinced they would be among the first, were they Let Loose, that would Joyn the Others." But he went on to countenance the holding and maintenance of Indian prisoners and Bouquet's use of Hudson as a spy.[45] By mid-July these "inoffensive" Indian prisoners were at Carlisle, and now Bouquet's immediate responsibility. Amid more white terror and resentment caused by recent attacks there, Bouquet reported that "It was with the utmost Difficulty, I could prevail with the enraged Multitude not to massacre them. I don't think them very safe in the Goal [*sic*]: They cannot be released as they would be torn to Pieces by our People, or forced to join the Enemy."[46] Before the end of the month, John Hudson was sent as a British courier to besieged Fort Pitt and as a spy beyond. His family and the Conaways were back in Fort Bedford again by September, and once again being threatened with death by the locals. The Conaways escaped up a chimney at night, leaving their child to be added to the family of the other sleeping hostage, Mrs Hudson. She and the children were still there seventeen months later. John Hudson was at Fort Niagara in 1764, with adequate provocation for his drinking excessive amounts of army rum.[47] According to a captive whose release he had brokered, Hudson later made regular and extended friendly visits in the Fort Bedford area until at least 1780.[48]

If the British Army treated its few captive Indian noncombatants with a mixture of severity, chicanery, and concern, the same could not be said of Indian combatants. In the wake of the fall of the nine garrisons in May and June 1763, Amherst hoped that Bouquet's relief force bound for besieged Fort Pitt would "soon take an adequate revenge on the Barbarians," and "I Wish to Hear of no Prisoners, should any of the villains be met with in Arms." We do not know whether this became a specific order. After the two-day battle at Bushy Run, a single Indian prisoner had been taken by a Highland soldier. "After a little Examination he received his Quietus," perhaps, as tradition has it, by being shot dead by a colonial ranger while in custody.[49] The British Army held a few noncombatant Indians and diplomatic hostages known to have been fighters, but it had no captured Indian combatants as prisoners in this or the previous war.

One unusual incident revealed the possibility of taking Indian captives, and the difficulty of keeping them. In August of 1763, a party of 114 Lancaster County volunteer scalp hunters set out to attack the Great Island Indian settlement on the West Branch of the Susquehanna.[50] Four were killed and four were wounded in a skirmish on the way, and, as has been mentioned, they accomplished little more than the burning of crops and dwellings of Captain Bull and his Delaware community. As the scattered volunteers retreated, a group of twenty-eight surprised three Indians who had come from trading at the Moravian settlement at Bethlehem. After trading and talking with the three, the volunteers took them captive. Leader George Allen said that the Indians should be delivered to the commander at Fort Augusta, but one volunteer objected that he was determined to avenge himself "on the first Indian I saw" and feared that the captives would be released or sent to Philadelphia, "where they would be better used than ourselves by the Quakers." While stopped to allow the Indians to eat their interrupted meal, the vengeful volunteer recruited five others who were willing to shoot the captives in cold blood. The resumed march had proceeded only thirty yards when the six militiamen fired on signal, and all three Indians fell and were immediately scalped. One of the three, who had earlier taken the name George Allen to honor the one who had now become his captor, managed to escape and survive the scalping. Even this large party in complete control of three known and unarmed Indians, and traveling merely to nearby Fort Augusta, did not refrain from killing and scalping their prisoners, telling the fort commander that they "thought proper to kill & scalp them, and brought all their Goods & Horses along with them here." One Philadelphia newspaper reported simply that, having found "a Quantity of Powder and other Indian Goods, our People killed and scalped the said Indians, after asking them what questions they tho't proper."[51] This incident never prompted either outrage like that provoked by the Paxton Boys, who slaughtered Conestoga Indians three months later, or distaste like that shown for renegade David Owens, who murdered five members of his Shawnee family in their sleep and brought their scalps in for a bounty the following spring. The leader of the firing squad could apparently retell his story, anonymously, without evident regret or embarrassment.[52]

Colonial troops, militia, or posses took no Indian captives once the borderland raids began. When Pennsylvania reinstituted bounties on enemy prisoners and scalps in July 1763, and again the following year, the premium on prisoners was much too modest to encourage captors to accept the risks or expenses involved with adult Indian male captives.[53] Moravians, Quakers, and the Pennsylvania government attempted to provide some asylum for Indian friends, but these unprotected refuges became inadequate defenses against surrounding hostility. From the murders of Teedyuscung and Zacharias, which expanded the war, through to the slaughter of the peaceable Conestoga by the Paxton Boys, there were few signs of borderland interest in keeping Indians as friends or refugees, to say nothing of taking prisoners. Although neighbors of these Indian victims were worried about Indian revenge, the perpetrators had ceased to see the value of Indian acquaintances as a buffer against Indian enemies.[54]

Indians took each other captive in traditional raiding that continued throughout this war, and apparently increased as it ended. Most of these raids pitted Cherokee and Catawba against Shawnee. Although justified to the English as being responses to their earlier invitations and encouragements during the Cherokee War, these raids were increasingly independent of English efforts.[55] Sir William Johnson's 1764 campaign against the Susquehanna Delaware was the glaring exception.

It was only when the English authorities attempted to impose peace on their disparate Indian enemies in 1764 that the taking of Indian hostages became of interest. Gladwin exchanged hostages, but simply demanding Indian hostages was the more usual British tactic. Late in 1759, South Carolina's governor, William Lyttleton, had held an entire Cherokee peace legation hostage as he launched a campaign to chastise this tribe and acquire the killers of a number of frontiersmen. When the commander of Fort Prince George was lured out and killed, his furious troops killed all twenty-two Cherokee hostages held inside, fuelling rather than preventing a wider war.[56] By 1764 British military commanders in North America knew the difficulties with taking hostages, including the pressure on hosts to keep them safe amid a community overflowing with resentment against the hostages and their people. Yet when discussing possible peace terms that spring, both Johnson and Bouquet included taking hostages to ensure compliance. Johnson himself began the hostage taking while negotiating with those embarrassing Chenussio Seneca before his huge Niagara council of July–August 1764. Insisting on an end to their attacks and the surrender of "ev'ry Prisoner, Deserter, Negro, or Frenchman they have," Johnson went on to demand, and receive, two Chenussio chiefs as hostages for the fulfillment of these conditions. Colonel John Bradstreet, who witnessed Johnson's conference, included the same condition a week later in his abortive Sandusky peace negotiations.[57]

Even before his expedition set out from Fort Pitt to the Muskingum River at the end of September, Bouquet began taking hostages. He took two Delaware diplomats, war captain Kageshquanohel (the Pipe) and prominent chief Welapachtschiechen (Captain Johnny), who had come to Fort Pitt to ward off the impending invasion and, Bouquet claimed, "as spies without anything to say." As his expedition left Fort Pitt, Bouquet instructed the commandant that these hostages were to be given provisions, tobacco, and needed clothing. They were not to be allowed to escape, but "You may allow them in the daytime to walk in the fort but only one at a time, and never without two centries." The two sentries would not only prevent escape, but also protect the hostages from angry locals.[58] This was not quite the freedom of the fort that Virginian hostages had been allowed on the same site a decade earlier, but it appeared relatively accommodating. However, as Mingo negotiators for the Delaware approached the advancing army just three days later, Bouquet began forcing concessions by threatening to kill his hostages. He told the Delaware that the hostages would die if the messenger he wanted to send to Detroit, accompanied by Delaware guides, did not return promptly and safely. He said the hostages would otherwise be treated well, but held until peace had been concluded. The Delaware response was prompt and clever, seemingly understanding, accepting, and exploiting Bouquet's taking of hostages. Captive trader John Gibson was enlisted to write a letter that complimented Bouquet on his recent speech to the Mingo messengers and promised that the Delaware would meet him at Tuscaroras (Tuscarawas) if they could see that Kageshquanohel and Welapachtschiechen were there and well.[59] At the mid-October meeting, Bouquet showed the hostages, demanded the return of white and negro captives held by the Indians, and required that four of the most prominent chiefs stay with his army in the meantime: Seneca chief Guyasuta; Delaware leaders Passquelonckamy (Custaloga's son) and Kitchi (Turtle Heart); as well as a James Smith of the Shawnee.[60]

The climax of Bouquet's hostage taking came with the negotiations at the Muskingum River in November 1764. Bouquet agreed to release Kageshquanohel and Welapachtschiechen but demanded more hostages to ensure that the raiding would end, all white captives would be returned, and empowered "deputies" would go to negotiate peace with Sir William Johnson. Six Delaware, six Shawnee, and two Mingo surrendered themselves as hostages and were escorted to Fort Pitt by twenty Kahnawake and Canadian captain Joseph-Hippolyte Hertel, with the infamous David Owens along as interpreter.[61] This Iroquois escort, sent to Bouquet that summer by Johnson, may not have been intended to demonstrate submission to the Six Nations and the Covenant Chain, but it would seem such to the hostages and knowing witnesses.

Bouquet had great difficulty in providing the right mixture of confinement, security, and comfort at Fort Pitt for these hostages. It was wise to use the Kahnawake to escort hostages who included hated war chiefs. A separate room was set aside in crowded Fort Pitt for the hostages, with planks provided for sleeping. Bouquet specified that hostages were to have no restriction on their rations, and to have tobacco and a gill of rum a day. "As those People can not be kept Confined without endangering their Healths" (an assumption that Johnson and Gage seem not to have shared), Bouquet ordered that half of the hostages at a time be allowed to hunt or walk freely beyond the fort, be given ammunition for hunting, and be permitted to sell their meat and furs. Bouquet wanted the hostages given necessary clothing, but warned against becoming "too familiar" with them, or giving them any presents, especially any additional alcohol. This hostage taking likely contributed to the coming of peace, but not because it was effective for any of the three tribes involved. Both Seneca hostages escaped almost immediately, taking some of the fort's best horses and eight guns with them. All six of the Shawnee hostages soon followed. Although Bouquet had instructed commanders that the hostages "are to be kindly used, & no Person allowed to affront them, much less do them any injury," this admonition proved impossible to enforce. A Maryland provincial soldier intimidated the hostages with a scalp, falsely said to have belonged to one of the Shawnee hostages killed while out hunting. The Shawnee hostages, who included Red Hawk and Cornblade, escaped the next morning, and Hertel, the Kahnawake, and Owens were unable to find them.[62] Two Delaware hostages disappeared in February 1765 when granted permission to visit Mrs John Hudson, their kin still held at Fort Bedford, and another Delaware named Simon Girty was also free before spring. By May of 1765, only three of the Delaware hostages were still in custody, and George Croghan met with all three communities to negotiate replacement of the other eleven hostages taken the previous November.[63]

The chances of being captured, rather than killed, in Pontiac's War can be estimated (see table 3). Indians and the British Army were the main protagonists of the Anglo-Indian War, and there were many more Indian victims per month in this war than in the Seven Years' War, though an Indian was more likely to become a captive or hostage than earlier.[64] During the twenty-six months of this second war, some 200 Indians are known to have been killed immediately or very soon after capture. The fate of 46 of the 84 who were taken is known. The British

Army released or exchanged 15 Indian captives, including 7 of its 20 hostages. Seventeen other hostages and Indian captives taken in Pontiac's War escaped, with much fewer consequences than had followed the escape of the Shawnee hostages held in Charles Town a dozen years earlier.

For all others except Indians, the chances of being captured rather than killed were better in Pontiac's War than in the Seven Years' War. More victims were killed in Pontiac's War than were captured or missing, but the difference was less than might have been expected, and much less than in the previous war (see table 2). If those killed or captured per month are a measure of the intensity of war, Pontiac's War was less intense, except among Indian communities. This was a much better war for British soldiers, though soldiers and white settlers were somewhat more likely to be killed than captured. In a comparison of the odds of capture over death, traders fared best despite this being by far their worst war. Traders, soldiers, and settlers were more likely to be captured rather than killed than was the case in the previous war, and the odds were even a little better than in the conflicts of the decade before 1754 (see table 1).

The Delaware prophet Neolin's increasingly influential nativist teachings, calling for all Indians to separate further from whites, did not yet translate into any new unwillingness of Indians to take and incorporate white captives during Pontiac's War.[65] Although Indian captors were not always identified clearly, it is possible to suggest some differences in their interest in taking captives. Mixed parties of Indians were more common than in the previous war, and these raiders killed many more than they captured (273:195). The dissident Seneca, though treated most generously by William Johnson, were the most deadly opponents of the British Army, killing 93 and taking only 5 captives. The Delaware, once again including communities resident on both sides of the Allegheny Mountains, were major antagonists who likewise killed more than they captured (110:71). The Wyandot, prominent in waterborne captures near Detroit, killed fewer than they captured (62:68). The Shawnee's role in Pontiac's War has been exaggerated, and, as in the previous war, they were noticeably more inclined to take captives than were other raiders. The much-maligned Shawnee took two captives for every victim they killed (44:24), nearly matching their record in the previous war (211:99). All that had happened in the meantime, to the Shawnee and their opponents, had not changed the Shawnee interest in taking captives. None of these Indian raiders were nearly as deadly as the English, who showed little interest in taking captives except as hostages to prompt compliance with demands. The British Army itself killed 86 Indians while taking only 3 captives and 20 hostages. British colonial forces killed 39 while taking 10 captives: 8 of these they turned over to the British Army, and the other 2 escaped. The English projected their own savagery onto their opponents and talked duplicitously about the exchange of prisoners as a civilized requirement for peace, but both claims were betrayed by the clear lack of English ability and interest in taking Indian captives for information, adoption, or exchange.

War had transformed attitudes towards the taking of white settlers, traders, soldiers, and Indians as captives. As the French and Indian War had exploded in the borderlands in the wake of the defeat of Braddock's army in July 1755, Delaware and Shawnee raiders declared war with ruses and raids on unsuspecting, unprepared, and isolated white settler communities. Capture was relatively easy, and Indians suddenly became interested in settlers as captives, initially taking more than they killed. As the European settlers "forted up" or fled, and their governments gradually mobilized garrisons and rangers, the war became a more deadly one between warriors and soldiers. Few prisoners were taken in major battles or skirmishes, though besieged or burning "garrison houses" proved to be places where white settlers, as well as soldiers, were much more likely to be captured than killed. The increasing readiness to send "hot pursuit" parties after Indian raiders and their captives caused more casualties among the latter, though captors usually abandoned their captives in these circumstances rather than killing them. After the surrender of Canada, an uneasy truce of broken promises suspended nearly all the cross-cultural violence in Allegheny country.

The Anglo-Indian War of 1763–65 was launched first against surprised traders and soldiers, and then against borderland white settlers, with ruses that were clearly designed to kill or take captives with few risks. English traders were killed on a scale not seen before, but, in a war that was only one-fourth as long as the earlier one, soldiers were nearly as likely to be captured or to go missing as to be killed. Indian warriors continued to take a surprising number of captives, despite the number of captives already held, the increased likelihood of hot pursuit, the accumulation of grievances on all sides, the disappearance of French support for raiders and the French market for captives, and Neolin's nativist teaching. As the white obsession with recovering captives finally spread to the British Army, captives became even more valuable to those Indians who were negotiating or resisting a truce or peace, or were seeking postwar trade.

The overall numbers, by status or category, of those killed and captured in this entire generation can be estimated (see table 4). The 3,343 killed were a small minority of people in all the cultures and occupations involved, though these horrid losses left more orphaned, bereft, or dispossessed than dead. Traders, the most exposed and vulnerable group, were the only ones consistently more likely to be captured than killed. They were also unlikely to have much opportunity to resist. Among soldiers, who could never forget what happened to Braddock's advance force, all the losses in these colonial sideshows were very light compared to the slaughters between Europe's civilized powers engaged in what they took to be the main events of their wars. The Allegheny borderlands would draw enough new white settlers in less than a single year to replace everyone's losses in these Allegheny wars, and thereby accelerate the physical, economic, and cultural invasion that Indians had hoped the wars would slow.

The methods of taking captives had changed little, though Indian raiders adapted quickly to garrison houses, hot pursuit, and the use of horses along new roads. Those victims who knew that they could not resist effectively, and those traumatized by the explosion of violence around them, were the easiest to capture. After the less belligerent had fled the region, and especially after so many captives of 1755–58 were not returned, women and teenage boys of the colonial backwoods seem to have offered more resistance, and more were killed.

The enduring white borderers insisted that "The Indian kills indiscriminately. His object is the total extermination of his enemies," but this claim was a deliberate projection of their own ferocity, and a self-justifying falsehood.[66] At least 2,873 who could have been killed immediately in these Allegheny wars were not. Amid the horrors and outrages crying to be avenged, amid burning hatreds borne by those sent to kill in a lawless borderland where martial conventions were as contested as everything else, the taking of captives continued to be a major objective and amelioration. Indian communities derived martial and cultural confidence from the obvious fact that they had taken so many captives, whereas their opponents held none of their people at all.

Perhaps captives, kin, neighbors, and officials should not be denounced for failing to admit that every captive taken was a person who could have been killed. In the battle for Allegheny country, every person gained by the enemy represented a weakening of control over recently occupied or reoccupied territory, and every person "stolen" left open wounds that could be more enduring than the loss of one killed. Those who told nightmarish tales of what happened to captives, as ghoulish fireside entertainment and reinforcement of folk resistance, fuelled a dread of captivity that was represented as worse than a quick death in defiance. Those going captive continued to ignore all the efforts to make them fight to the death. What happened to captives once taken, as well as what was thought to have happened to them, determined how humane captivity was, and how humane it was eventually seen to be.

PART 3

CAPTIVITY, CONVERSION, AND ESCAPE

Most Allegheny captives were taken by Delaware, Shawnee, and Mingo war parties as martial success and proof of individual prowess. Unlike European and colonial soldiers, who took prisoners for reciprocal exchange, these Indians took most of their prisoners to be incorporated into their own communities. Clearing former homelands of enemies could have been more readily accomplished by simply slaughtering the enemy, but adding captives to enlarge and strengthen your own community was a bolder display of cultural confidence.

The choice of captives to be taken was initially individual, but was soon subject to the harsh realities of the trail into captivity (chapter 9). Could optimistic war parties take too many prisoners to control them, or feed them on the trail? Infant captives who could not be silenced would betray the whereabouts of the returning war party, and their deaths often came swiftly. Those who had been misjudged as able to make a long journey, at the pace deemed necessary, became vulnerable and could be deliberately killed "for no reason." The perils of the trail into captivity prolonged the traumas of the initial attack, especially with the widely publicized additional possibility of torture. The noisy and sometimes maiming viciousness of a village gauntlet ended the journey, but gave no hint that these horrors were about to end.

The terrifying introduction to Indian life was the first phase of breaking and remaking a captive (chapter 10). With the heads of their families often killed and their livelihoods destroyed, most frightened captives were surprised and relieved by the offer of membership in an Indian family, including complete ceremonial adoption in many cases. Those lost to white colonial families by war were taken in to replace Indians lost in the same war. Adaptation would take time, but the orphaned and widowed were gradually taught a new language and way of life in a family setting, not unlike the life of a colonial indentured servant. How well did Indian acculturation work? A few white Indians became famous, and infamous, and many more are presumed to be among the hundreds of captives who never returned. The age at capture and the gender of these converts are worth exploring, as well as the length of their "captivity." Were there recognizable degrees or layers of acculturation? The alternative to accommodation was escape, and it is interesting to learn who escaped, how long they had been held, and from whom they escaped (chapter 11).

Captivity had less obvious victims whose lives would be changed dramatically (chapter 12). Some of the bereft who had been unable to protect their families from capture could go to great lengths in searching for missing kin, or could be obsessed with a desire for revenge against known or unknown captors. Pennsylvania's Quakers, in and out of government, were embarrassed, divided, and politically defeated by these wars. Prominent Quakers founded a redeeming charity to recover captives in a campaign that was initially ridiculed but eventually adopted by their more martial political enemies.

Adaptation to Indian life was producing cultural hybrids who came to be seen as particularly dangerous to their natal culture as these wars prompted clearer definitions of a colonial society that resisted and sought to destroy the Indians. Indian communities came closer together in the war of 1763–65, but this change did not cause any abatement in their interest in taking white captives. The battle to limit acculturation would be fought less by captives themselves than by nervous authorities convinced that Indian re-education was successful.

9

Trails into Captivity

Trails into captivity could be particularly dangerous places for both captors and captives. Most captors were Indians who had worked together in preparation, travel, and combat, and who had then claimed captives and loot as individuals. As has been seen, there were tactical limits to taking captives in the first strike of a two- or three-strike raid, and there were bound to be some individual and intertribal negotiations and disputes over captives on the trail. Captors could not calculate in advance exactly who should take how many captives, or faultlessly discern which captives would prove able and willing to travel quickly and quietly with or without heavy burdens. Nor could captors know exactly how many captives could be fed for days or weeks from looted stores, prepared caches, or hunting on the way home. The increasing likelihood that successful war parties would be closely pursued and attacked by colonial militias or mounted rangers meant that the hurried caravans were a grueling, and often gruesome, baptism into a different life for captives, and sometimes a final inglorious challenge for the captors. In examining the first days of captivity, from the perspectives of the captors and captives in turn, special attention will be given to those killed on the trail into captivity, and those who attempted escape.

Allegheny warriors who enthusiastically took captives could soon be provoked into killing some of these prizes. A total of 111 captives, 1 in 17 of those captured or missing, are known to have been killed within a week of their capture. This figure is much higher than the record of captors on the New England frontier, where only 1 in 66 captives was subsequently killed by their captors.[1] Inability to travel at the pace of the retreating war party accounted for many of these deaths. Raiders could be expected to kill the severely wounded, rather than take them captive at all. However, they took at least 29 wounded captives, and only 2 of these are known to have been killed on the trail.[2] One woman was killed because she could no longer travel after accidentally breaking her leg on the trail.[3] Indian captors feared the sick much more than the wounded, and were especially fearful of smallpox, which whites were known to carry. All but 1 of 24 people said to have been sick when attacked were killed immediately, and the other, an ill trader, was killed within hours of his surrender at Pickawillany.[4]

Age could affect survival on the trail as it had affected initial capture. Babes under two years of age, whose cries would betray their location, were innocents who were not slaughtered nearly as frequently as white propaganda claimed. Seven are known to have been killed in attacks, whereas thirty-five were captured. Six of the captured were killed on the trail, but the other twenty-nine survived their first week of captivity, and at least nineteen were eventually returned.[5] Some babies, who were presumably the quieter ones, were carried by warriors or strapped to the backs of older captured children for transport.[6] People over fifty were less numerous than infants in the borderlands and much more likely to be killed in raids, even though grey-haired scalps were considered unworthy war trophies.[7] Of the thirty-four people over fifty who were attacked, only eleven were taken captive, and four of these were killed within a week of their capture. Old Samuel Hunter, a laborer of York County, Pennsylvania, was killed on the trail because he "could not run," and a man taken at the surrender of Fort Granville, "being old and not able to travel," was similarly executed.[8] Although it was said in Kittanning "that the French buy their old Prisoners from them, for which they give a great Price, and employ them in their servile Work," there was little market for those too old for heavy work. Abraham Miller of Northampton County, Pennsylvania, reported that his overweight mother lasted two days before being killed because she could no longer keep up with the caravan. David Boyd reported that his pregnant mother, carrying a baby near term, was killed because she could not travel. Pregnant Elizabeth Fleming survived her brief captivity and escape, and at least four other women survived captivity after being taken in the late stages of pregnancy.[9]

The troublesome were also likely to be killed on the trail. The Hicks youth captured with William Fleming was an early and widely known example: "The unhappy Youth not being accustomed to such Treatment as he now met with; and not being apprized of the bad Consequences that might attend the least Resistance, discovered great Uneasiness, and could not be prevailed upon to keep silent."[10] He was killed within an hour of capture. Isham Bernat, one of twenty-six captured in a large multitribal raid on Irwin River, Virginia, early in 1758, saw his nephew killed at the Ohio River several days after capture "because he was cross

& troublesome."[11] This particular war party was uncommonly prone to killing captives on the trail, killing a total of four. There is no surviving evidence of intertribal disputes over ownership of any of these captives, but this place on the Ohio was a logical dispersal point for the raiders and their captors. It is not known whether the captives' masters killed them, or whether others did so in pique or calculation.

This particular intertribal war party chose not to return by way of Fort Duquesne, where commandants could sometimes arbitrate, offer compensating gifts and promises, provide food, or occasionally purchase or accept a captive as a gift. Mary Jemison, taken in the spring of 1758 by a party of six Indians and four "Frenchmen," spent one night in Fort Duquesne and then saw the other two captives go with the French. She was not returned to her Shawnee captors, but given instead to two mourning Seneca women from a nearby town.[12] The meanings, insurance, or ameliorations that came from baptism at Fort Duquesne are hard to recover, but Recollect friar Denys Baron baptized at least nine children of captives in 1755–56, five of them with at least one parent present. One of these children was in Commandant Jean-Daniel Dumas's own household, and another in that of Commandant François-Marie Le Marchand de Lignery. Baron recorded the artful claim of the parents of a two month old: "the father and mother being united in lawful wedlock, both being Irish Catholics, who were captured by the Shawanees in coming here to join the Catholics."[13] Captain Claude-Pierre Pécaudy de Contrecoeur stood as godparent for one child, and military officers, traders, local French women, and fellow captives provided the same spiritual connection for others. One eighteen month old was baptized in the last days of her fatal illness,[14] but young John Turner survived three years with the Shawnee after baptism before being returned, along with his adaptive mother, Mary Newton-Girty-Turner.[15] A stop at Fort Duquesne could be an opportunity to settle disputes about captives, acquire a convenient and supportive baptism, or endure another unsettling distraction for captives bound for an Ohio Indian settlement.

There is surprisingly little evidence of food shortages for those being transported by Indian captors, though escaped captives and colonial expeditions routinely had severe shortages while traversing the Allegheny Mountains. The two reported Indian difficulties with provisions both involved the Miami, who lived farther west than other raiders attacking these British colonial frontiers. In July 1755 they were involved in a war party that took fifteen captives, including Jane Fraser (Frasier), near Fort Cumberland. Fraser recalled, without any elaboration, that food ran out by the end of the three-week journey. These problems were minor compared to those ensuing from Fraser's escape thirteen months later, when her two male companions died of starvation and she lived on bark and roots for eleven days.[16] The only other identifiable Miami engagement in Allegheny raiding in this war was the capture of Vause's Fort, a major operation with active French leadership and supply, and with many captives. Again there were food shortages on the trail westward. For all the evidence of hardship for white captives who escaped from the Ohio Indians, there are no other accounts of Indian war parties being unable to feed themselves and their captives on the road into captivity. It is, however, impossible to tell whether anyone was killed because of anticipated food shortages.

Commanders of European forts and armies were also concerned with prisoners as a drain on supplies, and promptly forwarded most of their captives to population centers. French commandants at Fort Duquesne or Detroit could usually send adequately supplied and guarded prisoners from fort to fort down to Montreal throughout this period. Although supplies were very short at Fort Duquesne in the autumn of 1758, the French care of those captives taken in Major James Grant's failed attack was good enough to warrant commendation by the captives. The British Army could accept the surrender of a French garrison of 624 at Fort Niagara in June of 1759 and bring them to New York without provisioning difficulties.[17] When the Canadian garrison at Detroit surrendered in November of 1760, the forty-two prisoners and their substantial escort proceeded on a long backcountry winter march to Fort Pitt without food shortages, before going on to Philadelphia and New York. Whatever their limitations, European forts in Allegheny country were repositories of men and supplies that facilitated travel for armies, and for escorted prisoners.

Colonial forces transported very few captives any distance. Thirty militiamen had easily escorted six compliant Shawnees to Charleston in 1753, and volunteers could occasionally bring small groups of Indian captives short distances in safety.[18] The Pennsylvania volunteers who killed two Delaware captives at Muncie Hill in 1763, and attempted the killing of a third, were not facing food shortages. Like some warriors, these men were exacting personal revenge and pre-empting the power of those at home who were likely to be more humane to captives. The only major colonial raids into Allegheny country, the Sandy Creek and Kittanning expeditions of 1756, both dissolved amid severe food shortages. Although neither ended quite as disastrously as Major

Robert Rogers's raid on St Francis in October 1759, where some rangers ate their prisoners or died of starvation, these colonial raids illustrated problems of supply that large parties of Indians, even when accompanied by unexpectedly large numbers of captives, were routinely able to overcome.

"Hot pursuit," long conventional in intertribal raiding, became a major threat to both Indian captors and white captives on the trail after 1756. On some occasions, usually elusive war parties were willing to stand and fight to retain their captives. A year earlier, Delaware captain Tewea had taken the time to divide loot from the Fleming household into bundles for himself and his companion, order pregnant Elizabeth Fleming to carry a bundle of clothes, and require William to carry a sack of meal.[19] Captives did not carry sacks of meal after this war was underway. Raiders expected to be chased by parties that were organized with increasing promptness by local volunteers or provincial rangers and garrisons. Horses were initially incidental in the retreat of war parties. In 1755 Delaware captors had walked while allowing teen captive Barbara Leininger to ride a horse to Kittanning; Shawnee captors let Mary Draper Ingles ride on an even longer journey to Lower Shawnee Town; and the Miami captors of Jane Fraser let her ride for the entire three-week journey. By the next summer, some Wyandot warriors were bringing home captured and heavily loaded Virginian horses.[20] If horses could be caught quickly, and controlled well, they could speed the retreat with much more loot, especially along the newly cut British military roads, and provide food in extremity. However, horses were easy to track and follow on horseback, difficult to hide or silence, and hard to feed adequately in rough Allegheny country. Additionally, horses could be used by captives attempting to escape.

Captors and captives were occasionally killed as a direct result of close pursuit on the trail.[21] The terror of the Ryan children, held under cover and threatened with death as a pursuit party rode by, is easily imagined. One captive was killed accidentally in the firefight on Sideling Hill in the spring of 1756, when pursuing militiamen initially released twenty-six captives, but lost twenty-one of them again in the overwhelming Delaware counterattack. The Shawnee-French war party that captured Mary Jemison deep in York County in 1758 killed five of their seven captives and told Mary that "they should not have killed the family if the whites had not pursued them."[22] Colonel John Armstrong led a pursuit in November 1763 that was called off after fresh snow obscured the tracks, but not before they found the body of a child who had not been able to keep up the pace of the Indians' escape.[23] The next year, as a mounted pursuit party near Fort Bedford was closing in upon Indians "flying from our People, a white Boy, they had Prisoner, fell from his Horse, upon which they killed and scalped him, cut off his Head, and left it in the Road."[24] Colonel Armstrong led another pursuit that summer that both prompted and discovered a grisly scene: "the Enemy being Closely pursu'd Kill'd their Prisoners on the flight, to the number of six or seven then Scatter'd as usual & made their escape."[25] In total, a dozen captors were killed by pursuit parties that themselves lost more than forty-eight would-be rescuers. Although at least fourteen captives died during these rescue attempts, pursuers released at least forty-eight during firefights. These results could not have been tabulated then, but they might have justified the effort, and confirmed that captors were reluctant to kill their prizes even under duress.

Captors killed a few of their captives for reasons that were understood, but the most notorious and least comprehended was the deliberate torture of captives unto death, at the site of an attack or on the trail into captivity. For all the honor associated with bringing a live captive into a village, warriors were sometimes tempted to try the endurance of their enemies, and to take ferocious revenge before the fate of a captive could be decided by others. Because most Indian attackers were seeking a quick strike and a speedy retreat with loot and captives, the cases of sustained torture at the site of capture were very rare. Delaware captors of a Maryland farmer named Lowther evidently feared no pursuit in March 1756. Lowther, who had killed one of his attackers, was found "dead and scalped, and otherways terribly mangled; his Brains were beat out, as is supposed with his own Gun-barrel, which we found sticking in his Skull, and his Gun broken: there was an Ax, two Scythes, and several Arrows, sticking in him."[26] Fourteen-year-old Arthur Crawford left an even more detailed remembrance of this torture of his uncle. Lowther had been stripped and tied to his cabin wall. Finding reapers' sickles nearby, the Delaware "amused themselves for about an hour in Cutting Lowther in every part of his body and limbs they put out both of his eyes with the points of the sycles and when they had thus sattisfied their Hellish vengance they tomahocked scalped him & cut of[f] his head."[27] This was not ritual torture but, like the mutilation of bodies evident in the first days of war on the Susquehanna River, revenge and bonding violence by angry novice warriors who did not fear pursuit. Delaware warriors also tortured a Pennsylvania militiaman to death immediately after the battle of Sideling Hill, in which three Delaware had been killed.[28] These two incidents, and the roasting alive of Lieutenant Francis Gordon by the Seneca who captured Fort Venango in 1763, are the best-attested cases of deliberate torture of captives at the site of their capture. None of these tortures were performed in or near the captors' villages, and none were sanctioned by the leading women of their community, or involved the entire village as tormentors.

When a war party had pushed itself and its captives beyond the fury of the fight and likelihood of counterattack, torture was still possible on the trail. At least two captives were burned to death near Fort Duquesne after the Battle of the Monongahela.[29] Shawnee warriors tortured and burned a Virginia militiaman days after their costly participation in the capture of Vause's Fort. Given their admiration for the stoic endurance of pain, warriors could demonstrate their own superiority in exacting these tortures, even if they could eat the militiaman's heart to give themselves more courage.[30] Torture before arrival back in the tribal community was a rare and cruel display of ferocity, and the practice did not increase in frequency between 1755 and 1765. Captive William Fleming was recalling New England tales told before the war when he admitted fearing "the most cruel Torture" in 1755.[31] Such fear of torture on the trail at the hands of warriors was justified, though the numbers were small compared to incidents of torture upon arrival in Indian villages or in the large wartime camps near Fort Duquesne or Detroit.

Captives were often distraught and disoriented by the horror of the attacks that had uprooted them, and forced them to witness the killing of loved ones and friends, or fellow traders, soldiers, or warriors. Preexisting fears of torture and wanton killing had been realized, and were compounded by what seemed the studied barbarity of killing helpless captives on the trail. Knowing that their previous lives had been destroyed, many captives were numbed and fearful enough to accept their fate without further resistance, and to begin the painful initiation into a different existence.

However, there were good reasons to consider a quick escape. Escape was the duty of soldiers and warriors, and was their only route to full and speedy restoration of status. For all captives, immediate escape through familiar territory was much easier than any later effort, which could involve a hungry odyssey through the unknown. Attempted escape on the trail was a life-threatening risk that more than sixty-five captives judged to be worth taking.

Captives' fears of suffering and death should have been major incentives for speedy escape, but surviving information is surprising in several respects. First, there are very few reports of failed attempts to escape on the trail;[32] one is left wondering whether any of the killings portrayed as wanton and unprovoked were to thwart or punish attempted escapes. Second, though twenty people had been promptly and voluntarily released from captivity during the decade before General Edward Braddock's defeat, only two incidents during the following decade are reported as anything like voluntary release by individual captors. In March of 1759, a war party and their soldier-prisoner were stopped by the Delaware at Kushkushi; the hosting Delaware decided, after a long council meeting, that their recent truce with the English meant that no English prisoners should be brought through their town. This captured soldier was released and escorted back to Fort Pitt.[33] The freeing of Mary Means and her mother by Maiden Foot in 1763 deserves to be famous because it was a singular act of kindness.[34] It was not the captors who released any of these victims. These may have been the only instances of the prompt release of captives during these wars, though it would certainly have been tempting for any returnee to report such an occurrence as a heroic escape, whether talking to suspicious neighbors or commanding officers who were watchful for spies and deserters.

It is especially surprising that only sixty-five captives, or only 3 per cent of those taken, are known to have escaped within the week of capture during this entire generation of borderland war. The majority of the escaping thirty-five white settlers were men who had freed themselves after raids in 1756 and 1757. It is understandable that traders and soldiers were more likely than settlers to escape quickly. Nine of the ten traders who escaped promptly did so as Pontiac's War commenced, and eleven of the seventeen soldiers who escaped also did so in 1763.

Despite the widely publicized escape of Elizabeth Fleming, and the defiant heroics of Jennet Clendennin, only ten women are known to have escaped quickly, as did twelve children under sixteen. The story of Jennet Clendennin is suggestive. After helping to feed Cornstalk's party of sixty Ohio Shawnee in June of 1763, Clendennin saw her husband killed by her guests before she was led away into captivity, along with her three young children and at least twenty-five neighbors. This large caravan had gone only ten miles when Clendennin handed her infant to another captive woman and then escaped into the nearby brush. Although all the known captives with this party were eventually returned, except for two of Clendennin's own children, there are no recorded eyewitnesses to this event, and it was decades later before Clendennin first spoke of her exploits with a chronicler.[35] By one account, this feisty woman berated her captors until slapped in the face with her husband's bloodied scalp, and thereafter she tried, in vain, to convince her traumatized fellow captives to flee. By another report, an angry Indian grabbed Clendennin's abandoned babe and, when its bawling failed to bring its hiding mother back, the Indian smashed the infant against a tree. This may have been the angry reaction of a warrior who had taken two captives and now was going home with none. Not only could the child not survive without its mother, but the babe's crying would also attract the pursuit party that was already following.[36] In hiding, Clendennin probably did not see this killing, and the graphic image was an echo of a then-familiar biblical metaphor for ferocity.[37] On returning home, Clendennin supposedly buried her husband under fence rails, confronting a disappointed "heir at law," and even remarried, all within a week.[38] She had enduring personal reasons to emphasize both Indian ferocity and her own defiance.

The Flemings' widely available story emphasized the advantages of immediate and cheerful submission, but it also offered a useful guide on how to escape. The couple, taken early in the war, had two advantages that were less likely later: they were not tied at night and had been allowed to talk to each other. Waiting for their captors to fall asleep, the couple made some deliberate noise in getting up, ostensibly to tend the fire and warm themselves. Their two captors were not roused, and it is interesting that William did not grab his captors' guns, but instead took a tankard and headed for a nearby spring. He later explained that if discovered he would have claimed to be getting a drink; if undiscovered, he would wait there for his wife to come, and they would then flee together. The plan worked well until William smacked his head into a tree limb in the dark, knocked himself unconscious, and fell into the underbrush. Elizabeth could not find him, and they each escaped separately.[39]

Night was the favored time to escape on the trail, but adult captives were often tied at night, or at least made to sleep under a blanket held in place by two sleeping captors. A few managed to untie themselves and escape, and the redoubtable Virginian hunter John Lane reportedly had the foresight to pick up a piece of glass while being hurried along Braddock's Road, somehow hid the shard in his armpit even when being stripped, and apparently used it to cut his way out of ropes during his escape on the first night in captivity.[40] One wounded Cumberland County man was tied on each of the first five nights, but escaped when left untied on the sixth night.[41] The size of war parties did not noticeably affect chances of escape; the Flemings escaped from two captors, whereas Jennet Clendennin escaped in broad daylight from a group of sixty captors.[42] Despite their fears of death and torture and the desire to escape, twenty-nine of every thirty were still held after their first week of capture.

Vigilant captors were certainly one reason why a captive's chances of escaping within the first week were slim. Yet all captors were not equally vigilant, or fortunate. Mixed parties of Indians and Canadians were much more likely to have a captive escape than were Indian parties raiding without Canadians.[43] War parties described as being exclusively of a single tribe also showed marked differences in the number of captives who escaped on the trail. The Delaware, like the Wyandot, lost about one captive in twenty-five, but it must be remembered that many Delaware were involved in a war against neighbors, and the North Branch Delaware in particular held their captives within relatively easy reach of their former homes. The Shawnee, based in the middle of Ohio country, lost only 1 of 214 captives on the trail, a lad who escaped in the very first attack on Buffalo Creek, North Carolina, in 1754. Shawnee vigilance, and the distance between Shawnee towns and colonial settlements, may have been the main reason why Virginian captives were only half as likely as Pennsylvanians to escape on the trail.[44]

Did captors, or captives, learn anything in the decade after 1754 that affected the frequency of escapes by those recently captured? Captors soon came to apply what had been common in intertribal raiding; they tied up all adult captives, threatened them with death if they attempted to escape, and prevented them from talking to each other. Hot pursuit after 1756 freed at least forty-eight, and nine of these, including two children, escaped on their own amid the confusion. The advent of horses may have helped captors carry loot, but they also were vehicles of escape for a few captives. Barbara Leininger thought that being on horseback would let her escape; she failed and, remarkably, was not executed for her attempt.[45]

Certainly, captors were more successful in preventing escape on the trail during the Seven Years' War than in Pontiac's War, and one-third of all prompt escapes occurred in 1763.[46] This improvement in chances of escape in the first week of captivity cannot be attributed to the unique situation of Detroit, where captives were held in the nearby camps of the besieging Indians. Aside from the single Queen's Ranger who escaped overland from the Point Pelee disaster and entered Fort Detroit at night, and three of his fellows who escaped amid the bombardment of the captured remnant of their flotilla, no soldiers escaped in their first week of captivity near Detroit. The only other person to do so was a fur brigade worker, who spoke enough French to be mistaken for a Canadian and was able to escape and make his way to Detroit within six days.[47] For all the reported brutality, disorder, and drunkenness, and the efforts of some humane French settlers to buy and hide captives, none of the seventy-three captives taken to the Indian villages and camps at Detroit in 1763 were able to escape from there to the nearby fort during their first week of captivity. Seven of the Fort Presqu'île garrison managed to run for their lives all the way to Fort Pitt after a large intertribal army had accepted their surrender. Five captured traders escaped promptly from the Delaware during the first Ohio Valley attacks that May, but, of 110 white settlers captured that year, only three escaped promptly.[48] The speedy escapes of 1763 were from diverse captors, did not concentrate at Detroit, and still did not number 4 in 100 of those captured.

The first week on the trail into captivity was extremely trying, even if all the rumor-fed fears were not realized. Warriors killed at least eighty of their captives during the first week, and sixty-five escaped, meaning that one captive in twenty was lost, one way or another, by the end of the first week of captivity. The overwhelming majority of captives survived their first week, had not attempted to escape, and were near the end of the frightening and degrading first phase of their searing initiation into a new existence.

10

Allegheny White Indians

Knowledgeable writers during the first generation of Allegheny warfare, including Cadwallader Colden, Benjamin Franklin, and William Smith,[1] voiced concern that many captives rejected redemption and the return to Christianity and civilization, preferring to become white Indians. Pennsylvanians knew the adage about the ease with which a white person could become an Indian, and the near impossibility of making a white person out of an Indian. The sophisticated author of *Letters from an American Farmer* rather wildly suggested that thousands of Europeans became Indian, but that no Indians became European.[2] One modern commentator goes further in claiming, "One of the greatest scandals of the colonial, federal, and antebellum eras of American history was that the majority of those turned into 'white savages' flatly refused to return to 'civilization.'"[3] Whether captives' stories were preserved as tales of courage, adaptability, or adventure, or were infused with criticism of white society, they all imply that Indians had a method of re-education that could be very effective. The concern itself has always been Eurocentric, for it should not be surprising that traumatized and vulnerable orphans sought the protection of families that forcibly replaced the ones they had just seen destroyed. Eighteenth-century relatives and commentators, who presumed that heredity was an indelible determinant of character, were entitled to some surprise when environment and re-education clearly trumped genetics. Nonetheless, two linked questions are worth exploring: how was Indian incorporation of white captives undertaken, and how successful was it?

Those studying white Indians have relied on a few best-recorded cases scattered over great stretches of time and space.[4] Credible surviving sources are few, ambiguous, and usually skeletal. Captives taken in Allegheny country between 1745 and 1765 constitute a particularly intriguing study group because most were clearly intended for incorporation into Indian village life, and most were held beyond easy escape or speedy redemption. There was relatively little commercial and diplomatic transfer of captives to other tribes or French allies, certainly compared to battlegrounds nearer to New France. Of some 2,873 people captured or missing on the Allegheny frontier between 1745 and 1765, only one white Indian, Mary Jemison, has left what is an extensive second-hand account based upon interviews she gave sixty-six years after her captivity as a teenager. However, the sources and opportunities for analysis improve greatly if the subject is expanded to consider Indian acculturation as a cumulative process that affected most captives who were eventually returned.

The general process of re-educating captives was similar throughout the region, though details varied with tribe, location, and circumstance. It is useful to remember the psychological impact of witnessing an attack that killed loved ones or friends, and the fear of subsequent torture and the gauntlet, or *bastonade*.[5] Adoption marked a sudden and complete shift of attitude towards captives, and thereafter many were promptly and fully incorporated into working Indian communities, even before they understood the language. In considering torture, adoption, integration, and assimilation, certain common features will be recognized amid the differences in captors and circumstances. There were gradations of adaptation, especially for those who did not stay captive for long, but those who lived out their lives with their former captors were definitely not the only ones indelibly transformed by their captivity.

The threat and fear of torture were immediate and essential concerns for adult captives, and marked the beginning of their forced transformation. Torture had long been the ultimate test of personal courage for captured warriors, and the deliberate horrors were sublimated into an opportunity for an unsuccessful warrior to restore and enhance his own reputation and that of his people. The long, excruciating platform torture of the Iroquoians, and the pole burnings of the Shawnee, had become legendary long before 1745. Under torture, the bravest sang their defiance, mocked their tormentors for the inadequacy of their efforts, and sometimes taunted them into an angry or merciful blow that ended the macabre ritual. The Shawnee, for instance, preserved the memories of enemies who showed remarkable bravery under torture. The Savannah Shawnee, early in the eighteenth century, had captured and tortured a leading Creek warrior they called "Old Scarny," who mocked their tortures as inadequate and asked for free hands and a fire-heated gun barrel to show them how better to torment him. He then grabbed the offered gun by its red-hot barrel, wielded it as a weapon, and escaped to avenge himself repeatedly. In another instance, a Seneca warrior, tortured relentlessly by the Shawnee, showed no weakness, and eventually asked for a pipe and tobacco, and then sat deliberately in the fire, smoking until executed by a Shawnee warrior impressed by his gallant enemy.[6] Such accounts, elaborated in retelling to encourage both fighting to the death and the bearing of suffering, were parts of a history that were not reinforced by any direct reports of Indian torture of each other on the Allegheny frontier in the generation after 1745.[7]

While whites claimed that Indians were cowards because they would not expose themselves to be shot in battle, the Shawnee retorted that "the whites were cowards and would not stand fire."[8] There is no evidence that any of the twenty-six whites who were ritually tortured to death near Allegheny Indian villages in the generation after 1745 performed "well" by Indian standards.[9] White captives considered torture to be fiendish brutality, and fear of it inspired some to fight unto death, others to attempt to escape, and most to comply with what could be understood of captors' demands in the hope of being spared.[10] Although Europeans had witnessed routine judicial torture as a spectator sport at home, these cruelties were performed by a segregated caste of often-hooded executioners. In confronting comparable Indian torture, Europeans managed to be appalled that entire Indian communities, including women and children, joined in the torture.[11] Exaggerated claims of torture became easy accusations used to inspire white resistance, to degrade Indian enemies, to justify white brutalities, and to add lurid, morbid, and pornographic inventions to the appeal of both real and imaginary captivity narratives. Ritual cannibalism and other mutilations of bodies were not necessarily linked to torture, though they caused further revulsion among those accustomed to Christian death rituals.

The torture of white victims in the Allegheny borderlands often did not conform to what is presumed to be traditional Indian practices. For Iroquois, platform torture had been the climax of a community's celebration of those victories that had been complete enough to include the capture of an enemy warrior. Although the victorious warriors selected their intended victims, and marked them with black face-paint, eminent matrons met the returning war party outside the village to make the final decision on whether a victim would be tortured to death or spared for possible adoption.[12] Iroquois customs were evolving away from platform torture in villages. The only known Iroquois torture in Allegheny country in this period was the Seneca burning of Lieutenant

Francis Gordon at Fort Venango in 1763, which occurred in this fort rather than in a Genesee Valley Seneca village. This killing displayed a brutality that was neither a ritual nor an impromptu retaliation, for no Indian attackers are known to have been casualties in the capture of that fort.

The Shawnee were widely, if unreliably, reported as still practicing their comparable tradition, in which the peace matrons could save a captive at the edge of the village, but the touch of one of the matrons of the Miseekwaaweekwaakee society meant certain death. In the imagination of Robert Kirk and the distant recollection of Mary Jemison, mid-eighteenth-century Shawnee villages were still the sites of major ritual burnings.[13] The very few well-attested Shawnee burnings may have conformed to traditional tribal practice. After heavy losses during the 1756 siege of Vause's Fort, the returning Shawnee approached Lower Shawnee Town with their share of the captives, and captive-witness Peter Looney reported that the warriors "made a sacrifice of one Cole, whom they roasted alive, and tormented for a whole Night before he expired, cutting Pieces of his Flesh off his Body, and eating it."[14] Looney did not mention any visit by women from the town before Sergeant Cole was condemned, but the site suggests that the torture may have been more than a belated brutal revenge of warriors who had lost many companions to a resolute enemy. Looney and the other captives present were all shaken but otherwise unharmed. The later Shawnee reputation for torture derived from reports that they took and kept few prisoners in the latter stages of the American Revolution; this reputation has been too easily projected backwards to the Seven Years' War by those writing after 1780.[15]

Delaware village participation in torture was developed or rediscovered as they sought to reassert a largely moribund warrior ethic. Sixteen-year-old John Coxe was among some fifty captives in Kittanning in 1756 as war parties returned, and he did not know why they singled out Paul Broadly, "whom they, agreeable to their usual Cruelty, beat for half an hour with Clubbs and Tomahawks, and afterwards fastning him to a Post cropt his Ears close to his head and chopt his Fingers; that they called together all the Prisoners to be Witnesses to this Scene of their inhuman Barbarity."[16] If Coxe accurately described what he had seen, this might seem less a ritual torture than a ferocious beating that escalated into tying Broadly to a post and proceeding to a torture intended primarily to frighten other captives and warn them not to attempt escape. Marie Le Roy and Barbara Leininger were among the witnesses who understood Broadly's torture this way; they were convinced that Broadly had been trying to escape with the Pennsylvanians who had just attacked Kittanning. The somewhat-enhanced Le Roy–Leininger narrative of 1759 claims that this torture continued about three hours, ending only when the victim asked for water and – more inventively than traditionally – was forced to drink molten lead.[17]

Attempted escape was certainly the reason for the only torture of a woman reported on this frontier, also by the Delaware in the wake of the same Pennsylvanian attack. Mrs Alexander McAllister, who had been captured along with her husband in Cumberland County three months earlier, was initially recovered by the Pennsylvanian raiders, and then recaptured by the Delaware. Despite severe losses in the attack, the Delaware did not immediately vent their rage on Mrs McAllister. First, all the captives, including Hugh Gibson, Marie Le Roy, and Barbara Leininger, were gathered to witness this "lesson." The victim was then stripped, tied to a post, and tortured with hot irons until she died amid screams of pain.[18]

The Delaware of Kittanning had ritually tortured a third captive earlier that summer, but not because he had tried to escape. As the French and Indian conquerors of Fort Granville were returning westward through Kittanning at the end of July 1756, the captured fort's luckless commander, Sergeant John Turner, was reportedly identified and accused by a Delaware whom he had beaten several years earlier. A soldier serving under Turner, and captured with him, mentioned merely that all the prisoners were taken to Kittanning, "where they continued about three Hours in which Time John Turner one of the Prisoners was there burnt."[19] Prisoners rescued in the Kittanning raid a month later gave details that allowed the *Pennsylvania Gazette* to elaborate. The Delaware had tied Turner "to a Black Post, danced round him, made a great Fire, and having heated Gun-barrels red hot, they run them through his Body; they tormented him thus near three Hours, then scalped him alive; and at last held up a Boy, with a Hatchet in his Hand, to give him a finishing Stroke."[20] (Execution by a boy demonstrated that the victim had cried out, and was judged unworthy of execution by an adult).[21] The burning of Turner may have helped Pennsylvania to decide to target Kittanning for the raid that September, and the burnings of Broadly and McAllister were part of this raid's consequences. Turner, Broadly, and McAllister were all tortured in Kittanning, the substantial Delaware town led by Shingas and Tewea, which had become the main base for Ohio Delaware raiding parties and was full of white captives who had suddenly come within range of possible rescue.

The only other reported torture by the Delaware occurred farther west at Kuskuski in 1758, and is not as well attested. The victim was Daniel McManimy, a laborer working for Richard Bard when they were captured by Ohio Delaware. As the returning war party approached Kuskuski, McManimy was kept outside the town while the other captives, including Bard's wife, Ketty, reportedly ran a gauntlet. Ketty Bard did not witness McManimy's execution but assembled the story during her two years as a captive and recorded it soon after her return. Those trying to frighten her may have exaggerated some details, as might have Ketty herself, or her son, who used now-lost family papers in preparing the only account we have of this torture. McManimy was evidently encircled, beaten with sticks and tomahawks, and then tied to a post near a large fire. Then he was scalped alive, and tortured with hot coals, heated gun barrels, and bayonets until he died.[22] The similarities between this account and Coxe's story of what happened to Paul Broadly suggest that Delaware torture began with a severe beating, and then the victims were tied to a post, and then mutilated, and deliberately burned and wounded until they died. None of these victims were allowed the quicker death in a fire. The Ohio Delaware ritually tortured 4 of 433 prisoners in this period: 2 because they had tried to escape, 1 to avenge an old grievance, and another 1 to avenge the death of a warrior involved in the capture. Other Delaware captives were certainly threatened with burning or intended for burnings that did not occur. John McCullough, who was with the Delaware for eight years as a young captive, later recounted that if anyone was willing to pay thirty buckskins for a captive who had been painted for death, "he must be given up to him, alleging they would have bad luck if they refused to accept it; the one who makes the purchase, keeps him as a slave, to hunt & raise corn for him." McCullough knew one old Delaware who made three such purchases, treated his slaves kindly, and eventually returned all of them.[23]

By far the most notorious scenes of torture occurred in Pontiac's camp, then across the river from Fort Detroit, where at least two-thirds of all the known torture victims of this generation died. When the Ojibwa Kinonchamek rebuked Pontiac for cruelty to prisoners, he was making a valid charge, whatever the politics of the moment. The Delaware prophet Neolin, who was thought to be very influential with

Pontiac, was also known to oppose this abuse of captives.[24] The tortures at Detroit may have been part of an attempt to lure the garrison out of their defensible fort, but most were prompted by the dramatic escape of prisoners in the first bateau of the flotilla captured at Point Pelee. According to the journal of Robert Navarre, Canadian notary at Detroit, at least eleven of the Queen's Rangers captured at Point Pelee were tortured upon landing at Pontiac's camp on 29 May 1763. Navarre's account mentions several methods of torture, which may or may not have indicated different bands of torturers. Some captives were stripped, shot with arrows, and beaten with clubs and fists to keep them upright until they died of their wounds. Others were tied to stakes, tortured with fire, and cut with gun flints and knives until they bled to death. Navarre was understandably horrified both by the roasting and eating of some of the dead, and by bodies left exposed or thrown in the river. As described by this source, these killings lacked much evidence of being related to known tribal rituals.[25] Wherever he was on 29 May, and he was free to move within Pontiac's camp, Robert Navarre was better positioned to observe these seemingly spontaneous horrors than were the British in the garrison across the river. The killing of the former commander at Detroit, Captain Donald Campbell, after nearly two months as Pontiac's most prominent prisoner, was not a ritual killing either. Ojibwa chief Wasson, furious at the death and mutilation of his nephew in a skirmish two days earlier, demanded that Pontiac provide Campbell as a fit object for his revenge. Campbell was brought to the Ojibwa camp, where Wasson had him stripped of his clothing and then killed him with a single blow of his tomahawk, and had his body thrown in the river. Thomas Meares, a captured soldier of the Royal American Regiment who was forced to witness this killing, later described it as being "in a most barbarous and inhuman manner." The killing was deliberate revenge, and the victim was humiliated by being stripped naked, but Campbell was not tortured.[26] Pontiac's camp was a place of constant terror for captives like John Rutherfurd because even the adopted could not be protected from sudden killing by drunken warriors, or by those fulfilling the requirements of some gruesome dream.[27]

Captives suffering or fearing torture, or forced to witness it, were in no position to know how uncommon it was, nor would they have been greatly comforted by such knowledge. Aside from Pontiac's camp at Detroit on 29 May 1763, the torture of captives was rare. Captured children were not tortured, and Mrs McAllister was the only one of more than

242 captured women to be tortured.[28] The chances of an adult male captive being tortured were less than one in a hundred, and twenty-three of the twenty-six tortured to death were soldiers.[29] The torture of those who attempted to escape was a horrifying threat to captives, but it was the seemingly random tortures that would have been the most devastating. The searing and sustained terror felt by captives for days or weeks after capture, as well as the depression and despair caused by the family disaster that had just made one a widow or an orphan, was a major feature of what has to be called the forced conversion, or "involuntary detachment," of white captives.[30]

The gauntlet, or *bastonade*, was widely known as the worst of the routine brutalities of going into Indian captivity, and was presumed to be so common that it became a plausible feature to include in imaginary tales of captivity, or an easy addition to thrice-told stories of real captivities. David Zeisberger, Moravian missionary to the Iroquois and the Ohio Delaware, claimed that it was routine among all woodland Indians. As the warriors and their captives reached the village, the captives were required to dance. The entire village then gathered in two rows, and the captives, with or without their arms bound, were then ordered to go through the gauntlet to a designated safe point. "[A]s soon as they set out the people begin to strike at them with switches, clubs, hatchets and their fists." Fit captives could minimize the suffering by racing as fast as they could, and as close to one side of the gauntlet as possible. "Female prisoners are frequently rescued by the women who take them between their ranks and carry them to the town."[31] In portrayals of these savage beatings, little attention has been paid to the interest of the captor, who has brought his valued prize home in triumph to see it immediately reduced or ruined by kin, who might be acquiring an invalid instead of an additional working relative.

The surviving evidence from the Allegheny frontier before 1765 does not sustain the notion that the gauntlet Zeisberger described was a routine ritual of admission to an Ohio Indian community; the severest gauntlets were those inflicted by multitribal gatherings of warriors encamped at Fort Duquesne. The fullest and most vivid account is from James Smith's later remembrance of his own beating there. On 8 July 1755, the day before General Edward Braddock was attacked, Smith was captured and brought to Fort Duquesne for interrogation. Although he undoubtedly attempted to run fast through the quickly formed gauntlet, as he had been advised, he was flogged all the way by two long rows of warriors. He was knocked unconscious twice, and remembered waking up in the fort the second time, with a French doctor washing his wounds and a French officer asking questions. One of Smith's Delaware captors called the beating "only an old custom the Indians had, and it was like how do you do."[32]

Who beat Smith nearly to death and, as he asked in vain, why? The French, having sent out the scouting party that brought this prisoner for interrogation, could not have appreciated having Smith nearly killed before arrival. More than 600 Indians, predominantly Ottawa, Potowatomi, and "mission" Indians from Canada, had just arrived and were involved in a protracted council about whether to initiate hostilities against the British.[33] The beating may have been related to this council, which eventually decided to join the Canadians in attacking Braddock. The beating was an opportunity to develop enthusiasm for the next day's gruesome work. It is noteworthy that Smith reported no gauntlet when his captor later brought him into the Muskingum town of Tullihas, where he was adopted.[34] A Virginian girl named Rachel (Rachile) was, according to a French chronicler, also severely beaten in a *bastonade* at Fort Duquesne in 1755. She was then given to the fort's commander, and she took a month to recover from her wounds and months more to overcome a debilitating fear of all Indians.[35] Mary Jemison recalled being taken there early in 1758, and reported "some customs upon their prisoners which they deemed necessary," but she mentions only that captives' hair was combed, and their faces and hair painted red before they were presented at the fort.[36] In September of that year, however, captives taken in Major James Grant's failed raid on Fort Duquesne and its Indian encampments, were being beaten as they were brought to the fort. Fellow captive Thomas Gist, held in relative safety across the river, saw these prisoners attacked both by warriors returning from the battle and by others from the fort "with tomahawks, knives, swords and sticks, with the most horrid screaming and yelling that I ever heard, and was beat and drove from one side of the cleared ground to the other, till the unhappy men could not stand; then they were tomohawked, scelped and in short was massacred in the most barbarious manner that can be immajined."[37] The Indians inflicted unmitigated vengeance on those who had attacked them, though from his location Gist did not see any gauntlet being formed.

General reports of Delaware staging gauntlets for prisoners arriving at their villages are numerous enough. Charles Stuart was severely hurt going through a Kittanning gauntlet of about 200 armed Indians, but noticed that only the handles of tomahawks and the flat side of sabers were used and that captive children and young adults were not beaten.[38] Young John McCullough ran no gauntlet himself at Fort Duquesne or Shenango, but included a conventional description of this practice in an equally conventional ethnographic "Indian Manners and Customs" section added to his and other more pretentious narratives. Here he spoke of captives beaten in every town they passed through, and of men beaten more severely than women, who were sometimes shielded by sympathetic Indian women.[39] A missionary, proud of Moravian Delaware towns, stated that these Christian Delaware abhorred the gauntlet, and prevented it, while helping any captives paraded through their towns by others. Moravian Indians incurred the wrath of both sides as a result.[40] Mrs Jean Lowry, whose narrative emphasized her staunch Protestant resistance to the Delaware and the French and amply fulfilled her subtitle's claim to offer an "Account of the Hardships She Suffered," was severely beaten on entering a Delaware hunting encampment and again at another village, though she was spared a dreaded gauntlet at Kittanning. She arrived there while the warriors were away on raids, was instructed to carry a turkey feather through the gauntlet to show she was marked for adoption, and received only one blow.[41] Another party of prisoners, including John Craig, were beaten with hickory switches until bloodied in what might have been a gauntlet gathered as the captives were being presented to Shingas at Kittanning early in 1756.[42] Descendants of Ketty Bard seem to have elaborated her story in claiming that she and four captive children were beaten severely in a gauntlet at Kittanning.[43]

Other captives of the Delaware reported something very different. Like John McCullough, captives George Ebert, Hugh Gibson, and John Street all said nothing about being beaten. Marie Le Roy and Barbara Leininger, who arrived at Kittanning as captives in December 1755, would report, "As this was to be the place of our permanent abode, we here received our welcome, according to Indian custom. It consisted of three blows each, on the back. They were, however, administered with great mercy. Indeed, we concluded that we were beaten merely to keep up an ancient usage, and not with the intention of injuring us."[44] Isaac Hollister, captured by North Branch Delaware in the next war, reported a severe beating in running a gauntlet of fists, yet this was not upon his arrival, but six months later, when he was recaptured after attempting to escape. Although it took him two weeks to recover from the beating, he regarded the *bastonade* as a mercy afforded him because of his youth; he knew attempted escape was punishable by death.[45] The strangest, and most dubious, comment on the Delaware gauntlet was a third-party remembrance of the captivity of thirteen-year-old David Boyd, captured in 1756. Before being adopted, he supposedly was subjected to running gauntlets of sorts, either for others' amusement or to toughen him.[46]

On the Allegheny frontier in the mid-eighteenth century, the gauntlet seems to have been uncommon for captives and, except for Jean Lowry's experience and the occasional ferocious attacks near Fort Duquesne, less severe than has been assumed. Surviving accounts do not suggest that Allegheny captives ran or witnessed gauntlets on entering the villages of Wyandot, Mingo, Ojibwa, Ottawa, Miami, or Shawnee. From the surviving direct evidence, which is limited, a symbolic gauntlet was sometimes used by the Delaware early in the Seven Years' War.

Captives who survived or avoided the gauntlet experienced a sudden and marked improvement in circumstances, as they were then assigned to families or to individual masters or mistresses.[47] The captor, having been recognized for his accomplishment in the celebration at his return, usually relinquished control of his captive then, and seldom became the captive's master. The dominant matrons of Seneca, Mingo, and Shawnee communities were influential in determining how additions were made to their families, and their wishes likely coincided with the intentions of the war captain, who may have undertaken the raid with their encouragement. The same may have been true of the Delaware, who were also matrilineal, but Zeisberger claimed that the decisions on captives were made by a council.[48]

Ready adoption of alien prisoners into Indian societies, in Allegheny country and elsewhere, was in striking contrast to ideal European practices in the middle of the eighteenth century. Europeans, in theory, considered captured Christian and Indian enemies to be fellow humans but not intimates; they were not to be enslaved, or even put to work,[49] and were to be guarded, subsisted, and preserved for exchange. British officers who confined and provisioned Indian captives and hostages in forts regarded themselves as behaving most honorably, though the confined Indians would not have agreed. Indian adoption of captives has too often been regarded by white chroniclers as a part of kidnapping or wife-stealing, rather than a major amelioration of what was brutal, family-smashing warfare. Despite open hospitality to visiting strangers, Indians lived primarily in the company of their real or fictive kin, with very little responsibility toward, or trust of, those regarded as outsiders.[50] Some level of naming and adoption was key to the survival and prosperity of alien traders, travelers, and stray deserters, as well as war captives. Communities anxious to replace war dead were open to adopting many of their enemies brought home in triumph. Without adoption into a protecting family, a captive was marginal, effectively enslaved, often oppressed, and always vulnerable.[51]

Prompt adoption was admission to a family, but did not bring freedom. The adopted were refused contact with their natal community and forced to change their values, habits, and identities. They were subject to alien family authority, which brought considerable variety in treatment and assignments. They were seldom armed for protection or hunting, and remained under the threat of death if they attempted to escape. If slavery is defined as powerlessness originating as a substitute for death, alienation from one's natal culture, and loss of personal honor and identity, these war captives were slaves.[52] However, there were important features of the incorporation of white captives into Indian communities of the upper Ohio Valley that indicate that this condition should not be called slavery if compared with Amerindian captivity elsewhere. White women captives were taken as wives by prominent Indian males. Children of captives, and captured children, were not kept as servants. Captives were made to dress, eat, and live like their captors, but were not tattooed, dressed, or tonsured as a separate and recognizable servile group. War captives never became numerous enough to absolve their masters of their own work, or to create a separate laboring class to be controlled brutally at some personal distance. In these rather egalitarian societies, captives did not become personal attendants of the elite, or victims of ritual fertility cults or funereal practices. With few known exceptions, Allegheny captives of Indians were promptly considered to be kin in what were "open kinship" communities. Treatment varied by master, but slavery was the starting point of expected inclusion rather than the purpose of a capture.[53]

After nearly thirty years of trade and diplomacy with the Allegheny tribes, George Croghan responded to famous Scottish historian William Robertson's query about whether "any considerable number of their Prisoners [were] spared and adopted." Croghan confidently asserted, "most adopted."[54] Children between the ages of three and six years constituted over 40 per cent of the known adoptees. Those between seven and fifteen, and those over sixteen, accounted, equally, for most of the rest.[55] The age bias seems obvious, and those whites who accepted Lockean notions of the child as a *tabula rasa* could not have been very surprised. Nearly three-quarters of the adopted were under sixteen, but numerous adults were known to have been adopted as well. Despite the evocative insistence that the Indians were stealing women and children, men outnumbered women among adult captives known to have stayed with the Indians.

There were a few observable differences in adoption into various Indian communities. In most northern Iroquoian languages, including Seneca-Mingo, the word *enàsqua* was used to refer to a slave, a captive prisoner, or a domesticated animal like a horse or dog.[56] In all Iroquoian cultures, including Mingo, Caughnawaga, and Wyandot-Huron in Ohio country, adoption meant admission to a family, less often to a clan, and more rarely to a nation.[57] James Smith's recollections are the fullest surviving account of the prompt and elaborate adoption of a teenage male into a respected Kahnawake family. After his beating and partial recovery at Fort Duquesne, he was taken to Tullihas, a village of Kahnawake, Delaware, and Mohicans on the Muskingum River. The next day, he recalled, his hair was plucked, except for a decorated topknot, his nose and ears were pierced and decorated, and he was dressed in a breech cloth, painted, and given silver arm bands and a wampum belt around his neck. He was formally presented to the inhabitants, with an elder's speech that he did not understand, and three young women ensured his thorough dunking in the river. Then he was well dressed, repainted, and solemnly informed, in a speech with a translator, that his white blood had been washed away and he was now a Kahnawake, adopted in place of a great man. He then met his new Kahnawake kin, and the day was crowned with a feast of green corn and venison. Smith knew nothing of what had likely been a life-saving decision by women elders. He joined the family's hunters, after a suitable apprenticeship, and remembered approvingly his always being treated as an equal.[58]

Thomas Gist's account of his adoption by the Wyandot of Detroit in 1758 was similar. His gauntlet was without violence, he stood naked in the village for an hour before his adoption, and he was apparently assigned by a male council, dunked by women, and adopted into a family who immediately treated him as one of them and daily dressed his wounds until he recovered. The Wyandot gained a reputation for being particularly willing to adopt captives, including captured colonial officers like Gist, Peter Looney, and John Smith. The Iroquoians could adopt a male captive readily enough, and some adoptees, like the Catawba Tanaghrisson, could even rise in status, though they could not, of course, become hereditary league chiefs.

The adoption of a teenage Pennsylvania girl by the matrilineal Iroquois was another matter. By chance, the only other surviving detailed memoir of Iroquoian adoption on this frontier is that of Mary Jemison. Initially captured by a Shawnee war party that included Canadians, she was taken to Fort Duquesne, and there, likely with some compensation to the Shawnee, she was given to two Seneca women who had lost a brother in battle and had just come out of mourning to seek a prisoner or scalp in compensation. Arriving at a small Seneca settlement about eighty miles downriver, Mary waited in the canoe while these women went into their settlement and returned "with a suit of Indian clothing, all new, and very clean and nice." Mary was washed, dressed, and taken to the women's wigwam. The women of the village gathered there to inspect Mary, and proceeded with a traditional Iroquoian "requickening" ceremony, entirely in the hands of the women. One of them, likely a *gantowisa* (respected elder), made an impassioned speech lamenting the loss of a young warrior, while the other women wailed and wrung their hands. The mood then shifted abruptly to a happy welcoming of Mary, now Dickewamis – meaning handsome or pleasant girl. "I was ever considered and treated by them as a real sister, the same as though I had been born of their mother."[59] In Mary's account of her very long life as a worthy Seneca woman who had married a Delaware and a Seneca warrior in turn, and had had six children, she never suggested that she had, or missed having, the status of a clan matron. Jemison and Smith left the fullest of nine memoirs of Iroquoian captivity on the Allegheny frontier in this period, and it is noteworthy that all of them suggest full and prompt adoption.[60] Whatever the humiliation of being called an *enàsqua*, Allegheny captives of the Seneca, Mingo, Kahnawake, and Wyandot-Huron did not claim that they were kept as pets, servants, slaves, or beasts of burden.

The Delaware language had very different words for slave, prisoner, and servant, and none of them was at all similar to the word for dog, which was telling even if it did not prevent Delaware from occasionally calling their captives dogs.[61] In July 1756, eight-year-old John McCullough and his five-year-old brother, James, were captured by five Delaware and a Canadian. As the victorious war party approached Fort Duquesne, the boys had all the hair on their head plucked; as James Smith had, they were slapped about by an elder or shaman in what they did not recognize as a ceremony, and then they were decorated with hawk feathers and a wampum belt, and paraded through a harmless gauntlet of onlookers into Fort Duquesne. In a "French house," John recalled seeing his brother for the last time as he was given to a Frenchman by a Delaware chief. In the same room, John was given to Delaware Tom (a.k.a. Captain Tom), who spoke English well, and was grateful for this replacement for a brother killed a year earlier. After being introduced to the Delaware camp just across the Allegheny River, John was taken by canoe back into the river and washed so thoroughly by two young men that he thought he was being drowned. On wading out of the river, he was told he was now an Indian, and given a "new ruffled shirt." No Delaware women appear to have been involved in this stage of his adoption. John was promptly sent to live with an adoptive uncle at Shenango, on Beaver Creek. On arrival there, the family "set up a lamentable cry, for some time – when their lamentation was over, they came to me one after another and shook me by the hand." Young John's adoption process had resembled Mary Jemison's, though it came in two stages and included handshakes and what may have been other minor distinctions based on gender.[62]

Although adoption was usually as prompt and unconditional with the Delaware as with their Iroquoian neighbors, there were two reported cases of boys who were held captive for some time before being adopted by the Delaware. David Boyd was thirteen when captured from his father's Cumberland County farm in February of 1756, and claimed by the Delaware. His grandson's family history maintained that for the first year David "belonged to the tribes in common, to go and come as he was ordered by any one who chose to command him." Supposedly, this shy victim of bullying and neglect finally trounced a tormentor and, nearly a year after capture, was declared fit to be an Indian. If this is not an inventive addition to a tale, it is a rare case of a young captive needing to prove himself before adoption.[63] Thoroughly washed of his whiteness in a river, his hair removed except for a tuft on the crown, David was then painted and dressed appropriately, and was belatedly adopted by an older warrior who had treated him well from the day of his capture.[64] Teenage Hugh Gibson was also taken by Delaware the same year, and later remembered initial hunger and abuse; "however I did not remain long before I was adopted into an Indian family, and then I lived as they did, though the living was poor."[65] These cases, if accurately recounted, show some hesitation in adoption without challenging the general picture of prompt adoption.

There were also at least three young captives who were held but reportedly never adopted by the Delaware, and their experiences were markedly different. These captives mentioned having masters but no families. Barbara Leininger and Marie Le Roy were girls captured very early in the war and held for three and a half years by the Delaware; one would expect them to have been adopted. Both may have forfeited adoption by attempting to escape on the trail into captivity. "The Indians gave us enough to do. We had to tan leather, to make shoes (moccasins), to clear land, to plant corn, to cut down trees and build huts, to wash and cook." Food was short and strange, "and sometimes we were forced to live on acorns, roots, grass, and bark"; these girls were not being held among the starving refugees of Tioga, but amid better-provided Kittanning and Beaver River villagers. The girls were reportedly hired out to work for the French at Fort Duquesne for a couple of months, and also had to "clear the plantations of the Indian nobles, after the German fashion, to plant corn, and to do other hard work of every kind." This was more than Delaware women's arduous work. These girls were evidently not just sharing Indian hardships but, as they reported, "bearing the yoke of the heaviest slavery."[66] Although there is suspicion that the publication of their account was influenced by Pennsylvanians in support of the war, and a failed attempt to escape could have drastic consequences, Leininger and Le Roy indicated that captives could feel enslaved.

Another youth, named John Coxe, was a captive of the Delaware at Kittanning before being taken to Tioga, where life was much harder, hunger was more rampant, and some prisoners starved to death seeking food in the woods. An old chief he called "Makomesy" was John's master, but not his "father."[67] Young Isaac Hollister, another captive of the North Branch Delaware in 1763, remained a despised outsider, too. He recorded being famished most of the time, inadequately clothed to withstand winter, and made to "fetch wood every day upon my back half a mile."[68] Captivity meant sustained oppression for at least a few captives young enough to be remade as Delaware but old enough to escape and tell their stories.

There are no full surviving accounts of Ohio Shawnee adoption in this period, though they were notoriously resistant to repatriation of these adoptive kin. Like the Iroquois, the Shawnee reportedly respected the decisions of distinguished women elders about the fate of captives, though the Shawnee prophet Tenskwatawa later recalled that it was chiefs who assigned the saved captives "to such persons in the village as manifest a desire to have their services, or they are adopted as among other nations."[69] The word *kiikeenika* indicates, and conflates, a slave, a prisoner, and a servant.[70] At least forty-five white captives remained Shawnee for life, including at least three who came back to them after being forced to return to Pittsburgh. Both Mary Moore, wife of Sepettekenathe, and Joshua Renick grew up to become parts of remembered Shawnee history. Nancy Renick and Jacob Persinger were amongst the most reluctant of returnees, and Persinger was not the only one who went from being captured and adopted by the Shawnee in place of a dead relative to being forcibly captured and adopted by unrelated whites to replace a missing child.

The Miami were not very active in the mid-century Allegheny wars. Their process of prisoner adoption, as understood a lifetime later, varied somewhat from that of the other tribes. The warrior who led an expedition initially decided the fate of captives: those marked for adoption were painted red, and those chosen to die were painted black. On arrival in the Miami village, only those painted black apparently ran a gauntlet. A captive who survived the severe gauntlet reportedly still had no chance to escape, being then surrendered to the women of "the man eating society and is thereafter irrecoverable." Captives painted red were given to other tribes or Miami communities not in the war, but could also be kept as slaves of a chief, or could be fully adopted to replace a lost warrior.[71] The five mid-century Miami captives about whom anything is known would all suggest that such suitability was generously interpreted. Joshua Renick was a lad who grew up to become a prominent Miami leader. Mrs Jane Fraser was eight months pregnant when captured in 1755, was adopted into a leading Miami family to replace a warrior, and was treated well until her escape a year later. Two others taken at about the same time were adopted and prized for their work as tanners. John Slover, taken a few years later, may have been kept as a slave of a chief. His memoirs said nothing of his treatment, but he said that after six years with the Miami, he was sold to a Delaware, and that after being "put into the hands of a trader, I was carried amongst the Shawanese, with whom I continued six years."[72]

The Ojibwa, who used the word *awakân* for either a slave or a prisoner, were not adopting prisoners in or from Allegheny country during the Seven Years' War, and, when war came to their own country in 1763, the two captives who are known to have been adopted were incorporated very differently. Before this war, Ojibwa warrior Wawatam already regarded the suitably puzzled Michilimackinac trader Alexander Henry as his blood-brother, as the result of a dream. When Henry was taken captive by the Ojibwa, Wawatam claimed him as a relative, and protected him as a member of his immediate family for more than a year. Henry hunted with Wawatam, suspecting that "I could have enjoyed as much happiness in this, as in any other situation." It was only near the end of this period that, for safety's sake, Henry was shaved, painted, and dressed as an Ojibwa.[73]

Captivity was different for Lieutenant John Rutherfurd, taken on Lake St Clair on the first day of the siege of Detroit, and then taken home by his Ojibwa master, Peewash, without any ceremony. Peewash's aged father soon shaved, painted, re-dressed, and decorated the new captive. About a month later, Peewash conducted a ceremony at the grave of a dead son, whose spirit was to be appeased as Rutherfurd became his replacement. Rutherfurd had been led to believe that Ojibwa adoption would free him from the drudgery of assisting his new mother, but this was not the case. Because Peewash had "a particular regard for his wife, [he] chose that I should still assist her on many occasions," including what for the privileged officer was the humbling, hand-blistering pounding of corn. Nor did adoption ease Rutherfurd's fear of the spasmodic drunken killing of prisoners in and near Pontiac's camp, or preclude his sale to Monsieur Antoine Cuillerier. Rutherfurd had sought this sale/ransom, and had been surrendered, and Peewash had taken the £40 ransom in goods, before Pontiac intervened to veto the arrangement. In this reading of adoption, and at this stage in Ottawa-Ojibwa relations, Peewash was able to reclaim his new son and supposedly keep the goods that had been paid for him.[74] These two Ojibwa cases indicate both a range of captive experience and the limits on attempts to generalize about adoption.

It is difficult to estimate how many captives were adopted by Allegheny Indian communities between 1745 and 1765. Only twenty-seven surviving captivity accounts of any kind are reasonably clear on whether their subjects were adopted, and there may have been differing understandings or changing views about admitting such adoptions of military or civilian captives who subsequently attempted to re-enter colonial society, or about admitting the adoptions of those later celebrated in family memoirs and folklore. Nineteen of these twenty-seven captives are known to have been adopted promptly, and three were adopted after some delay.[75] If it is assumed that these few surviving records did not exaggerate the chances of adoption, there could have been as many as 1,500 adoptions among all those known to have been captured alive or those reported missing. Such adoptions would have numbered more than three times the 469 Allegheny Indians known to have been killed in battle with Europeans and Indians in this generation, though the number who died otherwise might have invited all of these adoptions. If, as is suspected, the Indian population of Ohio country continued to grow rapidly through this period, it was through immigration from the east by Indian refugees, through natural increase, and through the adoption of white captives. By 1765 the Ohio Indian communities contained more than 10,000 people, and perhaps 15 per cent of them were whites.[76] Although their distribution would have been very uneven, the adopted may have accounted for one-third of the population of some Allegheny Indian villages.

Adoption indicated both the breadth and narrowness of Indian perceptions of the alien and the family. In one sense, all who were not real or fictive kin were alien; Indians were not racist because many of their own "race" were seen as alien. While refusing sustained loyalty to broader "imagined communities," Allegheny Indians readily brought aliens into their families. Even a pious, pompous Christian minister, horrified at captives' preference for their new life as Indians, was impressed. William Smith wrote in 1764, "The perpetual slavery of those captivated in war, is a notion which even their barbarity has not suggested to them. Every captive whom their affection, their caprice, or whatever else, leads them to save, is soon incorporated with them, and fares alike with themselves."[77] Whatever captives had previously been told, adoption brought an abrupt shift from terror to acceptance that was part of the psychology of conversion. These adoptions came from Indian cultural restraints and requirements, but European colonials could seldom reach beyond their need to demonize the Indians, whom they were dispossessing, in order to acknowledge the Indian humanity that saved the lives of so many.

"White Indian" was a label that hid more than it revealed, and it may have been intended to do so. The term has been applied, belatedly and exclusively, to those who refused to be "redeemed" and lived the balance of their lives with the Indians. In the Allegheny borderlands of the mid-eighteenth century, 4 per cent of whites captured by Indians are known to have become white Indians, people who were at once puzzles for those who presumed the superiority of "Christianity and civilization" and prime exhibits for critics of white society. In a colonial society where differences of racial and familial lineage were increasingly thought decisive, and worth preserving, the white Indian was a particularly disturbing phenomenon. Nevertheless, missionary David Jones, amazed at just how Indian two Virginian sisters had become after growing up Shawnee, was encouraged to hope, "Might we not infer from hence, that if Indians were educated as we are, they would be like us?"[78]

The creation of white Indians only began with adoption, and was pursued immediately with thoroughgoing immersion. Prompt conformity in food, clothing, and shelter were unavoidable, and only the new clothes elicited much comment in subsequent narratives. The changed clothing, and the hair style of males, seemed the most notable change, even for those without mirrors. If clothing was a quick and obvious step to a new identity in Indian village life, it could also easily be reversed. To enforce immersion, captured families were usually deliberately scattered, talking to other European captives or visitors was censored, speaking European languages was forbidden, and attempted escape was punishable by death. Most adoptees had to learn a new language, a process that initially isolated and eventually integrated them.

Yet all was not alien for the captive. For all the colonials' pretensions about how entitled they were to confiscate the country from supposedly barbaric Indians, captives' accounts of their own lives in Ohio Indian communities are most remarkable for what was too familiar for comment. Once they joined Indian families, those who had lived on new subsistence farms on the east side of the Alleghenies began doing similar things on the west side of these mountains. For captive men, clearing new land for "settling" was hard but familiar work done more quickly and easily by using Delaware, and Scots-Irish, gird-and-burn methods than by using the thoroughgoing clearing common on small "German-style" farms of those suddenly immobile migrants who were busy fencing and excluding. There was every reason to appreciate the additional time Indian men spent hunting and fishing, though the long and sometimes desperate winter hunts on very short rations were trials worth recounting. Some of the famed "long-hunters" learned their skills in captivity. Tanners, smiths, and horse wranglers may have simplified their work because of fewer tools and equipment, but their work was valued and continued. Captive boys and youths likely had fewer chores in their new Delaware families, but were apprenticing as hunters and warriors, as they would have been in their natal families. When young Christopher Staffel was being sought among the Susquehanna Delaware, "he will not tell his Fathers name least he should be sent down to him and made to work like the white people." Quaker Nathaniel Holland, who "ransomed" this youth after nearly six years with the Delaware, confirmed this view when he reported being "afraid he is too slothful for much good."[79]

A second-hand remembrance of captive Thomas Armstrong shows how a thoroughly converted boy could still grow up curious about his origins. Captured in 1756, with his sister and mother, Thomas grew up Delaware and refused repatriation. However, he learned English, married an English captive, and inquired repeatedly into his origins. He eventually undertook the long journey to visit Elizabeth, his sister, who had been long since returned after only three years as a captive, "a gentle, sweet-faced woman, who eyed him with compassion" but did not recognize him. Elizabeth offered hospitality readily. Thomas was quiet throughout the hours he spent at her home, and chose not to identify himself. His later explanation, to a white man, was that he recognized how thoroughly Indian he was, how weak his English was, and how "every thing looked to him so grand and imposing in and around her dwelling." Overawed, he left without connecting with his only known blood relative.[80] Adam Brown, captured as an infant in Virginia in 1763, brought along his *métis* son and daughter when he visited his overjoyed mother after an absence of fifty years. Neither Adam nor his children could be induced to remain; he signed over his inheritance as eldest son to his younger brother Samuel, another former captive, and the three visitors returned home.[81]

When making explicit comparisons between their lives as Indians and their lives among the "civilized" to whom they returned, captives anxious to reintegrate still confessed that the Indians were scrupulous in the equality they afforded their adoptive kin, and that they were generous and persistent in their affections. Less frequently, returnees recorded their admiration for the simplicity and peace of the less-striving and more-accepting Indian way of life. A young man, captured and adopted years earlier by the Ohio Delaware but still remembering his Maryland family name, hesitated before deciding to return in 1772. He told missionary David McClure, "here, he says, I go and come as I please, and the King is my Uncle; (he was adopted into the Delaware 'royal family') but if I go among the white people they will make me a Slave." McClure was not alone in thinking that the "unknown charm" of Indian life included "uncontrouled liberty," "freedom from all anxiety and care for futurity," and "love of ease."[82]

The best candidates for complete conversion were children captured between the ages of three and six, who readily lost their native tongue and ways, and remembered little or nothing of their former lives to compare with their Indian families. George Brown, Joshua Renick, and William Ward, who later became famous Indian warriors and chiefs, were all captured at this age. At least one of every five children captured this young became white Indians. If this number seems low, it needs to be remembered that more than one-third of children captured at this age were with the Indians for less than two years. Nor do we know how free they were to stay or return. They were attached to the Indian family they had come to know, and then forcibly reclaimed in the name of a white parent they might have remembered only because of the tune of a lullaby. We do know that some returned youngsters who did not escape again were brought to Pittsburgh bound hand and foot, weeping, understandably convinced that they were being captured. Elizabeth Studebaker, taken at this age and having already lived almost all her life with the Delaware by 1764, was amongst those who promptly ran away to the only home they knew.[83]

Those captured between the ages of seven and fifteen could remember more of their names, families, neighborhoods, and birth languages but were still young enough to be made into white Indians, as were Fanny Barnett, Levy and Gershom Hicks, and Mary Jemison. Peter Weese, brought to the 1762 Lancaster conference after five years with the Seneca, was granted his wish: "Peter desired he might not now be detained among the White People, but left to his liberty to return to the Indians."[84] Fifteen-year-old Simon Girty Jr spent most of eight years with the Seneca before being returned against his will in November of 1764. Lewis Bingeman, captured at thirteen, became a prominent Shawnee warrior who, in 1768, led a party of thirty to avenge the peacetime murder of an Indian by a disreputable white hunter. Bingeman gained the white collusion that lured the murderer to hunt where he became the prey.[85] These youths could make comparisons between the two kinds of lives they had led to date and, in some cases, were old enough to decide which life they would lead. It is surprising that, in the admittedly unrepresentative group of 268 children in this age category, only 15 are known to have become white Indians, and that more than twice this many escaped. Although boys were twice as likely as girls to be captured, 10 of the 15 white Indians were girls. Admittedly, nearly half of this entire group were captured in Pontiac's War, and had less than two years to become Indians before the bullying "redemptions" of November 1764.

The lives of the Barnett sisters demonstrate extremes in the pace of adjustment for this age group. Fanny Barnett was a teen captured in 1756 along with her six-year-old sister, Susannah. Fanny promptly married a Shawnee and had five children within the next seven years. Susannah, who insisted on remembering her name and her infancy in Virginia, left the Shawnee after twelve years, promptly became a Baptist, married a white man, and settled near Pittsburgh.[86] Her prompt reconversion was regarded as miraculous.[87] In 1775, after nineteen years as a Shawnee, Fanny Barnett was finally "surrendered" as a family-tearing part of the peace settlement of 1774. She was the longest-held captive of the Seven Years' War in Allegheny country to be returned, and she stayed only a few days with her sister, "but not being reconciled to stay," she promptly returned to her Shawnee people.[88]

Captives taken beyond the age of sixteen were much less likely to become white Indians. Only twenty-three adults are definitely known to have been adopted, and eight of these chose to remain with their Indian captors.[89] Michael and Marie-Anne Shaw, and their young son, were captured in Virginian borderlands by a Kahnawake raiding party before these wars began. They seem to have been allowed to live in the same community, and all became permanent residents of Oka and then Two Mountains.[90] Soldiers Conrad Wagner and Thomas Robinson each stayed with their Indian captors, and were greatly outnumbered by the British and British colonial troops who were said to have deserted to the Indians. Captive Gower Sovereign was last reported as being with her four children in Lower Shawnee Town in 1764; all that is known of them thereafter is that her son Joseph was killed in a Shawnee hunting camp by American troops twenty-five years later.[91] Only one adult, an Irish farmer from Paxton named William Johnson, was thought to have converted so promptly, after being reported missing in the fall of 1757, that he was considered a traitor when taken by George Washington's patrol fourteen months later.[92]

Those who became white Indians sought to prove themselves in their new communities in various ways. Michel La Chauvignerie Jr, a young Canadian ensign who surrendered himself to the English in October 1757 after becoming lost near Fort Henry, Pennsylvania, was asked about French treatment of prisoners and gave a predictable and defensive response. He then went on to say,

> the Indians keep many of the Prisoners amongst them, chiefly young People whom they adopt and bring up in their own way, and says that those Prisoners whom the Indians keep with them become so well satisfied and pleased with the Way of Living that they don't care to leave them, and are often more brutish, boisterous in their Behaviour and loose in their Manners than the

> Indians, and thinks they affect that kind of Behaviour thro' Fear of and to recommend themselves to the Indians, and says the French who are mixed with the Indians seem also to behave in the like manner.[93]

Some converts sought to recommend themselves at the expense of other captives. One need not be fully converted to serve as a decoy who lured passersby on the Ohio River into death or captivity.[94] New captives might be drawn towards their converted countrymen, but these converts could be particularly abusive, and prone to discover real and fictitious escape plots by the new captives. One convert frankly admitted that other captives would not talk to him.[95]

Some white Indians grew up to become implacable enemies who fought against their former white families, proving to everyone that they were Indians. John Ward was only three when captured early in 1758, and he grew up to fight Virginian forces that included his birth father in 1774 and a brother in 1792, before John was mortally wounded the next year by Kentucky militia, including another of his brothers.[96] Child captives Joshua Renick of Virginia and George Brown of Pennsylvania both raided often and successfully enough for each to earn the status of Shawnee war chief.[97] Adam Brown grew up to become a notable Miami war chief who signed treaties with the United States government in 1805 and 1807.[98] Levy Hicks was a teen when captured in 1755 and, like his elder brother Gershom, was in raiding parties with the Delaware within a few years. Although they both "escaped" to Fort Pitt, Levy in 1762 and Gershom in 1764, they had become thoroughly Delaware. Narrowly escaping being hung as Indian spies or "rebels in arms," they were suspected for years.[99]

Spying and scouting near army posts were special tasks for which white Indians were well-suited and where they could either prove their conversion, or end it. British officers like Colonel Henry Bouquet were anxious to dub any white taken with the Indians as a spy, especially after the case of Gershom Hicks. James Bell was a teen when taken captive in Lancaster County in 1758, and he was a young Delaware brave when he "escaped" from his scouting party to enter Fort Pitt six years later.[100] He admitted he had intended to fight against the whites in 1763, but said he had been prevented by illness. Although he claimed to be with a war party stealing horses when he escaped to the British the next year, he was readily called a spy. On hearing of Bell's predicament, a former neighbor wrote a letter that touched on what he thought were the local markers of loyalty. Living near the farm from which James Bell was captured, the neighbor assured Colonel Henry Bouquet that "His father was killed at the same time & one of his unkels & his cussen a while before. I am well aquainted with many of his friends & knows them to be an Honest Cristen People. His brothers & cusens has been several times out with me I[n] pershute of the Indians & are well known to be loyal subjects to His Majesty."[101] None of this was very compelling evidence of James Bell's own loyalties. Young men who claimed they had escaped long Indian captivities in the course of the wars were feared as possible spies precisely because their conversion into white Indians was presumed.

The thorough transformation of male captives did not produce some uniform "white Indian," and the story of the Girty boys suggests a range of possibilities. Their father had been a popular trader with the Delaware from his home in Paxton, and his family grew up knowing the Delaware and their language. Four of his sons and their mother, Mary Girty-Turner, together with her infant son, John, and her second husband of two years, were all captured in the fall of Fort Granville in 1756. Three weeks after witnessing his stepfather's torture and death, eighteen-year-old Thomas Girty was retaken by the Pennsylvania forces that attacked Kittanning, but the other survivors in the Girty-Turner family, still in captivity, were then dispersed. Mary and her youngest were sent to one Shawnee town downriver, and twelve-year-old James was adopted into another. Fifteen-year-old Simon was sent north to be adopted by the western Seneca, and ten-year-old George was adopted by the Delaware. James, Simon, and George would all remain with the Indians for nearly eight years, and John Turner Jr was held for ten before these four white Indians were reluctantly returned in the major release of captives in 1764 and 1765.[102] Thomas, the eldest, had been held for only three weeks before rescue, despised Indians thereafter, and became a patriot in and after the American Revolution. Simon moved readily between white and Indian society and worked as a translator, messenger, and spy for the British, the patriots, and then the British once again. His famous defection to the British in 1778 was prompted in large part by his unfashionable sympathy for Indians, which had provoked numerous brawls. He went on to work for the British Department of Indian Affairs for the next forty years, as diplomat, spy, and soldier. Simon married former captive Catherine Malott in 1784, and they farmed near Fort Malden, Ontario. His younger brothers more decisively preferred life with the Indians, though both would work and fight alongside Simon during the American Revolution. James married a Shawnee and became a trader. George was assimilated fully into Delaware life, marrying and raising a family; he was the only brother who never returned, but all three "Indian Girtys" were recognized, and feared, as white Indians.[103]

Were Indian assumptions and requirements more alien and oppressive for white female captives than for males? Women on the German and Scots-Irish homesteads of Cumberland and Augusta Counties worked with their men in the fields, cooked, sewed, mended, tended children and animals, and also planted, harvested, and preserved garden crops. Young Mary Jemison seems to have been reasonably well prepared for her life as a Seneca woman, and was convinced that "their task is probably not harder than that of white women … and their cares are not half as numerous, nor as great."[104] Jane Fraser found her daily life among the Miami unremarkable. Mary Draper Ingles was apparently not adopted by the Shawnee, but was well treated during nearly seven months with them, and was busy making much-prized shirts. In her six years with the Shawnee, Hannah Dennis gained a reputation for the skills she used or developed as a wonderworker with herbal medicines and potions, though she still did what she called "squaw's work."[105] Although hauling meat and firewood, or making salt, seemed alien enough to be thought special burdens by captive women, the pounding of corn or wheat was the major daily task for all borderland women who had limited access to a grist mill.[106] "Squaw work" may have been a little harder, and seen by whites as more demeaning, but most of it was not alien, and some of it was lightened by the ways that it was shared.

Female captives became white Indians who seldom encountered white settlers, or their record keepers. Indian men were expected to act in "the woods" dealing with the outside world, whereas women dominated the domestic "clearing." We have only glimpses of some of them, who had lost their white names and identities. A Mohawk named Peter, "a sober sort of man" living near Pittsburgh in 1759, was "married in their way to a White woman I think taken from Virginia with whom he lives & it is not observable that she is much discontent."[107] Prominent Ohio Delaware Bisquittam "took a Dutch captive for his wife" in 1757.[108] Young Rhoda Boyd was seen once in Ohio country within a few years of her capture, and again as she and Elizabeth Studebaker escaped back to lives with the Delaware following their forcible return in 1764.[109] Captive Priscilla Ramsay, a "very handsome, good natured girl," married into a Seneca family, and then married a white man and lived with the Iroquois at Grand River, Upper Canada (Ontario).[110] Missionary David McClure, visiting the Ohio Delaware in 1772, described a Delaware woman named "Eliot" who had been captured as a child fourteen years earlier: "She appeared perfectly naturalized, and conformed to the Indian custom and dress. I saw her frequently at work with the squaws, pounding corn. She appeared to be a stout & healthy young woman. I believe she could not speak the english language, and knowing no condition other than savage life, probibly [*sic*] was as contented as her indian companions. It is not unlikely that the family were slain when she was taken, and no friends have appeared to reclaim her."[111] Female converts like Fanny Barnett or Mary Jemison lived as Indian villagers, marrying, raising families, and remembering their white names but usually escaping white inquirers.

Surviving evidence does not suggest that rape was part of the violence of these wars. The only reports of rape came from the imaginations of Peter Williamson and Robert Kirk, or were circulated in fevered colonial exhortations to more thoroughgoing resistance. The woodland Indian warrior ethic included sexual abstinence before and during campaigns in the belief that this ensured the highest military performance.[112] Rape was certainly not part of the fighting, either for captured white women or for Indian women, who were generally insulated from capture by whites. The complete silence about any subsequent sexual relations of captives outside marriage was predictable. Unprotected slaves, whether *panis*, Cherokee, or English, remained vulnerable to violation by their masters. Once adopted into Indian families, white women captives could join in the customs of serial monogamy, and there were some claims that Delaware communities required captives to do so.[113] Perhaps Mrs John Hudson, a Delaware in protective custody of the British garrison at Fort Bedford for more than a year, was never sexually abused. Perhaps two unadopted fifteen-year-old white captive girls, hired out by the Delaware to work in Fort Duquesne for two months, were neither sexually harassed nor molested. Although they preferred French food to that of the Delaware, they returned to the Delaware because they "could not, however, abide the French."[114] It is impossible to know whether rape of captives was nonexistent, as the records suggest, or merely unspeakable.

Four of Mary Moore's daughters provided varied and complicated tales of female adaptation. The Moores, farming on the Cinch River, Virginia, were attacked by a Shawnee war party in May of 1757, and Mary was captured, along with her seven children. She was released by the spring of 1763, and had heard something of Ann, her daughter by an earlier marriage, leading her to place a touching advertisement in the *Pennsylvania Gazette*:

> WHEREAS Ann Mullen, Daughter to the Subscriber, was taken Prisoner by the Shawanese Indians, from the Cow Pasture, Augusta County, in Virginia, six Years since, this Summer——About four Years ago, she, with one Lany Pussey, made their Escape from the Lower Shawanese Towns, and were afterwards taken by the Onandagoes, with whom they remained eleven Months, when they ran away from them, the said Ann Mullen about six Weeks before the said Lany Pussey, and were together in the Jerseys, about Rariton, where some Relations of the latter live. Ann Mullen is about 21 Years of Age, of a low Stature, dark Complexion, and brown Hair; her Mother is now at Fort Pitt, lately released by the Shawanese, waiting for her Children that are among them, to be brought in. Whoever can give Information of the said Ann Mullen, whether dead or alive, and will send a few Lines, directed to Mr. Josiah Davenport, at Philadelphia, or Fort Pitt, it will be taken extremely kind by her sorrowful Mother, who, out of seven Children taken, has not yet been able to receive one.
> MARY MOORE

We hear no more of Ann or of another sister who was last reported in Lower Shawnee Town after many other captives had been returned in 1764.

Two other Moore sisters have left more evidence of the power and limits of their thorough Shawnee conversion. Margaret was about nine when captured and grew up Shawnee.[115] She married Sepettekenathe (Blue Jacket), a warrior, chief, diplomat, and trader, with whom she had a son she called Joseph. Margaret was about eighteen, and pregnant again, when Sepettekenathe agreed that she visit her Virginian relations. She found her mother and was persuaded to stay well beyond the birth of her second child, Nancy. The family remembrance was that Margaret did not return to Ohio country until thirty-seven years later, when she accompanied her daughter Nancy and her Virginian son-in-law as they settled in a white farming community on the Miami River. Nancy supposedly saw her father for the first time shortly before he died in 1804, and her brother Joseph visited once before joining the British in the War of 1812. Nancy and her brother Joseph were both accepted as half-bloods by the Wapakoneta Shawnee chiefs, and each was given 640 acres of treaty lands in 1810. Margaret lived there with her daughter and son-in-law, plus four grandchildren, and the family was described a decade later as "very industrious, honest and well behaved," though troubled by Indian relations who were "living on them for weeks at a time, consuming in idleness their subsistence." Margaret, Nancy, and her husband all became active members of the Muddy Run Meeting House, a Christian church on the Mad River, where they were all eventually buried.[116]

Margaret's story included pieces her daughter did not record. Although Margaret's parting from Sepettekenathe was said to have been amicable, and son Joseph supposedly stayed with his father to encourage Margaret's return, it is very likely that the separation was intended to be permanent. Nancy would recall that her mother "dearly loved" Sepettekenathe, and never remarried. Sepettekenathe, however, promptly took another wife, the Shawnee-French daughter of prominent Canadian trader Jacques Dupéront Baby,[117] and the first of their four children was born within two years. Margaret's return to Ohio country was supposedly postponed by the wars of 1774 and 1776–95, and it was mere coincidence that she finally came back the year Sepettekenathe died. However, Nancy left no account of what should have been a memorable first meeting with her father, though she recalled details of her single visit with her brother, Joseph.

There is another loose-fitting piece to the Margaret Moore story. Thirty-one years before, in 1773, missionary David Jones visited the home of Shawnee trader Richard Connor, on the Muskingum River. At this time, when Sepettekenathe was a war chief in the area, Jones met Margaret and her sister, Peggy, and reported that Connor and a chief of the nearby town of Wakitomica had married two white sisters who had been taken captive as children: "they have the very actions of Indians, and speak broken English. It seems strange to me to see the captives have the exact gestures of Indians." After five years back in Virginia, Margaret Moore had been seen in Shawnee country near Sepettekenathe's town. We do not know how or why she was on the Muskingum in 1773, but this 800-mile trip suggests that she was very ambiguous about being a Virginian.

Here, in 1773, we meet Margaret's equally intriguing sister, Peggy, who grew up Shawnee. By one version of her story, she had been bought by white trader Richard Connor, on condition they stay with the tribe and have their first son raised as a Shawnee.[118] A year after

Jones's visit, Virginia militia burned Wakitomica as part of Dunmore's War, which ended in August 1774. The Shawnee formally "returned" Peggy and her husband to Pittsburgh as part of the imposed peace, but kept their young son. Within a few months, the couple was back on the Muskingum. Richard left Peggy with the Moravian Delaware at nearby Schonbrun before going on what proved a futile first mission to recover their son. Meanwhile, Peggy was very well received amongst the Moravians, and did not want to leave. Missionary David Zeisberger noted her comment about her previous winter, spent in Pittsburgh: "she did not like it at all there. She cannot fit in with the White people, especially people like those in the Fort, and she does not want to live among the savage Indians any more."[119] Although whites were not usually accepted into Moravian mission communities, Richard and Peggy were allowed to stay, and they ransomed their four year old. In the summer of 1777, while the Delaware and the Moravians were still neutrals in the Revolutionary War, a party of Mingo and Shawnee warriors, including Peggy's nephew Joseph, now a war captain, brought white captives through the new Moravian settlement of Lichtenau. Joseph was soon back, with a group of other relations, to retrieve Peggy, "because times were so dangerous now and he feared he would some day see his sister taken as a prisoner, which he would not like." Convinced that she was happy where she was, Joseph relented and vowed to warn warriors not to molest his sister's settlement. Richard and Peggy stayed with the Moravians, and the last two of her four sons were baptized there in 1777 and 1780.[120] Peggy Connors had found a place with the Christian Delaware, neither quite as white as sister Margaret, nor quite as Shawnee as nephew Joseph.

The Delaware Moravian communities might have provided a suitable compromise for a number of female captives who had become very acculturated, but only one other captive convert has been identified. Rachel Abbott and her infant child were captured by a Delaware war party in April of 1757 near the mouth of Conococheague Creek in Maryland, and her child was soon killed. Nineteen years later she was the wife of prominent Delaware chief Welapachtschiechen (Captain Johnny) of the Turtle phratry, and the mother of three of his children. She attended a Moravian service at Lichtenau, on the Muskingum, in the fall of 1776, and was apparently moved to say, "Oh, how happy I am that I am finally here and have heard God's word for the first time in 19 years ... I have often longed to come to you and live with you, and now God has granted my desire. I also woke up happier this morning than I can ever remember." After some hesitation and deliberation with fellow Delaware leaders, who were trying to preserve their neutrality in the new war between whites, Welapachtschiechen decided to live with the Moravians, convert, and take the name Isaac. Rachel and Isaac had a Christian marriage ceremony, as did their adult children after baptism. Their progeny, including an Isaac and a Rachel, grew up in the Moravian community, which also came to include Welapachtschiechen's sister, two cousins, and two grand-daughters. The Moravians may have served as a refuge as war came again to Ohio country, and for Rachel Abbott they provided the best of the two worlds she had come to know.[121]

As the Girtys, Moores, and Barnetts illustrate, acculturation was seldom a complete and permanent accomplishment, even for the minority of captives who never returned to the white part of this complex borderland. Becoming a white Indian often resulted in very hard choices or very cruel fates, especially as the white authorities became more determined to "redeem" every drop of white blood. However, varying levels of adaptation permanently affected almost all captives held for any length of time, and people reinvented themselves in a variety of ways. Some remained physically stalled between the cultures, like the unnamed hunter encountered by Felix Renick in a 1798 trip to the Muskingum. Renick's own family had included white Indians and at least one woman who chose to live on the edge of a remote Indian village, but this hunter seemed a sadder case that elicited Renick's sympathy. He was a former captive who had decided to live thirty miles away from his nearest neighbor, in a bark hut, "solitary and alone" except for his dog. "He raised a small patch of corn, potatoes, etc. without any fence, there being no animals to trespass on his premises but wild ones, and those that did so generally paid the penalty with their lives."[122] Others lived as hunters, traders, or near-neighbors to the Indian communities that were once their homes. Felix Renick also described a thinner layer of obvious acculturation that took years to suppress. His mother-in-law fought to "break those wild Indian boys" returned from captivity, including six children of her See (Sea) family who were returned in 1764. It "was utterly impossible, she said, to keep clothes on them; in the summer season she did not attempt it, as it was worse than useless to do so ... It took a number of years to root out this attachment [to Indian ways], and indeed it was thought by a part of their friends that some of the boys carried remnants of it to their graves."[123] Many of these returnees left Indian communities with skills, characteristics, habits, memories, and loyalties that were fruits of very effective Indian indoctrination.

The creation of white Indians was more difficult on the Allegheny frontier than might have been expected from the methods, from the circumstances, and from white folk memories. Acculturation was launched by the severe shock attending the destruction of family, by isolation from familiar captives, and by full adoption, which could be expected to succeed, especially with the young. The "endless mountains" between what, for a time, became the Indian and the white regions of this borderland, and the distance to New France should have encouraged a captive's reconciliation to life as an adopted Indian. Yet only 1 in 26 of the more than 1,700 captives taken by Indians in the Allegheny-Ohio borderlands between 1745 and 1765 are known to have become thoroughly and permanently "white Indians." Although the numbers seem low, and are far from reliable, it appears that more captives became white Indians in the Allegheny borderland in the middle of the eighteenth century than was the case with colonial New England captives, and especially with those New Englanders taken in the middle of the eighteenth century.[124] The cultural self-criticism of some white intruders, and an awareness that captivity transformed many who eventually left their adoptive Indian homes, helped create the fears and myths about the power of Indian culture.

The Indians of the upper Ohio region completely absorbed more captives than did the Canadians or Indians of New France during the same period. Although at least 168 Allegheny captives spent time in New France during this generation, many were soldiers held only until exchange, and no more than four Allegheny captives are known to have become Canadians.[125] This contrasts sharply with the fact that nearly half of the New England captives taken between 1675 and 1763 eventually stayed in New France. After 1745, Catholic New France was making little effort to convert Protestant captives from either New England or Allegheny country. Captives in New France were also being sustained in body and cultural identity by networks around the very generous and well-connected Colonel Peter Schuyler and influential former captives, including New England girls who had become Canadian nuns.[126]

There is another comparison that might help in evaluating the rate of transformation into white Indians, namely the fate of Indian, *métis*, and white youngsters captured by white society in the process of reclaiming their own. Most seem to have disappeared. Mrs Hannah Smith brought her two-year-old *métis* son with her when she returned to her husband in

Virginia after six years as a captive. Mr Smith welcomed his wife back but despised the boy, as did others. "The boy grew up to manhood, and exhibited the appearance and disposition of his sire. Attempts were made to educate him, but without success. He enlisted into the army of the Revolution, and never returned."[127]

Evidence of the success of Indian acculturation should include the habits and values that remained with many of those who were ostensibly redeemed. The unusually strenuous efforts of white authorities to recover captives in 1764 undoubtedly terminated the transformation of hundreds of potential white Indians. These partially acculturated people returned with Indian skills, habits, attitudes, and kin. They had seen some elements of white society amongst those of their captors who spoke English well, people who argued about religion, needed gunpowder, liked shirts and baked white bread, and came to value horses and cows, about which the captives knew more. These former captives joined the white Indians, inadvertently or deliberately, as agents of the relentless white invasion. The Indians of this generation had created many potential brokers between themselves and colonial British America, but could keep or reclaim fewer of them than did the white society, which was thereby better equipped to continue its invasion of Indian country.

11

Escaped

Too many escaped from captivity in Allegheny country to support exaggerated claims about the allures of becoming a white Indian, and too few escaped to indicate compelling cultural loyalty. Some captives knew that their previous life had just been completely destroyed. A Mrs Green, captured near Fort Dinwiddie in 1764 and retaken the same day, was asked why she had not resisted captivity. She replied, "I would as soon die as not; my husband is murdered, my children slain, my parents are dead; I have not a relative in America, everything dear to me is gone. I have no wishes, no hopes, no fears. I would not rise to my feet to save my life."[1] Other captives were too young to remember much of their previous life, and became dependents, accepting acculturation to Indian life or a new life in New France or British America. Of course, there were also severe deterrents to attempting escape from any of the region's captors. An escapee from a fort risked being killed in the attempt or falling victim to vengeful locals and scalp hunters, and escape could inflict further restrictions on all the prisoners still held. European armies regarded attempts at escape as brave games to test wits, and the likes of Captain Robert Stobo could be retaken twice without serious consequences. However, Indian captors made it very clear, by threat and occasional example, that an unsuccessful escape was punishable by death. James Bell claimed that his Seneca captors killed one captive who attempted to escape and another for expressing the wish to return to the white people.[2] Virginian soldier William Shaw claimed that his toes were cut off to prevent his escape, a parallel to the maiming some Virginians inflicted on runaway slaves after recapture.[3] Escapees were also in serious danger of becoming lost and starving or freezing to death in entirely unfamiliar territory, dangers that were greater for those taken the farthest, for children, and for alien soldiers or new immigrants. A further misfortune befell two young women who escaped from Shawnee only to be captured by Onondaga and held for eleven more months before they escaped together again, more permanently.[4]

Hugh Gibson was the only one who publicly admitted that he had become fainthearted while escaping and had returned to his captors, but he is unlikely to have been the only one who did so.

Most captives whose fate is known neither became white Indians nor escaped, but were returned by negotiation. Yet it is significant that more captives are known to have escaped than to have converted to their captors' societies, in part because record keepers had a purpose in celebrating escapees and ignoring those who clearly refused to return. The wish to recover a familiar way of life, lived in one's own language, needs no explanation. Escape, particularly in the first months of captivity, should have appealed to most of those still very uncomfortable in new identities. Captives of Indians were soon "held" unshackled in relatively open communities that lived by constantly moving to gather resources from nearby forests and by undertaking longer seasonal journeys to hunt, fish, gather, or trade. The dynamics of escape from captivity can best be examined by considering, in turn, who escaped and how, the length of their captivity, and where they were being held.

A total of 225 Allegheny captives are known to have escaped between 1745 and 1765, less than one in seven of those captured but three times as many as are known to have become white Indians. Almost all escapees were adults, and four of five were male. This can be read as evidence that females had less commitment to white society, but those numbers lose most of their significance when it is remembered that male captives outnumbered female by three to one. More interesting, boys between ages seven and fifteen were three times more likely to escape than were girls of this age.[5] This may reveal more about gender training in white colonial society than about gendered prospects in Indian society, and these numbers certainly challenge the repeated claims that Indian life seemed much more attractive to boy captives than to their sisters.

It might be assumed that the freedoms of Indian society were especially attractive to those captives who had been dependent in British colonial society, making them less likely to seek escape. Very few captives were identified as indentured servants, and the statistics on their fate are inconclusive. Nonetheless, of the eight whose fate is known, six escaped.[6] The differences between the lives and prospects of indentured servants and slaves are suggested by the frequency of escape from Indian captivity. At least twelve black slaves were captured by Indians, and the only one who escaped back to colonial slavery was very poorly rewarded; the attack in which he was captured had impoverished his uncaptured Virginian master, who promptly sold this dutiful slave on his return.[7] Most black slaves did not fear new Indian masters enough to prompt them to take risks to return to old European ones.

Of all captives taken in Allegheny country, Indians were by far the most likely to escape. Regarding captivity as both degrading and noxious, Indian captives took high risks and made extraordinary efforts to escape. Keeping Indian captives was taxing and dangerous, and was usually attempted only by the British military, who imposed closer control than did other captors. The only Indian captives known to have stayed with other captors were five Indian slaves captured, along with their English masters, by Ojibwa in 1763.[8] Nearly half of Indian captives mentioned in records escaped, and half of these escaped within six months. The longest known captivities of Indians who eventually escaped were the eight months a Piankashaw was held at Fort Chartres in 1752 and the nearly two years that twelve Cherokee were held captive by the Iroquois of Kahnawake.[9] The fourteen Delaware, Shawnee, and Mingo hostages held in Fort Pitt late in 1764 were a special category of captive. They were allowed some freedoms, including the liberty to hunt, and it is not surprising that eleven of them escaped within a season. Captured Indians did not become red Europeans; instead, they escaped in such numbers as to demonstrate an intense aversion to close confinement, and a strong attachment to their communities.

Among non-Indian captives, traders and soldiers were the most likely to escape. Although the records are particularly deficient concerning captured traders, one-third of whom remained "missing," nearly another one-third are known to have escaped. They had advantages over other captives. They were much more likely to know the language of their captors, have customers, friends, and lovers among them, and know something of the country through which they were attempting to escape. Most traders who escaped did so within three months of their capture. They were effectively joining all their fellow traders who were fleeing as war began. Most lost their trade goods, all had no immediate prospects of trading, and few of the survivors would re-enter this business after the war ended.[10]

Escaping soldiers lacked all three of the traders' advantages and had usually been captive longer, but they were just as likely to escape.[11] Eleven of the forty-seven soldiers who escaped had been held by French or Canadian captors, and the other thirty-six had been captives of Indians. Regular armies eventually paid soldiers for their time as captives, though soldiers were not usually promoted while captive. The captive soldier's conventional duty was to attempt escape and thus to distract the enemy. Captain Robert Stobo's escape from Quebec was celebrated, and Virginia's reward for him was soon extended to full pay for all Virginian soldiers during their captivity with either the French or the Indians. A soldier of the Virginia Regiment was eventually believed, and compensated, after reporting that he had escaped from fifteen months of Indian captivity only to fall ill on his way home and thus be unable to rejoin his regiment before it was disbanded.[12] Soldiers often escaped in pairs; fear of being betrayed to one's captors by a disloyal co-conspirator was weaker than the need for a witness to support one's claim to have been a prisoner, who was entitled to back pay and a new uniform and equipment, rather than a deserter, who forfeited all his pay and faced court martial and possible execution. Soldiers were also understandably cautious, even evasive, under examination. Other soldiers encountered during captivity are not usually named in depositions, for deserters were hard to distinguish from soldier-captives and any association with a suspected deserter was dangerous. Soldiers had the familiar, if hard, life of the regiment awaiting them on return, and perhaps an opportunity for some revenge, unlike the broken trader, the widowed spouse, or the orphaned child captive.

Although more white settlers escaped than did Indians, traders, or soldiers, fewer than one in five captured settlers escaped. Most settlers who were reported as escaping had been captive longer than other escapees, and six white settlers reportedly "escaped" after more than five years in captivity.[13] Male white settlers and their sons were twice as likely to escape as were their wives, mothers, or sisters. However, captive adult male settlers were somewhat less likely to escape than were traders and soldiers, who, in turn, were less likely to escape than were Indian captives, the majority of whom were also adult males.[14]

Captives' decisions, to reject or accept life with their captors, were better informed the longer they were held. More than one-quarter of escapees whose length of captivity is known were free within a week, reacting to the horrors they had just seen rather than knowledge of the life awaiting them as captives. Half the adult captives who escaped did so within six months, before most had full command of their captors' language or had seen more than half of the annual cycle of Indian life. Some adult captives held for a year, like Ensign Thomas Gist or trader Alexander Henry, expressed regret as they chose to escape the Indian way of life they had come to appreciate; only one of five escapees had been captive this long. Of fifty adult captives held for more than five years, only seven were said to have escaped the Indian communities they had come to know quite well.[15] The success of Indian acculturation can be appreciated by remembering that, of 242 captives still living with the Indians after five years, only 7 "escaped."

Opportunities to escape varied widely, and were not always related to levels of surveillance. Indian captives were held in garrisoned forts, if not in cells, yet were the most likely to escape; whites held by garrisons seldom escaped and were likely to do so in transit between posts. Soldiers held in and near Pontiac's camp were willing to run through a gauntlet of besiegers to gain refuge in nearby Fort Detroit. Captured white settlers were given to escaping in the first week on the trail when surveillance was closest. Hugh McSwain, too quickly assigned to oversee the horses taken in the same raid as himself, killed the two Delaware also given this task. On the trail into captivity white settlers escaped visual surveillance when sent to bring water or gather wood, and later escapes included those by prisoners sent out from the villages to assist hunters, make salt, gather herbs, or carry messages.[16] Four captives of the Delaware were able to plan and carry out their escape readily after pretending to be sick, at which time they were isolated from the many watchful eyes in the village.[17]

As older male captives became acculturated, their opportunities to travel increased. Mary Ingles reported that the Shawnee "suffered some Men to go out a Hunting, and let them have three Charges of Ammunition, but would allow them no more, for fear of their returning back to the English."[18] Making war against whites was a proof of white Indians' new loyalty that could occasionally be turned into an opportunity to escape, with the likelihood of their being suspected of spying for the Indians.[19] Two captives were included in Indian parties trading at British forts when they decided to stay and "escape."[20] Three Pennsylvania soldiers held captive at Logstown had another less fortunate prisoner to thank for their escape: "the Indians having sold a Prisoner to the French, receiv'd a Nine Gallon Cagg of Brandy; This deponent and George Hiley, another Prisoner, thought that wou'd be a good Time for them to escape, as it was customary for the Indians on such Occasions, to make a Frolick and get drunk."[21] Opportunities like this one were rare, but the rhythms of Indian village life brought increasing opportunities for those who remained determined to escape.

Where captives were held made an immense difference to their prospects for successful escape. Escape on the trail into captivity, as has been seen, involved a relatively short journey through country just seen, if not already familiar, with some prospect of encountering rescuers along the way and with little difficulty being recognized on return. Escaping the two miles from Pontiac's camp into Fort Detroit, or from the European frontier forts, was very different from escaping from the North Branch Delaware above Tioga or from Indian villages in Ohio country. The difference between escapes from Allegheny River sites like Kittanning and escapes from the villages on the Scioto or Wabash Rivers was a distance of more than 350 additional miles and required about three weeks of travel. The major forts that linked Fort Duquesne to the Quebec citadel until 1760, and became British posts thereafter, were not built expressly to hold or rescue captives, but came to do both. English and Indian captives from the *pays d'en haut* were taken from fort to fort on their way to imprisonment in Quebec or in France. After capture or rebuilding by the British, these sites were still prisons for Indian captives and hostages, but they now became landmarks and places of refuge and sustenance for those still escaping from captivity among the Indians.

From its creation, Fort Duquesne held captured traders and hostage soldiers to be sent on to Montreal and Quebec. Mixed forces of French and Indians returned there to apportion their human booty, with the French usually showing less interest in captives than the victims hoped. It was a major way-station for those going into Indian or French captivity. Whatever the defensive weaknesses of the fort, none of the more than 138 captives who passed through Fort Duquesne escaped from within it. Although a refuge for some British deserters, and even for some Acadians escaping through the wilderness from their special kind of captivity, Fort Duquesne was not the objective of many escaping captives.[22] After British Fort Pitt rose from the ashes of Fort Duquesne, it became the principal destination for European traders, soldiers, and settlers escaping Ohio Indian or French captivity. Its place at the forks of the Ohio River made it an obvious destination by water from three directions, and this bustling center of trade, war, and diplomacy had already created a network of footpaths and horse trails. This sprawling fort was not particularly secure, as at least twenty Indian captives and hostages escaped from there.

Detroit had long been the nearest center for French initiatives in the upper Ohio Valley and became the base at which captured British traders were secured. During the Seven Years' War, captives were not held in Fort Detroit for any length of time, and those few who were said to have escaped from Detroit actually escaped from the Indian villages in the vicinity. Those escaping from the Detroit area were undertaking a very long journey. Two men taken in multitribal raids on the Virginia frontier in the spring of 1758 stayed in a Wyandot village near Detroit for six months, and escaped only after being sent back across Lake Erie; even so, they still had a twenty-three-day trek to Fort Pitt.[23]

Ensign Thomas Gist, taken by Wyandot in 1758, was very well cared for within sight of Detroit for a year, and acknowledged his good treatment and his ingratitude on deciding to escape. As recounted later in a detailed "journal," his escape became possible once he heard that the British had captured Fort Niagara in July of 1759, giving him a specific reachable objective. Although his Huron was not fluent, he learned what he could from an old Huron about the challenging route along the north shore of Lake Erie. Upon resolving to escape, Gist first sought a companion, and, instead of a fellow soldier, he chose a young Virginian settler, John McCrary, "who I knew to be a lad I could depend on." They were both acculturated enough to seek ammunition and moccasin leather, rather than provisions, but ammunition was difficult to get in quantity. They approached a fellow captive, an "old Dutchman" who had gathered some ammunition and gunpowder as part of another group's preparation for escape. Fearing discovery as more people learned of his plans, Gist wisely became vague and shared less information. McCrary pressed for inclusion of his thirteen-year-old brother and fellow captive, and Gist reluctantly agreed on condition that the boy would be told only on the night before they left, and would be abandoned in the woods if he could not keep up. With a gun, some ammunition stolen from his Indian family, and at least one tomahawk and a bow and arrows, Gist set off as if merely hunting. Escape itself, for Gist or the McCrarys, had not been a serious problem, nor was there any known pursuit. The weeks of travel, through swamps along a shoreline that included misleading peninsulas like Long Point, was the most severe aspect of their escape. The three were several times reduced to living on grapes or tasting rotted carrion, though they killed one buck, several raccoons, a turkey, and an owl along the way. The three escapees finally reached Fort Niagara in twenty-four difficult days.[24]

After Detroit became a British fort, it had a unique, significant, and very different role for captives during Pontiac's War. The siege was itself rather new for Indian participants, as was Pontiac's need to hold captives with, or near, an Indian army that was initially within cannon range of a captive's place of refuge. Captives might be needed in negotiation, so closer confinement than usual was necessary, and terror was invited, if not required, to deter or punish escapees. Acculturation was hardly possible here, though only three escaped within the first week of their capture. For captive traders and soldiers, the escape itself was the desperate challenge, for there was no need to learn about elaborate routes to safety, to conspire with other captives, or to accumulate food, ammunition, or moccasin leather.[25] The French inhabitants around the fort, most treading carefully between their unwelcome new British overlords and their angry Indian acquaintances, might help captives by buying or hiring them to work nearer to the fort or, alternatively, might report such schemes to Pontiac. Ensign John Rutherfurd, though adopted by his Ojibwa captor and well treated, soon proposed his own purchase by his acquaintance Antoine Cuillerier, living and trading close to the fort. The successful negotiations, through an intermediary, gave Rutherfurd only one day of relative comfort before the Ottawa angrily confiscated him, fearing that such ransoming was becoming endemic. Returned to the Ojibwa, Rutherfurd soon enlisted another Frenchman who, for a price, paddled him past Pontiac's camp at night to the safety of a British ship anchored at the fort.[26] More than one-third of all captives who escaped anywhere during Pontiac's War came in to Detroit.[27]

Fort Niagara, in the early 1750s, offered Allegheny country captives being transported to French Canada their last opportunity for relatively easy escape. Two captured traders escaped from a ship just out of Niagara in 1750, making their way to nearby Fort Oswego.[28] Three years later, the much-traveled Nova Scotian captive Stephen Coffen could hardly have asked for a more convenient opportunity to escape. A tired crew of Canadian rowers who had spent a hard night paddling a bateau out of Fort Niagara, put ashore for breakfast within a mile of Fort Oswego, allowing Coffen and a French deserter to escape easily. French conquest of Oswego in August 1756 drastically altered the local landscape for English captives seeking to escape. A few weeks later a Scots immigrant, captured at Great Cove, was doing farm labor along with three other captives when they were able to escape in a canoe from near Fort Niagara. They paddled across the Niagara River and set off through the woods, starving, eating carrion, quarrelling, and dividing into pairs of disoriented and weakened wanderers. One pair managed to reach a white settlement in about two weeks, and a rescue party located the other two.[29] The next summer two more captives escaped near Fort Niagara and traveled a grueling 200 miles, through "bad, and mostly drowned" land, to the site of obliterated Oswego. From there, they proceeded up the abandoned, but traceable, British communication route up along the Oswego River to the Mohawk River, where Iroquois "gave them Victuals, of which they were in great Want," and saw them on their way to Albany.[30] Although no one escaped from Fort Niagara itself, escape from its vicinity had been easy before 1756, and was grueling to mid-1759, after which this fort became the objective of a long journey to freedom by Thomas Gist and the McCrary brothers.

Captives escaping by water down the North Branch of the Susquehanna River needed no compass, for they would eventually arrive at Fort Augusta, Pennsylvania's major fort located at the river's forks. As Teedyuscung's community went to war late in 1755, they migrated upriver from Wyoming to start a new settlement about twenty-five miles above Tioga. With the river as guide and conveyance, an escapee from there might hope to paddle to Fort Augusta in four or five days. Yet such escapes were rare. John Coxe had the easiest escape along part of this route. His master had brought him far downriver to collect some stored grain for the hungry new settlement, and then left Coxe unguarded while out hunting. Although malnourished and sick, Coxe was able to paddle his master's canoe downriver to Fort Augusta and freedom in a single day.[31] Coxe's escape by canoe was simpler than the only other successful one, undertaken a month later. Captives David McMullen and Thomas Moffit were bought by Catherine Montour, something of a trader in captives and daughter of noted borderland broker "French Margaret." While Catherine was away negotiating with Sir William Johnson about the ransom of another captive, McMullen and Moffit escaped. The pair were in the woods for three days before reaching the North Branch, stealing a canoe, and paddling for ten days that must have been primarily cautious night travel. Their depositions said nothing of how they fed themselves on the trip.[32] Catherine, making this same trip from Tioga to Fort Augusta herself two years later, voiced a broker's lament about these two escaped captives. She staved off the Friendly Society agent's entreaties about recovering captives by showing him her receipts for "Sundries given for some Men Prisoners which she bought to work for her as she could not plant corn herself. Who ran away from her & because she got Nothing for her Loss in them, she think[s] herself much injured. & said, shall I sell for others, & can get nothing for myself."[33]

Escape overland from the Tioga vicinity to Northampton County's outposts was much more difficult than escape by water. Desperate from hunger and cold, John Howell convinced Isaac Hollister to join him in an escape that proved disastrous in March of 1764. The conspirators each cached forty ears of corn and six small corn cakes, and then used their daily chore of wood gathering to cover their flight. This proved to be a false spring, and the weather soon turned severe. Without adequate footwear, they soon froze their feet; without adequate clothes, they had to make a fire each night, and even occasionally during the day. They risked discovery each time, but presumably they were not being pursued. According to Hollister, Howell was increasingly reluctant to continue, and their food ran out. They lived on tree bark for ten days, and their journeying had ceased by then. Before he died of starvation and exposure, Howell supposedly urged Hollister to be willing to eat his flesh to survive. Hollister provisioned himself with meat from his dead companion, and set off again. Four days later, and at least three weeks after his escape, Hollister was recaptured near an Indian town on the river. He was returned to his angry Delaware master, who had him run naked through a gauntlet that nearly killed him.[34] Hollister had been a captive for six months, and evidently had not learned enough during this time to escape successfully.

George Ebert and Samuel Miller had been captive in the same region only a few days when they escaped, but they had better fortune. Taken in May 1757, they soon escaped from their Delaware captors' settlement, a day's journey north of Tioga. Near Tioga, they were given shelter by French Margaret herself, who fed and hid them from their pursuers for four weeks before she urged the pair to proceed. They paddled down the North Branch for three days to Wyoming, were well received by the Indians they encountered, and were given directions to Fort Allen from there. The pair became lost in the woods, but arrived safely at Fort Hamilton six weeks after their capture, rightly expressing their gratitude to French Margaret.[35]

The most intriguing escape on the North Branch was that of sixteen-year-old Sally Wilkins, who had been a captive for six and a half years, and had become a white Indian who nevertheless decided to "escape." Late in 1763 her Delaware community had heard of the Paxton massacre of Conestoga Indians, at which news the Delaware women wailed and pulled their hair, the men vowed revenge, and all "began to be very cross to the Prisoners." At the time of her escape, the community was also very agitated and concerned about the "disappearance" of Captain Bull and his party at the end of February 1764. Sally waited longer for spring than the impatient Howell and Hollister, who probably understood less than she about Delaware language and politics. She waited until May, when, together with another captured young woman and her brother, Sally stole some "green powder" and fled. She reported that the powder consisted of ground corn, dried herbs and roots, and salt, and she said that a spoonful provided a day's sustenance, though it made one very thirsty. Eating only the powder and some roots, the three ran at night and hid during the day for the three weeks it took to reach her Northampton refuge, where she reportedly "looks very well."[36] What Sally knew of Delaware food and travel in the region made for a clean escape that averaged eight miles a night, needed no fires, involved no hunting, trusted no one, and kept the escapees out of sight in the daytime.

Only nine of the ninety-nine Northampton County captives held near Tioga escaped, though they were held less than 150 miles from Fort Allen, were invited to escape by the river, and suffered from harsher circumstances than most. The water route could be traveled safely only at night, or with whatever blessing or good fortune French Margaret could bestow. The overland route was slower, especially in harsh weather, and provisions were a major concern. No escapees reported hunting, which would risk discovery, and the safest food source was the "green powder," about which only a white Indian like Sally Wilkins was likely to be knowledgeable.

Escape from west of the Allegheny Mountains was inherently a more strenuous ordeal. The Iroquois rightly called the country west of the Susquehanna "Tyannuntasacta," meaning "the endless mountains."[37] A determined crow might have flown only 85 miles to reach Fort Cumberland from Fort Duquesne, or 150 miles to reach Carlisle, but the route for humans was much longer. The Appalachians crumpled into as many as six mountain ranges, creating broken country of heavily wooded slopes, fast streams, and swampy bottoms. Indians had developed more than a dozen major paths for trading and raiding through this rather barren waste where the hunting was hard and corn lands were rare. By the 1740s, Pennsylvania traders were using packhorses to negotiate two of these Indian trails: the Kittanning-Frankstown-Juniata route and the "Raystown path" from Shippensburg to the forks of the Ohio. The favored path from these forks south to Fort Cumberland on the Potomac River was still named after the Delaware chief Nemacolin. In 1755 Nemacolin's Path became Braddock's Road, and the Raystown path was "improved" somewhat that year as well.[38] All the Indian paths became warpaths between 1755 and 1758, and a captive escaping from Ohio country had to be well informed or fortunate to find and follow anything other than General Edward Braddock's overexposed road through the mountains.

One early escapee from Kittanning was well acquainted with the trail home, and his journey was relatively quick. John Baker, a servant of

George Croghan, was captured by warriors he knew near Croghan's trading station at Aughwick, on the Kittanning-Frankstown path, in January of 1756. Less than two months later, when sent on an errand some distance from Kittanning, Baker killed and scalped his single guard. With a weapon, and perhaps a bit of food carried for the day, he came home in just ten days. After reporting on captives held at Kittanning, and proving how near this Allegheny River Delaware base could be, Baker became a guide for the Pennsylvania force that would attack the town six months later. This well-equipped army followed the same route to reach Kittanning in ten days, though the commander complained of "a very bad road, abounded with Morasses and broken Hills difficult of passage." In their retreat, fleeing in fear they were being pursued, some of the army apparently raced to Fort Lyttleton, thirteen miles south of Aughwick, in half this time.[39]

For the inexperienced, the upper Ohio Valley was much farther away from the deserted lands of white colonial farmers, as was made terribly clear to teenagers Eleanor Ryan and her brother. They were captured near the South Branch of the Potomac in August of 1763 and, to evade mounted pursuers, were taken on a deliberately rugged route over the Alleghenies to the headwaters of the Monongahela River. After twelve days going west, the thoroughly exhausted pair feared execution and resolved to escape when sent to gather firewood. Without food or weapons, and without trails or rivers as guides, they merely "steered towards the sun-rising." After fifteen days of wandering, her brother starved to death; after five more days, Eleanor somehow managed to find Harness's Fort, back on the Potomac's South Branch, but she had "almost starved to death."[40] One could die of starvation in backwoods America, whether escaping on the upper Susquehanna River or in the mountains beyond Virginia.

After the raid on Kittanning, its residents put more distance between themselves and avenging Pennsylvanians by migrating west, either the 50 miles to Kuskuski, or the more than 100 miles to Delaware and Shawnee settlements near the forks of the Muskingum River. Escape from the Muskingum Valley was a particularly long journey in the two years between the Kittanning attack and the fall of Fort Duquesne, and it is not surprising that only one person is known to have accomplished this. Jenny McLean, a servant indentured to Indian trader and blacksmith John Fraser, was likely captured in the first raid near Fort Cumberland, even before Braddock's defeat in July 1755. McLean was in Shingas's community for thirteen months, where she improved upon her Delaware language and survival skills, which would have been some part of her previous life with Fraser. Unfortunately we know nothing of her escape except that she traveled over 200 miles, presumably avoiding Fort Duquesne and following at least some of Nemacolin's Path (Braddock's Road), to arrive at Fort Cumberland in November of 1756.[41]

For British captives escaping from farther down the Ohio, the river was an unfriendly guide: its waters relentlessly went west, and going against them meant going toward French Fort Duquesne before 1759. Those escaping the Shawnee followed a version of a major Shawnee raiding route from the Scioto River – or from the larger settlements of Lower and Upper Shawnee Town on the Ohio – into southwestern Virginia. Reversing their route into captivity, escapees went up the south side of the Ohio River as far as the Great Kanawha River, fording treacherous tributaries miles upstream and negotiating disorienting swamps. Travelling up a steep and wooded valley that the Great Kanawha cut into the Alleghenies, the escapee – or the raider – gained access to the vulnerable, isolated, and partially abandoned settlements on the upper reaches of the Greenbrier, James, and Shenandoah Rivers. Those who thought they were home found only burned farmsteads, and lifesaving turnip patches.

The first and most celebrated escape along this route back to Augusta County was that of Mary Draper Ingles and Katherine Bingeman. The two had been captured in separate Shawnee raids on the New River in July 1755, and this well-provisioned raiding party and their captives traveled only ten days to reach Upper Shawnee Town. Two months later, the pair met while working for a hunting party about 100 miles west of the town, where they cooked, stretched skins, and gathered salt. Left in camp while the hunters were out, the two women agreed to escape together. Because the river was their only guide, they walked for four days upriver to near Upper Shawnee Town itself, avoiding recapture there by hiding in a cornfield. They traveled up the Great Kanawha, living mainly on grapes and nuts. After a month on the exhausting journey, the starving and enfeebled women had a fight. Mary Draper Ingles, whose version of what happened has been well preserved and elaborated, feared that the stronger Mrs Bingeman was going to kill and eat her. Mary arrived home forty days after escaping, and Katherine returned a few days later.[42] This odyssey may have inspired courage and loyalty in some newspaper readers, but it was a poor advertisement for escape from Lower Shawnee Town.

Much less seems to be known about the escape from Shawnee captivity of two men the following year. Maurice Griffith was taken by Shawnee scouts near Vause's Fort in August 1755, escaped the following year, and was remembered as an organizer and potential scout for a group of "Associators" who planned an aborted attack on Shawnee towns in 1757.[43] Trader and militia captain Samuel Stalnacker of the new Holston River settlement had ignored earlier Shawnee warnings to leave his outpost, and he and his wife were captured by Shawnee even before Braddock's defeat initiated more generalized raiding. Stalnacker escaped in May 1756, and his report on French preparations was delivered to Williamsburg within a month.[44] These escapes were not publicized. Perhaps these men were expected to escape, and the women were not; perhaps it was simply that the men escaped in the summer, when the newspapers were full of the campaigning, whereas the autumn escape of Ingles and Bingeman helped fill a quieter February issue of the *New York Mercury*.

It is likely that Griffith and Stalnacker escaped from the Shawnee with Jane Fraser. Jane, the pregnant young bride of Fort Venango gunsmith John Fraser, was captured near Fort Cumberland at the end of June 1755 and taken on horseback into captivity, almost certainly along part of Braddock's newly cut road. They required an unanticipated three weeks to get to a town on the Miami River, and provisions failed. Jane had and lost her child a month after arrival and was adopted into a family that treated her well. A year later she, and two fellow captives, who were unnamed in the third-party remembrances of her adventure, stole a few days' food and escaped when the warriors were warring and the hunters were hunting. In Jane's remembered story, the two men are dismissed; they simply "foundered themselves" and could not travel after the food was gone. Jane traveled on alone, living on plants and bark. She must have avoided Fort Duquesne, but found her way home along Braddock's Road. Reportedly in good health when she met her neighbors within a few miles from home, she was paraded in triumph to meet her husband, who had remarried in the interim, presuming her dead. In local history a century later, Jane Fraser was remembered as another of those resourceful and heroic women celebrated as knowing enough to escape back to "civilization" from captivity deep in Ohio country.[45]

After the British Army built Fort Pitt, escapees from Ohio Indian country could avoid the long struggle for survival through "the endless mountains." Early in 1759, at least two escape plots were hatching among captives of the Delaware held on the West Branch of the Muskingum. These coalesced into a single plan to free Barbara Leininger, Marie Le Roy, Hugh "Owen" Gibson, and recently arrived David

Brackenridge. After gathering a bit of food stored by other plotters and feigning serious illness to allow separation from the village, the four skirted settlements along the river, rafted across, and then ran for nearly twenty-four hours. Gibson, who was handy with the gun he brought, sustained them by killing two deer. The group traveled four days, and about 100 miles, to reach the Ohio River. After crossing the river, they traveled east for a week, arriving at Fort Pitt after sixteen days. The escapees were in good enough condition to resume traveling eastward the next day.[46] The comparative ease of escape to Fort Pitt was confirmed by a seventeen year old held by the Delaware in a new settlement thirty miles inland from Upper Shawnee Town. Sent on an errand, he found four days' worth of provisions in an empty Shawnee cabin and set off for Pittsburgh. He traveled along the north shore of the Ohio and arrived within just eight days.[47]

The building of Fort Pitt did not in itself provoke or assist many escapes, and a Virginian captive from the New River region could still follow the more arduous Great Kanawha route that she had seen on her way into captivity. Hannah Dennis left no written record of her adventure but became a fabled strong woman who escaped on this route. Shawnee warriors killed her husband and child in the raid in which they captured Hannah near the forks of the James River in the summer of 1757. Taken to Chilicothe Town on the Scioto, she adapted well, learned Shawnee, followed Shawnee customs, reportedly "lived like a squaw," and gained a reputation for magic and medicine. The surviving stories all presume that this survivor adapted merely to gain freedom of movement in order to flee, but it was six years before she converted what would not have been her first search for medicinal herbs into her escape in June of 1763. No surviving accounts chose to notice that war had begun in the region the previous month, with the killing or scattering of all the English traders. If she was pursued as persistently as the accounts claim, was it because she brought news of war? Hannah Dennis crossed the Scioto at least once, recovered from an injured foot, crossed the Ohio on a log, and followed the Great Kanawha route into the mountains. She lived on wild berries, roots, herbs, and river mussels, but became too exhausted to proceed. After twenty days of traveling, she was found and rescued by someone from the Clendennin community at Greenbrier. She recovered amongst them, and then set off on horseback for her former home on Purgatory Creek with weeks to spare before the crushing Shawnee raid that seemed to come in her wake. Did she bring news of war that people ignored, and later forgot in favor of the story of a generous peacetime banquet provided by locals for the treacherous Shawnee? In any event, she apparently had been quicker in making a longer journey than Mary Draper Ingles and Katherine Bingeman, and would eventually join them and Jane Fraser in local annals.[48]

Hannah Dennis was not the most exotic or celebrated prisoner of the Shawnee said to have been saved from death entirely by a chance rescue in the Allegheny Mountains of Virginia in this period. In the interlude of relative peace, between 1759 and 1763, Samuel Givens of Augusta County was one of those who had been "long hunting," and his train of horses was already loaded with meat and skins when he saw an odd creature that he decided to investigate before shooting. It proved to be a starving, exhausted, and naked young man, covered in scabs and speaking what to Givens was an incomprehensible language. Givens fed and nursed the man and brought him to Captain Dickinson's place near Windy Cove. There the stranger recuperated for several months and learned enough English to reveal that his name was Selim, and that he was from Algiers and had been educated for several years in Constantinople. He had been on a ship returning home when it was captured by a Spanish man-of-war, and then he was transferred to a French ship bound for New Orleans. After some time there, he was sent up the Mississippi River, where he was eventually captured by or given to the Shawnee. There he had seen an English woman captive, and had learned through signs that she had been brought from farther east. Knowing even less of his undertaking than had the young Ryans, Selim escaped and set out for the rising sun.

After he recovered in health and learned some English, Selim was brought to an Augusta County court day at Staunton, where he attracted the attention of many, including Rev. John Craig. Craig took him home, and discovered that Selim could read the Greek New Testament fluently. Selim was an adaptable and engaging captive-refugee, and he soon became a Christian. Yet Selim remained anxious to go home to his wealthy family, and Craig raised funds to allow him to go to England. Supposedly Selim returned home, was disowned by his father for abandoning his faith, and somehow made his way back to Virginia. Although intermittently considered insane, the long-suffering Selim still elicited the sympathy of many, including Robert Carter, Captain Dickinson, and Governor John Page, a member of Congress who took Selim to Philadelphia with him in 1789 and had Charles Willson Peale paint his portrait (see illustration 3). Confined in the Williamsburg Lunatic

3 "Old Selim," engraved from a lost Charles Willson Peale portrait, 1789. William Meade, *Old Churches, Ministers and Families of Virginia*, 2 vols (Philadelphia, PA, 1857), vol. 1, 130.

Asylum for a time, the much-afflicted Selim reportedly was freed once again before he died.[49] Selim's story revealed the coincidences that were possible, the dangers of ignorance of the pitiless Alleghenies, the borderers' sympathy for escaped captives, and the stresses of conversion or being caught permanently between two worlds.

White captives who deliberately escaped their white rescuers have been given a significance far beyond their numbers. Quaker ladies, given charge of a thirteen-year-old girl returned at Easton in August 1761, reported overcoming her initial reluctance and dressing her in new clothes, but then heard that she had escaped and eluded those sent to track her. This white Delaware "spoke English well & remembered how her Parents were murdered by the Indians, when she and her brothers were taken captive, yet such is the influence they had obtain'd over her, that after all the assurances we could give of her being kindly receiv'd by her Uncle & other sorrowing relations she rather chose to live with the Indians & in which she does not appear to be singular, as most of the Children which have been restor'd to us have manifested the Same Disposition."[50] Two other girls escaped in November 1764, from an army that Colonel Henry Bouquet had warned to guard returned captives closely in order to prevent the embarrassment of their escape. In these cases, the immediate escape was the challenge, for Indian assistance was likely thereafter. Yet only three white captives, all of them girls, are known to have succeeded in escaping rescuers to rejoin their Indian families. At least two others, John McCullough and Jacob Persinger, escaped but were eventually "recovered." Many more are known to have been returned against their will.

Escape from captivity was dangerous, and the accounts of abortive plots that intersected with successful ones suggest that the impulse was much more widespread than the attempts. For captives held in forts or in Pontiac's camp, as well as the recently captured being taken into captivity, the greatest challenge was getting free of their captors. For those contemplating escape from remote Indian villages, it was easier to get free of close scrutiny than to cache enough food, know the way home, and endure the difficulties of the journey. One of the attractions of capturing children was that they were much less likely to escape than adults, and were less dangerous when doing so. Celebrating the vulnerable who managed to escape was, perhaps inadvertently, a condemnation of the lack of courage, ingenuity, or cultural loyalty in the vast majority of captives, who did not seem to try.

At least 225 captives did escape, and 171 of them were adults, 40 of whom were Indians. The warriors, soldiers, and traders all had lives to return to, and adult white male settlers were better able to recover their former livelihoods and legal rights than were their dependents. Four-fifths of those who escaped were leaving Indian captors, rejecting the purported attractions of acculturation. Nearly 80 per cent of escaping captives, whose captivity time is known, fled within their first year of captivity. Most of these people were still gripped by the horrors of the raids in which they were captured, were deliberately being kept from their own kind, and were still learning the language of the community they were being forced to join. Even after only one year as a captive, Virginian soldier Thomas Gist saw his escape as an unwarranted rejection of those who were now his Wyandot hosts. "All curiosity with regard to acting the part of an Indian, which I could do very well, being th[o]roughly satisfied, I was determined to be what I really was."[51] Trader Alexander Henry was close to the same mental state after a year of very generous treatment by his Ojibwa captor and blood-brother Wawatam: "By degrees, I became familiarized with this kind of life; and had it not been for the idea of which I could not divest my mind, that I was living among savages, and for the whispers of a lingering hope, that I should be one day released from it – or if I could have forgotten that I had ever been otherwise than as I then was – I could have enjoyed as much happiness in this, as in any other situation."[52] The determination to be who they had been, rather than become white Indians, seemed to fade after a year with the Indians. Of 421 captives known to have been held for more than a year, and whose fate is known, only 40 escaped. These few escapes fade into complete insignificance if it is remembered that more than 1,000 more captives were still missing after a year.

12

The Bereft

It is easy to empathize with those who suddenly lost their loved ones in borderland war, and lost the livelihoods they had built with spouses and children who were suddenly dead or stolen. Indian survivors usually fled west, crowding relatives, fellow tribesmen, and strangers, though 80 Ohio Indians sympathetic to the British fled east to George Croghan's place at Aughwick late in 1754, and spent most of the ensuing war there. By the next autumn, Moravians in Pennsylvania were sheltering 556 other Indian refugees.[1] Sheriff John Potter had a "family" of 100 white women and children at his home near Penn's Creek in the wake of the November 1755 attacks.[2] A Paxton commentator noted later that newly arrived destitute refugees from farther west were used to living without money most of the year, and brought "nothing to support them but a few cattle, for which they can hardly find range in the inner Parts of the Country."[3] Even frustrated military commanders, who saw needed militias dissolving, and refugees clogging their roads and eating their supplies, could be sympathetic, at least when seeking support from civilian authorities. Colonel Henry Bouquet wrote from Carlisle to Pennsylvania's governor about "The desolation of so many families reduced to the last Extremities of Want & Misery. The Despair of those who have lost their Parents, Relations & Friends, with the Cries of [des]tructed Women & Children who fill the Streets, form a scene of horror painful to Humanity & impossible to describe."[4] Missionary Charles Beatty, touring the Pennsylvania backcountry in 1766, found it "truly affecting to see, almost in every place on the frontiers, marks of the ravages of the cruel and barbarous enemy," and he heard from traumatized returned captives and survivors who had seen their parents murdered. "Women saw their husbands killed and scalped, while they themselves were led away by the bloody hands of the murderers. Others related that they saw the cruel scene, and that they themselves narrowly escaped."[5]

The bereft have left little surviving evidence of their difficulties, and three prevalent assumptions cause us to undervalue the agonies of those who lost kin in these borderlands. First is the debatable belief that the patriarchal and authoritarian early modern Christian family was not yet transformed into the "modern" affective family of romantic marriage and tender childrearing. In this view, marriages were family alliances rather than love matches, women were oppressed underlings, and parental devotion to children was tempered by the hovering dread that they would not survive infancy. Children also had good reason to fear the loss of their parents, as a sizable minority of children were orphaned by disease, maternal death, and warfare. Second is the claim that family losses were so common that survivors were or became numbed, tough, and resigned in order to cope with their essential helplessness.[6] Third is the idea that the overt and extended lamentations of Indian widows and mothers, routinely reported in white captives' accounts of their own adoption, were presented as theatrical preliminaries to the adoption rather than genuine feelings of loss.

It is also too easy to presume that borderland life attracted particularly hard people who chose to risk the life they were confiscating from the region's previous inhabitants, or to suspect that the coarse and difficult borderland life inured people to hardship and loss. Those who were not case-hardened on arrival could be taught by the brutalities of pioneering. Jennet Clendennin was celebrated for abandoning her young children in order to escape on the trail into captivity, covering her husband's body with fence rails, and supposedly remarrying immediately. What kind of people could parade the bodies of slain neighbors through Philadelphia in the spring of 1756 or dump bodies on the steps of the Lancaster County courthouse to disrupt those trying to negotiate an end to hostilities?[7] The steely brutality of the Paxton Boys, led by their Christian clergy in slaughtering innocent Conestoga women and children, had massive local complicity and support, while confirming other Pennsylvanians, white and Indian, in their belief that these frontiersmen were the real barbarians.

Three strategies for coping with loss in these wars have remained visible: grieving, avenging, and searching. The bodies of those killed were, where possible, taken through the consoling tribal burial rituals of Indian villages and Christian sects. The culturally sanctioned lamentations of Delaware and Shawnee women were recorded most often when, at the end of a full year of mourning, echoes of their grief were still heard in the wailing that was part of the rites for adopting replacements for the dead. War parties were routinely launched to avenge specific deaths and console particular survivors. Vengeance was the stated purpose of the raids that could sometimes target specific offending communities and even individuals. The entire bereft community would occasionally avenge themselves by participating in the beating, torture, and death of some captured enemy. Alternatively, captives could be kept as servants, subject to petty and persistent humiliations. Adoption of an enemy could sublimate the suffering and end vengeance, and it was this amelioration that sustained the hopes of those seeking their missing kin. For Indians, grieving and avenging were the only reported responses; searching for the missing was pointless, for those few captured by Indian enemies were considered dead.

Christian rituals and expectations were different. If sympathetic kin could provide temporary comfort and sympathy, the grieving Delaware and Shawnee had more kin nearby than did this first generation of intruding European settlers. Christians urged each other to emulate their founder in suffering, to hope for the hereafter, to perform their burial rituals in solemn resignation, and to avoid public displays of lamentation. Old Testament–sanctioned righteous anger and revenge could be vented by joining vigilante scalp hunters, militia and ranger companies, or colonial and regular regiments of full-time warriors. But private revenge against specific killers was seldom feasible for those who insisted that these wartime deaths were "murders"; perpetrators could seldom be identified or effectively pursued.

One additional response was the invention of mythical pioneer heroes, lone avengers who turned some personal tragedy into a mission to kill as many Indians as possible, guilty or innocent. Captain Jack reportedly was transformed into a nomadic white vigilante by an attack that had killed his wife and children in about 1754, near Aughwick. Protected from the law by locals, Captain Jack was associated with numerous unsolved Indian deaths, real or imagined.[8] In Minisink, on Pennsylvania's northeastern edges, a comparable legend of Tom Quick emerged. Quick was set on avenging the killing of his father, and did kill an Indian named Maudlin in 1761, when drinking and bantering in a tavern led to a fatal shot in the back outside. A legend grew wildly from there, in folklore that excused and accounted for scores of alleged murders of Indians, and even resulted in a statue to his memory that stood for a century.[9] Joseph Doddridge had already noted a general enthusiasm for tales "in which some captive virgin was released from captivity and restored to her lover."[10] This folklore answered a felt need for vengeance that was not satisfied by lame military counterstrikes or the terms of eventual peace. Some murderers may have escaped scrutiny by community collusion in attributing killings to a mythical avenger.

A generalized "Indian hating" grew among European borderers, reinforced by a coalescing Indian anger at whites, both of which would long outlive this war. The fierce antagonisms between Pennsylvania's ethnic and religious groups were trumped by a newer identity that derived much from this shared hatred of Indians. Quakers, Moravians, and Mennonites valiantly, and stubbornly, resisted this trend and would be marginalized in the political and social order of the subsequent revolutionary and republican Pennsylvania.

One bereft husband and father devised a desperate and unusual solution in the wake of his tragic loss. On 10 November 1756, the garrison at Cumberland County's Fort Lyttleton saw a one-eyed man riding furiously westward on a stallion, and they set off in pursuit. They caught up with Philip Bäder and found his overloaded horse was carrying "Boild Meat Butter and Sundry other provisions Suffit. to Carry Him to the Ohio, with a Kettle bedcloths Onions and Sundry Sorts of Garden Seeds – And provinder for his Stallion." He was also carrying a very suspicious letter, in German, to someone at Fort Duquesne. Bäder, who had come from Germany about 1742 and settled at Conococheague in 1750, was intent on finding his wife and two children, who had been taken in a raid two months earlier. Distraught, Bäder had consulted his neighbor Friederich Croft (Kraft), saying that "he could have no quiet, and must follow them, expecting if the Indians did not kill him on his way he might yet get his Wife and Children." Croft was apparently encouraging. A year earlier, a German deserter from Fort Duquesne had made his way to Croft's farm and had mentioned that two of Croft's kinsmen, a soldier and a cooper, had been recruited by the French in Germany and were then working at this French fort. Croft gave the distressed Bäder a letter to those kinsmen, and Bäder "Swapt a Still for a Stallion To Carry him out," and set off to the west. Given the suspicious circumstances, Bäder and Croft were both arrested, investigated, and sent to jail in Carlisle and then to Philadelphia. Both professed to be Protestants, though their German neighbors voiced some suspicions. Two months after his arrest, Bäder petitioned Lieutenant Governor William Denny from Philadelphia's jail seeking mercy. He explained that "between Cristmess and New Year, I was Brought before Mr. allen, and he Told me that I was Cleart from Your honnour," on condition that he post security or join the British or Pennsylvania regulars. His blindness prevented him from joining the forces, and his desperate venture had left him with no remaining property to post as security for his good behavior. He was judged harmless and released.[11]

Bäder's method is not known to have appealed to any other relatives of the nearly 2,500 people who were missing and initially presumed "taken" in these Allegheny wars. Kin had to wait for the rumors and unconfirmed reports that, in nearly half the cases, never came. The four per cent of captives who escaped became valued sources of news, though this was incomplete, inconclusive, unreliable, and out of date. Printed accounts by escapees like Barbara Leininger and Marie Le Roy included lists of those sighted, as did the newspaper accounts of a few released captives like Charles Stuart. These reports were unlikely to reach the anxious relatives of captives directly, and were already very dated before arrival. Indian traders and diplomats, the best sources for information on the missing, could not venture into the Allegheny Mountains amidst the fighting of 1755 to 1758, or 1763–64.

Richard Bard, a York County miller who had escaped five days after Delaware had captured his family, carried a particularly heavy burden of survivor guilt. His initial interviews were restrained and factual, revealing no particular angst about leaving his wife with captors who had already killed his child and another two of their nine captives.[12] Richard subsequently went to Fort Pitt to inquire about his wife's whereabouts, attempted one risky trip west from there with Delaware he did not trust, and "did little but wander from place to place in quest of information respecting her." He also wrote forty-eight verses of awkward couplets like:

Were all things of this spacious globe
  Offered to ease my mind,
Alas! all would abortive prove
  Whilst Ketty is confined.[13]

Richard persisted in his search for Ketty, eventually located her, and risked his life again to become a hostage in the final negotiation of her extravagant ransom. Richard was the only person known to have successfully negotiated a direct private ransom before 1764, taking high risks in the face of dire warnings and official bans on such undertakings. Philip Bäder and Richard Bard were husbands whose strenuous searches for lost wives and children have left some traces, and confirm what hardly needs confirming – that an intense and debilitating sense of loss and survivor guilt could drive at least some of those who escaped their own family's captivity.

Parents seeking their missing children, whom they had been unable to protect from capture, displayed similar feelings, pursued various search methods, and encountered even more problems, as the trials of the Martin family illustrate. John Martin described himself as "One of the Bereaved of my Wife & five Children, By Savage War at the Captivity of the Great Cove" in November 1755. Martin was an experienced Indian trader, which gave him some advantages in attempting to recover his family. Delaware captors had traded Mrs Martin to a prominent French trader at Logstown, Jacques Baby, and he or one of his brothers also bought the youngest Martin child, two-year-old Janet, from Delaware at Kittanning. It is likely that John Martin found an undisclosed way to "deal with the enemy" and help his wife repay Baby the price for her "ransom" and that of Janet. These two redeemed captives could not come home directly during the war, but were sent first to Quebec, and then to England in an exchange ship, before they managed to rejoin John in Pennsylvania.[14]

The reunited parents then tried to recover their three other surviving captive children, still held by the Delaware. In the relatively quiet spring of 1762, John Martin agreed to travel 130 miles west of Fort Pitt to Tuscarawas, carrying letters from Colonel Henry Bouquet and George Croghan to Delaware leaders Tamaqua and Shingas. Martin also carried Bouquet's letter to Thomas Calhoun, the most prominent British trader to have returned to Muskingum country, urging him to help Martin recover his children. These two traders met with Shingas several times to arrange his participation in the forthcoming conference at Lancaster, but Shingas clearly saw the captives as part of negotiations and therefore would not free any of them until then. John saw his daughter Martha, but Calhoun reported that he "must content himself with the expectation of seeing his children at Lancaster Which was all the sattisfaction they could now give him."[15]

The Lancaster conference of 1762, for which John Martin had carried messages, was much anticipated by Pennsylvanians seeking their captive kin. As the Delaware party, led by Tamaqua and accompanied by Christian Frederick Post, approached Carlisle, "The people ... were most all gathered to see the prisoners." Then "the white people carried one of the prisoners of[f] in the night; Beaver [Tamaqua] was much displeas'd about it." When the Delaware and their captives arrived in

Lancaster, "a multitude of people followed us to our Camp, & Crowded so close upon the Indians that they hardly could get air," and Post went to the magistrates for help in keeping the people back.[16] None of John Martin's children were among the seventeen captives returned at this Lancaster conference, and he was among a number of parents who, as the conference ended, petitioned Lieutenant Governor James Hamilton for "Benign Compassion to interpose Yr Excellencies Beneficient influence in favour of Yr Excellencies Most Obedient & Dutifull Servt."[17] Samuel Curtis told the lieutenant governor that he knew where his daughter was being held by the Seneca, and Hamilton likely provoked the Seneca by claiming that if Curtis "pleases to go and see her, and desires my Passports, he shall be furnished with them."[18] John Martin's efforts had failed, and his missing children would not be returned until the end of Pontiac's War more than two years later. Three children captured at 8, 10, and 12, would be returned as young Indians of 15, 17, and 19 years of age.

When John Martin finally recovered his children at Pittsburgh late in November 1764, he also brought another strenuous parental saga to an end. Eight-year-old John McCullough had been captured from Conococheague in the summer of 1756, and his parents heard nothing of him for four years. In 1760 Andrew Wilkins, among those traders venturing west again on the strength of the truce, saw John with his adoptive family on Beaver Creek and reported this to John's father back in Shippensburg. The father came out the next summer and found John, but, since his master was away, no ransom could be arranged. In 1762 the father returned to Venango better equipped, and he negotiated the ransom only to have John promptly run away to his Delaware life. If John's parents intended any further effort the following summer, a new war intervened. Neither of his parents was at the Muskingum River, Fort Pitt, or Carlisle in November of 1764 when this white Delaware of sixteen was finally returned. John Martin, with Bouquet's approval, brought John back to his parents. McCullough's fulsome account is notably silent on his parents' reaction to his return or his own cultural adjustment.[19]

Another man who was disappointed at the Lancaster conference, and not relieved until late in 1764, was Francis Innis. He had been captured with his wife, Margery, and their three young children at the surrender of Bigham's Fort in 1756. Within a year, Francis and Margery were imprisoned in Quebec, their youngest was dead, and their other two children were with the Ohio Indians. By 1759 the exchanged parents were back from captivity, and a now-disabled Francis and his wife journeyed to Fort Augusta that summer asking Quakers there for help in recovering Francis Jr and Jenny, then ten and eight years old. The parents were at the Lancaster conference three years later, joining John Martin in disappointment and in vainly petitioning George Croghan.[20]

Most families broken between 1754 and 1758 remained broken during the general cessation of hostilities between 1759 and 1762 and during the new war that lasted for nearly two years thereafter. Only a handful of captives held by the Indians were ransomed before 1764, very few of those exchanged were not soldiers, and only a small minority had escaped. Relatives might hear rumors about their own, but they would also hear horror stories of torture and death on the trail and in captivity. With each passing month, they had more reason to fear that their loved ones would never return, could not be recognized, or would become white Indians who could not be brought back anyway. It was a long time to wait, to fume, and to suffer, but it was not long enough to forget or to heal.

The suffering kin of captives taken in the borderlands did not have enough political influence to make the recovery of captives into a major war aim, but this objective appealed to Pennsylvania's political and moral leaders as a cause that could be understood and shared by all the squabbling factions of a diverse society. In contrast to Virginia, Pennsylvania had been slow to go to war and very quick to seek a peace that highlighted the return of captives. Suspect as a disloyal laggard in the war, the Pennsylvania government was initially alone in this preoccupation. Eventually, the British Army and its Indian commissioners would have their own reasons to champion and then monopolize this quest.

Indian acculturation worked so well that blood relatives feared the complete loss of their kin, and Indian warriors continued to take captives in great numbers throughout these wars in Allegheny country. The trauma of capture amid scenes of death, and the fear of torture or death on the trail into captivity, and in the village gauntlet, all brought most captives to an exhausted, if not calculating, acceptance of a very different life. Particularly for captives under sixteen, adoption into a new family led to new roles and, over time, the acquisition of a new language and perspective. Adult captives seldom became thoroughgoing white Indians, but only a small minority of captives resisted Indian acculturation to the point of risking death to escape. Age at capture and length of captivity joined personal differences in affecting the pace and depth of cultural transformation, but all those who did not escape quickly were proof that Indian acculturation was successful. For those anxious to redeem kin, time was among their enemies, and war made even the most audacious and persistent wait.

PART 4

SETTING ALL THE CAPTIVES FREE

The return of prisoners and captives played a significant part in the clash of cultures in Allegheny country, with the Indians generally resisting and the Europeans often insisting. Indians regarded any large-scale return of captives as a humiliation that implied that their capture had been a crime and their adoption insincere. The very idea of such a return as a precondition of peace was dismissed by the Susquehanna Delaware as absurd in 1755. Europeans regarded the return of prisoners as a welcome mark of shared humanity and an encouraging sign that a dispute had been settled, a truce strengthened, or a peace concluded. As has already been seen, there were two categories of captives who appear to have decided their own fate. The white Indians actively or passively chose to live the life of acculturated Indians, and joined with their new families in avoiding, resisting, or reversing their "redemption." Escapees, on the other hand, risked their lives in a dramatic refusal of transformation into Indians. They were resented by their captors but were understood to have behaved acceptably within both Indian and European military traditions. Despite the historical attention paid to both of these groups as sensitive markers in ongoing cultural warfare, it must be remembered that relatively few captives taken in Allegheny country decided their own fates in either of these ways.

Most captives were "freed" by the efforts of others, leaving enduring suspicions about their enthusiasm for redemption. A few prisoners were simply released by their captors, promptly or eventually, as acts of personal affection, generosity, or convenience. Many captives were returned as diplomatic gifts by Indian negotiators, which was conventional only if done in moderation. Regular gift exchange was understood as part of creating and maintaining a fictive kinship, a membership in an Indian family that was valued in diplomacy and trade. This gift giving easily became linked to the presents regularly offered to Indian delegations at the end of conferences with whites. These exchanges expanded to become thinly disguised trafficking in captives, a reality denied but understood by all participants (chapter 13). White military authorities made increasingly strident protests against the ransoming of captives, but diplomatic gift exchange through official conferences expanded greatly, and through them the British Army effectively paid for hundreds of ransoms.

The evolution of redemption by gift exchange was slow, and the initial results were poor, prompting private attempts to ransom kin from Indians in the meantime, and military exchanges of prisoners of war between Europeans (chapter 14). Private efforts at ransom were discouraged by the military, very difficult to arrange between suspicious parties, and subject to rejection by captor or adopted captive. The exchange of prisoners put a tangible value on captives, even if distinctions of status were carefully preserved. Indians did not exchange prisoners with their traditional enemies, and very rarely did so with the British Army. Europeans rarely exchanged prisoners with Indians, but came to insist that the release of all prisoners was a part of making peace. Whites exchanged prisoners among themselves during war and at its end, amid self-congratulation on their humanity and civility in doing so. For some British colonial civilians taken by Indians in Allegheny country, the route home involved becoming ransomed or purchased servants of French or Canadian soldiers, spending some time "working off" their purchase in Canada, and then being returned or exchanged as prisoners of war at Crown Point or in Europe.

Forcible recapture of prisoners always involved high risk for the captives and usually for the rescuers (chapter 15). "Hot pursuit" was effective for Indian communities retaliating against white raiders, and had enough success when employed by colonial militia and rangers to become routine by 1764. Direct attack on Indian villages known to house captives was very rare, and the outcome of Pennsylvania's raid on Kittanning helps explain why. The most expensive, elaborate, and dramatic forcible recovery of captives was Colonel Henry Bouquet's intimidating punitive expedition to the Muskingum River in the fall of 1764. Among the captives retaken were dozens of youths who were bound and guarded by their proclaimed rescuers, raising some questions about the value of the enterprise. British, Pennsylvania, Virginia, and Maryland troops had cooperated in a major operation that recovered 287 captives without ransom or bloodshed. Any broad celebration of this success was initially delayed to see if a firm peace would come from the truce concluded at the Muskingum (chapter 16). Even after this success became evident, and William Smith's celebratory history had been published, enthusiasm for this cooperative imperial success was smothered by the Stamp Act crisis.

The efforts made to recover captives had a wide variety of motives, and the extent of their success can be measured by the number of captives recovered, the compromises their recovery represented, and the peace it anticipated and confirmed. The return of captives may have seemed a clear cultural victory for Europeans, but the objections of some returning captives and the *métis* characteristics of so many more supported doubts about the attractiveness and superiority of the European invasion.

The various methods used to recover captives, from Europeans and from Indians, deserve separate examination and comparison. Most captives were held by Delaware, Shawnee, and Mingo communities that were reluctant to lose their new kin, and most were sought by an army that despised ransom and expected the surrender of captives as proof of an effective truce. The problems, the cost, and the relative success of each approach can be measured better in hindsight.

13

Diplomacy of Gift Exchange, 1756–62

Despite formidable Indian, European, and cross-cultural obstacles, and the intensifying poison of war itself, the freeing of captives through negotiation was a persistent theme between 1756 and 1762. Recovering captives as diplomatic gifts had been routine in the decade before war. During the years of active raiding, 1755–58, the Pennsylvania government and Quaker elite made somewhat frantic efforts to recover captives and make peace with the North Branch and Ohio Delaware. The evolution of this policy, which had no parallel in Virginia for a host of reasons, is revealing and instructive in itself. In the four years of truce that followed the fall of Fort Duquesne in 1758, the British Army took up the Pennsylvania priority on the return of captives through its Indian superintendency, and especially through George Croghan. This diplomacy of gift exchange, quietly funded by the British military, continued until it suddenly collapsed late in 1762. By examining the origins, successes, and limitations of this diplomatic approach to recovering captives, we come to understand more about the conventions observed, compromises made, the limits reached, and the consequences.

In the decade before 1755, the prompt and public release of captives was common. The Shawnee who captured Pennsylvania traders on the Allegheny River in 1745 robbed them and let them go within hours, without any apparent desire to keep them, and without realizing that the French commandant at Detroit was willing to pay to gain custody of English traders in Ohio country. As Anglo-French belligerence increased, a few Ohio Indians captured English traders to give or sell to the French, but had no interest in keeping or adopting any of these captives. The French arrested English traders in peacetime and punished them with imprisonment and deportation to France, but the victims were never tried, and all were eventually released without compensation or apology. Most European and colonial soldiers knew that they were not authorized to take prisoners of war in peacetime. Claude-

Pierre Pécaudy de Contrecoeur released Ensign Edward Ward's party after their surrender at the site of Fort Duquesne early in 1754, requiring nothing more than a promise not to return within a year. In this context, George Washington's capture of the survivors of the Jumonville incident in May 1754 was, like the attack itself, a provocative incitement to war. British authorities freed those of Washington's prisoners who were sent to England, and Louis Coulon de Villiers, in retaliating in Allegheny country, took only a pair of officers as well-treated hostages who were supposed to ensure the release of the prisoners whom the injudicious young Washington had taken.

A few other captives had been released as good-will gestures, even as tensions rose on what we now know was the edge of another Anglo-French war. Elizabeth Steal (Tell) was freed from Canada in 1754 as one such act of charity, and attendant spying.[1] Seneca speaker Thanayieson was comfortable in presenting captured Carolina trader William Brown to Conrad Weiser at the alliance-building Logstown meeting of 1748, and in apologizing for Brown's capture by young Nottaway warriors.[2] Brown's freedom had not been anticipated, and the gifts distributed at the end of this conference were not augmented because of his release.

It is not at all surprising that, when ferocious raids began in 1755, Pennsylvania officials, Quaker notables, and distraught relatives of captives all thought that diplomatic meetings were the obvious way to regain captives and restore peace. Backcountry war was quite new for the government of Pennsylvania and only an ancestral memory for that of Virginia. Both governments initially blamed the victims, but responded very differently to the captures of their people that began in the latter half of 1755.

The Virginia government made no direct effort to recover its captives and was much less active than the Pennsylvania government in pursuing peace. Lieutenant Governor Robert Dinwiddie had brought no military experience to governing Virginia, but he avidly promoted the fight with the French and their allies for control of the upper Ohio Valley. Although he exploited the death of the earliest victims to generate sympathy for his war, when fighting began he denounced the victims as cowards in the face of a paltry enemy and threatened those who fled with the loss of their land titles. The Virginia House of Burgesses contained more investors in Ohio lands than representatives of the new frontier counties, even before one of the latter was killed by Indians and the resulting by-election was canceled after the polling was disrupted by "tumultuous and riotous" locals who were angry at government inaction.[3] Dinwiddie urged Virginians to imitate New England bounty hunters, and promptly offered a scalp bounty of £10, equivalent to three months' wages for a laborer. Virginian soldiers, militiamen, and vigilantes were to hunt Indians profitably, as they would wolves, with no discrimination between friend, bystander, and foe, and with no premium for those captured alive. The Government of Virginia went to its kind of war with relative speed and ease, and the bounty came readily in a province without a prominent pacifist community or numerous resident Indian allies to reassure, placate, or protect.[4]

Although Cherokee allies were potential victims, there were no immediate incidents, and the Cherokee were soon included among those who could earn Virginia scalp bounties. The Virginian deputy superintendent of Indian affairs from 1757 to 1759 was former Ohio Company agent Christopher Gist, and his main function was to recruit and equip Cherokee and Catawba allies.[5] Diplomacy with Ohio Indians was left largely to the British superintendent for the northern department, William Johnson, and particularly to his lieutenant at Fort Pitt, George Croghan. The official Virginian response to the war may not have been very successful, but it had been relatively prompt and predictable. Once war began, the Virginian authorities showed no concern whatever, even in their rhetoric, for the return of captives.

The official Pennsylvanian response to the raids of 1755 was slower, more tortured and inconsistent, and, eventually, more successful both in ending raids and in recovering captives. Pennsylvanians made no martial preparations in the four months between the first terrifying accounts from neighboring Virginia and the first Indian attacks that hit Pennsylvania's Berks, Lancaster, and Cumberland Counties in October and November of 1755. Frontiersmen coalesced into angry and threatening crowds, one bearing the frozen bodies of their neighbors, that descended on Philadelphia to demand action.[6] When Lieutenant Governor Robert Hunter Morris, another war leader with no military experience, asked the Quaker-controlled assembly for action, they stalled, discussed possible Indian land grievances as the cause of the raids, and then linked any appropriation for war to the improbable taxing of all proprietary lands. The assembly did, however, promptly grant £10 each to two captives who had escaped the Indians, wishing "to furnish them with Necessaries, and enable them to return to Cumberland Country."[7] It was December, by which time two frontier "mobs" had visited Philadelphia, before the first painful political compromises were reached on some appropriations for war and a voluntary militia.

Some of the Pennsylvanian hesitancy derived from a wish to protect valued Indian friends and converts from intimidation by red or white vigilantes, and to limit the defection and migration of influential and knowledgeable Delaware and Shawnee to their more alienated Ohio-based kin. In December of 1755, Morris was still assuring Indians living at Wyoming, Nescopeck, and Shamokin that "The People of the Province have always considered you as their own Flesh and Blood."[8] In the new year he went to Carlisle to meet disappointingly few Ohio Iroquois, a small remnant of the community whose friendship and trade the Pennsylvanians had successfully cultivated for a decade and then failed to support against the intruding French between 1752 and 1754. The meeting's message, like the attendance, made it clear that Indian determination to fight the English was spreading. By March 1756 the friendly Indians were fewer and more desperate, including frightened refugees who had come to Philadelphia. Morris established a refugee camp for them on the proprietary Conestoga Manor in Lancaster County, but warned their overseer that local people may not be well disposed to the Indians, and that stragglers might be killed.[9] This voluntary protective custody became its own sort of captivity, as were the swelling Moravian Indian mission settlements.[10]

Pennsylvania finally went to war with the Delaware in April of 1756. Although several of the assembly's "Commissioners for Laying out £60,000 for the King's use" were linked to the Quaker party, this commission negotiated the transition to war. Benjamin Franklin, their clerk, had already been planning frontier forts and mobilizing volunteers who called him their colonel even before he was given this rank. Franklin drafted the commissioners' report that called for: a declaration of war on the enemy Delaware, attacks on their villages, and a generous bounty for the scalps of Indians over the age of ten. Civilian bounty hunters were to have $130 for a scalp of a male Indian, with an additional $20 premium for a live captive. Female Indian prisoners were to be valued at $130, and their scalps at $50. Conrad Weiser was among those who sensibly objected that there was no way to distinguish the scalps of friendly Indians, and that too small a premium was being offered for the risks attending capture of a live male prisoner. Although few bounties were ever paid, proclaiming the bounty was an attempt to "spirit up" the militia.[11]

Pennsylvania's proclamation of war followed the commissioners' recommendations closely, but there were significant modifications. Morris attempted to help those Delaware who had sought the province's protection or joined the Pennsylvanians in fighting the war, allowing the latter to collect full scalp bounties themselves. The proclamation raised the age, from ten to twelve years, of Indians who might profitably be scalped. Morris also proposed a radical initiative, perhaps derived from prominent Quakers. "AND for every English Subject, that has been taken and carried from this Province into Captivity, that shall be recovered and brought in, and delivered at the City of Philadelphia, to the Governor of this Province, the Sum of *One Hundred and Fifty Pieces of Eight [will be paid], but nothing for their Scalps*." In a footnote, the proclamation explained that nothing was given for the scalps of captives because "if killed by our friendly Indians they would claim the same reward as for Indian scalps." At least to the Philadelphia policy-makers, scalping whites was unacceptable, and they knew nothing as yet about the particularly feared and hated white Indians. Promising to use public money to redeem captives was entirely contrary to the "New England" policy preferred in Virginia and elsewhere, where it was feared that any prospect of ransom would prompt even more captures. No one publicly defended this Pennsylvania policy as possibly reducing the killing of captives, or undermining Indian insistence that their captives had become kin who could never be surrendered or abandoned.[12] There is no surviving evidence that this bounty on returned captives was ever paid.

The Quakers' power did not evaporate with the declaration of war. They were undergoing their own religious revitalization, and a group of influential Philadelphia Quakers combined vigorous opposition to the war with strenuous and expensive efforts to restore peace and redeem captives.[13] In the days immediately after the proclamation of war, leading Quakers met at the home of Israel Pemberton Jr, wealthy merchant, philanthropist, and combative opponent of war, slavery, and the weakening of Quaker practice. Non-Quakers Scarouady, Conrad Weiser, and Andrew Montour attended as invited advisors on making peace, as did Daniel Claus, who was Weiser's assistant and William Johnson's deputy secretary and future son-in-law. The Quakers insisted that they were prepared to pay and take risks, but said they would operate only "thro the assistance of the Governor who had been consulted on ye occasion." Scarouady, without declaring any conflict of interest, advised them to leave the actual negotiations to Iroquois like himself. The Quakers promptly pledged the impressive sum of £5,000 to support the effort, and organized the Association for Regaining and Preserving Peace with the Indians by Pacific Measures.[14]

From the very first days of the war, the return of captives became a central requirement for Pennsylvania authorities in making peace. Within ten days of formally declaring Pennsylvania's first war on the Delaware, the government of Robert Hunter Morris began peace overtures to the North Branch Delaware. In making war and peace simultaneously, and in emphasizing the humane purpose of setting free the approximately 267 colonists who had been captured in the nine months since General Edward Braddock's defeat in July 1755, the Pennsylvania government was attempting to mollify both pacifist Quakers and bellicose Scots-Irish frontiersmen. On the advice of Scarouady, Morris hired Kanuksusy, an Ohio Seneca diplomat well known to the Quakers as Captain Newcastle.[15] By choosing the eloquent Kanuksusy to lead an Indian legation to the North Branch Delaware at Tioga, Scarouady, the Quakers, and Morris were subtly invoking the increasingly uneasy Iroquois lordship over the Delaware. Going to war while the Iroquois remained neutral was, in itself, a major Delaware defiance of this dominance. Kanuksusy was to appear to act on his own, assisted by New Jersey Delaware translator Cawkeeponen (John Pumpshire), and was to suggest to the warring Delaware chief Teedyuscung that the Iroquois might be able to convince Pennsylvania to make peace if the Susquehanna Delaware ceased raiding and surrendered all their English captives to the Iroquois.[16]

Neither the Pennsylvanians nor the Six Nations had thus far done anything to intimidate these Delaware, but the persuasive Kanuksusy obtained a preliminary hearing at Tioga after agreeing to "go of[f] a little from the Governor's Instruction." During his next visit to Tioga, Kanuksusy formally delivered Morris's message, which was supposed to climax with, "Brethren: This last is a very Important article on what we absolutely depend, that all Prisoners taken on both sides shall be delivered up, as there can be no Sincerity on Either Side where this is not done, and that, in a most full and ample manner, without keeping Back a Single Prisoner; this Belt assures you that it shall be punctually performed by us, and we Expect the same punctually on your Side." Two long belts were then to be presented to emphasize this point.[17]

After reporting back to the Pennsylvania Council that Morris's speech had been well received, and urging a peace-making conference at Easton as soon as possible, Kanuksusy asked to see the lieutenant governor in private. There Kanuksusy reported that his friends at Tioga had discussed matters privately with the Delaware leaders in advance to ensure the success of their public meeting, and that everything was readily resolved, except the issue of returning prisoners, which his friends "advised him to drop" as more appropriate for the lieutenant governor to raise personally once a conference was convened. "[I]n these preparatory Conferences it would answer no Purpose, nor was it agreeable to Indian Forms." Morris excused Kanuksusy for ignoring this central instruction but was clearly disappointed, and insisted that "unless this Article should be complied with, and that without hesitation or Fraud, he would never consent to a Peace."[18]

It was already evident that the return of captives would be a serious barrier to negotiating a truce or peace. Indian views of adoption of captives was not the only problem. Any exchange of prisoners was bound to be entirely one-sided. Although at least forty-seven Indians had been killed in the nine months before Pennsylvania formally declared war, only one had been captured, and he was promptly killed by furious Berks County residents.[19] A third major deterrent was the Indian custom of using captives in their own dispute settlements. Within Indian societies, and in diplomatic dealings between allies, it was customary to offer a captive as compensation for an unfortunate and regretted murder. Any large-scale, one-sided offer of prisoners represented an admission of guilt, which was entirely unacceptable in ending what the Delaware considered a justified war.[20]

Why did Morris's advisors, who had guided him wisely in choosing Kanuksusy as negotiator, allow him to make the unpalatable return of captives into such an early and obvious objective? The Quakers, still on good terms with Morris, heartily supported the idea, and would subsequently provide valuable presents for all negotiations. The return of all captives was also supported without reservation by Six Nations advocates: the Mohawk-trained government interpreter Conrad Weiser, and Oneida chief Scarouady. Morris wrote Sir William Johnson, New York's chief negotiator with the Six Nations and superintendent of Indian affairs, claiming that Six Nations intermediaries should "have insisted on it as a Preliminary, and the only Test they could give of their Sincerity, that they should deliver up our People which they have taken Prisoners." Johnson knew the Iroquois conventions better than Morris, and had recently given his own Canadian prisoners to the Mohawk for adoption. Although he considered the Pennsylvania declaration of war to be a badly timed infringement on his own authority, Johnson and Six Nations delegates bullied the powerless titular Delaware leader, Nutimus, into accepting Morris's terms at a conference. Supposedly they extracted something similar in private from rising eastern Delaware spokesman Teedyuscung. In Johnson's odd translation, Teedyuscung agreed to return all English prisoners "who had fallen to the share of his people."[21] If this twice-translated phrase was a personal commitment to return captives taken by Teedyuscung's immediate family, it would be a negotiator's personal gift that was not at all uncommon. However, Johnson and others insisted on a broader interpretation. All these advocates of Iroquois overlordship favored forcing the Shawnee and Delaware to return all their prisoners through the Iroquois, apparently as an appropriate humiliation, or fine, for supposedly subordinate peoples who had begun war against the English without Six Nations approval. Once the prisoners had been given to the Six Nations, their return would have been a matter of gifts and ransoms paid to the Six Nations at a lavish conference.

Although a political revolution attended the withdrawal of the stricter Quakers from the assembly, Pennsylvania's diplomatic focus on the return of captives remained. At conferences with the North Branch Delaware over the next two years, Pennsylvanians reiterated that all prisoners must be exchanged as part of making peace, though the Delaware response was not at all encouraging. When Teedyuscung and Morris met at Easton late in July 1756, the former was anxious to establish that he, and not Chief Nutimus, was the spokesman of the Susquehanna Delaware. Without being given the status of chieftain by Delaware matrons, this dispossessed native of New Jersey and former Moravian convert had managed, within two years, to become a Delaware spokesman, approved by some dissident Iroquois. Pennsylvanians struggling to end the slaughter on their frontiers were willing to deal with this swaggering Delaware, in the hope that he would be able to secure peace. Morris was willing to accept Teedyuscung's leadership, but wanted a better-attended meeting to which the Delaware were to bring all their captives. Morris had been blunt again: "while you retain our Flesh & Blood in Slavery It cannot be Expected we can be friends with you, or that a Peace can come from our hearts. I repeat this Article of the Prisoners as a Necessary Condition of Peace, and desire you will Consider it as such."[22] In accordance with protocol, Teedyuscung replied to each paragraph of Morris's speech in turn, but deliberately avoided the one concerning the return of prisoners.[23] He and Morris agreed to a larger meeting in the fall, and both conceded that any agreement between them did not include the much more numerous Delaware now living on the upper Ohio River. This point was soon painfully clear; on the last day of this conference, Ohio Delaware and Shawnee captured and destroyed Fort Granville, and just over a month later, Pennsylvania troops retaliated with the attack on Kittanning. Teedyuscung had made a separate war, and now he was making a separate peace.

Teedyuscung had certainly not forgotten about prisoners. Having been encouraged to return his own prisoners for a sizable ransom, Teedyuscung prepared for his next meeting at Easton by sending four prisoners early in October of 1756. In addition to the ransom, he asked that his wife Elizabeth and their two youngest children be returned from Bethlehem, where they were staying at an inn, apparently with Pennsylvania government support and protection. His family declined this invitation when visited by Teedyuscung's messengers, but he was assured by the lieutenant governor, in a phrase that would later return to irritate many white Pennsylvanians, that "we will not keep them one Minute longer than they desire to stay."[24] At the meeting itself, Teedyuscung freed the fifth captive of his own.[25]

The novice Pennsylvania lieutenant governor, Colonel William Denny, "blundered" at this conference by asking Teedyuscung the causes of the war. Teedyuscung, with Quaker assistance but without the approval of the other Tioga leaders whose message he otherwise carried, declared that the problem was land fraud by both the Pennsylvania proprietors and the Six Nations overlords. Although the guilty proprietor and frightened Pennsylvania officeholders doctored the minutes and eventually outmaneuvered the Quakers and Teedyuscung on the land fraud issue, the patent injustice of the Walking Purchase had been established, and the non-Quaker committee of the assembly exposed this proprietary fraud.[26]

Teedyuscung had effectively proposed a plausible and very challenging exchange of land for prisoners by the end of his third conference at Easton in the summer of 1757. Easton was itself a small new village in the heart of the Walking Purchase.[27] Here the land fraud issue was aired, documents were copied, secure land and permanent housing for Teedyuscung's people at Wyoming were promised, and a peace belt was passed amid mutual congratulations. Then Denny stumbled again by mentioning that the peace would be confirmed once terms had been agreed to. Teedyuscung, apparently surprised, sought clarification. Denny explained, "It is a Rule among Nations, upon confirming a Peace, to deliver up all Prisoners on both sides," and he offered a belt of wampum. Denny had been misinformed. Conrad Weiser had drafted Denny's speech, in which he absurdly claimed that all Indian nations customarily released all prisoners as peace negotiations began.[28]

Teedyuscung rightly exploded at this violation of Indian diplomatic protocol. He rejected the belt, and insisted that the matter should have been brought up earlier. If Denny could suddenly bring up the prisoners as a precondition for confirming peace, then he would bring up justice in the matter of Delaware lands as another precondition.[29] As one who was known to violate protocol occasionally himself, Teedyuscung was objecting to the return of all prisoners, not just to the timing of Denny's remarks.

Although this storm eventually passed, Teedyuscung's resistance to the return of all prisoners was obvious, as were his linking of prisoner return and land claims, and his recognition that the return of captives remained unacceptable to those for whom he spoke. A frustrated Pennsylvania Assembly addressed Denny on the matter months later, in the midst of negotiations to get Teedyuscung to take a peace mission to the Ohio Indians. The assembly complained that the return of captives was not even in the minutes of recent meetings, that Teedyuscung had not delivered the prisoners he promised, and that he had not even been reminded of this promise.[30] At the July 1758 conference at Easton, Teedyuscung returned only one captive, Sarah Decker, a Northampton girl whom Christian Frederick Post had seen by chance in Teedyuscung's own house the previous month.[31] In more than two years of negotiation with Teedyuscung, accompanied by generous presents, Pennsylvanians had recovered only six captives, all of whom belonged to Teedyuscung personally.

In the summer of 1760 Teedyuscung joined Post and John Hays in a significant journey from Bethlehem north via Tioga, hoping to go through Seneca territory to a grand Indian council on the Allegheny River. Along the way Post and Hays watched for white captives and, in covering about 200 miles up the North Branch of the Susquehanna River, recorded seeing a total of twenty. The mission aborted there because the Seneca flatly refused to allow the emissaries to proceed through their territory.

Post, one of the most trusted and best-informed cultural brokers in Allegheny country, was so frustrated with the failure of this mission and the perceived oppression of captives that he wrote an uncharacteristically impassioned letter directly to General Jeffrey Amherst. Being assured by Indians that the Senecas had many captives in their "Back Towns," Post argued that the allied Six Nations should be forced to give up all their captives first, as an example for other Indians. In a thinly veiled criticism of William Johnson, Post said that Amherst was the only one with authority over the Indian superintendents, and that he would serve his own honor, his king, and Christianity by insisting on the return of all captives. Post argued against believing Indian claims that the captives did not want to return, insisting that all of them be brought down to a conference where they could speak for themselves in safety. He wrote that "those who refused to bring Down their Captives to be Declared as Enemies, & then everything would appear in its true light." He also objected to exempting those women who had married Indians, supposedly to bind the Indians to the English. Although he had twice married Indians himself, Post argued that leaving these captive women was "making the poor Women Slaves to such Indians, & Giving them a liberty to mock & Ridicule at our holy Christian Religion."[32] These were views that Post could not have revealed to his Indian friends, but they would eventually fit with the army's plans.

The mission of Teedyuscung, Post, and Hays had one notable success. At Wyalusing they had conferred with an impressive Delaware prophet named Papunahoal (Papunhank or Papoonan), leader of a small group of millenarian Munsee.[33] After recalling that his community had already returned all captured horses to Teedyuscung, and apologizing for being so tardy in returning their captives, Papunahoal presented three captives, all held in captivity for nearly five years. Post noted that Papunahoal had bought these three from others who had taken them, and Post commented that "The children cry'd, as if they would die, when they were presented to us."[34] Teedyuscung had recommended that the captives be returned, and now urged Papunahoal to deliver them personally to the Pennsylvania governor in council.

A month later, Papunahoal and a party of twenty-five from his community set out, with the three captives and several more horses to be returned. At least one of the horses was claimed by its former owner along the way, and the conversation there can only be imagined. Officials scurried to arrange credit with tavern keepers along the route, and the conference was held at the State House in Philadelphia. After hearing Papunahoal's conciliatory opening speech, the governor, councilors, and "Gentlemen of the city" heard something surprising from Toan-kakanan, the group's second designated speaker. "Tho' we are poor, we want no recompence for the prisoners and Horses; We do not return them to you from a desire of gain; you are welcome to them, and we are glad of this opportunity of obliging you." They asked only that a

British deserter living amongst them be granted a discharge, a wish the governor could not grant and about which he apparently neither said nor did anything subsequently. The next day, the governor did offer presents, which Papunahoal politely refused, explaining that he was a religious leader who could not accept gifts without irritating those Indian leaders "who transact publick Business." He could not accept presents, "which spoil and corrupt the receivers of them." He did urge fairer trade dealings, produced a worthless New Jersey bill of currency that he had been given in trade for furs, and accepted the governor's offer of total compensation for this fraud. Papunahoal concluded this second session with a "solemn Act of Prayer and thanksgiving." Four days later the conference resumed, now including "A Large Number of the People called Quakers," and the governor again offered presents, insisting that they were not a reward, would not corrupt Papunahoal, and would simply replace clothes and blankets ruined on the long trip home.[35] The three captives returned by Papunahoal were freed by the kindness of their Indian masters, but even the most sympathetic Quakers found this generosity surprising. If these three were released at the urging of Teedyuscung, it was the only known example of his successfully negotiating the release of any captives who were not in his own custody.[36]

The Pennsylvania government had undertaken peace talks with Teedyuscung very early in the war, talks that eventually brought a welcome truce and then a separate peace to the colony's northeastern frontier, while establishing a pattern for negotiations with the Ohio Indians. The Friendly Society had been very supportive of Teedyuscung and the Easton negotiations, providing funds and assistance in return for a place at the meetings and an opportunity to do justice while embarrassing their political enemies. The negotiations also proved that Europeans could be induced to make considerable concessions, including land concessions, in return for promises to return captives. Yet only ten captives, including one returned by a master fearing that Teedyuscung's peace would end any rewards for returning a captive, are known to have been returned for all this effort.[37] It became increasingly clear, to those willing to do more than denounce Indians for failure to return all captives, that Indian negotiators were powerless to fulfill terms that required others in their communities to return captives. Christian Frederick Post, at the end of yet another of his missions to the far-from-traditional community that Teedyuscung led, summarized the situation clearly:

> All that are taken are looked upon by the Indians as the Private Property of the Captors & are either given away to those families who have lost any Men in the War, or are sold & bought several times. Now, as the Indians have no public Fund to redeem them out of the Hands of private Persons & we have none of their People Prisoners to exchange for them, it will be next to impossible to procure the Return of the Captives without a price for them & redeeming them ourselves.[38]

Europeans had learned that a useful truce could be achieved by promising justice in exchange for captives, but that captives were not readily returned after peace had been concluded. Another lesson learned from the Pennsylvanian experience was that a truce that required the return of prisoners could stop the raids. However, Indian negotiators did not accept the return of captives as a precondition for a truce, and white negotiators who seriously intended to recover captives learned not to make a final peace until after the return of all the captives had proven that Indian acceptance of the settlement was widespread.

Negotiating for the return of captives held by the Ohio Delaware was a very different quest that began only in the summer of 1758. General John Forbes then called upon Pennsylvania's experts to explore a truce with those Ohio Indians who controlled the territory around, and helped defend, his military target of Fort Duquesne. When Christian Frederick Post went out to test the prospects for peace, he accompanied prominent Delaware chief Pisquetomen, a nephew of Sassoonan and close relative of Ohio Delaware leaders Tamaqua (Beaver), Shingas, and Menatochyard (Delaware George).[39] Pisquetomen and Post found a surprisingly hungry Delaware community that had fought as allies of the French on the assumption that provisions were more plentiful than they had proven to be. The Ohio Delaware were ready to consider alternatives when Post addressed their large gathering near Kuskuski. Although the Delaware voiced grievances and made it clear that Teedyuscung had no authority to negotiate for them, they seemed to react well to Post's reading of the 1757 agreement at Easton, "till I came to that part respecting the prisoners. This they disliked; for, they say, it appears very odd and unreasonable that we should demand prisoners before there is an established peace; such an unreasonable demand makes it appear as if we wanted brains."[40]

The British Army was not about to let the return of captives interfere with negotiating the truce it needed to get easier access to its military target; and it took a very pragmatic approach to recovering captives that would last as long as the truce. The next Easton meeting, of October 1758, was a grand assembly of more than 500 Six Nations, Delaware, and Shawnee, almost all of them from the east side of the Allegheny Mountains. They discussed terms with Pennsylvania's lieutenant governor and council, the governor of New Jersey and his Indian commissioners, Colonel Henry Bouquet in place of the ill General Forbes, and with George Croghan as William Johnson's deputy supervisor of Indian affairs. It needs to be remembered that this was a month after Major James Grant's complete defeat by Indians and French at Fort Duquesne. The proposed truce for the Ohio Valley included an Indian promise to withdraw their support from the French, and a British promise to withdraw from the Ohio Valley once the French were ousted. It is noteworthy that no English prisoners were brought to this conference, and nothing was said about captives of the Ohio Delaware and Shawnee, the tribes that were sent a peace proposal from this conference.

Evidently one of the main purposes of the governors and the Iroquois leadership at this conference was to use the occasion for a ferocious Iroquois denunciation of Teedyuscung's leadership. One reason for this became clear only later, when Lieutenant Governor James Hamilton reported that, though the demand had been excluded from the meeting's official minutes, Teedyuscung had insisted – in public and to the Quakers – that "the prisoners would never be deliver'd up, till the Indians were satisfied about the Lands."[41] His charge of land fraud, leveled against both the Pennsylvanians and the Six Nations, was behind this unsuccessful effort by both to destroy him. Teedyuscung had been supported and encouraged by the Friendly Society, which had earned a place by providing substantial gifts for the conferences at Easton. Croghan, who had earlier worked well with the Quakers and Teedyuscung, now joined the Six Nations representatives, the military officials, and the governors in a move that was less successful in ousting Teedyuscung than in pushing the Quakers aside. The Friendly Society would continue to fund messengers and work to redeem captives, but it had no further influence on the truce being negotiated with the Ohio Indians.[42]

The British certainly seemed to compromise on the return of captives during these successful negotiations. When a diplomatic mission took this conference's peace proposal to the Ohio Indians, they were refused any contact with captives by increasingly suspicious Delaware hosts. A Pennsylvania militia captain reportedly "told the Indians, the English should let all the prisoners stay amongst them, that liked to stay."[43] The Indians of the upper Ohio Valley withdrew their support from the French, and Fort Duquesne fell. In their first formal meeting with British officials, held a few weeks later at Fort Pitt, the Ohio Valley Delaware negotiated what they thought was an acceptable truce. Chief Custaloga later recalled that Colonel Bouquet had said: "I do not speak to you about the English prisoners you have adopted as your relatives and incorporated into your families. I only hope that, when peace is made, you will be willing to return those of advanced age, who would be in your way, or of very little use to you. As for the young children, who are pretty and able to serve you, I will not be angry if they stay among you."[44] George Croghan, who had a dubious Six Nations grant of 200,000 acres of Ohio lands, had compelling personal reasons to refuse to translate what was a clear Delaware demand of complete British withdrawal from the upper Ohio.[45] The official minutes of this meeting were entirely distorted by Croghan and Bouquet, who claimed that the Ohio Indians had agreed to return all their prisoners and to accept a permanent British presence in their valley. Christian Frederick Post's account, which he refused to alter on Croghan's direct demand, supported Custaloga's later testimony. Bouquet and Croghan had accepted a compromise that they immediately denied and misrepresented as complete Indian submission to British terms.[46] A calculated truce, not a peace, had been negotiated at Easton and Pittsburgh in 1758, and in neither case did the terms include any demand for the return of prisoners held in the west.[47] French emissaries to these same Ohio Indians confirmed these terms when they tried to encourage Indian resistance a few months later. The French tried to convince the Indians that the relentless insistence upon the return of captives meant the English did not value the Indians, and, at the same time, they tried to argue that the English now did not even care about their own captive people "since they so easily consented to giving up children which the savages had taken since the beginning of the war."[48]

The standard military view of the return of captives can be seen clearly from the perspective of the Pennsylvanian colonel who commanded at Fort Pitt early in 1759. When several Delaware offered to sell a captive girl for whiskey and trade goods, Lieutenant Colonel Hugh Mercer brushed them off with an insistence that the British were not going to behave like the French, and that captives must be surrendered freely to gain peace.[49] Mercer remained confident that many Delaware and other Indians would join the British as soon as a British Army arrived on the Ohio River, "unless we begin to squabble too soon about the Captives, who are civilly treated at present."[50] However, Mercer asked his superior officer, Colonel Bouquet, what he was to do about captives and Indians who were camped near the fort. "The Country People sollicit me to purchase their friends, but that method I detest, as most dishonourable." Bouquet agreed, replying firmly: "The Indians act a very bad part in respect of our Prisoners. You are upon no account to give them any consideration for their Liberty … I hope that we shall soon be able to force them to comply with their Treaty, Till then Patience, Art, and Dissimulation must be used."[51] It was clear that the military, which abhorred ransom, wanted neither to negotiate it or to pay for it. Bouquet was hoping that some strike could be made against the Ohio Indians in 1759, while the French were busy defending themselves elsewhere.

Whatever the military thought of ransom, it would pay plenty of it over the next three years. The central figures in this development were George Croghan and Tamaqua. Croghan was a subtle and resilient bankrupt trader and land speculator who had learned several Indian languages, married the daughter of a prominent Mohawk, and gained a reputation as the effective frontier negotiator who represented William Johnson and the Crown in Allegheny country. In a series of secret business partnerships that proved very expensive for his partners, Croghan promised great profits from any reopening of trade with the Indians, from the provisioning of army posts, and from the lucrative business of supplying him with presents for Indians who attended the conferences he conducted as deputy superintendent of Indian affairs. Croghan was able to decide what presents were warranted, sell these goods as a silent trading partner, buy them as deputy superintendent, and give them to appreciative Indians, who came to regard him as their most generous and commendable white friend.[52] Generosity bestowed status and prompted reciprocity, and Indian legates offered captives in what were generous gift exchanges that continued through 1761. White Seneca Mary Jemison was recalling what was believed by Seneca on the Genesee River at this time when she later reported that "the King of England offered a bounty to those who would bring in the prisoners that had been taken in the war, to some military post where they might be redeemed and set at liberty."[53] There was no such bounty, but the British Army, represented by a fiscally embattled General Jeffrey Amherst, was grudgingly funding the entire costs of Croghan's "very bountiful" transactions, after accepting William Johnson's lax review of these expenses.[54]

The other central figure in the exchange of captives for presents was Tamaqua (Beaver or King Beaver), who now emerged as the leading Ohio Delaware seeking peace. As brother and successor to Shingas, Tamaqua had much more influence than Teedyuscung, and had direct control over many more captives. At a major conference at Fort Pitt in July 1759, where Iroquois, Wyandot, Shawnee, and Delaware met George Croghan and Lieutenant Colonel Mercer, Tamaqua spoke for the Delaware and other tribes. He returned ten prisoners, and referred fondly to two of them whom he loved as his mother and sister, and asked that they would not be hidden, so that he might see them when he visited the "inhabitants." Croghan responded with lavish presents for the leaders, and clothing for all 375 Indians who attended the meeting. In less than a month he clothed 721 Indians in exchange for captives. He was actively, and profitably, pursuing a return of captives, and avoiding questions about British withdrawal from the lands that Croghan claimed for himself and his friends.[55] In May of 1760, when Tamaqua and 100 other Delaware brought him fourteen more captives, Croghan had temporarily run out of presents and could offer them only "4 Caggs of Rum as I had nothing else to give them." In the previous year he had clothed at least 1,632 Delaware, Shawnee, Ottawa, Ojibwa, Wyandot, and Miami and recovered 120 captives. In urging the new British commander at Philadelphia to fund more presents, Croghan reported that the Indians who came to trade often brought captives, for whom he was obliged to make presents of rum. He went on to claim that "Gineral Stanwix made itt a Custom I have nott been able to breake throw itt as yett tho itt is very Expenciff." Croghan had trumped both the military view of ransom and the Delaware resolve, voiced clearly the previous December, to exchange prisoners only for British withdrawal from Fort Pitt. Croghan had also gathered what he could claim were promises from the Delaware, Shawnee, and Wyandot that all their captives would be returned.[56]

As soon as Quebec fell, the British Army began insisting that all European prisoners had to be surrendered before a peace would be negotiated.[57] When the British took ceremonial possession of Detroit in December 1760, Croghan reminded the assembled Indians that General

Jeffrey Amherst, Major Robert Rogers, and Sir William Johnson all demanded fulfillment of that summer's promise to return all the prisoners.[58] At a major conference at Easton in the summer of 1761, eastern Delaware and Iroquois heard nothing but Pennsylvanian insistence on the return of captives. There were already signs of Indian hesitation. The Ohio Indians were not there at all, and only one captive was returned – a girl who promptly escaped.[59]

However, the Ohio Indians were not resisting, but following Croghan's urging to attend Sir William Johnson's massive and elaborate June conference at Detroit, where the mood was markedly more generous and conciliatory. By the summer of 1761, Detroit-area Indians had been receiving anti-British war belts and messengers from dissident Seneca, and were perceived by British officials as increasingly unreliable.[60] Johnson was personally embarrassed by any Six Nations defection and increasingly anxious about a possible alliance between dissident Seneca leaders and those of the Great Lakes and Ohio Valley nations. This conference combined lavish presents, conciliatory talk, and only a glancing reference to the return of prisoners.[61] At Detroit, and on his way home, Croghan was given seventy-two captives, almost as many as had been brought in to him at Pittsburgh by small parties of Delaware, Shawnee, and Mingo during the previous year.[62] Croghan was still getting results, with the support of Johnson's great parcel of gifts funded by the British Army.

Croghan was succeeding without bullying and was now anxious to soften the demands for the return of prisoners in discussions with the Shawnee.[63] Having been unable to convince a number of freed captives to return to Pennsylvania, Croghan expressed doubts about the value of continuing to press so hard for the remaining prisoners. Ohio Indian leaders also began to recognize that surrendering more adoptees would completely destroy the Indian position in the truce. As long as the English wanted these people back unharmed, there was still a chance to negotiate a British withdrawal from the Ohio Valley. There were also Indian fears, easily fanned by French traders and messengers, that once the prisoners were all returned, the British would resume hostilities.[64]

Nonetheless, the Ohio Delaware and Shawnee were cooperative enough to surrender some captives during this time of reduced British insistence on the matter. As Croghan returned from the Detroit conference, he stopped at Beaver's Town and was given sixteen more captives. Over the following six weeks, the Shawnee brought thirty-one captives to Croghan at Fort Pitt, and the Delaware brought twenty-two. Tamaqua led one group that brought in eight of these captives and a belt assuring Johnson that the rest of their captives would be returned in the spring; the Shawnee sent similar assurances.[65] Croghan mentioned nothing of the cost of ransom or presents, except to record that Bouquet had ordered that a gift of £5 worth of goods be given to one captive of the Delaware who had been returned.

Although the relaxation of British pressure and generous presents had coincided with the return of numerous captives, this policy was soon amended. In December 1761 Amherst, the unsympathetic overseer of the inflated Indian affairs budgets, received a list of New York prisoners still held by Delaware Indians. Knowing that Johnson was planning yet another major conference, Amherst forwarded this list to him together with the directive to "take Such measures, as might appear most Conducive for obtaining the Liberties of those miserable objects, Still remaining in the hands of the Indians."[66] However, Amherst made it clear that no ransom was to be paid. Johnson, needing to improve his relationship with his disgruntled superior, promptly ordered his deputies to insist, once again, on the return of all captives.[67]

As perceptive and popular a frontier fort commander as Lieutenant James Gorrell, at isolated Green Bay, could offer only befuddling genetics in trying to convince Menominee and Puan chiefs to return any remaining prisoners. On the one hand, he urged the Indians henceforward to view the defeated French as "our friends & Brothers As they are Subjects to his Majesty & we form One Body & Blood, & since we are Joyned by Friendship, that henceforth we shall be all one people." Here as elsewhere, the notion that the British, French, and Indians would form a single people was to become part of selling the surrender of Canada and the Peace of Paris. On the other hand, in the same speech, Gorrell called for the return of English prisoners, on the grounds that "they are our own Blood, and you know it wou'd grieve you to have your Blood with any Nation." While urging compliance as a sign of affection, Gorrell knew the idea was unpalatable, and threatened that "your great Father & our King … will be very angry if you don't Comply to this Request & is able to send as many men as there are trees in the Wood to Oblige you to a Compliance."[68] By August of 1762, Johnson, his deputies, and garrison commanders were pressing again for the return of all captives. When one Seneca messenger told Johnson that all prisoners who were willing to return were doing so, Johnson insisted that those who chose to stay with the Seneca must be forced to return as well.[69] This pressure would help forge the Seneca-Delaware alliance that Johnson had previously tried so hard to prevent.

British commanders were also developing another approach. From the summer of 1761, when Bouquet felt confident enough to implement a trade ban on the Shawnee until they returned their captives, the British Army was beginning to change its approach in the face of unwelcome new economies imposed on the army.[70] Small parties of Shawnee brought a few captives to Croghan and were allowed to trade. Bouquet anticipated more captives the following spring, and lamented to Amherst, "General Monckton had Authoris'd me to give them some Presents on these Occasions; but from the high Price of goods Purchas'd here I find the smallest Present Comes about £5. And at the same time Appears to me Unavoidable."[71] Amherst urged frugality, but also stated, "The English remaining in the hands of the Indians Must be Delivered up; for I would not have One left after this Summer; And I think the Indians will not Dare to Refuse to Comply with Our Demands."[72] When answering Bouquet's question directly, Amherst insisted that Indian failure to fulfill promises was reason enough to stop all presents, and he claimed that the Cherokee had returned all their prisoners and that "this was brought about merely by Laying a Restraint on the Trade, which accordingly produced the Desired Effect, when Treatys, Bribes, and all Other Methods had failed."[73]

Just as the British Army was giving up on the open-handed approach to recovering captives, the Pennsylvania government funded a major conference at Lancaster in August of 1762. Tamaqua led a cavalcade of Delaware and their captives, who had set out from Tuscarawas in June. Christian Frederick Post, who was one of several messengers sent out to promote the conference and the return of captives, came along with them. They met and talked with resistant masters of captives, persuading some to join the caravan. Tamaqua was soon complaining of captives escaping along the trail, and he agreed with Post: "I wish'd to have them once at the Council fire, if they then ran away nobody would be concern'd about them, but the Govr wanted to see them." By 3 July the parade had reached Fort Pitt, where Indians pressed the commander to accept the captives, but he insisted that the governor of Pennsylvania was at Lancaster to receive and care for the captives (and pay for presents). Bouquet, under Amherst's restraining orders on presents, confirmed the military's refusal and reported that the thirty Indians present had brought only 18 of the 200 to 300 captives the Delaware were thought to be holding, and that the Shawnee had brought none.[74] At least one Pittsburgh trader was approached with the offer of a captive for twenty gallons of rum, but "I told him that would be Selling them as Servants at a Dearer Rate than Negroes is Sold, & that ye General and our Governor expect'd they would bring them all in & deliver them according to promise."[75] Liquor traders farther east were less restrained. When the caravan reached Carlisle, trail-weary Indians were drinking to excess, and at least one more captive was spirited away by relatives. Finally, after forty-five days on the trail, the party arrived at Lancaster.[76]

This proved to be the awkward climax of Pennsylvania's formal efforts to recover captives by diplomatic negotiation. Pennsylvania's experienced Lieutenant Governor James Hamilton was not allowed to make peace, which was the army's business, and was permitted to discuss only the return of prisoners. Tamaqua surrendered seventeen captives, and claimed that the Delaware had returned all "your flesh and blood" as asked, and that only those who refused to return were still with the Ohio Delaware. He even added, "I hope they will come to you after some Time, because you live better than we do." Tamaqua had softened the Delaware position, but Hamilton was still insisting that there could be no lasting peace until every single English captive was returned. All prisoners were "born Subjects of our Great King, and as such, he has a Right to demand them."[77]

Hamilton, Croghan, and Johnson had expected the substantial Six Nations legation at Lancaster to support them in pressing for the complete submission of the Delaware on the matter of prisoners. The Seneca brought in a dozen prisoners, but Oneida diplomat Saghughsuniunt (Thomas King) spoke powerfully on behalf of the Delaware in their resistance to these demands. He spoke of his own earlier raiding against Catawba and Cherokee, where his prisoners were his own and "nobody had any right to meddle with them." When he fought the French, he said, the English took his French prisoners without any recompense, "which makes me think it was owing to the Evil Spirit." He noted that, though the English had insisted on the return of their "flesh and blood" over the past three years, they had also claimed that those returned would be free to do what they wished, including return to the Indians. However, he charged, the English made bound servants of these people: "This is the reason why I brought so few of them. No wonder they are so loath to come, when you make Servants of them." Saghughsuniunt took on the persona of the Delaware for whom he spoke, and went on to describe surrendering the girl at Easton the previous summer. She had immediately escaped from the English, and, by the time he arrived home, she was already there. He went on, "I have brought an English prisoner, who I love as my own Wife. I have a young Child by her. You know it is very hard for a man to part with his Wife. I have delivered her, therefore take care of her, and keep her safe, that she don't make her escape." The conference adjourned to the county courthouse, where Saghughsuniunt turned over twelve captives who had lived with the Munsee Delaware and the Seneca.[78] A week later, Hamilton attempted to reply to Saghughsuniunt's charges. He offered no peace and insisted that the proprietary purchases of Delaware land had been perfectly legal. He said nothing of separating wives from husbands, asserted that ransom was not a European custom, and claimed that white men who wanted to stay with the Indians were all deserters or criminals. He insisted that returned captives would be free, explaining that they were held in the courthouse only temporarily, until their relatives could come. He flatly, and falsely, denied making servants of returned captives: "We do no such thing."[79]

The treatment of one captive returned here was uncharacteristically generous, perhaps to counter Saghughsuniunt's charges, and it supported Post's earlier contention that the Pennsylvania lieutenant governor just wanted to see the captives, and was not obsessed with what happened to them afterward. Young Peter Weese had been captured by Mingos in a raid on the Potomac's South Branch in May of 1757. After more than five years with the Indians, Peter was among the twelve captives returned at Lancaster by Mingo chief Kinderuntie. Peter asked that he "might not now be detained among the White People, but left to his liberty to return to the Indians," and was interviewed privately to confirm that the desire was genuinely his own. Peter gave several reasons to stay with the Indians for the next winter, promised to visit a brother living near Pittsburgh on his way north with Kinderuntie, and also promised to return to the governor in the spring. Peter Weese, orphaned and now a white Indian, was the only captive who was formally granted permission to return to the Indians, and he stayed there.[80]

For the Indian legates, the Lancaster conference was as disappointing as it was for most of those white Pennsylvanians who had expected their kin to be returned there. In the face of a relentless Hamilton,

Tamaqua finally brought the painful meeting to a close, and prompted the distribution of presents by agreeing to return all prisoners to Pittsburgh in the autumn. One sign of the failure of the conference was the Seneca request that a chief's son, in Philadelphia to learn English and prepare for a diplomatic role, be returned. The disappointed Delaware had come to refurbish friendship and sign a peace, but found the Pennsylvanians so preoccupied with their captives that they would speak of nothing else. The Delaware did not know that captives were all that the Pennsylvanians were allowed to discuss. Croghan met Tamaqua and his companions as they were returning home through Fort Pitt, and probably enjoyed reporting that they were "seemingly much Disatisfy'd haveing lost most of thire horses & other Nesesaerys on thire way up from Lancaster."[81] Thomas McKee likely saw and heard even more. He reported that the disgruntled Indians had left most of their presents "on the road to Ohio" and invited Pennsylvania's lieutenant governor to gather them up for distribution at the next conference.[82] The captives that Tamaqua promised did not arrive. After the Lancaster conference, Tamaqua faded for a time as a leader of the Ohio Delaware. He had invested his reputation in a great effort to return captives, and those returned were too numerous to be his own captives. He had convinced other Delaware, and in so doing had encouraged British and colonial leaders, observers, and captives' kin to believe that the Ohio Delaware had no inviolable taboo against surrendering captives.

Although Indian negotiators returned many captives in the shifting and expensive diplomacy, there were also a number of Indian masters who simply freed their captives themselves. In March of 1759, Nathaniel Holland, storekeeper and energetic agent for the Friendly Society who had been cultivating Indian friendships at Shamokin, finally learned that a young woman captive had been held a mere six miles away. He and Captain Trump from the garrison at Fort Augusta promptly set out and "found the poor unhappy woman cutting wood" for her elderly Mingo husband. We cannot know whether Captain Trump's presence intimidated this Mingo, but with "much reluctance" he agreed, without ransom, to let the woman return to Shamokin with Holland. This gift was made even though Holland was known to be paying ransom for captives and the woman's older brother had been "sold to Gen. Johnson the fall following their captivity." Holland learned that she was Catherine Nicholson, who had been orphaned and captured, together with her two brothers, by Delaware and Shawnee near Patterson's Fort three years earlier and had later been given to the Mingos. Catherine, who spoke Seneca fluently, married Holland within seven months of her release.[83]

Ohio Delaware masters could be as generous as Papunahoal, as Nicholson's husband, or as those described by David Boyd and James Kenny. Young David Boyd had been captured by the Ohio Delaware and was eventually adopted by the old warrior who had captured him. According to a grandson, David had been captive for nearly four years when his Delaware "father" decided to return him, and even paid to have a letter sent to inform relatives. Under a flag of truce, a reluctant seventeen-year-old David and his Delaware "father" traveled to Carlisle, where this captor-benefactor was severely beaten by David's maternal uncle, and David ran away. The next day, as the story was remembered, David's Delaware father sold furs and horses to clothe David for his new life with the whites, and gave him some cash as well. Amid continuing tensions and suspicions, this generous old Delaware was denied permission to return David to his natural father personally, and could only release the youth and head back to the Ohio Valley.[84]

James Kenny, a Quaker trader at Fort Pitt, witnessed an even more impressive display of self-denying Delaware generosity. Jammy Willson and other former Delaware acquaintances were returning to trade at Fort Pitt in the summer of 1761. On 12 August, Kenny wrote that Jammy

> never went to War by report, but having obtain'd a White Woman & Boy, he kept ye Woman as his Wife, using her kindly; on finding she inclin'd to return to her own People he brought her & ye boy with ye Amount of his Estate to our Store & told ye Woman notwithstanding He Loved her, as she want'd to leave him, would let her go, so he divided his substance equally with her, giving half ye remaindr to ye Boy & set them both free & went with ye Woman home giving her a Horse to Ride; an Instance of more self denial than many men of great Christian professions shew their poor Negros.[85]

The marriage may not have been happy, but the divorce was exemplary.

If Tamaqua had made a promise at Lancaster that he would not be able to keep, the Pennsylvania authorities were even quicker to prove the hollowness of Hamilton's insistence that returned captives were not bound out as servants. An advertisement appeared in the *Pennsylvania Gazette* just two weeks after the end of this Lancaster conference. The

Pennsylvania Board of Commissioners, established to receive and care for returned captives and to compensate their Indian captors very well for their "travel expenses," described twelve of the recently returned young captives, none of whom had been claimed by relatives. Four teens remembered their English or German names and where they had been captured, but six others remembered less. This group of refugees was completed by Mary Todd, about twenty-five years old and taken in New Jersey in 1755, who was apparently the wife referred to in Saghughsuniunt's Lancaster speech. She had been returned together with her infant child. The ad called on relatives to claim these young people soon, stating that "otherwise the Boys will be bound out to Trades, and the Girls so disposed of, as to prevent their becoming a further Expence to the Public."[86] After a mere two weeks in a city distant from the place of capture or previous residence of these strays, the authorities were terminating their support. Here was a foretaste of the human cost of a policy that would soon bring more dislocating redemptions.

Another consequence of the Lancaster conference was the renewed military control over the return of captives. The Pennsylvania government appointed two commissioners to receive all the remaining captives who had been promised. The commissioners arrived at Pittsburgh with resources and instructions to negotiate, and a request that Bouquet and the garrison assist. Bouquet politely refused until he heard from Amherst, insisting that all Indian affairs there were conducted in the king's name. The military would conduct the conference, distribute the gifts in the king's name "in Consideration of their Loss of time & fatiques in bringing those Prisoners," receive the captives, and then turn them over to Pennsylvania's commissioners. Bouquet noted that the Crown had borne the entire expense for Indian diplomacy to date, and had brought back more than 400 captives, and he hoped Amherst would not allow any province to "interfere in their own name." Amherst supported Bouquet, and Lieutenant Governor Hamilton accepted Bouquet's agenda, but no Indians or prisoners arrived.[87]

Pennsylvania's elaborate and expensive diplomatic efforts to recover captives had been consistent through 1758, when it was taken over by Crown officials for the next three years, before being given back briefly in 1762. The Pennsylvanians had been lured along by promises, and had eventually achieved some success. In negotiating with and through Teedyuscung, a total of only ten captives of the Susquehanna Delaware had been returned. However, much more was achieved through Croghan's appropriation of the Pennsylvanian approach. Tamaqua and the Ohio Delaware brought in at least 165 captives between 1759 and 1762, the Shawnee had returned at least 79, and the Mingo at least 16. Croghan admitted that 31 additional captives had simply been released in the Ohio villages, but his claim to have received 411 returned captives by the fall of 1762 is entirely plausible.[88] No wonder Quaker James Kenny had to endure a "very conceited" young Shawnee who "told ye Prisoners in our House, that Geo. Croghan was ye Only Man amongst us they regard'd & only for him it might be war again, & that none of us knew how to please Indians but him."[89] Some Shawnee, refusing to negotiate the return of a captive wife held at Wakitomica in 1762, insisted, "Th[e]y Want Mr Croghan to Come & bring Goods to there [*sic*] Towns; then th[e]y Say th[ey] Will Deliver All the Captives amongst them up to him."[90] Whatever all such presents had cost the British military, Croghan, who at one point contributed £100 in gifts himself, had managed to appear as the sole source of fair and generous treatment. He had also thoroughly eliminated the threat that captives would be exchanged for British evacuation of disputed upper Ohio lands, including his own.

In contrast to the fairly consistent position of the Pennsylvanian government, the British Army and Indian superintendency had clouded and complicated negotiations by a more variable approach to the return of captives. If the Indians had revealed that they could surrender captives in some circumstances, the British officials had also indicated that, at least on occasion, they could overlook the continuing captivity of those whose supposed plight could be an obsession in diplomacy at other times. When Canada was conquered, and the British government demanded new economies in the British Army in America, there were funding cuts that prompted widespread anger and some mutiny in the army. Although it is clear enough that Amherst did not like Indians, nor like buying the compliance of those he thought were now British subjects, it is not hard to understand his growing impatience with a lavish Indian diplomacy that had gone well beyond token presents. Amherst never admitted to paying ransom for colonial captives, and now he could not afford it. How galling it would have been if he had known that self-serving Croghan had gained an undeserved reputation for generosity, whereas Amherst and the army that had paid for it all would be punished brutally for ending this extravagance.

Amherst's call for restraints on presents, which never became a complete ban, has long been seen as an ignorant provocation and major cause of the Indian war of 1763–64.[91] What has not been appreciated is that Croghan's extravagant and self-serving ransom of captives, disguised as diplomatic presents, had continued in spite of Amherst's calls for cuts in spending. The insistence upon the return of captives thereafter, without compensation, helped cause the eclipse of Tamaqua as peace leader of the Delaware. The trade ban on the Shawnee had also been implemented as an alternative to presents, provoking resentment and hardship. By the autumn of 1762, the return of captives had all but ended, and the path to renewed war had been cleared.

By the time the truce collapsed in the spring of 1763, Indian warriors and their opponents were well aware that there had been a sizable traffic in captives in Allegheny country. The return of some 411 captives was a worthy testimony to the industry and humanity of many. No one knew exactly how many more captives were still held, and it is not surprising that some people had, in the meantime, been pursuing other approaches in seeking their captured kin.

14

Redeemed and Exchanged, 1745–62

Before 1760 there had been little evidence that significant numbers of captives could be recovered through the diplomatic efforts of the Pennsylvania government or the British Army's deputy superintendent of Indian affairs, George Croghan.[1] Two other kinds of negotiation were also being undertaken: private redemptions and military exchanges. In the cultural and military borderlands of Allegheny country, each of these approaches encountered major difficulties derived from different conceptions of captivity and redemption. Although each method had successes of great consequence to those involved, it seems fair to ask why they did not accomplish more.

Ransom or sale of some captives was a well-established custom with the Delaware, Shawnee, and Iroquois, with European military and maritime communities, and with those who occupied the borderlands between New York, New England, and New France before 1745. The uses of ransom in Allegheny country varied with circumstances that can be distinguished as particular to the decade before 1754, to the active war years of 1755–58, and to the truce of 1759–62.

Ransom was not considered an honorable option for a captured Indian warrior. After raiding Cherokee communities for several months in 1747, a pair of Iroquois warriors were finally captured and condemned to death at Keeowee. As he faced death, the younger of the two Iroquois called to nearby English traders, supposed Iroquois allies, pleading with them to arrange his ransom. Although the traders did not respond, and may not have been free to do so, the victim's companion promptly upbraided him for his weakness, and the pair reportedly then met warriors' deaths, enduring fire with stoic bravery.[2] Although ransom was deemed unworthy for Indian warriors, it was not uncommon for other condemned captives to be ransomed by a member of the captor's community. John McCullough, who spent the years between eight and sixteen as an adopted captive of the Ohio Delaware, reported that they had a custom that anyone willing to pay thirty buckskins could buy a captive who had been condemned to be burned. The ransomed person then became a slave, "to hunt and raise corn" for his master. McCullough knew one old Delaware who had bought three such captives in this way, treated them "leniently," and eventually surrendered all of them to the British Army.[3] Those purchased in this manner can be forgiven for remembering their escape from death as a ransom, even though it was also a purchase of a slave.

Ransom had a very long and more honorable history in European warfare, where elite warrior captives had long been a special form of plunder. When seeking the recovery of several prominent citizens captured by northern Indians in 1748, Governor James Glen of South Carolina asked Pennsylvania authorities to "procure the Ransom" by approaching the governor of Canada or French-allied Indians.[4] Readers of the *Pennsylvania Gazette*, viewing the terms of the Aix-la-Chapelle peace a year later, might have wondered about the possibility of enforcing it in North America, but they understood what ransom was: "The prisoners made on all Sides, as well by sea and land, and the hostages required or given during the war, to this day, shall be restored without ransom in six weeks or sooner."[5]

The ransom of captives would become much more familiar to some Pennsylvanians over the next five years as their merchants became targets in the Anglo-French rivalry that the peace of Aix-la-Chapelle could not contain. Morris Turner and Ralph Kilgore were captured by the Miami in 1750 at the invitation of the French commandant at Detroit, who ransomed them for 10 gallons of brandy and 100 pounds of tobacco and considered them his servants until they escaped.[6] John Defever claimed that he had been captured by Wyandots early in 1752, ransomed by the French commandant at Vincennes, and then taken to Quebec and Louisbourg before being released.[7] These ransoms by French officials transformed captives into prisoners of the government of New France.

A most revealing ransom in the prewar period concerned the six Pennsylvanian traders captured by chance in Cherokee country by Kahnawake Iroquois early in 1753. The six traders were initially taken to Fort des Miamis and then to Detroit, where the Kahnawake sold Jacob Evans and Thomas Hyde to Commandant Pierre-Joseph Céloron de Blainville. Unlike the Ohio Indian communities, the Kahnawake were very experienced at trading captives profitably to the Canadian governors, to Canadian employers, or to the captives' New England relatives or countrymen. On returning to Canada, these Kahnawake attempted to sell their other four captives to the new governor, Ange Duquesne de Menneville, Marquis Duquesne. Duquesne's strong sense of military honor and his personal humanity to captives would become evident in other cases, but he would not buy these prisoners. Susanna, a Kahnawake trader, explained that the governor of Canada "made answer he would have nothing to do with those Prisoners, upon which they, the Indians, took them to their Towns, and three of them were given to an Indian living in Caghnawaga, one to the Indians at Canassategy, and two [Jacob Evans and Thomas Hyde] were imprisoned at Québec, for what reason she did not know." Evidently the two captives bought by Céloron, on behalf of the Canadian government, were jailed as illegal traders, and the other four were prisoners of the Indians alone.[8]

All six of these captives joined in writing letters seeking relief and redemption. Albany mayor Robert Sanders, the trilingual merchant prominent in the illicit trade between Albany and Montreal, forwarded the captives' appeals to Philadelphia, including one of 9 June 1753, addressed to "Loving and unacquainted Friends."[9] Sanders and the other Albany Indian Commissioners met with Pennsylvania's Mohawk-speaking negotiator Conrad Weiser, sent to Albany for this purpose. They all interviewed trader Susanna and sent her back to Kahnawake chief Anuchrakechty with a wampum belt and a promise to pay well for the maintenance and transport of the captive traders. This was already the euphemism used by white authorities trying to avoid the appearance of buying captives, which might encourage the taking of more. Sanders explained to the captives what was being done for their "releasement," and emphasized that "the buying of you from the Indians would parhaps be of a Bad Consiquence as you are Taken in time of peace but we will reward them well for keeping & Bringing you here which they already know and you may tell them again."[10] Sanders also wrote to thank a Madame Louisa Desrivieres Desmurseaux and her husband, who lived in Kahnawake, "for her kind treatment & Civilitys to the foresaid prisoners." A Kahnawake named Nissewndanie brought captive Alexander McGinty to Albany in September 1753 and, after hard bargaining, released him for goods valued at £17.19.1½.[11] Three Kahnawake sachems arrived in Albany the following month, arguing that friends of the remaining three captives should pay the cost of negro replacements. This suggestion neatly paralleled the Canadian government's practice of exchanging Indian slaves for English captives.[12] The commissioners again tried to avoid direct purchase and insisted that the price paid to care for and deliver McGinty was their final offer for each captive. A deal for two of the prisoners, David Hendricks and Jabez (Toby) Evans, was arranged by the end of October.[13] The last Kahnawake captive from the McGinty party, William Powell, was not returned for another seven months, when a prominent Onondaga and his wife from "Kanossadaga" brought Powell to Albany. They evidently knew the game, and "demanded a negro man in exchange for said Powel." Eventually they settled for 8,000 wampum, to which the commissioners added "a blancket of Strouds and a shirt, because he is a principal Indian belonging to ye Onondaga Castle."[14]

There is a stark difference between what is known of the fates of the four captives retained by the Kahnawake and the two sold to the French. All four captives in Kahnawake hands were ransomed within eighteen months of their capture, at a total cost of £72.5.1½. This was enough below the initial asking price to prompt a much-publicized and derided letter of complaint from Kahnawake chief Anuchrakechty.[15] The Pennsylvania government eventually paid the cost of these four ransoms, blurring Sanders's efforts to insist that the payment was for "expenses."[16] The two traders who had been ransomed by Commandant Céloron at Detroit, Jacob Evans and Thomas Hyde, likely fared worse. Like several Pennsylvania traders captured in Ohio country in 1750, Evans and Hyde were considered illegal alien traders captured in French-claimed territory that, by 1753, apparently included Kentucky. They were last heard of in Quebec City, awaiting transport to prison in France.[17]

Chief Anuchrakechty's letter alerted or reminded inhabitants throughout the British North American colonies that ransom from Indian captors was an established business in Canada, and the famous letters of Robert Stobo the following year confirmed that this traffic was also possible at the new Fort Duquesne. Amid the bravado of Stobo's widely publicized letters, he named the prisoners held at the fort and reported that those held by the Indians there could have been ransomed, though for an exorbitant 40 pistoles each – much higher than the average price of £18.1.3 New York currency paid that same summer in Albany to redeem the Pennsylvania traders.[18] Ransom was possible, and it is not too surprising that Lieutenant Governor Robert Hunter Morris would include a ransom for recovered captives in his declaration of war against the Delaware in April of 1756.[19]

Despite Lieutenant Governor Morris's naive hope, the direct ransom of Pennsylvanians from Indian captors was very rare once war began.

Only two Allegheny country captives might have been ransomed during the war, both by Sir William Johnson in New York. One was an unnamed woman taken with Daniel McMullen at Minisink in December 1755 by North Branch Delaware. McMullen later reported that he and the woman were both bought by "French Margaret's" daughter, Catherine Montour, who, together with her mother and sister, became a broker in the sale and ransom of captives. Although he was in no position to be sure of his story, McMullen said he escaped while his new mistress was taking the woman who had been captured with him off to be ransomed by William Johnson. There is some evidence that another Susquehanna Valley captive was also ransomed by Johnson the following year.[20] The possible sale of a single captive a year to an Indian broker who then resold that captive to William Johnson in New York represented a very slim chance for ransom; most Indian captors were not interested in negotiating ransoms with their enemies during war.

Once war began, the only redemptions possible were through French military commanders, soldiers, missionaries, or traders.[21] Some civilian captives understandably called these French interventions ransom, or at least opportunities to ransom themselves. Although trader-captives Turner and Kilgore had been put to work at Detroit back in 1750, while waiting to be transported to Quebec and France, they had not been "working off" a ransom price. French commanders saw numerous civilian captives during the war, but most were presented by their Indian masters as proof of success in raiding, and then carried off to Indian villages. General Edward Braddock's hired guide, John Walker, was one of the first civilian war captives deliberately acquired by the commandant at Fort Duquesne. After interrogation, Walker was incarcerated briefly and then sent on what amounted to a guided tour, in irons, of most French forts from there to Montreal.[22] Other captives were interrogated at Fort Duquesne or given medical attention before their Indian captors took them on to Ohio villages. Barbara Leininger and Marie Le Roy were reportedly hired out to the French at the fort by their Delaware masters. Captured Canadian ensign Michel Maray de La Chauvignerie Jr said that his father, commanding at Fort Machault in 1757, had been given a total of three captives and had bought two others, but that "The Indians have a great Number of Prisoners, But they can scarce be prevail'd with to part with any of them."[23] Commandants were given a few of these captives and bought a few others.[24]

In at least three cases, Canadian soldiers bought white women captives directly from their Indian captors. Two were women of the British regiments captured in Braddock's defeat, likely taken by Canadian mission Indians. A Mrs Miller was apparently sold by her Indian captors to a French officer at Fort Niagara. Although the price he paid is not known, she subsequently ransomed herself for two years of service plus the ten guineas she had sewn into her petticoat. After serving the officer at Fort Toronto, and his wife in Montreal, Mrs Miller was released in 1757 and sent back to her native England in a cartel ship.[25] The future of the other two women bought by French soldiers was different. One, another survivor of 9 July 1755, was bought by a French subaltern, whom she married; she was captured again in the 1759 French surrender of Fort Niagara and returned to her first husband.[26] A third white woman, taken in a raid early in 1756, was traded by her Indian captor to an accompanying Canadian soldier for his share of the loot. The soldier, who valued his share at 400 livres (approximately £19 Pennsylvania currency), may have had more than one reason to reconsider his bargain; he subsequently offered her to the governor at his buying price, promising to marry her if this was not acceptable. No reply has been found.[27]

French missionaries and traders in the west are also known to have occasionally bought British captives, who might work off their ransom, and then become prisoners of war in Canada. Charles Stuart and his wife were captured in the major Delaware-Shawnee-Mingo raid on Big Cove in October 1755 and given to Wyandots by Delaware chief Shingas. After eight months with the Wyandot, they were sold to two French priests and stayed with them in the Wyandot village near Detroit "Till they had Workt Out their Ransom money wch amtd To abt 24 Pennsylvania Moneys Worth of European Goods as they sell at retail in the Country Stores, The Ransom Money was work'd Out By the 1st of March 1757 After wch they workt one month for 30 French Livres." The couple had paid their modest ransom (about £8 sterling each) with eight months of work, and then they were sent, with other captives, as prisoners to Quebec. After two months in prison there, while their companion Captain John Smith of Vause's Fort enjoyed the liberties afforded captive officers, the Stuarts joined Smith, Mrs Miller, and a large company of released prisoners aboard a cartel ship that took them to Plymouth, England. The couple were back in Philadelphia, via Cork and New York, by December 1757, twenty-six months after their capture.[28]

Mrs John Martin and her five children were captured in the same Delaware-Shawnee-Mingo raid as the Stuarts, and French ransom became the way home for two of them. Two-year-old Janet, tethered outside the Kittanning hut of her new Delaware owner, caught the eye of a Canadian trader, who ransomed her for a blanket. Mrs Martin was also bought "by the French" and eventually taken to Quebec. Not only was she able to ransom herself by working, but she also rediscovered Janet there, and worked to ransom her for the initial price of the blanket. They both were sent to England, and later returned to Philadelphia. The reunion with her husband occurred just before he went out to Tuscarawas himself, as a courier to Shingas in 1762, seeking his other three surviving children, who would not be returned until November of 1764.[29]

The ransom of civilian captives by the French in Ohio country during the war was infrequent, and prices varied so much as to suggest that there was no sizable or established market for their labor there. Mrs Miller repaid about £21 sterling for her liberty, the Stuarts repaid only £8 each, at least two captives were bought for nine to ten gallons of liquor each, while a child was bought for a blanket. Logstown Delaware or Shawnee "sold a Prisoner to the French [and] received a nine gallon Cagg of Brandy."[30]

Upon reaching Montreal or Quebec, ransomed or purchased Allegheny civilian captives who had come into French hands joined thousands of military prisoners and civilian captives from all theatres. Some, like Mrs Miller or Jean Lowry, arrived with time yet to serve on their ransom, whereas others like the Stuarts arrived already freed from their ransom obligations. When John Walker arrived in Montreal, in irons, he said he was interrogated, spent a week in jail, and was then hired out to work "at 15 Livres a Month, 10 of Which the Governor was to have, and the Prisoner the Rest, which is done to all the English Prisoners, who won't renounce their Religion."[31]

Allegheny prisoners, military and civilian, indentured or not, found unexpected sources of assistance in Canada. An amazing number were helped by the generosity of wealthy fellow captive Colonel Peter Schuyler (1710–62), commander of the captured Oswego garrison (see illustration 4). Between 1756 and 1758 his lodgings in Quebec were an open house for English prisoners. He sent supplies to the sick in jail or hospital, lent money, endorsed notes, ransomed captives, and officially negotiated exchanges of prisoners. He was allowed to return home for a time in 1757, on parole, to arrange additional credit. Many of those he helped before his own exchange in October 1758, and through designated deputies for nine months thereafter, were from his New Jersey regiment, or from more northern British colonies, but the gratitude

4 "Colonel Peter Schuyler, Patron of Captives in Canada." Artist unknown. Collections of the New Jersey Historical Society, Newark, New Jersey.

expressed by Allegheny captives and their governments indicates the range and scale of his generosity. The Virginia House of Burgesses, in repaying Schuyler – with interest – for his expenses on behalf of Virginians, commended him "for his unparalleled Tenderness and Humanity to Captain Robert Stobo and several other Inhabitants of this Colony, who have been, and still are unfortunate Prisoners in Canada." Jean Lowry's gloomy and self-righteous account of her sufferings in Canada included a warm tribute to Schuyler, "who was singularly kind unto and careful of me and many others, for which I can never be sufficiently thankful."[32] There is very little surviving evidence that Allegheny captives were aided by the network of former New England captives who had become Canadian nuns, wives, and employers of English captives, though such assistance may have occurred.[33] Once they had repaid their ransom, civilian prisoners held in Canada could hope to be exchanged with soldiers via Crown Point, New York, or put aboard a cartel ship for Boston or England.

One group of "Thirteen Americans," who arrived aboard a cartel ship at Spithead in September of 1757, petitioned the British Admiralty for clothes and passage home and explained how they got there. They reported being taken from their homes on the frontiers of Pennsylvania and Virginia by French-allied Indians, who "Carried us to Canada and Sold us as Slaves to the French and kept our Children with them and we ourselves Oblig'd to work out our ransom with the French before they would allow us to become Prisoners of War, and at last had the good Fortune to be Exchang'd."[34] These thirteen, and the dozen others described above, were the only civilians known to have been ransomed out of more than 1,000 captured while the war continued in Allegheny country.

After a truce was negotiated at Easton and Fort Pitt, it was thought that the prospects for ransoming captives would improve. After their mission to the Susquehanna Delaware at Wyoming, in June of 1758, Christian Frederick Post and Charles Thomson laid out the obvious problem: captives were private property, and Indian communities had "no public Fund to redeem them out of the Hands of private Persons."[35] Post and Thomson were reporting to both the British Army's General John Forbes and Pennsylvania's lieutenant governor, William Denny, but they did not venture to suggest who should organize and pay for such ransoms.

There were major difficulties for individuals anxious to find and redeem their missing kin, in the wake of a savage war that caused hatred, impoverishment, and migrations on all sides. Traders at Fort Pitt and Shamokin could be urged to make inquiries of those Indians who first risked coming to trade there, and the first white traders venturing west again were asked to do likewise. Christian Frederick Post and Pisquetomen went west on a diplomatic mission in November of 1758 that was definitely too early for safe travel. The party was attacked near Loyalhanna, where five members of its military escort were killed, and five others were captured by the Shawnee. Captured Sergeant Henry Austin of the Virginia Regiment was to be burned to death, and Post and Pisquetomen joined Menatochyard (Delaware George) and Captain Bull in frantic negotiations that saved his life. Sergeant Austin became one of the first private redemptions at the end of the war: within a month his master returned him to Fort Pitt on Austin's promise to pay ten gallons of rum as ransom.[36]

The redemption of George Woods reveals a more complicated arrangement that may not have been unique. Cayuga John Hudson had already facilitated the return of at least one captive when, in July 1757, he acquired two more captives, who had already been held for a year. He took George Woods and Jenny Grey to Fort Duquesne, where, after several days of negotiation, he turned George Woods over to the French. Woods had done some negotiating on his own, promising Hudson ten pounds of tobacco a year when he got home. Woods was released by the French, and had annual visits from Hudson and his son that continued at least to 1780. On some of these visits they discussed Jenny Grey, a four year old when Hudson became her master and probably her adoptive father. He was proud to report to Woods that Jenny grew up Iroquois, married, and raised a family in the Mohawk Valley.[37] The case of John McCullough, explained earlier, reveals the additional difficulties in redeeming transformed and resistant child captives.

Despite strenuous efforts, the improved communications possible during the truce, and the evident willingness of a few Indians to consider some ransoms, Richard Bard, a miller in York County, Pennsylvania, was the only individual who redeemed anyone privately in this period. Bard had escaped in 1758 from the Delaware captors who still held his wife, Ketty, and he risked execution by venturing west the following winter with a party of Delaware negotiators, led by Coquetageghton (White Eyes).[38] After only a few miles, the Indians became drunk and very threatening, and Richard fled back to the fort. However, he had learned who held Ketty and where, and he managed to send a letter conveying his promise of a ransom of £40 Pennsylvania currency for her safe return. He later negotiated with one Indian who initially agreed to attempt a rescue but then declined, claiming that the risks were too high. Whether or not Richard had word from Ketty's captors, he went up to Shamokin and then headed west once again. He soon met a party, led by a Delaware known as John James, that included Ketty and other members of her adoptive family, presumably coming east to meet Richard. Even with his strenuous and persistent efforts, the willingness of Ketty's captors, and the good fortune or coincidence of this meeting, the concluding negotiations in December 1760 were tense. The captors were reluctant to go near garrisoned Fort Augusta at Shamokin, and Richard had been cautious enough to bring none of the ransom money along with him. He offered himself as hostage while his wife went to Shamokin for the money that apparently settled this large ransom quite amicably.[39]

The only group that actively pursued private ransoming of captives during the truce was the Quakers' Friendly Association, and its efforts were primarily with captives taken by the North Branch Delaware, who had made peace earlier than the Ohio tribes. Holland was at Shamokin in the spring of 1758, when he sent Israel Pemberton a detailed account of a frustrating conversation about captives that he had had with French Margaret's daughter, Catherine Montour, and a Delaware named William Sock, who had come downriver from Tioga. It was then that Catherine Montour showed receipts for what she had paid for captives David McMullin and Thomas Moffat – only to have them run away; she insisted that she would not lose more money to recover captives. Holland was surprised that she "seem'd to have no manner of Commisseration for the unhappy Captives," and he could learn little about specific captives, "those who have, or have had any will not be conversant about them."[40]

Nathaniel Holland persisted and soon strengthened his local influence by being appointed the provincial storekeeper at Shamokin.[41] When Teedyuscung visited in the spring of 1759 and heard of Holland's concern for captives, he asked why nothing had been done for a young woman captive living nearby. Holland, taking the captain of the garrison with him, promptly found Catherine Nicholson and gave an unspecified present in return for her freedom. Holland took it "extremely ill" that local Indians he had befriended had said nothing about her or other captives.[42] In May 1760 Holland noticed that French Margaret had brought a captive boy to within sight of Shamokin, and rightly assumed he was for sale. Holland balked at the asking price of £20, explaining to Israel Pemberton that this might be tolerable if the lad were the only captive, but Holland suspected that this was a price-setting experiment. Within two months, he had redeemed the boy for £9.7.6. The problems apparently did not end with the ransom. In October, Holland reported that when presented with a choice of going east or being indentured at Shamokin, the redeemed lad chose to become an indentured servant of the provincial government at Shamokin. He became visible proof of the repeated Indian claim, which Holland had somehow found outrageous, that captives who returned to the whites would become servants.[43]

Although Holland was assiduous in collecting information about the location of captives, and was active in attempting to redeem them, he also presented himself to the Friendly Association as shrewd and economical with its funds. Captive Thomas Lane, taken at Fort Niagara by French-allied Indians and severely used, was brought to Shamokin by his masters. Lane had promised £10 for his freedom, but could not raise the money. Holland thought to "put off" the captors with some flour, but was warned that these people held a girl captive as well, who might not be released unless the terms were seen as fair. "I gave them £7.10 – privately, with which they seem'd well satisfied."[44] Holland paid the same price for a captured trader's servant.[45]

The Friendly Association supported Holland's efforts at Shamokin, but it also tried to find and recover captives through the peripatetic and indefatigable Christian Frederick Post. In August of 1761 he reported to Pemberton from Tuscarawas that the Shawnee were reluctant to bring in what he thought were about 150 captives. He could report no ransoms among the Ohio Delaware, and rightly foresaw that they would not attend that summer's conference in Pennsylvania, preferring to take captives to the great Johnson-Croghan meeting at Detroit. The comparative generosity of the officials of the Indian Department, and the diplomatic value of these exchanges, were evident. All Post could do was distribute some combs, brooches, and buttons among the captives, odd gifts in light of his concluding lament that "Our prisoners amongst em go as if they were broke[n] down from the Gally, it makes any ones heart ache to see them so Ragged & naked."[46] The Quakers' Friendly Association achieved only a few ransoms, and demonstrated that even those with active agents, resources, and excellent information could not accomplish much.

The British Army's commanders were as unsympathetic to private ransom as were those Delaware and Mingos who so frustrated Nathaniel Holland.[47] Hugh Mercer, a Scottish doctor who was a veteran of Braddock's defeat and the Kittanning raid and was a lieutenant colonel commanding at Fort Pitt in the winter of 1758–59, displayed this view clearly and prophetically. A Delaware couple brought in a young girl captive, requiring whiskey for the man and a present for the woman "whose property" the girl was. Mercer "judged it necessary to sett them right in their Notions of delivering up our People; and told them, we were not come into their Country to purchase our People of them, but to offer them Peace, on the Condition of every one of the Captives being brought home & delivered up early in the Spring; otherwise there was No Peace, but I would demand them in the Mid[d]le of their Towns." Mercer then claimed that he took the girl, and gave the woman a matchcoat "out of charity." Since the Delaware couple made no further demands, Mercer judged them satisfied.[48] Within a few weeks Mercer was asking Colonel Henry Bouquet what to do about captives who were visiting the fort with their Indian families and wanted to stay: "May we not interfere – The Country People sollicit me to purchase their friends, but that method I detest, as most dishonourable." Bouquet agreed entirely and hoped that the 1759 campaign against Quebec would weaken the French in the Ohio Valley enough to allow a punitive expedition.[49] He could not have imagined that such an undertaking would be five years away. The question of what to do about captives brought in to Fort Pitt was soon solved, as has been seen. George Croghan, as deputy superintendent of Indian affairs, arrived that spring to begin three years of intense diplomacy – at the expense of the British Army – that recovered over 400 captives, in return for expensive presents that were seldom called ransom by either side.

Like Mercer, General Jeffrey Amherst found ransom dishonorable, and had all but banned it by the end of 1760. The sense of dishonor may have been linked either to grandiose presumptions that the military had already imposed a peace that had stipulated the surrender of captives or to military notions of exchange of prisoners. Amherst was also attempting to control his expenses by curbing Croghan, which was not accomplished before 1762. By then Amherst was drawing upon recent experience with the Cherokee to argue that a thorough trade embargo would force the return of captives. Yet great sums had been spent in the name of the king, and the military was also determined to maintain the royal monopoly on Indian diplomacy, while cutting costs. When the Pennsylvania government organized and funded the Lancaster conference of August 1762, Amherst insisted that the discussion could be exclusively about the return of captives, which was reportedly why the attending Indians were disgusted. When Pennsylvania commissioners subsequently attempted to distribute presents themselves, Colonel Bouquet objected and Amherst supported him.[50]

The generals did make some genuine efforts, short of ransom, to return captive children. After the capture of Canada, Amherst sent to Philadelphia six named children who had been captured in Pennsylvania and held in Canada. One of them was John Man, taken together with his mother and a brother and the Jemison family, almost all soon killed after the Shawnee attack on Marsh Creek in April 1758. John was sold to a French officer and brought to Montreal. At the British capture of this city, John was released and taken in, "almost naked," by recently arrived British merchants Finlay and Campbell. The next spring, these merchants advertised in the *Pennsylvania Gazette* for John's kin, asking that they either send an indenture for him to serve until maturity or, "on paying Charges, they may have him on Demand." Three months later, without either of these options materializing, John was sent to Philadelphia on Amherst's orders, and was at the state house awaiting his still-missing kin. The same issue carried another advertisement, likely placed on the order of Thomas Gage, military governor of conquered Montreal. In this ad Elizabeth Ball, a girl captured by Indians at Conococheague five years earlier, sought her parents, her uncle, or her mother's relations. If any of them would report "their desire of having the said Elizabeth Ball return to live with them," General Gage would have her sent promptly from the Montreal convent where she was living.[51]

Although ransoms ended when the truce died, and were not considered by either side during Pontiac's War,[52] there would be fortunate irony in two incidents during this war. The first involved the Ottawa capture/rescue of the Green Bay garrison and the survivors of the Michilimackinac garrison. The Ottawa negotiated with the Ojibwa to gain control of all the captive soldiers, without any known compensation, and then agreed to pay ransom for five traders. Thirty-four officers, soldiers, and traders, and what could be recovered of their goods, became unusual commodities in a cavalcade of Ottawa canoes that followed their traditional trade route down the Ottawa River, arriving at Montreal on 6 August 1763. In conference there, the astonished General Thomas Gage was determined to "reward them well," providing lavish presents and expressing "everlasting Esteem" for the L'Arbre Croche Ottawa. Gage revealed his reaction more frankly to William Johnson: "The whole Behavior of these People, has exceeded any thing that could be expected, from Nations much more polished & refined. It is indeed beyond Belief. They resisted the Menaces of the Chippawas and refused any share of the Plunder."[53] Neither the minutes nor the report of William Johnson's deputy gives any details of the presents/ransoms paid in gratitude to the Ottawa. The army that banned ransom and presents to the Indians had just made a major exception on its own behalf.

A final ransom of this war was the second ransom of George Croghan himself. In June of 1765, Croghan led a diplomatic mission to the

Illinois that was attacked by Kickapoo and Mascouten warriors near the mouth of the Wabash River. Three Shawnee deputies and two of Croghan's men were killed in the attack, and Croghan and two other whites were taken captive. Although robbed of all his presents, money, and equipment, Croghan was still able to arrange credit once they arrived at Fort Ouiatenon. Croghan was not released until the French commandant at Fort Chartres ordered it, and Croghan paid a ransom of sixty-four gallons of newly bought rum.[54] This last ransom, of himself, was at nearly seven times the quantity of rum that had ransomed Sergeant Henry Austin in 1758.

Private ransom was rare for Allegheny captives of the Ohio Valley peoples. Unlike the Kahnawake, they were neither familiar with, nor much interested in, returning captives this way. Those seeking to ransom kin faced major obstacles in even locating them or arranging meetings, especially when the military was uncooperative. During a truce in which at least 411 Allegheny captives had been returned through formal diplomacy with the Crown's representatives, only twenty-five captives are known to have been ransomed privately, or through French intervention. Croghan's presents were likely more valuable than some of the direct ransoms offered, and his method was viewed by all sides as a more honorable exchange of gifts and a legitimate part of negotiating or sustaining peace, trade, and alliance.

Exchange of prisoners was not within the martial assumptions or habits of the Delaware, Shawnee, or Mingo in Pennsylvania or Allegheny country. In intertribal war or peacemaking, the exchange of warrior captives would have been contrary to all expectations. Retained captives had become kin, or at least private possessions, and exchange violated these senses of belonging as well as perceptions of honor. Intertribal peace treaties that included an exchange of prisoners, like the Iroquois-Catawba and Iroquois-Cherokee treaties of the early 1750s, had been reluctantly negotiated under British pressure, and the prisoner exchange features of these agreements were minimal, contested, and never fulfilled. A commentator in 1761 remarked that Indians objected to "a Prisoner's fighting Against them A Second Time … and are mighty displeased with us for Exchanging Prisoners."[55]

In contrast, European or colonial regulars or militia captured while fighting each other had good prospects of eventual exchange. The exchange of prisoners of war in western Europe had evolved to include all military personnel, evaluated in the elaborate tables of their ranks. The majority of captured regular and militia officers in America were sought out and acquired by successful military commanders, almost certainly in exchange for gifts if the captors had been Indians. These professional peers became prisoners of war without any personal obligation to repay their ransom or work for their keep, and they could anticipate eventual exchange. Captured officers could be paroled and returned in anticipation that someone of comparable rank would be released in exchange. The two captains who became captives/hostages after the French prewar victory at Fort Necessity had been treated generously, and this standard was not abandoned because of the Virginians' abuse of Captain Michel Pepin *dit* La Force. Young Ensign La Chauvignerie Jr, in contrast, was free on his parole while a captive, and was sent aboard a flag of truce ship from Philadelphia to be released without designated exchange in Hispaniola in the spring of 1759.[56] Virginian ranger Captain John Smith, who had gained some notoriety from his spirited defense of doomed Vause's Fort, was given enough freedom in captivity to survey several upcountry French forts, estimate French and Indian manpower, and urge Indians near Detroit to defect to the English.[57] He was never imprisoned and was sent to England for exchange within a year of his capture.

In contrast, captured rank-and-file soldiers, regular or militia, whether taken directly or ransomed from Indian captors, became prisoners of a king, and were either jailed or sent to work in Canada or British America. Their subsistence was to be provided on account, and they were not required to pay off any ransom that had been paid to acquire them from Indian captors. One way home for such soldiers was the cartel ships that took prisoners of war from Canada to Boston and to England in 1757 and 1760, from Louisbourg to France in 1758, or from New York to France in 1761.[58] Such voyages presumed that French and British authorities would subsequently arrange appropriate exchanges.

The exchange of prisoners within the North American theatre of the Seven Years' War involved very few captives from the Allegheny war. The British, with a manpower advantage and better supply of provisions than their opponent, were not drawn to initiate exchanges, nor was the Canadian governor of New France. After the capture of Fort Niagara and Quebec, and serious impending food shortages for a country under siege, Governor Pierre-François Rigaud, Marquis de Vaudreuil, finally initiated negotiations for an exchange completed in December 1759. Although both sides agreed to use the new Convention of Sluis (Écluse) as a guide, there were predictable arguments about the status of colonial rangers and *troupes de la marine*. In a vague imitation of the cartel's "initial exchange," Vaudreuil sent 270 prisoners to Crown Point: 16 officers, 90 British regulars, 47 rangers, 48 colonial soldiers, and 69 civilians. Few of these returned prisoners were from the Allegheny theatre of war. One was James Smith, taken while road building for Braddock's army and finally escaping the Kahnawake at Montreal four years later, only to become a prisoner of the French. The others captured in the west were Major James Grant and two fellow officers in his failed raid on Fort Duquesne. Amherst carefully matched the officers in sending 211 prisoners: 53 French regulars, 35 marines, 107 Canadian militia, 14 military support staff, and 2 women.[59] Amherst did not accept the exchange of civilians, nor their status as prisoners of war. The two women he returned were not weighed in the exchange, but were those readily available from among the small group of wives of the captured Niagara garrison who had initially refused to return directly to Canada and were being maintained by the British Army under the specific terms of this surrender. Amherst deliberately refused his own commissary of prisoners' plea on behalf of the long-held Captain La Force and, due either to respect or contempt, excluded all the *troupes de la marine* officers taken at La Belle Famille, then living in comfortable parole on Long Island. The only captured officers from this incident who were exchanged were the colonel and major of the Detroit militia.[60]

With Indian and European conventions so different concerning prisoner exchange, it is interesting to notice any cross-cultural negotiations of this sort. In 1753 the Kahnawake were willing to sell or trade a captive English trader for a negro slave, but this was not a conventional exchange of captives. The same year, South Carolina's governor, James Glen, likely in innocent ignorance, called in vain for the Shawnee to exchange captives for the four Shawnee he held in jail. Something resembling an exchange occurred that year when George Croghan and Andrew Montour were captured from the party returning Glen's two other Shawnee captives. Upon recognizing their returning kin, the Shawnee captors released Croghan and Montour, despite the handsome price the French had put on their heads. As reported, this exchange was immediate, natural, and without ceremony – it was also while the Shawnee and British were still at peace.

There was only one fleeting and intriguing whisper of cross-cultural exchange of prisoners during the war. In Pennsylvania's earliest diplomatic approach to the warring North Branch Delaware in April of 1756, Iroquois intermediaries pressing Teedyuscung's followers to return white captives received the retort that the Delaware expected the return of all their people held captive. Pennsylvania's governor was surprised, and protested that only one Delaware was then in jail, for his own protection. It is not clear whether Teedyuscung had been referring to the Indian refugees gathered at Conestoga Manor, or to those with the Moravians who had refused to join him. In any case, his negotiating strategy would soon shift to the exchange of white captives for the return of Indian lands.[61]

Given the absence of prisoner exchange between the British and the Indians, the initial interactions between Ottawa chief Pontiac, British major Henry Gladwin, and Potawatomi negotiators in the early summer of 1763 are particularly interesting. When Pontiac invited a very suspicious Gladwin to negotiate at the house of Canadian Antoine Cuillerier, Gladwin understandably declined. Captain Donald Campbell, who had been the more genial previous commander at Detroit, and Lieutenant George McDougall then volunteered to go in Gladwin's stead. Gladwin demanded hostages before allowing his officers to parley, and Potawatomi chiefs Big Ears and No-Kaming were surrendered and held in the fort.[62] When Pontiac decided to hold the two negotiating British officers as prisoners, he thereby left the Potawatomi chiefs as prisoners of Gladwin. Although Pontiac had violated the understanding with Gladwin, he was well aware of the uses of an exchange of prisoners. When Antoine Cuillerier subsequently bought John Rutherfurd from his Indian captors early in June, likely as an indirect ransom, some Indian leaders interpreted this as an unwelcome sign that peace was being negotiated. Pontiac responded forcefully, reclaiming Rutherfurd, and reportedly said "that it was not good President [*sic*] to sell their Prisoners, that when things come to be accomodated they cou'd exchange them or give them up as they saw occasion."[63]

Not surprisingly, the Potawatomi were soon wavering in their support for Pontiac; they were talking peace at the fort, and brought three captured soldiers to exchange for their two chiefs held there. Gladwin readily accepted the return of the ensign and two soldiers, but exchanged only Chief No-Kaming, insisting that the more prominent Chief Big Ears would be returned only in exchange for all the other English captives of the Potawatomi. Over the ensuing weeks, the Potawatomi surrendered sixteen more captives in reclaiming Big Ears, bargaining that should have acutely embarrassed British officers who were so status-conscious in balancing ranks whenever exchanging prisoners with the French.[64] It is essential to notice that Big Ears and No-Kaming had not been captured in battle, but were betrayed hostages. Negotiating an exchange for them would not bring shame on them, or on those who negotiated their release.

There had been limited results from attempts to negotiate the return of Allegheny captives outside the formal diplomacy that centered on George Croghan at Fort Pitt. Private ransom of captives from Indians had very little success, as it was hampered by inherent difficulties in negotiating with enemies in a poorly understood cultural borderland, and was discouraged by the general refusal of British military authorities to help. The sale of captives to the French, with the price then considered as a ransom to be repaid in work, was a little more frequent. A total of seventy-three captives of the Allegheny war are known to have been ransomed directly, or through French purchase. The other mode of negotiating for captives was through the direct exchange of captives. Aside from the Potawatomi exchange at Detroit in 1763, there is no evidence of the cross-cultural exchange of prisoners. Although Europeans had well-developed practices for the exchange of prisoners, these were not applied in North America before 1759, and included only 104 who might be termed prisoners of the Allegheny war. Most of the Allegheny captives who were formally exchanged (82) were French and Canadians returned by the British Army. These results were modest, could not compare with the 411 recovered by Croghan by 1762, and still left about 1,500 Allegheny captives who would be thought of as missing at the end of October of 1764.[65] By then a more coercive method was being attempted.

15

Forced Return of Captives

The use of force to recover captives and prisoners was always a dangerous option. Not only did all cultures accept that prisoners could be used first as general deterrents against attack, and then as individual shields in such an attack, but they also believed that killing prisoners was acceptable when they could undermine or encumber their attacked captors. Despite these hazards, the English used three kinds of military initiative that could have the recovery of prisoners as a major objective: "hot pursuit" of the raiding parties who had taken prisoners, a deliberate raid on a community known to hold numerous captives, and a large-scale expedition undertaken expressly to force the release of captives. Each of these forceful methods had different risks, costs, and results that changed perceptions of their usefulness through the decade of war. Were there stages in the use of these methods, or was there some evolution in scale of forceful strategies used to recover captives?

All participants used hot pursuit as a form of counterattack. Raids by Indians on other Indians' communities have left very few records, but such raids routinely provoked immediate pursuit that frequently recovered some of the recently captured. The Delaware very effectively pursued the Pennsylvanians who attacked Kittanning in 1756, though the captives they sought to recover were English, not Delaware. Since the English took no Indian captives in raids, Indians were not pursuing to recover their own people. The French and Indians promptly counterattacked Major James Grant's raiders at Fort Duquesne in 1759, and again the captives taken were all English.

Only British colonial militia and rangers used hot pursuit expressly, and eventually routinely, to recover their own people. Local colonial forces, entirely frustrated by their inability to prevent raids and captures, or even to find their enemy, were drawn to hot pursuit as a purposeful outlet for anger that trumped fear and horror. Assembled from those who could respond quickly, and usually mounted in order to have any hope of overtaking the raiders, the rescuers seldom had any clear idea about the size of the force they pursued, or whether several related enemy raiding parties would coalesce on the trail and become more formidable than the tracks might suggest. In order to catch up with the raiders, who might be a day or two ahead of the mounted pursuers, the latter had to ride hard along one of the very few military roads or major trading paths through the forested mountains. Even if they had quickly assembled adequate food for more than a few days, they could not bring fodder in meaningful quantities, and were tempted to go farther than would allow them to preserve sufficient food and fodder for their return. Hungry and exhausted rescuers straggling through the woods were readily killed or captured.

As captive Elizabeth Ryan noticed, noisy rescuers were easily detected, and their fighting potential was readily assessed by observers from the hiding rearguard of the retreating Indian raiding party. If the rescuers were heavily outnumbered by the captors, a devastating ambush was easily executed. If the rescuers appeared too numerous, the raiders and their captives could hide until the danger passed. In the infrequent event that a superior force of rescuers managed to overtake and surprise a raiding party, the results were still unpredictable.

The risks of hot pursuit were clearly displayed in the "battle" of Sideling Hill in April of 1756. After burning McCord's Fort in Cumberland County, Shingas and his Delaware war party headed west with twenty-six captives. Four days later, evidently after the Delaware relaxed their vigilance, they were surprised on Sideling Hill by a party of what captive Jean Lowry called "Friends and Neighbours, who had Assembled so quickly and pursued so diligently for our Rescue." The neighbors, reinforced by militia and members of the provincial garrison at Fort Lyttleton to number about fifty, had approached the Delaware camp undetected and launched a dawn attack. In the initial volley, only one Indian was killed and one wounded, and the Delaware immediately scattered into the laurel shrubbery. The rescuers untied the captives from their overnight bonds and cautiously moved everyone to higher ground. Then the Delaware, who had reassembled in the dense shrubbery and surrounded the would-be rescuers and their rescued, counterattacked very effectively. In the ensuing two-hour skirmish, twenty rescuers and one captive girl were killed, as were three Delaware. Four children and Mrs John Thorn were the only captives who managed to escape or remain with their surviving rescuers, who broke out of the Delaware encirclement and retreated to Fort Lyttleton.[1] This failure was promptly represented as an unequal contest between the inaccurate, if more rapid-firing, smooth-bore muskets of the militia and the rifled guns well used by the Delaware.[2] The battle of Sideling Hill was not the last of the hot pursuits, but Pennsylvanian troops lost their appetite for this type of rescue for years. Seven years later, Pennsylvanians used it again, twice, and each time the chase ended in the discovery of the bodies of captives who had been killed to facilitate escape.[3]

It is not surprising that relatives of the captured were known to counsel against hot pursuit. Real or feared pursuit prompted captors to kill some noisy infants, as well as the wounded, weak, old, overweight, and pregnant. As has been seen, captives were driven hard to put distance between raiders and pursuers in the first days after capture. Mary Jemison eventually accepted the argument that it was close pursuit that caused her captors to kill five of the six who had been captured with her in 1758, and closely pursued captors were known to have killed six or seven captives before scattering in the face of hot pursuit by Pennsylvanians again in the summer of 1764.[4] If horses had been captured in a raid, as happened more frequently as the Ohio Indians came to use and sell horses in this period, the raiding party's initial retreat could be quicker. The underfed and hard-driven horses would likely fail and be abandoned, and the raiders then moved captives and themselves through the forested highlands without easy detection.

Hot pursuit, however, came to have some successes, especially for Virginians. As the Seven Years' War progressed and the no-man's-land widened, more garrisons became outposts located to the west of the raids, and the chances of overtaking retreating Indian captors improved. In October 1759 Virginia militia and rangers from Fort Dunlop chased a Shawnee war party and their fourteen captives taken from Carr's (Kerr's) Creek. In a night skirmish, ten of the captured were recovered, along with seventeen horseloads of plunder.[5] Virginia rangers overtook another war party two days after their attack on the South Branch of the Potomac River in August 1763. Two prisoners, eleven horses, and considerable plunder were recovered.[6] The following month Virginia militia recovered Mrs George Workman and her three children within a day of their capture, and David Cloyd's four slaves were recovered the following spring after a ten-day pursuit.[7]

Hot pursuit produced poor results in these Allegheny wars. Pennsylvanians tried it early in the Seven Years' War, abandoned it for a time after tragic results, and then revived this tactic again in Pontiac's War, with equally poor results. Virginians came to hot pursuit a little later in the Seven Years' War, and maintained this method of counterattack thereafter. In total, some thirty-nine captives were rescued by colonial forces and at least eight more were recovered in intertribal raiding in Allegheny country between the Cherokee, Shawnee, and Catawba in this period. It is not possible to specify how many captives were killed on the trail because of hot pursuit, but for most of the decade of war, they were not routinely killed as rescuers approached. Nonetheless, the number of captives and rescuers killed certainly exceeded the number of captives recovered by hot pursuit. Forcing the return of captives could be an ennobling venture, but the odds were against clear success.

The Kittanning raid of September 1756 was a unique, ambitious, and puzzling attempt to recover captives by force. What was expected would happen to the estimated 150 English captives held there when the Pennsylvanians attacked? Despite the large size of the attacking force, the advantage of an early morning surprise, and the insider information provided by escaped captive John Baker, the Pennsylvanians failed to destroy the town and recovered few captives. The efficient Delaware version of hot pursuit followed, encumbered neither by concern for the fate of Delaware captives – for the Pennsylvanians had taken none – nor by delays to gather supplies. In the rout of the Pennsylvanians, the Delaware recaptured several of their English captives. Thirty-three Pennsylvanian raiders were killed, and two more were captured and burned to death after an attack that had killed fourteen Delaware and recovered seven captives. The raid proved how far Pennsylvania could send a substantial force, and that it was willing to risk the lives of captives in order to make this counterstrike. Both sides celebrated victory in their own ways, but the Pennsylvanians had very good reasons not to repeat this reckless venture.

The most impressive and successful use of force to recover captives was the British Army's expedition to the Muskingum River in 1764, led by Colonel Henry Bouquet. The poor results of the Kittanning raid had been masked by propaganda, but better information should have prevented any serious consideration of another expedition into the Ohio Valley to recover captives. Certainly the British Army, remembering General Edward Braddock's defeat, had earlier shown little interest in such a project. General Jeffrey Amherst, like other army officers, felt that the conquest of New France had been a display of power that should have brought Indians to return all their captives, as they had repeatedly promised at Easton in 1758, at Fort Pitt in 1759, and at Lancaster in 1762. The return of more than 400 captives through George Croghan and William Johnson by 1762 may have looked like reassuring compliance, but it was actually brought about by paying expensive ransoms, a practice that ended with the increasing restrictions on spending imposed by Britain and enforced by Amherst. Indian failure to return all their captives had come to be seen as proof that Indian negotiations had been in bad faith, especially after the outbreak of the Anglo-Indian War in 1763.

By 1764 the British Army had come to show uncharacteristic enthusiasm in recovering captives by force when it was trying to bring the embarrassing and expensive new Indian war to an end. Punitive British expeditions that had burned Cherokee towns farther south in 1760 and 1761 were rightly credited with prompting a negotiated peace. Amherst planned expeditions into Ohio country, one via Lake Erie and the other moving west from Pennsylvania. If all went well, these efforts could project enough power for long enough to prompt Indian agreement to a truce. In negotiating such a truce, the assurances of Indian chiefs and war captains were no longer considered adequate, for they had little authority to control kin and neighbors who favored continuing raiding or keeping their captives. Taking hostages was one part of the army's tactics, but both the French and Indian War and the Cherokee War had demonstrated that Indian hostages were never so influential that all raiding ceased because of them, and hostages were hard to hold and protect, especially if given enough liberty to distinguish them from military criminals.[8] In its early stages, the British Army's commanders were planning punitive expeditions that would include taking hostages, but there was no mention of recovering captives.

Could the English insist upon the return of all captives in 1764 as a precondition that would demonstrate a wider Indian acceptance of a truce? Some prominent soldiers had thought so for some time, even before the punitive expeditions of the Cherokee War had brought negotiations. Lieutenant Colonel Hugh Mercer had reported to his commanding officer in February of 1759 that he had told Indians who wanted ransom for captives that if captives were not returned without compensation, he "would demand them from the Mid[d]le of their Towns."[9] Colonel Henry Bouquet had agreed with Mercer, answering his question about recovering captives with, "I hope that we shall soon be able to force them [the Ohio Indians] to comply with their Treaty."[10] Mercer and Bouquet were ahead of the army in this view, but five busy years later Bouquet could finally make a serious proposal on the matter. In May of 1764, he sent Amherst's successor, General Thomas Gage, suggestions for terms he thought appropriate to be demanded of the

Ohio nations. The second of his terms, after the surrender and execution of the killers of English traders in 1763, was: "That they deliver up all the white men, they have amongst them, either as Prisoners, or adopted, and the last to be absolutely insisted on, whether they themselves consent to it or not, as they [and some Frenchmen living with the Shawanese] have been very active against us." Bouquet was remembering the spying, deceptions, and robberies of a few adoptees, but likely recognized that a widespread return of captives would indicate a broader acceptance of peace.[11] This measure would avenge the honor of the army, demonstrate a humbling submission by the Indians, and, courtesy of the British Army, bring the captives back to increasingly disgruntled colonials. General Gage agreed with Bouquet's ideas, but deferred to William Johnson's knowledge and experience in Indian diplomacy for final judgment.[12]

As Bouquet prepared for his expedition, the Shawnee issued their own revealing call for peace with their "Friends and Brothers" the British, just as William Johnson was preparing for the conference that would seek, among other things, to isolate and target the Ohio Valley Delaware and Shawnee as the last remaining enemies of the war. A Shawnee letter addressed to Johnson was dictated to captive Thomas Smallman, who was Croghan's cousin and a former Pennsylvania major and trader with the Shawnee. He had been captured by Wyandots a year earlier and given to the Shawnee. Smallman was trusted to write and deliver the Shawnee letter at Fort Pitt, to arrange for negotiations, and to return to the Shawnee.[13] The letter explained the choice of messenger by pointing out that a delegation of Shawnee, Delaware, Wyandot, and Mingo had been fired upon with cannon when they approached Fort Pitt the previous summer, after which "our Foolish Young Men remained there to fight against the Fort." The Shawnee still considered themselves in a ten-year war triggered by the fate of Itawachcomequa's party: "don't blame us, but yourselves for our prosecuting the war against you as we have done."[14] The only Shawnee condition for peace that was mentioned in the letter was that "you must erect no more Forts on our Ground." Smallman did all that the Shawnee asked of him, and would be so employed again, but on this occasion he returned to captivity without bringing any hope of negotiation. British military leaders, who may have known nothing of the Itawachcomequa affair or its immediate consequences, made no sense of the letter and dismissed it as a taunting provocation to British armies preparing to attack; in later negotiations, Colonel John Bradstreet called the letter "impertinent," and Bouquet referred to it as "insolent."[15] Yet the Shawnee had been serious enough to approach Major Henry Gladwin at Detroit as well, only to be referred to Johnson or to Fort Pitt.[16] The Shawnee had also been wise in sending Smallman as intermediary, as the fate of Delaware leaders attempting to negotiate at Fort Pitt would demonstrate.

Sir William Johnson had, as early as 1756, supported forcing the Delaware to return all their captives as a humiliating punishment, and he had alternately preached and temporized on the subject ever since. He, like Bouquet, made return of captives a central part of making peace in 1764. Always very partial to the Six Nations, and embarrassed that he had not kept all of them loyal to the British during the previous year, Johnson had first settled with the rebellious Chenussio Seneca at the end of March 1764. Those Chenussio who had joined the war against the British agreed to give three chiefs as hostages to ensure that they would cease all raids, cede land around Fort Niagara, "stop up the Road to the Shawanese, and Delawares, and never treat with them without our Permission," and return "all ye Prisoners, Deserters, Frenchmen & Negroes" still held.[17] The seriousness with which Chenussio leaders took their promise is indicated by a dispute between an old chief and Mary Jemison's Seneca brother. Refusing to give Mary up, her Seneca brother eventually insisted he would rather kill her himself than see her returned. Mary and her Seneca sisters took his threat seriously enough that she and her son fled for their lives and hid for three days.[18]

Having settled terms with the Chenussio Seneca, Johnson sent Iroquois messengers throughout the *pays d'en haut* warning that a major army of British and Iroquois were preparing to come west, and inviting all to a major peace conference at Fort Niagara. Captive Alexander Henry heard this message as it was amplified and distorted on delivery to the Ojibwa at far-off Michilimackinac. The Ojibwa were concerned by the threat of an invasion and drawn by the promise that "Sir William Johnson will fill their canoes with presents; with blankets, kettles, guns, gun-powder and shot, and large barrels of rum, such as the stoutest of the Indians will not be able to lift." Two thousand representatives of nineteen nations gathered at Niagara in July 1764 to learn that the British wanted peace, and offered massive presents, valued at about £38,000, in a departure from the recent parsimony and restrictions on English trade in alcohol and gunpowder. In offering to all belligerents what he had offered to the Chenussio four months earlier, Johnson set both the method and the objectives of peacemaking, marked by a renewed concern for recovering captives.[19]

Colonel John Bradstreet and his force of 1,500 men decorated, strengthened, and witnessed Johnson's Niagara meeting, and Bradstreet repeated Johnson's demands to a delegation of ten Wyandot, Delaware, Shawnee, and Mingo who met him near the burned site of Fort Presqu'île soon thereafter.[20] Bradstreet, like Bouquet, had orders to attack the Ohio Delaware and Shawnee settlements on the Muskingum and Scioto Rivers, but he avoided this strenuous assignment by agreeing to negotiate a provisional peace when his force reached Sandusky. Six of the ten Indians who came to negotiate were to stay with Bradstreet as hostages to ensure the fulfillment of the terms. All captives, whether they wanted to return or not, were to be brought to Sandusky within twenty-five days, and all tribal chiefs were to accompany them to ratify the peace. An inspection team of eighteen would then tour the villages to ensure that all prisoners were returned, and eighteen hostages would be held during this process. Land was also to be ceded within cannon shot of all present and future British forts in the region. Bradstreet promised that Bouquet's expedition, already known to be delayed, would not proceed against the Ohio tribes if they accepted peace.[21]

Bradstreet had both avoided and exceeded his responsibility, but what mattered more was that he was deceived. Neither chiefs nor captives came to Sandusky. Indian raids into Virginia and Pennsylvania during the twenty-five-day waiting period may have been hard to stop, but two small raids into Virginia in September were taken as proof that the peace of Sandusky was not effective.[22] What became of Bradstreet's six hostages is not recorded; they may still have been with him when he returned to Sandusky, where he discovered that he was deceived, and sent out small raids and feints for weeks before breaking camp and undertaking what proved a disastrous return to Niagara. Bradstreet would be readily denounced by Gage, Johnson, and Bouquet, and his failure was additional evidence that hostages were not enough.

Some preparation for the other invasion of the Ohio Valley had begun, by both sides, the previous summer when Bouquet's relief force proved unable to exploit its limited victory at Bushy Run. Most of the Delaware and Shawnee had by then abandoned their settlements on the upper Ohio, Allegheny, and Beaver Rivers, moving themselves and their captives west once again, this time to join kin in the Muskingum and Scioto Valleys. These migrants had moved as far west as practicable without provoking the Miami or Illinois. Although food was plentiful enough there, British embargoes and French weakness meant that usable gunpowder was becoming scarce. Escaped Virginian captive Mathias Warren reported that, by the spring of 1764, Shawnee were killing most of their meat with bows and arrows, though he could not estimate the quantities of meat being dried in preparation for war.[23] Indian diplomatic messengers arriving at Fort Pitt were to receive nothing but provisions for their journey home, and were to be grilled about how many captives they had, their names, and where they were held. The Indians could only hope that the British would not sustain an effective invasion through the 130 miles of wilderness that now separated them from Fort Pitt, or that the invaders could be stalled by a negotiated peace.

Despite relentless efforts, Bouquet's own military preparations for the march to the Muskingum Valley did not go smoothly. Although recovering captives was now a stated objective of this campaign, the assemblies of Virginia and Pennsylvania were openly uncooperative, even in the face of Amherst's requisitions. Bouquet, in Philadelphia in the winter of 1763–64, was frustrated by difficulties in recruiting men, and in gathering wagons, horses, cattle, and supplies. He had supported Colonel Adam Stephen's project for Virginian volunteers to spearhead an invasion of the Ohio towns the previous fall, and had seen this effort flounder for lack of support from a wary Virginia Council and a thrifty House of Burgesses.[24] With fewer than 400 regulars available for his 1764 campaign, Bouquet again encouraged enthusiastic Virginian officers to recruit volunteers. Although he could not pay them, he promised arms, provisions, and other necessaries, and hoped, in vain, that they would eventually be paid by their own government. Bouquet also mentioned that Virginian volunteers could be rewarded by Pennsylvania's new scalp bounty, which soon offered up to $150 for an adult male captive – with a discount of only 10 per cent for delivering his scalp instead.[25]

Bouquet did not tell the Virginians that the Pennsylvanians were as yet doing very little to support his campaign, but he exploded angrily and uncharacteristically in a mid-July letter to John Harris, prominent trader and ferryman at Paxton. Asked to hire Harris's brother as a gunsmith, Bouquet replied that "After all the noise and bustle of your young men" in killing defenseless converted Indians, he had expected volunteers. Instead, "I see by your Letter that they go as Pack Horse drivers and waggoners, employs for which a coward is as fit as a brave man: Will not people say that they have found it easier to kill Indians in a gaol, than to fight them fairly in the woods?"[26] Bouquet mentioned the scalp bounty, which Paxton men had demanded but were not now volunteering in order to collect, and also mentioned that Virginians were volunteering to fight without pay, whereas not a single Pennsylvanian had come forward. Admitting that he was revealing his own sentiments, Bouquet went on: "For my own part I am so much disgusted at the backwardness of the frontier people in assisting us in taking revenge on the savages who murder them daily with impunity, that I hope this will be the last time I shall venture my reputation and life for their sake." Harris may have been stung by the letter, for he called a meeting of locals, and, whether or not he read them Bouquet's letter, he reported that most of the young men would join the expedition at Pittsburgh.[27] By then, both of the undermanned battalions of the Pennsylvania regiment, then totaling some 688 men, had already mustered with Bouquet's regulars at Carlisle.[28]

Former captives made surprisingly limited contributions to Bouquet's expedition. Recently escaped captive Mathias Warren was questioned about the location, numbers, and military preparations of the Shawnee and Delaware. John Prentice, a captive trader freed by the Wyandot at Sandusky in the spring of 1764, offered some useful information from that quarter.[29] On the other hand, recently returned James (Robert) Bell and Gershom Hicks were suspected as spies and traitors, and were repeatedly interrogated for information that was then considered worthless. None of the four guides for the expedition had ever been captives, though all had been Ohio traders.[30] James Smith, a returned Kahnawake white Indian with warrior skills, was a junior officer with the Pennsylvanians. Captain George Etherington, and possibly other members of his company, were with Bouquet, after having been captured by Ojibwa and rescued by Ottawa the previous year. Captives John Gibson and Thomas Smallman were captives used by the Delaware and Shawnee as scribes and/or messengers; Bouquet did not use escaped captives as messengers, translators, or guides.

Despite charming accounts suggesting the opposite, civilian relatives of captives were not able to accompany Bouquet's army beyond Fort Pitt. Bouquet deliberately and repeatedly excluded most women. The day before the army left Carlisle, Bouquet had already ordered that "no Women can be allowed to follow the Troops after they march from this Place," noting that the army was not allowed to provision them and that food could not be bought "beyond the Settlements." This order was evidently hard to enforce and was repeated twice in the following month, as the army made its way to Fort Pitt. Only one woman per company and two more for the field hospital were allowed to continue beyond Fort Pitt. Anticipating objections, Bouquet insisted, "It will be therefore in vain for any other women to attempt to follow the Troops." A civilian man who wanted to avenge or rescue kin was even less likely to be allowed to follow this army, unless he was shamed or bullied into volunteering. A ban on all hunting, which could facilitate desertion, alert enemies, or invite attack, meant that a civilian would need his or her own horse train of provisions to subsist for what would prove to be three months in the company of an army where hundreds of deserters would readily steal horses and provisions for their own escape. Virginians and Pennsylvanians who had lost relatives are known to have volunteered to join Bouquet.

Although the meticulous and energetic Bouquet had been prominent in building General John Forbes's wagon road from Carlisle to the site of Fort Pitt in 1758, and had retraced it in twenty-seven days with his bloodied relief expedition in 1763, it took him thirty-nine days to herd the 1764 expedition along this easiest and most familiar initial leg of their journey.[31]

The sensible Indian response to this approaching force, and one that had worked to deter Bradstreet, was to initiate talks. Ten Delaware chiefs arrived as Bouquet's army reached Fort Pitt. Three of these chiefs ventured across the Allegheny River to negotiate, or at least to delay the invaders and learn something of their strength and purpose. On Bouquet's orders, Welapachtschiechen (Captain Johnny) and Kageshquanohel (the Pipe) were immediately seized as spies and held as hostages, and the third chief was sent back with a threat that the two hostages would be killed if Bouquet's messengers to Detroit did not return safely with a message from Bradstreet, and Bouquet declared that if the Delaware "did not improve the clemency now offered to them, by returning back as soon as possible with all their prisoners, they might expect to feel the full weight of a just vengeance and resentment."[32]

Less than two weeks later, when the army and its herds of cattle and sheep had safely crossed the Allegheny, a self-identified Onondaga and an Oneida approached Bouquet, claiming to have come originally from William Johnson. They asked for a delay and talks with all the enemy tribes, adding that these peoples were all sorry for the war and were gathering their captives at Lower Shawnee Town to take them to Bradstreet. If captives were being concentrated at Lower Shawnee Town on the Scioto River, Bouquet could suspect that this was to put them farther away from his army, rather than to gather them for an easy trip to Sandusky.[33] Bouquet responded haughtily with a catalog of broken Indian promises and recent violence, and insisted that being sorry was not enough. The army would go to the Tuscarawas branch of the Muskingum River, and Delaware and Shawnee interested in negotiation could meet him there. He promised only that his soldiers would not kill anyone on the way unless attacked.[34]

This promise was inherently difficult to keep. The army Bouquet assembled was full of hatred and resentment against the Shawnee and Delaware. It included men like James Smith, a former captive and now a lieutenant with the Pennsylvania regiment, who had been active in the vigilante raids that disrupted trade to the Indians and had burned out the "friendly" Delaware of Grand Island the previous autumn. Richard Butler, later the US Indian commissioner who "browbeat" a Shawnee legation, was an ensign with the same Pennsylvania forces.[35] The Paxton Boys still had widespread support well beyond the recent protesters and their protectors.[36] More surprising than colonial hatred of Indians was the frank opinion of Colonel John Reid, the veteran regular commanding the Black Watch regiment. When the army left Fort Pitt, Reid discussed with others, and then proposed to Bouquet, undertaking a spoiling raid against a nearby Delaware village, "preventing the Ratification of a Peace, from it's nature, odious to almost every man under Your Command."[37] Despite Bouquet's own contempt for Indians, so evident in the infamous gift of smallpox-infected blankets at Fort Pitt in 1763, he managed to restrain those pressing for blood and scalps throughout this campaign.

The invasion proceeded as smoothly as planned over its first twelve days. Axe-men, covered by Virginian volunteers, cleared major obstructions for the three columns of soldiers and built a few narrow bridges that where essential. There was no "Bouquet's Road" because none was needed by a pack-train force that brought neither wagons nor artillery. The army of more than 1,200 marched at the easy pace of the herds and loaded packhorses they seemed organized to protect, averaging under ten miles a day (see illustration 5).[38] Only one white captive escaped to the protection of this moving army; John Palmer, taken by Delaware only six days before, joined the army at Beaver Creek on their fourth day out.[39] Five days later, at an intersection of Indian trails, the army filed past painted posts that celebrated the taking of numerous scalps and prisoners.[40] There were no military diversions to burn abandoned villages or crops, for the Indians had already done this at a number of sites, including Logstown, and the army camped each night in cautious

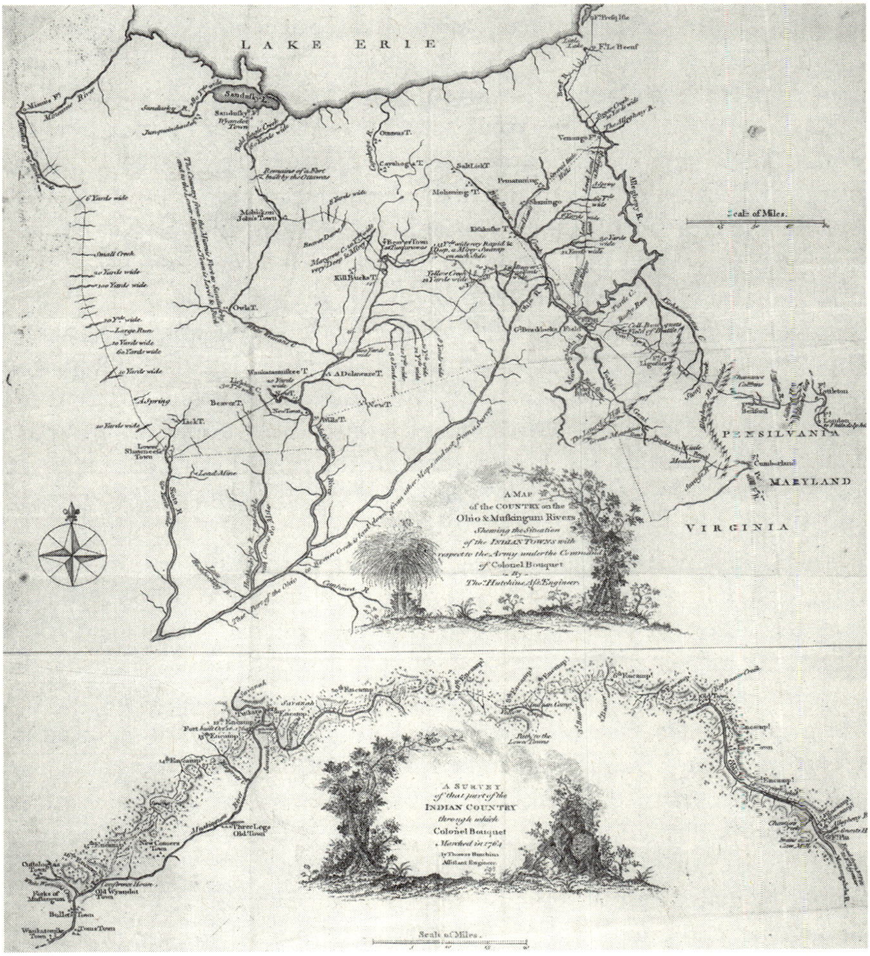

5 "A Survey of That Part of the Country through which Colonel Bouquet Marched in 1764," by Thomas Hutchins. Dechert Collection, Annenberg Rare Book and Manuscript Library, University of Pennsylvania.

good order on preselected and defensible hills. They were moving along a trail familiar to traders, like chief guide Alexander Lowery, though it was country most of the force had never seen. They encountered absolutely no resistance, no sniping at sentinels, no horse stealing, and no additional attempts to initiate negotiations. This huge herd and pack train, completely enveloped with troops, was watched by Delaware and Shawnee scouts, who "counted our Numbers, & ... were very surprised at them."[41] The calm may have been tense, but it suggested that even the "reckless young men," so often prone to bravado in such circumstances, were restrained or thwarted on both sides.

As the army confidently approached the Tuscarawas River, new negotiations were anticipated, and Bouquet issued new warnings to his troops. Expected Delaware and Shawnee legates were "not to be treated in a hostile manner till their Intentions are known," but he was equally clear that "no marks of Civility or Friendship is to be shown to them by Speaking or shaking hands with them, till they shall be compelled to give proper Satisfaction for the unjust War they have enter'd into, and the many & barbarous Cruelties they have committed." Anticipating some discontent with this restraint, Bouquet assured the army that the Indians would be regarded as enemies until they submitted and gave "such satisfaction as will be adequate to the Spirit now exerted by an Injured People, and equally consistent with the Honor and Dignity of the British Empire."[42]

The Delaware had been making their own preparations to meet Bouquet. The colonel's messenger had not been allowed to proceed to contact Bradstreet at Detroit, though the message had been forwarded. Bouquet's messenger was released on 14 October to return with a Delaware letter, written by captive trader John Gibson in the name of eleven Delaware leaders. The brief and conciliatory letter put a favorable interpretation on Bouquet's hostage taking of 2 October, and confirmed the meeting planned at the Tuscarawas River, where good intentions would be confirmed if the Delaware could see their two hostage chiefs. Whether or not Bouquet noticed that the letter was not written in the names of major chiefs Shingas, Tamaqua, or Custaloga, his reply was immediate and encouraging. Bouquet now pressed for separate talks with the Delaware, though the Delaware had assured Bouquet that they would come as soon as the Shawnee legates arrived.[43]

The intense and carefully managed diplomacy, conducted in the camp of an invading army, began on 17 October. Bouquet was attended by thirteen senior officers, representing every branch of the assembled army, together with Alexander McKee as Croghan's deputy, and the returned renegade David Owens as interpreter. The Indian legation was led by principal speaker Keyashuta, the Ohio Seneca war chief prominent throughout negotiations. The Anglo-Iroquoian format and style of conferences were thereby restored, though the Iroquois were represented here only by Mingo dissidents who had not made peace with William Johnson seven months earlier. The Shawnee were represented only by Chief Kisinoutha (Big Wolf), who was attended by six warriors. Kisinoutha did not speak, and was reported to have witnessed the proceedings "with abjected sullenness." The Delaware were represented by Tamaqua, the familiar head of the Turkey phratry and established leader of the Delaware peace party, and by the enduring Custaloga, head of the Wolf phratry, who had witnessed the effrontery of General Edward Braddock in 1755 and the duplicity of Bouquet and Croghan in negotiations in 1759. The Delaware also brought leading warrior Kitchi (Turtle Heart) as their own speaker, plus nineteen other warriors, but no captives. Keyashuta opened the meeting with a conciliatory speech supported by the presentation of one string and four belts of wampum and reinforced by the immediate return of eighteen captives.[44] Custaloga endorsed Keyashuta's speech, and presented forty-two small sticks, one for each captive in the Wolf phratry whom he promised to return. Tamaqua followed, presenting forty-one more sticks; perhaps it was not coincidental that this was exactly the number he had promised to return five years earlier.[45] Keyashuta, who mentioned negotiations with Bradstreet as an excuse for some confusion and delay in returning captives, concluded the opening presentations with a reading of Bradstreet's articles of peace as already agreed at Sandusky.

Bouquet's belligerent reply was delayed by bad weather and by what his revealing endorsement of the previous minutes called "on Account of one Tribe of the Delaware not being present." No leaders of the Turtle phratry had been there on 17 October, though both the Wolf and Turkey Delaware were properly represented. McKee and Owens certainly knew this, as would have Bouquet, but he was seeking a separate peace with these relatively cooperative Delaware. Despite the weather, Bouquet now moved the army encampment to the west bank of the Muskingum, in order to gain better grass for the livestock and to increase pressure on nearby Indian towns. On 20 October he brought a major contingent with him back across the river for talks in a "bower" constructed to stage his response. Skipping all the traditional Iroquoian courtesies, which he had previously witnessed and practiced, Bouquet exuded aggressive confidence, which his chronicler called a "firm and determined spirit." He first dealt with Bradstreet's peace, reading it to prove that it had expired because captives had not been delivered by the due date of 6 September, and noting that Bouquet's own first message to the Delaware had not been written until two weeks after this expiry. John Palmer was presented as proof that the Delaware were still taking captives as late as 28 September. Bouquet chastised the assembled for perfidy, again delivering a catalog of Indian duplicity and English grievances. He threatened them with the fury of soldiers who were relatives of the killed and captured, men "impatient to take Revenge of the Bloody Murderers of their Friends." He threatened the Delaware with attack from the Six Nations and from the other tribes who had recently made their peace with Johnson. He gave them twelve days to deliver all their captives to his camp, which would be close to the nearby Shawnee town of Wakitomica. All English, French, or negroes, whether men, women, or children, whether "married, or under any other Denomination whatever," were to be surrendered together with clothing, provisions, and stores for their journey to Fort Pitt. The terms upon which the Delaware, Shawnee, and Mingo might seek peace would be explained only if this preliminary demand was fully met.[46] Bouquet also required that the chiefs each appoint one man to stay with his army during the twelve days of waiting, though these men were not formally called hostages. Keyashuta, Kitchi, Custaloga's son, and a Shawnee warrior known as James Smith accepted this role. The Shawnee, centered at Lower Shawnee Town on the Scioto, could not meet this timetable; Kisinoutha could promise only to take the terms to the Shawnee chiefs, hoping to be back at Wakitomica in time, and urging that the Shawnee be treated like the Delaware.

Bouquet was still making his separate peace with the Delaware, and ensuring that the Shawnee could not comply. It was a week later before he sent a message to the Shawnee that insisted on the original timetable, demanded intercepted letters to Bouquet from the French commandant at Fort Chartres, and required provisions for the Shawnee and their prisoners during negotiations. Kisinoutha intervened to take the message to Lower Shawnee Town himself and promised to be back to deliver his own captives before the deadline.[47] He was back five days later, still ahead of Bouquet's deadline, when he joined seven other Shawnee in bringing Bouquet eight captives. The colonel thanked them, but there was a racial edge to his "I hope your chiefs will follow your Example, and deliver every drop of White blood in your Nation."[48] This was not hyperbole. With the whites on this frontier theoretically united as never before, this was a call to humiliating surrender of the Indians' own *métis* children. At the very least, this genetic talk did not fit well with rhetoric by which the nations of the Ohio Valley and Great Lakes now came to address the British monarch as their father.[49] King George was being represented as determined to separate Indians from whites much more rigorously than had the Proclamation Line of 1763.

Bouquet's deadline was 1 November, and the limited Indian response by then could be read as calculated defiance. On that day, he formally accepted thirty-two captives from Custaloga, and three additional ones brought in by Keyashuta. Although these captives were evidence of sincerity, Bouquet responded that "there is a number of prisoners amongst you; till the last of them are delivered up, I cannot proceed to the good work of peace."[50] Custaloga had delivered thirty-two of the forty-two captives he had promised on behalf of the Delaware Wolf phratry, but Tamaqua had not arrived with the promised forty-one Turkey phratry captives, and nothing at all had been heard from the Turtle phratry of the Delaware. Keyashuta had brought in only twenty-one Mingo captives. A mere eight Shawnee captives had arrived, and these were not from the major concentration of captives held in and near Lower Shawnee Town, but from local headman Kisinoutha. Neither Bouquet nor anyone else could have known precisely how many captives were being held, but he could be confident that the sixty-one received by the deadline were just a small minority of them.[51] For all his bluster in front of Indian legates and his own officers, Bouquet gave no signs to his army, to his superiors, or to Indian witnesses that he planned to attack anyone as his deadline passed.

Over the next two weeks, Bouquet managed to keep his forces under control, and his limited faith in Delaware compliance proved largely justified. Tamaqua's party arrived the next day, bringing the promised forty-one captives from the Turkey phratry. Because "some of them may attempt to run away," Custaloga, Tamaqua, and others turned fifty-seven captives over to Bouquet on 3 November, before any formal presentations.[52] Bouquet's suspicion that these leaders still had more captives was confirmed two days later when they delivered eleven more. In a private letter to Brigadier General John Stanwix, Bouquet now claimed that the Delaware had surrendered all their captives. The resulting conferences began on 9 November, when the same officers who had attended Bouquet twenty-four days earlier reassembled to meet with Keyashuta, Custaloga, and thirty of their warriors. Keyashuta began with Iroquoian condolences for the death of a British soldier whom he agreed had been "murdered" in the woods two days earlier. He presented three more captives, and offered assurances that the Seneca and "Custaloga's Tribes" had returned all their captives, and he used wampum belts and strings to cover the graves of all those killed and to reopen the path of friendship. Bouquet responded, without the usual one-day delay, leaving the surrender of the soldier's murderer to the chiefs, accepting the "three last prisoners," and figuratively covering the bones of the dead with a string. He then addressed them as brothers seeking peace. They were to provide Bouquet with hostages, two Seneca and two from Custaloga's tribe, who were to remain at Fort Pitt while fully empowered and acceptable deputies made peace with Sir William Johnson. Bouquet said he believed they had surrendered all their prisoners, but they were to bring in to Fort Pitt any additional ones, "as well as any of those now delivered up that might return to you." Bouquet returned Welapachtschiechen and Kageshquanohel, and he was thinking of Captain Bull and his companions when he claimed he would recommend to General Thomas Gage "to have them given to you when the peace is concluded." The meeting ended with previously withheld handshakes between Bouquet and the chiefs, which reportedly "occasioned great joy amongst them."[53]

The other phratries of the Ohio Delaware met with Bouquet separately the next day, with all the negotiators of the previous day in attendance. Tamaqua and twenty warriors represented the Turkey phratry, and Chief Kelipama and twenty-five warriors were there for the Turtle phratry. Tamaqua delivered thirteen more captives and promised to return any others discovered, including any surrendered captives who might run away. Bouquet repeated the terms of the previous day, including the demand for two new hostages and the selection of deputies from each group for his approval. Bouquet asked publicly, as he must have done privately, why Kelipama attended rather than his brother, Nettawatwee, the paramount chief of the Turtle phratry. In a private meeting the next day, Bouquet and Delaware chiefs agreed on the choices of hostages and deputies. Tamaqua then made a strange request that indicated a deliberate or pretended distancing between the reconciled Delaware and the Shawnee. He asked for a specific translator to accompany the Delaware deputies going to Johnson: "As Owens speaks our language so well, and is accustomed to the Woods, We should be glad that he could accompany them." As a final act of empty imperial bravado, Bouquet declared the nonattending paramount chief Nettawatwee deposed, ordered that his phratry should choose another, and stated, "I will confirm him, and he shall be King of the Turtle Tribe, and acknowledged as such by the English."[54]

Before considering Bouquet's final dealings with the Shawnee, it is helpful to consider his relations with another tribe that was largely beyond his immediate reach, the Wyandot. When Bouquet's army had set out from Fort Pitt, Iroquoian commentators thought that the Wyandot were among those being challenged. However, no Wyandot were on hand to hear Bouquet's ultimatum of 20 October, and he let his deadline pass before sending an officer and three Virginia volunteers to the Wyandot, with orders to bring in all their prisoners. Near the head of the Scioto River, the messengers located a lone Wyandot chief, Oterunque. His respectful written reply claimed that all the Wyandot chiefs had gone hunting, that a messenger would search them out, and that they would reply, and return all their prisoners, in the spring.[55] In the week that Bouquet's messengers were away, four Wyandot captives were apparently returned, without any formality. On 15 November, when Bouquet was concluding his operation on the Muskingum, he wrote Colonel Bradstreet that "The Wyandots have sent me Four Prisoners, & promised to deliver fourteen more in the spring."[56] On the basis of no recorded negotiations, no hostages, and what he knew was not a return of all their prisoners, Bouquet included the Wyandot among the tribes with whom he had concluded a truce.[57] In their case, nothing resembling full compliance had been required.

In contrast, relations between the Shawnee and Bouquet that month were guarded, and Bouquet's history of negotiating with them had not been encouraging. Kisinoutha of Wakitomica, whose town was within easy striking distance for Bouquet's army, had cooperated fully. However, Kisinoutha had stopped two of Bouquet's messengers from going to Lower Shawnee Town and admitted to the second that all of the Shawnee chiefs had gone to see the French at Fort Chartres. Bouquet's third messenger was a particularly provocative choice, the hated David Owens himself, who was accompanied by Delaware hostage Kitchi. By one report, Owens was immediately threatened with death as the notorious murderer of his Shawnee family, but his adoptive relatives were restrained by his insistence that Bouquet's army would attack to avenge his killing. Owens was released, and paramount chief Mesquepalathie (Red Hawk) soon wrote from Wakitomica, via captive Thomas Smallman, to report that his group, and "a great number of your Flesh and Blood," had arrived. In releasing Smallman, Mesquepalathie knew that this captive would report to Bouquet on fresh supplies of French gunpowder in Lower Shawnee Town and the presence there of "Joncaire," and Mesquepalathie may even have known that Smallman had learned from an English captive, married to a Frenchman, that Joncaire was attempting to incite the Shawnee to resist the English.[58]

Neither Smallman's written report nor Bouquet's journal of negotiations claimed that, on hearing of the British invasion, the Shawnee "had resolved to kill their prisoners and fight us." However, William Smith's Historical Account states that Smallman reported this Shawnee response, and that the execution of all the captives was narrowly averted twice by the timely arrival of messengers from Bouquet. Without mentioning his source of information, Bouquet wrote John Penn a week later: "The Shawanee have been very Obstinate, and nothing has prevented the Chastisement they deserved, but the certainty that if they were driven to despair they would massacre 150 Prisoners then in their hands."[59] The central limitation of forcible recovery of captives had emerged once again. The Delaware, who were more directly threatened by Bouquet and had been fairly united in their decision to seek peace, were not accused of making such a threat. Bouquet, who had vilified the Shawnee before and found them obstinate here, took the Shawnee threat seriously. Smallman had let Bouquet know that the Shawnee were not coming to make peace simply because they had no other option.

Mesquepalathie, six fellow chiefs, and forty warriors met Bouquet and his now familiar phalanx of officers on 12 and 14 November. Mesquepalathie opened the meeting by offering the conventional wiping of the eyes and clearing of the ears, and then mentioned the thirty-six captives brought in and others still remaining who would be returned in the spring. He did not retell the Shawnee story of a single war reaching back to the insult of 1753, but instead claimed that the Shawnee had made peace at Fort Pitt early in 1763, a peace that had been broken by Pontiac's foolish Ottawa. Since the Shawnee had not been major participants in Pontiac's War, this was a sensible line of argument. He went on to cover the bones of the killed, and presented well-preserved letters and treaty minutes reaching back to 1711 as reminders of an Anglo-Shawnee friendship that was now to be renewed. Bouquet did not reply for two days, during which he had a crucial private conference with leading Shawnee warriors and was thereafter able to tell what must have been a very restless army of his own that the "haughty" Shawnee would accept the same terms as the Delaware.[60] On 14 November, Bouquet reasserted his requirement of the return of all captives, as explained over the previous six weeks to those who had said they represented the Shawnee. He claimed that it was Kisinoutha's pledge on behalf of the Shawnee that had stayed Bouquet's recent plan to attack. He announced that the Delaware had already fulfilled their obligation entirely, whereas the Shawnee had brought in "only a small parcel of the prisoners ... What right have you to expect different terms?" Bouquet insisted that the Shawnee return all captives, Frenchmen, and negroes "taken from us either in this or in any other War," which erroneously implied that the thirty-six captives just returned had been those the Shawnee had taken in Pontiac's War.[61] He went on to demand six Shawnee hostages and a cessation of all hostilities. The immediate agreement, spoken by the familiar and conciliatory Chief Benevisica, had certainly been rehearsed. Six named hostages, led by Mesquepalathie, were provided and a promise given to gather the other captives and bring them to Fort Pitt. Bouquet then accepted the Shawnee submission, figuratively buried the bones of the victims, and urged tenderness in gathering up the captives. He sent a few Virginian volunteers, related to Shawnee-held captives, to help bring them from Lower Shawnee Town to Fort Pitt. Bouquet then announced, "I permit you to appoint Deputys to go to Sir William Johnson to make peace."[62] With the Wyandot, Bouquet had accepted as adequate compliance the submission of a few of their captives, as those still held and promised for the spring were thought to number only ten. Bouquet accepted the same level of compliance from the Shawnee, as he had reason to believe that he had recovered only 44 of what he thought were 150.[63] In the case of the Shawnee, however, he required six prominent hostages.

Perhaps the most amazing feature of this muscular diplomacy was that there was virtually no violence. Delaware warriors had watched while a huge enemy force marched right into the heart of their settlement. No sentries were killed, and no horses or cattle were reported stolen, though some resistance might have supported the negotiating chiefs. The sullen and resentful Pennsylvanians, watching the exchange of niceties with those who had killed their kin, did not even stage a disruption and blame it on the Indians. The murder of a single soldier in the woods was acknowledged and ignored, without any indication of what he had been doing there. The Shawnee did not raid the camp from their safe base eighty miles away, in an attempt to disrupt and delay the unwanted proceedings. During the long month of negotiations, including the tense days after Bouquet's deadline had been ignored, there were no signs that Pennsylvania or Virginia volunteers even plotted to take the scalps of nearby Indians in order to collect the new bounties. Even James Smith, bragging from the safety of Kentucky thirty-five years later, had no exploits to recount about his role as a Pennsylvania lieutenant at the Muskingum in 1764. Colonel John Reid and his regulars attempted no spoiling raid, and exacted no revenge. Uncommon discipline and restraint seem to have prevailed, among invaders who might have been aware of unrecorded threats to captives, and among defenders who were very short of gunpowder and may have been impressed and intimidated by the army, or who may have been much more subject to tribal authority than is generally believed.

Bouquet had certainly anticipated the return of numerous captives, but arrangements for their care evolved only as they arrived. During the one-sided initial negotiations, Bouquet had demanded that captors provide food, clothing, and bedding for the captives, and there is no evidence of any food shortages in the camp or on the return to Fort Pitt. Some Indians even stayed near the army, hunting and preparing food for their adopted kin, all the way to Fort Pitt. Clothing was an entirely different matter, and one of increasing consequence as the negotiations continued into November. The army had apparently not anticipated a need to clothe the returning captives, and it is not clear whether these captives were made to shed some clothing before being turned over to the army. Such minimal compliance may have indicated resentment, as had been the case elsewhere.[64] Lutheran minister Henry Melchior Muhlenberg, in a contemporary account, exaggerated in claiming that most captives had been returned without any clothing. He went on to say that Bouquet led his troops as they "cut off the flaps of their coats and waistcoats, and cut up their blankets and so on to cover the absolute nakedness of the poor creatures."[65] Bouquet would confirm that the captives remained without adequate clothing, or tents, on their trip to Fort Pitt, where the army distributed enough shirts, leggings, shoes, and blankets to reclothe almost all the captives as they arrived there.[66] This rather thorough reclothing, in army surplus, was unavoidable, but it was also part of the cultural reclamation of the captives, even if the result would have been visibly hybrid, and predominantly male.

The first eighteen captives returned by Keyashuta, and an unspecified number brought by the Delaware over the next three days, were not much of a test of the army's preparedness, but there was one rather surprising aspect. The orders of 21 October included: "The Remainder of the Captives will at their own request receive Arms & Ammunition and are to proceed wt the Troops." We do not know any more about these temporary soldiers. They were not the better-known, obstreperous white Indians returned against their will from a culture they preferred, but were they captives resenting their previous treatment and declaring their loyalty to their native culture?[67]

While waiting twelve days for the anticipated main group of returned captives, Bouquet's force of over 1,200 built redoubts, a storehouse, ovens, and mess cabins that made "Camp # 16" more bearable as the weather turned colder. In addition, "Three houses with separate apartments were also raised for the reception of the captives of the respective provinces, and proper officers appointed to take charge of them, with a matron to attend the women and children."[68] A detachment of guards was assigned to secure each house.

The dramatic, emotional climax of the expedition was the arrival of the captives in the camp, according to Bouquet's second-hand chronicler, Rev. William Smith, who described "a scene which language indeed can but weakly describe; to which the Poet or Painter might have repaired ... [and a person might] exercise all the tender and sympathetic feelings of the soul." Smith's exuberance has misled scholars into thinking that a caravan of relatives had followed the army to the Muskingum and now searched among the returning captives, with the fortunate ending their search in happy and tearful reunions, amid the distress of other returning children and women who fought to escape what for them was exile from their Indian and *métis* families and confinement in a cruel new captivity.[69]

There was no caravan of relatives at the Muskingum and no witnesses' accounts of family reunions in the camp, though a few emotional reunions occurred there. A Virginian volunteer named Kincade was delighted to be reunited with his wife, Eleanor, who had been pregnant when captured with their three children at Cowpasture seven months earlier. She had been adopted into Tamaqua's Delaware family, and well treated. She brought Kincade's three-month-old child back with her, but their emotions would have been very mixed, for she also had grief to share. Their four-year-old boy had not been able to keep up on the captive trail, and had been summarily killed, and their seven-year-old daughter had died of disease in her one summer of captivity. The two year old whom Eleanor had carried all the way into captivity had then been taken from her, and she had not seen her since. While Eleanor was still with her husband in Camp # 16, a three year old was returned whom she claimed as her own. The child had already forgotten her English, spoke only Delaware, and did not recognize her parents.[70]

Camp # 16 looked very different to the only returned captive who recorded his own remembrance of it. When brought there against his will, John McCullough had spent the most recent and interesting half of his young life as an adopted Delaware. His new family was then living only ten miles from the Muskingum camp, and apparently gave him up readily. Long after he had returned to white society, McCullough still could not recall this scene as happy: "they took all the prisoners to the camp, myself among the rest, and delivered us up to the army. We were immediately put under a guard, – a few days after, we were sent under a strong guard to Pittsburg." McCullough did not mention the cold or nakedness of the returning captives, though he was issued a shirt, a blanket, and leggings once they reached Fort Pitt. He added, "On our way two of the prisoners made their escape, to wit: one Rhoda Boyd and Elizabeth Studibaker, and went back to the Indians." Whether or not he remembered having envied those girls, John was still using the term "prisoners" to describe himself and the other captives of Bouquet's army.[71]

The trip from the Muskingum to Fort Pitt was more difficult now, as the weather worsened. By 9 November, Bouquet had prepared orders for those escorting, receiving, and releasing the next contingent of 110 returned captives, including Eleanor Kincade, John McCullough, Rhoda Boyd, and Elizabeth Studebaker. The escort of fifty Pennsylvania and Virginia troops, under Captain Thomas Buford of the latter, were issued provisions and cattle for troops and captives for their 128-mile trek. Horses were provided to haul provisions and to carry both the lame and the youngest captives who could not march. The pace was to be quick but tempered by a need to end each day's march early in order to gather plenty of firewood and build shelters, "to screen the prisoners as much as possible from the bad effects of the cold; & the bad state of their clothing which could not be remmedyed." The escort, which might have been larger, was also to ensure that no returned captives escaped, and was to "be extremely watchful & to take the utmost care to prevent any accident of this kind happening, as it would be disgracefull to yourself & the officers under your command."[72] Nonetheless, both Elizabeth Studebaker and Rhoda Boyd managed to escape near the end of this trip, and they would never be returned.[73]

Bouquet now ordered that all the "prisoners" be kept at Fort Pitt upon arrival, that the men be lodged separately from the women and children, and that all be well-guarded to prevent escape back to the Indians. Two issues that had emerged after the first return of captives to Fort Pitt could be expected to return. Only one of these first seventeen captives had not been claimed by someone at Fort Pitt, but there was no record of who had taken custody of them. Commandant Captain David Hay asked that he might have the one unclaimed girl to help with his own children, while promising to use "every method to find out her relations." Bouquet agreed, but moved to ensure that this would be an exception. Henceforth, he would insist that there be full-names lists of all captives, in duplicate, and receipts for any transfers of custody, and that no more captives be released until Bouquet arrived back at Fort Pitt himself.[74] He asked Pennsylvania's governor to help the returning captives when they reached Carlisle: "as several of them are not known, I beg you will appoint a Person to receive them at that Place, and provide them with the necessities of Life till they are claimed."[75]

The last ninety-five of the prisoners were thoroughly guarded and escorted to Fort Pitt by Bouquet's returning army, and all arrived there on 29 November, when a few captives met their kin. John McQueen was reunited with his captive wife, Mary, and newly released Susan Knox left her mark in accepting custody of herself and her four children. We do not know whether she was surrendered with these children, was reunited with them at the Muskingum camp, or discovered them only at Fort Pitt, but the five of them were clothed and released together the day the army returned to Fort Pitt. Michael Divers recovered two sons, and Pat Flaherty was reunited with his daughter or niece, Esther, gone from Virginia for eight years. John Martin, that most energetic of bereaved fathers who had been to the Tuscarawas Valley himself in 1762 in search of his missing children, was among those at Fort Pitt to meet the returning army. Martin, and perhaps his already-recovered wife and daughter, was reunited there with three more of his children who had been with the Delaware since their attack on Great Cove nine years earlier. Martin, a trader who knew at least some Delaware, also took custody of John McCullough and three other returned captives who had been taken from the same settlement.[76]

From Fort Pitt, the captives were escorted by returning provincial soldiers along one of two roads built when this fort was a British military objective. There was less concern about runaways now, given the distance traveled and the weather. Eighty-eight captives known to have been taken from Virginia were now able to ride home down Braddock's Road with this colony's volunteers, on horses that had been hired by the British Army for the campaign.[77] Only fourteen of these captives, including the Kincades, Seas, and Yocums, are known to have been taken in Pontiac's War. All the others had been captive for at least five years, and the majority had been captured as adults. William Smith tells of a young Mingo, forced to surrender his Virginian wife, who not only accompanied her from the Muskingum to Fort Pitt, but also insisted upon accompanying her beyond this point, though warned that he could be killed by "the surviving relations" of other Virginian victims. It is not known who his wife was, or what became of either of them. At least two other Virginian returnees each brought a *métis* child back with them.[78] "Peggy the mulatto" had been in the first group of captives returned by Keyashuta, had been signed for by John Martin at Fort Pitt, and was taken back to Virginia faster than the other returning captives, "gone home with her late Master's grandson." Just over two weeks after they left Fort Pitt, Captain Thomas Buford reported that he had returned the captives to their relatives, except for five whose relations were still being sought in Hampshire County. Buford's task had been easier because most of his charges had surnames, and were known to be from Virginia; orphans who remembered nothing of their native land went with the Pennsylvanian troops.[79] Perhaps some relatives may have gathered at Fort Cumberland to inspect and reclaim kin, but there was no public announcement of such an event. The Virginia government, which had done so much to ignite war a decade earlier, avoided all support for the 1764 campaign and likely did nothing for those returned, who were all civilians.

Ulrich Conrad heard that his daughter Barbara, captured seven years earlier, had been returned with Bouquet's army to Fort Pitt, but "cannot learn what, since that Time, is become of her." After waiting for nearly a year, Ulrich placed an advertisement offering a £3 reward for information:

> She is 26 Years of Age, her Name Barbara, and her Indian Name Attawa; she has probably light brown Hair, her Eyes between grey and brown; has lived with an old Indian woman, who has but half a Nose. Whoever will give an Account of the said Girl to either of the following Persons, viz. to Frederick Mouse, Stocking-weaver at Philadelphia; to John Adam Moser, at Tulpeherkein; to Jacob Hauseman, at Carlisle; to George Shafer, at Conecrecheague, to Michael Laubinger, at Winchester; or to her Father, on the South Branch [of the Potomac River], in Augusta County, in Virginia, so that, in all Probability, she may be had again, shall have the above Reward, and reasonable Charges, paid by me.[80]

Ulrich had a wide network of contacts, but he may well have been misinformed. It is not known whether Barbara Conrad ever came home, as her mother and brother had done earlier, or whether she returned to the Shawnee, where her younger sister still lived. The hunt for Barbara, and for others who had not come home, was now exclusively a family matter.

Pennsylvania's rescued captives, and those whose origins were not known, were mounted on returning Pennsylvania packhorses and escorted from Fort Pitt by the second contingent of Pennsylvanian troops along Forbes Road. The journey of nearly 200 miles from Fort Pitt was broken at each of four forts on the way to Carlisle. Here the Pennsylvania troops were to be paid and disbanded, and a provincial commissioner was to take charge of the "unclaimed" returning captives. On 6 December, the *Pennsylvania Gazette* had spread the news "that the Troops of this Government were to be sent immediately to Carlisle, and with them the Prisoners belonging to it." It was here at the end of December that many people, including refugees who had fled from frontier farms, gathered to meet the troops, as well as kin and neighbors returning from captivity. The widow Leininger, whose husband and son had been killed and whose two daughters had been captured at Penn's Creek nine years earlier, was there in search of her daughter, Regina. She found no recognition amongst the captives, and no help from asking about a daughter last seen at age nine or ten and now twice that age. At the suggestion of the commissioners, Mrs Leininger sang a German hymn that had been one of Regina's favorites. According to Rev. Henry Melchior Muhlenberg, who saw mother and daughter six weeks later, Regina had immediately recognized the hymn, and her mother through it.[81]

Although Bouquet's expedition ended there, the return of captives continued. Perhaps the worst return from captivity on this frontier was that of nine Virginia captives who were gathered by Alexander McKee and a group of six Virginia volunteers who, with the conciliatory Shawnee chief Benevisica, had gone to Lower Shawnee Town from Camp # 16. The party may have met some resistance in gathering captives, or at least objections to sending them off in mid-winter. Three of the rescued were reported as having been ransomed then by their father or brother, who were among those Virginia volunteers, and it is quite possible that all nine were their relatives or close neighbors.[82] Seven of these nine had been captive less than two years, and sixteen-year-old Elisabeth Filkison was the only one of them who had become a white Indian, after "about Seven Years" with the Shawnee.[83] Whatever their stories, three women, four teenage girls, and two younger children set off with their escort for Fort Pitt, more than 200 miles away, in the dead of winter. Deep snow and cold weather slowed them, and they ran out of food. Benevisica, who accompanied them, hunted with enough success to save their lives. Only two of the party arrived at Fort Pitt on their own, and a thirteen-man rescue party brought in the others. All the captives were frostbitten, and Margaret Byrd, "an old woman: taken 8 years ago from Jackson River Augusta County," died the day after she arrived at Fort Pitt.[84] Benevisica spoke reassuringly to Croghan, Major William Murray, and Six Nations representatives about his people's enthusiasm for peace and willingness to return captives, dismissing "Red Hawk & other foolish Men" who had run away from being Bouquet's hostages for this peace. The results to date had not been very convincing, and no one was pretending that the Shawnee had yet complied with the provision to return all captives. With the British Army gone, fresh supplies of French ammunition, their escaped hostages back home, and almost all their captives still with them, the Shawnee had some opportunity to consider options in the early months of 1765, and the British would suspect them of doing so.

The Shawnee response in the spring of 1765 was their carefully considered reaction to Bouquet's expedition. George Croghan came back to Fort Pitt at the end of February, and promptly sent a messenger to call the Shawnee, Delaware, Mingo, and Sandusky chiefs for a conference. Over the next two months Indian messengers arrived to ask about trade, which was still embargoed, and about possible Quaker participation in the talks, which was refused. The Delaware negotiators did not arrive until the end of April, the first Shawnee arrived on 2 May, and it was another week before the major conference formally opened. Croghan, Major Murray, and a few officers of the garrison hosted nearly 2,000 Delaware, Shawnee, Seneca, and Wyandot. In the name of General Gage, Croghan called for the return of all captives, the replacement of escaped hostages, and the sending of deputies to Johnson. Keyashuta echoed Croghan, and a Shawnee chief admitted, "We behaved wrong last Fall," promising an answer the next day.

On Friday, 10 May, the Shawnee answered impressively. They came in a body across the Allegheny River, "beating a drum and singing their peace song, agreeable to the Ancient Custom of their Nation, which they continued till they entered the Council House." Lawoughgua spoke to the English as "father" for the first time, agreed to all the previous terms, including the provision of hostages and deputies, and presented forty-two former captives.[85] There was reason for his noting that "they are now become unacquainted with your Customs and manners, and therefore, Fathers, we request you will use them tenderly and kindly, which will be a means of inducing them to live contentedly with you."[86] All but five of these returned captives had been taken when under sixteen, more than half of them had been with the Shawnee for more than five years, and at least thirty-six of them had been adopted. It is noteworthy that all but one of the captives returned by the Shawnee were Virginians, indicating the Shawnee focus upon Virginia and their previous reluctance to return captives.[87] The Shawnee peace treaty, negotiated at Johnson Hall in July 1765, was something of an anticlimax. The Shawnee deputies accepted the same humiliating subjection to the Six Nations and the British that the Delaware had accepted in June.[88]

Colonel Bouquet and his admirers, including the assemblies of both Virginia and Pennsylvania, were certainly entitled to consider the Muskingum expedition a great success. Without firing a shot, and without losing more than the one stray soldier murdered while off in the woods, the expedition could take credit for imposing a truce, and for recovering a total of 278 captives by May of 1765. No captives are known to have been killed to avoid surrendering them, only two are known to have escaped, and none died while being escorted home. Admittedly, the Shawnee had been accorded the terms of truce before they had complied, and the punishment of enemies had been confined to verbal abuse, some serious embarrassment, and the more painful surrender of adopted kin and a few blood relatives whose mothers were white. There had also been an effective ban on all trade until the terms of Bouquet's negotiations were fulfilled.[89] It had been a long winter of waiting for the Shawnee to endorse and complete negotiations.

The impact of forcing the surrender of captives upon the Delaware and Shawnee is hard to measure. Warriors who had earlier found the uncompensated return of captives entirely unacceptable, and the return of captives as a precondition of peace negotiations preposterous, had been brought to accept, assist, and legitimize both of these alien proceedings. Doing so had to be difficult in itself, even if the white witnesses did not fully understand the humiliation. Doing so in the presence of Keyashuta, who had suddenly been transformed from an anti-British ally into something of a British Six Nations representative, and before Kahnawake Mohawk witnesses, was an admission of guilt for going to war, and an acceptance of the impending restoration of the despised Iroquois empire of the "Covenant Chain," now enforced by British soldiers, and ratified by that white lord of the Mohawks, William Johnson. If the Delaware prophet Neolin's call for separation of Indians from whites had not affected the rate of capture during this war, perhaps it gained more support as the separation was being insisted upon by the white intruders. The women who wept, delayed, and harbored captives, who could be hidden before or after they ran away from the soldiers, now joined the bereft. Unlike those given up earlier after family discussion and anticipation of rewards, the captives surrendered at the Muskingum were largely white Indians who had spent years growing up in families they considered their own. Only intimidation could have brought about these sad and embarrassing surrenders, without compensation, and even before a peace was settled.

The well-executed military plan had offended not only Indians, but also angry white borderers who could claim that nothing resembling retribution had been exacted from those who had killed and captured more than 5,000 people. The British Army could exaggerate what was accomplished in the battle of Bushy Run as their revenge for the garrisons massacred in 1763. Virginian and Pennsylvanian volunteers in Bouquet's last campaign included some victims' kin and neighbors, as well as some who had been taunted into joining the "manly" fight against the Indians, but they were also made to witness the "humane" negotiation with enemies who had raided their farms and killed or captured their people.[90] People who had been offered revenge plus large scalp bounties gained neither, and there is no record of payment for the return of these captives, as had been true for the surviving Kittanning raiders in 1756. Individual vigilantes would attack Indians frequently after 1764, and attempts to apprehend the perpetrators were frustrated by a local conspiracy of silence. Virginia's Augusta Boys, and Pennsylvania's Black Boys would emerge quickly to attack those who reopened trade in arms to Indians farther west.

Another problem was that the negotiators, on both sides, had stated that all the captives had been returned, which effectively ended the official quest. It is hard to believe that anyone involved, or witnessing these events, could have genuinely believed this to be the case. Bouquet knew that the Shawnee still held dozens of captives, even before Alexander McKee gave him the names of eighty-four still in Lower Shawnee Town after his negotiations had concluded.[91] The returned "prisoners" knew they were leaving kin behind once again, especially if they were from the captured white clans of Armstrong, Barnett, Boyd, Renick, or Vause who managed to learn something of what happened to their still-captive blood relatives. Spouses and parents who had volunteered with the army also knew, and a few of them had gone on to Lower Shawnee Town themselves. Other spouses and parents who gathered to meet the army at Fort Pitt, Carlisle, or Fort Cumberland learned that all the captives had not been returned. More than 1,100 captives had not been returned, and most of them were never heard from again.[92]

It is also legitimate to consider the Muskingum expedition as a heavy-handed climax to an extended diplomacy. The Bouquet expedition was even more expensive than the hospitality and gifts offered by Croghan, though Pennsylvania shared the costs in 1764 by paying its own troops, and even paid the Virginia volunteers.[93] Negotiation by intimidation caused the surrender of long-since adopted captives who would never have been brought to Fort Pitt for something like Croghan's captives-for-presents conferences of 1759–62. Yet, in the case of most Shawnee, the 1764 negotiations had been conducted with Bouquet's army still distant enough to be no immediate threat to those who had adopted captives. It would have been extremely difficult to execute threats issued eighty miles away, after the Shawnee had gathered their harvests and begun to disperse for winter hunting.

Nonetheless, the Muskingum expedition was, by a wide margin, the most successful of the three English methods used to force the return of captives. Hot pursuit, financially the cheapest method, returned a total of only thirty-nine captives in a decade, and cost more lives than it recovered, though it was still used by both Virginia and Pennsylvania in 1764. The Kittanning raid was one of three such British colonial counterattacks attempted in 1756, and the only one to reach its target. Although hailed as a needed victory, it recovered only seven captives and resulted in the deaths of thirty-five raiders compared to fourteen Delaware defenders. The massive Muskingum expedition was by far the most expensive operation to recover captives and impose a truce, an effort possible and justifiable to the British Army and Pennsylvania government only in the context of 1764. It brought back 278 captives without killing or causing the death of anyone, or paying any ransom. The expedition was not an evolution of English methods for recovering captives, but a dramatic display of the effectiveness of intimidating force. This was certainly a humiliation for those Shawnee, Delaware, and Mingo who had resisted the return of captives, and it was a new captivity for a number of English who had become white Indians.

16

Imperial Moment, 1765

The army that marched to the Muskingum Valley in 1764 was composed of British regulars, two Pennsylvania regiments, and hundreds of volunteers from Virginia and Maryland. This was a successful display of the possibilities of imperial cooperation at a time of major political dissent within the empire caused by the Stamp Act crisis. The military campaign involved none of the anticipated fighting, and instead became an effective display of muscular diplomacy at the Muskingum River, coincidentally where the Shawnee trail to war with the English had begun twelve years earlier. Without firing a shot or burning a village, the expedition succeeded, as the Pennsylvania Assembly's formal address of thanks noted, "in laying a Foundation for a lasting as well as honourable Peace with them [the Indians]; and rescuing from Savage Captivity, upwards of Two Hundred of our Christian Brethren, Prisoners among them."[1] How was this nonviolent recovery of captives and negotiated truce, without the bloody sacrifices of Bushy Run or Kittanning, received then and afterwards?

Freeing 207 captives immediately without compensation was an achievement, but it was not at all certain that the truce made on the Muskingum would hold beyond the winter, or that the promised peace would materialize. There was no parade, commemorative medal, purse for the commander, or any conspiracy of exaggerations as had marked the return of Pennsylvania's own lackluster Kittanning expedition in 1756. White borderers could remain skeptical. They had not seen all their relatives returned in 1764 or deaths avenged; instead, the Indians they regarded as murderers had been treated with some courtesy, apparently left unpunished, and given the initiative to negotiate a peace or not. Farther east, where there was growing unease with aggressive new imperial legislation, there was little enthusiasm for celebrating empire. The Virginia government even refused to pay its volunteers who had gone with Colonel Henry Bouquet and scouted so effectively. After showing curiosity about the expedition's fate and reporting the agreed-upon terms in November 1764, the Pennsylvania newspapers said relatively little about the subject. John Penn's truce was printed early in December, and the full list of the returned captives was printed in January. The next month the papers gave some prominence to the Pennsylvania Assembly's fulsome address of thanks, and to Bouquet's response.[2]

The British Army moved with some speed to congratulate Bouquet and promote him to brigadier general, but was not accustomed to bloodless diplomacy or to the celebration of efficient naturalized foreign mercenaries who succeeded where Britons had failed. Bouquet's previously approved request for leave to go to England was denied, and he was instead made commander in the southern department. This promotion meant that he would not receive much attention in London and was removed from Allegheny country, where he had built a reputation with Indians as well as whites.

The Indian department was more visibly uncomfortable with Bouquet's success, for George Croghan and Bouquet had already become direct rivals. Bouquet snidely claimed that Croghan had gone to England to avoid joining his expedition,[3] and Croghan was quick to reassert himself on his return. He wrote from Philadelphia to his deputy, Alexander McKee at Fort Pitt, urging him to act on proposed changes that he knew were not yet approved in London. Croghan pronounced new arrangements for the Department of Indian Affairs that put all trade and diplomacy entirely in its hands, independent of the military, "which I make no doubt will be no small mortification to some people." McKee was to invite Indians to meet Croghan within a month to open trade, and McKee need not tell the commanding officer about these instructions. Bouquet heard of the letter and promptly ordered it intercepted, opened, and held at Fort Pitt if it contained anything regarding the Indians with whom he had treated. Finding that it did, Bouquet wrote General Thomas Gage, claiming to accept the proposed changes with relief, while complaining that he had not even been informed. He was surprised that "powers of so great importance to this country should in this instance have been trusted to a man so illiterate, impudent, and ill bred, who subverts to particular purposes the wise views of the government." The government decision to vest such power in the Indian department had been made months earlier, but Bouquet had reason to expect better treatment.[4]

Croghan and William Johnson also sought to recover authority and initiative by emphasizing the importance of Croghan's expedition to

Illinois country at the end of 1764. Johnson praised Bouquet in a letter to the Board of Trade, but indicated that the peace had begun with Johnson's own earlier Niagara conference and would not be achieved unless Croghan's Illinois mission was successful.[5] Croghan rewrote the story a year later in an unsolicited letter to Benjamin Franklin, Pennsylvania's agent in London. Putting the expeditions of Colonel John Bradstreet and Colonel Bouquet together, Croghan said, "How far they succeeded is unnecessary for me to relate," and he then claimed that Bouquet remained "not a little distressed – In that all his endeauvors had hitherto failed, with respect to gaining the Ilinois." Subduing Illinois country had not been Bouquet's assignment, but Croghan was busy insisting that his own survival there was more significant than Bouquet's campaign.[6]

Awareness of Bouquet's accomplishment suddenly surged in Pennsylvania in May of 1765. Perhaps the arrival at Fort Pitt of the Shawnee with their captives indicated the continuing impact of the expedition of the previous autumn. Or perhaps the new appreciation was orchestrated by Scottish-born Rev. William Smith (1727–1803), the ambitious, industrious, and political Anglican rector of the College of Philadelphia, who happened to be the most prolific published author in colonial America at the time.[7] Smith had built a reputation as an educator and preacher, an articulate supporter of the proprietors and the war, and an increasingly bitter political rival of his former friend Benjamin Franklin. Smith had also been bashing Quaker and German pacifists for a decade, and calling Christian soldiers to their "just war" duties.[8] Smith had sent copies of his patriotic *The American Magazine and Monthly Chronicle for the British Colonies* to a supportive Bouquet late in 1757, and two years later Bouquet remarked that Smith had "defeated the Philistins compleatly" in a legal battle with the Pennsylvania Assembly.[9] By 1762 Smith was also beginning speculations in frontier lands, an interest that reinforced his existing enthusiasm for effective military initiatives there.

Smith, who believed that history "is nothing more than religion and philosophy taught by examples,"[10] celebrated the expedition as clear proof of the need for force, and the possibility of its humane use. First, Smith oversaw the commencement proceedings at the College of Philadelphia on 30 May 1765. In a staged dialogue, a speaker asks,

> Can we forget how, thro' the trackless Wood,
> With Phalanx firm, and Sword unstain'd in Blood

Our brave Commander urg'd his glorious Way;
And bent the fierce Barbarians to his Sway;
Taught them our Power and Mercy both to Own,
And shook the haughty Chieftains on their Throne?

A footnote reminded those who might have forgotten, or failed to recognize, that this praise was for "General Bouquet in his Expedition to Muskingum." The rhyming continued,

The mournful Captives, hopeless and forlorn,
From Gospel-light, from Friends, from Freedom torn.
Restor'd by him, again behold their Home,
Rejoic'd – ... in savage woods no more to roam!
You heav'ns the Deed approve ... strike bold the Lyre
And let returning Peace the Strain inspire.[11]

These lines were spoken, and printed in the newspapers, for an audience that had just learned that all efforts to prevent the dreaded Stamp Act had failed. Smith privately opposed the Stamp Act, though he could not anticipate the level of resistance that subsequent autumn. Bouquet was back in Philadelphia in June, and advertised that those with accounts to settle with him were "to send them immediately to his House," as he was about to sail to take up his new post. The *Pennsylvania Gazette* had evidently rediscovered him, and found it newsworthy to report, on the Fourth of July, "Since our last, the Honourable Brigadier General Bouquet sailed for Pensacola, in the Schooner Pensacola, Captain Dyer."[12]

This item was certainly linked to a larger advertisement in the same issue, for William Smith's just-published *An Historical Account of the Expedition against the Ohio Indians, in the Year 1764, under the Command of Henry Bouquet, Esq.* Using Bouquet's papers and conversations, Smith wrote of the expedition extensively and sympathetically. In describing the diplomacy of the mission, Smith was at some pains to insist that Bouquet had been firm and demanding of the Indians, and to claim that the Shawnee had intended to kill all their captives on two occasions. Smith was celebrating a hero, and may have been consciously balancing the perceived virtues of resolute manliness and generous humanity, a stance that was at once an effective response to the Quakers and a distancing from the worst excesses of Smith's unsavory political allies, the Paxton Boys.[13] Smith exaggerated the pathos of the "most affecting scene" of the arrival of captives at the military camp, and, if he had known it, he would surely have included Regina Leininger's pious story. More significantly, Smith reveled in what were, to him, the unexpected displays of humanity and affection by the Indian relatives of the adopted captives. Smith, whose earlier bellicose writings had been appreciated by those in the Pennsylvania backcountry, seemed to reach well beyond the known boundaries of his own humanity here. Although he promptly turned to denouncing the adult captives who had to be forced to become "free" again, and he could not even speak of a marriage between white and Indian, he now recognized the attractiveness of Indian life and values. The account of the expedition was only the first half of the book; the other half was taken up with reflections on Indians and frontier war, a borrowed plan for creating and using "light troops" against Indians, and a scheme for settling disbanded troops defensively. Thomas Hutchins, who had been a volunteer and mapmaker on the expedition, seems to have been the source, if not the author, of the last section of the book.

An Historical Account did more than celebrate British military leadership in the service of European settlers and captives, an enthusiasm that was limited and about to evaporate entirely. Richard Slotkin considers the book "one of the most significant studies of wilderness life and warfare."[14] Smith's view of the Stamp Act colored his discussion "Of the temper and genius of the Indians." It was now timely to begin with a bow to Jean-Jacques Rousseau: "The love of liberty is innate in the savage; and seems the ruling passion of the state of nature." It was decidedly more imaginative to claim, "Jealous of his independency and of his property, he will not suffer the least encroachment on either; and upon the slightest suspicion, fired with resentment, he becomes an implacable enemy, and flies to arms to vindicate his right, or revenge an injury."[15] Smith and Hutchins implied that the hated and dreaded Indians could be models for Americans in warfare and in other virtues that Christians should imitate. Surprisingly, ten full paragraphs from the book, centering on the invented "affecting scene" of captives returning to the army and the tenderness of the Indians, were reprinted in the *Pennsylvania Gazette* a couple of weeks later, supposedly submitted by a reader who was "particularly affected" by them.[16]

Fate would be much kinder to Smith than to Bouquet. Smith was an adroit navigator of troubled political waters, and *An Historical Account* proved to be his most successful publication. William Bradford's Philadelphia printing sold well, as did a London reprint the following year, and abridged versions were published in Robert Dodsley's *Annual Register for the Year 1765* and in *The Gentleman's Magazine* the following spring. A Dublin edition bound together with Robert Rogers's *Journals* appeared in 1769, and by that time translated editions had appeared twice in Paris and once in Amsterdam. Smith and his book had fared better than Bouquet, who died of yellow fever within days of arriving at Pensacola. Captain Dyer's return to Philadelphia in November 1765 was noted in the newspapers,[17] both of which had suspended publication in protest against enforcement of the Stamp Act and had then resumed with full accounts of the stamp protests. Neither paper mentioned the passing of the "brave commander" of the verses they had printed six months earlier.

The 1766 London reprint of *An Historical Account* featured two interesting plates, drawn by Smith's successful young American protégé, Benjamin West. Although these are well known, and often reproduced, they have not been seen as much more than decorations donated by a grateful student. West was the son of prominent Chester County Quakers, and had been as far west as Lancaster before his talent and contacts took him to Philadelphia, Italy, and London. West was determined to be a historical painter at a time when classical and Biblical paintings were in vogue. Although he was already a much sought-after painter, West took the time to prepare two very detailed drawings for T. Jefferies's 1766 London edition of Smith's *An Historical Account*. Amid the ferocious Pennsylvania political battles in London, pitting Smith and the Penns against Franklin and the Pennsylvania Assembly, West drew these two pieces for Smith's version of Bouquet's success without compromising his reputation for neutrality in the politics of his native province.[18]

Guided by his mentor's second-hand account and his own imagination, West first drew what was labeled "The Indians Giving a Talk to Colonel Bouquet in a Conference at a Council Fire near His Camp on the Banks of Muskingum in North America, in Octr. 1764" (see illustration 6). The choice of subject deliberately invited comparison with classical orators, though all wore contemporary clothing, an innovation that West would champion in historical painting. The open-ended bower is tall and well lit, made of hewn and civilized boards attached to living trees. Colonel Bouquet, whom West had never known, is pictured facing the orator and is attended closely by an apprehensive scribe and three others. The whites are all listening attentively. The speaker, representing unpretentious Indian oratory, wears a blanket rather like

6 “The Indians Giving a Talk to Colonel Bouquet,” by Benjamin West, 1766. Dechert Collection, Annenberg Rare Book and Manuscript Library, University of Pennsylvania.

a toga, his right arm raised and finger pointing skyward while his left hand offers what appears to be the first wampum belt of the meeting. He wears a decorated headband and an unlikely topknot, worthy of John White's 1585 drawings.[19] The Indian seated nearest the viewer is muscular, lightly clad in a toga, and calmly smoking a pipe-tomahawk. Crowded behind the speaker are eight intense-looking Indian companions, not watching the speaker but carefully observing Bouquet. Two Indians appear to be interjecting or interrupting the speaker, which would not have been likely. The setting is a warm October afternoon, the trees are still in leaf, the Indians are lightly clad, and the fire is a symbolic welcome. Although the tents of the military are in the middle distance, the only weapons visible are the tip of Bouquet's sheathed sword, and the hilt of another being leaned upon by a man in civilian clothes, and that harmless-looking calumet-hatchet serving as a tobacco pipe.

Smith's evocation of the climactic return of captives to Bouquet's camp had included a call to a poet or painter "to enrich their highest colorings of a variety of human passions."[20] West's response was "The Indians Delivering Up the English Captives to Colonel Bouquet near His Camp at the Forks of Muskingum in North America in 1764" (see illustration 7). West sought to portray the intensity of the exchange rather than its scale. West has Bouquet seated on a stump, attended by his scribe and two young men who appear curious about the captives. A strong and intelligent-looking Indian is presenting two chubby children, one clinging to a kneeling Indian woman. A beautiful young white mother is close behind this couple, carrying a plump child tonsured with West's standard Indian haircut. Less distinct are several other captives and Indians, at least one of whom is weeping. A canopy of trees shelters everyone. Bouquet's sword is visible, as are a squad of shouldered muskets in the middle distance, and soldiers' tents are in the background beneath a very large flag. The Indians are portrayed as reluctantly submitting to imperial power.

Were West's detailed pencil drawings simply in preparation for major paintings of "the humane commander," which were then in vogue?[21] About this time he painted the related "General Johnson Saving a Wounded French Officer from the Tomahawk of a North American Indian."[22] Yet West did not paint canvases from the two drawings of Bouquet, either on commission for a Pennsylvanian or English patron, or on speculation.[23] Smith's affecting scene may have proven too difficult to portray to West's satisfaction, or it may not have appealed to

7 "The Indians Delivering Up the English Captives to Colonel Bouquet," by Benjamin West, 1766. Dechert Collection, Annenberg Rare Book and Manuscript Library, University of Pennsylvania.

any potential patrons. After all his fighting with Quaker pacifists, Smith reveled in a display of force that recovered captives without bloodshed. However briefly, Smith and West sought to make the Muskingum expedition into an iconic imperial event.

Evaluation of Bouquet's accomplishment at the Muskingum was varied and became particularly vulnerable to rapid changes of context. It was still possible for British soldier-historian Thomas Mante, whose *The History of the Late War in North-America* ... appeared in London in 1772, to view Bouquet's expedition as a satisfying climax and conclusion to his broad and detailed history of the British Army at war in America. Although Mante had been a supportive staff officer of Colonel Bradstreet, and felt that Bouquet was self-seeking and unfair to Bradstreet, Mante had no more attractive way to conclude his success story of the British Army in North America than to attach Pontiac's War directly to the Seven Years' War, and then climax the entire experience with Bouquet achieving a peace that Mante could still say, eight years later, had held "ever since."

The larger British imperial conquest was also passing away. Relentless white greed for Indian land, and occasional acts of unprovoked white savagery, would soon lead to Dunmore's War and the spread of the American Revolution into Allegheny borderlands. The brutal warfare, which would eventually be seen as a Sixty Years' War between the Shawnee and the "Long Knives," resumed. Patriots would ignore their own greed and savagery while considering Indian retaliation as unprovoked savagery in dishonorable violation of agreements, including the promises made to Bouquet and Johnson.

The Muskingum campaign would not work in most post-revolutionary histories of the United States the way it had for Mante. George Bancroft's patriotic *History of the United States of America*, expanding from three to six volumes in editions dating from the 1830s to the 1890s, merely mentions the "happy sagacity" of Bouquet at Bushy Run and does not mention the Muskingum expedition at all. The French at Illinois are credited with ending the Indian war, and Bancroft then hurries on to devote sixteen chapters to the origin, politics, and consequences of the Stamp Act.[24] Military historians have been more interested in Bouquet's tactics of survival at Bushy Run than in his adroit management of the following year's "affecting scene," where he restrained the angry soldiers he led, negotiated the uncompensated return of long-held captives, and established a truce that lasted a decade despite repeated provocation by white "pioneers."[25]

Efforts to set all the captives free had been strenuous and enduring, whatever the mixture of motives, and the cumulative results remained equivocal. Of the 2,873 captives taken on all sides, some 1,572 are known to have returned. This was "setting all the captives free" only if the more than 1,000 who were still missing were all presumed dead. Some 225 of those returning, including 40 Indians, had escaped. Most of the 104 who were formally exchanged were French and Canadian soldiers exchanged by the British Army. Seventy-three captives were ransomed, and 79 were retaken by force. The 278 captives eventually surrendered as a result of Bouquet's muscular diplomacy were far exceeded by those returned in the gift exchanges of William Johnson and George Croghan, who are known to have received 704 released captives. The British Army paid for much of Bouquet's expedition, for the formal exchanges of soldiers, and for all of the diplomacy of the Indian superintendency. The cost of attempting to impose cultural dominance in the matter of captives had been high, the results were incomplete and widely underappreciated, and those civilians returned by such intervention had not demonstrated any initiative of their own in returning. They would be called upon to prove themselves thereafter, and most would carry the legacy of their time with the Indians with some caution.

PART 5

AFTERWARDS AND AFTERWORDS

Whether they became white Indians, were rescued or escaped, or felt "redeemed" or forced into a new captivity by their return, most of the "freed" could never truly go home again. Traumas had been endured, families smashed, livelihoods destroyed, and identities had been lost, altered, or acquired. Although most had been through this trauma at captivity, many returned captives went through some radical change a second time upon their return (chapter 17). There was another way in which returned captives could not go home again. A generation of war had dethroned the Pennsylvania Quakers, destroyed much of the tolerance they had advocated for their multi-ethnic society, and built a new and more aggressive political culture in colonial Allegheny country. War had only momentarily reversed the invasion by white farmers, and peace saw the acceleration of the intrusion of the land-hungry. These invaders were increasingly suspicious of fellow whites who knew and liked Indians, to say nothing of those who spoke their languages, had acquired their behaviors, had friends among them, or brought back their own *métis* children. Mixed and blurred identities could still be necessary in some callings and useful in others, but were increasingly suspect.[1]

A few returned captives left depositions or memoirs that indicate what they remembered and forgot in recovering, adapting, or reinventing their identities. The accounts of captivity offered in depositions, newspapers, pamphlets, and more fulsome printed and unprinted narratives all benefit from being read in their precise context to understand the role of authors' needs and circumstances, deliberate or anticipated military and governmental censorship, the influence of narratives already available, and changing social, political, and literary conventions (chapter 18).

Some of the difficulties of "re-entry" can be illustrated in the immediate experience of the seven captives recovered by Pennsylvanians at

Kittanning in 1756, people who had been captive for a relatively short time. They had not won the honor due to those who had escaped, though Colonel John Armstrong and his fellow officers kindly donated their share of the scalp money to the rescued.[2] The recovered captives were paraded in what must have looked like a cross-cultural military triumph in Lancaster in mid-October, which included a display of Delaware scalps, wampum belts, and Tewea's fine powder horn and pouch. These former captives were held in custody while the scalp money for their recovery was negotiated and another public display arranged. The captives were still with Armstrong a month later when Governor William Denny arrived at Lancaster and formally welcomed the freed captives, who were again displayed and questioned before finally being released. Despite all the effort, cost, and sacrifice involved in recovering these few captives, they were not welcomed back very well.

Freedom would taste very different for each of these rescued captives. Sarah Kelly of Virginia came back knowing that her husband had been killed and believing that all six of her captured children were still missing. One of her sons had escaped shortly after capture, and she might have been able to learn of this and to find him, if he had become a servant somewhere near the site of their captivity.[3] Margaret Hood of Maryland, captured the previous November near the mouth of Conococheague Creek, left no traces after her return.[4] Seven-year-old Martha Thorn, taken in the fall of McCord's Fort five months before the Kittanning raid, readily remembered her name and the battle of Sideling Hill, during which her mother had escaped, carrying a luckier baby in her arms. Martha, whose father had been away the day she had been captured, likely returned to her reassembled, if traumatized, family. Mrs Ann McCord was with young Martha in the surrender of McCord's Fort, along with her own five children. Ann had seen her eldest daughter killed by friendly fire in this same battle, and may have known that two of her daughters managed to escape that day.[5] She came home from Kittanning to them and her husband after five months of captivity, but would have to wait more than two years for the return of her two other surviving children.

Young Catherine Smith was less fortunate. At five years of age, she had been captured with her mother near Shamokin in December of 1755, and was soon separated from her.[6] When rescued at Kittanning, Catherine had become blind. A fulsome newspaper advertisement by the Pennsylvania Hospital in May of 1760 revealed her situation:

> NOTICE is hereby given that Catherine Smith, a child of ten years of age, her parents unknown, has been at the Pennsylvania hospital almost for three years past, she having been taken captive by the Indians, during the time of her captivity having lost her sight, was taken into the hospital in hope of her being relieved; but the endeavour of the physicians proved ineffectual. It is now proposed she should be instructed in some business as may be proper for her circumstances; and the provincial commissioners are willing to give with her a competent sum of money. She is a child of a mild and tractable temper and pramiune [*sic*] genius. Wherefore any persons of approved character, and of a compassionate humane disposition who are willing to undertake the care of her education, and to give her the necessary instruction, may apply to the treasurer of the Pennsylvania hospital, or either of the managers, who will treat with them on the terms.[7]

We now know, as she did not, that her mother had already been redeemed and exchanged by way of France and England in 1757.[8] Catherine was not reunited with her mother. She was bound out soon after the ad appeared, and was still a servant six years later.[9] Even captives held briefly, and remembering their names and place of capture, had trouble reconnecting with their surviving families.

Two other captives recovered at Kittanning may not have been particularly grateful, and would come to feel the shunning imposed on those considered suspect. Barbara Hicks, whose husband and two children had been killed, had four surviving captured sons, two of whom would become notorious as suspected spies for the Delaware. The other two, who had also become thoroughly acculturated Delaware, would come back unwillingly eight years after Barbara was returned.

Eighteen-year-old Thomas Girty was also recovered at Kittanning, having been captive only a month, but in this time he had seen Fort Granville surrendered and his stepfather tortured to death. His mother, his three younger brothers, and his infant half-brother remained captive. Thomas had been back from Kittanning for nearly sixteen months when the Cumberland County Orphan's Court formally ordered him bound as an apprentice for six years, to the commander of his rescue party, John Armstrong.[10] Thomas somehow managed to preserve the Girty family property until his mother returned in 1759. Thomas's three younger brothers, finally brought back against their will by Colonel

Henry Bouquet's army in 1764, would become infamous among supporters of the American Revolution as the dreaded "Indian Girtys."[11] Thomas's half-brother, John Turner Jr, had spent eight of his nine years with the Shawnee when he was returned in May of 1765. He never learned to read or write, and evidently did not need to in his career as a trapper, trader, scout, farmer, and land speculator. He married, survived the social opprobrium associated with his Indian "origins" and three "traitorous" half-brothers, and eventually moved west to the Allegheny River Valley, where he lived out his long life.[12]

Captives were all marked for life. Although "post-traumatic stress disorder" would not be discovered or invented for another two centuries, those who had witnessed grotesque death or torture of loved ones, or had been threatened themselves, were likely to suffer distressing recollections, dreams, and hallucinations, and to become more withdrawn, suspicious, irritable, and hyper-vigilant. We cannot know whether a majority of captives suffered "clinically significant distress or impairment in social, occupational, or other important areas of functioning," which could be acute, chronic, or even "delayed onset."[13] Almost all captives were coping, or failing to cope, with very troubling memories.

Some captives became white Indians who fought to display and confirm their new identity. Some managed to hover between the polarizing worlds of white and red, as "long-hunters," hermits, cranks, traders, guides, interpreters, couriers, or as their wives, and a few gained comfort in the hybrid Delaware Moravian Christian communities. Others confirmed their clear commitment to white society by becoming prominent in "Indian hating" and fighting Indians. Telling their story, or withholding it, was part of a returned captive's negotiation of re-entry into what was increasingly seen as "white society."

17

Restoring and Revising Identities

Felix Renick was never a captive, but he came from one Greenbrier River family that knew much captivity, and he married into another. In 1798 he and two companions traveled west, in the calm that followed the Treaty of Greenville (1795), to view and claim fertile lands at Wakatomica Bottom on the Muskingum River. These rich lands had been worked by Itawachcomequa's people when he left on his fateful quest forty-five years earlier, but after four intervening wars this was becoming white American territory. Felix recorded an adage common among his people: "It is easy to make an Indian out of a white man, but hard, if not impossible to make a white man out of an Indian, or even to reclaim a white man after being converted into an Indian." He supported this claim by recalling his mother-in-law's lament at the effort needed to "break in" boys who had been captive, especially young John Sea, who had been captured in 1763, and returned in 1765, but had promptly ran away to live two more years with the Shawnee: "[I]t was utterly impossible, she said, to keep clothes on them; in the summer season she did not attempt it, as it was worse than useless to do so ... It took a number of years to root out this attachment, and indeed it was thought by a part of their friends that some of the boys carried remnants of it to their graves."[1]

Felix was also reminded of captives by the cultural hybrids he and his companions met in 1798. Near what would eventually become Bowling Green, Ohio, Felix and his friends met an old hunter living with his dog in a "bark camp" some thirty miles from his nearest neighbor. He raised a garden of corn and potatoes without any fences, killing all animal trespassers for food. This hunter had been a captive and, despite having chosen his isolation between cultures, enjoyed regaling his visitors with accounts of what he called his "scrapes" with the Indians.

Felix made a more surprising discovery on reaching a cluster of cabins at Johnson's Station in Wakatomica Bottom. The old widow they stayed with proved to be his relative by marriage, Mary Sea, who had been captured in Cornstalk's 1763 Greenbrier attack and had been returned in 1765.[2] Although a captive for less than two years, Mary went west again long before Felix, who nonetheless managed to be called "the pioneer." She evidently spoke Shawnee and had married a trader named William Johnson. Although she knew where her kin were, she stayed on alone on the Muskingum after William died.

Returned captives continued to recover, revise, or invent themselves as they chose or were pushed into various levels of reintegration into white society. Escape from captivity was considered the best demonstration of preference for one's natal culture, but relatively few had escaped. Family and property might be reclaimed or reassembled, and, for some, former work could be diligently resumed. Just as white Indians fought against the whites to prove their conversion, "red colonists" fought against Indians to prove they had come back. A few returnees also gave testimonials of their loyalty when providing initial depositions, writing accounts of their recent captivity, or recording what was remembered decades later. These memories will be examined in the next chapter. In the second round of acculturation for these captives, age and former status largely determined what was required and what was possible. Dependent children, youths, servants, slaves, and adult women each had distinctive problems, prospects, and requirements upon returning, as did captured men who had been traders, soldiers, or farmers. There is value in considering, in turn, the quest for identity by each of these kinds of returned captive.

Although the changing legal status of a child was still being debated by sophisticates of this period, the religious dissenters of the Pennsylvania frontier, their justices, and their orphan's courts were confident advocates of the newer and more thoroughgoing legal dependency of children.[3] Child captives had been dependents before capture, survived in captivity as dependents in adoptive Indian families, and were expected on their return to become dependents in their birth families, nuclear or extended, if they still had them. If the identity of their birth parents could not be remembered or found, and kin did not claim them, young orphans could be taken in by strangers, and older ones were cared for by putting them into the service of willing families.[4] In this and other ways, there was a distinction between younger children, captured under the age of seven, and the older ones.

Few young children could retain much independent memory of their life before captivity, such as their names, their native language, and where they had been captured. These things were better remembered by those young children who had been allowed to remain in the company of their mothers, siblings, or neighbors during captivity. Children born in captivity were not quite captives, but shared in their captive mother's identity, and were treated as captives as they were "returned." Robert Renick was born a few months after his mother was captured, spent his childhood as Pechyloothame, but also carried the name of his killed father and older brother, and was returned with his mother when he was seven. His youth would have been awkward, but he evidently accepted white settler society. He and his mother lived among kin, and Robert eventually married and inherited the rebuilt family estate from his unmarried elder brother and fellow captive, William.[5]

Uprooted *métis* children were also "returned" in 1764–65 in what must have been particularly trying circumstances. Officers compiling lists of returned captives entered the mother's name and then "her child" or "her children" without names, though it is possible that other *métis* children were amongst those identified only by their Shawnee, Delaware, or Seneca names, or by descriptive identifiers like "Soremouth," "Crooked legs," or "girl with a Sore Knee."[6] Of the sixteen *métis* children known to have accompanied their returning mothers, Hannah Smith's son is the only one about whom anything further is known. He was presented to a surprised Mr Smith, who accepted a wife who had been gone for six years and brought home an Indian chief's son, but he "had a most bitter aversion to the young chief." The boy apparently looked like his Indian father, grew up in the Smith house without accepting his re-education, joined the Continental Army as a young private, and never returned.[7]

When nineteen-year-old Catherine Jager returned from a decade with the Susquehanna Delaware, she brought her *métis* child with her, and both of them likely suffered the "Contempt and Derision" of the young women of Northampton County, Pennsylvania.[8] Most of the *métis* children accompanied young mothers, like Catherine, who had grown up and married as white Indians. Little is known of their fate, but something might be suggested by the presumed status of Mary Todd's child. Todd, whose entire immediate family had been killed when she was captured in December of 1755, was returned with her young *métis* child at the 1762 Lancaster conference. Despite being twenty-five, she was not considered free upon her return. With no white relatives to claim them, she and her child were listed in a public advertisement that concluded: "the Boys will be bound out to Trades, and the Girls so disposed of, as to prevent their becoming a further Expence to the Public."[9] And then there were the "Two Young Women, about 16, or 18 Years of Age, taken about 8 or 9 Years ago, supposed to belong to New-Jersey. Two

Children they had by Indians." William Johnson, who regarded Colonel Henry Bouquet's insistence upon the return of *métis* children as "highly judicious," listed these four people among twenty-five returned to him in 1765. In advertising these people "who will be delivered to their Relations upon Application," Johnson had no remembered name for any of these four, or for fifteen others. One can only wonder at the fate of "Bridget's son," who was under ten when he was surrendered to Bouquet's army without any record of an accompanying Bridget, and no other captive is known to have had her Christian name.[10]

The *métis* children of two other Allegheny captives are known to have had very different futures. Fanny Barnett had married a Shawnee and had five children, who were with her in Lower Shawnee Town in 1764. The two children grew up Shawnee, and Fanny stayed with them for another decade. She was "surrendered" in 1775, in the wake of Dunmore's War, but stayed with her white sister for only a few days before returning to her Shawnee family. Captive Margaret Moore's *métis* children, Joseph and Nancy, were both children of then-famous Shawnee chief Waweyapiersenwaw (Blue Jacket), formerly Sepettekenathe, but led dissimilar lives that eventually came together. Young Joseph was with his mother only until she became pregnant with Nancy. Margaret was then "allowed" to visit her mother, who had returned to Virginia from her own captivity in 1763, and Margaret stayed with her mother for an entire generation. Neither Margaret nor young Nancy, who "never saw the face of an Indian except when she looked in a mirror," was subjected to a still-valid Virginia law against miscegenation with blacks or Indians.[11] Nancy married James Stewart and, about 1804, she, her husband, her mother, and her four children all migrated to Ohio country. Nancy met her father and brother there for the first time. Joseph was remembered as then "a pretty fair specimen of the aborigines of the wild woods – dressed in their style, with buckskin leggins and mocassins, a blanket belted around the waist, and silver brooch for fastening over the breast." Their father was dead before 1810, when Joseph and Nancy were acknowledged as "half-bloods of their tribe" and each awarded 640 acres by treaty rights. Joseph joined Tecumseh's forces two years later, and never returned from that war. Nancy, her husband, and her mother, "a handsome old lady of some sixty years or upwards," lived out their lives on those granted lands, attending and eventually being buried in the cemetery of the Muddy Run Meeting House, a Christian church on the Mad River, below West Liberty, Ohio.[12]

At least 124 children were returned from an Indian life that had begun when they were less than seven years old.[13] For the thirty-one who were captive for less than a year, the acculturation would eventually be reversed without much trace, though the destruction of their families had likely altered their life prospects dramatically. The forty who spent more than five years with the Indians had been reshaped in ways that would be recognizable for the rest of their lives. Their first language and habits were Shawnee, Delaware, or Seneca, and many forgot their European language and their name and place in that society.

Young children who returned from short captivities accompanied by their mother would have obvious advantages in reintegration.[14] Infant Janet Martin was ransomed by her mother in New France, and then traveled with her to England and home again to her father in Cumberland County. Although captured at an impressionable age, she had been with the French for much less time than her older siblings were with the Indians.[15] Susan Knox and her four young children had been captive for only a year before they all came back with the Bouquet expedition.[16]

Returning to mother was no guarantee of smooth re-entry for youngsters coming back to white frontier society. After Jean Clendennin, age six, returned from two years in captivity, "it was a long time before the mother formed any attachment for this little waif, with all its Indian habits to be overcome." Perhaps Jean's mother was also troubled by her own abandonment of the girl at capture. Yet Jean would grow up to be a considerable local heiress, and she married "well," as did her children. Eve Eice of Virginia and six of her children, all under seven years of age when captured, were all returned together to Bouquet's army after living nine years with the Indians.[17] Son John promptly ran away to his former life, and was later presented to Sir William Johnson as an unredeemable renegade who was sold into Florida servitude. Seven members of the Sea clan, captive for less than two years, were returned in two groups; John Sea was one of two children returned with his mother, but promptly escaped to live two more years with the Shawnee.

Returning with mother did not bring much security in itself. Fathers had often been killed and farms abandoned and/or sold by kin, while widowed mothers often remarried promptly after returning. Stepfathers may have provided essential support to mothers and children, but only the occasional child with a preserved inheritance was officially assigned a guardian – who could be neither a remarried mother nor stepfather –

by the county orphan's court. Those captured as infants and living with the Indians for several years were often old enough to be indentured upon return, whether orphaned or not, and their acculturation to white colonial society, like their earlier acculturation to Indian society, was supervised in the family of an unrelated master.

Most of those captured before they were seven and subsequently returned were not accompanied by their mothers. Nonetheless, more than half of these children were promptly identified, not always correctly, by both Christian and family name. In some cases, they were returned with older siblings or neighbors, who could better tell them, or Bouquet's scribes, their names and where and when they had been captured.[18] David Hutchinson was captured at age two and returned by the Shawnee to Fort Pitt in May of 1765, when he was nine; perhaps his mother, whose captivity had ended five months earlier, was still there to meet and identify him.[19] Molly and Nalupua Byrd, under seven when their family was captured at Greenbrier, having lived longer than that with the Shawnee, were identified when returned, though Nalupua's Christian name – if she had one – had been forgotten. These teenage Byrds were known to be from Augusta County, Virginia, but they had little to recover of a former life: their father had been killed when they were captured, and his estate would have been long since settled. Their mother had died after a grueling return from captivity to Fort Pitt the previous winter, and two other siblings stayed with the Shawnee permanently. The returned sisters may not have had a chance to find their older brother John, who had been returned to Bouquet the previous November, before all three of them were put into the service of other white families.[20]

Accounts of the belated return of two very young captives, Thomas Ingles and Susannah Barnett, are illuminating and miraculous, respectively. Thomas Ingles was four when captured with his mother and younger brother in a well-known incident at the headwaters of the Roanoke River in August of 1755. His mother soon escaped, his brother soon died, and Thomas grew up Shawnee. About 1762 his uncle William hired a former Shawnee captive and trader, Thomas Baker, who succeeded in ransoming eleven-year-old Thomas. Despite Baker's vigilance, young Thomas escaped less than fifty miles into the homeward journey, and was sheltered by the Shawnee when Baker retraced the journey and inquired. Apparently Baker and his employer attempted the same mission again in 1763, but were turned back by the outbreak of Pontiac's War. In 1768 Baker and William Ingles made a third attempt, and this time successfully redeemed Thomas. His indulgent and prosperous family worked to teach him the English language and folkways, but the seventeen year old "would take fits at times and would start off and be gone 2 or 3 days at a time." The family sent him down country to Dr Thomas Walker's boarding school in Albemarle County. Three or four years there seemed to have improved Thomas's English, altered his manners, and completed his acculturation. He displayed his conversion by joining the Virginian forces in Dunmore's War, and served in the garrison left after the battle of Point Pleasant. Meeting Shawnee acquaintances who negotiated the peace, Thomas went back with them and, his nephew recalled, "stayed some time with them." Whatever the temptations there, Thomas eventually returned to the garrison and then to Virginia's frontier to farm in the New River region. He had married and had fathered three young children when, in 1782, his farmstead was attacked by Indians while he was in the fields. Thomas joined a pursuit party of militia, who persisted until they surprised the raiders a week later. When the Virginians attacked, the Indians tomahawked their captives; Thomas's wife and two older children were among those killed. Thomas Ingles's new life had ended in a tragic contest between the cultures he had come to understand. Although he is not known to have returned to the Shawnee, Ingles went west on his own, first to Tennessee and eventually to Mississippi.[21]

If Thomas Ingles was lost, Susannah Barnett was assuredly found. According to her pious Baptist chronicler, Virginian Susannah Barnett was captured by the Shawnee at age six and, unlike her older sister Fanny, "never could be reconciled to stay with them; she never forgot the white people, her own name, and the name of the place she was taken from, but thought that if ever an opportunity offered she would try to make her escape and get home." Twelve years later, in the peaceful year 1768, this eighteen-year-old Shawnee girl reportedly walked some 200 miles to Fort Pitt, being assisted and accompanied at a crucial time by a generous and unidentified Indian couple. The chronicler regarded Susannah's inspiration to leave on a specific day, and her timely meeting with the Indian couple, as special acts of Providence. At Fort Pitt she received appropriate white woman's clothing from sympathetic people and assistance in getting home to her family.[22] She soon had a Baptist conversion experience, married, and settled with her husband near Fort Pitt. Her futile effort to repatriate her elder sister was retold to reinforce her own miraculous story of white cultural survival and resistance.[23]

A third sizable group of child captives did not know their surnames upon their eventual return, or were misidentified. A young man known only as Tom, who had spent the years between five and twenty with the Shawnee, served as a courier for Sir William Johnson in 1768, but was Shawnee enough to be imprisoned on suspicion at Fort Niagara and jailed as a vagrant in Montreal.[24] A thirteen year old named George, who spoke no other English than his name, was returned to Fort Augusta in 1762: "Whoever knows any Thing of him, is desired to come and pay Charges, and take him away."[25] Some youths in this position were promptly claimed by unrelated people. Parents who failed to find their own child among the white-Indian orphans at Fort Pitt or Carlisle might, in unacknowledged imitation of Indian adoption of captives, acquire an approximate replacement. A thirteen-year-old girl "very much freckled, red hair'd" was, after nine years with the Mingo, initially claimed by Margaret Stuart of Great Cove as her daughter Mary, but this girl was turned over to the local magistrate when, upon the return of Mary herself, it was determined that Margaret "hath got one that certainly is her own."[26] The returned boy raised as Jacob Persinger claimed that he had become who he was in the same way.[27] Maria Christina Schmidt was eleven when returned at Lancaster, cared for by a Quaker family temporarily, and then, over her objections, taken by a man who claimed to be her father. It was another year before her own parents happened to discover her and take her home. One child of Francis Innis, claimed by a Philadelphian, was recovered only after a serious dispute.[28] The British commander at Fort Bedford, assisting an orphan's legal guardian equipped with a court order, forcibly recovered another returned captive girl from a trader and his wife. Captain Lewis Ourry reported being harassed by this would-be mother, but felt justified, "especially as the Child is almost ruined already by the bad Examples continuously before her Eyes, and is as abusive in her Language as her Tutoress, who has turn'd the Town upside down since she came. I am obliged to shut the Fort Gates to keep her out of it – but her Mouth, who can shut."[29]

An extensive legal case of false identity concerned Jane Grey, a three year old taken with her mother, Hannah, in the capture of Bigham's Fort in 1756. Jane's devastated father, John Grey, died after making a will that granted separate land to Hannah and Jane upon their return from captivity. Hannah escaped, and, when daughter Jane failed to be among those returned at the Muskingum River in 1764, Hannah deliberately chose an unclaimed child and raised her as Jane. Hannah admitted her fraud in private to several persons, and one garrulous woman denounced the girl as "a big black ugly Dutch lump, and not to be compared to the beautiful Jenny Grey." The real Jane Grey never returned, but grew up and married in Iroquoia, and her whereabouts were occasionally reported to her mother. Only after a series of colorful trials was it decided in 1823 that the woman who had been raised as Jane Grey was not the daughter of John Grey, and her land went to other claimants.[30]

Most of the unclaimed children were put in the care of Pennsylvania's commissioners appointed to help returning captives, and some were cared for over several months.[31] The commissioners gave more sustained support to blind Catherine Smith, but generally placed children briefly with willing families, and then sought longer-term solutions with advertisements like,

> NOTICE is hereby given, that six of the Captives, recovered by Col. BOUQUET from the Indians, in November last, are now at Philadelphia, under the Care of this Government, viz. three Boys, and three Girls, whose Descriptions are respectively as follow.
>
> BOYS, Stephen, about 14 Years old, fair Complexion, light brown Hair, and dark brown Eyes.
>
> William, about 12 Years of Age, brown Complexion, black Hair, and black Eyes.
>
> The other Boy, Name unknown, about the same Age, fair Complexion, brown Hair, and brown Eyes.
>
> GIRLS, Betty, Sister to William, about 9 Years of Age, dark Complexion, black Eyes, and black Hair.
>
> Rachel, about 10 Years of Age, fair Complexion, grey Eyes, and light brown Hair.
>
> Catherine, about 9 Years old, fair Complexion, light brown Eyes, and brown Hair.
>
> They have been several Years among the Indians and do not recollect their Surnames, nor from what Place they were taken.
>
> Such Persons therefore as have had their Children or other Relations carried into Captivity during the first Indian War, upon Application to the Provincial Commissioners in this City, within six Weeks, may see the above mentioned Children, and if they find any of their Relations amongst them, are requested to take them away, otherwise the Boys will be bound out to Trades, and the Girls so disposed of, that they may be no further Expence to the Publick.[32]

Whatever Indian orators had said against the practice of putting surrendered children out to be servants, which colonial officials had denied, it was the usual way to care for and train orphans and reintegrate stray young former captives.[33]

The county orphan's courts were not primarily there to arrange care for orphans, whether captive or not; their central function was to protect the property rights of orphaned children whose dead fathers had owned property but had not left a will. Surprisingly few cases of captive children and returned captives were recorded there. Mothers who had not promptly remarried, as so many did, could be guardians of their own children, but mothers who were still in captivity, or who had remarried, could not. Jane Cochrane, widowed in an attack in which she was captured with two of her children, reached out from captivity by urging someone she met to have the orphan's court appoint a particular man as guardian for her other two, uncaptured, children. Although the request was oral and second-hand, the Cumberland County Orphan's Court complied.[34] The orphan's courts were very patriarchal, and routinely allowed the eldest surviving son a double share of personal property and control of the entire landed estate if he promised allowances and legacies to his mother and siblings. The case of Caspar Walter's eldest daughter was different. Caspar had been killed, and his four children captured. Four years later, an orphan's court appointed an administrator, because Caspar's widow had remarried. Mary, now of full age and just back from captivity, asked the court for "a Dividend of the Estate." The court assigned Mary the role of the eldest son, giving her the entire preserved inheritance and responsibility to distribute the shares to her three siblings, all of whom were eventually returned.[35]

The most dramatic turn in the handling of heirs and estates by an orphan's court concerned Peter Sheaffer, who was reported killed in May of 1757. A year later the Northampton County Orphan's Court accepted his daughter's choice of guardian, and in August 1759 Peter's personal estate was settled between his widow, his son and namesake, and his two daughters. The fate of inherited land took longer to decide, as was usual. The orphan's court was surprised to learn, in March of 1761, that Peter had returned from captivity "and is returned to his Plantation in Plainfield Township." The guardian of his daughters gave Peter the money and records that had resulted from "his intermedling with his Estate" and was legally discharged.[36]

Most of the child captives who were returned are not known to have grown up with opportunities built upon their early grounding in Delaware, Shawnee, or Seneca culture and language. Theirs had been a child's grasp of Indian life, language, and geography. They were not called upon to give legal depositions upon their return. Their Indian childhood was overlaid with deliberate European acculturation, either in their birth families or during their service in other families. None of them became known as translators, interpreters, scouts, or guides. Nor did any of them rise to prominence in the civil or military structures of revolutionary America. Aside from the unpublished second- or third-person remembrances of Susannah Barnett and Thomas Ingles, none left surviving stories of their interlude with the Indians. Whether or not captivity had impaired their written command of English or German, none published memoirs at a time when these became popular and were thought to be instructive.

The 332 captives taken between ages seven and fifteen, if they stayed more than two years in captivity, could have become the most bicultural of Allegheny people. They had acquired considerable facility in at least two languages, had learned borderland survival skills and livelihoods, remembered a childhood identity to revisit, and had family ties and geographical knowledge that spanned the borderlands.[37] Of course, there were tensions, divided loyalties, and circumstances that kept some from such a role, or that helped decide which of the contending cultures they would live within and serve.

Only eleven of these youths are known to have stayed with their captors. Although they lived in an oral culture, they may have retained some ability to speak and even read English or German, and could help with translation in trade, with land dealings, and with a variety of other cross-cultural interactions. Margaret Moore was likely of such assistance to her Shawnee husband, becoming a practical and symbolic part of the complex life of Sepettekenathe. Mary Jemison told her interviewer of a long life lived without much evidence that her Pennsylvania childhood remained very relevant, except in giving her some of the retained language with which to tell her story to an English-speaking audience. White Indians Joshua Renick and Lewis Bingeman became warriors who were directly involved in diplomatic contacts with their former communities.

Stronger and more self-sufficient than younger captives, youths proved three times as likely to escape as to become white Indians, though a number of those who were returned came unwillingly.[38] Six of every seven of the returnees knew their surnames, and they were likely to remember their childhood neighborhoods, and even hymns heard in infancy. Although less likely to be returned with their mothers, some of these youths and adults could, like Elizabeth Tell and Hannah Burke, make their own efforts to find what remained of their families. These youths brought back appropriate survival skills for life in Allegheny country, were competent in an Indian language, and could recover and enhance their childhood English or German fairly quickly.

Girls who returned from their Indian lives as young women were competent and comfortable doing field work as well as the myriad domestic tasks of simple living. Some young women like Peggy Moore (Connor), Catherine Nicholson (Holland), Mary Sea (Johnson), and Sally Sea (Robinson) readily found a place between cultures as the wives of Indian traders. Another returned Virginian captive married and was back in Muskingum country by 1773, where she helped a visiting missionary with his Shawnee vocabulary.[39]

Young adult captives could also become cheap, or free, labor; they were returned at times of recovered farms and renewed agricultural expansion, whether with the truce of 1759 or the peace of 1765. Eve and Philipina Wampler, for instance, had been returned by 1760, but both promptly disappeared. When located two years later, Eve had somehow come into the custody of a trader's son, and Philipina had reportedly been given to a soldier by George Croghan.[40] Ten-year-old Elizabeth Countzmann was put out to service almost immediately after her return from captivity in January 1765, and within two months her master was summoned for neglect, perhaps at the insistence of her mother, who had recently been returned. These young women may have struggled with their two identities, as the younger captive Rachel Abbott did with her religion, but the surviving evidence of struggle is scarce. Abbott reported finding a haven of personal peace only when amongst the Moravian Delaware. It is possible that Susannah Vause returned to the Shawnee for a time, but she eventually became Mrs Abraham Inskip of Kentucky.[41] Local historians recount the otherwise undocumented story of Mary Painter, said to have been captured in Frederick County, Virginia, in 1758. Eighteen years later she was found among the Cherokee by a man who lured her back, married her, and raised a family with her at her parent's place. "Mary had lost her mother tongue, learned a little English afterwards, but always conversed with her husband in the Indian language. They finally removed to the West."[42] It is likely that a number of returned young women married and then migrated with their husbands to the Ohio Valley or to Kentucky, as Susannah Vause and both Nancy and Peggy Renick did. Given the opportunities that drew the adventurous farther west to "pioneer" on cheap land, it is easy to suspect that women who had been captured, had seen some of the country, and had learned Delaware or Shawnee were overrepresented amongst these migrants. They would have been more comfortable than others in moving west, away from creeping white sophistications at which they were likely less than adept. Marriageable-aged women were sought after on this predominantly male frontier, and the story of their Indian interlude could readily be lost in their new name and attendant social and cultural identities. On the other hand, three Clouser sisters taken at ages ten, seven, and five returned from a few months of captivity in 1764 to live out their long lives as brides, mothers, and widows in their natal community in the Valley of Virginia.[43]

Girls who returned as young women did not all adjust readily. According to her mother, Catherine Jager was "a very unhappy young Woman, having spent in the Indian Idleness those Days of her Life in which Girls learn to qualify themselves for Business, and is now unable to support herself." This suspicious wording, in a successful petition for assembly assistance in 1766, appealed to prejudices while garnering "a little Assistance for the Support of her unfortunate Daughter, with her innocent Babe."[44] Perhaps Northampton County had fewer young couples moving west than was the case from Cumberland, York, or Lancaster.

Captive male youths who returned as young men had more options than their sisters, and are certainly more likely to be traceable in surviving records. Those who became "long-hunters," gone for months in Kentucky and Ohio country, were continuing their quest for beaver and deerskins begun as Shawnee or Delaware youths. Like the woodsman noted by Felix Renick, these men lived relatively solitary and anonymous lives that required limited contact with Indians or with whites. The three "Indian Girtys" all began negotiating their forced return to white society in this way, and they each eventually settled upon identities that were, likely coincidentally, more Indian the younger they had been when captured.[45] James and Simon Girty moved on to become Indian traders, combining their skills and contacts with a capacity to borrow a "stake" from wholesale merchants. Simon would function in most of the roles available, as a hunter, a trader, an interpreter, a soldier fighting in turn for both sides in the American Revolution, and eventually an Indian agent for the British government in Canada. Other young men returning from captivity could use similar skills and contacts in working for Indian traders who were attempting to rebuild their business in postwar Allegheny country. Jonathan Nichols accepted an indenture with the commissioners of prisoners at Fort Pitt, and would go on to become an interpreter at the garrison and, at least occasionally, a guide for travelers.[46] Levy Hicks was another ex-captive who served as a guide for travelers going west from the Juniata River.[47]

Given the world they inhabited, these young men would be called upon to prove their restored identity, and loyalty, in fighting. After seven years with the Delaware, Arthur Crawford of Maryland had been back only a year when he became captain of a company of rangers in Pontiac's War.[48] John Slover, who returned in 1773 after nearly thirteen years with the Miami and Shawnee, did not participate in Dunmore's War against his Shawnee kin, which commenced almost immediately, but he did enlist in a Virginia regiment early in the Revolution and served as a guide, interpreter, and chronicler for the disastrous expedition of Colonel William Crawford in 1782.[49] William Renick, after nearly eight years with the Shawnee, succeeded as a farmer and became a major of militia in Greenbrier.[50]

William Renick's subsequent rise to local prominence invites two questions: what kind of farmers were men who had grown up with Indian understandings of agriculture; and were boys who had grown up Indian ever trusted with public office in their natal communities? William married, settled after a single move, and accumulated a substantial landed estate in Greenbrier. John McCullough, a very resistant returnee after eight years with the Delaware, eventually reported simply that he returned to his father's farm and spent the rest of his life there. William and James Martin, aged eight and ten when captured, spent part of their nine years of captivity on Big Sewickley Creek and eventually returned to that land after being freed, living and farming there most of their lives.[51] We cannot know whether these men were careful and industrious farmers, or able land speculators, but they did become rooted after a training that would have conditioned them to be more mobile. If William Renick's prosperity was based upon farming, he must have relearned it well. His election to major of militia may have been more social than martial, but it does suggest that he was trusted by those who had become his white adult male peers.[52]

Although re-entry into colonial communities did not come easily, only a few young captives are known to have given up on the process, and returned to live with the Indians. Thomas Armstrong was captured as an infant and was still a boy when recovered, but he soon ran away to live with the Seneca permanently.[53] Frances Barnett had been with the Shawnee for nineteen years and, after spending a few days with her sister Susannah, became convinced that she belonged with the Shawnee. Peter Wagner seems to have tried a little harder. In the spring of 1760, while he was held on the North Branch of the Susquehanna River, he managed to get his name, and something of his story, conveyed to a passing visitor. When Peter came in to Shamokin four months later, he provided a list of captives he knew were still being held. Two years later, at twenty-three, he was living in Philadelphia and was instructed and confirmed by Lutheran minister Henry Melchior Muhlenberg. Sometime thereafter Peter returned to live with the Shawnee, and his interlude in Philadelphia was forgotten.[54] The story of Susannah Vause is more obscure, and likely more complicated. She was returned in February of 1763 and was recognized as she passed through Pittsburgh. However, twenty months later she was listed among those still held by the Shawnee after the negotiations with Bouquet. There is no reliable evidence of another return, but she married in Virginia and settled in Kentucky.[55] What is known of these few captives indicates the unsettled identities that likely troubled many young returning captives.

Those captured between the ages of seven and fifteen became bicultural, and became hunters, guides, traders, land speculators, translators, and Indian agents, or knowledgeable wives of any of these. However reluctantly and belatedly, it was the expanding, conquering white colonial society that eventually gained the bicultural skills and knowledge of much of this group. The few depositions and narratives left by youths were heavily influenced by adults, and later memoirs range widely in their views of Indian life. Whatever their genuine ambivalence, these returned captives were inclined, or required, to support the fate that had brought them back to colonial society.

Dependent servants and slaves, whether youths or adults, were not numerous among the killed or captured in these borderlands, perhaps because they were not numerous on these fragile fringes of white settlement. Only thirty-four captives were identified as servants when taken, and ten of these are known to have come back. The small numbers make any comparisons with other groups dubious, but servants may have been less likely to return than even child captives. Only five captured servants were youths when taken, likely indentured and therefore serving part of their time as captives. It may be mere coincidence that only one of them is known to have returned.[56] Fifteen-year-old Frederick Fereich, a servant of Thomas Potter captured at Richard Bard's Mill, was one of these youths. Despite the efforts of an advocate for his widowed mother, an impoverished servant herself, who had somehow learned of her son's whereabouts five years after his capture, Frederick could not be found.[57] Four of the ten "servants" who did return had been working as traders' horse drivers when captured by Delaware near Fort Ligonier in April 1759, and may not have been indentured at all.[58] A total of five captured adult servants escaped, presumably to resume their service with masters who had been more fortunate than themselves in more ways than one. John Schilling could not return to his service. He had been captured in 1757 with his fascinating Dunker masters Israel and Gabriel Eckerle and was, with them, sold by the Ottawa to the French at Fort Duquesne, sent on to Montreal and Quebec as objects of particular curiosity, and shipped to La Rochelle. His masters died in a La Rochelle hospital, and Schilling was back in their native Strasbourg by 1761, recounting the details of the Eckerles' trials and fate.[59]

African slaves were the ultimate dependents and, ironically, were therefore particularly valued by all Allegheny communities. Five slaves are known to have been killed, and the fates of eight of the sixteen captured are known.[60] The four slaves of David Cloyd were recaptured by a pursuit party and returned to their owner, as were four other slaves surrendered to Colonel Bouquet.[61] For them, life after redemption would be a return to the routines of a more familiar captivity. This was not the case for Sam Tony, not likely a captive of the Delaware but rather a runaway slave who had escaped Maryland for a freer life with Indians. Suspected of spreading anti-white sentiments among the Indians, he was demanded by Sir William Johnson as part of the Seneca peacemaking, and then sold into West Indian slavery.[62] Five *panis* slaves of English merchants, captured by the Ojibwa in 1763, evidently stayed with their hosts, whether as slaves or adopted kin.[63] Only one slave is known to have escaped, or attempted to escape, from Indian captivity. Returning slaves, like servants, were made to know their place, but they were more likely to still have one than were captured and returned children or other returned youths. Their numbers were few, their culture was oral, and their remembrances perished more completely than those of other returned youths.

In the culturally polarizing Allegheny borderlands, returning adult captives had some explaining to do. Two adults had died for every one captured, and the returned were among those who clearly had not resisted unto death. Nor were they among the adult captives who had escaped or the small minority who were killed during captivity, perhaps for resisting their masters or attempting to escape. Being returned through diplomacy, whether in exchange for Croghan's presents or under the threat of Bouquet's army, was not convincing proof that an adult captive had wanted to return. Captivity left few adults fluently bicultural, or permanently marked with the habits and preferences of their captors, but the symbolic return to white folks' clothing was an inadequate sign of a redemption that could easily be reversed. Acceptance would have to be earned, in different ways, by returning adults of either gender.

Women captives have always been of special interest, and accounts of their experiences have gone from being brave and poignant tales of cultural loyalty to being exemplars of changing expectations of women as survivors, amazons, or frail flowers and, rather more fancifully, to being seen as coded subliminal accounts of momentary female liberation from the social and sexual restraints of Christian colonial life. A little can be added to our understanding of these women by seeking information on their lives after they returned from captivity. Admittedly, women are harder to trace than men, and subsequent marriage, with its attending name change, made it a little easier to leave an embarrassing captivity behind.

The fate of nearly a quarter of the women captured beyond their sixteenth birthday is unknown. Of the 154 women captives whose fate is known, only 4 died in captivity, 3 are known to have stayed with the Indians, and 1 stayed with the French.[64] Most were returned through negotiation (99) or escape (24), and fewer were retaken (13), ransomed (9), or exchanged (1). Women over sixteen who were taken into Allegheny captivity were just as likely as men to escape.[65] The twenty-four women captives who escaped had thereby exonerated themselves fully in their natal communities by this dangerous action, and were particularly celebrated. Nine of these women had been held for only a few days. As they escaped, some knew they were going back home, and others knew that they were not. Two were promptly reunited with their husbands, whereas at least four others had been widowed while being captured. Jennet Clendennin was one of the latter, and she promptly qualified as administrator of her husband's estate, and remarried to protect the property from predatory relatives.[66] Most of the fifteen women who escaped after a longer captivity faced weeks of grueling wilderness, which had been their most severe deterrent. Mary Draper Ingles, whose experiences of escape are the best recorded, would be reunited with her husband, and they eventually returned to their New River lands together and raised three sons and two daughters; she survived into her mid-eighties.[67] In contrast, we know nothing of the fate of the rarest kind of woman captive known to have escaped. Mrs Samuel Conaway was a Cayuga held in protective custody at Fort Bedford in 1763, along with her Cayuga husband. According to the fort commander, this peaceable couple were threatened and harassed by locals even within the fort until finally, after more than three months in custody, they left their child with a friend and escaped together up a chimney at night.[68]

The story passed on about the escape of Hannah Dennis was so distorted that it has caused even local folklore collectors a little pause. Dennis was by far the longest-held woman captive to "escape" and one of only two who escaped after a captivity of more than eighteen months.[69] She had seen her husband and child killed as she was captured in 1757, and reportedly lived for six years with the Shawnee at Chillicothe as an adaptive survivor, learning Shawnee well and eventually becoming a respected healer. The year 1763 did not afford her a first chance to escape. As war returned, she began to fear for her life and fled back to the upper James River, supposedly pursued by a war party all the way to the Clendennins' place at the Levels. All the retellings of this escape end just when it should have become particularly interesting. Perhaps that was all people wanted to hear at their firesides, and no one was tempted to add a moralizing postscript. We simply do not know what happened to Dennis after she returned, under very suspicious circumstances, to her former neighborhood on what had already been named Purgatory Creek.[70]

A clear majority of adult women captives who returned to white colonial society did so because of negotiations between their Indian masters and white men of authority: Croghan, Johnson, and Bouquet. Most of these women had lived with their captors for more than two years, and varied in their enthusiasm for returning. William Smith was horrified to hear that adult women captives had wept bitterly at being returned to Bouquet's army, and that some of them refused to eat for days.[71] There are no recorded stories of adult women immediately escaping back to the Indians, but there is some ambiguity in reports such as Ulrich Conrad's previously discussed advertisement offering £3 for information concerning his daughter, delivered up at Fort Pitt in the fall of 1764: "She is 26 Years of Age, her Name Barbara, and her Indian Name Attawa; she has probably light brown Hair, her Eyes between grey and brown; has lived with an old Indian woman, who has but half a Nose. Whoever will give an Account of the said Girl so that, in all Probability, she may be had again, shall have the above Reward, and reasonable Charges, paid by me."[72] Another woman captive, the British soldier's wife who thought she was a widow and married a French soldier, would not have seen her return to her first husband as an occasion characterized by the jovial, flippant irony supposed by the newspaper report.[73]

How did women fare who returned to white society from captivity? Those who had husbands to return to still had a place, whatever the suspicions that hounded those few who returned with *métis* children or convenient stories that captured women had been given only a month to choose an Indian husband or die. No women were captive long enough to be considered legally dead under the "seven year providential absence" of colonial legal convention, but they faced uncertainties. Jane Frasier had been away just over a year when, after escaping and traveling for fifteen grueling days, she returned to find that her husband of less than a year had presumed her dead and had remarried. On Jane's return, John Frasier sent his second wife, who "seemed a very nice woman," back home to her father, "as their marriage was illegal, but he would still support her as he promised." We do not know how happy the marriage of Jane and John Frasier was thereafter.[74]

Widows left with children were not allowed to resume frontier farming, either by plowing or by the less strenuous Indian methods they had learned. If they did not remarry, their eldest surviving male child was, in intestate cases, allowed to negotiate for control of the property, in return for offering modest annuities to his mother and siblings. Widowed Mrs Robert Renick returned from captivity to find her husband's personal property sold and her son William given legal control of the family land. Mary Girty-Turner and all five of her sons initially returned to live at Squirrel Hill near Pittsburgh, where the four-year-old son of her second husband joined them on his return, and inherited everything.[75] Widowed Barbara Hicks was the first of her family to be returned, and she managed to hold her husband's property for eight years before her children finally returned. Widows of frontier farmers, whose personal property had been stolen or sold to cover seasonal or mortgage debt, would be hard pressed to hire laborers to work their land. Remarriage was a very common occurrence given the preponderance of males in the population of frontier counties, and the best way for a widow to protect her legal part of the estate may have been to give it to a new husband, as Jennet Clendennin did.

Returning women captives had seldom been held long enough to become well versed in their captor's culture, and were less likely than younger female captives to have the skills or inclination to marry traders or hunters after captivity. Reconstructing a family that farmed in the colonial manner was a return to a livelihood that best fitted the skills and training of these women, and they were in demand whenever the peace that brought them home also invited farm reconstruction or expansion.

Despite all the suffering of women and children, the bride stealing and the kidnapping, Allegheny warfare primarily involved men. Maxims about how easy it was to make an Indian out of a white man, or about how much harder it was to reclaim young men than young women, were built upon the experiences of captured youths, not captured men over sixteen. More than 2,434 men were killed in battle, scouting, or defending their families, farmsteads, and villages. Some 589 men are known to have been captured, and only 6 of these are known to have stayed with their captors, whereas another 45 died in captivity, as often as not by torture. The 538 men who returned from captivity needed to explain why they had been captured and spared, and could be suspected of compromised loyalties. Even escape was not adequate proof of loyalty. On the other hand, because only one in ten captured men had been held for more than two years, they were less likely to become thoroughly acculturated than women or younger captives. This meant that very few returned men had a genuine facility in their captor's language or culture, or had strong links of adoptive membership in a captor's community. Returned men were twice as likely to be soldiers as farmers, and twice as likely to be farmers as traders. The problems of readmission and opportunities to recover status varied widely, and can usefully be considered in terms of these three occupations at capture.

Fewer than 300 soldiers are known to have returned from Allegheny captivity, compared to 2,042 killed or missing. Although few were promoted during captivity, the work, status, and regimental "family" of regular soldiers were there when they returned.[76] Regular army officers like Major William Grant, Captains John Rutherfurd and George Etherington, and Lieutenant James Gorrell resumed their commands and careers without evident prejudice.[77] The 86 soldiers who were formally exchanged between European enemies, and the 33 from the Great Lakes garrisons who were "redeemed" from the Ottawa in 1763, were promptly returned to their units. The same options were also there for the 47 soldiers who escaped, the 129 who were returned by the Indians, and the 3 who had been retaken by force. Only 20 regular and provincial soldiers were held captive for more than two years before being returned. Some officers, including those of the Royal American Regiment who had manned the outposts before, during, and after Pontiac's War, later became active as Indian traders. No Indian warrior or chief was held captive for more than eight months, and chiefs had no evident change in roles after being a hostage.

The epitome of the soldier-captive was Captain Robert Stobo, whose daring exploits, trial, and eventual escape were widely reported and well rewarded. Virginia treated this returned hero to a handsome gratuity, a 9,000-acre Ohio land grant, and a precedent-setting gift of full pay during his entire captivity, an unusual privilege for soldiers but one that was subsequently applied to all captured soldiers of the Virginia Regiment.[78] Stobo was bold and inconsistent enough to petition successfully for the double pay that he claimed was usually awarded to hostages, though he had acted as a prisoner of war in spying and escaping, and had claimed to be a prisoner of war rather than a hostage at his trial in Canada.[79] On the recommendation of William Pitt, Stobo was awarded a rare gift for a colonial officer, a captaincy without purchase in a regular British regiment – in this case, in the long-established and secure 15th Regiment of Foot. Stobo was in this position for a decade before he committed suicide in his barracks in Chatham, England.[80] Although we cannot know what brought him to suicide, we can assume that the rewards offered to this courageous escaped soldier represented the best re-entry that could be afforded to an escaped soldier.

The Virginia House of Burgesses refused to compensate another of its veterans of 1754, John Ramsey,[81] whose case suggests a wider issue with "captured" soldiers. In one of his letters smuggled from Fort Duquesne, Stobo had identified Ramsey as "the cause of our misfortunes" for deserting the day before the battle and informing the enemy of the location and numbers of George Washington's force.[82] Ramsey claimed, in petitioning for his back pay in 1763, that he had been taken prisoner in the battle of Fort Necessity and held in cruel captivity by Indians for five and a half years. On returning to Virginia in 1761, he had promptly rejoined the Virginia Regiment. Having investigated his claim, as they routinely did in such cases, a Burgesses' committee admitted his continued membership in the Virginia Regiment but reported that he had "behaved in a cowardly dastardly manner," had an earlier record of desertion, and had gone missing at Fort Necessity. In considering his petition unproven, the Burgesses recorded that it was not clear "whether he was taken prisoner, or voluntarily surrendered himself, or fled to the enemy."[83] Returning to the regiment meant an immediate recovery of status and livelihood for men like Ramsey. Another Virginian soldier, recovered after more than eight years in captivity, apparently joined the Virginia volunteers with Bouquet's forces on the same day.[84] Virginian ensign Thomas Gist returned to his regiment, as expected, after escaping from a year's captivity with the Wyandot.[85]

Some soldiers with the colonial regiments did well in civilian life after their return from captivity. Gist inherited and expanded his father's lands at Mount Braddock, and served repeatedly as a justice of the peace.[86] Arthur Campbell, an eighteen-year-old Virginian scout from a prominent Augusta County family, spent four years with the Wyandot before being released in 1760. On return he was given full pay and a sizable land grant. He built a mill, and became a justice of the peace, militia major, member of the 1775 House of Burgesses, and long-serving county lieutenant. He also led the Virginian campaign against the Cherokee in 1780, but this was twenty years after captivity, and not part of his initial re-entry and acceptance.[87] These relatively short captivities did not derail the subsequent success of young men "of good family" for whom military service was recognized as an adventurous stage of early adulthood. John Smith, the Virginian ranger captain and militia major taken in the surrender of Vause's Fort, had his moment of official recognition and celebrity in England after exchange. He had lost all three of his sons in the war, and, given his name, it is not clear what he did after being given free passage home, and a substantial cash reward by the Virginia government.[88] Peter Looney, who served under Smith at Vause's Fort, returned from captivity to receive a soldier's land grant, to marry, and to have a namesake son before dying young in 1760.[89] The returned soldiers fitted into colonial society fairly easily, if their captivity was considered genuine, without leaving evidence of divided identities or doubtful loyalties.

The sixty-eight "Indian traders" known to have returned from mid-century captivity in Allegheny Indian country did so with specific problems as well as specific advantages. Whether trading on their own account or as agents, they had been robbed in being captured, and had debts and credit problems that complicated their re-entry into trading. Few of these returned captives are known to have resumed their trade with Ohio Indians. Alexander Henry did resume trading, becoming prominent in the fur trade of the upper Great Lakes and investing in mining together with former fellow captive merchant Henry Bostwick.[90] Thomas Smallman, a former officer in the Pennsylvania forces, became a trader sponsored by his cousin, George Croghan, before and after being captured twice in Pontiac's War.[91] George Croghan continued with his own personal trading opportunities together with his official position as deputy superintendent of Indian affairs. He was also the spokesman for the well-organized and persistent lobby of the "suffering traders" who sought land grants in compensation for their trading losses. His transition from trader to land speculator was natural enough at a time when these borderlands were being confiscated.[92]

Although almost all returned traders had been adult male captives, and only six were held for more than six months, their previous work had left them better informed about Shawnee, Delaware, or Iroquoian languages, customs, and trade than were other adult captives. Who and what these returnees knew could be particularly useful as trade resumed, and reliable brokers, guides, translators, land agents, and specialists in Indian diplomacy were needed by local and imperial governments. Hugh Crawford had been in the Indian trade for twenty-five years when he was captured on the Maumee River in 1763; two years later he guided a British expedition up the Mississippi River and became a popular British Indian agent at Detroit.[93]

The most illustrious career after captivity for a trader was that of John Gibson. He had been a Pennsylvania soldier in the Seven Years' War before becoming an Indian trader. Captured by the Delaware as Pontiac's War commenced, he was adopted, held for the duration, and released to Bouquet late in 1764. Gibson resumed licensed trading at Pittsburgh, and even gained a passport from James Smith's Black Boys the following year because his trading cargoes did not include weapons for Indians. Gibson married the sister of a prominent Mingo chief and English ally, Soyechtowa (James Logan). In the spring of 1774, belligerent Virginian intruders led by Michael Cresap tricked and murdered thirteen members of Soyechtowa's family, including Gibson's wife. The murderers defiantly sent the only survivor, Gibson's daughter, to her father. Soyechtowa joined those seeking revenge in what became known as Dunmore's War, and Gibson recorded Soyechtowa's eloquent lament, made famous by its inclusion in Thomas Jefferson's *Notes on the State of Virginia*.[94] Despite lingering suspicions of him, Gibson joined the Revolution, and became a justice of the peace for West Augusta, a member of the local Committee of Correspondence, and the elected colonel of Virginia's 13th Regiment. The Delaware chose to have all their negotiation of the 1778 Treaty of Pittsburgh conducted through Gibson, and he went on to become a brigadier general and commander of the "Western Department." He was secretary, and occasionally acting governor, of the Indiana territory from 1800 to 1816.[95]

Gibson was exceptional as a captured trader who resumed trading, married a Mingo, and still managed to become a significant American officeholder.

Adult male farmers returned from captivity could be called upon to prove their commitment to their community by becoming soldiers. Hugh McSwain of the Coves was one white farmer who became a hero, a soldier, and a legend. In escaping from Tewea, he took two scalps, a horse, and a silver-mounted gun. At Fort Cumberland he was paid the scalp bounties, sold the horse and gun, and was immediately commissioned as a lieutenant. "After many dangerous enterprises," McSwain was killed in battle near Fort Ligonier.[96] Robert Eastburn was a civilian "artisan" from Pennsylvania when captured in New York in 1756; on his release in 1758, he published an account of his sufferings, and became a captain in a Pennsylvania regiment.[97]

The best-known civilian captive who went to war in these borderlands on his return was James Smith, an impressionable eighteen-year-old Pennsylvania road worker who spent more than four years as a captive with the Wyandot and Kahnawake on the Muskingum River. Because of his age at capture, his kin "were surprised to see me so much like an Indian, both in my gait and gesture," and he became known as "Indian Jimmie." He would go to considerable lengths to use what he had learned and particularly to prove that he did not sympathize with Indians. With the outbreak of Pontiac's War, Smith was elected captain of a company of fifty locally paid rangers, and he chose former captives as his lieutenants, training them in Indian hunting/fighting methods. With unfashionably short hair, red kerchiefs, and blackened faces, these became "the Black Boys." Smith's assignment was purely defensive, and he remained disappointed that it was so unlike the warfare of his Kahnawake mentors. He volunteered in the Pennsylvania regiment in the summer of 1763 and was also among those unauthorized volunteers who burned Indian crops and villages on the Susquehanna River that autumn. He was a lieutenant with the Pennsylvania troops who accompanied Bouquet to the Muskingum in 1764, though he wrote nothing about being a witness to diplomatic restraint that he likely found difficult. He was central as the Black Boys became an effective Conococheague vigilante group that disrupted convoys of Indian trade goods in 1764,[98] and even besieged a small garrison of regulars at Fort Loudoun who had been misled into aiding those traders.

In 1769 Smith again led vigilantes, this time to free men who had been arrested for a comparable attack on another convoy, and he was tried and acquitted in the death of an arresting officer. Smith's popularity repeatedly shielded him from provincial justices and British military authorities. He became a captain in Dunmore's War and a major with the Pennsylvanian forces in the Revolution, but he returned to his Cumberland County militia after George Washington refused his proposal of an irregular battalion of riflemen. Smith moved to Bourbon County, Kentucky, in 1788, where he became prominent in local and state politics and completed his substantial and often-reprinted memoirs. Methods of warfare were all that Smith had claimed to admire in his Kahnawake teachers and hosts, and he used the methods where he could in a subsequent career of fighting Indians.[99] In old age he undertook two trips west as a Presbyterian missionary to the Indians, about which it would be interesting to know more, and he was said to have died in 1812 while preparing to join the "Long Knives" in yet another borderland war.

Farming was the dominant livelihood of borderland white males, including those who were sometime soldiers or traders. The challenges facing returned farmers were serious, and many would find themselves as dispossessed as the robbed traders. Only seven had been captive for the seven years that would cause them to be legally declared "dead by absence,"[100] but most wives, children, and creditors had needs and demands that brought the personal and real property of the missing to sale much earlier than that. Virginian captive Christopher Hicks had been missing less than three years when an administrator of his estate was bonded.[101] David Brackenridge had likely been a Delaware captive for less than six months when he escaped in time to see the end of the auction of his personal property.[102] Peter Sheaffer had been captive three years and returned to find his personal effects sold and his children in the care of the Northampton County Orphan's Court, which had helpfully preserved his land, assuming it was the estate of his children. The Virginia government had tried to make borderers stay to defend their lands by legislating the resale of "abandoned" frontier farms.[103] In contrast, the Pennsylvania Assembly offered a little encouragement early in 1764, with a two-year tax exemption for those who "have been driven from their Settlements, and lost their Effects by the late Indian Ravages."[104] Men with farming experience and skills would, in the wake of peace, have no trouble finding work, and, if they did not recover lands held earlier, they could hope to farm new land by moving west once again. Most of them had not learned things in captivity that translated into a livelihood other than subsistence farming thereafter.

The adventures of Gershom Hicks display other possible futures for a captured young man. He had been nineteen, and living and working on his large family's borderland farm, when they were attacked in November of 1755. Gershom was among four captured with their mother, whereas three others died, including his father. These circumstances may have made it easier for Gershom to embrace the Delaware life more fully than other captives his age. Within five years he had become a white Delaware, and he was hired as a guide by the British commander at Fort Venango, who called him "a fellow who has been Prisoner with the Indians & just the same as one of themselves."[105] But Gershom had not entirely abandoned being Delaware. In the spring of 1764 he was raiding with the Delaware, and, on returning from a raid of the kind that had disrupted his birth family, Gershom undertook a brazen scheme for spying within Fort Pitt. Pretending to have been more recently captured and just escaped, he was readily admitted to the fort. His ruse was discovered, however, and he rather narrowly escaped execution by the military as a spy or by civil authorities as a traitor. On his release after the war, this white Indian apparently did not go back to live with the Delaware, but joined his mother and three younger brothers, who were all back in the white community. When Frederick Stump and his servant brutally murdered ten Delaware, Shawnee, and Iroquois early in 1768, the coroner of Cumberland County recruited Gershom to break the news to the Delaware of Grand Island, and he was successful in forestalling revenge killings.[106] Gershom also seems to have proven his reconversion by fighting in a Pennsylvania regiment of the Continental Line. He was still living, and presumably farming, with his brother Levy at Hicks Run, in Allegheny County, in 1800.[107]

The impact of longer captivity on two other young men of Cumberland County was equally marked and eventually very divergent. Both had been adopted captives of Iroquoians and returned to lives that would trade on this experience. Both became officers in the Pennsylvania militia, engaged in vigilante activity, and, like Gershom Hicks, initially joined the patriotic rebellion in 1776. James Smith became a farmer and a legend as a vigilante and Indian fighter. This "first rebel" also became a Kentucky pioneer, a legislator, and an author. Simon Girty was not held captive as long, but was a little younger when captured and was from a family of Indian traders. This background helps account for his fundamentally different set of subsequent identities, livelihoods, and loyalties. He was known to dress variously as an Indian, as a colonial, and, more defiantly, as a hybrid of both. Girty became a hunter, trader, interpreter, and an Indian agent. At the outbreak of Dunmore's War, he worked for the Virginians, and successfully negotiated with Indian leaders, including Guyasuta and Kageshquanohel, to prevent a wider war. Although he served the revolutionaries, he repeatedly found himself undervalued, and he disliked legitimizing the deceitful rebel policies toward the Indians. In the spring of 1778, Girty and two other Indian agents defected to the British and Indian side of the Revolutionary War, where Girty became active as an interpreter, scout, and ranger with Seneca and Wyandot war parties. He continued as an interpreter and auxiliary as this war merged with the Ohio Indian war, which lasted until 1794, and he remained on the British Indian department's payroll thereafter. Girty had married Catherine Malott, formerly a captive with the Delaware, and they worked a sizable farm at Amherstburg, Canada West (Ontario), where they raised their three children.[108] Girty and Smith both combined their experience as captives with some capacity to inspire and lead fighting men, but Girty's fighting men were Indians and Smith's were Virginians. These two ended their lives as farmers, one among the Loyalists in Canada West and the other among the "Long Knives" of Kentucky.

Returned captives were a varied lot, and what is known of them defies attempts to claim that their experience permanently marked them as different, whether as valued cultural brokers or despised hybrids. The length of captivity varied from a few hours to more than a decade, greatly affecting the impact of capture on identity. Age at capture was another crucial element. The capture itself was a traumatic and searing event for all, but would have a particularly powerful impact on young children, though their subsequent treatment and adoption would transform their view of Indian life. Most became Indians, and retained too little of their former cultures to be hybrids. Those who were brought back developed without visible harm or profit from what they learned in captivity. Many of the returned youngsters were forced from Indian families into lives as white orphans, and most were unable to return to the lives from which they had been plucked as babes. None of them ever published memoirs about their childhood with Indians, or about their life thereafter.

Most of those captured as youths came back, and these included a sizable group who had become competent in two contending cultures. In this elemental sense, colonial society captured most of the knowledge and skills of this group. Some became "long-hunters," guides, hermits, traders, interpreters, and Indian agents as peace allowed the resumption of much that had been normal life. Those who had escaped from captivity may have been prized in their natal culture, but they were limited as brokers by a continuing Indian resentment and distrust toward those who had fled. Other returned youths could use what and whom they knew in the subsequent trade and diplomacy of the British and American empires. Their thoughts were, and are, harder to discern. The returned youth captives, more than captured adults, had learned enough to dismiss several self-serving hypotheses of the white culture. They knew that the Allegheny and Ohio watersheds were not God's "empty lands" reserved for white pioneers. They knew that Indians were not unfeeling, ignorant, or improvident people needing Christianity and instruction in farming, or replacement by more efficient and industrious plowmen. These hybrid people did not automatically fear or hate Indians in Indian country, in the middle grounds at forts, conferences, and Moravian missions, or in isolated Indian enclaves. They knew that the Delaware and Shawnee had not been defeated in war in 1758, 1763, or 1765, and had not lost ownership of their land through some pretended right of conquest by Europeans then, or by Iroquois earlier. These cultural hybrids were unreliable as political or judicial "boosters" of white expansion, offering neither excuses nor justifications for the attending violence against Indians as some sort of deserved revenge. This perspective was not particularly welcome in frontier farmhouses, among the land-hungry venturers into Kentucky or Ohio, or among the non-Quaker elites consolidating power in a more aggressive Pennsylvania after 1765. Most of those who returned from a youth spent with the Indians were not particularly literate in adulthood, which may be why very few left memoirs. Like the recollections of captured servants who did not return, and of the captured slaves who did return, it would be fair to say that their views and remembrances were deemed unusable by the purposeful chroniclers of "founding" Allegheny families and neighborhoods.

Captured adults proved quite resistant to Indian acculturation. A quarter of those captured, whose fate is known, escaped. The stories of some escaped women were promptly publicized, though most disappeared into what can too easily be seen as a smooth re-entry into white colonial society. Soldiers may have had the easiest transitions back to their previous lives, and farmers may have lost their property but certainly not their way of life in the new borderlands. Dispossessed traders had sufficient knowledge of Indian languages and customs to become cultural brokers, and had the painful experience of loss that made some of them among the most trusted agents of white ambitions in Indian country. There were important exceptions, but most adult captives returned with their identities preserved. Most had less faith in Indians than they had before, and their perspective was exemplified and exaggerated in the subsequent life and writing of James Smith. The adults who returned from captivity would readily reinforce some prevailing views among those never captured. The cross-cultural experience of many returned captives, affected so differently, became channeled and truncated by subsequent needs, interests, and events. By the end of 1764 the Ohio Indians had lost most of their adopted kin, who could have been their most promising bicultural brokers. The white settlers had joined a fairly successful project to redeem "every drop of white blood," and they would proceed to marginalize the more ambivalent, tolerant, or hybrid amongst them, or to use them, with caution, only when necessary.

18

Captivating Accounts, 1755–1826

As thickets of subsequent literary and historical analysis can testify, a captivity narrative was seldom just a captivity narrative. These stories were much too popular to have merely satisfied the curiosity of those who wanted to know what happened to captives. Captivity accounts have long been published and studied as American adventures in suffering and redemption, captivity and freedom, exile and return. Although they may have needed no further justification, the emotional attractiveness of captivity themes has also made them irresistible, then and since, to those with various conscious or unconscious agendas.[1] This "escape" literature could be very potent and adaptable propaganda, appropriated to serve in the creation and preservation, or the questioning, of religious, cultural, and political solidarities. Such narratives were a familiar aspect of the early modern empires of Spain, France, and Britain.[2] Accounts from British America, India, and the Mediterranean formed part of the cultural binding of an ambitious English-speaking empire in the eighteenth century, and British migrants and imperial soldiers were featured in the captivities and recoveries that were part of integrating Allegheny country into that empire.[3] That imperial perspective lost out to a contending vision of an imagined American community that emerged within the lifetime of most early Allegheny captives, and their accounts could become iconic representations of a fight for freedom and a unique new American identity. Eighty-five-year-old Hugh Gibson gave the last returned captive's interview in 1826, and it serves as a sensible time to end this study of Allegheny captivity accounts. The remembered sufferings of captives would live on to serve as "justification by suffering" for the relentless nineteenth-century confiscation and destruction of Indian country, and then became the foundational genre for studies of American literature.

Little attention has been paid to early Allegheny captivity narratives in their more immediate context, the remaking of Pennsylvania. The lifetime of a youth captured in the Allegheny borderlands in the 1750s was one of astounding changes. The period from 1754 to 1765 brought a global war to comparatively peaceful Allegheny borderlands, together with a political convulsion that overturned Quaker dominance, helped provoke the province's first Indian war, and left unpunished the vigilante murderers of Indians. Over the next two decades, imperial solidarity evaporated, and the American War for Independence was fought against the region's Indians and their British allies. The victorious but fragile new republic promptly resumed a ferocious battle with the Shawnee and their allies for control of the Old Northwest.[4] Memoirs of a couple of the longest-lived Allegheny captives of the 1750s were not published until after all of these intervening wonders had passed. Captivity accounts could also challenge all of the tidy-minded categories, as well as Christian, white, and male assumptions, because they were essentially cross-cultural experiences. Admiration for the simple sharing of an Indian family and its adopted kin, for the generous communal values of an Indian village, or for the natural freedom of a hunter's life could be a telling critique of colonial life as well as a statement of longing for the same.

"Backcountry" captives taken in Allegheny borderlands were certainly not chosen because they could write, and publication in the Quaker capital of Philadelphia was farther away from their lives than was captivity on the Muskingum River. The first wars in the Allegheny borderlands occasioned hundreds of moving stories of suffering and adventure, but most survivors told their stories in taverns, or around kitchen and camp fires with their kin and acquaintances. Most of what they remembered, forgot, or invented has disappeared or been captured only obliquely in the remembrance of others. Yet twenty-five surviving captives, little more than one in a hundred, have left what appear to be their own accounts published in newspapers, in separately printed pamphlets, or in books. Cultural and literary scholars examine this harvest with relish, together with an attending crop of second- and third-person recollections, folklore, and the numerous contemporary novels built upon the same themes.

Historians who try to use the narratives to help reconstruct what happened are suspicious of eight of these narratives, published long after the event,[5] and dismiss four others as largely, if not entirely, fictitious.[6] The gap between what can be known and some of the dozen purveyed distortions seems to be much too large and consequential to be accepted with pious shrugs about how little can possibly be known for certain. Nor can they be favored with the insistence that perceptions were more important than what really happened, or be excused as all-but-inevitable "instruments of cultural self-definition."[7] Yet the understanding of the authentic narratives must include some sense of their uses, as well as some appreciation of their literary antecedents and competitors, and the tastes of their anticipated audience.

First-person captivity accounts are given some preference in studying what happened, but they certainly cannot be considered full, frank, or unbiased sources. Returned captives giving legal depositions were usually negotiating re-entry into their natal society during dangerous times, and needed to allay suspicions and display loyalty before civil magistrates or military commanders who had questions and purposes of their own. In depositions or narratives, returned captives could also engage in some conscious self-fashioning, for at least a second time in their lives. Captives or their questioners may have been anxious to strengthen wartime solidarity with reassuring stereotypes of innocent captives' sufferings, Indian savagery, and French complicity. Captives who wrote or told their memoirs much later in life usually lost or scrambled some details. As well, they were more enamored with exciting recollections of their youthful adventure, more generous to the "vanishing Indian," and more likely to indulge in outright fabrications that they or their publishers thought necessary to serve changing literary fashion.

Publication of a narrative in a newspaper, as a separate publication, or in an anthology introduced an additional cast of characters who influenced what was presented as captives' own accounts. With purposes of their own, interviewers initiated some narratives, sometimes editing them heavily, or even writing biographies disguised as autobiographies. Colonial newspaper publishers were primarily cautious reprinters of news that was safely from elsewhere. In exposing local stories of interest and significance, they were subject to censorship and self-censorship in a business that usually needed government printing contracts.[8] Wise Pennsylvania printers would seek the safety of official approval before printing captivity accounts that could affect morale and recruitment, question official versions of events, or reveal information of military value.

What of the supposed insatiable popular market for captivity narratives? Those who have confidently asserted that captivity accounts were always popular have not carefully examined the mid-Atlantic colonies in the last half of the eighteenth century. The hinterlands of Philadelphia were definitely not New England, where, for the previous lifetime, Puritan ministers had popularized captivity accounts as narratives of spiritual odyssey and cultural solidarity against Indian and Catholic enemies. When the Seven Years' War began, there had been very little interest in reprinting captivity narratives in Philadelphia. None of the famous New England Puritan accounts had been reprinted there. Two imported Quaker captivities, of Jonathan Dickinson in Florida and Elizabeth Hanson in New Hampshire, had been initially published in Philadelphia. Dickinson's 1699 account had been republished as recently as 1751, and Hanson's 1728 narrative had appeared again in 1754 and 1759.[9] The outbreak of war did not bring much public enthusiasm for published captivity accounts. Despite the official need for recruits and funds, only six of fourteen captives' legal depositions were printed, in whole or part, in the province's newspapers. At least three military officers' captivity journals are known to have survived, but only one was printed, and that in an amplified and distorted form thirty years later, in London, England.[10] Heroic hostage Robert Stobo offered something to the newspapers upon his escape in 1759, but he had been dead for thirty years before his memoirs were published, also in London. The rich, careful, and potentially important "An Account of the Captivity of Charles Stuart ..." was not published until 1926.[11] All these appeared to be cases of returned captives who did not find ready markets for their writing. Eventually an audience was built for some Allegheny captivity narratives, and its emergence is worth charting. To some extent, Allegheny captivity narratives were "bound and determined"[12] by their specific place and time of publication. A closer look at these narratives, in the order in which they were published, can suggest how well these accounts reflected and supported, or challenged, the intentions of those who would have them serve ethnic and religious communities, Pennsylvania, the British empire, or the American republic.

In the summer of 1755, Pennsylvania newspapers had to admit General Edward Braddock's defeat, but they seem to have deliberately avoided the first available account of an escaped captive. A man named Staut had been captured with his family in the Virginia backcountry in June of 1755. They were taken to Fort Duquesne, where they witnessed the build-up of French forces. Staut was still at the fort when the victorious Indian and French army returned from defeating Braddock, and he saw the plunder, the confiscated artillery, and a single captive taken from that battlefield. Staut escaped a couple of days later and arrived "almost famished" to tell what he knew at Fort Cumberland. His story appeared promptly in the *Maryland Gazette* and was reprinted, as might be expected, in the *New York Mercury* and the *South Carolina Gazette*, but it did not appear in either of Philadelphia's two newspapers.[13] The war was still far away from Pennsylvania's capital in August 1755, and there was still hope that this war would stay away.

Three months later, after the attacks on Penn's Creek and Great Cove, both Philadelphia newspapers printed the story of the escape of Hugh McSwain of Cumberland County. Within two weeks of his capture, he and "an old Dutchman" had been sent to drive stolen cattle westward, supervised by a single Delaware and a white Indian named Joseph Jackson. McSwain killed both his captors as they slept, "and brought in their scalps, Arms and Matchcoats to Fort Cumberland." The papers based their story on a letter from Winchester, written as soon as McSwain arrived there, but offered no subsequent details that could represent him as a Pennsylvania hero of this still-undeclared war. After being paid for a horse, gun, and the scalps, and being given a lieutenant's commission, McSwain went on to fight in "many battles and skirmishes with the Indians" before being killed in 1758.[14] He was not destined to be celebrated as a Hannah Dustin or Daniel Boone of this frontier, and, beyond the rather cryptic newspaper description of his escape, McSwain's heroic story was never published. Two other escaped captives gave depositions before the Pennsylvania Council in mid-November concerning a major attack on the Potomac River, and their incidental capture in Path Valley, Pennsylvania, led by very prominent Ohio Delaware and including two men "lately supported at the Expence of this Province at Augwick."[15] The testimony of these escaped captives was not made public. Both Philadelphia newspapers, though edited by strong supporters of the war party, were effectively muzzled.

In February of 1756, at least three Pennsylvania and New York papers carried a lengthy story about two unnamed Virginia women who had escaped from Shawnee captivity. Their capture itself was not discussed, and, after mention of their running an initial gauntlet, their treatment as captives of Indians was described in what would become the formulaic dismissal: "as well as could be expected from Persons of their Savage Disposition." The report centered on how these women, whom we now know were Mary Draper Ingles and Katherine Bingeman, survived their forty days of fatigue and hunger before reaching their New River homes. It was an anonymous tale as told in the newspapers and, frankly, might have served as an explanation of why more captives did not attempt to escape. Perhaps it was intended as an encouraging story of women willing to take great risks and endure severe suffering in order to reclaim their Virginia frontier lives. The Ingles family nurtured versions of the story for generations, but the first full memoir was not published until two centuries after the women had returned.[16]

In contrast, there was prompt and astonishing enthusiasm in Pennsylvania for the comparatively tame account of the very brief captivity of William and Elizabeth Fleming. They were recently married British immigrants farming in Great Cove, Pennsylvania, when they were captured in November of 1755. Less than twenty-four hours later, they escaped. They told of their passive compliance and civil conversations with the well-known and articulate Delaware chief Tewea (Captain Jacobs), who confirmed French complicity months before the Anglo-French war was formally declared. Elizabeth was one of only two returned Allegheny women captives who told their story in print in their lifetime. Pregnant, confused, and terrified "of falling a Prey to savage Fury, or torn to pieces by ravenous wild Beasts," she made her way home, only to find Indians still attacking there. She became foot-sore, lost, despairing, and repeatedly collapsed from exhaustion and hunger. Amid the sound of guns and "Indian holos," she hid beside a dying cow, in fodder, in a thicket, in a gum tree, and in a blackened outdoor oven. She portrayed herself as resourceful and enduring, yet also as the frail heroine popular in the imported English sentimental novels of the time, especially those of Samuel Richardson. Elizabeth's husband, William, presented himself as a rational, polite, and accommodating gentleman before he made his separate, nonviolent, escape.

The Flemings' accounts apparently interested several audiences in Pennsylvania in 1756. Their pamphlet was first printed in Lancaster eleven weeks after their return, and sold well there and in Philadelphia.[17] William Fleming's calm acceptance of capture and nonviolent escape pleased the colony's numerous pacifists much more than the war party led by Lieutenant Governor James Hamilton. Quakers were actively supported by Moravians, Mennonites, Amish, Dunkers, Schwenkfelders, and other German churches in opposition to war. Although these may have constituted only one-sixth of the 60,000 German speakers in the province, they were disproportionately more likely to be naturalized, to vote, and to buy reprinted European martyrologies. The two German editions of the Flemings' translated pamphlet were printed by pacifist Christopher Saur.[18]

Yet the Flemings' reports made a strong political and religious case against the French, and Elizabeth's moving voice of frail and sensitive motherhood could encourage support for militant and military action. The first edition appeared after Pennsylvania's scalp bounties had been set, and while the government was still debating whether to declare war against the Delaware. Even if authorities had not formally approved this timely publication, they were soon attempting to influence the pamphlet's growing readership. What was likely the second edition had "An INTRODUCTION To the Reader" that was much more belligerent than the Flemings' text. The pamphlet was now "to give an Idea of the Distress of such as are so unfortunate as to fall into the Hands of our Savage Enemies" and was to inform those "who may seem disinterested in these Matters, or make light of them." The authors now hoped to teach readers "to set a juster Value on the Liberties and Mercies we now perhaps unthankfully enjoy," and, rather incidentally, to invite readers to be grateful to God. A promptly published third, enlarged edition went even further, pointedly claiming that the French-inspired Delaware and Shawnee, "finding Pennsylvania the only defenceless province," focused their attacks there for this reason.[19] The Flemings were being drawn or pushed to reframe their captivity story to give direct support to those in favor of the war.

The Flemings' story was by far the most popular account of Allegheny captivity during the war, and it was one that consciously sought financial support for the victims. After the Lancaster printing by William Dunlap, there were at least two English editions printed in Philadelphia, perhaps both by "James Chattin, for the unhappy sufferers."[20] Within three months of their return, the Flemings were selling their enlarged third edition, in English, from their own lodgings in Philadelphia. In their second newspaper advertisement, they "hoped all well disposed people, who are curious to read this little pamphlet, will purchase from the Authors, having lost all they had in the world, and are now reduced to poverty."[21] There was also a New York edition in 1756 and one published by Green and Russell in Boston later that year. This Boston edition was likely taken from another lost Pennsylvania printing of 1756, offered as Pennsylvania's Kittanning expedition was assembling, since the Boston title page included "A NARRATIVE necessary to be read by all who are going in the Expedition, as well as every BRITISH Subject."[22] The two surviving German editions were printed in Germantown and distributed there, in Lancaster, and in Philadelphia. The *New York Mercury* is the only newspaper known to have printed the entire pamphlet, in two installments. The editor of the *Pennsylvania Gazette* printed the authors' ads and certainly saw their narratives, but declined to publish any part of them, perhaps to encourage local support for the Flemings' publication. Interest in the tract was intense, but proved quite fleeting. *A Narrative of the Sufferings and Surprizing Deliverances of William and Elizabeth Fleming* was perfectly attuned to the local political crosscurrents of 1756, but the authors' account of rational composure and unavenged discomfort was soon overwhelmed by events. Their pamphlet was not reprinted for 222 years.[23]

Both Benjamin Franklin's *Pennsylvania Gazette* and William Bradford's *Pennsylvania Journal and Weekly Advertiser* were justifiably full of horrific accounts of frontier attacks in 1756, but the newspapers avoided the Fleming narrative as well as the earlier account of the Staut escape. The *Pennsylvania Gazette* did show interest in the heavily edited deposition of escaped captive John Craig, published on 1 April 1756, just as the Pennsylvania Assembly was declaring war on the Delaware. Craig "informs us" of his capture by five Delaware, stating that he was driven with a rope around his neck, stripped and tied down at night, required to haul heavy loads of loot by day, whipped, and then adopted by Shingas. Exchanges of sensible questions and answers with leading Delaware, including Shingas, were features of his deposition that were not printed. Craig, rather than Shingas, was said to list nine tribes assembling for war, and to note that they "would carry on the War against them as long there was a Man of them alive." Here was an early version of the frequently published message of returning captives: the Indians were fusing into a powerful and determined unit, and colonists needed to do the same.[24] Lieutenant Governor Robert Hunter Morris and his council offered the press this sanitized, unambiguous account that could reconcile more Pennsylvanians to his declaration of war and rouse them to the dangers that were about to descend upon them.

Although there is no conclusive evidence that the government, rather than the newspapers, suppressed captivity accounts, it is hard to avoid the suspicion that the Pennsylvania government deliberately used the press to shape public perceptions of the Kittanning expedition in the late summer of 1756. The informative earlier deposition of John Baker, who had escaped from Kittanning and was a guide for the expedition, had been kept from the press.[25] While the expedition was making its way west, readers of both Philadelphia newspapers were given information brought in by a man named Nicholas Barnhold, who had been wounded and captured in the recent loss of Fort Granville. His was the first detailed account of the fall of this fort, its burning on the orders of the French officer "commanding," and the summary killing of one prisoner who could not keep up with the march.[26] Barnhold had escaped before this triumphant war party reached Kittanning and tortured John

Turner to death; certainly such lurid detail would have been useful as additional justification for Pennsylvania's counterstrike. On 9 September, just as the surviving Kittanning raiders were fleeing from Delaware pursuers, Philadelphia newspaper readers were presented with a rare treat: two depositions by Pennsylvania captives who had recently escaped. John Rowe had been a captive of the Delaware for two days, and his deposition before a Virginia magistrate described Indian fears of pursuit parties, and Indian preference for raiding settlements beyond the frontier forts, "for there they should find people enough straggling about carelessly and unarmed."[27]

Both Philadelphia papers also printed most of the detailed evidence that escaped captive John Coxe had presented to the Pennsylvania Council. Coxe estimated Kittanning's population, including about fifty "English Prisoners," and described the horrific torture of Paul Broadly. Coxe had also been taken to Tiahoga, where he counted the warriors and "about Twenty German Prisoners," saw the launch of frequent small raiding parties, and suffered food shortages. When Coxe's account was printed, the North Branch Delaware had ceased raiding and were in peace negotiations with Pennsylvania. Someone quietly excised part of what Coxe reported to the Pennsylvania Council, information that Tioga Delaware dissidents were still anxious to continue the war.[28] Earlier newspaper silence about the Flemings does not prove censorship, and the timing of Craig's account may have been fortuitous, but the careful excisions to moderate Coxe's report on Tioga belligerence could not have been accidental. The Philadelphia press was either censored or was censoring itself. The widely acknowledged broader propaganda uses of captivity accounts as cultural weapons did not overcome more complicated immediate political purposes.[29]

The Kittanning raid was carefully orchestrated for the press, before and after, and the recovered captives would say very little that was ever printed. On 23 September, Colonel John Armstrong's very optimistic dispatch had been summarized in both Philadelphia papers, which claimed that thirty to forty Delaware had been killed and eleven captives recovered; it was also mentioned that at least fourteen Pennsylvanians had been killed and that seventeen were missing, including Captain Hugh Mercer's party of twelve, plus their four recovered captives, who had not come in and may have been intercepted.[30] The final count, never reported, would exactly reverse Armstrong's claims, because thirty to forty Pennsylvanians were killed, and fourteen Delaware. Two weeks later the *Pennsylvania Gazette* proudly noted that Armstrong and his officers had selflessly given their loot to their own men and donated their scalp money to the recovered captives. In mid-October, readers were assured that Tewea had been killed in the raid, and that the governor had personally examined the returned captives at Lancaster. All that the captives told the press, indirectly, concerned the torture of John Turner at Kittanning. Four months later, Philadelphia's newspapers published the city's citation for Colonel John Armstrong, including the presentation of a gold medal and cash.[31] The illusion of victory at Kittanning had been carefully preserved.

If Pennsylvania's newspaper readers longed for stirring accounts of captivity and escape, or authorities were anxious to use captivity narratives to rouse more manly resolves, then neither was satisfied in the ten months after the Kittanning raids. There had been less raiding that fall, but there were sizable attacks again in the spring of 1757, all fully reported in the papers. In July of 1757, newspapers in Annapolis, Philadelphia, and then New York printed a second-hand account of the deposition of John Street, a drummer captured at Fort Granville, who had just escaped from Fort Duquesne with a negro slave named François. Street's description of increasing French strength, and his report of plans for an attack on Fort Cumberland, were all that was deemed of interest. François was not named, but "on a separate Examination confirms what Street says."[32] A couple of weeks later, readers were treated to the more compelling account of Peter Looney, ensign in the heroic, if futile, defense of Virginia's Vause's Fort, captive of the Shawnee, and witness to the torture of a fellow soldier, perpetrated with the supposed complicity of the French. Looney reported seeing Indian and French reinforcements bound for Fort Duquesne, and described his rather uneventful escape from Niagara to Albany and Philadelphia. The Philadelphia papers proudly noted that Looney had been born in Philadelphia, though he lived in Virginia.[33]

The winter of 1757–58 brought some relief from Indian raids, as well as a few published accounts of returned captives. John Kennedy, a Pennsylvania trader captured in 1754, finally returned from a short imprisonment in Fort Duquesne, and longer ones in Quebec and France. The point of his story, as carried by both Philadelphia papers early in December 1757, was that "he was sent in a very miserable condition to England, where, being an intire Stranger, he applied to the Honourable THOMAS PENN, Esq; one of our Proprietaries, who received and treated him with great Humanity, and not only supplied him with Clothes and Money for his Support during his Stay in England, but gave him wherewithal to defray the Expence of his Passage hither." The proprietary party, and the larger war party, did well by the press throughout the war.[34]

Newspaper readers never heard nearly as much as Charles Stuart (Stewart) wanted to tell them about his captivity, and that of his wife, both of whom surely deserved more celebrity than the Flemings as survivors of captivity. Admittedly they had not escaped, and they returned when there was no particular official need for their story. Taken in the initial raids on Great Cove in the autumn of 1755, they were eventually exchanged and arrived back in Pennsylvania at the end of 1757. The *Pennsylvania Gazette* cryptically summarized their intervening trials and adventures in a single brief paragraph, including their running a gauntlet at Kittanning, and being carried to Detroit, indentured to French missionaries, sent to England in a cartel ship, and then returned to New York in a troop transport. As much newspaper space was given to the names of the thirteen captives the Stuarts reported seeing in or near Detroit, and especially to one Agnes Hamilton, a surviving captive of Braddock's defeat. The *New York Mercury* had not picked up the story when the Stuarts were in that town, but reprinted most of what was told to the *Pennsylvania Gazette*.[35] These summaries were nowhere near all that the Stuarts had to say; "An Account of the Captivity of Charles Stuart ..." is an extremely rich and detailed document, amounting to twenty-three printed pages when finally published in 1926. This elaborate statement had certainly been prepared as a publishable captivity narrative, but it was likely given to, and held by, military authorities very soon after the Stuarts arrived in Philadelphia. The larger account begins with details of Stuart's losses, and those of his neighbors, at the hands of a war party headed by Shawnee captain John Peter, who "Talks very good English." After taking the Stuarts, the group continued to raid in the neighborhood for two days before setting off to rejoin parties led by Shingas, Captain Will, and Tewea. Stuart had learned promptly of Hugh McSwain's daring escape; his killing of two Delaware meant that Stuart was initially condemned to die in revenge. Shingas saved Stuart's life, recounting how the Stuarts had been well known for their previous hospitality to passing Indians. Shingas's endorsement not only saved Stuart's life but probably explained why the Stuarts were able to stay together throughout their captivity, though their children were taken away.

Stuart also provided details of a stirring speech by Shingas to the English prisoners, a speech that was destined never to reach its intended audience. Shingas said that he regretted the need for war, but roundly blamed Braddock, whose impolitic, if prescient, rebuff to an Indian legation had been "that No Savage Should Inherit the Land." According to Shingas, most of the Indians had waited to see Braddock's fate, after which the French drew them in with threats rather than promises. Even then, the Delaware sent a final legation under Tewea to Philadelphia in August 1755, but they had returned empty-handed. Only after this second rebuff, and more French encouragement, had the Ohio Indians begun raiding in Pennsylvania. Shingas could still propose peace in November 1755, but only with the unlikely condition that the English provide the Delaware with artisans who would make gunpowder, smelt lead, work iron, fix guns, and weave blankets. He also wanted the English to come and live in peace with the Indians, bringing ample trade, though not necessarily to intermarry. This speech to a captive audience was not written down and sent east, nor was it reported orally before being overtaken by events. In responding to Shingas, the attending captives, without any sense of irony, had apparently claimed that Pennsylvania authorities could not compel English settlers to live among the Indians. It is not surprising that this statement would not be published in English America during the war; it was much more sensible, sophisticated, and disarming than the arguments made in the widely advertised Flemings' conversations with Tewea just a day or two earlier.

Stuart went on to detail a gauntlet run at Kittanning, but his own injuries did not prevent him from mentioning in his fuller account that young captives were exempt from this gauntlet, and he noticed that the warriors did not utilize their weapons fully. Shingas gave the Stuarts as a present to the Wyandot, and they were allowed to ride horses all the way to Sandusky. From there, they went to Detroit, were kindly treated by the commandant, Claude-Pierre Pécaudy de Contrecoeur, and managed to observe the fort's size, strength, and approaches. Stuart then detailed traveling back to the Ohio and Muskingum Rivers with Wyandot hunters, observing good land for farming, meeting and parting with their son, and tasting buffalo meat. They visited several successful Wyandot hunting camps, and described the Wyandot and Ottawa villages above Detroit, and at Fort St Joseph. Little is said of their indenture with the Jesuits near Detroit or their passage to Quebec and Plymouth, England. The Stuart case is proof that an honest, balanced, intriguing, and well-written captivity narrative might not be published at all, especially while the war continued. Most accounts of captive life among the Indians were not terrifying enough to promote resistance unto death. For military and political leaders, surrender and desertion needed no encouragement.

Newspaper readers in Virginia and Pennsylvania were finally presented with a military hero of their own early in 1758, but public reports were surprisingly restrained. Two years earlier, Virginian ranger captain and militia major John Smith had commanded the small patrol that ferociously defended Vause's Fort, until he had only 3 able men left and finally had to surrender to a force reduced to 135. A bit of the story, told by Peter Looney, had been published in newspapers six months earlier, and Charles Stuart's more recently published account had listed Smith among captives still held near Detroit.[36] The *New York Mercury* reported its summary interview with the returned hero on 30 January 1758, and the *Pennsylvania Gazette* and the *Pennsylvania Journal and Weekly Advertiser* did so ten days later. Smith had been escorted to Fort des Miamis before being given to Potawatomi at Fort St Joseph. He mentioned some Indian discontent with the French, and prospects for the English in Indian diplomacy. After a brisk mention of "encountering innumerable Hardships," Smith noted that he arrived at Quebec, was generously assisted there by Colonel Peter Schuyler, and sailed to England in the summer of 1756.

John Smith was not a humble or reticent man, and what he did not tell the newspapers, or they chose not to report, was more interesting than what they offered. Smith had managed, according to Stuart's unpublished narrative, to stir up enough pro-English feelings to be cautioned by the French commandant at Detroit, who then sent him down to Quebec. Smith never mentioned that he was sent to England in a cartel ship, along with the Stuarts. On arrival in England, he was well received as a plain spoken patriot who had lost three sons in the war and regretted that he had no more who could serve his country. He attracted the attention of William Pitt, and presented what he called "Extract from the Journal of Major John Smith, 1756–1757." Here he exaggerated slightly in writing that Vause's Fort had been attacked by 230 men, of whom his party of 10 had killed 40; he exaggerated more in claiming he thereby prevented these raiders from penetrating to the heart of Virginia. As a captive, he noted the numbers of troops and guns at ten French forts from Fort des Miamis to Fort Frontenac. He then described the major Indian tribes he encountered: the Shawnee, "great Enimys of late of the English"; the formerly friendly Miami; the Twigtwees, whom he thought would follow the English if it was safe to do so; plus the pro-French Ottawa and Huron farther north. The Potawatomi of Fort St Joseph, who had adopted him and likely protected him from more severe French scrutiny, had "danced under English Colours, taken from Gen'l Braddock, and fired through French Colours" in his presence – a group portrait in sharp contrast to that of escaped trader-captive Cornelius Van Slyke, drawn nine years later after the intervening ferocities of Pontiac's War.[37] Smith was confident that the Indians from Ohio country to Illinois country could be won over, and the French ousted, "there not being one Great Gun" in any of their Ohio forts. He went on to propose, unsuccessfully, that 1,000 "Woods men" plus Cherokee and Catawba, carrying fifteen days' provisions, undertake a swift, fort-destroying expedition. Smith was paid his remaining back salary when he petitioned the Virginia House of Burgesses on his return, and was eventually paid for his time as a captive as well.[38] If Smith had been able to keep a journal, as his "extract" suggests, it was never published and does not seem to have survived. The only other Allegheny captivity described in the *Pennsylvania Gazette* in 1758 was a slightly garbled second-hand account of Richard Bard's escape.

Early in 1758 there had been another ripple of Philadelphia publishing interest in a captivity narrative, this time the story of Robert Eastburn, a blacksmith and pious deacon of the First Presbyterian Church of Philadelphia. His was not quite an Allegheny captivity; he had been captured in 1756 at the Wood Creek Carrying Place in New York very early in the Canadian siege of Fort Oswego, but his account was offered to his hometown Philadelphia audience. He had been adopted at Oswegatchie, hired out in Montreal, sent to England in a cartel ship, and returned home the following year. William Dunlap, the Flemings' first printer, who had just moved from Lancaster to Philadelphia, printed Eastburn's account, complete with an endorsing preface by Rev. Gilbert Tennent. As with the Flemings, the author sold his own story, at eight locations in Philadelphia and New Jersey.[39] Eastburn went on to answer his own patriotic call, to "be of good Courage, and play the Man, for our People, and the Cities of our God!" by becoming a captain in the second Pennsylvania regiment.[40] Eastburn's *A Faithful Narrative* was promptly reprinted by Green and Russell for Boston's established market in tales of captivity and redemption, but Eastburn was not reprinted in Philadelphia for seventy years.[41]

Ironically, the only full narrative of an Allegheny captivity that had been printed during the war years had been the fulsome account of the very brief and relatively easy detention of William and Elizabeth Fleming. Newspaper work did not include active pursuit of stories, even when they came to town, and editors were cautious about what they reprinted from other newspapers or from self-appointed correspondents. The depositions of John Craig, Nicholas Barnhold, and John Coxe became timely bulletins printed in support of Pennsylvania government initiatives. Newspapers printed only cryptic summaries of the fascinating adventures of Mary Draper Ingles, John Street, Peter Looney, Charles Stuart, John Kennedy, John Smith, or Richard Bard. More than 100 people had escaped from Allegheny captivities between 1754 and 1758, and the newspaper coverage showed severe restraint that suggests censorship. A government trying to rouse patriotic fervor to recover captives may have found news of good treatment in captivity, rational captors, or easy escapes to be less than helpful much of the time. However, it is hard to dismiss the possibility that, though the return of captives was a major stated government objective in wartime Pennsylvania, there was no irresistible public hunger at that time for accounts of returned captives.

During the truce of 1759–63 between the Ohio Indians and the British Army, fighting ceased, but neither side fulfilled its central promises. Three Allegheny captivity accounts were published separately in Pennsylvania during this time, and they can be studied as tests of interest among printers and readers. The first two were firm condemnations of French Catholic Canada and its Indian allies. The only Allegheny captivity account published in Pennsylvania in 1759 appeared in German and English versions as the patriotic story of Marie Le Roy and Barbara Leininger, German-speaking girls who escaped from what they saw as French-inspired cruelties. There is a sharp, and previously unnoticed, contrast between their printed narrative and their initial military examination. They were examined immediately after their escape to Fort Pitt, in March 1759, telling briefly what they thought mattered, or at least what the soldier recording their account found valuable. Of the 1755 attack on Penn's Creek, they said simply that fifteen were killed, without even mentioning that their fathers were among them. In contrast, they named all eight of those captured with themselves and all eight of the Delaware who captured them, as though the latter were being identified as criminals and the former called as witnesses. The girls noted having been taken to Kittanning for a year, until the Pennsylvanians attacked, and then briefly to Fort Duquesne.[42] After two months at the fort, the Kittanning Delaware and their captives migrated to the mouth of Beaver Creek, and, when word of General John Forbes's expedition arrived, they moved on up to Kuskuski, and finally to the relative safety of the Muskingum River. After the girls' brief travel sketch, their examination ends with the cryptic statement "On the 16th March made their Escape, & got into Pittsburgh on the 31st."

After outlining this story, the Le Roy–Leininger deposition added three comments, almost certainly prompted by a Pennsylvania officer interviewing them at what was then a precarious outpost. In any case, the girls thought these comments relevant, and so did their recorder. First, they mentioned that six "Huron" (Wyandot) had come to the Delaware settlement at the Muskingum, presumably in the winter of 1758–59, to suggest that their community would seek peace with the "English" if this was the Delaware inclination, but not otherwise. The Delaware's unyielding response was clear from the girls' second observation: "the Indians in conversation said the English were fatening at Pitsburg, & wou'd be fat by and by, & yn they wou'd kill them." The girls' third recorded comment was also intended to question the existing truce: Pisquetomen "does not appear to them to be hearty for ye English, but to be false hearted."[43] Although not published, or intended for publication, the girls' testimony asserted that these fifteen year olds, who had spent more than three years with the Delaware, had not been acculturated at all. Lieutenant Colonel Hugh Mercer was kind to the girls,[44] and found their testimony particularly timely and useful. His provincial garrison, left to hold the site of burned Fort Duquesne, was particularly uneasy in the wake of their own rash expedition to the northward, a recent failure that had violated the fragile truce. He had good reason to forward the examination of Marie and Barbara, and the girls themselves, promptly to Philadelphia.

Within six weeks, Marie and Barbara were in Philadelphia, telling a fuller and rather different story in a fourteen-page pamphlet, entitled *Erzehlungen von Marie Le Roy und Barbara Leininger*, "Written and Printed as dictated by them" and sold at the German Printing Office of Peter Miller and Lewis Weiss for a substantial six pence a copy.[45] Although it was generally true that, south of New England, authors were expected to pay the cost of printing, it was the printers or sponsors who invested in this publication.[46] In the pamphlet, the girls told the horrible details of their fathers' killing, but the names of neither the attackers nor the captured were included. Although they mentioned that their Delaware master was "tolerably kind" and that their running of the gauntlet was a playful ritual rather than a suffering, no space was given to describing Indian ways except in their cruelty. The torture and death of two captives who were retaken after the Kittanning raid are detailed, passing on to readers the Delaware message – and the girls' self-congratulation – that only those willing to face such a gruesome death can "run away with a brave heart." They certainly made it clear that the Kittanning raid was much less successful than previously reported, either in destroying this Delaware settlement or in recovering captives. The girls admitted enjoying French food during their brief stay at Fort Duquesne, but resisted all French invitations to stay with them, simply because these child patriots apparently "could not, however, abide the French." Perhaps by then they understood more Delaware than French. However, their choice of captor fitted uneasily with their insistence upon Delaware belligerence and brutality, and they knew it. They went with the Indians, they said, because these "would be more likely to make peace with the English than the French, and in as much as there would be more ways open for flight in the forest than in a fort."

There is nothing in the pamphlet about any of the three accusations of duplicity against the Delaware that were the conclusion of their earlier examination. The brave escape was much better described in the pamphlet, showing that it involved four captive conspirators who slipped by their captors' village at night. God has a place in the pamphlet version that was not in the military examination; God was thanked when the village dogs did not bark, and when an Indian raft was found. "If one could not believe there is a God, who helps and saves from death, one had better let running away alone." We learn here for the first time that two men escaped with the girls, men who have left no evidence of being examined on arrival at Fort Pitt, or subsequently. The four fugitives were sustained by the gun and hunting skills of Hugh Gibson, and he and fellow escapee David Breckinridge carried the girls on their shoulders as they waded across the Ohio just below Fort Pitt. Yet the helpful escaping men were entirely missing in the girls' first account, and remained very peripheral in the second.

The publication of their story was very purposeful; the escaped girls had been forwarded on an immediate mission by Lieutenant Colonel Mercer. They had spent only a single day at Fort Pitt before the four escapees headed east with a military escort. Gibson went no farther than Fort Bedford, and Breckinridge stayed at Lancaster, but the two girls promptly went on to Philadelphia. This, the pamphlet insists, "is not done in order to render our own sufferings and humble history famous" but to tell of other captives they met, so that relatives and friends might learn that they were still alive. The impressive finale of the pamphlet was a description of what the girls knew of thirty-eight named captives still scattered in Indian country, with some comments on where these had been captured and where they were being held. Like hostages and captives in all kinds of settings, they had been anxious to exchange names and promises to notify next of kin.[47] The girls' ability to learn the names of captives is notable, especially given Indian resistance to captives communicating with each other and in contrast to young Mathias Warren's complete ignorance on such matters.[48] They added that they met numerous additional captives, whose names they never knew or could not remember. Le Roy and Leininger ended with an assurance that they intended to go to Lancaster, where they could easily be found and would be happy to provide further information for anyone seeking people held among the Indians.

Puzzles remain about this full and quickly published youth captivity narrative. These two orphaned girls, whose mothers likely had fled eastward, mentioned nothing about seeking or finding their families. Their trip to Philadelphia may have been aided by the military, but the pamphlet was of little help to the military. There was an unknown male editor who intruded into their story on occasion, but his identity is hidden. The editing was religious and patriotic, and any one of three prominent clerical supporters of Pennsylvania's "war party" may have helped: Richard Peters, Henry Melchior Muhlenberg, or William Smith.[49] This was the very first publication for printers Peter Miller and Lewis Weiss, who had bought Benjamin Franklin's German Printing Office. Publication was too late to be part of any official attempt to rouse Germans to participate in a war that most hoped had ended. The account was published after Christian Frederick Post and Pisquetomen's peace mission to the Ohio Valley, which the girls mention obliquely and denigrate. The pamphlet appeared after the Ohio Delaware had abandoned the French and Fort Duquesne had fallen, and after the truce of December 1758 had been negotiated at Fort Pitt. We do not know whether the girls, who would be under death sentence with the Delaware for escaping, later advised anyone seeking captive relatives, but these runaways would have been anathema among the Ohio Delaware, and would have trouble gathering fresher information. However, the girls' primary purpose may well have been as stated, to offer details that would help relatives to recover their kin from what they had portrayed as the unending danger of death. Their story did not outlive this purpose and was soon forgotten, in contrast to the more stirring and pious tale about Barbara's younger sister, Regina, about which more later.[50]

Amid the shower of victories in 1759 and numerous released and escaped captives, the Philadelphia papers printed accounts of the adventures of only one escapee, the remarkable Captain Robert Stobo. On 28 June both Philadelphia papers related a bit of information from "a Gentleman who had been a Prisoner at Quebec for five Years; that he with four more had made their Escape in a Canoe." A week later both Pennsylvania papers identified him as Captain Stobo, "a Man of a most enterprizing Genius," and described his experience as a hostage at some length. Two months later the *Pennsylvania Journal and Weekly Advertiser* printed Stobo's brief account of his escape from Quebec, and exploits in the St Lawrence Valley, and his evaluation of the military strength of the citadel then being attacked.[51] Stobo's story was not assembled for separate publication, and the Le Roy–Leininger account and Stobo's were the only Allegheny narratives published anywhere that year.[52]

In the spring of 1760, the year Canada would surrender, a unique Allegheny captivity narrative was published in Philadelphia. William Bradford, printing rival of Benjamin Franklin, editor of the *Pennsylvania Journal and Weekly Advertiser*, and publisher of numerous political and religious books, printed *A Journal of the Captivity of Jean Lowry and Her Children*.[53] This tract was marked by a religious preoccupation and intensity reminiscent of earlier New England captivity narratives and absent from all other accounts from Allegheny borderlands. The pamphlet began with a factual account of the attack that killed her husband and burned McCord's Fort in 1756. Amid the flames, "divine Providence determined" that she surrender herself and her five children rather than be burned. The trials of the journey are detailed, including the dashed hopes after rescuers were successfully counterattacked. Lowry, like Le Roy and Leininger, recounted a constant expectation of being killed, "But God had mercifully ordered otherwise." This pious, scrupulous, and defiant Christian woman refused to work on Sunday for Indians or Frenchmen, and was beaten and nearly drowned for this unbending tenacity. Although she was helped across a swollen river by "a great-bodied Mingo squaw," her thanks were only for God, with whom, admittedly, she could better converse. Although she had "good usage" while a servant of the French at Fort Venango and Montreal, and could thank French people for kindnesses, she found her cause in thoroughgoing religious defiance. We are not surprised to hear that she was one of four women in a party of fourteen who attempted to escape from Montreal, or that she wanted to be imprisoned rather than returned to her decadent French Catholic mistress. Nonetheless, Governor Pierre-

François Rigaud, Marquis de Vaudreuil, not God, was thanked for freeing her from servitude, and Colonel Peter Schuyler for what must have been substantial financial assistance. By April of 1759, and page eighteen of her thirty-one-page account, she was back from two Atlantic crossings, with many more English people to thank, and waiting "to see if God in his adorable Providence, would favour me with any agreeable account from my five poor Fatherless Captives among the Savage Indians."

Perhaps because Jean Lowry was an assertive Irishwoman with a good Calvinist familiarity with the Bible, she had attracted a few clerics in Montreal to practice their English in religious disputation. Hers is the only surviving account to suggest that the French still made any serious attempts to convert English captives. Lowry devoted the final dozen closely printed, and closely argued, pages of her journal to "Several Disputes" with unidentified Catholic priests on baptism, transubstantiation, petitioning the Virgin Mary, apostolic succession, penance, the priesthood of all believers, and whether Christ descended into Hell for three days. Invariably, Lowry claimed to have won the arguments using scripture and logic, and the pamphlet ended with an unnamed Canadian witness reportedly conceding, "she has you now." Lowry saw herself as helpless but redeemed by God, ferociously defiant in faith, unbending in culture, and ultimately victorious where it mattered. Deacon Eastburn, Marie Le Roy, and Barbara Leininger all thanked God for being saved, and credited God for the kindness of Indian people, but Lowry was in a class of her own. It would be condescending for the modern reader to presume that her rather embarrassing religiosity could not have been genuine and must have been the result of distortion by some unknown clerical ghostwriter.[54] If Indian captivity narratives had a role in secularizing earlier "Providence tales," Jean Lowry's story defiantly rejected this function.[55] She had been back in Pennsylvania for a year when William Bradford published this unusual pamphlet in 1760. He was a supporter of the war, and may have thought that this tract would be of interest as a captivity narrative, as an anti-Catholic primer, or as another aspect of that year's conquest of New France. None of these appeals caused the pamphlet to be reprinted in the next two centuries.[56]

German printers Peter Miller and Lewis Weiss, of Philadelphia, had launched their business in 1759 with publications that included the Le Roy–Leininger narrative and an almanac, *Neu-eingerichteter americanischer Geschichts und Haus-Calender ... 1762*. Two years later they entertained their annual almanac readers with the eight-page "Story of an Indian Captive," Pennsylvania soldier Abraham Urssenbacher. Captured outside the fort at Raystown in July of 1759, Urssenbacher was taken to Fort Machault (Venango) and then apparently carried along on the disastrous French and Indian relief expedition sent from there to Fort Niagara. Urssenbacher had been captured by Potawatomi, and went home with those saddened returning warriors to Fort St Joseph. There he was purchased and well treated by the French commandant, until Urssenbacher escaped in March of 1760. There had been anxieties about Indian intentions, and gauntlets to be run, but the greatest trial of his captivity was the long and hungry journey across the southern Ontario wilderness back to now-British Fort Niagara. Here was a captivity narrative offered as an unelaborated and true adventure story.[57] It was never published separately, never translated into English for the larger Pennsylvania and American audience, and never reprinted in anthologies. The truce of 1759–62 had not seen any rush to print and market Allegheny captivity narratives in Pennsylvania. Lowry's quaint diatribe was only the fourth of these to be sold as a separate publication in Pennsylvania, and it would be the last of them to be published there for nearly half a century.[58]

Even amid the "paper blizzard" of sixty-three publications in Philadelphia throughout 1764, arguing for and against the brutal killing of the converted Conestoga Indians by the Paxton Boys, neither side sponsored publication of a single captivity narrative.[59] The only narrative of Allegheny captivity to be published during Pontiac's War was the brief newspaper account of the captivity and escape of Eleanor Ryan. Although Ryan "gives the following account," the papers printed nothing about the attack near Stony Creek, Virginia, in which she and her brother were captured. The main interest was in her five captors' reactions when followed by the "hot pursuit" of Virginian horsemen. The captives were then threatened with immediate execution and were forced to trek through very rough country. Without food, weapons, or much energy, these two escapees set off towards the rising sun. The one-paragraph story then closes abruptly: "After wandering in the mountains for 15 days, her brother perished by hunger; and in 5 days afterwards she got into Harness's fort, on the South Branch [of the Potomac River], almost starved to death." Although published in the official press of Virginia and Pennsylvania, this tale was no advertisement for either pursuit parties or attempted escape.[60]

A total of only three Allegheny captivity narratives had been published as separate pamphlets in Pennsylvania between 1745 and 1765, and all of them were by and about female captives taken in western Pennsylvania. When four times as many men as women are known to have returned from captivity, and more men than women were functionally literate, it seems more than coincidence that women wrote the only accounts published separately during these wars.[61] Although it needs to be remembered that William Fleming's account was published with his wife's, and that Robert Eastburn's narrative of a soldier's captivity in New York and New France was printed and sold in Philadelphia, it was four female captivities that dominated the very limited market in Pennsylvania for Allegheny captivity narratives. Was it easier for women to describe experiences of their own vulnerability?[62] Elizabeth Fleming, Jean Lowry, Marie Le Roy, Barbara Leininger, their patrons, and their publishers gambled that these accounts would sell. Although the three narratives varied enough to prevent easy generalization, they all proclaimed innocence in the face of unwarranted attack, and they all preferred their white communities without any ambiguity whatever. Jean Lowry presented herself as a thoroughly defiant Protestant polemicist, calling on and thanking her God without evident irony or gender politics.[63] Le Roy and Leininger were apparently patriotic girl scouts, who were not at all acculturated after three and a half years of captivity, and then risked death to escape the Delaware. The most popular account, that of Elizabeth and William Fleming, was about a couple who did not spend a single night in captivity. Elizabeth did not write about going into captivity, but was composed enough to draw her captor into a very serious conversation that showed how acculturated he had become. It was only after escaping that Elizabeth became the lost and frightened "frail flower" in imitation of romantic novels and later captivity accounts. There is no way of knowing whether her story sold so well because it could serve as a metaphor for a nonviolent and promising young society that was suddenly caught in a catastrophe for which it thought it was blameless, and from which it still hoped to escape promptly.

If the emotive power of captive wives and mothers could rouse the martial spirit of menfolk, or serve as "justification by suffering" for the land-hungry, it was a resource that was used enthusiastically only once in Philadelphia and its hinterlands in the generation after 1756. These initial accounts offered their readers no females who reported that they escaped white male oppression by being captured by Indians, none who explored Indian society as a welcome personal adventure, and none who used Indian customs as a conscious critique of their natal communities. These women wanted to get home, and risked their lives to do so; neither Fleming nor Lowry hinted that they left fascinating Indian communities to return to servitude as colonial wives, *femmes couvertes*.[64] It is possible that their domestic oppression prevented any such remarks, but much more likely that they did not feel this way.

The British Atlantic empire was coming closer together during the war of the 1750s, but there were clear differences in access to, and appetite for, Allegheny captivity stories. In contrast to the few and factual narratives of Allegheny captivity initially offered to Pennsylvania readers, or readers of Isaac Hollister's *A Brief Narration of the Captivity of Isaac Hollister, Who Was Taken by the Indians, Anno Domino, 1763* (New London, CT, 1767), British readers were offered more, and what they were offered was fictionalized from the beginning. Edward Kimber, a prolific London writer and editor, and once a tourist in America, included an Allegheny captivity in his popular sentimental romance *The History of the Life and Adventures of Mr. Anderson* (London and Dublin, 1754; London and Berwick, 1782; Glasgow, 1799). A London boy is abducted and sold into cruel servitude in Maryland, and, amid the gyrations of fortune, the whipped slaves, the fainting ladies, and love lost and found, Tommy Anderson is briefly an Indian trader captured west of Virginia and sent to Canada and France, everywhere charming his civil captors. Roy Harvey Pearce, a modern scholar who has argued that the "decline and fall" of the authentic captivity narrative had occurred by the end of the eighteenth century, does not consider British writers.[65] Although supposedly set earlier in the century, Kimber's novel caught elements of the Anglo-French commercial rivalry for Ohio country in the decade before its publication.[66] It also featured a villain named Williamson, and Kimber's novel was said to have prompted some to challenge the credibility of the most famous British writer of an Allegheny captivity narrative, Peter Williamson.

By 1757 the English were hearing of Allegheny frontier raids, including those in the anonymous *The Cruel Massacre of the Protestants in North America, shewing how the French and Indians joined together to scalp the English ...*, which reported that hundreds of families had been massacred or captured, and that the Crown was fighting back, and was supporting frontier refugees.[67] A newfound English appetite for Indian captivity narratives was cultivated by the lurid 103-page *French and Indian Cruelty: Exemplified in the Life and Various Vicissitudes of Fortune, of Peter Williamson*, printed in London, York, and Glasgow in 1757, and revised and reprinted frequently in Britain over the next forty years before becoming a staple of American anthologies of Indian captivity.[68] Eighteenth-century British readers, who were growing accustomed to identifying humane sensibility with civilization and cruelty with barbarism, could extract special satisfaction from evidence of French cruelty, while expecting such behavior from Aboriginals. Williamson insisted on the truth of his fabrication, though it is surprising that he was believed then, and inexcusable now.[69] He was evidently born near Aberdeen in 1730 and, whether kidnapped or not, claimed to have been shipped as a servant to Pennsylvania in 1743, where he married his master's daughter, and had become a farmer on the Berks-Northampton frontier by 1754. He declared that his farm was suddenly attacked by Indians, in what would have been a rare night attack, on 2 October 1754, at the beginning of an imaginary rampage sustained for an entire month without any retaliation whatever.

Such a raid, leaving at least thirty-three dead and five captured, would have been extremely important news if any of it had happened.[70] Specifying false dates and names of families scalped and burned, Williamson hurried on to offer lurid details of cannibalism, rape, and inventive tortures, culminating in a victim being buried to the neck, scalped, and, after several hours of torment, burned to death in a fire set by his head. Never clear on who his supposedly Delaware captors were, and never suggesting that they were neighboring Teedyuscung's Wyoming Valley Delaware, Williamson claimed to have been tortured and forced to carry loot all the way to "Alamingo," some 200 miles beyond the Blue Mountains.[71] He plagiarized paragraphs about moccasins and *werowances* (tribal chiefs), invented the ritual murder of elderly Indians, and never acknowledged any language barrier for a recent immigrant farmer held captive for less than three months. Then Williamson was purportedly taken along as a bearer on a Delaware raid, which became his opportunity to escape. Brazenly defying any doubters, he lied that he had been examined by Lieutenant Governor Robert Hunter Morris and the Pennsylvania Assembly, that he had signed a deposition, and that his adventure was widely reported in colonial and British papers. And so it certainly would have been, if what he invented had occurred, and especially if these events had occurred more than six months before Braddock's defeat in July 1755 and a full year before any raids in Pennsylvania. Williamson also claimed to be an avenger in a party that later rescued a naked New England beauty from lusting captors, and slaughtered fifty Indians without losing a man – a stunning success that authorities would have eagerly advertised amid the litany of English losses that marked the first years of the war. Williamson's account also included much more likely subsequent adventures: fort building in Pennsylvania early in 1756, surrender at Oswego that year, and prompt return to England in a cartel ship. He knew a good deal about Pennsylvania and the military affairs of that frontier, but he entirely invented his Indian captivity, as he went on to reinvent himself as "Indian Peter, King of the Delaware," traveling showman in Britain, collector of Indian artifacts, and proprietor of an Edinburgh coffee house where he displayed and often sported the Indian garb he had gathered, including a costume in which he was eventually buried.

Aficionados of harmless self-fashioning might applaud such creative adjustment, and wish there had been a market in America for such profitable forms of escape therapy for real captives.[72] Yet Peter Williamson's poisonous deceptions not only fuelled British hatred for Indian and French enemies and Quaker pacifists during the Seven Years' War, but would also go on to a long career as fodder for hate-mongering in Britain, and then join the purposeful anthologies of "true-tales" of Indian atrocity in the United States after 1793, by which time most of the witnesses to what had not happened in 1754 had died.[73] Although of little known influence on those recounting their own Allegheny captivities, Williamson's creation was a model of publishing success for the new secular captivity narrative, one that included white male vengeance and avoided the humble exhortations to the divine that had been so visibly punishing, sustaining, or redeeming for earlier New England captives and for Marie Le Roy, Barbara Leininger, and Jean Lowry. A couple of other captivity narratives, about Britons taken in what would become the Canadian maritime provinces, were published in England, but neither attracted much attention.[74] Williamson evoked, reflected, and justified the British appropriation of America, and he relished the savage violence of aliens.

Williamson's invention was eventually mocked by a clever hoax. A tantalizing two-part "Extract from an Account of the Captivity of William Henry in 1755, and of His Residence among the Senneka Indians Six Years and Seven Months till He Made His Escape from Them, Printed at Boston, 1766," was printed in two successive issues of the *London Chronicle* late in June 1768. William Henry was introduced as an indifferent student at an English dissenting academy before migrating to become an Ohio trader captured at the outbreak of war. Adopted by the Seneca, he quickly learned their language and, while mending guns, often spoke with "Canussatego," an elderly warrior, counselor, and chief. Canussatego told wondrous tales of the creation of the world and the Iroquois. Henry countered that these eloquent Iroquois stories depended upon memory passed from one generation to the next, whereas "the account I gave them was written down by direction of the great spirit himself." Henry's final facetious remark was that readers should pity the Indians for their ignorance compared with "the unerring oracles that we possess, and the histories contained in them." This playful and well-concealed hoax was almost certainly by Benjamin Franklin, who was Pennsylvania's agent in London at the time.[75] The attractive-sounding book, which would have been unique among captivity accounts for being in quarto format, has never been found, and no other excerpts or advertisements for it are known. No William Henry is listed among traders to the Ohio Valley, though a George Henry was a Pennsylvania trader to the Ohio who was captured at Pickawillany in 1752 and returned from France within a year.[76] No English traders were captured in Ohio country in 1755, for they had all fled. The author's Iroquois creation story was his own imaginary concoction. Although it was a minor misunderstanding to identify Canasatego (Canussatego) as Seneca rather than Onondaga, it was a major imposition to center the story on numerous conversations with a sachem who had died five years before this captivity was supposed to have begun. Imaginary Allegheny captivities had a market in Britain, especially when masquerading as real ones.

The exotic appeal of Allegheny captivity reached as far as the Irish provincial town of Limerick, where one J. Farrar hurriedly published a substantial volume called *The Memoirs and Adventures of Robert Kirk, Late of the Royal Highland Regiment*, in 1775, just as British troops were leaving Irish garrisons for a new war in America. The author reported that he was a Scot who had joined the Montgomery Highlanders, had gone to America with this regiment in 1757, and had been one of nine captured by the Shawnee in Major James Grant's failed raid on Fort Duquesne the following year. He said he saw five of the prisoners, none of whom he knew, burned to death horribly, but he was saved by his initial captor as a replacement for a brother recently killed by the Cherokee. Kirk was apparently immediately given a gun, ammunition, a scalping knife, and a tomahawk, as well as the late brother's wife and son. In the spring of 1759 Kirk and three other white captives were invited to join a Shawnee raid against the Cherokee. When raiders Kirk and David Owens found themselves alone in the woods, they decided to escape, coming into Fort Cumberland three weeks later. The pair were supposedly questioned, overcame brief suspicions that they were deserters, and were then supposedly very well treated. Kirk rejoined his regiment at Lancaster, Pennsylvania, receiving back pay, and a new uniform, and "was further particularly taken notice of by my officers."[77]

Kirk interrupted his own story to discuss the capture of David Owens, son of a substantial farmer on Conococheague Creek in Cumberland County. Shawnee reportedly attacked the family working in their fields in 1755, capturing Owens's two sisters and killing his two brothers and a servant. David and his father managed to defend the house for an hour before the father killed an Indian, whose enraged comrades set fire to the place and took the defenders captive. In what would have been a unique report from these borderlands, Kirk recounted Owens's claim that the Shawnee "satiated their lust on his sisters, and afterwards killed and scalped one of them." Owens is said to have seen his father disemboweled, and his intestines tied to a tree, and the unfortunate man was then chased around it until he died. David and his surviving sister were loaded with plunder and taken "to their town where his sister still remained."[78] The Owens story should provoke suspicions that either Kirk was imposed upon or he was imposing on his readers. The Shawnee did not attack Conococheague Creek in 1755, no people named Owens were reported killed, captured, or in captivity, and the rape of the sisters would be a unique violation of warrior ethics, even if the gruesome torture of their father had not been the invention of a fevered imagination. The real and infamous David Owens, who was never described as a captive elsewhere, was the son of an Indian trader, and was a man who murdered his Shawnee wife and kin to claim scalp bounties. If he ever told any of this story to Kirk, he certainly did not do so while escaping with him from the Shawnee.

Kirk's dubious adventures merely began with his fantastic Shawnee captivity tale. Later in 1759 he supposedly volunteered to go with Major Robert Rogers on the St Francis raid, "the carnage terrible, hardly any of the enemy escaping."[79] He was supposedly with Rogers's own party in the protracted retreat, and claimed to have eaten the flesh of a captured Abenaki woman whom Rogers had killed for that purpose. After recuperating, Kirk was supposedly engaged in the 1760 campaign to Montreal, and then went west with Rogers to the forts of the *pays d'en haut*. After campaigning in the West Indies in 1762 (he says 1761), he supposedly returned to Allegheny country to join Colonel Henry Bouquet in the battle of Bushy Run and the 1764 expedition to the Muskingum River, where the Indians "saw that our force was considerable, and that in all probability we would destroy their country entirely" and therefore made peace. Kirk reportedly visited his adoptive Shawnee family and friends, who received him kindly because he preserved their mistaken impression that he had not escaped from them but from the Cherokee. Kirk's martial marathon of the British regular soldier in America ended the following year, when he supposedly joined an expedition that went down the Ohio and Mississippi Rivers. His account then trailed off into borrowed description of birds, trees, fruits, and animals of the region and a price list for specific skins and hides.

Kirk's story was a clever piece of purposeful literature tied closely to recent history by someone with considerable knowledge of the experience of the British Army in America, and likely with access to Thomas Mante's *The History of the Late War in North-America …*, a 1772 publication that made vicarious understanding of this subject much easier. Stephen Brumwell, the historian who most wants Kirk's breathless tale to be true, has identified him as a Robert Kirkwood, a private who is known to have been imprisoned at Fort Ontario for desertion in 1761, pardoned to go on an expedition to Newfoundland, transferred from the Montgomery Highlanders to the Black Watch in 1763, and then sent to serve in Ireland with this regiment at least until 1767. Brumwell does hesitate at some of Kirk's "claims," considers some things "problematic," and admits that eating the squaw may be "a lurid figment of the author's imagination."[80] Kirk's *Memoirs* may well be a composite of stirring tales told around army campfires, and it was certainly padded with numerous pieces lifted verbatim from Baron Lahontan, a soldier from a different army and an earlier time. Published in at least 150 subscription copies, Kirk's tale of courage, wicked Indians, and a generous army could encourage and sustain soldiers who heard nothing of the author's own desertion, but read of many reasons not to desert. Kirk may be as fictitious as William Henry, or as incredible as Peter Williamson, but the author joined them in using a fabricated Allegheny captivity as an attention-getting device for a British audience.

The demands of a late-eighteenth-century British audience are made clearest in the case of the publication of the only genuine journal of Allegheny captivity to appear in the author's lifetime.[81] Captain Thomas Morris had been sent by Colonel John Bradstreet as emissary to Fort Chartres, late in August of 1764 and kept a travel diary of his dangerous mission through enemy territory, a trip that included a brief captivity among the Miami. He had set out from Cedar Point, Ohio, with an escort of twenty-one, including both the renowned Oneida orator

Saghughsuniunt (Thomas King) and Jacques Godfroi, a Canadian trader who had been accused of aiding in the capture of British-held Fort Miami, and was pardoned on condition he keep Morris safe.[82] Morris met Pontiac at the first Ottawa village on the Maumee River, and that chief afforded him some protection there and at two other villages, but Morris was repeatedly threatened. When his party reached Fort Miami, there were new threats and accusations from Miami who had just been aroused by visiting delegates of the warring Shawnee and Delaware. Here Morris was captured, stripped, bound, and repeatedly threatened with death. He was tied to a post by the neck until freed by the young village headman. Godfroi and his Miami connections repeatedly saved Morris's life, but the diplomatic mission was aborted, and the two of them had a harrowing journey back to Detroit. Morris sent Colonel Bradstreet his journal, which needed no elaboration to serve its primary purpose, showing clearly why he had not been able to complete his assignment.[83]

The fate of this simple journal in the literary atmosphere of late-eighteenth-century England is telling. Morris became a minor literary figure and patron after retiring from the army in 1775, and eventually he printed a revised and expanded version of his soldier's travel diary in *Miscellanies in Prose and Verse* (London, 1791). Morris ennobled his savages by softening his twenty-seven-year-old journal's denunciations of Shawnee and Delaware, whom he had initially accused of lies "such as the malice of savages only, could invent," and he eliminated a reference to their plan to negotiate in bad faith with Bradstreet: "A hellish plan, but not a foolish one; & well worthy of so detestable a race of mortals." If Morris was following the growing fashion of sensibility toward the primitive in editing out his earlier denunciations, he was also willing to add color with entirely imaginary details of Indian methods of torture, admitting "These modes of torture I should not have mentioned, if the gentleman who advised me to publish my journal, had not thought it necessary."[84] In his revised account, while tied by the neck to a Miami village post, Morris was supposedly thinking of Indians' propensity to: apply hot stones to the feet, run hot needles into the eyes, and shoot the same arrows repeatedly into a victim, yanking them out between shots. He had apparently not heard or remembered anything of real Allegheny tortures, which were certainly different, though they were sometimes as horrific as the ones he fabricated. A dramatist by 1791, Morris also added dialogue to his earlier journal, especially incidental bits of French conversation with Godfroi. There was a new flourish, as the captive was now visited by "two very handsome young Indian women," making him "Happy Don Quixote, attended by princesses!" These changes were all judged tolerable, if not necessary, improvements to the journal. Such dramatic adjustments, and clear fabrications, were thought excusable in marketing a drama of exotic imperial captivity to an English audience.[85] This brief diary, frankly documenting both a fortunate captive's legitimate fears and Indian willingness to protect an enemy emissary, had become an entertaining invention of passing interest in Britain.[86]

There was British interest in captivity narratives from the Allegheny borderlands, and this market was firmly in the hands of Edinburgh showman Peter Williamson. British officials were not using captivity narratives to encourage imperial unity during this global war. There was no need to orchestrate the publication or suppression of accounts of returned captives, as was quite obvious in Pennsylvania. No Allegheny captivity narratives were published during the American Revolution, which would reorder both British and American uses for these tales,[87] and little attention was paid to Captain Thomas Morris's elaborated journal. There was also limited interest in the amazing story of Captain Robert Stobo. He had been dead for thirty years before the *Memoirs of Major Robert Stobo of the Virginia Regiment* was published in London in 1800, when all its anti-French elements could serve a Britain at war with Napoleonic France. Stobo is not suspected of writing this boastful biography, but it had certainly been written before his death by someone who knew his story very well. The work correctly summarized his trials as a hostage-prisoner and his swashbuckling escape from Quebec. Despite the timing of the publication, and its patriotic fervor, the book had a modest reception. In post-revolutionary America, there was no enthusiasm for reprinting such stories about an earlier war with their new French ally, or about a British hero.[88]

British readers were now much more interested in Alexander Mackenzie's journal of North American travel, exploration, fur trading, and imperial land claiming. His *Voyages from Montreal to the Frozen and Pacific Ocean* appeared in London in 1801, and he was lionized and promptly knighted.[89] Alexander Henry the elder, captive of the Ojibwa at Michilimackinac in 1763, may have hoped for similar attention when he published his *Travels and Adventures in Canada and the Indian Territories between the Years 1760 and 1776* in London and New York in 1809, but there was no comparable achievement, interest, or applause.[90] Henry was unprecedented in revealing his powerful bond with his cannibalistic Ojibwa rescuer, captor, and kinsman Wawatam.[91] Henry and his publishers had read the times correctly in emphasizing travel and adventure, rather than the captivity among the Ojibwa of one who subsequently became a Loyalist émigré. The publication of Kimber in Dublin and Glasgow, Kirk in Limerick, and Williamson throughout Britain could suggest that Allegheny captivity helped develop an emerging sense of British cultural identity in the last half of the eighteenth century. Williamson and Kirk had painted their Pennsylvania political and military contexts quite knowledgeably. However, captives lost and recovered on an Allegheny frontier that had since been lost again were bound to be of limited interest in Britain after 1783.

Pennsylvania printers indicated no new enthusiasm for captivity narratives in the decade after 1765; these were not yet the vehicles to encourage or celebrate this colony's new political culture, or its renewed westward expansion. Although Mary Rowlandson's captivity of a century earlier was reprinted nine times in New England between 1770 and 1776, Philadelphia printers offered neither that narrative nor any Allegheny captivity accounts amid the nascent stirrings of an American quest for freedom.[92] None of the four Allegheny captivity narratives printed in this decade were printed in Pennsylvania: the two already discussed were printed in Ireland,[93] a third in Connecticut, and the fourth in Saxony. There was enough Connecticut interest in one of their own survivors of the ill-fated settlement in Pennsylvania's Wyoming Valley to justify publication of Isaac Hollister's *A Brief Narration of the Captivity of Isaac Hollister, Who Was Taken by the Indians, Anno Domino, 1763* in both New London and Hartford in 1767. Hollister had been captured in the North Branch Delaware retaliation for the killing of Teedyuscung. After a cold and hungry winter in captivity, Hollister and a "Dutchman" conspired to escape, and the latter insisted on the attempt being made in March. Hollister's toes froze badly, and his companion eventually collapsed and died, after giving Isaac permission to eat his flesh in that event.

Hollister showed no "survivor guilt" in being the only one saved in the initial attack, but sought to excuse himself while making a full confession of his unwitnessed cannibalism. After recapture, and a deserved gauntlet and recovery, he was sent away to the Seneca. After a few months in the Ohio Valley, he heard that all captives were to be returned. Hollister was stripped, in precise compliance with the terms, and delivered to the commander at what he still called Fort Duquesne. Thin and weak, he spent more than a year recovering there and in Philadelphia before coming home to his remaining family in Newborough, Connecticut. Away three and a half years, Hollister concluded his account by thanking "those gentlemen and ladies who were so generous as to contribute a considerable sum of money on my behalf." Here was a stirring, truthful account of suffering, cannibalism, and survival, seemingly safe in the past by the time Hollister returned home in 1767. Thomas Green could print it for bookseller Knight Sexton in Hartford, and it was printed by "the printing office" in New London, but it did not attract a publisher in Pennsylvania or elsewhere for the next thirty-six years.[94]

Although the inspiring story of Regina Leininger was published in Saxony in 1769,[95] it was one of only two emphatically Christian accounts of Allegheny captivity and return that entered Pennsylvania folklore during this period. Ten-year-old Regina, with her sister Barbara, had been among the Penn Creek captives of 1755, and she was returned to Bouquet's army nine years later. Although then impossible to recognize, she was dramatically reunited with her mother at Carlisle by recognizing the singing of a hymn. Less than two months later Regina and her mother traveled more than sixty miles to visit Lutheran missionary Rev. Henry Melchior Muhlenberg, purportedly in search of a Bible and hymnal. Muhlenberg did much more than give Regina a Bible and money for a hymnal. Like other ministers before and after him, Muhlenberg immediately took command of her moving story of captivity, faith, and redemption. He routinely kept a detailed journal intended to be transcribed and periodically sent back to the evangelical Lutheran mission center at Halle, in Saxony, where inspiring accounts were published in a series called *Hallische Nachrichten*. These, like the *Jesuit Relations*, were intended to raise spirits, donations, and recruits. Regina Leininger's story was entered, and appropriated, in Muhlenberg's journal.

Although he was son-in-law of Conrad Weiser, Muhlenberg had previously shown limited interest in frontier captives. His journal occasionally noted the depredations of Pontiac's War, he once raised money for German Lutheran refugees from the frontier, and he had given religious instruction to a couple of former captives.[96] Things changed with the visit of the Leiningers on 27 February 1765, when Muhlenberg recorded three related vignettes from his visitors, each a potentially publishable item for *Hallische Nachrichten*. The first was a predictable meditation on those captives who preferred to stay with the Indians. If less caustic than the Anglican William Smith on this subject, Muhlenberg was sure that this preference for barbarity reflected the fallen nature of men who would "rather live for themselves and their sinful passions than for Him who died and rose again for them." The second item was a rhapsodic account of how Bouquet and his soldiers gave their own spare clothes, and cut and altered what they were wearing, to cover those captives who had been returned naked. Muhlenberg presented this frenzied generosity as the exemplary practice of Christian religion.[97]

Regina Leininger's story was Muhlenberg's third, and best, morality story of that day. Taken in the 1755 attack in which her father and brother were killed, Regina and her older sister, Barbara, had soon been separated. Regina had somehow managed to carry a captured two-year-old girl on her back for much of the march into captivity, before both were adopted by an old Delaware woman, and Regina became the provider for all three of them for most of the ensuing nine years. Muhlenberg reported that prayers, hymns, and remembered bits of the Bible were "her chief delight" in the face of all this hardship. Upon her release, Regina was brought to Carlisle, and neither she nor her widowed mother recognized each other. Her mother eventually sang a hymn that Regina recognized, and the two embraced and went home together, along with the younger captive girl who had been cared for by Regina throughout their captivity, and had been unclaimed at Carlisle. When Muhlenberg gave Regina a Bible on her visit, she opened it and, in accordance with the divine intervention often associated with the resulting choice of text, immediately read an account of Tobit: "though a captive among strangers, yet he did not fall away from God's Word."[98] She was apparently as able to read German as when she went into captivity at the age of ten. Although Regina's religion had been conveyed to her entirely by her pious parents, Muhlenberg attempted to use her story to praise Christian schools as "necessary, profitable, and good" for instilling such piety. As printed at Halle, the account did not include a discussion of those who preferred to remain Indians, and the story of brave and kindly Colonel Bouquet was shortened, but four verses of the hymn that united mother and daughter were added. Even though Regina could still read and understand German, she may never have known how much Muhlenberg had filtered and bent her story as it appeared in *Hallische Nachrichten* in 1769, and neither can we.[99]

A similar Allegheny captivity story emerged in the same period, though it may have been folklore for nearly a century before being recorded. Young sisters Frances and Susannah Barnett were captured by the Shawnee on the Virginia frontier in 1756. The older one, Fanny, adapted well to her new life, married a Shawnee, and raised two children. Susannah, only six when captured, reportedly remained entirely unreconciled to Shawnee life through twelve years of captivity. In 1768 she was suddenly inspired to walk to Fort Pitt, aided by the timely appearance and generosity of a kindly old Indian couple. On arrival she "was then among her own people, who gave her clothes and dressed her like other white women, and assisted her so that she arrived safely at home. Shortly after her arrival, she presented a Christian experience to a Regular Baptist Church, was received and baptized." She married and, in 1775, welcomed her sister Fanny, who had just been surrendered by the Shawnee. Fanny "stayed a few days, but not being reconciled to stay, Cummins took her back to Fort Pitt, and she went off with the Indians." As eventually transmitted to frontier historian-archivist Lyman C. Draper, Susannah's return was a miracle, confirming a Baptist belief in predestination.[100] Such oral reports of Allegheny exile and redemption were irresistible to preachers, and they were the only obvious local users of these stories between 1765 and 1784.

After the American Revolution, there was a perceptible increase in American interest in Allegheny-Ohio country, and in real and imagined captivities there. The new republic's government was fighting a unifying war for this "first American west," and for the fiscal benefit of federally controlled lands. Regional differences, especially concerning slavery, could be overcome, and a national identity could be fostered, by a focus on freedom and a "manifest destiny" in the virgin lands of the west. New captive heroes came out of the War of Independence, anthologies of captivity narratives became popular literature, a new genre of novels took up these themes, and patriotic American historians and folklorists discovered this usable past. Those memoirs and family histories of colonial Allegheny captives that first appeared after 1783 were affected both by reaching back further and by looking forward to the promises of this new west.

The iconic American frontier hero was discovered, and invented, in the supposed autobiography of Colonel Daniel Boone, appearing as a fifty-three-page appendix to surveyor and land speculator John Filson's *The Discovery, Settlement, and Present State of Kentucke ...*, a promotional tract first printed in 1784, and promptly reprinted and translated. Boone, who was Filson's guide, had been a fellow native of Pennsylvania and a persistent "long-hunter" in Kentucky, where he was twice taken captive by the Shawnee during the War for Independence, and twice escaped. Aggressive in confiscating, settling, and fortifying Indian land, Boone is made to insist that the white invaders were innocent defenders of their own country, and that Indians were savage and dangerous wild animals. The builder of Boonesborough could even be surprised that the Shawnee "seemed determined to persecute us for erecting this fortification." Through the efforts of Boone the conqueror and avenger, Kentucky was supposedly transformed: "where the hand of violence shed the blood of the innocent; where the horrid yells of savages, and the groans of the distressed, sounded in our ears, we now hear the praises and adoration of our Creator."[101] The idealized self-reliant frontier hunter was well versed in Indian ways, but, in hot pursuit or pitched battle, he zealously and mercilessly fought to save captured maidens, defend peaceable farmers, and convert a savage land to a uniquely American civilization. The Boone myth gave a new purpose to western adventure, in captivity narratives, novels, and histories.

How would the rapidly propagated Boone myth influence the accounts of those eight Allegheny captives taken between 1745 and 1765 whose memoirs were first published after 1784? Captain Isaac Stewart's mistitled fabrication *A True and Faithful Narrative of the Surprizing Captivity and Remarkable Deliverance* ..., printed in 1786, was unique. Stewart's exhausting title, about 7 per cent of the entire pamphlet, claimed he was captured fifty miles west of Fort Pitt in 1764 "in Company with a great Number of others, who were all inhumanly and barbarously massacred and burnt alive by those cruel and blood-thirsty Savages." This exclamation of outrage was followed by a text in which he said only that he had been "carried away by them to the Wabash [River], with many more White Men, who were executed with circumstances of horrid Barbarity." Perhaps nothing more needed to be said in an account published in the year that Colonel William Crawford was defeated, captured, and burned in Ohio country. Stewart claimed he had been saved by "what is called the Good Woman of the Town," who ransomed him for a horse.[102] Stewart did not identify his captors or write anything about his "two Years in Bondage amongst the Indians" before he was easily redeemed, together with a Welshman named John Davey, by an unnamed Spaniard. The captivity merely opened Stewart's improbable little tale, published at a safe distance in time and space, in the captivity narrative capital of Boston, where it was included as a tailpiece to the much more substantial narrative of Frances Scott, taken on the Virginia frontier in 1785.[103] Perhaps because he was supposedly a captain, Stewart's tale would be reprinted much more often than it could possibly deserve, by those anxious to assemble nineteenth-century anthologies that denounced Indians or urged venturers to populate the lands west of the Mississippi that the new United States had formally ceded to the Spanish in 1783.[104]

One of the richest, most nuanced, and eventually most popular memoirs of colonial Allegheny captivity was *An Account of the Remarkable Occurrences in the Life and Travels of Colonel James Smith during His Captivity with the Indians, 1755–1759* (Lexington, KY, 1799). Whether this was written soon after Smith's return in 1759, or later with the aid of journals, his stirring and informative captivity account had the advantage of usually being precise in testable details and accurate in its grasp of the major events of that now-distant war. Smith had become a proud "Indian fighter" and "the Paxtoneers' fellow traveller"[105] who explained Indian methods of warfare in detail so that knowledge of these could be used to attack Indians and defend against them. His patriotic American account mythologized the colonial rifleman, and included one very dubious and unconfirmed story of Indians burning many soldier-captives within sight of Fort Duquesne on the day of Braddock's defeat.[106]

Why was Smith not the frontier icon, instead of Boone? Smith had preceded Boone by twenty years and had exceeded him in contributing to the revolutionary movement. He had also been with his captors much longer than had Boone, and was more religious and reflective in recounting his distant experiences. Smith could sound like a backwoods Montesquieu or Rousseau when describing the religious and social arrangements of the Kahnawake, Ottawa, and Wyandots with whom he had lived. Although a Presbyterian missionary by 1799, he still admired that Indians "have neither church or state erected as money-making machines." Indians were quoted as sources of wisdom that whites sorely lacked. He even confessed to aborting an excellent chance to escape captivity in order to bring meat to starving Indian companions for whom he felt responsible. He also offered an aside that made no friends in Lexington: he frankly denounced the Gnadenhütten massacre of 1782 as "an act of barbarity beyond any thing I ever knew to be committed by the savages themselves."[107] Smith paid for the publication of his ambivalent account, which "was little thought of in the log cabin town of Lexington, apparently did not sell rapidly or well, and as a result the cost of its printing became a great and unbearable burden to the author."[108] His book would eventually sell better on both sides of the Appalachian Mountains; it was anthologized during his lifetime, and would be repeatedly serialized and abridged, in addition to appearing in six full editions in the subsequent century.[109] It was in Lexington, in 1821, that Samuel L. Metcalf published *A Collection of Some of the Most Interesting Narratives of Indian Wars in the West*, which began with the Boone narrative, included a number of later western war stories, and ended with a 108-page reprint of Smith's entire account. By 1832, another author could assume that the accounts of Smith and Boone "are found upon the shelves of almost every Bookseller in the West."[110]

Yet Smith never rivaled Boone as an icon. One can only guess what difference it might have made if Smith's account had found an encouraging publisher in 1760 rather than a cautious one forty years later. In the interim, Smith had been a self-righteous vigilante against Indians, Indian traders, and the British Army, and had been part of the 1774 campaign against the Shawnee, as well as fighting in the Revolution and spending years of political prominence in Kentucky. Although a prototype for the Boone legend, Smith never rescued a captured maiden, and "Injun Jimmie" may have become too *métis* to be the avenging white "pioneer" of the first American west.[111]

Nonetheless, more than Boone, Smith became standard fare in serving a significant new market for anthologies of captivity accounts. The first of these, *Affecting History of the Dreadful Distresses of Frederic Manheim's Family* ..., was published in Exeter, New Hampshire, in 1793, and, though composed primarily of Pennsylvania captivity accounts of the revolutionary period, included the Allegheny captivity fantasies of Peter Williamson and Isaac Stewart set in the Seven Years' War. The stated purpose of the Manheim anthology was to advertise the "dreadful cruelties" of Indians. This anthology went through five more editions in the next seven years, including printings in Boston; in Leominster, Massachusetts; in New York; and two printings in Philadelphia, in 1794 and 1800, for prominent publisher Mathew Carey.[112] Evidently captivity narratives had finally come to sell well in Philadelphia.

Archibald Loudon, an enterprising Carlisle printer, drew several elders into publishing their memoirs of early Allegheny captivity for the first time in his *A Selection of Some of the Most Interesting Narratives of Outrages Committed by the Indians in Their Wars with the White People*, the first volume of which appeared in 1808. Loudon was not at all bashful about his purpose, which was to show that the Indians were not primitive innocents of "Jean Jacques Rousseau's, and other rhapsodies," but were "even worse than the most ferocious wolf or panther of the forest."[113]

Loudon's first volume was dominated by predictable reprints, including Peter Williamson, Isaac Stewart, and James Smith, but it also included the previously unpublished narratives of John Slover and John McCullough. "The Narrative of John Slover" was primarily about his later capture and escape in the wake of the defeat of William Crawford's ill-fated 1782 Virginian expedition against Indians in the Sandusky region. Slover interrupts his main story for a one-paragraph flashback to his earlier life as a white Indian. He had finally ended captivity when he met white relatives at Fort Pitt in 1774 (he thought it had been 1773), who urged him to return, "which I did with some reluctance, this manner of life having become natural to me, inasmuch as I had scarcely known any other."[114] Upon his return Slover soon proved his conversion by becoming a soldier, and then a scout, but a generation later he was still defending his choice to return in 1774, he was still fighting ferocious Indians, and he was excoriating the Indian Girty brothers, who were white Indians like himself.[115] Slover was less able than James Smith to put some distance between his vigilante phase and his account of earlier adventure.

By 1808 John McCullough had returned from captivity to live more than forty years on the family farm in the Conococheague Valley in Cumberland County, a place by then far from the bleeding borderlands. He vividly remembered his boyhood capture as an adventure in which he saw few people killed, was frightened by rituals that proved harmless, and was subjected to cold and privation supposedly "to make me hardy." He recounted being cared for in sickness and being sheltered by a Delaware woman who lied to save him from the consequences of his part in a fatal shooting, and who also later saved him from drowning.[116] He explained the purification message preached by the Delaware prophet Neolin, and also explained some Delaware habits and customs, both in his account and in a separate appendix. John had forgotten his English in captivity, except for his name and where he was captured, and was later bemused by what had been his own resistance to his father's efforts to redeem him, and by his forced return to Bouquet's army. He was grateful to "Providence," he said in conclusion, that the Indians captured him when a scalp would have done, carried him when they were slowed by doing so and in danger from pursuers, nursed him when he was ill, and saved him from drowning. Lest this sounded too much like praising God for the virtues of the Delaware, he balanced this cleverly by adding that he was also grateful to Providence for his escape from his father's attempt to rescue him in 1764, for that would have put him in Mr Enoch Brown's school to be "murdered" there, like his cousins, by the Indians he had come to know so well.

McCullough had recovered or acquired good English skills after the age of sixteen, later styled himself an esquire, and rather pretentiously added to his account a deliberately ethnographic "few observations on the manner and customs of the ABORIGENES of our country," perhaps in fashionable imitation of French travel accounts or the memoirs of James Smith, published a decade earlier and reprinted by Loudon in the same volume as McCullough's memoir.[117] McCullough recounted the Delaware's traditional belief in the soul and the hereafter, and told of their rituals in quest of good crops and hunts, just as a zealous French Jesuit missionary would have done earlier for more obvious purposes. He went on to what he declared were more interesting subjects. Delaware isolation of women before childbirth, and their ritual cleansing afterward, puzzled him: "How they became so far acquainted with the Mosaic law, as treats of uncleanness, is a mystery to me!" Indian warfare was supposedly a major topic, but McCullough had not been to war as a Delaware, and he confined himself entirely to what he had seen, namely the rituals of assembling and launching a war party and then of marking the party's return, including the adoption, ransom, or burning of prisoners. His remarks were about Indians in general, as was too common, as though all had the same customs as the Delaware he knew.[118] John McCullough's self-deprecating and generous memoir was possible from a confident older man who identified captivity rather fondly with his youth, who had lived a peaceable life in the interim, and who was touched by the sentimentality and romanticism that editor Loudon claimed he was attempting to counter but chose not to suppress in this instance.

Loudon had promised a second volume from all the accounts that he had gathered, if public interest warranted, and this second substantial volume appeared three years later. Robert Eastburn's *A Faithful Narrative* was reprinted here in its entirety, and there were numerous short second-hand accounts of events in the Allegheny borderlands in the Seven Years' War and the Revolution. The exploits of Hugh McSwain, John Armstrong, and David Owens were remembered, and an array of captivities and slaughters sketched. Archibald Bard's reconstruction of his parents' captivity appeared here, as did two first-person memoirs from the Seven Years' War that were published for the first time. Robert Robison (Robinson) provided a fragmented narrative that mixed tales he had heard with things he had seen, including none-too-flattering remembrances of being in the Kittanning raid. Hugh Gibson recounted being captured at fourteen in 1756 by the Delaware and, after initial abuse, being adopted. He had seen the Kittanning raid, which he regarded as a failure, and witnessed the resulting torture of Mrs Alexander McAllister. Gibson remembered becoming a "tolerably good hunter" and had eventually escaped with gun and horse after more than five years of captivity. Gibson noted that the Delaware had many sensible rules among themselves and a "tolerable good idea of the Supreme Being."

Gibson's brief account, written at age sixty-seven concerning what happened in his teens, was not his last word on the subject. In 1826, at age eighty-five, he was interviewed by Timothy Alden, linguist, college president, missionary, antiquary, and frontier enthusiast.[119] Gibson's story was enlarged, his parentage was described, and his capture was followed by a full account of his adoption into the Ohio Delaware "royal family." Gibson's view of the Kittanning raid, from the perspective of a captive held there, was unchanged, but the horror of Mrs McAllister's torture had been moderated from the work of "ruthless barbarians" and "hellish fiends" to the "tender mercies of the poor unenlightened savages."[120] In his last interview Gibson emphasized the Delaware concern that he might flee, and recounted an escape that was aborted by his fainthearted partner. He also mentioned that his refusal of a Delaware marriage had irritated his master, and that circumstance may have prompted him to consider the escape he now described more fully. He happened to meet fellow captives David Brackenridge, Barbara Leininger, and Marie Le Roy near the headwaters of the Muskingum. The escape of the four was sketched in less detail than in *Erzehlungen von Marie Le Roy und Barbara Leininger*, but was in conformity with that account. Whether prompted by a question from interviewer Alden or not, the account ended with the strong assurance "that Mr. Gibson had no inclination to spend his days with the Indians, although in general, with a few painful exceptions, he was treated kindly by them."[121] Alden wrote up the interview and read it back to Gibson, who reportedly approved it. Perhaps Gibson was more comfortable speaking rather than writing and perhaps his interviewer helped him remember things he had not thought of when writing his earlier account. Certainly much had changed in the fifteen intervening years, encouraging him to temper both fear and rage, and to remember the better attributes of what were thought to be the disappearing Indians. Hugh Gibson's last description of his captivity and escape was published posthumously. It was fuller than his first account, more accurate, and more generous. Nonetheless, it was not destined to attract much of an audience.

If most memoirs of former captives shared a comfortable assumption about the progress that had followed white conquest, there was one truly remarkable exception that challenged them all. *A Narrative of the Life of Mrs. Mary Jemison* (Canandaigua, NY, 1824), by James Everett Seaver, reached bestseller status soon after publication. Printer and bookseller James D. Bemis decided to print something of the unusual life of a remarkable elderly Seneca woman, "the white woman of the Genesee." Bemis arranged for James Everett Seaver, a local teacher and writer of verse, to interview Mary Jemison. The result cannot be regarded as a first-person narrative, but Seaver's stirring "as-told-to" biography was written in the form of an autobiography, rather like Filson's account of Boone. Seaver interviewed Mary Jemison for three days in English, a language Mary could not read, had tried to maintain, but had not spoken much in over sixty-five years.[122] Seaver wrote the account of Mary's long, arduous, and simple life as a Seneca as though it were in her words, including the supposedly verbatim recollection of substantial speeches, like that delivered at her adoption, in the Seneca language Mary did not then know. Seaver had Mary use phrases like "completely elude the sagacity of their pursuers," and had her offer romantic hymns of praise for "uncontaminated" Indian life threatened with "extermination."[123] The whole chapter on her second husband, Hiokatoo (1708?–1811), an acceptable husband but a ferocious enemy of the whites, was based entirely upon Seaver's interview with a "cousin," George Jemison, and was added to satisfy white stereotypes, and perhaps to ease white consciences.[124]

Historians can be frustrated by Seaver's "egregious" interference, and by his "gall to alter, ornament, and otherwise dress up poor Mrs. Jemison's interview."[125] Although the title page says that the book was "Carefully taken from her own words," Seaver called himself the author of what his preface called "a piece of biography." Readers are given the text as though Mary is speaking, but her words are often hard to distinguish from his. We cannot even be sure that Seaver challenged Mary, as he claimed,[126] on her clear and persisting error of dating her captivity in the spring of 1755, when she was twelve and the war had not begun in Pennsylvania, instead of the spring of 1758, when she was fifteen and a ferocious war had finally come to her neighborhood on Marsh Creek in York County. The conflation of the 1759 siege of Niagara and the slaughter at Devil's Hole in 1763 was more understandable in either the speaker or the interviewer of 1823.[127] It is hard to be sure that, after twenty-five years with the Seneca, she could still have been offered her "liberty," as though she were still a captive.[128] It is surely Jemison, rather than Seaver, who proclaimed her love for her first husband, showed a strong dislike for the Shawnee, and dreaded the impact of alcohol on Indians.[129] But was it Seaver who thought so well of William Crawford "and his brave band," who thought that colonel "a patriot and hero," and who denounced Simon Girty as a callous "traitor," all conforming to the contrived tales that Hugh M. Brackenridge had propagated in the 1790s?[130] The grandiloquent words of the conclusion are certainly Seaver's, and we cannot be sure which of them was worried about "reduction from a civilized to a savage state," or about "the nauseous dregs of the bitter cup of slavery." Mary had compelling personal reasons to denounce liquor, tobacco, and Indian men's drunken "frolics," which had cost her two sons.[131]

Seaver caught and reinforced an enduring countertrend of sentimental regard and respect for the "vanishing Indian" then current in captivity accounts and novels. This was the only Allegheny captivity narrative from the mid-eighteenth century that "explicitly valorize[d] the transculturation of captives."[132] The enthusiastic remembrance of Mary Jemison herself would eventually include the reverent transfer of her remains and dedication of a life-size statue in Letchworth Park, New York State (see illustration 8).[133] Other families had saved and nurtured recollections like those of Beatrice Byerly, who had been warned by a "good Indian" of an impending attack, and those of Mary Means and her mother, who had been freed by a friendly Delaware whose kindness was eventually repaid.[134] Thomas Jefferson published Mingo chief James Logan's famous speech in 1774, and the "pathetic eloquence" of Indian orators became a stock item in the rhetoric textbooks of the early republic.[135] From the 1790s, Ann Eliga Bleecker and Susannah Haswell Rowson were writing popular captivity romances, whereas Charles Brockden Brown offered more gothic tales of captivity.[136] Seaver's Mary Jemison narrative sold more than 100,000 copies in 1824 alone, competing well with two related novels of that year, James Fenimore Cooper's *The Last of the Mohicans* and Lydia Maria Child's *Hobomok*.[137] Although Child portrayed marriage between a white woman and an Indian sympathetically for the first time in American fiction, Jemison's life described it in fact.[138] Bemis printed copies before and after Seaver had obtained official copyright, but Bemis soon was challenged by

8 Statue of Mary Jemison at Letchworth Park, New York State, 1910. Mary Jemison, *A Narrative of the Life of Mary Jemison*, ed. C.D. Vail (New York: American Scenic and Historic Preservation Society, 1942), frontispiece.

printings in several New York State towns and particularly in New York City and in England. The Jemison narrative has been through more than thirty editions since, and has never been out of print for long. Although it is impossible to tell how much of the account is Jemison's, it has considerable value for historians and anthropologists studying the Seneca or woodland Indian women, and its wide readership has lasted long enough to secure its place in the afterlife that is the academic study of long-popular American literature.

Jemison and Gibson were the last surviving colonial Allegheny captives known to have told, or retold, a memoir that was promptly printed. Only three substantial original accounts, those of Charles Stuart, Thomas Gist, and John Rutherfurd, have been published subsequently – and these more than a century and a half after the events.[139] There were a number of posthumous family remembrances, fascinating stories have been gathered by local historians and folklorists,[140] and novelists and filmmakers have continued to draw on the power of frontier captivity themes.[141]

Printed accounts of colonial Allegheny captivity have served numerous purposes, and will continue to do so. Those few published during the colonial wars were directly or indirectly used to support Pennsylvania's war effort, though the only genuinely popular one was the Flemings' pamphlet, demonstrating the wisdom of passive accommodation and nonviolent escape by the innocent. The Flemings' accounts served, in English and German, a Pennsylvania that effectively died that year. It was the silencing of captives, rather than what they wrote, that served the war effort and initially preserved the myth of a great victory at Kittanning. The new Pennsylvania created by the war rejected Quaker leadership, and drew together Scots-Irish, Germans, Lutherans, Presbyterians, and Anglicans. It is hard to regard captivity accounts as contributing much to the emergence of this new identity. The captivity narrative of Marie Le Roy and Barbara Leininger was printed in both English and German, but it was not widely read in either language. The deliberate Christian uses of captivity were few, marginal, and sectarian. Christian themes of captivity and redemption were implied rather than celebrated in most accounts, and the most explicit were never popular. Revolutionary Pennsylvania's apparent lack of interest in its citizens' earlier captivities may have been caused by the untimeliness of anti-French and pro-British sentiments, or it may have been no more than a continuation of a regional aversion to the genre. In the 1790s, when captivity narratives came to be popular in Pennsylvania, they were confirming changes already accomplished, and sharing in a broader cultural reconstruction.

There is no evidence that Allegheny captivity accounts helped build an American revolutionary identity before the War of Independence ended. It is tempting to regard captivity narratives as indications of continuing support of an American regard for liberty as more precious than life, but the narratives were also about those who chose captivity over death, and displayed varying levels of transculturation. A growing regional market for anthologies of captivity narratives, and novels about captivity, had developed in the mid-Atlantic states from the 1790s. Although these were deliberately crafted to denigrate Indians and justify the unjustified confiscation of their country, it is equally true that the later accounts reflected increasing ambiguity about the values of the new republic. This was particularly the case with the most enduringly popular accounts of James Smith and Mary Jemison. By the time the last surviving captives of the earlier Allegheny war offered their oral and written memoirs, the romance of the disappearing Indian had become popular. If the captivity narrative had always allowed "audiences to indulge in that which they simultaneously disavow,"[142] the immense and enduring popularity of Mary Jemison's story was a safe victory for the captivity narrative as a criticism of the expanding white empire from which she had been snatched in 1758. In general, however, claims of a large and sustained audience for captivity accounts, suggested for a host of obvious or ingenious reasons, must be regarded as inapplicable to Philadelphia and its literary hinterlands before 1840.

CONCLUSION

The repeopling of the upper Ohio region was a multicultural scramble to fill a partial vacuum rather than extend any clear frontiers or negotiate a middle ground. Shawnee, Delaware, and Mingo communities on the upper Ohio River were created by seasoned refugees from white intrusion who were rebuilding identities while trading with the societies they resisted. They helped create and display their solidarity by endemic long-distance raids to the south for Cherokee and Catawba scalps and captives. Collisions with British colonials along the way were predictable, but infrequent, and white captives were very seldom taken. These venturing Indians clearly abhorred being taken captive themselves, and South Carolina's imprisonment of six Shawnee allies in peacetime caused outrage that provoked a Shawnee war with the "Long Knives" that lasted, intermittently, for sixty years. Canadian fort commanders in the region took white captives in peacetime, arresting rival Pennsylvania traders and sending them to jail in Quebec and France. Despite clear and substantial inducements, Ohio Indians were very reluctant to assist the French in what proved an effective assertion of trade monopoly.

As Anglo-French rivalry escalated into open military conflict, Canadian officers treated captured British colonial soldiers very differently than captured traders. When Virginians, Canadians, and Indians clashed in famous little peacetime parodies of European sieges and surrenders, contending views of war and captivity brought confusion. Some belligerents granted parole, some took prisoners or hostages in an undeclared war, and others killed those who had just been granted quarter by others. English- and French-speaking colonials, who had enjoyed rather peaceable relations with Native Americans in this region, pushed trade rivalry and land hunger far enough to draw transatlantic imperial intervention. Overreaching Atlantic empires collided with each other, and with Native Americans, all the way to the Muskingum

River; the British and the Indians both seemed to win briefly before they would both lose.

Taking captives, and choosing captivity rather than fighting to the death, were major ameliorations in wars that were not total in Allegheny country. At least 2,873 people who might have been killed were not. In the Seven Years' War, European and colonial troops took and exchanged prisoners according to their established conventions, but very seldom took Indian prisoners. Indians, engaged in their own wars or fighting in alliance with the French, took Indian and white captives to demonstrate individual martial prowess and, in Allegheny country, to add new members to their communities. Preoccupation with taking captives shaped Indian strategy and tactics in ways not appreciated by their allies, by their enemies, or by most historians. The number of captives taken could indicate the geography of a particular fight, the margin of victory, the anticipation of a second strike, and/or the logistics of the trek home. Contrary to accepted wisdom, the colonial garrison houses clearly justified their existence if survival of those they protected was their primary purpose. The chance of being captured rather than killed was much better in sieges of these fortified houses and mills than in surprise raids on farmhouses, and the odds of survival were much better in these raids than in open battles. Military historians of colonial North America, and the archives and indexes that serve them, might profitably pay more attention to captives and prisoners of war, rather than reflecting the view of authorities at the time, namely that captivity among the Indians was a form of surrender and a marginal and embarrassing subspecies of cowardice or desertion.

The Anglo-Indian War of 1763–65 was fought without significant French or Canadian assistance or influence, and featured both a new ferocity towards British colonial traders and a surprising new willingness to capture soldiers. Despite an increased rate of Indian losses crying for vengeance and a growing number of white captives already in their settlements, Ohio Indians sustained their preoccupation with taking captives throughout this war. Perhaps white preoccupation with recovering captives, which had led to profitable exchanges of gifts as well as embarrassing compromises, had ultimately served to reinforce Indian martial values. Even when "hot pursuit" became routine, Indian captors continued to take numerous captives and were usually reluctant to kill them even when counterattacked. Although the Delaware prophet Neolin was advocating the separation of Indians from whites, he also approved the humane treatment of captives. Whether they were following him or not, the Indian warriors fighting between 1763 and 1765 were somewhat more likely to take soldiers and settlers captive, rather than kill them, than was the case at any time between 1745 and 1762.

The willingness to go as a captive, rather than fight to the death or resist enough to provoke execution, had not changed much despite official efforts to make surrender sound horrid, painful, and fatal. Soldiers were more likely to go as captives in Pontiac's War than previously, and adult male settlers chose captivity over death as often as earlier. The increase in the number of women and teenage boys who were killed as opposed to being captured was the only significant change. The proportion of victims who became captives changed little, suggesting that, for captors and captives, the lines of cultural or racial difference were not hardening as much as a few notorious incidents might indicate.

Despite the alluring propaganda of the time, and the continuing interest in narratives by and about women captives, these wars were primarily between men. Although more than 2,525 soldiers, warriors, traders, and farmers were killed, 1,128 of them were captured. Capturing men did not bring the same opportunity to enlarge a community as capturing women of childbearing age, and adult male captives were more burdensome because they did not usually grow food in Indian societies, as women captives readily did. Adopting more hunters did not increase the supply of game. Yet women constituted fewer than one in five of the adults captured, though they were favored in being as likely to be captured as killed. One-third of the captives were children, and those between seven and fifteen were twice as likely to be captured as killed. Those captured were evidently not chosen because of some obvious social engineering by Indian captors.

Indian communities confidently incorporated captives quite effectively, though the success has been exaggerated. Captives had been traumatized by the initial attack, the death of people they knew, and the continuing terror and fears of the trail into captivity. Very few risked death to escape to their natal culture, and most gradually came to accept their new life with Indians. Time was needed to learn the required language, manners, and skills, and the transformation was incomplete for many of those who spent two years or less in captivity. Those captured under the age of six were most likely to become white Indians for life, and those taken between the ages of seven and fifteen were potential brokers, with some knowledge of both cultures and known kin on both sides. All captives held any length of time carried permanent signs of their adjustment to their captors' societies. The majority of captives returned, and, equally significant, the majority of the returned came back by the efforts of others. Most of the returned who had not escaped quickly would remain under some suspicion concerning their cultural loyalty for the rest of their lives.

The return of captives was a unifying priority in what was the first war to come to Quaker Pennsylvania, whereas recovering captives was of surprisingly little interest to Virginia authorities. The efforts to recover captives were led by unusual heroes. Quakers were central to the earliest negotiations, and promptly gained a truce with Teedyuscung, but they did so while supporting a peace that threatened to exchange white captives for some land previously lost by the Indians. Quakers were brushed aside by the British Army's deputy superintendent of Indian affairs, George Croghan, a rascally and self-serving bankrupt who became central to the return of more than 700 captives. General Jeffrey Amherst, who disliked Indians and abhorred ransom, approved payment for the presents that became the equivalent of ransom in Croghan's schemes. Amherst has never been credited with this reluctant generosity, but has routinely been denounced for provoking a new war when budget cuts brought him to stop most of these presents. By 1764 military commanders were finally convinced that Indian acceptance of a truce could be monitored only by their willingness to return captives.

Serious compromises were made on both sides. A British Army that put no priority on recovering civilian captives, and despised ransom, came to insist upon the first and pay for both. It even mounted a major expedition to intimidate Indians into eventually surrendering 278 more captives. Colonials who knew that all the captives had not been returned, and saw the welcome return of captives as very inadequate revenge for all the killing and destruction of the wars, were made to accept a bloodless resolution. Shawnee, Delaware, and Mingo were not conquered by Colonel Henry Bouquet's expedition of 1764, but they were forced to return captives without compensation, and before peace was made, something they had regarded as preposterous a few years earlier. This compromise may have been eased somewhat by the spread of Neolin's teaching on the separation of Indians and whites, but the forced return of captives also left resentments that soon resurfaced. Although a detailed study has not been made, it has been reported that Indians, and especially the Shawnee, were less likely to take and adopt white captives during the American Revolution.

The Muskingum campaign had forcibly ended the acculturation of some of those recently taken, and had confiscated many long-held captives who did not want to return and were effectively being captured a second time. Returning bicultural captives could, at a personal level, encourage peace and understanding between settlers and Indians who were their kin, and Pennsylvania's previous history had made it a good place for such an experiment. However, Pennsylvania's emerging post-war political society was not interested in this approach. The belligerent quest for revenge and land was powerful and enduring in the Pennsylvania and Virginia backcountry. Some returnees, like Simon Girty and his brothers, became agents for the settlers before eventually "deserting" to fight on behalf of the Indians and British in the American Revolution. Very few, like trader-captive John Gibson and Indian fighter and author James Smith, would overcome suspicion and become prominent in the subsequent American invasion of Ohio country. Most returned captives went back to the edges of what became revolutionary America.

For captives, telling their story was part of coming back, but only a few Allegheny captivity narratives were ever published. Wartime political or military censorship favored a few accounts, distorted others, and prevented the publication of some. Surprisingly few narratives were published in Pennsylvania in the generation after 1765, especially compared to New England, where the reprinted captivity narratives were popular and helped build a white nativist identity on the eve of the American Revolution. It was only in the 1790s that anthologies of captivity narratives, fictitious as well as genuine, began to appear in Pennsylvania. These narratives were chosen to vilify Indians for a generation that was rapidly confiscating Indian lands and confining Indians to captivities of their own on reservations farther west. The extraordinary memoirs of James Smith and Mary Jemison, which were sympathetic to the "vanishing Indian," became popular only in the 1820s, as the last of the early captives died. Captives were not writers, but their stories became iconic in American literature because they could be made to serve nativist solidarity despite their cultural ambiguity, and they have remained fashionable as exemplars of a peculiarly American preoccupation with personal freedom.

TABLES

TABLE 1 VICTIMS OF ALLEGHENY CONFLICT, BY STATUS, 1745–54

	Traders *N (%)*	*Soldiers* *N (%)*	*Settlers*[a] *N (%)*	*Indians* *N (%)*	*Total* *N (%)*
Known killed[b]	24 (33)	56 (52)	36 (63)	22 (46)	138 (50)
Known captured	40 (56)	34 (38)	8 (14)	26 (54)	108 (39)
Missing	8 (11)	11 (10)	13 (23)	0	32 (11)
Total (%)	*72 (26)*	*101 (36)*	*57 (21)*	*48 (17)*	*278 (100)*
Ratio of killed to captured or missing	1:2	1.2:1	1.7:1	1:1.2	1:1

a Including servants and slaves.
b Killed at capture or within five days.

Source: SPSS database.

TABLE 2 VICTIMS OF ALLEGHENY WARFARE, BY STATUS, 1755–62

	Traders *N (%)*	*Soldiers* *N (%)*	*Settlers*[a] *N (%)*	*Indians* *N (%)*	*Unknown* *N (%)*	*Total* *N (%)*
Known killed[b]	2 (40)	1,405 (77)	770 (46)	247 (76)	2 (22)	2,426 (63)
Known captured	3 (60)	188 (10)	461 (27)	24 (7)	0	676 (18)
Missing	0	221 (12)	463 (27)	57 (17)	7 (78)	748 (19)
Total (%)	*5 (.001)*	*1,814 (47)*	*1,694 (44)*	*328 (9)*	*9 (.002)*	*3,850 (100)*
Ratio of killed to captured or missing	1:1.5	3.5:1	1:1.2	3:1	–	1.7:1

a Including servants and slaves.
b Killed at capture or within five days.

Source: SPSS database.

TABLE 3 VICTIMS OF PONTIAC'S WAR, BY STATUS, 1763–65

	Traders *N (%)*	*Soldiers* *N (%)*	*Settlers*[a] *N (%)*	*Indians* *N (%)*	*Unknown* *N (%)*	*Total* *N (%)*
Known killed[b]	60 (36)	246 (53)	255 (52)	200 (73)	15 (30)	776 (55)
Known captured	43 (26)	126 (27)	160 (33)	41 (15)[c]	28 (56)	398 (26)
Missing	64 (38)	92 (20)	74 (15)	35 (13)[c]	7 (14)	272 (19)
Total (%)	*167 (12)*	*464 (32)*	*489 (34)*	*276 (19)*	*50 (3)*	*1,446 (100)*
Ratio of killed to captured or missing	1:1.8	1.1:1	1.1:1	2.6:1	–	1.2:1

a Including servants and slaves.
b Killed at capture or within five days.
c Including hostages.

Source: SPSS database.

TABLE 4 VICTIMS OF ALLEGHENY WARFARE, BY STATUS, 1745–65

	Traders *N (%)*	*Soldiers* *N (%)*	*Settlers*[a] *N (%)*	*Indians* *N (%)*	*Unknown* *N (%)*	*Total* *N (%)*
Known killed[b]	86 (35)	1,707 (72)	1,063 (43)	469 (72)	17 (4)	3,342 (55)
Known captured	86 (35)	355 (15)	810 (33)	91 (14)[c]	362 (92)	1,708 (28)
Missing	72 (30)	324 (13)	577 (24)	93 (14)[c]	15 (4)	1,077 (17)
Total (%)	*244 (4)*	*2,386 (39)*	*2,450 (40)*	*653 (11)*	*394 (6)*	*6,127 (100)*
Ratio of killed to captured or missing	1:1.8	2.5:1	1:1.3	2.5:1	–	1.2:1

a Including servants and slaves.
b Killed at capture or within five days.
c Including hostages.

Source: SPSS database.

ABBREVIATIONS

AN. Archives Nationales, Paris.

ANB. *American National Biography*. Ed. John A. Garraty et al. New York: Oxford University Press, 1999. Online.

BL, Add. Mss. British Library, London, Additional Manuscripts.

DAB. *Dictionary of American Biography*. Ed. Allen Johnson and Dumas Malone. 22 vols. New York: Scribner, 1928–44.

DCB. *Dictionary of Canadian Biography*. Ed. Frances Halpenny et al. 14 vols to date. Toronto: University of Toronto Press, 1966–.

Draper Mss. Draper Manuscripts in the State Historical Society of Wisconsin, Madison, WI.

EAID. *Early American Indian Documents: Treaties and Laws, 1607–1789*. Ed. Alden T. Vaughan. 20 vols. Washington, DC: University Publications of America, 1979–2004.

GWP. *The Papers of George Washington, Colonial Series*. Ed. W.W. Abbot. 10 vols. Charlottesville, VA: University Press of Virginia, 1983–95.

HBP. *The Papers of Henry Bouquet*. Ed. S.K. Stevens et al. 6 vols. Harrisburg, PA: Pennsylvania Historical and Museum Commission, 1951–94.

Historical Statistics of the United States. 2nd ed. 2 vols. Washington, DC: United States Bureau of the Census, 1975.

HL, AB. Huntington Library and Art Gallery, San Marino, CA. Abercromby Papers.

HL, LO. Huntington Library and Art Gallery, San Marino, CA. Loudoun Papers.

HL, MM. Huntington Library and Art Gallery, San Marino, CA. Miscellaneous Manuscripts.

HSP. Historical Society of Pennsylvania, Philadelphia, PA.

JP. *The Papers of Sir William Johnson*. Ed. James Sullivan. 14 vols. Albany, NY: University of the State of New York, 1921–65.

LAC. Library and Archives Canada, Ottawa, formerly National Archives of Canada.

Margry. *Découvertes et établissements de François dans l'ouest et dans le sud de l'Amérique septentrionale, 1614–1754: Mémoires et documents originaux*. Ed. Pierre Margry. 6 vols. Paris, 1876–86.

MPCP. *Minutes of the Provincial Council of Pennsylvania from the Organization to the Termination of Proprietary Government*. Ed. Samuel Hazard. 10 vols. Harrisburg, PA, 1838–53.

MVHR. *Mississippi Valley Historical Review*.

NYCD. *Documents Relative to the Colonial History of the State of New York*. Ed. Edmund B. O'Callaghan and Berthold Fernow. 15 vols. Albany, NY, 1856–87.

NYG. *New York Gazette*.

NYHS. New York Historical Society.

NYM. *New York Mercury*.

ODNB. *Oxford Dictionary of National Biography*. Ed. H.C.G. Mathew and Brian Harrison. 6 vols. Oxford, UK: Oxford University Press, 2004. Online.

PA. *Pennsylvania Archives*. Ed. Samuel Hazard et al. 138 vols. Philadelphia and Harrisburg, PA, 1852–1949.

PG. *Pennsylvania Gazette*.

PH. *Pennsylvania History*.

PJ. *Pennsylvania Journal and Weekly Advertiser*.

PMHB. *Pennsylvania Magazine of History and Biography*.

Preston Papers. Draper Mss, QQ, William Preston Papers. Manuscripts in the State Historical Society of Wisconsin, Madison, WI.

PRDH. Programme de Recherche en Démographie Historique. Online.

PUQAM. Parchemin: Banque de données notariales (1626–1784), Université de Québec à Montréal.

RAPQ. *Rapport de l'Archivistes de la Province de Québec*.

RAR. Royal American Regiment.

RCFFP. *Report of the Commission to Locate the Site of the Frontier Forts of Pennsylvania*. Ed. Thomas L. Montgomery. 2nd ed. 2 vols. Harrisburg, PA: W.S. Ray, 1916.

SCDIA. *Colonial Records of South Carolina: Documents Relating to Indian Affairs*. Ed. William L. McDowell Jr. 2 vols. Columbia, SC: South Carolina Archives Department, 1958–69.

SCG. *South Carolina Gazette*.

TNA. The National Archives, Kew, England, formerly the Public Record Office.

V&P. *Votes and Proceedings of the House of Representatives of the Province of Pennsylvania, PA*. 8th ser. 8 vols. Harrisburg, PA, 1931–35.

VG. *Virginia Gazette*.

VMHB. *Virginia Magazine of History and Biography*.

W&MQ. *William and Mary Quarterly*. Series 3.

WPHM. *Western Pennsylvania Historical Magazine*.

APPENDIX

Named Captives Taken on the Allegheny Frontier, 1745–65: A Tentative List

FIRST NAMES ONLY

Adam. Negro slave of John Trimble. Captured at Middle River, Frederick County, VA, 15 September 1764. RETAKEN by militiamen five days later. Norman L. Baker, *French and Indian War in Frederick County, Virginia* (Winchester, VA: Winchester-Frederick County Historical Society, 2000), 132; Joseph A. Waddell, *Annals of Augusta County, Virginia*, 2 vols (Richmond, VA, 1886–88), vol. 2, 433–8.

Betty. "about 9 Years of Age, dark Complexion, black Eyes, and black Hair" when RETURNED at Muskingum, 15 November 1764. Unclaimed *métis* child? Sister of William. *PG*, 21 February 1765; *WPHM* 39 (1956): 193, 196.

Betty. Taken at Tulpehocan, Berks County, PA, 1757. RETURNED by Munsee Delaware, 10 May 1765. *WPHM* 39 (1956): 198; *JP*, 11: 721.

Bridget's son. RETURNED at Muskingum, 15 November 1764. Sent to northern district of Virginia. A *métis* child? *PG*, 17 January 1765; *WPHM* 39 (1956): 189.

Catherine. "about 9 Years old, fair Complexion, light brown Eyes, and brown Hair" when RETURNED at Muskingum, 15 November 1764. Sent to Pennsylvania. *PG*, 21 February 1765.

Christina. RETURNED at Muskingum, 15 November 1764. Sent to Pennsylvania. *PG*, 17 January 1765; *WPHM* 39 (1956): 192.

Ebenezer. RETURNED at Muskingum, 15 November 1764. Sent to Virginia. *WPHM* 39 (1956): 196.

Esther. Taken near Easton, Northampton County, PA, 1756. "about 18" when RETURNED at Johnson Hall, NY, by Seneca and Susquehanna Delaware, May 1765. *NYG*, 4 July 1765; *NYM*, 19 August 1765; *PG*, 19 September 1765.

George. About thirteen when RETURNED "by a Party of Indians" to Fort Augusta. "says his Name is George, which is all the English he can speak." With Samuel Martin of Paxton country, who advertised for "Whoever knows any Thing of him." *PG*, 24 June 1762.

George. Soldier in Royal American Regiment. Taken at Detroit in May 1763 and still captive in September of that year. MISSING. Henry Gladwin, "The Gladwin Manuscripts: With an Introduction and a Sketch of the Conspiracy of Pontiac," *Michigan Pioneer and Historical Society Collections* 27 (1897): 648.

George. A second soldier in Royal American Regiment identified only by first name. Taken at Detroit in May 1763 and still captive in September of that year. MISSING. Gladwin, "Gladwin Manuscripts," 648.

Hannah. RETURNED at Muskingum, 15 November 1764. Sent to Virginia. *PG*, 17 January 1765; *NYG*, 21 January 1765; *WPHM* 39 (1956): 190.

Hans. RETURNED at Muskingum, 15 November 1764. Sent to Virginia. *WPHM* 39 (1956): 189; *PG*, 17 January 1765; 17 January 1765; *NYG*, 21 January 1765.

Henry. RETURNED at Muskingum, 15 November 1764. Sent to Pennsylvania. *WPHM* 39 (1956): 191; *PG*, 17 January 1765; *NYG*, 21 January 1765.

Irena. RETURNED at Muskingum, 15 November 1764. *PG*, 17 January 1765; *NYG*, 21 January 1765; *WPHM* 39 (1956): 193.

Jacob. About eight years of age. Taken at Greenbrier, Augusta County, VA, 1763. Brother of captive Mekethwa. RETURNED at Muskingum, 15 November 1764. *JP*, 11: 720; *WPHM* 39 (1956): 198.

John/Jacob. Boy taken at Tulpehoken, PA. Seen at Wyalusing, 20 April 1760. MISSING. "Journey on the Forbidden Path: Chronicles of a Diplomatic Mission to the Allegheny Country, March–September 1760," ed. Robert S. Grumet, *Transactions of the American Philosophical Society* 89, part 2 (1999): 49, 117.

Ketty/Kitty/Hetty. Girl of about seven. Taken near Shamokin, PA, 1756. RETURNED by Munsee Delaware at Muskingum, 15 November 1764. *JP*, 11: 720; *PG*, 17 January 65; *WPHM* 39 (1956): 198.

Kitty [Catherine]. Taken in Pennsylvania. RETURNED at Muskingum, 15 November 1764. *PG*, 17 January 1765; *WPHM* 39 (1956): 192 (given leggings, shoe pack, and blanket).

Magdalene/Pagothow. Virginian girl. RETURNED at Muskingum, 15 November 1764. *WPHM* 39 (1956): 196.

Marie-Victoire. Infant taken in "Ohio country" in 1759. Baptized in Montreal. Likely STAYED in Canada. Marcel Fournier, *De la Nouvelle-Angleterre à la Nouvelle-France: L'histoire des captifs anglo-américains au Canada entre 1675 et 1760* (Montreal, QC: Société Généalogique Canadienne-française, 1992), 236.

Mary. Born in Bedford, MA, and taken at Minisink by Delaware in 1755. "Journey on the Forbidden Path," ed. Grumet, 49, 51.

Mekethwa. Girl about five when taken at Greenbrier, Augusta County, VA, 1763. RETURNED at Muskingum, 15 November 1764. Sister of Jacob. *JP*, 11: 721; *WPHM* 39 (1956): 198.

Peggy. Mulatto taken in Virginia. RETURNED at Muskingum, 15 November 1764. *WPHM* 39 (1956): 188, 190, 192; *PG*, 17 January 1765. ("gone home with her late Master's grandson.")

Peter. Pennsylvanian. RETURNED at Muskingum, 15 November 1764. *WPHM* 39 (1956): 191; *NYG*, 21 January 1765.

Phebe. Pennsylvanian. RETURNED at Muskingum, 15 November 1764. *WPHM* 39 (1956): 193; *PG*, 17 January 1765; *NYG*, 21 January 1765.

Polly [Mary]. Virginian. RETURNED at Muskingum, 15 November 1764. *WPHM* 39 (1956): 190; *PG*, 17 January 1765; *NYG*, 21 January 1765.

Polly ["Not her real name"]. Pennsylvanian. RETURNED at Muskingum, 15 November 1764. *WPHM* 39 (1956): 193; *PG*, 17 January 1765; *NYG*, 21 January 1765.

Pompadour. Slave. Pennsylvanian. RETURNED at Muskingum, 15 November 1764. *WPHM* 39 (1956): 191; *PG*, 17 January 1765; *NYG*, 21 January 1765.

Pompey. Slave taken near Detroit, 13 May 1763. Servant of trader John Welch. MISSING. *HBP*, 6: 412; *JP*, 10: 694–6; *PG*, 22 December 1763.

Rachel. Pennsylvanian captive "about 10 Years of Age, fair Complexion, grey Eyes, and light brown Hair" when RETURNED at Muskingum, 15 November 1764. Unclaimed. *WPHM* 39 (1956): 193; *PG*, 17 January 1765, 21 February 1765.

Roger. Delaware warrior. Captured by Iroquois and William Johnson's agents in January 1764. Given to Johnson by the Seneca, and jailed in Albany. Likely sold in West Indies. MISSING. Gregory Evans Dowd, *War under Heaven: Pontiac, the Indian Nations and the British Empire* (Baltimore, MD: Johns Hopkins University Press, 2002), 183–4.

Sally [Sarah]. Taken from Frederick County, VA. RETURNED at Muskingum, 15 November 1764. *WPHM* 39 (1956): 190; *PG*, 17 January 1765; *NYG*, 21 January 1765.

Stephen. "about 14 Years old, fair Complexion, light brown Hair, and dark brown Eyes" when RETURNED at Muskingum, 15 November 1764. Unclaimed. *PG*, 21 February 1765.

Tamar. Mulatto taken from Augusta County, VA. RETURNED at Muskingum, 15 November 1764. *WPHM* 39 (1956): 195; *PG*, 17 January 1765; *NYG*, 21 January 1765.

Tom. Servant of trader named Knapp. Taken near Detroit, May 1763, and still held on 8 September 1763. MISSING. Gladwin, "Gladwin Manuscripts," 647.

William. "about 12 Years of Age, brown Complexion, black Hair, and black Eyes" when RETURNED at Muskingum, 15 November 1764. Brother of Betty. Unclaimed. *PG*, 21 February 1765.

FULL NAMES OR SURNAMES ONLY

Abbott, Rachel. Taken near mouth of Conococheague Creek, MD, 20 April 1757. Became a Delaware WHITE INDIAN. David Zeisberger, *The Moravian Mission Diaries of David Zeisberger*, ed. Herman Wellenreuther and Carola Wessel, trans. Julie Weber (University Park, PA: Pennsylvania State University Press, 2005), 339, 357, 390, 422, 443; John Heckewelder, *History, Manners, and Customs of the Indian Nations Who Once Inhabited Pennsylvania and the Neighbouring States*, rev. ed. (Philadelphia, PA, 1876), 341–2.

Adams, Hans. Brother of Peter and Simon. Taken at fall of Bigham's Fort, Cumberland County, PA, 11 June 1756. RETURNED at Muskingum, 15 November 1764. *WPHM* 39 (1956): 191; *PG*, 17 January 1765; *NYG*, 21 January 1765; *JP*, 11: 488.

Adams, James/Jemmy. Father or brother of Hans, Peter, and Simon. Taken at fall of Bigham's Fort, Cumberland County, PA, 11 June 1756. RETURNED at

Muskingum, 15 November 1764. *PG*, 17 and 24 June 1756, 17 January 1765; *NYM*, 21 and 28 June 1756; *WPHM* 39 (1956): 191; *JP*, 11: 488.

[Adams?], Peter. Brother of Hans and Simon. Taken in Pennsylvania at fall of Bigham's Fort, Cumberland County, PA, 11 June 1756. RETURNED at Muskingum, 15 November 1764. *WPHM* 39 (1956): 191; *PG*, 17 January 1765; *NYG*, 21 January 1765; *JP*, 11: 488.

[Adams?], Simon. Brother of Hans and Peter. Taken in Pennsylvania at fall of Bigham's Fort, Cumberland County, PA, 11 June 1756. RETURNED at Muskingum, 15 November 1764. *WPHM* 39 (1956): 191; *PG*, 17 January 1765; *NYG*, 21 January 1765; *JP*, 11: 488.

Albert, Kathrin. Taken from Bethel Township, Lancaster County, PA, 19 May 1757. MISSING. *PMHB* 32 (1908): 310.

Albert, Maria Margaretta/Magdalena. Girl of twelve to sixteen, light hair, and grey eyes, when taken from Bethel Township, Lancaster County, PA, in the spring of 1756 [or 1757?]. MISSING. Haverford College Library, Indian Committee Records, 824/11, vol. 4, n.p. A Maria Magdalena Albert had been born in Lancaster County, 22 July 1750. https://www.familysearch.org.

Anderson, George. Taken in Pennsylvania. RETURNED at Muskingum, 15 November 1764. *JP*, 11: 488; *PG*, 17 January 1765; *NYG*, 21 January 1765.

Andrews. Child of John Andrews. Taken in Hanover Township, Lancaster County, PA, 4 August 1757. MISSING. *PG*, 18 August 1757; *NYM*, 22 August 1757.

Andrews. Wife of John Andrews. Taken in Hanover Township, Lancaster County, PA, 4 August 1757. MISSING. *PG*, 18 August 1757; *NYM*, 22 August 1757.

Anthon/Antoine, Dr George Christian. Taken at Fort Ouiatenon, 8 June 1765, and FREED 11 July 1765. *JP*, 11: 853, 872, 958; *PG*, 15 August 1765; Nicholas B. Wainwright, *George Croghan, Wilderness Diplomat* (Chapel Hill, NC: University of North Carolina Press, 1959), 220–1.

Appleby, George. Soldier in second battalion of Pennsylvania regiment. Taken at Kittanning by Delaware, 9 September 1756. Likely RETURNED. *PA*, ser. 2, 2: 458–60; *PG*, 23 September 1756; *NYG*, 27 September 1756. Worked for Colonel Henry Bouquet in South Carolina in 1761. *HBP*, 5: 344–6, 653–4. A George Appley was rated in York County in 1779–83, and in Cumberland County in 1785. *PA*, ser. 3, 20: 685; *PA*, ser. 3, 21: 28, 192, 435, 530, 767.

Arants/Arrans, Jacob. Virginia soldier. "one of Capt. Trent's Men, Master of the Indian Language & perfectly acquainted with all the ways & Mountns betwn this and the Fork" according to George Washington. Taken at surrender of Fort Necessity, 4 July 1754. Sent via Fort Niagara to Montreal. MISSING. *GWP*, 1: 221; Robert Stobo, *The Memoirs of Major Robert Stobo of the Virginia Regiment*, ed. Neville B. Craig (Pittsburgh, PA, 1854), 91–2; Frank H. Severance, "The Tale of Captives at Fort Niagara," *Buffalo Historical Society Publications* 9 (1906): 238.

Archer. Daughter of John and Elizabeth Archer. Taken on 1 November 1756 with three brothers near McDowell's Mill, Cumberland County, PA. Mother killed. MISSING. *JP*, 5: 616–17; *PA*, ser. 1, 3: 40–1; *PG*, 11 November 1756; *NYM*, 15 November 1756.

Archer, George. Seven-year-old child of John and Elizabeth Archer. Taken with two brothers and a sister on 1 November 1756 near McDowell's Mill, Cumberland County, PA. Mother killed. *PA*, ser. 1, 3: 40–1; *PG*, 11 November 1756; *NYM*, 15 November 1756. WHITE INDIAN who in 1767, "if alive, is now 18, fair complexion, dark Eyes well grown when taken." *JP*, 5: 616–17.

Archer, Joseph. Child of John and Elizabeth Archer. Taken on 1 November 1756 with two brothers and a sister near McDowell's Mill, Cumberland County, PA. Mother killed. *PA*, ser. 1, 3: 40–1; *PG*, 11 November 1756; *NYM*, 15 November 1756. RETURNED at Muskingum, 15 November 1764. *JP*, 5: 616–17.

Archer, Thomas. Of Maryland. RETURNED in a flag of truce ship from Canada to Boston, 16 August 1747. *PG*, 3 September 1747.

Archer, Thomas. Three-year-old child of John and Elizabeth Archer. Taken on 1 November 1756 with two brothers and a sister near McDowell's Mill, Cumberland County, PA. Mother killed. *PA*, ser. 1, 3: 40–1; *PG*, 11 November 1756; *NYM*, 15 November 1756. WHITE INDIAN who in 1767 was "Aged 14 [and] his brother Joseph says [that when] he left him he was A Hearty well set Lad has dark Eyes, and That he Left him a prisoner in the Mingoe Nation." *JP*, 5: 616–17.

Arighwadaga. Chenussio Seneca chief. Taken hostage by William Johnson against the return of all prisoners, 5 August 1764. MISSING. *JP*, 11: 318, 321, 325.

Armstrong, Betty. Wife of James Armstrong. Taken with her children Elizabeth and Thomas, 27 January 1756, near Patterson's Fort on Juniata River, Cumberland County, PA, by a Delaware and Shawnee war party. ESCAPED to Fort Augusta, 26 June 1757. "Shamokin 3. Mo [May] 27 1759 from Nathaniel Holland," Haverford College Library, Indian Committee Records, 824/11, vol. 3, n.p.; *PA*, ser. 2, 2: 686, 799, 811; *PG*, 5 February 1756; William A. Hunter, *Forts on the Pennsylvania Frontier, 1753–1758* (Harrisburg, PA: Pennsylvania Historical and Museum Commission, 1960), 379.

Armstrong, Elizabeth. Two-year-old daughter of James and Betty Armstrong. Taken with her mother and brother Thomas, 27 January 1756, near Patterson's Fort on Juniata River, Cumberland County, PA, by a Delaware and Shawnee war party. RETURNED by the Delaware to William Johnson, 12 April 1759. *PG*, 2 February 1756, 31 May 1759; *NYG*, 4 June 1759.

Armstrong, Thomas. Son of James and Betty Armstrong. Taken with his mother and sister Elizabeth, 27 January 1756, near Patterson's Fort on Juniata River, Cumberland County, PA, by a Delaware and Shawnee war party. WHITE INDIAN who married an unidentified white captive who knew no English. They settled at Buffalo Creek, where he served as interpreter for the mission. Poignant third-person account of a later visit to a sister. Archibald Loudon, ed., *A Selection of Some of the Most Interesting Narratives of Outrages Committed by the Indians in Their Wars with the White People*, 2 vols (Carlisle, PA, 1808–11), vol. 2, 173; "Incidents in the Life of an Indian Captive," *American Historical*

Record 1 (1872): 409–10; *PG*, 5 February 1756; Hunter, *Forts*, 379; James Axtell, *The European and the Indian* (New York: Oxford University Press, 1981), 195.

Ashcroft, Daniel. MISSING after attacked while driving cattle near Colonel Thomas Cresap's Sawmill, MD, 30 June 1756. *PG*, 15 July 1756; *NYM*, 19 July 1756.

Ashley/Ashby, Nimrod. Captain in Virginia Regiment. Taken 4 June 1764 on South Branch of Potomac River, Augusta County, VA. Although his wife sought compensation, claiming he had been killed, the Virginia House of Burgesses judged, on 3 December 1766, that he had not been proven dead and was still MISSING. BL, Add. Mss, 21650, fol. 238; *PG*, 14 June 1764; *Journals of the House of Burgesses of Virginia, 1761–1765*, ed. John Pendleton Kennedy (Richmond, VA: Colonial Press, 1907), 346; *Journals of the House of Burgesses of Virginia, 1766–1769*, ed. John Pendleton Kennedy (Richmond, VA: Colonial Press, 1906), 29–30, 50. Compare Samuel Kercheval, *A History of the Valley of Virginia*, 4th ed. (Strasburg, VA: Shenandoah, 1925), 97.

Ashloff. Adult male. MISSING after Indian raid near Town Creek, Frederick County, VA, 4 October 1755. *PG*, 16 October 1755; *PJ*, 16 October 1755.

Aubry, Charles Philippe (d. 1770). Lieutenant in regular Régiment de Lionnois, captain of Louisiana marines in Illinois, and co-commander at battle of La Belle Famille, 24 July 1759, where he was captured by Iroquois, tortured, and acquired by William Johnson. Sent to France for EXCHANGE, December 1760. Commander in Louisiana (1763–65), governor under the French (1765–66), and co-governor under the Spanish (1766–69). Charles A. Brasseaux, *France's Forgotten Legion: Service Records of French Military and Administrative Personnel Stationed in the Mississippi Valley and Gulf Coast Region, 1699–1769*, indexed CD-ROM (Baton Rouge, LA: Louisiana State University Press, 2000); Brian Leigh Dunnigan, *Siege–1759: The Campaign against Niagara* (Youngstown, NY: Old Fort Niagara Association, 1986), 70, 103; *NYCD*, 10: 989; TNA, CO 5/1068, fol. 304.

Auger, Pierre. Canadian militiaman. Captured at battle of La Belle Famille, 24 July 1759. Hired out in Somerset County, NJ, that year. MISSING. Job Stockton Papers, NYHS.

Austin/Ostin, Henry. Sergeant of Virginia Regiment. Taken escorting Christian Frederick Post and Pisquetomen near Loyalhanna, PA, 16 November 1758. Condemned to be burned but RANSOMED at Fort Pitt, 23 December 1758, for ten gallons of rum. Ransom paid by Lieutenant Christopher Gist. *PG*, 7 and 21 December 1758; R.G. Thwaites, ed., *Early Western Travels, 1748–1846*, 32 vols (Cleveland, OH: Arthur H. Clark, 1904–07), vol. 1, 250, 287; *Letters to Washington and Accompanying Papers*, ed. Stanislaus Murray Hamilton, 5 vols (Boston, MA, 1898–1902), vol. 3, 148.

Babson, Mordecai. Virginian. RETURNED at Muskingum, 15 November 1764. *WPHM* 39 (1956): 190, 196; *JP*, 11: 485; *PG*, 17 January 1765; *NYG*, 21 January 1765.

Bacon, Catherine. Pennsylvanian. RETURNED at Muskingum, 15 November 1764. *WPHM* 39 (1956): 193; LAC, MG 19, F 35/2, lot 621, 5; *PG*, 17 January 1765;

NYG, 21 January 1765. A Catherine Bacon married Wendan Zerban in Tulpehocken Trinity Church, Lebanon County, PA, 24 March 1767. *PA*, ser. 2, 2: 20; https://www.familysearch.org.

Bäder, [Mrs Philip]. Taken near Conococheague, Cumberland County, PA, 20 September 1756, with two unnamed children. All three of them remained MISSING. Husband arrested attempting to join them. *NYM*, 11 October 1756; *PG*, 7 October 1756; Hunter, *Forts*, 415–17.

Baillie, Thomas. Soldier in Virginia Regiment. Taken in attack on a supply train near Fort Ligonier, PA, 23 May 1759. ESCAPED July 1761. *Journals of the House of Burgesses, 1761–1765*, ed. Kennedy, 39, 41, 42; Hunter, *Forts*, 95–6; BL, Add. Mss, 21644, 172.

Baker. Son of Mrs Jacob Baker. Taken near Fort Henry, Berks County, PA, 23 May 1764, with his unnamed brother. Mother and aunt killed in the attack. Both boys were KILLED and scalped within hours of being captured. *PG*, 31 May and 7 June 1764.

Baker, John. Servant of George Croghan. Taken by Ohio Delaware, 27 January 1756, near Aughwick, Cumberland County, PA. ESCAPED 10 March 1756. Guided Kittanning raid, in which he was killed. HSP, Penn Mss, Indian Affairs, vol. 2, no. 78; *PG*, 1 April 1756.

Baker, John. Soldier in Captain John Fenton Mercer's company of Virginia Regiment. Captured at Great Meadows, 4 July 1754. Sent to Canada. MISSING. Stobo, *Memoirs*, 91–2; *Travels in New France by J.C.B.*, ed. Sylvester K. Stevens, Donald H. Kent, and Emma Edith Woods (Harrisburg, PA: Pennsylvania Historical Commission, 1941), 64; Severance, "Tale of Captives," 238.

Baker, William. Soldier in second battalion of Pennsylvania regiment. MISSING in attack on Kittanning, 9 September 1756. *PA*, ser. 2, 2: 458–60; *PG*, 23 September 1756; William A. Hunter, "Victory at Kittanning," *PH* 23 (1956): 392–402.

Baldwin, Abraham. Taken by Delaware Captain Bull's party near Wyoming, Northampton County, PA, 4 September 1763. RETURNED to William Johnson by the Chenussio Seneca, 31 July 1764. *JP*, 4: 498; *PG*, 6 and 13 September 1764.

Baldwin, Daniel. Taken with wife, Jane, by Delaware Captain Bull's party near Wyoming, Northampton County, PA, 4 September 1763. MISSING, and said to have been burned to death in a report that was otherwise erroneous. *JP*, 4: 498; *PG*, 6 and 13 September 1764.

Baldwin, Jane. Taken with husband, Daniel, by Delaware Captain Bull's party near Wyoming, Northampton County, PA, 4 September 1763. DIED of starvation in winter of 1763–64 while prisoner of the Chenussio Seneca. *JP*, 4: 498; *PG*, 6 and 13 September 1764.

Ball, Elizabeth. Girl taken in Cumberland County, PA, June 1756. Advertised as in a convent in Montreal in June 1761, and interested in returning. *PG*, 2 July 1761. MISSING? An Elizabeth Ball married William Moore in Philadelphia, 12 January 1769. *PA*, ser. 2, 2: 21. An Elizabeth Ball had 400 acres surveyed in Northumberland County (formerly part of Cumberland) in 1784. *PA*, ser. 3, 25: 69.

Bard/Baird, Catherine/Ketty. Wife of Richard. Taken in York County, PA, 13 April 1758. RANSOMED in December 1760 for £40 Pennsylvania currency. *PG*, 11 May 1758; *NYM*, 15 May 1758; *PA*, ser. 1, 3: 396–7; Loudon, ed., *Selection*, vol. 2, 47–65; https://www.familysearch.org.

Bard/Baird, John. Infant son of Richard and Ketty. Taken with them on 13 April 1758 by Delaware. KILLED the same day. *PG*, 11 May 758; *NYM*, 15 May 1758; *PA*, ser. 1, 3: 396–7; Loudon, ed., *Selection*, vol. 2, 47–65; https://www.familysearch.org.

Bard/Baird, Richard. A miller. Taken with family in York County, PA, by Delaware, 13 April 1758. ESCAPED 18 April 1758. *PG*, 11 May 758; *NYM*, 15 May 1758; *PA*, ser. 1, 3: 396–7; Loudon, ed., *Selection*, vol. 2: 47–65; https://www.familysearch.org.

Barnett, Frances/Fanny. Taken, at about age ten, along with her younger sister, Susannah, in a Shawnee raid in Virginia in 1756. Married a Shawnee and had five children by 1763. Returned very briefly in 1775 but returned to her Shawnee family. WHITE INDIAN. *WPHM* 39 (1956): 202; Draper Mss, Kentucky Papers, 23CC98-103.

Barnett, Susannah. Taken at age six, along with older sister, Frances, in a Shawnee raid in Virginia in 1756. ESCAPED to Fort Pitt in 1768. Baptized, married Thomas Cummins, and settled near Fort Pitt. *WPHM* 39 (1956): 202; Draper Mss, Kentucky Papers, 23CC98-103.

Barnett, William. Taken in August 1757, at about age nine, in a Delaware raid into Lancaster County, PA. He was RETURNED to George Croghan, September 1759, escaped back to the Delaware for a few days, but was returned to Croghan by Kageshquanohel (the Pipe). *PG*, 25 August and 1 September 1757; *PMHB* 17 (1947): 351; Henry M.M. Richards, *The Pennsylvania-German in the French and Indian War* (Lancaster, PA: Pennsylvania-German Society, 1905), 295–303.

Barnhold/Barnholdt, Nicholas. Soldier wounded and captured by French and Indians in their conquest of Fort Granville, Cumberland County, PA, 31 July 1756. ESCAPED six days later. *PG*, 19 August 1756; *PJ*, 19 August 1756.

Barnoy, Sidney. Taken on Pennsylvania or Virginia frontier. Ransomed from Indians. Worked off ransom in New France. Sent to France. EXCHANGED September 1757. TNA, Adm. 1/4323, n.p.

Barrowly/Barrowelly, Martin. Taken in Cumberland County, PA, 31 July 1756, by Shawnee. ESCAPED to Potomac River with John Hogan, 1 April 1757. *PG*, 19 August 1756; HL, LO, 3758; *MPCP*, 7: 561–2.

Baskins/Basket. Taken, with his mother, Mary, elder brother, and aunt Peggy, in Delaware attack on family farmstead on Juniata River, Cumberland County, PA, 30 July 1756. Seen later at Kuskuski with his mother. MISSING. *NYM*, 8 September 1756; *PA*, ser. 2, 7: 437.

Baskins/Basket. Taken, with his mother, Mary, younger brother, and aunt Peggy, in Delaware attack on family farmstead on Juniata River, Cumberland

County, PA, 30 July 1756. Reported held in towns beyond Kuskuski. MISSING. *NYM*, 8 September 1756; *PA*, ser. 2, 7: 437.

Baskins/Basket, Mary. Taken, and widowed, in Delaware attack on family farmstead in Juniata Valley, Cumberland County, PA, 30 July 1756. Sister Nancy/Peggy and two sons taken with her. Seen at Kuskuski before 1759. RETURNED to George Croghan at Fort Pitt, 19 September 1759. *NYM*, 8 September 1756; *PA*, ser. 2, 7: 437; "George Croghan's Journal, April 3, 1759, to April [30], 1763," *PMHB* 71 (1947): 352.

Baskins, Nancy/Peggy. Taken with sister Mary and nephews in Delaware attack on family farmstead in Juniata Valley, Cumberland County, PA, 30 July 1756. RETURNED at Muskingum, 15 November 1764. *PA*, ser. 2, 7: 437; *PG*, 17 January 1765; *WPHM* 39 (1956): 193, 196.

Bell, James (1). Taken on 25 June 1756 in Augusta County, VA. RETURNED at Muskingum, 15 November 1764. Preston Papers, 1: 83; *PG*, 17 January 1765; *JP*, 11: 485; *WPHM* 39 (1956): 189. Served with Colonel Henry Bouquet immediately. F.B. Lyman Chalkley, *Chronicles of the Scotch-Irish Settlement in Virginia*, 3 vols (1912; reprint, Baltimore, MD: Genealogical, 1965), vol. 1, 209.

Bell, James (2). Taken by Seneca, 10 September 1758, in Hanover Township, Lancaster County, PA. Father and brother killed. Seen at Shamokin, 12 May 1760. ESCAPED to Fort Ligonier, PA, 25 May 1759, where he was imprisoned as a spy. MISSING. *PG*, 5 October 1758; Haverford College Library, Indian Committee Records, vol. 2, 4; BL, Add. Mss, 21651, fols 4–8; BL, Add. Mss, 21644, fol. 172; Hunter, *Forts*, 95–6.

Bell, Robert. Soldier in Lieutenant Thomas Bullitt's company of Virginia Regiment. Captured in Cumberland County, PA, 23 May 1758. RETURNED at Muskingum, 15 November 1764. *PG*, 23 August 1759; *WPHM* 39 (1956): 189; *NYG*, 21 January 1765; *HBP*, 6: 658.

Bernat/Barnett. Young nephew of Isham Bernat/Barnet. Taken with his family by Shawnee on South Branch of Potomac River, Augusta County, VA, 19 March 1758. KILLED on the trail as "cross & troublesome." *PA*, ser. 1, 3: 632–3.

Bernat/Barnett, Isham. Taken by Shawnee, with his family, on South Branch of Potomac River, Augusta County, VA, 19 March 1758. ESCAPED from Scioto River settlement. *PA*, ser. 1, 3: 632–3; Mathew C. Ward, *Breaking the Backcountry: The Seven Years' War in Virginia and Pennsylvania, 1754–1765* (Pittsburgh, PA: University of Pittsburgh Press, 2003), 211; Haverford College Library, Indian Committee Records, 824/11, vol. 4, 7.

Bernat/Barnett, Jesse. Child taken with family by Shawnee on South Branch of Potomac River, Augusta County, VA, 19 March 1758. RETURNED, with mother and sister, to William Johnson at Fort Niagara, July 1764, by Wyandot with whom they had lived. *PG*, 6 September 1764. See also *WPHM* 39 (1956): 202.

Bernat/Barnett, Lena. Child taken with family by Shawnee on South Branch of Potomac River, Augusta County, VA, 19 March 1758. RETURNED, with mother and brother, to William Johnson at Fort Niagara, July 1764, by Wyandot with whom they had lived. *PG*, 6 September 1764. See also *WPHM* 39 (1956): 202.

Bernat/Barnett, Sara. Taken with family by Shawnee on South Branch of Potomac River, Augusta County, VA, 19 March 1758. RETURNED, with her children Jesse and Lena, to William Johnson at Fort Niagara, July 1764, by Wyandot with whom they had lived. *PG*, 6 September 1764. See also *WPHM* 39 (1956): 202.

Big Ears. Potawatomi chief taken as hostage by Major Henry Gladwin at Detroit, 10 May 1763. EXCHANGED for sixteen captives of the Potawatomi. BL, Add. Mss, 21658, fols 88–90; Amherst Papers, TNA, WO 34/49, fols 214–15; Jehu Hay, *Diary of the Siege of Detroit in the War with Pontiac*, ed. Franklin B. Hough (Albany, NY, 1860), 26, 42–6; [Robert Navarre], "The Journal of Pontiac's Conspiracy," in *The Siege of Detroit*, ed. M.M. Quaife (Chicago, IL: Lakeside, 1958), 137–8.

Bighead, David. Boy said to be from Pennsylvania. RETURNED at Muskingum, 15 November 1764. *PG*, 17 January 65; *WPHM* 39 (1956): 193, 196; *JP*, 11: 490.

Bingeman, Katherine. Widowed and captured with her two children in Shawnee attack on North River, Augusta County, VA, 3 July 1755. ESCAPED from Lower Shawnee Town with Mary Draper Ingles, 17 February 1756. Petitioned Virginia House of Burgesses. *NYM*, 14 July 1755 (where she was reported killed); *Journals of the House of Burgesses of Virginia, 1758–1761*, ed. H.R. McIlwaine (Richmond, VA: Colonial Press, 1908), 239; F.B. Kegley, *Kegley's Virginia Frontier: The Beginning of the Southwest, the Roanoke of Colonial Days, 1740–1783* (Roanoke, VA: Southwest Virginia Historical Society, 1938), 256.

Bingeman, Lewis. Virginia boy. Captured on North River, Augusta County, VA, with mother and sister, 3 July 1755. WHITE INDIAN who led 1768 avenging party that killed murderer Jacob Price. Kercheval, *History of the Valley*, 85.

Bingeman, Lezy (Elizabeth). Virginia girl. Captured on North River, Augusta County, VA, with mother and brother, 3 July 1755. Still held in Lower Shawnee Town late in 1764. MISSING. *WPHM* 39 (1956): 202; "Register," Preston Papers, 1: 83.

Blankinship, Stephen. Soldier in Virginia Regiment. Captured on 28 April 1758. RETURNED at Muskingum, 15 November 1764. *PG*, 17 January 1765; *WPHM* 39 (1956): 194; *JP*, 11: 485; *Journals of the House of Burgesses, 1761–1765*, ed. Kennedy, 328.

Bodmore, Philip. Virginian in Captain Robert Stewart's troop of rangers. Taken about 1 October 1755. MISSING, and later reported deserted. *GWP*, 2: 306, 307.

Boggs. Infant taken with mother near Fort Swatara, Lancaster County, PA, 4 August 1756. KILLED on the trail. Hunter, *Forts*, 337; Israel Daniel Rupp, *The History and Topography of Dauphin, Cumberland, Franklin, Bedford, Adams and Perry Counties* (Lancaster, PA, 1846), 118.

Boggs, [Mrs]. Taken with infant near Fort Swatara, Lancaster County, PA, 4 August 1756. MISSING. Hunter, *Forts*, 337; Rupp, *History and Topography of Dauphin*, 118.

Boiford. Surgeon with Commandant François-Marie Le Marchand de Lignery. Taken at battle of La Belle Famille, 24 July 1759. MISSING. Dunnigan, *Siege–1759*, 103.

Bolton, William. Soldier in Royal American Regiment. Taken at fall of Fort Miami, 27 May 1763. RETURNED by 20 December 1763. Gladwin, "Gladwin Manuscripts," 649, 658.

Bonheur, Hilaire. Canadian in Captain Antoine-Gabriel-François Benoit's company of marines. Taken at battle of La Belle Famille, 24 July 1759. Held in Somerset County, NJ. EXCHANGED 17 December 1760. *JP*, 13: 115; Job Stockton Papers, NYHS.

Bonnenouvelle. Canadian corporal in Cabanac's company of marines. Taken in surrender of Detroit, 30 November 1760. Ordered aboard the *Fowey* to France for EXCHANGE, 4 May 1761. TNA, WO 1/5, 176; *PG*, 15 January and 5 February 1761; *NYM*, 30 March 1761.

Bonnet, Henry. Virginian. RETURNED at Muskingum, 15 November 1764. *WPHM* 39 (1956): 196.

Bonvouloir de Longueuil, Augustin. Canadian. Taken in Jumonville incident, 28 May 1754. RETURNED, via Martinique, 22 June 1755. *PG*, 13 and 27 June, 22 August, and 12 September 1754; *Collections des manuscrits contenant lettres, mémoires et autres documents historiques relatifs à la Nouvelle France*, 4 vols (Quebec City, QC, 1883–85), vol. 3, 521–2.

Bostwick, Henry. English trader at Michilimackinac. Taken by Ojibwa, 2 June 1763. RANSOMED at Montreal by General Thomas Gage. Alexander Henry, *Travels and Adventures in Canada and the Indian Territories between the Years 1760 and 1776*, ed. James Bain (1809; reprint, Toronto: G.N. Morang, 1901), 12n, 103; Gladwin, "Gladwin Manuscripts," 666–7.

Bouchard, Jean-Nicholas. Canadian in Captain Luc de La Corne's company of marines. Taken at battle of La Belle Famille, 24 July 1759. Held in Somerset County, NJ. EXCHANGED, 7 May 1760. *JP*, 13: 115; Job Stockton Papers, NYHS.

Boucher de Niverville de Montisambert, Louis (d. 1803). Canadian Marine lieutenant. Taken at battle of La Belle Famille, 24 July 1759. EXCHANGED in France, 4 May 1761. Quebec mill operator in 1765. Died in Boucherville, QC, 8 August 1803. Dunnigan, *Siege–1759*, 80, 103; *DCB*, 4: 653; PRDH.

Boucherville. Canadian marine cadet. Taken by Virginians in Jumonville incident, 28 May 1754. EXCHANGED in France via England, 22 June 1755. *PG*, 13 and 27 June, 22 August, 12 September 1754; *Collections des manuscrits ... Nouvelle France*, vol. 3, 521–2.

Bourguignon. Sergeant in Captain Paul-Louis Dazemard de Lusignan's company of Canadian marines. Taken in surrender of Detroit garrison, 30 November 1760. EXCHANGED in France in 1761. *PG*, 15 January and 5 February 1761; TNA, WO 1/5, 176; *NYM*, 30 March 1761.

Boyd. Two-year-old boy taken by Delaware, with his mother and siblings, at Shippensburg, Cumberland County, PA, 10 February 1756. KILLED the next day. David Boyd, *History of the Capture and Captivity of David Boyd from Cumberland County, Pennsylvania* (N.p., 1931), 29; J. Norman Heard, *Handbook of the American Frontier*, 5 vols (Metuchen, NJ: Scarecrow, 1987–98), vol. 2, 32.

Boyd, David (1743–1831). Thirteen year old taken by Delaware, with his mother and siblings, at Shippensburg, Cumberland County, PA, 10 February 1756.

RETURNED in 1760 and made several attempts to return to Delaware. Married Elizabeth Henderson in Shippensburg in 1771 and fathered ten children. Boyd, *History*; *PA*, ser. 2, 7: 437; Heard, *Handbook*, vol. 2, 32; https://www.familysearch.org.

Boyd, James. Taken by Delaware, with his mother and siblings, at Shippensburg, Cumberland County, PA, 10 February 1756. RETURNED. Boyd, *History*; *PA*, ser. 2, 7: 437.

Boyd, Nancy [Mrs John, nee Urie]. Taken by Delaware, with her six children, at Shippensburg, Cumberland County, PA, 10 February 1756. KILLED on the trail the next day. Boyd, *History*; https://www.familysearch.org.

Boyd, Rhoda. Child of John. Taken by Delaware, with mother and siblings, at Shippensburg, Cumberland County, PA, 10 February 1756. Returned at Muskingum, 15 November 1764, but escaped near Fort Pitt. WHITE INDIAN. *PG*, 17 January 1765; Boyd, History; *PA*, ser. 2, 7: 437.

Boyd, Sarah/Sallie. Eldest child of John. Taken by Delaware, with mother and siblings, at Shippensburg, Cumberland County, PA, 10 February 1756. Seen by brother David in 1757. RETURNED at Muskingum, 15 November 1764. *PG*, 17 January 1765; *WPHM* 39 (1956): 192; *PA*, ser. 2, 7: 437; Heard, *Handbook*, vol. 2, 32.

Boyd, Thomas. Child of John. Taken by Delaware, with mother and siblings, at Shippensburg, Cumberland County, PA, 10 February 1756. RETURNED at Muskingum, 15 November 1764. *PG*, 17 January 1765; *JP*, 11: 488; Boyd, *History*; *PA*, ser. 2, 7: 437.

Boyer. Daughter of Henry Boyer. Taken, with brother and sister, from Lehigh Gap, Northampton County, PA, by Delaware, 2 January 1757. MISSING. *PMHB* 32 (1908): 314; Richards, *Pennsylvania-German*, 383–4.

Boyer. Daughter of Henry Boyer. Taken, with brother and sister, from Lehigh Gap, Northampton County, PA, by Delaware, 2 January 1757. MISSING. *PMHB* 32 (1908): 314; Richards, *Pennsylvania-German*, 383–4.

Boyer, Frederick (1744–1813). Thirteen-year-old son of Henry Boyer. Taken, with sisters, from Lehigh Gap, Northampton County, PA, by Delaware, 2 January 1757. Taken to Canada. RETURNED after about five years. *PMHB* 32 (1908): 314; Richards, *Pennsylvania-German*, 383–4.

Boyl/Boyles. Boy of Mrs Charles Boyl/Boyles. Taken in attack on Jackson River, Augusta County, VA, 11 September 1756. Seen at Lower Shawnee Town late in 1764. MISSING. Preston Papers, 1: 83; *PG*, 7 October 1756; *WPHM* 39 (1956): 202.

Boyl/Boyles. Child of Mrs Charles Boyl/Boyles. Taken in attack on Jackson River, Augusta County, VA, 11 September 1756. MISSING. Preston Papers, 1: 83; *PG*, 7 October 1756.

Boyl/Boyles. Child of Mrs Charles Boyl/Boyles. Taken in attack on Jackson River, Augusta County, VA, 11 September 1756. MISSING. Preston Papers, 1: 83; *PG*, 7 October 1756.

Boyl/Boyles. Child of Mrs Charles Boyl/Boyles. Taken in attack on Jackson River, Augusta County, VA, 11 September 1756. MISSING. Preston Papers, 1: 83; *PG*, 7 October 1756.

Boyl/Boyles, Sally. Daughter of Mrs Charles Boyl/Boyles. Taken in attack on Jackson River, Augusta County, 11 September 1756. Seen at Lower Shawnee Town late in 1764. MISSING. Preston Papers, 1: 83; *PG*, 7 October 1756; *WPHM* 39 (1956): 202.

Brackenridge, David. Horse driver at Fort Ligonier, PA. Taken by Delaware at Loyalhanna, PA, 1758. ESCAPED with Hugh Gibson, Marie Le Roy, and Barbara Leininger, 16 March 1759. Home to see auction of his effects. *PA*, ser. 2, 7: 427–38; BL, Add. Mss, 21644, fol. 132; *Massachusetts Historical Society Collections*, ser. 3, 6 (1837): 153; Rupp, *History and Topography of Dauphin*, 110–12.

Bradshaw. Son of William. Taken at Craig's Creek, VA, March 1757. MISSING. Preston Papers, 1: 83.

Bradshaw, William. Taken at Craig's Creek, VA, March 1757. A William Bradshaw was mentioned in Augusta County court records on 14 March 1758 and 4 May 1767. Likely ESCAPED. Preston Papers, 1: 83; Chalkley, *Chronicles of the Scotch-Irish*, vol. 3, 351, 453.

Brake, [Mrs John]. Taken by Delaware on South Fork of South Branch of Potomac River, Augusta County, VA, 20 April 1756. Pregnant, unable to travel, and KILLED the same day. Baker, *French and Indian War*, 47.

Bratton, William. Virginian ranger. Wounded and captured in fall of Vause's Fort, Augusta County, VA, 25 June 1756. RETURNED. *PG*, 28 July 1757; Preston Papers, 1: 83.

Bready/Brady, Ann. Pennsylvanian. RETURNED at Detroit, 1 December 1760. *HBP*, 5: 210.

Bready/Brady, Mary. Pennsylvanian. RETURNED at Detroit, 1 December 1760. *HBP*, 5: 210. A Mary Brady married Thomas Short, 19 December 1772. *PA*, ser. 2, 2: 35.

Brennard/Brannin, Anne. Wife of James. Taken in Berks County, PA, 1757. Held in French Margaret's Town. Seen at Shamokin in May 1761. MISSING. *PG*, 3 July 1760; Haverford College Library, Indian Committee Records, 824/11, vol. 4, 115–18.

Brennard/Brannin, James. Youth taken in Berks County, PA, 1757. RETURNED to Philadelphia, 28 June 1760. *PG*, 3 July 1760; *HBP*, 6: 214–18.

Brennard/Brannin, Jesse. Daughter of James and Anne. Taken in Berks County, PA, 1757. Held in French Margaret's Town. Seen at Shamokin in May 1761. MISSING. *PG*, 3 July 1760; Haverford College Library, Indian Committee Records, 824/11, vol. 4, 115–18.

Breylinger. Child of Jacob and Hanna. Taken at Penn's Creek, Cumberland County, PA, 16 October 1755. DIED in captivity at Kittanning in 1756. C. Hale Sipe, *The Indian Wars of Pennsylvania* (Harrisburg, PA: Telegraph, 1929), 206.

Breylinger. Child of Jacob and Hanna. Taken at Penn's Creek, Cumberland County, PA, 16 October 1755. MISSING. Sipe, *Indian Wars*, 204–9.

Breylinger, Hanna. Wife of Jacob, and mother of two. All three taken at Penn's Creek, Cumberland County, PA, 16 October 1755. Seen at Kuskuski before March 1759. MISSING. Sipe, *Indian Wars*, 204–9; "The Narrative of Marie Le Roy and Barbara Leininger," *Proceedings of the Pennsylvania-German Society* 15 (1905): 125.

Broadly/Broadley, Paul. Taken in 1755. TORTURED to death at Kittanning, February 1756. *MPCP*, 7: 242–3; *NYM*, 9 June 1756.

Brown. Woman captured in Cumberland County, PA, 31 May 1764, when brother killed. ESCAPED the next day. *PG*, 7 and 14 June 1764; *NYM*, 11 June 1764.

Brown, Adam. Boy taken, with his younger brother Samuel, on James River, Augusta County, VA, October 1764. WHITE INDIAN who became a Miami chief. Died at Malden, Upper Canada, 1815. Baker, *French and Indian War*, 133; Alexander Scott Withers, *Chronicles of Border Warfare, or A History of the Settlement by the Whites, of North Western Virginia, and of the Indian Wars and Massacres, in that section of the state, with reflections, anecdotes, etc. …* (1831; reprint, New York: Arno, 1971), 96–7n; Waddell, *Annals of Augusta*, vol. 1, 121.

Brown, George, Jr. Boy taken by Shawnee near Conococheague, Cumberland County, PA, 20 September 1756. WHITE INDIAN who became a Shawnee chief. *PG*, 7 October 1756; *NYM*, 11 October 1756; M.M. Quaife, ed., *The Siege of Detroit* (Chicago, IL: Lakeside, 1958), xx–xxi.

Brown, John Wendell. Taken on South Branch of Potomac River, Augusta County, VA, April 1756. Taken to Fort Duquesne, New France, and France. RANSOMED September 1757. TNA, Adm. 1/4323, n.p.; *Journals of the House of Burgesses, 1758–1761*, ed. McIlwaine, 16.

Brown, Joseph. Canadian soldier from Montreal. Taken by George Washington, 28 May 1754. RETURNED via England, 22 June 1754. *Collections des manuscrits … Nouvelle France*, vol. 3, 521–2.

Brown, Margaret. Teenage daughter of John Wendell Brown. Taken on South Branch of Potomac River, Augusta County, VA, April 1756. Said to be with the "Oschaschi" in Prairie West, c. 1758. MISSING. "Narrative of Marie Le Roy and Barbara Leininger," *Proceedings of the Pennsylvania-German Society* 15 (1905): 125; *PA*, ser. 2, 7: 438; *Journals of the House of Burgesses, 1758–1761*, ed. McIlwaine, 16.

Brown, Samuel. Boy captured at Jackson River, Augusta County, VA, 11 September 1756. Likely RETURNED. A Samuel Brown was a courier for Colonel Henry Bouquet in 1764. Preston Papers, 1: 83; *PG*, 11 September 1756; *NYM*, 11 October 1756; *HBP*, 6: 855.

Brown, Samuel. Boy captured with his brother Adam on James River, Augusta County, VA, October 1764. RETURNED 1769. Became Colonel Samuel Brown of Greenbrier. Withers, *Chronicles* (1895), 96; Waddell, *Annals of Augusta*, vol. 1, 121–2.

Brown, William. Youth taken by Seneca in North Carolina in 1748. RETURNED at Logstown conference, 12 September 1748. *MPCP*, 5: 290–3, 304, 353; *PA*, ser. 1, 2: 16–17; Thwaites, ed., *Early Western Travels*, vol. 1, 20, 31–4.

Browne, Andrew. Pennsylvania trader. Captured at fall of Pickawillany, 21 June 1752. KILLED and cannibalized the same day. *VG*, 20 and 27 October 1752; Theodore C. Pease and Ernestine Jenison, eds, *Illinois on the Eve of the Seven Years' War* (Springfield, IL: State Historical Society, 1940), 811.

Bruce, William. Trader captured by the Ottawa at Michilimackinac, 15 June 1763. RANSOMED at Montreal, 15 August 1763. Gladwin, "Gladwin Manuscripts," 668–70.

Brumley, Charles. Volunteer in Montgomery Highlanders. Taken in Major James Grant's defeat at Fort Duquesne, 14 September 1758. RETURNED at surrender of Detroit, 1 December 1760. *HBP*, 5: 210, 262; *PG*, 28 September 1758.

Brumley/Bromley, William. Soldier in Captain Stuart's company of Virginia Regiment. Taken in Major James Grant's defeat at Fort Duquesne, 14 September 1758. EXCHANGED 14 September 1760. *Journals of the House of Burgesses, 1758–1761*, ed. McIlwaine, 188; HL, AB, 659; *PG*, 28 September 1758. Compare *GWP*, 6: 45–7.

Bryan, Rebecca. Virginia woman. Taken in Augusta County, VA. RETURNED at Muskingum, 15 November 1764. *JP*, 11: 487; *WPHM* 39 (1956): 190; *PG*, 17 January 1765.

Bull, Captain (Johann Jacob). Delaware headman and son of Teedyuscung. Taken near Auqvauge, PA, by Iroquois, 27 February 1764. Jailed in Albany and New York. EXILED to West Virginia in 1765. *PG*, 15 March and 12 April 1764; *JP*, 4: 739–40; *JP*, 11: 105, 118–20; Dowd, *War under Heaven*, 152; Jane T. Merritt, *At the Crossroads: Indians and Empires on a Mid-Atlantic Frontier, 1700–1763* (Chapel Hill, NC: University of North Carolina Press, 2003), 303.

Bullitt/Bullet, [Thomas?]. Captain in Virginia Regiment. Captured in Major James Grant's defeat at Fort Duquesne, 14 September 1758. RETURNED to claim land as a veteran. Draper Mss, Virginia Papers, 3ZZ48; George Mercer, *George Mercer Papers Relating to the Ohio Company* (Pittsburgh, PA: University of Pittsburgh Press, 1954), 611–12; Illinois Historical Society, *Collections* 11 (1916): 571.

Burk, [James?]. Taken at Holston River in October 1754. ESCAPED within a few days. Preston Papers, 1: 83; Baker, *French and Indian War*, 10.

Burk, Thomas. Trader from Lancaster County, PA. Captured by French officers at Sandusky, November 1750. Released in France, 27 January 1752, and RETURNED. *The Ohio Company Papers, 1753–1817, Being Primarily Papers of the "Suffering Traders" of Pennsylvania*, ed. Kenneth P. Bailey (Arcata, CA: N.p., 1947), 36–7; Howard N. Eavenson, *Map Maker and Indian Trader* (Pittsburgh, PA: University of Pittsburgh Press, 1949), 142–3; Charles A. Hanna, *The Wilderness Trail, Or the Ventures and Adventures of the Pennsylvania Traders on the Allegheny Path*, 2 vols (New York: Putnam, 1911), vol. 2, 327; Hunter, "Victory at Kittanning."

Burke. Child of Mary Burke. Taken by Shawnee in capture of Upper Tract Fort, 27 April 1758. MISSING. *WPHM* 39 (1956): 202; *VG*, 22 December 1774.

Burke, Hannah. Child of Mary. Taken by Shawnee in capture of Upper Tract Fort, 27 April 1758. RETURNED c. 1771. *WPHM* 39 (1956): 202; *VG*, 22 December 1774.

Burke, Mary [Mrs William]. Widowed and captured, with her two children, in Shawnee capture of Upper Tract Fort, 27 April 1758. RETURNED at Muskingum, 15 November 1764. *WPHM* 39 (1956): 202.

Burke, Thomas. Soldier in second battalion of Pennsylvania regiment. Captured on 9 September 1756, after Kittanning raid, and TORTURED to death. "Narrative of Marie Le Roy and Barbara Leininger," *PA*, ser. 2, 7: 401–12;

Hugh Gibson, "An Account of the Captivity of Hugh Gibson among the Delaware Indians of the Big Beaver and the Muskingum, from the Latter Part of July 1756 to the Beginning of April 1759," *Massachusetts Historical Society Collections*, ser. 3, 6 (1837): 141–53; *PA*, ser. 2, 2: 439, 458–60.

Burns, James. Soldier taken by Miami in surrender of Fort Miami, 27 May 1763. EXCHANGED for Potawatomi chief No-Kaming at Detroit, 15 June 1763. Hay, *Diary*, 26; *JP*, 10: 731–2; Gladwin, "Gladwin Manuscripts," 657–8.

Burns, Patrick. Farmer from Cumberland County, PA. Captured by the Delaware, 19 October 1755. ESCAPED 26 October 1755. Deposition in HSP, Penn Papers, Indian Affairs, vol. 2, no. 4.

Burton, Jonathan. Soldier in Virginia Regiment. Taken captive at Fort Presqu'île, 2 September 1760. Pensioned as disabled on RETURN, 1 December 1760. Still on pension in 1793. *HBP*, 5: 17, 210–11; Chalkley, *Chronicles of the Scotch-Irish*, vol. 1, 511–12.

Buss/Busz. Child of Johannes Adam Buss. Taken in Albany Township, Northampton County, PA, 6 November 1756. MISSING. *PG*, 18 November 1756; *PMHB* 32 (1908): 318; *NYM*, 22 November 1756; Hunter, *Forts*, 296.

Buss/Busz. Child of Johannes Adam Buss. Taken in Albany Township, Northampton County, PA, 6 November 1756. MISSING. *PG*, 18 November 1756; *PMHB* 32 (1908): 318; *NYM*, 22 November 1756; Hunter, *Forts*, 296.

Buss/Busz. Child of Johannes Adam Buss. Taken in Albany Township, Northampton County, PA, 6 November 1756. MISSING. *PG*, 18 November 1756; *PMHB* 32 (1908): 318; *NYM*, 22 November 1756; Hunter, *Forts*, 296.

Buss/Busz. Child of Johannes Adam Buss. Taken in Albany Township, Northampton County, PA, 6 November 1756. MISSING. *PG*, 18 November 1756; *PMHB* 32 (1908): 318; *NYM*, 22 November 1756; Hunter, *Forts*, 296.

Buss/Busz [Mrs Johannes Adam]. Taken with her four children in Albany Township, Northampton County, PA, 6 November 1756. MISSING. *PG*, 18 November 1756; *PMHB* 32 (1908): 318; *NYM*, 22 November 1756; Hunter, *Forts*, 296.

Butler, James. Pennsylvania trader. Captured in Ohio country in 1763. RETURNED at Muskingum, 15 November 1764. *WPHM* 39 (1956): 191, 196; *PG*, 17 January 1765.

Byrd. Child of Mary and John Byrd. Captured by Shawnee on Jackson River, Augusta County, VA, 11 September 1756. Seen in Lower Shawnee Town in 1764. MISSING. *WPHM* 39 (1956): 202; Preston Papers, 1: 83; *PG*, 7 October 1756; *PJ*, 7 October 1756.

Byrd. Child of Mary and John Byrd. Captured by Shawnee on Jackson River, Augusta County, VA, 11 September 1756. Seen in Lower Shawnee Town in 1764. MISSING. *WPHM* 39 (1956): 202; Preston Papers, 1: 83; *PG*, 7 October 1756; *PJ*, 7 October 1756.

Byrd. Child of Mary and John Byrd. Captured by Shawnee on Jackson River, Augusta County, VA, 11 September 1756. MISSING. Preston Papers, 1: 83; *PG*, 7 October 1756; *PJ*, 7 October 1756.

Byrd, John. Son of Mary and John Byrd. Captured by Shawnee on Jackson River, Augusta County, VA, 11 September 1756. RETURNED at Muskingum, 15 November 1764. Preston Papers, 1: 83; *PG*, 7 October 1756, 17 January 1765; *PJ*, 7 October 1756; *JP*, 11: 485.

Byrd, Mary [Mrs John]. Widowed and captured with her six children by Shawnee in attack on Jackson River, Augusta County, VA, 11 September 1756. RETURNED, 7 January 1765, to Fort Pitt but died within a few days. *WPHM* 39 (1956): 197, 202; Preston Papers, 1: 83; *PG*, 7 March 1765.

Byrd, Molly (1). Infant daughter of Mary and John Byrd. Captured by Shawnee on Jackson River, Augusta County, VA, 11 September 1756. RETURNED by Shawnee, 10 May 1765. *JP*, 11: 721; *WPHM* 39 (1956): 198, 202; Preston Papers, 1: 83.

Byrd, Molly (2). Young daughter of Mary and John Byrd. Captured by Shawnee on Jackson River, Augusta County, VA, 11 September 1756. RETURNED by Shawnee, 10 May 1765. *JP*, 11: 721; *WPHM* 39 (1956): 198, 202; Preston Papers, 1: 83.

Byrd, Nalupua (Nalupeia). Infant daughter of Mary and John Byrd. Captured by Shawnee on Jackson River, Augusta County, VA, 11 September 1756. RETURNED by Shawnee, 10 May 1765. *JP*, 11: 721; *WPHM* 39 (1956): 198, 202.

Cabe, Thomas. Captive seen at Lower Shawnee town in 1764. MISSING. *WPHM* 39 (1956): 202.

Calhoun, Thomas. Pennsylvania trader. Taken by Delaware on Muskingum River, 29 May 1763. ESCAPED three days later. *HBP*, 6: 413; *PG*, 16 June 1763; *NYG*, 4 July 1763.

Callender, Robert. Veteran Pennsylvania trader and onetime partner of George Croghan. Captured by Wyandot at Sandusky in May 1763. RETURNED by 11 March 1765. BL, Add. Mss, 21651, fols 210–11; *Ohio Company Papers*, ed. Bailey, 180. Compare *JP*, 10: 741–2 (where he was reported killed).

Cameron, Allan. Montgomery Highlander. Captured by Mingo in Major James Grant's defeat at Fort Duquesne, 14 September 1758. RETURNED at Detroit, 1 December 1760. *HBP*, 5: 210; *PG*, 28 September 1758.

Campbell. Youth from Cumberland County, PA. Taken by Mingo. Spoke Seneca when RETURNED by the Crow to George Croghan at Fort Pitt, 19 September 1759. "George Croghan's Journal," 352.

Campbell, Arthur (1743–1811). Taken at about sixteen by Wyandot near Fort Young, Augusta County, VA, in 1758. RETURNED (vs escaped) at British takeover of Detroit, 1 December 1760. Later justice of the peace, militia major, and member of the 1775 Virginia House of Burgesses. *HBP*, 5: 210; R.G. Thwaites and L.P. Kellogg, *Documentary History of Dunmore's War 1774* (Madison, WI: Wisconsin Historical Society, 1905), 39–40n; William Smith, *An Historical Account of the Expedition against the Ohio Indians, in the Year 1764, Under the Command of Henry Bouquet Esq.* (Philadelphia, 1766), 29; *Journals of the House of Burgesses, 1761–1765*, ed. Kennedy, 324, 328. See also H.L. Quinn, *Arthur Campbell: Pioneer and Patriot of the Old Southwest* (Jefferson, NC: McFarland,

1990), 10–12; and *Dictionary of Virginia Biography* (Richmond, VA: Library of Virginia, 1998), vol. 2, 554–6.

Campbell, Donald. Captain and former commandant at Detroit. Given to Pontiac as a hostage, 10 May 1763. KILLED by Ojibwa chief Wasson, 4 July 1763. BL, Add. Mss, 21649, fols 252–3.

Campbell, John. Likely husband of Mary. Taken in Cumberland County, PA, 31 March 1757. RANSOMED, and taken to Canada, France, and England. Freed by September 1757. TNA, Adm. 1/4323, n.p.

Campbell [Johnson], Margaret (c. 1749–c. 1783). Virginia girl. Likely captured with Arthur in 1758. Learned several Ohio Indian languages. RETURNED to William Johnson, c. 1764. Stayed with Mohawk, married Johnson's son Brant Kaghneghtago, and raised their four daughters in Mohawk Valley. Barbara J. Sivertsen, *Turtles, Wolves, and Bears: A Mohawk Family History* (Bowie, MD: Heritage, 1996), 133, 135, 302n12.

Campbell, Mary. Wife of John. Taken in Cumberland County, PA, 31 March 1757. RETURNED at Muskingum, 15 November 1764. *WPHM* 39 (1956): 193, 196; *PG*, 14 April 1757, 17 January 1765; *NYM*, 11 and 18 April 1757.

Campbell, Mary. Ten year old taken in Cumberland County, PA, 21 May 1758. RETURNED and known to be in Albany, NY, before October 1764. *PG*, 11 October 1764.

Campbell/Cammel, James. Pennsylvania trader. Captured by Delaware at Licking Creek, OH, 23 May 1763. RETURNED at Muskingum, 15 November 1764. *JP*, 11: 488; *WPHM* 39 (1956): 191; *PG*, 17 January 1765; C. Hale Sipe, *Fort Ligonier and Its Times* (Harrisburg, PA: Telegraph, 1932), 230.

Cannaberry, Terence. Soldier in second battalion of Pennsylvania regiment. MISSING in raid on Kittanning, 9 September 1756. *PA*, ser. 2, 2: 458–60; *NYM*, 27 September 1756; *PG*, 23 September 1756; Hunter, "Victory at Kittanning," 392–402.

Cantrell. One of two children MISSING in Indian attack on Cedar Creek, Frederick County, VA, September 1757. *NYM*, 10 October 1757; Baker, *French and Indian War*, 96; Cecil O'Dell, *Pioneers of Old Frederick County, Virginia* (Westminster, MD: Heritage, 2007), 44, 79, 131.

Cantrell. One of two children MISSING in Indian attack on Cedar Creek, Frederick County, VA, September 1757. *NYM*, 10 October 1757; Baker, *French and Indian War*, 96; O'Dell, *Pioneers*, 44, 79, 131.

Carpenter. One of five Carpenter children taken in Shawnee attack on Jackson River, Augusta County, VA, 11 September 1756. MISSING. Preston Papers, 1: 83; *PG*, 7 October 1756; *PJ*, 7 October 1756.

Carpenter. One of five Carpenter children taken in Shawnee attack on Jackson River, Augusta County, VA, 11 September 1756. MISSING. Preston Papers, 1: 83; *PG*, 7 October 1756; *PJ*, 7 October 1756.

Carpenter. One of five Carpenter children taken in Shawnee attack on Jackson River, Augusta County, VA, 11 September 1756. MISSING. Preston Papers, 1: 83; *PG*, 7 October 1756; *PJ*, 7 October 1756.

Carpenter. Young son of William Carpenter. Captured by Delaware on James River, Augusta County, VA, October 1764. RETURNED 1778. Preston Papers, 1: 83; *PG*, 7 October 1756; *PJ*, 7 October 1756; Withers, *Chronicles* (1895), 96; Baker, *French and Indian War*, 133; Waddell, *Annals of Augusta*, vol. 1, 121.

Carpenter, Jerry/Terry. One of five Carpenter children taken in Shawnee attack on Jackson River, Augusta County, VA, 11 September 1756. RETURNED 10 May 1765. *WPHM* 39 (1956): 198; *JP*, 11: 720; Preston Papers, 1: 83; *PG*, 7 October 1756; *PJ*, 7 October 1756.

Carpenter, Joseph. Taken in Shawnee attack on Jackson River, Augusta County, VA, 11 September 1756. ESCAPED before May 1763 and became a soldier. Preston Papers, 1: 83; *PG*, 7 October 1756; *PJ*, 7 October 1756; Chalkley, *Chronicles of the Scotch-Irish*, vol. 1, 326, 486, 499.

Carpenter, Solomon. One of five Carpenter children taken in Shawnee attack on Jackson River, Augusta County, VA, 11 September 1756. RETURNED at Muskingum, 15 November 1764. Preston Papers, 1: 83; *PG*, 7 October 1756, 17 January 1765; *PJ*, 7 October 1756, 17 January 1765; *NYG*, 21 January 1765.

Carr, Anne. Held captive in French Margaret's Town. RANSOMED for £15 at Shamokin, 17 May 1761. Friendly Society Records, Haverford College Library, Indian Committee Records, 824/11, vol. 4, 115–18.

Carroll. One of three children of Hugh. Captured near Juniata River, Cumberland County, PA, 30 July 1756. MISSING. *PG*, 5 August 1757; *NYM*, 9 August 1756.

Carroll. One of three children of Hugh. Captured near Juniata River, Cumberland County, PA, 30 July 1756. MISSING. *PG*, 5 August 1757; *NYM*, 9 August 1756.

Carroll. One of three children of Hugh. Captured near Juniata River, Cumberland County, PA, 30 July 1756. MISSING. *PG*, 5 August 1757; *NYM*, 9 August 1756.

Carroll, [Mrs Hugh]. Captured near Juniata River, Cumberland County, PA, 30 July 1756. MISSING. *PG*, 5 August 1757; *NYM*, 9 August 1756.

Carroll, Hugh. Captured in attack near Juniata River, Cumberland County, PA, 30 July 1756. ESCAPED two days later. KILLED in another attack three months later. *PG*, 5 August and 11 November 1756; *NYM*, 9 August and 15 November 1756; *PA*, ser. 1, 3: 40–1.

Carter. Girl captured in Delaware attack on Connecticut settlement at Wyoming, Northampton County, PA, 15 October 1763. MISSING. *JP*, 4: 497; *PG*, 20 and 27 October 1763.

Carter. Young boy captured in Delaware attack on Connecticut settlement at Wyoming, Northampton County, PA, 15 October 1763. MISSING. *JP*, 4: 497; *PG*, 20 and 27 October 1763.

Carter, Eliza[beth]. Ten year old captured by Delaware in attack on Connecticut settlement at Wyoming, Northampton County, PA, 15 October 1763. RETURNED by Chenussio Seneca to William Johnson at Fort Niagara conference, 31 July 1764. *JP*, 4: 496–7; *PG*, 6 September 1764; *NYG*, 17 September 1764.

Carter, Sara. Younger sister of Eliza. Captured with her in Delaware attack on Connecticut settlement at Wyoming, Northampton County, PA, 15 October 1763. RETURNED by Chenussio Seneca to William Johnson at Fort Niagara conference, 31 July 1764. *JP*, 4: 496–7; *PG*, 6 September 1764; *NYG*, 17 September 1764.

Cartmell, Molly. Youth captured by Shawnee in attack on Cowpasture, Augusta County, VA, 22 October 1757. RETURNED at Muskingum, 15 November 1764. Preston Papers, 1: 163; *WPHM* 39 (1956): 195, 196; *JP*, 11: 486; *PG*, 17 January 1765; *NYG*, 21 January 1765.

Cartmell, Peggy. Youth captured by Shawnee in attack on Cowpasture, Augusta County, VA, 22 October 1757. RETURNED at Muskingum, 15 November 1764. Preston Papers, 1: 163; *WPHM* 39 (1956): 195, 196, 202; *JP*, 11: 486; *PG*, 17 January 1765; *NYG*, 21 January 1765.

Castle, Mary. Woman from Augusta County, VA. RETURNED at Muskingum, 15 November 1764. *PG*, 17 January 1765; *WPHM* 39 (1956): 190, 195; *JP*, 11: 486 (where she is called "Elizabeth").

Cawacawache. Adult male thought to be from Virginia. White Indian RETURNED at Muskingum, 15 November 1764. *PG*, 17 January 1765; *NYG*, 21 January 1765; *WPHM* 39 (1956): 189; *JP*, 11: 485.

Chapman. Young daughter of Abigail. Captured with her mother and sisters in Delaware attack on Connecticut settlement at Wyoming (Cushietunk), May 1763. RETURNED to Johnson Hall, NY, May 1765. *PG*, 19 September 1765: *NYG*, 4 July 1765; *NYM*, 19 August 1765.

Chapman. Young daughter of Abigail. Captured with her mother and sisters in Delaware attack on Connecticut settlement at Wyoming (Cushietunk), May 1763. RETURNED to Johnson Hall, NY, May 1765. *PG*, 19 September 1765; *NYG*, 4 July 1765; *NYM*, 19 August 1765.

Chapman, Abigail. Captured with her three daughters in Delaware attack on Connecticut settlement at Wyoming (Cushietunk), May 1763. RETURNED at Fort Niagara, June 1764. *PG*, 6 September 1764; *NYG*, 17 September 1764; *JP*, 4: 496n.

Chapman, Abigail, Jr. Captured with her mother and sisters in Delaware attack on Connecticut settlement at Wyoming (Cushietunk), June 1763. RETURNED at Fort Niagara, May 1764. *PG*, 6 September 1763; *NYG*, 17 September 1764; *JP*, 4: 496n.

Chapman, Abraham. New York trader. Captured by Ojibwa at Detroit, 13 May 1763. Held for two months, torture begun, but RELEASED on 12 July when thought mad. Hay, *Diary*, 7, 47; BL, Add. Mss, 21649, fols 252–6; *JP*, 10: 741–2; Gladwin, "Gladwin Manuscripts," 642; John Heckewelder, *History, Manners, and Customs of the Indian Nations Who Once Inhabited Pennsylvania and the Neighbouring States*, rev. ed. (Philadelphia, PA, 1876), 257–8.

Chem. Trader captured by the Potowatomi at Fort St Joseph, MI, 27 May 1763. MISSING. *JP*, 10: 715; BL, Add. Mss, 21655, 214.

Cherry, Jane. Pennsylvania woman captive reported alive at Detroit in 1757. MISSING. *NYM*, 2 January 1758; *PG*, 22 December 1757.

Childs/Childes, Edward. Soldier in Captain Stuart's company of Virginia Regiment. Captured by Shawnee and French in Major James Grant's defeat at Fort Duquesne, 14 September 1758. Sent to Canada and France and EXCHANGED in July 1760. *Journals of the House of Burgesses, 1758–1761*, ed. McIlwaine, 18; *Journals of the House of Burgesses, 1761–1765*, ed. Kennedy, 179, 186; *PG*, 28 September and 19 October 1758; HL, AB, 659. Compare *GWP*, 6: 46.

Christie, John. Ensign in Royal American Regiment. Captured by Wyandot in surrender of Fort Presqu'île, 21 June 1763. RETURNED at Detroit, 9 July 1763. *PG*, 7 July and 18 August 1763; *NYM*, 8 and 15 August 1763; *NYG*, 8 August 1763.

Christman. Young son of Henry. Captured by Delaware in Northampton County, PA, 4 April 1756, and seen at Tioga. MISSING. *PMHB* 32 (1908): 313; *PA*, ser. 1, 3: 45.

Christopher, Molly. Captive still held in Lower Shawnee Town at end of 1764. MISSING. Likely a white Indian. *WPHM* 39 (1956): 202.

Cisney/Sisney. Young son of John. Taken with brother and father seven miles from Shippensburg, Cumberland County, PA, 8 July 1757. RETURNED at Detroit, 1 October 1761. *PA*, ser. 1, 3: 219–20; *HBP*, 5: 822; *PG*, 4 August 1757; *NYM*, 8 August 1757.

Cisney/Sisney. Young son of John. Taken with brother and father seven miles from Shippensburg, Cumberland County, PA, 8 July 1757. RETURNED at Detroit, 1 October 1761. *PA*, ser. 1, 3: 219–20; *HBP*, 5: 822; *PG*, 4 August 1757; *NYM*, 8 August 1757.

Cisney/Sisney, John. Captured by Indians, along with his two sons, seven miles from Shippensburg, Cumberland County, PA, 8 July 1757. Likely RETURNED. Owned farm near Shippensburg from 1771 to 1785. *PG*, 4 August 1757; *NYM*, 8 August 1757; *PA*, ser. 1, 3: 219–20; *PA*, ser. 3, 20: 58, 325, 755; Diane E. Greene, *Cumberland County, Pennsylvania Quarter Session Dockets, 1750–1785* (Baltimore, MD: Clearfield, 2000), 154.

Clamentine [nom de guerre]. Canadian marine in Commandant Pierre-Joseph Céloron de Blainville's company. Captured at battle of La Belle Famille, near Fort Niagara, 24 July 1759. Interned in Somerset County, NJ, and then EXCHANGED, 9 December 1760. *JP*, 13: 115; Job Stockton Papers, NYHS.

Clark, Andrew. Virginian. Captured by Shawnee, 15 July 1763. RETURNED by Shawnee to Fort Pitt, 10 May 1765. *JP*, 11: 720; *WPHM* 39 (1956): 198.

Clark, Rachel. Woman from Cumberland County, PA. Taken by two Shawnee, 2 November 1755. Reported seen in captivity. MISSING, but possibly returned. A Rachel Clark married John Aves in 1772, and was taxed for property in Bedford County in 1775. *MPCP*, 6: 673–4; *PG*, 13 November 1755; *NYM*, 17 November 1755; *PA*, ser. 2, 2: 51; *PA*, ser. 3, 20: 108; *MVHR* 13 (1926): 60.

Clayton. Captain of militia in Lancaster County, PA. Taken in Major James Grant's defeat at Fort Duquesne, 14 September 1758. RETURNED, likely by exchange, before 1763. Draper Mss, Virginia Papers, 3ZZ48; *PG*, 27 October 1763.

Clem, Daniel. Pennsylvania boy taken in 1755. RETURNED at Muskingum, 15 November 1764. *PG*, 17 January 1765; *NYG*, 21 January 1765, *WPHM* 39 (1956): 196.

Clem, Felty. Pennsylvania youth taken in 1755. RETURNED at Muskingum, 15 November 1764. *JP*, 11: 488; *PG*, 17 January 1765; *NYG*, 21 January 1765, *WPHM* 39 (1956): 191.

Clem, Ludvick. Pennsylvania youth taken in 1755. RETURNED at Muskingum, 15 November 1764. *JP*, 11: 486; *PG*, 17 January 1765; *NYG*, 21 January 1765, *WPHM* 39 (1956): 191.

Clendennin. Infant child of Jennet. Captured by Shawnee at Greenbrier, Augusta County, VA, 15 July 1763. KILLED the next day after mother escaped. Joseph Doddridge, *Notes on the Settlement and Indian Wars of the Western Parts of Virginia and Pennsylvania* (Wellsburgh, VA, 1824), 227; Draper Mss, Frontier Wars Papers, 21U136.

Clendennin. Young son of Jennet. Captured by Shawnee at Greenbrier, Augusta County, VA, 15 July 1763. DIED in captivity. Draper Mss, Frontier Wars Papers, 21U136-7; Doddridge, *Notes on the Settlement*, 227.

Clendennin, Jean/Jane (b. 1758). Five-year-old daughter of Jennet. Captured by Shawnee at Greenbrier, Augusta County, VA, 15 July 1763. RETURNED at Fort Pitt, 14 May 1765. *JP*, 11: 721; *WPHM* 39 (1956): 198; Draper Mss, Frontier Wars Papers, 21U136-7; Doddridge, *Notes on the Settlement*, 227.

Clendennin, Jennet/Anne [Mrs Archibald]. Widowed and captured with three children in Shawnee attack on Greenbrier, Augusta County, VA, 15 July 1763. ESCAPED next day. Chalkley, *Chronicles of the Scotch-Irish*, vol. 2, 93; Doddridge, *Notes on the Settlement*, 226–7.

Clifford, Samuel. Man from Cumberland County, PA. Captured by Delaware near Tioga, in July 1756, after having escaped from captivity after Colonel John Bradstreet's skirmish near Fort Oswego, NY, on 3 July 1756. RETURNED by Teedyuscung, 11 October 1756. *PG*, 2 November 1756; *NYM*, 18 October 1756; *MPCP*, 7: 284.

Clouser/Clowser. Infant girl KILLED soon after family captured in Frederick County, VA, 2 June 1764. Kercheval, *History of the Valley*, 97–8; *PG*, 14 June 1764; *NYG*, 18 June 1764.

Clouser/Clowser, Betty. Teenage daughter of Mary. Captured in Frederick County, VA, 2 June 1764. RETURNED at Muskingum, 15 November 1764. Kercheval, *History of the Valley*, 97–8; *PG*, 14 June 1764, 17 January 1765; *NYG*, 18 June 1764, 21 January 1765; *JP*, 11: 487; *WPHM* 39 (1956): 190.

Clouser/Clowser, Magdalene. Young daughter of Mary. Captured in Frederick County, VA, 2 June 1764. RETURNED at Muskingum, 15 November 1764. Kercheval, *History of the Valley*, 97–8; *PG*, 14 June 1764, 17 January 1765; *NYG*, 18 June 1764, 21 January 1765; *JP*, 11: 487; *WPHM* 39 (1956): 190.

Clouser/Clowser, Mary, Jr. Teenage daughter of Mary. Captured in Frederick County, VA, 2 June 1764. RETURNED at Muskingum, 15 November 1764. Kercheval, *History of the Valley*, 97–8; *PG*, 14 June 1764, 17 January 1765; *NYG*, 18 June 1764, 21 January 1765; *JP*, 11: 487; *WPHM* 39 (1956): 190.

Clouser/Clowser, Mary [Mrs Henry]. Widowed and captured with four daughters in attack in Frederick County, VA, 2 June 1764. RETURNED at Muskingum, 15 November 1764. Kercheval, *History of the Valley*, 97–8; *PG*, 14

June 1764, 17 January 1765; *NYG*, 18 June 1764, 21 January 1765; *JP*, 11: 487; *WPHM* 39 (1956): 190.

Cloyd. Teenage son of David Cloyd. Captured in raid in Augusta County, VA, 20 March 1764. MISSING. *PG*, 3 May and 14 June, 1764; *NYG*, 18 June 1764; Kercheval, *History of the Valley*, 97.

Cobble, Michael. Virginian. RETURNED at Muskingum, 15 November 1764. *WPHM* 39 (1956): 189, 196; *JP*, 11: 485; *PG*, 17 January 1765; *NYG*, 21 January 1765.

Cochran. Young son of Robert. Taken by Delaware in capture of Bigham's Fort, Cumberland County, PA, 11 June 1756. MISSING. *NYM*, 21 and 28 June 1756; *PG*, 17 and 24 June 1756; Loudon, ed., *Selection*, vol. 2, 185.

Cochran. Young son of Robert. Taken by Delaware in capture of Bigham's Fort, Cumberland County, PA, 11 June 1756. MISSING. *NYM*, 21 and 28 June 1756; *PG*, 17 and 24 June 1756; Loudon, ed., *Selection*, vol. 2, 185.

Cochran, John. Teenage son of Robert. Captured by Delaware in fall of Bigham's Fort, Cumberland County, PA, 11 June 1756. RETURNED at Muskingum, 15 November 1764. *JP*, 11: 487; *WPHM* 39 (1956): 191; *NYM*, 21 and 28 June 1756; *PG*, 17 and 24 June 1756, 17 January 1765.

Cockran, Denis. Soldier in Royal American Regiment. Captured near Pittsburgh and RETURNED at Fort Niagara, 15 August 1760. BL, Add. Mss, 21645, fol. 182.

Cody, Daniel. Captive of Shawnee seen at Lower Shawnee Town late in 1764. MISSING. *WPHM* 39 (1956): 202.

Cohoon. Child taken with mother and sibling in capture of Neally's Fort, Frederick County, VA, 23 April 1756. MISSING. Baker, *French and Indian War*, 51–2.

Cohoon. Child taken with mother and sibling in capture of Neally's Fort, Frederick County, VA, 23 April 1756. MISSING. Baker, *French and Indian War*, 51–2.

Cohoon, [Mrs]. Pregnant woman taken with two children in capture of Neally's Fort, Frederick County, VA, 23 April 1756. KILLED the same day. Baker, *French and Indian War*, 51–2.

Cole. Soldier in Virginia Regiment. Captured in fall of Vause's Fort, Augusta County, VA, 25 June 1756. TORTURED to death by Shawnee on trail near Lower Shawnee Town. *PG*, 28 July 1757; *NYM*, 1 August 1757.

Collet. Canadian soldier from Charlesbourg, QC. Captured by Virginians in Jumonville incident, 28 May 1754. RETURNED via Martinique, 24 October 1755. *Collections des manuscrits ... Nouvelle France*, vol. 3, 521–2; *PG*, 13 and 27 June, 22 August, and 12 September 1754.

Collett, Daniel. Pennsylvania packhorse man with Thomas Calhoun's crew. Captured by Delaware on Muskingum River, 29 May 1763. ESCAPED the next day. BL, Add. Mss, 21649, fol. 130.

Colley, Peggy [Margaret]. Virginian. RETURNED at Muskingum, 15 November 1764. *WPHM* 39 (1956): 190; *PG*, 17 January 1765; *NYG*, 21 January 1765.

Collins, Thomas. Virginian. Captured on 15 July 1763. RETURNED at Muskingum, 15 November 1764. *WPHM* 39 (1956): 189; *JP*, 11: 485; *PG*, 17 January 1765; *NYG*, 21 January 1765.

Conaway. Child of Cayuga Samuel Conaway. Captured by Pennsylvania militia, 1 June 1763. Held in protective custody at Carlisle and Fort Bedford. MISSING. BL, Add. Mss, 21642, fol. 477; BL, Add. Mss, 21649, fol. 143; *HBP*, 6: 214, 247–8, 250–2, 308, 332, 596.

Conaway, Mrs Samuel. Captured with Cayuga husband and child by Pennsylvania militia, 1 June 1763. Held in protective custody at Carlisle and Fort Bedford. ESCAPED 12 September 1763. BL, Add. Mss, 21649, fol. 143; BL, Add. Mss, 21642, fol. 477; *HBP*, 6: 247–8, 214, 250–2, 308, 332, 596.

Conaway, Samuel. Cayuga captured with his wife and child at their farm on Susquehanna River by Pennsylvania militia, 1 June 1763. Held in protective custody at Carlisle and Fort Bedford. ESCAPED 12 September 1763. BL, Add. Mss, 21649, fol. 143; BL, Add. Mss, 21642, fol. 477; *HBP*, 6: 247–8, 214, 250–2, 308, 332, 596.

Condon, John/Peter. Taken with wife, Sara, at Conococheague Creek, Cumberland County, PA, by Shawnee and Delaware, 2 November 1755. Signed as Catholic at baptism of his daughter Helaine at Fort Duquesne, 15 May 1756. Likely the Peter Condon RETURNED at Lancaster conference, 13 August 1762, by Tamaqua. *The Baptismal Register of Fort Duquesne*, ed. A.A. Lambing (Pittsburgh, PA, 1885), 70–1; *Minutes of Conferences Held at Lancaster in August 1762* ... (Pennsylvania, PA, 1763), 7.

Condon, Sara [Mrs John, nee Choisy]. Taken with husband, John, at Conococheague Creek, Cumberland County, PA, by Shawnee and Delaware, 2 November 1755. Gave birth to daughter Helaine in March 1756. MISSING. *Baptismal Register*, ed. Lambing, 70–1.

Conletoncontre, Sergeant. French marine in Lieutenant François-Xavier de St Ours's company. Taken by Major Robert Rogers in surrender of Detroit, 30 November 1760. Ordered to France aboard HMS *Fowey*, 4 May 1761. EXCHANGED. TNA, WO 1/5, 176; *PG*, 15 January and 5 February 176; *NYM*, 30 March 1761.

Connor, James. Soldier in Royal American Regiment. Captured by Huron at Detroit, 28 May 1763. RETURNED within five months. [Robert Navarre], *Journal of Pontiac's Conspiracy, 1763*, ed. C.M. Burton (Detroit, MI: Lakeside, 1912) 144n; TNA, WO 34/49, fol. 267.

Conogontony/Conogoniony. White Indian woman thought to have been from Virginia. RETURNED at Muskingum, 15 November 1764. *WPHM* 39 (1956): 190, 192; *PG*, 17 January 1765; *NYG*, 21 January 1765.

Conrad. Child of Ulrich. Captured with mother and four siblings on South Branch of Potomac River, Augusta County, VA, 19 March 1758. DIED in captivity. *PG*, 5 September 1765.

Conrad. Child of Ulrich. Captured with mother and four siblings on South Branch of Potomac River, Augusta County, VA, 19 March 1758. DIED in captivity. *PG*, 5 September 1765.

Conrad. Child of Ulrich. Captured with mother and four siblings on South Branch of Potomac River, Augusta County, VA, 19 March 1758. WHITE INDIAN. *PG*, 5 September 1765.

Conrad. Eldest son of Ulrich. Captured with mother and four siblings on South Branch of Potomac River, Augusta County, VA, 19 March 1758. RETURNED 1762. *PG*, 5 September 1765.

Conrad, Barbara ["Attawa"]. Nineteen-year-old daughter of Ulrich. Captured with mother and four siblings on South Branch of Potomac River, Augusta County, VA, 19 March 1758. Reportedly returned at Muskingum, 15 November 1764, but still MISSING a year later. *PG*, 17 January and 5 September 1765.

Conrad, Mrs Barbara. Wife of Ulrich. Captured with her five children on South Branch of Potomac River, Augusta County, VA, 19 March 1758. Catholic godparent at Detroit while a captive. RETURNED, together with her eldest son, in 1762. *PG*, 5 September 1765; *Baptismal Register*, ed. Lambing, 76–7.

Consola. Daughter of Emmanuel. Captured by Delaware in Northampton County, PA, September 1757. Reported in 1764 as "taken the war before last." WHITE INDIAN. *PMHB* 32 (1908): 314; *PG*, 6 September 1765.

Contracht. Girl captured with her mother and sister by Delaware in Northampton County, PA, December 1755. MISSING. *PG*, 1 January 1756; *PJ*, 1 January 1756; *NYM*, 5 January 1756.

Contracht. Girl captured with her mother and sister by Delaware in Northampton County, PA, December 1755. MISSING. *PG*, 1 January 1756; *PJ*, 1 January 1756; *NYM*, 5 January 1756.

Contracht [Mrs]. Widowed and captured with her two daughters in Delaware attack in Northampton County, PA, December 1755. MISSING. *PG*, 1 January 1756; *PJ*, 1 January 1756; *NYM*, 5 January 1756.

Cooley, Isaac. Fourteen when returned at Lancaster treaty in September 1762. *Minutes of Conferences … Lancaster, 1762*, 7; *PG*, 9 September 1762.

Coon, Anne. Teenager from Northampton County, PA. Taken near Delaware River, 1 January 1756. RETURNED by June 1761. *PMHB* 32 (1908): 315; *PG*, 2 July 1761.

Coon, Elizabeth. Teenager from Northampton County, PA. Taken near Delaware River, 1 January 1756. RETURNED at Muskingum, 15 November 1764. *PMHB* 32 (1908): 315; *WPHM* 39 (1956): 189; *PG*, 17 January 1765.

Coon, Jane. Teenager from Northampton County, PA. Taken near Delaware River, 1 January 1756. Seen at Pittsburgh in 1760 with one *métis* child. RETURNED at Muskingum, 15 November 1764, with her two *métis* children. Haverford College Library, Indian Committee Records, 824/11, vol. 3, n.p.; *PMHB* 32 (1908): 315; *PG*, 17 January 1765; *NYG*, 21 January 1765.

Coope, Sergeant. Soldier in Royal American Regiment. RETURNED at Fort Niagara, 15 August 1760. BL, Add. Mss, 21645, fol. 182.

Cooper, Thomas. Soldier in Royal American Regiment. Taken by Wyandot at "Depot of St. Cayler on Lake Erie," 28 May 1763. RETURNED before 21 December 1763. Gladwin, "Gladwin Manuscripts," 661.

Cooper, Thomas. Virginian boy. Captured near Potomac River, 16 October 1753. Seen on Ohio River, January 1754. RETURNED to William Johnson, c. September 1764. *PG*, 27 December 1753, 26 February 1754; *JP*, 4: 575.

Corken, James. Soldier in second battalion of Pennsylvania regiment. Captured in Cumberland County, PA, 1 November 1756. MISSING. *PA*, ser. 1, 3: 40–1; *PA*, ser. 2, 2: 459; *PG*, 11 November 1756.

Corn Blade [Tamimabuck]. Shawnee hostage given to Colonel Henry Bouquet at Muskingum, 14 November 1765. ESCAPED from Fort Pitt, 3 December 1764. HL, MM, 569, fols 37–8; *MPCP*, 9: 232; *HBP*, 6: 717.

Cotter, John. Captive last seen in Lower Shawnee Town late in 1764. MISSING. *WPHM* 39 (1956): 202.

Coulon de Villiers, François (1712–94). Canadian marine captain. Captured by William Johnson's army at battle of La Belle Famille, 24 July 1759. EXCHANGED in France, 24 January 1761. TNA, CO 5/1068, fol. 304; *DCB*, 4: 177–8.

Coulson. Trader captured by Delaware at Beaver Creek, 23 May 1763. ESCAPED the next day. Mary Carson Darlington, *Fort Pitt and Letters from the Frontier* (Pittsburgh, PA, 1892), 85.

Countzmann, Elizabeth. Age nine when taken at Carr's (Kerr's) Creek, VA, 17 July 1763. RETURNED by Shawnee to Fort Pitt, 5 January 1765. *PG*, 7 March 1765; *WPHM* 39 (1956): 197. In March 1765 the Augusta County court summoned a George Weaver who "has in his possession Elizabeth Countzmann and does not provide for her." Chalkley, *Chronicles of the Scotch-Irish*, vol. 1, 118.

Countzmann, Mrs. Taken with her daughter by Shawnee at Carr's (Kerr's) Creek, VA, 17 July 1763. RETURNED at Muskingum, 15 November 1764. BL, Add. Mss, 21651, fol. 127.

Cousler. Girl taken with her mother at Greenbrier River settlement, Augusta County, VA, September 1755. MISSING. Preston Papers, 1: 163.

Cousler, [Mrs]. Taken with her daughter at Greenbrier River settlement, Augusta County, VA, September 1755. MISSING. Preston Papers, 1: 83.

Cox, James. Virginian. Captured near Potomac River, 26 November 1757. ESCAPED, taking a scalp, two days later. *PG*, 8 and 15 December 1757, 2 March 1758; *NYM*, 19 December 1757.

Coxe, John. Captured with his brother and John Craig by Delaware near McDowell's Mill, Cumberland County, PA, 11 February 1756. ESCAPED to Fort Augusta, 14 August 1756. *MPCP*, 7: 242–3; *PG*, 19 February, 1 April, and 9 September 1756.

Coxe, Richard. Captured with his brother and John Craig by Delaware near McDowell's Mill, Cumberland County PA, 11 February 1756. MISSING. *MPCP*, 7: 242–3; *PG*, 19 February, 1 April, 9 September 1756.

Craig, John. Captured with the Coxe brothers by Delaware near McDowell's Mill, Cumberland County, PA, 11 February 1756. Adopted by Shingas. ESCAPED in March 1756. HSP, Penn Mss, Indian Affairs, vol. 2, no. 78; *PG*, 19 February and 1 March 1756.

Craven, Mary. Virginian. RETURNED at Muskingum, 15 November 1764. *WPHM* 39 (1956): 190, 196; *JP*, 11: 487; *PG*, 17 January 1765; *NYG*, 21 January 1765.

Crawford, Arthur. Maryland youth. Captured by Delaware, 26 February 1756. RETURNED 1762. Became a ranger captain, and was killed in 1763. Draper Mss, Pittsburgh and Northwest Virginia Papers, 6N77.

Crawford, Hugh. Pennsylvania trader. Captured by Ottawa and Mingo near Cedar Point, OH, 14 May 1763. ESCAPED to Fort Detroit, 7 November 1763. *HBP*, 6: 197, 412–13; *Ohio Company Papers*, ed. Bailey, 159; *PG*, 16 and 30 June 1763; *NYM*, 4 July 1763.

Croghan, George. Deputy superintendent of Indian affairs. Captured by the Ouiatenon, 8 June 1765. RANSOMED, for sixty-four gallons of rum, 11 July 1765. *JP*, 11: 836–41; Wainwright, *George Croghan*, 220–1; *PG*, 15 August 1765.

Crooked Legs. Pennsylvania boy. RETURNED at Muskingum, 15 November 1764. *WPHM* 39 (1956): 192, 196; *JP*, 11: 488; *PG*, 17 January 1765; *NYG*, 21 January 1765.

Crow. One of four children of Joseph captured with their mother in Cumberland County, PA, 3 June 1764. MISSING. *PG*, 14 June 1764.

Crow. One of four children of Joseph captured with their mother in Cumberland County, PA, 3 June 1764. MISSING. *PG*, 14 June 1764.

Crow, Jane. Teenage daughter of Joseph. Captured with her mother in Cumberland County, PA, 3 June 1764. RETURNED at Muskingum, 15 November 1764. *WPHM* 39 (1956): 193; *PG*, 17 January 1765; *NYG*, 21 January 1765.

Crow, [Mrs Joseph]. Wife of Joseph. Captured with four children in Cumberland County, PA, 3 June 1764. ESCAPED 11 June 1764. *PG*, 14 and 21 June 1764; *NYG*, 25 June 1764.

Crow, Polly. Daughter of Joseph. Captured with her mother in Cumberland County, PA, 3 June 1764. RETURNED at Muskingum, 15 November 1764. *WPHM* 39 (1956): 193; *PG*, 17 January 1765; *NYG*, 21 January 1765.

Crump, Francis. "A Dutchman" captured by the Shawnee. RETURNED to George Croghan, 28 December 1759. "George Croghan's Journal," 364.

Cunningham, Betsy. One of four children of Jacob captured by Shawnee in second "massacre" at Carr's (Kerr's) Creek, Augusta County, VA, 17 July 1763. Likely RETURNED. Chalkley, *Chronicles of the Scotch-Irish*, vol. 1, 164; Baker, *French and Indian War*, 126.

Cunningham, Henry. One of four children of Jacob captured by Shawnee in second "massacre" at Carr's (Kerr's) Creek, Augusta County, VA, 17 July 1763. MISSING. Baker, *French and Indian War*, 126.

Cunningham, James. One of four children of Jacob captured by Shawnee in second "massacre" at Carr's (Kerr's) Creek, Augusta County, VA, 17 July 1763. Likely RETURNED. Chalkley, *Chronicles of the Scotch-Irish*, vol. 2, 41, 122, 359, 410, 422, 424, 430; Baker, *French and Indian War*, 126.

Cunningham, John. Taken on South Branch of Potomac River, Augusta County, VA, 19 March 1758. MISSING but may have returned. Preston Papers, 1: 83; Chalkley, *Chronicles of the Scotch-Irish*, vol. 2, 449.

Cunningham, Margaret. Child scalped and captured by Shawnee at Greenbrier, Augusta County, VA, 17 October 1759. RETURNED. Captured again, with three other children of Jacob, by Shawnee, 17 July 1763. RETURNED 10 May 1765. Lived another forty years. *WPHM* 39 (1956): 198; *JP*, 11: 721; Baker, *French and Indian War*, 126.

Cunsarle. Young daughter of Manuel. Captured in Northampton County, PA, September 1757. MISSING. *PMHB* 32 (1908): 314.

Curtis. Daughter of Pennsylvanian Samuel Curtis. Held captive by Seneca in 1762. *Minutes of Conferences ... Lancaster, 1762*, 33.

Cutrides/[Cartwright?]. Child of Abraham. Taken with mother and a sibling in Northampton County, PA, November 1755. MISSING. *PMHB* 32 (1908): 314.

Cutrides/[Cartwright?]. Child of Abraham. Taken with mother and a sibling in Northampton County, PA, November 1755. MISSING. *PMHB* 32 (1908): 314.

Cutrides/[Cartwright?], [Mrs Abraham]. Captured with two children in Northampton County, PA, November 1755. MISSING. *PMHB* 32 (1908): 314.

Dagneau Douville de Lamothe, Guillame. Major in Detroit militia. Captured in battle of La Belle Famille, 24 July 1759. EXCHANGED at Crown Point, NY, 14 December 1759. Dunnigan, *Siege–1759*, 80; *DCB*, 3: 158–9.

Dagneau Douville de La Saussaye. Canadian ensign and trader. Captured by Cherokee and Virginians near Fort Cumberland, MD, 8 June 1757. KILLED by Cherokee the same day. *NYCD*, 7: 282; *DCB*, 4: 192; Hunter, *Forts*, 125–6; *PG*, 23 June 1757; *NYM*, 27 June 1757.

Dagneau Douville de Quindre, Louis-Césaire (1704–67). Colonel in Detroit militia. Captured in battle of La Belle Famille, 24 July 1759. EXCHANGED at Crown Point, NY, 14 December 1759. Dunnigan, *Siege–1759*, 80; *DCB*, 3: 158–9.

Dannal/Darnell. Teamster-sutler taken captive by Delaware near Fort Ligonier, PA, April 1759. RANSOMED by Nathaniel Holland at Shamokin for £8 Pennsylvania currency in 1760. BL, Add. Mss, 21644, fol. 132; Haverford College Library, Indian Committee Records, 824/11, vol. 4, n.p.; Hunter, *Forts*, 163–4.

Danvers, Sir Robert. With surveying party on Lake St Clair when captured by Ojibwa, 6 May 1763. KILLED and cannibalized the same day. BL, Add. Mss, 21649, fol. 252; *PG*, 7 July 1763, 11 and 18 August 1763.

Davidson, Agnes. Woman from Cumberland County, PA. Captured with daughter, 20 March 1763. RETURNED at Muskingum, 15 November 1764. BL, Add. Mss, 21650, fol. 103; *PG*, 5 April 1764, 17 January 1765; *NYG*, 5 April 1764, 21 January 1765; *WPHM* 39 (1956): 193.

Davidson, Molly (a.k.a. Nancy). Infant daughter of Agnes. Taken with her mother in Cumberland County, PA, 20 March 1763. RETURNED at Muskingum, 15 November 1764. BL, Add. Mss, 21650, fol. 103; *PG*, 5 April 1764, 17 January 1765; *NYG*, 5 April 1764, 21 January 1765; *WPHM* 39 (1956): 196.

Davies, Benjamin. Soldier taken in surrender of Vause's Fort, Augusta County, VA, 25 June 1756. MISSING. Reported dead before November 1759. *PG*, 28 July 1757, 9 February 1758; Preston Papers, 1: 83; https://www.familysearch.org.

Davies, Thomas. Virginian. Captured at Roanoke, Augusta County, VA, June 1756. ESCAPED. Preston Papers, 1: 83.

Davis, Owen. Maryland man. Taken "at Conagagee on Potomac," 5 June 1756. EXCHANGED at Crown Point, NY, 24 November 1759. TNA, CO 5/57, fols 119–21; *PG*, 23 June 1757.

Davis, William. Youth captured at Blackwater, VA, 1755. RETURNED to Fort Pitt by Shawnee, 10 May 1765. *WPHM* 39 (1956): 198; *JP*, 11: 720.

Davis, William [Mondeaticker]. Delaware hostage taken by Colonel Henry Bouquet at Muskingum, 11 November 1764. MISSING. HL, MM, 569, fol. 32; *JP*, 8: 459.

Dawson. One of four young children captured with their mother in Frederick County, MD, 23 June 1755. MISSING. *MPCP*, 6: 456; *PG*, 10 July 1755.

Dawson. One of four young children captured with their mother in Frederick County, MD, 23 June 1755. MISSING. *MPCP*, 6: 456; *PG*, 10 July 1755.

Dawson. One of four young children captured with their mother in Frederick County, MD, 23 June 1755. MISSING. *MPCP*, 6: 456; *PG*, 10 July 1755.

Dawson. One of four young children captured with their mother in Frederick County, MD, 23 June 1755. MISSING. *MPCP*, 6: 456; *PG*, 10 July 1755.

Dawson [Mrs]. Taken with her four young children in Frederick County, MD, 23 June 1755. MISSING. *MPCP*, 6: 456; *PG*, 10 July 1755.

Day. Child of Mrs Day. Taken with mother and three siblings in Augusta County, VA, 1 June 1764. RETAKEN the next day. *PG*, 14 June 1764; *NYG*, 18 June 1764; Kercheval, *History of the Valley*, 85–6.

Day. Child of Mrs Day. Taken with mother and three siblings in Augusta County, VA, 1 June 1764. RETAKEN the next day. *PG*, 14 June 1764; *NYG*, 18 June 1764; Kercheval, *History of the Valley*, 85–6.

Day. Child of Mrs Day. Taken with mother and three siblings in Augusta County, VA, 1 June 1764. MISSING. *PG*, 14 June 1764; *NYG*, 18 June 1764; Kercheval, *History of the Valley*, 85–6.

Day. Child of Mrs Day. Taken with mother and three siblings in Augusta County, VA, 1 June 1764. MISSING. *PG*, 14 June 1764; *NYG*, 18 June 1764; Kercheval, *History of the Valley*, 85–6.

Day, [Mrs]. Captured with her four children in Augusta County, VA, 1 June 1764. MISSING. *PG*, 14 June 1764; *NYG*, 18 June 1764; Kercheval, *History of the Valley*, 85–6.

Decker, Sarah. Teenage girl. Captured by Delaware in Northampton County, PA, December 1755. Seen at Wyoming. RETURNED by Teedyuscung at Easton, 11 July 1758. HL, AB, 368; Minutes for 10 July 1758, Haverford College Library, Indian Committee Records, 824/10, vol. 2, n.p.; HSP, Penn Mss, Indian Affairs, vol. 3, nos 52–3; William Fenton, *The Great Law and the Longhouse* (Norman, OK: University of Oklahoma Press, 1998), 505.

Deets/Deedt, [Mrs Benjamin]. Widowed and captured in Delaware attack in Northampton County, PA, December 1755. MISSING. *PMHB* 32 (1908): 315.

Delea. Virginian. Captured in Hampshire County, 30 August 1763. RETAKEN ten days later. *PG*, 15 September and 6 October 1763.

Dempsey, Hannah. Captive of Shawnee. Seen at Lower Shawnee Town late in 1764. MISSING. *WPHM* 39 (1956): 202.

Denite, John. Held some time by Indians near Venango. ESCAPED to New Jersey, 29 July 1756. *PG*, 9 September 1756.

Dennis, Joseph. Husband of Hannah. Captured by Shawnee at forks of James River, Augusta County, VA, 25 July 1757. KILLED eight days later. James B.

Finley, *Life among the Indians* (Cincinnati, OH, 1857), 45–7; Withers, *Chronicles* (1895), 92–3.

Dennis, Hannah. Captured by Shawnee at forks of James River, Augusta County, VA, 25 July 1757. Adopted, and became a medicine woman. ESCAPED June 1763. Withers, *Chronicles* (1895), 92–3; Finley, *Life among the Indians*, 45–7.

Desillets. Marine cadet with Louisiana forces in Illinois. Captured after battle of La Belle Famille, 24 July 1759. MISSING. Dunnigan, *Siege–1759*, 80, 103,

Deven [Dever?], Barnabas. Virginia soldier in Captain Jacob Van Braam's company. Captured by Abenaki after surrender of Fort Necessity, 4 July 1754. MISSING. Severance, "Tale of Captives," 249; *Travels in New France by J.C.B.*, ed. Stevens, Kent, and Woods, 64.

Devine, Morrice. Pennsylvanian. Captured in Ohio country, May 1763. RETURNED at Muskingum, 15 November 1764. *JP*, 11: 486; *WPHM* 39 (1956): 191; *PG*, 17 January 1765; *NYG*, 21 January 1765; LAC, MG 19, F 35, lot 621, 3.

Devins. Marine lieutenant with Louisiana forces in Illinois. Captured in battle of La Belle Famille, 24 July 1759. MISSING. Dunnigan, *Siege–1759*, 80, 103.

Devoy, James. Trader from Cumberland County, PA. Captured in fall of Pickawillany, 21 June 1752. Taken to Canada and France. RETURNED by 1 June 1753. *PG*, 23 November 1753; *VG*, 20 and 27 October 1752; Pease and Jenison, eds, *Illinois on the Eve*, 29, 811; Hanna, *Wilderness Trail*, vol. 2, 330–1; Mercer, *George Mercer Papers*, 419–20, 463.

Dickers. "under age" daughter of Andrew Dickers. Taken in Northampton County, PA, September 1757. MISSING. *PMHB* 32 (1908): 314.

Dickey. Child of Elizabeth. Captured with her mother in Lancaster County, PA, 18 August 1757. MISSING. *PG*, 25 August and 1 September 1757; *NYM*, 5 September 1757.

Dickey, Elizabeth. Captured with her child in Lancaster County, PA, 18 August 1757. MISSING. *PG*, 25 August and 1 September 1757; *NYM*, 5 September 1757.

Didon, Charles. Canadian marine in Mezierer's company. Taken in battle of La Belle Famille, 24 July 1759. Held in Somerset County, NJ. EXCHANGED at Crown Point, NY, 9 December 1759. *JP*, 13: 115; Job Stockton Papers, NYHS.

Dillinger. Infant boy. Captured with mother near Bowman's Fort, Frederick County, VA, 22 August 1764. KILLED the same day. Kercheval, *History of the Valley*, 100; Baker, *French and Indian War*, 143; *NYG*, 1 October 1764.

Dillinger, Rachel [Mrs John]. Widowed and captured with infant son near Bowman's Fort, Frederick County, VA, 22 August 1764. RETAKEN four days later by Virginia militia. Kercheval, *History of the Valley*, 100; Baker, *French and Indian War*, 143; *PG*, 20 September 1764; *NYM*, 1 October 1764; *NYG*, 1 October 1764.

Diven/[Diver?], Hans. Son of Christopher Diven. Orphaned and captured in attack near Denning's Creek, Cumberland County, PA, 17 June 1763. RETURNED at Muskingum, 15 November 1764. Sent to Michael Diver at Fort Pitt. *PG*, 30 June 1763, 17 January 1765; *JP*, 11: 488; *WPHM* 39 (1956): 188.

Diven/[Diver?], John. Son of Christopher Diven. Orphaned and captured in attack near Denning's Creek, Cumberland County, PA, 17 June 1763. RETURNED at Muskingum, 15 November 1764, and then sent to Michael Diver at Fort Pitt. *PG*, 30 June 1763, 17 January 1765; *JP*, 11: 488; *WPHM* 39 (1956): 188.

Doe, William. Soldier in Pennsylvania "Light Horse." Captured in summer of 1760. RETURNED in French surrender of Fort Detroit, 1 December 1760. *HBP*, 5: 210.

Donahue, Lawrence/John. Soldier in second battalion of Pennsylvania regiment. Captured in attack on Kittanning. RETURNED at Muskingum, 15 November 1764. *PA*, ser. 2, 2: 458–60; *PG*, 23 September 1756, 17 January 1765; Hunter, "Victory at Kittanning," 392–402; *WPHM* 39 (1956): 192, 196.

Dougherty, Johanna/Anna. Six year old taken with her older sister by the Delaware on Conecocheague Creek, Cumberland County, PA, November 1755. Seen at Kaschkaschkung. RETURNED at Lancaster conference, 19 August 1762. *PA*, ser. 2, 7: 437; *MPCP*, 8: 750; *Minutes of Conferences ... Lancaster, 1762*, 7.

Dougherty, Nancy. Ten year old taken with her younger sister by the Delaware on Conecocheague Creek, Cumberland County, PA, November 1755. MISSING. *PA*, ser. 2, 7: 437.

Doyle, James. Man from Philadelphia County, PA. Reported as DIED in captivity in Canada in 1747. *PG*, 27 August and 3 September 1747.

Drake, John. Captured in Northampton County, PA, 12 December 1755. RETURNED by July 1757. *PG*, 18 and 25 December 1755; *RCFFP*, 1: 297, 321.

Draper, Betty (d. 1774). Wife of John. Wounded and taken captive by Shawnee, 30 July 1755, at New River, Augusta County, VA. RANSOMED 1761. *NYM*, 26 January and 16 February 1756; Sipe, *Indian Wars*, 28–30, 99–100, 105–6; Waddell, *Annals of Augusta*, vol. 1, 75.

Druillon de Macé, Pierre-Jacques (1727–80). French officer in marines. Wounded and captured by Virginians in Jumonville incident, 28 May 1754. Sent to England in June 1755. RETURNED to France that month. *DCB*, 4: 226–7; *PG*, 13 and 27 June 1754, 22 August 1754.

Du Bois, Jean [nom de guerre "Vadiboncoeur"]. Canadian marine in Captain Charles Déschamps de Boishebert's company. Taken by British Army in battle of La Belle Famille, 24 July 1759. EXCHANGED at Crown Point, NY, 9 December 1759. *JP*, 13: 115; Job Stockton Papers, NYHS.

Dubreuil. French corporal in Villemonde's marine company. Taken by British Army in surrender of Fort Detroit, 30 November 1760. Sent to France. EXCHANGED 1761. TNA, WO 1/5, 176; *NYM*, 30 March 1760.

Ducharme. Canadian soldier from Lachine. Captured by Virginians in Jumonville incident, 28 May 1754. Released in England, 22 June 1755, and RETURNED. *PG*, 13 and 27 June, 22 August, and 12 September 1754; *Collections des manuscrits ... Nouvelle France*, vol. 3, 521–2.

Duchatelet, Joseph. Canadian soldier from L'Assomption parish. Captured by Virginians in Jumonville incident, 28 May 1754. Released in England, 22 June

1755, and RETURNED. *PG*, 13 and 27 June, 22 August, and 12 September 1754; *Collections des manuscrits ... Nouvelle France*, vol. 3, 521–2.

Duncan, John. Pennsylvania youth. Taken with his sister by Delaware near "Leckawecksein," May 1763. RETURNED by Chenussio Seneca at Fort Niagara, July 1764. *PG*, 6 September 1764; *NYG*, 17 September 1764.

Duncan, Sara. Pennsylvania youth. Taken with her brother by Delaware near "Leckawecksein," May 1763. RETURNED by Chenussio Seneca at Fort Niagara, July 1764. *PG*, 6 September 1764; *NYG*, 17 September 1764.

Dunning, James. Pennsylvania trader. Captured by Shawnee of Chartier's Town, 18 April 1745. FREED by captors the next day. *NYCD*, 10: 20; Hanna, *Wilderness Trail*, vol. 1, 311; *PG*, 16 May 1745.

Duplessis, Louis Victor. Assistant engineer in Royal American Regiment. Captured near French Creek, OH, 5 September 1760. MISSING. BL, Add. Mss, 21638, fol. 154; *GWP*, 6: 467, 470.

Duppell. Young son of Lawrence Duppell, of Berks County, PA. Captured in June 1756 and KILLED soon thereafter. *PG*, 17 and 24 June 1756; *NYM*, 21 and 28 June 1756.

Duppell. Older son of Lawrence Duppell, of Berks County, PA. Captured in June 1756. MISSING. *PG*, 17 and 24 June 1756; *NYM*, 21 and 28 June 1756.

Dusable. Canadian marine cadet. Captured by Virginians in Jumonville incident, 28 May 1754. Released in England, 22 June 1755, and RETURNED. *PG*, 13 and 27 June, 22 August, and 12 September 1754; *Collections des manuscrits ... Nouvelle France*, vol. 3, 521–2.

Dutch Jacob, [Mrs]. Captured by Shawnee at New River, Augusta County, VA, 3 July 1755. ESCAPED 20 December 1755. Preston Papers, 1: 83; *NYM*, 26 January and 6 February 1756.

Dyer. Daughter of William Dyer. Taken by Shawnee in capture of Seybert's Fort, Augusta County, VA, 28 April 1758. MISSING. Baker, *French and Indian War*, 108.

Dyer, James. Son of William Dyer. Taken by Shawnee in capture of Seybert's Fort, Augusta County, VA, 28 April 1758. ESCAPED to Fort Pitt, 28 February 1760. Preston Papers, 1: 83; Chalkley, *Chronicles of the Scotch-Irish*, vol. 1, 149, 191; Kercheval, *History of the Valley*, 91; *PG*, 11 and 18 May 1758; *NYM*, 15 and 22 May 1758.

Dyer, Roger. Son of William Dyer. Taken by Shawnee in capture of Seybert's Fort, Augusta County, VA, 28 April 1758. ESCAPED to Fort Pitt, 28 February 1760. Preston Papers, 1: 83; Chalkley, *Chronicles of the Scotch-Irish*, vol. 1, 149, 191; Kercheval, *History of the Valley*, 91; *PG*, 11 and 18 May 1758; *NYM*, 15 and 22 May 1758.

Eberhard, Margaret. Young daughter of George. Orphaned and captured on Shamokin Road, October 1755. RETURNED at Muskingum, 15 November 1764. *PMHB* 32 (1908): 311.

Ebert/Evers, George. Man from Northampton County, PA. Taken by Delaware, 11 May 1757. ESCAPED with Abraham Miller, hidden by French Margaret, and made his way to Fort Hamilton, 12 June 1757. *MPCP*, 7: 620–1; *PMHB* 32 (1908): 316; *NYM*, 16 May 1757; *PG*, 12 and 30 May 1757.

Eckerle, Gabriel [Jotham]. German Dunker hermit. Captured by Ottawa and Canadians on Cheat River in 1757. Taken to New France and France, where he DIED, 17 March 1758. *GWP*, 4: 366; *PG*, 26 October 1758; Dowd, *War under Heaven*, 100; Walter Conrad Klein, *Johann Conrad Beissel, Mystic and Martinet* (Philadelphia, PA: Porcupine, 1972), 152–64; E.G. Alderfer, *The Ephrata Commune* (Pittsburgh, PA: University of Pittsburgh Press, 1985), 136–8.

Eckerle, Israel [Onesimus]. German Dunker hermit. Captured by Ottawa and Canadians on Cheat River in 1757. Taken to New France and France, where he DIED, 17 March 1758. *GWP*, 4: 366; *PG*, 26 October 1758; Dowd, *War under Heaven*, 100; Klein, *Johann Conrad Beissel*, 152–64; Alderfer, *Ephrata Commune*, 136–8.

Eckinrod. Eight-year-old son of John. Taken in Linn Township, Northampton County, PA, 28 May 1757. MISSING. *PMHB* 32 (1908): 319; *PG*, 2 June 1757; *NYM*, 6 June 1757.

Edwards, John. British soldier. Captured in May 1763 and held near Detroit. RETURNED by 20 December 1763. Gladwin, "Gladwin Manuscripts," 658–60.

Eger, Crosby. Virginia soldier. Taken in General Edward Braddock's defeat, 9 July 1755. Sent to New France and England. EXCHANGED November 1758. Captured at sea on return, and imprisoned in Bordeaux for six months. *Journals of the House of Burgesses, 1758–1761*, ed. McIlwaine, 66, 68.

Eice/Eyce/Ice, Catherine. Young daughter of Eve. Captured with her mother on South Branch of Potomac River, Augusta County, VA, 1755. Held by Delaware at "Kaschkaschkung." RETURNED at Muskingum, 15 November 1764. *PA*, ser. 2, 7: 437; *WPHM* 39 (1956): 190; *PG*, 17 January 1765; *NYG*, 21 January 1765. Compare Kercheval, *History of the Valley*, 92.

Eice/Eyce/Ice, Christina. Woman captured with her family on South Branch of Potomac River, Augusta County, VA, 1755. RETURNED by Shawnee, 10 May 1765. *WPHM* 39 (1956): 198; *JP*, 11: 720.

Eice/Eyce/Ice, Elisabeth. Young girl captured with her family on South Branch of Potomac River, Augusta County, VA, 1755. RETURNED at Muskingum, 15 November 1764. *WPHM* 39 (1956): 190; *PG*, 17 January 1765; *NYG*, 21 January 1765.

Eice/Eyce/Ice, Eve. Woman captured with her family on South Branch of Potomac River, Augusta County, VA, 1755. Held by Delaware at "Kaschkaschkung." RETURNED at Muskingum, 15 November 1764. *PA*, ser. 2, 7: 437; *WPHM* 39 (1956): 190; *PG*, 17 January 1765; *NYG*, 21 January 1765.

Eice/Eyce/Ice, John. Child captured with his family on South Branch of Potomac River, Augusta County, VA, 1755. RETURNED at Muskingum, 15 November 1764. Back with the Delaware when captured by Iroquois in January 1764 and turned over to William Johnson. Deemed a renegade and sold into servitude in British West Florida. *WPHM* 39 (1956): 190; *PG*, 17 January 1765; *NYG*, 21 January 1765; *JP*, 4: 314; *JP*, 11: 165–6, 201.

Eice/Eyce/Ice, Lewis. Infant son of Eve. Captured with his family on South Branch of Potomac River, Augusta County, VA, 1755. Held by Delaware at "Kaschkaschkung." RETURNED at Muskingum, 15 November 1764. *PA*, ser. 2, 7: 437; *WPHM* 39 (1956): 190; *PG*, 17 January 1765; *NYG*, 21 January 1765.

Eice/Eyce/Ice, Thomas. Young boy captured with his family on South Branch of Potomac River, Augusta County, VA, 1755. RETURNED at Muskingum, 15 November 1764. *WPHM* 39 (1956): 190; *PG*, 17 January 1765; *NYG*, 21 January 1765.

Eice/Eyce/Ice, William. Young boy captured with his family on South Branch of Potomac River, Augusta County, VA, 1755. RETURNED at Muskingum, 15 November 1764. *WPHM* 39 (1956): 190; *PG*, 17 January 1765; *NYG*, 21 January 1765; *PA*, ser. 2, 7: 437.

Elliott. Young daughter of Charles Elliott. Orphaned and captured by Delaware in Path Valley, PA, 11 July 1763. WHITE INDIAN seen by missionary David McClure in 1772. *PG*, 21 July 1763; Dowd, *War under Heaven*, 141; Sipe, *Indian Wars*, 433–4; David McClure, *Diary of David McClure, Doctor of Divinity, 1748–1820* (New York, 1899), 86–7.

Ellis. Corporal in Royal American Regiment. Captured by Delaware and Shawnee while escorting Frederick Christian Post near Loyalhanna, PA, 16 November 1758. ESCAPED 11 May 1759. BL, Add. Mss, 21644, fol. 152; Thwaites, ed., *Early Western Travels*, vol. 1, 250; *PG*, 7 December 1757, 21 December 1758; *EAID*, 3: 490n119.

Ellison, Gabriel. Captured by Seneca in Bucks County PA, November 1762. RETURNED to Johnson Hall, NY, January 1764. *PG*, 9 February 1762; *NYM*, 6 February 1764.

Ely, Thomas. Soldier in George Washington's company of Virginia Regiment. Captured in Major James Grant's defeat at Fort Duquesne, 14 September 1758. ESCAPED the same day. BL, Add. Mss, 21682, fol. 13.

Enas. Thirteen-year-old boy. Captured in Berks County, PA, 8 November 1763. ESCAPED later the same day. *PJ*, 17 November 1763.

Erwin/Irwin, Luke. Pennsylvania trader. Captured by French at Sandusky, 27 January 1750. Taken to Fort Niagara, Quebec, and France. Released 27 January 1752 and RETURNED to native Ireland. Eavenson, *Map Maker*, 142–3; *Ohio Company Papers*, ed. Bailey, 36–7; Hanna, *Wilderness Trail*, vol. 2, 334.

Estill, Kitty Moffet. Captured by Shawnee in Augusta County, VA, 15 September 1764. RETAKEN five days later. Waddell, *Annals of Augusta*, vol. 2, 433–8; Baker, *French and Indian War*, 132.

Etherington, George. Captain in Royal American Regiment. Captured by Ojibwa in taking Fort Michilimackinac, 2 June 1763. Taken by Ottawa to Montreal. RANSOMED 15 August 1764. *PG*, 11 and 18 August 1763; *DCB*, 3: 262; David Armour, *Attack at Michilimackinac* (Mackinac Island, MI: Mackinac State Park Commission, 1971), 61, 63.

Evans. Child of Abigail by a Seneca. Surrendered with mother at Lancaster conference, 19 August 1762. MISSING. *MPCP*, 8: 750.

Evans, Abigail. Pennsylvania girl. Captured by Seneca at Stoney Creek, PA. RETURNED, with her *métis* child, at Lancaster conference, 19 August 1762. *MPCP*, 8: 750.

Evans, Jabez [Toby]. Pennsylvania trader. Captured by Kahnawake Iroquois in Kentucky, 26 January 1753. RANSOMED for £17 Pennsylvania currency, through Albany commissioners, September 1754. LAC, MG 19, F 35/2, lot 680, 13–14; *MPCP*, 5: 662–4; *PG*, 27 September 1753, 17 August 1754.

Evans, Jacob. Pennsylvania trader. Captured by Kahnawake Iroquois in Kentucky, 26 January 1753. Bought by Pierre-Joseph Céloron de Blainville as commandant at Detroit, imprisoned in Canada, and sent to France. RELEASED there, January 1754. *PA*, ser. 1, 2: 131–32; *MPCP*, 5: 663; *PG*, 27 September 1753, 17 August 1754.

Evans, John. Trader from Cumberland County, PA. Captured by Ottawa in surrender of Pickawillany, 21 June 1752. Taken to Canada and France. RETURNED to Philadelphia by 1 June 1753. *PG*, 23 November 1752; *VG*, 20 and 27 October 1752; Pease and Jenison, eds, *Illinois on the Eve*, 811; *MPCP*, 5: 663–4.

Ewechonmey [the Wrestler]. Shawnee chief taken hostage by Colonel Henry Bouquet at Muskingum, 14 November 1764. ESCAPED from Fort Pitt, 3 December 1764. HL, MM, 569, fols 37–8; *MPCP*, 9: 232; *HBP*, 6: 717.

Ewins, John. From Augusta County, VA. Taken by Shawnee, 14 May 1763. RETURNED to Fort Pitt, 15 May 1765. *WPHM* 39 (1956): 198; *JP*, 11: 720; Chalkley, *Chronicles of the Scotch-Irish*, vol. 2, 93.

Fager, Daniel Stuart. Soldier in Captain James MacKay's company of Virginia Regiment. Captured at Fort Necessity, 3 July 1754. MISSING. *MPCP*, 6: 143; Stobo, *Memoirs*, 91–2.

Faulkner (Fortiner), Joseph. Trader from New Jersey. Captured at Cuyahoga, September 1750. Sent to Fort Niagara, Montreal, and Quebec. Converted and STAYED in New France. Eavenson, *Map Maker*, 15; *Ohio Company Papers*, ed. Bailey, 36–7; Hanna, *Wilderness Trail*, vol. 2, 332.

Fell. Infant child of Martin. Captured in Berks County, PA, 3 November 1756. MISSING. *PMHB* 32 (1908): 316; *RCFFP*, 1: 126, 128; *PG*, 11 November 1756; *NYM*, 15 November 1756.

Fell. Son of Martin. Captured in Berks County, PA, 3 November 1756. MISSING. *PMHB* 32 (1908): 316; *RCFFP*, 1: 126, 128; *PG*, 11 November 1756; *NYM*, 15 November 1756.

Fell, [Mrs Martin]. Widowed and captured with two children in Berks County, PA, 3 November 1756. MISSING. *PMHB* 32 (1908): 316; *RCFFP*, 1: 126, 128; *PG*, 11 November 1756; *NYM*, 15 November 1756.

Fent/Feint, Joseph. Sergeant in Virginia Regiment. Captured by Shawnee and Delaware near Fort Duquesne, 29 December 1756. Presumed killed and a monument erected. ESCAPED by May 1757. *NYM*, 10 January and 25 April 1757; *PG*, 6 January 1757; *GWP*, 4: 161–3; *Journals of the House of Burgesses of Virginia, 1752–1755, 1756–1758*, ed. H.R. McIlwaine (Richmond, VA: Colonial Press, 1909), 479.

Ferrant. Lieutenant with Louisiana marines in Illinois country. Captured by the British at battle of La Belle Famille, 24 July 1759. MISSING. Dunnigan, *Siege–1759*, 80, 103; *JP*, 13: 115.

Ferrick, Frederick. Servant of Thomas Potter. Captured by Delaware at Richard Bard's Mill, York County, PA, 13 April 1758. Seen at Tuscarawas, April 1762. MISSING. *PA*, ser. 1, 3: 396–7; Loudon, ed., *Selection*, vol. 2, 47–65; BL, Add. Mss, 21648, fol. 128; *PG*, 11 May 1758; *NYM*, 15 May 1758.

Feulevant [nom de guerre?]. Private in the Gaspé marines. Taken in surrender of Fort Detroit to British, 30 November 1760. Sent to Fort Pitt, New York, and France, where he was EXCHANGED in 1761. TNA, WO 1/5, 176; *PG*, 15 January and 5 February 1761; *NYM*, 30 March 1761.

Filkison, Ann. Girl captured by Shawnee at Smith River, Augusta County, VA, 28 April 1758. MISSING. Last seen in Lower Shawnee Town late in 1764. *WPHM* 39 (1956): 202.

Filkison/Fulkis, Elisabeth. Girl captured by Shawnee at Smith River, Augusta County, VA, 28 April 1758. RETURNED to Fort Pitt, 5 January 1765. *WPHM* 39 (1956): 197; *PG*, 7 March 1765; *NYG*, 18 March 1765.

Fincher. Servant or young son of Quaker John Fincher. Orphaned, captured, and ESCAPED in Delaware attack in Berks County, PA, 8 September 1763. *NYM*, 19 September 1763.

Fincher, Rachel. Daughter of Quaker John Fincher. Orphaned and captured by Delaware in Berks County, PA, 8 September 1763. RETURNED at Muskingum, 15 November 1764. *MPCP*, 9: 40–1; *WPHM* 39 (1956): 189; *PG*, 15 September 1763, 17 January 1765; *NYM*, 19 September 1763; *NYG*, 19 September 1763, 21 January 1765; Sipe, *Indian Wars*, 453–4.

Finley. Son of John. Orphaned and captured near Shippensburg, 8 July 1757. MISSING. *PA*, ser. 1, 3: 219–20; *PG*, 4 August 1757; *NYM*, 8 August 1757; Cumberland County Orphan's Court Dockets, vol. 2, 1761–86, Cumberland County Courthouse, Carlisle, PA, entry for 25 May 1762.

Finley, Ann. Pennsylvanian. Said to have been captured in 1755. RETURNED at Muskingum, 15 November 1764. *WPHM* 39 (1956): 193, 196; *JP*, 11: 489; *PG*, 17 January 1765; *NYG*, 21 January 1765.

Finley, John (1722–74). Pennsylvania trader. Captured near Picts' Town on Miami River, 28 January 1753. RETURNED that year. *NYM*, 7 May 1753; *HBP*, 5: 414n.

Fishbach/Fishpough. Child of Walter. Captured with mother and siblings at Greenbrier River, Augusta County, VA, September 1755. MISSING. Preston Papers, 1: 83.

Fishbach/Fishpough. Child of Walter. Captured with mother and siblings at Greenbrier River, Augusta County, VA, September 1755. MISSING. Preston Papers, 1: 83.

Fishbach/Fishpough, [Mrs Walter]. Widowed and captured with four children at Greenbrier River, Augusta County, VA, September 1755. MISSING. Preston Papers, 1: 83.

Fishbach/Fishpough, Margaret. Teen captured with mother and siblings at Greenbrier River, Augusta County, VA, September 1755. RETURNED at Muskingum, 15 November 1764. Preston Papers, 1: 83; *WPHM* 39 (1956): 195, 196; *JP*, 11: 486; *PG*, 17 January 1765; *NYG*, 21 January 1765.

Fishbach/Fishpough, Susannah. Teen captured with mother and siblings at Greenbrier River, Augusta County, VA, September 1755. RETURNED at Muskingum, 15 November 1764. Preston Papers, 1: 83; *WPHM* 39 (1956): 195, 196; *JP*, 11: 486; *PG*, 17 January 1765; *NYG*, 21 January 1765.

Fisher. Young daughter of James Fisher, retired British soldier. Orphaned and captured by Wyandot near Detroit, 10 May 1763. DIED in captivity a few weeks later. Heard, *Handbook*, vol. 2, 115.

Fisher. Young daughter of James Fisher, retired British soldier. Orphaned and captured by Wyandot near Detroit, 10 May 1763. Taken to Saginaw village. MISSING. Heard, *Handbook*, vol. 2, 115.

Fisher, Betty. Young daughter of James Fisher, retired British soldier. Orphaned and captured by Wyandot near Detroit, 10 May 1763. KILLED on Pontiac's orders at his Maumee River community, 5 September 1764. *PG*, 11 and 18 August 1763; Richard White, *The Middle Ground: Indians, Empires, and Republics in the Great Lakes Region, 1650–1815* (New York: Cambridge University Press, 1991), 299; Dowd, *War under Heaven*, 354–6.

Fisher, John. Young son of James Fisher, retired British soldier. Orphaned and captured by Wyandot near Detroit, 10 May 1763. RETURNED at Muskingum, 15 November 1764. *WPHM* 39 (1956): 188; *NYM*, 13 August 1765; *PG*, 17 January 1765; *NYG*, 21 January 1765.

Fisher, Manning/Martin. Trader captured near Detroit in May 1763. ESCAPED to Detroit by 8 September 1763. Hay, *Diary*, 54; Gladwin, "Gladwin Manuscripts," 646–7.

Fisher, Tuenis. Trader at La Baye who went with the garrison to Michilimackinac. Captured by the Ojibwa, 15 June 1763. Likely RANSOMED with the garrison at Montreal, 16 August 1763. Gladwin, "Gladwin Manuscripts," 668–70.

Flaherty, Esther. Virginia girl. Captured, with her mother, by Delaware in 1756. Held at Kuskuski. RETURNED at Muskingum, 15 November 1764. Sent to Pat Flaherty at Fort Pitt two weeks later. *PA*, ser. 2, 7: 437; *WPHM* 39 (1956): 188; *JP*, 11: 490; *PG*, 17 January 1765; *NYG*, 21 January 1765.

Flaherty, Frances/Fanny. Virginian. Captured with her daughter Esther by Delaware in 1756. Had six-week-old daughter Marie-Louise baptized at Fort Duquesne, 9 July 1756. Said to have married a Frenchman and STAYED with the French. *Baptismal Register*, ed. Lambing, 74–5; *PA*, ser. 2, 7: 437.

Flat Nose. Girl thought to have been captured in Pennsylvania. RETURNED at Muskingum, 15 November 1764. *WPHM* 39 (1956): 193; *JP*, 11: 490; *PG*, 17 January 1765; *NYG*, 21 January 1765.

Fleming, Elizabeth. Taken with her husband by Delaware at Great Cove, Cumberland County, PA, 2 November 1755. ESCAPED the same night. William Fleming and Elizabeth Fleming, *A Narrative of the Sufferings and Surprizing*

Deliverances of William and Elizabeth Fleming (1756; reprint, New York: Garland, 1978); *NYM*, 17 November 1755, 8 and 15 March 1756.

Fleming, William. Taken with his wife by Delaware at Great Cove, Cumberland County, PA, 2 November 1755. ESCAPED the same night. Fleming and Fleming, *Narrative*; *NYM*, 17 November 1755, 8 and 15 March 1756.

Fontain, Louis. Canadian marine in Captain Louis Herbin's company. Captured at battle of La Belle Famille, 24 July 1759. Held in Somerset County, NJ. EXCHANGED at Crown Point, NY, 9 December 1760. Job Stockton Papers, NYHS; *JP*, 13: 115.

Forsyth, John. Boy captured at Carr's (Kerr's) Creek by Shawnee, 17 July 1763. RETURNED to Fort Pitt, 10 May 1765. *WPHM* 39 (1956): 198; *JP*, 11: 720.

Fouret, Bartholemew. Canadian marine in Michel Pepin *dit* La Force's company. Captured at battle of La Belle Famille, 24 July 1759. Held in Somerset County, NJ. EXCHANGED at Crown Point, NY, 9 December 1760. Job Stockton Papers, NYHS; *JP*, 13: 115.

Fox, George. Man from Northampton County, PA. Captured by North Branch Delaware, January 1756. RETURNED by Teedyuscung, 11 October 1756. *MPCP*, 7: 284; *PMHB* 32 (1908): 315; *PG*, 21 October 1756; *NYM*, 18 October 1756.

Fox, Jacob. Man from Northampton County, PA. Captured by North Branch Delaware, January 1756. RETURNED by 16 December 1757. *PMHB* 32 (1908): 315, 316; *The Journals of Henry Melchior Muhlenberg*, trans. Theodore G. Tappert and John W. Doberstein, 3 vols (Philadelphia, PA: Evangelical Lutheran Ministerium of Pennsylvania, 1942–58), vol. 2, 297.

Francis, Jean. Canadian marine in Debel's company. Captured at battle of La Belle Famille 24 July 1759. Held in Somerset County, NJ. EXCHANGED via Crown Point, NY, 9 December 1760. *JP*, 13: 115; Job Stockton Papers, NYHS.

[Francybly?]. Canadian marine in Montarin's company. Captured at battle of La Belle Famille, 24 July 1759. Held in Somerset County, NJ. EXCHANGED via Crown Point, NY, 9 December 1760. *JP*, 13: 115; Job Stockton Papers, NYHS.

Frantz/France, Christopher. One of four children of Hans. Taken with mother in Berks County, PA, 19 June 1758. RETAKEN in capture of Fort Niagara, 25 July 1759. *PA*, ser. 1, 3: 425–6; *PG*, 29 June 1758, 23 August 1759; *NYM*, 3 July 1758, 20 August 1759.

Frantz/France, Elizabeth. One of four children of Hans. Taken with mother in Berks County, PA, 19 June 1758. RETURNED at Muskingum, 15 November 1764. *PA*, ser. 1, 3: 425–6; *WPHM* 39 (1956): 192; *PMHB* 32 (1908): 318; *PG*, 29 June 1758, 17 January 1765; *NYM*, 3 July 1758; *NYG*, 21 January 1765.

Frantz/France, Hans. One of four children of Hans. Taken with mother in Berks County, PA, 19 June 1758. Sold to French at Fort Presqu'île. MISSING. Haverford College Library, Indian Committee Records, 824/10, vol. 4, n.p.; *PG*, 29 June 1758; *NYM*, 3 July 1758.

Frantz/France, Michael. One of four children of Hans. Taken with mother in Berks County, PA, 19 June 1758. RETAKEN in capture of Fort Niagara, 25 July 1759. *PA*, ser. 1, 3: 425–6; *PG*, 29 June 1758, 23 August 1759; *NYM*, 3 July 1758, 20 August 1759.

Frantz/France, [Mrs Hans]. Taken with her four children in Berks County, PA, 19 June 1758. “Weakly.” KILLED the same day. *PA*, ser. 1, 3: 425–6; *PG*, 29 June 1758; *NYM*, 3 July 1758.

Fraser, Alexander. Lieutenant in Royal American Regiment on mission down Ohio Valley. Taken in May 1765 by Ottawa and Potawatomi chiefs visiting at Kaskaskia. Released two days later on intervention by Pontiac. RETURNED via New Orleans. *PG*, 22 August 1765; *Collections of the Illinois State Historical Society* 10 (1915): 491–3.

Fraser, Jane. Pregnant wife of trader John. Captured by Miami near Fort Cumberland, MD, July 1755. ESCAPED with two men in August 1756. Husband had remarried. Jane Frasier, *Narrative of the Captivity of Mrs. Jane Frasier* (1930; reprint, New York: Garland, 1977); *PG*, 24 July 1755.

Frederick. One of three children of Noah. Orphaned and taken in Lancaster County, PA, 12 October 1756. MISSING. *PG*, 21 October 1756; *MPCP*, 7: 303.

Frederick. One of three children of Noah. Orphaned and taken in Lancaster County, PA, 12 October 1756. MISSING. *PG*, 21 October 1756; *MPCP*, 7: 303.

Frederick. One of three children of Noah. Orphaned and taken in Lancaster County, PA, 12 October 1756. MISSING. *PG*, 21 October 1756; *MPCP*, 7: 303.

Freeling/Freeland. One of five children of John and Peggy. Taken with parents by Shawnee in Augusta County, VA, 3 July 1755. Last reported in Lower Shawnee Town late in 1764. Likely WHITE INDIAN. William Preston Papers, 1: 83; *WPHM* 39 (1956): 202.

Freeling/Freeland. One of five children of John and Peggy. Taken with parents by Shawnee in Augusta County, VA, 3 July 1755. Last reported in Lower Shawnee Town late in 1764. Likely WHITE INDIAN. William Preston Papers, 1: 83; *WPHM* 39 (1956): 202.

Freeling/Freeland. One of five children of John and Peggy. Taken with parents by Shawnee in Augusta County, VA, 3 July 1755. Last reported in Lower Shawnee Town late in 1764. Likely WHITE INDIAN. William Preston Papers, 1: 83; *WPHM* 39 (1956): 202.

Freeling/Freeland. One of five children of John and Peggy. Taken with parents by Shawnee in Augusta County, VA, 3 July 1755. MISSING. William Preston Papers, 1: 83.

Freeling/Freeland. One of five children of John and Peggy. Taken with parents by Shawnee in Augusta County, VA, 3 July 1755. MISSING. William Preston Papers, 1: 83.

Freeling/Freeland, John. Captured with wife and five children by Shawnee in Augusta County, VA, 3 July 1755. RETURNED at Muskingum, 15 November 1764. William Preston Papers, 1: 83; Haverford College Library, Indian Committee Records, 824/10, vol. 1, n.p.; *PG*, 17 January 1765; *NYG*, 21 January 1765; *WPHM* 39 (1956): 194, 202.

Freeling/Freeland, Peggy. Captured with husband and five children by Shawnee in Augusta County, VA, 3 July 1755. RETURNED at Muskingum, 15 November 1764. William Preston Papers, 1: 83; *PG*, 17 January 1765; *NYG*, 21 January 1765; *WPHM* 39 (1956): 194, 196, 202.

Frichet, Thomas [Leclair]. Canadian marine in De Bonne's company. Taken by British at battle of La Belle Famille, 24 July 1759. Imprisoned in Somerset County, NJ. EXCHANGED at Crown Point, NY, 9 December 1760. *JP*, 13: 115; Job Stockton Papers, NYHS.

Frick, Betty. Eighteen-year-old Virginian. Taken by Delaware in 1756. Seen at Kuskuski. MISSING. *PA*, ser. 2, 7: 437.

Fried, Nicholas. Man from Northampton County, PA. Taken 17 January 1756. MISSING. *PG*, 15 January 1756.

Frim, Isera. Fourteen-year-old girl captured by Delaware in the Connecticut settlement at Lackawana, Northampton County, PA, 4 September 1763. RETURNED by Chenussio Seneca to Johnson Hall, NY, 31 July 1764. *JP*, 4: 498.

Fullerton, Nelly. Woman held at Lower Shawnee Town late in 1764. *WPHM* 39 (1956): 202.

Galliday. Young child of Joseph. Taken near Conococheague, Cumberland County, PA, 1 June 1758. MISSING and also reported killed. Loudon, ed., *Selection*, vol. 2, 198; *PG*, 22 June 1758; *NYM*, 26 June 1758.

Galliday, [Mrs Joseph]. Widowed and taken near Conococheague, Cumberland County, PA, 1 June 1758. MISSING and also reported killed. Loudon, ed., *Selection*, vol. 2, 198; *PG*, 22 June 1758; *NYM*, 26 June 1758.

Galloway. Young child of William. Captured with mother by Shawnee and Delaware at Great Cove, Cumberland County, PA, 2 November 1755. WHITE INDIAN seen with Shawnee seven years later. *HBP*, 6: 89; *PG*, 13 November 1755; *NYM*, 17 November 1755.

Galloway. Young child of William. Captured with mother by Shawnee and Delaware at Great Cove, Cumberland County, PA, 2 November 1755. WHITE INDIAN seen with Shawnee seven years later. *HBP*, 6: 89; *PG*, 13 November 1755; *NYM*, 17 November 1755.

Galloway, David. Captured at Jackson River, Augusta County, VA, 11 September 1756. ESCAPED. *PG*, 7 October 1756; *NYM*, 11 October 1756; Preston Papers, 1: 83.

Galloway, Elizabeth. Grandmother of William's children. Captured with them by Shawnee and Delaware at Great Cove, Cumberland County, PA, 2 November 1755. KILLED and her grey scalp burned the same day. Charles Stuart, "The Captivity of Charles Stuart, 1755–57," *MVHR* 13 (1926–27): 60.

Galloway, [Mrs William]. Captured with two children by Shawnee and Delaware at Great Cove, Cumberland County, PA, 2 November 1755. Seen with Shawnee seven years later. MISSING. *HBP*, 6: 89; *PG*, 13 November 1755; *NYM*, 17 November 1755.

Gamelin, Eustrache. Captain in Detroit militia. Taken by British in battle of La Belle Famille, 24 July 1759. RELEASED by General Jeffrey Amherst in October 1760 to accompany Major Robert Rogers in surrender of Detroit. Dunnigan, *Siege–1759*, 80, 103; Thwaites, ed., *Early Western Travels*, vol. 1, 109; "George Croghan's Journal," 391n.

Gamilon. Canadian marine in Captain Claude-Pierre Pécaudy de Contrecoeur's company. Taken in surrender of Detroit, 30 November 1760. EXCHANGED in

France in 1761. TNA, WO 1/5, 177; *PG*, 15 January and 5 February 1761; *NYM*, 30 March 1761.

Garcia, Louis. Canadian marine. Captured by Cherokee on Ohio River, May 1754. Taken to Charleston, SC. MISSING. Pease and Jenison, eds, *Illinois on the Eve*, 868–9, 912–13.

Garrah. Young child of "Dutch." Held in Lower Shawnee Town late in 1764. MISSING. *WPHM* 39 (1956): 202.

Garrah. Young child of "Dutch." Held in Lower Shawnee Town late in 1764. MISSING. *WPHM* 39 (1956): 202.

Garrah. Young child of "Dutch." Held in Lower Shawnee Town late in 1764. MISSING. *WPHM* 39 (1956): 202.

Garrah, "Dutch." Held with his three children in Lower Shawnee Town late in 1764. MISSING. *WPHM* 39 (1956): 202.

Geisinger, [Mrs George Peter]. Widowed and captured near Tulpehocken, Berks County, PA, December 1756. MISSING. *RCFFP*, 1: 108; *PMHB* 32 (1908): 312.

Georgealant. Canadian marine in Captain Jacques-François Legardeur de Courtemanche's company. Taken by British in surrender of Detroit, 30 November 1760. EXCHANGED in France in 1761. TNA, WO 1/5, 176; *PG*, 15 January and 5 February 1761; *NYM*, 30 March 1761.

Gibson, Hugh/Owen. Teen captured by Delaware in Cumberland County, PA, 29 July 1756. ESCAPED with three others, 16 March 1759. *PA*, ser. 2, 7: 427–38. Compare Gibson, "Account of the Captivity," 141–53, with Loudon, ed., *Selection*, vol. 2, 170, 181–4.

Gibson, John (1740–1822). Trader from Lancaster County, PA. Captured by Shawnee in Ohio Valley, 23 May 1763. RETURNED at Muskingum, 15 November 1764. Resumed trading. Married "Chief" Logan's sister and became colonel in a Virginia regiment during American Revolution. Commander and Indian agent at Fort McIntosh in 1778. Commander of the "Western Department" and a brigadier general. Secretary, and occasionally acting governor, of the Indiana territory from 1800 to 1816. BL, Add. Mss, 21655, fol. 265; *PG*, 17 January 1765; *NYG*, 21 January 1765; *HBP*, 6: 412; Thwaites and Kellogg, *Documentary History*, 10–11; Charles Beatty, *The Journal of a Two Month Tour* (London, 1768), 32, 59–60.

Gibson/Gibbons, Sarah. Youth captured by Shawnee at Capon River or North River, Augusta County, VA, 1 April 1756. RETURNED by Shawnee to Fort Pitt, 10 May 1765. *WPHM* 39 (1956): 198; *JP*, 11: 720; Kercheval, *History of the Valley*, 72.

Gilmore, Elizabeth [Mrs John]. Widowed and captured in Shawnee attack on Carr's (Kerr's) Creek, Augusta County, VA, 17 October 1759. RETURNED at Muskingum, 15 November 1764. *WPHM* 39 (1956): 195, 196; *PG*, 17 January 1765; *NYG*, 5 and 12 November 1759, 21 January 1765.

Gilmore, Elizabeth, Jr. Young daughter of Elizabeth and John. Captured with mother in Shawnee attack on Carr's (Kerr's) Creek, Augusta County, VA, 17 October 1759. RETURNED at Muskingum, 15 November 1764. *WPHM* 39

(1956): 195, 196; *PG*, 17 January 1765; *NYG*, 5 and 12 November 1759, 21 January 1765.

Gilmore, Jane/Jenny. Virginian woman. Captured by Shawnee at Carr's (Kerr's) Creek, Augusta County, VA, 17 July 1763. RANSOMED by her brother and returned to Fort Pitt, 10 May 1765. BL, Add. Mss, 21651, fol. 127.

Gilmore, John, Jr. Adult son of John and Elizabeth. Captured in Shawnee attack on Carr's (Kerr's) Creek, Augusta County, VA, 17 October 1759. RETURNED at Muskingum, 15 November 1764. *WPHM* 39 (1956): 194, 196; *PG*, 17 January 1765; *NYG*, 5 and 12 November 1759, 21 January 1765.

Girardin. Canadian soldier from Ile-Jesus, QC. Captured by Virginians in Jumonville incident, 28 May 1754. RETURNED via Martinique, 17 October 1755. *PG*, 13 and 27 June, 22 August, and 12 September 1754; *Collections des manuscrits ... Nouvelle France*, vol. 3, 521–2.

Giro/Girault, Pierre. Canadian marine in Michel Pepin *dit* La Force's company. Captured in battle of La Belle Famille, 24 July 1759. Held in Somerset County, NJ. EXCHANGED via France, 9 December 1760. *JP*, 13: 115; Job Stockton Papers, NYHS.

Girty, George. Eleven-year-old boy from Cumberland County, PA. Taken with his family by Delaware in fall of Fort Granville, PA, 31 July 1756. RETURNED at Muskingum, 15 November 1764. *PG*, 19 August 1756; *WPHM* 39 (1956): 191; *JP*, 11: 488; Phillip W. Hoffman, *Simon Girty, Turncoat Hero* (Franklin, TN: American History Imprints, 2009); J. Norman Heard, *White into Red: A Study of the Assimilation of White Persons Captured by Indians* (Metuchen, NJ: Scarecrow, 1973), 127–9.

Girty, James (1739–1817). Thirteen-year-old boy from Cumberland County, PA. Taken with his family by Delaware in fall of Fort Granville, PA, 31 July 1756. Sent to the Shawnee. RETURNED at Muskingum, 15 November 1764. *PG*, 19 August 1756; *WPHM* 39 (1956): 191; *JP*, 11: 488; Hoffman, *Simon Girty*; Heard, White into *White into Red* Red, 127–9.

Girty, Simon, Jr (1741–1818). Fifteen-year-old boy from Cumberland County, PA. Taken with his family by Delaware in fall of Fort Granville, PA, 31 July 1756. Sent to the Seneca. RETURNED at Muskingum, 15 November 1764. *PG*, 19 August 1756; *WPHM* 39 (1956): 191; *JP*, 11: 488; Colin Calloway, "Simon Girty: Interpreter and Intermediary," in *Being and Becoming Indian: Biographical Studies of North American Frontiers*, ed. James A. Clifton (Chicago, IL: Dorsey, 1989), 38–58; Hoffman, *Simon Girty*; Heard, *White into Red*, 127–9.

Girty, Simon [Killackchoker]. Delaware taken hostage by Colonel Henry Bouquet at Muskingum, 11 November 1764. ESCAPED before May 1765. HL, MM, 569, fol. 32; *MPCP*, 9: 250–64.

Girty, Thomas (1739?–1820). Oldest of Girty boys. Taken with his family by Delaware in fall of Fort Granville, Cumberland County, PA, 31 July 1756. RETAKEN in Kittanning raid, 8 September 1756. Apprenticed to John Armstrong. *PG*, 19 August and 23 September 1756; Consul Willshire Butterfield, *History of the Girtys* (Cincinnati, OH, 1890), 1–2; Hoffman, *Simon Girty*, 368–

70; Cumberland County Orphan's Court Dockets, vol. 2, 1761–86, Cumberland County Courthouse, Carlisle, PA, n.p.

Girty-Turner, Mary [nee Newton]. Captured by Delaware with husband and five sons in fall of Fort Granville, Cumberland County, PA, 31 July 1756. Taken to Kittanning and then to the Shawnee. RETURNED 1759. *PG*, 19 August 1756; Hoffman, *Simon Girty*, 11–13, 18–21.

Girty-Turner, John [Theecheapei]. Infant son of Mary. Taken with family in fall of Fort Granville, Cumberland County, PA, 31 July 1756. Sent to Kittanning and then to the Shawnee. RETURNED to Fort Pitt, 10 May 1765. American scout in Dunmore's War. *PG*, 19 August 1756; Heard, *White into Red*, 127–9; Hoffman, *Simon Girty*, 72–3, 409–10n2.

Gist, Thomas. Ensign in Virginia Regiment. Captured by Wyandot in Major James Grant's defeat at Fort Duquesne, 14 September 1758. Held near Detroit. ESCAPED 5 October 1759. "Thomas Gist's Indian Captivity, 1758–1759," *PMHB* 80 (1956): 285–311; HL, AB, 658, 659; *PG*, 28 September and 19 October 1758.

Goddard, Stanley. Trader taken by Ojibwa in capture of Fort Michilimackinac, 2 June 1763. RANSOMED from Ottawa later that year. Armour, *Attack at Michilimackinac*, 60; Henry, *Travels* (1901), 49; Francis Parkman, *The Conspiracy of Pontiac and the Indian War after the Conquest of Canada*, 6th ed., 2 vols (Boston, MA: Little, Brown, 1905), vol. 1, 344.

Good, Jacob. Reported held at Lower Shawnee Town late in 1764. *WPHM* 39 (1956): 202.

Gordon, Francis. Lieutenant in Royal American Regiment. Commander at Fort Venango when taken by Seneca, 16 June 1763. TORTURED to death three days later. *PG*, 7 July 1763; *NYG*, 11 July 1763; David Dixon, *Never Come to Peace Again: Pontiac's Uprising and the Fate of the British Empire in North America* (Norman, OK: University of Oklahoma Press, 2005), 147.

Gore, Rose. Woman captured by Shawnee at Blackwater, VA, 28 April 1758. RETURNED by Shawnee to Fort Pitt, 10 May 1765. *WPHM* 39 (1956): 198; *JP*, 11: 721.

Gorrell, James. Lieutenant in Royal American Regiment. Commander at Green Bay, WI. Taken by Ottawa at Fort Michilimackinac. RANSOMED at Montreal, 16 August 1763. *JP*, 10: 714; *DCB*, 3: 261–2.

Gould, Molly. Held in Lower Shawnee Town late in 1764. *WPHM* 39 (1956): 202.

Graham, John. Virginia soldier in Captain Adam Stephen's company. Captured in fall of Vause's Fort, 25 June 1756. Held by Wyandot and likely RETURNED. Lived in Fairfax County, VA. Preston Papers, 1: 83; *GWP*, 3: 256; *PG*, 28 July 1756, 9 February 1758; United States Bureau of the Census, *Heads of Families at the First Census of the United States Taken in the Year 1790: Records of the State Enumerations of 1782 to 1785: Virginia* (Baltimore, MD: US Bureau of the Census, 1966), 16.

Granier, Louis [Grand Jean]. Canadian marine in Captain Louis Herbin's company. Taken in Battle of La Belle Famille, 24 July 1759. Held in Somerset County, NJ. EXCHANGED at Crown Point, NY, 9 December 1760. *JP*, 13: 115; Job Stockton Papers, NYHS.

Grant, Alexander. Ensign in Montgomery Highlanders. Taken in Major James Grant's defeat at Fort Duquesne, 14 September 1758. RETURNED. Draper Mss, Virginia Papers, 3ZZ48.

Grant, James (1720–1806). Of Ballindalloch. Major in Montgomery Highlanders. Defeated and captured at Fort Duquesne, 14 September 1758. EXCHANGED at Crown Point, NY, 14 December 1759. Made war and peace with Cherokee in 1761. Promoted to colonel, and was governor of East Florida from 1763 to 1771. HL, AB, 655, 658; *PG*, 28 September and 19 October 1758, 6 December 1759; *ANB*.

Graves. Virginia soldier in Captain Robert Stobo's company. Taken after fall of Fort Necessity, 4 July 1754. RETURNED 30 August 1754. *Travels in New France by J.C.B.*, ed. Stevens, Kent, and Woods, 64; Robert C. Alberts, *The Most Extraordinary Adventures of Major Robert Stobo* (Boston, MA: Houghton Mifflin, 1965), 97.

Gray, Benjamin. Soldier in Royal American Regiment. Taken by Indians in surrender of Fort Presqu'île, 23 June 1763. ESCAPED to Fort Pitt the same day. William Trent, "William Trent's Journal at Ft. Pitt, 1763," *MVHR* 11 (1924–25): 402; *HBP*, 6: 299, 301n.

Green, [Mrs]. Captured by Shawnee near Fort Dinwiddie, Augusta County, VA, 26 May 1764. RETAKEN by militia the same day. BL, Add. Mss, 21650, fol. 238; *PG*, 14 June 1764; Lewis Preston Summers, *History of Southwest Virginia, 1746–1786, Washington County, 1777–1870* (Richmond, VA: J.L. Hill, 1903), 81.

Grey/Williams, Hannah. Taken with her three-year-old daughter in fall of Bigham's Fort, Cumberland County, PA, 9 June 1756. Seen at Kuskuski before early 1759. ESCAPED in wagon of furs at Fort Pitt, 16 October 1759. Married Enoch Williams and raised an adopted daughter as Jane Grey. *PG*, 17 and 24 June 1756; Severance, "Tale of Captives," 257; "James Kenny's 'Journal to Ye Westward,' 1758–59," ed. John W. Jordan, *PMHB* 37 (1913): 437; Sherman Day, *Historical Collections of the State of Pennsylvania*, 2 vols (Philadelphia, PA, 1843), vol. 2, 383–5; Samuel Hazard, *Hazard's Register of Pennsylvania*, 16 vols (Philadelphia, PA, 1828–35), vol. 1, 192. A principal in the famous "Grey property case," which was not settled until 1823 (see 10 Serg. & Rawle, 182).

Grey, Jane. Three year old taken in fall of Bigham's Fort, Cumberland County, PA, 9 June 1756. Lived with Cayuga John Hudson for several years from 1757. WHITE INDIAN who stayed with the Iroquois, married, and raised children in New York. *PG*, 17 and 24 June 1756; Day, *Historical Collections*, vol. 2, 383–5.

["Grey, Jane"]. Young German-speaking child. Taken in Pennsylvania, c. 1756. RETURNED at Muskingum, 15 November 1764. Raised by Hannah Grey as her missing daughter, Jane. Married a Mr Gillespie. Later exposed and dispossessed of Jane Grey's portion of her father's estate. Day, *Historical Collections*, vol. 2, 383–5.

Griffith, Maurice. Virginian. Captured by Shawnee near Vause's Fort, Augusta County, VA, 12 August 1755. ESCAPED 8 December 1756. Scout for Washington in 1758. Preston Papers, 1: 83; Kegley, *Kegley's Virginia Frontier*, 247; *GWP*, 5: 276–7.

Grissell, Andrew. Soldier in Captain Harbin's company of Royal American Regiment. Captured in Major James Grant's defeat at Fort Duquesne, 14 September 1758. ESCAPED the same day. BL, Add. Mss, 21682, fol. 13.

Grissy, Anthony. Soldier in second battalion of Pennsylvania regiment. Captured by Delaware after Kittanning raid, 9 September 1756. MISSING. *PA*, ser. 2, 2: 458–60; *PG*, 23 September 1756; *NYM*, 27 September 1756; Hunter, "Victory at Kittanning," 392–402.

Guinter. One of two young children of Philip. Captured in Cumberland County, PA, October 1756. MISSING. *PMHB* 32 (1908): 312.

Guinter. One of two young children of Philip. Captured in Cumberland County, PA, October 1756. MISSING. *PMHB* 32 (1908): 312.

Guinter. Older daughter of Philip. Captured in Cumberland County, PA, October 1756. MISSING. *PMHB* 32 (1908): 312.

Gunn, Catherine. Woman captured by Delaware and Mingo at Catawba Creek, Frederick County, VA, 1 October 1764. RETAKEN soon thereafter. Baker, *French and Indian War*, 134.

Guthrie, John. Captive held in Lower Shawnee Town late in 1764. MISSING. *WPHM* 39 (1956): 202.

Guttridge, William. Pennsylvanian. Seen at Detroit in 1757. *PG*, 22 December 1757; *NYM*, 2 January 1758.

Haig[h], John. Maryland youth. Captured by Shawnee near Fort Cumberland, MD, 25 May 1759. RETURNED at Fort Pitt, 5 May 1765. BL, Add. Mss, 21644, fol. 193; *WPHM* 39 (1956): 197.

Hailin, Cathrina. Child from Northampton County, PA. Captured by North Branch Delaware, 1 January 1756. MISSING. *PMHB* 32 (1908): 314. Compare *PG*, 22 January 1756 (where she was reported killed).

Haller/Holler, Henry. Pennsylvania ensign. Captured in Major James Grant's defeat at Fort Duquesne, 14 September 1758. Taken to Canada and EXCHANGED at Crown Point, NY, 12 December 1759. *PA*, ser. 2, 2: 481; *PG*, 28 September and 19 October 1758, 6 December 1759; HL, AB, 655, 658; *V&P*, 7: 5655, 5835.

Hambrough/Hambach, Frederick. Trader captured at Fort St Joseph, MI, 27 May 1763. RETURNED. Trading there again when killed in 1768. BL, Add. Mss, 21655, fol. 214; *JP*, 10: 715; Susan Sleeper-Smith, *Indian Women and French Men: Rethinking Cultural Encounter in the Western Great Lakes* (Amherst, MA: University of Massachusetts Press, 2001), 63.

Hamilton. Boy from Cumberland County, PA. Taken by Wyandot, 28 January 1756. RETURNED to George Croghan at Fort Pitt, 1 November 1760. "George Croghan's Journal," 356.

Hamilton. Nine-year-old boy. Captured by Delaware on Potomac River, 17 July 1763. RETURNED to Fort Pitt on his own in 1772. McClure, *Diary of David McClure*, 86–8.

Hamilton, Agnes. Woman of the regiment captured at General Edward Braddock's defeat, 9 July 1755. Seen near Detroit in 1757. MISSING. Merlin Stonehouse Transcripts, vol. 4, n.p., Huntington Library and Art Gallery, San Marino, CA; *PG*, 22 December 1757.

Hamilton, Archibald. Seven year old captured with two sisters by Shawnee at Carr's (Kerr's) Creek, 17 July 1763. RETURNED to Fort Pitt, 10 May 1765. Draper Mss, Kentucky Papers, 11CC291; *JP*, 11: 720.

Hamilton, Mary. Captured with sister and brother by Shawnee at Carr's (Kerr's) Creek, 17 July 1763. RETURNED to Fort Pitt, 10 May 1765. Said to have been ransomed by her father. *WPHM* 39 (1956): 197; *PG*, 7 March 1765; BL, Add. Mss, 21651, fol. 127.

Hamilton, Miriam. Captured with sister and brother by Shawnee at Carr's (Kerr's) Creek, 17 July 1763. RETURNED to Fort Pitt, 10 May 1765. Said to have been ransomed by her father. *WPHM* 39 (1956): 197; *PG*, 7 March 1765; BL, Add. Mss, 21651, fol. 127.

Hannel, Mary. Virginia teen. Taken by Shawnee at Blackwater, Augusta County, VA, 1755. RETURNED to Fort Pitt, 10 May 1765. *WPHM* 39 (1956): 198; *JP*, 11: 720.

Harmantrout, Christopher/Charles. Man taken in northern Virginia. RETURNED at Muskingum, 15 November 1764. *WPHM* 39 (1956): 189, 196; *PG*, 17 January 1765; *NYG*, 21 January 1765.

Harper, Eve. Taken with husband, Thomas, on South Branch of Potomac River, Augusta County, VA, 19 March 1758. RETURNED at Muskingum, 15 November 1764. *PG*, 17 January 1765; *NYG*, 21 January 1765; *WPHM* 39 (1956): 195, 196; Preston Papers, 1: 83.

Harper, Jane. Woman captured near Shippensburg, Cumberland County, PA, 8 July 1757. MISSING. *PA*, ser. 1, 3: 219–20; *PG*, 4 August 1757; *NYM*, 8 August 1757.

Harper, Thomas. Taken with wife, Eve, on South Branch of Potomac River, Augusta County, VA, 19 March 1758. RETURNED at Muskingum, 15 November 1764. *PG*, 17 January 1765; *NYG*, 21 January 1765; *WPHM* 39 (1956): 194; Preston Papers, 1: 83.

Harris. Surgeon with Pennsylvania forces. Captured in Major James Grant's defeat at Fort Duquesne, 14 September 1758. RETURNED. Draper Mss, Virginia Papers, 3ZZ48.

Harris, James. Virginian. RETURNED at Muskingum, 15 November 1764. *PG*, 17 January 1765; *NYG*, 21 January 1765; *WPHM* 39 (1956): 189; *JP*, 11: 485.

Harry, John. Pennsylvanian. RETURNED at Muskingum, 15 November 1764. *PG*, 17 January 1765; *NYG*, 21 January 1765; *JP*, 11: 489.

Hartinger, Catherine. Infant daughter of Peter. Orphaned in attack in Berks County, PA, 1 October 1758. Still captive on 14 August 1761. MISSING. Berks County Orphan's Court Dockets, Berks County Courthouse, Reading, PA, vol. 1, 15, 17, 20, 22.

Hartinger, George Henry. Young son of Peter. Orphaned in attack in Berks County, PA, 1 October 1758. Still captive on 14 August 1761. Likely RETURNED. Berks County Orphan's Court Dockets, Berks County Courthouse, Reading, PA, vol. 1, 15, 17, 20, 22; *U.S. Census of 1790, Pennsylvania*, 44.

Havener. Girl captured by Shawnee in fall of Seybert's Fort, Augusta County, VA, 28 April 1758. MISSING. Baker, *French and Indian War*, 109.

Hawes, Sarah. Woman captured by Shawnee in fall of Seybert's Fort, Augusta County, VA, 28 April 1758. MISSING. Baker, *French and Indian War*, 108.

Hay. Virginian. Captured on 3 July 1755. KILLED later the same day. *PG*, 3 July 1755.

Hays. Lieutenant in Pennsylvania forces. Captured in Major James Grant's defeat at Fort Duquesne, 14 September 1758. RETURNED. Draper Mss, Virginia Papers, 3ZZ48.

Hays. Pennsylvania trader. Captured by Wyandot at Sandusky in May 1763. MISSING. *HBP*, 6: 413.

Heiss, [Mrs Caspar]. Captured in Northampton County, PA, 12 December 1755. KILLED three days later. *PJ*, 18 December 1755; *PG*, 8 January 1756.

Henderson, Edward. Pennsylvanian. RETURNED at Muskingum, 15 November 1764. *JP*, 11: 488; *PG*, 17 January 1765; *NYG*, 21 January 1765.

Hendricks, David. Trader from Lancaster County, PA. Taken by Kahnawake in Kentucky, 26 January 1753. Ransomed for £17 Pennsylvania currency through Commissioners of Indian Affairs at Albany. Trading again in September 1764. *PG*, 27 September 1753, 17 August 1754; *NYM*, 7 May and 24 September 1753, 19 August 1754; Hanna, *Wilderness Trail*, vol. 2, 333.

Henry, Alexander (1739–1824). Captured by Ojibwa at Michilimackinac, 4 June 1763. Rescued by "blood-brother" Wawatam. RETURNED at Fort Niagara, 22 June 1764. Alexander Henry, *Travels and Adventures in Canada and the Indian Territories between the Years 1760 and 1776* (1809; reprint, Edmonton, AB: Hurtig, 1969), 76–174; *DCB*, 6: 316–19.

Henry, Elisabeth. Captured with her daughter by Delaware in Shearman's Valley, Cumberland County, PA, 29 July 1756. RETURNED at Muskingum, 15 November 1764. *WPHM* 39 (1956): 192; *JP*, 11: 488; *PG*, 17 January 1765; *NYG*, 21 January 1765.

Henry, Elizabeth/Betsy. Girl captured with her mother by Delaware in Shearman's Valley, Cumberland County, PA, 29 July 1756. Adopted and became a WHITE INDIAN. Gibson, "Account of the Captivity," 141–53; Loudon, ed., *Selection*, vol. 2, 170, 181–4; Beatty, *Journal*, 59–60.

Henry, George. Trader from Cumberland County, PA. Captured in Ohio Valley, 21 June 1756. Sent to Canada and France. RETURNED to Philadelphia by May 1753. *VG*, 20 and 27 October 1752; *NYM*, 28 May 1753; *PG*, 23 November 1752; Pease and Jenison, eds, *Illinois on the Eve*, 811; Hanna, *Wilderness Trail*, vol. 2, 334.

Hess, Henry. Brother of Peter. Captured by Delaware at Lower Smithfield, Northampton County, PA, 1 January 1756. MISSING. Anthony F.C. Wallace, *King of the Delawares: Teedyuscung, 1700–1763* (Philadelphia, PA: University of Pennsylvania Press, 1949), 83–5; Sipe, *Indian Wars*, 256–8.

Hess, Henry. Nineteen-year-old son of Peter. Captured by Delaware at Lower Smithfield, Northampton County, PA, 1 January 1756. ESCAPED. *PMHB* 32 (1908): 315, 316; *MPCP*, 7: 284; *NYM*, 18 October 1756; *PG*, 21 October 1756.

Hess, Peter. Captured with his brother and son by Delaware at Lower Smithfield, Northampton County, PA, 1 January 1756. KILLED the same day. *PMHB* 32 (1908): 315; Wallace, *King of the Delawares*, 83–5; Hunter, *Forts*, 277; Sipe, *Indian Wars*, 256–8.

Heysham, Molly. Captured in Blue Mountain region of Cumberland County, PA, October 1755. RETAKEN in capitulation of Fort Niagara, 25 July 1759. *PG*, 23 August 1759; *NYM*, 20 August 1759.

Hicks. One of two unnamed boys taken with family at Great Cove, Cumberland County, PA, 2 November 1755. RETURNED at Muskingum, 15 November 1764. *PG*, 17 January 1765; *NYG*, 21 January 1765.

Hicks. One of two unnamed boys taken with family at Great Cove, Cumberland County, PA, 2 November 1755. RETURNED at Muskingum, 15 November 1764. *PG*, 17 January 1765; *NYG*, 21 January 1765.

Hicks. Young man taken, with William Fleming, by Delaware at Great Cove, Cumberland County, PA, 2 November 1755. Resistant, and KILLED within an hour. Fleming and Fleming, *Narrative*; *NYM*, 8 March 1756.

Hicks, Barbara [Mrs John]. Widowed and captured with four of her sons at Great Cove, Cumberland County, PA, 2 November 1755. RETAKEN in Kittanning raid, 8 September 1756. *PA*, ser. 1, 2: 775; *PG*, 23 September 1756; *NYM*, 27 September 1756.

Hicks, Christopher. Soldier taken in fall of Vause's Fort, Augusta County, VA, 25 June 1756. MISSING and presumed dead. *PG*, 28 July 1757, 9 February 1758; *NYM*, 1 August 1757; Preston Papers, 1: 83; Chalkley, *Chronicles of the Scotch-Irish*, vol. 3, 54, 67.

Hicks, Gershom. Captured with mother and three brothers at Great Cove, Cumberland County, PA, 2 November 1755. Became Delaware WHITE INDIAN. Captured again by British at Fort Pitt when he "escaped," 14 April 1764. Released. *HBP*, 5: 381–2; *HBP*, 6: 514–16, 522–6, 540–1, 663; *JP*, 11: 169–70; BL, Add. Mss, 21638, fol. 385.

Hicks, Levy/Levi. Captured with mother and three brothers at Great Cove, Cumberland County, PA, 2 November 1755. Became Delaware white Indian but ESCAPED to Fort Pitt, 22 July 1762. "Journal of James Kenny, 1761–1763," ed. John W. Jordan, *PMHB* 37 (1913): 155–6; *HBP*, 6: 526; Beatty, *Journal*, 46, 49.

Hiley, George. Pennsylvania soldier. Captured by Indians in fall of Fort Granville, Cumberland County, PA, 31 July 1756. ESCAPED from Logstown, 1 April 1757. HL, LO, 3758; *MPCP*, 7: 561–2.

Hinds/Hynes, Thomas. Free negro who "belongs to Philadelphia." Captured in surrender of Fort William Henry, NY, 9 August 1757. Taken to Ohio. RETURNED at Detroit in 1760. *HBP*, 5: 210.

Hochstetler, Christian. Eleven-year-old son of Jacob. Captured with father and brother Joseph in Delaware and Shawnee attack in Bern Township, Berks County, PA, 28 September 1757. Still MISSING at end of May 1765. *PMHB* 32 (1908): 312, 317; *PA*, ser. 1, 4: 99; *JP*, 4: 451; *JP*, 11: 759; Hunter, *Forts*, 318.

Hochstetler, Jacob. Widowed and captured with two sons in Delaware and Shawnee attack in Bern Township, Berks County, PA, 28 September 1757. RETURNED by early August 1762. *PMHB* 32 (1908): 312, 317; *PA*, ser. 1, 4: 99; Hunter, *Forts*, 318.

Hochstetler, John. Man from Berks County, PA. Captured by Shawnee and Delaware, 12 October 1755. Held at Buckaloons. ESCAPED to Fort Augusta, 5 May 1758. *Wilderness Chronicles of Northwestern Pennsylvania*, ed. Sylvester K. Stevens and Donald R. Kent (Harrisburg, PA: Pennsylvania Historical Commission, 1941), 119–21.

Hochstetler, Joseph. Thirteen-year-old son of Jacob. Captured with father and brother Christian in Delaware and Shawnee attack in Bern Township, Berks County, PA, 28 September 1757. Held by Custaloga. RETURNED in 1763 via New York. *PMHB* 32 (1908): 317; *PA*, ser. 1, 4: 99; Hunter, *Forts*, 318; *JP*, 11: 757.

Hoeth/Huth/Head, Caroline. Orphaned and captured by Delaware in Northampton County, PA, 12 December 1755. Seen in Ohio country before March 1759. MISSING. *PA*, ser. 2, 7: 437; *PMHB* 32 (1908): 313; *PG*, 18 and 25 December 1755, 8 January 1756; *MPCP*, 6: 758–9.

Hoeth/Huth/Head, Catherine. Orphaned and captured by Delaware in Northampton County, PA, 12 December 1755. Seen in Ohio country before March 1759. RETURNED at Muskingum, 15 November 1764. *PA*, ser. 2, 7: 437; *PMHB* 32 (1908): 313; *PG*, 18 and 25 December 1755, 8 January 1756, 17 January 1765; *PJ*, 17 January 1765; *NYG*, 21 January 1765; *MPCP*, 6: 758–9.

Hoeth/Huth/Head, Mary. Orphaned and captured by Delaware in Northampton County, PA, 12 December 1755. Seen in Ohio country before March 1759. MISSING, but also reported killed on the trail into captivity. *PA*, ser. 2, 7: 437; *PMHB* 32 (1908): 313; *PG*, 18 and 25 December 1755, 8 January 1756; *MPCP*, 6: 758–9.

Hogan, John. Pennsylvania soldier. Taken in fall of Fort Granville, Cumberland County, PA, 31 July 1756. ESCAPED to Fort Pitt, 1 April 1757. *PG*, 19 August 1756; HL, LO, 3758; *MPCP*, 7: 561–2.

Holbert, Ebenezer. Fourteen year old captured in Northampton County, PA, late in 1755. "learned the delaware language perfectly." ESCAPED from near Lake Erie in November 1759. *PMHB* 32 (1908): 315; *PG*, 29 November 1759.

Hollister, Isaac. Youth captured by Delaware in Northampton County, PA, 4 September 1763. Escaped, retaken, and RETURNED in 1767. Isaac Hollister, *A Brief Narrative of the Captivity of Isaac Hollister, Who Was Taken by the Indians, Anno Domino, 1763* (New London, CT, 1767).

Holtiman/Holtomen, Christopher. Captured by Delaware in Virginia, 28 April 1758. RETURNED at Lancaster conference, 13 August 1762. *Minutes of Conferences ... Lancaster, 1762*, 7; Kercheval, *History of the Valley*, 84.

Homier. Canadian soldier from Montreal. Captured by Virginians in Jumonville incident, 28 May 1754. RETURNED via Martinique, 24 October 1755. *PG*, 13 and 27 June, 22 August, and 12 September 1754; *Collections des manuscrits ... Nouvelle France*, vol. 3, 521–2.

Hood, Margaret. Maryland woman. Captured by Delaware near mouth of Conococheague Creek, Cumberland County, PA, 2 November 1755. RETAKEN in Kittanning raid, 8 September 1756. *PG*, 23 September 1756; *PA*, ser. 1, 2: 775.

Hoops, Adam. Sergeant in Royal American Regiment. Captured in Major James Grant's defeat at Fort Duquesne, 14 September 1758. ESCAPED to Detroit, 6 August 1760. *PG*, 28 September and 19 October 1758; HL, AB, 659; BL, Add. Mss, 21638, fol. 126.

Horner, [Mrs George]. Captured by Delaware at Capon River, VA. MISSING. Kercheval, *History of the Valley*, 72.

Hout, Elizabeth. Thirteen-year-old girl. Captured near Easton, Northampton County, PA, 1756. RETURNED to Johnson Hall, NY, May 1765. *NYG*, 22 July 1765; *NYM*, 19 August 1765; *PG*, 19 September 1765.

Hover, Anton. Canadian marine in Montarin's company. Captured at battle of La Belle Famille, 24 July 1759. Held in Somerset County, NJ. EXCHANGED at Crown Point, NY, 9 December 1760. *JP*, 13: 115; Job Stockton Papers, NYHS.

Howard, Charles. Virginian. Captured on South Branch of Potomac River, Augusta County, VA. RANSOMED and returned in September 1757 via Canada and France. TNA, Adm. 1/4323, n.p.; Kercheval, *History of the Valley*, 50, 55.

Howard, Margaret. Virginian. Captured on South Branch of Potomac River, Augusta County, VA. RANSOMED and returned in September 1757 via Canada and France. TNA, Adm. 1/4323, n.p.; Kercheval, *History of the Valley*, 50, 55.

Howarth. Corporal in Captain John Joseph Schlosser's company of Royal American Regiment. Captured near Fort Ligonier, PA, 12 July 1759. MISSING. BL, Add. Mss, 21644, fol. 231; *HBP*, 3: 407.

Howell, Daniel. Connecticut settler at Wyoming, Northampton County, PA. Captured 4 September 1763. ESCAPED but became lost and died of starvation. *PG*, 13 September 1764.

Hubler. One of three young children of Mrs Franz Hubler. Captured with her by Delaware in Berks County, PA, 9 September 1763. MISSING. *MPCP*, 9: 44; *NYM*, 19 September 1763.

Hubler. One of three young children of Mrs Franz Hubler. Captured with her by Delaware in Berks County, PA, 9 September 1763. MISSING. *MPCP*, 9: 44; *NYM*, 19 September 1763.

Hubler. One of three young children of Mrs Franz Hubler. Captured with her by Delaware in Berks County, PA, 9 September 1763. MISSING. *MPCP*, 9: 44; *NYM*, 19 September 1763.

Hubler, [Mrs Franz]. Captured with three of her children by Delaware in Berks County, PA, 9 September 1763. MISSING. *MPCP*, 9: 44; *NYM*, 19 September 1763.

Hudson. Infant child of Cayuga John Hudson. Born in June 1763 in captivity at Fort Bedford. MISSING. *HBP*, 6: 214, 247–8, 250–2, 308, 332, 596; BL, Add. Mss, 21649, fol. 143.

Hudson. One of two young children of Cayuga John Hudson. Captured with parents, 1 June 1763, by Pennsylvania militia at his Susquehanna farm. Held at Fort Bedford. MISSING. *HBP*, 6: 214, 247–8, 250–2, 308, 332, 596; BL, Add. Mss, 21649, fol. 143.

Hudson. One of two young children of Cayuga John Hudson. Captured with parents, 1 June 1763, by Pennsylvania militia at his Susquehanna farm. Held at Fort Bedford. MISSING. *HBP*, 6: 214, 247–8, 250–2, 308, 332, 596; BL, Add. Mss, 21649, fol. 143.

Hudson, John. Cayuga captured with family, 1 June 1763, by Pennsylvania militia at his Susquehanna farm. Held at Fort Bedford. RELEASED to spy for the British in 1764. *HBP*, 6: 214, 247–8, 250–2, 308, 332, 596; BL, Add. Mss, 21649, fol. 143.

Hudson, [Mrs John]. Delaware wife of John Hudson. Captured with family, 1 June 1763, by Pennsylvania militia at his Susquehanna farm. Held at Fort Bedford. MISSING. *HBP*, 6: 214, 247–8, 250–2, 308, 332, 596; BL, Add. Mss, 21649, fol. 143.

Huff, Samuel. Held in Lower Shawnee Town late in 1764. MISSING. *WPHM* 39 (1956): 202.

Hugart, William. Virginia man. RETURNED by a Mohican to George Croghan at Fort Pitt, 1 August 1760. "George Croghan's Journal," 380.

Hughes, Joseph. Soldier in Captain Stuart's company of Virginia Regiment. Captured by Shawnee in Major James Grant's defeat at Fort Duquesne, 14 September 1758. EXCHANGED via Canada, France, and England before October 1760. HL, AB, 659; *Journals of the House of Burgesses, 1758–1761*, ed. McIlwaine, 188; *PG*, 28 September and 19 October 1758. Compare *GWP*, 6: 46–7.

Hunt, Thomas. Seventeen year old captured by Delaware in New Jersey in 1756. Seen at Tioga. RETURNED from Canada, 24 November 1759. *PA*, ser. 1, 3: 45–6, 56–7; TNA, CO 5/57, fols 119–21; *MPCP*, 7: 336.

Hunter, Samuel. Older laborer from York County, PA. Captured by Delaware, 13 April 1758. "could not run." KILLED the next day. *PA*, ser. 1, 3: 396–7; Loudon, ed., *Selection*, vol. 2, 47–65; *PG*, 11 May 1758; *NYM*, 15 May 1758.

Hunter, William. Soldier in second battalion of Pennsylvania regiment. Captured by Delaware in aftermath of Kittanning raid. Likely RETURNED by March 1759, when a William Hunter was a sutler at Fort Lyttleton. *PA*, ser. 2, 2: 458–60; *HBP*, 3: 225; *PG*, 23 September 1756; *NYM*, 27 September 1756; Hunter, "Victory at Kittanning," 392–402.

Huntzman, Adam. Man from Augusta County, VA. Captured in 1764. RETURNED at Muskingum, 15 November 1764. *WPHM* 39 (1956): 194; *PG*, 17 January 1765; *NYG*, 21 January 1765; *JP*, 11: 485; *NYG*, 24 December 1764.

Huntzman, Barbara. Woman from Augusta County, VA. Captured in 1764. RETURNED at Muskingum, 15 November 1764. *WPHM* 39 (1956): 195, 196; *PG*, 17 January 1765; *NYG*, 21 January 1765; *JP*, 11: 486.

Huntzman, John. Man from Augusta County, VA. Captured in 1764. RETURNED at Muskingum, 15 November 1764. *WPHM* 39 (1956): 194, 196; *PG*, 17 January 1765; *NYG*, 21 January 1765; *JP*, 11: 485; *NYG*, 24 December 1764.

Huss/Huse. Eighteen-year-old son of Jacob. Captured by Delaware in Northampton County, PA, likely in January 1756. RETURNED to Johnson Hall, NY, May 1765. *PG*, 19 September 1765.

Hutchinson, David. Infant taken by Shawnee at "Catapin," Augusta County, VA, 27 April 1758. RETURNED to Fort Pitt, 10 May 1765. *JP*, 11: 720; *WPHM* 39 (1956): 198.

Hutchinson, Florence [Mrs John]. Widowed and captured in Shawnee raid into Augusta County, VA, 27 April 1758. RETURNED at Muskingum, 15 November 1764. *WPHM* 39 (1956): 195, 196; *PG*, 17 January 1765; *NYG*, 21 January 1765; *JP*, 11: 486.

Hutchinson, George. Man from Cumberland County, PA. Captured by Delaware and Shawnee near Fort Cumberland, MD, 1 October 1755. ESCAPED three days later. HSP, Penn Mss, Indian Affairs, vol. 2, no. 42; *PA*, ser. 1, 2: 462–3.

Huth/Hold, Elizabeth. Thirteen year old captured by Delaware in Northampton County, PA, 17 January 1756. RETURNED at Johnson Hall, NY, May 1765. *PMHB* 32 (1908): 313; *PG*, 15 January 1756, 19 September 1765; *NYG*, 22 July 1765; *NYM*, 19 August 1765.

Hyde, Thomas. Trader from Lancaster County, PA. Captured by Kahnawake Iroquois in Kentucky, 26 January 1753. Bought by French, taken to Canada, and likely RELEASED in France. A Thomas Hyde married in Pennsylvania, 27 April 1772. *MPCP*, 5: 626, 663–4; *NYM*, 7 May and 24 September 1753, 19 August 1754; *PG*, 27 September 1753; *PA*, ser. 2, 2: 127.

Hyden, Samuel. Virginian. Captured in Augusta County, VA, 18 June 1756. Seen at Detroit the next year. MISSING. Preston Papers, 1: 83; *NYM*, 2 January 1758; *PG*, 12 December 1757.

Hyert/Hynd, Leonard. Virginian. Captured in 1764. RETURNED at Muskingum, 15 November 1764. *WPHM* 39 (1956): 189; *PG*, 17 January 1765; *NYG*, 21 January 1765; *JP*, 11: 485.

Ingles, George. Two-year-old son of John and Mary. Taken in Shawnee attack on New River, Augusta County, VA, 30 July 1755. DIED in captivity soon thereafter. *NYM*, 25 August 1755; Preston Papers, 1: 83; John Ingles Narrative, Draper Mss, Frontier Wars Papers, 12U112, 17; John P. Hale, *Trans-Allegheny Pioneers: Historical Sketches of the First White Settlements West of the Alleghenies, 1748 and After*, 3rd ed. (Raleigh, NC: Derreth, 1971), 39, 115.

Ingles, Mary [Mrs John]. Taken in fall of Vause's Fort, Augusta County, VA, 25 June 1756. RETURNED before March 1761. *PG*, 25 June 1756; *NYM*, 1 August 1756; Preston Papers, 1: 83; *Journals of the House of Burgesses, 1758–1761*, ed. McIlwaine, 221–9.

Ingles, Mary Draper (1732–1815) [Mrs William]. Taken in Shawnee attack on New River, Augusta County, VA, 30 July 1755. ESCAPED 30 September 1755. *NYM*, 25 August 1755, 1 March 1756; *PG*, 26 February 1756; Kercheval, *History of the Valley*, 106–7; Mary Draper Ingles, *The Story of Mary Draper Ingles and Son John Ingles*, ed. Roberta Inglis Steele and Andrew Lewis Ingles (Radford, VA: Commonwealth, 1969).

Ingles, Mathew. Taken in fall of Vause's Fort, Augusta County, VA, 25 June 1756. RETURNED and died soon thereafter. John Ingles Narrative, Draper Mss, Frontier Wars Papers, 12U112, 14.

Ingles, Thomas. Four-year-old son of Mary Draper Ingles and William. Taken in Shawnee attack on New River, Augusta County, VA, 30 July 1755. RANSOMED in 1768. Preston Papers, 1: 83; Thwaites and Kellogg, *Documentary History*, 179–80n; Waddell, *Annals of Augusta*, vol. 1, 75.

Innis. Infant taken with family at fall of Bigham's Fort, Cumberland County, PA, 9 June 1756. Reported KILLED later. *PG*, 17 and 24 June 1756; TNA, WO 34/10, 192–200.

Innis, Francis. Taken with family in fall of Bigham's Fort, Cumberland County, PA, 9 June 1756. Imprisoned in Quebec in 1757. EXCHANGED by 1759. *PG*, 17 and 24 June 1756; TNA, WO 34/10, 192–200; *PA*, ser. 1, 4: 106–7; *V&P*, 6: 5001, 5152; Haverford College Library, Indian Committee Records, 824/11, vol. 3, n.p.; "Journal of James Kenny, 1761–1763," ed. Jordan, 175.

Innis, Francis, Jr. Seven year old taken with parents in fall of Bigham's Fort, Cumberland County, PA, 9 June 1756. RETURNED at Muskingum, 15 November 1764. Either Francis Jr or his sister Jenny "a gentleman of Philadelphia had, and refused to give it up, until Innis proved the child his by a private mark." *WPHM* 39 (1956): 191; Day, *Historical Collections*, vol. 2, 384; *PG*, 17 and 24 June 1756, 17 January 1765; *V&P*, 6: 5001, 5152.

Innis, Jenny. Five year old taken with parents in fall of Bigham's Fort, Cumberland County, PA, 9 June 1756. RETURNED at Muskingum, 15 November 1764. *WPHM* 39 (1956): 192; *PG*, 17 and 24 June 1756; LAC, MG 19, F 35/2, lot 621, 4; *JP*, 11: 489.

Innis, Margery [Mrs Francis]. Taken with family in fall of Bigham's Fort, Cumberland County, PA, 9 June 1756. Imprisoned in Quebec in 1757. EXCHANGED by 1759. At Shemokin that year. *PG*, 17 and 24 June 1756; TNA, WO 34/10, 192–200; "Journal of James Kenny, 1761–1763," ed. Jordan, 175.

Ireny/Irena. Woman captured at Greenbrier River, Augusta County, VA, September 1755. RETURNED at Muskingum, 15 November 1764. Preston Papers, 1: 83; *WPHM* 39 (1956): 193; *JP*, 11: 490.

Istobe, William. Virginia soldier. Captured near Ashby's Fort, Augusta County, VA, 1 April 1756. Taken to Canada and EXCHANGED in England. *PG*, 15 April and 6 May 1756; *NYM*, 19 April and 3 May 1756; *Journals of the House of Burgesses, 1758–1761*, ed. McIlwaine, 84, 95.

Itawachcomequa [the Pride]. Prominent Shawnee. Captured by militia near Salkehatchie River, 15 June 1753. Jailed in Charlestown, where he DIED, 24 October 1753. *SCG*, 18 June and 29 October 1753; *SCDIA*, 1: 421–33; Ian K. Steele, "Shawnee Origins of Their Seven Years' War," *Ethnohistory* 53 (2006): 657–87.

Ivory, William. Virginia soldier. Captured in Major James Grant's defeat at Fort Duquesne, 14 September 1758. RETURNED by Wyandot to Detroit, 1 December 1760. *HBP*, 5: 210; *PG*, 28 September 1758.

Jack, Jeremiah. Captured near Potomac River, 17 April 1757. MISSING. Loudon, ed., *Selection*, vol. 2, 196.

Jackson, William. Ten year old captured in Berks County, PA, by Delaware in 1757. RETURNED at Lancaster conference, 13 August 1762. *PG*, 9 September 1756; *RCFFP*, 1: 69; *Minutes of Conferences ... Lancaster, 1762*, 7.

Jager. Catherine's *métis* child. RETURNED with her to William Johnson in June 1765. *PG*, 9 December 1756; *PMHB* 32 (1908): 319; *MPCP*, 7: 621; *V&P*, 7: 5883.

Jager, Catherine. Taken on 28 November 1756 from Heidelberg Township, Northampton County, PA, at age nine, by Susquehanna Delaware. White Indian who was nonetheless RETURNED, with her *métis* child, to William Johnson in June 1765. *PG*, 9 December 1756; *PMHB* 32 (1908): 319; *MPCP*, 7: 621; *V&P*, 7: 5883.

James. One of two children of Mr and Mrs James. Orphaned and captured in Sherman's Valley, PA, March 1763. MISSING. BL, Add. Mss, 21650, fol. 140; *HBP*, 6: 514–16, 522–6; *NYM*, 14 May 1764; *NYG*, 14 May 1764.

James. One of two children of Mr and Mrs James. Orphaned and captured in Sherman's Valley, PA, March 1763. MISSING. BL, Add. Mss, 21650, fol. 140; *HBP*, 6: 514–16, 522–6; *NYM*, 14 May 1764; *NYG*, 14 May 1764.

Jamieson. Woman from Cumberland County, PA. Captured near Fort Loudoun, PA, 25 July 1764. KILLED the next day. BL, Add. Mss, 21650, fol. 366; *PG*, 9, 13, and 30 August 1764; *NYG*, 13 August 1764; *NYM*, 13 August 1764.

Jamieson/Jemison. Child from York County, PA. Captured with her family by Shawnee, 5 April 1758. KILLED two days later. Mary Jemison, *A Narrative of the Life of Mrs. Mary Jemison*, ed. June Namias (Norman, OK: University of Oklahoma Press, 1992), 69–70; HL, AB, 143; *PG*, 13 April 1758; *NYM*, 17 April 1758.

Jamieson/Jemison, Betsy [Mrs Thomas]. Woman from York County, PA. Widowed and captured with her family by Shawnee, 5 April 1758. KILLED two days later. Jemison, *Narrative* (1992), 69–70; HL, AB, 143; *PG*, 13 April 1758; *NYM*, 17 April 1758.

Jamieson/Jemison, Betsy, Jr. Girl from York County, PA. Captured with her family by Shawnee, 5 April 1758. Still at Lower Shawnee Town late in 1764. MISSING. *WPHM* 39 (1956): 202; Jemison, *Narrative* (1992), 69–70; *PG*, 13 April 1758; *NYM*, 17 April 1758.

Jamieson/Jemison, Mary [Dickewamis] (1743?–1831). Fifteen year old from York County, PA. Captured with her family by Shawnee, 5 April 1758. Adopted by Seneca. Married a Delaware and then a Seneca. Interviewed 1823. WHITE INDIAN. Jemison, *Narrative* (1992), 69–70; *PG*, 13 April 1758; *NYM*, 17 April 1758.

Jamieson/Jemison, Mathew. Boy from York County, PA. Captured with his family by Shawnee, 5 April 1758. KILLED two days later. Jemison, *Narrative* (1992), 69–70; HL, AB, 143; *PG*, 13 April 1758; *NYM*, 17 April 1758.

Jamieson/Jemison, Robert. Boy from York County, PA. Captured with his family by Shawnee, 5 April 1758. KILLED two days later. Jemison, *Narrative* (1992), 69–70; HL, AB, 143; *PG*, 13 April 1758; *NYM*, 17 April 1758.

Jamieson/Jemison, Thomas. Man from York County, PA. Captured with his family by Shawnee, 5 April 1758. KILLED two days later. Jemison, *Narrative* (1992), 69–70; HL, AB, 143; *PG*, 13 April 1758; *NYM*, 17 April 1758.

Jarret de Vercheres. Lieutenant in Canadian garrison at Detroit. Surrendered 30 November 1760. Ordered to France in May 1761 and EXCHANGED. TNA, WO 1/5, 176; *PG*, 15 January and 5 February 1761; *NYM*, 30 March 1761.

Jenkins, Edward. Ensign in Royal American Regiment. Captured in Major James Grant's defeat at Fort Duquesne, 14 September 1758. Taken to Canada. EXCHANGED at Crown Point, NY, 13 December 1758. Promoted to lieutenant, and captured as commander of Fort Ouiatenon, 1 June 1763. Taken to Illinois, where he was RELEASED in January 1764. HL, AB, 655, 658; *HBP*, 2: 633; BL, Add. Mss, 21650, part 2, fol. 4; *PG*, 28 September and 19 October 1758, 11 and 18 August 1763; *NYM*, 8 August 1763.

Jew, Sally. Servant girl from Frederick County, VA. Captured by Shawnee, 25 July 1757. MISSING. Baker, *French and Indian War*, 93.

John, Captain. Delaware. Captured and held hostage by Colonel Henry Bouquet at Fort Pitt, September 1764. RETURNED 9 November 1764. *MPCP*, 9: 226; Sipe, *Fort Ligonier*, 221.

Johnson, David [Daniel?]. Militia captain from Northampton County, PA. Captured by Delaware in January 1756. Seen at Detroit in 1757. RETURNED at Muskingum, 15 November 1764. *WPHM* 39 (1956): 191; *PG*, 22 December 1757, 17 January 1765; *NYG*, 21 January 1765.

Johnson, William. Captured in Paxton, Lancaster County, PA, by Delaware, 19 September 1757. RETAKEN near Loyalhanna, PA, with two Delaware, by George Washington's troops, 12 November 1758. Considered a renegade, but his report on the weakness of Fort Duquesne proved true and was acted upon successfully. Nonetheless, likely executed. HL, AB, 824; *PG*, 6 October 1757, 30 November 1758; *NYM*, 10 October 1757, 4 December 1758.

Johnston, John. Soldier in Captain Thomas Bullitt's company of Virginia Regiment. Captured by Shawnee in Major James Grant's defeat at Fort Duquesne, 14 September 1758. Taken to Fort Duquesne, Canada, and France. EXCHANGED in England in July 1760. *Journals of the House of Burgesses, 1758–1761*, ed. McIlwaine, 188; HL, AB, 659. Compare *GWP*, 6: 46–7; and *PG*, 28 September and 19 October 1758.

Joliboir [nom de guerre]. Canadian marine in Captain Paul-Louis Dazemard de Lusignan's company. Taken in surrender of Detroit, 30 November 1760. Sent to New York and France. EXCHANGED in 1761. TNA, WO 1/5, 176; *PG*, 15 January and 5 February 1761; *NYM*, 30 March 1761.

Jolicour [nom de guerre]. Canadian marine in Captain Jean-Daniel Dumas's company. Taken in surrender of Detroit, 30 November 1760. Sent to New York and France. EXCHANGED in 1761. TNA, WO 1/5, 176; *PG*, 15 January and 5 February 1761; *NYM*, 30 March 1761.

Jordan. Widow. MISSING after Indian attack on Conococheague, Cumberland County, PA, 2 November 1755. *MPCP*, 6: 673–4; *PG*, 13 November 1755; *NYM*, 17 November 1755.

Kageshquanohel [Captain Pipe] (d. 1794). Wolf clan Delaware chief related to Shawnee Itawachcomequa. Taken hostage at Fort Pitt, September 1764. RETURNED by Colonel Henry Bouquet at Muskingum, 9 November 1764. Colin G. Calloway, "Captain Pipe," *ANB*; *MPCP*, 9: 226; Sipe, *Fort Ligonier*, 221.

Kamph, Diedrick. Soldier in Colonel Henry Bouquet's company of Royal American Regiment. Captured in Cumberland County, PA, 16 November

1758. RETURNED to Fort Niagara, 15 August 1760. BL, Add. Mss, 21645, fol. 182; BL, Add. Mss, 21654, fol. 9; Thwaites, ed., *Early Western Travels*, vol. 1, 250; *PG*, 7 and 21 December 1758; *NYM*, 1 January 1759.

Keighteighque. Shawnee. Taken hostage by Colonel Henry Bouquet at Muskingum, 14 November 1764. ESCAPED from Fort Pitt, 3 December 1764. HL, MM, 569, fols 37–8; *MPCP*, 9: 232; *HBP*, 6: 717.

Keller. Boy captured with mother and two brothers in Northampton County, PA, 16 September 1757. MISSING. *PMHB* 32 (1908): 316; *PG*, 22 September 1757.

Keller. Boy captured with mother and two brothers in Northampton County, PA, 16 September 1757. MISSING. *PMHB* 32 (1908): 316; *PG*, 22 September 1757.

Keller. Young boy captured with mother and two brothers in Northampton County, PA, 16 September 1757. MISSING. *PMHB* 32 (1908): 316; *PG*, 22 September 1757.

Keller, [Mrs Joseph]. "Mother Keller." Captured with three sons in Northampton County, PA, 16 September 1757. RETURNED. *PMHB* 32 (1908): 316; *PG*, 22 September 1757; *RCFFP*, 1: 242.

Keller/Kaller, Peter. Man from Northampton County, PA. Captured in February 1756. MISSING. May have returned. There was one Peter Keller in each of Bucks, Berks, Lancaster, and York Counties, PA, in 1790. *PMHB* 32 (1908): 313; *U.S. Census of 1790, Pennsylvania*, 45, 140, 290.

Kelly. Boy about fifteen. Captured by Shawnee with family of seven near Cunningham's Fort, Frederick County, VA, 22 April 1756. ESCAPED to Winchester the same day. *PG*, 13 May 1756; *NYM*, 17 May 1756.

Kelly. Young child. Captured by Shawnee with family of seven near Cunningham's Fort, Frederick County, VA, 22 April 1756. MISSING. *PG*, 13 May 1756; *NYM*, 17 May 1756.

Kelly. Young child. Captured by Shawnee with family of seven near Cunningham's Fort, Frederick County, VA, 22 April 1756. MISSING. *PG*, 13 May 1756; *NYM*, 17 May 1756.

Kelly. Young child. Captured by Shawnee with family of seven near Cunningham's Fort, Frederick County, VA, 22 April 1756. MISSING. *PG*, 13 May 1756; *NYM*, 17 May 1756.

Kelly. Young child. Captured by Shawnee with family of seven near Cunningham's Fort, Frederick County, VA, 22 April 1756. MISSING. *PG*, 13 May 1756; *NYM*, 17 May 1756.

Kelly, Edward/Teddy. Young child. Captured by Shawnee with family of seven near Cunningham's Fort, Frederick County, VA, 22 April 1756. RETURNED. Guide in 1774 campaign against Shawnee. *PG*, 13 May 1756; *NYM*, 17 May 1756; Kercheval, *History of the Valley*, 197; Doddridge, *Notes on the Settlement*, 242.

Kelly, Sarah [Mrs David]. Widowed and captured with her six children by Shawnee near Cunningham's Fort, Frederick County, VA, 22 April 1756. RETAKEN in raid on Kittanning, 8 September 1756. *PG*, 13 May and 23 September 1756; *PA*, ser. 1, 2: 775.

Kennedy, John. Pennsylvania trader. Captured by English John, a Delaware, at Christopher Gist's Ohio trading post at Redstone Creek, 23 April 1754. Taken to Fort Duquesne, Canada, and France. RETURNED to England by 18 August 1757. HSP, Penn Papers, Indian Affairs, vol. 3, nos 24–5; *PG*, 8 December 1757; *PJ*, 8 December 1757.

Ketakatwitche, [Jean/Jenny]. Girl captured by Shawnee on South Branch of Potomac River, Augusta County, VA, 1755. RETURNED to Fort Pitt, 10 May 1765. *WPHM* 39 (1956): 198.

Kighto. White boy. RANSOMED at Shamokin from Mohawk Peter by Nathaniel Holland, 30 July 1760. Haverford College Library, Indian Committee Records, 824/11, vol. 3, 4.

Kilgore, Ralph. Pennsylvania trader's man. Captured with Morris Turner by Indians west of Logstown, 27 May 1750. Taken to Detroit and then to Canada. ESCAPED at Fort Niagara, August 1750. *MPCP*, 5: 480–4; *JP*, 1: 302–4; Severance, "Tale of Captives," 266–7; *Ohio Company Papers*, ed. Bailey, 152, 153.

Kimberlain, Jacob. Virginian. Captured near New River, Augusta County, VA, 19 October 1763. KILLED when captors attacked by Virginia militia. *PG*, 18 December 1763; Withers, *Chronicles* (1895), 99.

Kincade. One of three young children of Eleanor. Captured by Shawnee in attack on Jackson River, Augusta County, VA, 11 September 1756. Seen in Lower Shawnee Town nine years later. WHITE INDIAN. *PG*, 7 October 1756; *NYM*, 11 October 1756; *WPHM* 39 (1956): 202.

Kincade. One of three young children of Eleanor. Captured by Shawnee in attack on Jackson River, Augusta County, VA, 11 September 1756. Seen in Lower Shawnee Town nine years later. WHITE INDIAN. *PG*, 7 October 1756; *NYM*, 11 October 1756; *WPHM* 39 (1956): 202.

Kincade. One of three young children of Eleanor. Captured by Shawnee in attack on Jackson River, Augusta County, VA, 11 September 1756. Seen in Lower Shawnee Town nine years later. WHITE INDIAN. *PG*, 7 October 1756; *NYM*, 11 October 1756; *WPHM* 39 (1956): 202.

Kincade, Eleanor/Aley [Mrs George]. Widowed and captured with her three young children by Shawnee in attack on Jackson River, Augusta County, VA, 11 September 1756. Seen in Lower Shawnee Town nine years later. Likely a WHITE INDIAN. *PG*, 7 October 1756; *NYM*, 11 October 1756; *WPHM* 39 (1956): 202.

Kincade/Kinkead. Four-year-old son of William. Captured with mother and two siblings by Delaware and Shawnee at Warm Springs, Frederick County, VA, 14 April 1764. KILLED three days later. *PG*, 3 May 1764; Draper Mss, Kentucky Papers, 16CC193-7.

Kincade/Kinkead. Seven-year-old daughter of William. Captured with mother and two siblings by Delaware and Shawnee at Warm Springs, Frederick County, VA, 14 April 1764. DIED in captivity, of illness, soon thereafter. *PG*, 3 May 1764; Draper Mss, Kentucky Papers, 16CC193-7.

Kincade/Kinkead, Isabella. Two-year-old daughter of William. Captured with mother and two siblings by Delaware and Shawnee at Warm Springs,

Frederick County, VA, 14 April 1764. RETURNED at Muskingum, 15 November 1764. *PG*, 3 May 1764; Draper Mss, Kentucky Papers, 16CC193-7; *WPHM* 39 (1956): 194; *PG*, 17 January 1765; *NYG*, 21 January 1765.

Kincade/Kinkead, Eleanor [Mrs William]. Captured with three children by Delaware and Shawnee at Warm Springs, Frederick County, VA, 14 April 1764. A child of William's was born in captivity and returned with her. RETURNED at Muskingum, 15 November 1764. *PG*, 3 May 1764; Draper Mss, Kentucky Papers, 16CC193-7; *WPHM* 39 (1956): 194; *PG*, 17 January 1765; *NYG*, 21 January 1765.

Kingon, George. Soldier in Captain Gavin Cochrane's company of Royal American Regiment. Captured in attack on convoy at Stony Creek, Cumberland County, PA, 12 July 1759. MISSING. BL, Add. Mss, 21644, fol. 231.

Kirk/Kirkwood, Robert. Possibly a soldier in Montgomery Highlanders who may have been captured by Shawnee in Major James Grant's defeat at Fort Duquesne, 14 September 1758, and claimed to have escaped, 22 June 1759. Robert Kirk, *The Memoirs and Adventures of Robert Kirk, Late of the Royal Highland Regiment* (Limerick, UK, 1775), 5–40, reprinted as *Through So Many Dangers: The Memoirs and Adventures of Robert Kirk, Late of the Royal Highland Regiment*, ed. Ian McCulloch and Timothy Todish (Fleischmanns, NY: Purple Mountain, 2004).

Klein. Daughter of Christian. Captured in Northampton County, PA, 19 April 1757. Seen near Tioga a week later. MISSING. *PMHB* 32 (1908): 316; *PG*, 12 May 1757; *MPCP*, 7: 493–4, 620.

Knox. Boy captured with parents and five siblings at Great Cove, Cumberland County, PA, 8 November 1763. RETURNED at Muskingum, 15 November 1764. Sent to mother at Fort Pitt two weeks later. *PG*, 15 December 1763, 17 January 1765; *NYG*, 21 January 1765; *WPHM* 39 (1956): 188.

Knox. Young child captured with parents and five siblings at Great Cove, Cumberland County, PA, 8 November 1763. KILLED the same day at Sideling Hill. *PA*, ser. 1, 4: 138; Sipe, *Indian Wars*, 462–3.

Knox. Young child captured with parents and five siblings at Great Cove, Cumberland County, PA, 8 November 1763. MISSING. *PA*, ser. 1, 4: 138; Sipe, *Indian Wars*, 462–3.

Knox, Jane. Girl captured with parents and five siblings at Great Cove, Cumberland County, PA, 8 November 1763. RETURNED at Muskingum, 15 November 1764. Sent to mother at Fort Pitt two weeks later. *PG*, 15 December 1763, 17 January 1765; *NYG*, 21 January 1765; *WPHM* 39 (1956): 188.

Knox, Mary. Girl captured with parents and five siblings at Great Cove, Cumberland County, PA, 8 November 1763. RETURNED at Muskingum, 15 November 1764. Sent to mother at Fort Pitt two weeks later. *PG*, 15 December 1763, 17 January 1765; *NYG*, 21 January 1765; *WPHM* 39 (1956): 188.

Knox, Susan. Girl captured with parents and five siblings at Great Cove, Cumberland County, PA, 8 November 1763. RETURNED at Muskingum, 15 November 1764. Sent to mother at Fort Pitt two weeks later. *PG*, 15 December 1763, 17 January 1765; *NYG*, 21 January 1765; *WPHM* 39 (1956): 188.

Knox, Susan/Susannah [Mrs William]. Captured with her husband and six children at Great Cove, Cumberland County, PA, 8 November 1763. RETURNED at Muskingum, 15 November 1764. *PG*, 15 December 1763, 17 January 1765; *NYG*, 21 January 1765; *WPHM* 39 (1956): 188.

Knox, William. Captured with his wife and six children at Great Cove, Cumberland County, PA, 8 November 1763. Likely RETURNED. Taxed by county in 1779. *PG*, 15 December 1763; *PA*, ser. 3, 17: 510.

L'Hotelier, Louis Maximilie. Canadian marine in Captain Luc de La Corne's company. Captured at battle of La Belle Famille, 24 July 1759. Held in Somerset County, NJ. EXCHANGED at Crown Point, NY, 16 December 1760. *JP*, 13: 115; Job Stockton Papers, NYHS.

La Bonte. Canadian marine in Captain Pierre Boucher de Boucherville's company. Surrendered with Detroit garrison, 30 November 1760. Sent to New York. EXCHANGED in France. *PG*, 15 January and 5 February 1761; TNA, WO 1/5, 177; *NYM*, 30 March 1761.

La Chauvignerie, Michel, Jr. Canadian marine ensign who surrendered himself at Fort Henry, Berks County, PA, 12 October 1757. Held in Germantown. Paroled and EXCHANGED via Hispanola, 28 April 1759. *PA*, ser. 1, 3: 294–6, 298, 305–8, 329–30; Hunter, *Forts*, 325, 338.

La Fleur. Canadian marine corporal in Captain François-Marie Picoté de Belestre's company. Surrendered with Detroit garrison, 30 November 1760. Sent to New York and France in 1761. EXCHANGED. *PG*, 15 January and 5 February 1761; TNA, WO 1/5, 176; *NYM*, 30 March 1761.

La Force, Michel Pepin *dit* (b. 1721). Canadian marine captain. Captured by George Washington's troops in Jumonville incident, 28 May 1754. Held in Williamsburg jail. Sent to New York and France for EXCHANGE in December 1760. TNA, WO 34/38, fol. 210; HL, LO, 5464, 5468; R.A. Brock, ed., *The Official Papers of Robert Dinwiddie, 1751–1758*, 2 vols (Richmond, VA, 1883–84), vol. 1, 297, vol. 2, 227–8; PUQAM; http://www.genealogie.umontreal.ca.

La Jeunesse. Canadian marine corporal in Captain François-Marie Le Marchand de Lignery's company. Surrendered with Detroit garrison, 30 November 1760. Sent to New York and France in 1761. EXCHANGED. *PG*, 15 January and 5 February 1761; TNA, WO 1/5, 176; *NYM*, 30 March 1761.

La Loup. Piankashaw warrior. Captured by French, 8 December 1751. Held at Fort Chartres. RETURNED 24 June 1752. Pease and Jenison, eds, *Illinois on the Eve*, 29, 574, 635–44, 660–1, 673.

La Mirande. French trader. Captured by Shawnee, October 1750. MISSING. Pease and Jenison, eds, *Illinois on the Eve*, 29, 362–5; *MPCP*, 5: 496–8.

La Mirande. Wife of French trader. Captured by Shawnee, October 1750. MISSING. Pease and Jenison, eds, *Illinois on the Eve*, 29, 362–5; *MPCP*, 5: 496–8.

La Mouelle. Canadian marine lieutenant. Captured at battle of La Belle Famille, 24 July 1759. MISSING. Dunnigan, *Siege–1759*, 80, 103.

La Noye/La Noix. Marine lieutenant with Illinois forces. Captured at battle of La Belle Famille, 24 July 1759. MISSING. Dunnigan, *Siege–1759*, 80, 103.

La Pensie. Marine in Captain Jean-Daniel Dumas's company. Surrendered with Detroit garrison, 30 November 1760. Sent to New York and France for EXCHANGE in 1761. *PG*, 15 January and 5 February 1761; TNA, WO 1/5, 177; *NYM*, 30 March 1761.

La Pierre. Canadian marine corporal in Captain Charles de Sabrevoix's company. Surrendered with Detroit garrison, 30 November 1760. Sent to New York and France for EXCHANGE in 1761. *PG*, 15 January and 5 February 1761; TNA, WO 1/5, 176; *NYM*, 30 March 1761.

La Plante, Charles. Canadian marine cadet. Captured near Fort Cumberland, MD, by the garrison there, 10 December 1757. EXCHANGED via Hispaniola, 28 April 1759. *PG*, 5 January 1758; HL, LO, 5049.

La Terreur. Marine in Captain La Nodiere's company and drummer for the Detroit garrison. Surrendered 30 November 1760. Sent to New York and France for EXCHANGE in 1761. *PG*, 15 January and 5 February 1761; TNA, WO 1/5, 176; *NYM*, 30 March 1761.

La Tourmentte. Canadian marine in Captain Charles de Sabrevoix's company. Surrendered with Detroit garrison, 30 November 1760. Sent to New York and France for EXCHANGE in 1761. *PG*, 15 January and 5 February 1761; TNA, WO 1/5, 177; *NYM*, 30 March 1761.

La Volonte. Canadian marine in Lieutenant François-Xavier de St Ours's company. Surrendered with Detroit garrison, 30 November 1760. Sent to New York and France for EXCHANGE in 1761. *PG*, 15 January and 5 February 1761; TNA, WO 1/5, 177; *NYM*, 30 March 1761.

Lafferty, Daniel. Soldier in Captain Andrew Montour's company of Virginia Regiment. Captured at fall of Fort Necessity, 4 July 1754. Taken to Fort Niagara. MISSING. Severance, "Tale of Captives," 267; Stobo, *Memoirs*, 91–2.

Lamore. Interpreter for the English. Captured by Shawnee and Mingo near Fort Robinson, NC, March 1762. ESCAPED soon thereafter. Henry Timberlake, *Lieut. Henry Timberlake's Memoirs, 1756–1765* (1765; reprint, Marietta, GA: Continental, 1948), 125–6.

Lander. Captain in Royal American Regiment. Captured by Indians in Major James Grant's defeat at Fort Duquesne, 14 September 1758. RETURNED. Draper Mss, Virginia Papers, 3ZZ48.

Lane, John. Noted Virginia woodsman. Captured by Indians near Potomac River, 25 November 1757. ESCAPED the next day. Accidentally killed by Virginia militia while in Indian disguise four months later. *PG*, 8 and 15 December 1757, 2 March and 27 April 1758; *NYM*, 19 December 1757.

Lanscisco. *Métis* child of Mary. Surrendered with her at Muskingum, 15 November 1764. *JP*, 11: 486; *PG*, 4 and 11 September, 9 October 1755; *NYM*, 8 and 15 September 1755; *WPHM* 39 (1956): 195, 196; *PG*, 17 January 1765; *NYG*, 21 January 1765.

Lanscisco, Eleanor. Girl captured with her sister near South Branch of Potomac River, Augusta County, VA, 24 August 1755. RETURNED at Lancaster conference, 13 August 1762. *Minutes of Conferences ... Lancaster, 1762*, 7; *PG*, 4 and 11 September, 9 October 1755; *NYM*, 8 and 15 September 1755.

Lanscisco, Mary. Girl captured with her sister near South Branch of Potomac River, Augusta County, VA, 24 August 1755. RETURNED, together with her *métis* child, at Muskingum, 15 November 1764. *JP*, 11: 486; *PG*, 4 and 11 September, 9 October 1755; *NYM*, 8 and 15 September 1755; *WPHM* 39 (1956): 195, 196; *PG*, 17 January 1765; *NYG*, 21 January 1765.

Larabel, Joseph. Canadian soldier "de Longue-Point." Captured in Jumonville incident, 28 May 1754. RETURNED to France via England, 22 June 1755. *Collections des manuscrits … Nouvelle France*, vol. 3, 521–2; *PG*, 13 and 27 June, 22 August, and 12 September 1754.

Large, Glote. Canadian soldier. Captured at battle of La Belle Famille, 24 July 1759. Held in Somerset County, NJ. MISSING. *JP*, 13: 115; Job Stockton Papers, NYHS.

Laurence, Pierre. Canadian marine in Captain Joseph-Gaspard Chaussegros de Lery's company. Captured at battle of La Belle Famille, 24 July 1759. Held in Somerset County, NJ. EXCHANGED at Crown Point, NY, 16 December 1760. *JP*, 13: 115; Job Stockton Papers, NYHS.

Lavigne. Canadian soldier "de Varennes." Captured in Jumonville incident, 28 May 1754. RETURNED via Martinique, 17 October 1755. *Collections des manuscrits … Nouvelle France*, vol. 3, 521–2.

Lawrence, Robert. Soldier in Royal American Regiment. Captured on Maumee River, 13 May 1763. RETURNED by 21 December 1763. Gladwin, "Gladwin Manuscripts," 661; *PJ*, 2 December 1763.

Le Coeur, Nicholas [*dit* "la Tendrisse"]. Canadian marine in De Bonne's company. Captured at battle of La Belle Famille, 24 July 1759. Held in Somerset County, NJ. EXCHANGED at Crown Point, NY, 16 December 1760. *JP*, 13: 115; Job Stockton Papers, NYHS.

Le Marchand de Lignery, François-Marie (1703–59). Canadian commander at battle of La Belle Famille, 24 July 1759. Wounded, captured, and DIED in captivity five days later. *DCB*, 3: 378–9.

Le Roy, John Jacob. Captured with sister by Delaware at Penn's Creek, Cumberland County, PA, 16 October 1755. RETURNED at Muskingum, 15 November 1764. *WPHM* 39 (1956): 191; *PG*, 17 January 1765; *NYG*, 21 January 1765; *JP*, 11: 486; *PA*, ser. 2, 7: 429.

Le Roy, Marie. Captured with brother by Delaware at Penn's Creek, Cumberland County, PA, 16 October 1755. ESCAPED 16 March 1759. "Narrative of Marie Le Roy and Barbara Leininger," *Proceedings of the Pennsylvania-German Society* 15 (1905): 111–27; *PA*, ser. 2, 7: 427–38; Sipe, *Indian Wars*, 204–9.

Leake/Leak, William. Pennsylvanian. RETURNED at Muskingum, 15 November 1764. *WPHM* 39 (1956): 192; *PG*, 17 January 1765; *NYG*, 21 January 1765.

Lee, John. Soldier of Maryland regiment. Captured by Wyandot in Major James Grant's defeat at Fort Duquesne, 14 September 1758. RETURNED at Detroit, 1 December 1760. *PG*, 28 September 1758; *HBP*, 5: 210.

Legardeur de Repentigny, Louis. Canadian marine officer. Captured at battle of La Belle Famille, 24 July 1759. Likely EXCHANGED. Married in Montreal, 9 January 1764. *DCB*, 4: 449; PRDH.

Legardeur de Repentigny, Pierre-Jean-Baptiste-Francois-Xavier (1719–76). Canadian marine officer. Captured at battle of La Belle Famille, 24 July 1759. EXCHANGED in France in 1761. *DCB*, 4: 448–9.

Leininger, Barbara. Captured with mother and sister by Delaware at Penn's Creek, Cumberland County, PA, 16 October 1755. ESCAPED 16 March 1759. "Narrative of Marie Le Roy and Barbara Leininger," *Proceedings of the Pennsylvania-German Society* 15 (1905): 111–27; *PA*, ser. 2, 7: 427–38; Sipe, *Indian Wars*, 204–9.

Leininger, Margaret [Mrs Sebastian]. Widowed and captured with two daughters by Delaware at Penn's Creek, Cumberland County, PA, 16 October 1755. RETURNED at Muskingum, 15 November 1764. *WPHM* 39 (1956): 192; *JP*, 11: 489; *PG*, 17 January 1765; *NYG*, 21 January 1765.

Leininger, Regina/Rachel. Captured with mother and sister by Delaware at Penn's Creek, Cumberland County, PA, 16 October 1755. RETURNED at Muskingum, 15 November 1764. *WPHM* 39 (1956): 192; *JP*, 11: 489; *PG*, 17 January 1765; *NYG*, 21 January 1765; *PA*, ser. 2, 7: 429; Henry Melchior Muhlenberg, "Regina, the German Captive," in *Proceedings of the Pennsylvania-German Society* 15 (1906): 82–9; Charles F. Snyder, "The Story of Regina Leininger, Indian Captive of the Penn Creek Massacre," Northumberland County Historical Society, Proceedings and Addresses 9 (1937): 73–82.

Leonard, Henry. Man from Augusta County, VA. Captured 30 July 1755. MISSING. Preston Papers, 1: 83.

Lepin, François [*dit* "La Foret"]. Canadian marine in Captain Jean-Daniel Dumas's company. Captured at battle of La Belle Famille, 24 July 1759. Held in Somerset County, NJ. EXCHANGED at Crown Point, NY, 16 December 1760; Job Stockton Papers, NYHS; *JP*, 13: 115.

Leslye, William. Lieutenant in Royal American Regiment. Captured by Ojibwa in taking Fort Michilimackinac, 2 June 1763. RANSOMED at Montreal, 15 August 1763. *PG*, 11 and 18 August 1763; *JP*, 10: 777–88.

Levy, Andrew [Little Levy]. Trader. Captured by Wyandot and Ojibwa at Sandusky, 20 May 1763. RETURNED by Wyandot at Detroit, 9 July 1763. *HBP*, 6: 412; *PG*, 11 August and 22 December 1763; *NYM*, 15 August 1763.

Levy, Solomon. New York trader. Captured on Lake Erie, May 1763. ESCAPED into Detroit the following month. *HBP*, 6: 413.

Lewis, Andrew. Major in Virginia Regiment. Captured in Major James Grant's defeat at Fort Duquesne, 14 September 1758. EXCHANGED at Crown Point, NY, 14 December 1759. HL, AB, 655, 658; *PG*, 28 September and 19 October 1758, 3 January 1760.

Lewis, John. Soldier in second battalion of Pennsylvania regiment. Captured by Delaware at Kittanning, 9 September 1756. MISSING. Several men of this name lived in Pennsylvania between 1779 and 1782. Hunter, "Victory at Kittanning"; *PA*, ser. 2, 2: 458–60; *PG*, 23 September 1756; *NYM*, 27 September 1756; *PA*, ser. 3, 18: 273; *PA*, ser. 3, 20: 587; *PA*, ser. 3, 21: 35, 110, 564; *PA*, ser. 3, 22: 197.

Lick, John. Captured with father and brother by Delaware at Penn's Creek, Cumberland County, PA, 16 October 1756. Seen at "Kitahohing" before March 1759. MISSING. Sipe, *Indian Wars*, 204–9; *PA*, ser. 2, 7: 438.

Lick, Peter. Captured with two sons by Delaware at Penn's Creek, Cumberland County, PA, 16 October 1756. MISSING. Sipe, *Indian Wars*, 204–9.

Lick, William. Captured with father and brother by Delaware at Penn's Creek, Cumberland County, PA, 16 October 1756. Seen at "Kitahohing" before March 1759. MISSING. Sipe, *Indian Wars*, 204–9; *PA*, ser. 2, 7: 438.

Lingefelter, Anna Kathrin. Older woman captured in Bethel Township, Lancaster County, PA, 19 May 1757. RETURNED at Muskingum, 15 November 1764. *WPHM* 39 (1956): 190; *PMHB* 32 (1908): 310; *PG*, 17 January 1765; *NYG*, 21 January 1765; Haverford College Library, Indian Committee Records, 824/11, vol. 4, n.p.

Lingefelter, Mary Catherine. Woman captured in Bethel Township, Lancaster County, PA, 19 May 1757. RETURNED at Muskingum, 15 November 1764. *WPHM* 39 (1956): 193, 196; *PMHB* 32 (1908): 310; *PG*, 17 January 1765; *NYG*, 21 January 1765; Haverford College Library, Indian Committee Records, 824/11, vol. 4, n.p.

Lloyd, John. Boy from Cumberland County, PA. Taken near Little Cove by Delaware and Shawnee, 2 November 1755. RETURNED at Lancaster conference, 13 August 1762. *Minutes of Conferences ... Lancaster, 1762*, 7; *PG*, 9 September 1762.

Lodick. White held in Lower Shawnee Town late in 1764. MISSING. *WPHM* 39 (1956): 202.

Long, John Adam. Older Virginia man. Captured near Winchester by Delaware, 3 April 1756. ESCAPED from Buckaloons, 15 August 1756. *PG*, 21 October 1756; *NYM*, 18 October 1756.

Looney/Lewney, Peter. Virginia soldier. Captured by Miami in fall of Vause's Fort, Augusta County, VA, 25 June 1756. ESCAPED at Fort Niagara, 12 July 1757. *NYM*, 25 July and 1 August 1757; *PG*, 28 July 1757; "Captivity of Peter Looney," *MVHR* 15 (1928): 95–6.

Lorash, Barbara. Captured in Bethel Township, Lancaster County, PA, 20 July 1757. MISSING. *PMHB* 32 (1908): 311.

Lorash, Christina. Captured in Bethel Township, Lancaster County, PA, 20 July 1757. MISSING. *PMHB* 32 (1908): 311.

Lorash, Jacob. Captured in Bethel Township, Lancaster County, PA, 20 July 1757. MISSING. A Jacob Lorash was taxed in Lancaster County in 1771. *PMHB* 32 (1908): 311; *PA*, ser. 3, 17: 157.

Lorash, Kathrin. Captured in Bethel Township, Lancaster County, PA, 20 July 1757. MISSING. *PMHB* 32 (1908): 311.

Louaveska. Young Virginia girl. Captured by Shawnee at South Branch of Potomac River, Augusta County, VA, 1755. White Indian RETURNED at Fort Pitt, 10 May 1765. *JP*, 11: 720; *WPHM* 39 (1956): 198.

Low, Isaac. Pennsylvania soldier. Captured by Ottawa in Major James Grant's defeat at Fort Duquesne, 14 September 1758. RETURNED at Detroit, 1 December 1760. *HBP*, 5: 210; *PG*, 28 September 1758.

Lowery, James. Trader from Lancaster County, PA. Captured by Kahnawake in Kentucky, 26 January 1753. ESCAPED two days later. *NYM*, 7 May and 24 September 1753; *PG*, 27 September 1753.

Lowry. Son of Jean. Captured with family by Delaware at Conococheague, Cumberland County, PA, 1 April 1756. RETURNED at Fort Pitt, 16 October 1759. Jean Lowry, *A Journal of the Captivity of Jean Lowry and Her Children* (Philadelphia, PA, 1760); "James Kenny's 'Journal to Ye Westward,' 1758–59," ed. Jordan, 437.

Lowry, Elizabeth/Eliza. Young daughter of Jean. Captured with family by Delaware at Conococheague, Cumberland County, PA, 1 April 1756. RANSOMED by Martin McDaniel for £20 Pennsylvania currency, 19 February 1962. Lowry, *Journal*; Haverford College Library, Indian Committee Records, 824/11, vol. 4, 357; *V&P*, 7: 5561.

Lowry, James. Son of Jean. Captured with family by Delaware at Conococheague, Cumberland County, PA, 1 April 1756. Seen at Kuskuski before March 1759. MISSING. Lowry, *Journal*; *PA*, ser. 2, 7: 438.

Lowry, Jean [Mrs John]. Widowed and captured with her five children by Delaware at Conococheague, Cumberland County, PA, 1 April 1756. Taken to Kittanning, Quebec, and Dartmouth, UK. RETURNED by 11 October 1758. Lowry, *Journal*.

Lowry, Jean/Jane. Daughter of Jean. Captured with family by Delaware at Conococheague, Cumberland County, PA, 1 April 1756. RETURNED at Muskingum, 15 November 1764. *WPHM* 39 (1956): 193, 196; *JP*, 11: 490; Lowry, *Journal*; *PG*, 17 January 1765; *NYG*, 21 January 1765.

Lowry, Mary. Daughter of Jean. Captured with family by Delaware at Conococheague, Cumberland County, PA, 1 April 1756. RETURNED at Muskingum, 15 November 1764. *WPHM* 39 (1956): 193, 196; *JP*, 11: 490; Lowry, *Journal*; *PG*, 17 January 1765; *NYG*, 21 January 1765.

Lowry, Susan. Daughter of Jean. Captured with family by Delaware at Conococheague, Cumberland County, PA, 1 April 1756. RETURNED at Muskingum, 15 November 1764. *WPHM* 39 (1956): 193, 196; *JP*, 11: 490; Lowry, *Journal*; *PG*, 17 January 1765; *NYG*, 21 January 1765.

Lowther. Maryland farmer. TORTURED to death by unidentified Indians near Stoddart's Fort, 26 February 1756. Draper Mss, Pittsburgh and Northwest Virginia Papers, 6NN78-80; *PG*, 25 March 1756; *NYM*, 29 March 1756.

Lucar, Pierre [*dit* "Tonneme"]. Canadian marine in Captain Paul-Louis Dazemard de Lusignan's company. Captured at battle of La Belle Famille, 24 July 1759. Jailed in Somerset County, NJ. EXCHANGED at Crown Point, NY, 16 December 1760. Job Stockton Papers, NYHS; *JP*, 13: 115.

Lynn. Of Maryland. MISSING near Stoddart's Fort, 22 February 1756. *PG*, 29 March 1756; *NYM*, 29 March 1756.

Lynn. Maryland man. MISSING with two of his family near Stoddart's Fort, 22 February 1756. *PG*, 29 March 1756; *NYM*, 29 March 1756.

Lynn, Isaac. Boy missing with family near Stoddart's Fort, 22 February 1756. WHITE INDIAN who never returned. *PG*, 29 March 1756; *NYM*, 29 March 1756; Draper Mss, Pittsburgh and Northwest Virginia Papers, 6NN78-80.

Mackendorie, Sarah. Girl from Cumberland County, PA. Captured by Delaware and Shawnee in attack on Little Cove, 2 November 1755. RETURNED at Lancaster conference, 13 August 1762. *Minutes of Conferences ... Lancaster, 1762*, 7; *PG*, 9 September 1762.

Mackey. Boy from Lancaster County, PA. Captured 18 August 1757. RETURNED. *PG*, 25 August and 1 September 1757; Richards, *Pennsylvania-German*, 295–303.

MacMahan, John. Soldier in Captain Donald Campbell's company of Royal American Regiment. Captured at Detroit, May 1763. RETURNED there by 24 November 1763. BL, Add. Mss, 21651, fol. 197.

Maconnie, John. Soldier in Royal American Regiment. Surrendered with Fort Presqu'île, 23 June 1763. RETURNED by 20 December 1763. Gladwin, "Gladwin Manuscripts," 658.

Mallo. Eldest daughter of Michael. Captured by Shawnee in fall of Seybert's Fort, Augusta County, VA, 28 April 1758. RETURNED with her mother in 1764. *PG*, 27 June 1765.

Mallo. One of five children of Michael captured by Shawnee in fall of Seybert's Fort, Augusta County, VA, 28 April 1758. DIED in captivity, likely of smallpox. *PG*, 27 June 1765.

Mallo. One of five children of Michael captured by Shawnee in fall of Seybert's Fort, Augusta County, VA, 28 April 1758. DIED in captivity, likely of smallpox. *PG*, 27 June 1765.

Mallo. One of five children of Michael captured by Shawnee in fall of Seybert's Fort, Augusta County, VA, 28 April 1758. DIED in captivity, likely of smallpox. *PG*, 27 June 1765.

Mallo, John Adam [Wannimen]. Five-year-old son of Michael. Captured by Shawnee in fall of Seybert's Fort, Augusta County, VA, 28 April 1758. Survived smallpox in captivity. Became WHITE INDIAN who was reported returned with Pennsylvania troops in 1764 but was still missing seven months later. *PG*, 27 June 1765.

Mallo, Michelle [Mrs Michael]. Captured with five children by Shawnee in fall of Seybert's Fort, Augusta County, VA, 28 April 1758. RETURNED 1764. *PG*, 27 June 1765; BL, Add. Mss, 21646, fols 65–6.

Man. Son of John. Captured with mother and brother by Shawnee at Marsh Creek, York County, PA, 5 April 1758. KILLED two days later. *PG*, 2 April 1761; Jemison, *Narrative* (1992), 69–70; HL, AB, 143.

Man, John. Son of John. Captured with mother and brother by Shawnee at Marsh Creek, York County, PA, 5 April 1758. Sold to a French officer, brought to Montreal, and after this city's capture, released and taken in by merchants Finlay and Campbell. RETURNED July 1761. *PG*, 2 April and 2 July 1761; Jemison, *Narrative* (1992), 69–70; HL, AB, 143.

Man, [Mrs John]. Captured with two sons by Shawnee at Marsh Creek, York County, PA, 5 April 1758. KILLED two days later. *PG*, 2 April 1761; Jemison, *Narrative* (1992), 69–70 (where she is recalled as Mrs William Mann); HL, AB, 143.

Mann, Moses. Virginia soldier. Captured at Ashby's Fort, Augusta County, VA, 1 April 1756. MISSING. Land conveyed to son and heir, John, 10 September

1763. *PG*, 15 and 29 April 1756, 6 May 1756; Preston Papers, 1: 83; Chalkley, *Chronicles of the Scotch-Irish*, vol. 3, 42, 416.

Manselle. *Métis* daughter of Dorothy. Surrendered with mother at Muskingum, 15 November 1764. MISSING. *WPHM* 39 (1956): 192, 193; *JP*, 11: 489; *PG*, 17 January 1765; *NYG*, 21 January 1765.

Manselle. *Métis* son of Dorothy. Surrendered with mother at Muskingum, 15 November 1764. MISSING. *WPHM* 39 (1956): 192, 193; *JP*, 11: 489; *PG*, 17 January 1765; *NYG*, 21 January 1765.

Manselle, Dorothy. Pennsylvanian. RETURNED, with her *métis* son and daughter, at Muskingum, 15 November 1764. *WPHM* 39 (1956): 192, 193; *JP*, 11: 489; *PG*, 17 January 1765; *NYG*, 21 January 1765.

Manselle, Margaret. Pennsylvanian. RETURNED at Muskingum, 15 November 1764. *WPHM* 39 (1956): 192; *JP*, 11: 489; *PG*, 17 January 1765; *NYG*, 21 January 1765.

Maray de La Chauvignerie, Michel. Canadian marine lieutenant. Captured at battle of La Belle Famille, 24 July 1759. MISSING. Dunnigan, *Siege–1759*, 80, 103.

Marin de La Malgue, Joseph [Marin *fils*] (1719–74). Canadian marine captain. Captured at battle of La Belle Famille, 24 July 1759. EXCHANGED in England in 1761. Captured off Newfoundland in 1762 and again sent to France. Died as lieutenant colonel of French troops in a Madagascar settlement. *DCB*, 4: 512–14.

Marit, Frans. Canadian marine in Debuson's company. Captured at battle of La Belle Famille, 24 July 1759. Held in Somerset County, NJ. EXCHANGED via Crown Point, NY, 9 December 1760. *JP*, 13: 115; Job Stockton Papers, NYHS.

Marle, Edmund. Captured near Fort Cumberland, MD, 30 September 1755. MISSING. *PJ*, 16 October 1755; *PG*, 16 October 1755; *NYM*, 20 October 1755.

Marshall, [Mrs Edward]. Widowed and captured in Northampton County, PA, June 1757. MISSING. *PMHB* 32 (1908): 316; *RCFFP*, 1: 315; Israel Daniel Rupp, *History of Northampton, Lehigh, Monroe, Carbon, and Schuylkill Counties* (Harrisburg, PA, 1845), 437–8.

Martin, James. Ten-year-old son of trader John. Captured with mother and siblings by Delaware and Shawnee at Great Cove, Cumberland County, PA, 2 November 1755. Taken to Kittanning. RETURNED at Muskingum, 15 November 1764, and sent to his father at Fort Pitt, 29 November 1764. *WPHM* 39 (1956): 188; *PG*, 13 November 1755, 17 January 1765; *NYG*, 21 January 1765; Sipe, *Indian Wars*, 225–6.

Martin, Janet. Two-year-old daughter of trader John. Captured with mother and siblings by Delaware and Shawnee at Great Cove, Cumberland County, PA, 2 November 1755. Sold to M. Baubee and REDEEMED by mother in Quebec. Returned with her via England before 1762. *PA*, ser. 1, 4: 100; *PG*, 13 November 1755; *NYM*, 17 November 1755; Sipe, *Indian Wars*, 225–6.

Martin, John. Old man captured at Maxwell's Fort in Cumberland County, PA, 23 April 1757. RETURNED to George Croghan at Fort Pitt, 20 August 1759.

"George Croghan's Journal," 344; Loudon, ed., *Selection*, vol. 2, 196; Hunter, *Forts*, 560.

Martin, Martha. Twelve-year-old daughter of trader John. Captured with mother and siblings by Delaware and Shawnee at Great Cove, Cumberland County, PA, 2 November 1755. RETURNED at Muskingum, 15 November 1764, and sent to her father at Fort Pitt, 29 November 1764. *WPHM* 39 (1956): 188; *PG*, 17 January 1765; *NYG*, 21 January 1765; Sipe, *Indian Wars*, 225–6.

Martin, Mary. Nineteen-year-old daughter of trader John. Captured with mother and siblings by Delaware and Shawnee at Great Cove, Cumberland County, PA, 2 November 1755. Reported KILLED at Kittanning soon thereafter, but a Mary Martin was charged as a runaway indentured servant on 22 April 1760. Greene, *Cumberland County*, 24; Sipe, *Indian Wars*, 225.

Martin, [Mrs John]. Captured with five children by Delaware and Shawnee at Great Cove, Cumberland County, PA, 2 November 1755. Taken to Kittanning. REDEEMED herself and daughter Janet in New France, and returned via England by 1762. *PG*, 17 November 1755; *PA*, ser. 1, 4: 100; Sipe, *Indian Wars*, 225–6.

Martin, William. Eight-year-old son of trader John. Captured with mother and siblings by Delaware and Shawnee at Great Cove, Cumberland County, PA, 2 November 1755. Taken to Kittanning. RETURNED at Muskingum, 15 November 1764, and sent to his father at Fort Pitt, 29 November 1764. *WPHM* 39 (1956): 188; *PG*, 13 November 1755, 17 January 1765; *NYG*, 21 January 1765; Sipe, *Indian Wars*, 225–6.

Mason, Robert. Pennsylvania man held captive near Detroit in 1757. MISSING. *PG*, 22 December 1757; *NYM*, 2 January 1758.

Matthews, John. Sixteen year old captured by Delaware at Minisink, Northampton County, PA. RETURNED at Lancaster conference, 18 August 1762. *PG*, 9 September 1762.

Maus/Mouse, Christina [Mrs George]. Widowed and taken with three children by Shawnee in fall of Seybert's Fort, Augusta County, VA, 28 April 1758. RETURNED at Muskingum, 15 November 1764. Remarried promptly. *WPHM* 39 (1956): 195, 196; *PG*, 17 January 1765; *NYG*, 21 January 1765.

Maus/Mouse, Elizabeth. Daughter of George. Captured with mother and two siblings by Shawnee in fall of Seybert's Fort, Augusta County, VA, 28 April 1758. RETURNED at Muskingum, 15 November 1764. Chose her own guardian, 21 May 1765. BL, Add. Mss, 21646, fol. 65; *WPHM* 39 (1956): 195; *JP*, 11: 486; Haverford College Library, Indian Committee Records, 824/10, vol. 1, n.p.; *PG*, 17 January 1765; *NYG*, 21 January 1765; Chalkley, *Chronicles of the Scotch-Irish*, vol. 3, 89.

Maus/Mouse, George, Jr. Twelve-year-old son of George. Captured with mother and two siblings by Shawnee in fall of Seybert's Fort, Augusta County, VA, 28 April 1758. Seen at "Sagunck," living with an Indian named Galasco. MISSING. BL, Add. Mss, 21646, fol. 65; Haverford College Library, Indian Committee Records, 824/10, vol. 1, n.p.

Maus/Mouse, John. Son of George. Captured with mother and two siblings by Shawnee in fall of Seybert's Fort, Augusta County, VA, 28 April 1758. Lived with Wyandot near Detroit. Sold to an English trader but not home by 1762. MISSING. BL, Add. Mss, 21646, fol. 65; Haverford College Library, Indian Committee Records, 824/10, vol. 1, n.p.

Maynard, Andrew/André. Captured by, or deserted to, a French and Indian party at Redstone Creek, Cumberland County, PA, March 1755. Likely RETURNED and worked as interpreter for William Johnson by 1764. *Papiers Contrecoeur et autres documents concernant le conflit anglo-français sur l'Ohio de 1745 à 1756*, ed. Fernand Grenier (Quebec City, QC: Laval University Press, 1952), 283, 306–7; Hunter, *Forts*, 42; *JP*, 4: 520.

McAdam, Elizabeth. Captured in Delaware-Shawnee attack on Little Cove, Cumberland County, PA, 2 November 1755. RETURNED at Lancaster conference, 13 August 1762. *Minutes of Conferences ... Lancaster, 1762*, 7; Sipe, *Indian Wars*, 222.

McAllister, Alexander. Captured with his wife in Delaware destruction of Bigham's Fort, Cumberland County, PA, 11 June 1756. MISSING, but one of this name was taxed in Westmoreland County in 1786. *PG*, 17 and 24 June 1756; *NYM*, 21 and 28 June 1756; *PA*, ser. 3, 22: 467.

McAllister, [Mrs Alexander]. Captured with husband in Delaware destruction of Bigham's Fort, Cumberland County, PA, 11 June 1756. Rescued but recaptured at Kittanning and TORTURED to death, 9 September 1756. Loudon, ed., *Selection*, vol. 2, 182; Hunter, "Victory at Kittanning," 399.

McBriar, Andrew. Pennsylvania trader. Captured by Delaware English John at Christopher Gist's Ohio trading post at Redstone Creek, 23 April 1754. Sent to Canada. MISSING. *Ohio Company Papers*, ed. Bailey, 61, 121; Stobo, *Memoirs*, 91–2.

McBride, Hannah. Eleven year old captured by Delaware in taking of Richard Bard's Mill, York County, PA, 13 April 1758. RETURNED to Fort Pitt, 16 December 1761. "Journal of James Kenny, 1761–1763," ed. Jordan, 25–6; *PA*, ser. 1, 3: 396–7; Loudon, ed., *Selection*, vol. 2, 47–65; *PG*, 11 May 1758; *NYM*, 15 May 1758.

McCammon, Jane. Captured seven miles from Shippensburg, Cumberland County, PA, 8 July 1757. MISSING. *PG*, 4 August 1757; *PA*, ser. 1, 3: 219–20.

McClanachan, Elijah. Old man captured near Fort Dinwiddie, Augusta County, VA, 26 May 1764. RETAKEN 11 June 1764. BL, Add. Mss, 21650, fol. 238; *PG*, 14 June 1764; Preston Papers, 2: 49.

McClelland. One of two children of David. MISSING after Delaware-Shawnee attack on Great Cove, Cumberland County, PA, 2 November 1755. A Robert McClelland scouted for General Anthony Wayne in 1794. *PG*, 2 November 1755; William Hintzen, *Sketchbook of the Border Wars of the Upper Ohio Valley, 1769–94* (Manchester, CT: Precision Shooting, 1999), 294–5.

McClelland. One of two children of David. MISSING after Delaware-Shawnee attack on Great Cove, Cumberland County, PA, 2 November 1755. A Robert

McClelland scouted for General Anthony Wayne in 1794. *PG*, 2 November 1755; Hintzen, *Sketchbook*, 294–5.

McClelland, [Mrs David]. Widowed and captured with her two children in Delaware-Shawnee attack on Great Cove, Cumberland County, PA, 2 November 1755. MISSING. *PG*, 2 November 1755.

McClung, James. Boy captured in Cowpasture, Augusta County, VA, September 1757. RETURNED. Preston Papers, 1: 83; Elizabeth Perkins, *Border Life: Experience and Memory in the Revolutionary Ohio Valley* (Chapel Hill, NC: University of North Carolina Press, 1998), 197.

McClure. Captured in Hanover Township, Lancaster County, PA, 19 September 1757. MISSING. Three McClures, Alexander, Charles, and John, were Indian traders at Fort Pitt and in the Ohio valley, 1763–65. *PG*, 29 September 1757, 16 June 1763; *JP*, 4: 734, 738; *HBP*, 6: 490.

McConnell, [Mrs]. Captured at Jackson River, Augusta County, VA, 11 September 1756. ESCAPED. Preston Papers, 1: 83; *PG*, 7 October 1756.

McCord. One of two young daughters of Ann. Captured by Delaware in burning of McCord's Fort, Cumberland County, PA, 1 April 1756. RETAKEN in battle of Sideling Hill four days later. *PG*, 22 April 1756.

McCord. One of two young daughters of Ann. Captured by Delaware in burning of McCord's Fort, Cumberland County, PA, 1 April 1756. RETAKEN in battle of Sideling Hill four days later. *PG*, 22 April 1756.

McCord. Son of Ann. Captured by Delaware in burning of McCord's Fort, Cumberland County, PA, 1 April 1756. RETURNED to George Croghan at Fort Pitt by Kageshquanohel (the Pipe), 14 September 1759. *PG*, 22 April 1756; "George Croghan's Journal," 351.

McCord. Young daughter of Ann. Captured by Delaware in burning of McCord's Fort, Cumberland County, PA, 1 April 1756. RETURNED at Fort Pitt, 16 October 1759. *PG*, 22 April 1756; *NYM*, 12 April 1756; "James Kenny's 'Journal to Ye Westward,' 1758–59," ed. Jordan, 437.

McCord, Mary. Eldest daughter of Ann. Captured by Delaware in burning of McCord's Fort, Cumberland County, PA, 1 April 1756. KILLED by friendly fire in battle of Sideling Hill four days later. *PG*, 22 April 1756; *NYM*, 12 April 1756.

McCord, [Mrs] Ann. Captured with five children by Delaware in burning of McCord's Fort, Cumberland County, PA, 1 April 1756. RETAKEN at Kittanning, 8 September 1756. *PA*, ser. 1, 2: 775; *PG*, 22 April 1756; *NYM*, 12 April 1756.

McCoy, John. Sergeant in Royal American Regiment. Captured by Potawatomi and Miami in fall of Fort Miami, 27 May 1763. ESCAPED to Detroit and promoted to captain by 21 December 1763. Hay, *Diary*, 83–4; Gladwin, "Gladwin Manuscripts," 660.

McCoy/McKay, James. Soldier in Captain Stuart's company of Virginia Regiment. Captured by Shawnee and French in Major James Grant's defeat at Fort Duquesne, 14 September 1758. EXCHANGED via Canada, France, and England by July 1760. *Journals of the House of Burgesses, 1758–1761*, ed. McIlwaine, 188; HL, AB, 659. Compare *GWP*, 6: 46–7.

McCracken. Orphaned daughter of James. Captured with her sister by Shawnee on Patterson's Creek, Frederick County, VA, October 1755. WHITE INDIAN seen in Lower Shawnee Town a decade later. *WPHM* 39 (1956): 202; Baker, *French and Indian War*, 28–9, 139. Compare K. Cartmell, *Shenandoah Valley Pioneers and Their Descendants* (Winchester, VA: Eddy, 1909), 74 (where she is reported returned in 1759).

McCracken, Jean. Orphaned daughter of James. Captured with her sister by Shawnee on Patterson's Creek, Frederick County, VA, October 1755. WHITE INDIAN seen in Lower Shawnee Town a decade later. *WPHM* 39 (1956): 202; Baker, *French and Indian War*, 28–9, 139. Compare Cartmell, *Shenandoah Valley*, 74 (where she is reported returned in 1759).

McCreery, John. Boy captured by Wyandots at Cowpasture, Augusta County, VA, 24 April 1758. Held near Detroit. ESCAPED with brother and Thomas Gist, 12 September 1759. Travelled twenty-four days to Fort Niagara. "Thomas Gist's Indian Captivity," 288.

McCreery, William. Boy captured by Wyandot at Cowpasture, Augusta County, VA, 24 April 1758. Held near Detroit. ESCAPED with brother and Thomas Gist, 12 September 1759. Travelled twenty-four days to Fort Niagara. "Thomas Gist's Indian Captivity," 288.

McCullough, James. Five year old captured with older brother by Delaware near Fort Loudoun, York County, PA, 26 July 1756. Sent to French at Fort Duquesne. MISSING. BL, Add. Mss, 21655, fol. 112; Loudon, ed., *Selection*, vol. 1, 259.

McCullough, John. Eight year old captured with younger brother by Delaware near Fort Loudoun, York County, PA, 26 July 1756. RETURNED at Muskingum, 15 November 1764. Entrusted to John Martin at Fort Pitt two weeks later. Loudon, ed., *Selection*, vol. 1, 252–301; *WPHM* 39 (1956): 188; BL, Add. Mss, 21655, fol. 112; *PG*, 17 January 1765; *NYG*, 21 January 1765.

McDonald. James. Soldier in Pennsylvania "Light Horse." RETURNED at Detroit, 1 December 1760. *HBP*, 5: 210.

McDonald, John. Ensign in Montgomery Highlanders. Taken in Major James Grant's defeat at Fort Duquesne, 14 September 1758. RETURNED by Wyandot at Detroit, 12 January 1760. HL, AB, 659, 794; TNA, CO 5/57, 450; BL, Add. Mss, 21643, fol. 225; "George Croghan's Journal," 365.

McDonnell, John. MISSING, and presumed captured by Delaware in fall of Bigham's Fort, Cumberland County, PA, 11 June 1756. *PG*, 17 and 24 June 1756; *NYM*, 21 and 28 June 1756.

McDougall, George. Lieutenant in Royal American Regiment. Negotiator taken captive by Pontiac at Detroit, 10 May 1763. ESCAPED 2 July 1763. BL, Add. Mss, 21649, fols 252–3.

McFerrin, William. Man captured at Catawba, Augusta County, VA, October 1757. MISSING. Preston Papers, 1: 83.

McGinty, Alexander. Trader from Lancaster County, PA. Captured by Kahnawake in Kentucky, 26 January 1753. RANSOMED for £20 Pennsylvania currency through the Commissioners of Indian Affairs in Albany, NY, September

1753. *MPCP*, 5: 627; Sanders Letterbook, 1742–43, 1753–58, LAC, MG 18, C6, 61; *PG*, 27 September 1753, 17 August 1754; *NYM*, 7 May and 24 September 1753.

McIlroy. Elizabeth's *métis* child. Returned with her at Muskingum, 15 November 1764. MISSING. *PG*, 22 September 1757, 17 January 1765; *WPHM* 39 (1956): 192.

McIlroy. Fourteen-year-old son of Henry. Captured in Paxton Township, Lancaster County, PA, 8 September 1757. MISSING. *PG*, 22 September 1757; *PMHB* 32 (1908): 309.

McIlroy. Mary's *métis* child. Returned with her at Muskingum, 15 November 1764. MISSING. *PG*, 22 September 1757, 17 January 1765; *WPHM* 39 (1956): 192, 196.

McIlroy, Elizabeth. Daughter of Henry. Captured in Paxton Township, Lancaster County, PA, 8 September 1757. RETURNED at Muskingum, 15 November 1764. *PG*, 22 September 1757, 17 January 1765; *WPHM* 39 (1956): 192; *NYG*, 21 January 1765; LAC, MG 19, F 35/2, lot 621.

McIlroy, Mary. Daughter of Henry. Captured in Paxton Township, Lancaster County, PA, 8 September 1757. RETURNED with her *métis* child at Muskingum, 15 November 1764. *PG*, 22 September 1757, 17 January 1765; *WPHM* 39 (1956): 192, 196; *NYG*, 21 January 1765.

Mckeasey/Mackesy. Son of Alexander. Captured in attack at Tom's Creek, MD, 27 July 1757. MISSING. *PJ*, 11 August 1757; *PG*, 11 August 1757; *NYM*, 22 August 1757.

McKeen/McKean. Daughter of John. Carried off by Indians in Cumberland County, PA, 8 August 1756. MISSING. *PG*, 19 August 1756.

McKenzie, Hugh. Captain in Montgomery Highlanders. Captured in Major James Grant's defeat at Fort Duquesne, 14 September 1758. EXCHANGED via Canada and England. Died on campaign in West Indies in 1762. HL, AB, 655, 658; *JP*, 3: 991.

McKey/McKay, John. Boy taken in Lancaster County, PA, 18 August 1761. MISSING. *PA*, ser. 1, 4: 99.

McKinney/McKenny, John. Captured by a Delaware at Little Cove, Cumberland County, PA, 29 February 1756. Taken to the French at Fort Duquesne. ESCAPED near Fort Niagara about 30 September 1756. *NYM*, 23 February and 22 March 1756; Draper Mss, Pittsburgh and Northwest Virginia Papers, 6NN77-8; *PG*, 18 March 1756; *PJ*, 18 March 1756; Hunter, "Victory at Kittanning," 378.

McLaughlin, James. Trader employed by John Fraser at Fort Venango. Captured there by Delaware, 15 August 1753, and given to Commandant Paul Marin de La Malgue. Taken to Canada and France. RETURNED by January 1754. *PA*, ser. 1, 2: 131–2; *MPCP*, 5: 659–60; *The Diaries of George Washington*, ed. Donald Jackson and Dorothy Twohig, 6 vols (Charlottesville, VA: University Press of Virginia, 1976–79), vol. 1, 138n.

McLean, Jenny. Servant of trader John Fraser. Captured by Delaware on Patterson's Creek, Frederick County, VA, 26 June 1755. ESCAPED September 1756. *MPCP*, 6: 641; *MPCP*, 7: 381; *SCG*, 31 July 1755.

McManimy, Daniel. Laborer captured by Delaware in taking of Richard Bard's Mill, York County, PA, 13 April 1758. TORTURED to death at Kuskuski, 22 April 1758. *PA*, ser. 1, 3: 396–7; Loudon, ed. *Selection*, vol. 2, 48–51; *PG*, 11 May 1758; *NYM*, 15 May 1758.

McManus. Sergeant in Captain Arthur Dobb's company of Virginia Regiment. Captured near Fort Cumberland, MD, 1 October 1755. KILLED the next day. HSP, Penn Papers, Indian Affairs, vol. 2, no. 42; *PJ*, 16 October 1755.

McMullen, Daniel. Captured by Delaware in Northampton County, PA, December 1755. Taken to Tioga. ESCAPED with Thomas Moffitt, September 1756. HSP, Penn Papers, Indian Affairs, vol. 2, no. 101; *MPCP*, 7: 282–4.

McQuaid, James. Young boy from Cumberland County, PA. Captured near McDowell's Mill, Cumberland County, PA, 1 November 1756. MISSING. *PA*, ser. 1, 3: 40–1; *PG*, 11 November 1756; *NYM*, 15 November 1756.

McQueen, Jane [Mrs John]. Pennsylvanian. RETURNED at Muskingum, 15 November 1764. Joined husband at Fort Pitt, 29 November 1764. *WPHM* 39 (1956): 189.

McSwain, Hugh/George. Captured by Shawnee in Cumberland County, PA, 19 October 1755. Given to Delaware and killed two in his ESCAPE to Fort Cumberland, MD, 3 November 1755. Commissioned in Virginia Regiment, and killed near Fort Ligonier, PA, 1758. *PG*, 13 November 1755; Rupp, *History and Topography of Dauphin*, 108.

Means, Mary. Eleven-year-old daughter of Richard. Captured by Delaware near Fort Ligonier, PA, June 1763. RELEASED by Maiden Foot the same day. After 1784, as Mrs Mary Kearney, she provided for Maiden Foot. Sipe, *Fort Ligonier*, 187–8.

Means, [Mrs Richard]. Captured with her daughter by Delaware near Fort Ligonier, PA, June 1763. RELEASED by Maiden Foot the same day. Sipe, *Fort Ligonier*, 187–8.

Medley, Ann/Hannah. Daughter of Jean. Captured by Miami in fall of Vause's Fort, Augusta County, VA, 25 June 1756. RETURNED via New France and Crown Point, NY, 15 November 1759. Preston Papers, 1: 83; TNA, CO 5/57, fols 119–21.

Medley, Betsy. Taken by Shawnee in fall of Vause's Fort, Augusta County, VA, 25 June 1756. WHITE INDIAN seen in Lower Shawnee Town late in 1764. Preston Papers, 1: 83; *WPHM* 39 (1956): 202.

Medley/Medlain, James. Son of Jean. Captured by Miami in fall of Vause's Fort, Augusta County, VA, 25 June 1756. RETURNED via New France, 24 November 1759. TNA, CO 5/57, fols 119–21.

Medley, Jean. Captured with her four children in fall of Vause's Fort, Augusta County, VA, 25 June 1756. RETURNED at Crown Point, NY, 15 November 1759. "Reduced to beg Relief from House to House." TNA, CO 5/57, part 1, fols 119–21; Preston Papers, 1: 83 (where she was reported as captured with two children); Nathaniel Turk McCleskey, "Across the First Divide: Frontiers of Settlement and Culture in Augusta County, Virginia, 1738–1770" (PhD diss., College of William and Mary, 1990), 317.

Medley, William. Taken by Shawnee in fall of Vause's Fort, Augusta County, VA, 25 June 1756. WHITE INDIAN seen in Lower Shawnee Town late in 1764. *WPHM* 39 (1956): 202.

Mercier. Canadian marine. Captured by Cherokee on lower Ohio River in May 1754. Taken to Charleston. MISSING. Pease and Jenison, eds, *Illinois on the Eve*, 868–9, 912–13.

Messett, Joseph. Canadian marine in Miziere's company. Captured in battle of La Belle Famille, 24 July 1759. Held in Somerset County, NJ. EXCHANGED at Crown Point, NY, 9 December 1760. Job Stockton Papers, NYHS; *JP*, 13: 115.

Meyer/Myer. Infant child of Frederick. Orphaned and captured in Bern Township, Berks County, PA, 29 June 1757. RETAKEN the same day. *NYM*, 11 July 1757; *PMHB* 32 (1908): 312; Rupp, *History of Northampton*, 468.

Meyer/Myer. One of four children of Frederick. Orphaned and captured in Bern Township, Berks County, PA, 29 June 1757. MISSING. *NYM*, 11 July 1757; *PMHB* 32 (1908): 312; Rupp, *History of Northampton*, 468.

Meyer/Myer. One of four children of Frederick. Orphaned and captured in Bern Township, Berks County, PA, 29 June 1757. MISSING. *NYM*, 11 July 1757; *PMHB* 32 (1908): 312; Rupp, *History of Northampton*, 468.

Meyer/Myer, Frederick. One of four children of Frederick. Orphaned and captured in Bern Township, Berks County, PA, 29 June 1757. RETURNED at Muskingum, 15 November 1764. *NYM*, 11 July 1757; *PMHB* 32 (1908): 312; Rupp, *History of Northampton*, 468; *WPHM* 39 (1956): 189; *PG*, 17 January 1765; *NYG*, 21 January 1765; Berks County Orphan's Court Dockets, Berks County Courthouse, Reading, PA, vol. 1, 34, 59.

Meyers, Patrick. Soldier in second battalion of Pennsylvania regiment. Taken by Delaware at Kittanning, 9 September 1756. MISSING. *PA*, ser. 2, 2: 458–60; *PG*, 23 September 1756; Hunter, "Victory at Kittanning," 392–402.

Miases. Son of Henry. Captured at South Fork, Augusta County, VA, 14 September 1764. MISSING. *PG*, 11 October 1764; *NYG*, 15 October 1764.

Miller. Child of Mrs George. Captured with mother and three siblings in Cumberland County, PA, 19 September 1757. MISSING. *NYM*, 3 October 1757; *PG*, 29 September 1757.

Miller. One of two daughters of Alexander. Captured by Delaware in Antrim Township, Cumberland County, PA, 30 June 1757. MISSING. *PG*, 14 July 1757; *NYM*, 18 July 1757; *MPCP*, 7: 632; Loudon, ed. *Selection*, vol. 2, 196.

Miller. Son of Leonard. Captured in Hanover Township, Lancaster County, PA, 6 August 1757. MISSING. *PG*, 18 August 1757; *NYM*, 22 August 1757.

Miller, Abraham. Captured with his mother at Philip Bosart's farm, Northampton County, PA, 1 May 1757. ESCAPED with George Ebert, hidden by French Margaret, and then went to Fort Hamilton, 12 June 1757. *MPCP*, 7: 620–1; *PMHB* 32 (1908): 316; *NYM*, 16 May 1757; *PG*, 12 and 30 June 1757.

Miller, Agnes. One of two daughters of Alexander. Captured by Delaware in Antrim Township, Cumberland County, PA, 30 June 1757. RETURNED at Fort Pitt, 16 December 1761. *PG*, 14 July 1757; *NYM*, 18 July 1757; *MPCP*, 7: 632;

Loudon, ed. *Selection*, vol. 2, 196; "Journal of James Kenny, 1761–1763," ed. Jordan, 25–6.

Miller, Beverley. Young daughter of Mrs George. Captured with mother and three siblings in Cumberland County, PA, 19 September 1757. RETURNED at Muskingum, 15 November 1764; *WPHM* 39 (1956): 192; *PG*, 29 September 1757 and 17 January 1765; *NYG*, 21 January 1765.

Miller, Margaret/Peggy. Child of Mrs George. Captured with mother and three siblings in Cumberland County, PA, 19 September 1757. RETURNED at Muskingum, 15 November 1764; *WPHM* 39 (1956): 192; *PG*, 29 September 1757 and 17 January 1765; *NYG*, 21 January 1765.

Miller, Michael. Soldier taken in attack on Royal American Regiment convoy at Stony Creek, Cumberland County, PA. Likely RETURNED. BL, Add. Mss, 21644, fol. 231; *PA*, ser. 3, 20: 120, 135, 176, 269, 311, 406.

Miller, [Mrs]. Captured in General Edward Braddock's defeat, 9 July 1755. Taken to Canada. RANSOMED herself for £10 sterling and two years of service. Returned to England. Merlin Stonehouse Transcripts, vol. 4, n.p., Huntington Library and Art Gallery, San Marino, CA.

Miller, [Mrs]. Captured with son Abraham at Philip Bosart's farm, Northampton County, PA, 1 May 1757. KILLED two days later. *PMHB* 32 (1908): 316; *PG*, 30 June 1757.

Miller, [Mrs George]. Woman from Cumberland County, PA. Captured with four of her children, 19 September 1757. MISSING. *NYM*, 3 October 1757; *PG*, 29 September 1757.

Miller, Nancy. Young child of Mrs George. Captured with mother and three siblings in Cumberland County, PA, 19 September 1757. WHITE INDIAN seen in Lower Shawnee Town late in 1764. *WPHM* 39 (1956): 202; *PG*, 29 September 1757; *NYM*, 3 October 1757.

Milles, Nicholas. French soldier. Captured by Virginians in Jumonville incident, 28 May 1754. RETURNED via England, 22 June 1755. *PG*, 13 and 27 June, 22 August, and 12 September 1754; *NYM*, 17 June 1754; *Collections des manuscrits ... Nouvelle France*, vol. 3, 521–2.

Minor, Mary. Captured near Shippensburgh, Cumberland County, PA, 8 July 1757. MISSING. *NYM*, 8 August 1757; *PG*, 4 August 1757; *PA*, ser. 1, 3: 219–20.

Minskey, Emmanuel. Soldier in second battalion of Pennsylvania regiment. MISSING day after attack on Kittanning, 9 September 1756. *PA*, ser. 2, 2: 458–60; *NYM*, 27 September 1756; *PG*, 23 September 1756; Hunter, "Victory at Kittanning," 392–402.

Misquepalothe/Mesquepalathie [Red Hawk]. Shawnee chief. Taken hostage by Colonel Henry Bouquet, 14 November 1764. ESCAPED from Fort Pitt, 3 December 1764. HL, MM, 569, fols 37–8; *MPCP*, 9: 232; *HBP*, 6: 717.

Mitch, Molly. Virginian. RETURNED at Muskingum, 15 November 1764. *WPHM* 39 (1956): 190, 196; *PG*, 17 January 1765; *NYG*, 21 January 1765.

Mitchell, Joseph. Three year old captured in Cumberland County, PA, 20 March 1764. MISSING. *PG*, 5 April 1764; *NYG*, 5 April 1764; *NYM*, 9 April 1764.

Moffit, Thomas. Captured by Delaware at Pokeepsie, Northampton County, PA, March 1756. ESCAPED with Daniel McMullen to Fort Augusta that September. *MPCP*, 7: 282–4.

Moore. Child of Mary Anne. Captured with mother and four siblings in Shawnee attack on Cowpasture, Augusta County, VA, 16 May 1757. MISSING. Preston Papers, 1: 83.

Moore/Mullen, Ann. Daughter of Mary Anne. Captured with mother and four siblings in Shawnee attack on Cowpasture, Augusta County, VA, 16 May 1757. Escaped in 1759, and then held by Seneca for eleven months. MISSING. Preston Papers, 1: 83; *PG*, 17 March 1763.

Moore, Margaret. Daughter of Mary Anne. Captured with mother and four siblings in Shawnee attack on Cowpasture, Augusta County, VA, 16 May 1757. WHITE INDIAN who married Sepettekenathe (Blue Jacket), and had two children with him (Joseph and Nancy). Returned to Virginia and eventually went back to Ohio. Preston Papers, 1: 83; John Sugden, *Blue Jacket: Warrior of the Shawnees* (Lincoln, NB: University of Nebraska Press, 2000), 3, 31, 255.

Moore, Mary Anne [Mrs John]. Widowed and captured with her five children in Shawnee attack on Cowpasture, Augusta County, VA, 16 May 1757. RETURNED before March 1763. Released her dower rights in 1765 to cover husband's debts. Preston Papers, 1: 83; *PG*, 17 March 1763; Chalkley, *Chronicles of the Scotch-Irish*, vol. 3, 422.

Moore, Molly/Mary. Daughter of Mary Anne. Captured with mother and four siblings in Shawnee attack on Cowpasture, Augusta County, VA, 16 May 1757. WHITE INDIAN reported in Lower Shawnee Town late in 1764. Preston Papers, 1: 83; *WPHM* 39 (1956): 202.

Moore, Moses. Captured by Wyandot at Jackson River, Augusta County, VA. ESCAPED 14 March 1759. Preston Papers, 1: 83; *PA*, ser. 1, 3: 632–3.

Moore, Peggy. Daughter of Mary Anne. Captured with mother and four siblings in Shawnee attack on Cowpasture, Augusta County, VA, 16 May 1757. White Indian who RETURNED and joined the Moravians in 1774 with trader-taverner husband, Richard Connor. Preston Papers, 1: 83; Zeisberger, *Moravian Mission Diaries*, 270; David Jones, *A Journal of Two Visits Made to Some Nations of Indians on the West Side of the River Ohio in the Years 1772 and 1773* (Burlington, NJ, 1774), 88.

Moore, Thomas. Captured near Potomac River in Maryland. RETURNED at Lancaster conference, 13 August 1762. *Minutes of Conferences ... Lancaster, 1762*, 7.

Morisseau. Canadian marine in Captain Pierre-Jean-Baptiste-François-Xavier Legardeur de Repentigny's company. Captured by Virginians in Jumonville incident, 28 May 1754. RETURNED via Martinique, 24 October 1755. *PG*, 13 and 27 June, 22 August, and 12 September 1754; *Collections des manuscrits ... Nouvelle France*, vol. 3, 521–2.

Morren, Ash. Canadian marine in Montarin's company. Captured by British at battle of La Belle Famille, 24 July 1759. Held in Somerset County, NJ.

RETURNED at Crown Point, NY, 9 December 1760. *JP*, 13: 115; Job Stockton Papers, NYHS.

Morris. Virginia soldier in Captain Robert Stobo's company. Taken after capitulation of Fort Necessity, 4 July 1754. RETURNED from Fort Duquesne, 30 August 1754. Alberts, *Most Extraordinary Adventures*, 97; *Travels in New France by J.C.B.*, ed. Stevens, Kent, and Woods, 64.

Morris, John. Soldier in Royal American Regiment. Captured in Cumberland County, PA, 20 February 1764. Seen on Muskingum River. Likely RETURNED. A John Morris was a landowner taxed in that county in 1779. BL, Add. Mss, 21650, fols 55, 56; *HBP*, 6: 514, 516n; *PG*, 8 March 1764; *NYG*, 9 April 1764; *PA*, ser. 3, 20: 170.

Morris, Thomas. Captain in the British Army's 17th Regiment of Foot. Captured by Miami while on mission for Colonel John Bradstreet to Fort Chartres, 7 September 1764. RELEASED three days later. "Captain Morris' Journal," *Old Fort News* 6 (1941): 3–11; Thomas Morris, *Miscellanies in Prose and Verse* (London, 1791).

Morris, Thomas. Soldier in Virginia Regiment. Captured by Wyandot at Loyalhanna, PA, 12 October 1759. RETURNED at Detroit, 1 December 1760. *PG*, 26 October 1758; *HBP*, 5: 210–11.

Morrow, Robert. Soldier in Lieutenant Colonel Hugh Mercer's company, second battalion of Pennsylvania regiment. MISSING at Kittanning, 9 September 1756. A Robert Morrow was taxed in Cumberland County in 1778. *PA*, ser. 2, 2: 458–60; *PG*, 23 September 1756; Hunter, "Victory at Kittanning," 392–402; *PA*, ser. 3, 20: 110.

Motzs, Bernard. Captured near Tulpehocken in October 1756. MISSING. *PMHB* 32 (1908): 312.

Moxom, Henry. Soldier in Virginia Regiment. Captured by Wyandot at Fort Presqu'île, 2 September 1760. RETURNED there 1 December 1760. BL, Add. Mss, 21655, fol. 99; *HBP*, 5: 17, 210.

Munro, Archibald. Lieutenant in Montomery Highlanders. Captured in Major James Grant's defeat at Fort Duquesne, 14 September 1758. RETURNED. Draper Mss, Virginia Papers, 3ZZ48.

Murphy, James. Soldier in Pennsylvania "Light Horse." Captured by Ottawa near Shippensburgh, Cumberland County, PA, 5 August 1758. RETURNED at Detroit, 1 December 1760. *HBP*, 5: 210; *PG*, 31 August 1758; *NYM*, 4 September 1758.

Nanning. New York trader. Captured at Detroit in May 1763. MISSING. *NYM*, 8 August 1763.

Naylshonoiwaes. Delaware hostage taken by Colonel Henry Bouquet, 11 November 1764. MISSING and likely escaped. HL, MM, 569, fol. 32.

Neculissika. Infant captured by Shawnee on James River, Augusta County, VA, 1758. White Indian RETURNED to Fort Pitt, 10 May 1765. *WPHM* 39 (1956): 198; *JP*, 11: 720.

Neely, Samuel. Boy captured near McDowell's Mill, Cumberland County, PA, 1 November 1756. MISSING. A Samuel Neely was taxed in York County in

1779. *PG*, 11 November 1756; *NYM*, 15 November 1756; *PA*, ser. 1, 3: 40–1; *PA*, ser. 3, 21: 44, 262.

Neff, [Mrs Leonard]. Captured by Delaware on South Branch of Potomac River, Augusta County, VA, 20 April 1756. ESCAPED the same day. Baker, *French and Indian War*, 47.

Neicheumata. Young boy captured by Shawnee in fall of Seybert's Fort, Augusta County, VA, 28 April 1758. White Indian RETURNED to Fort Pitt, 10 May 1765. *JP*, 11: 720; *WPHM* 39 (1956): 198.

Neros, Nicholas. Canadian marine in "Vergo" company. Captured in battle of La Belle Famille, 24 July 1759. Held in Somerset County, NJ. EXCHANGED at Crown Point, NY, 9 December 1760. *JP*, 13: 115; Job Stockton Papers, NYHS.

Neufang, Peter. Eight-year-old son of Balthasar. Captured by Delaware in Berks County, PA, 6 March 1756. RETURNED by Teedyuscung, 1 December 1759. *PMHB* 32 (1908): 311, 316; *PG*, 11 March 1756; *PJ*, 11 March 1756; Hunter, *Forts*, 307.

Newcomer[?]. Female white captive said to have murdered Kahnawake Eagle Feather, the husband of white Indian Mary Harris, near Muskingum River. She fled, but was caught by Wyandot and KILLED in December 1751. Mercer, *George Mercer Papers*, 13, 103, 492; Emma Lewis Coleman, *New England Captives Carried to Canada between 1677 and 1760 during the French and Indian Wars*, 2 vols (Portland, ME: Southworth, 1925–26), vol. 2, 87–8.

Newland, George. Soldier in Pennsylvania "Light Horse." Captured in 1760 and RETURNED at Detroit, 1 December 1760. *HBP*, 5: 210.

Nicholson, Owen. Pennsylvania trader. Captured in Canadian-Ottawa destruction of Pickawillany, 21 June 1752. Taken to Canada and France. RETURNED. Back in Philadelphia by March 1753. *PG*, 23 November 1752; *NYM*, 28 May 1753; Pease and Jenison, eds, *Illinois on the Eve*, 29, 811.

Nicholson/Nichols, Catherine. One of three children of Edward. Orphaned and captured by Delaware and Shawnee near Patterson's Fort, Cumberland County, PA, 27 January 1756. RETURNED to Nathaniel Holland at Shamokin, 20 March 1759. Married Holland. *PG*, 5 February 1756; Loudon, ed. *Selection*, vol. 2, 172–4; Hunter, *Forts*, 379; Haverford College Library, Indian Committee Records, 824/11, vol. 3, n.p.

Nicholson/Nichols, Jonathan. One of three children of Edward. Orphaned and captured by Delaware and Shawnee near Patterson's Fort, Cumberland County, PA, 27 January 1756. RETURNED September 1759. Guide and interpreter in 1772. *PG*, 5 February 1756; *NYM*, 9 February 1756; Hunter, *Forts*, 379; Haverford College Library, Indian Committee Records, 824/11, vol. 4, n.p.; McClure, *Diary of David McClure*, 55.

Nicholson/Nichols, Thomas. One of three children of Edward. Orphaned and captured by Delaware and Shawnee near Patterson's Fort, Cumberland County, PA, 27 January 1756. RETURNED. Guide in Cherokee country in 1769, and against the Shawnee in 1774. *PG*, 5 February 1756; *NYM*, 9 February 1756; Hunter, *Forts*, 379; *JP*, 12: 761; Kercheval, *History of the Valley*, 197.

Nitschmann, Susanna. Widowed and captured by Delaware in Northampton County, PA, 24 November 1755. KILLED in May 1756. *PMHB* 32 (1908): 313; *PA*, ser. 1, 2: 522–3; Sipe, *Indian Wars*, 241–3; Richards, *Pennsylvania-German*, 147–8.

No-Kaming. Potawatomi chief. Taken hostage by British Army at Detroit, 10 May 1763. EXCHANGED there five weeks later. Quaife, ed., *Siege*, 137–8; *PG*, 18 August 1763; *NYM*, 15 August 1763; Dowd, *War under Heaven*, 121.

Nosewelamah. Young girl captured by Shawnee in Blackwater, Augusta County, VA, 1755. White Indian RETURNED to Fort Pitt, 10 May 1765. *JP*, 11: 720; *WPHM* 39 (1956): 198.

Nutimus, Joseph. Susquehanna Delaware. Captured by Iroquois, 28 February 1764, and taken to William Johnson. EXILED to West Virginia, where he was killed in Bulltown massacre of 1774. *JP*, 11: 119–20; *PG*, 15 March and 12 April 1764; Dowd, *War under Heaven*, 152.

O'Brien, Henry. Soldier in Captain Andrew Montour's company of Virginia Regiment. Captured at Fort Necessity, 4 July 1754. Sent to Canada. RETURNED to Boston, 10 July 1755. Became an Ohio trader and was killed there in August of 1767. *PG*, 17 July 1755; Stobo, *Memoirs*, 91–2; *MPCP*, 9: 521.

Odweiler. Girl captured in Blue Mountains, Berks County, PA, October 1755. MISSING. *PG*, 6 November 1755; *PJ*, 6 November 1755.

Ogaghradarisha. Elderly Six Nations man. Captured by Ojibwa in Cumberland County, PA, 17 October 1756. Held for a few hours, questioned, and RELEASED the same day. HSP, Penn Papers, Indian Affairs, vol. 2, no. 103.

Old White Chief. Young boy orphaned and captured in Seneca attack on Susquehanna River in Seven Years' War. WHITE INDIAN who became a Seneca chief. Harriet Caswell, *Our Life among the Iroquois Indians* (Boston, MA, 1892), 51–6.

Oliver, Josiah. Virginian captured in 1756. RETURNED via New France, 24 November 1759. TNA, CO 5/57, fols 119–21.

Ormand, Abraham. White captive of Shawnee. Still in Lower Shawnee Town late in 1764. WHITE INDIAN. *WPHM* 39 (1956): 202.

Otter, Joannah. Girl captured with sister at Cushietunk, Northampton County, PA, May 1763. RETURNED to William Johnson at Fort Niagara by Chenussio Seneca, July 1764. *PG*, 6 September 1764; *NYG*, 17 September 1764.

Otter, Sarah. Girl captured with sister at Cushietunk, Northampton County, PA, May 1763. RETURNED to William Johnson at Fort Niagara by Chenussio Seneca, July 1764. *PG*, 6 September 1764; *NYG*, 17 September 1764.

Ouimet, Albert. Soldier from "de Milles Isles" in New France. Captured by Virginians in Jumonville incident. RETURNED via England to France, 22 June 1755. *Collections des manuscrits ... Nouvelle France*, vol. 3, 521–2; *PG*, 13 and 27 June, 22 August, and 12 September 1754; *NYM*, 17 June 1754.

Owens, David. Interpreter captured at Lower Shawnee Town, 6 November 1764. RELEASED three days later. Had earlier murdered his Shawnee wife and four children. Governor John Penn had refused him scalp bounties and forced him to join Colonel Henry Bouquet's expedition at the Muskingum River in November 1764. Heard, *Handbook*, vol. 2, 279.

Packs, John. British soldier. Captured by Ojibwa near Fort Michilimackinac, May 1763. RETURNED to Fort Detroit by 8 September 1763. Gladwin, "Gladwin Manuscripts," 652–3.

Packwood, Samuel. Virginia soldier. Captured near Fort Cumberland, MD, 23 January 1756. RANSOMED and returned via Detroit, New France, and France. TNA, Adm. 1/4323, n.p.; *GWP*, 2: 306, 307; "Journal of James Kenny, 1761–1763," ed. Jordan, 181.

Painter, Margaret. Likely captured in Cumberland County, PA, 2 April 1757. RETAKEN in capture of Fort Niagara, 25 July 1759. *PG*, 14 April 1757; *NYM*, 18 April 1757, 20 August 1759; *PJ*, 23 August 1759.

Palmer, John. Pennsylvanian. Captured by Ohio Delaware, 28 September 1764. ESCAPED to Colonel Henry Bouquet's army five days later. HL, MM, 569, fol. 8; *WPHM* 39 (1956): 189; *PG*, 17 January 1765.

Paquwesee. Young girl captured by Shawnee at Blackwater, Augusta County, VA, 1755. White Indian RETURNED by Shawnee to Fort Pitt, 10 May 1765. *JP*, 11: 720; *WPHM* 39 (1956): 198.

Paré, Louis. Canadian marine in "Cantsent" company. Captured by British at battle of La Belle Famille, 24 July 1759. Held in Somerset County, NJ. EXCHANGED at Crown Point, NY, 2 December 1760. *JP*, 13: 115; Job Stockton Papers, NYHS.

Parent, Joachim. French marine "de Soulanges." Captured by Virginians in Jumonville incident, 28 May 1754. RETURNED via England, 27 September 1755. *NYCD*, 10: 352–3; *PG*, 13 and 27 June, 22 August, and 12 September 1754; *NYM*, 17 June 1754.

Paris, François [*dit* "Velecoeur"]. Canadian marine in Vincent's company. Captured in battle of La Belle Famille, 24 July 1759. Held in Somerset County, NJ. EXCHANGED at Crown Point, NY, 16 December 1760. *JP*, 13: 115; Job Stockton Papers, NYHS.

Parks, Nathan. Connecticut settler in Wyoming Valley, Northampton County, PA. MISSING after Delaware attack of 12 December 1755. *PG*, 18 December 1755.

Parrot, Daniel. Soldier in Lieutenant Thomas Bullitt's company of Virginia Regiment. Captured in Major James Grant's defeat at Fort Duquesne, 14 September 1758. EXCHANGED via Canada, France, and England, July 1760. *Journals of the House of Burgesses, 1758–1761*, ed. McIlwaine, 188; HL, AB, 659; *PG*, 28 September and 19 October 1758. Compare *GWP*, 6: 46–7.

[Parsinger]. One of three young children captured with their mother at Jackson River, Augusta County, VA, 11 September 1756. MISSING. Preston Papers, 1: 83; *PG*, 7 October 1756; *NYM*, 11 October 1756.

[Parsinger]. One of three young children captured with their mother at Jackson River, Augusta County, VA, 11 September 1756. MISSING. Preston Papers, 1: 83; *PG*, 7 October 1756; *NYM*, 11 October 1756.

[Parsinger, Mrs]. Woman captured with three young children at Jackson River, Augusta County, VA, 11 September 1756. MISSING. Preston Papers, 1: 83; *PG*, 7 October 1756; *NYM*, 11 October 1756; Joseph Persinger, *The Life of Jacob Persinger* (Sturgeon, MO, 1861).

[Parsinger/Persinger, Jacob]. Later adoptive name of a young boy. One of three young children captured with their mother at Jackson River, Augusta County, VA, 11 September 1756. RETURNED in 1764 and adopted by Parsingers. A hunter, farmer, and soldier in the 1770s. Preston Papers, 1: 83; *PG*, 7 October 1756; *NYM*, 11 October 1756; Persinger, *Life of Jacob*.

Passquelonckamy. Custaloga's son. Delaware hostage taken by Colonel Henry Bouquet, 11 November 1764. MISSING. HL, MM, 569, fol. 32.

Patten, John. Trader from Wilmington, Delaware. Captured by the French at Fort des Miamis, 20 November 1750. Sent, by way of Fort Niagara, to New France and France. RELEASED 27 January 1752. Captured by French again at Logstown, 14 January 1754. RELEASED the same day by intervention of Scarouady. Eavenson, *Map Maker*, 5–27; *SCG*, 6 November 1754.

Patton. Son of William. Captured near Staunton, VA, 1 October 1764. MISSING. *PG*, 15 November 1764.

Paul, John/Andrew. Captured at Maxwell's Fort, Cumberland County, PA, 23 April 1757. ESCAPED two days later. Hunter, *Forts*, 560; *PG*, 26 May 1757; *NYM*, 30 May 1757.

Paul, Louis. Canadian soldier from Sorel, QC. Captured by Virginians in Jumonville incident, 28 May 1754. RETURNED via England to France, 22 June 1755. *Collections des manuscrits … Nouvelle France*, vol. 3, 531–2; *PG*, 13 and 27 June, 22 August, and 12 September 1754.

Pauli, Christopher. Ensign in Royal American Regiment. Captured by Wyandot and Ottawa in fall of Fort Sandusky, 16 May 1763. Taken to Pontiac's camp and adopted by Ojibwa. ESCAPED into Detroit, 3 July 1763. *JP*, 10: 730; *PG*, 9, 16, and 30 June 1763, 11 and 18 August 1763.

Payer, Frederick. Boy captured in Lower Bergen, NJ. RETURNED to General Jeffrey Amherst at Montreal and sent to Philadelphia in June 1761. *PG*, 2 July 1761.

Pearson, Abel. Sutler's driver. Captured by Delaware near Fort Ligonier, PA, 6 April 1759. ESCAPED nine days later. BL, Add. Mss, 21644, fol. 132; *HBP*, 3: 253–4; Hunter, *Forts*, 163–4; *NYG*, 30 April 1759.

Pearson, Jacob. Sutler's driver. Captured by Delaware near Fort Ligonier, PA, 6 April 1759. ESCAPED nine days later. BL, Add. Mss, 21644, fol. 132; *HBP*, 3: 253–4; Hunter, *Forts*, 163–4; *NYG*, 30 April 1759.

Peck, Marie. "German woman." Captured in Maryland, 20 August 1756. Seen in Ohio country within thirty months. MISSING. *PG*, 9 September 1756; *VG*, 3 September 1756; "Narrative of Marie Le Roy and Barbara Leininger," *Proceedings of the Pennsylvania-German Society* 15 (1905): 125.

Peeple/Peoples, James. Son of Robert. Captured near McClure's Gap, Cumberland County, PA, 21 July 1756. Seen at Detroit the next year. Likely RETURNED. A Mr Peebles was a volunteer wounded at Bushy Run in 1764, and a James Peebles was taxed in Westmoreland County in 1783. *PG*, 29 July 1756, 22 December 1757; *NYM*, 2 August 1756, 1 February 1758; *RCFFP*, 2: 531, 534; *PA*, ser. 2, 22: 416.

Peeple/Peoples, Sarah. Young daughter of Robert. Captured near McClure's Gap, Cumberland County, PA, 21 July 1756. Seen at Detroit the next year. Father still searching in December 1764. WHITE INDIAN. *JP*, 4: 630; *PG*, 29 July 1756, 22 December 1757; *NYM*, 2 August 1756, 12 January 1758.

Peller, Charles. Pennsylvania soldier in Colonel John Armstrong's company. "Bavarian" captured near Shippensburg, 6 June 1757. Interrogated at Fort Niagara six weeks later. MISSING. *PG*, 16 June 1757; *NYM*, 20 June 1757; Hunter, *Forts*, 466–7.

Pepper, William. Virginia soldier. Captured in fall of Vause's Fort, Augusta County, VA, 25 June 1756. RETURNED. *PG*, 28 July 1757, 9 February 1758; *NYM*, 1 August 1757; Preston Papers, 1: 83.

Perigord, Guillaume. Canadian marine in Berbin's company. Captured at battle of La Belle Famille, 24 July 1759. Held in Somerset County, NJ. EXCHANGED at Crown Point, NY, 16 December 1760. *JP*, 13: 115; Job Stockton Papers, NYHS.

Perry. Young son of Samuel. Taken near McDowell's Mill, Cumberland County, PA. MISSING. *PG*, 11 November 1756; *PA*, ser. 1, 3: 40–1.

Peter, John. Soldier in Lieutenant Thomas Bullitt's company of Virginia Regiment. Captured defending a convoy near Fort Ligonier, PA, 23 May 1759. RECOVERED in capture of Fort Niagara, 25 July 1759. *PG*, 23 August 1759; *NYM*, 20 August 1759; *NYG*, 27 August 1759.

Peter, John, Jr. Soldier in Virginia Regiment. Wounded and captured defending a convoy near Fort Ligonier, PA, 23 May 1759. Taken to Fort Niagara and RECOVERED in the surrender there, 25 July 1759. Awarded £15 by Virginia House of Burgesses. *Journals of the House of Burgesses, 1758–1761*, ed. McIlwaine, 209, 211; BL, Add. Mss, 21644, fol. 172; Hunter, *Forts*, 95–6; Kenneth G. Robison, "John Peter, Jr., of Early Albemarle County Virginia," unpublished ms. (1987), copy in Old Fort Niagara Association Library, Youngstown, NY.

Peters/Seiver, Ann Mary. Young daughter of Jacob. Orphaned and captured with five siblings on South Branch of Potomac River, Augusta County, VA, February 1757. MISSING. *NYM*, 14 March 1757; Preston Papers, 1: 83.

Peters/Seiver, Catharine. Young daughter of Jacob. Orphaned and captured with five siblings on South Branch of Potomac River, Augusta County, VA, February 1757. MISSING. *NYM*, 14 March 1757; Preston Papers, 1: 83.

Peters/Seiver, George. Young son of Jacob. Orphaned and captured with five siblings on South Branch of Potomac River, Augusta County, VA, February 1757. Blind when RETURNED to Fort Pitt in 1761 and under care of Colonel William Clapham. Haverford College Library, Indian Committee Records, 824/11, vol. 4, n.p.; Preston Papers, 1: 83.

Peters/Seiver, Hans Nicholas. Son of Jacob. Orphaned and captured with five siblings on South Branch of Potomac River, Augusta County, VA, February 1757. REDEEMED in Canada by Colonel Peter Schuyler in 1758. *NYM*, 14

March 1757; Preston Papers, 1: 83; Haverford College Library, Indian Committee Records, 824/11, vol. 4, n.p.

Peters/Seiver, Henry. Son of Jacob. Orphaned and captured with five siblings on South Branch of Potomac River, Augusta County, VA, February 1757. ESCAPED 1759. *NYM*, 14 March 1757; Preston Papers, 1: 83; Haverford College Library, Indian Committee Records, 824/11, vol. 4, n.p.

Peters/Seiver, Molly/Elizabeth. Six-year-old daughter of Jacob. Orphaned and captured with five siblings on South Branch of Potomac River, Augusta County, VA, February 1757. White Indian RETURNED by Shawnee to Fort Pitt, 10 May 1765. *NYM*, 14 March 1757; Preston Papers, 1: 83; *WPHM* 39 (1956): 198; *JP*, 11: 721; Haverford College Library, Indian Committee Records, 824/11, vol. 4, n.p.

Peterson, [Mrs Jacob]. Captured at South Fork, Augusta County, VA, 28 April 1758. RETURNED. Preston Papers, 1: 83; *PG*, 11 and 18 May 1758; *NYM*, 15 and 22 May 1758; Kercheval, *History of the Valley*, 91.

Petro, Nicholas. Virginian. RETURNED at Muskingum, 15 November 1764. *WPHM* 39 (1956): 189; *PG*, 17 January 1765; *NYG*, 21 January 1765; *JP*, 11: 485.

Petro, Philip. Virginian. RETURNED at Muskingum, 15 November 1764. *WPHM* 39 (1956): 189; *PG*, 17 January 1765; *NYG*, 21 January 1765; *JP*, 11: 485.

Phillipe, Pierre. Canadian soldier. Captured at battle of La Belle Famille, 24 July 1759. Held in Somerset County, NJ. EXCHANGED promptly. A Pierre Philipe married in Montreal, 29 November 1759. *JP*, 13: 115; Job Stockton Papers, NYHS; PRDH.

Phillips, Francis. Soldier in Lieutenant Colonel Hugh Mercer's company, second battalion of Pennsylvania regiment. Missing at Kittanning, 9 September 1756. Likely RETURNED by early 1759. Hauling flour at Fort Lyttleton in March 1759 and taxed in Bedford County in 1776. *PA*, ser. 2, 2: 458–60; *PG*, 23 September 1756; *HBP*, 3: 244; *PA*, ser. 3, 22: 132.

Phillips, Philip. Boy captive of the Iroquois who became a white Indian and "renegade." RETURNED. Salaried interpreter for the British by May 1764. *HBP*, 5: 416n; *JP*, 11: 207; *JP*, 12: 627; *JP*, 13: 708, 721.

Picoté de Belestre, François-Louis. Canadian ensign in *troupes de la marine*. Taken on 8 June 1757 in Maryland by the Cherokee. Active in promoting the Cherokee War (1759–61). RETURNED in 1761, and settled in Louisiana. *PG*, 23 June 1757; *NYCD*, 7: 282; HL, LO, 3838; *DCB*, 4: 634.

Picoté de Belestre, François-Marie (1716–93). Canadian captain in *troupes de la marine*, and commandant at Fort Detroit. Taken in surrender of Detroit, 30 November 1760. EXCHANGED in France in 1761. Back in Canada by 1764. *DCB*, 4: 633–6.

Pike, Joseph. Captured in fall of Fort Oswego, NY, 14 August 1756. Sent to Indians at Canesatego for two years, where he worked as a hunter and cleared land. Sold to Montreal merchant in 1758. Jailed there on death of this merchant. EXCHANGED at Crown Point, NY, 19 June 1760. *PG*, 24 July 1760.

Pittikanothy/Bittikanety. Infant boy captured by Shawnee at James River, Augusta County, VA, 1756. White Indian RETURNED to Fort Pitt, 10 May 1765. *WPHM* 39 (1956): 198; *JP*, 11: 720.

Poirot, Valentine. Canadian in the Gaspé marines. Captured in battle of La Belle Famille, 24 July 1759. Held in Somerset County, NJ. EXCHANGED at Crown Point, NY, 16 December 1760. *JP*, 13: 115; Job Stockton Papers, NYHS

Potter, Thomas. Captured by Delaware in taking of Richard Bard's Mill, York County, PA, 13 April 1758. KILLED within an hour. *PG*, 11 May 1758; Loudon, ed., *Selection*, vol. 2, 48.

Poulet. Ensign in Royal American Regiment. Captured in May 1763. RETURNED by 9 August 1764. Gladwin, "Gladwin Manuscripts," 640.

Powell, William. Pennsylvania trader. Captured by Kahnawake in Kentucky, 26 January 1753. RANSOMED through Indian affairs commissioners in Albany, September 1754. *PG*, 27 September 1753, 15 August 1754; LAC, MG 19, F 35/2, lot 680, 32–3.

Powers, Charles. Captured by Wyandot in 1754. Seen at Detroit in 1757. RETURNED to George Croghan at Fort Pitt, 26 January 1760. *PG*, 22 December 1757; *NYM*, 2 January 1758; *JP*, 10: 136–7; "George Croghan's Journal," 365.

Powers, Valentine. Captured at Powers Mill, Frederick County, VA, likely in December 1757. RETURNED 1763. Baker, *French and Indian War*, 152.

Prendergrass, Philip. Soldier in Lieutenant Colonel Hugh Mercer's company, second battalion of Pennsylvania regiment. MISSING after their attack on Kittanning, 9 September 1756. *PA*, ser. 2, 2: 458–60; *PG*, 23 September 1756; *NYM*, 27 September 1756.

Prentice, John. Pennsylvania trader. Captured by Wyandot at Sandusky, 10 May 1763. RETURNED at Detroit, 27 April 1764. Trading again by 1765. *PG*, 22 December 1763; Hay, *Diary*, 89; BL, Add. Mss, 21650, fol. 180; BL, Add. Mss, 21651, fol. 21; Commissioners of Indian Trade Accounts, Journal, 1763–65, Pennsylvania Historical Museum Commission, Harrisburg, PA.

Pretaboire, ["Drummer"]. Canadian marine in Captain Jean-Daniel Dumas's company. Taken prisoner with surrender of Detroit garrison, 30 November 1760. Sent to New York and France for EXCHANGE in 1761. *PG*, 15 January and 5 February 1761; TNA, WO 1/5, 176–7; *NYM*, 30 March 1761.

Price, Hannah. Captured in Virginia in 1756 or 1757. RETURNED at Muskingum, 15 November 1764. *WPHM* 39 (1956): 190; *PG*, 17 January 1765; *NYG*, 21 January 1765; *JP*, 11: 487.

Price, James. Captured in Virginia in 1756 or 1757. RETURNED at Muskingum, 15 November 1764. *WPHM* 39 (1956): 189; *PG*, 17 January 1765; *NYG*, 21 January 1765; *JP*, 11: 485.

Price, Sarah. Captured in Virginia in 1756. Godmother to John Turner at Fort Duquesne, 18 August 1756. RETURNED at Muskingum, 15 November 1764. *Baptismal Register*, ed. Lambing, 78–9; *WPHM* 39 (1956): 190; *PG*, 17 January 1765; *NYG*, 21 January 1765; *JP*, 11: 487.

Pringer. Young white child seen with mother and a sibling at Lower Shawnee Town late in 1764. MISSING. *WPHM* 39 (1956): 202.

Pringer. Young white child seen with mother and a sibling at Lower Shawnee Town late in 1764. MISSING. *WPHM* 39 (1956): 202.

Pringer, Mary. White woman seen with her two young children at Lower Shawnee Town late in 1764. MISSING. *WPHM* 39 (1956): 202.

Prints, Antoine. Canadian marine in Captain Jean-Daniel Dumas's company. Captured at battle of La Belle Famille, 24 July 1759. Held in Somerset County, NJ. EXCHANGED at Crown Point, NY, 16 December 1760. *JP*, 13: 115; Job Stockton Papers, NYHS.

Prunier. Canadian marine. Surrendered with garrison at Detroit, 30 November 1760. EXCHANGED in 1761 via Philadelphia, New York, and France. TNA, WO 1/5, 177; *NYM*, 30 March 1761.

Punnel/Punnet, Henry. Virginian. RETURNED with his wife at Muskingum, 15 November 1764. *JP*, 11: 485; *PG*, 17 January 1765; *NYG*, 21 January 1765.

Punnel/Punnet, Peggy. Virginian. RETURNED with her husband at Muskingum, 15 November 1764. *JP*, 11: 485; *WPHM* 39 (1956): 190; *PG*, 17 January 1765; *NYG*, 21 January 1765.

Pussey/Pusey, Lany. Captured with her father and brother by Shawnee in 1757. Escaped with Ann Mullen, and both were captured by the Seneca. ESCAPED again in 1759. *PG*, 17 March 1763.

Pussey/Pusey, Robert. Captured with his son and daughter by Shawnee in 1757. RETURNED to Fort Pitt, 22 September 1762. "Journal of James Kenny, 1761–1763," ed. Jordan, 163.

Pussey/Pusey/Puzy, Robert, Jr. Captured with his father and sister by Shawnee in 1757. WHITE INDIAN seen at Lower Shawnee Town late in 1764. *WPHM* 39 (1956): 202.

Queekqueekcomoochque. WHITE INDIAN girl with the Ohio Delaware. Loudon, ed., *Selection*, vol. 1, 264.

Quinn, Samuel. Man from Northampton County, PA. Captured by Delaware near Wyoming, 15 October 1763. Escaped to the Seneca and RETURNED by them to Johnson Hall, NY, May 1764. *JP*, 11: 175; *PG*, 20 and 27 October 1763, 17 May 1764.

Ramsay, Josiah/Joseph. One of two children orphaned and captured in Cumberland County, PA, 1 September 1756. Seen in Lower Shawnee Town late in 1764. RETURNED. *WPHM* 39 (1956): 202; Thwaites and Kellogg, *Documentary History*, 168n. Compare *PG*, 9 September 1756 (where it is claimed that he was killed).

Ramsay, Priscilla. One of two children orphaned and captured by Delaware in Cumberland County, PA, 1 September 1756. WHITE INDIAN who married twice and settled in Grand River, ON. Mary Jemison, *A Narrative of the Life of Mary Jemison*, ed. C.D. Vail (New York: American Scenic and Historical Preservation Society, 1942), 44. Compare *PG*, 9 September 1756 (where it is claimed that she was killed).

Ramsey, John. Soldier in Virginia Regiment. Captured by French at Fort Necessity. Accused of desertion. RETURNED by January 1760, and refused back pay. *Journals of the House of Burgesses, 1761–1765*, ed. Kennedy, 179, 186; *MPCP*, 6: 143; Stobo, *Memoirs*, 91.

Ramston/Ramstein, Nicholas. Man from Northampton County, PA. Captured by Delaware, 17 January 1756. RETURNED at Easton conference, 5 April 1757. *NYM*, 18 April 1757; *PG*, 14 April 1757; *PMHB* 32 (1908): 316; *MPCP*, 7: 474.

Rand, Joshua. Man from Charlestown, MA. Captured by Ottawa at Fort William Henry, NY, 9 August 1757. Taken west to above Michilimackinac. RETURNED 1763. *Boston Gazette*, 12 December 1763; Coleman, *New England Captives*, vol. 2, 357.

Rannoc. "Frenchman" with the British garrison at Fort Presqu'île. Captured in fall of this fort, 23 June 1763. MISSING. Gladwin, "Gladwin Manuscripts," 658.

Raughs/Rowse, Samuel. Pennsylvanian. Seen at Detroit in 1757. MISSING. *NYM*, 2 January 1758; *PG*, 22 December 1757.

Reager, Barbara. Girl captured with brother and sister in Augusta County, VA, 28 April 1758. RETURNED at Muskingum, 15 November 1764. Married John Caplenger Jr by 1772. *WPHM* 39 (1956): 194; *PG*, 17 January 1765; *NYG*, 21 January 1765; *JP*, 11: 485; Chalkley, *Chronicles of the Scotch-Irish*, vol. 3, 527.

Reager, Dorothy. Girl captured with brother and sister in Augusta County, VA, 28 April 1758. RETURNED at Muskingum, 15 November 1764. Married John Likens by 1772. *WPHM* 39 (1956): 194; *PG*, 17 January 1765; *NYG*, 21 January 1765; *JP*, 11: 485; Chalkley, *Chronicles of the Scotch-Irish*, vol. 3, 527.

Reager, John. Boy captured with two sisters in Augusta County, VA, 28 April 1758. Still MISSING in 1772. Chalkley, *Chronicles of the Scotch-Irish*, vol. 3, 527.

Reichard. Eight-year-old girl captured in Berks County, PA, 29 June 1757. MISSING. Rupp, *History of Northampton*, 468.

Reilly. Lieutenant with Maryland forces. Captured in Major James Grant's defeat at Fort Duquesne, 14 September 1758. RETURNED. Draper Mss, Virginia Papers, 3ZZ48.

Renick/Ranock, George. Son of Robert. Captured with family by Shawnee at forks of James River, Augusta County, VA, 25 July 1757. RETURNED to Fort Pitt, 10 May 1765. *WPHM* 39 (1956): 198; *JP*, 11: 720.

Renick/Ranock, Joseph or Robert Jr [Pechyloothame]. Posthumous son of Robert. Born in 1757 during mother's captivity. Seen in Lower Shawnee Town late in 1764. Eight-year-old white Indian when RETURNED to Fort Pitt, 10 May 1765. *WPHM* 39 (1956): 198; Draper Mss, Frontier Wars Papers, 21U129; *JP*, 11: 720.

Renick/Ranock, Joshua. Son of Robert. Captured with family by Shawnee at forks of James River, Augusta County, VA, 25 July 1757. Seen at Lower Shawnee Town late in 1764. WHITE INDIAN who became a war chief. Preston Papers, 1: 83; *WPHM* 39 (1956): 202; Draper Mss, Kentucky Papers, 4CC119.

Renick/Ranock, Margaret/Peggy. Daughter of Robert. Captured with family by Shawnee at forks of James River, Augusta County, VA, 25 July 1757. RETURNED at Muskingum, 15 November 1764. Married and moved to Ohio. Preston Papers, 1: 83; *WPHM* 39 (1956): 195, 196, 202; *PG*, 17 January 1765; *NYG*, 21 January 1765; Draper Mss, Frontier Wars Papers, 21U129.

Renick/Ranock, [Mrs Robert, nee Archer]. Widowed and captured with her seven children by Shawnee at forks of James River, Augusta County, VA, 25 July 1757. RETURNED to Staunton, 1767. Preston Papers, 1: 83; Baker, *French and Indian War*, 93; Withers, *Chronicles* (1895), 90; Waddell, *Annals of Augusta*, vol. 1, 125.

Renick/Ranock, Nancy. Daughter of Robert. Captured with family by Shawnee at forks of James River, Augusta County, VA, 25 July 1757. Seen at Lower Shawnee Town late in 1764. RETURNED to Greenbrier, married, and moved to Ohio. *WPHM* 39 (1956): 202; Preston Papers, 1: 83; Draper Mss, Frontier Wars Papers, 21U129.

Renick/Ranock, Robert Jr. Infant son of Robert. Captured with family by Shawnee at forks of James River, Augusta County, VA, 25 July 1757. KILLED on the trail a few days later. Draper Mss, Frontier Wars Papers, 21U127; Draper Mss, Kentucky Papers, 4CC120.

Renick/Ranock, William. Son of Robert. Captured with family by Shawnee at forks of James River, Augusta County, VA, 25 July 1757. Seen at Lower Shawnee Town late in 1764. RETURNED to Fort Pitt, 10 May 1765. Became prominent in Greenbrier and a militia major. *WPHM* 39 (1956): 202; Draper Mss, Frontier Wars Papers, 21U129.

Reynolds. Lieutenant in Pennsylvania forces. Captured in Major James Grant's defeat at Fort Duquesne, 14 September 1758. RETURNED. Draper Mss, Virginia Papers, 3ZZ48.

Rhodes. Daughter of John. Orphaned and captured with four siblings near Stover's Town, Frederick County, VA, 22 August 1764. KILLED on the trail. Baker, *French and Indian War*, 130; *PG*, 13 September 1764.

Rhodes. Daughter of John. Orphaned and captured with four siblings near Stover's Town, Frederick County, VA, 22 August 1764. KILLED on the trail. Baker, *French and Indian War*, 130; *PG*, 13 September 1764.

Rhodes. Four-year-old son of John. Orphaned and captured with four siblings near Stover's Town, Frederick County, VA, 22 August 1764. KILLED on the trail two days later. Baker, *French and Indian War*, 130; *PG*, 13 September 1764.

Rhodes, Daniel. Son of John. Orphaned and captured with four siblings near Stover's Town, Frederick County, VA, 22 August 1764. RETURNED at Muskingum, 15 November 1764. *WPHM* 39 (1956): 190; *PG*, 17 January 1765; *NYG*, 21 January 1765. Compare Baker, *French and Indian War*, 130; and Kercheval, *History of the Valley*, 102–3.

Rhodes, Michael. Son of John. Orphaned and captured with four siblings near Stover's Town, Frederick County, VA, 22 August 1764. RETURNED at Muskingum, 15 November 1764. *WPHM* 39 (1956): 190; *PG*, 17 January 1765; *NYG*, 21 January 1765. Compare Baker, *French and Indian War*, 130; and Kercheval, *History of the Valley*, 102–3.

Riddle, John. Man from Cumberland County, PA. Captured 10 July 1763. RETURNED at Muskingum, 15 November 1764. *WPHM* 39 (1956): 188; *PG*, 17 January 1765; *NYG*, 21 January 1765; LAC, MG 19, F 35/2, lot 621, 4.

Robertson. Daughter of Benjamin. Captive in Lower Shawnee Town late in 1764. MISSING. *WPHM* 39 (1956): 202.

Robertson. Son of Benjamin. Captive in Lower Shawnee Town late in 1764. MISSING. *WPHM* 39 (1956): 202.

Robertson, Archibald. Lieutenant in Montgomery Highlanders. Captured in Major James Grant's defeat at Fort Duquesne, 14 September 1758. RETURNED. Draper Mss, Virginia Papers, 3ZZ48.

Robinson, Thomas. Soldier in Lieutenant Thomas Bullitt's company of Virginia Regiment. Captured in Cumberland County, PA, 23 May 1758. Reportedly STAYED among the Indians. *PMHB* 32 (1908): 311; *PG*, 23 May and 23 August 1759; *NYM*, 20 August 1759.

Rodmon, Jonathan. Pennsylvania soldier. Captured in fall of Fort Granville, Cumberland County, PA, 31 July 1756. ESCAPED to Fort Augusta, 31 August 1756. Hunter, *Forts*, 392.

Roe, William. Captured in Northampton County, PA, 12 December 1755. MISSING. *PG*, 18 December 1755.

Rogers. Young child of Benjamin. Captured with family near Fort Cumberland, MD, 30 September 1755. MISSING. *PG*, 16 October 1755; *NYM*, 20 October 1755; *SCG*, 13 November 1755.

Rogers. Young child of Benjamin. Captured with family near Fort Cumberland, MD, 30 September 1755. MISSING. *PG*, 16 October 1755; *NYM*, 20 October 1755; *SCG*, 13 November 1755.

Rogers, Benjamin. Captured with wife and seven children near Fort Cumberland, MD, 30 September 1755. MISSING. *PG*, 16 October 1755; *NYM*, 20 October 1755; *SCG*, 13 November 1755.

Rogers, Betty. Eldest daughter of Benjamin. Captured with family near Fort Cumberland, MD, 30 September 1755. Seen in captivity. MISSING. *PA*, ser. 2, 7: 437; *PG*, 16 October 1755; *NYM*, 20 October 1755; *SCG*, 13 November 1755.

Rogers, Esther. Daughter of Benjamin. Captured with family near Fort Cumberland, MD, 30 September 1755. Seen in captivity. RETURNED at Lancaster conference, 13 August 1762. *PA*, ser. 2, 7: 437; *PG*, 16 October 1755; *NYM*, 20 October 1755; *SCG*, 13 November 1755; *Minutes of Conferences ... Lancaster, 1762*, 7.

Rogers, Jacob. Son of Benjamin. Captured with family near Fort Cumberland, MD, 30 September 1755. Seen in captivity. RETURNED at Lancaster conference, 13 August 1762. *PA*, ser. 2, 7: 437; *PG*, 16 October 1755; *NYM*, 20 October 1755; *SCG*, 13 November 1755; *Minutes of Conferences ... Lancaster, 1762*, 7.

Rogers, James. Son of Benjamin. Captured with family near Fort Cumberland, MD, 30 September 1755. Adopted Shawnee and WHITE INDIAN. Interpreter and spy for Americans in 1775. *PA*, ser. 2, 7: 437; *PG*, 16 October 1755; *NYM*, 20 October 1755; *SCG*, 13 November 1755; William J. Van Schreeven, ed., *Revolutionary Virginia: The Road to Independence*, 7 vols (Charlottesville, VA: University Press of Virginia, 1973–83), vol. 4, 140–1.

Rogers, [Mrs Benjamin]. Captured with husband and seven children near Fort Cumberland, MD, 30 September 1755. MISSING. *PG*, 16 October 1755; *NYM*, 20 October 1755; *SCG*, 13 November 1755.

Rogers, Richard. Son of Benjamin. Captured with family near Fort Cumberland, MD, 30 September 1755. Seen in captivity. RETURNED at Lancaster conference, 13 August 1762. *PA*, ser. 2, 7: 437; *PG*, 16 October 1755; *NYM*, 20 October 1755; *SCG*, 13 November 1755; *Minutes of Conferences ... Lancaster, 1762*, 7.

Roseboom, Garrit. Trader at La Baye. Accompanied garrison to Fort Michilimackinac. Captured there by Ojibwa, 15 June 1763. RANSOMED from Ottawa by General Thomas Gage at Montreal, 16 August 1763. Gladwin, "Gladwin Manuscripts," 668–70.

Rosenbarger, John. Captured in Bethel Township, Lancaster County, PA, 12 December 1755. Likely RETURNED. A John Rosenbarger was in Donegal Township in 1771. *PMHB* 32 (1908): 310; *PA*, ser. 3, 17: 89.

Ross, John. Virginian. RANSOMED by Canadians and returned via France and England, September 1757. Landowner and militiaman in Augusta County, VA. TNA, Adm. 1/4323, n.p.; Kegley, *Kegley's Virginia Frontier*, 452, 474, 477, 480–1, 587, 618.

Ross, Lawrence. Virginian. RETURNED at Fort Frederick, 17 August 1764. Likely in Hampshire County, VA, in 1782. BL, Add. Mss, 21650, fol. 406; *U.S. Census of 1790, Virginia*, 27.

Ross, Robert. Virginian. RANSOMED by Canadians and returned via France and England, September 1757. TNA, Adm. 1/4323, n.p.

Ross, Tavernor. Virginian who became a WHITE INDIAN. Returned at Muskingum, 15 November 1764, but rejoined the Shawnee and fought with them against the Virginians at Point Pleasant in 1774. Eventually returned to the "American settlements." *WPHM* 39 (1956): 190; Colin G. Calloway, ed., *The Shawnees and the War for America* (New York: Viking, 2007), 55–6.

Ross, William. Virginian seen at Detroit early in 1757. RANSOMED by Canadians and returned via New France, France, and England, September 1757. *PG*, 22 December 1757; TNA, Adm. 1/4323, n.p.

Rowe, John. Maryland man captured on 20 August 1756. ESCAPED to Virginia two days later. *VG*, 3 September 1756; *PG*, 9 September 1756; *PJ*, 9 September 1756.

Roy, André [Pacane]. Canadian trader and spy. Captured by Piankashaw Miami, August 1750. Given to Lowrey family in compensation for a death. RELEASED in Lancaster County, PA, three weeks later. *MPCP*, 5: 461–2; Pease and Jenison, eds, *Illinois on the Eve*, 202–3.

Russell, Isaac. Son of James. Captured near Stroudsburg, Northampton County, PA, 10 February 1764. RETURNED by Delaware and Seneca to Johnson's Hall, NY, May 1765. *PG*, 16 February 1764, 19 September 1765; Sipe, *Indian Wars*, 471.

Rutherfurd, John. Lieutenant in Royal American Regiment. Captured by Ojibwa on Lake St Clair, 6 May 1763. Adopted, and arranged a ransom that was revoked by Pontiac. ESCAPED into Fort Detroit, 4 August 1763. "John Rutherfurd's Captivity Narrative," in Quaife, ed., *Siege*, 219–74; Hay, *Diary*, 20, 21; *PG*, 7 July 1763, 11 and 18 August 1763; *NYM*, 15 August 1763.

Ryan. Brother of Eleanor. Captured with her at Stony Creek, VA, 20 August 1763. ESCAPED 4 September 1763. Starved to death while returning, 19 September 1763. *PG*, 8 December 1763.

Ryan, Eleanor. Captured with her brother at Stony Creek, VA, 20 August 1763. ESCAPED 4 September 1763. Arrived at Harness's Fort, 24 September 1763. *PG*, 8 December 1763.

Rychman, Garrit. New York trader. Captured near Detroit, 1 July 1763. RETURNED that month. *NYM*, 8 August 1763.

Ryder, William. Lieutenant in Royal American Regiment. Captured in Major James Grant's defeat at Fort Duquesne, 14 September 1758. EXCHANGED in England. *PG*, 28 September and 19 October 1758; HL, AB, 655, 658; *HBP*, 4: 421; *HBP*, 5: 356, 356n; *HBP*, 6: 53n; TNA, Adm. 97/106, fols 236–9.

Salmon. Old shoemaker. Captured ten miles from Carlisle, Cumberland County, PA, 21 July 1756. MISSING. *PG*, 29 July 1756.

Salvignac. French lieutenant in Régiment de Béarn. Captured at battle of La Belle Famille, 24 July 1759. MISSING. Dunnigan, *Siege–1759*, 103.

Sans Souci [nom de guerre]. Canadian marine in Captain François Lefebvre Duplessis Faber's company. Surrendered as part of Detroit garrison, 30 November 1760. EXCHANGED in France, 1761. TNA, WO 1/5, 176; *PG*, 15 January and 5 February 1761; *NYM*, 30 March 1761.

Sauvage, Louis ["St Esperance"]. Canadian marine in Verrier's company. Captured at battle of La Belle Famille, 24 July 1759. Held in Somerset County, NJ. EXCHANGED via Crown Point, NY, 16 December 1760. *JP*, 13: 115; Job Stockton Papers, NYHS.

Scarouady/Monacatoocha. Oneida chief, and Iroquoian Half-King in upper Ohio. Captured by a French and Indian scouting force near General Edward Braddock's camp, 19 June 1755. RETURNED the same day, after Iroquois objections. *SCG*, 8 July 1755; Hunter, *Forts*, 129–30.

Schilling, John/Robert. Servant of the Eckerle brothers. Captured with them by Ottawa and Canadians on Cheat River in 1757. Taken to New France and France. RETURNED to Strasburg, in Alsace, in 1761. *PG*, 26 January 1858; Pierre Pouchot, *Memoirs of the Late War in North America between England and France*, ed. B.L. Dunnigan (Youngstown, NY: Old Fort Niagara Association, 1994), 124–5, 377–9; Klein, *Johann Conrad Beissel*, 152–64; Alderfer, *Ephrata Commune*, 136–8.

Schlosser, Francis. Ensign in Royal American Regiment. Commander of garrison at Fort St Joseph, MI, when it was captured by Potawatomi, 27 May 1763. EXCHANGED at Detroit, 9 July 1763. BL, Add. Mss, 21658, fols 88–90; TNA, WO 34/49, fols 214–15; Hay, *Diary*, 26; *PG*, 11 and 18 August 1763; *NYM*, 15 August 1763.

Schmidt. Daughter of Balthasar. Captured at Adam Trump's in Berks County, PA, 23 June 1756. MISSING, and reported killed. *PMHB* 32 (1908): 317; Rupp, *History of Northampton*, 465–6.

Schmidt, Maria Christina. Captured at age nine at Graceham, MD, August 1755. RETURNED two years later, and assigned by court to wrong father for another year. *PMHB* 43 (1919): 284.

Schopffler. Man captured by Delaware near Nazareth, Northampton County, PA, 1 January 1756. ESCAPED the next day. *PG*, 22 January 1756; *NYM*, 26 January 1756.

Schrink/Schrenk. One of two young children of Christian. Captured in Berks County, PA, 8 July 1757. MISSING. *PG*, 14 July 1757; *NYM*, 18 July 1757; *RCFFP*, 1: 95.

Schrink/Schrenk. One of two young children of Christian. Captured in Berks County, PA, 8 July 1757. MISSING. *PG*, 14 July 1757; *NYM*, 18 July 1757; *RCFFP*, 1: 95.

Schuyler, Magdalen. Girl captured by Shawnee at Greenbrier, Augusta County, VA, 15 July 1763. RETURNED to Fort Pitt, 10 May 1765. *JP*, 11: 720; *WPHM* 39 (1956): 198.

Sea/See, Catherine [Mrs Frederick, nee Vanderpool] (1725–c. 1806). Widowed and captured with her six children by Shawnee at Muddy Creek, Augusta County, VA, 15 July 1763. RETURNED at Muskingum, 15 November 1764. *WPHM* 39 (1956): 195; *PG*, 17 January 1765; *NYG*, 21 January 1765; *JP*, 11: 486; Felix Renick, "A Trip to the West," *American Pioneer* 1 (1842): 73–80; https://www.familysearch.org.

Sea/See, George (1751–92). Twelve-year-old son of Frederick. Captured with family by Shawnee at Muddy Creek, Augusta County, VA, 15 July 1763. RETURNED at Muskingum, 15 November 1764. *WPHM* 39 (1956): 194; *PG*, 17 January 1765; *NYG*, 21 January 1765; *JP*, 11: 485; https://www.familysearch.org.

Sea/See, John (1757–c. 1834). Six-year-old son of Frederick. Captured with family by Shawnee at Muddy Creek, Augusta County, VA, 15 July 1763. RETURNED by Shawnee to Fort Pitt, 10 May 1765. Ran away to Shawnee and stayed two years. *WPHM* 39 (1956): 198; *JP*, 11: 720; Renick, "Trip," 78; https://www.familysearch.org.

Sea/See, Margaret/Peggy (1745–1815). Daughter of Frederick. Captured with family by Shawnee at Muddy Creek, Augusta County, VA, 15 July 1763. RETURNED by Shawnee to Fort Pitt, 10 May 1765. Married William Robinson, 1766. *WPHM* 39 (1956): 198; *JP*, 11: 720; https://www.familysearch.org.

Sea/See, Mary. Daughter of Frederick. Captured with family by Shawnee at Muddy Creek, Augusta County, VA, 15 July 1763. RETURNED at Muskingum, 15 November 1764. Married trader William Johnson and lived on Muskingum River again. *PG*, 17 January 1765; *NYG*, 21 January 1765; *WPHM* 39 (1956): 195, 196; *JP*, 11: 486, 720; Renick, "Trip," 78; https://www.familysearch.org.

Sea/See, Mary. Daughter of Michael Frederick. Captured by Shawnee at Muddy Creek, Augusta County, VA, 15 July 1763. RETURNED by Shawnee to Fort Pitt, 10 May 1765. *WPHM* 39 (1956): 198; Renick, "Trip," 78; https://www.familysearch.org.

Sea/See, Michael (1751–92). Son of Frederick. Captured with family by Shawnee at Muddy Creek, Augusta County, VA, 15 July 1763. RETURNED at Muskingum, 15 November 1764. *WPHM* 39 (1956): 194; *PG*, 17 January 1765; *NYG*, 21 January 1765; *JP*, 11: 485; https://www.familysearch.org.

Sea/See, Sarah/Sally (b. 1755). Daughter of Johann Frederick. Captured by Shawnee at Muddy Creek, Augusta County, VA, 15 July 1763. RETURNED by Shawnee to Fort Pitt, 10 May 1765. *WPHM* 39 (1956): 198; *JP*, 11: 720; https://www.familysearch.org.

Sebrai, Henri. Canadian marine in Captain Joseph-Gaspard Chaussegros de Lery's company. Captured at battle of La Belle Famille, 24 July 1759. Held in Somerset County, NJ. RETURNED via Crown Point, NY, 16 December 1760. *JP*, 13: 115; Job Stockton Papers, NYHS.

Seeger, John. Trader captured by Ojibwa at Grand River, ON, 2 June 1763. RETURNED before 8 September 1763. Gladwin, "Gladwin Manuscripts," 647, 652.

Severings, John. Soldier in Royal American Regiment. Captured by Wyandot at Detroit, 28 May 1763. RETURNED by 1 October 1763. Quaife, ed., *Siege*, 144n; TNA, WO 34/49, fol. 267.

Severn, John. Elderly servant. Captured at Cowpasture, Augusta County, VA, 19 March 1758. KILLED four days later. Preston Papers, 1: 83; *PA*, ser. 1, 3: 632–3.

Seybert/Seabert/Seivers, Catherine. Daughter of Jacob. Captured by Shawnee in surrender of Seybert's Fort, Augusta County, VA, 28 April 1758. Seen at Kuskuski or Muskingum in 1758–59. RETURNED at Muskingum, 15 November 1764. *PA*, ser. 2, 7: 437; *WPHM* 39 (1956): 194; *PG*, 17 January 1765; *NYG*, 21 January 1765; *JP*, 11: 486.

Seybert/Seabert/Seivers, Ebenezer/Henry. Son of Jacob. Captured by Shawnee in surrender of Seybert's Fort, Augusta County, VA, 28 April 1758. RETURNED by Shawnee to Fort Pitt, 10 May 1765. *PG*, 11 and 18 May 1758; Preston Papers, 1: 83; *JP*, 11: 720; *WPHM* 39 (1956): 198.

Seybert/Seabert/Seivers, Elizabeth. Daughter of Jacob. Captured by Shawnee in surrender of Seybert's Fort, Augusta County, VA, 28 April 1758. Seen at Kuskuski or Muskingum in 1758–59. RETURNED at Muskingum, 15 November 1764. *PA*, ser. 2, 7: 437; *WPHM* 39 (1956): 194; *PG*, 17 January 1765; *NYG*, 21 January 1765; *JP*, 11: 486.

Seybert/Seabert/Seivers, George. Son of Jacob. Captured by Shawnee in surrender of Seybert's Fort, Augusta County, VA, 28 April 1758. Seen at Kuskuski or Muskingum in 1758–59. MISSING. *PA*, ser. 2, 7: 437.

Seybert/Seabert/Seivers, John. Son of Jacob. Captured by Shawnee in surrender of Seybert's Fort, Augusta County, VA, 28 April 1758. RETURNED by Shawnee to Fort Pitt, 10 May 1765. *PG*, 11 and 18 May 1758; Preston Papers, 1: 83; *JP*, 11: 720. Compare *WPHM* 39 (1956): 198.

Seybert/Seabert/Seivers, Margaret. Daughter of Jacob. Captured by Shawnee in surrender of Seybert's Fort, Augusta County, VA, 28 April 1758. Seen at Kuskuski or Muskingum in 1758–59. RETURNED at Muskingum, 15 November 1764. *PA*, ser. 2, 7: 437; *WPHM* 39 (1956): 194; *PG*, 17 January 1765; *NYG*, 21 January 1765; *JP*, 11: 486; https://www.familysearch.org.

Seybert/Seabert/Seivers, Mary [Mrs Jacob]. Widowed and captured with her seven children by Shawnee in surrender of Seybert's Fort, Augusta County, VA, 28 April 1758. Seen at Kuskuski or Muskingum in 1758–59. MISSING. *PA*, ser. 2, 7: 437; https://www.familysearch.org.

Seybert/Seabert/Seivers, Nicholas. Son of Jacob. Captured by Shawnee in surrender of Seybert's Fort, Augusta County, VA, 28 April 1758. MISSING, though a Nicholas is in court records of 1778–82. Baker, *French and Indian War*, 108–9; Chalkley, *Chronicles of the Scotch-Irish*, vol. 3, 155, 554, 558, 572.

Sharl, Elizabeth. Captured in Bethel Township, Lancaster County, PA, 19 May 1757. MISSING. *PMHB* 32 (1908): 310.

Shaw, Patrick. Sergeant in Royal American Regiment. Captured by Ojibwa on Ste Claire River, 29 May 1763. MISSING. TNA, WO 34/49, fol. 5.

Shaw, William. Sergeant in Virginia Regiment. Captured by Shawnee and Delaware, 29 December 1756. Tortured. Monument built on assumption he was killed. EXCHANGED by November 1758. *Journals of the House of Burgesses, 1761–1765*, ed. Kennedy, 66, 68; *GWP*, 4: 163.

Shaw/Chat, Anne-Marie [Mrs Michael]. Captured with husband and son by Canadian Iroquois in Virginia, 1750. WHITE INDIAN at Oka and Two Mountains. Fournier, *De la Nouvelle-Angleterre*, 203.

Shaw/Chat, Louis-Andre. Son of Michael. Captured with his parents by Canadian Iroquois in Virginia, 1750. WHITE INDIAN at Oka and Two Mountains. Fournier, *De la Nouvelle-Angleterre*, 203.

Shaw/Chat, Michael. Captured with wife and son by Canadian Iroquois in Virginia, 1750. WHITE INDIAN at Oka and Two Mountains. Fournier, *De la Nouvelle-Angleterre*, 203.

Sheaffer, Peter. Captured by Indians in Northampton County, PA, 2 May 1757. Presumed killed but RETURNED to recover his children and estate in Lancaster County Orphan's Court, 25 March 1761. Northampton County Orphan's Court Records, Northampton County Courthouse, Easton, PA; *PG*, 12 May 1757; *NYM*, 16 May 1757; *MPCP*, 7: 620.

Shefer/Sheaffer. Young daughter of Balthazar. Captured in Berks County, PA, October 1755. MISSING. *PMHB* 32 (1908): 311.

Shelburger, Daniel. Soldier in Queen's Rangers. Captured by Wyandot at fall of Fort Presqu'île, 23 June 1763. RETURNED at Detroit, 9 July 1763. TNA, WO 34/49, 212–14; BL, Add. Mss, 21649, fols 242–3; Hay, *Diary*, 43–5; *PG*, 7 and 11 August 1763.

Shepherd, Benjamin. Connecticut settler at Wyoming, PA. Captured by Delaware, 4 September 1763. RETURNED by Chenussio Seneca to William Johnson at Fort Niagara, NY, 31 July 1764. *JP*, 4: 497; *JP*, 11: 318.

Sherby, Thomas. Captured in Cumberland County, PA, December 1755. ESCAPED from Fort Venango, 29 July 1756. *PG*, 9 September 1756.

Shillinge, Jean. Canadian soldier taken in battle of La Belle Famille, 24 July 1759. Held in Somerset County, NJ. RETURNED. *JP*, 13: 115; Job Stockton Papers, NYHS.

Shobrin, Dorothy. Captured by Shawnee and Delaware at Big Cove, Cumberland County, PA, 2 November 1755. RETURNED at Lancaster conference, 13 August 1762. *Minutes of Conferences ... Lancaster, 1762*, 7.

Silkpurse. One of at least two children of George. Captured with parents by Delaware and Shawnee in Cumberland County, PA, 2 November 1755. MISSING. *MVHR* 13 (1926): 60.

Silkpurse. One of at least two children of George. Captured with parents by Delaware and Shawnee in Cumberland County, PA, 2 November 1755. MISSING. *MVHR* 13 (1926): 60.

Silkpurse, George. Captured with wife and children by Delaware and Shawnee in Cumberland County, PA, 2 November 1755. MISSING. *MVHR* 13 (1926): 60.

Silkpurse, [Mrs George]. Captured with husband and children by Delaware and Shawnee in Cumberland County, PA, 2 November 1755. MISSING. *MVHR* 13 (1926): 60.

Silkspiner, Josua/Joseph. Boy captured by Shawnee at Greenbrier, Augusta County, VA, June 1763. RETURNED to Fort Pitt, 10 May 1765. *WPHM* 39 (1956): 198. Compare *JP*, 11: 720.

Silus/Silvias, Nicholas. Son of John George. Captured in Lynn Township, Northampton County, PA, 14 February 1756. RETURNED via New York, July 1761. *NYM*, 23 February 1756; *PMHB* 32 (1908): 313; *PG*, 2 July 1761.

Simard, Joseph. Sixteen-year-old Canadian. Captured by Cherokee and brought in to Fort Augusta, PA, February 1757. RANSOMED and EXCHANGED by 1759. *NYM*, 14 March 1757; *SCG*, 5 December 1757; Preston Papers, 1: 151; HL, LO, 5468; TNA, WO 34/38, fols 21–2.

Sims/Sipes, Andrew. Fourteen year old captured in Cumberland County, PA, 20 March 1764. RETURNED at Muskingum, 15 November 1764. *WPHM* 39 (1956): 191; *PG*, 5 April 1757, 17 January 1765; *NYG*, 21 January 1765; *NYM*, 9 April 1764; BL, Add. Mss, 21650, fol. 103.

Slover, Elisabeth [Mrs Jacob]. Captured with family in Augusta County, VA, 1763. RETURNED at Muskingum, 15 November 1764. *WPHM* 39 (1956): 195, 196; *PG*, 17 January 1765; *NYG*, 21 January 1765.

Slover, Elisabeth, Jr (b. 1759). Young daughter of Jacob. Captured with family in Augusta County, VA, 1763. RETURNED at Muskingum, 15 November 1764. *WPHM* 39 (1956): 195, 196; *PG*, 17 January 1765; *NYG*, 21 January 1765; https://www.familysearch.org.

Slover, Jacob. Captured with family in Augusta County, VA, 1763. RETURNED at Muskingum, 15 November 1764. *PG*, 17 January 1765; *NYG*, 21 January 1765.

Slover, John [Mannuchcothee] (b. 1755). Eight-year-old son of Jacob. Captured in Augusta County, VA, 1763. Several years with Miami and then with Shawnee. White Indian RETURNED to Fort Pitt, 1773. Guide for Colonel William Crawford's force in 1782, when he was captured and escaped. https://www.familysearch.org; Loudon, ed., *Selection*, vol. 1, 20–1, Heard, *White into Red*, 134.

Smallman, Thomas. Former major in Pennsylvania forces, and trader for George Croghan with Shawnee. Captured by Wyandot at fall of Fort Sandusky, 20 May 1763, and given to the Shawnee. Courier for Shawnee to Colonel Henry Bouquet. RETURNED 9 November 1764. Captured again with Croghan's party at Fort Ouiatenon, 8 June 1765. RELEASED 11 July 1765. *WPHM* 39 (1956): 203; *JP*, 10: 741–2; *JP*, 11: 169, 450–1, 488, 537, 836–41, 988; HL, MM, 569; *HBP*, 6: 103, 412–13; *PG*, 22 December 1763, 15 August 1765; Wainwright, *George Croghan*, 220–1; Richards, *Pennsylvania-German*, 229, 233, 239.

Smart, David. Soldier in Royal American Regiment. Captured in 1763. RETURNED to appear at an inquiry at Fort Pitt, 24 December 1763. Parkman, *Conspiracy of Pontiac*, vol. 1, 295–6n.

Smelliker, Andrew. Boy captured in Hanover Township, Lancaster County, PA, 30 September 1757. Seen with French Margaret. MISSING. *NYM*, 17 October

1757; Haverford College Library, Indian Committee Records, 824/11, vol. 4, n.p.

Smelliker, Godfrey. Youth captured in Hanover Township, Lancaster County, PA, 30 September 1757. RANSOMED from French Margaret in 1760. *NYM*, 17 October 1757; Haverford College Library, Indian Committee Records, 824/11, vol. 4, n.p.

Smelliker, Susannah/Barbara. Girl captured in Hanover Township, Lancaster County, PA, 30 September 1757. MISSING. *NYM*, 17 October 1757; Haverford College Library, Indian Committee Records, 824/11, vol. 4, n.p.

Smeltzer, Hans Adam. One of three young sons of Peter. Captured in Berks County, PA, 21 August 1757. RETURNED at Muskingum, 15 November 1764. *WPHM* 39 (1956): 191; *PG*, 1 September 1757, 17 January 1765; *NYG*, 21 January 1765; *PMHB* 32 (1908): 317.

Smeltzer, Jacob. One of three young sons of Peter. Captured in Berks County, PA, 21 August 1757. RETURNED at Muskingum, 15 November 1764. *WPHM* 39 (1956): 191; *PG*, 1 September 1757, 17 January 1765; *NYG*, 21 January 1765; *PMHB* 32 (1908): 317.

Smeltzer, Joseph. One of three young sons of Peter. Captured in Berks County, PA, 21 August 1757. RETURNED at Muskingum, 15 November 1764. *JP*, 11: 488; *PG*, 1 September 1757; *PMHB* 32 (1908): 317.

Smith. Daughter of Balthazar. Captured in Lancaster County, PA, April 1757. MISSING. *PMHB* 32 (1908): 312.

Smith, Catherine (1). Seven-year-old daughter of William. Captured with mother and infant sister by Delaware in Northampton County, PA, 10 December 1755. Became blind in captivity. RETAKEN in Kittanning raid, 8 September 1756. Unclaimed by relatives and put out to service with Thomas Hill in Philadelphia, until at least 1766. *PG*, 23 September 1756; *PA*, ser. 1, 2: 775; *V&P*, 7: 5655, 5944–5.

Smith, Catherine (2). One-year-old daughter of William. Captured with mother and sister by Delaware in Northampton County, PA, 10 December 1755. Baptized at Fort Duquesne, 10 August 1756, probably with mother absent. DIED there four days later. *PMHB* 32 (1908): 313; *Baptismal Register*, ed. Lambing, 76–7.

Smith, Cecilia/"Sessaly" [Mrs William]. Captured with two daughters by Delaware in Northampton County, PA, 10 December 1755. Sent to Canada and France. RANSOMED. *PMHB* 32 (1908): 313; TNA, Adm. 1/4323, n.p.; *Baptismal Register*, ed. Lambing, 76–7.

Smith, Elizabeth. Pennsylvania woman RETURNED at Muskingum, 15 November 1764. *WPHM* 39 (1956): 192; *PG*, 17 January 1765; *NYG*, 21 January 1765; *JP*, 11: 489.

Smith, Fisher. *Métis* son of Hannah. Effectively captured from Shawnee when mother returned at Muskingum, 15 November 1764. STAYED in unhappy captivity with whites. Became a soldier in the American Revolution and died c. 1777. *WPHM* 39 (1956): 192; *PG*, 17 January 1765; *NYG*, 21 January 1765; Kercheval, *History of the Valley*, 81; Cartmell, *Shenandoah Valley*, 74.

Smith, Hannah. Virginia woman. Captured by Shawnee in Virginia, 1758. RETURNED, with her *métis* son, Fisher, at Muskingum, 15 November 1764. *WPHM* 39 (1956): 192; *PG*, 17 January 1765; *NYG*, 21 January 1765; Kercheval, *History of the Valley*, 81.

Smith, James. Sixteen year old captured by Delaware and Kahnawake near Fort Bedford, 3 July 1755. Taken to Fort Duquesne, Detroit, Ohio, and Montreal. Escaped in Montreal and retaken there. EXCHANGED at Crown Point, NY, 15 November of 1759. With Colonel Henry Bouquet in 1764. Leader of Black Boys. James Smith, *An Account of the Remarkable Occurrences in the Life and Travels of Colonel James Smith during his Captivity with the Indians, 1755–1759* (Lexington, KY, 1799); Loudon, ed., *Selection*, vol. 1, 119–302; *PG*, 22 December 1757; TNA, CO 5/57, part 1, fols 119–21.

Smith, John. Ranger captain commanding at Vause's Fort, Augusta County, VA, when it was surrendered, 25 June 1756. With the Miami near Detroit and then sent to Canada and Britain. EXCHANGED. TNA, 30/8/95, fols 214–15; HL, LO, 4807, 4925, 5452, 5658; "Extract from the Journal of Major John Smith, 1756–1757," in *Colonial Captivities, Marches, and Journeys*, ed. I.M. Calder (New York: Macmillan, 1935), 137–40; *PG*, 28 July 1757, 9 February 1758; *NYM*, 1 August 1757.

Smith, John. Soldier in Captain John Fenton Mercer's company of Virginia Regiment. Captured by Indians at fall of Fort Necessity, 4 July 1754. Sent to Canada. MISSING. Stobo, *Memoirs*, 91–2; *Travels in New France by J.C.B.*, ed. Stevens, Kent, and Woods, 64; Severance, "Tale of Captives," 294.

Smith, John. Sutler from York County, PA. Captured in Cumberland County, PA, 5 August 1758. MISSING. *PG*, 31 August 1758; *NYM*, 4 September 1758.

Smith, Joseph. Son of ranger captain John. Captured in fall of Vause's Fort, Augusta County, VA, 25 June 1756. RETURNED by Wyandot and Mohicans to George Croghan at Fort Pitt, 21 May 1760. Died of smallpox a few days later. *PG*, 28 July 1757; "George Croghan's Journal," 370.

Smith, [Mrs Thomas]. Widowed and captured in Frederick County, VA, 25 July 1757. Baker, *French and Indian War*, 93.

Snell, Hannah. Daughter of Adam. Orphaned and captured in Delaware attack at Philip Bosart's farm, Northampton County, PA, 23 April 1757. Broke leg in a fall. KILLED three days later at Tioga. *PMHB* 32 (1908): 316; *MPCP*, 7: 620; *PG*, 28 April and 30 June 1757.

Snodgrass, Elizabeth. Girl captured in Augusta County, VA, 29 March 1758. RETURNED at Muskingum, 15 November 1764. Preston Papers, 1: 83; *WPHM* 39 (1956): 195; *PG*, 17 January 1765; *NYG*, 21 January 1765.

Snogan, Andrew. Soldier in Royal American Regiment. Taken in Major James Grant's defeat at Fort Duquesne, 14 September 1758. RETURNED at Detroit, 1 December 1760. *PG*, 28 September 1759; *HBP*, 5: 210.

Solomon, Ezekiel. Trader captured by Ojibwa at Michilimackinac, 2 June 1763. RANSOMED at Montreal, 15 August 1763. Henry, *Travels* (1901), 49, 50–1, 103; *DCB*, 4: 718–19.

Soning, Antoine. Canadian marine in Captain François-Marie Picoté de Belestre's company. Taken in battle of La Belle Famille, 24 July 1759. Held in Somerset County, NJ. EXCHANGED at Crown Point, NY, 9 December 1760. *JP*, 13: 115; Job Stockton Papers, NYHS.

"Sore Knee." Girl RETURNED at Muskingum, 15 November 1764. *WPHM* 39 (1956): 196.

"Sore Mouth." Pennsylvania boy RETURNED at Muskingum, 15 November 1764. *WPHM* 39 (1956): 192, 196; *PG*, 17 January 1765; *NYG*, 21 January 1765.

Sour Plums. Girl RETURNED at Muskingum, 15 November 1764. *WPHM* 39 (1956): 196.

Sourback, Hannah Maria. Pennsylvania woman. RETURNED at Muskingum, 15 November 1764. *WPHM* 39 (1956): 192; *PG*, 17 January 1765; *NYG*, 21 January 1765; *JP*, 11: 489.

Souwarraghyona. Chenussio Seneca hostage. Given to William Johnson at Fort Niagara, 5 August 1764. MISSING. *JP*, 11: 318, 321, 325.

Sovereign. One of four children of Gower. Held captive with her in Lower Shawnee Town late in 1764. MISSING. *WPHM* 39 (1956): 202.

Sovereign. One of four children of Gower. Held captive with her in Lower Shawnee Town late in 1764. MISSING. *WPHM* 39 (1956): 202.

Sovereign. One of four children of Gower. Held captive with her in Lower Shawnee Town late in 1764. MISSING. *WPHM* 39 (1956): 202.

Sovereign, Gower. Held captive with her four children in Lower Shawnee Town late in 1764. MISSING. *WPHM* 39 (1956): 202.

Sovereign, Joseph. One of four children of Gower. Held captive with her in Lower Shawnee Town late in 1764. WHITE INDIAN killed by Americans in 1789. *WPHM* 39 (1956): 202; Heard, *White into Red*, 453.

Spright. One of two children captured with Michelle in Berks County, PA, 1757. MISSING. *PMHB* 32 (1908): 317.

Spright. One of two children captured with Michelle in Berks County, PA, 1757. MISSING. *PMHB* 32 (1908): 317.

Spright, Michelle. Captured with two children in Berks County, PA, 1757. MISSING. *PMHB* 32 (1908): 317.

Springer, Benjamin. New Jersey captive. Taken at Swarthout's Fort, 22 May 1756. ESCAPED, with John Denite and Thomas Sherby, from Fort Venango, 29 July 1756. Thirty-two days getting home. *PG*, 9 September 1756.

Squissatego. Seneca youth. Captured by Virginia militia at Greenbrier, Augusta County, VA, 3 October 1755. Likely RETURNED by 1758. *EAID*, 3: 445; *VG*, 3 October 1756; *JP*, 12: 389, 899.

St Cyrian. French marine corporal in Naltrie's company. Surrendered with Detroit garrison, 30 November 1760. Sent to France in 1761 for EXCHANGE. *PG*, 15 January and 5 February 1761; *NYM*, 30 March 1761; TNA, WO 1/5, 176.

St Jean. Canadian marine. Captured by Cherokee on lower Ohio River, May 1754. MISSING. Pease and Jenison, eds, *Illinois on the Eve*, 868–9, 912–13.

St Ours. Canadian marine ensign. Captured by Cherokee and Virginians west of Fort Cumberland, MD, 8 June 1757. KILLED the same day. *PG*, 23 June 1757; *NYM*, 27 June 1757; *NYCD*, 7: 282; Hunter, *Forts*, 125–6.

Staffel, Christopher. Boy captured by Delaware in Bethel Township, Lancaster County, PA, 3 November 1756. Reported killed but RANSOMED and reluctantly returned, 7 August 1761. *PMHB* 32 (1908): 310; Haverford College Library, Indian Committee Records, 824/11, vol. 4, n.p.

Stalnacker, Samuel. Trader and militia captain. Captured with his wife by Shawnee on Holston River, Augusta County, VA, 18 June 1755. ESCAPED 10 May 1756. Preston Papers, 1: 83; *PG*, 24 July 1755, 1 July 1756; *NYM*, 28 July 1755, 16 February and 5 July 1756; Haverford College Library, Indian Committee Records, 824/10, vol. 2, n.p.

Stalnacker, [Mrs Samuel]. Captured with her husband by Shawnee on Holston River, Augusta County, VA, 18 June 1755. KILLED six days later. Preston Papers, 1: 83; *PG*, 24 July 1755; *SCG*, 9 November 1755.

Stample, Margaret. Captured in Bethel Township, Lancaster County, PA, 24 October 1756. MISSING. *PMHB* 32 (1908): 310.

Stan, Cornelius/Nelius. Mennonite or Dunker boy about ten years old. RETURNED by Shawnee at Fort Pitt, 26 February 1763. Sent to Philadelphia but unclaimed several weeks later. *PG*, 17 March 1763; "Journal of James Kenny, 1761–1763," ed. Jordan, 178.

Stanford, Archibald. Pennsylvania soldier. RETURNED from captivity and compensated by assembly, 17 September 1760. *V&P*, 7: 5658.

Staut/Stott/Stuart. Of Maryland. Captured with wife and three children, June 1755. Taken to Fort Duquesne. ESCAPED one day's travel north of the fort, 12 July 1755, and traveled to Fort Cumberland, MD. *NYM*, 11 July 1755; *SCG*, 11 September 1755.

Staut/Stott/Stuart. One of at least two children captured with parents in western Maryland, June 1755. MISSING. *NYM*, 11 July 1755; *SCG*, 11 September 1755.

Staut/Stott/Stuart. One of at least two children captured with parents in western Maryland, June 1755. MISSING. *NYM*, 11 July 1755; *SCG*, 11 September 1755.

Staut/Stott/Stuart, [Mrs]. Captured with husband and at least two children in western Maryland, June 1755. MISSING. *NYM*, 11 July 1755; *SCG*, 11 September 1755.

Ste Marie. French trader. Captured by Shawnee at Fort des Miamis, October 1750. MISSING. *MPCP*, 5: 496–8; Pease and Jenison, eds, *Illinois on the Eve*, 362–5.

Steal/Tell, Elizabeth. Young daughter of Richard. Captured by Canadian Iroquois in western Pennsylvania in 1740s. Servant in Canada for a decade. RETURNED by governor of Canada through Albany to Philadelphia, 20 September 1754. LAC, MG 19, F 35/2, lot 680; *PG*, 3 and 31 October 1754; *NYM*, 4 November 1754; *SCG*, 10 October 1754; https://www.familysearch.org.

Stedman, Nathaniel. Soldier in Major Andrew Lewis's company of Virginia Regiment. Captured by Indians near Fort Pitt, 14 May 1759. ESCAPED August 1761. *Journals of the House of Burgesses, 1761–1765*, ed. Kennedy, 100–1, 140; BL, Add. Mss, 21644, fol. 175.

Stephens/Stevenson, Margaret. Twelve year old captured in Cumberland County, PA, 20 March 1764. MISSING. *PG*, 5 April 1764; *NYM*, 9 April 1764; *NYG*, 5 April 1764; BL, Add. Mss, 21650, fol. 103.

Stettler, Alice. Virginia woman. RETURNED at Muskingum, 15 November 1764. *WPHM* 39 (1956): 190; *PG*, 17 January 1765; *NYG*, 21 January 1765.

Stevens, Joseph. Pennsylvania trader. Captured by French and Ottawa at Pickawillany, 21 June 1752. Sent to Canada and France. RETURNED to Philadelphia, 6 January 1753. *PG*, 23 November 1752; Pease and Jenison, eds, *Illinois on the Eve*, 811; *NYM*, 28 May 1753.

Stevens, Nehemiah. Pennsylvania trader. Captured by Delaware English John at Christopher Gist's Ohio trading post at Redstone Creek, 23 April 1754. Sent to Fort Duquesne, Canada, and England. RETURNED. Stobo, *Memoirs*, 91–2; *PG*, 22 December 1757; Hanna, *Wilderness Trail*, vol. 1, 177.

Stewart. Captain in Virginia Regiment. Captured in Major James Grant's defeat at Fort Duquesne, 14 September 1758. RETURNED. Draper Mss, Virginia Papers, 3ZZ48.

Stewart. Woman widowed and captured near Cuthbertson's Fort, Cumberland County, PA, 5 August 1758. MISSING. *PG*, 31 August 1758; *NYM*, 4 September 1758.

Stewart, James, Jr. Orphaned and captured at Cowpasture, Augusta County, VA, September 1759. RETURNED before 17 February 1762. *NYM*, 10 October 1757; Chalkley, *Chronicles of the Scotch-Irish*, vol. 3, 47–8, 78, 84.

Stillwell. Eight-year-old child of Richard. Captured at "Canalaways," Cumberland County, PA, 28 January 1756. MISSING. *PG*, 12 February 1756; *NYM*, 16 February 1756.

Stillwell. Three-year-old child of Richard. Captured at "Canalaways," Cumberland County, PA, 28 January 1756. MISSING. *PG*, 12 February 1756; *NYM*, 16 February 1756.

Stinson, Elizabeth. Pennsylvania woman. RETURNED at Muskingum, 15 November 1764. *WPHM* 39 (1956): 188; *PG*, 17 January 1765; *NYG*, 21 January 1765; *JP*, 11: 490.

Stirley, John. Pennsylvanian taken at "Sheppy" in 1757. RETURNED in Canada. TNA, CO 5/57, fols 119–21.

Stirley, Phebe. Pennsylvanian taken at "Sheppy" in 1757. RETURNED in Canada. TNA, CO 5/57, fols 119–21.

Stobo, Robert. Captain in Virginia Regiment. Taken hostage by Canadians at Fort Necessity, 4 July 1754. Sent to Fort Duquesne and Quebec. Tried for his life. ESCAPED on third attempt, 7 June 1759, and sailed with nine others in an open boat to Louisbourg. *PG*, 25 July and 24 August 1754, 28 June and 5 July 1759; Stobo, *Memoirs*.

Stockton, George. Virginia boy. Captured with his sister, 10 April 1756. RETURNED. Kercheval, *History of the Valley*, 73.

Stockton, Isabel. Virginia girl. Captured with her brother, 10 April 1756. RETAKEN in British capture of Fort Niagara, 25 July 1759. *PJ*, 23 August 1759; *PG*, 23 August 1759; *NYM*, 20 August 1759; *NYG*, 27 August 1759; Kercheval, *History of the Valley*, 73–4.

Stokl, Michel. Canadian marine in De Bonne's company. Captured in battle of La Belle Famille, 24 July 1759. EXCHANGED at Crown Point, NY, 9 December 1760. *JP*, 13: 115; Job Stockton Papers, NYHS.

Stomfield, Joannes. Canadian in the Gaspé marines. Captured in battle of La Belle Famille, 24 July 1759. EXCHANGED at Crown Point, NY, 9 December 1760. *JP*, 13: 115; Job Stockton Papers, NYHS.

Stover, Emmanuel. Connecticut settler in Wyoming Valley, Northampton County, PA. Captured by Delaware, May 1763. RETAKEN by Arthur Montour's war party, March 1764, and brought to Johnson Hall, NY. *PG*, 10 May 1764.

Street, John. Pennsylvania soldier. Captured by Shawnee in fall of Fort Granville, Cumberland County, PA, 31 July 1756. Taken to Kittanning and down Ohio River. ESCAPED 15 June 1757 and came into Fort Cumberland, MD, 11 July 1757. *PG*, 19 August 1756, 28 July 1757; HL, LO, 3925; *NYM*, 1 August 1757.

Stroudman, Catherine/Kitty. Pennsylvania girl. Captured at Conococheague Creek, Cumberland County, PA, 1755. RETURNED at Muskingum, 15 November 1764. *WPHM* 39 (1956): 192; *PG*, 17 January 1765; *NYG*, 21 January 1765; *JP*, 11: 489.

Stroudman, Mary. Pennsylvania girl. Captured at Conococheague Creek, Cumberland County, PA, 1755. RETURNED at Lancaster conference, 13 August 1762. *Minutes of Conferences ... Lancaster, 1762*, 7.

Stroudman, Uly. Pennsylvania girl. Captured at Conococheague Creek, Cumberland County, PA, 1755. RETURNED at Muskingum, 15 November 1764. *WPHM* 39 (1956): 192; *PG*, 17 January 1765; *NYG*, 21 January 1765; *JP*, 11: 489.

Stuart, Charles. Squatter on Indian land in Big Cove, Cumberland County, PA. Captured with family by Delaware, 2 November 1755. Sent to Detroit, Canada, and England. RETURNED via New York, December 1757. Charles recovered possession of his property on return but was killed in Pontiac's War. *NYM*, 17 November 1755, 2 January 1758; *PG*, 13 November 1755, 22 December 1757; "Captivity of Charles Stuart," 58–81; David L. Preston, *The Texture of Contact: European and Indian Settler Communities on the Frontiers of Iroquoia, 1667–1783* (Lincoln, NB: University of Nebraska Press, 2009), 142.

Stuart, Mary. Young daughter of Charles. Captured with family by Delaware at Big Cove, Cumberland County, PA, 2 November 1755. Father failed to recover her in trip of 1762. RETURNED at Muskingum, 15 November 1764. Claimed by a Margaret Stuart until her own child returned. *NYM*, 17 November 1755, 2 January 1758; *PG*, 13 November 1755, 22 December 1757, 17 January 1765; "Journal of James Kenny, 1761–1763," ed. Jordan, 172; *PJ*, 8 August 1765.

Stuart, [Mrs Charles]. Captured with family by Delaware at Big Cove, Cumberland County, PA, 2 November 1755. Taken to Detroit, and then to Canada, England, and New York. RETURNED December 1757. *NYM*, 17 November 1755, 2 January 1758; *PG*, 13 November 1755, 22 December 1757.

Stuart, William. Four-year-old son of Charles. Captured with family by Delaware at Big Cove, Cumberland County, PA, 2 November 1755. Seen at Lower Shawnee Town late in 1764. WHITE INDIAN. "Captivity of Charles Stuart," 59; *NYM*, 17 November 1755, 2 January 1758; *PG*, 13 November 1755, 22 December 1757; *WPHM* 39 (1956): 202.

Studebaker, Elisabeth. Young daughter of Henry. Captured by Delaware near Little Cove, Cumberland County, PA, October 1755. Returned at Muskingum,

15 November 1764, but escaped back to the Delaware ten days later. WHITE INDIAN. *PG*, 17 January 1765; *NYG*, 21 January 1765; Cumberland County Orphan's Court Dockets, vol. 2, 1761–86, Cumberland County Courthouse, Carlisle, PA, entry for 16 November 1762; Heard, *White into Red*, 138–9.

Studebaker, Joseph. Son of Henry. Captured by Delaware near Little Cove, Cumberland County, PA, October 1755. RETURNED at Muskingum, 15 November 1764. *WPHM* 39 (1956): 191; *PG*, 17 January 1765; *NYG*, 21 January 1765.

Studebaker, Philip. Five-year-old son of Henry. Captured by Delaware near Little Cove, Cumberland County, PA, October 1755. RETURNED at Lancaster conference, 13 August 1762. Estate protected by Cumberland County Orphan's Court, 16 November 1762. *Minutes of Conferences ... Lancaster, 1762*, 7; *PG*, 9 September 1762; Cumberland County Orphan's Court Dockets, vol. 2, 1761–86, Cumberland County Courthouse, Carlisle, PA, n.p.

Stuerfages[?], Daniel. Soldier in Captain James Mackay's company of Virginia Regiment. Captured by Indians at fall of Fort Necessity, 4 July 1754. Sent to Fort Niagara and Canada. MISSING. Severance, "Tale of Captives," 296.

Succomabe. Chickasaw warrior living with the Shawnee. Captured by Cherokee, 12 May 1757, and questioned at Fort Lyttleton. MISSING. *PG*, 19 May 1757; *MPCP*, 7: 531.

Sullivan, Nathaniel. Virginian captured 25 September 1758. RETAKEN in surrender of Fort Niagara, 25 July 1759. *NYG*, 27 August 1759; *PG*, 23 August 1759; *PJ*, 23 August 1759.

Sutten, Elizabeth. Sixteen year old captured at Swatara, Lancaster County, PA, 19 May 1757. Likely RETURNED and married William Bagnall, 19 October 1761. Haverford College Library, Indian Committee Records, 824/11, vol. 4, n.p.; *PA*, ser. 2, 2: 239.

Swain, Jonathan. Corporal in Virginia Regiment. Captured by Wyandot in Major James Grant's defeat at Fort Duquesne, 14 September 1758. RETURNED at Detroit, 1 December 1760. *PG*, 28 September 1758; *HBP*, 5: 210.

Swan, Thomas. Soldier in second battalion of Pennsylvania regiment. MISSING after attack on Kittanning, 9 September 1756. *PA*, ser. 2, 2: 458–60; *PG*, 23 September 1756; *NYM*, 27 September 1756.

Swarthout. One of three daughters of Anthony. Orphaned and captured by Delaware in western New Jersey, 22 May 1756. RETURNED, with her *métis* child, by Seneca and Delaware to Johnson Hall, NY, May 1765. *PG*, 9 September 1756, 19 September 1765.

Swarthout. One of three daughters of Anthony. Orphaned and captured by Delaware in western New Jersey, 22 May 1756. RETURNED, with her *métis* child, by Seneca and Delaware to Johnson Hall, NY, May 1765. *PG*, 9 September 1756, 19 September 1765.

Swarthout. One of two *métis* children of the Swarthout girls. Surrendered to William Johnson at Johnson Hall, NY, May 1765, and advertised for family to claim. MISSING. *PG*, 19 September 1765.

Swarthout. One of two *métis* children of the Swarthout girls. Surrendered to William Johnson at Johnson Hall, NY, May 1765, and advertised for family to claim. MISSING. *PG*, 19 September 1765.

Swarthout. Youngest of three daughters of Anthony. Orphaned and captured by Delaware in western New Jersey, 22 May 1756. KILLED the same day. *PG*, 9 September 1756.

Swobe. Young son of Joseph. Captured by Shawnee at Jackson River, Augusta County, VA, 11 September 1756. MISSING. Preston Papers, 1: 83; *PG*, 7 October 1756; *NYM*, 11 October 1756.

Talbot, William. Soldier in the Virginia Regiment. Captured in Major James Grant's defeat at Fort Duquesne, 14 September 1758. RETURNED to Fort Pitt, December 1759. *Journals of the House of Burgesses, 1761–1765*, ed. Kennedy, 68, 71–2; HL, AB, 659.

Tanner, Christopher. Pennsylvania man. RETURNED at Muskingum, 15 November 1764. *WPHM* 39 (1956): 191; *PG*, 17 January 1765; *NYG*, 21 January 1765.

Tawanima. Virginia boy. White Indian RETURNED at Muskingum, 15 November 1764. *WPHM* 39 (1956): 191, 196; *PG*, 17 January 1765; *NYG*, 21 January 1765; *JP*, 11: 488.

Taylor. One of two children of Robert. Captured with family in fall of Bigham's Fort, Cumberland County, PA, 11 June 1756. MISSING. *PG*, 17 and 24 June 1756; *NYM*, 21 and 28 June 1756.

Taylor. One of two children of Robert. Captured with family in fall of Bigham's Fort, Cumberland County, PA, 11 June 1756. MISSING. *PG*, 17 and 24 June 1756; *NYM*, 21 and 28 June 1756.

Taylor, Mary [Mrs Robert]. Captured with family in fall of Bigham's Fort, Cumberland County, PA, 11 June 1756. ESCAPED to Fort Pitt, 25 December 1761. *PG*, 17 and 24 June 1756; *NYM*, 21 and 28 June 1756; Haverford College Library, Indian Committee Records, 824/10, vol. 2, n.p.; "George Croghan's Journal," 419.

Taylor, Robert. Captured with family in fall of Bigham's Fort, Cumberland County, PA, 11 June 1756. MISSING. *PG*, 17 and 24 June 1756; *NYM*, 21 and 28 June 1756.

Teabolt/Tiebolt. One of two sons of Michael. MISSING near Ashby's Fort, Augusta County, VA, 1 April 1756. *NYM*, 19 April 1756; *PG*, 6 May 1756; *SCG*, 1 July 1756.

Teabolt/Tiebolt. One of two sons of Michael. MISSING near Ashby's Fort, Augusta County, VA, 1 April 1756. *NYM*, 19 April 1756; *PG*, 6 May 1756; *SCG*, 1 July 1756.

Teaff/Taafe, Michael. Veteran Pennsylvania trader. Captured by Wyandot at Sandusky, May 1763. MISSING and reportedly died that year. *HBP*, 5: 652n, 837n; *HBP*, 6: 412; https://www.familysearch.org.

Teller, Garrit. New York trader. Likely taken in May 1763. RETURNED to Detroit by 8 September 1763. Gladwin, "Gladwin Manuscripts," 649.

Testard de Montigny, Jean-Baptiste-Philippe (1724–86). Canadian marine officer. Captured by Iroquois at battle of la Belle Famille, 24 July 1759. Sold to British Army and EXCHANGED in France, 15 July 1761. *JP*, 13: 115; *NYCD*, 10: 989; *DCB*, 4: 733–4.

Thiechcapec/Theecheapei. Virginia boy. Captured by Shawnee in 1758 and RETURNED to Fort Pitt, 10 May 1765. *JP*, 11: 720. Less likely taken from the Coves in 1755 as reported in *WPHM* 39 (1956): 198.

Thomas. Daughter of Mary. Captured with her mother in Frederick County, VA, 2 June 1764. RETURNED. *PG*, 14 June 1764; *NYG*, 18 June 1764; Kercheval, *History of the Valley*, 97–9.

Thomas, Jacob. Pennsylvania youth. RETURNED by Shawnee to Fort Pitt, 26 February 1763. "Journal of James Kenny, 1761–1763," ed. Jordan, 178–9, 187.

Thomas, Mary [Mrs Owen]. Widow captured with her daughter in Frederick County, VA, 2 June 1764. ESCAPED two days later. *PG*, 14 June 1764; *NYG*, 18 June 1764; Kercheval, *History of the Valley*, 97–9; Baker, *French and Indian War*, 129.

Thompson, John. Ranger in Captain Perara's company. Captured near Fort Cumberland, MD, in spring of 1757. Taken to Fort Duquesne and Niagara. ESCAPED 13 September 1757. Merlin Stonehouse Transcripts, vol. 2, n.p., Huntington Library and Art Gallery, San Marino, CA.

Thorn. Young child of John. Taken with her mother and sister by Delaware at McCord's Fort, Cumberland County, PA, 1 April 1756. ESCAPED in skirmish at Sideling Hill, 5 April 1756. *PG*, 22 April 1756; *NYM*, 12 April 1756.

Thorn, Martha. Daughter of John. Taken with her mother and sister by Delaware at McCord's Fort, Cumberland County, PA, 1 April 1756. RETAKEN at Kittanning, 8 September 1756. *PG*, 22 April 1756; *NYM*, 12 April 1756; *PA*, ser. 1, 2: 775.

Thorn, [Mrs John]. Taken with two daughters by Delaware at McCord's Fort, Cumberland County, PA, 1 April 1756. ESCAPED in skirmish at Sideling Hill, 5 April 1756. *PG*, 22 April 1756; *NYM*, 12 April 1756.

Thoulouse. Soldier in Detroit garrison. Surrendered to British with the fort, 30 November 1760. Sent to New York and France, where he was EXCHANGED in 1761. *PG*, 15 January and 5 February 1761; *NYM*, 30 March 1761; TNA, WO 1/5, 176.

Tiebout, Bernard. Canadian marine in Captain Charles Deschamps de Boishébert's company. Captured by British Army at battle of La Belle Famille, 24 July 1759. Held in Somerset County, NJ, where he enlisted with the English forces, 27 March 1760. *JP*, 13: 115; Job Stockton Papers, NYHS.

Todd. *Métis* child of Mary. Surrendered with her to the Pennsylvania legation at Lancaster, 19 August 1762. MISSING. *Minutes of Conferences ... Lancaster, 1762*, 7; *PG*, 25 December 1755, 9 September 1762; *MPCP*, 8: 750.

Todd, Mary. Girl from Northampton County, PA. Captured by Delaware near Samuel Dupui's place, 12 December 1755. RETURNED at Lancaster conference, 19 August 1762, by Echgoheson, a Munsee Delaware. *Minutes of Conferences ... Lancaster, 1762*, 7; *PG*, 25 December 1755, 9 September 1762; *MPCP*, 8: 750.

Tony, Sam. Escaped slave from Maryland living with the Delaware. Captured in Iroquois raids on Susquehanna River in January 1764. Delivered to William

Johnson by the Seneca. Sold in the West Indies, January 1765. *JP*, 11: 165–6; *PG*, 17 May 1764; Dowd, *War under Heaven*, 183–5.

Toons, William. Allegheny captive of Indians. REDEEMED by the French, taken to Canada and France, and returned to England by September 1757. TNA, Adm. 1/4323, n.p.

Toople, Isaac. Boy captured near Fort Presqu'île. RELEASED to General Jeffrey Amherst at Montreal by summer of 1761. *PG*, 2 July 1761.

Tosher/Tesher, Elizabeth. Captured in Augusta County, VA. RETURNED at Muskingum, 15 November 1764. *PG*, 17 January 1765; *NYG*, 21 January 1765.

Tostee, Paul. Pennsylvania trader. Captured by Shawnee at Chartier's Town, 18 April 1745. FREED a few hours later. *PG*, 16 May 1745; *NYCD*, 10: 20; Hanna, *Wilderness Trail*, vol. 1, 311.

Towniss/Noondias, Andrew. Delaware hostage given to Colonel Henry Bouquet, 11 November 1764. MISSING, and likely escaped. HL, MM 569, fol. 32.

Tribolet, Jean. Canadian in the Gaspé marines. Captured in battle of La Belle Famille, 24 July 1759. Held in Somerset County, NJ. EXCHANGED at Crown Point, NY, 16 December 1760. *JP*, 13: 115; Job Stockton Papers, NYHS.

Trim, Ezra. Pennsylvanian. Captured at "Leckawecksein" by Delaware, May 1763. RETURNED by Chenussio Seneca at Fort Niagara, July 1764. *PG*, 6 September 1764; *NYG*, 17 September 1764.

Trimble, James (d. 1804). Youth captured in Augusta County, VA, 15 September 1764. RETAKEN five days later. Waddell, *Annals of Augusta*, vol. 2, 412, 433–8.

Trotter, John. Pennsylvania trader at Fort Venango. Captured by Delaware chief Custaloga, 15 August 1753, and given to the French. Taken to Canada and France. RETURNED by January 1754. *MPCP*, 5: 659–60; *PA*, ser. 1, 2: 131–2.

Trouin. Canadian marine in Captain Louis Legardeur de Repentigny's company. Captured in Jumonville incident, 28 May 1754. RETURNED via Martinique, 24 October 1755. *Collections des manuscrits ... Nouvelle France*, vol. 3, 351–2; *PG*, 13 and 27 June, 22 August, and 12 September 1754; *NYM*, 17 June 1754.

Trueax, Adreas. New York trader. Captured near Detroit, May 1763. RETURNED there 30 July 1763. Gladwin, "Gladwin Manuscripts," 646–7; Hay, *Diary*, 54.

Trump. Son of Adam. Taken with his mother near Allemangel, Berks County, PA, 22 June 1757. ESCAPED to Fort Lebanon the next day. *NYM*, 4 July 1757; *PG*, 30 June 1757.

Trump, [Mrs Adam]. Wife of Adam. Widowed and captured with her son near Allemangel, Berks County, PA, 22 June 1757. ESCAPED to Fort Lebanon the next day. *NYM*, 4 July 1757; *PG*, 30 June 1757.

Tuffs, John. Allegheny captive of Indians. REDEEMED by the French, taken to Canada and France, and returned to England in September 1757. TNA, Adm. 1/4323, n.p.

Turnbull. British soldier. Captured at Detroit, 10 May 1763. Still captive in September. RETURNED by 21 March 1766. Gladwin, "Gladwin Manuscripts," 649; *JP*, 5: 89.

Turner, John. Pennsylvania sergeant who surrendered Fort Granville, Cumberland County, PA, 31 July 1756. Taken by Delaware to Kittanning, where he was BURNED to death on 2 August. HL, LO, 3758; *PG*, 19 August and 14 October 1756.

Turner, John, Jr. Infant captured with family in fall of Fort Granville, Cumberland County, PA. Baptized at Fort Duquesne. With Shawnee until RETURNED with his mother in 1759. Hoffman, *Simon Girty*, 224; *Baptismal Register*, ed. Lambing, 78–9; Draper Mss, Frontier Wars Papers, 12U35-8.

Turner, Morris. Pennsylvania trader. Captured with Ralph Kilgore by Indians west of Logstown, 27 May 1750. Given to French commandant at Detroit. ESCAPED at Fort Niagara, August 1750. *MPCP*, 5: 480–4; *Ohio Company Papers*, ed. Bailey, 152–3; Severance, "Tale of Captives," 266–7.

Up de Graave, Catherine. Girl captured with her brother by Delaware near Cushietunk (Wyoming), Northampton County, PA, May 1763. RETURNED by Chenussio Seneca to William Johnson at Fort Niagara, July 1764. *PG*, 6 September 1764; *NYG*, 17 September 1764.

Up de Graave, Peter. Boy captured with his sister by Delaware near Cushietunk (Wyoming), Northampton County, PA, May 1763. RETURNED by Chenussio Seneca to William Johnson at Fort Niagara, July 1764. *PG*, 6 September 1764; *NYG*, 17 September 1764.

Urssenbacher, Abraham. Pennsylvanian soldier. Captured by Potawatomi on 27 July 1759 near Raystown, Cumberland County, PA. Taken to Fort St Joseph and purchased by fort commander there. ESCAPED 18 March 1760, traveling overland through what would become Michigan and Ontario, to arrive at Fort Niagara on 27 May. *Neu-eingerichteter americanischer Geschichts und Haus-Calender ... 1762* (Philadelphia, 1761).

Ustah. Canadian marine in Captain Joseph-Michel Legardeur de Croisille et de Montesson's company. Captured by British in battle of La Belle Famille, 24 July 1759. Held in Somerset County, NJ. EXCHANGED at Crown Point, NY, 9 December 1760. *JP*, 13: 115; Job Stockton Papers, NYHS.

Van Aiken [Van Ellen], Jancke/Yonica. Young daughter of Peter. Orphaned and captured by Delaware in Northampton County, PA, 12 December 1755. RETURNED to a surviving brother by Papoonan at Philadelphia, 12 December 1760. *PMHB* 32 (1908): 314; "Journey on the Forbidden Path," ed. Grumet, 49, 51, 117, 122; *PG*, 25 December 1755.

Van Braam, Jacob. Captain in Virginia Regiment. Hostage to French taken after fall of Fort Necessity, 4 July 1754. FREED at capitulation of Montreal, 8 September 1760. *PG*, 25 July 1754, 5 July 1759, 27 November 1760.

Van Eps, Abraham. New York merchant. Captured at Detroit early in summer of 1763. ESCAPED into the fort, 8 July 1763. *NYM*, 8 August 1763; *PG*, 7 July and 11 August 1763.

Van Slyke/Slyck, Cornelius. Young New York trader. Captured by Ojibwa at Detroit, 9 July 1763. Given to the Potawatomi. ESCAPED at Fort St Joseph, 21 July 1767. Became major trader. Deposition of 21 July 1767, Native American

Collection, Clements Library, University of Michigan, Ann Arbor, MI; *JP*, 8: 672–3.

Vasbas, Louis. Canadian marine in Captain Charles de Sabrevoix's company. Captured at battle of La Belle Famille, 24 July 1759. Held in Somerset County, NJ. EXCHANGED at Crown Point, NY, 9 December 1760. *JP*, 13: 115; Job Stockton Papers, NYHS.

Vatelet, Jean. Canadian marine in Captain Pierre-Jean-Baptiste-François-Xavier Legardeur de Repentigny's company. Captured at battle of La Belle Famille, 24 July 1759. Held in Somerset County, NJ. EXCHANGED at Crown Point, NY, 16 December 1760. *JP*, 13: 115; Job Stockton Papers, NYHS.

Vause, Elizabeth. Daughter of Ephriam. Captured in fall of Vause's Fort, Augusta County, VA, 25 June 1756. MISSING. Preston Papers, 1: 83; *PG*, 28 July 1757, 9 February 1758; *NYM*, 1 August 1757.

Vause, [Mrs Ephriam]. Captured in fall of Vause's Fort, Augusta County, VA, 25 June 1756. MISSING. Preston Papers, 1: 83; *PG*, 28 July 1757, 9 February 1758; *NYM*, 1 August 1757.

Vause, Susannah. Daughter of Ephriam. Captured in fall of Vause's Fort, Augusta County, VA, 25 June 1756. Returned to Fort Pitt by Shawnee warrior Wide Mouth, 26 February 1763. WHITE INDIAN back with the Shawnee a year later. Eventually became Mrs Abraham Inskip of Kentucky. Preston Papers, 1: 83; *PG*, 28 July 1757, 9 February 1758; *NYM*, 1 August 1757; "Journal of James Kenny, 1761–1763," ed. Jordan, 178; *WPHM* 39 (1956): 202; Draper Mss, Kentucky Papers, 11CC220.

Venable, William. Captured near McDowell's Mill, Cumberland County, PA, 8 March 1756. RANSOMED by the French, taken to Canada and France, and returned in England in September 1757. *PG*, 1 April 1756; *NYM*, 5 April 1756; TNA, Adm. 1/4323, n.p.

Vermet, Jean [Mrs John]. Widowed and captured with her daughter in Shawnee attack on Buffalo Creek, NC, September 1754. Sent to Fort Duquesne. MISSING. *SCG*, 3 and 17 October 1754; *SCDIA*, 2: 23, 79; Preston Papers, 1: 83; *Baptismal Register*, ed. Lambing, 56–7.

Vermet, Mary Jane. Infant child of Jean. Captured with her in Shawnee attack on Buffalo Creek, NC, September 1754. Baptized at Fort Duquesne. MISSING. *SCG*, 3 and 17 October 1754; *SCDIA*, 2: 23, 79; Preston Papers, 1: 83; *Baptismal Register*, ed. Lambing, 56–7.

Villars/Visla/Villa, Mary Ann. Girl captured in Delaware attack on Penn's Creek, Cumberland County, PA, 16 October 1755. Seen in captivity. RETURNED at Muskingum, 15 November 1764. *PA*, ser. 2, 7: 427–38; Sipe, *Indian Wars*, 204–9; *WPHM* 39 (1956): 192; *PG*, 17 January 1765; *NYG*, 21 January 1765.

Wagner [Waggoner], Conrad. Soldier captured at surrender of Fort Presqu'île, 21 June 1763. Still with the Potawatomi in July 1767. WHITE INDIAN? Van Slyke deposition of 21 July 1767, Clements Library, Native American Collection, University of Michigan, Ann Arbor, MI.

Wagner [Waggoner], Frederick. Son of Conrad. Captured in attack on Lebanon Township, Berks County, PA, 19 September 1757. RETURNED by Seneca and Susquehanna Delaware to Johnson Hall, NY, May 1765. *PG*, 19 September 1765; *NYG*, 4 July 1765; *NYM*, 18 August 1765.

Wagner [Waggoner], [Mrs Conrad]. Widowed and captured in attack on Lebanon Township, Berks County, PA, 19 September 1757. MISSING. *PMHB* 32 (1908): 309.

Wagner [Waggoner], Peter. Orphaned and captured by Shawnee in Virginia in 1758. Seen at Canestio in June 1760 and at Shamokin two months later. Returned by March 1762. Instructed and confirmed by Rev. Henry Melchior Muhlenberg. Went back to Shawnee as a confirmed WHITE INDIAN. "Journey on the Forbidden Path," ed. Grumet, 107; Haverford College Library, Indian Committee Records, 824/11, vol. 3, 4; *Journals of Henry Melchior Muhlenberg*, trans. Tappert and Doberstein, vol. 1, 496, 523–4; Sugden, *Blue Jacket*, 18.

Walker, John. Virginia scout for General Edward Braddock. Captured by Shawnee and French, 29 May 1755. Taken to Fort Duquesne and Montreal. ESCAPED 14 October 1756. *PG*, 1 July 1755; *NYM*, 5 July 1755; HL, LO, 2254B, 2401A.

Walker, John. Virginia soldier. Taken in surrender of Vause's Fort, Augusta County, VA, 25 June 1756. RETURNED to George Croghan at Fort Pitt, 15 November 1759. Preston Papers, 1: 83; "George Croghan's Journal," 361.

Walker, Peter. Pennsylvania soldier. Captured in surrender of Fort Granville, Cumberland County, PA, 31 July 1756. ESCAPED by 20 August 1756. *MPCP*, 7: 232; Richards, *Pennsylvania-German*, 286–7.

Wallace. Boy captured by Delaware in fall of Seybert's Fort, Augusta County, VA, 28 April 1758. KILLED the same day. Baker, *French and Indian War*, 108–9.

Wallace, Aaron. Youth captured in Cumberland County, PA, 3 July 1763. ESCAPED the next day. BL, Add. Mss, 21642, fol. 452; *HBP*, 6: 410.

Wallace/Wallis, Samuel. Pennsylvanian. RETURNED at Muskingum, 15 November 1764. Became successful land speculator. *WPHM* 39 (1956): 192; *PG*, 17 January 1765; *NYG*, 21 January 1765; *JP*, 11: 488; Paul B. Boyer, *Wild Yankees: The Struggle for Independence along Pennsylvania's Revolutionary Frontier* (Ithaca, NY: Cornell University Press, 2007), 94, 98.

Walter, Ephraim. Twelve-year-old son of Casper. Captured in Cumberland County, PA, 8 August 1756. RETURNED at Muskingum, 15 November 1764. *PG*, 19 August 1756, 17 January 1765; *PJ*, 19 August 1756; *WPHM* 39 (1956): 191; *NYG*, 21 January 1765; *JP*, 11: 486; Jonathan S. Walter, "Genealogical Records of Some Early Fayette County Brethren," unpublished ms. (1979).

Walter, John. Thirteen-year-old son of Casper. Captured in Cumberland County, PA, 8 August 1756. Returned at Muskingum, 15 November 1764, but said to have gone back to be a WHITE INDIAN. *PG*, 19 August 1756, 17 January 1765; *PJ*, 19 August 1756; *WPHM* 39 (1956): 191; *NYG*, 21 January 1765; *JP*, 11: 486; Walter, "Genealogical Records."

Walter, Mary. Eleven-year-old daughter of Casper. Captured in Cumberland County, PA, 8 August 1756. RETURNED 15 March 1762. Claimed inheritance before Cumberland County Orphan's Court, 26 May 1762. *PG*, 19 August 1756; *PJ*, 19 August 1756; Cumberland County Orphan's Court Dockets, vol.

2, 1761–86, Cumberland County Courthouse, Carlisle, PA, n.p.; Walter, "Genealogical Records."

Walter, Rebecca. Daughter of Casper. Captured in Cumberland County, PA, 8 August 1756. RETURNED at Lancaster conference, 8 August 1762. *Minutes of Conferences ... Lancaster, 1762*, 7; *PG*, 19 August 1756; *PJ*, 19 August 1756.

Wampler, Christina. Five-year-old daughter of Peter. Captured by Delaware at Swatara, Lancaster County, PA, 28 September 1757. Adopted by Custaloga. RETURNED at Muskingum, 15 November 1764. *PG*, 6 and 13 October 1757, 17 January 1765; *PMHB* 32 (1908): 310; *WPHM* 39 (1956): 193; *NYG*, 21 January 1765; Haverford College Library, Indian Committee Records, 824/11, vol. 4, n.p.

Wampler, Elizabeth. Three-year-old daughter of Peter. Captured by Delaware at Swatara, Lancaster County, PA, 28 September 1757. Reportedly DIED in captivity before 1762. *PG*, 6 and 13 October 1757; *PMHB* 32 (1908): 309; Haverford College Library, Indian Committee Records, 824/11, vol. 4, n.p.

Wampler, Eve. Ten-year-old daughter of Peter. Captured by Delaware at Swatara, Lancaster County, PA, 28 September 1757. RETURNED by 1760, but not to her family. In custody of a trader at Fort Frederick, MD, in 1762. *PG*, 6 and 13 October 1757; *PMHB* 32 (1908): 309–10; Haverford College Library, Indian Committee Records, 824/11, vol. 4, n.p.

Wampler, Peter. One-year-old son of Peter. Captured by Delaware at Swatara, Lancaster County, PA, 28 September 1757. Reported killed before 1762 but RETURNED at Muskingum, 15 November 1764. *PG*, 6 and 13 October 1757; *PMHB* 32 (1908): 309–10; Haverford College Library, Indian Committee Records, 824/11, vol. 4, n.p.; *PG*, 17 January 1765; *NYG*, 21 January 1765.

Wampler, Philipina. Six-year-old daughter of Peter. Captured by Delaware at Swatara, Lancaster County, PA, 28 September 1757. RETURNED to George Croghan at Fort Pitt in 1762, but promptly given by him to a soldier. *PG*, 6 and 13 October 1757; *PMHB* 32 (1908): 309–10; Haverford College Library, Indian Committee Records, 824/11, vol. 4, n.p.

Wapatenaqua. Infant girl taken on South Branch of Potomac River, Augusta County, VA, 11 September 1755. RETURNED at Muskingum, 15 November 1764. *WPHM* 39 (1956): 198; *JP*, 11: 721.

Wapekapa [White Legs]. Shawnee hostage taken by Colonel Henry Bouquet at Muskingum, 14 November 1764. ESCAPED 3 December 1764. HL, MM, 569, fols 37–8; *MPCP*, 9: 232; *HBP*, 6: 717; Michael N. McConnell, *A Country Between: The Upper Ohio Valley and Its Peoples, 1724–1774* (Lincoln, NB: University of Nebraska Press, 1992), 204.

Ward, John (d. 1793). Three-year-old boy. Captured by Shawnee near Fort Dinwiddie, Augusta County, VA, January 1758. WHITE INDIAN warrior who fought against his kin in 1774, 1792, and 1793. Preston Papers, 1: 83; Heard, *White into Red*, 120; Colin G. Calloway, "Neither White nor Red: White Renegades on the American Indian Frontier," *Western Historical Quarterly* 17 (1986): 51.

Warren. Mother of Mathias. Captured with him by Shawnee near Colonel Thomas Cresap's Sawmill, MD, 13 July 1763. Taken to Upper Shawnee Town. MISSING. BL, Add. Mss, 21650, fol. 116.

Warren, Mathias. Virginia teen. Captured with his mother by Shawnee near Colonel Thomas Cresap's Sawmill, MD, 13 July 1763. ESCAPED 22 March 1764 and traveled eight days to Fort Pitt. Deposition in BL, Add. Mss, 21650, fol. 116.

Watson, [Mrs John]. Captured in Peters Township, Cumberland County, PA, 26 May 1756. MISSING. *PG*, 10 June 1756; *PJ*, 10 June 1756.

Wauntaupenny. Shawnee warrior. Captured by the Cherokee in the spring of 1757. Interrogated at Fort Lyttleton, 12 May 1757. MISSING. *MPCP*, 7: 531; *PG*, 19 May 1757.

Webster. Captain with Maryland forces. Captured in Major James Grant's defeat at Fort Duquesne, 14 September 1758. EXCHANGED. Draper Mss, Virginia Papers, 3ZZ48.

Wechquessinah. Virginia boy. Captured by Shawnee in 1755. RETURNED to Fort Pitt, 10 May 1765. *WPHM* 39 (1956): 197; *JP*, 11: 720.

Weese. Son of George. Orphaned and captured by Shawnee at South Branch of Potomac River, Augusta County, VA, 16 May 1757. MISSING. Preston Papers, 1: 83.

Weese, Peter. Son of George. Orphaned and captured by Shawnee at South Branch of Potomac River, Augusta County, VA, 16 May 1757. Returned at Lancaster conference by Seneca, August 1762, but allowed to return to them. WHITE INDIAN. *Minutes of Conferences ... Lancaster, 1762*, 7, 34–5.

Weeser, Leonard. Son of Nicholas. Captured by Delaware in Northampton County, PA, 1 January 1756. RETURNED at Easton meeting, 11 October 1756. Affidavit of 9 November 1756, *PA*, ser. 1, 3: 45–6; *PMHB* 32 (1908): 315; Sipe, *Indian Wars*, 257.

Weeser, William. Son of Nicholas. Captured by Delaware in Northampton County, PA, 1 January 1756. RETURNED at Easton meeting, 11 October 1756. *PMHB* 32 (1908): 315; *MPCP*, 7: 284; Sipe, *Indian Wars*, 257.

Weidner, George, Jr. Captured in Northampton County, PA, 15 October 1756. Likely RETURNED by 1767, when taxed in Berks County, PA. *PMHB* 32 (1908): 316; *PA*, ser. 3, 18: 56; *U.S. Census of 1790, Pennsylvania*, 32, 41.

Weighthakina. Shawnee hostage given to Colonel Henry Bouquet at Muskingum. ESCAPED from Fort Pitt, 3 December 1764. HL, MM, 569, fols 37–8; *HBP*, 6: 717; *MPCP*, 9: 232.

Welch, John. Pennsylvania trader. Captured by Wyandot and Canadians on Maumee River, 13 May 1763. Taken to Detroit, where he was KILLED the next day by the Ottawa. TNA, WO 34/49, fols 205–6; *HBP*, 6: 412; *PG*, 22 December 1763.

Weldrum. New York trader. Captured between Forts Miami and Ouiatenon in 1763. MISSING. Hay, *Diary*, 65.

West, Christopher. Virginia soldier. Captured by Indians at Reed Creek, VA, February 1756. Given to French, taken to Canada, and sent to England in a flag of truce ship in October 1758. EXCHANGED and rejoined his regiment by November 1759. Compensated by Virginia House of Burgesses. Preston Papers, 1: 83; *Journals of the House of Burgesses, 1758–1761*, ed. McIlwaine, 141, 147–8.

West, Margaret. Captured by Delaware in New Jersey, 26 February 1756. RETURNED by Cayuga John Hudson, 5 September 1756. *New York Historical Society, Collections for 1921* (New York: New York Historical Society, 1922), 94–7; BL, Add. Mss, 21655, fols 208–10; *HBP*, 6: 214–18.

Westbrook, Catherine/Kitty. Captured in Northampton County, PA, 17 November 1763. RETURNED at Muskingum, 15 November 1764. *WPHM* 39 (1956): 190, 196; *PG*, 17 January 1765; *NYG*, 21 January 1765.

Whealand. Man captured by Delaware in Northampton County, PA, 17 November 1763. MISSING. *PG*, 1 December 1763, *NYM*, 5 December 1763.

Wheat, Thomas. Captured by Indians in Augusta County, VA. RETURNED at Muskingum, 15 November 1764. *WPHM* 39 (1956): 194; *PG*, 17 January 1765; *NYG*, 21 January 1765; *JP*, 11: 485.

Wheeler, Marian. Captured by Delaware in Cumberland County, PA, 16 October 1755. MISSING. Sipe, *Indian Wars*, 204–9.

White, William. Nine year old captured by Delaware at Richard Bard's Mill, York County, PA, 13 April 1758. MISSING. *PA*, ser. 1, 3: 396–7; Loudon, ed. *Selection*, vol. 2, 48; *PG*, 11 May 1758; *NYM*, 15 May 1758.

Whitehead. Female thought to be from Virginia. RETURNED at Muskingum, 15 November 1764. *WPHM* 39 (1956): 196.

Wig[g], Tommy. Thought to be from Virginia. RETURNED at Muskingum, 15 November 1764. *WPHM* 39 (1956): 196.

Wilcox. One of four young children of William. Orphaned and captured in a Delaware-Shawnee attack near Patterson's Fort, Cumberland County, PA, 27 January 1756. MISSING. *PG*, 5 February 1756; *NYM*, 9 February 1756; Hunter, *Forts*, 379.

Wilcox. One of four young children of William. Orphaned and captured in a Delaware-Shawnee attack near Patterson's Fort, Cumberland County, PA, 27 January 1756. MISSING. *PG*, 5 February 1756; *NYM*, 9 February 1756; Hunter, *Forts*, 379.

Wilcox. One of four young children of William. Orphaned and captured in a Delaware-Shawnee attack near Patterson's Fort, Cumberland County, PA, 27 January 1756. MISSING. *PG*, 5 February 1756; *NYM*, 9 February 1756; Hunter, *Forts*, 379.

Wilcox, John. One of four young children of William. Orphaned and captured in a Delaware-Shawnee attack near Patterson's Fort, Cumberland County, PA, 27 January 1756. Likely RETURNED to farm in Rye Township, Cumberland County, PA. *PG*, 5 February 1756; *NYM*, 9 February 1756; Hunter, *Forts*, 379; *PA*, ser. 3, 20: 359.

Wilkey, Andrew. Pennsylvania trader. Captured by Delaware near Fort Venango, May 1763. ESCAPED soon thereafter. *HBP*, 6: 413; Hanna, *Wilderness Trail*, vol. 2, 364.

Wilkey, Robert. Pennsylvania trader. Captured by Wyandot at Sandusky in May 1763. MISSING. A Robert Wilkey was taxed for fifty acres and livestock owned in Bedford County, PA, in 1779. *HBP*, 6: 412; *PA*, ser. 3, 22: 186.

Wilkins. Brother of Sally. Captured with her by Delaware near Wind Gap, Northampton County, PA, 27 October 1757. ESCAPED shortly thereafter but not heard of. *PG*, 24 May 1764; *NYG*, 28 May 1764.

Wilkins, Mary. Daughter of James. Captured in Cumberland County, PA, 5 June 1764. RETURNED at Muskingum, 15 November 1764. *WPHM* 39 (1956): 192; *PG*, 17 January 1765; *NYG*, 21 January 1765; *JP*, 11: 489.

Wilkins, Sally. Captured with her brother by Delaware near Wind Gap, Northampton County, PA, 27 October 1757. White Indian who ESCAPED 19 May 1764. *PG*, 10 November 1757, 24 May 1764; *NYG*, 28 May 1764.

Williams. Infant daughter of Richard. Captured with him near Fort Cumberland, MD, 23 June 1755. White Indian RETURNED in 1765. *PG*, 10 July 1755; *MPCP*, 6: 456; Kercheval, *History of the Valley*, 92.

Williams. Young daughter of Richard. Captured with him near Fort Cumberland, MD, 23 June 1755. RETURNED within nine months, but captured in burning of Williams's Fort, Frederick County, VA, 7 March 1756. MISSING. *PG*, 10 July 1755, 15 April 1756; *MPCP*, 6: 456; Kercheval, *History of the Valley*, 97; Baker, *French and Indian War*, 193.

Williams, Catherine [Mrs Daniel]. Widowed and captured with her children by Delaware in Northampton County, PA, 12 December 1755. RETURNED at Muskingum, 15 November 1764. *WPHM* 39 (1956): 192; *PG*, 18 December 1755, 9 September 1756, 17 January 1765; *NYG*, 21 January 1765.

Williams, Daniel. Son of Daniel. Captured with family by Delaware in Northampton County, PA, 12 December 1755. Taken to Tioga and seen at Wyalusing, 28 May 1760. MISSING. *PG*, 18 December 1755; *PMHB* 32 (1908): 315; Sipe, *Indian Wars*, 258; "Journey on the Forbidden Path," ed. Grumet, 67.

Williams, David. Young son of Mary. Captured with her by Shawnee at Greenbrier, Augusta County, VA, 15 July 1763. RETURNED to Fort Pitt, 5 January 1765. *PG*, 7 March 1765; *WPHM* 39 (1956): 197.

Williams, Elizabeth. Daughter of Daniel. Captured with family by Delaware in Northampton County, PA, 12 December 1755. Seen at Wyalusing, 28 May 1760. RETURNED by Mussause, a Munsee Delaware, at Lancaster conference, 19 August 1762. *Minutes of Conferences ... Lancaster, 1762*, 7; *PG*, 18 December 1755; *PMHB* 32 (1908): 315; *MPCP*, 8: 750; "Journey on the Forbidden Path," ed. Grumet, 67, 71, 71n.

Williams, Elizabeth. Pennsylvania trader. Captured by Delaware English John at Christopher Gist's Ohio trading post at Redstone Creek, 23 April 1754. Likely RETURNED. Hanna, *Wilderness Trail*, vol. 1, 177. An Elizabeth Williams was on a Canadian list of prisoners, ready to be exchanged, dated at Montreal, 1 November 1758. TNA, WO 34/10, fol. 56.

Williams, Henry. Son of Daniel. Captured with family by Delaware in Northampton County, PA, 12 December 1755. RETURNED by Conyhochevatoquin, a Munsee Delaware, at Lancaster conference, 19 August 1762. *Minutes of Conferences ... Lancaster, 1762*, 7; *PG*, 18 December 1755; *PMHB* 32 (1908): 315; *MPCP*, 8: 750.

Williams, Jenny. Young daughter of Mary. Captured with her by Shawnee at Greenbrier, Augusta County, VA, 15 July 1763. RETURNED by Shawnee at Fort Pitt, 10 May 1765. *WPHM* 39 (1956): 198; *JP*, 11: 720.

Williams, Mary. Daughter of Daniel. Captured with family by Delaware in Northampton County, PA, 12 December 1755. Sent to Canada. RELEASED to General Jeffrey Amherst in Montreal, July 1761. *PG*, 18 December 1755, 2 July 1761; *PMHB* 32 (1908): 315.

Williams, Mary. Mother of David and Jenny. Captured with them by Shawnee at Greenbrier, Augusta County, VA, 15 July 1763. RETURNED to Fort Pitt, 5 January 1765. Died there within days. *PG*, 7 March 1765; *WPHM* 39 (1956): 197; *HBP*, 6: 754; BL, Add. Mss, 21651, fol. 127.

Williams, Richard. Captured with daughter twelve miles from Wills Creek, Frederick County, VA, 23 June 1755. ESCAPED early the next year, and built Williams's Fort, which was attacked and burned in March 1756. A Richard Williams was trading at Fort Pitt on 4 December 1761. *PG*, 10 July 1755; *MPCP*, 6: 456; *HBP*, 5: 404–5; Baker, *French and Indian War*, 193.

Williamson. Ten-year-old daughter of James. Captured near North Mountain, Cumberland County, PA, 7 November 1763. MISSING. *PG*, 24 November 1763; *NYM*, 28 November 1763; *NYG*, 28 November 1763.

Willson, [Mrs Jammy]. Pennsylvanian. Taken by Delaware and then bought and married by Delaware Jammy Willson. RETURNED, with her *métis* son and some resources, to Fort Pitt, 12 August 1761. "Journal of James Kenny, 1761–1763," ed. Jordan, 7.

Willson. *Métis* son of Jammy. Surrendered with his mother at Fort Pitt, 12 August 1761. MISSING. "Journal of James Kenny, 1761–1763," ed. Jordan, 7.

Wilson, Thomas. Teenage son of John. Captured in Augusta County, VA, July 1764. Taken to Chillicothe Town, where he DIED "of fever" several years later. Baker, *French and Indian War*, 130; Waddell, *Annals of Augusta*, vol. 2, 419.

Winston, Richard. Trader captured by Potawatomi at Fort St Joseph, 27 May 1763. RETURNED by 1 August 1763. Trading at Fort Vincenes in 1766–67. *PG*, 22 December 1763; BL, Add. Mss, 21655, fol. 214; *JP*, 5: 340, 367, 423, 515; *JP*, 10: 715; *JP*, 11: 614; *JP*, 12: 284; *JP*, 13: 296, 405–6.

Wiseman, John. Virginian. Captured on South Branch of Potomac River, Augusta County, VA, 19 March 1758. RETURNED at Muskingum, 15 November 1764. Preston Papers, 1: 83; *WPHM* 39 (1956): 190; *PG*, 17 January 1765; *NYG*, 21 January 1765.

Woleback. Daughter of Andrew. Captured in Berks County, PA, 2 November 1756. MISSING. *PMHB* 32 (1908): 317.

Wood, Experience. Virginia woman. RETURNED at Muskingum, 15 November 1764. *WPHM* 39 (1956): 190; *PG*, 17 January 1765; *NYG*, 21 January 1765; *JP*, 11: 487.

Wood, Sally. Teen captured by Shawnee at Greenbrier, Augusta County, VA, 31 August 1755. Seen at Sackum before March 1759. MISSING. *NYM*, 6 October

1755; *PG*, 9 October 1755; *SCG*, 16 October 1755; "Narrative of Marie Le Roy and Barbara Leininger," *Proceedings of the Pennsylvania-German Society* 15 (1905): 126.

Woods, Archibald. Virginia captive of Delaware. RETURNED at Lancaster conference, 13 August 1762. *Minutes of Conferences ... Lancaster, 1762*, 7.

Woods, George. Captured by Delaware in fall of Bigham's Fort, Cumberland County, PA, 11 June 1756. Bought by John Hudson. Ransomed himself for ten pounds of tobacco a year, and was turned over to the French at Fort Duquesne, July 1757. RETURNED by 1762. Paid ransom at least until 1780. *PG*, 17 and 24 June 1756; *HBP*, 6: 279n; *RCFFP*, 1: 589.

Woods, Martha. Captured at Goose Creek, VA. RETURNED to George Croghan by Wyandoughala, 31 July 1760. "George Croghan's Journal," 380.

Wooley, Martin. Canadian soldier and wagoner. Captured by Delaware party with one white near Fort Venango, February 1759. EXCHANGED 28 April 1759. *PG*, 5 April 1759; *NYG*, 9 April 1759; Hunter, *Forts*, 94.

Workman. One of three young children of George. Captured with their mother at Smith River, Halifax County, VA, 12 September 1763. RETAKEN by Virginia militia the same day. *PG*, 10 and 17 November 1763.

Workman. One of three young children of George. Captured with their mother at Smith River, Halifax County, VA, 12 September 1763. RETAKEN by Virginia militia the same day. *PG*, 10 and 17 November 1763.

Workman. One of three young children of George. Captured with their mother at Smith River, Halifax County, VA, 12 September 1763. RETAKEN by Virginia militia the same day. *PG*, 10 and 17 November 1763.

Workman, [Mrs George]. Captured with her three children at Smith River, Halifax County, VA, 12 September 1763. RETAKEN by Virginia militia the same day. *PG*, 10 and 17 November 1763.

Worley. One of three young children of John. Orphaned and captured in Northampton County, PA, December 1755. MISSING. *PMHB* 32 (1908): 314.

Worley. One of three young children of John. Orphaned and captured in Northampton County, PA, December 1755. MISSING. *PMHB* 32 (1908): 314.

Worley. One of three young children of John. Orphaned and captured in Northampton County, PA, December 1755. MISSING. *PMHB* 32 (1908): 314.

Wotton, John. Pennsylvania trader. Captured by French about 1746. STAYED with the French, and was interpreting for them in July 1756. *PG*, 9 February 1758.

Wunsch. Young daughter of Felix and Orshel. Captured with mother in Bethel Township, Lancaster County, PA, 8 June 1756. MISSING. *PMHB* 32 (1908): 310; *PG*, 17 June 1756.

Wunsch, Orshel [Mrs Felix]. Widowed and captured with her daughter and two of her sister's children in Bethel Township, Lancaster County, PA, 8 June 1756. MISSING. *PMHB* 32 (1908): 310; *PG*, 17 June 1756; *RCFFP*, 1: 64.

Yeth. Son of William. Captured near Hereford, Berks County, PA, 22 March 1756. MISSING. *PG*, 1 April 1756; *PMHB* 32 (1908): 319.

Yoakum/Yocum, Elizabeth. Ten year old captured by Shawnee at Greenbrier, Augusta County, VA, 15 July 1763. RETURNED by Shawnee to Fort Pitt, 5 January 1765. *WPHM* 39 (1956): 197; *PG*, 7 March 1765; *NYG*, 18 March 1765; https://www.familysearch.org.

Yoakum/Yocum, George. Five year old captured by Shawnee at Greenbrier, Augusta County, VA, 15 July 1763. RETURNED at Muskingum, 15 November 1764. *WPHM* 39 (1956): 194; *PG*, 17 January 1765; *NYG*, 21 January 1765; *JP*, 11: 485; Draper Mss, Kentucky Papers, 12CC149-50; https://www.familysearch.org.

Yoakum/Yocum, Margaret [Mrs Felty]. Widowed and captured with three of her children by Shawnee at Greenbrier, Augusta County, VA, 15 July 1763. RETURNED at Muskingum, 15 November 1764. *WPHM* 39 (1956): 194; *PG*, 17 January 1765; *NYG*, 21 January 1765; *JP*, 11: 486; https://www.familysearch.org.

Yoakum/Yocum, Sally/Sarah. Three year old captured by Shawnee at Greenbrier, Augusta County, VA, 15 July 1763. RETURNED by Shawnee to Fort Pitt, 10 May 1765. *WPHM* 39 (1956): 198; *JP*, 11: 720; https://www.familysearch.org.

Young. One of two young sisters captured in Frederick County, VA, August 1758. RETAKEN by Virginia militia after pursuit. Baker, *French and Indian War*, 159–60.

Young. One of two young sisters captured in Frederick County, VA, August 1758. RETAKEN by Virginia militia after pursuit. Baker, *French and Indian War*, 159–60.

Young, Betty. Daughter of Samuel Young. Captured in Lancaster County, PA, 18 August 1758. RETURNED at Muskingum, 15 November 1764. *WPHM* 39 (1956): 192; *PG*, 25 July 1757, 17 January 1765; *NYG*, 21 January 1765.

Young, Nelly [Helen] [Mrs Samuel Young]. Captured in Lancaster County, PA, 20 August 1757. ESCAPED to Fort Augusta the next day. *PA*, ser. 2, 2: 696; *PG*, 25 August and 1 September 1757; *NYM*, 5 September 1757.

Young, John. Soldier in Pennsylvania "Light Horse." Captured in 1760. RETURNED at Detroit, 1 December 1760. *HBP*, 5: 210.

Young, William. Virginian. Taken in 1757. RETURNED at Muskingum, 15 November 1764. *WPHM* 39 (1956): 189; *PG*, 17 January 1765; *NYG*, 21 January 1765; *JP*, 11: 485.

Zaslov. Son of John George. Orphaned and captured near Allamingal, Lynn Township, Northampton County, PA, 14 February 1756. MISSING. *PMHB* 32 (1908): 319; *PG*, 19 February and 1 April 1756.

NOTES

INTRODUCTION

1 For a much broader comparison concerning death rituals, see Erik R. Seeman, *Death in the New World: Cross-Cultural Encounters, 1492–1800* (Philadelphia, PA: University of Pennsylvania Press, 2010).

2 "The Narrative of Marie Le Roy and Barbara Leininger," *PA*, ser. 2, 7: 429.

CHAPTER ONE

1 James H. Merrell, *Into the American Woods: Negotiators on the Pennsylvania Frontier* (New York: Norton, 1999), 146.

2 Leroy V. Eid, "'A Kind of Running Fight': Indian Battle Tactics in the Late Eighteenth Century," *WPHM* 71 (1988): 148–71; Richard Aquila, "Down the Warrior's Path: The Causes of the Southern Wars of the Iroquois," *American Indian Quarterly* 4 (1978): 211–22.

3 David Zeisberger, "David Zeisberger's History of the Northern American Indians," *Ohio Archaeological and Historical Publications* 19 (1910): 101–2.

4 An 1824 interview with Tenskwatawa, the Shawnee prophet and brother of Tecumseh, reported in *Shawnee Traditions: C.C. Trowbridge's Account*, ed. Vernon Kinietz and Erminie W. Voegelin (Ann Arbor, MI: Michigan University Press, 1939), viii–x, 11–12. For a similar claim, alluding to the Chickasaw, see James Adair, *Adair's History of the American Indians* (1775; reprint, Johnson City, TN: Watauga, 1930), 416.

5 Verner W. Crane, *The Southern Frontier, 1670–1732* (Ann Arbor, MI: Michigan University Press, 1929), 12–21; J. Leitch Wright, *The Only Land They Knew: The Tragic Story of the American Indians of the Old South* (New York: Free Press, 1981), 105–7; James Merrell, *The Indians' New World: Catawbas and Their Neighbors from European Contact through the Era of Removal* (Chapel Hill, NC: University of North Carolina Press, 1989), 40–1, 118–19, 135; Marvin T. Smith, "Aboriginal Population Movements in the Early Historic Period Interior Southeast," in *Powhatan's Mantle: Indians in the Colonial Southeast*, ed. Peter H. Wood, George A. Waselkov, and M. Thomas Hatley (Lincoln, NB: University of Nebraska Press, 1989), 30. See also Dwight L. Smith, "Shawnee Captivity Ethnohistory," *Ethnohistory* 2 (1955): 29–57. On the Miseekwaaweekwaakee, see Richard White, *The Middle Ground:*

Indians, Empires, and Republics in the Great Lakes Region, 1650–1815 (New York: Cambridge University Press, 1991), 325.

6 Eid, "'A Kind of Running Fight,'" 158.

7 Daniel K. Richter, "War and Culture: The Iroquois Experience," *W&MQ* 40 (1983): 528–59; José António Brandâo, *"Your fyre shall burn no more": Iroquois Policy toward New France and Its Native Allies to 1701* (Lincoln, NB: University of Nebraska Press, 1997), esp. 72–8; Susan Johnston, "Epidemics, the Forgotten Factor in Seventeenth-Century Native Warfare in the St. Lawrence Region," in *Native People, Native Lands*, ed. Bruce A. Cox (Ottawa, ON: Carleton University Press, 1987), 14–31. On Tanaghrisson, see "Journal de Joseph-Gaspard Chaussegros de Léry, Lieutenant des troupes, 1754–1755," in *RAPQ, 1927–1928* (Quebec City, QC: Quebec Archives, 1928), 367; and William A. Hunter, "Tanaghrisson," *DCB*, 3: 613–15.

8 Richter, "War and Culture," 528–59; Richard Aquila, *The Iroquois Restoration: Iroquois Diplomacy on the Colonial Frontier, 1701–1754* (Detroit, MI: Wayne State University Press, 1983), 205–32; Bruce G. Trigger, *The Children of Aataentic*, 2 vols (Montreal, QC, and Kingston, ON: McGill-Queen's University Press, 1976), vol. 2, 789–840; James Lynch, "The Iroquois Confederacy and the Adoption and Administration of Non-Iroquoian Individuals and Groups Prior to 1756," *Man in the Northeast* 30 (1985): 83–99; Laurence M. Hauptmann, "Refugee Havens: The Iroquois Villages of the Eighteenth Century," in *American Indian Environments: Ecological Issues in Native American History*, ed. Christopher Veesey and Robert Venables (Syracuse, NY: Syracuse University Press, 1980), 128–39.

9 Amy Turner Bushnell, "Ruling 'the Republic of Indians' in Seventeenth-Century Florida," in *Powhatan's Mantle: Indians in the Colonial Southeast*, ed. Peter H. Wood, George A. Waselkov, and M. Thomas Hatley (Lincoln, NB: University of Nebraska Press, 1989), 136; Ramón A. Gutiérrez, *When Jesus Came, the Corn Mothers Went Away: Marriage, Sexuality, and Power in New Mexico, 1500–1846* (Stanford, CA: Stanford University Press, 1991), 149–56, 180–90; James F. Brooks, *Captives and Cousins: Slavery, Kinship, and Community in the Southwest Borderlands* (Chapel Hill, NC: University of North Carolina Press, 2002), esp. 1–19; Brett Rushforth, "'A Little Flesh We Offer You': The Origins of Indian Slavery in New France," *W&MQ* 60 (2003): 777–808. On the Pawnee "Morning Star" female sacrifices, see James R. Murie, *Ceremonies of the Pawnee* (Lincoln, NB: University of Nebraska Press, 1989), 114–36.

10 Eric Hinderaker, *Elusive Empires: Constructing Colonialism in the Ohio Valley, 1673–1800* (New York: Cambridge University Press, 1997), 16; Marcel Trudel, *L'esclavage au Canada français* (Quebec City, QC: Laval University Press, 1960), 61–7, 77, 99–103. Seventy-nine *panis* died in the Montreal General Hospital between 1754 and 1799, according to J.C. Hamilton, "The Panis – An Historical Outline of Canadian Indian Slavery in the Eighteenth Century," *Proceedings of the Royal Canadian Institute*, ns, 1 (1909): 24.

11 Brooks, *Captives and Cousins*, 15n, raises this possibility. In the surrender of Canada, *panis* and African slaves were to stay with their masters and be raised as Catholics, though General Jeffrey Amherst rather ambiguously excluded "Those we may assume were carried off as spoils of war" in clause 47 of capitulation. See *Memoires et Documents relatifs a l'histoire du Canada* (Montreal, QC, 1859), 9. The Ottawa sold a Pawnee at Fort Oswego in 1750, and he was still a slave in Albany in 1771. Sir William Johnson accepted a *panis* slave as a personal gift, negotiated the return of *panis* slaves of English merchants, attempted to trade a *panis* for an English captive, and became involved in the case of two *panis* who murdered their English master. See *JP*, 8: 153–4; *JP*, 10: 161, 269, 409–15, 431–2, 519–21, 690; and *JP*, 11: 280, 287, 310. Johnson claimed that the Ottawa had been selling such captives at Oswego since 1728. See *JP*, 1: 260–1. On Indian slaves in New France, see Brett Rushforth, *Bonds of Alliance: Indigenous and Atlantic Slaveries in New France* (Chapel Hill, NC: University of North Carolina Press, 2012).

12 Crane, *Southern Frontier*, 12–21; Wright, *Only Land They Knew*, 105–7; Merrell, *Indians' New World*, 36–43; Smith, "Aboriginal Population Movements," 30; Alan Gallay, *The Indian Slave Trade: The Rise of the English Empire in the Southeast; 1670–1717* (New Haven, CT: Yale University Press, 2002), esp. 294–305; Patricia K. Galloway, *Choctaw Genesis, 1500–1700* (Lincoln, NB: University of Nebraska Press, 1995), 356; Steven C. Hahn, *The Invention of the Creek Nation, 1670–1763* (Lincoln, NB: University of Nebraska Press, 2004), 52–4, 76–9.

13 Stanford Winston, "Indian Slavery in the Carolina Region," *Journal of Negro History* 19 (1934): 434.

14 Rushforth, "'A Little Flesh,'" 777–808. The population of Illinois country in a 1752 census was 1,380, 446 of whom were black slaves, and 149 Indian slaves. See Carl Ekberg, *French Roots in the Illinois Country: The Mississippi Frontier in Colonial Times* (Urbana, IL: University of Illinois Press, 1998), 152. See also Frank Raymond Secoy, *Changing Military Patterns on the Great Plains* (Locust Valley, NY: J.J. Augustin, 1953), 78–9; Daniel H. Usner Jr, *Indians, Settlers, and Slaves in a Frontier Exchange Economy: The Lower Mississippi Valley before 1783* (Chapel Hill, NC: University of North Carolina Press, 1992), 56–9; and Hinderaker, *Elusive Empires*, 118.

15 *NYCD*, 10: 114–16, 141, 145, 149–52, 156–7; White, *Middle Ground*, 76–82.

16 Aquila, "Down the Warrior's Path."

17 For the massive demands on the Canadian militia after 1745, see Louise Dechêne, *Le Peuple, l'État et la Guerre au Canada sous le régime français* (Montreal, QC: Boreal, 2008). See also former prisoner Enos Bishop's acerbic remarks in *NYM*, 11 August 1755.

18 LAC, MG 19, F 35/2, lot 680, 76; *PG*, 3 and 31 October 1754, where she is described as the daughter of Richard Tell. Charles Cook, Elizabeth's Caughnawaga *métis* guide, reported that Duquesne expected an "ambassador" to come to Fort Ste Frédéric.

19 Without official approval, George Croghan equipped four war parties, totaling about 100 men, who went against the Cherokee in the spring of 1760. See "George Croghan's Journal, April 3, 1759, to April [30], 1763," *PMHB* 71 (1947): 369.

20 Gage to Stuart, 27 January 1764, Thomas Gage Papers, American Series, 1755–75, p. 13, Clements Library, University of Michigan, Ann Arbor, MI; *NYCD*, 7: 777–8; *JP*, 4: 279–80, 296; *JP*, 12: 21; James H. Merrell, "'Their Very Bones Shall Fight': The Catawba-Iroquois Wars," in *Beyond the Covenant Chain: The Iroquois and Their Neighbors in Indian North America, 1600–1800*, ed. Daniel K. Richter and James H. Merrell (Syracuse, NY: Syracuse University Press, 1987), 130–1.

21 Merrell, *Into the American Woods*, 167–75; Aquila, *Iroquois Restoration*, 186–7; Warren R. Hofstra, *The Planting of New Virginia: Settlement and Landscape in the Shenandoah Valley* (Baltimore, MD: Johns Hopkins University Press, 2004), 17–49. Trader Thomas McKee witnessed the Great Island meeting and, at the urging of a white captive then with the Shawnee, fled for his life.

22 Pennsylvania Historical and Museum Commission, Harrisburg, RG 21; "Witham Marshe's Journal of the Treaty Held with the Six Nations by the Commissioners of Maryland, and Other Provinces, at Lancaster, in Pennsylvania, June, 1744," *Massachusetts Historical Society Collections*, ser. 1, 7 (1800): 171–201; *The Treaty Held with the Indians of the Six Nations at Lancaster, in Pennsylvania, in June, 1744* (Williamsburg, VA, 1744); Francis Jennings, *The Ambiguous Iroquois Empire* (New York: Norton, 1984), 356–75.

23 For signs and survivors of early eighteenth-century raids, see John Lawson, *A New Voyage to Carolina*, ed. Hugh Talmage Lefler (Chapel Hill, NC: University of North Carolina Press, 1967), 29, 50–6, 59.

24 Merrell, "'Their Very Bones,'" 115–33; quotation from *SCDIA*, 1: 144–5.

25 Merrell, "'Their Very Bones,'" 115–33. See also D. Peter MacLeod, *The Canadian Iroquois and the Seven Years' War* (Toronto, ON: Dundurn, 1996), 37–60.

26 The traders' later testimony mentions no Cherokee companions, but six Cherokee, two men, two women, and two children were reported captured by "Northern Indians" about this time. See Preston Papers, 1: 72.

27 *MPCP*, 5: 643–4; J. Lunn, "The Illegal Fur Trade out of New France, 1713–60," *Canadian Historical Association Annual Report* (1939): 61–79.

28 John Faulkner deposed, before Samuel Smith on 24 April 1756, that he was with the party captured 26 January 1753 and was the only one who escaped being captured. See *The Ohio Company Papers, 1753–1817, Being Primarily Papers of the "Suffering Traders" of Pennsylvania*, ed. Kenneth P. Bailey (Arcata, CA: N.p., 1947), 40; Randolph C. Downes, *Council Fires on the Upper Ohio* (Pittsburgh, PA: University of Pittsburgh Press, 1940), 65; and *MPCP*, 5: 627. In what was likely a related incident, trader John Finley escaped capture near the Kentucky River, but three of his servants were killed. See *PG*, 10 May 1753; and Charles A. Hanna, *The Wilderness Trail, Or*

the Ventures and Adventures of the Pennsylvania Traders on the Allegheny Path, 2 vols (New York: Putnam, 1911), vol. 2, 212–38. Lowery had a French price of $1,000 on his head in 1750. See *MPCP*, 5: 480–4.

29 *MPCP*, 5: 627, 643–4; *NYM*, 7 and 14 May 1753; *PG*, 10 May and 27 September 1753.

30 *NYM*, 24 September 1753. Alexander McGinty petitioned the Pennsylvania Assembly on 15 October 1753, mentioning that he had been ransomed by the mayor of Albany for about £20, was broke, needed clothes, and required money to get home to Cumberland County. He was granted £6 for the last of these purposes. See *PA*, ser. 8, 5: 3625; and *MPCP*, 5: 663–4.

31 *SCDIA*, 1: 126–7.

32 *SCG*, 11 April, 28 May, and 12 June 1753; *SCDIA*, 1: 414–20.

33 Helen H. Tanner, *Atlas of Great Lakes Indian History* (Norman, OK: University of Oklahoma Press, 1987), map 9, dates the settlement from 1756. See also Thomas Pownall, *A Topographical Description of the Dominions of the United States of America*, ed. Lois Mulkearn (1784; reprint, New York: Arno, 1976), 143: "Though the Quantity of good Land on Ohio, and its Branches, is vastly great, and the Conveniencies attending it so likewise; we may esteem that on Muskingum the Flower of it all."

34 George Croghan had a "trading place" there and flew an English flag during a visit in the fall of 1750. See Nicholas B. Wainwright, *George Croghan, Wilderness Diplomat* (Chapel Hill, NC: University of North Carolina Press, 1959), 37–8.

35 *SCDIA*, 1: 424; *SCG*, 18 June 1753. On a black wampum belt for doomed captives, see "The Narrative of John Slover," in *A Selection of Some of the Most Interesting Narratives of Outrages Committed by the Indians in Their Wars with the White People*, ed. Archibald Loudon, 2 vols (Carlisle, PA, 1808–11), vol. 1, 17–32. On prisoners ties, see Thomas Ridout, "Narrative of the Captivity among the Shawanese Indians, in 1788, of Thomas Ridout, afterwards Surveyor-General of Upper Canada, from the Original Manuscript in Possession of the Family," in *Ten Years of Upper Canada in Peace and War, 1805–1815*, ed. Matilda Edgar (Toronto, ON, 1890), 354. On the Shawnee use of medicine bundles, see Charles Johnston, *A Narrative of the Incidents Attending the Capture, Detention, and Ransom of Charles Johnston* (New York, 1827), 166.

36 Itawachcomequa was from the prestigious Chalahgawtha (Chillicothe) Shawnee division, and was related to Munsee Delaware war captain Kageshquanohel (the Pipe), who would later lead the Ohio Wolf phratry of the Delaware. See Hanna, *Wilderness Trail*, vol. 1, 232, 280–1, 287–8, 309, 311, 325, 331; *NYCD*, 10: 20; *The Appalachian Indian Frontier: The Edmond Atkin Report and Plan of 1755*, ed. Wilbur R. Jacobs (Lincoln, NB: University of Nebraska Press, 1967), 65, 65n; Jennings, *Ambiguous Iroquois Empire*, 269–70; and Merrell, *Into the American Woods*, 73–5. See also Francis Jennings, "Bisaillon (Bezellon, Bizaillon), Peter," *DCB*, 3: 65–6; White, *Middle Ground*, 190–2; and Michael N. McConnell, *A Country Between: The Upper*

Ohio Valley and Its Peoples, 1724–1774 (Lincoln, NB: University of Nebraska Press, 1992), 53–4.

On Captain Pipe, who was loaned to the Shawnee after the killing of Itawachcomequa, see *PA*, ser. 1, 3: 83. He was one of the "chief warriors" at the Fort Pitt treaty in May 1764 and still prominent in 1775. See *MPCP*, 9: 256; and R.G. Thwaites and L.P. Kellogg, eds, *The Revolution on the Upper Ohio, 1775–1777* (Port Washington, NY: Kennikat, 1970), 88. See also Colin G. Calloway, "Captain Pipe," *ANB*; and C.A. Weslager, *The Delaware Indians: A History* (New Brunswick, NJ: Rutgers University Press, 1972), 64, 250, 298.

37 In the 8 February 1752 letter, his name was rendered "Loawaghcomico." See Hamilton to Glen, 30 October 1753, *MPCP*, 5: 570, 685, 696–8.

38 *MPCP*, 6: 153; Hanna, *Wilderness Trail*, vol. 2, 139, 159; "Conrad Weiser's Journal of a Tour of the Ohio, August 11–October 2, 1748," in *Early Western Travels, 1748–1846*, ed. R.G. Thwaites, 32 vols (Cleveland, OH: Arthur H. Clark, 1904–07), vol. 1, 32; White, *Middle Ground*, 243. In 1753 he was married to the sister of Lepechkewe, called "the Young King." See *MPCP*, 6: 153, 160.

39 *SCDIA*, 1: 421; *SCG*, 18 June 1753. On the Bull family, and on James Glen, see W. Stitt Robinson, James Glen, from Scottish Provost to Royal Governor of South Carolina (Westport, CT: Greenwood, 1996).

40 Reprinted in *PG*, 26 July 1753; and in *NYM*, 30 July 1753.

41 *Appalachian Indian Frontier*, ed. Jacobs, 43; *SCDIA*, 1: 421–7, 433.

42 On Iroquois held by the French, see W.J. Eccles, "Denonville et les galériens iroquois," and Jean Leclerc, "Denonville et ses captifs iroquois," both in *Revue d'Histoire de l'Amérique Française* 14 (1960–61): 408–29, 545–58; and Jon Parmenter, *The Edge of the Woods: Iroquoia, 1534–1701* (East Lansing, MI: Michigan State University Press, 2010), 252–4n24. For evidence that execution was more acceptable than imprisonment, see Jan Grabowski, "French Criminal Justice and Indians in Montreal, 1670–1760," *Ethnohistory* 43 (1996): 405–29.

43 *SCDIA*, 1: 456.

44 Glen to Hamilton, 12 October 1753, *MPCP*, 5: 699–700; Glen to Hamilton, 3 October 1753, *SCDIA*, 1: 462–4.

45 Two years earlier, the Shawnee had threatened the Miami with war following the capture of a Shawnee woman and a boy. See *Christopher Gist's Journals*, ed. William M. Darlington (Pittsburgh, PA, 1893), 46. See also Lawrence H. Keeley, *War before Civilization* (New York: Oxford University Press, 1996), 85–8; and Theda Perdue, *Slavery and the Evolution of Cherokee Society, 1540–1866* (Knoxville, TN: University of Tennessee Press, 1979), 6.

46 Hamilton to Glen, 30 October 1753, *MPCP*, 5: 685, 696–8; Dinwiddie to Glen, 26 October 1753, *SCDIA*, 1: 466–7; Benjamin Franklin, *The Papers of Benjamin Franklin*, ed. Leonard W. Labaree, 29 vols (New Haven, CT: Yale University Press, 1959–92), vol. 5, 105–6. Compare Francis Jennings,

Empire of Fortune: Crowns, Colonies, and Tribes in the Seven Years' War in America (New York: Norton, 1988), 57–9.

47 *JP*, 9: 755; *SCG*, 29 October 1753; *SCDIA*, 1: 468; *NYM*, 30 July 1753; *MPCP*, 5: 706.

48 *SCDIA*, 1: 464–5, 467–8; *JP*, 9: 755; *SCG*, 29 October 1753; *NYM*, 30 July 1753.

49 Howard N. Eavenson, *Map Maker and Indian Trader* (Pittsburgh, PA: University of Pittsburgh Press, 1949); *MPCP*, 5: 698–700, 704. According to Croghan, Patten was paid £50 Pennsylvania currency to undertake the trip. See *PA*, ser. 1, 2: 209–10.

50 This town, of approximately 150 houses and 300 warriors, dated from the 1730s, had been destroyed by flood the previous summer, and was being rebuilt farther up the Scioto River. See Matthew C. Ward, "La guerre sauvage: The Seven Years' War on the Virginia and Pennsylvania Frontier" (PhD diss., College of William and Mary, 1992), 21; and Tanner, *Atlas of Great Lakes*, map 9. Three years later, escaped captive Samuel Stalnacker estimated that there were only 220 warriors in these Shawnee towns on the Muskingum River. Quoted in Chester Raymond Young, "The Effects of the French and Indian War on Civilian Life in the Frontier Counties of Virginia, 1754–1763" (PhD diss., Vanderbilt University, 1969), 13.

51 Hamilton to Glen, 6 December 1753, *SCDIA*, 1: 471; *MPCP*, 5: 704–9; Eavenson, *Map Maker*, 154–5.

52 *PA*, ser. 1, 2: 209–10.

53 "Croghan's Journal, 1754," in *MPCP*, 5: 732; and in R.G. Thwaites, ed., *Early Western Travels, 1748–1846*, 32 vols (Cleveland, OH: Arthur H. Clark, 1904–07), vol. 1, 74–5; *Papiers Contrecoeur et autres documents concernant le conflit anglo-français sur l'Ohio de 1745 à 1756*, ed. Fernand Grenier (Quebec City, QC: Laval University Press, 1952), 99–101, 128; Eavenson, *Map Maker*, 52–61; Hanna, *Wilderness Trail*, vol. 2, 3; William A. Hunter, *Forts on the Pennsylvania Frontier, 1753–1758* (Harrisburg, PA: Pennsylvania Historical and Museum Commission, 1960), 35, 103. On French commander Michel Maray de La Chauvignerie, see *DCB*, 2: 126, 625; and *DCB*, 3: 101, 320, 401, 614.

54 *Papiers Contrecoeur*, ed. Grenier, 99–101, 128; *MPCP*, 5: 734.

55 There is some confusion about whether Newcomer (Netawatwees) signed as a Delaware or a Shawnee, but he was definitely the former. See "Journal of James Kenny, 1761–1763," ed. John W. Jordan, *PMHB* 37 (1913): 187; and David McClure, *Diary of David McClure, Doctor of Divinity, 1748–1820* (New York, 1899), 61. See also BL, Add. Mss, 21655, fol. 251; Earl P. Olmstead, *Blackcoats among the Delaware* (Kent, OH: Kent State University Press, 1991), 10; and Gregory Evans Dowd, *A Spirited Resistance: The North American Indian Struggle for Unity, 1745–1815* (Baltimore, MD: Johns Hopkins University Press, 1991), 68–9.

56 Croghan's surprisingly candid translation is printed in *MPCP*, 5: 734. See also Hanna, *Wilderness Trail*, vol. 1, 360, 375; and compare Wainwright, *George Croghan*, 57–60.

57 HSP, Thomas Penn Letterbooks, vol. 3, 295; *MPCP*, 5: 730–5, 750–1, 760–3; Eavenson, *Map Maker*, 52–70; Howard N. Eavenson, "Pattin's Map of the Road to Shannopin Town," *WPHM* 27 (1944): 21–8.

58 "Journal de Joseph-Gaspard Chaussegros de Léry," 409–10; F.J. Thorpe, "Chaussegros de Léry, Joseph-Gaspard," *DCB*, 4: 145–7.

59 The fullest account is Ian K. Steele, "Shawnee Origins of Their Seven Years' War," *Ethnohistory* 53 (2006): 657–87. For another representation of Indian agency in the coming of war, see Fred Anderson, *Crucible of War: The Seven Years' War and the Fate of Empire in British North America, 1754–1766* (New York: Knopf, 2000), 5–21. The Shawnee captivity is not considered in Matthew C. Ward, *Breaking the Backcountry: The Seven Years' War in Virginia and Pennsylvania, 1754–1765* (Pittsburgh, PA: University of Pittsburgh Press, 2003), but there are a few words on the subject in Ward, "La guerre sauvage," 292. Part of the Shawnee story is mentioned in White, *Middle Ground*, 243–4; and in McConnell, *Country Between*, 120.

60 Deposition of 18 August 1757, in HSP, Penn Mss, Indian Affairs, vol. 3, nos 24–5.

61 Haverford College Library, Indian Committee Records, 824/10, vol. 1, n.p.

62 *JP*, 9: 755; *MPCP*, 7: 540.

63 *MPCP*, 8: 197–8; *PA*, ser. 1, 3: 548–50. A Delaware prisoner contended in 1757 that his people went to war by accepting a Shawnee war belt. See *PA*, ser. 1, 3: 147.

64 Henry Gladwin, "The Gladwin Manuscripts: With an Introduction and a Sketch of the Conspiracy of Pontiac," *Michigan Pioneer and Historical Society Collections* 27 (1897): 671.

65 *MPCP*, 7: 531–2.

66 BL, Add. Mss, 21655, fol. 91.

67 *MPCP*, 6: 153.

68 *SCG*, 3 and 17 October 1754; *PJ*, 24 October 1754; *The Baptismal Register of Fort Duquesne*, ed. A.A. Lambing (Pittsburgh, PA, 1885), 56–7. Two "white children," said to be taken at the Broad River, accompanied twenty Shawnee families who came from the Ohio Valley to Cherokee country in August of the next year. See *SCDIA*, 2: 79. In March 1755 the nineteen-month-old child of captives "Jeanes Voleenbork" and "John Vermet" of North Carolina was baptized at Fort Duquesne. Vermet, of French origin, was reportedly killed by the Shawnee "while coming to join the Catholics of these parts." See *Baptismal Register*, ed. Lambing, 56–7. See also Croghan to Johnson, 15 May 1755, *JP*, 1: 496.

69 See Ian K. Steele, "The Shawnee and the English: Captives and War, 1753–1765," in *The Boundaries between Us: Natives and Newcomers along the Frontiers of the Old Northwest Territory, 1750–1850*, ed. Daniel Barr (Kent, OH: Kent State University Press, 2006), 1–24.

70 *PA*, ser. 1, 3: 83.

71 *PG*, 27 December 1753; *NYM*, 31 December 1753.

72 Preston Papers, 1: 83; *NYM*, 18 March 1754; *PG*, 5 September 1754; Alexander Scott Withers, *Chronicles of Border Warfare, or A History of the Settlement by the Whites, of North Western Virginia, and of the Indian Wars and Massacres, in that section of the state, with reflections, anecdotes, etc. ...* (1831; reprint, New York: Arno, 1971), 74–5. The Foyles are called the "Files" in Otis K. Rice, *The Allegheny Frontier: West Virginia Beginnings, 1730–1830* (Lexington, KY: University Press of Kentucky, 1970), 30.

73 *The Diaries of George Washington*, ed. Donald Jackson and Dorothy Twohig, 6 vols (Charlottesville, VA: University Press of Virginia, 1976–79), vol. 1, 150; *PG*, 26 February 1754.

74 *Diaries of George Washington*, ed. Jackson and Twohig, vol. 1, 156.

75 *PG*, 12 March 1754; *SCG*, 26 March 1754.

76 Arent Stevens to Commissioners, 20 March 1754, LAC, MG 19, F 35/2, lot 680, 24–5.

77 LAC, MG 19, F 35/2, lot 680, 91; *PJ*, 14 January 1755; *PA*, ser. 1, 2: 244–5.

78 Thomas King, speaking at Easton, 18 October 1758, *EAID*, 3: 445. The incident had been reported in *VG*, 3 October 1755, and in *NYM*, 20 October 1755, where the Seneca were called "Northern Indians." King was asking about the fate of the captured Seneca youth, Squissatego, three years after the incident.

79 "Journal of James Kenny, 1761–1763," ed. John W. Jordan, *PMHB* 37 (1913): 154–6.

CHAPTER TWO

1 See Sylvia van Kirk, *Many Tender Ties: Women in Fur-Trade Society in Western Canada, 1670–1870* (Winnipeg, MB: Watson and Dwyer, 1980); Jennifer Brown, *Strangers in Blood: Fur Trade Company Families in Indian Country* (Vancouver, BC: UBC Press, 1980); and Susan Sleeper-Smith, *Indian Women and French Men: Rethinking Cultural Encounter in the Western Great Lakes* (Amherst, MA: University of Massachusetts Press, 2001). George Croghan's marriage to the daughter of Mohawk chief Nickus, in 1757, was part of his New York connection with William Johnson and with the Iroquois overlords of Allegheny and Ohio country. See Nicholas B. Wainwright, *George Croghan, Wilderness Diplomat* (Chapel Hill, NC: University of North Carolina Press, 1959), 138.

2 James H. Merrell, *Into the American Woods: Negotiators on the Pennsylvania Frontier* (New York: Norton, 1999), 47–53; Luther Reily Kelker, *History of Dauphin County, Pennsylvania*, 3 vols (New York and Chicago, IL: Lewis, 1907), vol. 1, 38–40.

3 Francis Jennings, "The Indian Trade of the Susquehannah Valley," *Proceedings of the American Philosophical Society* 110 (1966): 406–24.

4 *PA*, ser. 1, 1: 328. On Chartier, see William A. Hunter, *Peter Chartier, Knave of the Wild Frontier* (Carlisle, PA: Cumberland County National Bank, 1973); Merrell, *Into the American Woods*, 73–5; Francis Jennings, "Bisaillon

(Bezellon, Bizaillon), Peter," DCB, 3: 65–6; Lawrence Henry Gipson, *The British Empire before the American Revolution*, 15 vols (Caldwell, ID, and New York: Caxton and Knopf, 1936–70), vol. 4, 156–60; and Richard White, *The Middle Ground: Indians, Empires, and Republics in the Great Lakes Region, 1650–1815* (New York: Cambridge University Press, 1991), 190–2.

5 *PA*, ser. 5, 1: 371–2; Penn to Thomas, 21 August 1743, HSP, Thomas Penn Letterbooks, vol. 2, 47.

6 Penn to Thomas, 21 August 1743, HSP, Thomas Penn Letterbooks, vol. 2, 47, 138; Charles A. Hanna, *The Wilderness Trail, Or the Ventures and Adventures of the Pennsylvania Traders on the Allegheny Path*, 2 vols (New York: Putnam, 1911), vol. 1, 311; *MPCP*, 4: 757–8. Chartier's 600-acre plantation was confiscated in 1746 and sold for £520 to cover a debt of £647.13.5 owed to trader Thomas Lawrence, partner of Edward Shippen. See Hunter, *Peter Chartier*, 15.

7 Frederick B. Tolles, *James Logan and the Culture of Provincial America* (Boston, MA: Little, Brown, 1957), 168–70; Shawnee chiefs' message to Governor Patrick Gordon, c. 7 June 1732, *PA*, ser. 1, 1: 329–30, and see also 302–6, 325–8. For James Logan's version of the story, see "A Quaker Imperialist's View of the British Colonies in America, 1732," *PMHB* 60 (1936): 124–6; Hanna, *Wilderness Trail*, vol. 1, 232, 280–1, 287–8, 309, 311, 325, 331; White, *Middle Ground*, 189–93; and Hunter, *Peter Chartier*, 5–9. Jacques Legardeur de St Pierre, at Fort des Miamis in 1742, reported three separate approaches by the Shawnee, evidently seeking alliance and trade. See Joseph L. Peyser, *Jacques Legardeur de Saint-Pierre: Officer, Gentleman, Entrepreneur* (East Lansing, MI: MSU Press, 1996), 53.

8 Hanna, *Wilderness Trail*, vol. 1, 232, 280–1, 287–8, 309, 311, 325, 331.

9 The petition of "James Dinnen and Peter Tostee," claiming losses of £1,600, is reported in *PA*, ser. 8, 4: 3041. See also *MPCP*, 4: 757–8; *PG*, 16 May 1745; Hanna, *Wilderness Trail*, vol. 1: 232, 280–1, 287–8, 309, 311, 325, 331; *NYCD*, 10: 20; *The Appalachian Indian Frontier: The Edmond Atkin Report and Plan of 1755*, ed. Wilbur R. Jacobs (Lincoln, NB: University of Nebraska Press, 1967), 65, 65n; Francis Jennings, *The Ambiguous Iroquois Empire* (New York: Norton, 1984), 269–70; and Merrell, *Into the American Woods*, i, 73–5. See also Jennings, "Bisaillon," DCB, 3: 65–6; Gipson, *British Empire*, vol. 4, 156–60; White, *Middle Ground*, 190–2; and Michael N. McConnell, *A Country Between: The Upper Ohio Valley and Its Peoples, 1724–1774* (Lincoln, NB: University of Nebraska Press, 1992), 53–4. Croghan was then packing up his own winter's proceeds at Cuyahoga; he, too, was confronted, but only by a single Canadian from Detroit accompanied by a warrior. The Mingo refused to allow the arrest. See Wainwright, *George Croghan*, 7.

10 Pennsylvania's governor, George Thomas, reported, in general, to the assembly on Chartier's "infidelity" on 25 April 1745. See *PA*, ser. 8, 4: 3032, 3034.

11 Andrew Rodger, "Le Moyne de Longueuil, Paul-Joseph," DCB, 4: 463–5.

12 *Papiers Contrecoeur et autres documents concernant le conflit anglo-français sur l'Ohio de 1745 à 1756*, ed. Fernand Grenier (Quebec City, QC: Laval University Press, 1952), 1–10; *NYCD*, 10: 20–1.

13 *Appalachian Indian Frontier*, ed. Jacobs, 43; *SCDIA*, 1: 421–7, 433. James Adair claimed that he led a party of Catawbas intent on apprehending Chartier in 1747, but he and his family had already fled south. See James Adair, *Adair's History of the American Indians* (1775; reprint, Ann Arbor, MI: University of Michigan Press, 1966), 4n; and Hunter, *Peter Chartier*, 10–11. By 1750 Chartier was regarded by the Canadian governor of Louisiana as a Shawnee chief; in 1759 his community migrated north again to the Wabash Valley, and the sixty-five-year-old Chartier soon moved yet again, west of the Mississippi. See Randolph C. Downes, *Council Fires on the Upper Ohio* (Pittsburgh, PA: University of Pittsburgh Press, 1940), 39–41; Merrell, *Into the American Woods*, 73–5; Gipson, *British Empire*, vol. 4, 156–60; White, *Middle Ground*, 190–2; and *Mississippi Provincial Archives, French Dominion*, ed. Dunbar Rowland, A.G. Sanders, and Patricia Kay Galloway, 5 vols (Jackson and Baton Rouge, LA: Press of the Mississippi Department of Archives and History, 1927–84), vol. 5, 48. Conrad Weiser counted only 162 Shawnee warriors in the Logstown area in 1748. See Conrad Weiser, "Conrad Weiser's Journal of a Tour of the Ohio, August 11–October 2, 1748," in *Early Western Travels, 1748–1846*, ed. R.G. Thwaites, 32 vols (Cleveland, OH: Arthur H. Clark, 1904–07), vol. 1, 30–1. For the suggestion that there were more than 1,500 Shawnee warriors in the entire Ohio Valley in 1759, see James H. Howard, *Shawnee! The Ceremonialism of a Native Indian Tribe and Its Cultural Background* (Athens, OH: Ohio University Press, 1981), 31–3.

14 American Philosophical Society, Mss Class B, no. L82, vol. 4, fols 116–17; *MPCP*, 4: 780–1; Paul A.W. Wallace, *Conrad Weiser, Friend of Colonist and Mohawk* (Philadelphia, PA: University of Pennsylvania Press, 1945), 218–22.

15 American Philosophical Society, Mss Class B, no. L82, vol. 4, fol. 117; Edward J. Cashin, *Lachlan McGillivray, Indian Trader: The Shaping of the Southern Colonial Frontier* (Athens, GA: University of Georgia Press, 1992), 81–103; David H. Corkran, *The Creek Frontier, 1540–1783* (Norman, OK: University of Oklahoma Press, 1967), 118; White, *Middle Ground*, 198–207.

16 William A. Hunter, "Orontony," *DCB*, 3: 495–6; McConnell, *Country Between*, 62–3.

17 *NYCD*, 10: 83–8, 114–16, 119–20, 140–1, 150, 181–5; *Collections of the State Historical Society of Wisconsin* 17 (1906): 474–7; White, *Middle Ground*, 202–8. There is one unconfirmed report that, in their attack on the bateaux the Ottawa took the commanding officer prisoner, whom they have resolved to "return in place of a great trader from Philadelphia who was killed 4 years ago by the french or by his directions." See TNA, CO 5/1065, fol. 431.

18 Stewart Rafert, *The Miami Indians of Indiana: A Persistent People, 1654–1994* (Indianapolis, IN: Indiana Historical Society, 1996), 6, 23–4, 30–3; Harvey

Lewis Carter, *The Life and Times of Little Turtle: First Sagamore of the Wabash* (Urbana, IL: University of Illinois Press, 1987), 31–2.

19 On the Miami, see Bert Anson, *The Miami Indians* (Norman, OK: University of Oklahoma Press, 1970), 1–57; *NYCD*, 10: 83–8, 114–16, 119–20, 140–3, 150, 181–5; *Collections of the State Historical Society of Wisconsin* 17 (1906): 474–7; White, *Middle Ground*, 202–8; and Rafert, *Miami Indians*, 30–1.

20 Orontony and the majority of his community migrated southeast to the town of Kuskuski; seventy others went west to establish Coshocton (Conchaké).

21 White, *Middle Ground*, 220–34.

22 *PA*, ser. 1, 1: 737–8; Eric Hinderaker, "Declaring Independence: The Ohio Indians and the Seven Years' War," in *Cultures in Conflict: The Seven Years' War in North America*, ed. Warren R. Hofstra (Lanham, MD: Rowman and Littlefield, 2007), 105–25.

23 Wainwright, *George Croghan*, 29.

24 *NYCD*, 10: 114–16, 141, 145, 149–52, 156–7; White, *Middle Ground*, 76–82.

25 *NYCD*, 10: 116, 161–2.

26 *NYCD*, 10: 184; White, *Middle Ground*, 202–7.

27 Thanks to Linda Sabbathy-Judd for noting the connection between the British chartering of the Ohio Company and the decision of the French Ministry of Marine to transfer the oversight of the upper Ohio Valley from Louisiana to Canada.

28 Malcolm MacLeod, "Philippe-Thomas Chabert de Joncaire," *DCB*, 3: 101–2.

29 Margry, 6: 686–7. For the statement that there were only five English at this place, see Joseph-Pierre de Bonnécamps, S.J., "Relation du voyage de la Belle Rivière faite en 1749, sous les ordres de M. de Céloron," in *The Jesuit Relations and Allied Documents*, ed. R.G. Thwaites, 73 vols (Cleveland, OH, 1896–1901), vol. 69, 170–1. See also W.J. Eccles, "Céloron de Blainville, Pierre–Joseph," *DCB*, 3: 99–101.

30 Bonnécamps, "Relation du voyage," 177. William Trent's commentary of 1758, pp. 2–3, Clements Library, University of Michigan, Ann Arbor, MI; Doug MacGregor, "The Shot Not Heard around the World: Trent's Fort and the Opening of the War for Empire," *PH* 74 (2007): 358.

31 Margry, 6: 704–5; Bonnécamps, "Relation du voyage," 178–9.

32 Margry, 6: 713–14; Bonnécamps, "Relation du voyage," 182–3; Céloron to Hamilton, 16 August 1749, *MPCP*, 5: 425.

33 Bonnécamps, "Relation du voyage," 180–1. Céloron misleads here. See Margry, 6: 706–8.

34 Bonnécamps, "Relation du voyage," 186–7.

35 "1749: Céloron's Expedition down the Ohio," *Collections of the State Historical Society of Wisconsin* 18 (1908): 36–58; Bonnécamps, "Relation du voyage," 184–5; La Jonquière to Minister of Marine, 20 September 1749, Margry, 6: 727–8.

36 R. David Edmunds, "Pickawillany: French Military Power versus British Economics," *WPHM* 58 (1975): 175–6.

37 AN, C11A, vol. 119, fols 93–4; Theodore C. Pease and Ernestine Jenison, eds, *Illinois on the Eve of the Seven Years' War* (Springfield, IL: State Historical Society, 1940), xxx, 178, 190, 202–55; William Trent to Richard Peters, 18 August 1750, *MPCP*, 5: 461–2; Hanna, *Wilderness Trail*, vol. 1, 177. Pacane was also known as André Roy and may well have been the "Roy" who attempted to serve Céloron as Miami interpreter in 1749.

38 The firm Trent, Croghan, Callendar, and Teaffe lost more than £300 here. See Wainwright, *George Croghan*, 30.

39 *MPCP*, 5: 480–4; *PG*, 1 November 1750; Hanna, *Wilderness Trail*, vol. 2: 265–7; *JP*, 1: 302–4. Turner and Kilgore appeared before the Pennsylvania Assembly in October 1750, and they were granted £10. See *PA*, ser. 8, 2: 3361, 3364.

40 *Christopher Gist's Journals*, ed. William M. Darlington (Pittsburgh, PA, 1893), 41; Emma Lewis Coleman, *New England Captives Carried to Canada between 1677 and 1760 during the French and Indian Wars*, 2 vols (Portland, ME: Southworth, 1925–26), vol. 2, 87–8.

41 Howard N. Eavenson, *Map Maker and Indian Trader* (Pittsburgh, PA: University of Pittsburgh Press, 1949), 5–6, 122; *First Explorations of Kentucky: Doctor Thomas Walker's Journal and Colonel Christopher Gist's Journal*, ed. J. Stoddard Johnson (Louisville, KY, 1898), 118.

42 Louis Coulon de Villiers had been specifically instructed to enforce an ordinance forbidding trade with the English and to seize persons trading or corresponding with the English. See Pease and Jenison, eds, *Illinois on the Eve*, 223–4. The ordinance is in AN, C11A, vol. 95, 266. See also W.J. Eccles, "Coulon de Villiers, Louis," *DCB*, 3: 148–9.

William Perry, held in the New Orleans jail in 1757–58, reported that "in the Jayl, where he was, he saw one Thomas Morris, who told him he was an Indian Trader, and had traded with an Officer belonging to a large Fort that the French had, Four or Five Hundred Leagues up the Mississippi, near the Mouth of the Carolina River, and went there to demand the Money due to him; but, instead of being paid, he was arrested, put into Confinement, and sent to New Orleans." See "Examination of William Perry," in *Colonial Captivities, Marches, and Journeys*, ed. I.M. Calder (New York: Macmillan, 1935), 146–7.

43 Céloron to Vaudreuil, 23 April 1751, refers to them as five English traders taken at Sandusky. See Pease and Jenison, eds, *Illinois on the Eve*, 245. See also Eavenson, *Map Maker*, 10–26. Burk traded on behalf of Michael Teaffe of Philadelphia, and both Erwin and Faulkner were hired men who had contracts that included the clause that they would be paid for their time until they returned home. See *The Ohio Company Papers, 1753–1817, Being Primarily Papers of the "Suffering Traders" of Pennsylvania*, ed. Kenneth P. Bailey (Arcata, CA: N.p., 1947), 36–7.

44 Petition to Pennsylvania Assembly in October 1753, *PA*, ser. 8, 4: 3539–40; Eavenson, *Map Maker*, 7–11, 142.

45 Eavenson, *Map Maker*, 12–15, 113–16; Neville B. Craig, *The Olden Times*, 2 vols (Pittsburgh, PA, 1846–48), vol. 2, 180–7.

46 La Jonquière to Clinton, 10 August 1751, *NYCD*, 10: 732; *MPCP*, 5: 553–8.

47 Eavenson, *Map Maker*, 17–18; Pease and Jenison, eds, *Illinois on the Eve*, 498; *NYCD*, 10: 240–1.

48 *NYCD*, 10: 240–1. These five, John Howard, Josiah Howard, Peter John Salley, John Pateet, and Charles Sinclair, explored the Ohio and Mississippi Rivers with Virginia government support. Salley escaped after two years of imprisonment in New Orleans, and his journal/memoire is in TNA, CO 5/1327, fols 174–80. Pierre-François Rigaud, Marquis de Vaudreuil, sent three of the other prisoners to France in 1745, but the French ship carrying them was captured, and they were taken to England, and they evidently returned to Virginia. See TNA, Adm. 98/2, fol. 119; Pease and Jenison, eds, *Illinois on the Eve*, 19–20; and Fairfax Harrison, "The Virginians on the Ohio and the Mississippi in 1742," *VMHB* 30 (1922): 203–22.

49 Eavenson, *Map Maker*, 140.

50 *PA*, ser. 8, 4: 3539–40; Eavenson, *Map Maker*, 19–45, 126–46.

51 *MPCP*, 5: 496–8; Pease and Jenison, eds, *Illinois on the Eve*, 362–5, 773. La Mirande was trading on the Wabash River later that year. See *Gist's Journals*, ed. Darlington, 46.

52 The captives turned out to be two Illinois and pro-French Piankashaw chief La Loup, all of whom were eventually released; the single captured Piankashaw warrior had escaped. See Peters, "Detail of Indian Affairs," quoted in William A. Hunter, *Forts on the Pennsylvania Frontier, 1753–1758* (Harrisburg, PA: Pennsylvania Historical and Museum Commission, 1960), 5; R.G. Thwaites, ed., *Early Western Travels, 1748–1846*, 32 vols (Cleveland, OH: Arthur H. Clark, 1904–07), vol. 1, 58–71; Hanna, *Wilderness Trail*, vol. 2, 271–9; and Anson, *Miami Indians*, 47–8. The Canadian traders among the Shawnee were Pierre-Louis Boucher de Niverville, Sieur de Montizambert; Philippe Dagneau Douville, Sieur de La Saussaye, and his son; and Jacques Duperont Baby and his brother François. See Hunter, *Forts*, 21, 99, 129. Peters held mortgages on a number of George Croghan's frontier properties from 1749. See Wainwright, *George Croghan*, 12, 28.

53 Pease and Jenison, eds, *Illinois on the Eve*, esp. 381–93, 414–22, 444, 465, 487, 507, 572–86, 600, 627–48; HL, LO, 373; *NYCD*, 10: 239–41; R. David Edmunds, "Old Briton" and "Pickawillany," both in *American Indian Leaders*, ed. R. David Edmunds (Lincoln, NB: University of Nebraska Press, 1980), 1–20, 169–84; White, *Middle Ground*, 223–30. In 1750 La Jonquière had offered 100 ecus per captive, and 50 ecus per scalp, delivered to Céloron at Detroit. See AN, C11A, vol. 97, 42, vol. 98, 171–2, 271–2.

54 Michael A. McDonnell, "Charles-Michel Mouet de Langlade: Warrior, Soldier, and Intercultural 'Window' on the Sixty Years' War for the Great Lakes," in *The Sixty Years' War for the Great Lakes, 1754–1814*, ed. D.C. Skaggs and L.L. Nelson (East Lansing, MI: Michigan State University Press, 2001), 79–103; Paul Trap, "Mouet de Langlade, Charles-Michel," *DCB*, 4: 563–4. The Frenchman accompanying Langlade is identified as St Ours in Gipson, *British Empire*, vol. 4, 222. See also J.R. Turnbull, "Saint-Ours, François-Xavier de," *DCB*, 3: 577–8.

55 Robert Callender to Hamilton, 30 August 1752, *MPCP*, 5: 599; William Trent's journal, TNA, CO 5/1327, fols 250–5; Trent's account in *VG*, 20 and 27 October 1752, not printed in the *PG* until 23 November 1752. On 10 October 1754 Governor Duquesne described Langlade as acting under La Jonquière's orders on this mission. See Pease and Jenison, eds, *Illinois on the Eve*, 904–5. For the claim that Memeskia was executed after the surrender, see Edmunds, "Old Briton," 17.

56 John Defever, whose own captivity story needs confirming, claimed he was captured by Wyandots at Cuyahoga on 18 March 1752, taken to Fort Vincennes where the garrison commander redeemed him, and then taken through all the French forts to Quebec, where he simply took ship for Louisbourg and Boston. He claimed that, while he was at Detroit, he saw the commandant summon neighboring Wyandots, Tauwaus, and Pouce and invite them to attack the Miami. He said they would find English traders there and "promised a reward of Thirty livres for every English Prisoner or scalp." See TNA, WO 55/1817, fols 10–12; and HL, LO, 198B.

57 The five surviving captives were James Devoy, Joseph Stevens, John Evans, George Henery, and Owen Nicholson. All but Stevens petitioned the Pennsylvania Assembly in May 1753 for expenses to get back to their homes in Cumberland County and were granted £16. See *PA*, ser. 8, 4: 3555–6; Pease and Jenison, eds, *Illinois on the Eve*, 811–13; *NYM*, 28 May 1753; and Dinwiddie to Board of Trade, 16 June 1753, TNA, CO 5/1327, fol. 293.

58 The intent was to return these belts to the French and thereby terminate all existing agreements. See J. Frederick Fausz, "'Engaged in Enterprises Pregnant with Terror': George Washington's Formative Years among the Indians," in *George Washington and the Virginia Backcountry*, ed. Warren R. Hofstra (Madison, VA: Madison House, 1998), 126; and *The Diaries of George Washington*, ed. Donald Jackson and Dorothy Twohig, 6 vols (Charlottesville, VA: University Press of Virginia, 1976–79), vol. 1, 147.

59 McConnell, *Country Between*, 102, citing *NYCD*, 10: 256, and William Trent, *Journal of Captain William Trent from Logstown to Pickawillany a.d. 1752*, ed. A.T. Goodman (Cincinnati, OH, 1871), 18–21; Hunter, *Forts*, 140–1, 143, 159, 161. Captive Stephen Coffen, who was with Marin's forces, claimed that the Delaware had absconded with supplies they were transporting. See *NYCD*, 6: 836. More generally, see C.A. Weslager, *The Delaware Indian Westward Migration* (Wallingford, PA: Middle Atlantic, 1978), 3–34; and C.A. Weslager, *The Delaware Indians: A History* (New Brunswick, NJ: Rutgers University Press, 1972), esp. 200–4.

60 The pair somehow made their way to Bordeaux, where MacLaughlin was left for lack of passenger space in the *Betty and Sally* of Philadelphia, which brought Trotter home within seven months of his capture. See *MPCP*, 5: 659–60. In a deposition of 22 March 1754, Trotter said they were captured by 160 Frenchmen at Fort Venango, though bound with "Indian Hopples, made of wild Hemp." See *PA*, ser. 1, 2: 131–3; *Diaries of George Washington*,

ed. Jackson and Twohig, vol. 1, 138n; Hunter, *Forts*, 140; and W.J. Eccles, "Marin de La Malque, Paul," *DCB*, 3: 431–2.

61 Robert Stobo, *The Memoirs of Major Robert Stobo of the Virginia Regiment*, ed. Neville B. Craig (Pittsburgh, PA, 1854), 91–2. Between September 1746 and August 1747, some ninety-two prisoners and fifty-six scalps were paid for at Montreal. Captives sold for 120 to 140 livres. Scalps sold for an average of 33 livres. See D. Peter MacLeod, *The Canadian Iroquois and the Seven Years' War* (Toronto, ON: Dundurn, 1996), 15. The price Stobo mentions would be roughly 606.6 livres, using European exchange rates for that year. See John J. McCusker, *Money and Exchange in Europe and America, 1600–1775: A Handbook* (Chapel Hill, NC: University of North Carolina Press, 1978), 311.

62 *PG*, 8 December 1757; *PJ*, 8 December 1757; Hanna, *Wilderness Trail*, vol. 1, 179, vol. 2, 334; *Ohio Company Papers*, ed. Bailey, 121.

63 Forty-eight traders were captured and twenty-four others killed. The apparent murder of trader Joseph Campbell is not included in these calculations. He was killed by a Six Nations Indian, known as Israel, in the Tuscarawas Valley in Cumberland County, Pennsylvania, in September of 1754. See Croghan to Hamilton, 27 September 1754, printed in Israel Daniel Rupp, *The History and Topography of Dauphin, Cumberland, Franklin, Bedford, Adams and Perry Counties* (Lancaster, PA, 1846), 71–2. Thirty-two captured English traders were returned; John Wotton and Joseph Faulkner (Fortiner) stayed in Canada. The fate of four captured Canadian traders – André Roy (a.k.a. Pacane), La Mirande and his wife, and Ste Marie – is not known, nor is that of Pennsylvania trader Andrew McBriar.

64 For a French propaganda version of the saga of the merchants, see [A Patriot], *The Mystery Reveal'd, or Truth Brought to Light* (London, 1759).

65 On Vause's Fort, see chapter 5; and Anson, *Miami Indians*, 54.

66 Sixteen Pennsylvania traders wrangling a hundred packhorses could bring more goods to the upper Ohio Valley than a hundred Canadians paddling twenty canoes. Moreover, the Pennsylvanians could do this twice a year, whereas the Canadians could make only one annual trip. See Claiborne A. Skinner, *The Upper Country: French Enterprise in the Colonial Great Lakes* (Baltimore, MD: Johns Hopkins University Press, 2008), 167.

CHAPTER THREE

1 The force consisted of 2,100 militiamen, 300 *troupes de la marine*, and 200 "domiciled" Indians. The next spring 1,100 more militiamen were added. See Louise Dechène, *Le Peuple, l'État et la Guerre au Canada sous le régime français* (Montreal, QC: Boreal, 2008), 498–9.

2 W.J. Eccles, "Marin de La Malque, Paul," *DCB*, 3: 431–2; Claiborne A. Skinner, *The Upper Country: French Enterprise in the Colonial Great Lakes* (Baltimore, MD: Johns Hopkins University Press, 2008), 168–71; *The Diaries of*

George Washington, ed. Donald Jackson and Dorothy Twohig, 6 vols (Charlottesville, VA: University Press of Virginia, 1976–79), vol. 1, 138n.

3 See Hamilton to Dinwiddie, 6 May 1753, quoted in William A. Hunter, *Forts on the Pennsylvania Frontier, 1753–1758* (Harrisburg, PA: Pennsylvania Historical and Museum Commission, 1960), 15.

4 Ensign Edward Ward, quoted in Lawrence Henry Gipson, *The British Empire before the American Revolution*, 15 vols (Caldwell, ID, and New York: Caxton and Knopf, 1936–70), vol. 4, 188.

5 Fernand Grenier, "Pécaudy de Contrecoeur, Claude-Pierre," *DCB*, 4: 617–18. The summons is printed in Neville B. Craig, *The Olden Times*, 2 vols (Pittsburgh, PA, 1846–48), vol. 1, 83–4.

6 *Papiers Contrecoeur et autres documents concernant le conflit anglo-français sur l'Ohio de 1745 à 1756*, ed. Fernand Grenier (Quebec City, QC: Laval University Press, 1952), 117–19; Alfred Proctor James and Charles Morse Stotz, *Drums in the Forest* (Pittsburgh, PA: Historical Society of Western Pennsylvania, 1958), 124–6; *Travels in New France by J.C.B.*, ed. Sylvester K. Stevens, Donald H. Kent, and Emma Edith Woods (Harrisburg, PA: Pennsylvania Historical Commission, 1941), 54–6; Gipson, *British Empire*, vol. 4, 300–10; Edward Ward's deposition of 7 May 1754, TNA, CO 5/1328, fols 101–2.

7 Charles A. Hanna, *The Wilderness Trail, Or the Ventures and Adventures of the Pennsylvania Traders on the Allegheny Path*, 2 vols (New York: Putnam, 1911), vol. 1, 177–9; *The Ohio Company Papers, 1753–1817, Being Primarily Papers of the "Suffering Traders" of Pennsylvania*, ed. Kenneth P. Bailey (Arcata, CA: N.p., 1947), 121; *PG*, 9 May 1754, 8 December 1757; *NYM*, 13 May 1754; *SCG*, 4 June 1754.

8 For Dinwiddie's instructions to Washington (January 1754) and Tanaghrisson's message, see *GWP*, 1: 65, 105. William Trent's commission of 26 January 1753 had very similar wording; quoted in Doug MacGregor, "The Shot Not Heard around the World: Trent's Fort and the Opening of the War for Empire," *PH* 74 (2007): 366.

9 Washington's diary was captured at Fort Necessity. The initial translation, by Governor Duquesne's secretary, is the best surviving version, one that varies little from *Mémoire contenant le Précis des Faites, avec leurs pièces justificatives pour servir de réponse aux observations envoyées par les ministres d'Angleterrs dans les cours d'Europe* (Paris, 1756), published by the French government. The texts are compared in *Papiers Contrecoeur*, ed. Grenier, 133–81 (see esp. 155–7).

10 Washington to Dinwiddie, 18 May 1754, and answer dated 25 May and received 27 May, *GWP*, 1: 100, 102–4.

11 *GWP*, 1: 107–17, 124. Washington's initial reports did not claim the French fired first. Compare Fred Anderson, *Crucible of War: The Seven Years' War and the Fate of Empire in British North America, 1754–1766* (New York: Knopf, 2000), 6.

12 Druillon to Dinwiddie, 31 July 1754, in *The Official Records of Robert Dinwiddie, 1751–1758*, ed. R.A. Brock, 2 vols (Richmond, VA, 1883–84), vol. 1, 225. The Canadian Morceau, who was likely a runner sent back to Fort Duquesne as soon as the confrontation commenced, gave an account that Contrecoeur sent to Duquesne on 2 June 1754, printed in *Mémoire contenant le Précis des Faites*, 107. On English deserter Denis Kaninguen (Cunningham?), see "Journal de Joseph-Gaspard Chaussegros de Léry, Lieutenant des troupes, 1754–1755," in *RAPQ*, 1927–1928 (Quebec City, QC: Quebec Archives, 1928), 372–3.

13 Reprinted in *PG*, 27 June 1754.

14 Deposition of 21 August 1754, *SCDIA*, 2: 4.

15 Anderson, *Crucible of War*, 5–7; "Journal de Joseph-Gaspard Chaussegros de Léry," 372ff. See also Marcel Trudel, "L'Affaire Jumonville," *Revue d'histoire de l'Amerique française* 6 (1952–53): 331–73, translated in abridged form by Donald H. Kent as "The Jumonville Affair," *PH* 21 (1954): 351–81. Tanaghrisson's execution of Jumonville deserves attention as contributing to the launch of war between the Europeans, but it should be noted that only eighty Ohio Valley Indians joined him and Scarouady on the English side; most resisted their subsequent recruiting tour, complete with French scalps and new hatchets, and instead allied with the French. See *GWP*, 1: 122–3.

I have ignored Captain Adam Stephen's account, in *PG*, 19 September 1754, which is fictional about his own presence, and offers an implausible regular officer's vision of some other regiment in claiming that, because the French had been better at keeping their muskets dry than had the Virginians, "we could not depend on ours, and therefore keeping up our Fire, advanced as near as we could with fixt Bayonets, and received their Fire … our Bayonets gave us an Advantage over them."

16 *Official Records of Robert Dinwiddie*, ed. Brock, vol. 1, 201–7, 227–8.

17 Ibid., vol. 1, 298, 313, 347, vol. 2, 227–8, 367–8; LAC, MG 5, A1, vol. 439, 155.

18 He eventually claimed expenses for helping his fellow captives during their thirteen months of detainment in Virginia. See LAC, MG 5, A1, vol. 439, 155; AN, Col. E, vol. 139, n.p.; F.J. Thorpe, "Druillon de Macé, Pierre-Jacques," *DCB*, 4: 226–7; E.Z. Massicotte, "Pierre-Jacques Druillon, Seigneur de Macé," *Bulletin des Recherches Historiques* 26 (1920): 125–6; and *GWP*, 1: 110–11, 119.

19 LAC, MG 1, E, vol. 27, n.p.; *NYCD*, 10: 352–3; *Collections des manuscrits contenant lettres, mémoires et autres documents historiques relatifs à la Nouvelle France*, 4 vols (Quebec City, QC, 1883–85), vol. 3, 521–2. News of Braddock's defeat was printed in London on 26 August 1755. See *Gentleman's Magazine* 25 (1755): 378. On 20 October 1755, the British Navy's Commissioners for Sick and Wounded Seamen were still seeking admiralty orders concerning a reported twenty-one prisoners from Virginia expected aboard various merchantmen. See TNA, Adm. 98/5, fols 118–19.

An official French *Précis des faits*, translated and printed in Philadelphia in 1757, claimed that only seven of the prisoners were sent to England and that "Upon their Arrival, they implored the Assistance of the Duke de Mirepoix, who sent them over to France at the Expence of the King. What is become of the rest we are altogether ignorant?" See *A Memorial Containing a Summary View of Facts, with Their Authorities, in Answer to the Observations Sent by the English Ministry to the Courts of Europe* (Translated from the French) (Philadelphia, PA, 1757), 25–6.

20 *Papiers Contrecoeur*, ed. Grenier, 157n; *Collections des manuscrits ... Nouvelle France*, vol. 3, 521.

21 The Convention of Sluis (Écluse) of 6 February 1759, concerning prisoners, was reprinted in English, and in French as *Traité et convention pour les malades, blessés et prisonniers de guerre* ... by W. Dunlap in Philadelphia in 1759. This convention revived, elaborated, and improved upon the convention signed at Frankfurt am Main on 18 July 1743 between the French and the Austrians. See *The Genuine Cartel in French and English, faithfully compared with the original, which was signed at Frankfort, July the 18th 1743* (London, 1746). Thanks to Maureen Ryan for this reference. See also Francis Abell, *Prisoners of War in Britain, 1756 to 1815* (Oxford, UK: Oxford University Press, 1914).

22 Michel Pepin *dit* La Force, son of surveyor Pierre Pepin *dit* La Force and wife Michelle Leber, was born at Fort St Joseph-des-Illinois on 16 March 1721. He married Agathe Limoge Amand in 1744 and had become a captain in the *troupes de la marine* by 1750. He was involved in the fur trade in the early 1750s, and his wife managed their business and legal affairs until her death in 1772. See PUQAM; and http://www.genealogie.umontreal.ca. Thanks to José Igartua for these references.

23 Washington to Dinwiddie, 29 May 1754, *GWP*, 1: 111, 201–2; R. Stobo to Dinwiddie, 28 July 1754, in Robert Stobo, *The Memoirs of Major Robert Stobo of the Virginia Regiment*, ed. Neville B. Craig (Pittsburgh, PA, 1854), 87–8. On La Force, see also *SCG*, 11 June and 8 August 1754.

24 *Official Records of Robert Dinwiddie*, ed. Brock, vol. 1, 297.

25 Ibid., vol. 1, 297, vol. 2, 227–8.

26 Virginia's lieutenant governor, Francis Fauquier, wrote Amherst on 17 January 1760 that Virginians "were desirous to set him at Large in order to be eased of the Expence of Maintaining him." See Amherst Papers, TNA, WO 34/38, fols 32–3, 207, 210.

27 Wheelock to Amherst, 29 November 1759, TNA, WO 34/98, fols 35–6; HL, LO, 5468; Fauquier to Amherst, 17 March 1759, TNA, WO 34/98, fol. 21–2.

28 Amherst Papers, TNA, WO 34/38, fol. 210; HL, LO, 5464, 5468; *Maryland Gazette*, 26 August 1756; Pierre Pouchot, *Memoirs of the Late War in North America between England and France*, ed. B.L. Dunnigan (Youngstown, NY: Old Fort Niagara Association, 1994), 515; *Official Records of Robert Dinwiddie*, ed. Brock, vol. 2, 227–8, 367–8; Robert C. Alberts, *The Most*

Extraordinary Adventures of Major Robert Stobo (Boston, MA: Houghton Mifflin, 1965), 183.

29 In 1760 Quebec notary S. Sanguinet noted that La Force was a prisoner "en la Nouvelle Angleterre," and in 1771 notary J.-C. Panet observed that he had been away in foreign countries for a number of years. Another Michel Pepin *dit* La Force was buried in Quebec City on 2 December 1767. See PUQAM; and PRDH. Other marine officers sent to France with La Force did return. Captain Charles Philippe Aubry and Captain François Coulon de Villiers went to Louisiana, and Jean-Baptiste-Philippe Testard de Montigny and Joseph Marin de La Malgue fil were captured aboard ships bound for Newfoundland early in 1762, and were repatriated. See *DCB*, 4: 513–14, 733–4.

30 D. Peter MacLeod, *The Canadian Iroquois and the Seven Years' War* (Toronto, ON: Dundurn, 1996), 42–50; Stobo's letter of 28 July 1754, *MPCP*, 6: 162.

31 *Papiers Contrecoeur*, ed. Grenier, 200, not in the printed version of the journal in the *Précis des faits*; John Shaw's affidavit, *SCDIA*, 2: 3–7.

32 W.J. Eccles, "Coulon de Villiers, Louis," *DCB*, 3: 148–9.

33 Jean Pariseau, "Le Mercier (Mercier), François-Marc-Antoine," *DCB*, 4: 458–61.

34 John E. Ferling, *The First of Men: A Life of George Washington* (Knoxville, TN: University of Tennessee Press, 1988), 20.

35 Captain Adam Stephen vigorously defended Washington, and accused Van Braam, in his account for *PG*, 22 August 1754. Whatever Washington misunderstood of this French document, it should not have been the word "l'assasin."

36 *Papiers Contrecoeur*, ed. Grenier, 201. The *Précis des faits* excised Villiers opinion about prisoners as a wartime drain on provisions.

37 *GWP*, 1: 165–7.

38 Theodore C. Pease and Ernestine Jenison, eds, *Illinois on the Eve of the Seven Years' War* (Springfield, IL: State Historical Society, 1940), 362–5; Joseph L. Peyser, *Jacques Legardeur de Saint-Pierre: Officer, Gentleman, Entrepreneur* (East Lansing, MI: MSU Press, 1996), 26, 51–2.

39 *European Treaties Bearing on the History of the United States and Its Dependencies*, ed. F.G. Davenport and C.O. Paullin, 4 vols (Washington, DC: Carnegie, 1917–37), vol. 4, 74.

40 Carl E. Swanson, *Predators and Prizes: American Privateering and Imperial Warfare, 1739–1748* (Columbia, SC: University of South Carolina Press, 1991), 203–5; Peter Earle, *Sailors: English Merchant Seamen, 1650–1775* (London: Methuen, 1998), 123.

41 See Trudel, "L'Affaire Jumonville." Villiers's journal and the unadulterated French text of the surrender are printed in *Papiers Contrecoeur*, ed. Grenier, 196–205. The author of Stobo's memoirs hinted that his popularity provoked the "suspicion and envy of his superior officers, and this may, with some probability, be suspected for the reason of his being delivered up an hostage." See Stobo, *Memoirs*, 6. Stobo was a distant but favored re-

lation of Robert Dinwiddie, and it seems unlikely that Washington made the choice that Stobo, the senior captain, go as hostage. See ibid.

42 *Papiers Contrecoeur*, ed. Grenier, 204.

43 Ibid., 223–4.

44 Ibid., 202: "pour obvier au desordre qui Seroit infalliblement arrivé." In having the artillery smashed, Villiers was speeding his withdrawal and likely fulfilling a private concession to the defeated that went beyond the second article of the capitulation. In *PG*, 22 August 1754, Captain Adam Stephen claimed this was the case.

45 Paxton to Governor, 16 July 1754, HSP, Penn Official Correspondence, vol. 6, 203. Aside from this letter, reprinted in *NYM*, supplement of 22 July 1754, none of the other reports in the colonial press, even those insisting that the French violated the terms by allowing the Amerindians to pillage, mention these five deaths. See *PG*, 25 July 1754; *NYM*, 29 July 1754; and *SCG*, 19 September 1754. The official report by Washington and MacKay does not mention this incident (see *GWP*, 1: 159–68), though they may have left before it occurred. See *Travels in New France by J.C.B.*, ed. Stevens, Kent, and Woods, 63. See also MacLeod, *Canadian Iroquois*, 49.

46 Stobo's letter of 28 July 1754, in Stobo, *Memoirs*, 91–2; *Travels in New France by J.C.B.*, ed. Stevens, Kent, and Woods, 63–4.

47 Those carried to Canada were Jacob Arants (Arrans), John Baker, Barnabas Deven (Dever?), Daniel Stuart Fager, Daniel Lafferty, Henry O'Brien, and John Smith. See Stobo, *Memoirs*, 91–2; *Travels in New France by J.C.B.*, ed. Stevens, Kent, and Woods, 64; and Frank H. Severance, "The Tale of Captives at Fort Niagara," *Buffalo Historical Society Publications* 9 (1906): 237–307.

48 *Official Records of Robert Dinwiddie*, ed. Brock, vol. 1, 293. See also John R. Alden, *Robert Dinwiddie, Servant of the Crown* (Charlottesville, VA: Colonial Williamsburg Foundation, 1973), 47.

49 *NYM*, 26 August 1754; *Journals of the House of Burgesses of Virginia, 1752–1755, 1756–1758*, ed. H.R. McIlwaine (Richmond, VA: Colonial Press, 1909), 221.

50 They were Moses the Song, who was Scarouady's brother-in-law, and Delaware George. See Dinwiddie to Innes, 20 July 1754, in *Official Records of Robert Dinwiddie*, ed. Brock, vol. 1, 233. In transit the letters were opened by George Croghan at Aughwick, who sent copies to the Pennsylvania governor, and allowed enough to circulate to compromise Stobo's safety.

51 Eight Quakers who refused to guard the French prisoners at Winchester were jailed, as was the leader of a local protest that was disrupted by soldiers. It was a year before the eight Quakers were released. See Chester Raymond Young, "The Effects of the French and Indian War on Civilian Life in the Frontier Counties of Virginia, 1754–1763" (PhD diss., Vanderbilt University, 1969), 344–5.

52 Innes to Contrecoeur, *Papiers Contrecoeur*, ed. Grenier, 254; *Official Records of Robert Dinwiddie*, ed. Brock, vol. 1, 297–8, 347, vol. 2, 227–8.

53 See instructions in *Official Records of Robert Dinwiddie*, ed. Brock, vol. 1, 298ff; and Alberts, *Most Extraordinary Adventures*, 107–15.

54 Alberts, *Most Extraordinary Adventures*, 122.

55 See Duquesne to Contrecoeur, 25 July 1754, in *Papiers Contrecoeur*, ed. Grenier, 223; and Stobo, *Memoirs*, 10–12.

56 See, for instance, Ian K. Steele, "Susannah Johnson, Captive," in *The Human Tradition in Colonial America*, ed. Nancy L. Rhoden and Ian K. Steele (Wilmington, DE: Scholarly Resources, 1999), 262–4.

57 *Whitehall Evening Post*, 11 January 1755, quoted in Alberts, *Most Extraordinary Adventures*, 140n; Stobo, *Memoirs*, 12.

58 See "Procès de Robert Stobo et de Jacom Wambram pour crime de haute trahison," in *RAPQ, 1922* (Quebec City, QC: Quebec Archives, 1923), 299–347; LAC, MG 17, A 7–1, 4; Stobo, *Memoirs*; and Alberts, *Most Extraordinary Adventures*, 153–69. At his trial, Stobo said he understood no French, and a "Sieur Piot de Langloiserie" served as his interpreter; Van Braam claimed his French was better than his English. See Draper Mss, Frontier Wars Papers, 12U66, 69.

59 Louis Antoine de Bougainville, *Adventure in the Wilderness: The American Journals of Louis Antoine de Bougainville, 1756–1760*, trans. and ed. Edward P. Hamilton (Norman, OK: University of Oklahoma Press, 1964), 67.

60 Vaudreuil to Argenson, 1 November 1756, *NYCD*, 10: 492.

61 On 8 October 1760, having bestowed £1,000 on Stobo in addition to back pay, the Virginia House of Burgesses granted seven petitioning veterans "and all others who shall hereafter appear in the same Circumstances, the common allowance and pay of soldiers, during their absence in captivity." See *Journals of the House of Burgesses of Virginia, 1758–1761*, ed. H.R. McIlwaine (Richmond, VA: Colonial Press, 1908), 150, 188 (quote). In 1759 the New Jersey government established a commission to pay all arrears to any soldiers of the province who had been taken captive and returned, or who had died in captivity. See *PG*, 14 June 1759.

62 Alberts, *Most Extraordinary Adventures*, 170–340, 387n; Simon Stevens, *Journal of Lieut. Simon Stevens, From the Time of His Being Taken, near Fort William Henry, June the 25th, 1758* (Boston, MA, 1760); "L'Évasion de Stobo et de Van Braam de la prison de Québec en Mai 1757," *Bulletin des Recherches Historiques* 14 (1908): 154. In January 1764, however, the House of Burgesses refused Stobo's petition for his salary as a major during a year's leave of absence in England. See *Journals of the House of Burgesses of Virginia, 1761–1765*, ed. John Pendleton Kennedy (Richmond, VA: Colonial Press, 1907), 212.

63 Captain in the 15th Regiment of Foot for a decade, Stobo committed suicide in his barracks in Chatham, England, on 19 June 1770. See Alberts, *Most Extraordinary Adventures*, 317–18.

64 This despite the Burgesses having censured Van Braam in October 1754. See *Journals of the House of Burgesses, 1752–1755, 1756–1758*, ed. McIlwaine, 221; and Amherst Papers, TNA, WO 34/38, fols, 32–3, 38, 210. Virginia was paying Van Braam's bills as a prisoner in Canada as late as November 1759.

See Amherst Papers, TNA, WO 34/38, fol. 207; *Journals of the House of Burgesses, 1758–1761*, ed. McIlwaine, 227, 238; and Alberts, *Most Extraordinary Adventures*, 334.

65 He was not the John Ramsay killed in a raid on 27 April 1758 on the South Branch of the Potomac River. See Preston Papers, 1: 83.

66 Stobo, *Memoirs*, 91–2. Denis Kaninguen (Cunningham) was another English deserter who was a French witness of the Jumonville incident. See "Journal de Joseph-Gaspard Chaussegros de Léry," 372–3.

67 *Journals of the House of Burgesses, 1761–1765*, ed. Kennedy, 179, 186.

68 In February 1760, notary S. Sanguinet, at Quebec, mentioned that La Force was then a prisoner "en la Nouvelle Angleterre," and in 1771 notary J.-C. Panet observed that he had been away in foreign countries for a number of years. See PUQAM.

PART TWO

1 See John Grenier, *The First Way of War: American War Making on the Frontier* (Cambridge, UK: Cambridge University Press, 2005).

2 For comparison with Canadian borderlands, see especially John Demos, *The Unredeemed Captive: A Family Story from Early America* (New York: Knopf, 1994); William Henry Foster, *The Captors' Narrative: Catholic Women and Puritan Men on the Early American Frontier* (Ithaca, NY: Cornell University Press, 2003); Evan Haefeli and Kevin Sweeney, *Captors and Captives: The 1704 French and Indian Raid on Deerfield* (Amherst and Boston, MA: University of Massachusetts Press, 2003); Daniel K. Richter, "War and Culture: The Iroquois Experience," *W&MQ* 40 (1983): 528–59; and Alden T. Vaughan and Daniel K. Richter, "Crossing the Cultural Divide: Indians and New Englanders, 1605–1763," *American Antiquarian Society Proceedings* 90 (1980): 23–99.

On the South, see James F. Brooks, *Captives and Cousins: Slavery, Kinship, and Community in the Southwest Borderlands* (Chapel Hill, NC: University of North Carolina Press, 2002); and Alan Gallay, *The Indian Slave Trade: The Rise of the English Empire in the American South, 1670–1717* (New Haven, CT: Yale University Press, 2002).

3 André Corvisier, *Armies and Societies in Europe, 1494–1789* (Bloomington, IN: Indiana University Press, 1979), 183–6.

4 Regarding 1763, see *PG*, 18 August and 1 September 1763; *NYM*, 15 August 1763, and M.M. Quaife, ed., *The Siege of Detroit* (Chicago, IL: Lakeside, 1958), 137–8.

5 Canadian governor Pierre-François Rigaud, Marquis de Vaudreuil, attempted to include captured women in exchanges with the British Army, which would count only those who were "women of the regiments."

6 John Defever reported that the price at Detroit was 30 livres for either a scalp or a prisoner. See TNA, WO 55/1817, fol. 11. Scalp bounties were common in New France, and were readily extended to this frontier.

CHAPTER FOUR

1 *PA*, ser. 1, 3: 548–50. Escaped captive John Craig reported that in February 1756, Shingas spoke of a grand alliance of ten tribes that would raise 1,600 men. See HSP, Penn Mss, Indian Affairs, vol. 2, no. 78.

2 Matthew C. Ward, *Breaking the Backcountry: The Seven Years' War in Virginia and Pennsylvania, 1754–1765* (Pittsburgh, PA: University of Pittsburgh Press, 2003), 51

3 On captives versus scalps, see Charles Johnston, *A Narrative of the Incidents Attending the Capture, Detention, and Ransom of Charles Johnston* (New York, 1827), 167.

4 Ten Indians were living in McKee's Fort in April 1756, as was one young "Frenchman." See *PA*, ser. 1, 2: 634–5. The same month, Lieutenant Governor Robert Hunter Morris claimed he had only one Indian in jail, and by June he had a few in custody. See *MPCP*, 7: 97–100, 145–8. See also Albert H. Tillson Jr, "The Militia and Popular Culture in the Upper Valley of Virginia, 1740–1775," *VMHB* 94 (1986): 285–306.

5 *MPCP*, 6: 763; Theodore Thayer, *Israel Pemberton, King of the Quakers* (Philadelphia, PA: Historical Society of Pennsylvania, 1943), 59.

6 See chapter 18.

7 *SCG*, 3 and 17 October 1754.

8 *SCDIA*, 2: 23, 79. The following spring, the Shawnee showed reluctance to be recruited, which was explained as fear of revenge for the Carolina raid. See Croghan to William Johnson, 5 May 1755, *JP*, 1: 496.

9 "Journal de Joseph-Gaspard Chaussegros de Léry, Lieutenant des troupes, 1754–1755," in *RAPQ, 1927–1928* (Quebec City, QC: Quebec Archives, 1928), 409–10; Duquesne to Minister Machault, 31 May 1755, AN, C11A, vol. 100, fol. 3, printed in *Extraits des Archives des Ministres da la Marine et de la Guerre á Paris*, ed. H.-R. Casgrain (Quebec City, QC, 1890), 9–10. Duquesne had encouraged Shawnee revenge in a letter to Captain Claude-Pierre Pécaudy de Contrecoeur of 25 July 1754, who in turn had urged only defensive action before October. See *Papiers Contrecoeur et autres documents concernant le conflit anglo-français sur l'Ohio de 1745 à 1756*, ed. Fernand Grenier (Quebec City, QC: Laval University Press, 1952), 216–18, 220, 222–3, 266, 289.

10 *SCDIA*, 2: 23, 79; Preston Papers, 1: 83.

11 Preston Papers, 1: 83. The August murders were evidently not reported in the newspapers, whereas the Foyle murders were still thought to be of interest in *PG*, 5 September 1754.

12 Chester Raymond Young, "The Effects of the French and Indian War on Civilian Life in the Frontier Counties of Virginia, 1754–1763" (PhD diss., Vanderbilt University, 1969), 36–8, 42. Stalnacker was captured on 18 June 1755 in an attack in which his son, Adam, and a man servant were killed, and his wife was killed soon after capture. See *PG*, 24 June 1755, 1 July 1756; *NYM*, 28 July 1755, 16 February 1756, 5 July 1756; and Preston Papers, 1: 83.

13 Samuel Kercheval, *A History of the Valley of Virginia*, 4th ed. (Strasburg, VA: Shenandoah, 1925), 38, 43–4, 50, 55. "Potomac" is believed to be a corruption of the Shawnee name "Wappatomica."

14 *Hopewell Friends History, 1734–1934, Frederick County, Virginia ...* (Strasburg, VA: Shenandoah, 1936), 113–25. None of this community were killed in the war, but their appeal to Philadelphia Quakers for assistance for refugees prompted a serious inquiry into the purchase of the land beyond payments to Six Nations overlords.

15 James Adair, *Adair's History of the American Indians* (1775; reprint, Johnson City, TN: Watauga, 1930), 2n.

16 Jane T. Merritt, *At the Crossroads: Indians and Empires on a Mid-Atlantic Frontier, 1700–1763* (Chapel Hill, NC: University of North Carolina Press, 2003), 169–97.

17 Maldwyn A. Jones, "The Scotch-Irish in British America," in *Strangers in the Realm*, ed. Bernard Bailyn and Philip Morgan (Chapel Hill, NC: University of North Carolina Press, 1991), 284–313; David H. Fischer, *Albion's Seed: Four British Folkways in America* (New York: Oxford University Press, 1989), 665–71; Colin G. Calloway, *White People, Indians, and Highlanders: Tribal Peoples and Colonial Encounters in Scotland and America* (New York: Oxford University Press, 2008), 8.

18 Robert G. Crist, "Cumberland County," in *Beyond Philadelphia: The American Revolution in the Pennsylvania Hinterland*, ed. John B. Frantz and William Pencak (University Park, PA: Pennsylvania State University Press, 1988), 108.

19 *Papiers Contrecoeur*, ed. Grenier, 306–7. The deposition, in captivity, of Andrew Maynard, is in ibid., 283; and *PA*, ser. 1, 2: 288–9.

20 James Smith, *An Account of the Remarkable Occurrences in the Life and Travels of Colonel James Smith during His Captivity with the Indians, 1755–1759* (Lexington, KY, 1799), 6–9; *MPCP*, 6: 466–7; *MPCP*, 7: 282–4.

21 *Papiers Contrecoeur*, ed. Grenier, 364–7; William A. Hunter, *Forts on the Pennsylvania Frontier, 1753–1758* (Harrisburg, PA: Pennsylvania Historical and Museum Commission, 1960), 129–30. For speculation that this capture was a staged opportunity for Scarouady to negotiate with the French, see Ward, *Breaking the Backcountry*, 42.

22 John Walker escaped after eighteen months. See examinations at Fort Johnson, 21 November 1756, HL, LO, 2401A, and at New York, 25 December 1756, HL, LO, 2254B.

23 *Papiers Contrecoeur*, ed. Grenier, 364–7.

24 "Journal of James Kenny, 1761–1763," ed. John W. Jordan, *PMHB* 37 (1913): 183; *MVHR* 13 (1926): 63–4.

25 The account of a raid by sixty Ottawa into Virginia in May 1755 cannot be corroborated, and is here considered a conflation of later accounts and itself apocryphal. There is no record of such an Ottawa raid at any time during the war. The account appears in *Travels in New France by J.C.B.*, ed. Sylvester K. Stevens, Donald H. Kent, and Emma Edith Woods (Harrisburg, PA: Pennsylvania Historical Commission, 1941), 69–72.

26 Preston Papers, 1: 83; *PG*, 24 July 1755. Captive Samuel Hyden was seen two years later with Indians at Detroit. See *PG*, 22 December 1757. On Stalnacker, see *PG*, 1 July 1756; and F.B. Kegley, *Kegley's Virginia Frontier: The Beginning of the Southwest, the Roanoke of Colonial Days, 1740–1783* (Roanoke, VA: Southwest Virginia Historical Society, 1938), 117, 118, 121, 185.

27 *PG*, 10 July 1755; *MPCP*, 6: 456, 459.

28 Preston Papers, 1: 83; Kercheval, *History of the Valley*, 85–8. A more fantastic "Narrative of John Bingeman" is preserved in Draper Mss, Virginia Papers, 1ZZ36. On Katherine Bingeman's horrific escape adventure, see *Journals of the House of Burgesses of Virginia, 1758–1761*, ed. H.R. McIlwaine (Richmond, VA: Colonial Press, 1908), 239; and Draper Mss, Frontier Wars Papers, 12U112.

29 At least three of their children evidently remained with the Shawnee, with whom they had by then spent most of their young lives. See Preston Papers, 1: 83; *WPHM* 39 (1956): 194, 202; *PG*, 17 January 1765; and *NYG*, 21 January 1765.

30 "M'Aden's Journal," in William Henry Foote, *Sketches of North Carolina* (New York, 1846), 162.

31 Warren R. Hofstra, *The Planting of New Virginia: Settlement and Landscape in the Shenandoah Valley* (Baltimore, MD: Johns Hopkins University Press, 2004), 41, 44–5, 167, 176–7, 239; James Titus, *The Old Dominion at War: Society, Politics, and Warfare in Late Colonial Virginia* (Columbus, SC: University of South Carolina Press, 1991), 11 (re. Patton's lands).

32 *NYM*, 25 August and 8 September 1755. Seven settlers were killed in an even bolder Shawnee strike farther east, into Halifax County.

33 Mary Draper Ingles, *The Story of Mary Draper Ingles and Son John Ingles*, ed. Roberta Inglis Steele and Andrew Lewis Ingles (Radford, VA: Commonwealth, 1969); *NYM*, 16 February 1756; Joseph A. Waddell, *Annals of Augusta County, Virginia*, 2 vols (Richmond, VA, 1886–88), vol. 1, 75; Mary Musselwhite DeNoya, "Massacre at the Meadows," *Daughters of the American Revolution Magazine* 106 (1972): 132–6, 230.

34 For an analysis of the issues earlier, see Virginia DeJohn Anderson, *Creatures of Empire: How Domesticated Animals Transformed Early America* (New York: Oxford University Press, 2004); and Hofstra, *Planting of New Virginia*, 94–142.

35 *PG*, 13 November 1755. See also a less reliable account in Archibald Loudon, ed., *A Selection of Some of the Most Interesting Narratives of Outrages Committed by the Indians in Their Wars with the White People*, 2 vols (Carlisle, PA, 1808–11), vol. 2, 178–80.

36 *The Official Records of Robert Dinwiddie, 1751–1758*, ed. R.A. Brock, 2 vols (Richmond, VA, 1883–84), vol. 2, 198, 218; Preston Papers, 1: 83; *NYM*, 25 August and 8 September 1755.

37 *Official Records of Robert Dinwiddie*, ed. Brock, vol. 2, 235, 259; *GWP*, 2: 72–3, 104; *PG*, 16 and 30 October 1755.

38 *Maryland Gazette*, 9 October 1755; *PG*, 16 October 1755; *MPCP*, 6: 641; *MPCP*, 7: 381.

39 A premium of £5 was added when the act was renewed in 1757. See *The Statutes at Large: Being a Collection of All the Laws of Virginia, from the First Session of the Legislature in the Year 1619*, ed. William Waller Hening, 13 vols (Charlottesville, VA: University Press of Virginia, 1969), vol. 6, 550–2, vol. 7, 121–3; Dinwiddie to Colonel James Patton, 1 August 1755, and Dinwiddie to Colonel Buchanan, 14 August 1755, Preston Papers, 1: 84, 86; and Matthew C. Ward, "La guerre sauvage: The Seven Years' War on the Virginia and Pennsylvania Frontier" (PhD diss., College of William and Mary, 1992), 111–26.

40 Of 277 killed or taken by Shawnee between 1745 and 1765, 164 were in Virginia, 44 in the Ohio Valley, and only 20 in Pennsylvania. Only 15 of some 254 well-dated killings and captures by the Shawnee occurred between the months of November and April.

41 John Van Meter accompanied Delaware on an unsuccessful raid against the Catawba in 1725. A 1748 raid on the Catawba by thirty Delaware, in which they took a prisoner, ended with the group being counterattacked by ten Catawba, who reportedly killed the entire Delaware raiding party and recovered their captive. See Hofstra, *Planting of New Virginia*, 31, 94.

42 Charles Stuart, "The Captivity of Charles Stuart, 1755–57," *MVHR* 13 (1926–27): 63. Tewea not only corroborated this explanation for the coming of the Delaware war, but also added that Braddock "threatened to destroy all the Indians on the Continent, after they had conquered the French." See William Fleming and Elizabeth Fleming, *A Narrative of the Sufferings and Surprizing Deliverances of William and Elizabeth Fleming* (1756; reprint, New York: Garland, 1978).

43 Stuart, "Captivity," 63–4; *MPCP*, 6: 522–4; HSP, Penn Mss, Indian Affairs, vol. 2, no. 42. For Tewea's remarks to the Flemings early in November 1755, see *NYM*, 8 March 1756. For Vaudreuil's general summary, see AN, C11A, vol. 101, fol. 88.

44 James H. Merrell, *Into the American Woods: Negotiators on the Pennsylvania Frontier* (New York: Norton, 1999), 25–30.

45 The consultant was Tohashwughtoniont (a.k.a. Belt of Wampum or Old Belt). See Dunbar to Robert Hunter Morris, 27 August 1755, *PA*, ser. 1, 2: 385; and Merrell, *Into the American Woods*, 230.

46 *MPCP*, 6: 645–6; Anthony F.C. Wallace, *King of the Delawares: Teedyuscung, 1700–1763* (Philadelphia, PA: University of Pennsylvania Press, 1949), 69–71.

47 C. Hale Sipe, *The Indian Wars of Pennsylvania* (Harrisburg, PA: Telegraph, 1929), 204–9.

48 The attackers included Pisquetomen. See Wallace, *King of the Delawares*, 71; and *MPCP*, 5: 648–9. Seven years later Harris made a claim, which was denied, that he had hired thirty-two men for eighteen days late in 1755 on instruction from George Croghan. See *V&P*, 6: 5386, 5390.

49 *The Narrative of Marie Le Roy and Barbara Leininger* (Philadelphia, PA, 1759), reprinted in *PA*, ser. 2, 7: 427–38, and compare their deposition in *PA*, ser. 1, 3: 633–4. See also Michael N. McConnell, *A Country Between: The Upper*

Ohio Valley and Its Peoples, 1724–1774 (Lincoln, NB: University of Nebraska Press, 1992), 120–1; and Merrell, *Into the American Woods*, 227–33.

50 Patrick Burns, captured by Shawnee in Path Valley on 19 October 1755, reported that a war party of more than ninety, mostly Delaware led by Shingas and Tewea, were twenty miles west of Raystown on 22 October and resolved to attack Big Cove and Conococheague Creek. See HSP, Penn Mss, Indian Affairs, vol. 2, no. 44.

51 This attack was reported much later (1821–22). See C.A. Weslager, *The Delaware Indians: A History* (New Brunswick, NJ: Rutgers University Press, 1972), 94.

52 Patrick Burns had been take earlier that day and escaped. See *PA*, ser. 1, 2: 462–3.

53 *NYM*, 8 March 1756.

54 Ibid.

55 The Hicks family were attacked while heading for the nearest fortified house: two were reported killed and the rest captured. Mrs Barbara Hicks was recovered in the Kittanning raid ten months later, and one now-adult male was returned to Bouquet in November of 1764. See *PA*, ser. 1, 2: 775; and *PG*, 13 November 1755, 23 September 1756, 17 January 1765.

56 *NYM*, 8 March 1756.

57 *NYM*, 15 March 1756.

58 James H. Merrell, "Shamokin, 'the very seat of the Prince of darkness': Unsettling the Early American Frontier," in *Contact Points: American Frontiers from the Mohawk Valley to the Mississippi, 1750–1830*, ed. Andrew R.L. Cayton and Fredrika J. Teute (Chapel Hill, NC: University of North Carolina Press, 1998), 16–59.

59 For John Hockstetler's deposition after his escape, see *Wilderness Chronicles of Northwestern Pennsylvania*, ed. Sylvester K. Stevens and Donald R. Kent (Harrisburg, PA: Pennsylvania Historical Commission, 1941), 119–21. On Margaret Eberhardt, see *PMHB* 32 (1908): 311; and Sipe, *Indian Wars*, 240. Only three of thirty-four Berks County captives whose place of captivity is known were taken northward into New York, rather than west to Ohio country. Hockstetler's personal captor may well have been a migrating Delaware unsupported by the French or Shingas. Captor and captive settled at the pro-French Seneca village at Buckaloons (a.k.a. La Paille Coupée or Brokenstraw).

60 In 1742 Iroquois had enforced the terms of the infamous 1737 Walking Purchase, making Delaware leave the lower Lehigh Valley for Shamokin and Wyoming. See Weslager, *Delaware Indians*, 173–95.

61 Merritt, *At the Crossroads*, 96, 155–6; Earl P. Olmstead, *David Zeisberger: A Life among the Indians* (Kent, OH: Kent State University Press, 1997), 79–80; Wallace, *King of the Delawares*, 47–9; Weslager, *Delaware Indians*, 173–95, 211–12.

62 Merritt, *At the Crossroads*, 42, 155, 182, 190.

63 Deposition of Captain Jacob Morgan, in *PG*, 20 November 1755; and *NYM*, 24 November 1755. The original Morgan deposition specified that "his

privities [were] cut off and put into his mouth." On sexual features of mutilation, see Merritt, *At the Crossroads*, 178–9.

64 See Jacob Morgan deposition on Tulpehoken, in *NYM*, 24 November 1755. For the claim that the Wyoming Delaware were involved, see Ward, "La guerre sauvage," 134–5. See also Wallace, *King of the Delawares*, 80–6.

65 Captain Jachebus, a Munsee warrior from Assinisink, is said to have led the raid. Mrs Susanna Nitschmann's captivity indicates the origin of the raid. She was taken first to Wyoming, where she was cared for by a convert until taken north to Tioga. See Wallace, *King of the Delawares*, 77; and Henry M.M. Richards, *The Pennsylvania-German in the French and Indian War* (Lancaster, PA: Pennsylvania-German Society, 1905), 147–8.

66 The Indians seeking refuge numbered 205 at Bethlehem, 134 at Nazareth, and 104 at Friedensthall. See Olmstead, *David Zeisberger*, 96. The 315 refugees counted at Nazareth on 17 December 1755 were promptly redistributed. See "Six Months on the Frontier of Northampton County, Penna., during the Indian War, October 1755–June 1756," *PMHB* 39 (1915): 345–52. The Iroquois diplomats reporting from Tioga added, "if they have told us a pack of lies, we cannot help it." See *JP*, 9: 335.

67 *PA*, ser. 1, 2: 595.

68 *MPCP*, 6: 736–7; Sipe, *Indian Wars*, 241–2; Weslager, *Delaware Indians*, 229.

69 John Woolman had seen signs of migration out of Wyoming in September, but these may have been people unsympathetic to Teedyuscung. See John Woolman, *A Journal of the Life, Gospel Labours, and Christian Experiences of That Faithful Minister of Jesus Christ, John Woolman* (London, UK, 1847), 117, 123.

70 For depositions of captives Leonard Weeser and Henry Hess, see *PA*, ser. 1, 3: 45–6, 56–7. Margery West "saw no french or french Indians" during her captivity in 1756. See *New York Historical Society, Collections for 1921* (New York: New York Historical Society, 1922), 96. Prisoner John Coxe did see evidence of visiting with and by the Ohio Delaware. See *MPCP*, 7: 242–3. Concerning the fourteen men of Captain "Haysis's" company and the five Indians killed in the encounter, see *PMHB* 32 (1908): 315.

71 In the 1755 raids on Berks and Northampton Counties, more than four people died for every one captured (147:33).

72 *NYM*, 8 September 1755.

73 Ward, "La guerre sauvage," 427–40.

74 *MPCP*, 7: 242–3. A raid in November 1756 was likely an Ohio-based raid to disrupt the negotiations between Pennsylvania and Teedyuscung. See *PG*, 18 November 1756; and *PMHB* 32 (1908): 318.

75 *MPCP*, 7: 171–2; HL, LO, 757, 1265.

76 By the end of June 1756, a shortage of supplies was already evident at Fort Niagara. See Wallace, *King of the Delawares*, 96–7.

77 Young, "Effects of the French and Indian War," 432.

78 *MPCP*, 7: 242–3. Lieutenant Colonel John Armstrong reported 374 plantations had been evacuated beyond the Blue Mountains and 554 in the longer-settled Cumberland Valley. See Hunter, *Forts*, 211.

79 *NYM*, 29 March 1756; *PG*, 25 March 1756.
80 *MPCP*, 7: 242–3; *NYM*, 5 April 1756; *PG*, 19 February 1756.
81 Dumas exaggerated wildly when claiming to have six or seven parties out constantly, each including two Frenchmen. See Dumas to Minister of Marine, 24 July 1756, quoted in F.-J. Audet, *Jean-Daniel Dumas, le héros de la Monongahéla; esquisse biographique* (Montreal, QC: G. Ducharme, 1920), 78; *PG*, 19 and 29 April 1756; *NYCD*, 10: 396; and *GWP*, 2: 334–7.
82 *GWP*, 2: 137; *GWP*, 3: 23–4.
83 *PG*, 15 April and 6 May 1756; *GWP*, 3: 18, 84. John Adam Long, captured by the same party a few days earlier, described the event in *NYM*, 18 October 1756.
84 *Maryland Gazette*, 8 April 1756; *PG*, 15 April 1756.
85 In the "battle of Sideling Hill," some twenty-three soldiers and militiamen were killed, as were captive Mary McCord and three Delaware. See *PG*, 22 April 1756; *NYM*, 19 April 1756; Loudon, ed., *Selection*, vol. 2, 160; *PA*, ser. 2, 2: 463; Vaudreuil to Minister, 8 August 1756, AN, C11A, vol. 101, fol. 88; Hunter, *Forts*, 561.
86 *PG*, 17 and 24 June 1756; Frank H. Severance, "The Tale of Captives at Fort Niagara," *Buffalo Historical Society Publications* 9 (1906): 257.
87 François was brother to Louis and Jumonville. See *DCB*, 4: 177–8.
88 Dinwiddie to Board of Trade, 23 February 1756, TNA, CO 5/1328, fols 183–9.
89 Ward, *Breaking the Backcountry*, 95. Seventy-one Virginians identified as soldiers were killed or taken in 1756, including eleven involved in the siege of Vause's Fort.
90 Louis K. Koontz, *The Virginia Frontier, 1754–1763* (Baltimore, MD: Johns Hopkins University Press, 1925), 108 and appendix 1; Waddell, *Annals of Augusta*, vol. 1, 95.
91 *PG*, 8 January 1756, and reprinted in every issue throughout the next three months.
92 Proclamation in *PG*, 15, 22, and 29 April 1756; Yoko Shirai, "The Indian Trade in Colonial Pennsylvania, 1730–1768: Traders and Land Speculation" (PhD diss., University of Pennsylvania, 1985), 91–2.
93 Hunter, *Forts*.
94 Preston Papers, 1: 96–123; Ward, *Breaking the Backcountry*, 104–6.
95 During 1757 the Cherokee were reported in newspapers as killing twenty-three "enemy" Indians and "Frenchmen" and capturing eleven others.
96 The force was led by Colonel Thomas Cresap Jr. See *Maryland Gazette*, 6 May 1756; and Ward, *Breaking the Backcountry*, 106.
97 In March 1756, escaped captive John Baker estimated that "more than one hundred English Boys and Girls" were held at Kittanning, and that the town had eighty to ninety warriors. See HSP, Penn Mss, Indian Affairs, vol. 2, no. 78. On killing prisoners, see Thomas Brown, *A Plain Narrative of the Uncommon Sufferings and Remarkable Deliverance of Thomas Brown of Charlestown, in New England* (Boston, MA, 1760); Henry Timberlake, *Lieut.*

Henry Timberlake's Memoirs, 1756–1765 (1765; reprint, Marietta, GA: Continental, 1948), 113–16; and Ian K. Steele, *Betrayals: Fort William Henry and the "Massacre"* (New York: Oxford University Press, 1990), 74–5.

98 In his letter to Lieutenant Governor William Denny of 14 September 1756, John Armstrong asked for orders so "that I may know whether to send them to Philadelphia, or deliver them to their relatives, as your Honour shall think fit." See MPCP, 7: 263.

99 On Armstrong, and on his optimistic view of the expedition's fortunes, see "John Armstrong," in *Law Making and Legislators in Pennsylvania: A Biographical Dictionary*, ed. Craig Horle et al., 3 vols (Philadelphia and Harrisburg, PA: University of Pennsylvania Press, 1991–2005), vol. 3, 280–300.

100 Daniel P. Barr, "Victory at Kittanning? Reevaluating the Impact of Armstrong's Raid on the Seven Years' War in Pennsylvania," *PMHB* 131 (2007): 17–18.

101 Armstrong to Denny, 14 September 1756, *MPCP*, 7: 257–63.

102 Barr, "Victory at Kittanning?" 5–32; William A. Hunter, "Victory at Kittanning," *PH* 23 (1956): 376–407; James P. Myers Jr, "Pennsylvania's Awakening: The Kittanning Raid of 1756," *PH* 66 (1999): 399–420. Armstrong reported seventeen killed, thirteen wounded, and nineteen missing. At least three of the missing, Samuel Chambers, Thomas Burke, and Ensign John Scott, were killed by the Delaware. See *MPCP*, 7: 257–63. The records of the second battalion of the Pennsylvania militia, in *PA*, ser. 2, 2: 458–60, are erroneous. Three men – John Reynolds, John Layson (Lasson), and John Kelly – reported as killed at Kittanning had actually been killed at the battle of Sideling Hill in April. See *PG*, 22 April 1756.

103 On the capture of Mrs Alexander McAllister, see *PG*, 24 June 1756. This account of the torture follows Hugh Gibson's first telling of the incident. Compare Loudon, ed., *Selection*, vol. 2, 182, with Hugh Gibson, "An Account of the Captivity of Hugh Gibson among the Delaware Indians of the Big Beaver and the Muskingum, from the Latter Part of July 1756 to the Beginning of April 1759," *Massachusetts Historical Society Collections*, ser. 3, 6 (1837): 144.

104 *MPCP*, 7: 242–3, printed in *NYM*, 9 September 1756. The Le Roy–Leininger narrative does not name the captive, but the timing suggests Paul Broadly was much more likely the victim than John Turner. See *PA*, ser. 2, 7: 431.

105 "The Narrative of Marie Le Roy and Barbara Leininger," *PA*, ser. 2, 7: 401–12; Gibson, "Account of the Captivity," 141–53. An earlier version is in Loudon, ed., *Selection*, vol. 2, 192–5; and in William Fleming and Elizabeth Fleming, *A Narrative of the Sufferings and Surprizing Deliverances of William and Elizabeth Fleming* (1756; reprint, New York: Garland, 1978).

106 *PA*, ser. 2, 2: 458–60; Hunter, "Victory at Kittanning"; *PG*, 23 September 1756, 17 January 1765. Two other Pennsylvania soldiers, George Appleby and William Hunter, likely returned from captivity as well.

107 *PJ*, 21 October 1756.

108 A Delaware captive later reported that only one Frenchman, out of a patrol of five in the vicinity, fought with the Delaware in defense of Kittanning. See *PA*, ser. 1, 3: 147–8.

109 Helen H. Tanner, ed., *Atlas of Great Lakes Indian History* (Norman, OK: University of Oklahoma Press, 1987), map 9.

110 Near the end of September, a Delaware reportedly killed a man and was killed near Fort Dinwiddie. See *NYM*, 11 October 1756.

111 *PG*, 7 October 1756; *NYM*, 11 October 1756; Ward, *Breaking the Back Country*, 161.

112 For the claim that three Shawnee were killed, see Pierre Pouchot, *Memoirs of the Late War in North America between England and France*, ed. B.L. Dunnigan (Youngstown, NY: Old Fort Niagara Association, 1994), 110–11. In contrast, the colonial newspapers claimed it was four. See *PG*, 6 January 1757; *NYM*, 10 January 1757, 25 April 1757; and *SCG*, 17 February 1757. The Virginia Regiment's Sergeant Joseph Fent and a Catawba taken with him both escaped, and Sergeant William Shaw was later returned. See *GWP*, 4: 161–3; and *Journals of the House of Burgesses, 1758–1761*, ed. McIlwaine, 66. He was awarded £60 (see ibid., 68).

113 Four Indians were reported captured: two Indian servants were captured in the fall of Vause's Fort; Iroquois chief Ogaghradarisha was held very briefly by Ojibwa captors before being released (see HSP, Penn Papers, Indian Affairs, vol. 2, no. 103); and one Catawba captured by the Shawnee or the Delaware is known to have escaped (see Pouchot, *Memoirs*, 110–11; and *GWP*, 4: 161–3).

114 Fewer women and children had been involved in 1756, and the proportion of women killed rather than captured fell from 43 per cent to 34 per cent. There were no major battles, and the North Branch Delaware war had effectively ended in April. The uneasiness of the ceasefire is demonstrated in militia captain John Van Etten's report of 22 July 1756 on the killing of a Delaware after a testy conversation. See *PA*, ser. 1, 2: 720–1. This incident is illuminated by Peter Silver, *Our Savage Neighbors: How Indian War Transformed Early America* (New York: Norton, 2008), 143–6.

115 There were 102 raids in 1756 and 100 in 1757. See Ward, "La guerre sauvage," appendix C.

116 McConnell, *Country Between*, 122; Pouchot, *Memoirs*, 113.

117 Pouchot, *Memoirs*, 112.

118 *GWP*, 4: 194, 215–17; AN, C11A, vol. 102, fol. 53; *MPCP*, 7: 601, 603–5; Ward, "La guerre sauvage," 199–202. The three young Canadian ensigns were La Saussaye, Saint Ours (son of a captain), and François-Louis Picoté de Belestre (son of another *troupes de la marine* captain). The last survived the attack and was taken captive. After interrogation, he lived with the Cherokee and influenced the Cherokee movement toward war with the English. See Pierre Tousignant and Madeleine Dionne-Tousignant, "Picoté de Belestre, François-Marie" [the father], *DCB*, 4: 634.

119 HL, LO, 4648, 4706; *PA*, ser. 1, 3: 294–6, 298, 305–8, 329–30; Hunter, *Forts*, 325, 338.

120 HL, LO, 3925; *PG*, 28 July 1757; *NYM*, 1 August 1757; *Executive Journals of the Council of Colonial Virginia*, 6 vols (Richmond, VA: Virginia State Library, 1925–66), vol. 6, 66. See also Larry G. Bowman, "Virginia's Use of Blacks in the French and Indian War," *WPHM* 53 (1970): 63, 63n.

121 *PG*, 11 August 1757.

122 James Caull was killed by Delaware in Northampton County in November 1755, and another black was reported captured in New Jersey that year. See *PMHB* 32 (1908): 315; and *PG*, 9 September 1756. One black Pennsylvania soldier was reported missing in the attack on Kittanning. See Hunter, "Victory at Kittanning," 392–402; and *PG*, 23 September 1756.

123 Demeré to Bouquet, 21 February 1758, BL, Add. Mss, 21643, fols 58–9; *PG*, 23 February 1758.

124 Forbes to Abercromby, 4 May 1758, HL, AB, 230.

125 *Letters to Washington and Accompanying Papers*, ed. S.M. Hamilton, 5 vols (Washington, DC, 1898–1902), vol. 2, 296–8, 308–9.

126 HL, MM, 613.

127 Pierre Pouchot, commanding at Fort Niagara, sent marine ensign François Mouet de Louvigny out with a party that raided in Berks County early in April 1758. He recorded that fourteen had been killed or captured, whereas English colonial newspapers said that nine had died and one had gone missing. See Pouchot, *Memoirs*, 129; *PG*, 13 April 1758; and *NYM*, 17 April 1758.

128 One woman and four children were taken from a house in one attack, and a boy on horseback was captured. See *PG*, 14 July and 11 August 1757. On York County participation in the war, see Hunter, *Forts*, 173–4, 177, 184–5, 203, 404, 420, 440, 451, 555, 564.

129 Sixteen children under the age of sixteen are known to have been killed within a week of capture: four in 1755, two in 1756, two in 1757, and eight in 1758.

130 *PA*, ser. 1, 3: 396–7; *PG*, 11 May 1758. Compare these reports with the second-hand account in Loudon, ed., *Selection*, vol. 2, 47–65. The raiding party included James Linganoa (a.k.a. Delaware Jamy). See Hunter, *Forts*, 422.

131 *PA*, ser. 1, 3: 632–3.

132 Samuel Davies, *The Curse of Cowardice: A Sermon Preached to the Militia of Hanover County in Virginia at a General Muster, May 8, 1758* (London, UK, 1759); *PG*, 27 July 1758.

133 The total for 1756 was 888, whereas 782 were killed or taken in the eighteen months between January 1757 and June 1758.

134 *GWP*, 4: 306–8, 321–2; *SCDIA*, 2: 406–8.

135 Bouquet Papers, BL, Add. Mss, 21640, fol. 94.

136 Bouquet Papers, BL, Add. Mss, 21641, fol. 9; *PG*, 3 August 1758; *NYM*, 31 July 1758.

137 Bouquet Papers, BL, Add. Mss, 21640, fols 145–6.
138 *HBP*, 2: 493.
139 Thirty-one of the English were reported missing. Only one of them, Thomas Morris of Virginia, can be confirmed as captured. See *HBP*, 5: 210–11.
140 *Writings of General John Forbes Relating to his Service in North America*, ed. Alfred Proctor James (Menasha, WI: Collegiate, 1938), 232–3; Lawrence Henry Gipson, *The British Empire before the American Revolution*, 15 vols (Caldwell, ID, and New York: Caxton and Knopf, 1936–70), vol. 7, 273n.
141 On their return, the French and Indian force under de Corbière encountered a ten-man detail of the Royal American Regiment, under Lieutenant Hayes, returning from escorting Frederick Christian Post to negotiate with the Ohio Delaware. Five of these soldiers, including Hayes, were killed, and five were taken captive and brought to Fort Duquesne, becoming the last captives brought in there. See R.G. Thwaites, ed., *Early Western Travels, 1748–1846*, 32 vols (Cleveland, OH: Arthur H. Clark, 1904–07), vol. 1, 250; Bouquet Papers, BL, Add. Mss, 21645, fol. 182, and 21654, fol. 9; and *PG*, 7 and 21 December 1758.
142 A William Johnson of Paxton was reported "killed or carried off" fourteen months earlier. See *PG*, 6 October 1757; echoed in *NYM*, 10 October 1757. He may have been the same William Johnson who had given a deposition in Maryland in November 1756 describing Fort Duquesne, Fort Machault, and the Delaware he lived with there. See *MPCP*, 7: 342.
143 *GWP*, 6: 121–3n; *Writings of General John Forbes*, ed. James, 255–6; *PG*, 30 November 1758; *NYM*, 4 December 1758; *SCG*, 8 December 1758.
144 The main expedition, comprising 200 men under Lieutenant Colonel Hugh Mercer, never reached its destination, and a convoy of supporting bateaux was attacked early, leaving ten dead and two captured in a related incident. The Delaware of Kuskuski reportedly freed the two captives. See *NYG*, 7 May 1759.
145 *PG*, 3 May 1759; *NYG*, 7 May 1759; *NYM*, 30 April 1759.
146 *SCG*, 24 November 1759; *PG*, 1 and 8 November 1759; *NYG*, 5 and 12 November 1759. Four Gilmores were returned: Elizabeth, Elizabeth Jr, Jane, and John. See *PG*, 17 January 1765; and *WPHM* 39 (1956): 194–7. Herbert McClure was injured in the rescue and was eventually awarded £30. See *Journals of the House of Burgesses, 1758–1761*, ed. McIlwaine, 194.
147 There were incidents throughout the truce that lasted until the spring of 1763, most notably the renewed Iroquois and Shawnee raids against the Cherokee, encouraged by British authorities as adjuncts to their own war with the Cherokee. At least thirty-five were killed, with ten more presumed captured. Among the Delaware, Dr John and three of his family were also murdered in February 1760.
148 The Delaware killed 236, captured 443, and had 38 of these escape. Among the captives, 285 were returned, 24 are known to have stayed with the Delaware, and 96 remained missing. Mingo raiders were very seldom distin-

guished from Iroquois in general, which included Canadian Iroquois and Genesee Seneca. Only 18 were clearly identified as victims of the Mingo; 2 were killed, 6 were returned, 2 stayed with the Mingo, and 8 remained "missing."

149 James H. Howard, *Shawnee! The Ceremonialism of a Native Indian Tribe and Its Cultural Background* (Athens, OH: Ohio University Press, 1981), 31–3, estimates that there were about 1,500 Shawnee in the Ohio Valley in 1759. In September 1748, Conrad Weiser had been given a stick-count of 162 Shawnee warriors, incomplete but representing about 800 Shawnee. See *MPCP*, 5: 351. In 1765 David Jones estimated that there were about 600 Shawnee living in the Scioto and Muskingum Valleys. See McConnell, *Country Between*, 210.

150 The Shawnee killed 117 and captured 358. Among the captives, 210 were returned, 29 escaped, 34 are known to have stayed with the Shawnee, and another 85 remained "missing."

151 Indians known to have been killed totaled 31 in 1755, 95 in 1756, 26 in 1757, 30 in 1758, and 14 in 1759.

152 Among white civilians, 36 are known to have been captured, and 26 killed.

CHAPTER FIVE

1 Louis K. Koontz, The *Virginia Frontier, 1754–1763* (Baltimore, MD: Johns Hopkins University Press, 1925), 111–48; James Titus, *The Old Dominion at War: Society, Politics, and Warfare in Late Colonial Virginia* (Columbus, SC: University of South Carolina Press, 1991), 94; William A. Hunter, *Forts on the Pennsylvania Frontier, 1753–1758* (Harrisburg, PA: Pennsylvania Historical and Museum Commission, 1960).

2 *NYM*, 29 March 1756; *PG*, 25 March 1756. On an alarm horn, see "Deposition of Margery West Concerning Her Captivity by the Indians," *New York Historical Society, Collections for 1921* (New York: New York Historical Society, 1922), 94–7.

3 *MPCP*, 7: 242–3; *NYM*, 5 April 1756; *PG*, 19 February 1756. McDowell's Mill survived and had become a provincial magazine by early 1757. See *MPCP*, 7: 444–6.

4 *GWP*, 3: 23–4n; Preston Papers, 1: 83; *PG*, 15 and 29 April 1756; *NYM*, 19 April and 3 May 1756; Petition of William Istobe, *Journals of the House of Burgesses of Virginia, 1758–1761*, ed. H.R. McIlwaine (Richmond, VA: Colonial Press, 1908), 84.

5 *GWP*, 2: 137; *GWP*, 3: 23–4.

6 *GWP*, 2: 334–7; *PG*, 19 and 29 April 1756. Douville was urged to encourage humane treatment of captives. Although Douville was not an Indian, George Washington successfully sought a scalp bounty to be shared by all the militiamen involved.

7 Shingas himself was among those wounded. See *GWP*, 3: 18, 77–9, 81–4; *PG*, 15 April and 6 May 1756; *NYM*, 18 October 1756.

8 PG, 25 March 1756; Norman L. Baker, *French and Indian War in Frederick County, Virginia* (Winchester, VA: Winchester-Frederick County Historical Society, 2000), 147.

9 Widow Coxe was burned out of her home, near McDowell's Mill, on 11 February 1756. See *NYM*, 23 February 1756; and *MPCP*, 7: 242–3. Raiders failed in attempting to burn Coombes's Fort, near Stoddart's Fort, later in February. See *NYM*, 29 March 1756.

10 John Craig's account is in *PG*, 19 February 1756, and in *NYM*, 5 April 1756. See also *Maryland Gazette*, 8 April 1756; and *PG*, 15 April 1756. Compare Matthew C. Ward, "La guerre sauvage: The Seven Years' War on the Virginia and Pennsylvania Frontier" (PhD diss., College of William and Mary, 1992), 155. It is not clear whether the burning of Warden's Fort, in which the two men there died, occurred in the spring of 1756 or 1758. See Samuel Kercheval, *A History of the Valley of Virginia*, 4th ed. (Strasburg, VA: Shenandoah, 1925), 87, 115.

11 Henry M.M. Richards, *The Pennsylvania-German in the French and Indian War* (Lancaster, PA: Pennsylvania-German Society, 1905), 286–7.

12 Edward Shippen to Morris, 24 April 1756, *PA*, ser. 2, 2: 463; Jean Lowry, *A Journal of the Captivity of Jean Lowry and Her Children* (Philadelphia, PA, 1760); *PG*, 8, 15, and 22 April 1756; *NYM*, 12 and 19 April 1756; Hunter, *Forts*, 412, 561; Archibald Loudon, ed., *A Selection of Some of the Most Interesting Narratives of Outrages Committed by the Indians in Their Wars with the White People*, 2 vols (Carlisle, PA, 1808–11), vol. 2, 160.

13 AN, C11A, vol. 101, fol. 88; *PG*, 17 and 24 June 1756; Hunter, *Forts*, 124, 381, 389, 401, 556. See also *Wilderness Chronicles of Northwestern Pennsylvania*, ed. Sylvester K. Stevens and Donald R. Kent (Harrisburg, PA: Pennsylvania Historical Commission, 1941), 94n11. Seven of those captured (three women, one man, one teen, and two children) are known to have become prisoners of the Ohio Delaware, including Mrs Alexander McAllister. See Frank H. Severance, "The Tale of Captives at Fort Niagara," *Buffalo Historical Society Publications* 9 (1906): 257. Twelve captives eventually returned, seven remained "missing," and young Jane Gray is known to have stayed with the Six Nations.

14 A few Potawatomi and Wyandot may have joined as well.

15 Morris Griffith was captured there on 12 August 1755. See F.B. Kegley, *Kegley's Virginia Frontier: The Beginning of the Southwest, the Roanoke of Colonial Days, 1740–1783* (Roanoke, VA: Southwest Virginia Historical Society, 1938), 193–4, 214–15.

16 On Captain, self-styled major, John Smith, see TNA, 30/8/95, fols 214–15; HL, LO, 4791, 4807, 4925, 5452, 5658; and *NYM*, 30 January 1758. On Peter Looney, see *PG*, 28 July 1757, reprinted in *NYM*, 1 August 1757, reprinted in *London Chronicle, or Universal Evening Post*, 6–8 September 1757, reprinted in *The Military History of Great Britain, for 1756, 1757: Containing a Letter from an English Officer at Canada, Taken Prisoner at Oswego* (London, UK, 1757), 86–8, and reprinted in *MVHR* 15 (1928): 95–6. See also Preston Papers, 1:

131–5; *PG*, 9 February 1758; and *GWP*, 3: 260–1. Governor Pierre-François Rigaud, Marquis de Vaudreuil, exaggerated wildly in claiming that 300 Virginians were killed or captured, and 120 horseloads of booty carried off. See *NYCD*, 10: 486.

17 *PG*, 28 July 1757.

18 James Bell, William Bratton, Arthur Campbell, and William Pepper all returned, and Peter Looney escaped.

19 Preston Papers, 1: 83; William S. Ewing, "Indian Captives Released by Colonel Bouquet," *WPHM* 39 (1956): 189, 194, 202. When the Shawnee returned James Bell and Elizabeth Vause in November 1764, after more than eight years as captives, Elizabeth's sister Susannah was still among eighty-eight captives held by the Shawnee and the only one remaining from the capture of Vause's Fort.

20 This speech was reportedly given on 10 July 1756, and was interpreted by John Wotton, "who was taken Prisoner about Ten Years ago at the Lower Shawanese Town, and has been with the French ever since." See *PG*, 9 February 1758.

21 On the strategy, see Louis M. Waddell, "Defending the Long Perimeter: Forts on the Pennsylvania, Maryland, and Virginia Frontier, 1755–1765," *PH* 62 (1995): 171–95.

22 On Tewea, see Daniel P. Barr, "Victory at Kittanning? Reevaluating the Impact of Armstrong's Raid on the Seven Years' War in Pennsylvania," *PMHB* 131 (2007): 17–18; and W.J. Eccles, "Coulon de Villiers, Louis," *DCB*, 3: 148–9. Villiers recruited at least one Illinois, who accompanied him as a guide. See Jean-Bernard Bossu, *Travels through That Part of North America Formerly Called Louisiana*, trans. J.R. Forster, 2 vols (London, UK, 1771), vol. 1, 186–8. A year later, captive soldier John Hogan recalled the number of assailants as 100 Indians and 50 Frenchmen. See HL, LO, 3758.

23 Bossu, *Travels*, vol. 1, 185–7.

24 *PG*, 5 August 1756. On Fort Granville, see Hunter, *Forts*, 383–94.

25 Bossu, *Travels*, vol. 1, 186; Le Chevalier de la Pause, "Memoire et observation sur mon voyage en Canada," in *RAPQ, 1931–1932* (Quebec City, QC: Quebec Archives, 1933), 43.

26 Bossu, *Travels*, vol. 1, 187.

27 *PG*, 19 August 1756; depositions of John Hogan and John Street, HL, LO, 3758, 3925; Phillip W. Hoffman, *Simon Girty, Turncoat Hero* (Franklin, TN: American History Imprints, 2009); Colin Calloway, "Simon Girty: Interpreter and Intermediary," in *Being and Becoming Indian: Biographical Studies of North American Frontiers*, ed. James A. Clifton (Chicago, IL: Dorsey, 1989), 38–58.

28 A wounded soldier named Nicholas Barnhold, who escaped after six days, claimed that the French had taken the young adults, leaving the elderly and the children with the Indians. This may have been the arrangement for the trip west, but it was not the way the captives were eventually distributed. See *PG*, 19 August 1756; and *PJ*, 19 August 1756.

29 *MPCP*, 7: 242–3.

30 Kercheval, *History of the Valley*, 91–2, follows local folklore to claim that these raids were led by prominent Delaware war captain Killbuck (Bemineo Killbuck Sr), one of Kercheval's favorite villains.

31 The captives were: Florence Hutchinson and her son David, Mary Burke and her two children, and a daughter of William Elliott.

32 *WPHM* 39 (1956): 194; *PG*, 17 January 1765; *JP*, 11: 485; *Journals of the House of Burgesses of Virginia, 1761–1765*, ed. John Pendleton Kennedy (Richmond, VA: Colonial Press, 1907), 328.

33 Kercheval, *History of the Valley*, 91–2; *PA*, ser. 2, 7: 437; *GWP*, 5: 155, 160; Preston Papers, 1: 83.

34 The fate of twenty-four of these prisoners is known: eighteen were returned after captivity of at least four years; three young children of Mrs Michael Mallo reportedly died in captivity, and one stayed with the Indians; and youths Roger Dyer and James Dyer both escaped early in 1760.

35 Joseph Doddridge, *Notes on the Settlement and Indian Wars of the Western Parts of Virginia and Pennsylvania* (Wellsburgh, VA, 1824), 144.

36 Attacks on Ashby's, Coombes's, Coxe's, and Edward's Forts were aborted.

CHAPTER SIX

1 André Corvisier, *Armies and Societies in Europe, 1494–1789* (Bloomington, IN: Indiana University Press, 1979), 186. I am grateful to Tim Cook of the Canadian War Museum for access to his work in progress on surrender and the killing of prisoners on the Western Front in the First World War. See also Roger Noble, "Raising the White Flag: The Surrender of Australian Soldiers on the Western Front," *Revue Internationale d'Histoire Militaire* 72 (1990): 48–79; Niall Ferguson, "Prisoner Taking and Prisoner Killing in the Age of Total War: Towards a Political Economy of Military Defeat," *War in History* 11 (2004): 148–92; and Joanna Burke, *An Intimate History of Killing: Face-to-Face Killing in Twentieth-Century Warfare* (London: Basic Books, 1999).

2 On five June raids out of Fort Duquesne, see *Papiers Contrecoeur et autres documents concernant le conflit anglo-français sur l'Ohio de 1745 à 1756*, ed. Fernand Grenier (Quebec City, QC: Laval University Press, 1952), 364–7. On the capture of John Walker, on 29 May 1755, see HL, LO, 2401A, 2254B; and "An Account of the Remarkable Occurrences in the Life and Travels of Col. James Smith," in *A Selection of Some of the Most Interesting Narratives of Outrages Committed by the Indians in Their Wars with the White People*, ed. Archibald Loudon, 2 vols (Carlisle, PA, 1808–11), vol. 1, 121–4. On Scarouady (Monacatootha), see William A. Hunter, *Forts on the Pennsylvania Frontier, 1753–1758* (Harrisburg, PA: Pennsylvania Historical and Museum Commission, 1960), 129–30; and the peculiar announcement in *SCG*, 7 August 1755. The Delaware attack in Sussex County, New Jersey, on 21 and 22 May

1755, in which seven were killed and four captured, seems unrelated to a French quest for information. See *PG*, 9 September 1756.

3 Paul E. Kopperman, *Braddock at the Monongahela* (Pittsburgh, PA: University of Pittsburgh Press, 1977), 26; R. David Edmunds, *The Potawatomi: Keepers of the Fire* (Norman, OK: University of Oklahoma Press, 1978), 50–1. Among the 637 Indians, 407 were allies, and 230 were from the mission villages of Canada. See Louise Dechêne, *Le Peuple, l'État et la Guerre au Canada sous le régime français* (Montreal, QC: Boreal, 2008), 501. Black Hoof (d. 1831) was a Shawnee who later claimed to have been there. See John Sugden, "Black Hoof," *ANB*.

4 Captain Robert Orme, recovering from his wounds, claimed 714 of 1,100 men were killed or wounded, plus 63 of 86 officers. See Robert Orme to B. Franklin, 27 July 1755, *W&MQ* 66 (2009): 284. For casualties rates among losers, including those at Breitenfeld (1631) (19–24%), at Rocroi (1634) (29–54%), and at Poltava (1709) (33–49%), see George Raudzens, "Firepower Limitations in Modern Military History," *Journal of Society for Army Historical Research* 67 (1989): 130–53.

5 Fred Anderson, *Crucible of War: The Seven Years' War and the Fate of Empire in British North America, 1754–1766* (New York: Knopf, 2000), 94–107; Charles Hamilton, ed., *Braddock's Defeat* (Norman, OK: University of Oklahoma Press, 1959), 30. For claims that the Indians generally shot too high, and that an estimated 400 were killed and another 100 wounded too badly to escape scalping, see *The Life, Adventures and Surprising Deliverances of Duncan Cameron, Private Soldier in the Regiment of Foot, Late Sir Peter Halkett's* (Philadelphia, PA, 1756), 11.

6 Account of Cholmley's batman, reprinted in Paul E. Kopperman, *Braddock at the Monongahela* (Pittsburgh, PA: University of Pittsburgh Press, 1977), 183.

7 See Captain Orme's journal, the Morris journal, as well as the anonymous "Rélation du Combat" and "Rélation depuis le Départ de la Troupes," all in Winthrop Sargent, ed., *The History of the Expedition against Fort Duquesne in 1755* (Philadelphia, PA, 1855), 356, 387, 410, 412.

8 Braddock's orders of 18 June 1755 were obeyed. See *PA*, ser. 1, 2: 348. At several points thereafter, the order was given that only two women per company were to be allowed. See Charles Morse Stotz, *Outposts of the War for Empire* (Pittsburgh, PA: University of Pittsburgh Press, 1985), 41. One woman was killed in a raid on the baggage train on 6 July 1755 and at least one on the battlefield. See Hamilton, ed., *Braddock's Defeat*, 22, 25, 31.

9 Jean-Guillaume Plantavit de Lapause du Margon, "Les 'memoires' du chevalier de La Pause," in *RAPQ, 1932–1933* (Quebec City, QC: Quebec Archives, 1934), 305–95. For the suggestion that M. Roucher was the author of the account, see Kopperman, *Braddock*, 265–73; and Jeannine Pozzo-Laurent, "Plantavit de LaPause de Maron, Jean-Guillaume," *DCB*, 5: 676–8.

10 *Travels in New France by J.C.B.*, ed. Sylvester K. Stevens, Donald H. Kent, and Emma Edith Woods (Harrisburg, PA: Pennsylvania Historical Commission, 1941), 84. The supposed deserter-spy William Johnson may have been honestly reporting the part of the story he knew, namely that only three women were taken captive, two of whom were being carried to Canada and the other kept by the commandant at Fort Machault. See *MPCP*, 7: 342. M. Belestre, a prisoner examined in Winchester on 20 June 1757, may similarly be excused for claiming that three of the eight prisoners taken were soldiers, and that the other five were women. See *NYCD*, 10: 282.

11 *NYM*, 2 January 1758.

12 Merlin Stonehouse Transcripts, vol. 4, n.p., Huntington Library and Art Gallery, San Marino, CA. The tale of Colonel Thomas Gage's horse may well have been a fabrication of a lone male captive. See Gage to Albemarle, 24 July 1755, BL, Add. Mss, 32857, fols 342–3.

13 Brian Leigh Dunnigan, *Siege–1759: The Campaign against Niagara* (Youngstown, NY: Old Fort Niagara Association, 1986), 100.

14 *PG*, 6 September 1759. In what could be a related report, a French soldier claimed a beautiful English woman as his share of 400 livres, in a successful raid. See *NYCD*, 10: 530.

15 Staut (Stuart), taken earlier and escaping from Fort Duquesne a few days after the battle, saw no burnings, but learned that "after the Engagement the Indians pursued our People to the Monongahela, scalped and plundered all that were left upon the Field, except for five or six, who not being able to keep pace with the Victors in their return to the Fort, were all treated in the same Manner, one Virginian only surviving it." See *NYM*, 11 August 1755.

16 *Journals of the House of Burgesses of Virginia, 1758–1761*, ed. H.R. McIlwaine (Richmond, VA: Colonial Press, 1908), 66, 68.

17 *An Account of the Remarkable Occurrences in the Life and Travels of Col. James Smith, during His Captivity with the Indians, in the Years 1755, '56, '57, '58 and '59* (Lexington, KY, 1799); Sargent, ed., *History of an Expedition*, 259. Francis Parkman incorporated Smith's unquestioned account into his immensely popular *Montcalm and Wolfe*, 3 vols (Boston, MA: Little, Brown, 1905), vol. 1, 231.

18 *NYM*, 11 August 1755; *SCG*, 9 November 1755; HL, MM, 1717. There is a story that Alexander McKee, son of Irish trader Thomas McKee and his Shawnee wife, was a Pennsylvania trader with provincial forces and captured at Braddock's defeat. He was supposedly rescued from burning by a young Shawnee who became his wife. See Draper Mss, Pittsburgh and Northwest Virginia Papers, 6NN176. Compare Reginald Horsman, "McKee, Alexander," *DCB*, 4: 499–500.

19 *Shawnee Traditions: C.C. Trowbridge's Account*, ed. Vernon Kinietz and Erminie W. Voegelin (Ann Arbor, MI: University of Michigan Press, 1939), 19–21. Of some 755 British troops who were killed or captured in Allegh-

eny country between 1755 and 1765, fully 707 (93.6%) were killed. Of these, 20 were killed after capture, and 4 were "eaten" in Pontiac's War: 2 at Pontiac's camp at Detroit, 1 at Michilimackinac, and 1 near Fort Bedford, Pennsylvania.

20 This chapter of Jemison's narrative was derived from a relative, not Mary herself. See Mary Jemison, *A Narrative of the Life of Mary Jemison*, ed. C.D. Vail (New York: American Scenic and Historic Preservation Society, 1942), 103–8, 131.

21 Kopperman, *Braddock*, 31, 47, 137.

22 Grant to Forbes, 30 October 1758, BL, Add. Mss, 21652, fol. 64; Bouquet to Forbes, 17 September, BL, Add. Mss, 21640, fol. 169; HL, AB, 794; *HBP*, 2: 489–95, 513–22; Washington to George W. Fairfax, 25 September 1758, *GWP*, 6: 38–41; Lawrence Henry Gipson, *The British Empire before the American Revolution*, 15 vols (Caldwell, ID, and New York: Caxton and Knopf, 1936–70), vol. 7, 268–70; *PJ*, 28 September 1758; *PG*, 14 and 28 September 1758, 19 October 1758.

23 *HBP*, 2: 520.

24 The soldier, Thomas Ely, was among several confined for losing their weapons in this battle. Andrew Grissel of the Royal American Regiment told a similar story. All those accused of losing their muskets were acquitted. See BL, Add. Mss, 21682, fol. 13.

25 C.J. Russ, "Le Marchand de Lignery, François-Marie," *DCB*, 3: 378–9.

26 Ensign John MacDonald, of the Montgomery Highlanders, was with the Wyandot. Evidently Lignery did not know that Ensign Thomas Gist, of the Virginia Regiment, was also taken by the Wyandot in this battle. See "Thomas Gist's Indian Captivity, 1758–1759," *PMHB* 80 (1956), 285–311.

27 HL, LO, 3838; *NYCD*, 7: 282.

28 *HBP*, 2: 540 (quote), 525–6, 533–5, 539–41; *PG*, 28 September and 19 October 1758.

29 HL, LO, 6153; *PG*, 6 December 1759.

30 David Boyd, "History of the Capture and Captivity of David Boyd from Cumberland County, Pennsylvania," *WPHM* 14 (1931): 36.

31 "Thomas Gist's Indian Captivity," 285–311.

32 For a fuller discussion, see Ian K. Steele, "Over Niagara: Captives and Conventions in Colonial War, 1759–1761," *Journal of Canadian Studies* 39 (2005): 9–39. As soon as word of the defeat, and the subsequent surrender of Fort Niagara, reached upper Ohio country, Shawnee, Delaware, and Ottawa chiefs sent legations to treat with George Croghan. See Bert Anson, *The Miami Indians* (Norman, OK: University of Oklahoma Press, 1970), 60.

33 Minutes of George Croghan's meeting of 7–11 July 1759 are in the American Philosophical Society, Philadelphia, PA, Indian and Military Affairs of Pennsylvania, Mss Class 974.8, P19, 731–46. See also Pierre Pouchot, *Memoirs of the Late War in North America between England and France*, ed.

B.L. Dunnigan (Youngstown, NY: Old Fort Niagara Association, 1994), 174, 177, 183–6; and *NYM*, 20 August 1759.

34 The few Indians who had stayed to support Lignery, including Osages and Ojibwa, also lost at least six killed, straining their relations with the Six Nations for years. See "Thomas Gist's Indian Captivity," 302; and Frank H. Severance, *An Old Frontier of France: The Niagara Region and Adjacent Lakes under French Control*, 2 vols (New York: Dodd, Mead, 1917), vol. 2, 343.

35 Captain Charles Lee to Bunbury, 9 August 1759, *Collections of the New York Historical Society for 1871* (New York, 1872), 20–2; Pouchot, *Memoirs*, 219; Captain James De Lancey letter, 25 July 1759, *NYCD*, 7: 402; Severance, *Old Frontier*, vol. 2, 312.

36 Pouchot, *Memoirs*, 232.

37 Richard Huck-Saunders to Loudoun, 4 August 1759, HL, LO, 6134. On French casualties, see Pouchot, *Memoirs*, 232, 232n.

38 *PG*, 23 August 1759.

39 Amherst to James Wolfe, 7 August 1759, TNA, WO 34/46B.

40 Macarty to Kerlerec, 30 August 1759, AN, C11A, vol. 41, fol. 103; Haldimand Papers, BL, Add. Mss, 21687, fol. 12; Pouchot, *Memoirs*, 232, 232n; *JP*, 13: 121; Dunnigan, *Siege–1759*, 102–5. Amherst was told that there were 160 prisoners plus 17 officers taken at La Belle Famille. See *The Journal of Jeffrey Amherst*, ed. John Clarence Webster (Toronto, ON, and Chicago, IL: University of Chicago Press, 1931), 152.

41 *JP*, 13: 115. The ransom money for an unspecified number of the officers was £160. See *JP*, 3: 174. One officer was sold to Johnson. See David A. Armour, "Testard de Montigny, Jean-Baptiste-Philippe," *DCB*, 4: 733. Four years earlier Johnson had readily given captured French soldiers to the Iroquois to "cover their dead" after the battle of Lake George, while extending generous hospitality to captured soldier-aristocrat Jean-Armand, Baron de Dieskau. See Ian K. Steele, *Betrayals: Fort William Henry and the "Massacre"* (New York: Oxford University Press, 1990), 54.

42 *NYM*, 20 August 1759; *PG*, 23 August 1759. Compare *NYG*, 27 August 1759: "Our Indians at Niagara took near 500 scalps, and almost as many Prisoners, who are still to be brought down; these are mostly Canadians and Indians."

43 Amherst to Haldimand, 14 January 1760, BL, Add. Mss, 21661, fols 36–7; Severance, *Old Frontier*, vol. 2, 341. There is no surviving report of the agent, John Lottridge, but he was back at Oswego early in May 1760. See *JP*, 10: 143.

44 Three of these escaped from the Iroquois and, on coming to Fort Ontario, were promptly made British prisoners. See Alexander Duncan to Amherst, 19 April 1761, TNA, WO 34/19, fol. 41. Two others taken at Niagara, Étienne Desgroix and Jean Denny, had escaped from the Iroquois the same summer, and Amherst ordered them sent to England for exchange in their native France. See Amherst to Wheelock, 21 July 1761, TNA, WO 34/98, fol. 195.

45 *Our Revolutionary Forefathers: The Letters of François, Marquis de Barbé-Marbois, during His Residence in the United States as Secretary to the French Legation, 1779–1785*, ed. Eugene Parker Chase (New York: Duffield, 1929), 175–215. Thanks to Alan Taylor for this reference. The Chevalier de Pontgibaud, on the same trip, may have been remembering the same man, but claimed, "he had almost forgotten French." See *A French Volunteer of the War of Independence: The Chevalier de Pontgibaud*, ed. and trans. Robert Douglas (New York: New York Times, 1969), 48–9. Other Frenchmen of influence with the Oneidas in the 1780s were Angel De Ferriere, Lewis Denny, John Denny, and Peter Penet, none of whom can be linked to Niagara. See Lawrence M. Hauptman, *Conspiracy of Interests: Iroquois Dispossession and the Rise of New York State* (Syracuse, NY: Syracuse University Press, 1999), 53–5.

46 Captain François Coulon de Villiers (1712–94) was a victor at Fort Granville and the younger brother of Louis de Villiers and of Joseph Coulon de Villiers de Jumonville. See W.J. Eccles, "Coulon de Villiers, Louis," *DCB*, 3: 148–9.

47 Célene Cyr, "Legardeur de Repentigny, Pierre-Jean-Baptiste-François-Xavier," *DCB*, 4: 448–9.

48 Donald Chaput, "Marin de La Malgue, Joseph," *DCB*, 4: 512–14.

49 Armour, "Testard de Montigny."

50 Colonel Louis-Césaire Dagneau Douville de Quindre, and his brother Major Guillame Dagneau Douville de Lamothe, led the Detroit militia contingent. See Donald Chaput, "Dagneau Douville de Quindre, Louis-Césaire," *DCB*, 3: 158–9.

51 Captain Wheelock later sympathetically compared Lieutenant Boucher de Niverville de Montisambert to impoverished fellow prisoner Philippe-Thomas Chabert de Joncaire. See Wheelock to Amherst, 27 October 1760, TNA, WO 34/98, fols 84–5: "Monsr. Montizimbert a Lieutenant is much in the same situation with regard to his family – his children are at Detroit. His wife (an Englishwoman whom with his sister he bought of the Indians) is near Montreal."

52 On Lieutenant Michel Maray de La Chauvignerie, see Dunnigan, *Siege–1759*, 103.

53 Christopher Duffy, *The Military Experience in the Age of Reason* (London: Routledge and Kegan Paul, 1987), 277. In *The Gentleman's Compleat Military Dictionary*, 19th ed. (reprint, Boston, 1759), a partisan is described simply as "a Person who is very dexterous in commanding a Party, and knows the Country very well: he is employed in surprising the Enemies Convoys, or in getting intelligence."

54 Pouchot, *Memoirs*, 246–8n, 500–2; *Travels in New France by J.C.B.*, ed. Stevens, Kent, and Woods, 121–33.

55 Legardeur de Repentigny and Marin de La Malgue *fils* had each accumulated debts of $1,600 in fourteen months of captivity, expenses that both sides thought exorbitant. See Wheelock to Amherst, 29 September and 27 October 1760, and Amherst to Wheelock, 14 October 1760, TNA,

WO 34/98, fols 79–81, 84–5, 175–7; Amherst to Barrington, 6 January 1761, TNA, WO 1/5, fols 149–50; and Steele, "Over Niagara," 20–1. The Convention of Sluis (Écluse) of 6 February 1759 is printed, in French and English, in *The Journal of Captain John Knox*, ed. Arthur D. Doughty, 3 vols (Toronto, ON: Champlain Society, 1914–16), vol. 3, 258–88.

56 *Travels in New France by J.C.B.*, ed. Stevens, Kent, and Woods, 128–35; Wheelock to Amherst, 25 September, 6, 14, and 27 October, and 13 November 1760, TNA, WO 34/98, fols 72–3, 77–8, 84–8, 94–7, 175–7. On shipping negotiations, see TNA, WO 34/98, fols 92–9, 104, 182–4. The *troupes de la marine* were dissolved in 1761.

57 Hunter, *Forts*, 164–5; Nicholas B. Wainwright, *George Croghan, Wilderness Diplomat* (Chapel Hill, NC: University of North Carolina Press, 1959), 163–6; BL, Add. Mss, 21655, 56–8, 73–5 (re. the August meeting); Anson, *Miami Indians*, 60.

58 The killed are estimated as: 516 out of 1,450 (35.6%) with Braddock; 257 out of 800 (32.1%) with Grant; and 250 out of 600 (41.7%) with Lignery.

59 Peter Shafer, an "old Indian trader," was killed in the Tuscarora Valley, late in October 1755. See *PG*, 13 November 1755. William Clapham was killed in 1762 by his *panis* slaves, in an incident that related only obliquely to the war. See *HBP*, 6: 107–8; BL, Add. Mss, 21648, fol. 292; and *PG*, 2 December 1762. Three traders were captured by "northern Indians" near Fort Robinson (near Kingsport, Tennessee) in the spring of 1762, but promptly escaped. See Henry Timberlake, *Lieut. Henry Timberlake's Memoirs, 1756–1765* (1765; reprint, Marietta, GA: Continental, 1948), 125–6.

CHAPTER SEVEN

1 Henry Gladwin, "The Gladwin Manuscripts: With an Introduction and a Sketch of the Conspiracy of Pontiac," *Michigan Pioneer and Historical Society Collections* 27 (1897): 671–2.

2 Richard Peters to Henry Bouquet, 22 February 1760, BL, Add. Mss, 21645, fol. 59; James Burd to Henry Bouquet, 1 March 1760, BL, Add. Mss, 21645, fols 63–4.

3 BL, Add. Mss, 21638, fols 119, 242, 244–5; Gregory Evans Dowd, *War under Heaven: Pontiac, the Indian Nations and the British Empire* (Baltimore, MD: Johns Hopkins University Press, 2002), 58.

4 *HBP*, 5: 17, 210; BL, Add. Mss, 21655, fol. 99; *PG*, 15 January and 5 February 1761.

5 Michael N. McConnell, *A Country Between: The Upper Ohio Valley and Its Peoples, 1724–1774* (Lincoln, NB: University of Nebraska Press, 1992), 151, 156, 217.

6 Bouquet to Mercer, from Fort Bedford, 16 August 1761, Bouquet Papers, BL, Add. Mss, 21652, fol. 146; Mercer to Bouquet, reply of 20 August 1761, BL, Add. Mss, 21655, fols 84–5; Bouquet to Monckton, from Fort Pitt, 12

June 1761, BL, Add. Mss, 21638, fol. 228; Bouquet to Monckton, from Fort Pitt, 24 July 1761, BL, Add. Mss, 21638, fol. 244; Dowd, *War under Heaven*, 84–5 (re. the 1762 embargo). It is noteworthy that the French reported similar problems in Illinois country. See St Ange to D'Abbadie, 12 August 1764, *Collections of the Illinois State Historical Society* 10 (1915): 295.

7 BL, Add. Mss, 21646, fol. 305; BL, Add. Mss, 21655, fols 119–21; *JP*, 13: 255.

8 Croghan to Bouquet, 1 August 1761, BL, Add. Mss, 21655, fol. 129; Monckton to Bouquet, 5 July 1761, and Bouquet to Monckton, 11 August 1761, BL, Add. Mss, 21638, fols 235, 247. On Hamilton, see *PA*, ser. 1, 4: 65; and BL, Add. Mss, 21655, fols 162–7.

9 James H. Merrell, *Into the American Woods: Negotiators on the Pennsylvania Frontier* (New York: Norton, 1999), 200–2.

10 Eight Cherokee were reported killed and two captured by Mingos. The Wyandots lost four who were killed and two who were captured by the Cherokee. See BL, Add. Mss, 21647, fol. 184; BL, Add. Mss, 21648, fols 1–2; "Journal of James Kenny, 1761–1763," ed. John W. Jordan, *PMHB* 37 (1913): 154–6.

11 *JP*, 10: 543–4, 578.

12 On Amherst's reaction to an Oneida killing of a settler, see Alan Taylor, *The Divided Ground: Indians, Settlers, and the Northern Borderland of the American Revolution* (New York: Knopf, 2006), 28–33.

13 Donald Campbell to Bouquet, from Detroit, 4 August 1762, BL, Add. Mss, 21648, fol. 292; Pauli to Bouquet, BL, Add. Mss, 21648, fol. 302; Johnson to Amherst, 19 September 1762, *JP*, 10: 519–21; Amherst to Gladwin, 15 September 1762, TNA, WO 34/49, fol. 313; Amherst to Johnson, 23 May 1763, *JP*, 10: 690; Gladwin to Amherst, 26 October 1762, 26 January 1763, 20 April 1763, TNA, WO 34/49, fols 126–7, 146, 177; Gladwin, "Gladwin Manuscripts," 674–5.

14 Amherst to Gladwin, TNA, WO 34/49, fol. 322, underlining in Amherst's copy.

15 McConnell, *Country Between*, 183.

16 Donald Campbell to Bouquet, from Detroit, 10 February 1762, BL, Add. Mss, 21648, fols 28–9; Bouquet to Amherst, from Fort Pitt, 7 March 1762, *HBP*, 5: 53; Dowd, *War under Heaven*, 86.

17 The rumors were from Forts Ouiatenon and Miami. See *JP*, 10: 546–8; McKee to Bouquet, from Lower Shawnee Town, 8 November 1762, BL, Add. Mss, 21648, fol. 446; Croghan to Bouquet, from Fort Pitt, 4 February and 30 March 1763, BL, Add. Mss, 21649, fols 42, 98–9; Larry L. Nelson, *A Man of Distinction among Them: Alexander McKee and the Ohio Country Frontier, 1754–1799* (Kent, OH: Kent State University Press, 1999), 34, 37–9; Lieutenant Edward Jenkins to Major Gladwin, from Ouiatenon, 28 March 1763, BL, Add. Mss, 21655, fols 211–12; and Robert Holmes to Major Gladwin, 30 March 1763, BL, Add. Mss, 21634, fol. 221. James Kenny reported a Delaware warning to Juniata settlers in January 1763. See "Journal of James Kenny, 1761–1763," ed. Jordan, 184.

18 Anthony F.C. Wallace, *King of the Delawares: Teedyuscung, 1700–1763* (Philadelphia, PA: University of Pennsylvania Press, 1949), 258–61; "Journal of James Kenny, 1761–1763," ed. Jordan, 187; Nelson, *Man of Distinction*, 38–9.

19 Gregory Evans Dowd, "The French King Wakes Up in Detroit: 'Pontiac's War' in Rumor and History," *Ethnohistory* 37 (1990): 254–78.

20 On the Anishinabeg, see especially Michael Witgen, *An Infinity of Nations: How the Native New World Shaped Early North America* (Philadelphia, PA: University of Pennsylvania Press, 2012).

21 Discussion based upon David H. Corkran, *The Creek Frontier, 1540–1783* (Norman, OK: University of Oklahoma Press, 1967), 142–272; Lawrence Henry Gipson, *The British Empire before the American Revolution*, 15 vols (Caldwell, ID, and New York: Caxton and Knopf, 1936–70), vol. 9, 55–87; Gary C. Goodwin, *Cherokees in Transition: A Study of Changing Culture and Environment prior to 1775* (Chicago, IL: Department of Geography, University of Chicago, 1977); and Russell Thornton, *The Cherokees: A Population History* (Lincoln, NB: University of Nebraska Press, 1990), 1–37.

22 The raids continued after an Anglo-Cherokee peace agreed to on 17 December 1761, when the Cherokee countered with raids on Ohio tribes. See Lieutenant Elias Meyer to Bouquet, from Sandusky, 30 September 1761, BL, Add. Mss, 21647, fol. 184; Thomas Hutchins report, Lower Shawnee Town, c. 5 April 1762, BL, Add. Mss, 21655, fol. 181; and Edward St Leger (a trader) to Bouquet, from Salt Lick, 22 June 1762, *HBP*, 6: 98–9. See also Croghan to Bouquet, from Fort Pitt, 8 January 1763, *HBP*, 6: 139–40; and "Journal of James Kenny, 1761–1763," ed. Jordan, 155–6.

23 Christina Snyder, *Slavery in Indian Country: The Changing Face of Captivity in Early America* (Cambridge, MA: Harvard University Press, 2010), 137.

24 Ecuyer to Bouquet, at Fort Pitt, 29 May 1763, BL, Add. Mss, 21649, fol. 129; "Journal Kept at Fort Augusta, 1763," *PA*, ser. 2, 7: 459; *PJ*, 30 June 1764.

25 In February 1765 West Florida governor George Johnstone told the British Board of Trade that securing the Mississippi trade was "of the highest importance" since 700,000 skins were shipped out of New Orleans this year "in consequence of the Session of Canada by which most of the Furs have come to Illinois, and so by the Mississippi." See *Collections of the Illinois State Historical Society* 10 (1915): 439.

26 One exception was Warren Tracy, who was killed in the defense of the garrison at Michilimackinac. See Etherington to Gladwin, 12 June 1763, TNA, WO 34/49, fol. 207–9; *PG*, 11 and 18 August 1763; and *NYM*, 15 August 1763.

27 The five killed were Thomas Ormsby, Thomas Green, Edward St Leger, John Tool, and one McFarlane. See *HBP*, 6: 412, 490; BL, Add. Mss, 21649, fol. 136–7; Charles A. Hanna, *The Wilderness Trail, Or the Ventures and Adventures of the Pennsylvania Traders on the Allegheny Path*, 2 vols (New York: Putnam, 1911), vol. 2, 381; Archibald Loudon, ed., *A Selection of Some of the Most Interesting Narratives of Outrages Committed by the Indians in Their Wars with the White People*, 2 vols (Carlisle, PA, 1808–11), vol. 1, 278–9; and *PG*, 30 June 1763.

28 Calhoun's report of 1 June 1763, BL, Add. Mss, 21649, fols 130, 136–7, 490; BL, Add. Mss, 21655, fol. 275; *HBP*, 6: 412, 490; *PG*, 16 and 30 June 1763. Compare *NYG*, 4 July 1763.

29 John Pilers and three servants were killed on the river, and Lazarus Lowery Jr and four servants were killed in Lower Shawnee Town, as were three servants of John Gibson. Gibson was taken by the Delaware and later given to the Shawnee. See Hanna, *Wilderness Trail*, vol. 2, 381; and *HBP*, 6: 413.

30 On Abraham Chapman's five bateaux, see Jehu Hay, *Diary of the Siege of Detroit in the War with Pontiac*, ed. Franklin B. Hough (Albany, NY, 1860), 7, 47; BL, Add. Mss, 21649, fols 252–6; and *JP*, 10: 741–2. On Thomas Smallman and Andrew Levy's party of five, see *PG*, 22 December 1763.

31 Everet Wendell led this group, and was among the dead. Eleven other survivors fled to their boats and returned to Fort Niagara. See *JP*, 4: 134; *PG*, 23 June 1763; and Dowd, *War under Heaven*, 133.

32 John Prentice, Micheal Teaffe, and fellow trader Robert Wilkey were missing. See BL, Add. Mss, 21654, fols 177, 183–5; and *HBP*, 6: 412.

33 Hay, *Diary*, 11, 38, 46; *HBP*, 6: 197, 412–13; *PG*, 16 and 30 June 1763.

34 TNA, WO 34/49, fols 205–6; BL, Add. Mss, 21655, fols 210–11; *JP*, 10: 694–6. Welch's peltry was later assessed as worth £6,000. See Hanna, *Wilderness Trail*, vol. 2, 364.

35 His name was Abraham Chapman. See John Heckewelder, *History, Manners, and Customs of the Indian Nations Who Once Inhabited Pennsylvania and the Neighbouring States*, rev. ed. (Philadelphia, PA, 1876), 257–8.

36 Richard Winston wrote the merchants of Detroit on 19 June 1763, mentioning that Frederick Hambrough (Hambach) and one Chem had been taken prisoner. See BL, Add. Mss, 21655, fols 214–15.

37 On Langlade, see Paul Trap, "Mouet de Langlade, Charles-Michel," *DCB*, 4: 563–4; Michael A. McDonnell, "Charles-Michel Mouet de Langlade: Warrior, Soldier, and Intercultural 'Window' on the Sixty Years' War for the Great Lakes," in *The Sixty Years' War for the Great Lakes, 1754–1814*, ed. D.C. Skaggs and L.L. Nelson (East Lansing, MI: Michigan State University Press, 2001), 79–103.

38 William Trent's table of traders' losses, prepared at Fort Pitt on 5 September 1763, included eighty-eight killed or taken "this side of Detroit" and estimated losses at £45,000. See BL, Add. Mss, 21654, fol. 177. For the suggestion that nearly 100 Pennsylvania traders were killed or captured, a figure that likely excludes hired men and servants, see Hanna, *Wilderness Trail*, vol. 2, 368. For the claim that "Out of one hundred and twenty of them, among the different nations, only two or three escaped being murdered," which is closer to exaggerated frontier remembrances, see Joseph Doddridge, *Notes on the Settlement and Indian Wars of the Western Parts of Virginia and Pennsylvania* (Wellsburgh, VA, 1824), 222. By February of 1765, when traders' losses were presented as a claim against the Six Nations in hope of compensation in land, the figure was £80,862.12.4¾. See Hanna, *Wilderness Trail*, vol. 2, 364.

39 Their eventual victory came in an extortionist land grant that was part of the 1768 Treaty of Stanwix.

40 Fort Augusta survived, and the new Fort Penn (Stroudsburg) was likely not a fort at all. See William A. Hunter, "Provincial Defense in Pontiac's War," 26, 27a–d, unpublished draft paper, Pennsylvania State Archives, Manuscript Group 364, Carton 5.

41 M.M. Quaife, ed., *The Siege of Detroit* (Chicago, IL: Lakeside, 1958), 103–4, 241 (quote).

42 *PG*, 11 and 18 August 1763; *NYM*, 8 August 1763; Hay, *Diary*, 26; *JP*, 10: 731–2.

43 A Canadian trader named Charles Maisonville helped supply the Detroit garrison on 8 July 1763. See William R. Nester, *"Haughty Conquerors": Amherst and the Great Indian Uprising of 1763* (Westport, CT: Praeger, 2000), 131.

44 Jenkins to Gladwin, 1 June 1763, TNA, WO 34/49, fol. 204. Jenkins was still there on 29 July 1763. See BL, Add. Mss, 21655, fol. 211. See also Lieutenant Colonel Robertson, at Pensacola, to General Thomas Gage, 8 March 1764, *Collections of the Illinois State Historical Society* 10 (1915): 220: "I directed eighteen of the first battalion, who had been taken prisoners by the Indians on the lakes, and are now residing among the inhabitants of Illinois to join the 22nd."

45 Thomas Hutchins gathered information in 1762 that led him to estimate 400 Ojibwa and 250 Ottawa warriors at Michilimackinac. See TNA, WO 34/49, fol. 180; and Charles A. Bishop, *The Northern Ojibwas and the Fur Trade: An Historical and Ecological Study* (Toronto, ON: Holt, Rinehart and Winston, 1974).

46 Alexander Henry, *Travels and Adventures in Canada and the Indian Territories between the Years 1760 and 1776*, ed. James Bain (1809; reprint, Toronto, ON: G.N. Morang, 1901), 78.

47 Etherington certificate for Langlade, 10 June 1763, State Historical Society of Wisconsin, Madison, WI; Etherington to Gladwin, 12 June 1763, TNA, WO 34/49, fols 207–9; Henry, *Travels*, 42, 77–110; David A. Armour, "Du Jaunay, Pierre," *DCB*, 4: 240–2; David A. Armour, "Henry, Alexander," *DCB*, 6: 316–19; Dowd, *War under Heaven*, 126–7, 131.

48 Henry, *Travels*, 102, says that Ojibwa leader Le Grand Sable, who had missed the attack, later killed seven prisoners held in a lodge.

49 Etherington to Gladwin, 12 June 1763, *JP*, 10: 694–6. Du Jaunay (Jauny) was at the Ottawa mission from 1741 to 1765. See George Paré, *The Catholic Church in Detroit, 1701–1888* (Detroit, MI: Gabriel Richard,, 1951), 191; and Armour, "Du Jaunay, Pierre."

50 Etherington to Gorrell, at Michilimackinac, 11 June 1763, printed in Francis Parkman, *The Conspiracy of Pontiac and the Indian War after the Conquest of Canada*, 6th ed., 2 vols (Boston, MA: Little, Brown, 1905), vol. 1, 378.

51 Dowd, *War under Heaven*, 74–5, describes a 1762 portentous exchange between hungry Mingo and Seneca and Lieutenant Gordon. Restrained

from giving presents, Gordon did exchange provisions for a keg of rum he knew had been stolen from a nearby trader. See Gordon to Bouquet, 1 August 1763, BL, Add. Mss, 21648, fol. 183.

The Oneida, after visiting the victorious Chenussio, told William Johnson on 9 July 1763 that two officers had been taken captive and killed in the woods nearby, and that the sentinel at the gate had escaped. See *JP*, 10: 768–9. This cannot be confirmed. Gordon's list of Seneca grievances was rather enthusiastically reported to Johnson by Mohawk chief Soghsonowana (Thomas). See *JP*, 10: 769.

52 Price to Bouquet, 26 June 1763, BL, Add. Mss, 21649, fols 193–4; "William Trent's Journal at Ft. Pitt, 1763," *MVHR* 11 (1924–25): 401.

53 Christie to Gordon, 3 June 1763, BL, Add. Mss, 21649, fol. 141.

54 BL, Add. Mss, 21658, fols 88–90; Amherst Papers, TNA, WO 34/49, fols 214–15. See also *JP*, 10: 730.

55 Parkman, *Conspiracy of Pontiac*, vol. 1, 292, says there were twenty-seven men, including six of Cuyler's Queen's Rangers. Gipson, *British Empire*, vol. 9, 102, says Christie had twenty-four soldiers. Dowd, *War under Heaven*, 127, says perhaps sixty.

56 Christie to Bouquet, 10 July 1763, BL, Add. Mss, 21649, fols 242–3.

57 The soldier was Daniel Schelburgher of Cuyler's Queen's Rangers, who confirmed Christie's account on 9 July 1763. See Amherst Papers, TNA, WO 34/49, fols 212–14. On Wagner, see Van Slyke deposition of 21 July 1767, Native American Collection, Clements Library, University of Michigan, Ann Arbor, MI.

58 Hay, *Diary*, 84–5, 91–2, 238.

59 *PG*, 7 July 1763.

60 *HBP*, 4: 413; *HBP*, 6: 259–60; "William Trent's Journal," 402.

61 John Bremner journal and diary, 22 July 1763, NYHS, BV section. A fanciful deception by the commander, rather than any siege at all, was a preferred folk memory in the region. See Sherman Day, *Historical Collections of the State of Pennsylvania*, 2 vols (Philadelphia, PA, 1843), vol. 1, 314–15.

62 Quaife, ed., *Siege*, 229; Gladwin, "Gladwin Manuscripts," 663. A *panis* slave escaped with Sir Robert Davers's canoe. The Ojibwa hunter Wawatam offered a similar justification for cannibalism. See Henry, *Travels*, 103.

63 Sergeant Patrick Shaw, eighteen soldiers of the Royal American Regiment and boatmen, and one women were returning from a trip to deliver supplies to Fort Michilimackinac. See TNA, WO 34/49, fol. 5; and Howard H. Peckham, *Pontiac and the Indian Uprising* (Princeton, NJ: Princeton University Press, 1947), 158.

64 Amherst to Gladwin, 22 June 1763, TNA, WO 34/49, fol. 328. George Croghan proposed a massive hostage taking, of all the Indians in the colonies, with the threat of their execution if the raiding did not stop. He asserted, "I know that all Indians have a Great Regard for Each other," and "I know the Indians think more of the Loss of a Man then we do of fifty." See Croghan to Bouquet, 18 June 1763, BL, Add. Mss, 21649, fols 182–3.

65 Accounts of Cuyler's casualties cannot be fully reconciled. See Dowd, *War under Heaven*, 315n37. Christie, presumably hearing from Cuyler, counted 59 killed or missing out of 97, plus a woman and a child. Captain James Macdonald, hearing from 3 survivors who escaped, had 47 killed or taken out of 75. See BL, Add. Mss, 21649, fol. 141. William Trent, also at Detroit, heard that 58 were killed, including a woman and a child. See "William Trent's Journal," 398. If 97 men had arrived in ten bateaux, the average was nearly 10 per bateaux. After the assault, survivors scrambled into five of these bateaux, overcrowded and without adequate oars. Estimating these survivors as numbering at least 12 per bateaux, we can conclude that they would have initially numbered about 60. By such an estimate, 37, plus a boy, had died in the skirmish on the beach. Thirty-seven escaped in two bateaux, meaning that approximately 23 men were caught in the three other bateaux and were used to paddle the entire eight bateaux taken to Pontiac at Detroit. In this rough estimate, of the 97 soldiers, 37 escaped, 37 were killed, and 23 were taken. Of these prisoners, 4 escaped, 1 died attempting to escape, 7 were eventually freed, and 11 were tortured to death that day at Pontiac's camp.

66 This had been demonstrated in the overwhelming of Colonel John Parker's expedition on Lake George in 1757. I am grateful to canoeists Jack Hyatt and Rod Stingle for independently confirming that canoes can travel the fifty yards of effective musket range in less than the forty seconds it takes to reload that musket.

67 Quaife, ed., *Siege*, 257–8. Rutherfurd considered, but did not date, one killing of ten prisoners to be a frolic undertaken to fulfill a woman's dream that the bodies of ten scalped Englishmen were floating down the Detroit River (ibid., 259–60).

68 Ibid., 141–5, 241–2.

69 Ibid., 140–6; Louis Chevrette, "Pontiac," *DCB*, 3: 529. It remains possible that the recorded speeches were embellished by the anonymous author of "The Journal of Pontiac's Conspiracy," thought to be Robert Navarre, then French notary at Detroit. See Dowd, *War under Heaven*, 6, 97; Burton Historical Collections Staff, "Navarre, Robert," *DCB*, 4: 579–80; and [Robert Navarre], *Journal of Pontiac's Conspiracy, 1763*, ed. C.M. Burton (Detroit, MI: Lakeside, 1912).

70 BL, Add. Mss, 21658, fols 88–90; Amherst Papers, TNA, WO 34/49, fols 214–15; Hay, *Diary*, 26, 42–6; Quaife, ed., *Siege*, 137–8. Compare Dowd, *War under Heaven*, 124.

71 Hopkins to Amherst, 11 July 1763, TNA, WO 34/49, fols 216–17. The Potawatomi brought in five captives, and an Ojibwa surrendered trader Abraham Chapman.

72 In addition to Rutherfurd's aborted negotiations, at least five members of Captain Joseph Hopkins's ranger company were bought "as slaves" by French at Detroit. See TNA, WO 34/49, fols 218, 221, 227.

73 Campbell relayed this warning as a deterrent to fellow captive Rutherfurd in June. See Quaife, ed., *Siege*, 240–1.

74 Upon Pauli's escape, Rutherfurd was targeted but escaped. See ibid., 246–8.

75 Ibid., 257–8.

76 Thirty-five warriors and twenty-five soldiers were killed.

77 Hay, *Diary*, 56, 65; Robert Rogers letter of 8 August 1763, *PG*, 8 September 1763; Peckham, *Pontiac*, 201–9. I have found no evidence for Peckham's claim that "Others were taken prisoner" (208).

78 *PG*, 1 September 1763; Bouquet to Gladwin, 28 August 1763, BL, Add. Mss, 21649, fols 313–15; Peckham, *Pontiac*, 210–13.

79 *NYCD*, 7: 562; Peckham, *Pontiac*, 221–5. It is possible that the two prisoners whom Mary Jemison remembers being burned to death by the Seneca at Fallbrook were taken at Devil's Hole. See Mary Jemison, *A Narrative of the Life of Mary Jemison*, ed. C.D. Vail (New York: American Scenic and Historical Preservation Society, 1942), 55–7.

80 The known killed were 258 soldiers, 255 settlers, 200 Indians, and 60 traders.

81 Fifteen soldiers escaped, and Conrad Wagoner stayed with his Potawatomi captors. See Van Slyke deposition of 21 July 1767, Native American Collection, Clements Library, University of Michigan, Ann Arbor, MI.

CHAPTER EIGHT

1 The declaration of war was recognized by Captain Simeon Ecuyer on 30 May 1763, when Indians killed and scalped two men at the sawmill that served the garrison at Fort Pitt. See Ecuyer to Bouquet, BL, Add. Mss, 21649, fol. 130. The assault of 28 July to 1 August 1763 left roofs burned, but twenty warriors were killed in wounding eight soldiers, one of whom died later. Major Henry Gladwin indicated how thoroughly the British separated the Ohio war from the northern one when he refused to talk to the Shawnee and Delaware at all in July 1764, referring them to Fort Pitt or Sir William Johnson, "as they do not belong to his department." See George McDougall to Bouquet, 18 July 1764, BL, Add. Mss, 21650, fol. 348.

2 For the claim that more than fifty people were back on the Greenbrier River, see Otis K. Rice, *The Allegheny Frontier: West Virginia Beginnings, 1730–1830* (Lexington, KY: University Press of Kentucky, 1970), 55–6. See also James B. Finley, *Life among the Indians* (Cincinnati, OH, 1857), 45–7; and Joseph A. Waddell, *Annals of Augusta County, Virginia*, 2 vols (Richmond, VA, 1886–88), vol. 1, 111. For a report of the erroneous settlers' tale of Dennis being taken in a supposed Shawnee raid in 1761, amid peacetime, see Alexander Scott Withers, *Chronicles of Border Warfare, or A History of the Settlement by the Whites, of North Western Virginia, and of the Indian*

Wars and Massacres, in that section of the state, with reflections, anecdotes, etc. ... (1831; reprint, New York: Arno, 1971), 89–90. A report carried into North Carolina suggested that Hannah was with the raiding party, and escaped from it. See *Records of the Moravians in North Carolina*, ed. Adelaide L. Fries et al., 13 vols (Raleigh, NC: Edwards and Broughton, 1922–2006), vol. 1, 289.

3 Felix Renick, "A Trip to the West," *American Pioneer* 1 (1842): 77.

4 This return to Carr's (Kerr's) Creek gives support to the notion that Cornstalk was involved in the earlier attack. Compare John Sugden, "Cornstalk," *ANB*.

5 Mrs Archibald Clendennin escaped promptly, her infant was killed, and one of her boys died in captivity. See Waddell, *Annals of Augusta*, vol. 1, 111; Joseph Doddridge, *Notes on the Settlement and Indian Wars of the Western Parts of Virginia and Pennsylvania* (Wellsburgh, VA, 1824), 226–7; Draper Mss, Frontier Wars Papers, 21U136; and Draper Mss, Virginia Papers, 2ZZ.

6 William Clapham Sr had been notorious as a rather self-indulgent commander at Fort Augusta. See Matthew C. Ward, *Breaking the Backcountry: The Seven Years' War in Virginia and Pennsylvania, 1754–1765* (Pittsburgh, PA: University of Pittsburgh Press, 2003), 117–18; *PG*, 9 and 16 June 1764; BL, Add. Mss, 21654, fol. 171; "William Trent's Journal at Ft. Pitt, 1763," *MVHR* 11 (1924–25): 394; and "Journal of James Kenny, 1761–1763," ed. John W. Jordan, *PMHB* 37 (1913): 199. Two soldiers of the Royal American Regiment were killed at the mill at Fort Pitt the next day. See *PG*, 9 and 16 June 1763; and *HBP*, 6: 410.

7 According to the story, Maiden Foot took Mary's autographed handkerchief. After the battle of Fallen Timbers in 1794, a Captain Kearney found an old Indian sitting on a log waving a white handkerchief. He was Maiden Foot, the handkerchief was autographed "Mary Means," and Captain Kearney happened to be her husband. Maiden Foot reportedly lived out his last years in their home in Cincinnati and was buried there. See C. Hale Sipe, *Fort Ligonier and Its Times* (Harrisburg, PA: Telegraph, 1932), 187–8. For an example of current interest in this story, see http://www.buxtonart.com.

8 *PG*, 30 June 1763; *HBP*, 6: 410; Sipe, *Fort Ligonier*, 190. The Indian prisoners were John Hudson, Samuel Conaway, and their families.

9 *PG*, 21 July 1763; *PJ*, 21 July 1763.

10 In addition to Mary Means and her mother, James Beatty was taken while looking for a horse near Fort Bedford. He was returned to Colonel Henry Bouquet's troops on 15 November 1764, and given a shirt, leggings, shoes, and a blanket, all of which he apparently needed. See *WPHM* 9 (1956): 191; *PG*, 17 January 1765; and *NYG*, 21 January 1765. Aaron Wallace was taken nearby five days after Beatty, and was released or escaped the following day. See BL, Add. Mss, 21654, fol. 171; BL, Add. Mss, 21642, fol. 452; and *HBP*, 6: 410.

11 This account, which presumes three attacks, is reconstructed from reports of those claiming the success of three pursuits. It is most likely that the first attack was at Cape Capunt on 10 August 1763 and that a larger one was at Welton Meadows on Looney Creek on 20 August. See PG, 1, 8, and 15 September 1763, 6 October 1763.

12 PG, 8 December 1763.

13 MPCP, 9: 42–3.

14 PG, 15 September 1763; MPCP, 9: 40–1; HBP, 6: 393; NYM, 19 September 1763; NYG, 19 September 1763. Two of the three scalped children of Frantz Hubler died soon thereafter.

15 PG, 24 November and 15 December 1763.

16 Paul B. Moyer, *Wild Yankees: The Struggle for Independence along Pennsylvania's Revolutionary Frontier* (Ithaca, NY: Cornell University Press, 2007), 19–22.

17 MPCP, 9: 27–30; RCFFP, 1: 166; Earl P. Olmstead, *David Zeisberger: A Life among the Indians* (Kent, OH: Kent State University Press, 1997), 1[illegible]7.

18 Gregory Evans Dowd, *War under Heaven: Pontiac, the Indian Nations and the British Empire* (Baltimore, MD: Johns Hopkins University Press, 2002), 144; Anthony F.C. Wallace, *King of the Delawares: Teedyuscung, 1700–1763* (Philadelphia, PA: University of Pennsylvania Press, 1949), 252–64; Paul Moyer, "'Real' Indians, 'White' Indians, and the Contest for Wyoming Valley," in *Friends and Enemies in Penn's Woods*, ed. William A. Pencak and Daniel K. Richter (University Park, PA: Pennsylvania State University Press, 2004), 221–37; Peter Silver, *Our Savage Neighbors: How Indian War Transformed Early America* (New York: Norton, 2008), 167–8.

19 The first two companies of troops raised in Northampton County were led by brothers Nicholas and Jacob Wetterholt. The four Delaware were killed by members of Nicholas's company, but it was Jacob Wetterholt and his officers who were the victims of the revenge. See William A. Hunter, "Provincial Defense in Pontiac's War," 15–22, unpublished draft paper, Pennsylvania State Archives, Manuscript Group 364, Carton 5.

20 PG, 27 October 1763. The report on the incident was by a frustrated party of Lancaster scalp and booty hunters, and the tortures may have been "elaborated." On the accusation against a Christian Mohican named Renatus in the "murder" of John Stenton, and his acquittal, see Jane T. Merritt, *At the Crossroads: Indians and Empires on a Mid-Atlantic Frontier, 1700–1763* (Chapel Hill, NC: University of North Carolina Press, 2003), 280–2.

21 Isaac Hollister, *A Brief Narration of the Captivity of Isaac Hollister* (New London, CT, 1767); PG, 27 October 1763, 13 September 1764. Hollister claimed sixteen or seventeen were killed, whereas initial newspaper reports put the number at ten, as did reports at Fort Augusta. See "Journal Kept at Fort Augusta, 1763," PA, ser. 2, 7: 475. On the skirmishes, see PG, 1 December 1763; NYM 30 April 1764; and NYG, 23 April 1764. Two boys were attacked near Stroudsburg in February 1764, one of whom was killed, and

his brother, Isaac Russell, was captured. See *PG*, 16 February 1764, 19 September 1765; C. Hale Sipe, *The Indian Wars of Pennsylvania* (Harrisburg, PA: Telegraph, 1929), 470; and Merritt, *At the Crossroads*, 274–7.

22 On the Paxton Boys, see Alden T. Vaughan, "Frontier Banditti and the Indians: The Paxton Boys' Legacy, 1763–1775," *PH* 51 (1984): 1–29; Alison Olson, "The Pamphlet War over the Paxton Boys," *PMHB* 123 (1999): 31–55; Dowd, *War under Heaven*, 192–9; and Merrit, *At the Crossroads*, 285–92.

23 *PG*, 12 April 1764 (quote); *JP*, 4: 336–8, 365; *JP*, 11: 23–35, 108; *NYM*, 9 April 1764; Dowd, *War under Heaven*, 151.

24 *JP*, 4: 349; *JP*, 11: 103, 110; *PG*, 15 March and 12 April 1764; Dowd, *War under Heaven*, 151–2.

25 *JP*, 11: 315, 318–19.

26 *JP*, 11: 108. Johnson's will included enough servants and slaves to be divided into four separate bequests. See *JP*, 12: 1065.

27 *JP*, 11: 105, 119–20.

28 *MPCP*, 9: 277. See also Gage to Johnson, 12 May 1765, *JP*, 4: 739–40.

29 Gage to Johnson, 12 May 1765, *JP*, 4: 739–40.

30 Johnson to Elliot, 28 April 1764, *JP*, 11: 165–6; Johnson to Gage, 3 and 26 May 1764, *JP*, 11: 165–6, 174–5, 201; *PG*, 17 May 1764; Dowd, *War under Heaven*, 183–5. On Frederick Eice, see Bouquet Papers, BL, Add. Mss, 21655, fols 179–80; and *JP*, 10: 522. On the captivity of his family, see *WPHM* 39 (1956): 190; *PG*, 17 January 1765; Samuel Kercheval, *A History of the Valley of Virginia*, 4th ed. (Strasburg, VA: Shenandoah, 1925), 92.

31 Deposition of 30 March 1764 at Fort Pitt, BL, Add. Mss, 21650, fol. 116; Thomas Hutchins to Bouquet, 10 April 1764, BL, Add. Mss, 21650, fols 126–7.

32 Captain John Brady to Bouquet, 26 March 1764, BL, Add. Mss, 21650, fol. 113; *PG*, 5 April 1764.

33 *PG*, 3 May 1764. See also F.B. Lyman Chalkley, *Chronicles of the Scotch-Irish Settlement in Virginia*, 3 vols (1912; reprint, Baltimore, MD: Genealogical, 1965), vol. 1, 344; and F.B. Kegley, *Kegley's Virginia Frontier: The Beginning of the Southwest, the Roanoke of Colonial Days, 1740–1783* (Roanoke, VA: Southwest Virginia Historical Society, 1938), 277–88.

34 *PG*, 26 April 1764. The Kincades were captured near Warm Springs, east of the abandoned Jackson River settlement.

35 *PG*, 26 April 1764. The Kincade attack is mentioned in *PG*, 3 May 1764, and described in detail by Mrs Kincade's grandson in Draper Mss, Kentucky Papers, 16CC193-7.

36 On the raids, see BL, Add. Mss, 21650, fol. 238; *PG*, 14 June 1764; Preston Papers, 2: 49; and Kercheval, History of the Valley, 97–8. Delaware chief Killbuck mentioned the Canadian raider to Johnson. See Johnson's memo for 2 March 1765, *JP*, 11: 618. A sentry was mortally wounded on Grant's Hill, at Fort Pitt, and one soldier was killed and another captured near Fort Bedford. See BL, Add. Mss, 21650, fol. 234; *PG*, 14 June 1764.

37 BL, Add. Mss, 21650, fol. 240–1; *PG*, 14 June 1764.

38 *PG*, 9 and 30 August 1764; *NYM*, 13 August 1764; *NYG*, 13 August 1764; Sipe, *Indian Wars*, 473–4.

39 At least 258 soldiers and at least 255 settlers (including servants and slaves) were killed, the latter being 61 per cent of the 415 settlers whose fate is known. The fate of 74 settlers remains unknown. In the sixty-one months between September 1755 and October 1759, at least 714 settlers were killed, an average of 11.7 per month. In the fifteen months between May 1763 and July of 1764, at least 221 settlers were killed, an average of 14.7 per month.

40 Of those white civilians whose gender and fate are known, 135 of 199 males (68%) were killed, and 51 of 135 females (38%) were killed.

41 Two girls aged seven to fifteen were killed for every fifteen captured between 1755 and 1762. In 1763–64, 1 was killed for every 2.7 taken. The comparable figure for boys the same age fell from 1:2.1 to 1:1.5.

42 Thirty-four children known to be under age seven were killed, and 36 captured; in the Seven Years' War, the comparable numbers were 23 killed and 58 captured.

43 BL, Add. Mss, 21655, fols 208–10; *HBP*, 6: 214–18.

44 Ourry to Bouquet, 20 June 1763, BL, Add. Mss, 21642, fol. 440.

45 Amherst to Bouquet, 25 June 1763, *HBP*, 6: 257.

46 Bouquet to Hamilton, 13 July 1763, BL, Add. Mss, 21649, fol. 256, and *HBP*, 6: 308. There was another attempt to attack the Indian prisoners on 16 July 1763. See BL, Add. Mss, 21649, fol. 266.

47 Bouquet to Ecuyer, 26 July 1763, BL, Add. Mss, 21653, fol. 197; Bouquet to Amherst, 26 July 1763, *HBP*, 6: 326–7; Ecuyer to Bouquet, 2 and 5 August 1763, BL, Add. Mss, 21649, fols 282, 286–7; "William Trent's Journal," 409–10; Ourry to Bouquet, 23 September 1763, BL, Add. Mss, 21642, fol. 477; Dow to Bouquet, from Fort Niagara, 22 July 1764, *HBP*, 6: 596. If the four children were issued half rations, and Mrs Hudson one ration, they were almost certainly the three rations being issued to Indian prisoners by the reduced garrison at Fort Bedford mentioned in George MacIntosh to Bouquet, 27 August 1764, BL, Add. Mss, 21650, fol. 416. The Hudsons were likely still there in February 1765. See Bouquet to Gage, 12 February 1765, *HBP*, 6: 754.

48 Sherman Day, *Historical Collections of the State of Pennsylvania*, 2 vols (Philadelphia, PA, 1843), vol. 2, 384–5; *RCFFP*, 1: 589.

49 Amherst to Bouquet, 29 June 1763, *HBP*, 6: 277; *PG*, 1 September 1763; Sipe, *Fort Ligonier*, 210. Andrew Byerley recalled one of Barrett's rangers asking the Highlander, "What are you going to do with that fellow?" The Highlander replied, "I am taking him to Colonel Bouquet. If you want one, there are plenty of them running yonder in the woods, and you may catch one for yourself." The ranger then shot the captive dead, which "greatly incensed the brave Highlander and called forth the indignant rebuke of Bouquet." See Cyrus Cort, *Colonel Henry Bouquet and His Campaigns of 1763 and 1764* (Lancaster, PA, 1883), 42–3.

50 Pennsylvania did not formally reinstitute a scalp bounty until 7 July 1764, but payments of £10 each were made by the Provincial Commissioners for three scalps on 19 August 1763. See Hunter, "Provincial Defense," 10–11.

51 Archibald Loudon, ed., *A Selection of Some of the Most Interesting Narratives of Outrages Committed by the Indians in Their Wars with the White People*, 2 vols (Carlisle, PA, 1808–11), vol. 2, 175–7; "Journal Kept at Fort Augusta, 1763," *PA*, ser. 2, 7: 469; *PJ*, 8 September 1763.

52 For the claim that the leader was Captain William Patterson, see Kevin Kenny, *Peaceable Kingdom Lost: The Paxton Boys and the Destruction of William Penn's Holy Experiment* (New York: Oxford University Press, 2009), 212. On David Owens, see John Penn to Bouquet, 26 April 1764, BL, Add. Mss, 21650, fol. 164; Johnson to John Penn, 18 June 1764, *JP*, 11: 224–5; *NYG*, 23 April 1764; Charles A. Hanna, *The Wilderness Trail, Or the Ventures and Adventures of the Pennsylvania Traders on the Allegheny Path*, 2 vols (New York: Putnam, 1911), vol. 2, 386; and Sipe, *Fort Ligonier*, 209–10.

53 The bounty on adult male captives was 150 Spanish dollars, compared to 134 for a scalp. The bounty on adult female captives was 134 Spanish dollars, with only 50 for her scalp. See Hanna, *Wilderness Trail*, vol. 2, 385. The rates were unchanged the following year, but eligibility expanded to accommodate Virginian volunteers going west with Bouquet. See *MPCP*, 9: 188–9, 191–2; and Bouquet to William Rutherford, 5 July 1764, BL, Add. Mss, 21650, fols 313–14.

54 Silver, *Our Savage Neighbors*, 60–4.

55 In six known incidents reported in colonial newspapers between May 1763 and July 1765, twenty-six Indians were killed and nineteen captured. Fourteen of the killed and sixteen of the reported captured were Cherokee. See *SCG*, 16 July 1763, 24 September 1763; and *PG*, 15 November 1764, 25 April 1765, 6 and 13 June 1765, 15 August 1765.

56 David H. Corkran, *The Creek Frontier, 1540–1783* (Norman, OK: University of Oklahoma Press, 1967), 163–66; Lawrence Henry Gipson, *The British Empire before the American Revolution*, 15 vols (Caldwell, ID, and New York: Caxton and Knopf, 1936–70), vol. 9, 63–9.

57 *JP*, 11: 155, 318 (quote), 321, 325, 337; Bouquet to Gage, 2 May 1764, *HBP*, 6: 532–3. On Bradstreet's terms, see *JP*, 11: 328–33; and *MPCP*, 9: 195–6.

58 Bouquet to Captain David Hay, 30 September 1764, BL, Add. Mss, 21650, fols 533, 535.

59 BL, Add. Mss, 21655, fol. 258. The letter was signed by eleven prominent Delaware, including Chief Wingenum, war captains Jacobs, Killbuck, and Will, as well as the prophet Neolin. The "Simon Girty" in this list was Delaware war captain Katepakomen.

60 *MPCP*, 9: 219; *HBP*, 6: 674.

61 Bouquet to John Penn, 15 November 1765, BL, Add. Mss, 21651, fol. 52; HL, MM, 569, fol. 32; *MPCP*, 9: 220, 224–6, 228; Thomas-M. Charland, "Hertel de Saint-Francois, Joseph-Hippolyte," *DCB*, 4: 347–8.

62 Angered by a killing that threatened his peace negotiations, Bouquet attempted to have John Bow of Maryland captured and prosecuted for this killing. See *HBP*, 6: 738–9, 746.

63 Bouquet to Gage, 12 February 1765, *HBP*, 6: 754; *MPCP*, 9: 250–64.

64 In Pontiac's War the British Army killed at least 86 Indians, colonial forces 38, and warring Indians 33. In the Seven Years' War in Allegheny country, the British Army killed 30 Indians, British colonials killed 124, Canadians killed 6, and Indian opponents killed 53.

65 Dowd, *War under Heaven*, esp. 94–105.

66 Doddridge, *Notes on the Settlement*, 217 (quote), 218, 228.

CHAPTER NINE

1 Alden T. Vaughan and Daniel K. Richter, "Crossing the Cultural Divide: Indians and New Englanders, 1605–1763," *American Antiquarian Society Proceedings* 90 (1980): 64, 93.

2 Charles Stuart's report, *PG*, 22 December 1757.

3 *MPCP*, 8: 620; *PG*, 30 June 1757. The woman was Hannah Snell.

4 Theodore C. Pease and Ernestine Jenison, eds, *Illinois on the Eve of the Seven Years' War* (Springfield, IL: State Historical Society, 1940), 29, 811; *PG*, 23 November 1752; *VG*, 20 and 27 October 1752. The ill trader was Alexander MacDonald.

5 According to family history, the first infant killed was Robert Renick Jr, aged about eighteen months, who died by being dashed against a tree on the trail. See Draper Mss, Frontier Wars Papers, 21U127. Mary Draper Ingles reported another such killing. One baby died later in captivity, and the fate of three others is not known. For the suggestion that such killings were more routine than they were, see David Zeisberger, "David Zeisberger's History of the Northern American Indians," *Ohio Archaeological and Historical Publications* 19 (1910): 105.

6 Regina Leininger, aged ten, reportedly carried a two year old into captivity, who "clung to Regina and looked to her for comfort." See Henry Melchior Muhlenberg, "Regina, the German Captive," in *Proceedings of the Pennsylvania-German Society* 15 (1906): 84–5.

7 Captive and witness Charles Stuart reported that raiders killed "old Mrs. Galloway and her Scalp Being Gray they did not take it with the rest but Burnt it." See *MVHR* 13 (1926): 60.

8 *PA*, ser. 1, 3: 396–7; Archibald Loudon, ed., *A Selection of Some of the Most Interesting Narratives of Outrages Committed by the Indians in Their Wars with the White People*, 2 vols (Carlisle, PA, 1808–11), vol. 2, 47–65; *PG*, 28 July 1757, 11 May 1758.

9 On Mrs Miller, see *PG*, 30 June 1757; and *NYM*, 4 July 1757. See also *PMHB* 32 (1908): 316; and David Boyd, *History of the Capture and Captivity of David Boyd from Cumberland County, Pennsylvania* (N.p., 1931), 29. The other four

were Jane Fraser (Frasier), Jean Lowry, Mrs Robert Renick, and Eleanor Kinkade (Kinkead).

10 *NYM*, 8 March 1756.

11 *PA*, ser. 1, 3: 632–3.

12 Mary Jemison, *A Narrative of the Life of Mary Jemison*, ed. C.D. Vail (New York: American Scenic and Historical Preservation Society, 1942), 74–6.

13 *The Baptismal Register of Fort Duquesne*, ed. A.A. Lambing (Pittsburgh, PA, 1885), 70–1. The parents were Sara and John Condon.

14 Catherine Smith, daughter of William and Cecilia Smith, was baptized on 10 August 1756, and buried on the 14th. See ibid., 76–7. Another young daughter, of the same name, was also captured, and retaken at Kittanning.

15 On the nine baptisms, see ibid., 56–7, 70–1, 74–5, 76–7, 78–9 (John Turner Jr), 80–5.

16 Jane Fraser, *Narrative of the Captivity of Mrs. Jane Frasier* (1930; reprint, New York: Garland, 1977).

17 See Ian K. Steele, "When Worlds Collide: The Fate of Canadian and French Prisoners Taken at Fort Niagara, 1759," *Journal of Canadian Studies* 39 (2005): 9–39.

18 Three Indian captives were brought to General Edward Braddock's successor and eight to Captain Lewis Ourry.

19 *NYM*, 8 March 1756; William Fleming and Elizabeth Fleming, *A Narrative of the Sufferings and Surprizing Deliverances of William and Elizabeth Fleming* (1756; reprint, New York: Garland, 1978).

20 On Leininger, see "The Narrative of Marie Le Roy and Barbara Leininger," *PA*, ser. 2, 7: 429. On Mary Draper Ingles, see *PG*, 26 February 1756; and Draper Mss, Frontier Wars Papers, 12U112. See also "An Account of the Remarkable Occurrences in the Life and Travels of Col. James Smith," in Loudon, ed., *Selection*, vol. 1, 158.

21 In 1748 a party of thirty Delaware who had taken a Catawba captive were pursued, the captive was recovered, and all the Delaware were reportedly killed. See Warren R. Hofstra, *The Planting of New Virginia: Settlement and Landscape in the Shenandoah Valley* (Baltimore, MD: Johns Hopkins University Press, 2004), 31.

22 Jemison, *Narrative* (1942), 71.

23 *PA*, ser. 1, 4: 138; *PG*, 15 December 1763. A young Kinkade boy died the same way the next year. See *PG*, 3 May 1764; and Draper Mss, Kentucky Papers, 16CC193-7.

24 *PG*, 28 June 1764. A captured young Virginian boy died on the trail in March 1758, after slipping under the horse he was riding and being trampled. See *PA*, ser. 1, 3: 632–3.

25 *HBP*, 6: 567.

26 *PG*, 25 March 1756; *NYM*, 29 March 1756.

27 Draper Mss, Pittsburgh and Northwest Virginia Papers, 6NN78-80.

28 Jean Lowry, *A Journal of the Captivity of Jean Lowry and Her Children* (Philadelphia, PA, 1760), 5–6.

29 James Smith described at least one, and perhaps as many as twelve, being burned at what would have been an encampment of warriors rather than a village. The claim that Seneca warrior Hiokatoo burned two captives then does not specify where this occurred. See Jemison, *Narrative* (1942), 13.

30 PG, 28 July 1757, reprinted in *NYM*, 1 August 1757, reprinted in *London Chronicle, or Universal Evening Post*, 6–8 September 1757, reprinted in *The Military History of Great Britain, for 1756, 1757: Containing a Letter from an English Officer at Canada, Taken Prisoner at Oswego* (London, UK, 1757), 86–8, and reprinted in *MVHR* 15 (1928): 95–6. The militiaman's name was Cole.

31 *NYM*, 8 March 1756.

32 Barbara Leininger, allowed to ride while her captors walked, attempted to escape and was recaptured, threatened with burning, and reprieved. See *PA*, ser. 2, 7: 430.

33 *PG*, 3 May 1759.

34 The next month, Aaron Wallace was captured near Fort Bedford and "returned the next day." He may have been released, but it is more likely that he escaped. See BL, Add. Mss, 21654, fol. 171. According to family remembrance, an Indian warned Mrs Beatrice Byerly of Bushy Run of an impending attack and thereby allowed her and her four children to find refuge in Fort Ligonier. See Cyrus Cort (a descendant of Byerly), *Colonel Henry Bouquet and His Campaigns of 1763 and 1764* (Lancaster, PA, 1883), 17–18, 23–4.

35 Colonel John Stuart of Greenbrier gathered local stories in his "Memo 1798 July 15 by John Stuart," in Draper Mss, Virginia Papers, 2ZZ. This memo was copied in Samuel G. Drake, *Indian Captivities, or Life in the Wigwam* (Buffalo, NY, 1854), 284–6.

36 Other cases included Robert Renick Jr and the infant sons of Mrs Henry Clouser and Rachel Dillinger. See respectively Draper Mss, Frontier Wars Papers, 21U126-35; and Samuel Kercheval, *A History of the Valley of Virginia*, 4th ed. (Strasburg, VA: Shenandoah, 1925), 97–8, 100–1.

37 Alden T. Vaughan and Edward W. Clark, eds, *Puritans among the Indians: Accounts of Captivity and Redemption, 1676–1724* (Cambridge, MA: Belknap, 1981), 21, 143, 232. Readers of the Bible would have been familiar with curses that threatened enemy children with being dashed against rocks or the ground. See Psalm 137:8–9; 2 Kings 8:12; Isaiah 13:16; Hosea 13:16, and Nahum 3:10. Thanks to Rev. Michael Perry of Ottawa for these references.

38 Jennet's legal name was Ann. On 16 August 1763 she qualified as administrator of her husband's estate. She married John Rogers in 1767. Compare the claim that she remarried within a week of returning home from captivity in 1763. See F.B. Lyman Chalkley, *Chronicles of the Scotch-Irish Settlement in Virginia*, 3 vols (1912; reprint, Baltimore, MD: Genealogical, 1965), vol. 1, 108, vol. 2, 93.

39 *NYM*, 8 and 15 March 1756.

40 On John Lane, see *PG*, 2 March 1758. George Ebert and Abraham Miller were tied for nine nights, until they were beyond Tiahoga, and escaped the first night they were not tied. See *MPCP*, 7: 621.

41 This man was Nicholas Barnhold. See *PG*, 19 August 1756.
42 Twenty-seven of fifty-five escapees on the trail were taken either alone, or with one or two fellow captives.
43 "French and Indian" parties lost 7 of 164 captives in the first week of capture; intertribal parties of Indians lost only 27 of 926.
44 Twenty-two of 751 Pennsylvania captives escaped on the trail, whereas only 8 of 565 Virginians did so.
45 "Narrative of Marie Le Roy and Barbara Leininger," 113.
46 Twenty-nine of 1,240 captives (2.3%) escaped promptly in the Seven Years' War, whereas 25 of 646 (3.9%) did so in Pontiac's War. In 1763, 21 of 462 captives (4.5%) escaped in their first week. In 1757, the next best year for such escapees, 7 of 388 (1.9%) escaped in their first week.
47 Jehu Hay, *Diary of the Siege of Detroit in the War with Pontiac*, ed. Franklin B. Hough (Albany, NY, 1860), 11; *HBP*, 6: 412–13; *PG*, 16 and 30 June 1763.
48 One of three Catawba women captured by a Cherokee war party had escaped the same day. See *SCG*, 16 July 1763. Young Aaron Wallace of Cumberland County escaped the day after his capture in July 1763. See *HBP*, 6: 410; and BL, Add. Mss, 21642, fol. 452.

CHAPTER TEN

1 Cadwallader Colden, *The History of the Five Nations of Indians* (London, UK, 1747), 203; Franklin to Peter Collinson, 3 May 1753, in Benjamin Franklin, *The Papers of Benjamin Franklin*, ed. Leonard W. Labaree, 29 vols (New Haven, CT: Yale University Press, 1959–92), vol. 4, 481–2; William Smith, *An Historical Account of the Expedition against the Ohio Indians, in the Year 1764, Under the Command of Henry Bouquet Esq.* (Philadelphia, 1766), 29.
2 Felix Renick, "A Trip to the West," *American Pioneer* 1 (1842): 79; J. Hector St John de Crèvecoeur, *Letters from an American Farmer* (London, UK, 1782), 295.
3 B.E. Johansen and B.A. Mann, eds, *Encyclopedia of the Haudenosaunee* (Westport, CT: Greenwood, 2000), 4. Scholars of "white Indians" include J. Norman Heard, *White into Red: A Study of the Assimilation of White Persons Captured by Indians* (Metuchen, NJ: Scarecrow, 1973); and James Axtell, "The White Indians of Colonial America," in *The European and the Indian: Essays in the Ethnohistory of Colonial North America* (New York: Oxford University Press, 1981), 168–206, which goes beyond his seminal article by the same title in *W&MQ* 32 (1975): 55–88. Axtell has been challenged, in part, by Alden T. Vaughan and Daniel K. Richter, "Crossing the Cultural Divide: Indians and New Englanders, 1605–1763," *American Antiquarian Society Proceedings* 90 (1980): 23–99. June Namias, *White Captives: Gender and Ethnicity on the American Frontier* (Chapel Hill, NC: University of North Carolina Press, 1992), is intriguing.
4 John R. Swanton, "Notes on the Mental Assimilation of Races," *Journal of the Washington Academy of Sciences* 16 (1926): 493–502; Erwin H. Ack-

erknecht, "Psychological and Physiological Peculiarities of White Children Abducted and Reared by North American Indians," *Bulletin of the History of Medicine* 15 (1944): 15–36; Heard, *White into Red.*

5 For discussion of a Texas captivity in 1836 in which a young child, recaptured within a day, could not recognize its mother, see Heard, *White into Red*, 107–8. See also Leo Eitinger, "The Effects of Captivity," in *Victims of Terrorism*, ed. Frank M. Ochberg and David A. Soskis (Boulder, CO: Westview, 1982), 73–93.

6 James Adair, *Adair's History of the American Indians* (1775; reprint, Johnson City, TN: Watauga, 1930), 420–1.

7 In ibid., 410–12, Adair recounts the story of two Mohawk who, after four months of raiding and scalping in Cherokee country in 1747, were caught and tortured to death.

8 Joseph Persinger, *The Life of Joseph Persinger* (Sturgeon, MO, 1861), 3.

9 For an earlier account of a stoic white victim, see *PG*, 20 January 1730, discussed in Nicole Eustace, *"Passion Is the Gale": Emotion, Power and the Coming of the American Revolution* (Chapel Hill, NC: University of North Carolina Press, 2008), 252–3. See also Gordon M. Sayre, *Les Sauvages Américains: Representations of Native Americans in French and English Colonial Literature* (Chapel Hill, NC: University of North Carolina Press, 1997), 296–304.

10 Jesus Christ was a model for the converted but not a model of an Amerindian torture victim. Although the Moravian missionaries' term "Marter Geschichte" can be translated into English as either "Passion Story" or "Torture Story," their favored Delaware word for the passion was *amachchawelenda* or variants, meaning "agony" or "suffering," but not *apchinala*, meaning tortured to death. Thanks to Ray Whitenour, Jim Rementer, and Darryl Stonefish for their help with my strange inquiries.

11 Thomas S. Abler, "Scalping, Torture, Cannibalism and Rape: An Ethnohistorical Analysis of Conflicting Cultural Values in War," *Anthropologica* 34 (1992): 11–12.

12 For a 1677 eyewitness account of the Seneca burning four men, four women, and a boy, all Amerindian captives from the "Gulf Coast," see Wentworth Greenhalgh's journal, *NYCD*, 3: 251–2. Robert Rogers provided a vivid description of the burning of a captive on an elevated frame of poles, a sight he had never seen but described as typical. See Robert Rogers, *A Concise Account of North America* (London, UK, 1765), 233–6.

13 *Shawnee Traditions: C.C. Trowbridge's Account*, ed. Vernon Kinietz and Erminie W. Voegelin (Ann Arbor, MI: Michigan University Press, 1939), 19–21, 53–4. David Jones recounts hearing of gruesome torture of all Shawnee prisoners who were not adopted. See David Jones, *A Journey of Two Visits Made to Some Nations of Indians on the West Side of the River Ohio in the Years 1772 and 1773* (New York, 1865), 76.

David Zeisberger retells a dramatic, undated, story of a Shawnee warrior, captured by the Cherokee and prepared for burning: "a Cherokee woman arrived with a parcel of goods, and throwing them down at the feet of the warrior to whom the prisoner belonged begged for his release, alleging that she was a widow and wished to adopt him as her son. Her request was granted, the captive was released and delivered over to her, and on the same day he walked up and down the village well dressed. He was so grateful to his protectress that he remained faithful to her, even returning in due time from a visit he paid to his own people." See David Zeisberger, "David Zeisberger's History of the Northern American Indians," *Ohio Archaeological and Historical Publications* 19 (1910): 107.

14 Peter Looney's report after being released, *PG*, 28 July 1757, reprinted in *NYM*, 1 August 1757, reprinted in *London Chronicle, or Universal Evening Post*, 6–8 September 1757, reprinted in *The Military History of Great Britain, for 1756, 1757: Containing a Letter from an English Officer at Canada, Taken Prisoner at Oswego* (London, UK, 1757), 86–8, and reprinted in *MVHR* 15 (1928): 95–6.

15 Colin G. Calloway, *The American Revolution in Indian Country: Crisis and Diversity in Native American Communities* (New York: Cambridge University Press, 1995), 172–3.

16 *NYM*, 9 September 1756; *MPCP*, 7: 242–3. Charles Stuart, saved from torture by Shingas, claimed that he was scheduled to eat his own fingers and eyes and then to be tied to a post or tree and burned directly. See *MVHR* 13 (1926): 61–2.

17 The Le Roy–Leininger narrative does not name the captive, but the timing suggests Broadly was much more likely the victim than John Turner. See "The Narrative of Marie Le Roy and Barbara Leininger," *PA*, ser. 2, 7: 431.

18 *PG*, 17 and 24 June 1756; Hugh Gibson, "An Account of the Captivity of Hugh Gibson," in *A Selection of Some of the Most Interesting Narratives of Outrages Committed by the Indians in Their Wars with the White People*, ed. Archibald Loudon, 2 vols (Carlisle, PA, 1808–11), vol. 2, 182; Hugh Gibson, "An Account of the Captivity of Hugh Gibson among the Delaware Indians of the Big Beaver and the Muskingum, from the Latter Part of July 1756 to the Beginning of April 1759," *Massachusetts Historical Society Collections*, ser. 3, 6 (1837): 143–4. In Gibson's account, McAllister is tied to a sapling, and a fire is set and then extinguished by "a heavy thunder-gust." Mrs McAllister was shot and her body thrown on the embers. The torture is described entirely differently in "Narrative of Marie Le Roy and Barbara Leininger," 431. McAllister was first scalped, and then burned with wooden firebrands and forced to eat her own ears and fingers. She suffered from nine in the morning until near sunset, when a French officer took pity on her and "put her out of her misery." An English deserter, who had escaped from the Lancaster prison and joined the French, supposedly ate some of her flesh; the Indians cut her body in two at the waist and left it for the dogs.

A comparable brutal killing of an unidentified woman captive, who "had deserted" at the Muskingum River on 26 January 1751, was reported by

Christopher Gist. See *Christopher Gist's Journals*, ed. William M. Darlington (Pittsburgh, PA, 1893), 43–4.

19 John Hogan's deposition, 1 June 1757, HL, LO, 3758, printed in *MPCP*, 7: 561–2.

20 *PG*, 14 October 1756; *PA*, ser. 2, 7: 431.

21 Brett Rushforth, *Bonds of Alliance: Indigenous and Atlantic Slaveries in New France* (Chapel Hill, NC: University of North Carolina Press, 2012), 44.

22 Archibald Loudon, ed., *A Selection of Some of the Most Interesting Narratives of Outrages Committed by the Indians in Their Wars with the White People*, 2 vols (Carlisle, PA, 1808–11), vol. 2, 50.

23 Ibid., vol. 1, 292.

24 Gregory Evans Dowd, *War under Heaven: Pontiac, the Indian Nations and the British Empire* (Baltimore, MD: Johns Hopkins University Press, 2002), 100.

25 [Robert Navarre], *Journal of Pontiac's Conspiracy, 1763*, ed. C.M. Burton (Detroit, MI: Lakeside, 1912), 140–5.

26 For Meares's cryptic description, see Amherst Papers, TNA, WO 34/49, fol. 267; and Henry Gladwin, "The Gladwin Manuscripts: With an Introduction and a Sketch of the Conspiracy of Pontiac," *Michigan Pioneer and Historical Society Collections* 27 (1897): 650–1. See also [Navarre], *Journal*, 208–10.

27 Eight soldiers of the Royal American Regiment are said to have been killed in May 1763 in response to a woman's dream. See M.M. Quaife, ed., *The Siege of Detroit* (Chicago, IL: Lakeside, 1958), 259.

28 The story of the torture of Jacob Fisher, a corpulent twelve year old captured in Frederick County, Virginia, in 1758, cannot be traced back further than Samuel Kercheval, *A History of the Valley of Virginia*, 4th ed. (Strasburg, VA: Shenandoah, 1925), 80–1. See also Alice Nash, "'None of the women were abused'; Indigenous Contexts for the Treatment of Women Captives in the Northeast," in *Sex without Consent: Rape and Sexual Coercion in America* (New York: New York University Press, 2001), 10–26.

29 Vaughan and Richter, "Crossing," 64, found that one captive in sixty-six was killed by the Indians after capture. The comparable number on the Allegheny frontier, including all those killed on the trail as well as the tortured, was much higher at one in seventeen.

30 On the "Stockholm syndrome," see, for instance, James F. Campbell, *Hostage: Terror and Triumph* (Greenwood, CT: Greenwood, 1992). On "involuntary detachment," see A. Irving Hallowell, "American Indians, White and Black: The Phenomenon of Transculturation," *Current Anthropology* 4 (1963): 519–31, esp. 524.

31 Zeisberger, "David Zeisberger's History," 105. Horatio Jones, who was taken by the Seneca in 1781, escaped injury by running very close to one side of a gauntlet. See Joseph A. Francello, *The Seneca World of Ga-no-say-yeh* (Lanham, MD: University Press of America, 1980), 14–15.

32 Loudon, ed., *Selection*, vol. 1, 125.

33 D. Peter MacLeod, *The Canadian Iroquois and the Seven Years' War* (Toronto, ON: Dundurn, 1996), 52–3.

34 Loudon, ed., *Selection*, vol. 1, 123–5, 128.

35 *Travels in New France by J.C.B.*, ed. Sylvester K. Stevens, Donald H. Kent, and Emma Edith Woods (Harrisburg, PA: Pennsylvania Historical Commission, 1941), 70.

36 Mary Jemison, *A Narrative of the Life of Mary Jemison*, ed. C.D. Vail (New York: American Scenic and Historical Preservation Society, 1942), 72–3. For the claim that there were no warriors there to *bastonade* captives early in 1758, but matters were worse for captives who came in later that year, see *Travels in New France by J.C.B.*, ed. Stevens, Kent, and Woods, 99.

37 "Thomas Gist's Indian Captivity, 1758–1759," *PMHB* 80 (1956): 294.

38 Charles Stuart, "The Captivity of Charles Stuart, 1755–57," *MVHR* 13 (1926–27): 66.

39 Loudon, ed., *Selection*, vol. 1, 291.

40 Kenneth G. Hamilton, "Cultural Contributions of Moravian Missions among the Indians," *PH* 18 (1951): 14.

41 Jean Lowry, *A Journal of the Captivity of Jean Lowry and Her Children* (Philadelphia, PA, 1760), 9.

42 *NYM*, 5 April 1756.

43 Loudon, ed., *Selection*, vol. 2, 50.

44 "Narrative of Marie Le Roy and Barbara Leininger," 430.

45 Isaac Hollister, *A Brief Narration of the Captivity of Isaac Hollister* (New London, CT, 1767).

46 David Boyd, "History of the Capture and Captivity of David Boyd from Cumberland County, Pennsylvania," *WPHM* 14 (1931): 31.

47 The "Stockholm syndrome" is said to be triggered by the combination of persisting fear of death and small acts of kindness. See *FBI Law Enforcement Bulletin* 76 (July 2007): 1–10.

48 Zeisberger, "David Zeisberger's History," 106.

49 The captured Niagara and Detroit garrisons were rented out to work. See Ian K. Steele, "When Worlds Collide: The Fate of Canadian and French Prisoners Taken at Fort Niagara, 1759," *Journal of Canadian Studies* 39 (2005): 9–39; and *NYG*, 30 March 1761.

50 This anthropological view is ultimately rooted in E.E. Evans-Pritchard, *The Nuer: A Description of the Modes of Livelihood and the Political Institutions of a Nilotic People* (Oxford, UK: Clarendon, 1940), esp. 183. In Allegheny diplomatic relations, the members of allied Indian and European tribes were referred to as male relatives – grandfather, brother, father, cousin, or nephew. Exchange of gifts sustained this fictive kinship. See Jane T. Merritt, *At the Crossroads: Indians and Empires on a Mid-Atlantic Frontier, 1700–1763* (Chapel Hill, NC: University of North Carolina Press, 2003), 57–9.

51 Christina Snyder, *Slavery in Indian Country: The Changing Face of Captivity in Early America* (Cambridge, MA: Harvard University Press, 2010), 127–51.

52 William A. Starna and Ralph Watkins, "Northern Iroquoian Slavery," *Ethnohistory* 38 (1991): 34–57; Orlando Patterson, *Slavery and Social Death: A Comparative Study* (Cambridge, MA: Harvard University Press, 1982), 1–14.

53 Fernando Santos-Granero, *Vital Enemies: Slavery, Predation and the Amerindian Political Economy of Life* (Austin, TX: University of Texas Press, 2009), esp. 218–28.

54 "The Opinions of George Croghan on the American Indian," *PMHB* 71 (1947): 157.

55 Of 83 known adopted, 3 were under two years, 35 were three to six, 23 were seven to fifteen, and 22 were sixteen and older.

56 David Zeisberger, *Zeisberger's Indian Dictionary*, ed. Eben Norton Horsford (Cambridge, MA, 1887), 97, 149, 175. I am grateful to Professor Marianne Mithun, of the University of California at Santa Barbara, for this understanding of Zeisberger's words *enàsqua* and *agozene*, the latter rendered in modern Seneca as *agoshé:në*. The related Wyandot-Huron word *ňdask8* applied to prisoners and domestic animals. See John Steckley, *A Huron-English/English-Huron Dictionary* (Lewiston, NY: Edwin Mellen, 2007), 365. There are similar links in Ottawa, Illinois, Ashinabi, and Miami. See Brett Rushforth, "'Like Negroes in the Islands': Indians and the Making of Racial Slavery in French North America," paper read at the Omohundro Institute of Early American History and Culture, Williamsburg, VA, 20 October 2009; and Frederick Baraga, *A Dictionary of the Ojibway Language* (St Paul, MN: Minnesota Historical Society, 1992).

57 Barbara Alice Mann, *Iroquoian Women: The Gantowisas* (New York: Peter Lang, 2000), 175–7; William N. Fenton, *The Great Law and the Longhouse* (Norman, OK: University of Oklahoma Press, 1998), 31, 308; Johansen and Mann, eds, *Encyclopedia of the Haudenosaunee*, 3–7.

58 Loudon, ed., *Selection*, vol. 1, 199–302.

59 *PG*, 13 April 1758; HL, AB, 143. On requickening, see Daniel K. Richter, *The Ordeal of the Longhouse* (Chapel Hill, NC: University of North Carolina Press, 1992), 32–5.

60 The other seven accounts concern Adam Brown, Isaac Hollister, Louis Andre Shaw, Marie Anne Shaw, Michael Shaw, Tassewachwe (Noah), and Peter Weese.

61 The Delaware words were: *nihillālgussu* or *wachtschānerd* (slave); *techthunind* (prisoner); and *allogácan* (servant). See Zeisberger, *Zeisberger's Indian Dictionary*, 175, 149, 169, respectively.

62 Loudon, ed., *Selection*, vol. 1, 252–60. On John's captor, and his father's attempt to ransom him in 1762, see BL, Add Mss, 21648, fol. 231.

63 Heard, *White into Red*, 97, found delayed adoption of child captives, and unwillingness to adopt children, to be more common with tribes west of the Mississippi.

64 Boyd, "History of the Capture," 28–34.

65 Loudon, ed., *Selection*, vol. 2, 181. The only other reported late adoption, which occurred within a couple of months of capture, was soldier John Rutherfurd's adoption by the Ojibwa in 1763. See Quaife, ed., *Siege*, 243.

66 "Narrative of Marie Le Roy and Barbara Leininger," 430–2.

67 *MPCP*, 7: 242–3.

68 Hollister, *Brief Narration*, 2.

69 *Shawnee Traditions*, ed. Kinietz and Voegelin, 19–21, 53–5; Charles Callender, "Shawnee," in *Handbook of North American Indians*, vol. 15, Northeast, ed. Bruce G. Trigger (Washington, DC: Smithsonian Institution, 1978), 627–8.

70 Thomas Ridout rendered the word as *kikenecaw*. See Thomas Ridout, *Ten Years of Upper Canada in Peace and War, 1805–1815: Being the Ridout Letters*, ed. Matilda Edgar (Toronto, ON, 1890), appendix. See also C.F. Voegelin, "Shawnee Stems in the Jacob P. Dunn Miami Dictionary," *Indiana Historical Society Prehistory Research Series* 1 (1938–39): 63–108, 135–67. I am grateful to Professor David Costa's personal communication of 2 January 2010 for guidance on this matter.

71 C.C. Trowbridge, *Meearmeear Traditions*, ed. Vernon Kinietz (Ann Arbor, MI: University of Michigan Press, 1938), 23–4.

72 Loudon, ed., *Selection*, vol. 1, 17–32.

73 Alexander Henry, *Travels and Adventures in Canada and the Indian Territories between the Years 1760 and 1776*, ed. James Bain (1809; reprint, Toronto, ON: G.N. Morang, 1901), 73–6, 98, 111, 127 (quote). On *awakân*, see Friedrich Baraga, *A Dictionary of the Ojibway Language* (St Paul, MN: Minnesota Historical Society, 1992).

74 Quaife, ed., *Siege*, 228, 233, 242–3, 245 (quote), 251–4.

75 Three of these were long-held child captives who are here considered as very likely adopted: Peggy Moore Connor, John Slover, and Isaac Hollister.

76 Estimates of Ohio Indian populations are unavoidably speculative. Conrad Weiser's very specific, if incomplete, count of 1748 was 789 warriors: 165 Delaware, 398 Mingo, 162 Shawnee, and 64 others. See Conrad Weiser, "Conrad Weiser's Journal of a Tour of the Ohio, August 11–October 2, 1748," in *Early Western Travels, 1748–1846*, ed. R.G. Thwaites, 32 vols (Cleveland, OH: Arthur H. Clark, 1904–07), vol. 1, 30–1. The Delaware undoubtedly grew the fastest over the next decade, when Robert Stewart estimated there were 800 Delaware fighters. See *GWP*, 6: 361. If Weiser fully reported the Mingo, and underreported the Shawnee and the others, and if all of these groups doubled their numbers by 1759, the total would be about 2,048 warriors, or about 10,240 people, in 1759. See also Michael N. McConnell, *A Country Between: The Upper Ohio Valley and Its Peoples, 1724–1774* (Lincoln, NB: University of Nebraska Press, 1992), 23, 210; and James H. Howard, *Shawnee! The Ceremonialism of a Native Indian Tribe and Its Cultural Background* (Athens, OH: Ohio University Press, 1981). This study's database indicates that 2,135 are known to have been captured or missing in attacks by Ohio Indians to the end of 1765.

77 Smith, *Historical Account*, 28.

78 Jones, *Journey of Two Visits*, 88.

79 Holland to Israel Pemberton, from Shamokin, 30 September 1761, Haverford College Library, Indian Committee Records, vol. 4, n.p.

80 Loudoun, ed., *Selection*, vol. 2, 173; "Incidents in the Life of an Indian Captive," *American Historical Record* 1 (1872): 409–10; *PG*, 5 February 1756, 31 May 1759; *NYG*, 4 June 1759; William A. Hunter, *Forts on the Pennsylvania Frontier, 1753–1758* (Harrisburg, PA: Pennsylvania Historical and Museum Commission, 1960), 379; James Axtell, *The European and the Indian* (New York: Oxford University Press, 1981), 195.

81 Joseph A. Waddell, *Annals of Augusta County, Virginia*, 2 vols (Richmond, VA, 1886–88), vol. 1, 121–2.

82 David McClure, *Ohio Country Missionary: The Diary of David McClure, 1748–1820* (Waterville, OH: Rettig's Frontier Ohio, 1996), 87, 88.

83 *PG*, 17 January 1765; Heard, *White into Red*, 97, 138; Dale Van Every, *Forth to the Wilderness: The First American Frontier, 1754–1774* (New York: Morrow, 1961), 217–18.

84 *Minutes of Conferences Held at Lancaster in August 1762* ... (Philadelphia, PA, 1763), 34–5.

85 Kercheval, *History of the Valley*, 85, 106–7.

86 Draper Mss, Kentucky Papers, 23CC98-103. Susannah Barnett married Thomas Cummins, born in Virginia about 1738, and they settled fourteen miles from Pittsburgh. See https://www.familysearch.org. Thomas Cummins had represented himself as a newly arrived gentleman traveler in New York in a letter to William Johnson, dated 14 July 1750, *JP*, 1 289.

87 Henry Melchior Muhlenberg, "Regina, the German Captive," in *Proceedings of the Pennsylvania-German Society* 15 (1906): 86–8.

88 *WPHM* 39 (1956): 202; Draper Mss, Kentucky Papers, 23CC98-103.

89 Mary Girty-Turner, captured with her five children and second husband in the fall of Fort Granville, witness to her second husband's torture, and captive of the Shawnee, is said to have resisted being returned in 1759. Phillip W. Hoffman, *Simon Girty, Turncoat Hero* (Franklin, TN: American History Imprints, 2009), 11–13, 18–21.

90 Marcel Fournier, *De la Nouvelle-Angleterre à la Nouvelle-France: L'histoire des captifs anglo-américains au Canada entre 1675 et 1760* (Montreal, QC: Société généalogique canadienne-française, 1992), 203.

91 *WPHM* 39 (1956): 202; Richard White, *The Middle Ground: Indians, Empires, and Republics in the Great Lakes Region, 1650–1815* (New York: Cambridge University Press, 1991), 453.

92 *PG*, 6 October 1757, 30 November 1758; same in *NYM*, 10 October 1757, 4 December 1758.

93 *PA*, ser. 1, 3: 306.

94 The cautious reception of the pleas of Nelly Young at Fort Augusta in August 1757 illustrate the suspicion. See "Journal of Col. James Burd, while Building Fort Augusta at Shamokin, 1756–7," *PA*, ser. 2, 2: 696.

95 Deposition of James Bell, 4 October 1764, BL, Add. Mss, 21651, fols 6–7.

96 Colin G. Calloway, "Neither White nor Red: White Renegades on the American Indian Frontier," *Western Historical Quarterly* 17 (1986): 51; Heard, *White into Red*, 120.

97 On Joshua Renick, see Draper Mss, Frontier Wars Papers, 21U126-35. For letters by several descendants to Draper, see Draper Mss, Kentucky Papers, 4CC117-20, 4CC129. On George Brown, see *PG*, 7 October 1756; and Matthew C. Ward, "La guerre sauvage: The Seven Years' War on the Virginia and Pennsylvania Frontier" (PhD diss., College of William and Mary, 1992), 161.

98 Alexander Scott Withers, *Chronicles of Border Warfare, or A History of the Settlement by the Whites, of North Western Virginia, and of the Indian Wars and Massacres, in that section of the state, with reflections, anecdotes, etc. ...* (1831; reprint, New York: Arno, 1971), 96–7.

99 Although General Gage dismissed the charges of spying that Colonel Henry Bouquet suggested, the brothers were threatened with a trial in civil courts. See Gage to Bouquet, 15 October 1764, BL, Add. Mss, 21638, fol. 385: "Rebels in Arms are tried by the Civil Courts. At least I saw this practiced in Scotland, both by General Hawley and the Duke of Cumberland."

100 There may have been three James Bells who were captured in this borderland. A second was a Virginian soldier, said to have been captured at the fall of Vause's Fort in 1756 (see Preston Papers, 1: 83) and returned in November 1764 (see *JP*, 11: 485). An escaped Virginian soldier of the same name reported that he had been captured at Fort Ligonier in May 1759 and had escaped a year later. See Nathaniel Holland to Ian Pemberton, 16 May 1760, Haverford College Library, Indian Committee Records, 824/11, vol. 3, n.p. These two captivities could have befallen the same soldier, but only if he was captured three times: captured in 1756, and freed (no evidence); captured again in 1759, and escaped in 1760; and captured again after 1760 (no evidence), and returned in 1764.

101 Timothy Green to Bouquet, 4 October 1764, BL, Add. Mss, 21651, fol. 4.

102 *WPHM* 39 (1956): 191; *JP*, 11: 488.

103 Phillip W. Hoffman, *Simon Girty, Turncoat Hero* (Franklin, TN: American History Imprints, 2009); Colin G. Calloway, "Simon Girty: Interpreter and Intermediary," in *Being and Becoming Indian: Biographical Studies of North American Frontiers*, ed. James A. Clifton (Chicago, IL: Dorsey, 1989), 38–58.

104 Namias, *White Captives*, 84.

105 James B. Finley, *Life among the Indians* (Cincinnati, OH, 1857), 45–7n; Withers, *Chronicles* (1912), 92–3.

106 The claim by Catherine Jager's mother that her daughter had spent her captivity in Indian idleness at an age when "Girls learn to qualify for Business" was a petitioner's special pleading that worked. See *V&P*, 7: 5883, 5901–2. See also Lois Green Carr, Russell R. Menard, and Lorena Seebach Walsh, *Robert Cole's World: Agriculture and Society in Early Maryland*

(Chapel Hill, NC: University of North Carolina Press, 1991), 71 (re. pounding corn).

107 Samuel Lightfoot to Israel Pemberton, 22 April 1759, Haverford College Library, Indian Committee Records, vol. 3, n.p.

108 Gibson, "Account of the Captivity," *Massachusetts Historical Society Collections*, ser. 3, 6 (1837): 145.

109 *PG*, 17 January 1765; Loudon, ed., *Selection*, vol. 1, 285.

110 Jemison, *Narrative* (1942), 43–4.

111 McClure, *Ohio Country Missionary*, 86. A William Elliott and his wife were killed in the fall of Upper Tract Fort on the South Branch of the Potomac River. See Preston Papers, 1: 83; "Narrative of Robert Robison," in Loudon, ed., *Selection*, vol. 2, 168–70; and *PG*, 11 and 18 May 1758.

112 Peter Williamson, *French and Indian Cruelty: Exemplified in the Life and Various Vicissitudes of Fortune, of Peter Williamson* (London, York, and Glasgow, 1757), 47–9; Robert Kirk, *The Memoirs and Adventures of Robert Kirk, Late of the Royal Highland Regiment* (Limerick, UK, 1775), 38–40; Samuel Davies, *The Curse of Cowardice: A Sermon Preached to the Militia of Hanover County in Virginia at a General Muster, May 8, 1758* (London, UK, 1759) 5; Charles Johnston, *A Narrative of the Incidents Attending the Capture, Detention, and Ransom of Charles Johnston* (New York, 1827), 125.

113 Loudon, ed., *Selection*, vol. 2, 52.

114 "Narrative of Marie Le Roy and Barbara Leininger," 432.

115 Preston Papers, 1: 83.

116 Joshua Antrim, *The History of Champaign and Logan Counties* (Bellefontaine, OH, 1872), 327–8; John Sugden, *Blue Jacket, Warrior of the Shawnees* (Lincoln, NB: University of Nebraska Press, 2000), 32, 254–5 (quotes).

117 Sugden, *Blue Jacket*, 32.

118 Peggy is misidentified as one Mary Myers in J. Norman Heard, *Handbook of the American Frontier*, 5 vols (Metuchen, NJ: Scarecrow, 1987–98), vol. 2, 80; and in Dale Van Every, *Ark of Empire: The American Frontier, 1784–1803* (New York: Morrow, 1963), 137–8.

119 David Zeisberger, *The Moravian Mission Diaries of David Zeisberger*, ed. Herman Wellenreuther and Carola Wessel, trans. Julie Weber (University Park, PA: Pennsylvania State University Press, 2005), 259, 270 (quote), 308, 396n.

120 Ibid., 384, 392, 393 (quote), 525.

121 Ibid., 339 (quote), 390, 422, 443; John Heckewelder, *History, Manners, and Customs of the Indian Nations Who Once Inhabited Pennsylvania and the Neighbouring States*, rev. ed. (Philadelphia, PA, 1876), 341–2.

122 Renick, "Trip," 73–80, 79 (quote).

123 Ibid., 79. Archibald Hamilton was another boy captive remembered as preferring a breechcloth to the clothes offered returning captives. See Draper Mss, Kentucky Papers, 11CC291.

124 The proportion of New England captives taken by Indians who are known to have become white Indians was a little lower, at 3.2 per cent, though

the number of unknowns in both groups makes both calculation and comparison dubious. See Vaughan and Richter, "Crossing," 23–99, esp. 60, 97, tables 8 and 9.

125 Thomas and Katherine McLaughlin of Philadelphia were reported "Turn'd to the French." See *PG*, 3 September 1747. Trader Joseph Faulkner (Fortiner), taken in November 1750, converted. See Frank H. Severance, "The Tale of Captives at Fort Niagara," *Buffalo Historical Society Publications* 9 (1906): 237–307; *The Ohio Company Papers, 1753–1817, Being Primarily Papers of the "Suffering Traders" of Pennsylvania*, ed. Kenneth P. Bailey (Arcata, CA: N.p., 1947), 36–7; and Howard N. Eavenson, *Map Maker and Indian Trader* (Pittsburgh, PA: University of Pittsburgh Press, 1949), 142–3. Fanny Flaherty was said to have married a Frenchman (see "Narrative of Marie Le Roy and Barbara Leininger," 437), as had the unnamed wife of a French soldier captured with him in the fall of Fort Niagara and returned to her British first husband. See *PG*, 6 September 1759.

126 Lowry, *Journal*, is the only Allegheny narrative that claims heroic resistance against French priests' efforts to convert her. See also Vaughan and Richter, "Crossing," 62, 70; and Barbara E. Austen, "Captured ... Never Came Back: Social Networks among New England Female Captives in Canada, 1689–1763," in *New England/New France, 1600–1850*, ed. Peter Benes (Boston, MA: Boston University, 1992), 28–38. *PJ*, 7 December 1758, reporting upon Peter Schuyler's recent return to Edward's Fort with 114 prisoners, mentioned that these included "25 Women and Children, which he purchased from the French at very high prices," and noted that "During Colonel SCHUYLER's Captivity in Canada, his Gratitude to his unfortunate Countrymen, was without Bounds, his Table being ever open and free to those in distress; and we hear he has, out of his own private Purse, expended upwards of 20,000 Livers among his distressed Countrymen, in redeeming them from Captivity."

127 Kercheval, *History of the Valley*, 81. Lewis Ourry's list of returned captives, published in *PG*, 17 January 1765, included "Hannah Smith, and her Child." Although most children are named in the list, six others are referred to in this way. They are "Mary Lancisco, and her Child," "Eleanor Kincade, and two Children," "Elisabeth McElroy, and her Child," and "Elisabeth Coon, and two Children."

CHAPTER ELEVEN

1 Lewis Preston Summers, *History of Southwest Virginia, 1746–1786, Washington County, 1777–1870* (Richmond, VA: J.L. Hill, 1903), 81.

2 Nathaniel Holland to I. Pemberton, from Shamokin, 16 May 1760, Haverford College Library, Indian Committee Records, 824/11, vol. 3, n.p.

3 *Journals of the House of Burgesses of Virginia, 1758–1761*, ed. H.R. McIlwaine (Richmond, VA: Colonial Press, 1908), 188; *Journals of the House of Bur-*

gesses of Virginia, 1761–1765, ed. John Pendleton Kennedy (Richmond, VA: Colonial Press, 1907), 179. Noting that his feet had not healed, and that he had already been given £60, he was awarded the rest of his back pay of £22, plus £10 a year for life. See ibid., 186. John Kennedy, Hugh Gibson, Barbara Leininger, and Samuel Clifford suffered little recorded punishment for failed attempts to escape.

4 The two women were Ann Mullen and Lany Pussey. See *PG*, 17 March 1763.

5 Of those who were captured between ages seven and fifteen, 35 of 206 eventually escaped: 27 of 115 boys and 8 of 91 girls. No girls escaped on the trail, and women were a little less likely to do so than men.

6 Of 29 servant-victims, 12 remained missing, 9 are known to have been killed, 6 escaped, 1 was ransomed, and 1 was returned.

7 William Wiston claimed to have lost 14 slaves captured by Indians in July 1763, and he admitted that he had sold the only one who managed to escape. See *Journals of the House of Burgesses, 1761–1765*, ed. Kennedy, 209. Of the other 17 slaves captured by Indians, 5 (*panis*) stayed with the Indians, 4 were retaken, 3 were returned, 4 were missing, and Sam Tony was sold in the West Indies.

8 *JP*, 10: 287.

9 Forty-four of eighty-seven Indian captives escaped. Little is known about the 1753 Cherokee escapees, except that they successfully reached Albany and enlisted official assistance to continue their long journey home. See Arent Stevens to Commissioners, 20 March 1754, LAC, MG 19, F 35/2, lot 680, 91. On the Piankashaw held at Fort Chartres, see Theodore C. Pease and Ernestine Jenison, eds, *Illinois on the Eve of the Seven Years' War* (Springfield, IL: State Historical Society, 1940), 29, 574, 635–44, 660–1, 673.

10 Of those traders whose fate is known, 24 of 76 escaped. The captivity time of 19 traders who escaped is known: 7 escaped within a week, and 16 escaped within three months.

11 Of those captured soldiers whose fate is known, 47 of 151 escaped. The captivity time of 41 escaped soldiers is known: 16 escaped within a week, 23 within three months, and 36 within two years. Robert Stobo's escape after nearly five years as a hostage-prisoner, and two failed attempts, was by far the longest soldier captivity before escape.

12 The soldier was Nathaniel Stedman. See *Journals of the House of Burgesses, 1761–1765*, ed. Kennedy, 100–1, 140.

13 The captivity time of 60 settlers who escaped is known: 20 escaped within a week, 29 within a month, 40 within a year, and 47 within two years.

14 Of those settlers whose fate is known, 90 of 493 escaped: 28 of 318 captured females (8.8%) and 62 of 354 males (17.5%). The escape rate for adult males was: 24% for settlers, 31% for soldiers, 32% for traders, and 47% for Indians.

15 The seven escapees were: Hugh Gibson (held 1,947 days); Hannah Dennis (2,181); Levy Hicks (2,219); Sally Wilkins (2,397); Arthur Crawford (2,556); James (Robert) Bell (2,578); and Susannah Barnett (4,383).

16 The Flemings, Hollister, and Howell escaped while on such errands. Mary Ingles and Katherine Bingeman escaped while making salt, Hannah Dennis while gathering medicinal herbs, and Mathias Warren when sent between settlements.

17 These escapees were Hugh Gibson, Barbara Leininger, Marie Le Roy, and Hugh Breckenridge.

18 *NYM*, 16 February 1756.

19 On the escape of James (Robert) Bell, see BL, Add. Mss, 21651, fols 1–2.

20 These captives were James Dyer at Fort Pitt and Henry Alexander at Fort Niagara.

21 *MPCP*, 7: 561–2; HL, LO, 3758; *PG*, 19 August 1756.

22 Three Acadians traveling overland from South Carolina to Fort Duquesne were intercepted by Virginia forces and shipped to Britain by Lieutenant Governor Robert Dinwiddie. See Journal of the Commons House of Assembly, November 20, 1755–July 6, 1757, xvii n.

23 These escapees were Isham Bernat and Moses Moore. See *PA*, ser. 1, 3: 632–3. Sergeant Adam Hoops was almost certainly a captive of the Wyandot of Detroit; he escaped across Lake Erie to Fort Presqu'île after two years in captivity. See BL, Add. Mss, 21638, fol. 126.

24 "Thomas Gist's Indian Captivity, 1758–1759," *PMHB* 80 (1956): 285–311.

25 At least two escaped captives arrived in Detroit in starving condition: a trader who was four days in the woods after escaping from a Potawatomi town, and a captive who was eight days coming from Saginaw. See Jehu Hay, *Diary of the Siege of Detroit in the War with Pontiac*, ed. Franklin B. Hough (Albany, NY, 1860), 65, 89.

26 M.M. Quaife, ed., *The Siege of Detroit* (Chicago, IL: Lakeside, 1958), 251–5, 261–7. A month later, "At Half past nine this Evening a Negro made his Escape from one Marsacks who had bought him from the Indians." Two weeks later, "a Soldier sav'd himself by running off from a Chibbawa [*sic*] who brought him to Cuesieres to sell." See Hay, *Diary*, 64, 77.

27 Of those who escaped, 28 of 77 came in to Detroit.

28 The traders were Morris Turner and Ralph Kilgore. See *MPCP*, 5: 482–4.

29 John McKenny (McKinney) was back in Philadelphia by 17 November 1756, just under a year after his capture. See *Papiers Contrecoeur et autres documents concernant le conflit anglo-français sur l'Ohio de 1745 à 1756*, ed. Fernand Grenier (Quebec City, QC: Laval University Press, 1952), 230; and Draper Mss, Pittsburgh and Northwest Virginia Papers, 6NN77.

30 These escapees were Peter Looney and William Philips. See *PG*, 28 July 1757, reprinted in *Manuscripts and Records from the Burton Historical Collection* 1 (1917): 113–15, and reprinted in *MVHR* 15 (1928): 95–6.

31 *MPCP*, 7: 242–3.

32 *MPCP*, 7: 282–4. French Margaret was a niece of legendary Madame Isabel Montour (1667–1753), accomplished cultural intermediary in the region. See Jon Parmenter, "Isabel Montour, Cultural Broker on the Frontiers of New York and Pennsylvania," in *The Human Tradition in Colonial America*,

ed. Nancy L. Rhoden and Ian K. Steele (Wilmington, DE: Scholarly Resources, 1999), 141–59; and Nancy Hagedorn, "'Faithful, Knowing, and Prudent': Andrew Montour as Interpreter and Cultural Broker, 1740–1772," in *Between Indian and White Worlds: The Cultural Broker*, ed. Margaret C. Szasz (Norman, OK: University of Oklahoma Press, 1994), 44–60.

33 Nathaniel Holland to Israel Pemberton, from Shamokin, 13 April 1758, Haverford College Library, Indian Committee Records, 824/10, vol. 1, n.p.

34 Isaac Hollister, *A Brief Narration of the Captivity of Isaac Hollister* (New London, CT, 1767).

35 *MPCP*, 7: 620–1.

36 *PG*, 10 November 1757, 24 May 1764.

37 James H. Merrell, *Into the American Woods: Negotiators on the Pennsylvania Frontier* (New York: Norton, 1999), 131.

38 Paul A.W. Wallace, "Historic Indian Paths of Pennsylvania," *PMHB* 76 (1952): 1–29; Charles Morse Stotz, *Outposts of the War for Empire* (Pittsburgh, PA: University of Pittsburgh Press, 1985), 25. For a general description of the Pennsylvania backcountry in 1757, see *MPCP*, 7: 444–6.

39 James P. Myers Jr, "Pennsylvania's Awakening: The Kittanning Raid of 1756," *PH* 66 (1999): 406.

40 *PG*, 8 December 1763.

41 *PA*, ser. 1, 3: 83; *MPCP*, 7: 381.

42 *NYM*, 16 February 1756; *PG*, 26 February 1756. Two puzzles remain, based upon the separate petitions, seemingly by each woman, to the Virginia House of Burgesses in March 1761. Katherine Bingeman said nothing of her escape, and reported that William Byrd had paid money for her redemption, which she could not repay. Did the Shawnee get redemption money despite her escape? See *Journals of the House of Burgesses, 1758–1761*, ed. McIlwaine, 239. The petition of Mary Ingles was that of a relation, the wife of John Ingles, who lost her husband and was captured in the fall of Vause's Fort in 1756. Her petition was denied. See ibid., 221–2, 229.

43 Preston Papers, 1: 83; F.B. Kegley, *Kegley's Virginia Frontier: The Beginning of the Southwest, the Roanoke of Colonial Days, 1740–1783* (Roanoke, VA: Southwest Virginia Historical Society, 1938), 247.

44 *PG*, 24 July 1755, 1 July 1756; *NYM*, 28 July 1755, 16 February and 5 July 1756; Raymond Young, "The Effects of the French and Indian War on Civilian Life in the Frontier Counties of Virginia, 1754–1763" (PhD diss., Vanderbilt University, 1969), 13.

45 Jane Frasier, *Narrative of the Captivity of Mrs. Jane Frasier* (1930; reprint, New York: Garland, 1977).

46 "The Narrative of Marie Le Roy and Barbara Leininger," *PA*, ser. 2, 7: 427–38.

47 Deposition of Mathias Warren, 30 March 1764, BL, Add. Mss, 21650, fol. 116.

48 For accounts, see Alexander Scott Withers, *Chronicles of Border Warfare, or A History of the Settlement by the Whites, of North Western Virginia, and of the*

Indian Wars and Massacres, in that section of the state, with reflections, anecdotes, etc. ... (1831; reprint, New York: Arno, 1971), 89–93; James B. Finley, *Life among the Indians* (Cincinnati, OH, 1857), 45–47; and Joseph A. Waddell, *Annals of Augusta County, Virginia*, 2 vols (Richmond, VA, 1886-88), vol. 1, 111.

49 William Meade, *Old Church Ministers and Families of Virginia*, 2 vols (Philadelphia, PA, 1857), vol. 1, 341–8; Waddell, *Annals of Augusta*, vol. 1, 126–8.

50 Haverford College Library, Indian Committee Records, 824/11, vol. 4, n.p.

51 "Thomas Gist's Indian Captivity," 302.

52 Alexander Henry, *Travels and Adventures in Canada and the Indian Territories between the Years 1760 and 1776*, ed. James Bain (1809; reprint, Toronto, ON: G.N. Morang, 1901), 127.

CHAPTER TWELVE

1 *PA*, ser. 1, 2: 214–15, 218–19.

2 John Potter to Richard Peters, from Conegogig, 3 November 1755, *MPCP*, 6: 673–4; Earl P. Olmstead, *David Zeisberger: A Life among the Indians* (Kent, OH: Kent State University Press, 1997), 96.

3 *PG*, 21 July 1763.

4 BL, Add. Mss, 21649, fol. 256, printed in *HBP*, 5: 308.

5 Charles Beatty, *The Journal of a Two Month Tour* (London, 1768), 11–13.

6 Lois G. Carr, "The Development of the Maryland Orphans' Court, 1654–1715," in *Law, Society, and Politics in Early Maryland*, ed. Aubrey Land, Lois Green Carr, and Edward C. Papenfuse (Baltimore, MD: Johns Hopkins University Press, 1977), 41–62; Darrett B. and Anita H. Rutman, "'Now-Wives and Sons-in-Law': Parental Death in a Seventeenth-Century Virginia County," in *The Chesapeake in the Seventeenth Century: Essays on Anglo-American Society*, ed. Thad W. Tate and David L. Ammerman (Chapel Hill, NC: University of North Carolina Press, 1979), 153–82; Daniel Smith, "Autonomy and Affection: Parents and Children in 18th Century Chesapeake Families," in *Growing Up in America: Children in Historical Perspective*, ed. N. Ray Hiner and Joseph M. Hawes (Urbana, IL: University of Illinois Press, 1985), 45–58; John Demos, *Past, Present, and Personal: The Family and the Life Course in American History* (New York: Oxford University Press, 1986); Helena M. Wall, *Fierce Communion: Family and Community in Early America* (Cambridge, MA: Harvard University Press, 1990).

7 On the March 1756 incident, see Robert Daiutolo Jr, "The Role of Quakers in Indian Affairs during the French and Indian War," *Quaker History* 77 (1988): 6.

8 Sherman Day, *Historical Collections of the State of Pennsylvania*, 2 vols (Philadelphia, PA, 1843), vol. 1, 264; *RCFFP*, 1: 574–6.

9 Peter Silver, *Our Savage Neighbors: How Indian War Transformed Early America* (New York: Norton, 2008), 125–7; Vernon Leslie, *The Tom Quick Leg-*

ends (Middletown, NY: T.E. Henderson, 1977); James Eldridge Quinlan, *Tom Quick, the Indian Slayer, and the Pioneers of Minisink* ... (Monticello, NY, 1851).

10 Joseph Doddridge, *Notes on the Settlement and Indian Wars of the Western Parts of Virginia and Pennsylvania* (Wellsburgh, VA, 1824), 177.

11 *PA*, ser. 1, 3: 59; William A. Hunter, *Forts on the Pennsylvania Frontier, 1753–1758* (Harrisburg, PA: Pennsylvania Historical and Museum Commission, 1960), 415–17. A Philip Bäder was rated for 150 acres, one horse, and three cattle in Berwick Township, York County, Pennsylvania, in 1782. See *PA*, ser. 3, 21: 561.

12 Deposition in *PA*, ser. 1, 3: 396–7; *PG*, 11 May 1758; interview reported in [N. Holland] to Israel Pemberton, 20 May 1758, Haverford College Library, Indian Committee Records, 824/10, vol. 1, n.p.

13 Archibald Loudon, ed., *A Selection of Some of the Most Interesting Narratives of Outrages Committed by the Indians in Their Wars with the White People*, 2 vols (Carlisle, PA, 1808–11), vol. 2, 47–65, quote at 59.

14 *MPCP*, 5: 468–9; Yoko Shirai, "The Indian Trade in Colonial Pennsylvania, 1730–1768: Traders and Land Speculation" (PhD diss., University of Pennsylvania, 1985), 24–5. On Baby, see Dale Miquelon, "Baby, *dit* Dupéront (Dupéron, Duperron), Jacques," in *DCB*, 4: 38–40.

15 BL, Add. Mss, 21648, fol. 152, printed in *HBP*, 6: 85–6.

16 *PA*, ser. 1, 4: 92–8.

17 Calhoun to Bouquet, 14 May 1762, BL, Add. Mss, 21648, fol. 152, printed in *HBP*, 6: 85–6. John's petition of 12 August 1762 is in *PA*, ser. 1, 4: 100. The petitions of Catherine Mackay and Jacob Hockstetler are in ibid., 99.

18 *Minutes of Conferences Held at Lancaster in August 1762* ... (Philadelphia, PA, 1763), 33.

19 Loudon, ed., *Selection*, vol. 1, 252–302, esp. 268, 274, 285–6.

20 *PG*, 17 and 24 June 1756; *PA*, ser. 1, 4: 106–7; TNA, WO 34/10, 193–200; *V&P*, 6: 5001, 5152. On the Innises at Fort Augusta, see Haverford College Library, Indian Committee Records, 824/11, vol. 3, n.p. On the Innises at Lancaster, see "Journal of James Kenny, 1761–1763," ed. John W. Jordan, *PMHB* 37 (1913): 175.

CHAPTER THIRTEEN

1 *PG*, 31 October 1754; Minutes of the Albany Commissioners, LAC, MG 19, F 35/2, lot 680, 76.

2 R.G. Thwaites, ed., *Early Western Travels, 1748–1846*, 32 vols (Cleveland, OH: Arthur H. Clark, 1904–07), vol. 1, 20, 31, 33–4; *PA*, ser. 1, 2: 13; *MPCP*, 5: 353.

3 *Journals of the House of Burgesses of Virginia, 1752–1755, 1756–1758*, ed. H.R. McIlwaine (Richmond, VA: Colonial Press, 1909), 347, 348, 381, 383.

4 In a revision of April 1757, an adult male scalp was valued at £10 and a prisoner at £15. See *The Statutes at Large: Being a Collection of All the Laws of*

Virginia, from the First Session of the Legislature in the Year 1619, ed. William Waller Hening, 13 vols (Charlottesville, VA: University Press of Virginia, 1969), vol. 6, 550–2, 557, vol. 7, 121–3. Peter Wood estimates that in 1745 there had been 600 Indians living "east of the mountains" in Virginia, and this number fell to 400 by 1760. See Peter H. Wood, "The Changing Population of the Colonial South: An Overview by Race and Region, 1685–1790," in *Powhatan's Mantle: Indians in the Colonial Southeast*, ed. Peter H. Wood, George A. Waselkov, and M. Thomas Hatley (Lincoln, NB: University of Nebraska Press, 1989), 38.

5 Gist, a former Baltimore merchant, was a guide for George Washington in 1754 and General Edward Braddock in 1755, and he became deputy in the southern department, under Edmond Atkin. See David B. Trimble, "Christopher Gist and the Indian Service in Virginia, 1757–1759," *VMHB* 64 (1956): 143–65.

6 Sally Schwartz, *"A Mixed Multitude": The Struggle for Toleration in Colonial Pennsylvania* (New York: New York University Press, 1987), 214–16; William Smith, *A Brief View of the Conduct of Pennsylvania for the Year 1755* (London, 1756).

7 See Eugene R. Sheridan, "Morris, Robert Hunter," *ANB*; *V&P*, 5: 4120, 4132 (quote); and C. Hale Sipe, *The Indian Wars of Pennsylvania* (Harrisburg, PA: Telegraph, 1929), 230. The assembly voted a modest £60,000 toward both pay and fortification. See William A. Hunter, *Forts on the Pennsylvania Frontier, 1753–1758* (Harrisburg, PA: Pennsylvania Historical and Museum Commission, 1960), 194, 197.

8 *MPCP*, 6: 753. More generally, see William A. Hunter, "Provincial Negotiations with the Western Indians, 1754–1758," *PH* 18 (1951): 213–19.

9 Morris to John Ross, 8 March 1756, *PA*, ser. 1, 2: 595.

10 The neutral Shawnee chief Paxnous, speaking for the Delaware at Tioga in June of 1756, told Pennsylvania's negotiators, "There are a great Number of our People among you, and in a manner confined; we desire you will set them at Liberty, or rather give them a safe Conduct to Wyomink, where we intend to settle." See *MPCP*, 7: 141.

11 *PA*, ser. 1, 2: 619; *MPCP*, 7: 78–9; Yoko Shirai, "The Indian Trade in Colonial Pennsylvania, 1730–1768: Traders and Land Speculation" (PhD diss., University of Pennsylvania, 1985), 91–2. The commissioners ran out of funds by October 1757, and were unable to offer anything to widow Margaret Mitchell, who had been given the scalp of an Indian killed in a raid that killed her husband and son. See *PA*, ser. 1, 3: 308. On the limited impact of bounties, see Peter Silver, *Our Savage Neighbors: How Indian War Transformed Early America* (New York: Norton, 2008), 161–4.

A New York objection to scalp bounties called for the mutilation of captured raiders, who would lose a thumb, an eye, or their testicles, but regarded scalping, especially of women and children, as barbaric. See *Proposal to Prevent Scalping, etc. Humbly Offered to the Consideration of a Council of War* (New York, 1755).

12 Morris to the commissioners, 13 April 1756, *PA*, ser. 1, 2: 625–6, emphasis in original. The proclamation was printed in *PG*, 15, 22, and 29 April 1756; and in *NYM*, 19 April 1756.

The Virginian scalp bounty of £10 currency was, when granted, worth £7.13.10 sterling, whereas Pennsylvania's 150 pieces-of-eight were worth approximately £29.18.0 sterling. See John J. McCusker, *Money and Exchange in Europe and America, 1600–1775: A Handbook* (Chapel Hill, NC: University of North Carolina Press, 1978), 10, 211.

13 Jack D. Marietta, "Conscience, the Quaker Community, and the French and Indian War," *PMHB* 95 (1971): 3–27; Ralph L. Ketcham, "Conscience, War, and Politics in Pennsylvania, 1755–1757," *W&MQ*, ser. 3, 20 (1963): 316–439; Robert L.D. Davidson, *War Comes to Quaker Pennsylvania* (New York: Columbia University Press, 1957).

14 Minutes of meetings of 19, 21, and 23 April 1756, Haverford College Library, Indian Committee Records, 824/10, vol. 1, 103–7. Formal organization was approved at a meeting of 4 December 1756 (see ibid.) See also Jack D. Marietta, *The Reformation of American Quakerism, 1748–1783* (Philadelphia, PA: University of Pennsylvania Press, 1984); Theodore Thayer, *Israel Pemberton, King of the Quakers* (Philadelphia, PA: Historical Society of Pennsylvania, 1943); E.B. Bronner, "Pemberton, Israel," *ANB*; Douglas Leighton, "Claus, Christian Daniel," *DCB*, 4: 154–5; Theodore Thayer, "The Friendly Association," *PMHB* 67 (1943): 356–76; Robert Daiutolo Jr, "The Role of Quakers in Indian Affairs during the French and Indian War," *Quaker History* 77 (1988): 1–30; and Michael Goode, "A Failed Peace: The Friendly Association and the Pennsylvania Backcountry during the Seven Years' War," *PMHB* 136 (2012): 472–4.

From November 1756, through its Meeting for Sufferings, the Philadelphia Yearly Meeting assisted numerous Quakers displaced by fear of Indian attacks. See Haverford College, Quaker Collection, Philadelphia Yearly Meeting, Meeting for Sufferings, Minutes 1756–75, 28–32, 68, 84–5, 94–5, 102–3, 108–9, 124–5, 167, 177.

15 James H. Merrell, *Into the American Woods: Negotiators on the Pennsylvania Frontier* (New York: Norton, 1999), 65–9, 236–49 (re. Kanuksusy [Kos Showweyha]). On Kanuksusy, see also William N. Fenton, *The Great Law and the Longhouse* (Norman, OK: University of Oklahoma Press, 1998), 488–90; and *GWP*, 1: 140n20. For the claim that Kanuksusy's dying request to be buried in a Quaker cemetery is proof that he was a Quaker, see Anthony F.C. Wallace, *King of the Delawares: Teedyuscung, 1700–1763* (Philadelphia, PA: University of Pennsylvania Press, 1949), 109.

16 *MPCP*, 7: 97–100, 137–41. Morris and Conrad Weiser also sought the approval of Scarouady (see ibid., 106). On Pumpshire, see James H. Merrell, "'I Desire all that I have said ... may be taken down aright': Revisiting Teedyuscung's 1756 Treaty Council Speeches," *W&MQ* 63 (2006): 792–8, 801–2, 813–20. On the diplomatic role of the Iroquois, see Michael J. Mullin, "Sir William Johnson's Reliance on the Six Nations at

the Conclusion of the Anglo-Indian War of 1763–1765," *American Indian Culture and Research Journal* 17 (1993): 69–90.

17 *MPCP*, 7: 97–100.

18 *MPCP*, 7: 105–10.

19 *MPCP*, 6: 763.

20 Dwight L. Smith, "Shawnee Captivity Ethnohistory," *Ethnohistory* 2 (1955): 36–7; Merrell, *Into the American Woods*, 42–53, 302–15; Richard White, *The Middle Ground: Indians, Empires, and Republics in the Great Lakes Region, 1650–1815* (New York: Cambridge University Press, 1991), 202–8; *JP*, 10: 523.

21 *MPCP*, 7: 97–100, 193–4; Wallace, *King of the Delawares*, 97–101. On Johnson's gift of French prisoners after the battle of Lake George, see Ian K. Steele, *Betrayals: Fort William Henry and the "Massacre"* (New York: Oxford University Press, 1990), 54.

22 *MPCP*, 7: 212.

23 *MPCP*, 7: 204–20. Quaker minutes of the meeting are in Haverford College Library, Indian Committee Records, 824/10, vol. 1, n.p.

24 Wallace, *King of the Delawares*, 122–5; *MPCP*, 7: 284–9.

25 This fifth captive was Nicholas Ramston. The four initially released were George Fox, William Hess, Henry Weeser, and Samuel Clifford. See *PMHB* 32 (1908): 315, 316; *NYM*, 18 October 1756; *PG*, 21 October 1756; *MPCP*, 7: 284, 474; and Hunter, *Forts*, 243, 245. At this time, Teedyuscung claimed that he personally had only two captives left. See *MPCP*, 7: 334.

26 PA ser. 8, 6: 4502–6; Benjamin Franklin, *The Papers of Benjamin Franklin*, ed. Leonard W. Labaree, 29 vols (New Haven, CT: Yale University Press, 1959–92), vol. 7, 112–14. The fullest statement of this case was [Charles Thomson], *An Inquiry into the Causes of the Alienation of the Delaware and Shawanese Indians from the British Interest* (London, 1759). The Friendly Association paid L. Weiss £2 on 28 February 1758 "for engrossing Enquiry into the Grounds of the Indians Complaints &c. sent to England." See Haverford College Library, Indian Committee Records, 824/10, vol. 1, n.p.

27 Liam Riordan, *Many Identities, One Nation: The Revolution and Its Legacy in the Mid-Atlantic* (Philadelphia, PA: University of Pennsylvania Press, 2007), 38–30. The link between returning captives and reclaiming land was also made by Abenaki chief Atecouando, at Montreal on 5 July 1752, when addressing Captain Phineas Stevens, who had come to recover New England captives. See Thomas-M. Charland, "Atecouando," *DCB*, 3: 20–1.

28 *PA*, ser. 1, 3: 204–5.

29 *MPCP*, 7: 649–714, quote at 703.

30 Assembly address of 24 March 1758, Haverford College Library, Indian Committee Records, 824/10, vol. 1, n.p.

31 C.F. Post's journal, HL, AB, 368; Fenton, Great Law, 505.

32 Post to Amherst, 30 October 1760, *Records of the Moravian Mission among the Indians of North America*, 40 reels (New Haven, CT: Yale University Press, 1970), reel 28, Personalia Post 1746–67, box 219, folder 7.

33 On John Woolman's visit with Papunahoal, see John Woolman, *A Journal of the Life, Gospel Labours, and Christian Experiences of That Faithful Minister of Jesus Christ, John Woolman* (London, 1847), 120–2; and Thomas P. Slaughter, *The Beautiful Soul of John Woolman, Apostle of Abolition* (New York: Hill and Wang, 2010), 258–60.

34 The three captives were: a New England woman named Mary, likely taken from the Wyoming settlement in 1755; a boy named Jacob from Tulpehoken, taken the same year; and Mary Van Ellen, a girl from Minisink. See Post's draft of conference minutes, 20 May 1760, Haverford College Library, Indian Committee Records, 824/11, vol. 3, n.p.

35 "Journey on the Forbidden Path: Chronicles of a Diplomatic Mission to the Allegheny Country, March–September, 1760," ed. Robert S. Grumet, *Transactions of the American Philosophical Society* 89, part 2 (1999): 121–31, derived from *MPCP*, 8: 484–500; Silver, *Our Savage Neighbors*, 104–6.

36 Charles Thomson wrote *Some Account of the Behaviour and Sentiments of a Number of Well-Disposed Indians Mostly of the Minusing Tribe* (1760), a copy of which has not been located. In December of 1760 Lieutenant Governor James Hamilton reported that Teedyuscung had just delivered four captives to him, "two elderly women, and two Boys, who are quite naked and destitute." See *V&P*, 6: 5081, 5084.

37 Margery West stated in her deposition that her "son" was convinced to return her to Sir William Johnson for this reason. See "Deposition of Margery West Concerning Her Captivity by the Indians," *New York Historical Society, Collections for 1921* (New York: New York Historical Society, 1922), 94–7.

38 Post to William Denny, c. 18 June 1758, Haverford College Library, Indian Committee Records, 824/10, vol. 2, n.p.; copy in HSP, Penn Mss, Indian Affairs, vol. 3, nos 49–51; and printed in *PA*, ser. 1, 3: 419.

39 Pisquetomen happened to be at Teedyuscung's new settlement at Wyoming as Post went through. See Michael N. McConnell, "Pisquetomen and Tamaqua: Mediating Peace in the Ohio Country," in *North Eastern Indian Lives, 1632–1816*, ed. Robert S. Grumet (Amherst, MA: University of Massachusetts Press, 1996), 273–94; and Merrell, *Into the American Woods*, 242–9. Pisquetomen reported at the Easton conference on 13 October 1758 that he had been sent west by Pennsylvania's lieutenant governor, by Teedyuscung, and by Israel Pemberton. See *EAID*, 3: 438.

40 Christian Frederick Post, "Two journals of Western Tours ... [July–September 1758; October 1758–January 1759]," in Thwaites, ed., *Early Western Travels*, vol. 1, 199, 213–14.

41 Hamilton to Thomas Penn, 21 November 1760, HSP, Penn Mss, Official Correspondence, vol. 9, nos 184–6. In a private meeting at Easton, Cayuga and Mohawk speakers promised to return all their captives. See *EAID*, 3: 439–40.

42 The Friendly Society was struggling to keep its place in negotiations as early as the previous September, when it printed an address *To William Denny* ... (Philadelphia, PA, 1757).

43 Post, "Two journals," in Thwaites, ed., *Early Western Travels*, vol. 1, 247–9.

44 *HBP*, 2: 626.

45 In 1770 Croghan claimed these lands ran for fifteen miles back from the Ohio River between the mouth of Beaver Creek and Raccoon Creek. See *The Diaries of George Washington*, ed. Donald Jackson and Dorothy Twohig, 6 vols (Charlottesville, VA: University Press of Virginia, 1976–79), vol. 2, 281–2.

46 *Wilderness Chronicles of Northwestern Pennsylvania*, ed. Sylvester K. Stevens and Donald R. Kent (Harrisburg, PA: Pennsylvania Historical Commission, 1941), 134–8; Stephen F. Auth, *The Ten Years' War: Indian-White Relations in Pennsylvania, 1755–1765* (New York: Garland, 1989), 52–61. James Kenny reported that the British promise to withdraw was repeated at a conference at Fort Pitt on 9 September 1759. See "James Kenny's 'Journal to ye Westward,' 1758–59," ed. John W. Jordan, *PMHB* 37 (1913): 428–9.

47 *EAID*, 3: 427–66. On the twisting of the minutes of the Pittsburgh meeting of 4–5 December 1758, see Auth, *Ten Years' War*, 52–61.

48 Vaudreuil to the Minister, 15 February 1759, *Wilderness Chronicles*, ed. Stevens and Kent, 131–3.

49 Mercer to Bouquet, 7 February 1759, *HBP*, 3: 107–8.

50 Mercer to Bouquet, 24 April 1759, BL, Add. Mss, 21644, fol. 134.

51 *HBP*, 3: 213, 241.

52 General Amherst to William Johnson, 22 February 1761, and reply of 7 January 1762, *JP*, 3: 345, 601; William J. Campbell, "An Adverse Patron: Land, Trade, and George Croghan," *PH* 76 (2009): 117–40; William J. Campbell's forthcoming book *Negotiating the Oneida Carry: Empire and Speculation in Iroquoia*, esp. ch. 3; Walter S. Dunn Jr, *Frontier Profit and Loss: The British Army and the Fur Traders, 1760–1764* (Westport, CT: Greenwood, 1998).

53 Mary Jemison, *A Narrative of the Life of Mary Jemison*, ed. C.D. Vail (New York: American Scenic and Historical Preservation Society, 1942), 58, 388–91.

54 William Johnson's own expenses ran to approximately £23,000 between March of 1755 and 1757, and to another £17,000 between November 1758 and December 1759. See Gail D. MacLeitch, *Imperial Entanglements: Iroquois Change and Persistence on the Frontiers of Empire* (Philadelphia, PA: University of Pennsylvania Press, 2011), 67–8.

55 American Philosophical Society, Philadelphia, PA, Indian and Military Affairs of Pennsylvania, Mss Class 974.8, P19, 731–46; BL, Add. Mss, 21655, fols 73–5.

56 *MPCP*, 8: 389; "George Croghan's Journal, April 3, 1759, to April [30], 1763," *PMHB* 71 (1947): 316–70, 370n104; McConnell, "Pisquetomen and Tamaqua."

57 *JP*, 13: 163–4; Auth, *Ten Years' War*, 52–61, 123–4.

58 *JP*, 10: 198–206.

59 Minutes of Easton conference, 12 August 1761, Haverford College Library, Indian Committee Records, 824/11, vol. 4, n.p.; Bouquet Papers, BL, Add.

Mss, 21655, fols 131–69; *Minutes of Conferences Held at Easton in August 1761* ... (Philadelphia, PA, 1761).

60 "George Croghan's Journal," 409–11.

61 Auth, *Ten Years' War*, 152–3.

62 Between 22 May 1760 and the end of August 1761, Croghan had received ninety-seven captives. See "George Croghan's Journal," 369–415.

63 *JP*, 10: 317–18.

64 *JP*, 3: 550; *JP*, 10: 317–18; White, *Middle Ground*, 261–3.

65 See "George Croghan's Journal," 415–19. Christian Frederick Post had estimated that the Ohio Shawnee held as many as 150 captives, and the Delaware somewhat more. See Post to Friendly Society, 18 August 1761, Haverford College Library, Indian Committee Records, 824/11, vol. 4, n.p.

66 *JP*, 3: 566, 589–91; *JP*, 10: 343.

67 Johnson to Croghan, 8 January 1762, *HBP*, 6: 669–71.

68 *JP*, 10: 702.

69 *JP*, 10: 490–1.

70 Bouquet to Monckton, 10 and 24 July 1761, BL, Add. Mss, 21638, fols 236–7, 244, and reply of 24 August 1761, ibid., fol. 249.

71 Bouquet to Amherst, 30 March 1762, BL, Add. Mss, 21634, fol. 111.

72 Amherst to Bouquet, 2 May 1762, *HBP*, 6: 83.

73 Amherst to Bouquet, 25 July 1762, BL, Add. Mss, 21634, fol. 133.

74 *HBP*, 6: 100. On the costs of recovering prisoners, see Bouquet to Amherst, 30 March 1762, and Amherst to Bouquet, 25 July 1762, BL, Add. Mss, 21634, fols 111, 133.

75 "Journal of James Kenny, 1761–1763," ed. John W. Jordan, *PMHB* 37 (1913): 156.

76 *PA*, ser. 1, 4: 92–8. Post and the young John Heckewelder had been sent out to Tuscarawas in March 1762. See Earl P. Olmstead, *David Zeisberger: A Life among the Indians* (Kent, OH: Kent State University Press, 1997), 107–8.

77 *Minutes of Conferences Held at Lancaster in August 1762* ... (Pennsylvania, PA, 1763); *JP*, 10: 498–9; Auth, *Ten Years' War*, 174–8.

78 *MPCP*, 8: 742–50, quote at 745.

79 *MPCP*, 8: 760–1.

80 *Minutes of Conferences Held at Lancaster in August 1762*, 34–5.

81 "George Croghan's Journal," 426–7. On Kisheta and his son, see *HBP*, 2: 241, 305–6, 355, 448, 458, 648; *MPCP*, 8: 656, 770; and Merrell, *Into the American Woods*, 73.

82 *JP*, 3: 921.

83 Holland to I. Pemberton, 27 March and 11 October 1759, Haverford College Library, Indian Committee Records, 824/1l, vol. 3 , n.p.

84 David Boyd, "History of the Capture and Captivity of David Boyd from Cumberland County, Pennsylvania," *WPHM* 14 (1931): 28–42.

85 "Journal of James Kenny, 1761–1763," ed. Jordan, 7.

86 *PG*, 9 September 1762. On 13 November 1762, the assembly's committee on disbursement of military expenses paid a Joseph Conlin £8.0.6 for "boarding Indian captives." See *V&P*, 7: 5662.

87 *HBP*, 6: 118–20, 127, 139.

88 Croghan's list of 9 October 1762, Bouquet Papers, BL, Add. Mss, 21655, fol. 192, printed in *HBP*, 6: 121. According to Croghan's own Pittsburgh journal, kept by himself and his assistants, the total number of captives returned to him personally was 357 by the end of 1762. See "George Croghan's Journal."

89 "Journal of James Kenny, 1761–1763," ed. Jordan, 186.

90 William Galloway had traveled to Wakitomica to negotiate for his captured wife. See BL, Add Mss, 21648, fols 196–7; and *HBP*, 6: 89.

91 With his *Diplomacy and Indian Gifts: Anglo-French Rivalry along the Ohio and Northwestern Frontiers, 1748–1763* (Stanford, CA: Stanford University Press, 1950), esp. 180–6, Wilbur Jacobs established the argument without documenting the ban, but he noted Amherst's hope that presents would cease when trade was established. Despite his emphasis on economy in all respects, Amherst continued to allow William Johnson to decide on all of Croghan's accounts. See Amherst to Johnson, 22 February and 6 December 1761, *JP*, 3: 345, 581.

Croghan's instructions to Thomas Hutchins of 25 October 1761, concerning recovering captives, called for economy but presents. See Bouquet Papers, BL, Add. Mss, 21655, fols 172–4. Bouquet explained to Amherst, 24 May 1762, "Our Indian agents are a kind of Loadstone attracting the Indians who reciprocally attract presents, for when they are absent, the savages and the expence cease; after all in several cases we can not do without them, but if any address is required, It consists rather I think in managing the Manager than the Indians." See BL, Add. Mss, 21653, fol. 126.

In November of 1762 Amherst was still instructing Bouquet to negotiate the return of "those poor captives" by distributing presents. See BL, Add. Mss, 21634, fol. 164.

CHAPTER FOURTEEN

1 Captain Robert Stewart reported from Pittsburgh on 28 September 1759 that Indians had "brought us near Fifty of their Captives." See *Letters to Washington and Accompanying Papers*, ed. Stanislaus Murray Hamilton, 5 vols. (Boston, MA, 1898–1902), vol. 3, 165.

2 James Adair, *Adair's History of the American Indians* (1775; reprint, Johnson City, TN: Watauga, 1930), 410–12.

3 Archibald Loudon, ed., *A Selection of Some of the Most Interesting Narratives of Outrages Committed by the Indians in Their Wars with the White People*, 2 vols (Carlisle, PA, 1808–11), vol. 1, 291–2. Alexander McKee was said to have been saved from being burned by the Shawnee when a woman claimed and untied the man she would later marry. See Draper Mss, Pittsburgh

and Northwest Virginia Papers, 6NN176. John Gibson was also saved by being adopted by a Shawnee woman. See R.G. Thwaites and L.P. Kellogg, *Documentary History of Dunmore's War 1774* (Madison, WI: Wisconsin Historical Society, 1905), 10–11.

4 Glen to Anthony Palmer, President of the Pennsylvania Council, 9 April 1748, *MPCP*, 5: 303–4. On ransom, see William E.S. Flory, *Prisoners of War: A Study in the Development of International Law* (Washington, DC: American Council of Public Affairs, 1942), 111–12.

5 *PG*, 20 April 1749.

6 *MPCP*, 5: 482–4.

7 Deposition of 27 June 1753, TNA, WO 55/1817, fols 11–12.

8 *MPCP*, 5: 643–4.

9 LAC, MG 19, F 35/2, lot 680, 2–4.

10 Robert and John Sanders Letterbook, 1742–43, 1753–58, LAC, MG 18, C6 (photostat from NYHS), 76.

11 LAC, MG 19, F 35/2, lot 680, 5, 7–9; *NYM*, 24 September 1753; Charles A. Hanna, *The Wilderness Trail, Or the Ventures and Adventures of the Pennsylvania Traders on the Allegheny Path*, 2 vols (New York: Putnam, 1911), vol. 2, 252–6.

12 Brett Rushforth, *Bonds of Alliance: Indigenous and Atlantic Slaveries in New France* (Chapel Hill, NC: University of North Carolina Press, 2012), 297.

13 LAC, MG 19, F 35/2, lot 680, 11.

14 Ibid., 32–3.

15 The letter was variously ascribed to "Ononraguirte," "Ononeaguiete," or "Ononeaouis" in the *PG* of 15 August 1753, in the *SCG* of 3 October 1753, and in the *NYM* of 19 August 1753. The asking price of 400 livres, or £20 sterling per head, would have come to a total of £143.10 New York currency, plus travel expenses home. See John J. McCusker, *Money and Exchange in Europe and America, 1600–1775: A Handbook* (Chapel Hill, NC: University of North Carolina Press, 1978), 97, 164. In a letter from Montreal, dated 10 May 1755, a captive claimed that the French were buying captives at 300–400 livres worth of trade goods. See *NYM*, 11 August 1755.

16 LAC, MG 19, F 35/2, lot 680, 42.

17 *NYM*, 24 September 1753.

18 Robert Stobo, *The Memoirs of Major Robert Stobo of the Virginia Regiment*, ed. Neville B. Craig (Pittsburgh, PA, 1854), 91–2. The pistole, or doblon, was about 40 pence sterling in 1754, making such a ransom about £26 sterling, £46.8 New York currency, or £43.6 Pennsylvania currency. See McCusker, *Money and Exchange*, 100, 106, 164, 184.

19 *PG*, 15, 22, and 29 April 1756.

20 *MPCP*, 7: 282–4. Catherine Nicholson (Nichols) reported that her brother was also sold to William Johnson in 1757. See Nathaniel Holland to I. Pemberton, "Shamokin 3. Mo [May] 27 1759 from Nathaniel Holland," Haverford College Library, Indian Committee Records, 824/1l, vol. 3, n.p. Early in 1756 French Margaret's daughter bought a female captive from

Teedyuscung, who used the proceeds to buy a horse. See Anthony F.C. Wallace, *King of the Delawares: Teedyuscung, 1700–1763* (Philadelphia, PA: University of Pennsylvania Press, 1949), 100.

21 The purchase of captives by Europeans was already familiar in the Ohio Valley. François Morgane de Vincennes, commanding the fort that would be named for him, reported in 1733 that Illinois and Miami allies, upon returning from war with the Chickasaw, would present him with their captives and that "it is necessary to pay for this sort of thing." See *Indiana Historical Society Publications*, 3: 302–7, quoted in Eric Hinderaker, *Elusive Empires: Constructing Colonialism in the Ohio Valley, 1673–1800* (New York: Cambridge University Press, 1997), 118.

22 Deposition of 21 November 1756, HL, LO, 2254B.

23 Interrogation of 16 October 1757, *PA*, ser. 1, 3: 294–6.

24 Jean Lowry was given to the French commander at Fort Machault (whom she said was "Lisshn Vingrie"), treated well, and sent on to be a servant of the commander's wife in Montreal. She worked as a freed seamstress for several months before being sent to England, and then returned to Philadelphia. See Jean Lowry, *A Journal of the Captivity of Jean Lowry and Her Children* (Philadelphia, PA, 1760), 14–18.

For an unconfirmed account of a pretty Virginian girl given to the commandant, see *Travels in New France by J.C.B.*, ed. Sylvester K. Stevens, Donald H. Kent, and Emma Edith Woods (Harrisburg, PA: Pennsylvania Historical Commission, 1941), 69–73. The Dunker hermits Gabriel and Israel Eckerle, and their servant John Schilling, were captured in 1757 and sold to the commandant at Fort Duquesne. See Pierre Pouchot, *Memoirs of the Late War in North America between England and France*, ed. B.L. Dunnigan (Youngstown, NY: Old Fort Niagara Association, 1994), 124–5, 124–5n, 377–9.

25 Merlin Stonehouse Transcripts, vol. 4, n.p., Huntington Library and Art Gallery, San Marino, CA.

26 *PG*, 6 September 1759.

27 *NYCD*, 10: 530.

28 Charles Stuart, "The Captivity of Charles Stuart, 1755–57," *MVHR* 13 (1926–27): 58–81, quote at 78.

29 C. Hale Sipe, *The Indian Wars of Pennsylvania* (Harrisburg, PA: Telegraph, 1929), 224–7. The Canadian trader was either Jacques Baby, *dit* Dupéront, or one of his brothers, Louis or Antoine. See *DCB*, 4: 38–40.

30 John Hogan, deposition of 1 June 1757, HL, LO, 3758; *MPCP*, 7: 561–2. The average price for an Indian slave in New France, where the market was larger and quite stable, was about 350 livres, approximately £16 sterling. See Rushforth, *Bonds of Alliance*, 292–3.

31 Deposition of 21 November 1756, HL, LO, 2254B. Walker's claim that Governor Vaudreuil hired out civilian captives would have referred only to those redeemed with public money. Another captive reported, more optimistically, that in 1757 English prisoners in New France were "very well

used, and allowed to Work abroad at 15 livres per Month & provisions." See *JP*, 2: 718.

32 Schuyler is known to have ransomed at least one Virginian, teenager Hans Nicholas Peters. See Merlin Stonehouse Transcripts, vol. 4, n.p., Huntington Library and Art Gallery, San Marino, CA; *Journals of the House of Burgesses of Virginia, 1758–1761*, ed. H.R. McIlwaine (Richmond, VA: Colonial Press, 1908), 112; and Lowry, *Journal*, 17. He also arranged credit for Virginian officer Andrew Lewis. See *GWP*, 6: 101. On Peter Schuyler, see the 1763 affidavits of Dr Benjamin Stokes and William McDonald in F. Aston De Peyster Mss, box 8, no. 5, NYHS; John David Krugler, "Schuyler, Peter," *DCB*, 3: 587–9; and Robert C. Alberts, *The Most Extraordinary Adventures of Major Robert Stobo* (Boston, MA: Houghton Mifflin, 1965), 200–3, 332. He was eventually reimbursed: by the British Army (£592.8.0, plus £123.6.8 for mariners and artisans) (see F. Aston De Peyster Mss, box 8, no. 5, NYHS; and HL, AB, 972); by New Jersey (£6,000, or £3,726.14.0 sterling) (see F. Aston De Peyster Mss, box 8, no. 4); by New Hampshire (£172.6.4) (see Provincial Papers of New Hampshire, 6: 716, 719–20, 738–9); and by Pennsylvania (£83.6.6, plus £132.0.6) (see *V&P*, 6: 4912–13, 5065). The total sum, of £4,780.2.10 sterling, does not include his accounts with Massachusetts or Virginia.

33 Elizabeth Ball, captured at Conococheague Creek in June 1756, was in a convent in Montreal when she and General Gage advertised, in the *PG* of 2 July 1761, for her relatives to claim her. See Barbara E. Austen, "Captured ... Never Came Back: Social Networks among New England Female Captives in Canada, 1689–1763," in *New England/New France, 1600–1850*, ed. Peter Benes (Boston, MA: Boston University, 1992), 28–38, and William Henry Foster, *The Captors' Narrative: Catholic Women and Puritan Men on the Early American Frontier* (Ithaca, NY: Cornell University Press, 2003).

34 Petition of 29 September 1757, TNA, Adm. 1/4323, n.p.

35 *PA*, ser. 1, 3: 419; Haverford College Library, Indian Committee Records, 824/10, vol. 2, n.p.

36 Christian Frederick Post, "Two journals of Western Tours ... [July–September 1758; October 1758–January 1759]," in R.G. Thwaites, ed., *Early Western Travels, 1748–1846*, 32 vols (Cleveland, OH: Arthur H. Clark, 1904–07), vol. 1, 250, 254, 287. Apparently Lieutenant Christopher Gist paid the ransom. See *Letters to Washington*, ed. Hamilton, vol. 3, 148.

37 Sherman Day, *Historical Collections of the State of Pennsylvania*, 2 vols (Philadelphia, PA, 1843), vol. 2, 384–5; *RCFFP*, 1: 589. The payments were ended by the 1781 "massacre of the Bedford scouts," where the sons of Hudson and Woods recognized each other on opposite sides. See *RCFFP*, 1: 589.

38 On the meeting, see *Wilderness Chronicles of Northwestern Pennsylvania*, ed. Sylvester K. Stevens and Donald R. Kent (Harrisburg, PA: Pennsylvania Historical Commission, 1941), 134–8.

39 Loudon, ed., *Selection*, vol. 2, 47–65, quote at 59; Nathaniel Holland to I. Pemberton, 16 April 1761, Haverford College Library, Indian Committee Records, 824/11, vol. 4, n.p.

40 For Holland's letter of 13 April 1758 and his second-hand account of an interview with Richard Bard, in an unsigned letter of 20 May 1758, see Haverford College Library, Indian Committee Records, 824/10, vol. 1, n.p.

41 I. Pemberton to Isaac Zane, 6 June 1758, Haverford College Library, Indian Committee Records, 824/10, vol. 1, n.p.

42 "Shamokin 3. Mo [May] 27 1759 from Nathaniel Holland," Haverford College Library, Indian Committee Records, 824/1l, vol. 3, n.p. Thanks to Diana Franzusoff Peterson for a transcription of pages 2–3 of this letter, missing on the microfilm.

43 Holland to Pemberton, 6 and 16 May 1760, 2 October 1760, Haverford College Library, Indian Committee Records, 824/11, vol. 3, n.p.; accounts for 30 July 1760, ibid., vol. 4, 82.

44 Holland to Pemberton, 21 August 1760, Haverford College Library, Indian Committee Records, 824/11, vol. 4, n.p.

45 Holland to Pemberton, 16 April 1761, Haverford College Library, Indian Committee Records, 824/11, vol. 4, n.p.

46 Post to Pemberton, 18 August 1761, Haverford College Library, Indian Committee Records, 824/11, vol. 4, n.p.

47 Military ransom had disappeared in early Stuart England, but was revived during the Civil War. See Barbara Donagan, *War in England, 1642–1649* (Oxford, UK: Oxford University Press, 2008), 143–4, 376–9.

48 Mercer to Bouquet, 7 February 1759, BL, Add. Mss, 21644, fol. 44.

49 Mercer to Bouquet, April 1759, and reply of 13 April 1759, *HBP*, 3: 213–14, 241.

50 The ban on ransom was referred to explicitly in Burd to Bouquet, from Wakatomica, 8 June 1762, *HBP*, 6: 89. On a trade embargo against the Shawnee, and the Cherokee precedent, see Bouquet to Amherst, 30 March 1762, and reply of 25 July 1762, BL, Add. Mss, 21634, fols 111, 133. On Bouquet's insistence on the military monopoly of diplomacy, see BL, Add. Mss, 21634, fols 119–20, 127–8, 144; and James Hamilton to Bouquet, 11 November 1762, BL, Add. Mss, 21648, fol. 430.

51 *PG*, 2 April and 2 July 1761.

52 At Fort Michilimackinac in 1763, trader Stanley Goddard became the only known captive ransomed in the west during the war. See Alexander Henry, *Travels and Adventures in Canada and the Indian Territories between the Years 1760 and 1776*, ed. James Bain (1809; reprint, Toronto, ON: G.N. Morang, 1901), 49. On 22 September 1764 Father Pierre Du Jaunay presented the arriving British garrison with a captive soldier whom his servant had ransomed from Indian captors. See *JP*, 10: 287.

53 Claus to Johnson, 6 August 1763, conference of 9–11 August 1763, and Gage to Johnson, 12 August 1763, *JP*, 10: 777–88; "Lieut. James Gorrell's Journal," *Collections of the State Historical Society of Wisconsin* 1 (1903): 24–48.

54 *JP*, 11: 836–41; Nicholas B. Wainwright, *George Croghan, Wilderness Diplomat* (Chapel Hill, NC: University of North Carolina Press, 1959), 220–1; *PG*, 15 August 1765.

55 *JP*, 13: 189.

56 Flags of truce ships were notorious for engaging in illicit trade. Pennsylvania's lieutenant governor, William Denny, authorized seven such flags of truce ships in 1759, allegedly selling such permissions for £10 each. See William Hamilton to William Pitt, 1 November 1760, in *Correspondence of William Pitt*, ed. Gertrude Selwyn Kimball, 2 vols (New York: Macmillan, 1906), vol. 2, 351–2; and Pennsylvania State Archives, RG 21, Proprietary, Miscellaneous Papers 1664–1775, Register of Flags of Truce, n.p.

57 Major John Smith, "Extract from the Journal of Major John Smith, 1756–1757," in *Colonial Captivities, Marches, and Journeys*, ed. I.M. Calder (New York: Macmillan, 1935), 137–40.

58 *PG*, 26 July 1759, reported that eight French ships had been converted into cartel ships in 1758, to save the ships from capture and to take 300 prisoners from Quebec. Anthony Wheelock's ads recalling working prisoners are in *NYM*, 4 and 17 November 1760; and in *NYG*, 10 November 1760.

59 For Vaudreuil's list, see TNA, CO 5/57, part 1, fols 119–21. For Wheelock's list, see TNA, CO 5/57, part 1, fol. 76. Compare Amherst's list in TNA, WO 34/98, fol. 68.

60 Ian K. Steele, "When Worlds Collide: The Fate of Canadian and French Prisoners Taken at Fort Niagara, 1759," *Journal of Canadian Studies* 39 (2005): 9–39; Donald Chaput, "Dagneau Douville de Quindre, Louis-Césaire," *DCB*, 3: 158–9.

61 Morris to William Johnson, 24 April 1756, *MPCP*, 7: 97–100. On Johnson's trading a *panis* for a captive, see *JP*, 10: 262, 269, 409–15, 431–2.

62 Amherst to Gladwin, 22 June 1763, TNA, WO 34/49, fol. 328.

63 Jehu Hay, *Diary of the Siege of Detroit in the War with Pontiac*, ed. Franklin B. Hough (Albany, NY, 1860), 20, 21. Ojibwa successfully demanded Rutherfurd back.

64 BL, Add. Mss, 21658, fols 88–90; Amherst Papers, TNA, WO 34/49, fols 214–15; Hay, *Diary*, 26, 42–6; M.M. Quaife, ed., *The Siege of Detroit* (Chicago, IL: Lakeside, 1958), 137–8. Compare Gregory Evans Dowd, *War under Heaven: Pontiac, the Indian Nations and the British Empire* (Baltimore, MD: Johns Hopkins University Press, 2002), 124. By early July, the Wyandot had also brought in captives as part of their own discussions of peace with Gladwin. See Hopkins to Amherst, 11 July 1763, TNA, WO 34/49, fols 216–17.

65 These 1,494 captives included: 1,078 who remained missing, 320 who were subsequently returned, 65 who stayed with their captors, and 31 who died in captivity.

CHAPTER FIFTEEN

1 Jean Lowry, *A Journal of the Captivity of Jean Lowry and Her Children* (Philadelphia, PA, 1760), 5–6; Vaudreuil to Minister, 8 August 1756, AN, C11A, vol. 101, fol. 88; William A. Hunter, *Forts on the Pennsylvania Frontier, 1753–1758* (Harrisburg, PA: Pennsylvania Historical and Museum Commission,

1960), 561. Mary McCord was the child killed accidentally in the skirmish; two McCord girls, Mrs Thorn, her infant child, and an unnamed boy escaped then or were rescued.

2 Edward Shippen to Lieutenant Governor Morris, 24 April 1756, *PA*, ser. 1, 2: 642–3.

3 *PG*, 28 June 1764; *HBP*, 6: 567.

4 Mary Jemison, *A Narrative of the Life of Mary Jemison*, ed. C.D. Vail (New York: American Scenic and Historical Preservation Society, 1942), 71; *HBP*, 6: 567.

5 *SCG*, 24 November 1759; *PG*, 1 and 8 November 1759; *NYG*, 5 and 12 November 1759. Four Gilmores were returned: Elizabeth, Elizabeth Jr, Jane, and John. See *PG*, 17 January 1765; and *WPHM* 39 (1956): 194–7. Herbert McClure was injured in the rescue, and was eventually awarded £30. See *Journals of the House of Burgesses of Virginia, 1758–1761*, ed. H.R. McIlwaine (Richmond, VA: Colonial Press, 1908), 194.

6 *PG*, 1 and 8 August 1763.

7 *PG*, 10 and 17 November 1763, 3 April 1764.

8 See John Oliphant, *Peace and War on the Anglo-Cherokee Frontier, 1756–1763* (Basingstoke, UK: Palgrave, 2001).

9 Mercer to Bouquet, 7 February 1759, BL, Add. Mss, 21644, fol. 44.

10 Henry Bouquet to H. Mercer, 13 April 1759, *HBP*, 3: 241.

11 *HBP*, 6: 514–16, 522–6, 533 (quote), 534, 540–1, 586, 663.

12 *HBP*, 6: 532–3.

13 *JP*, 11: 402–3; *MPCP*, 9: 219; *HBP*, 6: 604.

14 Henry Gladwin, "The Gladwin Manuscripts: With an Introduction and a Sketch of the Conspiracy of Pontiac," *Michigan Pioneer and Historical Society Collections* 27 (1897): 671–2.

15 *HBP*, 6: 604; *MPCP*, 9: 218.

16 George McDougall to Bouquet, from Detroit, 18 July 1764, BL, Add. Mss, 21650, fol. 348.

17 *NYCD*, 7: 621–2, 718; *JP*, 4: 386–7; *JP*, 11: 155–7.

18 Jemison, *Narrative* (1942), 59–60.

19 *JP*, 11: 276–324; Alexander Henry, *Travels and Adventures in Canada and the Indian Territories between the Years 1760 and 1776*, ed. James Bain (1809; reprint, Toronto, ON: G.N. Morang, 1901), 156–64, quote at 162; Fred Anderson, *Crucible of War: The Seven Years' War and the Fate of Empire in British North America, 1754–1766* (New York: Knopf, 2000), 620. Johnson had assured Gage, in his letter of 1 June 1764, that he would do "every thing towards getting all the rest out of the Enemy hands." See *JP*, 11: 215.

20 *Wilderness Chronicles of Northwestern Pennsylvania*, ed. Sylvester K. Stevens and Donald R. Kent (Harrisburg, PA: Pennsylvania Historical Commission, 1941), 280–3; *JP*, 11: 328–33; *MPCP*, 9: 195–6.

21 *JP*, 4: 503–8; *JP*, 11: 328–33; William G. Godfrey, *Pursuit of Profit and Preferment in Colonial North America: John Bradstreet's Quest* (Waterloo, ON: Wilfrid Laurier University Press, 1982), 199–204.

22 On the raids, see *PG*, 20 September, 11 October, and 15 November 1764.

23 Bouquet to Major William Grant, 19 January 1764, BL, Add. Mss, 21653, fols 205–6, 249, 251–2; *HBP*, 6: 491. On Shawnee at Fort Chartres and purchases of gunpowder there, see St Ange to D'Abbadie, 9 November 1764, *Collections of the Illinois State Historical Society* 10 (1915): 253, 356; and Examination of Warren by Thomas Hutchins, BL, Add. Mss, 21650, fols 126–7.

John McCullough remembered that a Delaware council concluded "that they were scarce of ammunition, and were not able to fight him, that they were then destitute of clothing, and that, upon the whole, it was best to come to terms of peace with the white people." See Archibald Loudon, ed., *A Selection of Some of the Most Interesting Narratives of Outrages Committed by the Indians in Their Wars with the White People*, 2 vols (Carlisle, PA, 1808–11), vol. 1, 284.

24 Stephen-Bouquet correspondence of 15, 30 September, 10 October, and 7 November 1763, BL, Add. Mss, 21649, fols 334–5, 343–4, 371–2, 451–2.

25 Bouquet letters of 5 July 1764, BL, Add. Mss, 21650, fols 313–14, 317–18; Governor Fauquier's response of 9 July 1764, ibid., fol. 327. On the bounties, see *MPCP*, 9: 188–92. Bouquet's advertisement for volunteers, dated 11 August 1764, mentioned the bounties. See *HBP*, 6: 602. Fifty-seven Maryland volunteers arrived at Fort Pitt on 9 October, much ahead of Bouquet. See BL, Add. Mss, 21651, fol. 15. A corps of Maryland volunteers, under Captain McLelland, joined the army on 20 October, at "Camp # 13." See "The Orderly Book ...," *WPHM* 42 (1959): 190.

26 *HBP*, 6: 604; *MPCP*, 9: 218.

27 Bouquet to Harris, 15 July 1764, and reply of 17 August 1764, BL, Add. Mss, 21650, fols 349–50, 405. For an intriguing discussion of Bouquet's emotional manipulation of backwoodsmen and Indians, see Nicole Eustace, *"Passion Is the Gale": Emotion, Power and the Coming of the American Revolution* (Chapel Hill, NC: University of North Carolina Press, 2008), 373–80.

28 Henry Bouquet, "Orderly Book I of Colonel Henry Bouquet's Expedition against the Ohio Indians, 1764," *WPHM* 56 (1973): 389–94. About one-third of the Pennsylvania troops deserted before the expedition even reached Fort Loudoun. Compare Draper Mss, Pittsburgh and Northwest Virginia Papers, 1NN1, which puts the total number at 922 soldiers, plus officers.

29 Warren's deposition of 30 March 1764 is in BL, Add. Mss, 21650, fol. 116. John Prentice's letter to Bouquet, from Fort Loudoun, of 15 October 1764, is in BL, Add. Mss, 21651, fol. 21. See also Jehu Hay, *Diary of the Siege of Detroit in the War with Pontiac*, ed. Franklin B. Hough (Albany, NY, 1860), 89.

30 The chief guide was Alexander Lowery, of that trading clan. See BL, Add. Mss, 21656, fol. 27. He was assisted by Thomas Mitchell, Andrew Boggs, and James Brown. See BL, Add. Mss, 21651, fol. 113. On them as traders, see *WPHM* 42 (1959): 28n6.

31 Bouquet, "Orderly Book 1," *WPHM* 56 (1973): 402–28, continued in *WPHM* 57 (1974): 68–83, 89, 99. The cavalcade included herds of cattle, sheep, and 1,152 packhorses.

32 BL, Add. Mss, 21655, fols 227–8, and HL, MM, 569, printed in William Smith, *An Historical Account of the Expedition against the Ohio Indians, in the Year 1764, Under the Command of Henry Bouquet Esq.* (Philadelphia, 1766); in *HBP*, 6: 649–50; and in *MPCP*, 9: 208–9. See also Bouquet to Captain David Hay, 21 September 1764, BL, Add. Mss, 21650, fols 533, 535. These hostages were held until 9 November.

Bouquet had made two earlier attempts to contact Bradstreet. The first pair of messengers, sent to Sandusky, found him gone. The second pair had turned back when they found the severed head of a man stuck on a post in the middle of the path. See *HBP*, 6: 651–5.

33 Five or six captives had been acquired by Bradstreet's army by early October, and two women escaped to this army on 14 October. These two reported that their captors still held thirty captives, though they claimed to have none. Their chief, who was likely Kageshquanohel (the Pipe), was said to have led a major raid into Virginia in May, taking thirty scalps and prisoners, and was presently held by "the general." See John Bremner journal and diary, 6 and 14 October 1764, NYHS, BV section.

34 HL, MM, 569, fols 3–4, 7–8; *MPCP*, 9: 209–12.

35 Paul David Nelson, "Smith, James (1737–1814)," *ANB*; Patrick G. Williams, "Butler, Richard," *ANB*.

36 A petition to the Pennsylvania Assembly in March 1764, urging the Paxton agenda to oust all remaining Indians, restore all captives, pay frontier volunteers, and exclude Quakers from voting, was signed by more than 1,200 residents of Cumberland County. The list of names is lost. See *V&P*, 7: 5580–3.

37 BL, Add. Mss, 21650, part 2, 117–18; Peter Silver, *Our Savage Neighbors: How Indian War Transformed Early America* (New York: Norton, 2008), 132–3. On Colonel Reid, see *HBP*, 6: 535n; and David Dixon, *Never Come to Peace Again: Pontiac's Uprising and the Fate of the British Empire in North America* (Norman, OK: University of Oklahoma Press, 2005), 235. In 1763, Reid had been on a commission to judge Pennsylvanian civilians' claims for war losses.

William Johnson, writing General Gage on 1 September 1764, voiced his own wish that the Shawnee and Delaware be punished, while deleting his drafted comment that a peace would be a disappointment to the army. See *JP*, 4: 419.

38 Reports, in the *PJ* of 25 October and 1 November 1764, put the final numbers at 400 regulars, 400 Pennsylvania volunteers, 100 Pennsylvania "Light Horse," 250 Virginia volunteers, and 60 Maryland volunteers.

39 HL, MM, 569, fol. 8; "New Light on Bouquet's Ohio Expedition: Nine Days of Thomas Hutchins's Journal, October 3–October 11, 1764," *WPHM* 66 (1983): 276.

40 Smith, *Historical Account*, 11–12.

41 "New Light on Bouquet's Ohio Expedition," 276.

42 Orders of 13 October 1764, BL, Add. Mss, 21655, fol. 273; "The Orderly Book …," *WPHM* 42 (1959): 184–5.

43 Smith, *Historical Account*, 13. No note from Detroit to Bouquet survives from this specific period. Meanwhile, Bradstreet, at Sandusky, apparently received Bouquet's message on 13 October 1764, carried by two Indians who had seen Bouquet on 2 October, and he replied on 17 October. See *HBP*, 6: 667–8. On the exchange of 16 October, see *HBP*, 6: 665–6; and *MPCP*, 9: 213–14.

44 The orderly book for 17 October 1764 included: "The Captives delivered up this day by the Indian Deputys at the Congress to be Immediately furnished wt a Sufficient Quantity of Tents Kettles & Provisions —— A Guard of a Corporal & six Men to be detached from ye reserve to protect & assist them." See "The Orderly Book …," *WPHM* 42 (1959): 189.

45 *HBP*, 6: 670–1; Stephen F. Auth, *The Ten Years' War: Indian-White Relations in Pennsylvania, 1755–1765* (New York: Garland, 1989), 123–4.

46 BL, Add. Mss, 21655, fol. 241; draft in ibid., fols 239–40, 245–6; printed, with some variations, in *HBP*, 6: 671–5; in *JP*, 11: 441–6; in *MPCP*, 9: 216–19; and in Smith, *Historical Account*, 16–17.

47 *HBP*, 6: 681.

48 *HBP*, 6: 681–2; *MPCP*, 9: 220–1.

49 Jon William Parmenter, "Pontiac's War: Forging New Links in the Anglo-Iroquois Covenant Chain, 1758–1766," *Ethnohistory* 44 (1997): 617–54.

50 *HBP*, 6: 682–3; *MPCP*, 9: 221.

51 *PG*, 15 November 1764, reported the initial return of seventeen or eighteen and promises of returning "367 Captives they had in all, which they were quickly to bring in." Back on 24 July 1761, Bouquet had estimated that the Delaware then had about 100 captives, and the others about 150. See BL, Add. Mss 21638, fol. 244.

52 *MPCP*, 9: 222.

53 *MPCP*, 9: 223–6. Johnson understood Bouquet's meaning, and he pledged to help with gaining the release of Captain Bull and his companions in a letter of 17 December 1764. See BL, Add. Mss, 21651, fol. 94–5.

54 *MPCP*, 9: 226–9. William Smith was impressed: "Smile not reader at this transaction … [for] to frown them from their throne … will be found to require both resolution and firmness; and their submitting to it clearly shews to what degree of humiliation they were reduced." See Smith, *Historical Account*, 23.

55 Iroquois message of 2 October 1764, HL, MM, 569, fols 3–4; Oterunque to Bouquet, 8 November 1764, *MPCP*, 9: 227.

56 BL, Add. Mss, 21651, fol. 55. Prisoners returned by Wyandot are mentioned in Major John Small to Captain Thomas Buford, from the Muskingum, 9 November 1764, BL, Add. Mss, 21651, fols 40–2.

57 Orders of 29 November 1764, BL, Add. Mss, 21638, fol. 394, printed in *HBP*, 6: 710.
58 On Owens's challenge, see C. Hale Sipe, *Fort Ligonier and Its Times* (Harrisburg, PA: Telegraph, 1932), 223–4. See also Bouquet to Shawnee, 27 October 1764, *MPCP*, 9: 220–3; and Smallman to Bouquet, 8 November 1764, BL, Add. Mss, 21651, fol. 38, printed in *HBP*, 6: 706–7.
59 Smith, *Historical Account*, 20–1; Bouquet to Penn, 15 November 1764, BL, Add. Mss, 21651, fol. 52, printed in *MPCP*, 9: 207–8.
60 BL, Add. Mss, 21653, fol. 364; Bouquet to Colonel McNeil, 15 November 1764, BL, Add. Mss, 21651, fol. 50.
61 The Shawnee had not been major participants in Pontiac's War. Only seven of the twenty-four captives they returned at this time, whose date of capture is known, had been captured in this war, and three of these had not been captured by the Shawnee.
62 *HBP*, 6: 700–3; *MPCP*, 9: 229–33.
63 Bouquet said that 150 were still held when he wrote to T. Penn, 15 November 1764, BL, Add. Mss, 21651, fol. 52. Bouquet had one table that located 84 captives still held in Shawnee towns, and by the end of the month he had an additional list of 88 named captives still in Lower Shawnee Town. See BL, Add. Mss, 21655, fols 251, 296.
64 *MPCP*, 9: 219. In July 1764, at Detroit, George McDougall wrote Bouquet about salvaging 120 hats, 12 coats, and 50 pairs of breeches from Fort Niagara, which he had brought with him to Detroit "& have served them out to the men that was prisoners, as they stood most in need of them, which I hope you will approve of." See BL, Add. Mss, 21650, fol. 344.
65 Henry Melchior Muhlenberg, "Regina, the German Captive," in *Proceedings of the Pennsylvania-German Society* 15 (1906): 86.
66 The army distributed 213 shirts, 203 pairs of leggings, 168 blankets, and 263 packs of shoes, which evidently included more than one pair. See *WPHM* 39 (1956): 188–95. The bill paid to J.F. Davenport, the official Pennsylvania storekeeper at Fort Pitt, came to £121.11.0 Pennsylvania currency. See BL, Add. Mss, 21651, fol. 222.
67 "The Orderly Book …," *WPHM* 42 (1959): 191.
68 Smith, *Historical Account*, 18. There were no Maryland captives returned here. The matron was Margerite Peters. See *HBP*, 6: 859.
69 Smith, *Historical Account*, 26.
70 Draper Mss, Kentucky Papers, 16CC193-7; *PG*, 3 May 1764. The story, without identification of the Kincades, was recounted in Cyrus Cort, *Colonel Henry Bouquet and His Campaigns of 1763 and 1764* (Lancaster, PA, 1883), 69–70.
71 Loudon, ed., *Selection*, vol. 1, 285.
72 Brigade major Small to Buford, 9 November 1764, BL, Add. Mss, 21651, fols 40–2. The instructions also included, "It is unnecessary to mention to you to prevent any Intercourse between the young females and your Young males, particularly don't trust Ward with them." Bouquet repeated

this specific warning to Captain David Hay the same day (see ibid., fol. 42).

73 J. Norman Heard, *White into Red: A Study of the Assimilation of White Persons Captured by Indians* (Metuchen, NJ: Scarecrow, 1973), 4, 138–9; David Boyd, "History of the Capture and Captivity of David Boyd from Cumberland County, Pennsylvania," *WPHM* 14 (1931): 437; *PG*, 17 January 1765.

74 Hay to Bouquet, 29 October 1764, BL, Add. Mss, 21651, fol. 28; Colonel John Neill to Bouquet, 29 October 1764, ibid., fols 11, 26–7; Bouquet to Hay, 9 November 1764, ibid., fols 42–3. The first twenty-three people taken to Fort Pitt included John Palmer. See *WPHM* 39 (1956): 189. Bouquet's orders to Captain Charles Lewis, drafted on 4 November but dated 15 November 1764, are in BL, Add. Mss, 21658, fols 104–5, and printed in *HBP*, 6: 683–4.

75 Bouquet to J. Penn, 15 November 1764, BL, Add. Mss, 21651, fol. 52, printed in *MPCP*, 9: 207–8.

76 The others were John Fisher, Mary Stewart, and "Peggy a Mullato." See *WPHM* 39 (1956): 188–9.

77 Pennsylvanian packhorses were to carry the captives as far as Fort Cumberland, where Colonel John McNeill was to hire local horses, at the army's expense, to see the captives home from there. See Bouquet to McNeill, 15 November 1764, BL, Add. Mss, 21651, fol. 50.

78 Mary Lanscisco and Hannah Smith, both living with the Delaware for more than nine years, each brought a child with them. See *WPHM* 39 (1956): 188, 190, 194, 196.

79 Buford to Bouquet, 16 December 1764, BL, Add. Mss, 21651, fol. 91. The list of those sent to Virginia, under Buford's Colonel McNeill, is in *WPHM* 39 (1956): 194–5. It includes males named "Cawacawachi" and "Hans" and a female named "Conogoniony."

80 *PG*, 5 September 1765.

81 Muhlenberg, "Regina, the German Captive," 87–8.

82 John D. Shane, undated and confused interview, from the 1840s, with Alexander Hamilton, Draper Mss, Kentucky Papers, 11CC291.

83 BL, Add. Mss, 21651, fol. 127.

84 Murray to Bouquet, 5 January 1764, BL, Add. Mss, 21651, fol. 127. Benevisica's speech is, in part, in BL, Add. Mss, 21655, fol. 261, printed in *HBP*, 6: 761–2. The ransomed, Mary and Miriam Hamilton, and Jane Gilmore, had all been taken at Carr's (Kerr's) Creek in July of 1763. On the Hamiltons, see Draper Mss, Kentucky Papers, 11CC291; and Bouquet to Gage, 5 January 1765, *Collections of the Illinois State Historical Society* 10 (1915): 397, where he claims fourteen other Shawnee captives were returned at the end of November 1764.

85 The Shawnee deputies met with Johnson in July 1765, and agreed to peace. See HSP, Indians, Treaty of Peace of 13 July 1765 (microfilm Iroquois diplomacy, reel 28). In these negotiations, the Susquehanna Delaware and Seneca surrendered twenty-three captives taken on the Allegheny frontier. See *PG*, 19 September 1765.

86 *EAID*, 5: 702–11, quote at 708; *MPCP*, 9: 254–64.
87 *NYG*, 22 July 1765; *NYM*, 19 August 1765; *PG*, 19 September 1765.
88 TNA, CO 5/66, fols 276–90. The Delaware treaty is printed in *MPCP*, 9: 277–80.
89 Indiana Historical Society, *Collections* 11 (1916): 2, 6.
90 Nicole Eustace, "The Sentimental Paradox: Humanity and Violence on the Pennsylvania Frontier," *W&MQ* 65 (2008): 29–64.
91 BL, Add. Mss, 21650, fol. 296, printed in *WPHM* 39 (1956): 202.
92 Some 1,196 were not known to have returned. Of these, at least 31 died in captivity and 83 remained as white Indians.
93 The Virginia House of Burgesses eventually awarded £40 to nine militia officers who served with the expedition. See *Journals of the House of Burgesses of Virginia, 1766–1769*, ed. John Pendleton Kennedy (Richmond, VA: Colonial Press, 1906), 63.

CHAPTER SIXTEEN

1 *PG*, 14 February 1765; William Smith, *An Historical Account of the Expedition against the Ohio Indians, in the Year 1764, Under the Command of Henry Bouquet Esq.* (Philadelphia, 1766), 30–2.
2 *PG*, 15 and 29 November 1764, 6 December 1764, 17 January, 7 February, and 14 February 1765.
3 As early as February 1763, Croghan had resolved to go to England to press for compensation for his earlier trade losses. Croghan had, however, disobeyed Bouquet's direct order to accompany his 1763 relief expedition to Fort Pitt. See Nicholas B. Wainwright, *George Croghan, Wilderness Diplomat* (Chapel Hill, NC: University of North Carolina Press, 1959), 195, 200.
4 Murray to Bouquet, 14 December 1764, enclosing copy of Croghan to McKee, 6 December 1764, BL, Add. Mss, 21653, fols 330–1; draft of Bouquet to Gage, 22 December 1764, ibid., fols 333–5; Wainwright, *George Croghan*, 211.
5 Johnson to Board of Trade, 26 December 1764, TNA, CO 5/66, fols 187–96.
6 Croghan to Franklin, 12 December 1765, TNA, CO 5/66, fols 83–6.
7 Smith had fourteen titles printed between 1751 and 1760, well ahead of Jonathan Mayhew with eleven and Benjamin Franklin with eight. See "A Note on Statistics," in *A History of the Book in America*, vol. 1, *The Colonial Book in the Atlantic World*, ed. Hugh Amory and David D. Hall (Cambridge, UK, and New York: Cambridge University Press, 2000), 518. On Smith, see Albert Frank Gegenheimer, *William Smith: Educator and Churchman, 1727–1803* (Philadelphia, PA: University of Pennsylvania Press, 1943); Thomas Firth Jones, *A Pair of Lawn Sleeves: A Biography of William Smith (1727–1803)* (Philadelphia, PA: Chilton, 1972); Nancy L. Rhoden, "William Smith, Philadelphia Minister and Moderate," in *The Human Tradition in the American Revolution*, ed. Nancy L. Rhoden and Ian K. Steele (Wilmington, DE: Scholarly Resources, 2000), 61–80; and Ralph L. Ketcham,

"Benjamin Franklin and William Smith: More Light on an Old Philadelphia Quarrel," *PMHB* 88 (1964): 142–63.

8 William Smith, *A Brief State of the Province of Pennsylvania* (London, 1755); *A Brief View of the Conduct of Pennsylvania for the Year 1755* (London, 1756); and *A Christian Soldier's Duty: ... a Sermon Preached ... to the First Battalion of the Royal American Regiment ...* (Philadelphia, PA, 1757). In a letter to Thomas Barton, Smith was already very sensitive to "our poor back settlers" forced to flee leaving victims "bleeding beneath the unrelenting Hand of a Merciless Barbarian." Printed in lieu of a dedication, the letter appeared in Smith's *Unanimity and Public Spirit: A Sermon Preached at Carlisle and Some Other Episcopal Churches in the Counties of York and Cumberland, Soon after General Braddock's Defeat* (Philadelphia, PA, 1755), quote at xiv.

9 *HBP*, 1: 310–12; *HBP*, 4: 167. On this successful libel suit by Smith, see William Renwick Riddell, "Libel on the Assembly: A Prerevolutionary Episode," *PMHB* 52 (1928): 176–92, 249–79.

10 Quoted in Jones, *Pair of Lawn Sleeves*, 7.

11 *PG*, 13 June 1765.

12 *PG*, 20 June and 4 July 1765.

13 Nicole Eustace, "The Sentimental Paradox: Humanity and Violence on the Pennsylvania Frontier," *W&MQ* 65 (2008): 29–64. Bouquet's use of the phrase "just resentments" in reference to the frontiersmen did not, as suggested, indicate his social rehabilitation of the Paxtonites. The phrase was used by proprietor and governor John Penn in addressing the troops at Carlisle on 5 August 1764. See Smith, *Historical Account*, 3.

14 Richard Slotkin, *Regeneration through Violence: The Mythology of the American Frontier, 1600–1860* (Middletown, CT: Wesleyan University Press, 1973), 231–5, 252–4, quote at 231.

15 Smith, *Historical Account*, 38; Eustace, "Sentimental Paradox," 57–64. The Stamp Act became law on 22 March 1765, which was known in Philadelphia before the end of May.

16 *PG*, 25 July 1765.

17 *PG*, 14 November 1765.

18 Ann Uhry Abrams, *The Valiant Hero: Benjamin West and Grand-Style History Painting* (Washington, DC: Smithsonian Institution, 1985), 108–9; Robert C. Alberts, *Benjamin West: A Biography* (Boston, MA: Houghton Mifflin, 1978).

19 West provided a similar coif of feathers for the Indian featured in "General Johnson Saving a Wounded French Officer from the Tomahawk of a North American Indian" (1764–68) and in "The Death of General Wolfe" (1770). See also Nancy Shoemaker, *A Strange Likeness: Becoming Red and White in Eighteenth-Century North America* (New York: Oxford University Press, 2004), 62–4, 77–8.

20 Smith, *Historical Account*, 26.

21 Edward Penny's (1714–91) paintings of the Marquis of Granby and Robert Clive were among the best known.

22 The painting, dated between 1764 and 1768, is in the Derby Museum and Art Gallery, Derby, England.

23 There was no discussion of the drawings in John Galt's exhaustive *The Life, Studies, and Works of Benjamin West, Esq.*, 2 vols (London, 1820).

24 George Bancroft, *History of the United States of America*, rev. ed., 6 vols (Boston, MA, 1879), vol. 3, 387–588, quote at 385. An exception is I[srael] D[aniel] Rupp, *Early History of Western Pennsylvania and of the West* (Harrisburg, PA, 1846), 164–78. He devoted most of a chapter on Pontiac's War to the Bouquet expedition and its success.

25 J.W. Fortescue, *A History of the British Army*, 13 vols (London: Macmillan, 1899–1930), vol. 3, 16–18, 21, has three pages on Bushy Run, and a single complimentary sentence on the Muskingum expedition's "difficult task well done." Lawrence Henry Gipson, *The British Empire before the American Revolution*, 15 vols (Caldwell, ID, and New York: Caxton and Knopf, 1936–70), vol. 9, 123–6, regards Bouquet's expedition as "faultlessly executed" (vol. 9, 126). Reginald Hargreaves, *The Bloodybacks: The British Serviceman in North America and the West Indies* (London: Hart Davis, 1968), 179–83, offers detail on Bushy Run, while granting that the Muskingum expedition "broke the insurrectionary movement's back" (182). Douglas Edward Leach is balanced in his brief discussion of Bouquet's expedition, which is presented in a postscript to his *Arms for Empire: A Military History of the British Colonies in North America, 1607–1763* (New York: Macmillan, 1973), 501, 503. Compare Alexander V. Campbell, *The Royal American Regiment: An Atlantic Microcosm, 1755–1772* (Norman, OK: University of Oklahoma Press, 2010), 181–5.

PART FIVE

1 One mistress, seeking a runaway servant girl in the fall of 1762, claimed that she "passes through the country for an Indian Prisoner, and by that means it is supposed she has changed her Clothes." See *PG*, 14 October 1762.

2 *PG*, 7 October 1756. They also donated their share of the booty to their men, "An instance of Generosity this, which shows these Gentlemen did not go against the Enemy from a mercenary Motive, but from a regard for the Service of their King and the bleeding Country."

3 *PG*, 13 May and 23 September 1756; PA ser. 1, 2: 775.

4 *NYM*, 27 September 1756; *PG*, 23 September 1756; PA ser. 1, 2: 775.

5 Jean Lowry, *A Journal of the Captivity of Jean Lowry and Her Children* (Philadelphia, PA, 1760), 5–6; William A. Hunter, *Forts on the Pennsylvania Frontier, 1753–1758* (Harrisburg, PA: Pennsylvania Historical and Museum Commission, 1960), 561.

6 Cecilia Smith had two children with her when captured and may have come to think that Catherine was dead. See *PMHB* 32 (1908): 313. There is an entry for the baptism, on 10 August 1756, of "the daughter of Wil-

liam Smith and Cecilia Bangarnoz, her father and mother," in *The Baptismal Register of Fort Duquesne*, ed. A.A. Lambing (Pittsburgh, PA, 1885), 76–7. On 14 August this child, also named Catherine, died at age eighteen months.

7 *PG*, 8 May 1760.

8 *PMHB* 32 (1908): 313, where she is called "the Smith Wife"; TNA, Adm. 1/4323, n.p., where she is called "Sessaly"; *Baptismal Register*, ed. Lambing, 76–7. George Peters was another child captive who returned blind.

9 Her master, Thomas Hill of Philadelphia, was allowed £6 Pennsylvania currency per year, and an initial payment of £24.5.0 made on 7 June 1760. See *V&P*, 7: 5655, 5944–5.

10 The order is uncommon, for children fourteen and over were usually permitted to choose their guardian, and the orphan's court did not assign or supervise apprenticeships. See Cumberland County Orphan's Court Dockets, vol. 1, 1751–61, Cumberland County Courthouse, Carlisle, PA, 17.

11 Phillip W. Hoffman, *Simon Girty, Turncoat Hero* (Franklin, TN: American History Imprints, 2009); Colin G. Calloway, "Simon Girty: Interpreter and Intermediary," in *Being and Becoming Indian: Biographical Studies of North American Frontiers*, ed. James A. Clifton (Chicago, IL: Dorsey, 1989), 38–58; J. Norman Heard, *White into Red: A Study of the Assimilation of White Persons Captured by Indians* (Metuchen, NJ: Scarecrow, 1973), 127–9; Consul Willshire Butterfield, *History of the Girtys* (Cincinnati, OH, 1890).

12 John Turner (1755–1840), Draper Mss, Frontier Wars Papers, 12U35-8; Butterfield, *History of the Girtys*.

13 Anthony J. Marsella et al., eds, *Ethnocultural Aspects of Posttraumatic Stress Disorder: Issues, Research and Clinical Applications* (Washington, DC: American Psychological Association, 1996), 12, 14, 31–2 (quote), 50–1.

CHAPTER SEVENTEEN

1 Felix Renick, "A Trip to the West," *American Pioneer* 1 (1842): 73–80. Felix married Hannah Rachel. His companions were Joseph Harness and Leonard Stump.

2 *JP*, 11: 470, 485; *WPHM* 39 (1956): 194; *PG*, 17 January 1765; *NYG*, 21 January 1765.

3 On this issue, see Holly Brewer, *By Birth or Consent: Children, Law, and the Anglo-American Revolution in Authority* (Chapel Hill, NC: University of North Carolina Press, 2005). Brewer proves that Virginian law, in its defense of slavery, held more to the earlier emphasis upon status as determining rights and competence.

4 Y. Kawashima, "Adoption in Early America," *Journal of Family Law* 20 (1982): 677–96.

5 Draper Mss, Frontier Wars Papers, 21U129; *JP*, 11: 720; *WPHM* 39 (1956): 198.

6 *WPHM* 39 (1956): 192, 196.

7 Samuel Kercheval, *A History of the Valley of Virginia*, 4th ed. (Strasburg, VA: Shenandoah, 1925), 81.

8 *V&P*, 7: 5883. Catherine and her child were among those advertised by Johnson for disposal. See *PG*, 10 and 19 September 1765.

9 In *PG*, 9 September 1762, she is called Mary "Tudds." The other eight *métis* children accompanying their mother were: two children of Elizabeth Coon, Abigail Evans's child, Mary Lanscisco's child, Elizabeth McIlroy's child, the son and daughter of "Dorothy" (Manselle or Rigar?), and Jammy Willson's son.

10 Johnson to Bouquet, 17 December 1764, BL, Add. Mss, 21651, fols 94–5, printed in *HBP*, 6: 731; *PG*, 9 September 1756, 19 September 1765. For reference to "Bridget's son," see *WPHM* 39 (1956): 189.

11 The 1691 law prescribed banishment for such marriages, a heavy fine or servitude for having a *métis* child, and thirty years servitude for that child. The law was re-enacted in 1696, 1705, and 1753. See James Hugo Johnston, *Race Relations in Virginia and Miscegenation in the South, 1776–1860* (Amherst, MA: University of Massachusetts Press, 1970), 171–3.

12 S.M. Moore, "Early Recollections of Nancy Stewart," in Joshua Antrim, *The History of Champaign and Logan Counties* (Bellefontaine, OH, 1872), 327–8; John Sugden, *Blue Jacket, Warrior of the Shawnees* (Lincoln, NB: University of Nebraska Press, 2000), 3, 31, 255. None of Nancy's four children married.

13 They were little more than a third of the 323 captives known to have been taken at this age. Another 165 remained "missing," and 38 more are known to have stayed in, or promptly returned to, their Indian lives.

14 Agnes Davidson and her daughter Molly were returned together to Bouquet after eight months of captivity. See BL, Add. Mss, 21650, fol. 103; *PG*, 5 April 1764, 17 January 1765; and *WPHM* 39 (1956): 193, 196. Eleanor Kincade and her infant daughter were likewise returned. See *PG*, 3 May 1765; and Draper Mss, Kentucky Papers, 16CC193-7.

15 *PG*, 13 November 1755; C. Hale Sipe, *The Indian Wars of Pennsylvania* (Harrisburg, PA: Telegraph, 1929), 225–6.

16 *PG*, 15 December 1763, 17 January 1765; *WPHM* 39 (1956): 188.

17 On Jean Clendennin and her mother, see Draper Mss, Frontier Wars Papers, 21U136-7; *PG*, 17 January 1765; *WPHM* 39 (1956): 190; *PA*, ser. 2, 7: 437; F.B. Lyman Chalkley, *Chronicles of the Scotch-Irish Settlement in Virginia*, 3 vols (1912; reprint, Baltimore, MD: Genealogical, 1965), vol. 2, 93. Christina Eice, an adult, was not returned by the Shawnee until May 1765. See *WPHM* 39 (1956): 198; and *JP*, 11: 720, where she is called "Christian Fee."

18 Young Beverley Miller was returned with her older sister, Margaret, after seven years with the Indians. Her father, George Miller of Chambersburg, Cumberland County, Pennsylvania, had been killed in their capture; her mother and young sister never returned. See *WPHM* 39 (1956): 192, 202; Archibald Loudon, ed., *A Selection of Some of the Most Interesting Narratives of Outrages Committed by the Indians in Their Wars with the White People*, 2 vols

(Carlisle, PA, 1808–11), vol. 2, 197; *PG*, 29 September 1757, 17 January 1765; *NYM*, 3 October 1757; and *NYG*, 21 January 1765.

19 Preston Papers, 1: 83; *JP*, 11: 486, 720; *WPHM* 39 (1956): 195–6, 198; *PG*, 17 January 1765.

20 *WPHM* 39 (1956): 194, 197, 198, 202; *JP* 11: 485, 721; Preston Papers, 1: 83; *PG*, 17 January 1765, 7 March 1765; *NYG*, 18 March 1765.

21 The twenty-five-page memoir of John Inglis Jr is in Draper Mss. Frontier Wars Papers, 12U112. See also R.G. Thwaites and L.P. Kellogg, *Documentary History of Dunmore's War 1774* (Madison, WI: Wisconsin Historical Society, 1905), 179–80n.

22 *JP*, 6: 409.

23 Draper Mss, Kentucky Papers, 23CC98-103; *WPHM* 39 (1956): 202.

24 *JP*, 6: 409.

25 *PG*, 24 June 1762.

26 *PJ*, 8 August 1765. A daughter of Charles and Margaret Stuart, of Great Cove, was reported released at Pittsburgh on 16 December 1761. See "Journal of James Kenny, 1761–1763," ed. John W. Jordan, *PMHB* 37 (1913): 25–6. It is possible that this child was taken in as Mary Stuart until Mary Stewart was returned with Bouquet's army three years later. The magistrate was William Smith, Esq., of the Fort Loudoun district, brother of the more famous James Smith, who could help with translating what little the Mingo girl could remember of her white family and capture.

27 Joseph Persinger, *The Life of Jacob Persinger* (Sturgeon, MO, 1861).

28 Sherman Day, *Historical Collections of the State of Pennsylvania*, 2 vols (Philadelphia, PA, 1843), vol. 2, 384.

29 Ourry to Bouquet, 25 May and 17 June 1761, BL, Add. Mss, 21642, fols 179–80 (quote), 192–3.

30 Day, *Historical Collections*, vol. 2, 383–5; Samuel Hazard, *Hazard's Register of Pennsylvania*, 16 vols (Philadelphia, PA, 1828–35), vol. 1, 192. It was other features of John Grey's will that made it the famous "Grey property case." See 10 Serg. & Rawle, 182.

31 In her claim of 9 September 1766, Elizabeth Robinson, who had been "applied to" to care for the children, sought £5.5.6. See *V&P*, 7: 5894–5, 5905–6.

32 *PG*, 21 February 1765. For a similar ad, concerning James Brennard of Minisink, see *PG*, 3 July 1760.

33 *Conductor Generalis, or The Office, Duty, and Authority of Justices of the Peace* ..., 2nd ed. (Philadelphia, PA, 1749), 14–15; Farley Ward Grubb, "Babes in Bondage? Debt Shifting by German Immigrants in Early America," *Journal of Interdisciplinary History* 37 (2006): 1–34; John Demos, *A Little Commonwealth: Family Life in Plymouth Colony* (New York: Oxford University Press, 1970), 73, 88–9.

34 Minutes of 3 June 1761, Cumberland County Orphan's Court Dockets, Cumberland County Courthouse, Carlisle, PA, vol. 1, 1751–61, 47. A contemporary summary of the duties of orphan's courts is provided in Robert

Proud, *The History of Pennsylvania* ..., 2 vols. (Philadelphia, PA, 1797–98), vol. 2, 288–89. There is no proof that Jane Cochran, taken in the capture of Bigham's Fort, ever returned. Her son John, captured with her, was returned to Bouquet's army. See *WPHM* 39 (1956): 191; and *PG*, 17 and 24 June 1756, 17 January 1765.

35 *PG*, 19 August 1756; Minutes of 2 September 1760 and 26 May 1762, Cumberland County Orphan's Court Dockets, Cumberland County Courthouse, Carlisle, PA, vol. 1, 1751–61, 40–1, 68. Sister Rebecca was returned at the Lancaster conference in August 1762, and brothers Ephraim and John were returned to Bouquet's army in 1764. See *Minutes of Conferences Held at Lancaster in August 1762* ... (Philadelphia, PA, 1763); and *WPHM* 39 (1956): 191; *PG*, 17 January 1765.

36 *MPCP*, 7: 620; *PG*, 12 May 1757; Northampton County Courthouse, Easton, PA, Northampton County Orphan's Court Records, B, [1758–62], 5, 22, 26, 32.

37 Whereas 27 of 325 (8%) of children captured under the age of seven are known to have stayed with their captors, only 12 of 321 (4%) taken between the ages of seven and fifteen are known to have done so. While a statistics-destroying 49 per cent of those captured under the age of seven remained "missing," only 25 per cent of those captured between the ages of seven and fifteen did so.

38 Of those who returned, 34 of 219 (15.5%) had escaped. William Barnett, David Boyd, and the three Girty boys, George, James, and Simon, were captives taken as youths who are known to have resisted their return.

39 David Jones, *A Journey of Two Visits Made to Some Nations of Indians on the West Side of the River Ohio in the Years 1772 and 1773* (New York, 1865), 55–6.

40 "Some Account of Prisoners to Be Sent to Pittsburgh 1762," Haverford College Library, Indian Committee Records, 824/11, vol. 4, n.p.

41 Alternatively, there may have been two Susannah Vauses, one the aunt of the other. One was seen on her return through Pittsburgh on 26 February 1763. See "Journal of James Kenny, 1761–1763," ed. Jordan, 178. A Susannah Vause was reported as among the captives with the Shawnee late in 1765. See *WPHM* 39 (1956): 202. On her married name, see Draper Mss, Kentucky Papers, 11CC220.

42 Kercheval, *History of the Valley*, 80–1. Kercheval claims that Mary Painter was captured in an attack on her father's fortified house in 1758, and that forty-eight captives were taken there. The only two major attacks of that year into Virginia were the destruction of Upper Tract Fort, where twenty-three were killed and three taken, and of Seybert's Fort, where seventeen were killed and twenty-six captured. Details of these well-attested attacks do not include any family named Painter.

43 Betty, Magdalene, and Mary Clouser became Mrs Shultz, Mrs Snapp, and Mrs Fry, elderly widowed neighbors of Samuel Kercheval. See Kercheval, *History of the Valley*, 97–9.

44 *V&P*, 7: 5883.

45 Simon, taken at fifteen, married white captive Catherine Malott, and they lived as whites in a cabin near Detroit. James, taken at thirteen, became an Indian trader and married into the Shawnee community. George, taken at eleven, married into the Delaware, raised a family amongst them, and was known for urging white captives to accept the Delaware way of life. See J. Norman Heard, *White into Red: A Study of the Assimilation of White Persons Captured by Indians* (Metuchen, NJ: Scarecrow, 1973), 127–9.

46 Holland to Pemberton, 2 October 1759, Haverford College Library, Indian Committee Records, 824/11, vol. 3, n.p.: "I wrote to the Commissioners about the Lad & they agreed to have him bound to them; when I rec'd these Letters I read to him what you both propose, & he chose to stay here and be bound to them." Jonathan's surname was variously remembered as Nichols, Nicholas, and Nicholson. See David McClure, *Ohio Country Missionary: The Diary of David McClure, 1748–1820* (Waterville, OH: Rettig's Frontier Ohio, 1996), 55.

47 Charles Beatty, *Journals of Charles Beatty, 1762–1769* (University Park, PA: Pennsylvania State University Press, 1962), 49.

48 Draper Mss, Pittsburgh and Northwest Virginia Papers, 6NN78-80.

49 "The Narrative of John Slover," in Loudon, ed., *Selection*, vol. 1, 17–32.

50 Lyman C. Draper, unpublished account of the Renicks, Draper Mss, Frontier Wars Papers, 21U126–35; William Renick narrative, 26 January 1867, Draper Mss, Kentucky Papers, 4CC118; James H. Renick narrative, Draper Mss, Kentucky Papers, 4CC129.

51 Sipe, *Indian Wars*, 224–7.

52 He had apparently been chosen lieutenant by lot in 1777. See John Stuart, *Memoirs of Indian Wars and Other Occurrences by the Late Colonel Stuart of Greenbrier, as part of the Eyewitness Accounts of the American Revolution*, 3rd ser. (New York: New York Times, 1971), 59.

53 Loudon, ed., *Selection*, vol. 2, 173; "Incidents in the Life of an Indian Captive," *American Historical Record* 1 (1872): 409; *PG*, 5 February 1756; William A. Hunter, *Forts on the Pennsylvania Frontier, 1753–1758* (Harrisburg, PA: Pennsylvania Historical and Museum Commission, 1960), 379; James Axtell, *The European and the Indian* (New York: Oxford University Press, 1981), 195.

54 "Journey on the Forbidden Path: Chronicles of a Diplomatic Mission to the Allegheny Country, March–September, 1760," ed. Robert S. Grumet, *Transactions of the American Philosophical Society* 89, part 2 (1999): 107; Holland to Pemberton, 12 August 1760, Haverford College Library, Indian Committee Records, 824/11, vol. 3, 511–12; *The Journals of Henry Melchior Muhlenberg*, trans. Theodore G. Tappert and John W. Doberstein, 3 vols (Philadelphia, PA: Evangelical Lutheran Ministerium, 1942–58), vol. 1, 496, 523–4; Sugden, *Blue Jacket*, 18.

55 On the initial return of Susannah Vause, see "Journal of James Kenny, 1761–1763," ed. Jordan, 178. On her continuing captivity, see *WPHM* 39 (1956): 202. John D. Shane interviewed a Mrs Shanklin in the 1840s, and

noted, "Memory gone, and mind broken; so that she can scarcely connect her ideas." Her account suggests that she was either Susannah or her sister Elizabeth, and that they both eventually returned and married. One became Mrs Shanklin and the other a Mrs Abraham Inskip. See Draper Mss, Kentucky Papers, 11CC220.

56 Two of the four youths were "Indian servants" captured, or perhaps recaptured, in the fall of Vause's Fort in 1756. See Preston Papers, 1: 83; *PG*, 28 July 1757; *NYM*, 1 August 1757.

57 James Potter to Bouquet, 3 May 1762, BL, Add. Mss, 21648, fol. 128.

58 Holland to Pemberton, 16 April 1761, Haverford College Library, Indian Committee Records, 824/11, vol. 4, n.p.; *NYG*, 30 April 1759; Hunter, *Forts*, 163–4; BL, Add. Mss, 21644, fol. 132.

59 Walter C. Klein, *Johann Conrad Beissel, Mystic and Martinet, 1690–1768* (Philadelphia, PA: Porcupine, 1942), 163; Emmert F. Bittinger, *Allegheny Passage: Churches and Families, West Marva District, Church of the Brethren, 1752–1990* (Camden, ME: Penobscot, 1990), 19–22.

60 Two slaves of the French were reported killed by the Miami in 1751. See Richard White, *The Middle Ground: Indians, Empires, and Republics in the Great Lakes Region, 1650–1815* (New York: Cambridge University Press, 1991), 229. Some of the missing negroes may have belonged to someone David Jones called a rich Shawnee woman chief who "has several negroes who were taken from Virginia in time of last war, and now esteemed as her property." See Jones, *Journal of Two Visits*, 87.

61 On Cloyd's slaves, see F.B. Kegley, *Kegley's Virginia Frontier: The Beginning of the Southwest, the Roanoke of Colonial Days, 1740–1783* (Roanoke, VA: Southwest Virginia Historical Society, 1938), 287–8. Slaves Pompadour, Henry, and Peggy were returned to Bouquet in November 1764, and a Joseph Colbourne of Boston was returned in December 1760. See *HBP*, 5: 210; and *PG*, 15 January 1765.

62 Gregory Evans Dowd, *War under Heaven: Pontiac, the Indian Nations and the British Empire* (Baltimore, MD: Johns Hopkins University Press, 2002), 183–5; *JP*, 11: 165–6; *PG*, 17 May 1765.

63 *JP*, 10: 287.

64 In comparison, between 30 and 37 per cent of New England colonial women who became captives of the French and Indians stayed with their captors. See Alden T. Vaughan and Daniel K. Richter, "Crossing the Cultural Divide: Indians and New Englanders, 1605–1763," *American Antiquarian Society Proceedings* 90 (1980): 64.

65 The escapees numbered 34 of 141 women (24.1%), compared to 138 of 554 men (24.9%).

66 Chalkley, *Chronicles of the Scotch-Irish*, vol. 1, 108, vol. 2, 93. The other two women known to have escaped promptly were a Catawba woman who escaped Red Horse's party of Cherokee and a woman with the British garrison at Fort Presqu'île who escaped to Fort Pitt. See respectively *SCG*, 16

July 1763; and "William Trent's Journal at Ft. Pitt, 1763," *MVHR* 11 (1924–25): 402.

67 John Inglis Jr's memoir, Drapers Mss, Frontier Wars Papers, 12U:12.

68 Bouquet to Lieutenant Governor Hamilton, 13 July 1763, BL, Add. Mss, 21649, fol. 256, printed in *HBP*, 6: 308; Ourry to Bouquet, 23 September 1763, BL, Add. Mss, 21642, fol. 477.

69 Mary Taylor, taken by the Delaware at Fort Granville in July of 1756, was the other.

70 Alexander Scott Withers, *Chronicles of Border Warfare, or A History of the Settlement by the Whites, of North Western Virginia, and of the Indian Wars and Massacres, in that section of the state, with reflections, anecdotes, etc. ...* (1831; reprint, New York: Arno, 1971), 92–3; James B. Finley, *Life among the Indians* (Cincinnati, OH, 1857), 45–7; Joseph A. Waddell, *Annals of Augusta County, Virginia*, 2 vols (Richmond, VA, 1886–88), vol. 1, 111. See also Raymond Young, "The Effects of the French and Indian War on Civilian Life in the Frontier Counties of Virginia, 1754–1763" (PhD diss., Vanderbilt University, 1969), 133–5.

71 William Smith, *An Historical Account of the Expedition against the Ohio Indians, in the Year 1764, Under the Command of Henry Bouquet Esq.* (Philadelphia, 1766), 29.

72 *PG*, 5 September 1765.

73 *PG*, 6 September 1759.

74 Jane Frasier, *Narrative of the Captivity of Mrs. Jane Frasier* (1930; reprint, New York: Garland, 1977), 9–10.

75 Colin G. Calloway, "Simon Girty: Interpreter and Intermediary," in *Being and Becoming Indian: Biographical Studies of North American Frontiers*, ed. James A. Clifton (Chicago, IL: Dorsey, 1989), 42.

76 Captain Robert Stobo became a major in captivity. James Smith's similar advance may have been self-promotion. Sergeant John McCoy, of the Royal American Regiment's garrison at Fort Miami, evidently became a captain immediately upon his escape. See Jehu Hay, *Diary of the Siege of Detroit in the War with Pontiac*, ed. Franklin B. Hough (Albany, NY, 1860), 83–4; and Henry Gladwin, "The Gladwin Manuscripts: With an Introduction and a Sketch of the Conspiracy of Pontiac," *Michigan Pioneer and Historical Society Collections* 27 (1897): 660.

77 David A. Armour, "Gorrell, James," *DCB*, 3: 261–2.

78 On 8 October 1760, the Virginia House of Burgesses granted a petition of seven veterans "and all others who shall hereafter appear in the same Circumstances, the common allowance and pay of soldiers, during their absence in captivity." See *Journals of the House of Burgesses of Virginia, 1758–1761*, ed. H.R. McIlwaine (Richmond, VA: Colonial Press, 1908), 150, 188 (quote).

79 Robert C. Alberts, *The Most Extraordinary Adventures of Major Robert Stobo* (Boston, MA: Houghton Mifflin, 1965), 170–340, 387n; *Journal of Lieut.*

Simon Stevens, From the Time of His Being Taken, near Fort William Henry, June the 25th, 1758 (Boston, MA, 1760); "L'Évasion de Stobo et de Van Braam de la prison de Québec en Mai 1757," *Bulletin des Recherches Historiques* 14 (1908): 154. In January 1764, however, the House of Burgesses refused Stobo's petition for his salary as a major during a year's leave of absence in England. See *Journals of the House of Burgesses, 1758–1761*, ed. McIlwaine, 212.

80 Alberts, *Most Extraordinary Adventures*, 317–18.

81 He was not the John Ramsay reported killed in a raid of 27 April 1758 on the South Branch of the Potomac River. See Preston Papers, 1: 83.

82 Robert Stobo, *The Memoirs of Major Robert Stobo of the Virginia Regiment*, ed. Neville B. Craig (Pittsburgh, PA, 1854), 91–2. Louis Coulon de Villiers mentioned, but did not name, a deserter whom he questioned before the attack on Fort Necessity. See *Papiers Contrecoeur et autres documents concernant le conflit anglo-français sur l'Ohio de 1745 à 1756*, ed. Fernand Grenier (Quebec City, QC: Laval University Press, 1952), 199. Ramsey's case was not as clear as that of Denis Kaninguen (Cunningham), an English deserter who certainly had additional incentive to flee Jumonville Glen quickly, though he claimed to have witnessed the entire incident. See "Journal de Joseph-Gaspard Chaussegros de Léry, Lieutenant des troupes, 1754–1755," in *RAPQ, 1927–1928* (Quebec City, QC: Quebec Archives, 1928), 372–3.

83 *Journals of the House of Burgesses of Virginia, 1761–1765*, ed. John Pendleton Kennedy (Richmond, VA: Colonial Press, 1907), 179, 186.

84 This recovered soldier was James Bell. See Chalkley, *Chronicles of the Scotch-*Irish, vol. 1, 209.

85 "Thomas Gist's Indian Captivity, 1758–1759," *PMHB* 80 (1956): 285–311.

86 Ibid.; Lawrence A. Orrill, "Christopher Gist and His Sons," *WPHM* 15 (1932): 191–218.

87 Thwaites and Kellogg, *Documentary History*, 39–40n. Arthur Campbell's accumulated pay amounted to £41. See Kegley, *Kegley's Virginia Frontier*, 255.

88 *PG*, 9 February 1758; *NYM*, 30 January 1758; Kegley, *Kegley's Virginia Frontier*, 255; Charles Mullett, "Military Intelligence on Forts and Indians in the Ohio Valley, 1756–1757," *W&MQ*, ser. 3, 3 (1946): 398–410.

89 Kegley, *Kegley's Virginia Frontier*, 176, 232–3, 280, 349. Looney sought £46.16.0 for his losses and as a reward for his bravery. See *Journals of the House of Burgesses, 1758–1761*, ed. McIlwaine, 221, 229.

90 David A. Armour, "Henry, Alexander," *DCB*, 6: 316–19; David A. Armour, "Cadot (Cadotte), Jean-Baptiste," *DCB*, 5: 128–30.

91 Nicholas B. Wainwright, *George Croghan, Wilderness Diplomat* (Chapel Hill, NC: University of North Carolina Press, 1959), 190–1, 250, 254, 261, 279, 282, 308; Charles A. Hanna, *The Wilderness Trail, Or the Ventures and Adventures of the Pennsylvania Traders on the Allegheny Path*, 2 vols (New York: Putnam, 1911), vol. 2, 374–5; Henry M.M. Richards, *The Pennsylvania-*

German in the French and Indian War (Lancaster, PA: Pennsylvania-German Society, 1905), 229, 233, 239.

92 The "suffering traders" were predominantly men who had not been captured themselves. See *The Ohio Company Papers, 1753–1817, Being Primarily Papers of the "Suffering Traders" of Pennsylvania*, ed. Kenneth P. Bailey (Arcata, CA: N.p., 1947), 34–5. George Croghan was active in this cause of his own for more than a decade. See his letter to the Board of Trade, 8 June 1764, where he claimed traders lost at least £100,000 of goods in 1763, printed in *NYCD*, 7: 603; and in *Collections of the Illinois State Historical Society* 10 (1915): 256–63. Croghan wrote Benjamin Franklin on 12 December 1765, continuing the lobbying, and there claiming he had lost £1,500 in currency when captured in Illinois country earlier that year. See TNA, CO 5/66, fols 83–6. Of the ten firms petitioning William Johnson, on 10 February 1765, for Indian land to compensate for trading losses in 1763, Robert Callender and Thomas Smallman were the only principals who had been captured themselves. See *JP*, 11: 565–6.

93 *Collections of the Illinois State Historical Society* 10 (1915): 483–4; Hanna, *Wilderness Trail*, vol. 2, 373; Dowd, *War under Heaven*, 221, 250, 252.

94 Gibson claimed losses of £3,384.8.4. from the 1763 "robbery." See *JP*, 11: 614. See also Commissioners of Indian Trade Accounts, Journal, 1763–65, Pennsylvania Historical Museum Commission, Harrisburg, PA; and Francis Jennings, "James Logan," *ANB*.

95 Thwaites and Kellogg, *Documentary History*, 10–11; Charles Beatty, *The Journal of a Two Month Tour* (London, 1768), 32, 59–60.

96 Israel Daniel Rupp, *The History and Topography of Dauphin, Cumberland, Franklin, Bedford, Adams and Perry Counties* (Lancaster, PA, 1846), 108.

97 *A Faithful Narrative of the Many Dangers and Sufferings, as well as Wonderful Deliverances, of Robert Eastburn, during His Late Captivity among the Indians* … (Philadelphia, PA, 1758).

98 Wainwright, *George Croghan*, 214–16, attempts a defense of Croghan in this scheme.

99 Neil H. Swanson, *The First Rebel* (New York and Toronto, ON: Farrar and Rinehart, 1937); Wilbur S. Nye, *James Smith: Early Cumberland Valley Patriot* (Carlisle, PA: Cumberland County Historical Society, 1969); Leroy V. Eid, "'Their Rules of War': The Validity of James Smith's Summary of Indian Woodland War," *Register of the Kentucky State Historical Society* 86 (1988): 4–23.

100 The seven were: James Adams, Solomon Carpenter, John Freeling, Francis Innis, David (Daniel) Johnson, James Price, and William Young.

101 It was nearly three more years before the appraisement of Hicks's estate was recorded. See Chalkley, *Chronicles of the Scotch-Irish*, vol. 3, 54, 67.

102 Rupp, *History and Topography of Dauphin*, 156.

103 Robert Kirk's adventures may be apocryphal, but his account mentions a need for a returning fellow captive to get a magistrate's confirmation of his

landholdings in Cumberland County, Pennsylvania. See Robert Kirk, *The Memoirs and Adventures of Robert Kirk, Late of the Royal Highland Regiment* (Limerick, UK, 1775), 40.

104 *V&P*, 7: 5532.

105 Baillie to Bouquet, from Fort Venango, 1 April 1761, *HBP*, 5: 381–2, 407.

106 *MPCP*, 9: 444, 453–4, 480; James H. Merrell, *Into the American Woods: Negotiators on the Pennsylvania Frontier* (New York: Norton, 1999), 353n129; Lily Lee Nixon, *James Burd, Frontier Defender, 1726–1793* (Philadelphia, PA: University of Pennsylvania Press, 1941), 137.

107 *HBP*, 6: 526n.

108 Douglas Leighton, "Girty, Simon," *DCB*, 5: 345–7.

CHAPTER EIGHTEEN

1 For a thoughtful overview, see Annette Kolodny, "Among the Indians: The Uses of Captivity," *New York Times Books Review*, 31 January 1993. My own agenda is still not clear to me, though enthusiastically pursuing this subject for longer than the captivity of any Allegheny captive must constitute a happy captivity of some kind.

2 Lisa Voigt, *Writing Captivity in the Early Modern Atlantic: Circulation of Knowledge and Authority in the Iberian and English Imperial Worlds* (Chapel Hill, NC: University of North Carolina Press, 2009). The *Jesuit Relations* (1632–73) were a major French repository of French suffering and martyrdom in America. See Gordon M. Sayre, *Les Sauvages Américains: Representations of Native Americans in French and English Colonial Literature* (Chapel Hill, NC: University of North Carolina Press, 1997), esp. 264–304.

3 See especially Joe Snader, *Caught between Worlds: British Captivity Narratives in Fact and Fiction* (Lexington, KY: University Press of Kentucky, 2000); and Linda Colley, *Captives* (New York: Pantheon, 2002).

4 Colin G. Calloway, *The Shawnees and the War for America* (New York: Viking, 2007).

5 These were the accounts of Hugh Gibson, Alexander Henry, Mary Jemison, John McCullough, Thomas Morris, John Slover, James Smith, and Robert Stobo.

6 These were the accounts of Robert Kirk, Charles Saunders, Isaac Stewart, and Peter Williamson.

7 Jane Tompkins, *Sensational Designs: The Cultural Work of American Fiction, 1790–1860* (New York: Oxford University Press, 1986), xvi.

8 The debate about freedom of the press has centered on political dissidence and seditious libel, rather than on wartime restraints. See Leonard Levy, *Legacy of Suppression: Freedom of Speech and Press in Early American History* (Cambridge, MA: Harvard University Press, 1960), versus Jeffrey A. Smith, *Printers and Press Freedom: The Ideology of Early American Journalism* (New York: Oxford University Press, 1988), and especially Stephen Botein, "'Meer Mechanics' and an Open Press: The Business and Political

Strategies of Colonial American Printers," *Perspectives in American History* 9 (1975): 125–225. It was not a colonial printer, but a London one, who published Robert Stobo's brazen 1754 letters from Fort Duquesne, and helped put this captain in danger of death at the hands of a Canadian court.

The printers of the *Pennsylvania Gazette* derived almost 60 per cent of their income from this paper, with an average weekly circulation of approximately 2,500, and 10 per cent from government printing. Government displeasure was seldom risked. See Botein, "'Meer Mechanics,'" 143, 148, 167. Between 1740 and 1765 thirty-six newspapers were started in colonial North America, and twenty-two closed. See William David Sloan and Julie Hedgepeth Williams, *The Early American Press, 1690–1783* (Westport, CT: Greenwood, 1994), 103–4.

9 In 1759 Elizabeth Hanson's account was reprinted, by William Dunlap, in *The Journals of the Lives and Travels of Samuel Bownas, and John Richardson*. There were at least seventeen editions of Jonathan Dickinson's *God's Protecting Providence* ..., including those in: Philadelphia (1699, 1751, 1868), London (1700, 1759, 1790), Leyden (1707), Germantown, Pennsylvania (1756), Leipzig (1774), and Burlington, New Jersey (1811). Elizabeth Hanson's *God's Mercy Surmounting Man's Cruelty* ..., under several titles, appeared in fourteen editions, including those in: Philadelphia (1728, 1754), London (1760), Stanford, New York (1803), Leeds, England (1810), and Dover, New Hampshire (1824). See also *Held Captive by Indians: Selected Narratives, 1642–1836*, ed. Richard VanDerBeets (Knoxville, TN: University of Tennessee Press, 1973), 130–50.

10 Thomas Morris, *Miscellanies in Prose and Verse* (London, 1791).

11 Charles Stuart, "The Captivity of Charles Stuart, 1755–57," *MVHR* 13 (1926–27): 58–81.

12 This application of the phrase is from Christopher Castiglia, *Bound and Determined: Captivity, Culture-Crossing, and White Womanhood from Mary Rowlandson to Patty Hearst* (Chicago, IL: University of Chicago Press, 1996).

13 The stories appeared on 31 July, 11 August, and 11 September 1755, respectively.

14 *PG*, 13 November 1755; *PJ*, 13 November 1755; *NYM*, 17 November 1755. See also *PA*, ser. 1, 2: 462–3, 474–5; and Israel Daniel Rupp, *The History and Topography of Dauphin, Cumberland, Franklin, Bedford, Adams and Perry Counties* (Lancaster, PA, 1846), 107–8.

15 Depositions of George Hutchinson and Patrick Burns, 15 and 17 November 1755, HSP, Penn Mss, Indian Affairs, vol. 2, nos 42 and 44.

16 Lyman Draper gathered an array of Ingles family remembrances in Draper Mss, Frontier Wars Papers, 12U112. Local historian Joseph A. Waddell told a version of the story in his *Annals of Augusta County, Virginia*, 2 vols (Richmond, VA, 1886–88), vol. 1, 75. More recent interest began with Gary Jennings, "An Indian Captivity," *American Heritage* 19, no. 5 (1968): 64–71, and this interest includes: *The Story of Mary Draper Ingles and Son John Ingles*, ed. Roberta Inglis Steele and Andrew Lewis Ingles (Radford,

VA: Commonwealth, 1969); Mary Musselwhite DeNoya, "Massacre at the Meadows," *Daughters of the American Revolution Magazine* 106 (1972): 132–6, 230; Mary Rodd Furbee, *Shawnee Captive: The Story of Mary Draper Ingles* (Greensboro, NC: Morgan Reynolds, 2001); and Joan Vannorsdall Schroeder, "An Extraordinary Woman and Equal to Any Emergency: Mary Draper Inglis' Return to Virginia's New River Valley" (1 March 1998), http://blueridgecountry.com.

17 The advertisement in *PG*, 2 January 1756, promised publication on 17 January, to be sold by the printer, W. Dunlap in Lancaster, and by bookbinder Henry Sandy in Laetitia Court, Philadelphia. Dunlap moved to Philadelphia in 1758. See Charles R. Hildeburn, *A Century of Printing: Issues of the Pennsylvania Press, 1685–1784*, 2 vols (Philadelphia, PA, 1885), vol. 1, xii.

18 Jan Stievermann, "A 'plain, rejected little flock': The Politics of Martyrological Self-Fashioning among Pennsylvania's German Peace Churches, 1739–65," *W&MQ*, ser. 3, 66 (2009): 287–324. Printer Christopher Saur (1693–1758) was sympathetic to the pacifist Church of the Brethren, and his son Christopher (1721–84), who assisted and succeeded him in the Germantown printing business, was a member. See Peter Brock, *Pacifism in the United States: From the Colonial Era to the First World War* (Princeton, NJ: Princeton University Press, 1968), 173–5.

19 William Fleming and Elizabeth Fleming, *A Narrative of the Sufferings and Surprizing Deliverances of William and Elizabeth Fleming* (1756; reprint, New York: Garland, 1978). The Boston edition of 1756, presumably copying a Pennsylvania edition published between April and August of that year, was without the introduction and included none of the information or argument described in this paragraph.

20 The 1978 Garland edition was from a copy in the Newberry Library, Chicago, IL, Ayer 256.F5.1756b. It has a different title page, which does not name a printer, but reads, "*PHILADELPHIA*: Printed for the Benefit of the unhappy Sufferers, and Sold by them only. Price 6d." On William Dunlap, see Nicole Eustace, *"Passion Is the Gale": Emotion, Power and the Coming of the American Revolution* (Chapel Hill, NC: University of North Carolina Press, 2008), 43–5.

21 *PG*, 19 February 1756.

22 On the basis of the Flemings' ad, Peter Silver concludes that there were at least three Philadelphia editions sold within the first six weeks of 1756. See Peter Silver, *Our Savage Neighbors: How Indian War Transformed Early America* (New York: Norton, 2008), 196. The surviving three editions are in Charles Evans, *American Bibliography*, 14 vols (New York: P. Smith, 1941–59), vol. 1., nos 7662 (Boston), 7663, and 40824 (Germantown).

23 Eight months later *PG*, 13 November 1756, mentioned, in a list of those killed or captured in the Great Cove attack, that "William Fleming and Wife were taken Prisoners, but made their Escape." Christopher Saur printed and sold a German translation of the Flemings' accounts twice that year, in Germantown and Philadelphia. See Evans, *Bibliography*, nos

7658–63 and 40824; and Alden T. Vaughan, *Narratives of North American Indian Captivity: A Selective Bibliography* (New York: Garland, 1983), 25–6. Perhaps because it was not subsequently popular, Elizabeth Fleming's account is not considered in June Namias, *White Captives: Gender and Ethnicity on the American Frontier* (Chapel Hill, NC: University of North Carolina Press, 1992). The relatively helpless Fleming would be an exception to Namias's model of colonial women as "survivors." The Flemings' narrative was reprinted in 1978 as part of the Garland series.

24 HSP, Penn Mss, Indian Affairs, vol. 2, no. 78. This was reprinted in the *NYM*, 5 April 1756. On captives and "fusion," see Ed White, *The Backcountry and the City: Colonization and Conflict in Early America* (Minneapolis, MN: University of Minnesota Press, 2005), esp. 111.

25 Deposition of 31 March 1756, HSP, Penn Mss, Indian Affairs, vol. 2, no. 78.

26 *PG*, 19 August 1756; *PJ*, 19 August 1756.

27 *PG*, 9 September 1756; *PJ*, 9 September 1756. *VG*, 3 September 1756, included a few details from a Conococheague man who "made his Escape from them, and came to Conococheague last Saturday [28 August]." He was almost certainly John Rowe.

28 Compare *MPCP*, 7: 242–3, with *PG*, 9 September 1756, and *PJ*, 9 September 1756.

29 See, for instance, Richard VanDerBeets, "The Captivity Narrative as Propaganda," in *The Indian Captivity Narrative: An American Genre* (Lanham, MD: University Press of America, 1984), 13–23.

30 On the same date, 23 September 1756, the *Pennsylvania Gazette* reported that Mercer and twenty-three others had returned, though a week later, on 30 September, the paper carried the story that Mercer had returned alone, wounded and hungry, to Fort Lyttleton after fourteen days in the woods.

31 *PG*, 17 February 1757; *PJ*, 17 February 1757. John Armstrong continued to play along with the theme. Two decades later, when he was granted Appleby Manor at Kittanning, he renamed the tract "Victory." See Daniel P. Barr, "Victory at Kittanning? Reevaluating the Impact of Armstrong's Raid on the Seven Years' War in Pennsylvania," *PMHB* 131 (2007): 28.

32 *PG*, 28 July 1757; *NYM*, 1 August 1757.

33 *PG*, 28 July 1757; *PJ*, 28 July 1757. Six weeks later, Looney's story was reprinted, almost verbatim, in the *London Chronicle, or Universal Evening Post*. The London paper added a bit to give English readers context, but also made two interesting changes. Looney had reported that a French officer ordered Detroit Indians to join a planned attack on Fort Cumberland and then attack inhabitants. Londoners were told that the Indians were "afterwards to destroy all the English Inhabitants." More intriguing, although both Pennsylvania papers reported that a soldier named Cole had been "tormented for a whole Night before he expired, cutting Pieces of his Flesh off his Body, and eating it," Londoners learned only that Cole was "roasted alive." See *Manuscripts and Records from the Burton Historical Collection* 1 (1917): 113–15; and "Captivity of Peter Looney," *MVHR* 15 (1928): 95–6.

34 *PG*, 8 December 1757; *PJ*, 8 December 1757.

35 Compare *PG*, 22 December 1757, and *NYM*, 2 January 1758.

36 Looney's account was in *PG*, 28 July 1757, and *PJ*, 28 July 1757, and Charles Stuart's was in *NYM*, 2 January 1758.

37 Van Slyke deposition of 21 July 1767, Native American Collection, Clements Library, University of Michigan, Ann Arbor, MI.

38 TNA, Chatham Papers, GD8/95, no. 16, printed in *Colonial Captivities, Marches, and Journeys*, ed. I.M. Calder (New York: Macmillan, 1935), 137–9; *Journals of the House of Burgesses of Virginia, 1752–1755, 1756–1758*, ed. H.R. McIlwaine (Richmond, VA: Colonial Press, 1909), 499, 505; and *Journals of the House of Burgesses of Virginia, 1761–1765*, ed. John Pendleton Kennedy (Richmond, VA: Colonial Press, 1907), 330, 339–40. Charles Mullett, "Military Intelligence on Forts and Indians in the Ohio Valley, 1756–1757," *W&MQ*, ser. 3, 3 (1946): 398–410; F.B. Kegley, *Kegley's Virginia Frontier: The Beginning of the Southwest, the Roanoke of Colonial Days, 1740–1783* (Roanoke, VA: Southwest Virginia Historical Society, 1938), 109, 233–4, 255.

39 The pamphlet was printed by William Dunlap. The ad read, "Just Published, by Robert Easburn [sic], Narative of his late captivity &c. And to be sold in Philadelphia by David Hall, William Bradford, James Chattin, and by the author at his house. At Trenton by Alexander Chambers. At Prince Town by Elias Boucinot. At New Brunswick by John Lile [sic]." See *PJ*, 9 February and 2 March 1758.

40 *A Faithful Narrative of the Many Dangers and Sufferings, as well as Wonderful Deliverances, of Robert Eastburn, during His Late Captivity among the Indians* ... (Philadelphia, PA, 1758), 10; *PA*, ser. 2, 2: 482. Eastburn was paid £200 on 22 May 1758 for recruiting his complete company. See *V&P*, 6: 5051.

41 See Evans, *Bibliography*, no. 8117. Robert Eastburn's narrative was included in his son's *Memoirs of the Rev. Joseph Eastburn* (Philadelphia, PA, 1828; Hartford, CT, 1843). The 1758 edition of Robert Eastburn's narrative was reprinted in Cleveland in 1904.

42 Michel La Chauvignerie Jr confirmed that the Delaware and their captives were fed at Fort Duquesne for two months in the fall of 1756. See *PA*, ser. 1, 3: 305–8.

43 *PA*, ser. 1, 3: 633–4.

44 On Lieutenant Colonel Hugh Mercer's "giving them (and providing us with a peek at sutler stores) each a new chemise, petticoat, pair of stockings, garters and knife before having them escorted east," see Holly A. Mayer, "From Forts to Families: Following the Army into Western Pennsylvania, 1758–66," *PMHB* 130 (2006): 19.

45 Quotations are from "The Narrative of Marie Le Roy and Barbara Leininger," *PA*, ser. 2, 7: 427–38. No copy of the English version, "The Narrative of Marie Le Roy and Barbara Leininger who spent three and one half years as prisoners among the Indians and arrived safely on the city on the sixth of May," printed by the same house, has survived. See R.W.G. Vail,

The Voice of the Old Frontier (Philadelphia, PA: University of Pennsylvania Press, 1949), 267–9.

46 Botein, "'Meer Mechanics," 144.

47 Leo Eitinger, "The Effects of Captivity," in *Victims of Terrorism*, ed. Frank M. Ochberg and David A. Soskis (Boulder, CO: Westview, 1982), 81.

48 Deposition of Mathias Warren, 30 March 1764, BL, Add. Mss, 21650, fol. 116.

49 For a gendered reading of the pamphlet, see Ruth Ann Denaci, "The Penn's Creek Massacre and the Captivity of Marie Le Roy and Barbara Leininger," *PH* 74 (2007): 307–32. The three clerics, and Benjamin Franklin, were all accused, by passivist Christopher Sauer, of trying to Anglicize and militarize the Pennsylvania-German community. Peters and Muhlenberg are obvious suspects. The level of William Smith's command of German is unclear, but he was active in ventures among the Pennsylvania-Germans by the Society for Promoting Christian Knowledge, was secretary of the Pennsylvania-German Society, and worked with German printers and translators of some of his own work. See Stievermann, "'A plain, rejected little flock,'" 311; and Don Roy Byrnes, "The Pre-revolutionary Career of Provost William Smith, 1751–1780" (PhD, Tulane University, 1969), esp. 34, 38, 38n7, 47n23, 107–8. Thanks to Nancy Rhoden for these references.

50 For an alternative reading, see Denaci, "Penn's Creek Massacre," 307–22.

51 *PG*, 28 June and 5 July 1759; *PJ*, 28 June, 5 July, and 23 August 1759. Except for the truncated final paragraph, the last is a verbatim transcript of Stobo's deposition to Brigadier General Edward Whitmore, commandant at Louisbourg, dated 7 June 1759, printed in Robert C. Alberts, *The Most Extraordinary Adventures of Major Robert Stobo* (Boston, MA: Houghton Mifflin, 1965), 351–3.

52 The first American edition, *The Memoirs of Major Robert Stobo of the Virginia Regiment*, ed. Neville B. Craig (Pittsburgh, PA, 1854), was from a transcript of a British Library copy of the London edition of 1800, and was issued to mark the centenary of Stobo's capture.

53 The first advertisement appeared in Bradford's *Pennsylvania Journal and Weekly Advertiser* of 24 April 1760, and it was advertised again on 15 and 29 May, on 12, 19, and 26 June, on 10, 17, and 24 July, and finally on 11 September 1760. Apparently it was moving slowly. In 1765 Bradford would go on to print William Smith's *An Historical Account of the Expedition against the Ohio Indians, in the Year 1764, under the Command of Henry Bouquet, Esq.* and to reprint John Entick's *The General History of the Late War*. See *PJ*, 18 April and 27 June 1765.

54 Gary L. Ebersole, *Captured by Texts: Puritan to Postmodern Images of Indian Captivity* (Charlottesville, VA: University Press of Virginia, 1995), 15–60, 264–73, examines this issue carefully in relation to Mary Rowlandson's account, though Lowry's account is not considered in his chapter on

"Religious Captivities and the Attenuation of the Providential Interpretive Frame," ibid., 146–51.

55 See James Hartman, "The Birth of the Indian Captivity Narrative," in *Providence Tales and the Birth of American Literature* (Baltimore, MD: Johns Hopkins University Press, 1999), 128–63.

56 Thanks to Marjorie Bardeen at the Lancaster County Historical Society for access to "Lowery, Lazarus, Type copy of Samuel Evans script," which confirms that there was no known link between the trading clan of Lowerys and Jean Lowry. Lowry's journal was reprinted by Garland Publishing of New York in 1978.

57 Thanks to David R. Whitesell of the American Antiquarian Society for a copy of the Urssenbacher narrative from the *Neu-eingerichteter americanischer Geschichts und Haus-Calender ... 1762* (Philadelphia, PA, 1761), which was reprinted by Garland Publishing of New York in 1978. Thanks to Frederick A. Dreyer for a translation.

58 The Flemings' accounts were reprinted in Boston in 1760, and Charles Saunders's very unlikely tale, *The Horrid Cruelty of the Indians, Exemplified in the Life of Charles Saunders, Late of Charles-Town, in South Carolina*, was published in Birmingham, England, in 1763.

59 See Alison Olson, "The Pamphlet War over the Paxton Riots," *PMHB* 123 (1999): 31–55; Silver, *Our Savage Neighbors*, 190–1; Kevin Kenny, *Peaceable Kingdom Lost: The Paxton Boys and the Destruction of William Penn's Holy Experiment* (New York: Oxford University Press, 2009).

60 The account in *PG*, 8 December 1763, is a story datelined Williamsburg, 28 October 1763. Although a copy of the *Virginia Gazette* of that date has not been seen, the story is almost certainly from that paper.

61 Of adult women captives, 141 of 246 (57%) are known to have returned, compared to 554 of 1,139 adult men captives (49%). See also Michelle Burnham, *Captivity and Sentiment: Cultural Exchange in American Literature, 1682–1861* (Hanover, NH: University Press of New England, 1997).

62 See Linda Colley, "Going Native, Telling Tales: Captivity, Collaboration and Empire," *Past and Present* 168 (2000): 170–93, esp. 176.

63 For an inventive probing of Elizabeth Hanson, *God's Mercy Surmounting Man's Cruelty* (Philadelphia, PA, 1728), see William J. Sheick, *Authority and Female Authorship in Colonial America* (Lexington, KY: University Press of Kentucky, 1998), 85–93.

64 The rich literature on colonial women's captivity, and their narratives, includes Annette Kolodny, *The Land before Her: Fantasy and Experience of the American Frontiers, 1630–1860* (Chapel Hill, NC: University of North Carolina Press, 1984); Susan Howe, *The Birth-mark: Unsettling the Wilderness in American Literary History* (Hanover, NH: University Press of New England, 1993); Namias, *White Captives*; Castiglia, *Bound and Determined*; Sheick, *Authority and Female Authorship*; Kathryn Zabelle Derounian-Stodola, ed., *Women's Indian Captivity Narratives* (New York: Penguin, 1998); and Teresa A. Toulouse, *The Captive's Position: Female Narrative, Male Identity, and Royal*

Authority in Colonial New England (Philadelphia, PA: University of Pennsylvania Press, 2007).

65 Roy Harvey Pearce, "The Significances of the Captivity Narrative," *American Literature* 19 (1947): 1–20.

66 This novel, one of seven, was republished in London (1782), Berwick (1782), and Glasgow (1799). On Kimber, see Jeffrey Herrle, "Kimber, Edward," *ODNB*; Edward Kimber, *Itinerant Observations in America*, ed. Kevin J. Hayes (Newark, DE: University of Delaware Press, 1998); and Ebersole, *Captured by Texts*, 109–16.

67 This eight-page item, "printed and sold in Aldermary Church-Yard, Bow Lane, London," put its hopes on the soon to be reinforced Fraser Highlanders, which occurred in 1757. See J.R. Harper, *The Fraser Highlanders*, 2nd ed. (Montreal, QC: David M. Stewart Museum, 1979), 41–5, 122–31. For the plausible suggestion that *The Cruel Massacre* was published in 1758, and that it was based upon Williamson, see Richard C. Simmons, *British Imprints Relating to North America, 1621–1760: An Annotated Checklist* (London: British Library, 1996), 233. See also Troy Bickham, *Savages within the Empire: Representations of American Indians in Eighteenth Century Britain* (New York: Oxford University Press, 2005), 65–109.

68 John Thomson, *The Travels and Surprising Adventures of John Thomson* ... ([Falkirk?], 1761), so closely parallels Williamson's account that it can be considered a chapbook edition of Williamson. See Vail, *Voice of the Old Frontier*, 38.

69 Peter Williamson, *French and Indian Cruelty: Exemplified in the Life and Various Vicissitudes of Fortune, of Peter Williamson* (London, York, and Glasgow, 1757), 1. See also Peter Williamson, *Memorial, and Abstract of the Proof, in the Process, Poor Peter Williamson, against Alexander Cushnie, and Others, Magistrates of Aberdeen* (Edinburgh, Scotland, 1761), 1. On Williamson, see Timothy J. Shannon, "King of the Indians: The Hard Fate and Curious Career of Peter Williamson," *W&MQ*, ser. 3, 66 (2009): 3–44; P.J. Anderson, "Williamson, Peter," *ODNB*; Ferenc M. Szasz, "Peter Williamson and the Eighteenth Century Scottish-American Connection," *Northern Scotland* 19 (1999): 47–61; J. Bennet Nolan, "Peter Williamson in America, a Colonial Odyssey," *PH* 31 (1964): 23–9; William Roughead, "Indian Peter," *Juridical Review* 36 (1924): 1–32; and John Kay, "James Bruce, Esq., of Kinnaird, and Peter Williamson," in *A Series of Original Portraits and Caricature Etchings*, new ed., 2 vols (Edinburgh, Scotland, 1877), vol. 1, 128–39. For British views of Indians, see Tim Fulford, *Romantic Indians: Native Americans, British Literature and Transatlantic Culture, 1756–1830* (New York: Oxford University Press, 2006); and Bickham, *Savages*.

70 Misdating wartime attacks into peacetime was a common enough error or deliberate improvement on captivity narratives, having the effect of making the Indian raiders seem blatant violators of agreements. Mary Jemison insisted that she was captured in the spring of 1755, before any raiding had occurred into Pennsylvania, rather than in 1758. The year 1761,

again a time of truce that could be called peace, became a particularly common misdating in later Allegheny accounts. See the Renick family's attribution of an attack of July 1757 to "about the year 1761," Draper Mss, Kentucky Papers, 4CC120; and the story of Hannah Dennis told by several, including Elizabeth Fries Ellet, *Pioneer Women of the West* (New York, 1852), 110–11. For the estimate that John Slover was captured by Miami in 1761, though 1758 is most likely, see "The Narrative of John Slover," in *A Selection of Some of the Most Interesting Narratives of Outrages Committed by the Indians in Their Wars with the White People*, ed. Archibald Loudon, 2 vols (Carlisle, PA, 1808–11), vol. 1, 21. Some of these false memories were reinforced, if not induced, by Alexander Scott Withers, *Chronicles of Border Warfare, or A History of the Settlement by the Whites, of North Western Virginia, and of the Indian Wars and Massacres, in that section of the state, with reflections, anecdotes, etc.* ... (1831; reprint, New York: Arno, 1971).

71 Williamson, *French and Indian Cruelty*, 10–23. Allimingey was within Teedyuscung's land claim in northeastern Pennsylvania, and Allemangel was a German settlement in nearby Northampton County. See *JP*, 3: 839; and Shannon, "King of the Indians," 14.

72 See, for instance, J. Bennet Nolan, "Peter Williamson in America: A Colonial Odyssey," *PH* 31 (1964): 23–9, where a plea for tolerance of exaggeration and invention ends with the reminder that "he had a book to sell."

73 Williamson's narrative appeared in America first in the *Affecting History of the Dreadful Distresses of Frederick Manheim's Family* (Exeter, NH, 1793), and was included in the 1808 volume of Loudon, ed., *Selection*, vol. 1, 74–87. His narrative was also featured in Samuel L. Metcalf, *A Collection of Some of the Most Interesting Narratives of Indian Warfare in the West* (Lexington, KY, 1821); and in Samuel G. Drake's popular *Tragedies of the Wilderness* (Boston, MA, 1844) and *Indian Captivities, or Life in the Wigwam* (Buffalo, NY, 1854).

74 Henry Grace, *The Life and Sufferings of Henry Grace* ... (Reading, UK, 1764); Gamaliel Smethurst, *A Narrative of an Extraordinary Escape out of the Hands of Indians* ... (London, 1774).

75 Benjamin Franklin, *The Papers of Benjamin Franklin*, ed. Leonard W. Labaree, 29 vols (New Haven, CT: Yale University Press, 1959–92), vol. 15, 145–57; Bruce E. Johansen, *Forgotten Founders: Benjamin Franklin, the Iroquois, and the Rationale for the American Revolution* (Ipswich, MA: Gambit, 1982), 91–2. Thanks to Enid McFadden for the latter reference.

76 Charles A. Hanna, *The Wilderness Trail, Or the Ventures and Adventures of the Pennsylvania Traders on the Allegheny Path*, 2 vols (New York: Putnam, 1911), vol. 2, 334; *PA*, ser. 1, 2: 234; *NYM*, 28 May 1753.

77 Robert Kirk, *The Memoirs and Adventures of Robert Kirk, Late of the Royal Highland Regiment* (Limerick, UK, 1775), 40–1; a new edition, entitled *Through So Many Dangers: The Memoirs and Adventures of Robert Kirk, Late of the Royal Highland Regiment*, edited by Ian McCulloch and Timothy Todish, was published in New York in 2004. When this regiment went into winter quarters in January 1759, scattered at various Pennsylvania and

Delaware posts, including Lancaster, it reported twenty private soldiers still missing from the 1758 campaign. See *PJ*, 8 February 1759.

78 Kirk, *Memoirs*, 38–40.

79 Ibid., 45–6.

80 Enlistment of 25 October 1763, TNA, WO 12/5478, part 1, fol. 96; Stephen Brumwell, *White Devil: An Epic Story of Revenge from the Savage War That Inspired The Last of the Mohicans* (London: Weidenfeld and Nicholson, 2004), 223, 230, 298. See Brumwell's additional information in his "A Scottish Soldier's Story: Robert Kirkwood and His Memoirs," in Kirk, *Through So Many Dangers*, 13–27.

81 Captain John Rutherfurd and Ensign Thomas Gist kept or reconstructed journals published much later, in 1958 and 1956 respectively. Two captives held in Quebec prison between 1745 and 1748 managed to keep diaries that have survived. On the first, see George MacBeath, "Pote, William," *DCB*, 3: 531–2; and *The Journal of Captain William Pote, Jr., during His Captivity in the French and Indian War from May 1745, to August 1747*, ed. J.F. Hurst and Victor Paltsits (New York, 1896). On the second, see the anonymous "The Journal of a Captive, 1745–1748," in *Colonial Captivities*, ed. Calder, 3–136.

82 Gregory Evans Dowd, *War under Heaven: Pontiac, the Indian Nations and the British Empire* (Baltimore, MD: Johns Hopkins University Press, 2002), 219–20. On Thomas Morris, see Patrick Waddington, "Morris, Charles," *ODNB*; and Howard H. Peckham, "Captain Thomas Morris on the Maumee," *Ohio State Archeological and Historical Quarterly* 50 (1941): 49–57.

83 The original is in the Thomas Gage Papers, American Series, 1755–75, Clements Library, University of Michigan, Ann Arbor, MI. Morris received a copy back from Bradstreet's secretary, Thomas Mante, and had it in preparing his 1791 version. The original has been printed as "Captain Morris' Journal," *Old Fort News* 6 (1941): 3–11, with only one transcription error, the deletion of "not" on page 9, line 9, which should read that the Cygne said "that he would not have led me to my death."

84 The quotations are from the 1791 edition, page vi, and from the 1941 printed version of the original diary, page 7.

85 Morris's worst addition was the cursory entry of 11 September, "Continued our march," which contains a long celebration of the superiority of French Indian policy over English, entirely plagiarized from Thomas Mante, *The History of the Late War in North-America* … (London, 1772), 479–80. I am grateful to Richard Cargill Cole's unpublished paper "Thomas Morris, Soldier, Writer, Philanthropist" (1996) for discovering this connection.

86 There were no reprints between 1791 and 1978, when Morris's "Journal" was printed in the extensive series the Garland Library of Narratives of North American Indian Captivities.

87 On a continuing American literary interest in being English, see Leonard Tennenhouse, *The Importance of Feeling English: American Literature and*

the British Diaspora, 1750–1850 (Princeton, NJ: Princeton University Press, 2007), esp. 7–12.

88 Robert Stobo, *The Memoirs of Major Robert Stobo of the Virginia Regiment*, ed. Neville B. Craig (Pittsburgh, PA, 1854); *PJ*, 23 August 1759. Aside from the newspaper accounts of his escape and hero's reception in Virginia back in 1759–60, there was nothing published in America concerning Stobo before Neville B. Craig marked the hundredth anniversary of his capture with this Pittsburgh edition of Stobo's *Memoirs*. See also Alberts, *Most Extraordinary Adventures*; and Robert C. Alberts, "Stobo, Robert," *DCB*, 3: 600–2.

Tobias Smollett knew Stobo, and it is possible that he became fictionalized as Captain Obadiah Lismahago in Tobias Smollett, *The Expedition of Humphrey Clinker* (London, 1771). Stobo certainly had the title role in Gilbert Parker's *The Seats of the Mighty: Being the Memoirs of Captain Robert Moray, Sometime an Officer in the Virginia Regiment, and afterwards of Amherst's Regiment* (New York and Toronto, ON, 1896). See also Benjamin Matthias Nead, *Some Hidden Sources of Fiction: A Paper Read before the Historical Society of Dauphin County, Pennsylvania* (Philadelphia, PA: G.W. Jacobs, 1909).

89 W. Kaye Lamb, "Mackenzie, Sir Alexander," *DCB*, 5: 537–43; Elizabeth Biagent, "Mackenzie, Alexander," *ODNB*. The following year, a second London edition appeared, plus editions published in New York and Philadelphia, two German translations, and one French.

90 See L.G. Thomas, "Introduction to the New Edition," in Alexander Henry, *Travels and Adventures in Canada and the Indian Territories between the Years 1760 and 1776* (1809; reprint, Edmonton, AB: Hurtig, 1969), vii–xii.

91 Richard Slotkin, *Regeneration through Violence: The Mythology of the American Frontier, 1600–1860* (Middletown, CT: Wesleyan University Press, 1973), 328–9.

92 Greg Sieminski, "The Puritan Captivity Narrative and the Politics of the American Revolution," *American Quarterly* 42 (1990): 35–56; Robert J. Denn, "Captivity Narratives of the American Revolution," *Journal of American Culture* 2 (1979–80): 575–82.

93 An edition of Peter Williamson's account was printed in Dublin in 1766, and Robert Kirk's account was printed in Limerick in 1775.

94 Another edition of Hollister's account was published in Suffield, Connecticut, in 1803; in Townsend, Massachusetts, in 1855; and in William Henry Egle, *Contributions to Pennsylvania History* (Harrisburg, PA, 1890).

95 Thanks to Dr Wolfgang Splitter, of Martin Luther University of Halle-Wittenberg, for a full reference to the original publication, which appeared in the eleventh installment of *Hallische Nachrichten*, ed. Johann Georg Knapp, old ed. (Halle, Germany: Francke Orphanage, 1769), vol. 11, 1029–34.

96 *The Journals of Henry Melchior Muhlenberg*, trans. Theodore G. Tappert and John W. Doberstein, 3 vols (Philadelphia, PA: Evangelical Lutheran Min-

isterium of Pennsylvania, 1942–58), vol. 1, 386–9, 496, 523–4, 633, 655, 671, 692, vol. 2, 84.

97 Ibid., vol. 2, 204.

98 The first chapter of the apocryphal *Book of Tobit* was the source, though modern English translations do not now include this phrasing.

99 *Hallische Nachrichten*, vol. 11, 1029–34. A third American edition of Reuben Weiser (1807–85), *Regina, the German Captive Girl, or True Piety among the Lowly* survives. It was published in Baltimore in 1860, and reprinted by Garland Publishing of New York in 1977.

100 Draper Mss, Kentucky Papers, 23CC98-103, appendix 3; *WPHM* 39 (1956): 202. The Susannah Barnett (Cummins) story survives at several family history sites on the Internet.

101 The quotations are at pages 60 and 50 respectively. Filson's account was translated into German and French in 1785, and was separately printed in Norwich, Connecticut, in 1786, and in New York and Windsor, Vermont, in 1793. See especially Slotkin, *Regeneration*, 268–327.

102 This recognizable reference to a Shawnee matron's assigned role was promptly corrupted, in the Manheim anthology (1793), page 6, to become a woman named "Rose." This was repeated in Loudon, ed., *Selection*, vol. 1, 66, with the additional corruption of claiming the ransom was a "house" rather than a "horse."

103 Frances Scott, *A True and Wonderful Narrative of the Surprising Captivity and Remarkable Deliverance of Mrs. Frances Scott* (Boston, MA: E. Russell, 1786). See Evans, *Bibliography*, no. 19979. Although nothing remotely resembling Stewart's story occurred in Ohio country in 1764, and it is fair to dismiss the tale as one of fantasy, a Captain Stewart of Virginia had been taken in Major James Grant's raid of 1758, and was eventually returned. A Jonathan Davis, also of Virginia, was reported killed there. See Draper Mss, Virginia Papers, 3ZZ48.

104 Derounian-Stodola, ed., *Women's Indian Captivity*, 23–4.

105 White, *Backcountry and the City*, 113. Smith remembered enough things incorrectly to suggest either a later writing or deliberate errors.

106 When the account of the burnings was published separately in Pittsburgh-based magazine *Olden Times* 1 (1846): 72–5, the editor suggested that Smith had witnessed all the burnings, rather than the one he claimed, and also insisted that Smith's "veracity was unimpeachable" and offered "this melancholy tale, which, we believe, has never been contradicted."

Nor has it ever been confirmed. No other witnesses at Fort Duquesne that day, including a Virginian captive named Stuart and a British Army wife named Mrs Miller, mentioned the incident. See *NYM*, 11 August 1755; *SCG*, 9 November 1755; HL, MM, 1717. There is a story that Alexander McKee, son of Irish trader Thomas McKee and his Shawnee wife, was a Pennsylvania trader with provincial forces and captured at Braddock's defeat. He was supposedly rescued from burning by a young Shawnee who became his wife. See Draper Mss, Pittsburgh and Northwestern Virginia Papers, 6NN176. See also Reginald Horsman, "McKee, Alexander," *DCB*, 4: 499–500. This burning would have been at the edge of a Shawnee town, not at a warrior camp at Fort Duquesne. It is curious that British regulars left no tales of this event to fuel their revenge or to discourage desertion, and nothing is said of this incident by anyone else anxious to vilify or denounce the French or Indians in the next forty-five years. Possibly Smith was conflating some later event, and a couple of generations of fighting to take Kentucky from Indians would seem a little more justified if these burnings had occurred.

107 The quotations are from pages 82 and 88. In his *A Treatise on the Mode and Manner of Indian War* … (Paris, KY, 1812), 46, James Smith added, "except the burning of prisoners." For a particularly insightful meditation on Smith, see White, *Backcountry and the City*, 82–97.

108 Willard Rouse Jillson, *A Bibliography of the Life and Writings of Col. James Smith of Bourbon County, Kentucky, 1737–1812* (Frankfort, KY: N.p., 1947), 22.

109 On Smith, see Neil H. Swanson, *The First Rebel* (New York and Toronto, ON: Farrar and Rinehart, 1937); Jillson, *Bibliography*; Wilbur S. Nye, *James Smith: Early Cumberland Valley Patriot* (Carlisle, PA: Cumberland County Historical Society, 1969); and Leroy V. Eid, "'Their Rules of War': The Validity of James Smith's Summary of Indian Woodland War," *Register of the Kentucky State Historical Society* 86 (1988): 4–23. Smith published what he always considered the practical part of the work, as *A Treatise on the Mode and Manner of Indian War* … in Paris, Kentucky, in 1812.

110 John A. McClung, *Sketches of Western Adventure* (Philadelphia, PA, 1832), viii.

111 Filson's account of Boone and Smith's *Life and Travels* were both included in Metcalf, *Collection of Narratives*, but it is telling that Boone was featured on the title page and Smith was not. See Slotkin, *Regeneration*, 3–24, 268–369.

112 See Early American Imprints Series, online; and James N. Green, "Carey, Mathew," *ANB*.

113 Preface to Loudon, ed., *Selection*, vol. 1, 3–5.

114 Loudon, ed., *Selection*, vol. 1, 17–32, quote at 21.

115 Demonizing former captive Simon Girty as a white-Indian anti-hero seemed to emerge with the Boone myth. A popular example was Uriah James Jones, *Simon Girty, the Outlaw: An Historical Romance* (Philadelphia, PA, 1846).

116 On the cult of motherhood and captivity narratives in the nineteenth century, see Ebersole, *Captured by Texts*, 211.

117 Sayre, *Les Sauvages Américains*, offers an intriguing explanation of why French writers were more given to ethnography than were English. Neither McCullough nor James Smith are considered there, but their discussion fits well with Washburn's comment that this was a nineteenth-century

fashion. See Wilcomb E. Washburn, "Introduction," in *Narratives of North American Indian Captivity: A Selected Bibliography* (New York: Garland, 1983), xxxix.

118 Loudon, ed., *Selection*, vol. 1, 252–301.

119 "Alden, Timothy," DAB.

120 Compare Loudon, ed., *Selection*, vol. 2, 182, with Hugh Gibson, "An Account of the Captivity of Hugh Gibson among the Delaware Indians of the Big Beaver and the Muskingum, from the Latter Part of July 1756 to the Beginning of April 1759," *Massachusetts Historical Society Collections*, ser. 3, 6 (1837): 144.

121 Gibson, "Account of the Captivity," 153.

122 On Bemis's initiative, see Kolodny, *Land before Her*, 71, 75. Seaver claimed that Mary "speaks English plainly and distinctly, with a little of the Irish emphasis, and has the use of words so well as to render herself intelligible on any subject with which she is acquainted." See Mary Jemison, *A Narrative of the Life of Mary Jemison*, ed. C.D. Vail (New York: American Scenic and Historical Preservation Society, 1942), xi. When missionary Mrs Asher Wright visited Mary a decade later in 1833, an interpreter was taken along because Mrs Wright did not understand Seneca and, at least by that time, a conversation in English was not presumed. See Harriet Caswell, *Our Life among the Iroquois Indians* (Boston, MA, 1892), 56–7.

123 Original as reprinted in the fulsome Jemison, *Narrative* (1942), 29–30, 64; on Seaver, see 302–3.

124 Ibid., 103–8.

125 Richard VanDerBeets, *The Indian Captivity Narrative: An American Genre* (Lanham, MD: University Press of America, 1984), 26–7, 34.

126 Jemison, *Narrative* (1942), 41n.

127 Ibid., 55.

128 Ibid., 92.

129 As the recently captured Mary was being carried past what she thought was a Shawnee village on the upper Ohio River in April of 1758 in a Seneca canoe, she saw what she thought were recently burned human body parts on a pole, "a spectacle so shocking, that, even to this day, my blood almost curdles in my veins when I think of them." Seaver and later editors lamented that they could not identify this village, and no Shawnee attacks are reported around that time. See ibid., 55, 96–102.

130 Ibid., 103–9. See Silver, *Our Savage Neighbors*, 234–7, 281–5 (re. Brackenridge).

131 Jemison, *Narrative* (1942), 48, 139–40.

132 The phrase is from Voigt, *Writing Captivity*, 27n.

133 Charles D. Vail's edition of 1942 was also a monumental tribute, complete with attending essays, photographs of the earlier celebrations, details of the reinternment, and so forth.

In a noteworthy contrast, twenty-one years before the erection of the Jemison statue, more than 1,000 people gathered in tiny Milford, Pennsylvania, for the raising of an eight-foot Passaic zinc monument to legendary Indian-slayer Tom Quick. See Vernon Leslie, *The Tom Quick Legends* (Middletown, NY: T.E. Henderson, 1977). It was attacked and damaged in 1997, and removed for repair, and its restoration has been resisted.

134 On Mary Means, see C. Hale Sipe, *Fort Ligonier and Its Times* (Harrisburg, PA: Telegraph, 1932), 187–88. According to descendants, an Indian who remembered past kindnesses had warned Mrs Beatrice Byerly of Bushy Run of an impending attack and thereby allowed her and her four children to find refuge in Fort Ligonier. See Cyrus Cort, *Colonel Henry Bouquet and His Campaigns of 1763 and 1764* (Lancaster, PA, 1883), 17–18, 23–4.

135 Carolyn Eastman, "The Indian Censures the White Man: 'Indian Eloquence' and American Reading Audiences in the Early Republic," *W&MQ* ser. 3, 65 (2008): 535–64.

136 Ann Eliga Bleecker, *The History of Maria Kittle* (1793); Susannah Haswell Rowson, *Reuben and Rachel* (1798); Charles B. Brown, *Edgar Huntly* (1799). These were preceded by the anonymous delightful fantasy "A Surprising Account of the Discovery of a Lady Who Was Taken by the Indians in the Year 1777, and after making her escape, she retired to a lonely Cave, where she lived nine years," in Bickerstaff's *Almanack, for the Year ... 1788* (Norwich, CT, 1787). See also Steven Watts, *The Romance of Real Life: Charles Brockden Brown and the Origins of American Culture* (Baltimore, MD: Johns Hopkins University Press, 1994); David T. Haberly, "Women and Indians: *The Last of the Mohicans* and the Captivity Tradition," *American Quarterly* 28 (1976): 431–43; Frances Row Kestler, *The Indian Captivity Narrative: A Woman's View* (New York: Oxford University Press, 1990); and Lorrayne Carroll, "'Affecting History': Impersonating Women in the Early Republic," *Early American Literature* 39 (2002): 511–52.

137 See Mary Jemison, *A Narrative of the Life of Mrs. Mary Jemison*, ed. June Namias (Norman, OK: University of Oklahoma Press, 1992), 3–45.

138 Kolodny, *Land before Her*, 70–83. Catherine Maria Sedgewick featured a similar intercultural marriage in her novel *Leslie Hope, or Earlier Times in the Massachusetts*, 2 vols (New York, 1827).

139 Stuart, "Captivity," is a copy of a manuscript in the Force Collection of the Library of Congress. The original of "Thomas Gist's Indian Captivity, 1758–1759" is in the HSP. "John Rutherfurd's Captivity Narrative" was first printed in *American Heritage* 9 (1958): 65–81, and reprinted in M.M. Quaife, ed., *The Siege of Detroit* (Chicago, IL: Lakeside, 1958), 219–74. Rutherfurd's manuscript "Relation of a Captivity among the Indians of North America" is in the National Army Museum, Acc. 6003/17, London, England. A "J. C——R" left *A Short History and Description of Fort Niagara ... written by an English prisoner, 1758*, ed. Paul Leicester Ford (New York, 1890).

140 John Stuart, "Memoirs of Indian Wars and Other Occurrences," *Collections of the Virginia Historical and Philosophical Society*, 1st ser., 1 (1833): 37–68, first published the story of Mrs Clendennin of Greenbrier, a story spread

widely after 1839 in the numerous editions of Samuel G. Drake's *Tragedies of the Wilderness*. Joseph Persinger, *The Life of Jacob Persinger* (Sturgeon, MO, 1861), is hard to authenticate, though Abraham, Jacob, and Philip Parsinger were rangers between 1757 and 1759. See Virgil A. Lewis, *The Soldiery of West Virginia* (Baltimore, MD: Genealogical, 1967), 21. *A History of Allegheny County, Pennsylvania* (Chicago, IL, 1889) was the source for the 1930 pamphlet *Narrative of the Captivity of Mrs. Jane Frasier*. "History of the Capture and Captivity of David Boyd from Cumberland County, Pennsylvania," *WPHM* 14 (1931): 28–42, was a long-cherished family memoir.

Early local histories of note in this connection include: John Filson, *The Discovery, Settlement and Present State of Kentucky* (Wilmington, DE, 1784); Joseph Doddridge, *Notes on the Settlement and Indian Wars of the Western Parts of Virginia and Pennsylvania* (Wellsburgh, VA, 1824); John A. McClung, *Sketches of Western Adventure* (Philadelphia, PA, 1832); Samuel Kercheval, *A History of the Valley of Virginia* (n.p., 1833); Joseph Martin, ed., *A New and Comprehensive Gazeteer of Virginia* (Charlottesville, VA, 1835); Israel Daniel Rupp, *History of Northampton, Lehigh, Monroe, Carbon and Schuylkill Counties* (Harrisburg, PA, 1845); Willis De Haas, *History of the Early Settlement and Indian Wars of Western Virginia* (Wheeling, VA, 1851); and Neville B. Craig's monthly magazine *The Olden Time* (Pittsburgh, PA, 1846–47).

141 Better-known novels set in colonial Allegheny country include Gilbert Parker, *The Seats of the Mighty* (Toronto, ON, and New York, 1896); William K. Evans, *Isabella Stockton* (Boston, MA: Christopher, 1929); Hervey Allen, *The City at Dawn* (New York: Rinehart, c. 1950); and Conrad Richter, *The Light in the Forest* (New York: Knopf, 1953). Donald Clayton Porter published twenty-five novels for Bantam's White Indian Series between 1981 and 1994.

Between 1903 and 1970 there were ninety-two films about white captives. See Ralph E. Friar and Natasha Friar, *The Only Good Indian … The Hollywood Gospel* (New York: Drama Book Specialists, 1972), 302–5. More recent major films include *Little Big Man* (1970), *Lonesome Dove* (1985), *Dances with Wolves* (1991), and the 1992 remake of *The Last of the Mohicans*.

142 Burnham, *Captivity and Sentiment*, 176.

INDEX

See the alphabetized appendix for every named captive

Abbott, Rachel, 227–8, 366
Ackowanothio (Mingo chief), on Shawnee captives, 28
adoption of captives, 208–17; Croghan on, 209
Agouachimagand (Saginaw Ottawa chief), 39, 40, 41
Aix-la-Chapelle peace, 291
Albany, NY, Canadian trade to, 20
Alden, Timothy, 423
Aliquippa (Seneca "queen"), 42
Allen, George (PA militiaman), patrol kills Delaware captives, 177
Allegheny country, definition, 3
Amherst, Jeffrey (British general), and Canadian marine officers, 61–2, 306; and Clapham murder, 144; exchange of prisoners, 306; and Indian affairs budget, 281, 288–9, 303, 634n91; on Indian prisoners, 175–6; and return of captives, 281, 287–8, 302–3, 312–13
Anishinabeg, 145–6. *See also* Ojibwa; Ottawa; Potawatomi
Anuchrakechty (Kahnawake chief), 292–3
Armstrong, John (PA lieutenant colonel), 103, 352, 353; Kittanning account, 392–3; and raid on Big Island, 168
Armstrong, Thomas (white Indian), 368; visits sister, 218
Ashby, James (VA ranger captain), fort attacked, 118
Atkin, Edmond (Indian superintendent), 112
Aubry, Charles Philippe (French captain), 113, 136
Augusta County, VA, abandoned, 87, 99
Austin, Henry (RAR sergeant), ransomed, 298–9

Bäder, Philip, follows captured family, 253–4
Baker, John, 103; escape of, 241–2
Bard, Ketty, 203, 207, 254; ransom of, 299–300
Bard (Baird), Richard, mill attacked, 110; ransoms wife, 299–300
Barnett, Frances, 219–20, 368–9; account of, 417
Barnett, Susannah, 219–20, 361; account of, 417
Barnhold, Nicholas, account by, 391
battles, in French and Indian War, 127–41; in Pontiac's War, 160–1
Beatty, Charles, on war damage, 250
Beaver (King Beaver). *See* Tamaqua
Bell, James, 221–2, 620n100
Bemis, James D. (printer), 424, 425
Benevisica (Shawnee chief), 329, 335–6
bereft relations, 250–8
Berks County, PA, captives, 580n59; first raids in, 94, 167, 581n71
Big Ears (Potawatomi chief), hostage, 158, 160, 307
Big Island (Great Island), raided, 168
Bigham's Fort, PA, burned, 101, 119–20
Bingeman, John, family attacked, 85–6
Bingeman, Katherine, 625n42; account of, 388; escape, 243

Bingeman, Lewis (white Shawnee chief), 219
blacks, 107–8, 171, 174; escape of, 232–3
Bloody Run, battle, 161
Boone, Daniel, compared to James Smith, 419–20; myths of, 417–18
Boucher der Niverville de Montisambert, Louis (Canadian lieutenant), 107, 595n51
Bougainville, Louis-Antoine de (French captain), on hostages, 68
Bouquet, Henry (British colonel), 161, 161; vs Croghan, 341; distorts truce terms, 277; and Grant's raid, 133–4; and hostages, 178–80; on Indians, 320, 322; legacy, 337–9; on ransom, 278, 302; on refugees, 250; on returning captives, 287, 313–14
Bouquet's expedition, 312–39; belligerence in, 320; Camp # 16, 330–2; care of captives, 330–3; compared to Kittanning raid, 340; diplomacy of, 322–9; evaluations, 340, 349
Boyd, David, adoption of, 212; return of, 286
Boyd, Rhoda, 223, 332
Brackenridge, David, escape of, 244–5, 379, 400
Braddock, Edward (British general), 127–32; captives taken with, 129–32; casualties, 128; news of defeat, 61; Ohio chiefs, 88–9, 92
Braddock's Road, 75, 241, 243,
Bradford, William (printer), 402, 403
Bradstreet, John (British colonel), 178, 314, 316
British Admiralty, and captives, 298
British Army, in battles of Pontiac's War, 160–2, 181; and Braddock's defeat, 133; in Ohio forts, 146, 151; and ransom, 260, 277–9; and return of captives, 257, 275–6, 279–80, 287–8, 313
Broadly, Paul, torture of, 201
Brown, Adam (white Miami chief), visits kin, 218, 221
Brown, Enoch, school attacked, 173
Brown, George (white Shawnee chief), 106, 221
Brown, William (SC trader), returned, 264
Buffalo Creek, SC, attacked, 29, 81–2
Buford, Thomas (VA captain), 332, 334
Bull, William (SC lieutenant governor), 19; and Itawachcomequa, 22
Bushy Run, battle, 161; Indian captive at, 176, 607n49
Byrd, Mary, and children, 360
Byrd, Nalupua, 360

Calhoun, Thomas (PA trader), 149, 255
Campbell, Arthur (VA soldier), subsequent career, 376
Campbell, Donald (RAR captain), 307, attempts escape, 160; executed, 204
Canada (New France), becomes responsible for Ohio, 41; Indian slaves in, 16; invades Ohio, 20; trade to Albany, 20
Canada, traders, attacked in 1747, 38–41, 52, 71; and forts, 54–5; with Shawnee, 566n52
Canadian Iroquois, Kahnawake raid of 1752–53, 20–1; southern raids, 16–17
Canadian marine officers, and Grant's defeat, 134; leading raids, 98–100, 107; taken at La Belle Famille, 137–8
Canasatego (Onondaga chief), 18–19, 408–9
Captain Bull (Johann Jacob) (North Branch Delaware leader), captured, 169; exiled, 170; leads raids, 168–9
Captain Jack, avenger, 252
Captain Johnny. *See* Welapachtschiechen
captives, ages of, 188; in battles, 127–41; in Canada, 16–17; as compensation for murders, 40; going as, 80, 231; intertribal, 9, 13–20; as martial success, 14, 79; and slave trades, 15–16; taking, 5–6, 52, 73–116, 127–41, 183, 187–8; transforming, 6, 198–230; words for, 210–14, 617n56, 617n61. *See also appendix for named individuals*;

Indians; soldiers; traders; white settlers
captivity narratives, 7–8, 384–428; and American Revolution, 417; British audiences for, 406–14; colonial audiences for, 386–7, 389–90; early anthologies of, 420–4; in films, 673n141; in novels, 406, 426, 672n136; Pennsylvania appetite for, 389–90, 398, 404, 414, 427; by women, 371, 388–91, 398–406
Carey, Mathew (printer), 420
Carlisle, PA, captives return to, 335
Carr's (Kerr's) Creek, attacked, 114–15, 164, 311
cartel ships, 130, 295, 305
Catawba, 13, 14, 19–20; peace with Iroquois, 19–20; raid Chartier's Creek, 106; as slaves, 212–13; women escape Onondaga, 31
Céloron de Blainville, Pierre-Joseph (Canadian captain), 21; buys captives, 291, 293; and Pickawillany, 48; 1749 expedition of, 41–3
Chartier, Peter, 34–8, 563n13
Chenussio Seneca, 280; attack at Devil's Hole, 161; and Captain Bull, 168–9; and Delaware refugees, 170–1; and Johnson, 162, 169, 178, 272–3, 315; and prisoners, 162, 181; take Ohio forts, 154; and Teedyuscung, 96
Cherokee, 16, 107; escape Kahnawake, 31–2; and Johnson, 162, 169, 178; raids, 108, 178; Sandy Creek expedition, 102; and Virginia war, 265
Cherokee War, 146–7
children as captives, 30, 79–80, 83, 109–10, 112, 174, 188, 585n129; adopted, 209–10, 218–19; escape, 248; *métis*, 7, 229–30, 357–8, 622n127; ransom, 255; return of, 256, 356–65, 381
Christie, John (RAR ensign), 154–5
Clapham, William, Jr, murder of, 144
Clapham, William, Sr, 164–5, 604n6
Clendennin, Jean, return of, 359
Clendennin, Jennet (Anne), 194–5, 251, 371
Clouser sisters, 367
Cloyd, David, plantation attacked, 172
Cochrane, Jane, and orphan's court, 364
Conaway, Samuel (Cayuga), captivity of family, 175–6; escape of, 176, 372
Conestoga, Indians attacked, 159, 251; manor, 96, 266
Conrad, Barbara, 334, 372–3
Conrad, Ulrich, 334, 372–3
Contrecoeur. *See* Pécaudy de Contrecoeur
Cornstalk (Shawnee chief), leads raid on Greenbrier, VA, 164
Coulon de Villiers, Louis (Canadian captain), on prisoners, 63, 65, 71; takes Fort Granville, 122–4; takes Fort Necessity, 62–5
Coulon de Villiers de Jumonville, Joseph (Canadian ensign), 58–60
Countzmann, Elizabeth, indentured, 366
Cowpasture, VA, raided, 110, 331
Coxe, John, account edited, 392; escape, 239; at Tioga, 213
Craig, John, deposition edited, 391
Crawford, Arthur, 368
Crawford, Hugh (PA trader), 150, 377
Croft (Kraft), Frederich, and Bäder, 253–4
Croghan, George, 39, 278, 376–7, 561n1; and Amherst, 302; bounty on, 44; vs Bouquet, 341; Illinois expedition, 341–2 ; vs Quakers, 276; ransom of, 303–4; reputation with Indians, 278, 288; and return of captives, 278–81, 288–9, 302; secret business partnerships, 278; and Shawnee, 25–7, 29, 336–7; Six Nations land grant to, 277; and "suffering traders," 151, 599n38; and truce of 1758, 139, 277, 279
Cuillerier, Antoine, 307, 624n26; and Rutherfurd, 215
Cumberland County, PA, abandoned, 89, 99, 581n78; attacked, 91, 172–3;

orphan's court, 353, 364, 649n10; Scots-Irish in, 83
Custaloga (Pankanke) (Munsee Delaware chief), 50–1; and Bouquet's expedition, 323, 325; and truce of 1758, 277
Cuyler, Abraham (British lieutenant), 158

Dalyell, James (British captain), 160–1
database (SPSS), xiv
Davies, Samuel (VA minister), sermon of, 111
Decker, Sarah, returned, 272
Defever, John, 291, 567n56
Delaware George. *See* Menatochyard
Delaware Indians, 4, 113; adoption of captives, 211; and Anishinabeg allies, 146; and captives, 181; and gauntlet, 206–8; green powder of, 239–40; vs Pennsylvania, 83, 93; torture rituals, 201–3; trade embargoed, 143; warrior culture, 104; word for captives, 211. *See also* North Branch Delaware; Ohio Delaware
Dennis, Hannah, adaptation, 223; escape of, 163–4, 245–6, 372
Denny, William (PA lieutenant governor), and Teedyuscung, 271–2
Detroit, and captives, 236–8; conference of 1761, 280; siege of, 157–60
Dinwiddie, Robert (VA lieutenant governor), and forfeit of land, 99; and Fort Necessity, 65–6; and Jumonville incident, 60–2; promotes war, 30–1, 264–5; and return of captives, 264–5; war measures, 101
diplomatic barter for captives, 263–89
Doddridge, Joseph (PA minister), 252–3; on forts, 125
Douville, Alexandre Dagneau (Canadian ensign), instructions, 118
Druillon de Macé, Pierre-Jacques, 58–60
Du Jaunay, Pierre (Jesuit missionary), 153, 159
Dumas, Jean-Daniel (Canadian captain), 100, 582n81
Duquesne de Menneville, Ange, Marquis, 17, 67–8; and Buffalo Creek attack, 82; not buying captives, 292
Dunbar, Thomas (British colonel), and Indians, 89
Dunlap, William (printer), 390, 397
Dunning, James (PA trader), 36–7

Eastburn, Robert, 378, 397
Easton conferences, of 1756, 270–1; of 1757, 271–2, 275; of 1758, 28, 142, 276; of 1761, 280
Eckerle, Gabriel, 370
Eckerle, Israel, 370
Edward's Fort, skirmish near, 100, 118
Eice, Frederick, 170–1
Eice, John (adopted by Delaware), to servitude, 171, 359
Eger, Crosby (VA soldier), captivity of, 131
English John (Delaware), and Fort Necessity, 62; takes captives, 51
escape, of captives, 231–49; promptly, 193–6, 234; from rescuers, 247–8
Etherington, George (RAR captain), 152–3; and Bouquet's expedition, 318
exchange of prisoners, 305–8; at Detroit, 159–60, 175, 307

farmers as captives, 77–116, 163–84, 378–81. *See also* white settlers
Fereich, Frederick, 369–70
Fleming, Elizabeth, 195; account by, 389–91, 427; and Tewea, 91–3
Fleming, William, 91–3; account by, 389–91, 427; on compliance, 188; escape of, 195
Forbes, James (British general), 112; and Ohio Indians, 275–6
Forbes's Road, 75, 319
Fort Bedford, garrison protecting Indians, 165
Fort Chartres, 304; fur mart at, 148, 598n25

Fort Cumberland, MD, 55, 84–5, 87; Virginians at, 101
Fort des Miamis (Kekionga), captured, 38–9, 152; Morris at, 412
Fort Dinwiddie, attacked, 173
Fort Duquesne, 51, 57, 77, 133; baptism of captives, 189; and captives, 236, 400, 669n106; captives hired out to, 213; demolished, 114; negotiations, 111, 123, 134–5, 141, 189; reputation, 98; Stobo at, 65–7
Fort Granville, taken, 101, 122–3
Fort Le Boeuf, taken, 154
Fort Loudoun (Venore, TN), 148
Fort Machault, attacked, 114
Fort Michilimackinac, taken, 152–3
Fort Necessity, captured, 62–5; terms at, 62–3
Fort Niagara, escape from, 238–9; Johnson conference of 1764, 315
Fort Ouiatenon, taken, 152
Fort Pitt, conference of 1758, 277; conference of 1759, 279; siege of, 165–6
Fort Presqu'île, 26, 50, 55; abandoned, 107, 139; siege of, 154–6, 197
Fort St Joseph, taken, 152
Fort Sandusky, Bradstreet at, 316; captured, 151–2
Fort Trent, terms at, 57
forts, and Indians, 55–6, 118–19; and prisoners, 190, 236
Foyle, Robert, family killed, 30
Franklin, Benjamin, and Henry hoax, 408–9; as printer, 391, 401; and war, 266, 342
Fraser (Frasier), Jane, 189–90, 214; return of, 244, 373
Freeling, John, family attacked, 86
French and Indian War, 77–8; battles, 127–41; captives in 140–1, 435; map, 75; phase one (1755), 81–97; phase two (1756–57), 97–106; phase three (1757–58), 106–12; phase four (1758–59), 112–15; raids, 77–116; sieges, 117–26; as single contest, 77–8

Gage, Thomas (British general), and Bouquet-Croghan contest, 341; and Elizabeth Ball, 303; and Sam Tony, 171
garrison houses, 99–100, 102, 117–19
gauntlet, captives running, 205–8
Gibson, Hugh (Owen), 212, 232; accounts by, 423–4; escape of, 244–5, 400
Gibson, John (PA trader), 179; Delaware scribe, 322; subsequent career, 377–8
Girty, George, 222–3
Girty, James, 222, 367
Girty, Simon, 222, 367; compared to James Smith, 380–1; reputation, 421, 425
Girty, Thomas, 222; return of, 353
Girty-Turner, Mary, 122–3
Gist, Christopher, 47, 265
Gist, Thomas (VA ensign), account by, 427; on captives, 206; return of, 237, 248–9, 376
Gladwin, Henry (British major), and Clapham murder, 144; and Pontiac, 158–60, 307
Glen, James (SC governor), and Buffalo Creek attack, 81–2; and Itawachcomequa, 21–5; and ransom, 291
Gnadenhütten, 94; attacked, 95–6; 1782 massacre, 419
Gordon, Francis (RAR lieutenant), 154, 193
Gorrell, James (RAR lieutenant), 153–4, 281
Grant, James (British major), raid, 133–5
Great Cove, PA, attacked, 91, 167
Greenbrier River, settlement attacked, 86–7, 164, 245
Grey, Jane, 299; case, 362–3
Griffith, Maurice, escape of, 243–4

Hamilton, Agnes, on Braddock's defeat, 129

Hamilton, James (PA lieutenant governor), 22, 56; Céleron's letter to, 42; instructions for Patten, 28; and Itawachcomequa, 25–7; at Lancaster conference of 1762, 256, 283–5
Harris, John, and Bouquet, 317–18; party ambushed, 90
Hays, John (PA captain), trip with Teedyuscung and Post, 272
Henry, Alexander (trader), 150, 249, 376; on Ojibwa at Michilimackinac, 153; *Travels*, 413–14; and Wawatam, 214–15
Henry, William, hoax, 408–9
Hertel de Montcour, Pierre (Canadian officer), killed as rescue, 136
Hicks, Barbara, 353, 373, 580n55
Hicks, family attacked, 91–2, 188
Hicks, Gershom, 221, 380
Hicks, Levy, 221, 368
Holland, Nathaniel, 217; frees Catherine Nicholson, 285–6; and ransoms, 300–1
Hollister, Isaac, captivity, 213; escape of, 239–40; *Brief Narration*, 414–15
Holmes, Robert (RAR ensign), 152
Holston River settlement, attacked, 82, 85, 86
honors of war, 57, 63–4
horses, 191; in raids, 166–7, 311; return of, 273; stealing, 143
hostages, 40, 43, 64, 67, 70; Bouquet's, 178–80; Bradstreet's, 316; Chenusio Seneca, 315; of French, 64; Johnson and, 178; Potawatomi, 158, 160; Shawnee as, 24–5; of Shawnee, 47; traders as, 33
hot pursuit, 166, 173, 191–2, 196, 309–12, 339; Ingles and, 361; Ryans and, 166–7, 404; tactic against, 172, 182
Hudson, John (Cayuga), captivity of family, 175–6
Hudson, Mrs John (Delaware), 175–6, 180
Hutchins, Thomas, and Smith's *An Historical Account*, 321, 344
Illinois (tribe), and Pawnee captives, 15
Indians, 64–5, 78, 425; in Braddock's defeat, 84, 128, 206; at Bushy Run, 161; as captives, 73–4, 161, 175, 229–30, 584n113; casualties, 106, 112, 180, 182, 435–6; escape captivity, 24, 180, 233; in Grant's defeat, 133–5; at La Belle Famille, 136; refugees, 250; taking captives, 70–2, 73–9, 185; taking Presqu'île, 155; at Vause's Fort, 121–2; vigilance as captors, 196. *See also individual tribes*
Ingles, Mary Draper, accounts of, 387–8; adaption, 223; captured, 86–7; escape of, 243, 371
Ingles, Thomas, fate of, 360–1
Innes, Francis, recovering family, 256–7, 362
Iroquois, adoption among, 210–11; in Allegheny country, 4; mourning war of, 14–15; torture rituals, 200–1; words for captives, 210. *See also* Canadian Iroquois; Chenussio Seneca; Kahnawake; Mingo; Six Nations
Itawachcomequa (the Pride), 22, 36, 557–8n3; raid, 21–30

Jackson River, settlement attacked, 105, 172
Jager, Catherine, 357, 367
James, John (Delaware), and ransom of Ketty Bard, 299–300
Jemison, Mary (Dickewamis), 109–10, 132, 199, 365; adoption, 211; facility in English, 424, 671n122; into hiding, 315; *A Narrative*, 424–6; on Shawnee, 425, 671n129
Jenkins, Edward (RAR lieutenant), 152
Johnson, William (captive of Delaware, spy?), 113–14, 220
Johnson, William (Indian superintendent), 137; and Chenussio Seneca, 162, 169, 178, 272–3; and Croghan's accounts, 279; Detroit conference of 1761, 280; Niagara conference

of 1764, 178, 315; organizes raids, 169–70; and renegades, 171; and return of captives, 281–2, 315–16; and wartime ransoms, 294
Joncaire, Philippe-Thomas Chabert de (Nitachinon), 41, 47
Jonnhaty (Onondage), raid of 1742, 18
Jordan, Nicholas (Oneida adoptee), 138
Jumonville incident, 58–62

Kageshquanohel (the Pipe) (Delaware chief), 381, 557–8n36; hostage, 178, 319, 326; leads Shawnee, 30
Kahnawake, captures in 1753, 291–3; Smith among, 132
Kanuksusy, and North Branch Delaware, 268–9
Kennedy, John, 51, 393–4
Kenny, James, and Cherokee captive, 32; and Jammy Willson, 286
Keyashuta (Mingo war chief), 322–3, 325; as hostage, 324; transformed, 337
Kickapoo, 152; capture Croghan, 304
Kilgore, Ralph, 43–4; ransom of, 291
killing captives, when attacked, 309
Kimber, Edward (novelist), 406
Kincade, Eleanor, return of, 331
Kinderuntie (Mingo chief), returns captives, 284
Kinonchamek (Ojibwa leader), and torture, 159, 203
Kirk, Robert, dubious memoirs, 409–11
Kisinoutha (Big Wolf) (Shawnee chief), 323–5, 327
Kitchi (Turtle Heart) (Delaware chief), 149, 323; hostage, 179, 324
Kittanning, escape from, 241–2; evacuation of, 104; migrants to, 91, 93
Kittanning raid, 102–5, 312, 339; failure of, 400, 423; fate of recovered captives, 352–4; medal, 105; propaganda for, 392–3, 661n30; revenge for, 104
Kuskuski, 242; Post at, 275

La Belle Famille, battle of, 135–9; casualties, 136–7
La Chauvignere, Michel (Canadian ensign), 107; on captives, 220, 294
La Force, Michel Pepin *dit*, 58, 59, 61–2, 70, 571n22
La Galissonière, Roland-Michel Barrin, Marquis de (Canadian governor), 40–1
La Jonquière. *See* Taffanel
Lancaster conferences, Amherst limits, 302; and return of captives, 262–3, 282–5; of 1744, 19; of 1762, 219, 255, 282–5, 302, 357
Lancaster County, PA, first attacks in, 94
Lane, Thomas, ransom of, 301
Langlade. *See* Mouet de Langlade
Le Marchand de Lignery, François-Marie (Canadian captain), 134; and captives (1758), 134; gathering information, 112–13; at Fort Machault, 114, 135; at La Belle Famille, 135–9
Le Mercier, François (Canadian captain), 63
Le Moyne de Longueuil, Paul-Joseph, 37, 40; buys captives, 44; and Pickawillany, 43
Le Roy, Jean Jacques, family attacked, 90
Le Roy, Marie, 224; escape of, 244–5; narrative, 398–401, 663n49; work as captive, 213
Legardeur de Saint-Pierre, Jacques (Canadian captain), and Cooper boy, 31
Leininger, Barbara, 90, 224; escape of, 244; narrative, 398–401, 663n49; work as captive, 213
Leininger, Regina, 90, 335; narrative, 415–16
Leininger, Sebastian, family attacked, 90
Léry, Joseph-Gaspard Chaussegros de (Canadian lieutenant), 27
Lignery. *See* Le Marchand de Lignery
Logan, James, and Chartier, 34–5
Logstown, Céleron at, 42; council fire, 40

Looney, Peter (ranger ensign), account by, 393, 661n33; return of, 376; at Vause's Fort, 120–1
Loudon, Archibald (PA printer), *A Selection*, 420–4
Louisbourg, impact of 1745 fall, 38
Lower Shawnee Town, 559n50; captives at, 319–20, 338, 644n63; Céleron at, 42; Virginians to, 329, 335
Lowery, Alexander, 321
Lowery, James, bounty on, 44; escape of, 20–1
Lowery, John, death of, 43
Lowry, Jean, captivity, 296, 310, 636n24; and gauntlet, 207; *Journal*, 402–3; religious disputation of, 403; and Schuyler, 297

Maiden Foot (Delaware), and Mary Means, 165, 604n7
Malott, Catherine, 222, 381
Man, John, captivity of, 302–3
Mante, Thomas, 411; on Bouquet, 349
Marin de La Malgue, Paul (Canadian captain), and Ohio, 50–1, 55
Martin, Janet, ransom of, 255
Martin, John, 255–6, 295–6, 333
Martin, Mrs John, 255, 295
Maryland, attempts raid, 102. *See also* Fort Cumberland
Mascouten, 152; capture Croghan, 304
McAllister, Mrs Alexander, tortured, 104, 202, 423, 614n18
McCord's Fort, burned, 100, 402
McCullough, John, adoption of, 211–12; on buying condemned captives, 203, 290–1; narrative, 421–2; return of, 256, 331–2
McDougall, George (RAR lieutenant), 307; escaped, 160
McDowell's Fort, 118
McGinty, Alexander, petition, 557n30; ransom of, 292
McKee, Alexander, and Bouquet, 322; and captives of Shawnee, 145, 338; and Croghan, 341
McLean, Jenny, escape of, 242–3
McManimy, Daniel, tortured, 203
McMullen, David, 294; escape of, 239
McSwain, Hugh, 87, 235, 378; account of, 388
Means, Mary, 165, 425
Memeskia (Old Briton or La Damoiselle) (Piankashaw Miami chief), 39; and Céleron, 42–3; demonized, 48; killed, 48–9
men, as captives, 431; return of, 374–81. *See also* farmers as captives; traders as captives; soldiers as captives
Menatochyard (Delaware George) (Delaware chief), 144, 275, 299
Mennonites, resist Indian hating, 253
Mercer, Hugh (PA colonel), 399, 400; and Kittanning raid, 392, 661n30; and Leininger and Le Roy, 399–401, 662n44; on return of captives, 277–8, 301–2, 313
Mesquepalathie (Red Hawk) (Shawnee paramount chief), 327; hostage, 329, 336
Metcalf, Samuel L. (KY printer), 420
Miami, 152, 156; adoption of captives, 214; and John Smith, 396; and Pennsylvania alliance, 40; at Vause's Fort, 120–2
Miller, Mrs, 295; on captives in Braddock's defeat, 129–30
Miller, Peter (PA printer), 401, 403
misdating of attacks, 424, 665n70
missing captives, xiv, 140, 142, 249, 338, 350, 435–6
Mingo, 24–5, 32, 78; and Pennsylvania alliance, 40. *See also* Keyashuta; Scarouady; Tanaghrisson
Moffat, Thomas, escape of, 239
Montisambert. *See* Boucher der Niverville de Montisambert
Montour, Andrew, bounty on, 47; raids Delaware, 169
Montour, Catherine, and captives, 239, 294
Montour, Margaret (French Margaret), 240, 300, 624–5n32
Montreal, captives in, 296

Moore, Ann, 224–5
Moore, Joseph (Shawnee warrior), 225–6, 227
Moore, Margaret, 225–6, 365
Moore, Mary, 224–5
Moore, Nancy, 225–6
Moore (Connor), Peggy, 226–7, 366
Moravians, attacked, 95–6; Indian refugees with, 227–8, 581n66; resist Indian hating, 253
Morris, Robert Hunter (PA lieutenant governor), and Indian refugees, 96; Kanuksusy and, 268–9; and Teedyuscung, 268–70; and war, 265–7
Morris, Thomas (British captain), journal of, 411–13
Mouet de Langlade, Charles-Michel (Canadian ensign), and Michilimackina captives, 153; and Pickawillany, 48–9
Muhlenberg, Henry Melchior (PA minister), 330, 335; and Leininger narrative, 415–16
Muskingum, 21; escapes from, 125, 242–3
Muskingum expedition, 312–39

Navarre, Robert, 204
Neolin (Delaware prophet), 157, 159, 181, 337; and torture of captives, 203–4
Netawatwees (Newcomer) (Ohio Delaware leader), and Bouquet, 326; and Peace of Paris, 145
New England captivities, 16–17; compared, xiii, 187, 229, 267, 621–2n124, 654n64
New France, captives in, 229, 622n125
newspapers, 386–98; and censorship, 386, 388, 391, 392, 658n83
Nicholson (Holland), Catherine, 285–6
Nissewndanie (Kahnawake), sells McGinty, 292
No-Kaming (Potawatomi chief), hostage, 160, 307
North Branch Delaware, 89–91; captured and killed, 177, 190; captured in raids, 169–70; divided, 93–5; Pennsylvania diplomacy with, 268–9; raids by, 95–7, 167–9. *See also* Captain Bull; Teedyuscung
Northampton County, PA, 367; captives, 241; orphan's court, 379; raids in, 95, 96, 581n71
Nucheconer (Neucheconno) (Shawnee chief), 36, 37
Nutimus (Susquehanna Delaware "king"), 94; bullied, 269

Ohio Company of Virginia, 41, 54–5
Ohio Delaware, and Bouquet, 322, 641n23; as captors, 88; and English traders, 52, 149; and French, 50, 89, 277; leadership shift, 144; migration, 105, 146, 171, 316; raids by, 87–8, 165, 167; resisting peace, 399; and return of captives, 275, 337. *See also* Custaloga; Shingas; Tamaqua; Tewea
Ojibwa, 150; adoption of captives, 214; at Detroit, 157, 160; at Grand River, 150; and Niagara conference of 1764, 315; take Michilimackinac, 152–3, 156; take Pickawillany, 48; word for captives, 214
Old Scarny (Creek), escaped from torture, 199–200
Orontony (Wyandot-Huron chief), vs Canadians, 38–9
orphan's courts, 364
Ottawa (tribe), and Clapham murder, 144; desert Fort Duquesne, 113; escort garrisons to Montreal, 303; of L'Arbre Croche, 153, 159; and Pawnee captives, 15; and Pickawillany, 48–9; supposed raid of May 1755, 577n25
Ourry, Lewis (RAR captain), and Indian prisoners, 171, 175; recovering child, 362
Owens, David (interpreter), 322, 326, 327; Kirk's tale of, 410, murders his Shawnee family, 177

Pacane, hostage, 43, 565n37
Painter, Mary, 366, 652n42
Palmer, John, escape of, 320
panis, 15–16; and murder of Clapham, 144
Papunahoal (Papunhank or Papoonan) (Munsee leader), 273–4
parole, 60, 64, 135, 296, 305
Patten, John, (DE trader), capture of, 45–6; and Shawnee captives, 25–7
Patterson's Creek, PA, attacked in 1755, 85, 87, 100; attacked in 1756, 118
Patton, James (PA colonel), killed, 86
Pauli, Christopher (RAR ensign), 151–2, 158, 160
Pawnee, as slaves, 15, 555n11
Paxinosa (Shawnee chief), 94,
Paxton Boys, 169, 177, 178, 251, 320, 343, 404, 606n22
Peace of Paris, Indian reaction to, 145
Pécaudy de Contrecoeur, Claude-Pierre (Canadian captain), 84, 189, 395; and Dinwiddie, 66–7; seeking captives in 1755, 84, 132; and Shawnee, 84; takes Fort Trent, 57
Peewash (Ojibwa), and Rutherfurd, 215
Pemberton, Israel, Jr, 267; and Holland, 300
Penn, Thomas (proprietor), and Kennedy, 393–4
Penn's Creek, attack, 90
Pennsylvania, vs Delaware, 83, 265; first raids on, 89; Kittanning raid, 102–5, 352–4, 392–3; regiment, 102, 318; remaking of, 384–5; and return of captives, 268–70, 287–8, 335, 363–4; war measures, 101–2. *See also individual counties*
Pennsylvania Gazette, 17, 130, 169, 343, 390–1
Pennsylvania Journal and Weekly Advertiser, 391
Pennsylvania traders, 33–4; captured, 20–1, 43–6, 49–53, 148–51; and Céleron, 42–3; and Chartier, 35–8; competitive advantage, 568n66
Persinger, Jacob, 362
Pickawillany, 39–40, 42–3; taken, 49–50
Picoté de Belestre, François-Louis (Canadian ensign), 584n118
Picoté de Belestre, François-Marie (Canadian lieutenant), raids Pickawillany, 48; takes Vause's Fort, 120–3
Pisquetomen (Delaware chief), 144, 399; with Post to Ohio, 275
Point Pelee, skirmish, 158, 160–1, 602n65
Pontiac (Shawnee chief), and Canadians, 150; at Detroit, 74, 150, 157–60, 237–8; and Gladwin, 158–60, 307; and torture, 158–9
Pontiac's War, 74–6, 142–84; map, 147
population of Indians, in Ohio Valley, 216, 618n76; Shawnee, 587n149; in Virginia, 628n4
Post, Frederick Christian (PA diplomat), 145, 298; and Lancaster conference of 1762, 282; and Ohio captives, 301; to Ohio Delaware, 275, 282; returning captives, 255–6, 274–5; on Seneca captives, 272–3; trip with Teedyuscung and Hays, 272; and truce of 1758, 277
Potawatomi, take Fort St Joseph, 152; and Gladwin, 159–60; and John Smith, 396–7
Powell, William, ransom of, 293
printers, and censorship, 386, 388, 391, 392, 658n8
prisoners of war, conventions, 73, 79, 208; expenses of, 61; parole of, 61, 64. *See also* captives

Quakers, 170, 186; assist Teedyuscung, 271, 276; Friendly Association, 267, 276, 300–1; resist Indian hating, 253
Quebec, captives in, 296
Quick, Tom (avenger), 252; monument, 671n133

raids, 77–116, 163–84. *See also* Kittanning raid

Ramsay, Priscilla, 223–4
Ramsey, John (VA soldier), 69, 70; return of, 375
ransom of captives, 51, 255, 262, 290–304, 635n15; barriers to, 298–9, 308; British Army and, 260, 277–9, 302; Croghan and, 278–81, 288–9, 302–4; garrisons, 303; from Lower Shawnee Town, 335–6; Tamaqua and, 278–81; Thomas Ingles, 360–1; vs travel expenses, 287, 292; during war, 293–4
Redstone Creek, 56–7, 83
redemption of captives, 290–304; through the French, 294–6. *See also* ransom of captives
Reid, John (British colonel), and Indians, 320
release of captives, 6–7, 165, 285–6, 288
Renick, Felix, 228, 355–6
Renick, Joshua (white Shawnee chief), 221
Renick, Mrs Robert, Sr, 373
Renick, Robert (Pechyloothame), 357
Renick, William, 368
return of captives, 259–350; adults, 370–83; British Army and, 257; children, 256, 356–65; and identity, 356; for land, 271–2; obstacle to peace, 269; and Pennsylvania politics, 6, 257, 268, 386; Post on, 274–5; as servants, 283–4, 286–7, 300–1; before 1755, 263–4; youths, 256, 356–65. *See also* Bouquet's expedition; escape; exchange; hot pursuit; Kittanning raid; parole; ransom of captives; release of captives
Rigaud de Vaudreuil, Pierre-François (governor of New France), 68, 78, 402–3; and exchange of prisoners, 305–6
Robineau de Portneuf, Pierre (Canadian captain), 139
Roger (captured Delaware), 171
Rutherfurd, John (RAR lieutenant), 157–8, 238; "Captivity Narrative," 427; and Peewash, 215
Ryan, Eleanor, 166–7; escape of, 242, 404

Saghughsuniunt (Thomas King) (Oneida chief), on captives, 283–4; leads raid, 169; on Shawnee war, 28
Salt Licks, OH, traders killed at, 149
Sanders, Robert, 292–3
scalp bounties, 628n11; Canadian, 566n53, 568n61, 575n6; Pennsylvanian, 101–2, 177, 266, 317–18, 608n50, 629n12; Virginian, 38, 579n39, 608n53, 627n4, 629n12
Scarouady (Mingo chief), 24–5, 40, 90, 267–9; capture of, 84, 128
Schilling, John, 370
Schlosser, Francis (RAR ensign), 152
Schmidt, Maria Christina, return of, 362
Schuyler, Peter (NJ colonel), aids captives, 296–8, 403, 622n126, 637n32; parole of, 296
Sciota Valley, escapes from, 243–4
Scots-Irish, 77, 83, 117, 217, 223
Sea, John, 355
Sea (Johnson), Mary, 355–6
Sea family, re-education of, 228, 355
Seaver, James Everett, 424–6
Selim (Algerian captive), 245–6
Sepettekenathe (Blue Jacket) (Shawnee chief), 214, 225–6, 358, 365
servants, captured, 150, 232–3, 369–70
settlers. *See* white settlers
Seven Years' War. *See* French and Indian War
Seybert, Jacob (VA ranger captain), fort burned, 125
Shamokin, PA, 89–90
Shemokin Daniel (Delaware), raid, 165
Shaw, William (VA soldier), toes cut off, 231
Shawnee, 4, 29, 115, 143, 328; adoption of captives, 213–14; and Anishinabeg

allies, 146; and Bouquet's expedition, 323–5, 327–9; and captives, 115, 181, 336–7; and Catawba, 4, 14, 21–30; and Cherokee, 4, 108–9, 586n147; hold French hostages, 47; kept archive, 328; migrations of, 37–8; 316; peace proposal, 314; and Pennsylvania traders, 52, 149; raids of, 105–6, 111, 114–15, 124–6; torture by, 201; vs Virginia, 82; to war with English, 27–9; vs Westo, 6; word for captive, 213–14. *See also* Benevisica; Chartier; Itawachcomequa; Mesquepalathie
Sheaffer, Peter, return of, 364, 379
Shingas (Ohio Delaware "king"), 88–9, 144, 255; bounty on, 101; Braddock and, 395; speech by, 394–5
Sideling Hill, skirmish, 119, 310–11
sieges, in French and Indian War, 117–26; in Pontiac's War, 151–60
Six Nations of Iroquois, captives among, 272–3; Cayuga as captives, 175–6; at La Belle Famille, 136; neutrality of, 40; as overlords, 24, 38, 179–80, 270; peace with Catawba, 19; raid North Branch Delaware, 169. *See also* Chenussio Seneca
slaves, captives as, 15–16, 208–11, 291, 213–14, 216, 291; taken captive, 107–8, 174, 232–3, 292, 370. *See also panis*
Slotkin, Richard, on Smith's *An Historical Account*, 344–5
Slover, John, 214, 368; narrative of, 421
Sluis (Écluse), Convention of, 305, 571n21
Smallman, Thomas, 376; and Shawnee peace proposals, 314, 327–8
Smith, Catherine, return of, 352–3
Smith, Fisher (*métis*), 229–30, 357
Smith, Hannah, 229–30
Smith, James, 84, 378–81; *An Account*, 419–20; adoption of, 210; Black Boys, 338, 377, 378; and Bouquet's expedition, 318, 320; burning captives at Fort Duquesne, 131–2, 669n106; compared to Boone, 419–20; compared to Simon Girty, 380–1; and gauntlet, 205–6
Smith, John (VA ranger captain), 120–3, 210, 305, 376; accounts of, 396–7
Smith, William (Anglican cleric), 342; *An Historical Account*, 343–4; and Bouquet's reputation, 342–3; on Camp # 16, 331; on Indian adoption, 216
soldiers as captives, 11, 54–72, 151–62, 435–6; escape of, 233–4, 623n11; return of, 374–6
South Carolina, 15, 16, 19–25, 29, 178. *See also* Glen, James
Soyechtowa (James Logan) (Mingo chief), 377
Squash Cutter. *See* Yaghkapoose
Staffel, Christopher, resists return, 217
Stalnaker, Samuel, captured, 85; escaped, 244; warned, 82
Stamp Act, 7, 261, 342–5, 349
Staut, account by, 387–8
Steal, Elizabeth, return of, 17
Stephen, Adam (VA colonel), 317; account by, 570n15, 572n35
Stewart, Isaac (British captain), fabrication, 418–19
Stobo, Robert (VA captain), account of, 402; hostage, 64–9, 572–3n41; *Memoirs*, 387, 413; and ransoms, 293; rewards for, 68–9, 375; trial of, 68
Street, John, account by, 393
Stuart, Charles, 295; accounts of, 394–6, 427
Stuart, Margaret, 295
Stuart, Mary, 362, 651n26
Studebaker, Elizabeth, returns to Delaware, 219, 332
Stump, Frederick, murders by, 380
Succomabe (Chickasaw), on Shawnee war, 29
"suffering traders," 151, 377, 657n92
surrender, 125, 137, 138, 152–7; in battle, 58–9, 127–8. *See also* Fort Granville; Fort Necessity; Fort Niagara; Fort Presqu'île; Fort Trent

Susanna (Kahnawake trader), 20, 292

Taffanel de La Jonquière, Jacques-Pierre de (governor of New France), 45–7
Tamaqua (Beaver or King Beaver) (Delaware chief), 89, 139, 144, 255; and diplomatic ransom, 278–81; and Lancaster conference of 1762, 282–5; returns captives, 255–6, 279, 281–8, 323, 325
Tanaghrisson (Half-King) (Mingo chief), 14, 210; and captured Shawnee, 25–7; and French forts, 56–8; and Washington, 58–60, 71, 570n15
Tattamy, Moses (Delaware interpreter), on cause of Shawnee war, 28
Teedyuscung (Wyoming Delaware chief), 94–5, 98, 270, 276; and Denny, 271–2; ends raids, 98, 107; with Hays and Post, 272; and Johnson, 269–70; and Kanuksusy, 268–9; killed, 145, 167–8; land for captives, 271–2, 276; and Morris, 270; returns captives, 271, 287
Tewea (Captain Jacobs) (Ohio Delaware chief), 89; bounty on, 101; and Braddock, 579n42; burns forts, 119–20, 122; and Flemings, 91–3, 389; settlement attacked, 103–4
Ticasso (Thomas Hickman) (Delaware), death of, 143–4
Tioga, NY, 96, 268–9, 392; escape from, 239–41; hunger at 98, 213
Todd, Mary, 287, 357
Tony, Sam, 171
torture, 95, 104, 121, 132, 158–9, 192–3, 199–205; at Detroit, 203–4
Tostee, Peter (PA trader), 36–7
trade embargoes, and return of captives, 143, 282
traders as captives, 10–11, 34–52, 69–70, 148–51, 435–6; return of, 233, 376–8
trail into captivity, 187–97; escape on, 235–6; food on, 189–90
Trent, William (VA captain), 56
Tulpehocken, PA, attacked, 95
Turner, John (PA sergeant), tortured, 122–3, 202
Turner, John, Jr, 189, 354
Turner, Morris, 43–4; ransom of, 291

upper Ohio Valley, 16, 33, 43; escape from, 241–2; French into, 25–6, 53, 56; 1749 transfer to Canada, 41
Upper Tract Fort, burned, 124–5
Urssenbacher, Abraham (PA soldier), 404

Van Braam, Jacob (VA captain), 61, 63–6, 69; on hostages, 67
Vaudreuil. *See* Rigaud de Vaudreuil
Vause, Susannah, 366, 369, 652n41, 653n55
Vause's Fort, attacked, 101, 120
Villiers, Louis. *See* Coulon de Villiers, Louis
Virginia, 87, 101, 110, 164; return of captives, 264–5, 333–4; Sandy Creek expedition, 88, 102, 190; and Schuyler, 297; vs Shawnee, 82; volunteers with Bouquet, 317; "woodboys," 83–4. *See also* Augusta County; Cowpasture; Greenbrier River; Jackson River; Vause's Fort

Wakitomica, 21, 226–7, 557n32; Bouquet at, 324, 327
Walker, John (VA scout), captivity of, 84, 294
Walking Purchase, 96, 271
Walter, Mary, 364
Wampler, Eve and Philipina, 366
Ward, Edward, 54, 57
Ward, John (white Shawnee warrior), 221
Warren, Mathias, on Delaware, 171–2, on Shawnee, 318
Warriors' Path, 9, 13, 18–19, 22, 32–3; map, 10
Washington, George (VA colonel), diary, 58, 569n9; to Fort Le Boeuf, 26, 30, 50; and Fort Necessity, 62–6;

and Jumonville incident, 58–62, 71, 264
Wasson (Ojibwa chief), executes Campbell, 160, 204
Wauntaupenny (Shawnee), on war, 29
Wawatam (Ojibwa warrior), and Henry, 214–15
Weese, Peter, returns to Delaware, 219, 284
Weiser, Conrad, 38; and Paxton captive, 79; and return of captives, 271, 292; and scalp bounties, 101–2, 266
Weiss, Lewis (PA printer), 401, 403
Welapachtschiechen (Captain Johnny) (Delaware chief), 178, 227–8; hostage, 319, 326
Welch, John (PA trader), 150, 158
West, Benjamin, drawings, 345–9
Wheelock, Anthony (British captain), and La Force, 61, 70
white Indians, 198–230; surrendered to Bouquet, 338
white settlers, escapes of, 234; war on, 77–116, 163–84, 435–6
Wilkins, Sally, escape of, 240–1
Williams's Fort, burned, 100, 119
Williamson, Peter, fabrication of, 406–8
Willson, Jammy, releases family, 286
women captives, 79–80, 112, 129–30, 132, 174, 188; adaption of, 223–8; avoid gauntlet, 205; bought by French, 294–5; escape of, 194–5, 232, 243–4; narratives of, 404–6; and Niagara surrender, 130, 306; rape of, 224; return of, 273, 287, 366–7, 371–4; as wives, 209, 224–6, 295, 373–4
Woods, George, ransom of, 299
Wyandot, 38–9, 155, 158, 399; adopting captives, 210; and Bouquet, 326–7; desert Fort Duquesne, 113; Stuarts and, 395; taking captives, 150, 157, 181
Wyoming, PA, 94; attacks from, 95–6, 168; burned, 145, 167–8

Yaghkapoose (Squash Cutter) (Delaware leader), 169, 170
York County, PA, raided, 109–10
youths captured, 214, 219–20; as brokers, 365; escape of, 232, 365; return of, 365–9, 381–2

Zeisberger, David, 14, 208, 227; on gauntlets, 205; on release of condemned, 613n13